Mouldmade Bowls of the Black Sea Region and Beyond

Monumenta Graeca et Romana

Editor-in-Chief
Troels Myrup Kristensen (*Aarhus University, Denmark*)

Editor-in-Chief Emeritus
John M. Fossey FRSC (*Musée des beaux-arts de Montréal, Canada*)

Associate Editor
Beaudoin Caron (*Université de Montréal*)

Assistant Editors
Laure Sarah Ethier & Marilie Jacob (*Université de Montréal*)

Editorial Board
Anna Collar (*University of Southampton, UK*)
Søren Handberg (*University of Oslo, Norway*)
Kathleen M. Lynch (*University of Cincinnati, USA*)

Editorial Advisory Board
Andreas Konecny (*Universität Graz, Austria*)
Duane Roller (*Ohio State University, USA*)
Massimo Osanna (*Ministry of Culture, Italy*)
Peter Stewart (*University of Oxford, UK*)
Lea Stirling (*University of Manitoba, Canada*)

VOLUME 28

The titles published in this series are listed at *brill.com/mgr*

Mouldmade Bowls of the Black Sea Region and Beyond

From Prestige Object to an Article of Mass Consumption

By

Pia Guldager Bilde

Edited by

Susan I. Rotroff
(*Washington University in St. Louis*)

BRILL

LEIDEN | BOSTON

Cover illustrations: (front) The distinctive underside of a bowl of the Meter Medallion Workshop (KYB-129), with the bust of the goddess, in profile, and the signature of the potter Kirbeis; (back, top) Bowl with acanthus-ivy-flower scroll (AIB-39); (back, bottom) Bowl with Amazonomachy (EPH-82). Photos from the author's archive.

Library of Congress Cataloging-in-Publication Data

Names: Bilde, Pia Guldager, author. | Rotroff, Susan I., 1947– editor.
Title: Mouldmade bowls of the Black Sea region and beyond : from prestige object to an article of mass consumption / by Pia Guldager Bilde ; edited by Susan I. Rotroff.
Description: Leiden ; Boston : Brill, 2024. | Series: Monumenta Graeca et Romana, 0169–8850 ; volume 28 | Includes bibliographical references and index.
Identifiers: LCCN 2024009479 (print) | LCCN 2024009480 (ebook) | ISBN 9789004549098 (hardback) | ISBN 9789004680463 (ebook)
Subjects: LCSH: Black Sea Region—Antiquities. | Pottery, Hellenistic. | Bowls (Tableware)—Black Sea Region. | Bowls (Tableware)—Mediterranean Region. | Mediterranean Region—Antiquities. | Excavations (Archaeology)—Black Sea Region. | Excavations (Archaeology)—Mediterranean Region.
Classification: LCC DJK64 .B47 2024 (print) | LCC DJK64 (ebook) | DDC 939/.5—dc23/eng/20240315
LC record available at https://lccn.loc.gov/2024009479
LC ebook record available at https://lccn.loc.gov/2024009480

Typeface for the Latin, Greek, and Cyrillic scripts: "Brill". See and download: brill.com/brill-typeface.

ISSN 0169-8850
ISBN 978-90-04-54909-8 (hardback)
ISBN 978-90-04-68046-3 (e-book)
DOI 10.1163/9789004680463

Copyright 2024 by Pia Guldager Bilde and Susan I. Rotroff. Published by Koninklijke Brill NV, Leiden, The Netherlands by kind permission of the heirs of Pia Guldager Bilde.
Koninklijke Brill NV incorporates the imprints Brill, Brill Nijhoff, Brill Schöningh, Brill Fink, Brill mentis, Brill Wageningen Academic, Vandenhoeck & Ruprecht, Böhlau and V&R unipress.
Koninklijke Brill NV reserves the right to protect this publication against unauthorized use. Requests for re-use and/or translations must be addressed to Koninklijke Brill NV via brill.com or copyright.com.

This book is printed on acid-free paper and produced in a sustainable manner.

Contents

Foreword VII
Introduction by the Editor VIII
Acknowledgements XII
List of Illustrations XIV
General Information Concerning the Catalogue Entries XXII

PART 1
General Considerations

1 Introduction 3
2 History of Research 7
3 Methodology 17
4 Production and Distribution 38
5 Supplementary Shapes 53
   Catalogue to Chapter 5 63
6 Iconography and Interpretation 104

PART 2
Mediterranean Productions

7 Athens 135
   Catalogue to Chapter 7 137
8 Aiolis: Introduction 146
   Catalogue to Chapter 8 149
9 Pergamon 153
   Catalogue to Chapter 9 158
10 Kyme (i) 168
   Catalogue to Chapter 10 174
11 Kyme (ii): The Meter Medallion Workshop 192
   Catalogue to Chapter 11 216
12 Aiolis A: Elaia or Pitane? 261
   Catalogue to Chapter 12 263
13 Aiolis B: Elaia, Pitane, Gryneion or Pergamon? 267
   Catalogue to Chapter 13 273
14 Ephesos 286
   Catalogue to Chapter 14 327
15 Knidos 431
   Catalogue to Chapter 15 433
16 Vessels from Unidentified Production Sites 442

PART 3
Pontic Productions

17 Mouldmade Bowls in the Black Sea Region: Introduction   453
18 Myrmekion and Pantikapaion: (Pontic) Demetrios   459
    Catalogue to Chapter 18   468
19 Getic Productions   489
    Catalogue to Chapter 19   490

PART 4
Pontic Sites

20 Olbia Pontike   493
21 Istros   510
22 Chersonesos   516
23 The Chersonesean chora and Bol'šoj Kastel'   520
24 Pantikapaion   522
25 Myrmekion   528
26 Porthmion   532
27 Tyritake   538
28 Kepoi   540
29 Ruminskoe (Za Rodinu)   542
30 Volna 1 (Severo Zelenskoe)   544

Appendices

1 Getting Started   549
2 Laumonier 1977 Concordance   551
3 Revised Attributions of Vessels in Laumonier 1977   584
4 Moulds as Evidence of Production Places   591

   Bibliography   599
   Recent Bibliography on Mouldmade Bowls   615
   Index to the Text   619

Plates

Plates 1–245   631

Foreword

The present volume is the posthumous *magnum opus* of Pia Guldager Bilde, who served as Director of the Danish National Research Foundation's Centre for Black Sea Studies from 2002 to 2010. The manuscript was at an advanced state of completion at the time of her premature death in January 2013.[1] Pia's husband, Per Bilde, handed the relevant files (electronic and otherwise) over to Kristina Winther-Jacobsen with the express wish that her work be published. Kristina brought Troels Myrup Kristensen and John Lund in on this enterprise, which has now come to fruition.

The three of us began by identifying what needed to be done before the manuscript could go to press. As far as the text was concerned, the major – but not the only – challenge was that Pia had only finalized one part of the crucial Chapter 14 (on the mouldmade bowls from Ephesos). Moreover, she had drawn, described and photographed several thousands of mainly fragmentary vessels during her journeys in the Black Sea Region and visits to museums. She planned to use these as illustrations, but her original drawings needed to be scanned and cleaned up, and this was also the case with the photographs. Our aim was to complete her vision to the fullest extent possible, but for reasons of space, we were obliged to extract a chapter on the shared iconography of some of the mouldmade bowls and the so-called Tarentine terracotta altars. It will be published separately elsewhere, which, incidentally, was what Pia had originally planned to do.

The immediate task was to find a publishing house that was capable of taking on such a voluminous and complex publication, and we extend our sincere thanks to Brill for having accepted to do so in August 2018. Then, in April 2020, Susan Rotroff generously volunteered to assist in the endeavour, an offer which we accepted with great gratitude. As editor of the volume, Susan has worked tirelessly and with the greatest of care on completing the text, by filling out gaps and correcting inconsistencies. The volume would never have seen the light of day without her invaluable assistance. We extend our sincerest thanks to Susan for turning Pia's unfinished manuscript into a publishable book.

Our focus then shifted to readying Pia's drawings and photographs for publication. To that end, Pia's archive was transferred from Aarhus to the National Museum in Copenhagen in 2019 with the assistance of Jakob Munk Højte, our colleague from the Black Sea Centre, who had been the first guardian of the archive. In May 2020, we succeeded in obtaining a grant from the Aarhus University Research Foundation, and in December a further grant from Elisabeth Munksgaard Fonden. We are most grateful to both foundations for these donations, which enabled us to have all of Pia's drawings expertly scanned – and cleaned up – by Marie-Louise Jahn Hansen. We are no less grateful to Torben Jacobsen, who graciously undertook the gargantuan task of cleaning up the photographs. A final grant from the New Carlsberg Foundation for which we are also most grateful allowed the high quality reproduction of the plates.

We are thankful to Patricia Kögler and Renate Heginbottom-Rosenthal for providing valuable assistance in checking and filling out gaps in Pia's bibliography, and for assembling a separate bibliography of scholarship on mouldmade bowls published from 2012, when illness prevented Pia from continuing the study, to the present. This also applies to Valentina Mordvintseva, who kindly checked the transcriptions of names in the bibliography written in the Cyrillic alphabet. Our final task was to contact the copyright holders in order to obtain permission to reproduce the text figures, and we gratefully acknowledge the help of Jacklyn Burns, John McKesson Camp II, Søren Handberg, Jakob Munk Højte, Sarah Japp, Alexander Karjaka, Ulrich Mania, Erica Martin, Stella Miller-Collett, Rasmus Holst Nielsen, Meg Sneeringer, Marina Vachtina, Valentin Verardo, Leif Erik Vaag, Nina Zimmermann-Elseify and Denis Žuravlev in this respect. Unless otherwise indicated, the photos have been taken by Pia, who was also responsible for the vast majority of the drawings with the occasional assistance of collaborators at the Black Sea Centre.

Our guiding principle has been to preserve Pia's text as intact as we could, in order to publish a volume as close as possible to what she intended. If we succeeded, it is thanks to the assistance and support by Pia's many friends and colleagues. We dedicate our collective efforts to her memory.

Troels Myrup Kristensen
John Lund
Kristina Winther-Jacobsen
Aarhus and Copenhagen
9th of August 2023

---

1 An obituary for Bilde (in Danish) authored by colleagues Vinnie Nørskov and Birte Poulsen can be found here: https://arts.au.dk/aktuelt/nyheder/nyhed/artikel/mindeord-1/ (last accessed 25 October 2022).

Introduction by the Editor

I first became aware of Pia's manuscript in the Summer of 2018, at the IARPotHP conference in Croatia, when John Lund told me that Pia's friends and colleagues were exploring means to achieve its publication. The following Spring John sent me the good news that Brill had expressed interest in the project, and he asked me to read and evaluate the manuscript for the press.

Three things about the work especially excited me. The first was its general approach to the iconography of the mouldmade bowl. For almost a century and a half, ever since the bowls emerged as a distinct ceramic category, scholars had generally assumed that their decoration was purely ornamental. One could search for models and *Vorbilder*, but there was no point in interrogating the bowls for deeper meaning. Pia vehemently rejected this conventional wisdom, as least as concerns the bowls in their earliest formulations, and presented a convincing and very revealing reading of one complex piece, the Olbia situla (Guldager Bilde 2005). I had myself been among the sceptics, but I found Pia's interpretation convincing; her approach opens whole a new window into the Hellenistic world.

A second exciting contribution was an analysis of the long-known but elusive oeuvre of the potter Kirbeis – a man with clear Black Sea connections, both in his name and in the distribution of his products. The protracted debate about the location of his workshop – in the Black Sea or in western Asia Minor – had recently been resolved in favour of the latter by chemical analysis. But the products of the shop were difficult to study, scattered throughout the Black Sea region and the museums of Europe. I had gotten to know Kirbeis through publishing a single fragment found on Samothrace, and in that publication, I had commented on the need for a full examination of this workshop, a task that "calls for someone with command of Slavic languages and the ability to travel widely on the coasts of the Black Sea" (Rotroff 2010, 62). I had not known that such a person was already at work on the project, and it was exciting to have my wish granted, as it were, by Pia's work. Her astute analysis of the works of Kirbeis and his colleagues in what will now be known as the Meter Medallion Workshop, as well as other production centres in Aiolis, sheds light on an area that has heretofore been very shadowy indeed.

The third reason for my excitement was Pia's Chapter 14, a restudy of the Ephesian workshops, which not only undertook to place the Black Sea finds in context, but also proposed a complete revision of the workshop structure as presented in Laumonier's monumental *La céramique hellénistique à reliefs. Ateliers "Ioniens"* (1977). Since the Ephesian bowls enjoyed a very wide distribution, a better understanding of the conditions of their production held out the hope of a better understanding of trade networks in the late Hellenistic period.

And so I wrote an enthusiastic evaluation, which I hoped would help to speed the publication of what I felt was destined to be a landmark in the study of Hellenistic ceramics.

But there was a problem: the manuscript was unfinished. There were many small lacunae and missing references, easy enough to remedy. But Chapter 14 on the Ephesian bowls had been left in the early stages of composition. The basic conclusions about workshop structure were there, but much was expressed only in the form of lists or sketchy drafts. Along with Pia's colleagues in Denmark, I wondered who could be induced to take on the task of completing her work.

Then came COVID. I found myself isolated in the American Midwest, cut off from my research projects in Athens for the foreseeable future, and it occurred to me that I might put this otherwise empty time to good use by helping to get the manuscript into publishable form. My first offer was just to edit the prose. But as I worked my way through the text, I became convinced that I could take on the task of Chapter 14, which remained the main stumbling block to publication. My Danish colleagues accepted my offer to do so, and I found myself in the position of editor, with the responsibility of filling in the blanks, remaining as true as possible to Pia's intentions as I understood them.

Here's what I've done. Throughout the manuscript, I've completed, checked, or supplied references at points that Pia had marked for further attention. Whenever my interventions have gone further, I have said so in an editorial footnote. I have added references to more recent scholarship only in those rare cases where it has a direct impact on the manuscript; that is, had Pia been able to read it, she would have written differently. Otherwise, I have not updated her references; readers are directed to the bibliography of works on mouldmade bowls published in the last decade, prepared by Patricia Kögler and Renate Rosenthal-Heginbottom (see p. 615). I have reworded much of the manuscript with an eye to producing a text in more idiomatic English, but I have tried to stay close to the original text and to preserve its meaning as well as Pia's unmistakable tone. Chapter 14 has presented the greatest challenge, since much remained unwritten; the extent of my contribution is indicated by the footnotes. My guide here was the data base that Pia had constructed in the preparation of the book, which included all of the Ephesian bowls and fragments from the Black Sea region as well as those published by Laumonier, along with Pia's changes to Laumonier' attributions. Beyond this, I was sometimes able to supply information from published sources; at other times I tried to guess at the ways in which ideas that Pia mentioned briefly might have been developed. But I did not progress very far along that path, and in particular took care to present Pia's ideas, not my own.

It was also left to me to construct catalogues of the Ephesian and unassigned material (depending almost entirely on the data base), and here I departed radically from Pia's procedure. Her catalogues include *all* the fragments of Athenian, Pergamene, Aiolian, and Knidian bowls from the 11 sites basic to the study. She also included all the works of Kymean Workshop A and unassigned Kymean bowls. The catalogue for the Meter Medallion Workshop was restricted to 86% of the Black Sea collection but was expanded with many bowls from outside the Black Sea, as part of her program to draw as complete a portrait of the workshop as possible. She was more selective with the very repetitive works of Demetrios, including only 60% of the finds from the 11 sites. In contrast, my catalogue of the Ephesian bowls includes only 42% of the corpus she assembled from the 11 sites. The numbers were simply too large for complete inclusion, and many fragments were small and without significant decoration, or repeated well-known themes, or lacked illustrations, and no purpose would have been served by granting them a catalogue number. I aimed to include the following: pieces with the best examples of any given motif; all attributed pieces, whether illustrated or not; items that Pia had drawn (taking this as an indication of her sense of the significance of the piece); those she had mentioned in the text; and as large a sample as feasible from little-known sites (Bol'šoj Kastel', Kepoi, Porthmion, Ruminskoe, Tyritake, Volna 1), even if some of the fragments were minimal and/or lacked illustration. At the same time, I excluded many fine pieces that had already appeared in accessible publications such as Domăneanţu 2000 and Guldager Bilde 2010. For the catalogue of the vessels from unknown production places (Chapter 16), my approach was draconian: I limited it to bowls mentioned in the text and a few others of special interest, only 14% of the collection that Pia had amassed. The present situation in Ukraine, where many of the sites are located and some of the pottery is stored, only makes me wish I had included more.

I believe that Pia would ultimately have made more attributions in her Ephesos catalogue than currently appear; I have found reference to some in her text and in annotations on her drawings, and these I have added. Almost twice as many bowls attributed to Menemachos as to the PAR Monogram potter are included in her data base, while on Delos, for example, the proportions are reversed. This difference might reflect the two workshops' export patterns, but it could also point to missing attributions. I was often tempted to assign a bowl to a workshop (usually to the PAR Monogram Workshop), but with access only to photographs, it seemed risky, and Pia's distrust of the 'attribution game' also suggested it was better to be conservative in this matter.

Like everything else in 2020, this process has been complicated by the strictures of the pandemic, and particularly the lack of normal access to libraries. But many helpers came to my assistance. I must first thank the librarians of Washington University and their colleagues in the Interlibrary Loan system, who developed a system of contactless delivery that gave me access to several essential books. I also thank Bettina Schwarz, of the Austrian Archaeological Institute, who scanned an important section of the unwieldy *FiE* VIII/4 for me. Very often, however, when I encountered a problem, I turned to my knowledgeable friends. I would like especially to thank William Bubelis, Jan Jordan, Sabine Ladstätter, Bob Lamberton, Mark Lawall, Margaret Miles, Olga Palagia, Paul Scotton, Andrew Stewart, and Denis Žuravlev for their willingness to contribute their expertise to the project. I am grateful also to Gera van Bedaf at Brill for the care that she has expended on the preparation of the book for publication. It goes without saying that my Danish colleagues, and especially John Lund, provided abundant practical and intellectual support, and I am humbled by their faith in my ability to perform the task.

As I worked my way through Chapter 14, I found myself substantially in agreement with Pia's vision of the Ephesian workshop structure. There are so many details that one could take as guides to the identity of workshops – medallions, rim patterns, the form of an acanthus, and so forth – but the division of the material into two large groups using the criterion of form – a flat-bottomed bowl with a plain underside (Workshop Circle 1) vs. a more hemispherical one with a rosette medallion (Workshop Circle 2) – is very convincing. The unusual flat-bottomed shape is, in effect, a new form altogether, something one could imagine as beginning as a 'proprietary' item, and thus a promising foundation for a new analysis. Pia was not able to follow this proposal to its conclusions, especially as concerns the later material, but I hope that Chapter 14 and Appendix 3 (which presents her revision of many of Laumonier's attributions) will serve as a substantial foundation for others to build upon.

There is one area, however, in which I cannot follow Pia so confidently, and that is chronology. She accepted Laumonier's workshop sequence, placing Menemachos near the beginning of the series. This may be right, but I am troubled by the absence of his products in some early contexts: at Entremont, in the fill of the Temple of Castor and Pollux in Rome, and in the Südtor deposit at Ephesos (Benoit 1947, 82–83; Guldager Bilde 2008, 188; Gassner 1997, 71–88). His products are also absent from Cistern Л and Bothos 11 at Olbia, which were probably closed in the late 140's. The assemblages are small, and chance may be at work here, but C. Rogl, on the basis of her work with material at Ephesos, displaced Menemachos from the beginning of the series, as she explained in a paper at a conference organized by Pia and by Mark Lawall in 2008 and then published in a volume which they edited (Rogl 2014a; cf. also Rogl 2011, 547; 2021). Pia must have been aware of Rogl's position, but without the full exposition of Rogl's chronology and the evidence upon which it was based (only recently published, in Rogl 2021), there was no way she could respond to it. It will be the work of future scholars to resolve this dilemma. At the other end of the sequence, the presence of a nearly complete, signed bowl of Menemachos with large-scale figured decoration in a context of 88 or 69 BCE (destruction debris of the F/NIP building at Delos; Chatzidakis 2000, 116, pl. 64.b, c) seems to document more vigour in the late work of this shop than Pia suggests. I also stand by my contention that moulds, and through this medium, stamps and designs, had an improbably long life. Products of the Monogram PAR potter are documented both in some of the earliest contexts (Cistern F 5:1 in Athens and at Entremont; Rotroff 1982a, 89 cat. 377; Benoit 1947, 82–83) and also in some very late ones. According to P. Chatzidakis, most of the mouldmade bowls in the debris of a Delian tavern destroyed in 88 can be assigned to PAR and Menemachos, and he concludes that both workshops were still in operation in at that date. For the PAR Monogram Workshop, in particular, this is substantially longer than the ca. 25 years Pia allotted to its activity (see Fig. 67).

The reader will immediately notice that this book lacks a conclusion. Of this, Pia completed only the following, single paragraph:

"As we have seen, the bowls are good indicators not just of trade and economy, but also of exchange of technology, ideology, and societal values. In the late 3rd and especially in the 2nd century, the MMB played an important role in the 'elegant living' (Davies 1984, 311 n. 341; Davies 2001, 33) of significant parts of Hellenistic society. Inspired – even repeatedly so – by Ptolemaic court vessels in precious metal (and perhaps glass) they came to spread to the entire Hellenistic world ideas of *tryphe* which were first formulated in the aristocratic milieu of a culturally mixed setting. Increased wealth and increased trade in this period (Gibbins 2001; Morris et al. 2007) made the bowls available to yet larger parts of society. The bowls' imagery celebrated Dionysos, and especially the prominence on the bowls of scenes which we also find on the so-called Tarentine altars takes us to a sphere where some members of society distinguished themselves as initiates into a cult which may have promised, if not a better destiny in this world, then a better one in the next. In Aiolis, the celebration of Dionysos on the bowls obtained its own character, because in this part of the Greek world, probably with Pergamon as the driving force, bowls were decorated as short-hand sanctuary representations, as we can see from the ubiquitous garlands suspended from boukrania and other implements connoting the sacral sphere."

As this brief text makes clear, her study went well beyond the transition from prestige object to object of mass consumption, but I would like to dwell for a moment upon that central theme. There is no doubt that the *Vorbilder* of the mouldmade bowl arose in the cosmopolitan courts of Hellenistic royalty, the highest echelon of contemporary society. These monarchs had adopted the use of precious tableware and the custom of distributing it as gifts from their Persian predecessors (Rotroff 2019; 2020), and the third century was not the first time that those luxurious forms had made the leap from precious metal to clay and from the East to the West. A notable example occurred in late sixth- and fifth-century Athens, where select citizens made use of clay vessels that imitated and emulated Persian silverware (M.C. Miller 1993), even the Achaemenid cup – in shape much like the later mouldmade bowl. But their use was restricted to a small number of drinkers; at least, excavation has recovered only small numbers of fragments of these vessels. Conditions in the 3rd century, however, were different. Contact with the royal courts was closer; diplomatic exchange between the Greek cities and the royal courts was constant, and the kings themselves were even known upon occasion to visit the Greek cities. Opportunities to observe their luxurious lifestyle were more abundant.

The transition from silver to clay seems, on the present evidence, to have taken place at Athens in the last quarter of the 3rd century. Whether the instigator was a visionary craftsman with an eye purely to profit, or a wealthy owner who commissioned copies of his silverware, perhaps with a political or social motive (as gifts for his supporters at a lower level of society?), the mouldmade bowl began to travel slowly down the social ladder. For a generation or so it didn't get far, limited to a small group, presumably of well-to-do Athenians; large numbers of MMB fragments are not found at Athens before the early 2nd century. It was also slow to move laterally outside this geographical area. By the late 3rd century, Athenian ceramics had long lost their cachet and were rarely exported beyond a small radius. But the mouldmade bowl did travel, and a fragment of an early one at the artisans' village on the Rachi ridge at Isthmia (Anderson-Stojanović 1996, 72 cat. 17, pl. 17) suggests we are not talking about rich people moving with their pots. These were commercial exports, probably spearheaded by the potters themselves (or possibly wealthy owners of the potteries, if such existed). A next step was the replication of the type elsewhere, beginning around 200 and accelerating in the following decades. Ultimately, as Rostovcev imagined, "there was hardly any place in the Hellenistic world which had not its own Megarian bowls" (1967, 616). This must ultimately have resulted in a more accessible product, and the mouldmade bowl progressed further towards a product of mass consumption. But, as Pia and others have pointed out, it was not 'mass produced'. Despite the fact that they were made in moulds, each bowl was individually fashioned and finished. P. Kögler, examining products of a workshop dump at Knidos, has developed a theory that the bowls were specifically crafted for people of the middle rank of society – those unable to afford silverware, but far above the 'everyman' of mass consumption. Noting the very rare occurrence of bowls made in the same mould, she postulates a deliberate intention to make bowls that were unique. A potter would produce only one bowl, or at most a set of a few, from each mould, contributing to their desirability as prestige objects (Kögler 2010, 302–303).

Ephesos changed all that. A good harbour, access to pre-existing shipping routes, clay good enough for an attractive product, skilled potters, and presumably wealthy investors made possible the development of the manufactory that lay behind the explosion of Ephesian products in the second half of the 2nd century. They show up in large numbers, and in such humble settings as the homes of artisans and fishermen in Olbia, but they were still precious to some, as the many mended bowls of the Black Sea remind us. As these bowls travelled to the ends of the Hellenistic earth, the transformation from king's chalice to working man's beaker was complete.

Susan I. Rotroff
St Louis, Missouri
1 January 2023

Acknowledgements

It is with great pleasure and deep gratitude that I extend my heartfelt thanks to a multitude of colleagues and institutions which have provided me with access to material and have patiently answered my many questions concerning mouldmade bowls in the Black Sea region and beyond:

Bowls

Bulgaria:
Nessebre Archaeological Museum, Mesambria: A. Bozhkova, P. Kiashkina, T. Marvakov

France:
Paris, Louvre: J. Becq
Lyon, Université Lumière Lyon 2: P. Dupont

Germany:
Berlin, Altes Museum: U. Kästner; DAI *Eurasia Abteilung*: U. Schlotzhauer
Köln, Römisch-Germanisches Museum: F. Naumann-Steckner; *Antikensammlung, Universität zu Köln*: N. Fenn
Bonn: Akademisches Kunstmuseum: W. Geominy

Greece:
Athens, Agora Excavations: S. Dumont; *archive of École Française d'Athènes*: C. Pottet-De Boel, V. Boura, L. Yann, and M. Leclercq
Samothrace: S. Rotroff

Rumania:
Bucharest, Institute of Archaeology, Rumanian Academy of Sciences, Istros: C. Domăneanțu, V. Lungu, F. Matei-Popescu
Constanta, National Museum of Archaeology, Istros, Tomis: L. Buzoianu

Russia:
Bolšoj Kastel', Ďangul', Panskoe I: V.F. Stolba, A.N. Ščeglov
Golubickoe: D. Žuravlev
Moscow, Puškin Museum: Pantikapaion: V.P. Tolstikov, S.A. Kovalenko, N. Astašova; *State Historical Museum: Ruminskoe and collections of Uvarov, Buračkov, and Bertier de la Garde*: D. Žuravlev
Phanagoreia and surroundings: N.J. Lemberis, I.I. Marčenko
St Petersburg, IIMK RAN *archives*: G.V. Dlužnevskaja; IIMK RAN, *Myrmekion*: J.A. Vinogradov; *Porthmion*: M.J. Vachtina; *State Hermitage Museum, Chersonesos*: J.P. Kalashnik; *Myrmekion*: A.M. Butjagin; *Olbia*: A.G. Bukina; J.I. Il'ina; *Pantikapaion*: N.Z. Kunina, D.E. Čistov; *Volna I*: S.S. Solovjov

ACKNOWLEDGEMENTS XIII

Ukraine:
Kiev, Institute of Archaeology, National Academy of Sciences of Ukraine, Olbia in general: V.V. Krapivina, S.D. Kryžiskij; *Olbia Sector NGS*: A.V. Karjaka, N.A. Lejpunskaja; *Olbia Western Temenos*: V.I. Nazarčuk, A.S. Rusjaeva; *Sector R25*: V.V. Krapivina
Parutine, storeroom of the National Preserve of Olbia: Tatiana Shevchenko
Nikolaev Museum: V.A. Michajlov

Altars

Athens: N. Vogeikoff-Brogan; *DAI Athens photo archive*: M. Krumme
Boston, Museum of Fine Arts: B.K. Breed; C. Kondoleon
Chersonesos: J. Carter
Corinth: I. Romano
Kiev, Archaeological Museum: N.A. Lejpunskaja
Olbia: V.V. Krapivina
Oxford, Ashmolean Museum: M. Vickers
Paris, Louvre: J. Becq, A. Couliers
St Petersburg, State Hermitage Museum: J.I. Ilina; J.P. Kalašnik
Taranto, museo archeologico: A. dell'Aglio and A. d'Amicis
Vani: D. Akhvelidiani; V. Licheli; G. Kvirkvelia

Logistics

The following institutions have provided me with shelter during my research: The Danish Institute in Rome, the Danish Institute at Athens, the Danish Culture Institute in St Petersburg (R. Helms), Bikubenfonden, Olbia Archaeological Preserve (V.V. Krapivina). For this I am truly grateful.

Drawings and Photographs

Drawings and photographs are from the author's personal archive, and, except for some of the finds from Olbia, they are the work of the author. Some MMB from Olbia have also been drawn by: S.I. Boldyreva, S. Handberg, T.S. Meršavka, M.M. Zaikin, and L.L. Zaikina and photographs have also been taken by: S. Handberg, J.M. Højte, J.K. Jakobsen, and A.V. Karjaka. I should like to thank all the above-mentioned for their contributions. The inking of a number of bowls from Olbia was done by Hans Joachim Frey. Images are at a scale of 2:3 unless otherwise indicated.

Illustrations

Figures in the Text

1.a–b	Maps of the Black Sea region and the Kimmerian Bosporos	4
2	Table giving the most important corpora of MMB and other significant publications	8–9
3	Workshop attributions according to Laumonier 1977	13
4	MMB found on Delos and their production places	15
5	Hierarchy of elements used for identifying production places and workshops	18
6	Comparison of the size and proportions of Athenian, Kymean, and Ephesian bowls	19
7	Model of the relationship amongst the various elements characterizing a workshop and its circle	20
8	Diagram illustrating the Standard Normal Distribution	22
9	Diagram illustrating the relationship of sample size to the Normal Distribution curve	22
10	Life-cycle model of pottery	23
11	The mouldmade bowls found at Entremont	24
12	E.M. Rogers' adopter categories and the Normal Distribution Curve	27
13	First wave of influence from Alexandria: Athenian and Atticizing productions, first half of 2nd century	27
14	Silver bowl from Bulgaria (British Museum, inv. 1989,0724.1)	28
15	Gold-glass bowl from Canosa (British Museum, inv. 1871,0518.2)	30
16	Drawing of the Canosa gold-glass bowl	30
17.a–b	Silver bowl (J. Paul Getty Museum, inv. 96.AM.160)	31
18	Production places of bowls featuring a filled 'nelumbo'	34
19	Model of diffusion of the filled 'nelumbo' iconography according to current scholarship	34
20	A new model of the diffusion of the filled 'nelumbo' iconography	35
21	Modes of production in the Roman period	39
22	Structure of the 'Mainzer Workshop' as indicated by the punches	41
23	Signatures of the Meter Medallion Workshop	42
24	Names and signing practices in Workshop Circle 1	44
25	Map of Athens showing primary find locations of moulds	46
26	Map of Ephesos showing primary find locations of moulds	47
27	Revised version of Peacock's production model, adapted for the MMB	48
28	Self-sufficiency: the numerical relationship between local products and imports at selected sites	49
29	Distribution of bowls of Argos and Pontic Demetrios at the production site(s) and beyond	50
30	Division of supplementary shapes according to function	54
31	Comparative representation of supplementary shapes in the Pontic assemblages	54
32	Find contexts with supplementary shapes on Delos	55
33	Supplementary shapes present in the Pontic assemblages	62
34	Drawing of *Nelumbo nucifera*	105
35	Photograph of *Nelumbo nucifera*	105
36	Drawing of *Nymphaea lotus*	105
37	Photograph of *Nymphaea lotus*	105
38	Detail of the Nilotic mosaic from the grotto-nymphaeum in the Forum of Praeneste	107

39	Hathor's crown (PER-15)	108
40	Wadjet symbol (EPH-33)	109
41	Charioteer (XXX-3)	109
42	Table of the geographical distribution of 'Tarentine' altars	111
43.a–d	'Tarentine' altar in the Ashmolean Museum, Oxford	113
44	The main corpora of MMB with altar scenes	114
45	Frequency of individual altar stamps	115
46	Mantled dancing women (PER-2)	117
47	Frontal dancing women (KYX-10)	117
48	Silver tetradrachm of Ptolemy IV Philopator, r. 222–205 BCE	119
49	Cake stamp from Alexandria	120
50	Drawing of Myrtle, *Myrtus communis*	121
51	Mosaic in cella of temple of Hera Basileia at Pergamon	123
52	Mosaic in the Altar Room, Palace V, Pergamon	124
53	Tomb of Lyson and Kallikles, south wall	126
54	Coin of Demetrios II, r. 239–229 BCE	126
55	Silver tetradrachm of Antigonos Gonatas, r. 277–239 BCE	126
56	Silver tetradrachm probably struck in Thessaloniki, 183/2–174 BCE	126
57	Comparison of the occurrence of PSC, net-pattern, and long-petal decoration in the Pontic assemblages	127
58	Map of Western Asia Minor	147
59	Frieze dividers on Kymean vessels	169
60	Kymean vessels showing a scene of ritual preparation	171
61	Distribution of products of the Meter Medallion Workshop amongst the artisans of the workshop	192
62	Rim patterns in the Meter Medallion Workshop	196
63	Individual and shared stamps in the Meter Medallion Workshop	198
64	Geographical distribution of vessels of the Meter Medallion Workshop	214
65	Bronze coin of Kyme, 3rd century CE	215
66	Distribution of reduced and oxidized firing amongst Aiolis B vessels	268
67	Ephesian workshops documented in the Black Sea region and their relationships	288
68	Monogram PAR signature from Delos	299
69	Monogram PAR signature from Entremont	299
70	Monogram PAR signature from Istros (EPH-1251)	299
71	Monogram PAR signature from South Russia (Ashmolean Museum, inv. 1966.268)	299
72	Relative and absolute frequency of Ephesian rim patterns in single rim friezes	302
73	Nike racing a two-horse chariot (EPH-54)	308
74	Eagle and winged thunderbolt (EPH-129)	309
75.a–b	Gold octadrachm issued by Ptolemy IV Philopator	311
76	Decorative patterns of the second frieze of multiple rim friezes of Ephesian bowls	314
77	Pine-cone decoration in the Pontic assemblages	315
78	Ephesian calyces	317
79	Rosettes of Ephesian base medallions	322
80	Numbers and percentages of mouldmade bowls from the Pontic sites that form the basis for this study	455
81	Repair with lead clamp in place (EPH-857)	457
82	Repaired MMB in the Pontic assemblages	457
83	Repaired bowls in Olbian sectors with the largest assemblages	457
84	Proportions of Demetrios bowls according to decoration type	460
85	Base types of Demetrios bowls and their frequency	461
86	Bird in calyx of Aiolian bowl (AIB-83)	462

87	Bird in calyx of bowl of Demetrios (DEM-12)	462
88	Frequency of types of decoration of Demetrios bowls	463
89	Correlation between base types and decoration types of Demetrios bowls	464
90	Relative and absolute frequency of Demetrios vessels	466
91	Frequency of the various types of decoration on Demetrios bowls and their distribution	467
92	Map of Olbia indicating the main sectors where MMB studied in this book have been found	494
93	Sector AGD and the Western Temenos at Olbia	496
94	MMB from Bothros 11 at Olbia	497
95	Location of Cistern Л at Olbia	499
96	Chronological distribution of the Rhodian amphorae found in Cistern Л at Olbia	499
97	Chronological distribution of the Rhodian amphorae unearthed in Sector NGS at Olbia	500
98	Distribution of MMB found at Olbia according to production place	503
99	Find places of MMB at Istros	511
100	Distribution of MMB according to production place; Istros compared with Olbia	512
101	Distribution of MMB at Chersonesos according to production place	517
102	Distribution of MMB at Pantikapaion according to production place	523
103	Distribution of MMB at Myrmekion according to production place	529
104	Schematic plan of Hellenistic Porthmion	533
105	Composition of the assemblages at Porthmion and at Myrmekion	535
106	Composition of the assemblage of MMB at Tyritake compared with those at Myrmekion and Porthmion	539
107	Distribution of MMB at Kepoi according to production place	540
108	Distribution of MMB at Ruminskoe according to production place	543
109	Distribution of MMB at Volna 1 according to production place	544
110	Find places of moulds for the production of MMB	592

Plates

1	Athens. Figural decoration (ATH-3 – ATH-15)	631
2	Athens. Figural decoration (ATH-16 – ATH-32)	632
3	Athens. Pine-cone decoration; calyx (ATH-33 – ATH-38)	633
4	Athens. Calyx (ATH-39 – ATH-44)	634
5	Athens. Imbricate decoration; rim fragments (ATH-46 – ATH-58)	635
6	Athens. Rim fragments (ATH-60 – ATH-69)	636
7	Athens. Rim fragment; small bowl; juglet (ATH-70 – ATH-76)	637
8	Aiolis. Figural decoration; garlands (AIX-1 – AIX-8)	638
9	Aiolis. Garlands; calyx (AIX-9 – AIX-16)	639
10	Aiolis. Calyx; imbricate decoration; net pattern; long petals; rim fragment (AIX-17 – AIX-31)	640
11	Aiolis. Rim fragments; supplementary shapes (AIX-32 – AIX-35)	641
12	Pergamon. Figural decoration (PER-1 – PER-10)	642
13	Pergamon. Figural decoration (PER-11 – PER-22)	643
14	Pergamon. Figural and scroll decoration; myrtle wreath (PER-23 – PER-31)	644
15	Pergamon. Wreath decoration; calyx (PER-32 – PER-40)	645
16	Pergamon. Calyx (PER-41 – PER-52)	646
17	Pergamon. Calyx (PER-53 – PER-62)	647

ILLUSTRATIONS

18	Pergamon. Calyx; imbricate decoration; pendent-semicircle design (PER-63 – PER-73)	648
19	Pergamon. Net pattern; long petals; rim fragment (PER-75 – PER-84)	649
20	Pergamon. Supplementary shapes (PER-86 – PER-90)	650
21	Pergamon. Situla (PER-91, PER-92)	651
22	Kyme, Workshop A. Figural decoration (KYA-1 – KYA-8)	652
23	Kyme, Workshop A. Figural decoration (KYA-9 – KYA-15)	653
24	Kyme, Workshop A. Figural and scroll decoration; myrtle wreath (KYA-16 – KYA-24)	654
25	Kyme, Workshop A. Myrtle wreath; garlands (KYA-25 – KYA-36)	655
26	Kyme, Workshop A. Garlands; rim fragments; skyphos with ring handles (KYA-40 – KYA-53)	656
27	Kyme, Workshop A. Skyphos with ring handles; juglet (KYA-54 – KYA-58)	657
28	Kyme, unattributed. Figural decoration (KYX-1 – KYX-8)	658
29	Kyme, unattributed. Figural decoration (KYX-11 – KYX-20)	659
30	Kyme, unattributed. Figural decoration (KYX-21 – KYX-38)	660
31	Kyme, unattributed. Figural and scroll decoration (KYX-39 – KYX-47)	661
32	Kyme, unattributed. Scroll decoration; garlands (KYX-49 – KYX-54)	662
33	Kyme, unattributed. Garlands (KYX-55 – KYX-60)	663
34	Kyme, unattributed. Garlands; calyx with 'nelumbo' (KYX-63 – KYX-71)	664
35	Kyme, unattributed. Calyx (KYX-72 – KYX-77)	665
36	Kyme, unattributed. Calyx; imbricate decoration; pendent-semicircle design (KYX-78 – KYX-88)	666
37	Kyme, unattributed. Long petals; rim fragments; small bowl (KYX-89 – KYX-100)	667
38	Kyme, Meter Medallion Workshop (MMW) (Kyrbeis). Figural decoration (KYB-1)	668
39	Kyme, MMW (Kyrbeis). Figural decoration (KYB-2 – KYB-8)	669
40	Kyme, MMW (Kyrbeis). Figural decoration (KYB-10 – KYB-23)	670
41	Kyme, MMW (Kyrbeis). Figural decoration (KYB-24 – KYB-36)	671
42	Kyme, MMW (Kyrbeis). Figural decoration (KYB-37 – KYB-46)	672
43	Kyme, MMW (Kyrbeis). Calyx with figural decoration (KYB-47 – KYB-54)	673
44	Kyme, MMW (Kyrbeis). Calyx with figural decoration (KYB-56 – KYB-61)	674
45	Kyme, MMW (Kyrbeis). Calyx with figural decoration (KYB-67 – KYB-69)	675
46	Kyme, MMW (Kyrbeis). Calyx with figural decoration (KYB-70 – KYB-85)	676
47	Kyme, MMW (Kyrbeis). Calyx with figural decoration (KYB-86 – KYB-97)	677
48	Kyme, MMW (Kyrbeis). Calyx with figural decoration (KYB-99 – KYB-120)	678
49	Kyme, MMW (Kyrbeis). Calyx with figural decoration (KYB-124, KYB-127)	679
50	Kyme, MMW (Kyrbeis). Vine scroll (KYB-128)	680
51	Kyme, MMW (Kyrbeis). Garlands (KYB-129)	681
52	Kyme, MMW (Kyrbeis). Garlands (KYB-130)	682
53	Kyme, MMW (Kyrbeis). Garlands (KYB-132 – KYB-134)	683
54	Kyme, MMW (Kyrbeis). Garlands (KYB-136 – KYB-145)	684
55	Kyme, MMW (Kyrbeis). Garlands (KYB-146 – KYB-151)	685
56	Kyme, MMW (Kyrbeis). Garlands (KYB-152 – KYB-157)	686
57	Kyme, MMW (Kyrbeis). Garlands (KYB-158 – KYB-171)	687
58	Kyme, MMW (Kyrbeis). Myrtle wreath; calyx (KYB-172 – KYB-178)	688
59	Kyme, MMW (Kyrbeis). Calyx (KYB-179 – KYB-193)	689
60	Kyme, MMW (Kyrbeis). Calyx (KYB-198 – KYB-204)	690
61	Kyme, MMW (Kyrbeis). Calyx (KYB-206)	691
62	Kyme, MMW (Kyrbeis). Calyx (KYB-207 – KYB-228)	692
63	Kyme, MMW (Kyrbeis). Calyx (KYB-230 – KYB-243)	693

64	Kyme, MMW (Kyrbeis). Calyx; imbricate decoration; net pattern (KYB-245 – KYB-255)	694
65	Kyme, MMW (Kyrbeis). Base and rim fragments (KYB-258 – KYB-278)	695
66	Kyme, MMW (Kyrbeis). Rim fragments (KYB-284 – KYB-311)	696
67	Kyme, MMW (Kyrbeis). Rim fragments; small bowl (KYB-312 – KYB-319)	697
68	Kyme, MMW (Kyrbeis). Juglet (KYB-320)	698
69	Kyme, MMW (Kyrbeis). Amphora (KYB-322)	699
70	Kyme, MMW (Kyrbeis). Amphora (KYB-325)	700
71	Kyme, MMW (Kyrbeis). Amphora (KYB-325)	701
72	Kyme, MMW (Kyrbeis). Amphora (KYB-326, KYB-327)	702
73	Kyme, MMW (Possis). Calyx with figural decoration (KYB-330)	703
74	Kyme, MMW (Possis). Calyx with figural decoration (KYB-331)	704
75	Kyme, MMW (Possis). Calyx with figural decoration (KYB-332 – KYB-343)	705
76	Kyme, MMW (Possis). Calyx with figural decoration (KYB-344, KYB-345)	706
77	Kyme, MMW (Possis). Calyx with figural decoration (KYB-346, KYB-347)	707
78	Kyme, MMW (Possis). Calyx with figural decoration (KYB-348, KYB-350)	708
79	Kyme, MMW (Possis). Calyx with figural decoration (KYB-351)	709
80	Kyme, MMW (Possis). Calyx with figural decoration; scroll (KYB-352 – KYB-354)	710
81	Kyme, MMW (Possis). Scroll; garlands; calyx (KYB-355 – KYB-363)	711
82	Kyme, MMW (Possis). Calyx (KYB-364 – KYB-370)	712
83	Kyme, MMW (Possis). Calyx (KYB-371)	713
84	Kyme, MMW (Possis). Calyx; linear decoration (KYB-373 – KYB-386)	714
85	Kyme, MMW (Possis). Linear decoration; base and rim fragments; small bowl (KYB-387 – KYB-411)	715
86	Kyme, MMW (Zenodotos). Calyx with figural decoration (KYB-412)	716
87	Kyme, MMW (Zenodotos). Garlands (KYB-413)	717
88	Kyme, MMW (Zenodotos). Calyx (KYB-416 – KYB-422). Unattributed. Base fragments (KYB-424 – KYB-427)	718
89	Kyme, MMW (unattributed). Figural and scroll decoration; calyx (KYB-428 – KYB-438)	719
90	Kyme, MMW (unattributed). Calyx; rim fragments (KYB-439 – KYB-455)	720
91	Aiolis, Workshop A. Figural and scroll decoration (AIA-1 – AIA-5)	721
92	Aiolis, Workshop A. Myrtle wreath; multiple rim friezes; vegetal and linear decoration (AIA-6 – AIA-13)	722
93	Aiolis, Workshop A. Long petals; rim fragments (AIA-14 – AIA-19)	723
94	Aiolis, Workshop A. Rim fragments (AIA-22 – AIA-36)	724
95	Aiolis, Workshop B. Figural decoration (AIB-1 – AIB-3)	725
96	Aiolis, Workshop B. Figural decoration (AIB-4 – AIB-8)	726
97	Aiolis, Workshop B. Figural decoration (AIB-10 – AIB-25)	727
98	Aiolis, Workshop B. Scroll decoration (AIB-28 – AIB-38)	728
99	Aiolis, Workshop B. Scroll decoration (AIB-39 – AIB-41)	729
100	Aiolis, Workshop B. Scroll decoration; garlands; wreaths (AIB-50 – AIB-65)	730
101	Aiolis, Workshop B. Myrtle wreath; calyx, some with 'nelumbo' and long petals (AIB-66 – AIB-76)	731
102	Aiolis, Workshop B. Calyx with long petals (AIB-77 – AIB-91)	732
103	Aiolis, Workshop B. Long petals; rim fragment; bowl with shell feet (AIB-93 – AIB-115)	733
104	Aiolis, Workshop B. Chalice (AIB-116)	734
105	Aiolis, Workshop B. Bowl with shallow body and high collared rim (AIB-118 – AIB-122)	735
106	Aiolis, Workshop B. Bowl with shallow body and high collared rim (AIB-124 – AIB-130)	736

107	Aiolis, Workshop B. Bowl with shallow body and high collared rim; cup; beaker (AIB-131 – AIB-137)	737
108	Ephesos. Erotes (EPH-1-EPH-9)	738
109	Ephesos. Erotes (EPH-11 – EPH-23)	739
110	Ephesos. Erotes; Eros racing two-horse chariot (EPH-24 – EPH-45)	740
111	Ephesos. Eros racing two-horse chariot (EPH-46 – EPH-52)	741
112	Ephesos. Eros or Nike racing two-horse chariot; hunt (EPH-53 – EPH-61)	742
113	Ephesos. Hunt; animal friezes (EPH-63 – EPH-74)	743
114	Ephesos. Hunt; rabbit and eagle; mantled dancing women; Amazonomachy (EPH-75 – EPH-81)	744
115	Ephesos. Amazonomachy (EPH-82 – EPH-91)	745
116	Ephesos. Battle; mythological figures (EPH-94 – EPH-100)	746
117	Ephesos. Judgement of Paris; labors of Herakles (EPH-101 – EPH-106)	747
118	Ephesos. Scylla; symplegma; feline phallus; dolphins (EPH-107 – EPH-119)	748
119	Ephesos. Dolphins; thunderbolt (EPH-120 – EPH-131)	749
120	Ephesos. Thunderbolt; miscellaneous figures; inanimate motifs (EPH-133 – EPH-150)	750
121	Ephesos. Inanimate motifs; full-body acanthus scroll (EPH-151 – EPH-161)	751
122	Ephesos. Full-body acanthus scroll (EPH-162 – EPH-168)	752
123	Ephesos. Full-body acanthus and acanthus-vine scroll (EPH-169 – EPH-177)	753
124	Ephesos. Acanthus-vine scroll (EPH-182 – EPH-187)	754
125	Ephesos. Acanthus-vine scroll (EPH-189)	755
126	Ephesos. Acanthus-vine scroll (EPH-190 – EPH-195)	756
127	Ephesos. Acanthus-vine scroll (EPH-196 – EPH-199)	757
128	Ephesos. Acanthus-vine scroll (EPH-200, EPH-204)	758
129	Ephesos. Acanthus-vine scroll (EPH-206 – EPH-222)	759
130	Ephesos. Acanthus-vine scroll (EPH-223 – EPH-240)	760
131	Ephesos. Acanthus-vine and acanthus-vine-ivy scroll (EPH-242 – EPH-249)	761
132	Ephesos. Acanthus-vine-ivy and acanthus-flower scroll (EPH-250 – EPH-260)	762
133	Ephesos. Acanthus-flower scroll (EPH-261 – EPH-266)	763
134	Ephesos. Acanthus-flower scroll; stylized acanthus scroll (EPH-267 – EPH-277)	764
135	Ephesos. Stylized acanthus scroll (EPH-279 – EPH-285)	765
136	Ephesos. Stylized acanthus scroll (EPH-287 – EPH-304)	766
137	Ephesos. Stylized acanthus scroll (EPH-306 – EPH-314)	767
138	Ephesos. Stylized acanthus-vine scroll; ultra-stylized acanthus scroll (EPH-315 – EPH-320)	768
139	Ephesos. Ultra-stylized acanthus scroll; myrtle wreath (EPH-321 – EPH-325)	769
140	Ephesos. Myrtle wreath (EPH-326 – EPH-343)	770
141	Ephesos. Myrtle wreath (EPH-344 – EPH-349)	771
142	Ephesos. Myrtle wreath (EPH-352 – EPH-363)	772
143	Ephesos. Myrtle wreath (EPH-364 – EPH-380)	773
144	Ephesos. Myrtle wreath; ivy wreath (EPH-382 – EPH-388)	774
145	Ephesos. Garlands (EPH-389 – EPH-392)	775
146	Ephesos. Garlands (EPH-394 – EPH-398)	776
147	Ephesos. Garlands; suspended wreath; multiple rim friezes (EPH-399 – EPH-407)	777
148	Ephesos. Multiple rim friezes (EPH-408 – EPH-417)	778
149	Ephesos. Multiple rim friezes (EPH-419 – EPH-435)	779
150	Ephesos. Multiple rim friezes (EPH-436 – EPH-444)	780
151	Ephesos. Multiple rim friezes (EPH-445 – EPH-457)	781
152	Ephesos. Multiple rim friezes (EPH-458 – EPH-469)	782
153	Ephesos. Multiple rim friezes (EPH-470 – EPH-481)	783
154	Ephesos. Multiple rim friezes (EPH-483 – EPH-492)	784

155	Ephesos. Multiple rim friezes (EPH-493 – EPH-504)	785
156	Ephesos. Multiple rim friezes (EPH-505 – EPH-515)	786
157	Ephesos. Multiple rim friezes; pine-cone decoration (EPH-516 – EPH-534)	787
158	Ephesos. Pine-cone decoration; calyx A1 (EPH-535 – EPH-550)	788
159	Ephesos. Calyx A1 and A2 (EPH-552 – EPH-569)	789
160	Ephesos. Calyx A2 (EPH-571 – EPH-579)	790
161	Ephesos. Calyx A with filled 'nelumbo' (EPH-580 – EPH-588)	791
162	Ephesos. Calyx A with filled 'nelumbo'; other calyces with 'nelumbo' (EPH-589 – EPH-604)	792
163	Ephesos. Calyx B1 and B2 (EPH-606 – EPH-612)	793
164	Ephesos. Calyx B2 (EPH-618 – EPH-630)	794
165	Ephesos. Calyx B2 (EPH-631 – EPH-643)	795
166	Ephesos. Calyx B; other calyces (EPH-645 – EPH-657)	796
167	Ephesos. Other calyces; calyx C (EPH-659 – EPH-669)	797
168	Ephesos. Other calyces (EPH-670 – EPH-674)	798
169	Ephesos. Other calyces (EPH-675 – EPH-683)	799
170	Ephesos. Other calyces (EPH-684 – EPH-699)	800
171	Ephesos. Other calyces; imbricate rounded petals (EPH-700 – EPH-717)	801
172	Ephesos. Imbricate rounded petals (EPH-718 – EPH-725)	802
173	Ephesos. Imbricate rounded petals (EPH-726 – EPH-731)	803
174	Ephesos. Imbricate rounded petals (EPH-732 – EPH-742)	804
175	Ephesos. Imbricate rounded petals (EPH-746 – EPH-751)	805
176	Ephesos. Imbricate rounded petals (EPH-752 – EPH-757)	806
177	Ephesos. Imbricate rounded petals (EPH-758 – EPH-769)	807
178	Ephesos. Imbricate rounded petals (EPH-770 – EPH-779)	808
179	Ephesos. Imbricate rounded petals (EPH-780 – EPH-792)	809
180	Ephesos. Imbricate rounded and pointed petals (EPH-793 – EPH-807)	810
181	Ephesos. Imbricate pointed petals (EPH-808 – EPH-816)	811
182	Ephesos. Imbricate pointed petals (EPH-820 – EPH-837)	812
183	Ephesos. Imbricate pointed petals (EPH-840 – EPH-859)	813
184	Ephesos. Imbricate pointed petals (EPH-860 – EPH-870)	814
185	Ephesos. Imbricate pointed petals (EPH-873 – EPH-892)	815
186	Ephesos. Imbricate pointed petals (EPH-894 – EPH-900)	816
187	Ephesos. Imbricate pointed petals (EPH-903 – EPH-931)	817
188	Ephesos. Imbricate pointed petals; other imbricate designs (EPH-932 – EPH-947)	818
189	Ephesos. Other imbricate designs; pendent-semicircle design (EPH-948 – EPH-955)	819
190	Ephesos. Pendent-semicircle design (EPH-957 – EPH-973)	820
191	Ephesos. Pendent-semicircle design; net pattern (EPH-975 – EPH-991)	821
192	Ephesos. Net pattern (EPH-993 – EPH-1006)	822
193	Ephesos. Net pattern; plastic long petals (EPH-1007 – EPH-1016)	823
194	Ephesos. Plastic long petals (EPH-1017 – EPH-1032)	824
195	Ephesos. Plastic and stylized long petals (EPH-1033 – EPH-1046)	825
196	Ephesos. Stylized long petals (EPH-1047 – EPH-1062)	826
197	Ephesos. Stylized long petals (EPH-1063 – EPH-1080)	827
198	Ephesos. Stylized long petals (EPH-1081 – EPH-1106)	828
199	Ephesos. Stylized long petals; vertical fluting; rim fragments (EPH-1107 – EPH-1128)	829
200	Ephesos. Rim fragments (EPH-1129 – EPH-1150)	830
201	Ephesos. Rim fragments (EPH-1152 – EPH-1171)	831
202	Ephesos. Rim fragments (EPH-1174 – EPH-1194)	832

203	Ephesos. Rim fragments (EPH-1195 – EPH-1217)	833
204	Ephesos. Rim fragments (EPH-1218 – EPH-1241)	834
205	Ephesos. Rim and base fragments (EPH-1242 – EPH-1258)	835
206	Ephesos. Base fragments; small bowl (EPH-1260 – EPH-1273)	836
207	Ephesos. Small bowl; juglet (EPH-1274 – EPH-1299)	837
208	Ephesos. Juglet; kantharos (EPH-1300, EPH-1301)	838
209	Ephesos. Skyphos; amphora (EPH-1302, EPH-1303)	839
210	Ephesos. Amphora (EPH-1305, EPH-1306)	840
211	Ephesos. Amphora (EPH-1307)	841
212	Ephesos. Amphora; jug (EPH-1311 – EPH-1321)	842
213	Ephesos. Lagynos(?); situla (EPH-1322 – EPH-1328)	843
214	Ephesos. Situla; krater (EPH-1329, EPH-1330)	844
215	Ephesos. Krater; dinos (EPH-1331 – EPH-1335)	845
216	Ephesos. Lentoid guttus; unidentified large shapes (EPH-1336 – EPH-1351)	846
217	Knidos. Figural decoration (KNI-1 – KNI-4)	847
218	Knidos. Figural decoration (KNI-5 – KNI-14)	848
219	Knidos. Concentric circles; myrtle wreath; garlands (KNI-15 – KNI-25)	849
220	Knidos. Multiple rim friezes and calyx (KNI-26)	850
221	Knidos. Multiple rim friezes (KNI-28, KNI-29)	851
222	Knidos. Multiple rim friezes; calyx with figural decoration (KNI-30 – KNI-36)	852
223	Knidos. Calyx with figural decoration; calyx (KNI-38 – KNI-50)	853
224	Knidos. Calyx; imbricate and linear decoration (KNI-51 – KNI-60)	854
225	Knidos. Rim fragments; supplementary shapes (KNI-61 – KNI-75)	855
226	Unidentified production sites. Figural decoration (XXX-1 – XXX-9)	856
227	Unidentified production sites. Scroll; myrtle wreath; garlands; multiple rim friezes (XXX-11 – XXX-21)	857
228	Unidentified production sites. Calyx; imbricate pointed petals; pendent-semicircle design (XXX-22 – XXX-34)	858
229	Unidentified production sites. Pendent-semicircle design; net pattern; long petals; other linear designs; rim fragments (XXX-35 – XXX-47)	859
230	Unidentified production sites. Small bowl; other supplementary shapes (XXX-48 – XXX-61)	860
231	Unidentified production sites. Amphora; lagynos (XXX-63, XXX-68)	861
232	Unidentified production sites. Lagynos(?); krater (XXX-69 – XXX-72)	862
233	Unidentified production sites. Lentoid guttus; large closed shapes (XXX-73 – XXX-77)	863
234	Demetrios. Moulds (DEM-1 – DEM-6)	864
235	Demetrios. Moulds; decoration 1 (DEM-8 – DEM-30)	865
236	Demetrios. Decoration 1 (DEM-32 – DEM-46)	866
237	Demetrios. Decoration 1; decoration 1, 2, or 4 (DEM-49 – DEM-61)	867
238	Demetrios. Decoration 1, 2, 4, or 5; Decoration 2 (DEM-62 – DEM-91)	868
239	Demetrios. Decoration 2 (DEM-92 – DEM-106)	889
240	Demetrios. Decoration 2 and 3 (DEM-107 – DEM-144)	870
241	Demetrios. Decoration 3 (DEM-145 – DEM-166)	871
242	Demetrios. Decoration 3 and 4 (DEM-168 – DEM-192)	872
243	Demetrios. Decoration 4 and 5 (DEM-193 – DEM-214)	873
244	Demetrios. Decoration 5 (DEM-215 – DEM-244)	874
245	Demetrios. Decoration 7 and 8; base and rim fragments (DEM-245 – DEM-257). Getic productions (GET-1 – GET-3)	875

General Information Concerning the Catalogue Entries

Inventory Number

The Russian and Ukrainian inventory numbers are retained. Please note that several localities use the same prefix letter.

А, В, К, Л	Tyritake sectors A, B, K, L
Ке	Kepoi
М	Pantikapaion ('Mithridat', that is, Mithridates Hill, the city's acropolis); Myrmekion
О and Ол	Olbia
Olbia sectors	АГД: AGD. НГС: NGS. НГФ: NGF. P25: R25. СЗ: Sever-Zapad ('northwest'). ЮзА: JuzA ('south A')
П	Pantikapaion; Porthmion
Пан	Pantikapaion
Рум	Ruminskoe (alternative name: Za Rodinu)
СЗ	Severo Zelenskoe, the former name of the site today known as Volna 1
Х	Chersonesos
Ч	Čaika

Measurements

All measurements are in cm unless otherwise stated.
[Ed.: Vessel height and diameter are the most significant figures, but Pia Guldager Bilde (PGB) often includes measurements of fragments. Sometimes these do not precisely match the apparent sizes of the photographic images, discrepancies that stem chiefly from curvature of the fragments, photographic angle, and the point at which measurements were taken.]

Standard Abbreviations

D	Depth
H	Height
H:ø	Ratio between vessel height and rim diameter
RH	Rim height
W	Width
WT	Wall thickness
ø	Diameter

Particular Abbreviations

ccw	Counter clockwise
cw	Clockwise
EC	Ephesos, classical production
EE	Ephesos, early production
EL	Ephesos, late production
LP	Long-petal design

MMB	Mouldmade bowl(s)
PSC	Pendent-semicircle design
WC1	Workshop Circle 1
WC2	Workshop Circle 2
WSl	West Slope

Publication

Unless otherwise stated, the fragments have not been previously published.

Dates and Illustrations

All dates are BCE unless otherwise stated.

An asterisk (*) after the catalogue number, both in the catalogue and in the text, indicates that the piece is illustrated.

PART 1

General Considerations

∴

CHAPTER 1

Introduction

First invented in the 220s in Athens as an outburst of Egyptomania, in all likelihood occasioned by the celebration of the first Ptolemaia in 224/3 (Chapters 3 and 7), the mouldmade bowl some decades later became a popular piece of sympotic equipment, and, after the middle of the 2nd century, an item of mass production and consumption. The bowls have been found all over the Hellenistic world, from Spain in the west to Afghanistan in the east, and from Tanais in the north to Libya in the south (Pierobon 1985, 83; Guldager Bilde 1993; Rogl 2008a, 26). After their introduction at Athens they were soon produced in most of the larger cities of the Mediterranean and of the Black Sea region, and they were also copied in Hellenized, non-Greek areas such as Central Italy and amongst the Getes north of the Danube (Appendix 4). When the supply did not meet local demand, bowls were acquired from outside sources, be they local, regional or long-distance. Therefore, at most sites, the corpus of bowls will attest to a multitude of different sources. Because our understanding of the individual production places is still relatively crude, this has led to an 'attribution game' which has often blurred our understanding of trade and exchange rather than furthered it.

To date, research on MMB has primarily been concerned with the finds of individual sites occasioned by what has come to light by chance at the given place (Chapter 2). Comparative studies are rare. Moreover, much research on MMB has been influenced by the common negative attitude to Hellenistic art in general and to minor arts in particular which has prevailed during large parts of the 20th century. Their ornamentation has been considered almost exclusively decorative and hence without any potential meaning. Surely, were our bowls products of an earlier epoch, we would never have allowed ourselves to approach such a large body of material with such an off-hand attitude. And by doing so, we miss a golden opportunity to consider the social and religious life of the late Hellenistic period.

Our understanding of the chronology of the MMB is still coarse, and a good synchronization of the various production places is yet to be created. We know that they were produced over a relatively short time span: from the 220s to sometime in the first half of the 1st century, but the end date in particular is still imperfectly known. By and large, the MMB was a product of the 2nd century, and these vessels are thus a convenient dating tool for field archaeologists. But they are more than that: they can inform us of networks of trade and communication, of social networks, and they offer us the possibility of studying first-hand the lives of the people who made and used them: their taste and choices and their social and religious behaviour (e.g., Chapters 3, 4).

It was as a student in the 1980s in the excavation of the Temple of Castor and Pollux in the Roman Forum that I first encountered a small group of MMB – three fragments of the same bowl produced in the Ephesian workshop of the Monogram PAR potter and five small fragments of Italo-Megarian bowls – and I have been fascinated by this category of pottery ever since (Guldager Bilde 1993; 2008). For many intervening years, I worked on other matters, which had little to do with Hellenistic pottery, but in 2003, when, as director of the Danish National Research Foundation's Centre for Black Sea Studies, I initiated a collaboration with colleagues of the Institute of Archaeology of the Ukrainian Academy of Sciences in Kiev on the publication of the excavations of the houses in Olbia's Sector NGS carried out between 1985 and 2002 (Chapter 20), I seized the opportunity to work with the MMB once more. It was clear to me how little Western scholars know about the MMB found in the Black Sea region (and vice versa). The main aim of the Black Sea Centre was to provide a forum where Eastern and Western scholars could meet, so that knowledge could flow between the two regions, which for a large part of the 20th century had been kept apart for political reasons. My work with the Olbian MMB fitted this aim. Over the following years it became possible for me, through the help of many Eastern colleagues who were willing to share their material with me, to study the MMB found at further Black Sea sites too.

The main data of the book comes from my first-hand study of the MMB found in 11 different towns and cities of the northern and northwestern part of the Black Sea region (Fig. 1.a, b). The analysis of this material constitutes the core of this book (Chapters 21–31). The Black Sea assemblages I have had access to vary a great deal in size. The largest body of material comes from Olbia and Istros in the northwestern part of the region. Another large group of finds comes from the Bosporan Kingdom, from its capital, Pantikapaion, and from a number of larger and smaller sites located within the kingdom on both the

© PIA GULDAGER BILDE AND SUSAN I. ROTROFF, 2024 | DOI:10.1163/9789004680463_002

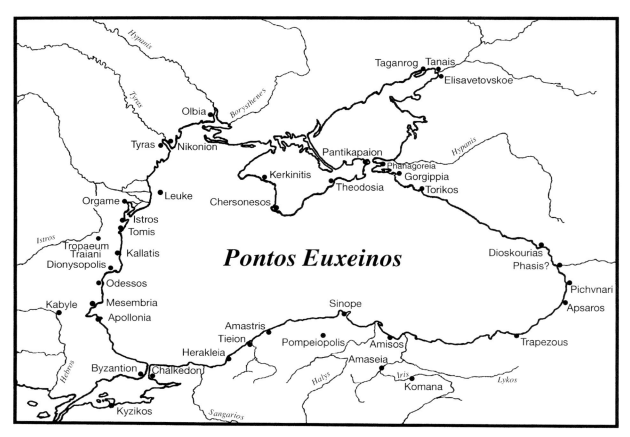
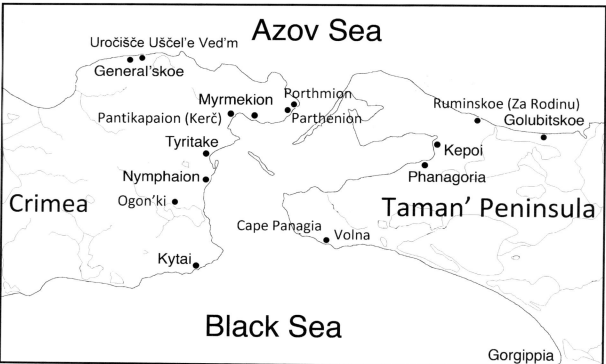

FIGURES 1.A, B   Maps of the Black Sea region and the Kimmerian Bosporos with sites discussed in this book. Adapted from Guldager Bilde et al. 2007–2008, figs. 1 and 19 and reproduced with the kind permission of Jakob Munk Højte

European and Asiatic side of the Kerč Strait. The smallest group comes from Western Crimea, from Chersonesos and from Bol'šoj Kastel', a fortified farmhouse in Chersonesos' distant chora. These two sites bridge the geographical gap between the Greek poleis of Istros and Olbia on the one hand and the Bosporan Kingdom on the other. I have incorporated all the material from the 11 sites that I have been able to lay my hands on and I have studied most of the fragments and vessels first hand. The majority of these have never been published before. However, in order to be as complete as possible, I have also included published material – even if I have not seen it myself. The corpus of MMB from any of the 11 sites thus consists of a heterogeneous body of material. In the statistical analyses employed throughout the book, I have divided the data into three categories depending on the trustworthiness of the identification of the individual pieces:

- Evidence category A (abbreviated ECA): fragments which I have studied first-hand (ca. 4,000 vessels).
- Evidence category B (abbreviated ECB): fragments which are published with illustration, or which are otherwise documented with photographs and/or drawings in various archives (ca. 900 vessels).
- Evidence category C (abbreviated ECC): fragments which are mentioned in publications without illustrations (ca. 400 vessels).[1]

In most cases, ECB fragments can and will be used in the statistics as primary data; at least the description of shape and decoration should be valid and, in most cases, also the ascription to a production place. ECC is more problematic, because I have not had the opportunity to verify the author's ascription and because some of these pieces may overlap with fragments in one of the two other groups. Therefore, they are included only as complementary material in statistics and catalogues; they will not be discussed any further.

I have several aims in the present book. Firstly, I want to present primarily to a Western audience a comprehensive corpus of MMB which have come to light in the northern and northwestern Black Sea region. This will fill a gap in the knowledge of Hellenistic pottery in the region as well as demonstrate, through the analysis of Mediterranean imports, how and to what degree this region was part of the Hellenistic ceramic koine and belonged to contemporary trade networks. Secondly, I want to employ this very large corpus to draw some general conclusions concerning the major production places represented in our assemblages: the Aiolian workshops, including the Kymean ones, the Ephesian workshops, and the Knidian workshops. Thirdly, I want to use the same material to consider in more general terms issues such as production, workshop organization, distribution and trade, and iconography and 'meaning'.

I should like to underline that I will not discuss production places and workshops unrelated to the Pontic assemblages. Thus, the prolific Greek mainland, Macedonian and Levantine workshops will just be touched upon only very briefly in passing.

In order to realize the above-mentioned aims, the following five-step procedure will be followed:

- The first step is concerned with the proper identification of the individual fragments and vessels. This part of the book is heavy on empirical material, and because I have chosen to document all data used, catalogues will necessarily take up a considerable amount of space.[2] Nevertheless, this part of the book constitutes the necessary basis for drawing any kind of historical conclusions.
- The second step is an analysis of some of the best-represented production places. This is done by viewing all of the Pontic assemblages, as well as finds from other sites – be they Pontic or Mediterranean – which are of relevance for the appropriate workshop, as *one assemblage*. Only by doing so can we obtain enough material to meet minimum requirements in terms of statistical validity, and, through statistical analysis, side-step some of the biases individual assemblages may have in terms of, for example, chronology. This is the reason why the main catalogue of the individual fragments is given in the chapter on the production place rather than in the chapter on the find place.
- The third step is an analysis which cuts across the production places. This is where we consider the more general and overarching questions such as workshop organization and production as well as iconography.
- The fourth step is an analysis of the finds at the 11 individual Pontic sites. This will be done in order to characterize the assemblage and its composition in terms of production places represented and the chronology. A list of catalogued vessels is appended to each site

---

1 The majority of these are fragments listed in Bernhard 1959 (Myrmekion) and in Kovalenko 1989 (only fragments ascribed to the production of Demetrios or the Meter Medallion Group are taken into account).

2 Ed. With the exception of the catalogues of the Ephesian and the unattributed material (Chapters 14 and 16), left uncompleted by PGB; only a selection of the total corpus is presented in these two cases.

chapter, arranged by production and then by decorative scheme, to provide a quick overview of each assemblage.
- The fifth and final step is a comparative analysis of the Black Sea assemblages. This part of the book allows us to consider overall questions such as distribution and trade.

The order of the chapters will not follow the order of the procedural steps. Even though it is an aim of the book to present the empirical material, the MMB, it is not an end goal in itself: it is a tool with which we can create an understanding of the men and women who made them, who moved them, who used them, who repaired them, and who in the end discarded them, and how these actions took place in time and space.

Throughout the present book, fragments of MMB are treated as bulk material, not as individual art objects. Therefore, more weight is given to tables with statistics than to lengthy descriptions of fragments which have the same decoration as the sherd preceding and following them in the catalogues. Nevertheless, decoration is also considered.

The cognitive process behind producing a mould is not unlike writing: stamps are like letters or words, selected individually and placed in context with further stamps, most commonly in horizontal registers, creating the final 'document' with its own internal hierarchy consisting of 'paragraphs', 'headers', and 'footers'. Therefore, we may approach the moulded object as we would approach a written text, by looking at the 'words' and the structure or 'syntax' with which they are grouped in order to convey 'language' and ultimately 'meaning'. Moreover, the bowls follow local and regional patterns of syntax and grammar. 'Loan words' may occur, but by and large the individual production places follow their own individual development. A semiotic reading of MMB as we would read a language can therefore help us to establish local productions, and to understand how they were related to other productions; we will also employ this type of reading in order to investigate 'meaning'.[3]

With few exceptions, MMB did not travel far beyond the place of their production and its immediate surroundings, and regionalism prevailed (Chapter 4). A good case is the only major Pontic production, that of Demetrios in the Bosporan Kingdom (Chapter 17). Of course, there are exceptions: Athenian bowls are found in discrete numbers throughout the Mediterranean and Black Sea region, whereas the Aiolian workshops are well-documented in the Black Sea region throughout the 2nd century – much more so than in the Mediterranean. A special case will be the investigation of one of the Kymean workshops, which I have termed the Meter Medallion Workshop. Its products primarily went to the Pontic area, and in previous research it was believed that this was also the home of the workshop's main potter, Kirbeis (Chapter 11).

I have also been able to verify the presence of Knidian MMB at most Pontic sites – at hand, in fact, in slightly larger numbers than Athenian bowls in the same area. But the largest production place of all was Ephesos, which after the middle of the 2nd century came to dominate the market throughout the Hellenistic world (Chapter 14). This is the only production place which can be classified as a true manufactory, as an attentive analysis of signatures will show (Chapter 4). The dominance of Ephesian workshops in the Black Sea region, where on average 65% of the assemblages comes from Ephesos, has occasioned a closer analysis of this production site and not least of A. Laumonier's *La céramique hellénistique à reliefs. Ateliers 'Ioniens'* (Exploration archéologique de Délos XXXI), published in 1977, in which the largest corpus known to date of Ephesian vessels has been published (Chapters 2 and 14, Appendix 2).

---

3 A good introduction to the theoretical frame for reading pictures as signs can be found in Hölscher 2000, 160–164.

CHAPTER 2

History of Research

MMB and the other shapes that were made in the same moulds pose a diverse array of questions. What was the name of the vessel in antiquity? And if this cannot be established, what term can we employ to describe the vessel as correctly (but also as economically) as possible? Where and when was the MMB first produced? And what inspired its first production? Where was it emulated? At what pace and to what extent did this take place? What were the patterns of trade in these products? And because the bowls were made in moulds, thus involving an element of mechanical reproduction, to what extent did copying of stamps and moulds and even trade in the same take place? How do we interpret their decoration? Was it purely ornamental? Or did it have an intended meaning? When did the production cease?

Many of the above questions have been addressed in past and current research, but most still lack an adequate answer. In the following, we shall briefly discuss the main trends within research on MMB.

Terminology

Terminology first. The bowl's ancient name has not been established with certainty, although numerous suggestions have been brought forward, such as *gyalas*, a bowl employed by the Megarians (Ath. Deip. 11.467c; Benndorf 1883, 117–118; Zahn 1940, 57), *skaphion*, *mastos*, or *skyphos* (Robert 1890, 3–4), *kymbe/kymbion* or *kotyle* (Courby 1922, 278), *hemitomos* (Ath. Deip. 11.470d; Edwards 1956, 83–84) or *kondy* (Ath. Deip. 11.477f–478a; Rotroff 1982a, 3), and in the infancy of the study, the vessels were identified with the *vasa Samia*[1] mentioned by many Roman authors (references in Waagé 1937). Below, in Chapter 6, I will argue for *kiborion*. However, as long as the ancient name eludes us, we are in want of a descriptive term. 'Megarian bowl' has had a long life and general acceptance, but we know it is wrong. It was coined by O. Benndorf in 1883, when he published a number of plaster casts of relief bowls; since they were believed to come from Megara, he therefore identified them with the Megarian *gyalas*. However, the vessels published by Benndorf are Athenian (Rotroff 1982a, 2). Rotroff has argued – and rightly so – that we ought not to perpetuate the use of an inaccurate term, even though it is tempting, because a truly almost-all-encompassing term is somewhat cumbersome: Hellenistic hemispherical mouldmade ceramic relief bowl, in short mouldmade bowl (Rotroff 1982a, 2–3). Throughout the book, I follow Rotroff's terminology (abbreviated MMB), even though the term is somewhat awkward when it comes to describing the supplementary shapes, many of which were *not* intended for drinking (Chapter 5).

Main Trends in the Study of Mouldmade Bowls

For most of the 20th century, Hellenistic pottery has not been particularly in vogue. This is mirrored in the relatively small number of publications devoted to MMB prior to the 1970s.[2] Publications of MMB have primarily been occasioned by finds made at individual sites and subsequently published as part of the field documentation. However, four monographs of the late 1970s and early 1980s contributed to a change in the scholarly community's attitude to the MMB: Laumonier 1977 on the Ephesian MMB found on Delos, Siebert 1978 on Peloponnesian MMB, Sinn 1979 on Macedonian MMB, and Rotroff 1982a on MMB from the Athenian Agora. These four publications spurred further attention to the subject, and since they saw the light, we can note an accelerated interest in the MMB, as witnessed by the number of publications devoted to them.

Moreover, the 1980s saw a new interest in the Hellenistic world. This was before the fall of the Iron Curtain and in the 'infancy' of globalization, when the many parallels between past and current society occasioned considerable interest in the period and its material culture, including its pottery. Thus, in the mid-1980s, Thessaloniki-based scholars, of whom S. Drougou was the driving force, initiated a series of very successful international conferences devoted entirely to Hellenistic pottery. The first was held in 1986, and to date, eight have taken place and a ninth is scheduled for 2012 (*Synantisi gia tin ellinistiki keramiki*). Of the eight conferences, at the time of this writing, six

---

[1] Robert 1890, 3 n. 2; Mahler 1924, 3–7 still argued for its use.

[2] The Black Sea literature will be discussed in Chapters 17–30; for the sake of overview, the main Black Sea contributions are also included in Fig. 2.

\multicolumn{3}{c	}{Mediterranean}	Year	\multicolumn{3}{c}{Black Sea region}
General study	Regional study	Site study		General study	Regional study	Site study
	Robert ('Homeric')		1890			
	Siebourg (I-M)		1897			
			1902	Latyčev (Kirbeis)		von Stern (Olbia situla)
		Zahn (Priene)	1904			
			1908			Boehlau and Zahn (Olbia; Vogell collection)
		Conze (Pergamon)	1912			
		Pagenstecher (Alexandria)	1913			
Courby			1922	Courby		
			1924	Mahler (dissertation)		
		Paribeni (Tivoli moulds)	1927			
Zahn (PSC)			1940			
		Schwabacher (Athenian Kerameikos), Baur	1941			
		Waagé (Antioch)	1948			
		Jones (Tarsos)	1950			
		Kraus (Mainz)	1951			
Byvanck-Quarles van Ufford (chronology)			1953			
Parlasca (rel. to Alexandria)	Ohlenroth (I-M)		1955			
		Edwards (Pnyx)	1956			
	Avilés (Spain)		1957			
	Jones (I-M)		1958			
Byvanck-Quarles van Ufford	Hausmann (Athens, Boeotia)	Arribas & Arribas (Pollentia)	1959			Blavatskij (Pantikapaion)
			1962		Šurgaja, Loseva (BK)	
Greifenhagen			1963			
			1964	Jentel (Louvre)		
		Hellström (Labranda)	1965			
	von Vacano (I-M)		1967		Casan-Franga (Geto-Dacian)	
		de Luca (Pergamon, Asklepieion), Jentel (Louvre), Schäfer (Pergamon)	1968			
	Arena (I-M)	Metzger (Eretria)	1969		Ocheseanu (Rumania)	Šelov (Tanais)
		Christensen (Hama)	1971			
Byvanck-Quarles van Ufford		Bouzek & Jansová (Kyme)	1974			Platek (Myrmekion)
		Edwards (Corinth), de Luca (Pergamon, Asklepieion)	1975			
			1976	Turcu		Vulpe & Gheorghiță (Popești)
		Laumonier (Delos), Siebert (S. Sabina wreck)	1977			

FIGURE 2   The most important corpora of MMB, and other significant publications. BK: Bosporan kingdom; I-M: Italo-Megarian. Contributions in the series Συνάντηση για την ελληνιστική κεραμική are not included.

HISTORY OF RESEARCH

	Mediterranean		Year		Black Sea region	
General study	Regional study	Site study		General study	Regional study	Site study
Callaghan (PSC)	Siebert (Peloponnesos)	Isler (Samos)	1978			Usačeva (Kepoi)
	Sinn (Macedonia)		1979			
Callaghan (myrtle)		Marabini Moevs (Cosa)	1980			
Callaghan (chronology)		Edwards (Corinth)	1981			
Callaghan (long petal), Rotroff (chronology)		Rotroff (Athens Agora), Heimberger (Thebes)	1982			
			1984			Samojlova (Tyras), Zabelina (Pantikapaion)
		Pierobon (Iasos)	1985	Bouzek		
		Edwards (Corinth), Negev (Oboda)	1986			
			1987			Kovalenko (Kirbeis)
	Brusić (Liburnia)	Hidri (Durrachium)	1988			
			1989	Kovalenko (habilitation)		
		Kossatz (Milet), de Luca (Pergamon)	1990	Bouzek		
		Mitsopoulos-Leon (Ephesos)	1991			
		Massa (Hephaistia, Lemnos)	1992			
Guldager Bilde		Akamatis (Pella)	1993			
			1994			Samojlova (Olbia)
	Puppo (Italy)	Rosenthal-Heginbottom (Tel Dor)	1995			
		Hausmann (Olympia), Rogl (Elis)	1996		Kovalenko (BK)	
		Gassner (Ephesos), Kraniotis (Abdera), Cornell (Tell Anafa), Leotta (Tivoli)	1997			
			1998	Kovalenko		Vnukov & Kovalenko (Kara Tobe)
		de Luca (Pergamon, altar sounding)	1999			
			2000			Domăneanțu (Istros)
Rogl (Signatures)		Krinziger et al. (Ephesos)	2001			
		Künzl ('Mainzer Werkstatt')	2002			Batizat, (Tyras)
		Rotroff (Sardis)	2003			
			2004			Tolstikov & Žuravlev (Pantikapaion)
			2005	Bouzek		
Rotroff (innovation)		Körpe (Assos)	2006		Irimia (Rumania)	Kropotov & Leskov (Krinički), Rusjaeva & Nazarčuk (Olbia)
			2007		Maslennikov (chora of BK)	Kovalenko (Čaika)
		Rogl (Lousoi)	2008			Šapcev (Bulganak)
		Kögler (Knidos)	2010		Grzegrzółka (BK)	Guldager Bilde (Olbia)

have been published and two more are in press.[3] They furnish us with a wonderful corpus of recent discoveries and discussions concerning Hellenistic pottery in general, and a multitude of articles include or are completely devoted to MMB. Archaeologists' interest in the Hellenistic world in the 1980s reached its zenith when the 13th International Congress of Classical Archaeology was held in Berlin and entirely devoted to the Hellenistic period (published in 1990).

From this time on, it has been more 'mainstream' to work with Hellenistic pottery and, therefore, also with MMB. And as we can see from Fig. 2, which sketches the development of scholarship with the indication of the more important contributions, the corpus of bowls brought to the attention of the scholarly community is rapidly expanding our knowledge of various production places.

In addition to the site-specific investigations which dominate the study of MMB, some more comprehensive publications have espoused a regional approach, such as Siebert 1978 (Peloponnese), Sinn 1979 (Macedonia), Brusić 1988 and 1999 (Liburnia), and Bouzek 1990 (Black Sea region). Similarly, the so-called Italo-Megarian bowls have mostly been studied in their entirety as a group, no matter where they were produced (e.g., Puppo 1995). One further regional study merits mention, S.A. Kovalenko's Habilitation, defended at the State University of Moscow in 1989, *Antičnaja rel'efnaja keramika III–I vv. do n.e. v Severnom Pričernomor'e*. Unfortunately, this important work, which is concerned with the MMB in the Black Sea region, remains unpublished.[4]

From Fig. 2, it is clear that we possess a rich corpus of material from many sites. What are scarce are more overall, synthetic and comparative studies. Two very old studies, both from the 1920s, are the only ones I know of which endeavour to consider the MMB in their entirety. The first is *Les vases grecs à reliefs*, published by F. Courby in 1922. This is the first major monograph dedicated to all kinds of vessels with relief decoration. Its long chapter V *La céramique à reliefs hellénistique: les bols* (pp. 277–447) concerns the MMB. Because the book was written when the study of the MMB was in its infancy, many of Courby's conclusions have not stood the test of time. This is first of all true concerning his attributions to production places. For example, Courby was of the opinion that the bowls found on Delos, which he had studied first-hand, were also produced there (1922, 378–398); they are, in fact, Ephesian (see Chapter 14). He also discussed the 'Crimean workshops' (1922, 408–413 [our Meter Medallion Workshop, see Chapter 11]) primarily based on Zahn 1908. His placement of Olbia in the Crimea is clearly a mistake, and so, as we shall see, is the attribution of the Meter Medallion Workshop to the Black Sea region.

Almost contemporary was Else Mahler's dissertation, *Die Megarischen Becher*, defended at the University of Basel in 1924.[5] The dissertation, which was supervised by Olbia's excavator, B.V. Farmakovskij (see Chapter 20), is based mainly on unpublished material in German museums and in St Petersburg (collections of the former Archaeological Commission and the State Hermitage Museum). The dissertation was never published, and it has therefore been completely forgotten.[6]

From the infancy of the study until today, an art historical approach has been the main method with which to address the bowls. This was especially clear in the 1950s, when debate centred on the origin of the MMB and its relationship chiefly to Alexandrian vessels of precious metal and glass (e.g., Byvanck-Quarles van Ufford 1953; Parlasca 1955; Byvanck-Quarles van Ufford 1959). If we leave aside publications which are either site-specific or synthetic, of what Orton, Tyers & Vince have coined 'the big three' of ceramic study – chronology, trade, and function/status (Orton et al. 1993, 23; Orton & Hughes 2013, 24–32) – chronology has been the main battle ground in research on MMB. In 1968, two important studies of Hellenistic pottery found in Pergamon were published: J. Schäfer's general study and the first volume of G. de Luca's publication of the pottery from the Asklepieion. While the first went unnoticed amongst scholars working with MMB, the latter with its stratigraphical approach soon became much cited. In the late 1970s and early 1980s, P.J. Callaghan wrote a series of articles on the chronology of various decorative motifs employed on the MMB: the pendent-semicircle motif (1978), the myrtle wreath (1980), and the long-petal motif (1981; 1982). His publications were chiefly dependent on the Pergamene publications; in fact, Callaghan was the first to notice the importance of the small group of MMB excavated in the foundation fill of the Great Altar in Pergamon and published in Schäfer 1968 (Callaghan 1981; 1982). In response to Callaghan's articles on the Pergamene chronology, the excavators of Pergamon undertook new excavations in the foundation of the Great Altar in order to obtain more

---

3 [Ed. As of 2020, 9 volumes have been published: A'–Θ'.].
4 I am grateful to S. Kovalenko for lending me his personal copy of the habilitation.
5 I am grateful to the University Library of Basel for lending me the original dissertation. Regrettably, it is incomplete; there are no plates (and not even a list of plates) and no bibliography.
6 It is mentioned in Parlasca 1955, 130.

material with which to refute Callaghan's low chronology (de Luca & Radt 1999). We shall return to the arguments in Chapter 6. The contextual approach in Rotroff's 1982a publication of the finds from the Athenian Agora added further fuel to the issue of chronology, and it underlined the potential of wells and cisterns as closed deposits (also Braun 1970; Rotroff 1988; Rotroff 1994b; Hausmann 1996; Ladstätter et al. 2003; Tolstikov & Zhuravlev 2004).

The last two of Orton, Tyers & Vince's 'big three' – trade and function/status – have received much less attention. The latter has not been addressed in a systematic way at all, even though several scholars mention in passing their view of how the bowls were perceived by their ancient users (e.g., Thompson 1934, 456; Edwards 1956, 90). The study of trade is an obvious one, but because we lack comparative studies, it is difficult to evaluate patterns of distribution; nevertheless, we do have some contributions which touch upon this aspect (e.g., Siebert 1978; Bouzek 1985; 1990; Guldager Bilde 1993; Rogl 2008a; Kögler 2010).

The Study of MMB in the 21st Century

Where do we stand today? The most pressing issue, of course, is the correct identification of the production place of any given fragment as well as its proper chronology, because this constitutes the baseline for any use we may want to make of it as a source for the history of economy, distribution and consumption, and without it, any attempt to answer questions of the kind mentioned above is bound to fail. Even though many production places and workshops are well described today, there are still significant gaps in our knowledge. For example, we are still in want of a definitive characterization of Pergamon as a production place and of the Pergamene workshops (see also Chapter 9), and even when it comes to Ephesos, the largest producer of all, we still have to lean on Laumonier's publication of the Delian corpus from 1977.[7] A way for the future is a more intensive use of archaeometric investigations. This has already been done at a small scale with interesting results (Kerschner et al. 2002; see also Chapters 12 and 13).

Moreover, research on MMB has had difficulty moving beyond its art-historical roots; thus, MMB are almost completely unexploited as sources for social and intellectual history. This has perhaps primarily to do with the generally low regard scholars have for 'copies' in contrast to 'originals' – and being objects of repeated production in a material as base as fired clay has not lent much prestige to the bowls. However, a study such as S. Rotroff's article from 2006, "The Introduction of the Moldmade Bowl Revisited: Tracking a Hellenistic Innovation" (*Hesperia* 75, 357–378) breaks new ground.

Before we end this discussion of the history of research, I should like to offer a more detailed consideration of a monograph which is of the highest importance for the current study: Alfred Laumonier's *La Céramique héllénistique à reliefs* 1. *Ateliers "ioniens"* (*Exploration archéologique de Délos* XXXI) from 1977. It belongs to the site-specific corpora and its approach is exclusively art historical.

Delos XXXI: A Reassessment

Delos XXXI is a monolith in the research on MMB. The book is concerned exclusively with what Laumonier terms the 'Ionian' bowls, which we now know were of Ephesian production, as eminently attested by the more than 100 moulds discovered in that city (Chapters 4 and 14 and Appendix 4). Laumonier 1977 is the main corpus one must consult if one wants to understand the Ephesian production. And since at any given site in the Black Sea region, Ephesian bowls constitute from 50 to more than 90% of the MMB, it is obviously of vital importance to understand this important production place.

In *Delos* XXXI, Laumonier published complete bowls and fragments of ca. 6,000 individual vases, of which two-thirds are illustrated with a black-and-white photograph, mostly at a scale of 1:2. Because the book is so monumental, it has enjoyed not just enormous use – but also considerable misuse. It is therefore appropriate to take a closer look at it and at the unpublished volume 2, which was planned to supplement it.

Alfred Laumonier (1896–1988) was trained as an ancient historian, and he was promoted from Casa de Velázques in Madrid in 1917–1918. In 1920 he was a member of the École Française d'Athènes under the direction of Ch. Picard. His earliest works were concerned with terracotta figurines. In 1921 he published his *Catalogue de Terres cuites du Musée Archéologique de Madrid*, and in 1956 he issued his first contribution to the *Exploration archéologique de Délos*, namely vol. XXIII, *Les figurines de terre-cuite*. In the 1930s he made his first exploratory trip to Caria, which resulted in his monograph *Les Cultes indigènes en Carie* published in 1958. The *Ateliers "ioniens"* was the last major work from his hand, published in 1977 when he was 81. This was preceded by three lesser studies: on MMB in Spain

---

7 [Ed. Note the recent publication of two important books that address these gaps: Rogl 2021 on the MMB of Ephesos and de Luca 2021 on the MMB of Pergamon.]

(Laumonier 1962) and in Toulouse (Laumonier 1967) and a general article on MMB (Laumonier 1973).

Delos XXXI is a corpus of MMB deriving from the French excavations on the island during the years 1904–1936, 1946-mid-50s, and 1958–1968. It is based on and supplements Courby 1922, and it also takes over its methodology in arranging the catalogue according to workshops (Laumonier 1977, 1). Its lack of consecutive catalogue numbers makes it extremely difficult to use.[8] In order to provide for myself an overview of the material (not to speak of a key to the book), I have entered Laumonier's table of the different 'workshops, series and categories' into a database (Laumonier 1977, 489–512).[9] A summary of this database with a complete concordance to Laumonier's text and plates is furnished as my Appendix 2.

Laumonier's Methodology

Volume 1 (and 2, see below) is organised according to heterogeneous classificatory principles, partly by 'workshop', partly by iconographic features (e.g., 'Floral'), and partly by technological features ('Vases gris'). Laumonier does not consider formal elements, such as shape, and he is sceptical of technical criteria such as fabric and coat (Laumonier 1977, 14), so when it comes to classification, he takes his point of departure in isolated elements, such as the rim pattern or the acanthus leaf of the lower body, instead of considering the sum total of the decorative elements, or at least the main decoration. A good example is his treatment of the potter signing My(…). His production is very characteristic in terms of shape, vessel proportions, and decoration. Nevertheless, Laumonier distributes bowls of My(…)'s production among no less than seven different workshops and two unclassified groups, because he took the rim pattern as his point of departure when defining the workshops in question. Consider, however, that the stamp for making the rim was used perhaps 30 times to make the rim pattern of a single bowl (e.g., 30 stamped ovules of the Ionian kyma), while the base stamp was used just once on the same bowl. This implies that the stamp for the rim pattern became worn more quickly and may have been discarded as much as 30 times as frequently as the stamp for the base medallion! Clearly, it is a much more 'economical' solution to group the vessels by the overall formal and iconographic criteria mentioned above, and this leads to a much more logical grouping of the vessels within the production of a single mould maker (more on My(…) in Chapter 14).

Workshops (Ateliers) *According to Laumonier*

Laumonier defined 14 major workshops (1977, 13):
- Apollonios
- Athenaios
- Belles Méduses
- CI [with lunate sigma: the transliteration ought to be Si(…)]
- Comique à la canne (and his circle)
- Doubles filets épais
- Hera(ios)
- Menemachos (and his circle)
- Monogram PAR (and his circle)
- NI (and his circle)
- Petite rose spiralée
- Philon (and his circle)
- Plagiaire
- Vases gris

According to Laumonier, the products of the Monogram PAR Workshop constitute almost one fourth of the entire Delian corpus (23.3% according to his attributions). In addition, there are two more large workshops making up ca. 9% of the corpus each: Hera(…), which Laumonier reconstructs as Hera(ios) (8.8%), and Menemachos (8.8%), as well as two smaller but still significant workshops, both making up slightly less than 6% of the corpus each: Philon (5.5%) and the Plagiaire (5.7%). 1,604 vessels, over one-fourth, were either not classified, or classified in small series, and many rim fragments were left out completely (Laumonier 1977, 13).

With such a large corpus at hand, there is no reason to compromise on methodology. In order to define the workshops, the best point of departure is analysis of the complete vessels, because only then are we completely certain of the relationship between the individual elements of the vessel. Of the ca. 6,000 individual vases in Laumonier's corpus, only 255 are complete in the sense that we have all elements of the vessel preserved in joining fragments, so that the overall decorative scheme can be assessed, as can the relationship between height and rim diameter. It is quite interesting to see how his workshops are represented by complete vessels, and as can be seen, there seems to be no relationship between number of complete vessels preserved and number of vessels attributed to the particular workshops (figures are summarized in Fig. 3). The workshops of the Vases gris, Belles Méduses and Monogram PAR are underrepresented among the complete pieces; the number of complete vessels attributed to Menemachos corresponds well with the number

---

8 The same is the case with the manuscript for volume 2, which employs the same methodology.
9 The tedious work of preparing this concordance was done by Line Bjerg and Elin Wanting, whom I thank heartily.

HISTORY OF RESEARCH

Laumonier 1977	Main workshop				Circle (*annexe*)			
	# of vessels	% (100%=5,993)	# of complete vessels	% of complete vessels	# of vessels	% (100%=255)	# of complete vessels	% of complete vessels
24 small series[a]	196	3.3	9	3.5				
Animés	124	2.1	3	1.2				
Apollonios	78	1.3	4	1.6	8		1	
Athenaios	92	1.5	8	3.1	5		1	
Belles Méduses	151	2.5	3	1.2				
CI	104	1.7	16	6.3	62	1.0	5	2.0
Comique à la canne	156	2.6	9	3.5	89	1.5	2	
Doubles filets épais	74	1.2	9	3.5	6			
Geometric decoration	130	2.2	2					
Écailles aigues	147	2.5						
Écailles arrondies	93	1.6	3	1.2				
Écailles ogivales	50		1					
Étoiles carrées à 6 branches creuses	60	1.0	2					
Floral	125	2.1	1					
Hera(ios)	530	8.8	27	10.6				
Imitations	11		2					
Long petal	238	4.0	3	1.2				
Menemachos	530	8.8	22	8.6	65	1.1	1	
MEP	25		3	1.2	4		1	
Monogram PAR	1,394	23.3	29	11.4	36			
NI	95	1.6	12	4.7	1			
Philon[b]	329	5.5	25	9.8	10		1	
Plagiaire	342	5.7	32	12.5				
Petite rose spiralée	99	1.7	3	1.2				
Rapace	60	1.0						
Rosette à 5 pétales échanchrés	52		2					
Signatures	66	1.1	7	2.7				
Vases gris	121	2.0	2		5			
Vegetal	160		4	1.6				

FIGURE 3   Workshop attributions according to Laumonier (1977)
Notes:
a. The 24 small series encompass from two to 24 fragments each;
b. Items ascribed to Philon include Ra-, My-, and imitations.

of attributed vessels (again according to Laumonier's identifications); whereas the workshops of CI, NI, Philon and the Plagiaire are much overrepresented among the complete vessels. This may point to a catastrophic event, such as one of the 1st-century sacks of the island, following which the (complete) late bowls were deposited.

Chronology according to Laumonier

The individual pieces published by Laumonier are rarely furnished with contextual information. At most the general locality, such as 'Kabirion' or 'Samothrakeion', is mentioned, but this does not suffice to help us clarify issues of relative or absolute chronology.

Laumonier discusses the applicability of stylistic dating, which he rejects (1977, 11) but in fact cannot avoid. His maxim *plus le vase est réussi du point de vue esthétique et technique, plus il a de chance d'être ancient* is applicable, but difficult to handle, and he therefore also resorts to the development of, e.g., the acanthus as the main defining criterion of the individual workshops. In general, he is not much concerned with matters of date. Nevertheless, he proposes a brief relative chronology (1977, 11–12), which we paraphrase below:

(1) Menemachos seems to represent the oldest current, as suggested by his more naturalistic acanthus leaves and more refined taste. The technique of his motifs is more assured, the motifs livelier and more original than those of the other makers, with a great variety of nelumbo with animated scenes and very few long petals. His many figured subjects recall Attic and Boeotian vessels, but an Ionian spirit can be detected in the foliage teeming with birds and Erotes and a general Dionysiac and erotic exuberance. Belle Méduses and Vases gris are also among the early workshops.

(2) Monogram PAR is in the centre of the production, with vegetal decoration already stylized and an eclectic repertoire.

(3) Philon with long petals and Heraios with imbricate petals mark the return to simple decorations and signal the end of the production.

(4) CI and Plagiaire date to the 1st century, the Plagiaire between 89 and 69.

The remaining workshops are not placed in the relative sequence.

Concerning absolute chronology, Laumonier himself writes that records of the contexts of the old finds are too vague or lacunose to be useful, but he observes that MMB are generally absent from 3rd-century strata. He therefore believes that the production could be placed between the years 166 and 69, the time when the island was a free port (Laumonier 1977, 7).

Laumonier 1977 is difficult to circumvent in terms of the size of the catalogue alone. In many ways, however, it has been a stumbling block rather than a help for past research, and today its many formal and methodological weaknesses makes it difficult to use as anything but a pool of illustrations. In fact, the best thing to do would be to re-classify the entire corpus and also include the fragments from other production places and of other shapes found on the island. But who will undertake such an immense task? Until someone does, I suggest that the publication be used with the utmost care, especially as regards its ascription of individual fragments to workshops. In Chapter 14 we shall return to the Ephesian workshops.

Volume 2: The Manuscript in L'École Française d'Athènes

The volume on the 'Ionian' bowls that appeared in 1977 was published as *La Céramique héllénistique à reliefs* **volume 1**, and, as we can glean from p. 13, at least one successive volume was planned. In this, vessels from other production places (Athens, Pergamon, Argos, Antioch, the production of Kirbeis, etc.) found on the island were to be published together with the vessels of other shapes, such as 'grandes vases' (skyphoi, kraters, filter-vases) and 'petites vases' (jugs and lagynoi), which had not been ascribed to the workshops of the first volume.

Regrettably, the planned volume has never seen the light of day. This is deplorable, because, even though of monumental proportions, volume 1 remains incomplete because it concerns only the finds of a single production place – we simply do not know the context of the Ephesian bowls when we are unaware of the other productions.

In March 2011 I had the opportunity to study Laumonier's hand-written manuscript for the second volume.[10] The manuscript is kept in the archive of the École Française d'Athènes. It was deposited there in July 2009 by G. Siebert, who had been entrusted by Laumonier with its publication.[11] The material consists of three boxes with notes, some sketches, rubbings of the decoration of most of the fragments, a handwritten manuscript, and layout

---

10   I am very grateful to the director and collaborators of the archive, C. Pottet-De Boel, V. Boura, L. Yann, and M. Leclercq for access to the archive.

11   I am grateful to G. Siebert, who readily answered my questions on the manuscript (March 2011).

for plates (archival reference *Delos 3-H (5)*). Non-Ionian bowls are rendered in 11 plates (marked I–XI), whereas the remainder is given in 33 plates (marked 1–33). According to the manuscript (p. 3), the organization of the second volume is as follows:

I *Grandes vases variés*
II *Skyphoi à queue d'aronde* [skyphoi with 'swallow-tail' handles; a mix of different productions, techniques and chronology, few of which are MMB]
III *Vases-filtres*
IV *Lagynoi* [gutti]
V *Vases à barbotine* [late Republican Thin-walled Ware, mostly dot-festooned beakers]
VI *Vases cannelés: amphores, bols, skyphoi, fragments* [black-gloss vessels with vertical ribbing, not MMB]
VII *Petits vases fermés*
VIII *Bols guillochés* [mostly Knidian bowls with rouletting]

To this are added the non-Ionian bowls. As is clear from the above, volume 2 was quite mixed in its content and was not restricted to vessels made in the mouldmade technique. My study of the manuscript made it clear that an additional 502 MMB were intended for publication – very few, in fact, considering the ca. 6,000 Ephesian bowls published in volume 1. Laumonier attributed relatively few of these to a production place; most were simply classified according to their decoration, such as 'végétaux et animés', 'atelier à décor végétal de belle qualité' or 'Macedoine'.

Of the 26 bowl fragments which Laumonier suggested were Attic, in my opinion, only five actually are so (nos. 5478, 9468, 9719, 9722; 68E 9318), whereas one fragment which he classifies as Pergamene must be Attic (no. 1376, pl. V, a very fine early piece surely moulded directly from a metal vessel). Three fragments were ascribed to Argos (nos. 362, 3173, 3419, pl. IV). The last-mentioned is signed by Demetrios-Iason, so its attribution is unproblematic. He ascribed only eight fragments to the Pergamene production, and of these, perhaps three actually come from Pergamon (nos. 4113, 8458, 9168), whereas he attributes 28 fragments to Antioch. I am not certain that any of these pieces actually came from there; two are Ephesian (nos. 1190, 3207) and one is perhaps Knidian (no. 3434). Conversely, one fragment which he ascribes to Italy seems to be Levantine, to judge from the occurrence of the Levantine version of the heart-bud ornament as rim pattern (no. 1548). He attributed no more than six fragments to the workshop of Kirbeis (nos. 482, 483, 1372, 2206, 3281, 9546, pl. III). Of these, two were signed (nos. 2206 [KYB-106], 9546 [KYB-215]); one further fragment (no. 1372 [KYB-192]) securely belongs to the MMW, and one most likely belongs to the same workshop (3281 [KYB-78]), whereas two cannot qualify as belonging to this workshop (nos. 482, 483).

Laumonier grouped a considerable number of fragments (51 in all) together as products of the *atelier des Abeilles* (the bee workshop). He does not suggest a production place for this group, even though he (correctly) mentions that two fragments (nos. 2056, 3106, pl. 1) which he considers related to this workshop could be Knidian, based on a fragment in the British Museum (59–12.26.209) excavated in the Temenos of Demeter in Knidos. It is beyond doubt that most of these fragments can be ascribed to the Knidian production (possible exceptions: nos. 3104, 8016, 9098). This may even be true of the four fragments which he attributes to a workshop which he baptized *atelier à la Grue* (nos. 1386, 3048, 3303, 3304, pl. IV).

If we turn to the supplementary shapes, it is first of all striking that a considerable number of filter jugs were found on the island (see Chapter 5), of which no less than 73 were recorded in the manuscript. Some were probably

Production place	Sum	%
?	336	5.2
Aiolis? (grey)	1	
Argos	1	
Argos?	3	
Athens	6	0.1
Athens?	46	0.7
Elis	1	
Ephesos	6,005	92.5
Ephesos?	28	0.4
Knidos	40	0.6
Knidos?	13	0.2
Kyme	5	0.1
Kyme?	1	
Levant?	1	
Pergamon	3	
Pergamon?	5	0.1
Grand total	6,495	

FIGURE 4
The number of MMB found on Delos and their production places, based on Laumonier 1977 and the unpublished manuscript in the École Française d'Athènes; the ascriptions have been emended by me. The high number of items from "Athens?" is due to the uncertainty as to whether the filter jugs Laumonier assigned to an Attic provenance are really Attic.

manufactured at Athens, some at Ephesos and some, undoubtedly, on Delos – at least, a mould with long petals separated by circles found on the island corresponds well to the main decoration of the filter jugs.[12] Also quite prominent are large kraters decorated with long-petal pattern (plastic and stylized), many of them in a grey fabric. I do not know where these were produced.

In terms of MMB productions represented on Delos, the overwhelming majority, 92.5%, is Ephesian (Fig. 4). The same had already been noted by F. Courby, who wrote: *Les bols du type que j'appellerai 'délien', parce qu'ils constituent la presque totalité de la collection de Délos …* (1922, 378). It is strange that Athenian vessels dating to before, say, 150 are virtually absent.[13] It is also interesting to note that, by and large, the Aiolian products did not go west, but north towards the Black Sea region (Chapters 9–13), whereas Knidian production is slightly better represented, but again, in lesser relative numbers than we find in the Black Sea region (Chapter 15).

---

12 Courby 1922, 392–393 cat. 159, pl. IX.d; Laumonier 1973, 254; Laumonier 1977, 2; Chatzidakis 1997, 302, pl. 223.a; Künzl 2002, 77 cat. 9.

13 [Ed. In addition, missing from Fig. 4 are at least 366 Attic bowls which were found in the early excavations on Delos and were studied by Laumonier, but, mysteriously, are not included in the manuscript of his second volume. They can be seen in the excavation storerooms on the island, and a selection have now been published (Rotroff 2018). Quite a few date before 150.]

CHAPTER 3

Methodology

In this chapter, we shall discuss some overall issues related to the study, analysis, and interpretation of production, identification, and dissemination of MMB as well as general considerations concerning the construction of chronologies. The chronology of individual production places is discussed in the appropriate chapters, and the date of individual decorative patterns occurring at more than one production site is discussed in Chapter 6.

The data upon which the book is built comes from a multitude of assemblages excavated at 11 different Black Sea localities. These assemblages are of a heterogeneous character in as much as they can be anything from individual closed contexts, such as finds from a grave or a pit, to finds from an entire site. Moreover, the fragments have been brought to light throughout the 20th century (and some vessels were even found in the late 19th century). Therefore, the fragments represent many excavators and their (or their superiors') individual field strategies. Indication of an object's context may be recorded, but, regrettably, in most cases, this information is not available.

Representativity and Quantification

Because of their easily recognizable decoration, most excavators have tended and tend to consider fragments of MMB as 'diagnostic', even if only body fragments are preserved. Therefore, in most of the assemblages I have been working with, the fragments of MMB seem to have been retained for analysis instead of being discarded, even though the size of the fragments can be very small, often as little as 1 cm². Accordingly, we do not face the problem of how representative a given body of fragments is of an original 'parent population'; on the contrary, I believe that we can be relatively confident that what was found, was kept.

Breakage patterns follow the overall size and wall thickness of the individual vessels; obviously, smaller vessels break in fewer pieces, and the thicker the vessel wall, the larger the fragments (Orton & Tyers 1992, 172). Preservation and fragment size also reflect depositional and post-depositional processes. Only in the case of primary deposits, where the fragments have not been moved after they were deposited (e.g., tombs and deposition resulting from 'catastrophic events'), are fragments large; complete (or near-complete) vessels characterize this type of deposit, whereas small, battered fragments suggest a different deposition story, namely that they could have been moved several times. This is often the case with secondary fills, for example. Thus, the relative size of the fragments will reflect the character of the deposit (see Orton & Tyers 1992, 172).

In order to evaluate workshop output and the relationship between the distribution of various workshops and production places in time and space, it is necessary to have comparable figures which allow us to calculate relative proportions. There are four basic methods which can be applied for quantifying pottery (and glass) (Orton et al. 1993, 168–171; Orton & Hughes 2013, 203–218.):

(1) Count of fragments
(2) Weight of fragments
(3) Estimated vessel equivalents (EVE)
(4) Estimated minimum number of vessels represented (EMN or EVRep) (Orton et al., 21, 172, 178; Orton & Hughes, 2013, 21–22, 207, 208–213, 215–216, 218).

The first two are self-explanatory and of little use if one wants to consider how the fragments of a given assemblage can be taken to represent an original number of vessels.

The calculation of the EVE is quite complicated, and it can be based on weight, surface area, or proportions. Calculating the EMN or EVRep is much simpler: fragments with the same properties are considered part of a single vessel even though no join can be established. The drawback , however, is that identification is intuitive and cannot be objectively verified, and that the sample size will influence the number of estimated vessels. Nevertheless, I have chosen to operate with the EMN or EVRep. Thus, I do not count individual fragments as one vessel, but attempt to attribute each fragment to a complete vessel. When in doubt, I count one sherd as one vessel. According to this method, the number of fragments will be considerably larger than the number of estimated vessels represented. However, the moulded decoration often makes the ascription of fragments to a single vessel easier and the result thus more plausible than in the case of fragments of undecorated wares.

© PIA GULDAGER BILDE AND SUSAN I. ROTROFF, 2024 | DOI:10.1163/9789004680463_004

Identifying Production Centres and Workshops

One of the fundamental challenges when working with a heterogeneous body of MMB is to identify the production place of individual fragments, not to speak of individual workshops. If we want to use the MMB for discussing issues such as chronology and trade, the proper identification of the individual fragment's production place is of paramount importance. However, since our knowledge of many productions is still coarse, the 'attribution game' can lead to many misidentifications. I endeavour to apply a relatively minimalistic approach to attributions. Thus, if in doubt, I do not ascribe the given piece to a production place. This has the effect that in every assemblage we must accept a certain proportion of unclassified fragments. In the Black Sea assemblages, such fragments range from a few percent to around 11%; the occasional higher percentages given in Fig. 80 (summarizing figures for all 11 sites) are due to the fact that, when part of the data comes from publications, correct attribution is less certain than in the cases where I have studied the material myself.

Basically, two sets of methodologies can be employed in order to localize a pottery production: one is the spatial distribution of resources, ceramic styles and/or artefacts (Orton & Hughes 2013, 235–245); the second is archaeometric analyses (Rice 2015, 100, 249, 376, 384–387; Orton & Hughes 2013, 18–20). The first, which is the dominant one, is also the most problematic because of its subjective character, whereas the second is costly and therefore sparingly applied. However, archaeometric analyses are becoming more and more common, and, as we shall see, they have the potential to answer many of the questions that scholars have struggled with (Chapter 11).

G. Siebert, in his 1978 book on the Peloponnesian workshops, has discussed the conditions which he believes are necessary for the reliable definition of workshops. These are commonsensical and therefore worth repeating (Siebert 1978, 8; see also Rogl 2008a, 32):

(1) A certain number of inscriptions
(2) A certain number of fragments
(3) Access to the actual fragments

The first condition is difficult to meet in the case of the many workshops which did not have the habit of signing their products (see Chapter 4). Concerning the number of fragments, Siebert is of the opinion that 100 vessels and fragments are the minimum necessary for establishing a workshop. I think this is a good rule of thumb, but workshops differed. Some used a large number of individual stamps; others were more repetitive. It goes without saying that the more stamps used in a workshop, the more fragments are needed to provide an understanding of the

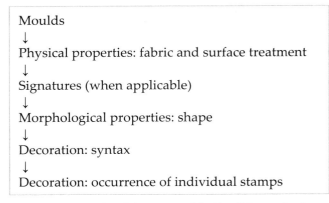

FIGURE 5   Hierarchy of elements used for identifying production places and workshops

workshop. The discussion in Chapters 11 and 12 concerning the Kymean workshops fully illustrates this point. Siebert's third condition is also important. Much material can be identified from photographs when the workshop has already been well defined through previous research, though colour photographs are obviously of more use than the more common black-and-white ones. However, illustrations do not do full justice to the physical properties – the fabric and surface treatment – of a ceramic fragment. So access and especially repeated access to the vessels is important.

The criteria for identifying production places and individual workshops employed throughout this book are based on a hierarchy of individual features of the single vessel (Fig. 5).

Moulds

Most important, of course, is the discovery of moulds, which beyond doubt attests to a production site. Moulds have been found at more than 80 localities (Appendix 4). They are the best evidence we have for identifying a production place. Although moulds could be and were traded and exchanged between workshops and between sites, the presence of a mould, even an imported one, at a site is a robust indication of production.

Physical Properties

The vessels' physical properties, that is, their fabric and surface treatment, have been and can be adduced as evidence for production places. However, to date in the scholarly literature, fabric and surface descriptions are almost exclusively based on visual inspection of the fragments (as also in this book) – if they are mentioned at all. Naturally, such descriptions are subjective and thus quite coarse, and they can only lead to broad classifications. Amongst most Black Sea scholars, for example, the

	Date range	Rim diameter Range	Rim diameter Average	Height Range	Height Average	H:Ø Range	H:Ø Average
Athens[a]	220-100(?)	12-17	14-15	7.3-9.6	7.7-8.8	1:1.6-1:1.9	1:1.7
MMW	175-130	12-14	13	7.1-8.8	7.8-8.5	1:1.5-1:1.9	1:1.7
Ephesos	150-100	12-13	12	6-7.3	6.5-7.2	1:1.8-1:2.2	1:1.8

FIGURE 6   Comparison of the size and proportions of Athenian, Kymean, and Ephesian bowls. Figures are based on the data in Rotroff 1982a and in the present book

presence of 'mica' is normally taken as an indication of an Asia Minor provenance of any given sherd. Once archaeometric analyses become more common, this defect will be remedied.

Even though there is considerable local and regional variation, there was a general tendency for the colour of the surface of oxidized vessels to evolve over time from black to red. This is in line with the development of late Hellenistic fine wares in general. Thus, Athenian bowls were (and remained) black, and the early workshops outside Athens imitating the Attic production also produced vessels with a black surface finish (e.g., Argive, early Pergamene and Ephesian vessels, Kymean vessels). In the kiln, the vessels were stacked inside one another but separated by a small clay ring.[1] In many cases, the ring prevented the interior of the bowl from being fully fired black, leaving a red medallion on the vessel's floor. In some workshops, beginning before the middle of the 2nd century, vessels were fired while stacked inside each other without the use of such devices. This gave the vessels a bi-colour appearance. For example, ca. 15% of the Kymean vessels show signs of being stacked in this way during firing. In all likelihood, the classical Ephesian workshops cultivated this effect by deliberately manipulating firing conditions. Thus, the vessels became very characteristically bicolour, with a black band at the rim on the exterior and a red interior and lower external body.

Workshops producing vessels with a reduced, hence grey, finish existed throughout the 2nd century. This kind of finish was most popular in Aiolis, where in fine wares, grey fabrics had centuries of tradition preceding the manufacture of MMB. However, a grey finish was also frequently encountered further south. Thus, almost one third of the Ephesian vessels of the Black Sea assemblages are of a reduced fabric, and even the Knidian production excelled in a fabric which was grey at the core with a thin oxidized coat (Chapter 15). Amongst the latest workshops employing this type of finish are Aiolis B (Chapter 13) and Pontic Demetrios (Chapter 18).

Signatures

When present, signatures are obviously of importance for assigning individual vases to a particular potter. However, as we shall see in Chapter 4, far from all workshops had the habit of signing their moulds or bowls – rather the contrary. And even when a signature is present, we cannot be certain that the same signature necessarily refers to the same person (see, for example, Chapter 11 on signatures starting with Pos- and Chapter 18 on multiple potters by the name of Demetrios).

Morphological Properties

Even though the MMB were all potted inside hemispherical moulds, their shape varied over time and space (Fig. 6). Variables are the way the rim was shaped and the height of the rim over the moulded part, as well as the diameter of the rim and the vessel's height. Whereas the first two are landscape specific, the latter two vary with time.

The point of departure was the Athenian bowls, the first ones to be made. They were quite deep, mainly between 7.3 and 9.6 cm (mostly 7.7–8.8 cm), and their rim diameters were also relatively large, between 12 and 17 cm, most commonly 14–15 cm.[2] Accordingly, the ratio between height and rim diameter was between 1:1.6 and 1:1.9, with an absolute peak at 1:1.7. The rim was straight and everted, and only the shape of the lip varied. Not surprisingly, the Athenian shape was widely imitated in the early workshops outside Athens, such as at Argos (Siebert 1978), Kyme (Chapters 11–12), and Knidos (Chapter 15), in the Levant, and in the early Ephesian Südtor Workshop (Chapter 14).

The Kymean Meter Medallion Workshop shows the development of the Athenian shape in the 2nd quarter of the 2nd century (Chapter 11). Bowls have a rim diameter predominantly between 12 and 14, with 13 cm being the most common; the height is mostly from 7.8 to 8.5 cm,

---

1 Such rings are reported, for example, from the Athenian Agora (Rotroff 1982a, 93 cats. 414–415, pl. 72; Rotroff 1994b, 19), from the Pnyx (Edwards 1956, 88–89, figs. 3, 5, pl. 50), and from Hephaistia in Lemnos (Massa 1992, pl. 84; 1997, 346).

2 Measurements derive from Rotroff 1982a and from bowls in the Pontic assemblages.

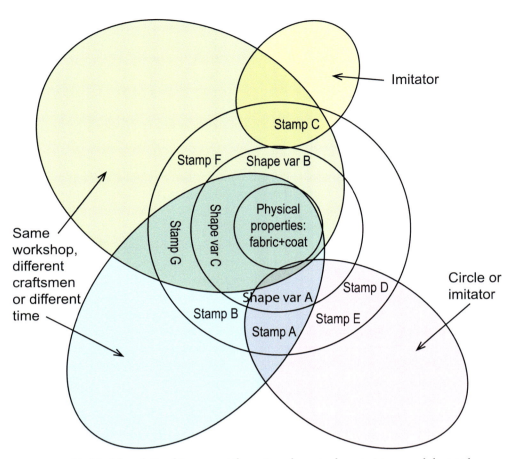

FIGURE 7 Model of the relationship amongst the various elements characterizing a workshop and its circle

and the ratio of height to diameter ranges from 1:1.5 to 1:1.9 with 1:1.7 being the most common.

After the formative years of production and imitation of MMB, roughly the first half of the 2nd century as illustrated by the Kymean MMW, the shapes of the bowls in the different workshops became much more diverse. A good example is the Ephesian workshops. In contrast to the Athenian bowls, Ephesian bowls of the classical and late production (see Chapter 14) became first of all very standardized and secondly, they became smaller: lower and with a smaller rim diameter. Their height was normally between 6 and 7.3 cm (mostly 6.5–7.2 cm) and their rim diameter between 12 and 13 cm, with 12 cm being most common. Accordingly, the ratio between height and rim diameter was higher than that of the Athenian bowls, namely 1:1.8–1:2.2, most commonly 1:1.8. With time, Ephesian bowls grew lower and lower, and the H:ø ratio accordingly larger. After the middle of the 2nd century, the shape of the rim also differed from the Athenian shape: now it became slightly in-turned with a plain rounded lip, and over time, the height of the rim over the moulded section diminished. Other workshops also excelled in new rim shapes, for example Aiolis B with a tall, concave rim. A similar shape was employed by the Central Italian workshops (Puppo 1995).

Decoration

The very technology of making mouldmade vessels has induced scholars to believe that the decoration says relatively little about the production place, because, as Laumonier writes of the acquisition of stamps: *on s'imitait, on se copiait, on se surmoulait, on s'empruntait des poinçons, ou on se les achetait, ou même sans doute on se les volait* (Laumonier 1973, 256). Trade in moulds has been suggested (Laumonier 1973, 254), but it is difficult to prove. The moulds found on Lemnos, both at Hephaistia (Massa 1992; 1997) and at Myrina (Archontidou-Argyri 1994), which at first appear to be Athenian, nevertheless turn out to have a local flavour when considered in detail. Therefore, they are to be considered Lemnian, but Atticizing. Only because the Lemnian assemblage of moulds is so large (Appendix 4) is it possible to reach this conclusion. If only a single or a few fragments were at hand, we would probably have considered them Athenian. Similarly, a mould found at Sardis with a very fine and detailed representation of a saluting Pan flanking a Dionysiac three-figure group (Chapters 6 and 11) could be imported (from Kyme? or from Ephesos?); at the least, it is strikingly different from the other moulds found in the same city (Rotroff 2003, 102 cat. 402, pl. 67). Also on Samos, some fragments of moulds have been excavated which could be copies or imitations of Ephesian moulds, or even imports from Ephesos (Tsakos 1994). Three of them (Tsakos 1994, pls. 229.b, c, 330.g) are very close to the Ephesian production, but a fourth (pl. 230.a) should teach us that matters on Samos were as complicated as on Lemnos, for this fragment combines a calyx of undoubtedly Ephesian imprint with a frieze which seems to be original to Samos – at least, the large archer depicted there does not find any Ephesian parallels I know of. The best example of an imported mould seems to be the one found at Lousoi, which on account of its fabric is ascribed to a non-local source, perhaps Corinth (Rogl 2008a, 41 cat. 24, pl. 30; 88–89 Scherbentyp 7). Rogl ascribes one further mould fragment to a non-local source, perhaps Patras, though on the basis of more ambiguous characteristics of the fabric (Rogl 2008a, 45 cat. 46, pl. 31). The way in which physical properties, decoration, craftsmen, and workshops may be interrelated is modelled in Fig. 7.

We shall return to this argument in more detail below. In general, I am sceptical as to large-scale copying of stamps, since it must have been so much easier to produce a fresh stamp than to copy one. What may have been copied (and I would rather say imitated or emulated) were overall ideas. Examples could be the lines of fine dots, ultimately inspired by punches on metal vessels, which were very common on Athenian vessels, and which were imitated in earlier workshops, for example at Ephesos (e.g., EPH-204*, EPH-719*), but (mostly) abandoned in the later ones with the exception of Aiolis B. Also probably of Athenian inspiration are the birds and minute flying Erotes in the Meter Medallion workshop, for example, (Chapter 11), and similarly, a number of figural elements, such as hunting scenes in early Ephesian workshops. In the cases mentioned, however, it was the idea rather than the stamps themselves which was copied (more on the common pool of decoration in Chapter 4). When it comes to the secondary decoration of rims and bases, I do not find it likely that copying took place (Rotroff 1982a, 25–26 is of the same opinion). A multitude of workshops could share the same element, such as the box meander (mainly employed in Ephesian workshops, but also found at Pergamon); again, it was the general design, not the stamp that was emulated. The same holds true of the Ephesian medallion, where the same type of rosette could be used by several potters, but not the same stamp.

Even though stamps and figural elements may ultimately have been borrowed from other workshops, in terms of decoration syntax, most workshops developed their own language. We cannot go further into the issue of decoration in this chapter; instead, I refer to Chapter 6 for decoration used at multiple production places and Chapters 8–15, 18–19 for the particular decoration of the individual production places.

Distribution

In this section we shall discusses various issues related to the distribution of the pottery. First we discuss its distribution in time: Normal Distribution and chronology. Then we discuss distribution in space, which draws on network analysis and agency and also on the diffusion of innovations.

The Central Limit Theorem and Normal Distribution

Throughout the book I will be using the *Central Limit Theorem* and its expression in the *Standard Normal Distribution*, also called the Gaussian distribution. This theorem operates with a theoretical finite average or mean (μ) and a finite variance (σ_3), and it gives us a theoretical distribution of probability. The resulting graph will always be bell-shaped, with a peak at the mean. Thus, theoretically, ca. 68% of a given data set (in dark blue) will be less than one standard deviation from the mean, while two standard deviations from the mean (medium + dark blue) account for about 95%, and three standard deviations (light + medium + dark blue) account for about 99.7% of any given data set (Fig. 8).

The Central Limit Theorem demonstrates mathematically that the larger the dataset, the closer the distribution of the average will be to the Normal Distribution (Fig. 9).

We will meet the Normal Distribution in the following sections, where we shall use it for predicting, for example, the chronological variation in a deposit. The underlying assumption is that the use of any type of pottery follows a regular pattern: Not in use → increasing use → steady use → decreasing use → no longer in use. Orton & Hughes (2013, 226–228) write that "it is not necessary to assume that the chronological distribution of a type follows a normal distribution, although there may be superficial similarities"; I am less sceptical, and the discussions in this book will show why.

The Normal Distribution can also be employed for considering the output over time within a workshop or

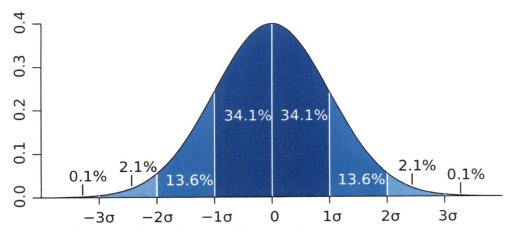

FIGURE 8   The Standard Normal Distribution (diagram by M.N. Toews).
http://en.wikipedia.org/wiki/Normal_distribution (accessed 2/12/22)

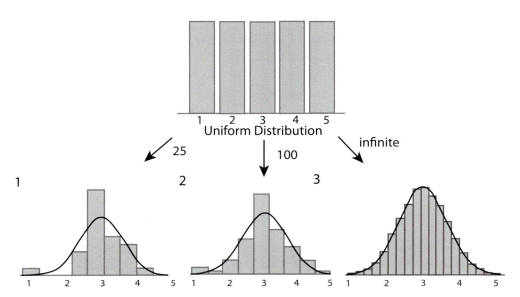

FIGURE 9   The larger the sample size, the closer its distribution comes to the Normal Distribution.
After http://www.wadsworth.com/psychology_d/templates/student_resources/workshops
/stat_workshp/cnt_lim_therm/cnt_lim_therm_09.html (accessed 10/11/20)

production site, provided that production was continuous and not subject to an abrupt change, such as sudden destruction.[3] Rhodian amphorae, which were stamped throughout the 2nd century with the annually changing name of the Halios priest, are valuable for dating purposes and will be used whenever applicable. Their overall distribution in time also follows the Normal Distribution curve (Lund 2011, fig. 3), as does their chronological distribution within a given deposit (a good example is the Olbian Cistern Л, Fig. 96). Even the pace of adoption of innovations within various adopter categories follows the Normal Distribution (Fig. 12).

Distribution in Time: Chronology

As already mentioned, MMB were produced over a relatively limited period, from sometime in the 220s, when they were first introduced in Athens,[4] until they finally disappeared sometime during the first half of the 1st century. Thus, they were made over considerably less than 200 years and perhaps not even over 150 years. The chronology of many productions of MMB is still relatively

---

3 This is also hinted at by Orton et al., 190; Orton & Hughes 2013, 226–228.

4 Rotroff 1982a, 9–13; Rotroff 1982b, 331; Rotroff 2005, 23–24; Rotroff 2006b.

coarse and the relationship between individual production places and workshops is known in broad terms only. In this section we shall discuss chronology from a methodological point of view, whereas the particular chronology of different production places and workshops will be considered in the chapters devoted to them.

Chronology is a thorny issue; it is a man-made construct, which we can liken to a building structure (Rotroff 2005, 17) or a web (Lawall 2005, 31). No matter how precise and appealing it may appear, it is nevertheless a modern construct. It is never better than the current state of knowledge; therefore, it is constantly being negotiated and renegotiated. But how do we define 'date'?

According to C. Orton, P. Tyers and A. Vince, there are at least two senses in which 'date' is used with reference to an artefact in archaeological literature (Orton et al. 185; Orton & Hughes 2013, 220–222):

(i) The date at which an artefact was made and
(ii) The range of dates within which artefacts of the same type were commonly in use.

Whereas the first date will have a short chronological span, the latter can cover a significant number of years. The distinction is therefore important, but in much research this is rarely made clear. J. Poblome has expanded the definition of 'date' to include three key elements (1999, 272):

[i] When an artefact first came to the market,
[ii] When it was most popular, and
[iii] When it became part of the stratigraphy in which it was found.

With this definition, the evidence of the depositional and post-depositional history of the artefact comes into play, and the time span further increased.[5] The discussion of chronology became even more complicated, when in 2007, J.T. Peña introduced the life-cycle model of the 'life' of a pot (2007, 6–16; Fig. 10):

	Use life	Discard	Time
[i] Manufacture	↓	→	↓
[ii] Distribution	↓	→	↓
[iii] Prime use	↓	→	↓
[iv] Re-use	↓	→	↓
[v] Maintenance	↓	→	↓
[vi] Recycling	↓	→	↓
[vii] Discard	↓		↓
[viii] Reclamation	↓		↓

FIGURE 10   Life-cycle model of pottery, based on Peña 2007

According to Peña, discard can take place any time during the first six 'phases' of the pot's 'life'. Thus, if deposit dates are employed, their chronology may depend on the 'stage' in the life cycle of the relevant objects. To my mind, it is extremely important to keep the different types of dates in mind, because when all types of date are employed indiscriminately, they result in very long – and often too long – and incompatible chronologies (see also Lund 2009). The dating of the classical phase of the Ephesian bowls can serve as an example (see also Chapter 14). At Entremont, destroyed in 125, a small, homogenous group of Ephesian MMB of the Monogram PAR Workshop came to light – one even with a signature (Benoit 1947, 82–83, fig. 2; Fig. 11). In a nearly contemporary context, the foundation fill of the Temple of Castor and Pollux in the Roman Forum, fragments of another Monogram PAR bowl, with acanthus-vine scroll, were found (Guldager Bilde 2008, 188 cat. R-1, fig. 178, pl. 81). The temple was dedicated in 117, but since the fill must have been in place when the foundations were constructed and before the entire superstructure was erected, it is hardly likely that the date of the fragments is as late as 117. At the other end of the spectrum, a bowl of Menemachos decorated with well-rounded imbricate petals with central and side veins was found on board the Antikythera shipwreck (Parlasca 1955, fig. 8). The wreck is dated as late as around 80–70 (Parker 1992, 55). The bowl was hardly part of the cargo but must have belonged to a member of the crew.[6] It is inconceivable that its date of manufacture was as late as the ship, and since it was a personal possession, it is difficult to estimate how long it had been in use before it was deposited on the bottom of the sea. 50 years would be my guess (Chapter 14).

P. Chatzidakis' discussion of a Delian wine shop is of importance for the date of the latest phase of the Ephesian MMB, because a significant number of complete or near-complete bowls of the late phase of Menemachos' workshop have been found in the shop, which was in operation from ca. 110 until it was destroyed, probably in 88 (Chatzidakis 1997), but this context cannot be employed for down-dating the Ephesian production as a whole.

So what are we dating? The moment when the mould was made? When a bowl was thrown inside the mould? When it was distributed, used or discarded? Or do we date a bowl by the date of the deposit in which it was found? These questions are connected to further sub-questions:

---

5   I owe this reference to J. Lund.

6   [Ed. Fragments of six more have now been reported, opening up the possibility that they were objects of trade; the question requires more study. For all seven, see Kavvadias 2012, 190–193 cats. 219–225.]

FIGURE 11   The mouldmade bowls found at Entremont, captioned "Poterie à reliefs hellénistiques avec marque délienne", in Benoit 1947, fig. 2. Reproduced with the permission of *Gallia*

how long were individual moulds (and stamps) in use? And how long were the bowls in use?

Because the manufacturing process involved the infrequent but repeated use of a mould over a long period of time, the date range could in principle be quite significant. The same argument can be employed concerning the stamps: were they workshop heirlooms which were passed on from father to son? Rotroff is of the opinion that the Athenian Workshop of Bion and Workshop A worked for ca. 50 years without change (Rotroff 1982a, 27, 28). This is an alarming perspective from a chronological point of view! Of course, I cannot argue against Rotroff, who has the grand overview over the Athenian production, but I must admit, I find her conclusion difficult to accept. Stamps became worn and were replaced, and with each replacement a slight change could take place in style, if copied free hand, and in size, if the copy was mechanical.

Deposit dates are obviously later than the dates of production and distribution. Moreover, even 'closed' deposits may contain finds with a significant date range. A good example is given by Rotroff, who comments that, taking as a point of departure finds of red-figured pottery in the Agora wells, the date range in most such deposits was 30–50 years (Rotroff 2005, 16–17, fig. 2). Let me once more mention Cistern Л in Olbia (Chapter 20). The fill in this deposit contained stamped Rhodian amphorae with a date range from period 2 to 5, that is, from ca. 234 to 144. However, more than 90% were confined to period 3c–3e (181–161). From a methodological point of view, I find it likely that the dating profile of the MMB followed that of the amphorae, which we can date more precisely.

The longevity of fine-ware pottery is a matter of scholarly dispute – but clearly one we need to reckon with. I have already mentioned the Menemachos bowl on board the Antikythera shipwreck, which may have been as old as 50 years. This was hardly the norm. But why should the ancients have discarded their pottery sooner than we do? For example, in my cupboard I have no porcelain newer than 10 years – and much of it is significantly older, for example, inherited from my grandparents, who bought it in the 1940s. J. Lund has discussed this matter, and his suggestion is that we should reckon with a period from 1 to 25 years for the use-life of fine-ware pottery (2009, 69).

The number of vessels with a given type of decoration at a particular site has been taken as an indicator of the date of the site or the longevity/brevity of the decorative type. This is not always so easy to discover, however, because by and large we lack quantifications of individual decorative patterns (the only exception is Rotroff 2003, 177–178) as well as a comparative inter-site analysis of this data. Thus, arguments derived from numbers are bound to be problematical. This is especially true of the Corinthian deposits and the discussion of the date of the introduction of important decorative patterns such as the PSC and the net pattern; the arguments are bound to fail, because the small numbers which have been adduced as proof of 'short time in existence' (e.g., Edwards 1975; Edwards 1981, 193; Callaghan 1982, 63) say nothing about time, but only confirm what we can see from other localities, namely that those patterns in general *are* scarce (see Chapter 6).

Because the present book pays attention to quantification of pottery styles and decorations and because it operates with a comparative perspective, it is possible to undertake what we may call a 'site or assemblage seriation'. This leads to a relative sequence of workshops and their moulds, and through cross-linking with other workshops and production places we can discover some overall patterns and trends in the decoration, not just at the level of individual workshops and production places, but also at a more general level.

Admittedly, what has been argued above hardly clarifies matters concerning chronology, but once more illustrates how difficult an issue it is. In the present book, I will endeavour to operate with an ideal production date, thus, I will look for the earliest possible date of any given piece. Anything else I view as hazardous (as Lund 2009, 70).

Distribution in Space, Networks, and the Diffusion of Innovations
The last part of this chapter will be devoted to a discussion of the invention of the MMB and the spread of the technology used to produce the bowls. Today there is consensus amongst scholars that the MMB was invented in Athens in the 220s, when an innovative local potter first emulated Ptolemaic court vessels made of precious metal. But how the technique and the bowls first came to be spread to other areas of the Greek world and at what pace is not yet satisfactorily understood.

The following will draw on network theory and the theory of the diffusion of innovations (Brughmans 2010; Knappett 2011). The main points will be that the MMB will allow us to study not just networks of trade and exchange, but also social networks and human agency. I will demonstrate that we can distinguish not just one but two distinct waves of Ptolemaic influence, and I will argue that the motor was the exchange of diplomatic gifts through the social network of the Ptolemaic court.

The Invention of the Mouldmade Bowl and the First Wave of Egyptian Inspiration
Royal courts commonly strengthened bonds with their peers, with sanctuaries, and with cities through gifts of, for example, silver plate (Treister 1996, 326; Panagopoulou 2007). As a result, silver vessels circulated in significant numbers in the Hellenistic period. Regrettably, the majority of these vessels have been lost over the centuries; those that have survived mostly derive from the art market, and thus are devoid of the contextual information which could clarify their provenance and date. This is also true for 'Alexandrian' metal ware, which is notoriously difficult to grasp (Treister 1996, 310–315).

In earlier research, the Egyptian connection of the mouldmade bowl was hotly debated, first of all in the 1950s, 60s and 70s.[7] R. Zahn had already pointed out that the deep hemispherical bowl with everted lip was an old Egyptian shape, which was produced in metal, faience and light clay (Zahn 1904, 416; see also Pagenstecher 1913, 64, 70). The latter could be painted or even gilded (Edgar 1911, pls. XXI–XXII). Also the decoration with a vegetal calyx and the Nilotic elements with water birds and swamp vegetation had a long history in Egypt. Therefore, in past research the bowls' Egyptian ancestry has never been seriously challenged (Zahn 1904; Pagenstecher 1913; Parlasca 1955; Byvanck-Quarles van Ufford 1959). The Egyptian connection led R. Zahn and later R. Pagenstecher to suggest that the MMB was invented, not in Megara, as was believed in the 19th century (see Chapter 2), but in Egypt. However, none of the MMB found in Egypt support this suggestion. We now know that the MMB published by Pagenstecher (1913, figs. 79–82) are mostly Ephesian. Today, our knowledge of the mouldmade bowl, its many production places, their individual style and their chronology, is much more sophisticated than it was in the 1950s, 60s and 70s. Therefore, many arguments concerning the relationship between Greek MMB and their Ptolemaic predecessors in metal and glass are outdated. Moreover, after Susan Rotroff published *Agora XXII* in 1982, it has been an established fact that the mouldmade bowl was first invented in the 220s in Athens following the first celebration in 224/3 of the Athenian Ptolemaia (Rotroff 1982a, 13; 1982b, 331; Rotroff 2006b). Rotroff's theory goes that on that occasion, Ptolemaic court vessels were displayed in Athens. This occasioned a local demand to possess such vessels, and a visionary Athenian potter started copying the bowls, first by means of moulds taken direct from metal vessels, later by making moulds which

---

7 Byvanck-Quarles van Ufford 1953; Parlasca 1955; Byvanck-Quarles van Ufford 1959; Adriani 1967; Byvanck-Quarles van Ufford 1970.

were stamped with a number of individual stamps. In the beginning, the style was sombre and delicate; the decoration always covered the entire body, frieze decoration was not used. Decoration was primarily figural or vegetal or combinations of the two. In addition to an Ionian kyma and/or a guilloche, the rim often featured a frieze of horizontal S-spirals of alternating direction topped by small palmettes and/or rosettes; this rim pattern without doubt was copied from the metal(?) predecessor of the so-called Tarentine altars (more on these in Chapter 6),[8] which may have made up part of the Ptolemaic silver displayed at the Ptolemaia.

Adoption of Innovations

Rotroff is to be commended for introducing the concept of innovation in her study of the earliest phases of the MMB at Athens, because this leads to a new understanding about the processes at work (Rotroff 2006b). Her primary use of innovation theory is to explain why MMB were so scarce in Athenian deposits prior to period IIId of the Rhodian amphorae (which begins ca. 175, according to the new chronology of G. Finkielsztejn (2001); Rotroff 2006b, fig. 5). Athenian deposits earlier than this date contained on average less than five MMB per deposit; this is in stark contrast to the time after 175, when deposits contained on average 27.5 MMB per deposit (Rotroff 2006b, 367). She explains this discrepancy by using the British archaeologist D.A. Spratt's theories about innovation processes (Spratt 1982; 1989). Spratt is an exponent of a linear innovation model; his model divides innovation into six phases, which either follow each other or happen simultaneously:

A) Discovery [technical knowledge, here the use of a mould]
B) Invention [practical use of technical knowledge]
C) Development
D) Investment
E) Production & Distribution
F) Obsolescence

Rotroff combines this model with Spratt's cash flow model (Rotroff 2006b, fig. 9) in order to explain why it took several generations before the Athenian MMB caught the attention of the market.

Diffusion of Innovations

I think we can take Rotroff's ideas one step further, because it is most likely not the cash flow model which explains the varying depositional patterns (though it can constitute part of it): they follow a much more general pattern, which we find in the diffusion of innovations not explained solely by the economy.

The American sociologist Everett M. Rogers has been the main exponent for developing a theory of the diffusion of innovation. His seminal book, *Diffusion of Innovations*, was published in 1962 and has subsequently appeared in several updated versions (I employ the 2003 edition). To Rogers, diffusion is *the process by which an innovation is communicated through certain channels over time among the members of a social system* (Rogers 2003, 5). His study clearly shows that it takes time to reach the 'tipping point', when an innovation becomes common property, no matter what kind of innovation is considered. Sometimes this has to do with the economy, but it can also have to do with, for example, tradition and general inertia in social systems.

Because the individuals in a social system do not adopt innovations at the same pace, Rogers has divided the adopters, as he calls them, into five adopter categories (Rogers 2003, 267–299):

(1) Innovators
(2) Early adopters
(3) Early majority
(4) Late majority
(5) Laggards

He later added a sixth category, the resisters.

By and large, these categories mirror social categories, with the innovators being persons with more social and economic capital than the remainder, and with laggards representing the socially and economically weakest individuals in the given society. Their number and the speed of adoption follows the Normal Distribution (Fig. 12).

One of Rogers' main points is that for most members of a social system, the decision whether to adopt or reject an innovation depends heavily on the innovation decisions made by other members of the same system. In fact, observation shows that the successful spread of an innovation, that is, the rate of adoption, follows an S-shaped curve (e.g., Rogers 2003, fig. 6-3; fig. 7-1).[9] We shall return to Rogers' diffusion of innovations below, but before we leave Athens and the first wave of Ptolemaic influence, we shall briefly consider how and at what pace the spread of the production of MMB took place in the years prior to 175, when the bowls became well represented in the Athenian deposits.

I have already mentioned the existence of Atticizing moulds found on Lemnos, at Hephaistia (Massa 1992; 1997) and at Myrina (Archontidou-Argyri 1994). Rotroff has suggested that the Hephaistia moulds were made locally by an immigrant Athenian potter (Rotroff 2013, 20–22, following Massa 1992, 244); I believe she is right, and this may also be the case concerning the single mould

---

8 Mahler already saw this connection (1924, 84).

9 This is also represented in Rotroff's fig. 10 plot x (2006, 374).

METHODOLOGY

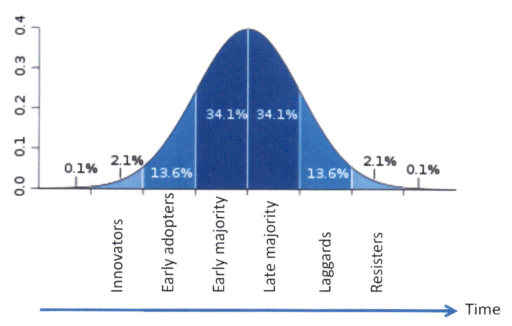

FIGURE 12 E.M. Rogers' adopter categories and the Normal Distribution Curve

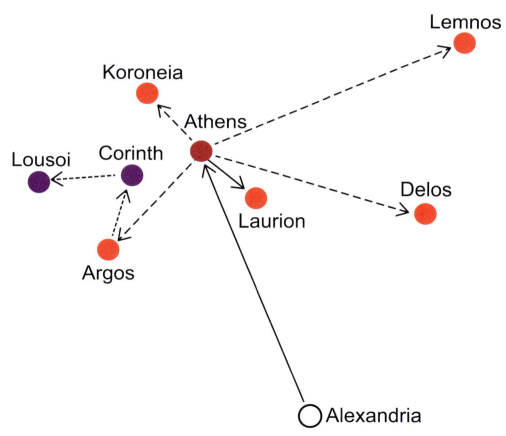

FIGURE 13 First wave of influence from Alexandria: Athenian and Atticizing productions, first half of 2nd century

FIGURE 14 Silver bowl from Bulgaria (British Museum, inv. 1989,0724.1)
PHOTO © THE TRUSTEES OF THE BRITISH MUSEUM

fragment found at Myrina. I should also like to mention a mould fragment found at Laurion, which seems to be Atticizing rather than Attic (Salliora-Oikonomakou 1979, 169 pl. 74c), as well as a mould fragment found in the Koroneia survey, which is Attic or more likely Atticizing (Appendix 4). The same may be the case with the one or more moulds with long-petal decoration which have been found on Delos (Courby 1922, 392–393 cat. 159, pl. IX.d; Chatzidakis 1997, 302, pl. 223.a). These examples should teach us that perhaps the potters travelled rather than the moulds.

The spread of Athenian influence on MMB as suggested above is summarized in Fig. 13. The reconstruction is hardly surprising, for the spread was primarily to areas located in the geographical vicinity, such as Laurion, or to areas within Athens' political orbit in the 160s, such as Lemnos and Delos. Outside these areas, the influence was also felt in the Peloponnesian workshops as well as in the early Asia Minor workshops. In the case of the former, copying and emulation took place (Siebert 1978), and it is possible that potters travelled between the two areas too, as recently suggested by Rotroff (Rotroff 2013). In Asia Minor, the inspiration is more on the general level (see Chapter 11).

The Second Wave of Egyptian Inspiration

We shall now turn our attention to what I see as the second wave of inspiration from Egypt. As this phenomenon has not been recognized before, we will need to discuss it in more detail than we did the first phase.

In 1968, the Munich Antikensammlung acquired three gilded silver vessels from the Fayoum.[10] Two were almost identical silver bowls. They are both decorated with four so-called 'nelumbo' petals[11] and four acanthus leaves with a bent tip; in front of the acanthus is a low 'nelumbo' (in the case of Ahrens 1968, no. 3 furnished with scales), whereas in front of the 'nelumbo' is a low acanthus leaf. Two of the large 'nelumbos' are ribbed internally and two are filled with flowers on stems. They are all furnished with a cabled outline. The acanthus and 'nelumbo' are separated by vertical looped stems with flowers and buds. An almost identical bowl appeared in 1992 on the New York art market

---

10 Inv. 4336–4338; Ahrens 1968, 232–233, nos. 3–5; Pfrommer 1987, 263 cats. KBk 117–118. The third vessel is a silver plate with a relief representation of Harpokrates on the interior.

11 The use of the term is conventional: in all likelihood, the floral element is the sepal of the *Nymphaea lotus*, which features the characteristic vertical ribbing. Therefore, I use 'nelumbo' between inverted commas.

METHODOLOGY

(Pfrommer 1996, fig. 20) and it was sold again at Christie's New York auction 16 June 2006.[12] This bowl too is said to derive from Egypt. A very closely related silver bowl, since 1989 in the British Museum, was found in Bulgaria (Fig. 14; Kraus 1951, 18–20, pls. 4–5). It has exactly the same shape and the double rosette of lotus petals of its base medallion is identical to those of the bowls in Munich and New York, so it is difficult not to ascribe this vessel to Egypt too. These four bowls make up a tight-fitting group in terms of shape and decoration.[13]

In Egypt, we find the same decoration emulated on clay vessels. The best – and frequently cited – example is a fragmentary clay relief bowl, the so-called Schreiber bowl, found in Alexandria and evidently moulded from a metal vessel.[14] But even closer, in particular, to the two bowls in Munich are the famous gold glass bowls from Canosa in the British Museum (Figs. 15, 16).[15] These bowls feature the 'nelumbo' filled in alternation with papyrus stems and floral stems separated by acanthus leaves with bent tips. We also find the low acanthus leaf in front of the 'nelumbo' and 'nelumbo' (with scales) in front of the acanthus, and in between are floral stems. Moreover, the base is the same as on all four silver bowls, namely a double rosette of lotus petals. The origin and date of the Canosa bowls is hotly debated.[16] Their context, a chamber tomb with several depositions and plundered in the 19th century, cannot answer the question. Very close to the Canosa bowls, in shape as well as decoration, is a silver bowl in the Toledo Museum of Art, and a similar, though more stylized, bowl can be found in the J. Paul Getty Museum in Malibu (Fig. 17).[17]

It is evident that there is not very much stylistic resemblance between these bowls and the early Athenian vessels. The Athenian bowls are much more sombre than the metal bowls described above, and the 'nelumbo' is never encountered amongst the Athenian products.[18] In fact, only a few vessels with a 'nelumbo' have ever come to light at Athens. One is a fragment of an imported MMB excavated in Agora deposit A 18:1, a cistern where the latest dateable objects are Rhodian stamped handles with Xenophantos as eponym (Rotroff 1982a, 88 cat. 375, pls. 66, 94; p. 96). With the new, lower chronology of G. Finkielsztejn, the deposit is dated ca. 210, not as originally published by Rotroff, third and early fourth quarter of the 3rd century (Finkielsztejn 2001, 191; Rotroff 2006a, 343). However, I am sceptical of this piece, because as also mentioned by Rotroff, an almost complete bowl made in the same mould was found in Deposit F 15:2 (Thompson's Group E; Thompson 1934, 406–409 cat. E 79, figs. 96a, 96b), which according to Rotroff was deposited at the end of the 2nd century (1982a, 110). Because this bowl is almost complete, it is hardly likely that it was 100 years old when it was deposited. I am sure that Rotroff's cat. 375 must be intrusive.[19]

Did this baroque type of decoration not appeal to the Athenian mould makers? Or did it not exist when the Athenian production was formed? In short, is its absence a feature of taste or of chronology? I find it likely that the latter is the case. In fact, if we once more consider the Egyptian Schreiber bowl,[20] it is clear that the acanthus leaf displays a mannerism also known from the architecture of the first half of the 2nd century, namely distinct 'eyes' created by the lobes of the leaf. This style in architecture is normally connected with the name of the architect Hermogenes of Priene. Good examples of this style in acanthus leaves are, for example, the akroteria of the temple of Artemis Leukophryene at Magnesia and the propylon of the bouleuterion in Miletos, the latter securely dated to the years 175–164 on the basis of the two

---

12   http://www.christies.com/LotFinder/lot_details.aspx?intObjectID =4722555 [accessed 10/11/20].
13   Munich inv. 4337: Ø 15.4; British Museum inv. 1989,0724.1: Ø 15; Munich inv. 4336: Ø 14.4; New York: Ø 13.6. We find the same decoration on a silver jug in the Allard Pierson Museum, inv. 3397, Amsterdam equally from Egypt: Pfrommer 1987, 262 cat. KBk 110, pl. 52 with references, and on a silver cup from the Artijukov kurgan in the Taman' Peninsula (Strong 1966, 114, pl. 31B; second half of the 2nd century).
14   Pagenstecher 1913, fig. 83.4; Pfrommer 1987, 263 cat. KBk 119 with references; Byvanck-Quarles van Ufford (1959, 61 n. 25) refers to Parlasca, who notes that it is not faience, as commonly believed, but brown clay. It is currently kept in the University Museum of Tübingen; its curator, N. Kreutz, confirms that it is made of clay.
15   Inv. 1871,0518.1–2, Harden 1968, 23–25, figs. 1–8; Pfrommer 1987, 264 cats. KBk 121, KBk 122; Gudenrath & Tatton-Brown 2003, with further references; Ø 20.1 and 19.3.
16   von Saldern 2004, 121. Pfrommer has already connected the Munich silver bowls and the Canosa glass vessels, all of which he dates in the early 2nd century (1987, 112).
17   Toledo Museum of Art inv. 75.11; Oliver 1977, 78–79 cat. 43; Pfrommer 1987, 265 cat. KBk 128, pl. 58.a with references. J. Paul

Getty Museum in Malibu (inv. 96.AM.160). Both silver bowls are from the art market.
18   As also mentioned by Rotroff (1982b, 333–334), the gold glass bowl from Hama formerly in the Rothschild Collection (von Saldern 2004, 122 with references), is identical in decoration to the early Athenian vessels, with slender acanthus leaves, slender sepals with twisted tip and floral stems. Clearly the gold glass bowls should be dated stylistically on the basis of the MMB (also Rotroff 1982b, 335).
19   This has been confirmed orally by Rotroff, February 2011; see also Rotroff 1997a, 434.
20   Parlasca has dated this bowl very late: ca. 100 (1955, 143–145); Byvanck-Quarles van Ufford (1959, 64) places it around 150.

FIGURE 15 Gold-glass bowl from Canosa (British Museum, inv. 1871,0518.2)
PHOTO © THE TRUSTEES OF THE BRITISH MUSEUM

FIGURE 16 Drawing of the Canosa gold-glass bowl (Rostovcev 1967, pl. XLIII.3)
© THE TRUSTEES OF THE BRITISH MUSEUM

METHODOLOGY 31

FIGURES 17.A–B   Silver bowl (J. Paul Getty Museum, inv. 96.AM.160). Gift of Barbara and Lawrence Fleischman; Bruce White Photography
REPRODUCED WITH PERMISSION OF THE J. PAUL GETTY MUSEUM

dedication inscriptions preserved on the architrave of the bouleuterion itself and the architrave of the propylon.[21]

The baroque style, which, accordingly, was not adopted at Athens, was especially popular in the Ephesian MMB of Menemachos' workshop. We shall discuss this workshop more fully in Chapter 14 on Ephesos. Here we shall consider only his earliest vessels with filled 'nelumbo'. On a number of vessels signed by Menemachos we find the same elements discussed above: the S-curved acanthus leaf with a small 'nelumbo' in front alternating with a large 'nelumbo' with a small acanthus leaf in front, separated by buds or flowers on looped stems. A related calyx – but never with a 'nelumbo' in front of the acanthus leaf and never with a filled 'nelumbo' – can also be found on some of the earliest bowls of the Monogram PAR workshop.[22] I believe that they were inspired by the Menemachos bowls.

Menemachos also occasionally depicted a 'nelumbo' filled with various figural scenes (e.g., EPH-580*). He employed three different stamps with an amorous couple on a *kline*: one with a female who stretches her right arm up to clasp the neck of the male, drawing his head down in order to kiss him,[23] and two versions of a *coitus a tergo* between a woman to the left holding her right hand on her head and a man to the right.[24] Menemachos' 'nelumbo' may also feature a dancing satyr (only one instance is known) and Nilotic elements with swamp vegetation and water birds (of which several stamp generations are known).[25]

When were these bowls made? And what was their background? In order to answer these questions, let us turn to Olbia. In Bothros 11, excavated between 1987 and 1988 in a small walled-in open-air sanctuary in the Western Temenos (see Chapter 20), a fragmentary grey-ware kantharos, which was very worn and heavily repaired, was unearthed (EPH-1301*). It is decorated in the same baroque style of the metal and glass vessels discussed above. We find the lush vegetation with fleshy acanthus leaves and flowers on looped stems, and a 'nelumbo' with cabled edges shows the same scene which we saw on the bowls signed by Menemachos: a kissing couple lying on a *kline*.[26]

This stamp, however, is much more detailed than most of Menemachos' representations. The 'nelumbo' is also larger and draperies are suspended in the background.[27] It is easy to identify the male as Eros, because his wings can clearly be distinguished. The woman embracing him is undoubtedly Psyche. The kantharos was clearly made in a mould taken directly from a metal bowl – as is also suggested by the spidery guilloche of its rim. In fact, the kantharos' closest parallel is the Toledo bowl mentioned several times already. Even though the filled 'nelumbo' there does not feature the kissing couple but floral stems instead, it is, nevertheless, very close in decoration, style, and size – and it even features the fine guilloche running right and set between two friezes of fine dots.

Considering its fabric, there can hardly be any doubt that the kantharos is an Ephesian product. Whether we want to assign it to Menemachos or (as I prefer) to the workshop of the Vases gris, it must at any rate be regarded as the source of inspiration for the Monogram PAR potter when he made his simplified version of this design. The fact that the kantharos is much worn and heavily repaired makes it certain that the vessel was older than the other vessels in the bothros. The bothros was probably filled in sometime in the 140s, after the temenos was destroyed (see Chapter 20). So, in all likelihood, the kantharos was crafted sometime in the second quarter of the 2nd century. This date would accord well with the date of the earliest production of Menemachos known from other sources (see Chapter 14).

Exactly the same scene that we saw on the Olbia kantharos, including the suspended draperies, is found on bowls produced in places as distant as Central Italy and Olympia (Siebert 1978, pl. 90.5; Hausmann 1996, 73 cats. 127–128, pl. 28). Unfortunately, the Olbia kantharos preserves only one filled 'nelumbo', so it is not possible to reconstruct the original metal vessel it was copied from. On one of the Olympia bowls (Hausmann 1996, cat. 127), the stamp with Eros and Psyche alternates with a 'nelumbo' filled with vegetation, whereas on a bowl from Elis, the scene alternates with the *coitus a tergo* (Proskynetopoulou 1992–1993, 116–117 cat. 263, pl. 33).

Even more illuminating in terms of bowl composition are the so-called Italo-Megarian bowls (Puppo 1995). A completely preserved bowl from Vulci in the Vatican signed by C. Popilius features six filled 'nelumbos' with three different scenes: the kissing couple with drapery in

---

21   Rumscheid 1994, I, 202; II, pl. 82.1–3 (Magnesia on the Meander); I, 31 [date]; II, pl. 99 (Miletos).
22   E.g., Laumonier 1977, 160 cats. 1224, 1281–1284, pls. 36, 124, 125.
23   E.g., Laumonier 1977, 34 cats. 1345, 1980, pls. 3, 116.
24   E.g., Laumonier 1977, 35–36 cats. 1340, 1342, 2264, pls. 4, 116 (*coitus a tergo* A); 34–35 cat. 1343, pl. 3 (*coitus a tergo* B).
25   Laumonier 1977, 36–37 cat. 1958, pls. 4, 117 (dancing satyr); 32–33 cats. 1327, 1328, 2318, 1238+2033, 1356+2058, pls. 3, 115 (Nilotic elements).
26   Cf. Laumonier 1977, 34 cats. 1345, 1980, pls. 3, 116.

27   In fact, the draperies can also be distinguished on a Menemachos bowl from Pantikapaion (EPH-580*).

METHODOLOGY

the background; the *coitus a tergo*;[28] and, third, rampant goats around an *agyieus* set in a floral calyx (an aniconic form of Dionysos; see p. 121).

Moulds and fragments of moulds featuring exactly the same scenes have been found at Tivoli: rampant goats around an *agyieus* and a kissing couple in front of suspended draperies.[29] Even though their similarity to the Vatican bowl has been recognized, they have not been connected with the workshop of Popilius, despite the signature PILI M on one of the Tivoli moulds found at Tivoli,[30] surely an erroneous rendering of Popilius. Italo-Megarian bowls are notoriously ill-dated, and in past and current research their chronology wanders from the 4th to the 1st century. In general, scholars have paid more attention to the epigraphy of the signed vessels than to establishing a credible development of shape and style. As of this writing, the best overall discussion is still Marabini Moevs 1980, which is based on the Cosa stratigraphy.[31] Marabini Moevs and Puppo date the Tivoli moulds in the second half of the 2nd century, and – to quote Marabini Moevs – they reveal "an intentional return to the past after the lapse of a few generations ..." (Marabini Moevs 1980, 194; repeated by Puppo 1995, 69). I see absolutely no reason for such a reconstruction, and I do not believe that stamps could lie around for generations to pop up again. Accordingly, I consider the Popilius bowl and the Tivoli mould fragments more or less contemporary with the Olbia kantharos.

The rampant goats inside a 'nelumbo' can also be found on several bowls from Achaia: on a complete bowl from Patras (Siebert 1978, cat. Pat. 4, pl. 54), on an identical bowl from Ithaka (Benton 1938–1939, 34 cat. 36, pl. 16), on a very similar one found at Lousoi but, according to C. Rogl, produced at Aigion (Rogl 2008a, 107–108 cat. 54, pls. 6, 31), as well as fragments from Aigion itself and from Elis (Kolia 2011, 55 cat. AMA 2246, pl. 9; Katsarou & Mourtzini 2011, 753 cat. 25, pl. 304). We even find the rampant goats on a fragment of a grey-ware bowl unearthed at Sardis (Rotroff 2003, 145 cat. 610, pl. 106). Strangely enough, the motif has not been attested amongst the Ephesian vessels, unless we can attribute the fragment from Sardis to the early Ephesian production.

On a bowl fragment from Corinth, the *coitus a tergo* inside a 'nelumbo' was rendered together with other figural scenes, and a stamp for the 'nelumbo' was even found there.[32] Also on a grey-ware bowl in Berlin from Asia Minor, probably from Aiolis (Hausmann 1990, 315, pl. 42.3), the stamp with *coitus a tergo* occurs together with a stamp where Eros engages a sleeping woman. The latter stamp I do not know from any further representations. The same is true for the dancing satyr known from a single Ephesian bowl and the woman undressing seen from behind recorded on a mould from Hierapolis (d'Andria 2003, 216, fig. 192). Finally, we should not fail to notice three vessels made in Elis, where inside the 'nelumbo' are rendered at least two of the scenes from the so-called Tarentine altars: the kithara-playing Orpheus (altar figure C1) known from Lousoi (Rogl 2008a, 101 cat. 21, pls. 3, 30, 44), and the Dionysiac trio (altar scene D)[33] found at Elis (alternating with a 'nelumbo' filled with a depiction of a krater) (Proskynetopoulou 1992–1993, 118 cats. 272, 273, pl. 34) and on Delos.[34]

We can conclude that relatively few different types of filled 'nelumbo' were in circulation, and, interestingly enough, the same stamp (or same representation) can be found in several productions. The most popular stamps were Psyche and Eros and the *coitus a tergo*, and almost as popular were the rampant goats around an *agyieus*. As is clear from Fig. 18, the most varied repertoire is found at Ephesos and at Elis.

In past research, the occurrence of the filled 'nelumbo' in a number of different productions has been explained by way of diffusion: according to Marabini Moevs, it was the 'Delian', that is, Ephesian, products which inspired the Italo-Megarian production (Marabini Moevs 1980, 184), and according to Siebert (1978, 112–114, 176) and Hausmann (1996, 74–75, 106), the Italo-Megarian bowls, in turn, inspired the Peloponnesian bowls (Fig. 19). I am sceptical of such a reconstruction.

---

28 Misunderstood by those drawing and describing the bowl: Siebourg 1897, 42: "zwei sitzenden Eroten, der r. bläst die Querflöte, der l. erhebt den r. Arm"; Puppo repeats the same erroneous description (1995, 48–49). For good photographs, see Marabini Moevs 1980, pl. 18.

29 Paribeni 1927, fig. 6; Marabini Moevs 1980, pl. 22.3 and 6; Puppo 1995, 70 cats. T6, T7, pl. XXXVI.

30 Paribeni 1927, 375, fig. 4; Puppo 1995, 69 cat. T2, pl. XXXV.

31 Her gazetteer of find contexts all too clearly shows how little foundation there is for the dating of most pieces, because many come from chamber tombs which were in use over considerable lengths of time. [Ed. See now Leotta 2017 for a recent wide-ranging study of the Italo-Megarian production, superceding Marabini Moevs 1980 and Puppo 1995.]

32 Edwards 1986, 407, 413–414 cat. 20 (C-1926–32 a-d), figs. 4.E, F, pl. 87; MF 13676, fig. 4.F, pl. 90. Here the figures are altered to represent banqueters, the woman holding a rhyton and bowl, the man a bowl!

33 See Chapter 6 for the nomenclature of the Altar scenes and figures.

34 Laumonier 1977, 427 cat. 1940, pl. 99. Even though Laumonier published this fragment in his book on the 'Ionian' bowls, he remarks that it is a *bol d'un caractère assez spécial* which should perhaps be grouped with the 'non-Ionian' bowls.

Filled 'nelumbo' with:	Ephesos	Asia Minor	Hierapolis	Tivoli and other Italo-Megarian	Olympia	Elis	Corinth	Aigion?
Psyche kissing Eros+draperies	X			X	X	X		
Coitus a tergo A	X							
Coitus a tergo B	X	X		X		X	X	
Eros revealing sleeping woman		X						
Woman undressing			X					
Rampant goats and *agyieus*		X		X				X
Dionysiac trio (altar group D)					X			
Orpheus (altar figure C1)					X			
Dancing satyr	X							
Nilotic flora/fauna	X				X			
Krater						X		

FIGURE 18   Production places of bowls featuring a filled 'nelumbo'

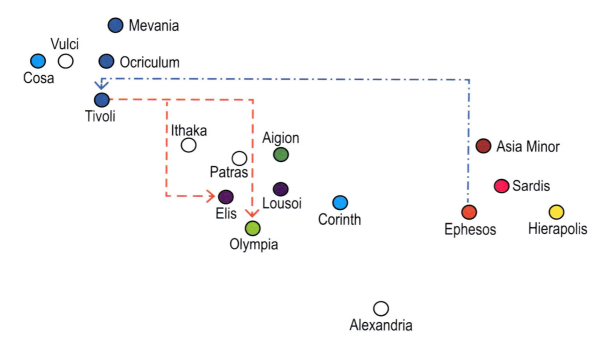

FIGURE 19   Model of diffusion of the filled 'nelumbo' iconography according to Marabini Moevs, Siebert, and Hausmann

Our analysis has shown that a particular baroque style of calyx with alternating 'nelumbo' and acanthus leaf was created in Egypt in the first half of the 2nd century and disseminated on pottery, metal and glass vases. It must have been quite commonplace, because two complexes contained more than one vessel of the same style, as we saw with the silver bowls from Fayoum in Munich and the two gold glass bowls in Canosa.[35] This style arrived in the Greek and Latin world sometime in the second quarter of the 2nd century, probably as part of a new, second wave of Egyptomania.

This was the turbulent time when Ptolemy VI Philometor ruled Egypt (181–145 BCE). For years, war was threatening between Egypt and the Seleucid Kingdom over control of Koile Syria, and in 169 Philometor was temporarily deposed from the throne by his siblings and co-regents. In order to secure his own position as well as the position of his kingdom, Philometor cultivated relations with the Greek world. He and members of the royal family and court participated in the Great Panathenaic games, where

---

35   Also a similar glass bowl in Geneva is perhaps made up of fragments from two similar bowls (von Saldern 2004, 122 and n. 9, pl. 107).

they won victories in 182, 170, 162, and 158 (Habicht 1992, 78–79). A long-term ally of the Ptolemies was the Achaean League in the northern Peloponnese, and in 169, Philometor requested their military support against the Seleucids. Philometor also cultivated relations with Rome. In 170/69 and again in 169/8, Egyptian embassies were sent to Rome asking for help in his struggles (Heinen 1972, 654–655; Hölbl 1994, 130, 132). In 168, the Romans sent Gaius Popillius Laenas, the consul for 172 and 158, to the Aegean. He was on a longer diplomatic voyage, with stops at Delos and Rhodes. After the news of Perseus' defeat in summer 168, he continued to Alexandria, where he drew his famous circle in the sand around the Seleucid King, whereupon Antiochos returned with his army to Syria.

I have already mentioned how silver vessels circulated in significant numbers in the Hellenistic period, not least in the form of royal diplomatic gifts and donations to pan-Hellenic and other sanctuaries (Panagopoulou 2007). We can only guess how Egyptian silverware of Philometor's court with the baroque style we have discussed reached the Mediterranean: we know that the Ptolemaic kings donated statues at Olympia (Bringmann & Steuben (eds.) 1995, 101–104) – but did Philometor also donate precious metal vessels? The occurrence of bowls with similar decoration in a number of cities, all members of the Achaean League, could very well be explained by Philometor's diplomatic activity in 169, when he asked the League for help against the Seleucids. And what about C. Popilius? Did he acquire similar vessels in 168 as a token of gratitude from the king for securing his throne? If so, were they copied back in Italy upon Popillius' return? In short, were the vessels signed C. Popili somehow connected with the Roman diplomat personally and his Egyptian voyage? To my mind, this is not unlikely. Incidentally, such a straightforward reconstruction would provide us with a very precise date for the origin(?) of the Italo-Megarian bowl, namely 168. This date agrees well with the Cosa stratigraphy, according to which the production of Italo-Megarian bowls was initiated in the second quarter of the 2nd century (Marabini Moevs 1980, 171–172), and also with the date of the Olbia kantharos and the early Menemachos vessels.

Let me sum up: in the second quarter of the 2nd century, a new, second wave of inspiration from Egypt can be noticed in the Greek world and in Italy. This time, the models were Ptolemaic precious metal vessels of the court of Ptolemy VI Philometor. The repeated and seemingly identical stamps of the kissing couple, Eros and Psyche, of the *coitus a tergo*, and of the rampant goats around an *agyieus* in the productions of Tivoli, the Greek mainland, Ephesos, and elsewhere in Asia Minor attest to how widespread such bowls must have been. Because the stamp

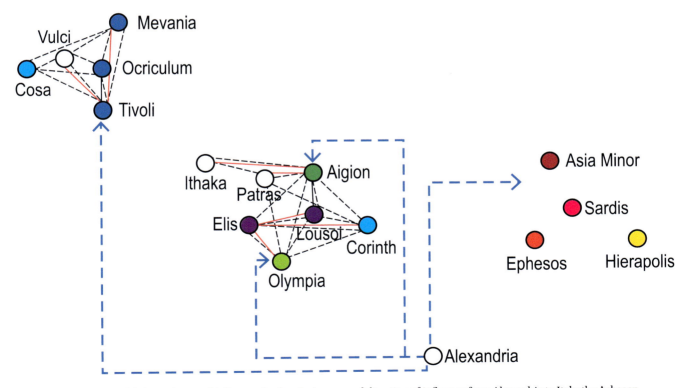

FIGURE 20 A new model. Second wave of influence (in the 160s): proposed direction of influence from Alexandria to Italy, the Achaean League, and to Asia Minor. Filled dots are production places; thin red line marks pottery-style network; thin black dotted line marks political network (Achaean League)

with the kissing couple, in particular, is so detailed that it also renders the suspended draperies, I find it likely that it was metal bowls (or plaster casts of metal bowls) that circulated rather than clay bowls or stamps which were copied. This seems to be supported by the Olbia kantharos. Moreover, it was not just the filled 'nelumbo' that arrived from Egypt during this period; it was the specific style of calyx, with a curved acanthus with bent tip and small 'nelumbo' in front alternating with a 'nelumbo' with a small acanthus leaf in front, often with buds or flowers on looped stems between them. This baroque style was emulated in an even larger number of Mediterranean workshops than the ones already mentioned. It is difficult to know whether these more general references to the Ptolemaic type of decoration were based on direct or indirect access to original Alexandrian models. I find the latter most likely; at least, this best explains the many contemporary varying representations with only a general resemblance to the originals (e.g., AIB-76*, KYB-365*, KYX-67*).

My reconstruction is represented in Fig. 20. It shows three clusters where we find the same reflections of Egyptian inspiration in the local MMB: an Italian cluster, one in the area of the Achaean League in the northwestern Peloponnese, and one in Asia Minor. It is difficult to know how many persons/cities/sanctuaries in these three clusters obtained precious metal vessels from the Ptolemaic court. My guess is that if too many vessels were in circulation, they would have lost their status as prestige objects. So an educated guess is, as argued above, that the main receivers in the Italian cluster were Popilius and perhaps other members of the Roman elite; in the Achaean cluster it is likely that recipients were the city of Aigion, the central meeting place of the league, and Olympia, the major pan-Hellenic sanctuary in the league's area. At our current level of knowledge, it is difficult to reconstruct the course of transmission to Asia Minor. It is likely that Pergamon played a decisive role, but this cannot be proved given the current state of our knowledge. In all three areas, further and interrelated workshops produced local MMB which to a greater (and later lesser) degree were inspired by the Ptolemaic originals – or perhaps rather by MMB of neighbouring areas emulating them.

The above reconstruction allows us to detect three levels of networks which are interlocked, but nevertheless, independent:
(i) The social network of the elite, linking individuals or states on a diplomatic level
(ii) The trade network
(iii) The local network of pottery production and emulation of pottery styles

Together they demonstrate the exchange of objects, taste and social practices. If we consider the second wave of inspiration from Egypt as a new wave of innovation, perhaps in the form of 're-invention' (Rogers 2003, 180–183), it provides an excellent illustration of Rogers' main conclusion: that the diffusion of innovations takes place primarily through the network of the elite ('opinion leaders', see Rogers 2003, 316–342). The second wave of influence from Egypt may have been as important as the first one, which had hit Athens half a century earlier, and it perhaps even led to the establishment of new workshops, as did the first. As was the case in Athens, after an initial phase of recognizably 'Egyptian' style and/or imagery, decoration on Mediterranean MMB soon followed different local trajectories, and before long, the Egyptian inspiration was just a distant memory.

Social Distribution and Function: From Prestige Object to an Item of Mass Consumption

The above reconstruction demonstrates that the MMB recurrently emulated Ptolemaic court vessels in precious metals, and because they were furnished with figural decoration, at the same time they became vehicles for the transmission of Ptolemaic ideology centred on the veneration of Dionysos and the Ptolemaic king. Laumonier has called their decoration *decor "paradisiaque"* (Laumonier 1977, 32 and 33). This is very accurate: the bowls' lush vegetation and Nilotic elements reflect the Ptolemaic *paradeisos tes tryphes*. They illustrate the abundance and prosperity which the Ptolemaic King promised to his subjects, a trope in Ptolemaic propaganda (Heinen 1983; Dunand 2007, 256). The symplegma scenes depicted inside a 'nelumbo', which became a frequent element in the MMB and other relief vessels of the late Hellenistic period (but which to my knowledge did not occur in Athens), are part and parcel of the same world. One has only to remember a relief rhyton found in Athribis, which prominently features a *coitus a tergo*. The rhyton is dated to the reign of Philometor by its excavator K. Myśliwiec, based on its stratigraphic context (Myśliwiec 2000a; Myśliwiec 2000b, 208).

The function of the MMB was primarily as a drinking vessel, and, as Rotroff has pointed out, the MMB replaced the kantharos, at least in Athens. The way the bowl was manipulated constituted a break with the past: neither stem nor handle was present for the Greek symposiast to grip, as s/he had been wont to do for centuries. The bowl was designed to be held with one hand with the bottom resting on the palm (see also further discussion in Chapter 5). From a functional point of view the form is not very practical, because a shape without a foot was not particularly stable. In other respects, the bowls represent a return to the past, because after almost 100 years of vessels decorated with floral motifs or, at the most, with images of jewellery in the West Slope tradition, the bowls once more featured figural decoration. The presence of pictures was an important element in Greek sympotic culture. Apart from their role as mirrors of social practices, they could also function at a very low, practical level as objects of conversation. The drinking and talking were social lubricants which created bonds between the symposium guests and their host.

MMB have been found in all types of contexts: public and private, domestic, funerary and religious. Most vessels were made for drinking purposes, but some were probably made for the grave. After the middle of the 2nd century, the MMB became a wide-spread commodity, and clearly, as it trickled down the social groups (or the adaptor categories, to phrase it with Rogers), it changed character from a prestige object emulating Ptolemaic court vessels to an item of mass production and mass consumption. In this period, most workshops no longer invested time, resources and mental creativity in the design of their moulds; instead they reproduced thousands and thousands of bowls with either a long-petal design or with small imbricate petals. So when we evaluate the significance of the vessels, it is important to do so with an eye on the time factor (see also Kögler 2010, 302).

CHAPTER 4

Production and Distribution

In the previous chapter, we discussed methodological issues concerning production and distribution, including the theoretical basis for the identification of workshops and production places. In this chapter, we shall turn to the finds themselves. The discovery of moulds testifies beyond doubt to places of production, and a closer scrutiny of signatures will help us to understand the mode and scale of workshop organization. In the first part, we will look at the production and the organization of workshops, whereas in the second part, we shall turn our attention to distribution. Both issues are related to discussions of the ancient economy: What kind of production are we dealing with? Is it mass production for mass consumption? Or was it small family enterprises potting for a local market? Or both? How were MMB distributed outside their place of production and to what degree – if at all? Were they objects of trade proper? Or were they just space-fillers in cargoes with agricultural and other products? Or are MMB found outside the place of production simply evidence of people moving with their pots?

Workshop Organization and the Scale of Production

Workshop Organization: Peacock's Model
In order to understand how the ancient workshops were organized, apart from the finds themselves, including signatures, we have pictorial and literary descriptions. However, the latter are mostly either late (e.g., Athenaios' *Deipnosophistai*, or *Geoponica*, a Byzantine treatise on agriculture) and/or anecdotal in nature, and the former are dependent on the adequate preservation and interpretation of the finds. Therefore, at least since the 1950s it has been a common trend in pottery studies to turn to ethnographical parallels as a supplementary source in establishing a theoretical framework for the interpretation of the archaeological material. R. Hampe's and A. Winter's studies of pottery workshops in Greece, Cyprus, and Southern Italy in the 1950s and early 1960s (Hampe & Winter 1962; 1965) are seminal. The two scholars are chiefly concerned with the technical side of the production process – installations, clay preparation, firing methods, etc. – but they also consider workshop organization to some extent. This issue has been more thoroughly discussed by D.P.S. Peacock (1982). He is concerned with the Roman period, and even though the method of production in this period is not completely congruent with that of the Hellenistic period (see below), his models are important, because they constitute a necessary corrective to the ethnographical investigations, which are mostly biased towards the more primitive end of the production spectrum (Peacock 1982, 6). So let us briefly look at Peacock's model (1982, 6–11).

Peacock distinguished eight different modes of production, with a gradually increasing level of complexity and number of people involved (summarized in Fig. 21). The production of MMB was a specialized craft and it involved a certain level of investment in equipment, especially in moulds. We can immediately exclude household production and probably also household industry as the mode of producing MMB. At the other end of the spectrum, the factory, the estate, and the military/official production are not relevant in the Hellenistic period. This leaves us with the individual and nucleated workshops as well as with the manufactory. So let us look briefly at these as explained by Peacock.

Individual Workshops
Individual workshops involve individuals working singly or with a small group of assistants, perhaps family members, and are either sedentary or adopt an itinerant mode in order to serve dispersed communities. The use of kilns and potter's wheels is usual. The workshop output constitutes a major source of the potter's subsistence. Small-scale production.

Nucleated Workshops
A group of individual workshops which form a more or less tightly clustered 'industrial' complex (*kerameikos*). The highest available technology will be exploited, and permanent installations, such as wheel houses and drying sheds, will normally be at hand. The workshop output is the primary means of subsistence for its staff. A wide variety of types of ware, conforming to set standards, is produced, with some specialisation within the individual workshops. Nucleation is favoured at places where raw materials, labour and/or markets are at hand. The output supplies widespread markets and often a middleman is engaged in distributing the products. Medium-scale production.

© PIA GULDAGER BILDE AND SUSAN I. ROTROFF, 2024 | DOI:10.1163/9789004680463_005

Production mode	Location	Craftsman	Engagement	Specialization	Purpose	Middlemen
Household production	home	women	sporadic	household pottery	private consumption	n.a.
Household industry	home, peripatetic	women (men)	sporadic/ part-time	household pottery	private consumption/market	no
Individual workshop	home/outside home, peripatetic	(women) men	part-time/ full-time	household pottery (fine-ware pottery)	market	no
Nucleated workshops	outside home	men	(part-time) full-time	standardized production of household/fine-ware pottery/lamps/terracottas	market	no/yes
The manufactory	outside home	men	full-time	specialized product	market	yes
The factory	outside home	men	full-time	specialized product	market	yes
Estate production	home	men	full-time	specialized product, often ceramic building materials	private consumption/market	yes
Military and other official production	special-purpose installation	men	full-time	specialized product	special purpose	yes

FIGURE 21 Modes of production in the Roman period, based on Peacock 1982, 8–11

The Manufactory
A group of craftsmen working in a single building or place, producing a single and highly specialized product. The main contrast to the workshops is the scale of the enterprise and the investment required. The owner either takes part in the work himself or supervises it, or it is run by one or more overseer slaves. The output supplies widespread markets, and a middleman is always engaged in distributing the products. Somewhat misleadingly, Peacock identifies the manufactory with the ancient *ergasterion*. This was just a 'workshop', which could be organized in many different ways and at many scales (Monaco 2000). Large-scale production.

An Item of Mass Production?: The Evidence of Moulds
Let us now turn to the MMB. It is frequently assumed that the MMB was an item of mass production (Akamatis 1993, 380; Brusić 1999, 4) – because the bowls were made in moulds which allowed 'mechanical' copying – and, because they emulated metal vessels, they are viewed as cheap substitutes for vessels in more precious materials (e.g., Rotroff 1982a, 13). Both assumptions are open to question. First, the use of a mould did not speed up the production process, but rather the contrary. After throwing the vessel in the mould, the potter was obliged to leave it in the mould for some time, so that it would dry and shrink enough to be lifted from the mould without damage to the relief decoration. The drying process must have been rather slow, because the thick-walled mould would have absorbed water from the wet clay, and this would have slowed the drying. So most likely, only one vessel could be made per mould per day. It was therefore necessary to have a substantial number of moulds on hand in order to secure a certain daily output. Unfortunately, it is difficult to establish how many moulds were available in individual workshops. Most of the finds of moulds are isolated pieces or fragments (Appendix 4). Only three assemblages provide us with an idea of the original number of moulds in use at the same time in a single workshop.

The largest batch of moulds ever found was excavated between 1980 and 1981 in the destruction level of two adjacent rooms in the east stoa of the agora of Pella, in Macedonia. In these rooms and in the gutter outside, 320 complete and fragmentary moulds were excavated (Akamatis 1993). The destruction of the workshop probably took place at the beginning of the 1st century, as indicated by the coins and stamped amphora handles found in the same contexts. The destruction was sudden and probably due to a natural disaster, perhaps an earthquake. Akamatis assigns the moulds to four different craftsmen (A to D) based on the shape of the moulds, but most of the bowls were made by craftsman A. It is of interest that only five individual stamps were common property. None of the moulds were signed.

The most important find is the debris of a workshop at Hephaistia on Lemnos (Massa 1992; Massa 1997). This is a kiln dump southeast of the Archaic sanctuary, excavated by L. Beschi from 1979 to 1984. A workshop building as well as kilns were unearthed. The production, which was probably instigated by an immigrant Attic potter (Massa 1992,

244; Rotroff 2013, 20–22), was in operation in the second quarter of the 2nd century. Altogether, 297 complete and fragmentary moulds were found, as well as various tools such as turning tables, stacking rings and a punch. None of the moulds were signed.

The third-largest batch of moulds is a group of 114 complete and fragmentary moulds which derive from the art market. At the end of the 1970s, they were sold to a number of German collections and are now divided between museums in Munich, Mainz, Tübingen, and Frankfurt (Künzl 2002). The moulds were furnished with a variety of Turkish provenances by their sellers. However, S. Künzl has drawn together this group and has demonstrated beyond doubt that they belong to a single production place, which she somewhat misleadingly calls the 'Mainzer Workshop'. From a stylistic and morphological point of view, the production site must be placed somewhere within the orbit of Pergamene influence, most likely at an inland location.[1] Künzl dates the moulds to the late 2nd or early 1st century, a date which is probably somewhat too late, but this need not concern us here. Based on a cluster analysis of the shape of the mould, on punches, and on style as well as on signatures, Künzl finds that the 114 moulds represent four individual production units or groups. No vessels produced in these moulds have ever been identified, so most likely the workshop's products served exclusively local needs. Since the moulds derive from the art market, it is not possible to estimate the size of the original assemblage.

Scale of Production and Workshop Organization: The Evidence of Signatures

Around 300 moulds were probably available at the same time in the workshops at Pella and Hephaistia, since they were deposited together. As already mentioned, on the basis of formal criteria (the shape of the moulds), Akamatis assigned the Pella moulds to four different craftsmen, of whom one, craftsman A, was the one most prolific. Massa observes that the Hephaistia moulds are very repetitive, and she does not distinguish multiple mould makers.

Even though the absence of archaeological context for the 'Mainzer Workshop' material makes it impossible to be sure that the 114 known moulds constitute the entire original assemblage, they are nevertheless very useful for our inquiry, because they document varying signing practices. With the aid of the signatures, we can reach a more refined understanding of workshop organization – and on more secure grounds – than if we were to rely solely on formal or stylistic criteria (Chapter 3). So, before we consider this workshop in more detail, a few comments on the practice of signing are appropriate.

The presence of signatures on MMB is very uneven from place to place and from time to time, and in past research, the purpose of these signatures has been the subject of controversy (e.g., Siebert 1978, 216–220). This fascinating subject has been discussed several times by C. Rogl, who in 2001 published a list of more than 160 individual signatures (Rogl 1999; 2001a), to which more can now be added (e.g., Rotroff 2002; Zavvou 2005). Signatures could be stamped or, more commonly, incised into the wet clay of the mould or of the vessel before firing. Inscriptions made after firing are normally unrelated to the workshop and are rather owner's marks, price marks, or evidence of use in a social or ritual context. When spelled out, signatures are normally given in the genitive, but the nominative also occurs. Names can also appear in abbreviated form or as monograms. Signatures can be located in different places on the vessel; practice varies from place to place. When the base was undecorated or was furnished with a small device only, the signature was normally placed under the base, but it could also be woven into the decoration of the body (as EPH-731*, Posei …) or it could be placed horizontally or, more commonly, vertically on the wall of the vessel.

In her 1999 article, Rogl summarizes the interpretation of such signatures in current research (1999):
– They guarantee quality
– They are a kind of declaration
– They have to do with internal affairs of workshop organization or the organization of the firing
– They have to do with the self-representation of the potter

Ever since the Archaic period, Greek potters and painters (and other artisans and artists) had signed their products, and clearly there was not just a single reason for doing so;[2] this is also true concerning the late Hellenistic period. In the case of the MMB, however, it should be noted that the identity of the person signing and his/her place in the *chaîne opératoire* is not completely clear. Signatures in the moulds most probably refer to the person crafting the mould rather than, e.g., the workshop owner. Whether the mould maker was also the potter is debatable; undoubtedly he could be, but the mechanical throwing of bowls in the moulds could also have been carried out by other, anonymous members of the workshop. However, two arguments

---

1 [Ed. A cache of similar moulds excavated at Kremna, in Pisidia, now reveals the point of origin; see Metin 2017; see also Metin 2014; 2015a–c.]

2 The same was discovered by Hampe and Winter when they interviewed Greek potters (1962, 97–98).

speak in favour of the mould maker and the potter (by and large) being the same person. Moulds are few compared with vessels turned in the moulds; if a mould maker's task was restricted to making moulds, he would soon be out of work. Moreover, it is well-documented that several workshops employed moulds which can be attributed to a number of individual hands, and a single shop would hardly need multiple specialist mould makers. An additional argument comes from the products of the Ephesian Workshop of Menemachos, where the signature in the mould is used alongside and in the same way as signatures on the vessels (Fig. 24).

We shall now turn to three different cases: the small-scale 'Mainzer Workshop', where signatures unmistakably must have had to do with the internal affairs of the workshop; the medium-scale Kymean Meter Medallion Workshop; and the large-scale Ephesian Workshop of Menemachos and his associates.

The 'Mainzer Workshop' as Evidence for Nucleated Workshops

Künzl's analysis of shape, punches, style, and signatures led her to conclude that the 114 moulds of the 'Mainzer Workshop' represent four individual production groups (Fig. 22). Group 2, furthermore, has three 'annexes': one which employs its own punches but also copies punches from Groups 1 and 3, one which copies Group 2 punches, and one which is related to the group stylistically. In addition to the four groups, there are 17 unclassified moulds. Even though each group has its own profile, they are nevertheless interrelated. This becomes even clearer when we look at Group 1.

This group, which is by far the largest, is remarkable because 25 of its moulds carry a signature. Two names occur: Artemis (ΑΡΤΜΕΟΥΣ) and Kra(...) (ΚΡ, ΚΡΑ, ΧΚ, or ΧΚΡΑ). On 22 of the signed moulds, the signature is located on the outside of the mould and, accordingly, had importance only within the workshop. Also, in this workshop, there is only a single punch that was used by mould makers of several groups, but there is evidence for the mechanical copying of punches (Künzl 2002, 26, 28). In this group, in which at least two craftsmen worked, 15 stamps of a total of 54 were employed by both, whereas 12 were employed exclusively by Artemis and 17 by Kra(...), and 10 are found only on the unsigned moulds. On two further moulds signed by Kra(...) on the exterior, an A has been incised in the calyx on the interior and thus visible on the finished product. Because the letter style differs from that of the Artemis stamps, Künzl suggests that a third person is evidenced (2002, 11). Similarly, Kra(...) signed once on the inside of the mould.

Künzl's attentive analysis of the morphological and stylistic properties of the moulds in addition to the personal signatures in the 'Mainzer Workshop' is important for our

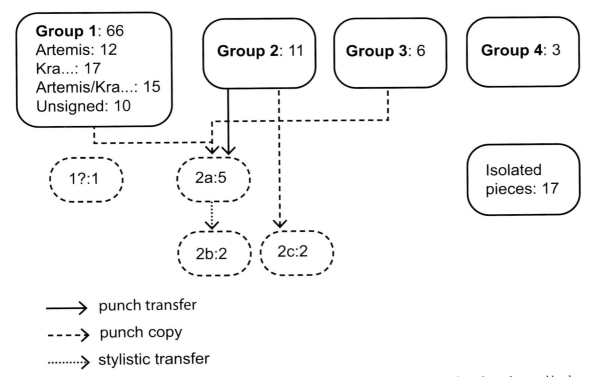

FIGURE 22 The 'Mainzer Workshop', based on Künzl 2002, figs. 3, 6, and 12. In Group 1, the number of punches used by the potters individually or shared (or occurring on unsigned moulds) is given.

understanding of workshop organization. If we consider Peacock's models of production, the 'Mainzer Workshop' clearly illustrates nucleated workshops, where some degree of collaboration exists even though the individual workshops (corresponding to Künzl's groups) retain a certain measure of individuality.

The Meter Medallion Workshop and the Nucleated Workshops of Kyme

Four individuals belonging to the same workshop are recorded in signatures on bowls of the MMW: Kirbeis, Possis, Zenodotos, and Zenodoules. They will be treated at greater length in Chapter 11; here, we shall discuss them solely as evidence for workshop organization.

From Fig. 23, we can see that it was the norm of this workshop to use a Meter bust as a device, but each potter had his own version of this bust (see Chapter 11). The Meter bust must have served as the workshop 'logo'. It was also general practice to sign the vessels; more than 90% of the bases feature a signature, which could either be part of the stamp (Kirbeis) or be incised directly in the mould. The mode differed from potter to potter. Kirbeis, Possis, and Zenodotos signed around the base medallion, whereas Zenodoules signed with a rectangular stamp on the body of the vessel. Zenodotos, in contrast to Kirbeis and Possis, signed with the latter part of the signature (-tou) in retrograde.

The relationship between the craftsmen and their use of individual stamps corresponds very well to what we saw in the 'Mainzer Workshop'. One potter (Kirbeis) dominates in number of signatures and output (Figs. 23 and 61); he is represented four times as often as the second-most important potter in the workshop, Possis. Signatures of Zenodotos and Zenodoules are both rare. If we exclude the stamps employed for the rim pattern and for stamping of the medallion, we can distinguish no less than 163 individual stamps in the Meter Medallion Workshop. Some of these stamps are personal, others are shared with one or more members of the same workshop (Fig. 63).

However, matters become even more complicated when we contextualize the MMW in Kyme and within the Kymean workshops. As will be discussed in Chapter 10, moulds and bowls unearthed in Kyme induced Bouzek and Jansová to distinguish at least five different workshops and their circles: the workshops of Paniskos, of Little Eagles, of Erotes, of Birds and Imbrications, and the Smyrna Workshop (1974). Even though I am somewhat sceptical about whether the fragments can be said to represent an equal number of actual 'workshops' rather than individual hands, it is certain that several workshops in addition to the Meter Medallion Workshop were functioning in Kyme at the same time. Thus, in addition to the 'workshops' distinguished by Bouzek and Jansová, I have identified a group of Kymean bowls which in terms of morphology and iconography must correspond to an individual potter. Although the numbers are too small for the reconstruction of an independent establishment, in view of its distinctive character I have, nonetheless, termed it Workshop A.

From the table in Chapter 11 (Fig. 63) it becomes clear that, while 132 of the 163 stamps employed in the MMW were used exclusively within this workshop, 31 stamps were shared by one or more members of the MMW and one or more Kymean workshops *outside* the MMW. Thus, the Kymean material reveals an intricate web of relationships most likely attesting to a group of nucleated

	Form of signature	Number of bases (ECA+ECB)		Device
		Signed	Unsigned	
Kirbeis	Genitive (Kirbei)	97		Meter bust, right
			2[a]	Wreath with *tainia*
			3[b]	Rosette
			1[c]	Comic mask
Possis	Genitive (Possidos)	22		Meter bust, right
		1[d]	3[e]	Comic mask
Zenodotos	Genitive (Zenodotou)	7		Meter bust, left
Zenodoules	Nominative (Zenodoules)	1		Meter bust, right
MMW?			4[f]	Meter bust, var. right

FIGURE 23 Signatures of the Meter Medallion Workshop. Bases which are either very worn or where only a tiny part of the medallion is preserved are not included.
Notes: a. KYB-268, KYB-324; b. KYB-123, KYB-317, KYB-318; c. KYB-320; d. KYB-350; e. KYB-348, KYB-363, KYB-364; f. KYB-424–KYB-427

workshops, where some have more to do with each other than others. Moreover, the Kymean workshops teach us the interesting lesson that the practice of signing could be something which distinguished one workshop from the other, even though they were contemporary and worked at the same place – and even shared stamps. Accordingly, whether to sign or not to sign was probably a deliberate choice made by the workshop.

From Nucleated Workshops to Manufactory: Ephesian Workshops

Two large workshops dominated Ephesian production: the workshop of the Monogram PAR potter (Workshop Circle 2) and that of Menemachos (Workshop Circle 1). We find much the same practice as we saw in the 'Mainzer Workshop' and in Kyme: some workshops employ signatures to a greater or lesser extent, others do not – or only sparingly. If we start with the latter, the best example of an enterprise with an enormous output, but which signs exceedingly rarely, is the Monogram PAR Workshop. This workshop takes its name from a monogram combining the letters ΑΔΠΡ as well as an I or T (or both) and perhaps an M and/or an N, which – to my knowledge – is documented on no more than ten vessels (see Chapter 14). There can be absolutely no doubt that these vessels pertain to one of the most widely exporting workshops, both in terms of quantity and spatial distribution (e.g., Guldager Bilde 1993). We must conclude that his signing practice was incidental, and it is therefore difficult to interpret the ten signed pieces as anything other than a mere whim, which may have been a 'response' to the signing practice of the second workshop circle operating contemporaneously in the same city, namely WC1 of Menemachos, his collaborators and followers.

In contrast to the Monogram PAR Workshop, which normally employed various rosettes as a base medallion device, almost all members of Menemachos' workshop employed the same undecorated base, occasionally with a wide, low false ring foot (Chapter 14). It provided ample space for a signature, and it is possible that this base type was chosen *because* it gave space for signing. However, unsigned bases of this type were also almost exclusively undecorated. Laumonier was of the opinion that each particular signature was evidence of an individual workshop. To my mind, this interpretation is wrong. As we shall see, the bowls which I have grouped together in WC1 also share other features, such as particular stamps and styles, beyond the shape of the base and the frequent use of a signature. So, there can be no doubt that they belonged to the same workshop or workshop circle.

In total, of the 565 bases of the Menemachean shape which I have recorded, 217 (38%) were signed. Of these, 52 were signed by Menemachos, so almost three fourths of the signed vessels were signed by his associates. The signatures come in a number of variants (Fig. 24; see also Laumonier 1977, 404, fig. 1 and 408, fig. 2): they can be written in the mould or in the wet clay of the vessel; the name can be spelled out (and then mostly in the genitive) or it can be abbreviated (with or without ligature), and the name can also be given in the form of a monogram, again, incised either in the mould or in the vessel. Finally, an isolated letter can also be given. Whether this is a letter proper or is to be understood as a numeral is difficult to decide.

How many persons do the signatures in WC1 represent? In some cases, the same person signs in a different way on different vessels: Menemachos himself mostly spells out his name, but on three vessels he signs Me(...)[3] in ligature, and Philon(nios) certainly also signs just with a Ph(...). Perhaps Apollonios also gives his name in monogram form (Laumonier 1977, 223) and Di(...) is probably the abbreviation used either by Dias or Dionysios. If we employ a very cautious approach and count the above four names, not as seven, and if we exclude the single letters (except for the Ph of Philon(nios)), we nevertheless reach the impressive number of 25–26 persons who for a shorter or longer period were engaged in Menemachos' workshop. To these can be added the mould maker My(...), who belonged to the orbit of the same workshop. His signature is known from four signed bases on Delos, where it is incised in the mould over the rosette of the base medallion in the form of My(...) in ligature[4] (see Chapter 14).

Of course, not all of these 25+ persons worked contemporaneously, because the workshop was in operation for perhaps as much as half a century (Chapter 14); nevertheless, this is the only workshop producing MMB where we can document more than a mere handful of artisans. I should therefore like to propose that the Ephesian workshops can be classified as Peacock's manufactory, more than just nucleated workshops. This corresponds well to the picture we obtain in general from the study of the Ephesian workshops, which dominated the overseas

---

3 This could also be an abbreviation of Melidon, but since that name occurs just once, Me(...) most likely is an abbreviation of the much more common Menemachos.
4 Laumonier 1977, 266–267 cat. 634, pl. 61; 270–271 cats. 2004, 4578, and 8675, pl. 63. The signature was overlooked by Laumonier on cats. 2004 and 8675. Rogl mentions a bowl signed by My(...) in Heraklaia Minoa (Falco 2000, 384, fig. 3.5 [mentioned in Rogl 2001a, 150 no. 10]).

Full name in genitive incised in:		Name abbreviation incised in:	Name monogram incised in:		Single letter incised in:
Mould	Bowl	Mould	Mould	Bowl	Mould
		Ad(…) or Da(…)	Ad(…) or Da(…)		
		Anti(…)			
		An(…) or Na(…) (lig.)			
Apollonios			Ap(…) or Pa(…)		A
Arkesilaos (also Arkesilas!)					
	Athenaios				
Damokles(?)		Da(…)			
	Dias	Di(…)			D
	Dionysios				
		Ei(…)			
Gorgias					
				Hera(…)	
					K
			Ly(…); can also contain M and A or D instead of L!		L
	Melidon	Me(…) (lig.)			
Menemachos					M
Moiragenes (also signing Moragenes)					
		My(…) (lig.)			
		Ni(…)			N
					X [Greek Ξ]
		Pe(…) (lig.)			
	Philon (also Philonnios!)	Ph(…)			Ph [Greek Φ]
Posei[...]					
Posid[...]					
Posi[...]					
		Si(…)			
					Ch [Greek X]
	Zoilos				
	[...]onu[...] or [...]ont[…]				
	[...]rinos				
	[…]on				

FIGURE 24   Names and signing practices in Workshop Circle 1 (the workshop of Menemachos and his circle). Cells linked by light grey indicate signatures probably of the same artisan

markets, especially in areas with a little or no local production of MMB, such as large parts of the Black Sea region (Fig. 80) as well as on Delos (Fig. 4). These workshops had a very large, standardized production with a very wide distribution.

Signatures: Summing Up

Before we return to the question of the scale of production and the moulds, let me briefly sum up my conclusions concerning the signatures. The occurrence of signatures in individual workshops varies from zero to over 90% with any numbers in between; apparently, this has to do with personal preferences, probably of the owner of the individual workshop, because, as we saw in the case of the Kymean and the Ephesian workshops, some of the city's workshops practiced signing, others not. In most workshops, signing appears to have been sporadic: a good example is the Athenian workshop of Bion, where only two of the up to 84 bowls in *Agora* XXII ascribed by Rotroff to this workshop are signed (Rotroff 1982a, 62, 64 cats. 154, 168, pls. 28, 31). Of course, this also has to do with preservation, because the signature is located on the wall of the bowl, not under its base; nevertheless, this example shows that signing was hardly habitual.

The intended meaning of the signatures may have to do with the self-representation of the signing artisans, as I suggest in the case of Kirbeis and perhaps Pontic Demetrios. Moreover, one should not overlook the fact that the signatures came to substitute for decoration, being 'word-pictures'. This may be inferred in the case of several of the Ephesian signatures of WC1, where we find three prominent examples of spelling errors, which can teach us that perhaps in some cases the true content of the letters was of less importance than their 'pictorial' quality:[5]

(a) A simple spelling error is probably the reason for the occurrence of Moiragenes and Moragenes.
(b) One and surely the same mould maker signed Arkesilaou and Arkesialos. It may be a simple error, switching the letters A and Λ, but the differing endings, which, in fact, gives two names (Arkesilas and Arkesilaos), hint at some uncertainty about the proper spelling.
(c) Equally extreme is the case where, again undoubtedly, the same mould maker signed Philonos and Philonniou, thus two different names (Philon and Philonnios), with different endings in the genitive.

Scale of Production

With the exception of the Ephesian case, most workshops seem to have been relatively small. In the 'Mainzer Workshop' and the MMW, we can identify two to four artisans by name; the same number was established at Pella. From a logistical point of view, +/- 300 moulds, the number documented at Pella and Hephaistia, could be used on a daily basis by a similar number of potters and their assistants. The greatest challenge for the workshops was probably to find the space to dry so many moulds at the same time – provided that all moulds were in use every day. Even though the MMB was a specialized product, it is not certain that it was the only product of the workshops; at least in the case of Hephaistia, it is clear that the shop also produced other mouldmade items, such as lamps and terracottas (Massa 1992, 31); the same combination of MMB and mouldmade lamps can also be found at Ephesos (Mitsopoulos-Leon 1985, 249). There is some limited evidence at Athens to suggest that lamps, terracottas, and mouldmade bowls were at least sometimes made in the same shops there as well (Rotroff 1982a, 31–32).

Single- or Multi-locality Workshops: A Question of Scale?

The moulds of Pella and Hephaistia were found at one centrally located place in the city: southeast of the Archaic sanctuary at Hephaistia and in the central agora of Pella. The Hephaistia workshop served a local market, and another production centre for MMB is attested in the neighbouring town of Myrina (Appendix 4), so perhaps this one workshop was adequate for local needs. The Pella workshop probably served a regional market (Akamatis 1993, 339–342), and it is possible that more workshops will come to light.

Cities with a medium- to large-scale production could have multiple workshops/manufactories in operation simultaneously at several localities in and around the city.

A good example is Athens (Fig. 25), where moulds have been found in the Agora (Rotroff 1982a), on the Pnyx (Edwards 1956), in the Kerameikos (Schwabacher 1941, pl. VIIa.11–14), and in Syntagma Square,[6] though most of them are in secondary and/or late contexts. The earliest contexts are located south of the Agora, immediately northeast of the Areiopagos (Satyr Cistern and Komos Cistern), and many moulds were found to the northwest of the Areiopagos, in an area with traces of a wide range of industrial activities (Rotroff 1982a, 27, 31). It is likely that production took place in the vicinity of all five find places.

Also in Ephesos, where at least 108 moulds have come to light (Rogl 2014a, 116), moulds have been found at a number of localities (Fig. 26). Most were excavated in a fill in the southern gate tower of the Magnesia Gate, but some come from the northern tower of the same gate as well (partially published: Seiterle 1981; 1982; Rogl 2001b; Tuluk 2001; Kerschner et al. 2002). Apart from this major batch, isolated mould fragments have been found in the Agora: at the basilica,[7] the prytaneion (Mitsopoulos-Leon 1985, 249, pl. 28.5), in a well (Meriç 2002, 34 cat. K 50, pl. 92), and at an unspecified find spot (Rogl 2008b, 528, fig. 10). In addition, two mould fragments were unearthed in Hanghaus 2 (Dereboylu 2001, 44 cats. 1–2, pl. 23.219 and 220).

Several findspots are also known from Tivoli, where, in 1926, 25 fragmentary moulds were found in the locality

---

5 Similarly, the abbreviated rendering of Pili M on a mould from Tivoli (Puppo 1995, 69 cat. T2, pl. XXXV) is probably to be understood as an erroneous rendering having to do with Popilius, whether this signature emulates or connotes its more famous predecessor.

6 Andreiomenou 1968, 80, pl. 84c–d; Daux 1968, 749, 753, fig. 9; Zaganiari-Phrantzi 1970, 137, fig. 1.

7 Laumonier 1977, 132; Mitsopoulos-Leon 1985, 249, pl. 28.6; Mitsopoulos-Leon 1991, 70 cat. D1, pl. 76; 74 cat. D 56, pl. 87.

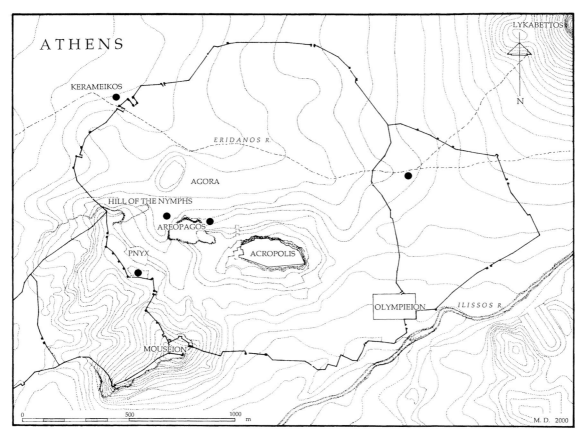

FIGURE 25   Athens. Primary location of finds of moulds. Agora Excavations, American School of Classical Studies, adapted from Camp 2001, fig. 1 with the kind permission of John M. Camp

S. Anna (Paribeni 1927), the site of a bath establishment in antiquity, and later, between 1991 and 1995, 104 fragmentary moulds came to light in a single *cuneus* in the amphitheatre (Leotta 1993; 1995; 1997). The distance between the sites is just a few hundred meters. Apart from the sites mentioned above, in most cases, mould fragments have come to light in secondary deposits and in fills unrelated to a workshop and are therefore few in number.

Workshop Organization and Scale: Summing Up
The MMB was a specialized product, and production took place at a number of scales (summarized in Fig. 27):
(a) Small-scale production: intended for local consumption and a local market. Example: Pontic Demetrios; probably mostly individual workshops.
(b) Medium-scale production: intended for local consumption as well as for regional and long-distance trade. Examples: Athens, Knidos, Kyme; probably mostly nucleated workshops.
(c) Large-scale (mass) production: intended for local consumption as well as for regional and long-distance trade. Example: Ephesos; the Ephesian workshops developed from (nucleated) workshops to manufactory over time.

In so far as our material allows us to draw any major conclusions, it appears that in general workshops were small, with only a handful of craftsmen, and the daily output was limited too. However, the individual workshops probably benefitted from a certain nucleation, which we can see at several production sites. Thus, 'mass production' does not necessarily imply large-scale production units: many smaller units could together produce large quantities of a given product.

An organization and an output which reflect a true manufactory with mass production and mass distribution is attested only at Ephesos. The simultaneous existence of several workshops in one urban centre is documented at least at Athens, Ephesos, and Tivoli.

Distribution and Trade

Most assemblages will constitute a mix of MMB from various production places. When the provenance of the

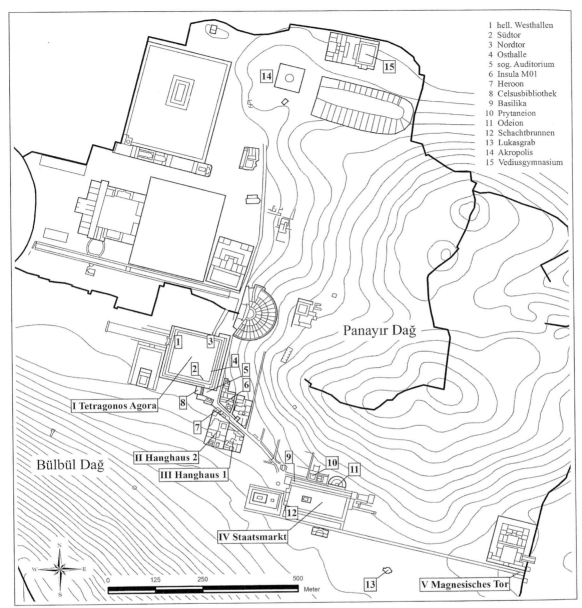

FIGURE 26 Ephesos. Primary location of finds of moulds, after Rogl 2021, fig. 1 with the kind permission of Christine Rogl

vessels is properly identified, any assemblage found at any given site will provide an indication of the degree of self-sufficiency of the locality as well as the opposite pole, an indication of the degree of contact with other production places. However, even though we can observe the actual relationship between vessels of local, regional and/or extra-regional provenance, we do not automatically obtain an understanding of why bowls of foreign provenance came to be part of a local assemblage. It is tempting to understand this as evidence of trade, and most likely, this was the main reason for the distribution of the MMB beyond their place of production. But there are other possibilities as well, such as:

– People moving about with their pots
– Gift-giving and gift-exchange
– Dedications in sanctuaries

And even if we could prove that trade was the reason for their distribution, this does not answer the question of the strategy behind it. It is obvious that, depending on the size of the output, the mode of trade could be anything from homebase reciprocity over central place redistribution or market exchange to freelance trading and port of trade, to use the terminology of C. Renfrew (1975, 41–43, fig. 10), because trade could be anything from entire shiploads of pottery to single pots employed as space-fillers in cargoes of other goods ('parasitic goods'). Even the down-the-line

Production mode	Location	Crafts-man	Engage-ment	Specialization	Purpose	Scale of production	Middlemen	Distribution
Individual workshop	home, outside home, peripatetic	(women) men	part-time, full-time	household pottery (fine-ware pottery)	market	small-scale	no	local (regional)
Nucleated workshops	outside home	(women)[a] men	(part-time) full-time	standardized production of household/fine-ware pottery/lamps/terracottas	market	medium-scale	no/yes	local, regional, long-distance
The manufactory	outside home	men	full-time	specialized product	market	large-scale	yes	local, regional, long-distance

FIGURE 27 Revised version of Peacock's production model adapted for the MMB
Note: a. The signatures of an Artemis in the 'Mainzer Workshop' attest to a female 'craftsman' in the context of nucleated workshops.

kind of exchange is a possibility – perhaps in areas off the main trading routes. Another approach is to consider the degree of self-sufficiency documented by the bowls found at a given site.

Self-Sufficiency
By and large, in most of antiquity and in any part of the ancient world, with the exception of the largest cities, self-sufficiency in agriculture went hand in hand with self-sufficiency in manufacturing. Most scholars who deal with the ancient economy are in agreement on this point (Hopkins 1983). This is also true concerning MMB, because in all likelihood, most centres of the late Hellenistic world had their own MMB industry, no matter in which corner of the Hellenistic world they were located, be it long- or short-lived and with a larger or smaller production output. In 1993, I noted more than 45 towns and cities where moulds had been found. In her 2002-publication, Künzl was able expand the list to 54 localities (Künzl 2002, 77–79). Today, we can assert that moulds were found at more than 80 localities (Appendix 4). With increased focus on Hellenistic pottery, more and more moulds will surely turn up in the coming years, and, thus, the number of sites where MMB are known to have produced will become higher yet. If we were to add places where the MMB have a particular local flavour (e.g., Cyprus and the Levant) and therefore may suggest the presence of a local production unattested by moulds, this would make the net of production sites even more fine-meshed. If in theory 'every' Greek town and city had its own production of MMB, to a certain extent they would be self-sufficient. In many places this also seems to have been the case.

A good example is Athens, where relatively few 'foreign' MMB have been found. Of the 353 bowls published in *Agora* XXII, Rotroff counts only 45 bowls as imports. A fair number of these are Ephesian and probably Ephesian,[8] one is probably from Knidos (Rotroff 1982a, 88 cat. 370, pl. 65), and one is from the Peloponnesos (Rotroff 1982a, 89 cat. 382, pls. 66, 88). Most, however, are of unknown production places, perhaps originating in local or regional sources which have not (yet) been identified.[9] The ratio between local products and imports in this one Athenian assemblage is, accordingly, 7.8:1.

Siebert's list of imports to Peloponnesian sites and exports of Peloponnesian bowls beyond the region of production (1978, 192–193) contributes to this inquiry. The largest body of material comes from Argos, where Siebert records 906 bowls; of these, 848 are local products made in four+ workshops, and the remainder are imports. Of these, seven come from the regional production of Athens, whereas 48 derive from a long-distance source, namely Ephesos; three are unidentified. Thus, Argos shows an extreme degree of self-sufficiency: 14.6:1. Another Peloponnesian example, namely Lousoi, has been analysed recently by C. Rogl (2008a). Lousoi was also a production place, as demonstrated by the discovery of five moulds (Rogl 2008a, 102 cat. 24, 106 cat. 46, 113 cats. 76–78). Of the 346 bowls found, she counts 270 as local; thus, the degree of self-sufficiency is 3.6:1. The

---

8 Rotroff 1982a, cats. 365, 376–379, 384–385, 388, 391–392, 395, 406, 369; Rotroff 1982a, 92, ref. to cat. 406.
9 Rotroff 1982a, cats. 364, 366–368, 371–375, 380, 383, 386–387, 389–390, 393–394, 396–405, 409.

	Source	Local	Local or regional	Regional	Long-distance	?	Grand total	Degree of self-sufficiency
Argos	Siebert 1978	848		7	48	3	906	14.6:1
Sardis	Rotroff 2003	207		21			228	9.9:1
Athens	Rotroff 1982a	308		1	15	29	353	6.8:1
Lousoi	Rogl 2008a	270	12	58	1	5	346	3.6:1
Pantikapaion	Chapter 25	37			347		383	1:9.4
Myrmekion	Chapter 26	85			199		284	1:2.3

FIGURE 28 Self-sufficiency: the numerical relationship between local products and imports at selected sites

remaining bowls derive from local or regional sources in the vicinity (Argos, Corinth, Elis and Achaean workshops); no Athenian bowls are attested and only one bowl from Ephesos was identified. The picture we obtain from Lousoi is of a town with a high degree of self-sufficiency, but apparently not with a production output which was large enough to meet the local demand. Therefore, local production was supplemented by a considerable number of imports from the home region, the Peloponnesos.

In Asia Minor, not surprisingly, Ephesos shows an almost complete self-sufficiency, whereas Miletos gives a more mixed picture. Of the 749 vessels found at Miletos, the largest part are local products; however, there are a significant number of regional imports, chiefly of Ephesian bowls (Kossatz 1990, 104–111) and other Asia Minor products;[10] long-distance trade is attested by Athenian bowls, amounting to around 20 pieces (Kossatz 1990, 111–112). Further inland, at Sardis, we find a situation where the local production made the site almost self-sufficient (Rotroff 2003); there is no evidence of bowls deriving from long-distance trade, and any supplement to local production was by regional products, primarily from Aiolis and Pergamon as well as from Ephesos (Fig. 28).

If we turn to the Black Sea region, to Pantikapaion and Myrmekion, we find a high degree of dependence on goods from long-distance sources and a very low degree of self-sufficiency, despite the fact that Demetrios produced MMB at both localities. At Myrmekion, the ratio between local products and imports is 1:2.3, whereas at Pantikapaion the ratio is as low as 1:9.4. The extremely low degree of self-sufficiency at Pantikapaion is puzzling; it may have to do with the fact that Pantikapaion was the capital of the Bosporan Kingdom and therefore was a hub in the region's trade network. Even so, the contrast with Myrmekion, which was a suburb of Pantikapaion, is remarkable. It cannot be excluded that chronology plays a role (Chapter 25).

Some productions were very limited in their output. Examples are Istros and Olbia, where only one mould has been documented in each city (Appendix 4); moreover, I have been unable to identify MMB of local production at either site. Instead, as far as the finds can tell us, the inhabitants relied (apparently almost) exclusively on imported vessels.

Exchange Networks and Trade
We shall now turn to a discussion of the variety of exchange mechanisms which may have been in operation in distributing the products of the workshops. In general, large-scale trade operations in anything but agricultural products are unlikely (also Pucci 1983, 111–112).

Small-Scale Production and Local Exchange Networks
Workshops which mainly catered to local consumption had a limited distribution. Siebert's analysis (1978) suggests Argos as an example. He identified three Argive bowls in the local area (at Tiryns and Mycenae), while regional distribution amounts to one bowl at Athens and one on Aigina. Concerning long-distance trade, not surprisingly, four bowls have been found on Delos; moreover, one was found aboard the Santa Sabina shipwreck and one in a tomb in Etruria (Siebert 1978, 193). Subsequent excavation and publication now requires the revision of these figures; at Lousoi alone, for instance, Rogl has now identified 19–20 Argive bowls (Rogl 2008a, 97–101 cats. 1–20). Nonetheless, the balance between Siebert's numbers may represent something close to the original one – and if we add Rogl's numbers to Fig. 29 without taking into account new finds made at Argos and perhaps elsewhere, the Rogl bowls would bias the picture.

The best case for assessing the distribution of a smaller workshop is, I believe, the workshop of Bosporan Demetrios, which had a limited production and a limited distribution (Chapter 18). The majority of the vessels have turned up within the local market area, up to 20 km from the sites of production (Fig. 29). Thus, beyond Pantikapaion and Myrmekion, where the bowls were

---
10 The way the book is organized inhibits a complete overview of the exact numbers.

	Source	Production site(s)	Local	Regional			Long-distance	?
Argos	Siebert 1978	848 vessels	6 vessels/ 2 sites	2 vessels/2 sites			6 vessels/ 3 sites	
Pontic Demetrios	Chapter 18			Bosporan kingdom, more than 20 km from production sites	Bosporan kingdom, location?	Northwestern BSR beyond Bosporan Kingdom		
		124 vessels/ 2 sites	89 vessels/ 3 sites	28 vessels/7 sites	5 vessels	12-13 vessels/6 sites	1	2

FIGURE 29   Distribution of bowls at the production site(s) and beyond: the examples of Argos and Pontic Demetrios

produced, significant numbers of Demetrios bowls have been found at Porthmion, Tyritake, and Ogon'ki. The percentage of Demetrios bowls at Porthmion is 16.5%; at Tyritake it is 23%, whereas at Ogon'ki, located in Tyritake's hinterland, the local Demetrios bowls constituted 92.3% of the assemblage.[11] This is in stark contrast to all other Bosporan localities, where the amounts are small in number as well as percentages. In fact, the number of Demetrios' bowls drops dramatically beyond 20 km from the production sites. Beyond the Bosporan Kingdom, Demetrios bowls are few, and outside the northern Black Sea region, to my knowledge, only one Demetrios bowl has been found – at Kyzikos (DEM-154), which is located geographically as close as can be to the Black Sea.

Medium-Scale Production and Distribution
Athenian vessels were widely distributed in both the Mediterranean and the Black Sea region, but outside the immediate environs of Athens, their numbers are limited (Guldager Bilde 1993, 197). No more than 76 (1.6%) are present among the over 4,600 vessels on our Black Sea sites. Whether the spread of the Athenian vessels followed a definite export strategy or the bowls moved around with their owners is difficult to decide.

If we consider the products of the Meter Medallion Workshop and other Kymean workshops, it is likely that their spread chiefly to the Black Sea region, where 97% of them have been found, was dependent on the location of Kyme on a major north-bound sailing route. We also find an indicator in their iconography that part of the production was made with a Pontic clientele in mind. One may point to the fact that the only bowls which employed a full-body figural decoration depicted an Amazonomachy, a theme which since the 4th century had been very much favoured in the Black Sea region, as we can see from the enormous imports of Attic red-figured pelikai (e.g.,

Fless 2002). But even more particular is the occurrence on two of Kirbeis' vessels of a very fine and detailed stamp of a gorytos (KYB-54*, KYB-55), which had an emblematic use in the Pontic region.

Large-Scale Production and Distribution
The heyday of the MMW was in the second quarter of the 2nd century. It is clear from a study of deposits at Olbia that from the middle of the century or slightly thereafter, Ephesian products supplanted Kymean ones (Chapters 12 and 20). The complete dominance of Ephesian MMB in the second half of the 2nd century throughout the Mediterranean and the Black Sea region (with the exception of the Greek mainland) seems to be a fact. In the Pontic region alone, Ephesian vessels account for more than 65%. However, this percentage reflects different situations. It is obvious that the later a given assemblage, the larger the proportion of Ephesian vessels. Good examples in the Black Sea region are Istros, Myrmekion and Porthmion, and in the Mediterranean the dominance of Ephesian vessels on Delos, with over 90% of the MMB, cannot be overlooked (Fig. 4). From the time of WC1 and WC2, the Ephesian production was at the scale of mass production for mass consumption.

Why did Ephesos come to dominate the market to the extent it did? Clearly it filled the gap at sites where no or only a sparse local production of MMB took place. But this is not an explanation. Ephesos was not a natural site for large-scale production, because the local clay was not particularly well suited for making pottery.[12] This is why so much lime was added to the clay: to produce a fabric which was sufficiently workable to serve the potter's need. In many ways, the question of the popularity of the Ephesian MMB recalls discussions concerning the widespread popularity of Rhodian amphorae, with which they are often found. Enormous numbers of Rhodian amphorae have been found throughout the Mediterranean and

---

11   On the site, see Zin'ko 2006, 294, 296–298, 302; for the MMB, see Grzegrzółka 2010, 17, 214–226.

12   Oral information from S. Ladstätter.

the Black Sea: 5,000 on Rhodes, 15,000 in the Pontic region (Lund 2007), 40,000 in Athens, and 100,000 in Alexandria. In contrast to the MMB, the amphorae carried a commodity, namely wine. Even though Rhodes still boasts today of being one of Greece's foremost wine regions, the popularity of its wine cannot explain its vast distribution. Rather, it is probably the auspicious coincidence of a good product, good organization, and the right logistics, primarily a good harbour, good ships, and the right location in the trade network.

Turning to Ephesos, it is clear that, for a period, Ephesos boasted a world-class harbour. However, throughout the centuries, the Ephesians fought the Kaystros River, which time and again silted the harbour. From Strabo we know that Attalos II Philadelphos (r. 159–138) ordered the harbour protected 'once and for all' with a mighty pier (Strabo 14.1.24) – according to the same author, with little result.[13] Nevertheless, it is conceivable that the measures had an – albeit temporary – effect, which may have boosted Ephesos' trade in the mid- and third quarter of the 2nd century. At any rate, the coincidence in time between the renovation of the harbour and the booming export in MMB is of note.

A.J. Parker's study of ancient shipwrecks has made it clear that fine pottery was almost exclusively secondary goods on board sunken ships (1992, 16; see also Pucci 1983, 111–112 and Gibbins 2001).[14] In his catalogue, Parker mentions a single wreck which carried MMB: the Apollonia B (or Apollonia II) shipwreck (Parker 1992, 57 cat. 48; Gibbins 2001, cat. 8). This wreck has never been more than summarily published (Laronde 1987; Long 1992). According to L. Long, the finds included amphorae of the following types: Rhodian (21%), Greco-Italic (9%), Koan (8%), Dressel 1 (7%), Lamboglia 2 (3%), Dressel 26 and Punic (1% each), in total 50% of the cargo. Plain ware (*ceramique commune*) made up 21% of the cargo, 14% was Campana ware, 11% red-glazed, 4% MMB.[15] The Rhodian amphorae are stamped by Ariston (unclear whether as fabricant or eponym; if the latter, dated to ca. 167/165) and the fabricant Drakontidas, active from ca. 140 through the 130s. Laronde published the MMB as of "Menemachos' workshop or other Ephesian workshop" (1987, 328–329). Unfortunately, no pictures have ever been published, so his attributions are impossible to confirm. The mixed date has made Lawall consider whether it is a single wreck or a dumped cargo (2005, 36), and one should probably not build too much on this wreck. A single MMB was found on the Grand Congloué 2 wreck and another on the Mahdia wreck but they were clearly not part of the cargo.[16]

The only other wreck I know of in which MMB have been recorded in significant numbers is the one which sank off Torre di Santa Sabina close to Brindisi in Apulia (not in Parker). The wreck was investigated by Italian archaeologists directed by N. Lamboglia between 1972 and 1976. On board were found 136 fragments from slightly over 100 individual MMB, which have been published by G. Siebert (1977). According to A. Antonazzo of the Italian antiquities authority, the ship mostly contained amphorae (Greco-Italic, Lamboglia 2, ovoid Adriatic of Salentine production, Rhodian, and Tripolitan). On board were also other fine wares such as black-gloss and thin-walled pottery, plain ware (*ceramica d'uso commune*), and lamps.[17]

As was the case with the amphorae and other fine wares of both the Apollonia and the S. Sabina wrecks, the MMB from the S. Sabina shipwreck came from a multitude of different production places. According to Siebert, 'Ionian' (i.e., Ephesian) bowls dominated, with 70% of the vessels, but 4% were Peloponnesian, 3% perhaps Athenian, and 1% northern Greek; 22% were unattributed.

Even though we cannot distinguish between the cargo and the personal belongings of the men on board the ship, and even though the question of whether the amphorae were reused and thus no longer related to their original places of production remains unanswered,[18] the two wrecks nevertheless bring the same story to light: ships carried out coastal tramping, where cargo was loaded and unloaded throughout the sailing route rather than moved exclusively from point A to point B (Davies 2001, 28; Gibbins 2001, 294–295; Horden & Purcell 2004, 137–152, 368–372). Logistics were therefore of high importance for the success of a given product: where on the trade network was the producer located? Whereas the dissemination of

---

13   A good discussion concerning Ephesos' harbour and the problem of keeping it functioning can be found in Kraft et al. 2007, which is based on recent sedimentological and geomorphological investigations in and around the city.

14   An exception is the Grand Congloué 1 wreck, dated at the beginning of the 2nd century; its cargo consisted of around 400 Greco-Italic amphorae, around 30 Rhodian amphorae, and a few other Greek amphorae, as well as no fewer than 7,000 pieces of black-gloss Campana ware (Parker 1992, 200–201 with references).

15   Strangely enough, Gibbins mentions the MMB as the "main cargo" (2001, 297 cat. 8); this is clearly wrong.

16   Benoit 1952, 252 fig. 15; Long 1987, fig. 2.7 (misleading) and p. 14 (Grand Congloué 2); Rotroff 1994a, 135–136, fig. 6 (Mahdia). The handful of MMB on the Antikythera wreck have already been mentioned (Chapter 3 n. 29).

17   [Ed. See now Antonazzo 2014 (189–190), with a brief discussion of the mouldmade bowls, now estimated as at least 300 vessels.]

18   See recent discussion by Lawall (2011, 43–44).

the Kymean workshops may have been more accidental and based on an excellent geographical location in a south-north trade network along the coast of Asia Minor to the Black Sea, the spread of the Ephesian products, which took place at a time when the MMB had caught the attention of the market, may have been on board ships predominantly carrying Rhodian amphorae. At any rate, the Ephesian producers seem to have pursued a conscious production and export strategy which exploited Ephesos' position as a 'world-class' harbour to the full.

CHAPTER 5

Supplementary Shapes

The dominant shape of MMB production was, of course, the handleless, footless bowl, thrown directly inside a hemispherical mould and of a fairly uniform size (rim diameter 10–19 cm, most commonly 12–14). These standard bowls will be the focus of the chapters on individual production places (Chapters 8–15, 18). In this chapter, however, we shall consider the other, much rarer shapes, many of them made using the same moulds used for the standard bowls but fitted with additional elements to create more complex open or closed shapes.

In order to gain a clearer understanding of these supplementary shapes, their morphology, and the frequency with which they occur, I have gathered as many examples as possible, both from the Black Sea region and elsewhere. The catalogue below encompasses more than 600 vessels; of these, 175 come from the 11 Pontic assemblages that form the basis of my study, the remainder from other Black Sea and Mediterranean sites.

Strangely enough, this subject has been little studied. The first scholar to consider the supplementary shapes was F. Courby. Based on the vessels found on Delos, Courby distinguished 12 shapes, designated with Roman numerals and illustrated with line drawings in a figure of his book (1922, fig. 62; note that the vessels are not represented at a uniform scale): a kyathos-like one-handled hemispherical bowl (V);[1] a hemispherical bowl with one(?) pinched handle (VI); a small, footless pitcher (VII); a footed, two-handled skyphos (VIII); a funnel (IX; only the tube and a trace of the body are pictured); a filter jug (X); a lagynos (XI); a guttus with a ring handle (XII); a krater (XIII); a globular vessel with collared neck (XIV); an amphora (XV); and another type of globular vessel with collared neck (XVI). In 1986, J. Raeder discussed a corpus of 17 amphorae made in the mouldmade technique. T.L. Samojlova considered the supplementary shapes found at Olbia in an article published in 1994. V. Mitsopoulos-Leon did the same in 1996, when she published a series of vessels excavated at Lousoi (see also Rogl 2008a), and in an article from 2004, S.G. Schmid published a relief amphora and two kraters found at Eretria. In addition, there are publications in which a single vessel of supplementary shape is treated, e.g., a hydria from the art market (Parlasca 1982), and three vessels from Olbia: a situla (von Stern 1902; Guldager Bilde 2005), another situla (Samojlova & Batizat 1994), and a krater (Samojlova 1998).

The supplementary shapes can be roughly divided into three groups based on the mould(s) employed:
– Mould of the standard hemispherical bowl
– Small mould (maximum diameter 5.5–9.5 cm)
– Special-purpose mould

The first group of moulds was employed for making a variety of shapes, such as drinking vessels with handles and/or feet, amphorae, kraters, filter jugs, and funnels.

The second group was used for making an array of small shapes, first of all a small bowl and a small one-handled juglet, but also other forms of drinking cups, dippers, small amphorae, amphoriskoi, lagynoi, oinochoai and other jugs, unguentaria, kraters, and bell-shaped lids.

The third group comprises moulds which were made particularly for vessels of different shapes: for example, tall, cylindrical moulds for making situlae, jugs, and rhyta, or shallow moulds, often with the decoration placed upside-down, for making the mouldmade shoulders of gutti and, occasionally, lagynoi.

Fig. 30 lays out the distribution of the supplementary shapes according to function. Most were intended for the mixing and serving of wine and are hence to be understood as symposium equipment supplementing the standard bowls. In addition, there is a comprehensive group of vessels, namely gutti and filter jugs, which most likely also had a function at the symposium: they were intended for the drop-wise pouring of a substance, probably perfumed oil. The vessels made in small moulds are more enigmatic. It is difficult to decide whether they were used in the same way as their larger equivalents, or whether the small shape implies a different function. It would be reasonable to view them as symbolic items made for funerary use, for example, and some of them have, in fact, been found in tombs. However, most of the pieces of known provenance seem to come from either domestic or public contexts (see below).

How common were the supplementary shapes? In the Pontic assemblages, they constitute 3.8% of all of the MMB found. However, this number covers significant variation, because at some sites, supplementary shapes have not been recorded at all, whereas at other sites they

---

1 Nos. I–IV are profile variations of standard hemispherical bowls.

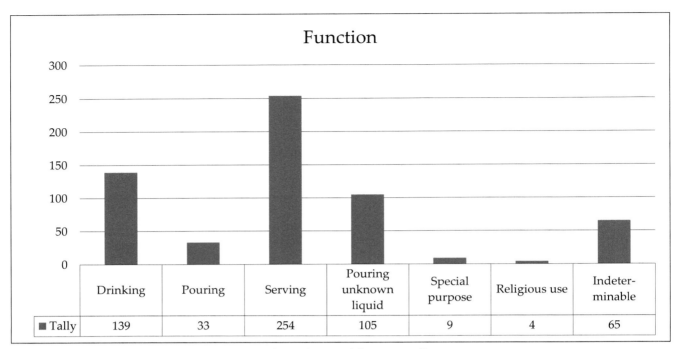

FIGURE 30   Division of the supplementary shapes according to function, following Rotroff 1997a

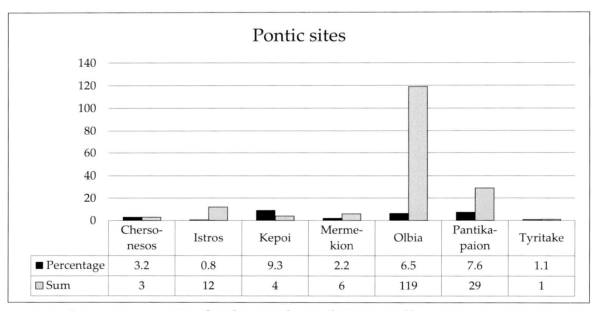

FIGURE 31   Comparative representation of supplementary shapes in the Pontic assemblages

constitute up to 10% of the MMB (Fig. 31). We shall return to the Pontic sites at the end of this chapter.

If we look at a number of representative publications, the percentage of additional shapes at other sites corresponds more or less to the Pontic figure. For example, Rotroff writes that of the 353 MMB published in Agora XXII (the moulds are subtracted from the total), only about 20 vessels (5.7%) were of supplementary shapes (1982a, 39). We find the same figure at Lousoi, where Rogl reports that the standard bowls constitute 94% of the assemblage of 354 vessels which she studied. Among the remaining 6% are 11 krateres/krateriskoi (SHA-379, SHA-380, SHA-395, SHA-396, SHA-424–SHA-430), four amphorae (SHA-267–SHA-269), four funnels (SHA-311), two oinochoai (SHA-285, SHA-286), one plate (SHA-437) and one small bowl (Rogl 2008a, 67). Similarly at Sardis, out

Laumonier 1977	Location	Total no. of fragments	Filter jugs	%	'Grands vases'	%	'Petits vases'	%
p. 7	South terrace of the Samothrakeion	287			5	1.7		
p. 8	Maisons Chamonard	44	1	2.3	5	11.4		
p. 9	House excavated in 1958	109	10	9.2	4	3.7		
p. 9	Maison de Fourni	183	2	1.1	3	1.6		
p. 10	Skardana living quarter	1,477	23	1.6			17	1.2

FIGURE 32 Find contexts with supplementary shapes on Delos, according to Laumonier 1977, 7–10

of 219 vessels in Rotroff's catalogue, only six vessels (2.7%) are of supplementary shapes (Rotroff 2003).[2] These vessels include a situla (SHA-318), a footed juglet (SHA-116), a footless juglet (SHA-104), an amphora (SHA-221), another closed vessel (SHA-561), and a spectacular lidded funerary urn with white slip and painted decoration as well as a plastic attachment on the shoulder (SHA-542). Only the situla seems to be an import (from Ephesos), whereas the remainder are probably local.

On Delos, of 6,495 vessels, 200 (3.1%) were of supplementary shapes. The number found in various contexts is, of course, open to some variation, as we can gather from Laumonier's introduction, where he lists a number of contexts in which supplementary shapes have been found (Laumonier 1977, 7–10; Fig. 32).

Based on the above, we can conclude that supplementary shapes – if present or identified at all – hardly made up more than a few percent of any given assemblage. With the exception of the small bowl, the juglet, the filter jug, and perhaps the krater and the amphora, all other shapes occur very sporadically in any production and they may, therefore, represent a whim of the potter crafting the vessel.

In terms of chronology, not all supplementary shapes were made at the same time. We can follow the earliest occurrence of such shapes in the deposits of the Athenian Agora, where two deposits are of particular interest. One is Deposit H-K 12–14, the building fill of the Middle Stoa, deposited before ca. 170, where the largest single batch of supplementary shapes was found. This consists of two amphorae of Athenian type (SHA-209, SHA-210), a jug(?) with a band handle (SHA-283), and no less than five Athenian-type kraters (SHA-331, SHA-336, SHA-339–SHA-341). In the contemporary Deposit M 21:1, the Komos cistern, four small bowls came to light (SHA-2, SHA-5–SHA-7; the first by the Workshop of Bion). In other workshops as well, the small vessels, the kraters, and the amphorae seem to be early, and few were made after the third quarter of the 2nd century. In fact, Ephesian kraters and situlae were probably not made after about the mid-2nd century, and the same is most likely the case of the Corinthian kraters too, at least of the type with applied feet, which seem to be a feature of the second quarter of the 2nd century, but perhaps also of the long-petal kraters.

Drinking vessels in supplementary shapes other than the small ones were few; in the second quarter of the 2nd century, in Kyme and elsewhere in Aiolis, a skyphos with ring handles and a low, stemmed foot was produced; the same basic shape but with pinched handles and a higher stem was made in the third quarter of the same century in the Ephesian Monogram PAR Workshop. A shallow cup with a high collared rim was common in the late Aiolis B production of the last quarter of the 2nd century and perhaps later.

In the second quarter of the 2nd century, a lentoid guttus with a tall, slender neck and a ring handle was produced at Ephesos. This shape was the first to employ moulds for the shoulder which were especially designed for this shape: shallow, so as to create a nearly straight or gently convex shoulder, and with the stamps positioned upside down. Its function was probably taken over by the filter jug, which characterizes the deposits of the abandonment fills on Delos (e.g., Fig. 32). The filter jug may have been sporadically produced in the second half of the 2nd century, but its heyday was the beginning of the 1st century. The lagynos, which in plain ware and white-slipped wares was so common in the second half of the 2nd century, was produced to only a limited extent in mouldmade technique. Two fragments have been found at Carthage (SHA-298, SHA-299), so they may date before 146; otherwise, however, the lagynos in the mouldmade technique seems to be a shape of the second half of the century.

I have already mentioned the shallow cup with a high collared rim of the Aiolis B production. In this production we find a whole new range of shapes, such as a chalice, a

---

[2] This figure does not include the finds from the Butler expedition listed in the end of Rotroff's book.

cup with band handles, and a beaker; they all point away from the tradition of the MMB and toward the red-gloss shapes of the latest Hellenistic period.

In what follows, we shall consider the individual shapes. We shall begin with the small shapes. Then follow the many shapes which were based on the mould of the standard bowl as well as the special-purpose moulds. The division of the material will be in terms of function following the terminology employed by S. Rotroff in Agora XXIX (1997a).

Shapes Made Using a Small Mould

Small Bowl
In addition to the standard-sized bowl, many workshops also produced a bowl with a diameter ranging from 7.5 to 9.1 cm (SHA-1–SHA-63). In fact, this was the single most common supplementary shape. Most were produced at Ephesos, both in oxidized and especially in reduced fabrics, but they were also made at Athens, in a number of Aiolian workshops, as well as in the Meter Medallion Workshop. It is likely that what was drunk from the small bowls differed from what was drunk from the standard bowl, or maybe they served a different purpose altogether. In Athens, the small bowl was occasionally furnished with a low foot (SHA-75). Second to third quarter of the 2nd century?

Small Bowl with One Handle (Dipper?)
A one-handled version of the small bowl was produced mostly in Ephesos and again especially in reduced fabrics (SHA-64–SHA-71). It may have served as a dipper. Second to third quarter of the 2nd century?

Juglet
A one-handled juglet with a biconical neck and a plain everted rim is second in numbers only to the small bowl (SHA-76–SHA-120). It is normally footless, but isolated footed pieces are known from the Ephesian and Sardian productions as well as from an unknown production (SHA-115–SHA-117). Since the form was based on a mould with a very small diameter (6–8 cm), the jugs are correspondingly quite small (5–7 cm high). They were made in a number of different places, chiefly at Ephesos, but also at Pergamon, Kyme, Sardis, and perhaps Myrina, as well as at Athens. Consequently, we find some slight variations in the morphology. For example, jugs with double handle joined with a clay ring (SHA-85–SHA-87) seem to be Pergamene, and up-turned rims with a slight offset on the interior appear to be Ephesian (e.g., SHA-93, SHA-95, SHA-97).

The shape's popularity makes it likely that it served a special purpose which escapes us today. Maybe these little jugs were dippers, or perhaps one could even drink from them. Or maybe their content was of a particular kind – Rotroff has suggested honey (2010, 60). Even though a few of them have been found in tombs, e.g., at Kepoi (SHA-90) together with an Ephesian bowl of the Monogram PAR Workshop (EPH-188), on Samothrace (SHA-88), at Sardis (SHA-106), and at Ancona (SHA-110), more have been found in domestic or public contexts (SHA-76–SHA-82, SHA-84, SHA-89, SHA-92, SHA-114, SHA-115, SHA-119). Because of their small size, decoration is normally a simple affair: either a calyx, imbricate petals, or vertical fluting, though there are a few slightly more ambitious vessels with figural elements. Second to third quarter of the 2nd century.

Small Amphora
Just one small amphora is attested (SHA-122). Its provenance and its place of production are unknown. Its shape is of hybrid Pergamene/Ephesian type (see below); it is decorated with a crude net pattern made of dots. Second to third quarter of the 2nd century?

Small Lagynos
Two small lagynoi of two different and unidentified productions are known (SHA-123, SHA-124). Second half of the 2nd century?

Small Oinochoe with Trefoil Mouth
One small oinochoe from Rhodes has been published, and two more are mentioned in the literature (SHA-125–SHA-127). They may be from the Kyme-Myrina area, because they are very similar to other small shapes made in that region, such as amphoriskoi and small bell-shaped lids (see below). Second quarter of the 2nd century?

Small Jug
Just two small jugs are known (SHA-128, SHA-129). One with extremely fine decoration in many friezes is known from the Italo-Megarian production, unfortunately without context. The second was found in a Macedonian tomb and since it features stylized long-petal decoration, most likely it dates to the second half of the 2nd century.

Unguentarium?
One shoulder fragment of a possible unguentarium is the only occurrence of this shape (SHA-130).

SUPPLEMENTARY SHAPES

Amphoriskos with Pointed Toe
I know of just two amphoriskoi made partially in a hemispherical mould (SHA-131, SHA-132). Both have a pointed toe and from the complete vessel in Kassel (SHA-131) has two vertical round handles from neck to shoulder. These are missing from the vessel from Myrina (SHA-132) but attested by handle scars. The vessel in Kassel is decorated with masks between low columns and it is probably Kymean (or Myrinean). The decoration of the vessel from Myrina is a bound myrtle wreath. The fact that one was found in Myrina and that the other has a decoration well known from the same area may induce us to believe that the two amphoriskoi were a local phenomenon of the Kyme-Myrina area. Second quarter of the 2nd century?

Small Krater
Just one small krater is documented, unfortunately of unknown provenance and production (SHA-133).

Lid with Ring Handle
Two small, bell-shaped lids have been found in the Kyme-Myrina area (SHA-134, SHA-135). They most resemble thymiaterion lids (also Schäfer 1968, 107), but they lack the perforations which such lids normally have. Second quarter of the 2nd century?

Shapes Made Using Standard and Special-Purpose Moulds

Kantharos
There was occasional experimentation with the kantharos shape in Athenian, Ephesian, and Italo-Megarian productions (SHA-136–SHA-142). Two shapes, a kantharos (SHA-137) and a volute krater, were furnished with a net pattern made of interlacing circles, which Rotroff has termed daisy bowls. Since several fragments have been found at Athens (one signed [...]TO[...]), Rotroff considers them to be of Attic production. I have not seen the Delian vessels myself, but I follow Rotroff's ascription (for other vessels with a daisy network, see SHA-337, SHA-348, SHA-383–SHA-386). Second half of the 2nd century and perhaps later.

Skyphos with Ring Handles
Especially at Kyme (Workshop A), but perhaps also at Pergamon (SHA-143), we find a skyphos with a high, undecorated, collared rim, a ridged band handle, and a low, stemmed foot (SHA-143–SHA-152). Second quarter of the 2nd century.

Skyphos with Pinched Handles
A skyphos with a high, undecorated, collared rim, a shallow body, a stemmed foot, and pinched band handles (SHA-153–SHA-156) is probably a development of the skyphos with ring handles described above. The few documented specimens were all produced in the early classical phase of the Ephesian Monogram PAR Workshop (Chapter 14). Mid-2nd to third quarter of the 2nd century.

Stemmed Bowl
A few stems (especially the Ephesian ones) may belong to skyphoi with pinched handles, but since only the tall stem is preserved, the shape of the vessel cannot be determined with certainty (SHA-157–SHA-165). Mid-2nd to third quarter of the 2nd century.

Globular Bowl
Three globular vessels with a rounded shoulder and a strongly projecting rim are attested at Athens (SHA-166–SHA-168); one preserves part of a handle. First half of 1st century?

Krateriskos
Some krater-shaped vessels with and without handles and with a rim diameter of less than 18 cm must have been intended for drinking rather than mixing (SHA-169–SHA-176). Such krateriskoi were mostly produced in the Central Italian workshops. 2nd century.

Shallow Cup with High Collared Rim
This cup has a shallow body topped by a wheel-made shoulder, the profile contracting below the high, collared rim. Vertical band handles (probably two and at least sometimes ridged) run from the shoulder to the middle of the rim; the foot is broad and flat. This shape was produced almost exclusively in the Aiolis B workshop (SHA-177–SHA-192; see Chapter 13). Late 2nd–early 1st century.

Chalice
Two types of chalice were made in Aiolis. One with a strongly S-curved rim related to the standard bowl shape of the Aiolis B production was probably made at Pergamon (SHA-193). It has a foot with a low, broad stem. Related chalices in Pergamene sigillata date from sometime between the first half of the 1st century BCE and the beginning of the following century (Meyer-Schlichtmann 1988, 167–168, form Kg 1, pl. 40). According to Meyer-Schlichtmann, the form was in general rare and never carried relief decoration, and he viewed it as a local development (1988, 168).

The second shape is found in the production of Aiolis B (SHA-194, SHA-195). It features a pronounced vertical hanging rim and a slightly profiled, hollow foot on a low, broad stem. The same shape (though with a much shallower bowl) was still being made in the local or nearby Çandarli ware of the early Empire (Loeschcke 1912, pl. 28.10). There can hardly be any doubt that the chalice, especially the second variant, is the forerunner of the mid- to late Augustan chalices of terra sigillata, especially form *Conspectus* R 2 (168, pl. 53) and Dragendorff Form 11, and we also find it in contemporary glazed pottery (Hochuli-Gysel 1977, 35–42). However, much more research is needed in order to understand the relationship between the development of the earliest terra sigillata and the Aiolian MMB. Late 2nd–early 1st century.

Cup with Band Handle
This rare shape, with a low foot and a band handle attached at the bottom of the wall, is also found only in the Aiolis B production (SHA-196, SHA-197). Late 2nd–early 1st century.

Beaker
A fragment of a cylindrical cup with a vertical rim is known from a single instance of the Aiolis B production (SHA-198). Late 2nd–early 1st century.

Rhyton
The rhyton required a special-purpose mould, which was more cylindrical (and narrower) than the bowl shape (SHA-200–SHA-203). The shape is very rarely attested. Of great interest are the two rhyta from Athribis (SHA-201, SHA-202), which are precious evidence for the promulgation of Ptolemaic ideology by means of mouldmade pottery. Late 3rd to early 1st century.

Amphora
Not surprisingly, the amphora was one of the more popular supplementary shapes, and it was produced in many different workshops (SHA-204–SHA-277). According to S. Rotroff, Hellenistic amphorae fall into two distinct groups: the Attic one, with rope handles and an out-turned or moulded rim, and the Pergamene one, with strap handles and a splayed rim (Rotroff 2010, 67). The Pergamene amphorae usually feature small rotellae at the junction of the handles and the shoulder, while many Athenian amphorae feature satyr masks in that position. On both, the shoulder and neck are usually decorated with West Slope decoration. These two types are also prominently present amongst the mouldmade amphorae, with the Pergamene type by far the most common.

We can distinguish one further type, which is related to the Pergamene one (and also used in Pergamon). I have termed it the Ephesian type, because several early Ephesian vessels are of this type. The rim shape is the same as the Pergamene one, but it is undercut; the base has an up-turned edge.

In addition to these three main types, there are also hybrids between them, as well as local Macedonian types (SHA-244, SHA-245), which follow their own trajectory. Furthermore, a large number of fragments which we can ascribe to large, closed vessels (mostly without coat on the interior) must belong to amphorae as well. First to third quarter of the 2nd century.

Oinochoe
Just one oinochoe with a tall, slender neck is attested (SHA-278). It was found at Corinth, but its place of production is unknown. Before 146?

Jug
A few jugs of various productions are known (SHA-279–SHA-286).

Lagynos
Lagynoi were produced in a number of different workshops, but always in small numbers (SHA-287–SHA-305). Most were made using the standard hemispherical mould for the lower body. Occasionally, however, the relief work is on the shoulder, created using a special, shallow mould, and, as on moulds for the lentoid guttus, with stamps positioned upside-down in order for the decoration to be 'readable' (SHA-287, SHA-298, SHA-299). Second half of the 2nd century.

Funnel
A small group of funnels was produced in the Ephesian Monogram PAR Workshop, formed by adding a narrow, tubular element to the bowl-shaped moulded part (SHA-306–SHA-310, with a few examples produced elsewhere, SHA-311, SHA-312). In all likelihood, these vessels served for pouring wine into a vessel with a slender neck, probably a lagynos or a vessel of similar shape. Second half of the 2nd century.

Situla
This rare shape (SHA-313–SHA-330) reproduced bronze vessels of the ovoid, bucket shaped type, which probably originated in Macedonia or Thrace in the 5th century and became quite common in late Classical and Hellenistic courts and noble households throughout the Mediterranean. The double, moveable handles of the

bronze original could not be imitated in clay; accordingly, the vessel lacks handles, though the handle attachments are reproduced. The bucket shape required a special-purpose mould which was used exclusively for making situlae. The situla exists in one basic type, with an everted, angular rim, but the rim exhibits three varieties: plain everted, undercut, and strongly undercut. On the basis of the available material, it is difficult to know whether this typological variation is a matter of chronology; it does not seem to be related to the production place, because the same rim shapes occur on both Pergamene and Ephesian situlae. Only two or three situlae preserve the entire profile (SHA-316, SHA-320, and perhaps SHA-323). On SHA-316 and SHA-320 we find the same low and wide bell-shaped, grooved foot which is also used on Aiolian amphorae (e.g., SHA-214–SHA-220, SHA-240, SHA-241). SHA-323 either did not have a foot or the foot is lost.

The situla is a large shape: 21.5–22.5 cm high and with a rim diameter ranging from 18 to 24 cm, most commonly 20–22 cm. Most situla fragments are without a particular provenance. Three fragments from Olbia derive from domestic contexts (SHA-313, SHA-321, SHA-326), whereas the completely preserved SHA-320, also from Olbia, most likely comes from the necropolis. The situla probably functioned as a krater and perhaps as a funerary urn.

The main producer seems to have been Ephesos, where most situlae were made in a reduced fabric. It is conceivable that production of the situla was short-lived. In this respect it is of note that many of them have a box meander as a rim frieze (SHA-314–SHA-316, SHA-324, SHA-325). Second quarter of the 2nd century.

Krater

A number of different types of vessels have been identified as kraters in the archaeological literature. Some of these, however, have a rim diameter of less than 18 cm, and it is therefore likely that they served as drinking vessels rather than for mixing wine with water. Consequently, some types published as kraters or krateriskoi are here termed chalices; chalices and krateriskoi are classified as drinking vessels.

The krater, which for centuries had been an integral part of symposium equipment, almost completely disappeared from the Greek shape repertoire in the Hellenistic period (Edwards 1975, 45; Rotroff 1997a, 14–15). This may have to do with ceramic vessels being supplanted by metal ones, or it may even reveal a change in sympotic practices (Rotroff 1997a, 14–15, 135–139). However, a number of different workshops produced kraters with the mouldmade technique from time to time (SHA-331–SHA-417), and many fragments from large vessels which are preserved only as body fragments may attest to a relatively wide-spread use of relief kraters (SHA-419–SHA-434). Nevertheless, the preserved fragments can hardly fill the void. The only place where the relief krater remained in vogue was in Liburnia, where it was by far the most popular shape, accounting for at least 86% of the finds (Brusić 1999, 11; Rogl 2008, 526). The Liburnian kraters were large bell kraters with lug handles on a tall, moulded base. An example found in Apulia (SHA-381) attests to their success outside their place of production.

Because kraters were produced in many different workshops, a number of individual morphological developments can be followed. Here we will consider just the most important ones.

Attic mouldmade kraters have a wide and flaring rim with a down-turned, moulded edge. The foot is relatively simple, and if SHA-338 is Attic and not Atticizing, it can also be profiled and relatively tall. Some of the Attic kraters carry West Slope decoration on the interior as well as on the exterior. A krater from Eretria with horizontal ear-shaped handles placed immediately above the moulded part is either Attic or Atticizing (SHA-343). The daisy pattern of several kraters found on Delos (SHA-337, SHA-348, SHA-383–SHA-385) allows us to attribute one further krater shape to Athens, namely a volute krater on a tall, profiled foot. A variant of this pattern is found on a large krater-like but footless bowl (SHA-386).

The Ephesian (and probably other Asia Minor) kraters had a projecting, club-shaped rim and there is a characteristic offset on the inside at the junction between bowl and neck. Occasionally the inside and outside of the rim are also decorated with moulded relief (SHA-351, SHA-397). Horizontal ear-shaped handles are placed immediately above the moulded part; the foot is tall and profiled, and its edge can be up-turned. A development can be noted from the kraters of the Vases gris and Menemachos to those of the Monogram PAR potter.

Bowls were sometimes furnished with three mouldmade feet, either stamped into the mould or applied to the bowl, and often in the form of satyr masks (on some early Athenian bowls, e.g., ATH-33*) or shells (e.g., Schwabacher 1941, pl. X.20; Kögler 2010, 520 cat. F.125, Pl. 28). They are not included in this chapter, but they are probably the forerunners of a series of large-format vessels, probably kraters, with applied feet in the form of comic or tragic masks or heads of Athena (SHA-412–SHA-416). These vessels seem to have been a specialty of the Corinthian workshops. They have been studied by G.R. Edwards, who listed 24 Corinthian examples and noted the presence of further imported fragments at Corinth (SHA-414;

Edwards 1975, 171–175; see also Edwards 1986, 404–405). According to him, the production of these vessels took place in the short interval of the second quarter of the 2nd century, just before the Mummian destruction of 146. Another group of Corinthian kraters feature plastic long-petal design (SHA-388–SHA-390). A number of long-petal kraters have also been found on Delos, but it is difficult to form an opinion concerning their place of production based on Laumonier vol. 2 alone (SHA-347, SHA-377, SHA-405–SHA-410, SHA-432). 2nd century.

Kalathos
A single kalathos is known from a Macedonian tomb at Kozani (SHA-418). Its production place is unknown. Like the situla, the kalathos was made in a special-purpose mould, which was cylindrical and deeper than moulds for bowls. Second quarter of 2nd century?

Dinos
Two vessels of a peculiar shape resembling a dinos (or a globular situla) have been found, one produced in Aiolis, the second in Ephesos (SHA-435, SHA-436). The form suggests a mixing bowl, but both are rather small for that function. Zimmer (2005, 114) labels the Aiolian vessel a pyxis, but there is no provision for a lid. Second to third quarter of the 2nd century.

Plate or Lid?
Mitsopoulos-Leon has published a fragment from Lousoi with moulded decoration on the inside of the rim as a plate; it could also be a lid (SHA-437).

Lentoid Guttus
Lentoid flask with tall, collared neck, conical ring base, and plain ring handle (SHA-438–SHA-449). The shoulder was thrown in a shallow mould with the relief decoration stamped upside-down, so that it would be properly oriented when the vessel was in use. On a vessel from Delos, plastic elements (comic slave and old-woman masks) were applied to the shoulder (SHA-443). The latter clearly points to Alexandria and the festival of the lagynophoria. Two of these vessels are covered with a yellow substance which may have functioned as primer for gilding (SHA-438, SHA-444).

The shape is very rare. Four gutti come from the Black Sea region – from Kepoi (SHA-447), a Myrmekion farmhouse (SHA-439), Olbia (SHA-438), and Pantikapaion (SHA-448) – and seven have been found on Delos. Most were made in the early Ephesian workshops. Second quarter of the 2nd century.

Tea-Pot Shaped Guttus
Two tea-pot shaped vessels in the Louvre may come from Myrina (SHA-450, SHA-451). Both have a rounded shoulder, a collared neck, and a conical foot, and the best-preserved (SHA-450) also retains a high-swung loop handle and a spout. A vessel of basically the same shape has also been found at Argos (and was produced there) (SHA-452).

Hydria
Just one hydria is documented in the mouldmade technique (SHA-453). Its neck is tall and biconical, the foot equally tall and bell-shaped. The vessel is furnished with a vertical band handle as well as two horizontal ear-shaped handles. The mould was signed with the otherwise unattested signature ΜΕΝΙΣΚΟΥ (Rogl 2001a, 141). Fabric and coat are not mentioned in Parlasca 1982, but the decoration points towards Aiolis.

Filter Jug
This shape has a globular, conical or baggy body with a strainer in the neck, a tubular spout, and a (ridged) ring handle (SHA-454–SHA-540). The upper part of the body was made in a mould, which was turned upside-down; the decoration was not accommodated to this position, but for the linear motifs that adorn the majority, this makes little difference. The lower part of the body, neck, rim, spout, handles, and foot were made separately. This form comes in two basic variants. One, termed the Athenian type, has a foot and a funnel-shaped neck. This variant usually has an incurved rim, but a finely decorated overhanging rim also occurs (SHA-472, SHA-473); the latter is probably earlier. The height is 11–14.5 with a maximum diameter of 11–14 cm. The second variant, termed the Ephesian type, is baggy and has no foot. In contrast to the first variant, this one has a short, collared neck. The height is 9.5–13 cm with a maximum diameter of 11.5–12 cm.

At least 73 fragmentary or complete filter jugs have been found on Delos, as documented in the plates for Laumonier's unpublished second Delos volume. It is a great pity that, with a few exceptions (SHA-456, SHA-465, SHA-467, SHA-483), this large collection has never been published. Laumonier divided the Delian material into to three main groups: Attic, Ionian grey ware, and oxidized and reduced vessels of unknown production place(s). He believed that the majority of the Delian filter jugs were Attic. A fair number of filter jugs have, in fact, been found at Athens (SHA-454, SHA-455, SHA-471–SHA-474, SHA-489, SHA-490, SHA-494, SHA-526, SHA-538, SHA-539), but, in all likelihood, the shape was also produced on Delos.

A significant number of the vessels are decorated with stylized long petals separated by a column of tiny circles topped by a small stylized palmette (SHA-464, SHA-465, SHA-467, SHA-468, SHA-533–SHA-536). A mould for producing vessels with precisely this pattern has been found on Delos.[3] Laumonier considered it an Athenian mould, and the same decoration can be found at Athens (e.g., Rotroff 1982a, cats. 336, 340–341, 353, 355–357). However, whether the mould was imported or not, it shows that in all likelihood at least some of the filter jugs could have been produced on the island. This may also explain why they are so well-represented on Delos and not elsewhere.

At least one potter signed moulds for making filter-jugs: at least three were signed by Ariston (SHA-456, SHA-473, SHA-495) and one bears the letters AION (almost certainly also representing the name Ariston, the missing letters obscured by the attached spout and handle) (SHA-474). The filter jugs were mostly decorated with various types of long-petal decoration. Their function is not entirely clear (see the discussion in Rotroff 1997a, 181), but the fact that they were made in mouldmade versions indicates that they belonged to the sympotic setting. The thin, tubular spout must have been intended for the slow and careful pouring of the liquid it contained. Most likely, this was perfumed oil. The large holes in the 'strainer', which would have strained away little material if used as such, allowed the perfumed smell to evaporate into the room.

In general, the mouldmade filter jug seems to be a late shape. It is not documented at the Athenian Agora earlier than the beginning of the 1st century (Rotroff 1997a, 39 n. 6; 183). This date is in tune with its massive presence on Delos, where the large number of complete vessels indicates that it was in use when the settlement was brusquely interrupted, probably by the attack by Mithridates in 88. I am not aware that this shape has been found in the Black Sea region. Early 1st century.

Lid
The figures are oriented upside-down on a bowl found on Delos (SHA-541). Since it apparently preserves the lip and since the shape is hemispherical and without the addition of a neck, it is unlikely that it is a fragment of a lentoid guttus or a lagynos, the only other shapes using a reversed decoration. Laumonier tentatively identifies it as a cover (1977, 415) and I have no better suggestion.

Funerary Urn
A small group of single pieces of basically the same shape are grouped together here (SHA-542–SHA-545). They feature a more or less globular body with a collared neck, a conical base of varying type, and horseshoe-shaped handles placed at the shoulder at varying heights. The collared neck is well suited to receive a lid, and, in fact, two of these vessels from Sardian tombs preserve a domed lid (SHA-542, SHA-543). They clearly served as funerary urns.

Supplementary Shapes in the Pontic Assemblages

On the basis of the above, let us take a look at the constellation of vessel shapes present in the Black Sea region. As already mentioned, 175 complete and fragmentary vessels in the Pontic assemblages belong to supplementary shapes; they constitute 3.8% of all of the MMB found there. However, as we can see from Fig. 33, these shapes are not found in equal proportions at all the sites (and at sites with small assemblages, they are not documented at all, see also Fig. 31). Not surprisingly, the two shapes which are found at most sites are the small bowl and the juglet.

It is striking that not only is the majority in terms of number and shape variety found at Olbia, but also, if we consider the relative proportions, the representation of supplementary shapes there is well over the average, not just compared with other Black Sea sites, but also compared with the Mediterranean. In fact, only at Kyme do we find (incidentally exactly) the same proportion of supplementary shapes: out of 123 vessels of the corpus published by Bouzek & Jansová (1974), eight (6.5%) are shapes other than hemispherical bowls; this is perhaps not so astonishing, since Olbia and Kyme seem to have the same chronological profile. The Olbia evidence underlines the fact that an assemblage needs to be very large for the supplementary shapes to surface. It also probably attests to the early date of much of the Olbian material. This is especially evident when we compare the Olbia figures with the frequency of supplementary shapes found at Istros, where they constitute less than 1%. Pantikapaion, which has the highest proportion of supplementary shapes, seems to be a special case. This is probably due to the fact that a considerable number of these shapes come from funerary contexts, a situation mirrored in the Kepoi assemblage. But it can of course also reflect the city's status as a royal capital, which contributed to an import pattern that varies from the regional norm (Chapter 24).

---

3 Courby 1922, 392–393 cat. 159, pl. IX.d; Laumonier 1973, 254; Laumonier 1977, 2; Chatzidakis 1997, 302, pl. 223.a; Künzl 2002, 77 cat. 9.

	Olbia	Istros	Chersonesos	Pantikapaion	Myrmekion	Tyritake	Kepoi
Small bowl	30	7	1	11	1	1	
Small bowl with one handle	2						
Juglet	10	1		1	1		2
Unguentarium?	1						
Amphoriskos	1						
Kantharos	1						
Skyphos with ring handles	4			1	1		
Skyphos with pinched handles	1						
Stemmed bowl	1			1			
Shallow cup with high collared rim	9		1	1	2		
Chalice	1						
Cup with band handle	2						
Beaker	1						
Cup?	1						
Amphora	22			7			1
Jug	1						
Lagynos	3						
Situla	6		1	3			
Krater	6	1		2			
Dinos	1						
Guttus	1			1			1
Large closed vessel	12	3		1	1		
Large vessel	2						
Sum	**119**	**12**	**3**	**29**	**6**	**1**	**4**
% of vessels at site	6.5	0.8	3.2	7.6	2.2	1.1	9.3

FIGURE 33 Supplementary shapes present in the Pontic assemblages

SUPPLEMENTARY SHAPES

CATALOGUE TO CHAPTER 5

Please note that descriptions are reduced to a minimum in this catalogue. For vessels from the Pontic assemblages, see the catalogue under the individual production places for full description of decoration and fabric. Illustrations of starred items may be found in the plates devoted to the individual production centers.

SMALL BOWL

Athens

SHA-1   ATH-72*
Olbia, O-63-106, 106[A], Kiev, Institute of Archaeology storeroom. Two non-joining frs. of base and lower body. H 4.6 × W 4.6, WT 0.25.

SHA-2
Athens, Agora, M 21:1 (Komos cistern), P 18671.[1] Largely complete. ⌀ rim 8.5; vessel H 5; H:⌀ 1:1.7. Main decoration: Erotes over low calyx. Workshop of Bion.
– Rotroff 1982a, 56 cat. 102, pls. 17, 92.

SHA-3
Athens, Agora, Area I 14, P 2308. Complete profile; half bowl. ⌀ rim 9; vessel H 5.8; H:⌀ 1:1.6. Main decoration: Erotes over low calyx.
– Rotroff 1982a, 55 cat. 95, pl. 16.

SHA-4
Athens, Agora, N 20: 7, P 12059. Complete profile; fragmentary. ⌀ rim 9; vessel H 5.7; H:⌀ 1:1.6. Main decoration: Erotes over low calyx.
– Rotroff 1982a, 55 cat. 98, pl. 17.

SHA-5
Athens, Agora, M 21:1 (Komos cistern), P 18655. Complete profile; fragmentary. ⌀ rim 8.3; vessel H 5.5; H:⌀ 1:1.5. Main decoration: altar fig. B1, C1 alternating with wreaths and Nikai as space fillers.
– Rotroff 1982a, 71 cat. 219, pl. 43.

SHA-6
Athens, Agora, M 21:1 (Komos cistern), P 20267. Complete profile; fragmentary. ⌀ rim 8.4; vessel H 5.6; H:⌀ 1:1.5. Calyx.
– Rotroff 1982a, 50 cat. 52, pl. 9.

SHA-7
Athens, Agora, M 21:1 (Komos cistern), P 18675. Complete profile; fragmentary. ⌀ rim 9.1; vessel H 5.5; H:⌀ 1:1.7. Calyx.
– Rotroff 1982a, 53 cat. 77, pl. 14.

SHA-8   ATH-73
Olbia, Frankfurt am Main, Kunst und Gewerbemuseum (formerly Vogell collection). Complete; under lip groove with miltos. ⌀ rim 9.1; vessel H 4.6; H:⌀ 1:2. Workshop of Bion.
– Zahn 1908, 49 cat. 3; Boehlau 1908, 29 no. 264.

Pergamon

SHA-9   PER-86*
Pantikapaion, П-1867-7, St Petersburg, State Hermitage Museum. Complete. ⌀ rim 8.5; vessel H 5.

Kyme

SHA-10   KYA-51
Olbia, Bonn, Akademisches Kunstmuseum (formerly Vogell collection). Complete. ⌀ rim 8.8; vessel H 5.6; H:⌀ 1:1.6. Workshop A.
– Zahn 1908, 59 cat. 12; Boehlau 1908, 29 no. 265; Zimmer 2005, 110 cat. A49.

SHA-11   KYB-317*
Olbia(?), inv. 54791 Uvarov 643, Moscow, State Historical Museum (Uvarov collection). Complete. WT 0.4, ⌀ rim 7.6, RH 3, ⌀ base 3.3; vessel H 5; H:⌀ 1:1.5. Kirbeis.

SHA-12   KYB-411*
Olbia, Sector E6, square 415e, yellow clay layer, O-E6-56-993, Kiev, Institute of Archaeology storeroom
Two large joining frs. of rim and bowl; almost half bowl preserved. H 6.2 × W 8, WT 0.4, ⌀ rim 8, 37%, RH 1.7. Possis.

SHA-13   KYB-318*
Pantikapaion, П-1868-254, St Petersburg, State Hermitage Museum. Complete. ⌀ rim 7.5; vessel H 5.2. Kirbeis.
– Kovalenko 1989, 374 cat. 26.

---
1   This and all other items from the Agora Excavations are kept in the Stoa of Attalos in Athens, which houses the museum, storerooms, and offices of the Excavations.

SHA-14 KYB-319*
Olbia, Sector E, square 250, O-E-49-2895, Kiev, Institute of Archaeology storeroom. One-third of bowl preserved, lacking base; interior covered with lime. WT 0.35, ⌀ rim 8.5, 12%, RH 2; vessel H 4.5; H:⌀ 1:1.9. Kirbeis.

SHA-15 KYB-316
Olbia, Göttingen (formerly Vogell collection). Complete. ⌀ rim 8.5. Kirbeis.
– von Stern 1902, 113 additional note; Boehlau 1908, 30 no. 274; Zahn 1908, 64–65 cat. 21; Rotroff 2010, 69 cat. 39.

SHA-16 KYX-100*
Istros, His-V 19429, Bucharest, Institute of Archaeology storeroom. Fr. of rim and upper body. H 5.2 × W 4.2, WT 0.3, ⌀ rim 9, 14%, RH 2.5.
– Domăneanţu 2000, 138 cat. 687, pl. 49.

SHA-17
Campania(?), inv. 8375, Capua, Museo Campano. Complete. ⌀ rim 8.5; vessel H 6.5. Rim frieze: Ionian kyma. Main decoration: altar scene D between saluting Pans, Eros pouring wine into *Pokalkantharos* from amphora, Eros with torch left, Dionysos(?) with cornucopia left, tree. Medallion: rosette A. Saluting Pan Group.
– Patroni 1897–1898, 124 cat. 1015, pl. XIX; Wuilleumier 1929, 64 cat. h; Schwabacher 1941, 186 no. 8; 189 no. 11; Pochmarski 1990, 285 RK 87.

SHA-18
Mesambria, necropolis, Nessebar, Archaeological Museum inv. 2008–38. Complete. ⌀ rim 8.8; vessel H 5.5; H:⌀ 1:1.6. Oxidized. Rim frieze: Ionian kyma. Main decoration: altar group D flanked by antithetical, saluting Pans, Eros left *aposkopein*, winged Dionysos-Eros on panther, Eros pouring wine from amphora into *Pokalkantharos*, Eros with torch, Dionysos(?) with cornucopia. No calyx. Medallion: rosette C. Saluting Pan Group.

SHA-19
Torbali-Metropolis, tomb, Ephesos Museum inv. 34/15/74. Complete. ⌀ rim 8.2; vessel H 4.8; H:⌀ 1:1.7. Oxidized. Rim frieze: Ionian kyma. Main decoration: altar group D flanked by antithetical, saluting Pans. No calyx. Medallion: rosette C. Saluting Pan Group.
– Erdemgil et al. 1989, 111; Tuluk 2001, 61–62 cat 3, pl. 30; and perhaps Siebert 1978, 245 n. 3.

SHA-20 KYX-99
Pantikapaion, Tomb N 14/60-27/IV-1960, Kerč History and Culture Reserve inv. KMAK 1895 (1960). Complete. ⌀ rim 9.5, ⌀ base 3.7; vessel H 7. Saluting Pan Group.
– Grzegrzółka 2010, 49–50 cat. 18.

Aiolis

SHA-21 AIX-34*
Pantikapaion, tomb, П-1908-82, St Petersburg, State Hermitage Museum. Complete. ⌀ rim 7.6; vessel H 5; H:⌀ 1:1.5.
– St Petersburg, IIMK RAN photo archive neg. III 12089.

Ephesos

SHA-22
Delos. Half bowl, lacking base. Reduced. Rim frieze: Ionian kyma. Main decoration: altar group D flanked by antithetical, saluting Pans.
– Laumonier 1977, 92 cat. 3247, pls. 20, 131 (Belles Méduses); Pochmarski 1990, 284 RK 82.

SHA-23 EPH-1265*
Olbia, Sector NGS, О-НГС-94-498, Parutine, Olbia National Preserve storeroom. Fr. of rim and body. H 4.2 × W 6, WT 0.2, ⌀ rim 8, 25%, RH 1.2.

SHA-24 EPH-1266*
Olbia, Sector I, West, ash clay layer, О-И-48-2100, Kiev, Institute of Archaeology storeroom. Fr. of rim and upper body. H 4.6 × W 4.8, WT 0.3, ⌀ rim 9, 14%, RH 1.8.

SHA-25 EPH-1267
Olbia, V.I. 4954, Antikensammlung, Staatliche Museen zu Berlin (formerly Vogell collection); lost in WW II. Complete. ⌀ rim 7.9; vessel H 5.1; H:⌀ 1:1.5.
– Zahn 1908, 62 cat. 18; Boehlau 1908, 31 no. 283.

SHA-26 EPH-1268*
Olbia, Sector E6, squares 408s, 413n, grey clay layer, O-E6-61-52, Kiev, Institute of Archaeology storeroom. Fr. of rim and upper body. H 3.8 × W 7.1, WT 0.1, ⌀ rim 9, 25%, RH 1.4.

SHA-27 EPH-1269
Olbia, Sector NGS, О-НГС-02-136, Parutine, Olbia National Preserve storeroom. Fr. of rim and upper body. H 3.1 × W 3.3, WT 0.25–0.44, ⌀ rim 8, 10%, RH 1.6.

SUPPLEMENTARY SHAPES

SHA-28 EPH-1270*
Olbia, Sector E6, square 413, 414, north and west of Cistern (128?), O-E6-59-2271, Kiev, Institute of Archaeology storeroom. Fr. of base and lower body.

SHA-29 EPH-1271*
Istros, His-1086, Bucharest, Institute of Archaeology storeroom. Fr. of rim and upper body. H 3.2 × W 2.2, WT 0.3, ⌀? (small), RH 1.2.

SHA-30 EPH-1272*
Olbia, Sector NGS, House IV-2 B 302/182, O-НГС-94-116, Parutine, Olbia National Preserve storeroom. Fr. of rim and upper body. H 3.7 × W 4.2, WT 0.25–0.43, ⌀ rim 8, 13%, RH 1.6. Menemachos.
– Guldager Bilde 2010, 276 cat. F-6, pl. 169.

SHA-31 EPH-1273*
Pantikapaion, П-1902-129, St Petersburg, State Hermitage Museum. Complete. H 3.5, ⌀ rim 8.5.

SHA-32 EPH-1274*
Olbia, O-no no. D, Kiev, Institute of Archaeology storeroom. Fr. of rim and upper body. H 2.8 × W 4.9, WT 0.24, ⌀ rim 8, 15%, RH 1.3.

SHA-33 EPH-1275*
Olbia, Sector E, square 117, humus layer, O-E-49-143, Kiev, Institute of Archaeology storeroom. Fr. of rim and body. H 3.6 × W 4.3, WT 0.2, ⌀ rim 9, 14%, RH 1.5. Menemachos.

SHA-34 EPH-1276
Istros, His-275, Bucharest, Institute of Archaeology storeroom. Body fr.

SHA-35
Delos. Complete. ⌀ rim 8.3; vessel H 4; H:⌀ 1:2.1. Calyx: imbricate.
– Laumonier 1977, 473 cat. 3805, pls. 109, 134.

SHA-36 EPH-1277*
Olbia, Sector R25, O-P25-93-1363, Parutine, Olbia National Preserve storeroom. Fr. of rim and upper body. H 3.5 × W 4.6, WT 0.33, ⌀ rim 9, 12%, RH 1.8.

SHA-37 EPH-1278
Pantikapaion(?), inv. CA 2286, Paris, Louvre (formerly collection of Messaksoudy, 1920). Complete. ⌀ rim 9.3; vessel H 5.5; H:⌀ 1:1.7. Philon.
– Jentel 1964, 116 cat. 2, pl. XII.

SHA-38 EPH-1279
Chersonesos, X-1900-1, St Petersburg, State Hermitage Museum. Complete profile, but lacks a few minor fragments. WT 0.2, ⌀ rim 8.5, RH 1.9, ⌀ base 3.8; vessel H 5.5; H:⌀ 1:1.6. Menemachos?
– IAK 2, p. 11.

SHA-39 EPH-1280
Tyritake, Kerč History and Culture Reserve inv. KMAK 10397 (1933?). Complete profile; two large frs. of rim, body and base. ⌀ rim 8.8, ⌀ base 3.2; vessel H 5.4.
– Grzegrzółka 2010, 114 cat. 146.

SHA-40 EPH-1281*
Olbia, Sector AGD, Bothros 11, О-АГД-88-209+214, 87–893, Kiev, Institute of Archaeology storeroom. Complete profile; two joining frs. of rim and most of body; one similar non-joining fr. preserving part of base; the sherds from 1987 and 1988 do not join but are from the same vessel. H 5.6 × W 8.3, WT 0.35–0.45, ⌀ rim 9, 25%, RH 1.7; vessel H 4.9; H:⌀ 1:1.8. Monogram PAR.
– Rusjaeva & Nazarčuk 2006, pl. 193.6.

SHA-41 EPH-1282*
Olbia, Sector R25, O-P25-04-3260, Parutine, Olbia National Preserve storeroom. Fr. of upper body.

SHA-42 EPH-1283
Olbia, V.I. 4998, Antikensammlung, Staatliche Museen zu Berlin (formerly Vogell collection), lost in WW II. Complete. ⌀ rim 9.5; vessel H 5.7; H:⌀ 1:1.7.
– Zahn 1908, 67 cat. 24; Boehlau 1908, 31 no. 282.

SHA-43 EPH-1284*
Olbia, Sector R25, O-P25-98-2143, Parutine, Olbia National Preserve storeroom. Fr. of rim and upper body. H 3.2 × W 3, WT 0.2, ⌀ rim 7.5, 12%, RH 1.3.

SHA-44 EPH-1285*
Olbia, Sector R25, O-P25-93-1297, Parutine, Olbia National Preserve storeroom. Rim fr. H 2.3 × W 3.3, WT 0.2, ⌀ rim 8.5, 12%, RH 1.1.

SHA-45 EPH-1286
Istros, His-1073, Bucharest, Institute of Archaeology storeroom. Fr. of lower body and part of base. H 2 × W 2.3, WT 0.3.

SHA-46 EPH-1287
Istros, His-166, Bucharest, Institute of Archaeology storeroom. Fr. of lower body.

SHA-47 EPH-1288*
Pantikapaion, palace foundation trench, M-84-56, Moscow, Puškin Museum of Fine Arts. Fr. of rim and upper body. H 3.9 × W 5, WT 0.1, ⌀ rim 8, 18%, RH 1.8.

SHA-48 EPH-1289*
Olbia, Sector R25, O-P25-92-836, Parutine, Olbia National Preserve storeroom. Rim fr. H 2.8 × W 2.8, WT 0.25, ⌀? (small), RH 1.35.

SHA-49 EPH-1290*
Olbia, Sector E2, square 55, Room [Cistern] Л, western part, grey clay layer, O-E2-48-4977, Kiev, Institute of Archaeology storeroom. Rim fr. H 3.2 × W 1.8, WT 0.5.

SHA-50 EPH-1291
Myrmekion, M-53-19, St Petersburg, IIMK RAN. Rim fr. H 2.9, WT 0.35, ⌀ rim 8, 15%, RH 1.3.

SHA-51 EPH-1292
Istros, His-403, Bucharest, Institute of Archaeology storeroom. Rim fr.

SHA-52 EPH-1293
Olbia, Sector R25, O-P25-95-111b, Parutine, Olbia National Preserve storeroom. Rim fr. H 2.7 × W 2.7, WT 0.21, ⌀? (small), RH 1.25.

SHA-53 EPH-1294
Olbia, Sector NGS, O-НГС-02-399, Parutine, Olbia National Preserve storeroom. Rim fr. H 2.5 × W 3.5, WT 0.2–0.39, ⌀ rim 8, 12%, RH 1.9.

SHA-54 EPH-1295*
Olbia, Sector NGS, O-НГС-02-738, Parutine, Olbia National Preserve storeroom. Rim fr. H 3.2 × W 5.4, WT 0.18–0.38, ⌀ rim 9, 14%, RH 1.9.

Knidos

SHA-55 KNI-73*
Olbia, Sector R25, O-P25-98-2806, Parutine, Olbia National Preserve storeroom. Fr. of rim and upper body. H 5.1 × W 4.4, WT 0.3–0.4, ⌀ rim 8, 15%, RH 1.7.

SHA-56 KNI-74*
Olbia, Sector R25, O-P25-00-1703, Parutine, Olbia National Preserve storeroom. Fr. of upper body. H 3.8 × W 2.5, WT 0.35.

Production Place?

SHA-57 XXX-48*
Pantikapaion, П-1902-128, St Petersburg, State Hermitage Museum. Complete. ⌀ rim 8.9; vessel H 5.

SHA-58 XXX-49*
Pantikapaion, П-1847-21, St Petersburg, State Hermitage Museum. Complete. ⌀ rim 8; vessel H 4.6; H:⌀ 1:1.7.

SHA-59
Alexandria. One third of bowl preserved. ⌀? (small). Rim frieze: astragal. Main decoration: altar group D flanked by antithetical, saluting Pans.
– Pagenstecher 1913, fig. 97c; Wuilleumier 1929, 65 cat. j; Schwabacher 1941, 186 no. 1; Pochmarski 1990, 285 RK 84.

SHA-60 XXX-50
Olbia, Giessen (formerly Vogell collection). Complete; holes for ancient repair. H 4,5, ⌀ rim 8.9.
– Zahn 1908, 62 cat. 17; Boehlau 1908, 29 no. 266.

SHA-61 XXX-51
Istros, Tumular necropolis, Tomb XXVI, His-58-V 19663, present whereabouts unknown. Complete profile; fragmentary bowl, ca. half preserved. ⌀ rim 8.4; vessel H 5.3.
– Alexandrescu 1966, 190 cat. XXVI.1, pls. 79, 94; Domăneanțu 2000, 135 cat. 666, pl. 48.

SHA-62 XXX-52
Pantikapaion, Mithridates Hill, Kerč History and Culture Reserve inv. KMAK 2144 (1962). Five joining frs. of rim and body. ⌀ rim 8.6.
– Grzegrzółka 2010, 73–74 cat. 60 (identified as Pergamene).

SHA-63 XXX-53
Pantikapaion, Gagarin Str. П-77-no.(?), Kerč History and Culture Reserve inv. KMAK 1701. Complete profile; almost half bowl preserved, joined from a number of frs. ⌀ rim 8.6.
– Grzegrzółka 2010, 79–80 cat. 71 (identified as Pergamene).

SMALL BOWL WITH ONE HANDLE (DIPPER?)

Aiolis B

SHA-64 AIB-135*
Olbia, Sector E6-7, squares 598e, 608e, grey clay layer, O-E6-7-61-256, Kiev, Institute of Archaeology storeroom. Fr. of rim

and body; attachment of band handle, 2.3 cm wide. H 6 × W 7.3, WT 0.3, ⌀ rim 9, 32%, RH 3.8.

Ephesos

SHA-65
Delos. Complete with exception of base. ⌀ rim 8; vessel H 4.6; H:⌀ 1:1.7, reduced. Rim frieze: Ionian kyma. Main decoration: heraldic Erotes around krater.
– Laumonier 1977, 417 cat. 1965, pls. 98, 134 (unassigned).

SHA-66
Delos. Upper half of vessel. Reduced. Multiple rim friezes: astragal; rosettes with four petals. Calyx: vertical floral stems.
– Laumonier 1977, 212 cat. 8930, pl. 17.

SHA-67
Ephesos. Complete. ⌀ rim 8. Reduced. Rim frieze: guilloche right. Calyx: straight acanthus alternating with sepals bent backwards.
– Gassner 1997, 78 cat. 229, pl. 17.

SHA-68
Bosporan Kingdom, Kerč History and Culture Reserve inv. KMAK 2088. Complete, though handle broken off. ⌀ rim 8.5, ⌀ base 2.4; vessel H 5.2. Rim frieze: rosette 2/4. Calyx: imbricate, large pointed petals with central vein. Medallion: rosette B.
– Grzegrzółka 2010, 41–42 cat. 10 (identified as Kymean).

SHA-69
Crimea, Kerč History and Culture Reserve inv. KMAK 2498. Complete with exception of handle. ⌀ rim 7.6, ⌀ base 2.6; vessel H 3.7. Reduced. Rim frieze: rosette 2/4. Calyx: imbricate, pointed petals with central vein.
– Grzegrzółka 2010, 36–37 cat. 3.

SHA-70
Delos. Fr. of upper body with handle. Rim frieze: S-spirals, horizontal. Main decoration: stylized long petals.
– Laumonier 1977, 451 cat. 4939, pls. 104, 134 (unassigned).

Production Place?

SHA-71   XXX-54*
Olbia, Sector R25, O-P25-95-1124, Parutine, Olbia National Preserve storeroom. Fr. of body with attachment of band handle. H 5.2 × W 3, WT 0.3.

OVOID SMALL CUP

Athens

SHA-72
Athens, Agora, Area A–D 14–17, P 25544. Body fr. Main decoration: stylized long petals.
– Rotroff 1997a, 308 cat. 621, fig. 45, pl. 59.

FOOTED SMALL BOWL

Athens

SHA-73, SHA-74
vacat.

SHA-75
Athens, Agora, Area C 17, P 18446. Fr. of base and lower body. Main decoration: swirling stylized long petals.
– Rotroff 1997a, 307 cat. 613, fig. 45, pl. 59.

JUGLET

Athens

SHA-76   ATH-75*
Olbia, Sector E6, square 432w, foundation of Room "O", O-E6-59-2080, Kiev, Institute of Archaeology storeroom. Fr. of body with part of shoulder; almost half of vessel. H 4.5 × W 6.5, WT 0.25

SHA-77   ATH-74*
Olbia, Sector Sever-Zapad, O-C3-77-43, Parutine, Olbia National Preserve storeroom. Fr. of shoulder and mid-body. H 4.3 × W 3.2, WT 0.4.

SHA-78   ATH-76*
Olbia, Sector NGS, O-НГС-02-352, Parutine, Olbia National Preserve storeroom. Fr. of base and body; very worn. H 4.3 × W 5.1, WT 0.29–0.45, ⌀ base 2.

SHA-79
Athens, Agora, N 20: 6 (lower fill), P 12032. Body fr. Calyx.
– Rotroff 1997a, 297 cat. 516, fig. 38, pl. 50.

SHA-80
Athens, Agora, P 21:4, P 28601. Almost complete shape; fragmentary; WSl decoration on shoulder and neck. ⌀. rim 9; vessel H 7.6. Calyx: imbricate, large, rounded petals with central vein.
– Rotroff 1997a, 297 cat. 515, fig. 38, pl. 50.

SHA-81
vacat.

SHA-82
Athens, Agora, M 21:1, P 17864. Complete; double handle knotted at top. WSl decoration on shoulder. Vessel H 7.2. Rim frieze: Lesbian kyma. Calyx: imbricate, small, pointed petals, birds flying left above. Medallion: rosette. Frieze separators: dots.
– Rotroff 1982a, 92 cat. 406, pls. 69, 89.

Pergamon

SHA-83   PER-90*
Istros, His-1147, Bucharest, Institute of Archaeology storeroom. Fr. of shoulder and upper body. H 4.3 × W 3.2, WT 0.35.

SHA-84   PER-89*
Olbia, Sector AGD, О-АГД-86-334, Kiev, Institute of Archaeology storeroom. Almost complete profile, lacking rim and part of handle, ca. 60% of vessel preserved. H 4, WT 0.3.

SHA-85   PER-88*
Olbia, V.I. 4857, Antikensammlung, Staatliche Museen zu Berlin (formerly Vogell collection). Complete. Double handle joined by clay ring. ⌀ rim 5.5; vessel H 7.5.

SHA-86
Northern Black Sea, Moscow, State Historical Museum? Complete. Double handle(?) joined by clay ring. Rim frieze: Ionian kyma. Main decoration: hunt? Animal left. Calyx: type cannot be distinguished. Medallion: small rosette?
– Usačeva 1978, fig. 3.3.

SHA-87
Art market, inv. 129, Frankfurt am Main, Universität und Liebighaus. Complete. Double handle joined by clay ring. ⌀ rim 4.6; vessel H 6.1. No rim frieze. Calyx: very detailed with 'nelumbo' and straight naturalistic acanthus; birds sit on tip of acanthus. Medallion: small rosette.
– CVA Frankfurt am Main 4 [Germany 66], 51–52, fig. 14, pl. 24.7–8, Beil. 3.6.

SHA-88
Samothrace, grave H 20, inv. 55.84. Complete except for handle. Main decoration: plastic long petals surrounded by dots and separated by vertical line of petals.
– Rotroff 2010, 59–60, fig. 5.1, 5.2.

Kyme

SHA-89   KYA-58*
Olbia, Sector AGD, О-АГД-91-202, Parutine, Olbia National Preserve storeroom. Two joining frs., complete except for rim and handle. WT. 0.35; vessel H 5.5. Workshop A.

SHA-90   KYB-320*
Kepoi, Tomb 43, Ке-60-43/14, Moscow, State Historical Museum, inv. 97173. Complete though lacking part of rim; no handle. ⌀ rim 5.7; vessel H 7.3. Kirbeis.
– Usačeva 1978, fig. 2.22.

Aiolis

SHA-91
Delos. Almost completely preserved, lacking rim and handle. ⌀ rim 8.5; vessel H 8.5. Reduced. Rim frieze: palmette, upside-down. Main decoration: *agyieus* in palmette, flowers on wavy stems. Medallion: rosette. Frieze separators: dots.
– Laumonier vol. 2, cat. 3505, pl. 28.

Ephesos

SHA-92   EPH-1296
Olbia, Sector AGD, О-АГД-87-660, Kiev, Institute of Archaeology storeroom. Fr. of shoulder and upper part of body; attachment of band handle. H 5 × W 7, WT 0.4.

SHA-93
Ephesos. Complete. ⌀ rim 5.6; vessel H 6.9. Reduced. Rim frieze: astragal. Main decoration: Erotes, *tropaion*. Medallion: small rosette.
– Gassner 1997, 75 cat. 217, pl. 15.

SHA-94   EPH-1297*
Myrmekion, M-49-631, St Petersburg, State Hermitage Museum. Fr. of shoulder and body. H 4.3, WT 0.35.

SHA-95
Delos. Complete profile lacks handle. Vessel H 5.2. Reduced. No rim frieze. Calyx: ovoid petals.
– Laumonier 1977, 83 cat. 313, pls. 18, 131.

SHA-96   EPH-1298
Olbia, present whereabouts unknown (formerly Vogell collection). Complete except for handle. Vessel H 7.4.
– Boehlau 1908, 27 no. 254, pl. VII.7.

SHA-97
Delos. Complete, lacking handle. Reduced. Vertical fluting. Plain, flat base. Menemachos?
– Laumonier vol. 2, cat. 3507, pl. 28.

SHA-98
Delos. Complete, lacking handle. Reduced. Main decoration: vertical fluting. Plain, flat base. Menemachos?
– Laumonier vol. 2, cat. 3508, pl. 28.

SHA-99
Delos. Lower part of vessel. Reduced. Main decoration: vertical fluting. Small disc base. Menemachos?
– Laumonier vol. 2, cat. 3509, pl. 28.

SHA-100
Delos. Lower part of vessel. Reduced. Main decoration: vertical fluting. Small disc base. Menemachos?
– Laumonier vol. 2, cat. 3510, pl. 28.

SHA-101
Delos. Body fr. Reduced. Main decoration: vertical fluting. Menemachos?
– Laumonier vol. 2, cat. 3511 pl. 28.

SHA-102
Delos. Complete, lacking handle. Reduced. Main decoration: vertical fluting. Plain, flat base. Menemachos?
– Laumonier vol. 2, cat. 3533, pl. 28.

SHA-103
Ephesos. Upper part of vessel including handle. ⌀ rim 5.8. Rim frieze: Ionian kyma.
– Gassner 1997, 86 cat. 268, pl. 20.

Sardis

SHA-104
Sardis. Fragmentary, one-fourth of lower part preserved. Rim frieze: dots. Main decoration: multi-petalled rosettes. Medallion: small rosette.

– Rotroff 2003, 116 cat. 483, pl. 83.

Production Place?

SHA-105
Crimea, Kerč History and Culture Reserve inv. KMAK 1612. Complete profile, lacking part of rim; surface much worn. ⌀ base 3. Reduced. No rim frieze. Main decoration: garland. Calyx: imbricate, pointed petals.
– Grzegrzółka 2010, 44–45 cat. 14 (identified as Kymean).

SHA-106
Sardis, Tomb 1007, P1757. Complete, lacking handle and part of rim. Vessel H 7.9. Rim frieze: bosses. Main decoration: wreaths. Medallion: rosette.
– Rotroff 2003, 202.

SHA-107
Art market, German private collection. Complete. Vessel H 6. Rim frieze: large dots. Calyx: widely spaced straight acanthus alternating with ovoid petals.
– ANTIKEN 1973, 78 no. 110, pl. 48.

SHA-108
Art market, German private collection. Complete. Vessel H 6.6. Rim frieze: Ionian kyma. Calyx: straight acanthus.
– ANTIKEN 1973, 78 no. 111, pl. 48.

SHA-109
Crimea, Kerč History and Culture Reserve inv. KMAK 1517. Complete profile, lacking part of rim. ⌀ rim 5.5, ⌀ base 2; vessel H 7.2. Reduced. No rim frieze. Calyx: palmettes separated by bud on dotted stem; birds left, as space filler. Medallion: small rosette.
– Grzegrzółka 2010, 43 cat. 12 (identified as Pergamene).

SHA-110
Ancona, Tomb 6, inv. 21505, Ancona, Museo Nazionale. Complete. Double handle joined by clay ring. ⌀ rim 6.1; vessel H 8. Calyx.
– Mercando 1976, 164, fig. 23; Puppo 1995, 157 cat. X20, pl. LXXI.

SHA-111   XXX-55*
Olbia, O-1909-no no., present whereabouts unknown. Complete.
– St Petersburg, IIMK RAN, photo archive neg. II 18228.

SHA-112   XXX-56
Kepoi, Moscow, State Historical Museum? Upper part of vessel lacking handle and base.
– Usačeva 1978, fig. 3.2.

SHA-113

Provenance unknown, inv. 1702, Bonn, Akademisches Kunstmuseum. Complete except for handle and part of rim. Vessel H 9.2. Calyx: imbricate, large, pointed petals with central vein.
– Zimmer 2005, 115 cat. A62, fig. 39.

SHA-114

Athens, Agora, Area D 17, P 20350. Fr. of body and base. Main decoration: stylized long petals.
– Rotroff 1997a, 426 cat. 1788, fig. 105, pl. 139.

JUGLET ON FOOT

Ephesos

SHA-115 EPH-1299*

Olbia, Sector E7, squares 783, 782s, 764s, 710s, House 12, O-E7-69-489+492, Kiev, Institute of Archaeology storeroom. Two joining frs. of base and lower body. H 3.2 × W 4.2, WT 0.35, ⌀ base 2.6.

Sardis

SHA-116

Sardis. Lower half of vessel. ⌀ base 4.9. Rim frieze: astragal. Calyx: frond alternating with vertical floral scroll; dolphins as spacers. Medallion: small rosette.
– Rotroff 2003, 111 cat. 446, pl. 75.

Production Place?

SHA-117

Alexandria, Würzburg, Martin von Wagner Museum der Universität Würzburg. Complete except for part of neck and handle. Vessel H 9.4. Rim frieze: ivy-berry clusters (or rosettes?). Calyx: ovoid petals.
– Langlotz 1932, 162 cat. 916, pl. 252.

JUGLET?

Myrina?

SHA-118

Kyme. Shoulder fr. with attachment of band handle. Rim frieze: heart guilloche left.
– Bouzek & Jansová 1974, 74 cat. MB 136, fig. 16, pl. 14.

Ephesos

SHA-119 EPH-1300*

Pantikapaion, palace foundation trench, M-84-33, Moscow, Puškin Museum of Fine Arts. Fr. of shoulder and upper part of body. H 4.2 × W 5.5, WT 0.5.

SHA-120

Delos. Almost completely preserved, lacking neck and rim and handle. ⌀ rim 7; vessel H 4.8. Calyx: lotus petals. Medallion: rosette of lotus petals.
– Laumonier vol. 2, cat. 314, pl. 28.

FEEDER

Macedonia?

SHA-121

Provenance unknown, inv. 1701, Bonn, Akademisches Kunstmuseum. Complete except for spout. Vessel H 11.7. Main decoration: standing Greek warriors.
– Zimmer 2005, 115–116 cat. A63, fig. 40.

SMALL AMPHORA

Production Place?

SHA-122

Provenance unknown, Bonn, Akademisches Kunstmuseum. Complete. Vessel H 8.5. Main decoration: net pattern made of crude dots. Hybrid Pergamene/Ephesian type.
– Zimmer 2005, 104, 106 cat. A23, fig. 18.

SMALL LAGYNOS

Production Place?

SHA-123

Provenance unknown, inv. 1472, Krakow. Complete. Vessel H 13.5. Rim frieze: multi-petalled rosettes. Main decoration: myrtle wreath with berries left. Medallion: rosette.
– CVA Cracow [Poland 2], III N, pl. 14.

SUPPLEMENTARY SHAPES

SHA-124
Provenance unknown, no no., Istanbul Museum. Complete except for handle. Vessel H 11.5. Rim frieze: Ionian kyma. Calyx: vegetal calyx.
– Schäfer 1968, 101, 108, fig. 8.1.

SMALL OINOCHOE

Myrina?

SHA-125
Rhodes, inv. 2111, Istanbul Museum. Complete. Vessel H 9. Rim frieze: Ionian kyma. Calyx: straight acanthus with flowers as spacers.
– Schäfer 1968, 101, 103, 108, fig. 8.2.

SHA-126
Rhodes, inv. 2106, Istanbul Museum. Preservation not mentioned. Vessel H 9.
– Schäfer 1968, 108 (not illustrated).

SHA-127
Rhodes, inv. 2047, Istanbul Museum. Preservation not mentioned. Vessel H 9.
– Schäfer 1968, 108 (not illustrated).

SMALL JUG

Production Place?

SHA-128
Kozani, Tomb 9. Complete except for handle. Vessel H: 19.9. Main decoration: stylized long petals.
– Batalis 2004, 230 pl. 80.

Italo-Megarian

SHA-129
Vulci, inv. 15460, Rome, Vatican Museum. Complete. ⌀ 8; vessel H 15. Main decoration: garlands, many small friezes.
– Puppo 1995, 140–141 cat. IT17, pl. LIX.

UNGUENTARIUM?

Production Place?

SHA-130   XXX-57*
Olbia, Sector NGS, О-НГС-06-487, Parutine, Olbia National Preserve storeroom. Shoulder fr. H 2.1 × W 3.9, WT 0.35, ⌀ max. 6.

AMPHORISKOS WITH POINTED TOE

Kyme?

SHA-131   KYX-101
Olbia, inv. T 462, Kassel Antikensammlung (formerly Vogell collection). Complete. Vessel H 17.4.
– CVA Kassel 2 [Germany 38], 64–65, fig. 41, pl. 87.5.

Myrina or Kyme?

SHA-132
Myrina, inv. Myr 591, Paris, Louvre. Complete but lacking handles. Vessel H 17.7. Rim frieze: Ionian kyma. Main decoration: bound five-petalled myrtle wreath left.
– Courby 1922, pl. X.c; Jentel 1968, 14, pl. 12.5.

SMALL KRATER

Production Place?

SHA-133
Art market, inv. 1917.990, Hamburg, Museum für Kunst und Gewerbe. Complete. ⌀ rim 8.6; vessel H 11. Multiple rim friezes: Calyx: imbricate, pointed petals with central vein.
– von Vacano 1966–1967, 85, pl. 36.3–4.

LID WITH RING HANDLE

Myrina?

SHA-134
Kyme, no no., Istanbul Museum. Complete. White-painted bands on body. Vessel H 10.8. Rim frieze: Ionian kyma. Calyx:

straight acanthus; rosettes as fillers. Schäfer considered it to be a lid for a thymiaterion.
– Pottier & Reinach 1885, 203; Schäfer 1968, 107, fig. 9.1.

SHA-135
Myrina, inv. Myr 419, Paris, Louvre. Complete. White-painted bands on body. Vessel H 10. Rim frieze: Ionian kyma. Calyx: straight acanthus; rosettes as fillers.
– Pottier & Reinach 1885, 203–204, fig. 17; Courby 1922, pl. X.d; Jentel 1968, 14.

KANTHAROS

Athens

SHA-136
Athens. Complete. WSl decoration on neck. Vessel H 21. No rim frieze. Main decoration: plastic pine cone.
– Watzinger 1901, 69 cat. 4, pl. IV.

SHA-137
Delos. Non-joining frs. of handle and body. Incised vegetal ornaments on neck. Main decoration: pendent-semicircle design combined with daisy network. On handle, relief dolphin.
– Laumonier vol. 2, cat. 2531, pl. 10.

Ephesos

SHA-138   EPH-1301*
Olbia, Sector AGD and Bothros 11, O-АГД-88-195, 208, Kiev, Institute of Archaeology storeroom. Four rim fragments (one with handle) and one body fr., all joining; one non-joining body fr. WT. 0.3–0.5, ⌀ rim 14.5, 38%; vessel H 11. VG Workshop?
– Samojlova 1994, fig. 1.3.

Italo-Megarian

SHA-139
Central Italy, inv. 545, Boston, Museum of Fine arts. Complete. Main decoration: calyx; stylized long petals. Lapius.
– Marabini Moevs 1980, 206, 208 pl. 19.6; Puppo 1995, 37 cat. L8, pl. V.

Production Place?

SHA-140
Delos. Complete profile; joined from numerous frs. WSl decoration on neck, incised vegetal ornaments. ⌀ rim 12.5; vessel H 16.5. Main decoration: stylized long petals separated by dots. On handle, relief dolphin.
– Laumonier vol. 2, cat. 2502 pl. 10.

KANTHAROS?

Athens

SHA-141
Delos. Six non-joining body frs. Main decoration: pendent-semicircle design and daisy network.
– Laumonier vol. 2, cat. 9333.

Production Place?

SHA-142
Delos. Body fr. Main decoration: stylized long petals.
– Laumonier vol. 2, cat. 2501.

SKYPHOS WITH RING HANDLES

Pergamon?

SHA-143
Laodikeia at Lykos, inv. H 3203, Würzburg, Martin von Wagner Museum der Universität Würzburg. Complete. Vessel H 13.3. Rim frieze: wave meander. Main decoration: Herakles with Hydra, centaur with long object, Nike with wreath left. Calyx: straight fleshy acanthus alternating with more stylized acanthus and ovoid petals; Aphrodite with Eros as spacers.
– Langlotz 1932, 162 cat. 911, pl. 252; Kotitsa 1998, 127–131 cat. 95, pls. 55–56; Künzl 2002, 25, fig. 11.

Kyme

SHA-144   KYA-52
Olbia, inv. T 493, Kassel Antikensammlung (formerly Vogell collection). Complete. Two grooves below lip. ⌀ rim 12.6; vessel H 12.6; H:⌀ 1:1. Workshop A.

– Zahn 1908, 68 cat. 30; Boehlau 1908, 27 no. 252; CVA Kassel 2 [Germany 38], 63–64, fig. 39–40, pl. 87.3–4.

SHA-145   KYA-55
Pantikapaion, area of 2 Lenin Str., Kerč History and Culture Reserve inv. KMAK 2381 (1961). Two joining frs. of rim and body with remains of handle attachment. Workshop A.
– Grzegrzółka 2010, 68 cat. 51 (identified as Pergamene).

SHA-146   KYA-54*
Olbia, Bonn, Akademisches Kunstmuseum (formerly Vogell collection). Complete. Scraped groove below lip. WSl decoration on rim, shadow of superposed white-painted horizontal Z's; two scraped grooves below them. ⌀ rim 10.5; vessel H 12. Workshop A.
– Zahn 1908, 68 cat. 31; Boehlau 1908, 27 no. 253; Zimmer 2005, 111 cat. A51.

SHA-147   KYA-53*
Myrmekion, M-57-339, St Petersburg, IIMK RAN. Fr. of rim and upper body. Two grooves below lip. H 5.5, WT 0.32, ⌀ rim 10, 10%. Workshop A.

SHA-148   KYA-56*
Olbia, Sector E2, square 55, Room [Cistern] Л, western part, grey clay layer, O-48-119+4982, Kiev, Institute of Archaeology storeroom. Two joining frs. of rim and body; remains of handle attachment. Scraped groove below lip. Shadow of superposed white-painted zigzag line on rim, two scraped grooves below. H 6.5 × W 8.7, WT 0.25, ⌀ rim 10, 27%, RH 2.8. Workshop A.

Aiolis?

SHA-149
Pergamon, inv. CA 1570, Paris, Louvre. Complete except for one handle. Two incised grooves below lip. WSl decoration on collar. ⌀ rim 7.5, ⌀ base 5; vessel H 7.5. Calyx.
– Jentel 1968, 12–13, pls. 11.2, 12.2 and 5.

Production Place?

SHA-150   XXX-58*
Olbia, Sector NGS, O-НГС-91-555, Parutine, Olbia National Preserve storeroom. Fr. of lower body. WSl decoration on interior. H 4.1 × W 4.1, WT 0.18–0.36.

SHA-151
Cerveteri(?), inv. 52468, Rome, Villa Giulia. Complete. ⌀ rim 11.4; vessel H 11.2. Main decoration: myrtle. Calyx.

– Ohlenroth 1959, 36, fig. 7; Puppo 1995, 142–143 cat. IT21, pl. LXIII.

SHA-152
Myrina, inv. 2159, Istanbul Museum
– Jentel 1968, 13 (not illustrated).

SKYPHOS WITH PINCHED HANDLES

Ephesos

SHA-153
Gorgippia, House 15, room 42, present whereabouts unknown. Complete. Main decoration: myrtle wreath with five bound leaves right. Monogram PAR.
– Alekseeva 1997, pl. 87.

SHA-154
Delos. Fr. of rim and upper body. Rim frieze: star rosettes. Main decoration: acanthus-vine scroll left. Monogram PAR.
– Laumonier 1977, 170 cat. 1458, pl. 35.

SHA-155
Delos. Fr. of rim and upper body. ⌀ rim 13. Rim frieze: star rosettes. Main decoration: pendent-semicircle design. Monogram PAR.
– Laumonier 1977, 201 cat. 4336, pls. 45, 132.

SHA-156   EPH-1302*
Olbia, Sector I, West, ash clay layer, О-И-48-2103, 3827, Kiev, Institute of Archaeology storeroom. Two non-joining frs. of rim and upper body. H 5.5 × W 6.3, WT 0.28, ⌀ rim 13, 15%, RH 3.3. Monogram PAR.

STEMMED BOWL

Athens?

SHA-157
Athens, Pnyx. Fr. of stem and lower part of body. Calyx: imbricate, small plastic leaves. Perhaps Ephesian.
– Edwards 1956, 102 no. 92, fig. 4, pl. 47.

SHA-157 bis
Athens, Agora, Area C 16, P 19430. Fr. of base and lower body. Main decoration: stylized long petals.
– Rotroff 1997a, 307 cat. 612 fig. 45, pl. 59.

SHA-157 ter
Athens, Agora, F 13: 3, P 6766. Fr. of base and lower body. Main decoration: stylized long petals separated by dots.
– Rotroff 1997a, 306–307 cat. 611, fig. 45, pl. 59.

Ephesos

SHA-158
Delos. Fr. of lower part of bowl and foot. ⌀ base 6.5. Calyx: calyx B.
– Laumonier 1977, 140 cat. 589, pls. 31, 132 (Monogram PAR).

SHA-159
Delos. Fr. of lower part of bowl and foot. Calyx: straight acanthus leaf alternating with tall ovoid petals; at transition to foot a row of small ovoid petals.
– Laumonier 1977, 176 cat. 588, pl. 38 (Monogram PAR).

SHA-160
Corinth. Fr. of stem and lower part of body. Calyx: imbricate, pointed petals with central and side veins. Ephesos?
– Edwards 1975, 170 cat. 850, pl. 75.

Cyprus?

SHA-161
Kition. Fr. of lower part of bowl. Main decoration: dancing figures (maenad? satyrs?). Published as ESA; one of the depictions is reversed.
– Salles 1995, 405 cat. 7, fig. 3, 4.

Macedonia?

SHA-162
Herakleia Lynkestis. Large part of bowl and part of foot. Rim frieze: rosettes. Main decoration: rounded petals separated by three dots; high and low rounded petals. Calyx: acanthus leaves with tip bent forwards.
– Keramopoullos 1932, 71, fig. 30.

Production Place?

SHA-163   XXX-59
Olbia, O-1929-872, present whereabouts unknown. Fr. of lower body and part of base.
– St Petersburg, IIMK RAN, photo archive neg. II 4825.

SHA-164
Kyme. Lower part of bowl. Calyx: imbricate, large rounded petals with central vein.
– Bouzek & Jansová 1974, 71 cat. MB 112, figs. 5, 14, pl. 14.

SHA-165   XXX-60
Pantikapaion, Cistern N 179, 96-no.(?), Kerč History and Culture Reserve. Fr. of stem and lower part of bowl.
– Tolstikov & Zhuravlev 2004, pl. 101.15.

GLOBULAR BOWL

Athens

SHA-166
Athens, Agora, D 11:4, P 10880. Body fr. with part of round handle. Calyx.
– Rotroff 1997a, 307 cat. 616, fig. 45, pl. 59.

SHA-167
Athens, Agora, D 12: 2, P 25534. Body fr. Main decoration: stylized long petals.
– Rotroff 1997a, 307 cat. 614, fig. 45, pl. 59.

SHA-168
Athens, Agora, Area D 17, P 20349. Body fr. Main decoration: stylized long petals.
– Rotroff 1997a, 307 cat. 615, fig. 45, pl. 59.

KRATERISKOS

Athens

SHA-169
Athens, Agora, Area D 16, P 19377. Fr. of rim, neck and upper body. ⌀ rim 16. Calyx: lotus petals with imbricate field in between. Ariston? [PGB].
– Rotroff 1997a, 307 cat. 617, fig. 45, pl. 59.

Macedonia

SHA-170
Kozani, Tomb 4. Complete. Max. ⌀ 18.2; vessel H 20.5. Multiple rim friezes: Ionian kyma, guilloche. Main decoration: figural, Homeric.
– Batalis 2004, 223, pl. 77a.

SUPPLEMENTARY SHAPES

Budva?

SHA-171
Budva, Beograd NM inv. 270/1. Complete. Horizontal ear-shaped handles. ⌀ rim 18, ⌀ base 7; vessel H 28. No rim frieze. Main decoration: incised crude scroll. Calyx: straight plastic acanthus. Dated far too early in publication: late 4th century.
– CVA Serbia and Montenegro 1, 29, pl. 30.1.

Italo-Megarian

SHA-172
Telamon, temple, inv. 93508, Firenze, Museo Archeologico. Complete; joined from numerous fragments. ⌀ rim 14.9; vessel H 12.6. Multiple rim friezes. Main decoration: figural. Calyx.
– von Vacano 1966–1967, pl. 35.1–3; Puppo 1995, 135–137 cat. IT11, pl. LVIII.

SHA-173
Art market. Complete. Multiple rim friezes. Calyx.
– von Vacano 1966–1967, 84, pl. 37.1.

SHA-174
Populonia, Buche delle Fate, chamber tomb, inv. 1076, Populonia, Museo Archeologico. Complete. ⌀ rim 17.9; vessel H 15.3. Multiple rim friezes. Calyx.
– von Vacano 1966–1967, pl. 36.1–2; Puppo 1995, 133–134 cat. IT9a.

SHA-175
Central Italy, present whereabouts unknown. Base fr. Calyx.
– Marabini Moevs 1980, 172, 177, 195, 225 n. 57, pls. 3, 14; Puppo 1995, 85 cat. C12, pl. XLIII.

SHA-176
Tibur, inv. 108717, Rome, Museo Nazionale. Fr. of base and lower body. Calyx.
– Marabini Moevs 1980, 210–211, pl. 23.9; Puppo 1995, 69 cat. T1, pl. XXXV.

SHALLOW CUP WITH HIGH COLLARED RIM

Aiolis B

SHA-177   AIB-122*
Olbia, O-64-1686, 1689(?), Kiev, Institute of Archaeology storeroom. Fr. of neck and body with part of base, non-joining fr. of base and lower body. H 5.4 × W 6, WT 0.35, ⌀ base 7.

SHA-178   AIB-124*
Olbia, Sector R25, O-P25-93-554, Parutine, Olbia National Preserve storeroom. Fr. of lower body. H 3, WT 0.3.

SHA-179   AIB-119*
Myrmekion, M-57-97, St Petersburg, State Hermitage Museum. Two joining frs. of base and lower body. W 12, WT 0.35, ⌀ base 5.6.

SHA-180   AIB-125*
Olbia, Sector E, "B", Pit 3, O-E-51-1906, Kiev, Institute of Archaeology storeroom. Fr. of neck, shoulder and body. H 3.4 × W 6.5, WT 0.25.

SHA-181   AIB-118*
Olbia, Sector E3, square 63, pit, O-E3-54-2851, Kiev, Institute of Archaeology storeroom. Complete profile; three frs. of rim and neck and two frs. of base and body, all joining; attachment of vertical band handle, width 1.7. W 11.5, WT 0.3, ⌀ rim 11, 26%, ⌀ base 5; vessel H 7.

SHA-182   AIB-129*
Olbia, Sector R25, O-P25-02-1421, 1422, Parutine, Olbia National Preserve storeroom. Two non-joining body frs.; tiny part of handle attachment. H 3.2, WT 0.4.

SHA-183   AIB-130*
Olbia, Sector R25, O-P25-99-2321+2321a, Parutine, Olbia National Preserve storeroom. Two joining frs. of base and lower body, one non-joining body fr. H 6 × W 8.8, WT 0.27, ⌀ base 7.

SHA-184   AIB-131*
Myrmekion, M-57-1391, St Petersburg, IIMK RAN. Fr. of shoulder and body. H 4.6, WT 0.4.

SHA-185   AIB-126*
Chersonesos, X-1959-20, St Petersburg, State Hermitage Museum. Body fr. H 4.2, WT 0.26.

SHA-186   AIB-123
Pantikapaion, M-63-392, Moscow, Puškin Museum of Fine Arts. Body fr.
– Zabelina 1984, 163, fig. 10d (identified as Pergamene); Bouzek 1990, pl. 21.9.

SHA-187   AIB-120
Kara Tobe, K-97-187. Fr. of body and shoulder.
– Vnukov & Kovalenko 1998, fig. 6.1 (identified as Pergamene); Petrova 2014, 230 n. 36.

SHA-188   AIB-121
Kara Tobe, K-97-187, present whereabouts unknown. Large fr. of rim and body with handle attachments.
– Vnukov & Kovalenko 1998, fig. 4.6 (identified as Pergamene); Petrova 2014, 230 n. 36.

SHA-189   AIB-132*
Olbia, Sector R25, O-P25-99-2072, Parutine, Olbia National Preserve storeroom. Fr. of lower body with tiny part of base.

SHA-190   AIB-128
Olbia, O-1909-1582, present whereabouts unknown. Fragmentary; complete profile except for base; one ridged band handle preserved.
– St Petersburg, IIMK RAN, photo archive neg. III 3430.

Production Place?

SHA-191   XXX-61*
Olbia, Sector R25, O-P25-99-2886, Parutine, Olbia National Preserve storeroom. Fr. of lower body. H 2 × W 2.5, WT 0.38.

SHA-192
Tomis, necropolis, Constanta Archaeological Museum. Complete profile; joined from numerous fragments. Calyx: imbricate.

CHALICE

Pergamon

SHA-193   PER-87*
Olbia, Odessa, Historical Museum. Complete.

Aiolis B

SHA-194   AIB-116*
Pergamon, V.I. 5863, Berlin, Antikensammlung (formerly Mavrogordato collection, 1910). Complete. ⌀ rim 14.1, ⌀ base 9.6; vessel H 15.8.
– Grüßinger et al. 2011, 476 cat. 3.96.

SHA-195   AIB-117
Libknechtovka village near Kerč, present whereabouts unknown. Fragmentary vessel; complete profile. ⌀ rim 19; vessel H 15.
– Smirnova 1967, figs. 55, 56 (fig. 55 is reversed); Petrova 2014, 220 n. 20.

CUP WITH BAND HANDLE

Aiolis B

SHA-196   AIB-134*
Olbia, Sector R25, O-P25-03-1913, Parutine, Olbia National Preserve storeroom. Fr. of rim and upper body with handle attachment starting at rim. H 4.5, WT 0.15.

SHA-197   AIB-133*
Olbia, Sector R25, O-P25-93-1706+1708, Parutine, Olbia National Preserve storeroom. Two joining frs. of mid- and lower body; attachment of flat handle. H 5.3, WT 0.3.

BEAKER

Aiolis B

SHA-198   AIB-137*
Olbia, Sector Sever-Zapad, O-C3-81-14, Parutine, Olbia National Preserve storeroom. Fr. of rim and body. H 5.7 × W 4.7, WT 0.35, ⌀ rim 7, 13%, RH 3.5.

CUP?

Aiolis B

SHA-199   AIB-136*
Olbia, Sector R25, O-P25-09-3548, Parutine, Olbia National Preserve storeroom. Fr. of base and lower body. H 3.1 × W 3.5, WT 0.2.

RHYTON

Ephesos

SHA-200
Ephesos. Preservation and decoration not mentioned.
– Rogl 2008b, 528 (not illustrated); a mould fragment found in the Agora which Rogl believes was intended for the production of rhyta (fig. 10).

Egypt

SHA-201
Athribis. Fragmentary vessel. Main decoration: male with radiate crown seated between two eagles with outspread wings; in his left arm he holds a sceptre; under the feet is a thunderbolt. Myśliwiec reads the sceptre as a thyrsos and therefore interprets the enthroned male as Dionysos or rather, a Ptolemaic king in the guise of Dionysos. Over this main scene is a frieze of frontal Nikai in a flaring dress with equally flaring *apoptygma* and large, outspread wings. According to Myśliwiec, the context in which the rhyton fragments were found dates to the end of the 3rd century; consequently, the enthroned male must be Ptolemy IV Philopator, who had the epithet Neos Dionysos.
– Myśliwiec 2000a, 257, pl. 127.

SHA-202
Athribis. Fragmentary vessel. Main decoration: symplegma, kithara-playing Erotes, dolphin-riding Erotes.
– Myśliwiec 2000a, 257–258, pls. 128–130a.

Production Place?

SHA-203
Delos. Fragmentary vessel. Main decoration: grotesque?
– Chatzidakis 2004 pl. 171. upper right.

AMPHORA, ATHENIAN TYPE

Athens

SHA-204
Athens, Agora, Q 11:3, P 7038. Fragmentary. WSl decoration on neck. Vessel H 22.7. Main decoration: Hunt over calyx. Workshop of Bion.
– Rotroff 1997a, 292 cat. 459, fig. 33, pl. 45.

SHA-205
Athens, Agora, Area N 16, P 27714. Fr. of base and large part of body. Main decoration: hunt over calyx. Workshop A.
– Rotroff 1997a, 292 cat. 458, fig. 33, pl. 45.

SHA-206
Athens, Agora, F 17: 3 (middle fill), P 25986. Fr. of base and large part of body. Main decoration: mythological. Workshop A.
– Rotroff 1997a, 292 cat. 455, fig. 33, pl. 45.

SHA-207
Athens, Agora, E 6:1, P 8557. Complete profile, lacking parts of body and neck. Twisted handles. WSl decoration. Vessel H 23. Rim frieze: Ionian kyma. Main decoration: ships, rider, lion, Nike. Calyx: straight acanthus with kneeling figures as spacers. Medallion: small rosette. Workshop A.
– Rotroff 1982a, 92 cat. 407, pls. 70, 89.

SHA-208
Athens, Agora, Area C 17, P 19860. Fr. of base and lower body. ⌀ base 12. Calyx.
– Rotroff 1997a, 292 cat. 454, fig. 33, pl. 45.

SHA-209
Athens, Agora, H-K 12–14 (Middle Stoa, building fill, before ca. 170), P 21030. Fr. of base and lower body. ⌀ base 8.8.
– Rotroff 1997a, 292 cat. 456, fig. 33, pl. 45.

SHA-210
Athens, Agora, H-K 12–14 (Middle Stoa, building fill, before ca. 170), P 1951. Fr. of base and lower body. ⌀ base 10. Workshop of Bion.
– Rotroff 1997a, 292 cat. 457, fig. 33, pl. 45.

Production Place?

SHA-211
Eretria. Upper part of vessel. Main decoration: chariot, Potnia theron, warrior?
– Schmid 2004, 496 cat. 7, pl. 238.

AMPHORA, PERGAMENE TYPE

Pergamon?

SHA-212
Pergamon. Fragmentary; most of body and one handle missing. Handles with rotellae, clay pellets on shoulder. WSl decoration on neck and shoulder. Multiple rim friezes: Ionian kyma; astragal. Calyx: vegetal, type cannot be identified.
– Schäfer 1968, 62 cat. D71, pl. 20; Raeder 1986, 204 cat. 7.

SHA-213
Pergamon. Complete except for upper part of neck and rim. Handles with rotellae. Multiple rim friezes: two grooves; guilloche left. Calyx: alternating naturalistic acanthus bent at tip

and jewelled ovoid petals. Medallion: double rosette. Frieze separators: dots.
– Schäfer 1968, 19, 46, 50, 62, fig. 14.1–2; Raeder 1986, 204 cat. 6; Hübner 1993b, 337, fig. 10.

Kyme

SHA-214   KYB-322*
Olbia, V.I. 4952, Antikensammlung, Staatliche Museen zu Berlin (formerly Vogell collection). Complete. Handles with rotellae. ⌀ rim 13.9, ⌀ base 12.8; vessel H 17.2. Kirbeis.
– von Stern 1902, 113 additional note; Zahn 1908, 68 cat. 28; Boehlau 1908, 26–27 no. 249; Neugebauer 1932, 188–189; Raeder 1986, 205 cat. 16; Rotroff 2010, 69 cat. 40.

SHA-215   KYB-325*
Olbia, Sector E6-7, squares 493, 473, grey clay layer, O-E6-7-63-762, Kiev, Institute of Archaeology storeroom. Complete profile lacking tip of rim, one handle and part of foot. Handles with rotellae. WSl decoration on neck and shoulder. WT 0.4, ⌀ ca. 12 (reconstructed); vessel H at least 17. Kirbeis.
– Samojlova 1984, 126, fig. 4.7.

SHA-216   KYB-321
Olbia, V.I. 5862, Antikensammlung, Staatliche Museen zu Berlin (formerly Mavrogordato collection, 1909), lost in WW II. Complete. Handles with rotellae. Vessel H 19.5. Kirbeis.
– Neugebauer 1932, 188; Verluste 2005, 205.

SHA-217   KYB-324
Olbia, Odessa, Historical Museum. Complete. Handles with rotellae; on the neck applied clay blobs (leaves of a garland added in paint). Vessel H 18. Kirbeis.
– Samojlova 1994, fig. 3.1 (identified as Pergamene).

SHA-218
Art market (Izmir 1914), V.I. 30351a, Antikensammlung, Staatliche Museen zu Berlin. Complete, apart from base, which is in modern plaster. WSl decoration. ⌀ rim 16.5; vessel H 19.5. Workshop of Paniskos?

SHA-219
Kyme. Lower part of bowl. ⌀ base 5.3. Calyx: straight acanthus leaves alternating with kantharoi. Medallion: rosette with six petals and pointed sepals. Workshop of Paniskos, circle.
– Bouzek & Jansová 1974, 54 cat. MB 25, figs. 1, 9, pl. 5.

SHA-220
Kyme. Base fr. ⌀ base 8.8. Calyx: acanthus alternating with ovoid petals. Medallion: small rosette with eight petals. Little Eagles Workshop, circle.
– Bouzek & Jansová 1974, 74 cat. MB 133, figs. 6, 16, pl. 15.

Aiolis

SHA-221
Sardis. Fragmentary; part of lower half preserved. Reduced. Rim frieze: bud. Main decoration: swans and bulls' heads carrying suspended garlands. Calyx: straight stylized acanthus alternating with altars.
– ANTIKEN 1973, 75 no. 104, pl. 54; Raeder 1986, 204 cat. 8.

Ephesos

SHA-224   EPH-1303*
Pantikapaion, П-1909-140, St Petersburg, State Hermitage Museum. Joined from numerous frs., preserving almost complete profile except for base. ⌀ rim 14; vessel H 17.8. Monogram PAR.

SHA-225   EPH-1304
Olbia, present whereabouts unknown, probably Odessa, Historical Museum. Complete. Vessel H 19. VG Workshop.
– Samojlova 1994, fig. 3.2.

Production Place?

SHA-226
Art market, inv. 3149, Bonn, Akademisches Kunstmuseum. Complete. Crude WSl decoration on shoulder. Vessel H 20. Calyx with dolphins as space fillers.
– Zimmer 2005, 104–105 cat. A22, fig. 17.

SHA-227
Kyme. Base fr. ⌀ base 4.8. Medallion: small rosette.
– Bouzek & Jansová 1974, 74 cat. MB 132, figs. 6, 16, pl. 15.

SHA-228
Kyme. Base fr. ⌀ base 7.5. Medallion: double rosette.
– Bouzek & Jansová 1974, 74 cat. MB 134, fig. 16, pl. 15.

SUPPLEMENTARY SHAPES

AMPHORA, EPHESIAN TYPE

Pergamon

SHA-229
Art market, inv. 2003,0721.1, London, British Museum (acquired from J. Schottlander). Complete. Crude WSl decoration on shoulder. ⌀ rim 15.5, ⌀ base 11.8; vessel H 23.5. Main decoration: hunting Erotes?

SHA-230
Provenance unknown, Bonn, Akademisches Kunstmuseum (on loan from private collection in Köln, inv. V 184). Complete. Vessel H 16.5. Main decoration: Aphrodite diadoumene frontal and from back twice, Eros celebrating krater, lotus petals in between.
– Hübner 1993a, 126, pl. 38; Zimmer 2005, 104–105 cat. A21, fig. 16.

SHA-231
Art market, inv. 3003, Bonn, Akademisches Kunstmuseum. Complete. Vessel H 19.5. Main decoration: ivy wreath. Calyx: palmettes and small palmettes on looped stems.
– Zimmer 2005, 103–104 cat. A20, fig. 15.

Aiolis

SHA-232
Art market, inv. 39505. Mainz, Römisch-Germanisches Zentralmuseum. Complete. ⌀ rim 16; vessel H 20.4. Rim frieze: Ionian kyma. Main decoration: frieze with one hunter [interpreted as Eros, but this is not likely], rabbits left, dogs left and deer(?). Calyx: naturalistic, lush acanthus bent at tip alternating with looped stems. Medallion: comic mask.
– CVA Mainz 2 [Germany 43], inv. O 39505, 80, pl. 40.1–3; Raeder 1986, 204 cat. 2.

SHA-233
Art market, inv. 39644, Mainz, Römisch-Germanisches Zentralmuseum. Complete. Handles with rotellae. ⌀ rim 16.4; vessel H 20.3. Rim frieze: Ionian kyma. Main decoration: hunt: hunters, dogs, lions, deer, rabbits. Calyx: vertical floral stems. Medallion: rosette; signed M or Σ.
– CVA Mainz 2 [Germany 43], 80, pls. 40.4–5; 41 (inv. O 39644); Raeder 1986, 204 cat. 3.

Ephesos

SHA-234   EPH-1305*
Pantikapaion, П-1850-20, St Petersburg, State Hermitage Museum. Complete. ⌀ rim 16, ⌀ base 12.4; vessel H 22.5.
– Schwabacher 1941, 187 no. 16; Pochmarski 1990, RK 90.

SHA-235   EPH-1306*
Pantikapaion, П-1852-5, St Petersburg, State Hermitage Museum. Complete. ⌀ rim 15.8, ⌀ base 12.5; vessel H 20.9. VG workshop.

SHA-236   EPH-1307*
Pantikapaion, П-1842-41, St Petersburg, State Hermitage Museum. Complete. ⌀ rim 15.9, ⌀ base 13.4; vessel H 21.5.
– Reinach 1892, 101 pl. XLVII.1–3; Raeder 1986, 204 cat. 10.

SHA-237   EPH-1308
Kepoi, Ке-62-192/39, Moscow, State Historical Museum. Complete. ⌀ rim 13, ⌀ base 13.5; vessel H 17.5. Pan mask medallion.
– Sorokina 1967, fig. 39.3–4; Usačeva 1978, 105, fig. 3.1; 4; Raeder 1986, 204 cat. 12.

SHA-238
Art market, inv. 1974–22, Hannover, Kestner Museum. Complete. ⌀ rim 15.7, ⌀ base 13; vessel H 24. Reduced. Rim frieze: Ionian kyma. Main decoration: two identical, superposed friezes with one hunter (interpreted as Eros, but this is not likely), rabbits left, dogs left and deer(?). Calyx: vertical floral stem alternating with pointed petal.
– Raeder 1986, 203–205 n. 1, cat. 1, fig. 1, pl. 37.1; CVA Hannover 2 [Germany 72], 84 9–12, Beil. 13.3; pl. 63.9–12.

SHA-239   EPH-1309
Olbia, present whereabouts unknown. Complete.
– Farmakovskij 1906, 157, fig. 315a–b; Raeder 1986, 204 cat. 13.

AMPHORA, HYBRID ATHENIAN/PERGAMENE TYPE

Kyme

SHA-240   KYB-326*
Olbia, necropolis, O-1901-3070/inv. Ол-519, St Petersburg, State Hermitage Museum. Complete profile, lacking some fragments. Handles with rotellae; separately applied foot is lost but can be seen as a faint line across the decoration. ⌀ rim 12.3, ⌀ base 3.8; vessel H 14.5. Kirbeis.
– Farmakovskij 1903a, 58, fig. 64; Farmakovskij 1903b, 18, fig. 35; IIMK RAN photo archive neg. II 17935; Raeder 1986, 204 cat. 11.

SHA-241   KYB-323
Olbia, inv. 2122, Tübingen, Antikensammlung des Instituts für Klassische Archäologie. Complete. Handles with rotellae. Vessel H 16. Kirbeis.
– Zahn 1908, 68 cat. 29 (attributed probably to Kirbeis); Boehlau 1908, 27 no. 250; Watzinger 1924, 70 cat. G 30, pl. 49; Watzinger 1926, 205 cat. 30; Raeder 1986, 204 cat. 15, pl. 37.3; Rotroff 2010, 69 cat. 41.

Production Place?

SHA-242   XXX-62
Olbia, inv. 1315, Bonn, Akademisches Kunstmuseum (formerly Vogell collection). Complete. Handles with rotellae. WSl decoration on neck and shoulder. Vessel H 24.3.
– Boehlau 1908, 26 no. 248; Raeder 1986, 205 cat. 17; Zimmer 2005, 103 cat. A21, fig. 16.

AMPHORA, HYBRID ATHENIAN/EPHESIAN/PERGAMENE TYPE

Ephesos

SHA-243   EPH-1310
Olbia, Odessa, Historical Museum. Complete. Vessel H 20.5.
– Samojlova 1994, fig. 1.1.

AMPHORA, MACEDONIAN TYPE

Macedonia

SHA-244
Herakleia Lynkestis. Fragmentary; preserves most of profile including handle attachments. Rim frieze: two grooves. Main decoration: figural, Homeric. Calyx?
– Keramopoullos 1932, 70, figs. 27–28.

SHA-245
Selitsa. Fragmentary; complete profile including handle attachments. Rim frieze: grooves. Calyx: type cannot be identified from photograph.
– Keramopoullos 1932, 123, figs. 80–81.

AMPHORA, TYPE?

Kyme

SHA-246   KYB-327*
Olbia or Pantikapaion, Buračkov 173b, Moscow, State Historical Museum (formerly Buračkov collection). Fr. of base and lower body. Separately applied foot lost, but location revealed by discolouration of lower part of vessel. ø base 3.5. Kirbeis.
– Žuravlev & Žuravleva 2014, 259, figs. 4.1, 5.1.

Ephesos

SHA-247   EPH-1311*
Olbia, Sector R25, O-P25-92-3227, Parutine, Olbia National Preserve storeroom. Fr. of mid- and lower body. H 6 × W 6.7, WT 0.4. VG Workshop.

SHA-248   EPH-1312*
Olbia, Sector R25, O-P25-93-896, 990b, Parutine, Olbia National Preserve storeroom. Shoulder fr. H 2.7 × W 7.8, WT 0.31–0.36, ø max. 18. VG Workshop.

SHA-249   EPH-1313*
Olbia, Sector NGS, О-НГС-06-113, 471, 484, Parutine, Olbia National Preserve storeroom. Shoulder fr., two joining body and two non-joining body frs. H 4.5 × W 14.7, WT 0.26, ø max.18.

SHA-250   EPH-1314
Olbia, Sector NGS, О-НГС-88-136, Parutine, Olbia National Preserve storeroom. Shoulder fr. H 4.1 × W 6.4, WT 0.3, ø ca. 20.

SHA-251   EPH-1315*
Pantikapaion, Zabelina 1247 26/3 [B], Moscow, State Historical Museum (Zabelina collection). Body fr. H 7 × W 9, WT 0.5.

SHA-252   EPH-1316
Olbia, Sector NGS, О-НГС-92-240, Parutine, Olbia National Preserve storeroom. Shoulder fr. with handle attachment. H 3 × W 3.3, WT 0.4.

SHA-253   EPH-1317*
Olbia, Cliff, square 285, O-70-148+149, Parutine, Olbia National Preserve storeroom. Two joining frs. of shoulder and body; scar of handle attachment. H 5.5 × W 10.5, WT 0.31.

SHA-254   EPH-1318
Pantikapaion, M-64-43, Moscow, Puškin Museum of Fine Arts. Fr. of base and lower body. H 6.5 × W 7. VG Workshop.

SHA-255
Delos. Shoulder fr. with handle attachment. Reduced. Rim frieze: Ionian kyma. Main decoration: figural (only heads preserved). Frieze separators: dots.
– Laumonier 1977, 103 cat. 6200, pl. 23 (Vases gris).

SHA-256   EPH-1319
Olbia, Sector E7, squares 475, 495, 515, yellow clay layer, O-E7-62-152, Kiev, Institute of Archaeology storeroom. Shoulder fr. with band handle with low rotellae.

SHA-257
Delos. Lower half of vessel. ⌀ base 11. Reduced. Multiple rim friezes: not preserved; large rosettes. Calyx: straight acanthus. Frieze separators: dots. VG Workshop.
– Laumonier 1977, 99 cat. 6003, pls. 22, 131 (Vases gris).

SHA-258
Delos. Lower half of vessel. ⌀ base 12.5. Reduced. Calyx: tall, straight acanthus (acanthus X). VG Workshop.
– Laumonier 1977, 98 cat. 6010, pl. 21 (Vases gris).

SHA-259   EPH-1320
Olbia, O-38-796, Kiev, Institute of Archaeology storeroom. Shoulder fr.

SHA-260
Delos. Fr. of shoulder. Closed vessel with vertical band handle starting at shoulder. Reduced. Rim frieze: Ionian kyma.
– Laumonier 1977, 104 cat. 6170, pl. 24 (Vases gris); Raeder 1986, 204 cat. 5.

Knidos

SHA-261
Knidos. Fr. of base and lower body. Main decoration: figural?
– Kögler 2010, 521 cat. F.139, pl. 29.

SHA-262
Knidos. Fr. of base and lower body. Calyx.
– Kögler 2010, 521 cat. F.138, pl. 29.

SHA-263
Knidos. Base fr.
– Kögler 2010, 479 cat. E.254, pl. 16.

SHA-264
Knidos. Base fr.
– Kögler 2010, 521 cat. F.140, pl. 29.

SHA-265
Knidos. Base fr.
– Kögler 2010, 521 cat. F.141, pl. 30.

SHA-266
Knidos. Fr. of base and lower body.
– Kögler 2010, 594 cat. Kn.346, pl. 60.

Lousoi

SHA-267
Lousoi. Several non-joining frs. of rim and body. Oxidized. Calyx: ovoid lotus petals alternating with crude, straight acanthus.
– Rogl 2008a, 150 cat. 329, pl. 22.

SHA-268
Lousoi. Shoulder fr. Oxidized. Multiple rim friezes: wave meander(?); astragal? Main decoration: stylized long petals.
– Rogl 2008a, 154 cat. 348, pl. 25.

SHA-269
Lousoi. Shoulder fr. Oxidized. Rim frieze: vertical S-spirals, crude.
– Rogl 2008a, 154 cat. 349, pl. 25.

Production Place?

SHA-270
Knossos. Large part of body and some of shoulder. Rim frieze: Ionian kyma. Main decoration: horseman right (type with gorytos), centaurs throwing rocks; Ionian kyma below. Frieze separators: dots.
– Eiring 2001, 102, fig. 3.4.k.

SHA-271   XXX-63*
Olbia, Sector NGS, O-НГС-97-508, Parutine, Olbia National Preserve storeroom. Two joining frs. of lower part of neck, shoulder and upper (moulded) part of body. Handles with rotellae. Parallel filled oblique triangles painted on shoulder; white dot on rotella. H 4.9 × W 11.2, WT 0.19–0.45.

SHA-272   XXX-64
Olbia, Sector R25, O-P25-93-169, Parutine, Olbia National Preserve storeroom. Shoulder fr. Shadow of wavy line originally painted white on shoulder. H 3.1 × W 3, WT 0.3.

SHA-273
Naxos. Fr. of base and lower body. Main decoration: myrtle wreath left.
– Kolia 2006, cat. Th 43, fig. 197.

SHA-274
Phanagoreia. Fr. of shoulder and upper body and attachment for band handle. No rim frieze? Calyx: imbricate, rounded petals with central and side veins.
– Kobylina 1956, 49, fig. 14.

SHA-275   XXX-65
Olbia, Sector E3, O-E3-64-2400, present whereabouts unknown. Base fr.
– St Petersburg, IIMK RAN, photo archive neg. I 56357.

SHA-276   XXX-66
Pantikapaion, Cistern N 179, 96-no.(?), Kerč History and Culture Reserve. Part of neck and shoulder with attachment of band handle with rotella.
– Tolstikov & Zhuravlev 2004, pl. 101.8.

SHA-277   XXX-67
Olbia, O-1924-257b, present whereabouts unknown. Shoulder fr.
– St Petersburg, IIMK RAN, photo archive neg. II 19333.

OINOCHOE

Production Place?

SHA-278
Corinth. Fragmentary; complete profile. Rim frieze: Ionian kyma. Main decoration: net pattern. Rouletting on shoulder.
– Weinberg 1949, 149, pl. 13.1 right; Edwards 1975, 50 n. 37; Romano 1994, 68 cat. 15, fig. 2, pl. 16 (Romano suggests Peloponnesian or East Greek).

JUG

Athens

SHA-279
Athens, Agora, Area O 15, P 22135. Body fr. WSl decoration on shoulder. Main decoration: plastic pine cone.
– Rotroff 1997a, 298 cat. 517, fig. 38, pl. 50.

Kyme

SHA-280   KYA-57
Crimea, Kerč History and Culture Reserve inv. KMAK 1605. Almost complete profile, lacking rim and part of handle. Workshop A.
– Grzegrzółka 2010, 42 cat. 11.

Ephesos

SHA-281   EPH-1321*
Olbia, O-1909-2407, present whereabouts unknown. Complete except for missing lip and part of handle.
– St Petersburg, IIMK RAN, photo archive neg. III 3426.

JUG?

Athens

SHA-282
Athens, Agora, Area A-B 19–20, P 25828. Body fr. WSl decoration on rim. Main decoration: satyrs, Erotes.
– Rotroff 1997a, 307 cat. 619, fig. 45, pl. 59.

SHA-283
Athens, Agora, H-K 12–14 (Middle Stoa, building fill, before ca. 170), P 21052. Body fr. Main decoration: plastic pine cone.
– Rotroff 1997a, 307–308 cat. 620, pl. 59.

SHA-284
Athens, Agora, Area D 17, P 20230. Body fr. Main decoration: vertical fluting.
– Rotroff 1997a, 307 cat. 618, fig. 45, pl. 59.

Lousoi

SHA-285
Lousoi. Base fr. Reduced. Calyx: lotus petals alternating with crude acanthus. Medallion: gorgoneion.
– Rogl 2008a, 150–151 cat. 332, pls. 23, 41, 46.

SHA-286
Lousoi. Fr. of base and lower body. Reduced. Calyx: long petals or lotus petals alternating with acanthus? Medallion: Gorgoneion.
– Rogl 2008a, 150 cat. 331, pls. 23, 41.

LAGYNOS

Pergamon?

SHA-287
Art market (Paris), V.I. 4881, Antikensammlung, Staatliche Museen zu Berlin. Complete. ⌀ rim 5.5, ⌀ base 9.3; vessel H 16.5. Fabric: fine, light red, non-micaceous. Thin reddish-brown coat not covering surface well. Oxidized. Relief decoration on body and shoulder. Body. Rim frieze: grooves. Main decoration: boukephalion carrying bound garland tied with *tainia*; small boukranion, pointed transport amphora, and small Eros right over garland; dolphin rider (same as on shoulder), Aphrodite diadoumene, dancing woman with swirling pony tail, separated by straight acanthus. Shoulder (all upside-down): dolphin rider, small Eros right, vertical horse, warrior with shield and spear, small boukranion. Medallion: double rosette with eight petals. Identical Aphrodite stamp on MMB amphora in Köln (Hübner 1993a, 126, pl. 38) and on small body fr. at Istros (**PER-9**).
– Hausmann 1977–1978, 221, pl. 57.1–2.

Myrina?

SHA-288
Myrina, inv. Myr 592, Paris, Louvre. Complete. WSl decoration. ⌀ base 5.5; vessel H 13.3. Rim frieze: Ionian kyma. Main decoration: dolphins left alternating with palmettes. Calyx: 'tulip' alternating with rosettes. Medallion: small rosette.
– Jentel 1968, 12, pls. 11.1, 16.1 and 3.

SHA-289
Myrina, inv. 2089, Istanbul Museum. Preservation not mentioned. WSl decoration. Main decoration: dolphins left alternating with palmettes. Medallion: small rosette.
– Jentel 1968, 12 (not illustrated).

SHA-290
Kyme, inv. 2230, Istanbul Museum. Preservation not mentioned. WSl decoration. Main decoration: dolphins left alternating with palmettes.
– Jentel 1968, 12 (not illustrated).

SHA-291
Kyme, inv. 2238, Istanbul Museum. Preservation not mentioned. WSl decoration. Main decoration: dolphins left alternating with palmettes.
– Jentel 1968, 12 (not illustrated).

Italo-Megarian

SHA-292
Central Italy, inv. 01.8115, Boston, Museum of Fine arts. Complete except for neck. Main decoration: ivy wreath; stylized long petals. Lapius.
– Marabini Moevs 1980, 206, 208, pl. 19.3; Puppo 1995, 37 cat. L7, pl. V.

SHA-293
Provenance unknown, inv. 5274, Ascoli Piceno, Museo Archeologico. Complete except for handle. Vessel H 19. Multiple rim friezes, calyx.
– Puppo 1995, 131 cat. IT5, pls. LV–LVI.

Antioch?

SHA-294
Antioch. Shoulder fr. with small part of body. WSl decoration on shoulder. Rim frieze: ivy. Frieze separators: dots.
– Waagé 1948, 28, fig. 8.13; Raeder 1986, 204 cat. 4 (erroneously identified as an amphora).

Macedonia?

SHA-295
Anthedon, inv. 161a, Antikensammlung, Staatliche Museen zu Berlin. Complete. Vessel H 26. Rim frieze: Ionian kyma. Main decoration: lush vine branch with leaves and bunches of grapes left; Autolykos and Sisyphos myth. Dionysios [A].
– Robert 1890, 90–96; Leroux 1913, 63 cat. 124; Hausmann 1959, 31, 56 cat. 33, pl. 44.1–2.

SHA-296
vacat.

Production Place?

SHA-297
Art market, inv. 1929,1014.6, London, British Museum (acquired from S.B. Burney). Complete except for handle. Main decoration: figural.

SHA-298
Carthage. Shoulder fr. Calyx: imbricate palmettes with superposed figure, on shoulder. Probably same vessel as **SHA-299**.
– Morel 1990, 23, pl. 2.d, left.

SHA-299
Carthage. Shoulder fr. with part of lower body. Calyx: imbricate palmettes with superposed figure on shoulder; imbricate pointed petals on body. Probably same vessel as **SHA-298**.
– Morel 1990, 23, pl. 2.d, right.

SHA-300
Sardis, Tomb 356, P744, lost. Fragmentary. Mouldmade body, thin neck, band handle. Rim frieze: dots. Main decoration: pendent-semicircle design with five-rayed sun wheel in centre.
– Rotroff 2003, 194.

SHA-301   XXX-68*
Olbia, V.I. 4955, Antikensammlung, Staatliche Museen zu Berlin (formerly Vogell collection). Complete. Vessel H 23.
– Zahn 1908, 68–72 cat. 32; Boehlau 1908, 27 no. 251; Leroux 1913, 67 cat. 133a; Zahn 1940, pl. 1.2.

SHA-302
Art market, German private collection. Complete. Vessel H 20. Rim frieze: Ionian kyma. Main decoration: plastic long petals.
– ANTIKEN 1973, 81 no. 118, pl. 54.

LAGYNOS?

Ephesos

SHA-303   EPH-1322*
Olbia, Sector R25, O-P25-95-902.1+96-1439, 95-902.2, 3, 4, 1161 (join across years), Parutine, Olbia National Preserve storeroom. Two joining body frs. (96-1439+95-902.1) and four non-joining body frs. H 8.7 × W 6, WT 0.42, ⌀ max. 21.

Production Place?

SHA-304   XXX-69*
Olbia, O-64-2498, St Petersburg, State Hermitage Museum. Lower half of vessel. H 9.5, ⌀ base 11.

SHA-305
Kyme, inv. 29.45.16, Philadelphia University Museum. Fragment. Lower body in relief; upper part covered with white coat. Main decoration: not mentioned.
– Rotroff 2003, 80 (mentioned, not illustrated).

FUNNEL

Ephesos

SHA-306
Ephesos, Südtor. Complete. ⌀ rim 14; vessel H 10.6. Multiple rim friezes: box meander ccw; small rosettes. Main decoration: acanthus-vine scroll left. Calyx: calyx B1.
– Gassner 1997, 78 cat. 226, pl. 17; Tuluk 2001 63 cat. 9, pl. 33.6a, b.

SHA-307
Delos. Spout and part of lower body. Main decoration: plastic pine cone.
– Laumonier vol. 2, cat. 2797, pl. 21.

SHA-308
Ephesos. Complete profile; fragmentary. ⌀ rim 17; vessel H 13.2. Reduced. Multiple rim friezes: guilloche right; astragal. Calyx: ovoid petals, palm fronds, 'nelumbo'; birds on twisted sticks.
– Gassner 1997, 76 cat. 220, pl. 15; Rogl 2008b, fig. 9.

SHA-309
Delos. Spout and part of lower body. Calyx: imbricate, pointed petals with central vein.
– Laumonier vol. 2, cat. 2798, pl. 21.

SHA-310
Delos, B 18831. Complete. Rim frieze: rosette 5. Calyx: imbricate, pointed petals with double outline. Menemachos or follower.
– Chatzidakis 2000, pl. 70a–b.

Lousoi

SHA-311
Lousoi. Several non-joining frs. of rim and body. Oxidized. Rim frieze: grooves. Calyx: ovoid lotus petals alternating with crude, straight acanthus.
– Rogl 2008a, 150 cat. 327, pls. 22, 41.

Production Place?

SHA-312
Delos. Spout and decorated clay ring at junction to body.
– Laumonier vol. 2, cat. 2799, pl. 21.

SITULA WITH EVERTED ANGULAR RIM

Ephesos

SHA-313 EPH-1323*
Olbia, Sector E3, O-E3-54-2014+2017, St Petersburg, State Hermitage Museum. Two joining frs. of rim and upper body of situla. H 8, ø rim 20. Menemachos?
– St Petersburg, IIMK RAN, photo archive neg. II 57144.

SHA-314 EPH-1324*
Pantikapaion, M-46-89(?), 2250, Moscow, Puškin Museum of Fine Arts. Two non-joining frs. of rim and body. H 7, ø rim 22, 18%.
– Loseva 1962, fig. 3.1.

SHA-315 EPH-1325
Pantikapaion, M-47-3645, Moscow, Puškin Museum of Fine Arts. Two frs. of rim and upper body; another rim fr. with heart-shaped handle attachment must belong. H 4.7 × W 9, ø rim 18, 12%.
– The fragment in Loseva 1962, fig. 3.2 must belong to this vessel (not seen).

SHA-316 EPH-1326
Olbia, inv. 23808, Odessa, Historical Museum. Complete profile, fragmentary. ø rim 24, ø base 10.2; vessel H 21.5. Menemachos.
– Samojlova 1994, fig. 1.2; Samojlova & Batizat 1994, fig. 1.

SHA-317 EPH-1327
Chersonesos, year and no. unknown, present whereabouts unknown. Fr. of rim and upper body. ø rim 22. Judgement of Paris.
– Ushakov & Strukova 2009, 431, fig. 2.

SHA-318
Sardis. Fr. of rim and upper part of body. ø rim 20.5. Multiple rim friezes. Ionian kyma; astragal.
– Rotroff 2003, 137 cat. 573, pl. 100.

SHA-319
Delos. Fr. of rim and upper body including broad band handle attached to lip. Reduced. Main decoration: pine cone.
– Laumonier 1977, 392 cat. 6007, pls. 86, 134 (unassigned, Series 3.2).

SITULA WITH EVERTED ANGULAR UNDERCUT RIM

Pergamon

SHA-320 PER-91*
Olbia, inv. Б.3274, St Petersburg, State Hermitage Museum (1899). Complete. ø rim 21; vessel H 22.5.
– von Stern 1899, 123–125, fig. 235; von Stern 1902; Bobrinskij 1904, 7 and 8, fig. 7; Wuilleumier 1929, 65 cat. s; Schwabacher 1941, 186 no. 15; 189 no. 10; 191, no. 4; 192, no. 9; AGSP 1984, pl. CXLV; Pochmarski 1990, RK 89; Finoguenova 1991, 132–133 (identified as Pergamene); Samojlova 1994, 90, fig. 2.1; Guldager Bilde 2005.

Ephesos

SHA-321 EPH-1328*
Olbia, Cliff "B-VIII", square 285, yellow clay layer, O-70-214, Parutine, Olbia National Preserve storeroom. Fr. of rim and upper body. H 6.3 × W 11.6, WT 0.4, ø rim 21, 19%, RH 3.3.
– Samojlova 1994, fig. 1.5.

SHA-322 EPH-1329*
Pantikapaion, M-46-1107, Moscow, Puškin Museum of Fine Arts. Rim fr. H 7.2 × W 8, ø rim 22.5, 14%.

SHA-323
Delos. Fragmentary, almost complete profile; lacking foot. ø rim 20; vessel H 15.5, reduced. No rim frieze. Calyx: large overlapping petals with marked mid- and side veins.
– Laumonier 1977, 473 cat. 6174, pls. 109, 134 (unassigned).

SITULA WITH EVERTED ANGULAR STRONGLY UNDERCUT RIM

Pergamon

SHA-324
Pergamon, Antikensammlung, Staatliche Museen zu Berlin. Fr. of rim and upper body. Reduced. Rim frieze: box meander cw.
– Conze et al. 1913, Beibl. 43.9.

Ephesos?

SHA-325
Delos. Fr. of rim and upper body. Rim frieze: box meander cw.
– Laumonier vol. 2, cat. 6022, pl. 9.

SITULA, TYPE?

Pergamon

SHA-326 PER-92*
Olbia, Sector NGS, O-НГС-05-149, Parutine, Olbia National Preserve storeroom. Body fr. H 5.8 × W 9.4, WT 0.5, ⌀ max. 20.

SHA-327 PER-93
Olbia, O-1912-556, present whereabouts unknown. Lower half of vessel preserved.
– St Petersburg, IIMK RAN, photo archive neg. III 3428.

Ephesos

SHA-328
Delos. Fr. of rim and upper body including broad band handle attached to lip. Reduced. Rim frieze: Ionian kyma. Main decoration: figural (only heads preserved). Frieze separators: dots.
– Laumonier 1977, 392 cat. 6008, pls. 86, 134 (unassigned, Series 3.2).

SHA-329
Ephesos. Fr. of upper part of body. Rim frieze: astragal. Main decoration: Erotes carrying garlands on which rings are suspended. Frieze separators: dots.
– Mitsopoulos-Leon 1991, 71 cat. D23, pl. 80.

SHA-330
Delos. Fr. of rim and upper body including broad band handle attached to lip. Reduced. Rim frieze: Ionian kyma.
– Laumonier 1977, 222 cat. 6097, pl. 49.

KRATER; ATHENIAN TYPE

Athens

SHA-331
Athens, Agora, H-K 12–14 (Middle Stoa, building fill, before ca. 170), P 1448. Large fr. of rim, neck and upper part of body. Rope handle. ⌀ rim 30.5. Main decoration: Erotes with wreaths. Workshop A?
– Rotroff 1997a, 306 cat. 604, fig. 44, pl. 58.

SHA-332 ALC-54
Athens, Agora, O 17: 5, P 26037. Complete profile. Horizontal rope handle. WSl decoration on upper part of neck. ⌀ rim 28.4.
– Rotroff 1982a, 70 cat. 211, pls. 41, 81; Pochmarski 1990, RK 58.

SHA-333
Athens, Agora, Area J 13, P 1495. Complete profile except for foot; much of rim missing. Horizontal rope handles. WSl decoration. ⌀ rim 31; vessel H 16.5. Multiple rim friezes: dolphins flanking rosette over horizontal S-spirals; Ionian kyma. Main decoration: satyrs flanking krater, Pegasos, masks. Calyx: imbricate, rounded petals with central vein. Medallion: small rosette surrounded by ferns and imbricate petals. Frieze separators: dots. Workshop A.
– Rotroff 1982a, 92 cat. 408, pls. 71, 90, 91.

SHA-334
Athens, Agora, M-N 15: 1, P 23403 a-c. Large fr. of rim and body. WSl decoration on rim int. and ext. ⌀ rim 33.5. Main decoration: mythological. Workshop A.
– Rotroff 1997a, 305–306 cat. 603, fig. 44, pl. 58.

SHA-335
Athens, Agora, M-N 15: 1, P 22895. Fr. of base and lower body. ⌀ base 10.8. Calyx with figural decoration.
– Rotroff 1997a, 306 cat. 607, fig. 44, pl. 58.

SHA-336
Athens, Agora, H-K 12–14 (Middle Stoa, building fill, before ca. 170), P 21035. Fr. of rim and body, attachment of horizontal handle. Main decoration: plastic pine cone.
– Rotroff 1997a, 305 cat. 601, fig. 44, pl. 57.

SHA-337
Delos. Fr. of body and part of foot. Reduced. Main decoration: daisy network.
– Laumonier vol. 2, cat. 6037, pl. 5.

SHA-338
Delos. Complete. Horizontal rope handles. ⌀ rim 18.5; vessel H 12.4. Reduced. Rim frieze: groove. Calyx: imbricate, small pointed petals. Ascription to Attica is open to question.
– Laumonier 1977, 467–468 cat. 6002, pls. 108, 134 (unassigned).

SHA-339
Athens, Agora, H-K 12–14 (Middle Stoa, building fill, before ca. 170), P 22837. Large fr. of rim and rim. WSl decoration on rim int. and ext. ⌀ rim 24.
– Rotroff 1997a, 306 cat. 605, fig. 44, pl. 58.

SHA-340
Athens, Agora, H-K 12–14 (Middle Stoa, building fill, before ca. 170), P 21029. Rim fr. ⌀ rim 23.
– Rotroff 1997a, 306 cat. 606, fig. 44, pl. 58.

SHA-341
Athens, Agora, H-K 12–14 (Middle Stoa, building fill, before ca. 170), P 21031. Fr. of base and lower body. WSl decoration on int. ⌀ base 9.5.
– Rotroff 1997a, 306 cat. 608, fig. 44, pl. 58.

Production Place?

SHA-342
Eretria. Non-joining frs. of rim and body. Main decoration: battle.
– Schmid 2004, 496 cat. 5, pl. 237.5.

SHA-343
Eretria. Upper part of vessel. Main decoration: seated deities? Attic or Atticizing.
– Schmid 2004, 496 cat. 6, pl. 238.6.

SHA-344
Beljaus, Bel-2000-45. Fr. of neck and upper part of body. Rim frieze: dots. Calyx: imbricate, rounded petals with central vein; upper row upside-down.

SHA-345
Athens, Agora, Area F 12, P 4576. Fr. of body with rope handle. Reduced. Main decoration: stylized long petals.
– Rotroff 1997a, 404 cat. 1625, pl. 127.

SHA-346
Athens, Agora, Area D 17, P 19917. Body fr. Reduced. Main decoration: stylized long petals.
– Rotroff 1997a, 404 cat. 1626, pl. 127.

SHA-347
Delos. Fr. of lower body and part of foot. Reduced. Main decoration: stylized long petals.
– Laumonier vol. 2, cat. 6017, pl. 3.

VOLUTE KRATER

Athens

SHA-348
Delos. Joined from numerous frs., lacking neck and foot. Vertical volute handles. Main decoration: daisy network.
– Laumonier vol. 2, cat. 6146, pl. 5.

SHA-349
Delos. Handle fr. of volute krater.
– Laumonier vol. 2, cat. 6014.

KRATER, EPHESIAN TYPE

Ephesos

SHA-350   EPH-1330*
Olbia, Sector NGS, House IV-4 B 351/218, O-НГС-92-677+93-539, 92–673, 678, 93–533, 539 (join across years), Kiev, Institute of Archaeology storeroom. Five rim frs. and seven body frs.; three of the rim frs. and three of the body frs. join. H 7.1 × W 12.5, WT 0.5–0.6, ⌀ rim 36. Menemachos.
– Samojlova 1994, 90, fig. 2.2; Samojlova 1998; Guldager Bilde 2010, 284 cat. F-95, pl. 188.

SHA-351   EPH-1331*
Olbia, Sector NGS, O-НГС-06-149, Parutine, Olbia National Preserve storeroom. Rim fr. H 4 × W 5.7, WT 0.3, ⌀ rim 20, 8%.

SHA-352
Delos. Complete. ⌀ rim 24, ⌀ base 10.1; vessel H 15.8. Reduced. Rim frieze: Ionian kyma. Main decoration: Erotes, centauromachy, Amazons. Calyx: straight acanthus alternating with Wadjet symbol. Frieze separators: dots. VG Workshop.
– Laumonier 1977, 100 cat. 6201, pls. 22, 131 (Vases gris).

SHA-353
Delos. Fr. of rim and upper body including horizontal ear-shaped handle. Reduced. Rim frieze: Ionian kyma. Main decoration: dogs (hunt?). Frieze separators: dots.
– Laumonier 1977, 103 cat. 6021, pl. 23 (Vases gris).

SHA-354
Delos. Lower half. Reduced. Main decoration: Herakles fighting lion, repeated. Calyx A. Menemachos.
– Laumonier 1977, 73 cat. 6088, pl. 16.

SHA-355
Delos. Fr. of rim and upper body. Tall horizontal ridged loop-handle. ⌀ rim 36. Reduced. Rim frieze: Ionian kyma. Main decoration: satyr playing aulos.
– Laumonier 1977, 101 cat. 6005, pl. 23 (Vases gris).

SHA-356
Delos. Rim fr. Reduced. Rim frieze: Ionian kyma. Main decoration: lion left.
– Laumonier 1977, 77 cat. 6040, pl. 16 (NI).

SHA-357
Delos. Rim fr. Reduced. Rim frieze: Ionian kyma. Main decoration: figural (only tops of heads preserved).
– Laumonier 1977, 77 cat. 6042, pl. 16 (NI).

SHA-358
Delos. Three joining body frs. Reduced. Main decoration: acanthus-vine scroll left. Monogram PAR.
– Laumonier vol. 2, cat. 6019+6041, 1516, pl. 7.

SHA-359
Tyras. Fr. of rim and upper part of body. Ear-shaped horizontal handle. Rim frieze: rosettes. Main decoration: groups of ivy leaves alternating with ivy-berry clusters. Frieze separators: dots.
– Samojlova 1984, 126, fig. 4.11.

SHA-360
Delos. Fr. of lower part of bowl and foot. ⌀ base 5.5. Main decoration: plastic pine cone.
– Laumonier 1977, 479 cat. 6082, pls. 111, 134 (unassigned).

SHA-361
Delos. Complete. ⌀ rim 26.5, ⌀ base 11.5; vessel H 15.2. Reduced. Rim frieze: rosette 1. Calyx: tall, folded acanthus alternating with floral stems.
– Courby 1922, pl. XIV.2; Laumonier 1977, 66 cat. 6000, pls. 14, 131.

SHA-362
Ephesos, Südtor. Fr. of rim and upper body including one horseshoe-shaped handle. ⌀ rim 3. Reduced. Rim frieze: box meander cw. Calyx: imbricate, rounded petals with central and side veins.
– Gassner 1997, 81 cat. 243, pl. 18; Rogl 2008b, fig. 8.

SHA-363
Delos. Fr. of rim and upper body. Reduced. Rim frieze: wave meander. Main decoration: plastic long petals separated by dots.
– Laumonier 1977, 218 cat. 6020, pl. 48 (Petite rose spiralée).

SHA-364
Delos. Fr. of shoulder and horizontal ear-shaped handle. Rim frieze: box meander cw.
– Laumonier vol. 2, cat. 6023, pl. 9.

SHA-365
Delos. Fr. of upper body close to rim; handle attachment. Reduced. Rim frieze: Ionian kyma.
– Laumonier 1977, 104 cat. 6026, pl. 24 (Vases gris).

SHA-366
Delos. Rim fr. Reduced. Rim frieze: Ionian kyma.
– Laumonier 1977, 104 cat. 6039, pl. 24 (Vases gris).

Production Place?

SHA-367
Delos. Fr. of neck and body. Reduced. Main decoration: dogs.
– Laumonier vol. 2, cat. 6031, pl. 7.

SHA-368
Miletos. Fr. of rim and upper body. Main decoration: scroll.
– Kossatz 1990, 59 cat. M 422, pl. 26.

SHA-369
Delos. Two joining frs. of rim, neck, and body. Reduced. Calyx.
– Laumonier vol. 2, cat. 6045, 6052, pl. 1.

SHA-370
Delos. Fr. of rim, neck, and body. Reduced. Calyx.
– Laumonier vol. 2, cat. 6172, pl. 1.

SHA-371
Delos. Base fr.
– Laumonier vol. 2, cat. 6118.

KRATER, MACEDONIAN TYPE

Macedonia?

SHA-372
Petres. Almost complete profile, lacking base; fragmentary. Main decoration: figural; plastic long petals.
– Adam Veleni 1997, pl. 114.b.

SHA-373
Selitsa. Fragmentary; preserves most of profile. Rim frieze: grooves. Calyx: tall pointed petals alternating with floral stems and spiral tendrils.
– Keramopoullos 1932, 122 fig. 79.

SHA-374
Kozani. Fragmentary, only lower half preserved; part of foot missing. Calyx: tall pointed petals alternating with floral stems and spiral tendrils.
– Petsas 1963, 58, pl. 41b.

SUPPLEMENTARY SHAPES

BELL KRATER

Production Place?

SHA-375
Sparta. Complete profile; lacking minor fragments. Main decoration: crude wreath.
– Zavvou 2005, 115–116 cat. 8, fig. 7.

KRATER WITH SHORT, CONCAVE NECK

Macedonia?

SHA-376
Petres. Complete profile; fragmentary. Main decoration: stylized long petals.
– Adam Veleni 1997, pl. 114.a.

Production Place?

SHA-377
Delos. Fr. of rim, neck and shoulder. Reduced. Main decoration: plastic long petals separated by circles.
– Laumonier vol. 2, cat. 6004, pl. 2.

KRATER WITH HORIZONTAL EAR-SHAPED HANDLE

Ephesos?

SHA-378
Miletos. Handle fr. with part of body. Rim frieze: Ionian kyma. Frieze separators: dots.
– Kossatz 1990, cat. without no., pl. 21.

KRATER WITH HANGING U-SHAPED HANDLES

Lousoi

SHA-379
Lousoi. Fragmentary; lacking foot and large part of wall. Multiple rim friezes: Ionian kyma, upside down; astragal. Main decoration: birds flying right alternating with rosettes. Calyx: ovoid petals alternating with flowers on stems and female figures. Rouletting on entire neck exterior above moulded part.
– Mitsopoulos-Leon 1996, 187, 190 K78/1985, figs. 1–4.

SHA-380
Lousoi. Fr. of body and part of neck with horseshoe-shaped handle. Rim frieze: S's.
– Mitsopoulos-Leon 1996, 187 K84/1985, fig. 5.

KRATER, LIBURNIAN TYPE

Liburnia

SHA-381
South Italy, Colosso Collection, Ugento. Complete. Rim frieze: rouletting. Main decoration: boukrania, wolf's head, calyx, dolphins.
– PUGLIA 1979, 354 fig. 633; Yntema 1995, 395 fig. 6.20.

SHA-382
Art market, inv. 3143, Bonn, Akademisches Kunstmuseum. Complete. Vessel H 16.3. Main decoration: wreath (type?), scene with Herakles?
– Zimmer 2005, 115, 117 cat. A64, fig. 41.

KRATER, TYPE?

Athens

SHA-383
Delos. Fr. of body and part of foot. Reduced. Main decoration: daisy network.
– Laumonier vol. 2, cat. 6036, pl. 5.

SHA-384
Delos. Fr. of body and part of foot. Reduced. Main decoration: daisy network.
– Laumonier vol. 2, cat. 6038.

SHA-385
Delos. Fr. of body and part of foot. Reduced. Main decoration: daisy network.
– Laumonier vol. 2, cat. 6138.

SHA-386
Delos. Complete profile; joined from many frs. Vessel H 12.5. Rim frieze: Ionian kyma. Main decoration: daisy network, variant.
– Laumonier vol. 2, cat. 6103, pl. 5; Rotroff 2018, 641 cat. 210, fig. 49.

SHA-387
Athens, Agora, Q 8–9, P 20188. Part of rim, upper wall, and handles. Upturned rope handles. WSl decoration on rim int. and ext. Multiple rim friezes: rosettes and leaves, S-shaped spirals, jewelling. Main decoration: chariots; Theseus.
– Hausmann 1959, 110 n. 128; Rotroff 1997a, 305 cat. 602 fig. 44, pl. 57.

Corinth

SHA-388
Corinth. Fr. of rim and upper body. Multiple rim friezes: Ionian kyma; guilloche left. Main decoration: plastic long petals. No measurements are given, but the vessel must have been large judging from the scale of the published photograph.
– Edwards 1981, 204 C-63-490, pl. 48.

SHA-389
Corinth. Four non-joining body frs. Trace of appliqué support. Main decoration: plastic long petals.
– Edwards 1986, 393, 415 cat. 29, pl. 88.

SHA-390
Corinth. Three non-joining frs. of mid- and lower body. Rim frieze: incised ivy. Main decoration: plastic long petals.
– Edwards 1986, 393, 415 cat. 30, pl. 88.

Pergamon?

SHA-391
Delos. Fr. of rim, neck and part of body. Reduced. Main decoration: garland.
– Laumonier vol. 2, cat. 6032, pl. 7.

Knidos

SHA-392
Knidos. Body fr. with horizontal ear-shaped handle.
– Kögler 2010, 521 cat. F.142, pl. 30.

Apollonia-Dyrrachium Area?

SHA-393
Valesio. Fragmentary; joined from numerous fragments. Rim frieze: grooves. Main decoration: hunt.
– Yntema 1995, 395 fig. 3.11.

Macedonia

SHA-394
Olympia, well north of building C. Numerous fragments. Hanging U-shaped handle. Main decoration: symplegma between columns.
– Hausmann 1959, pl. 39; Hausmann 1996, 72–73 cat. 125, pl. 28.

Lousoi

SHA-395
Lousoi. Three non-joining frs. of rim and body. Oxidized. Rim frieze: crude rouletting. Main decoration: ivy-vine scroll; bulls running right.
– Rogl 2008a, 153 cat. 343, pls. 24, 43.

SHA-396
Lousoi. Base fr. Reduced.
– Rogl 2008a, 154 cat. 347, pls. 25, 43.

Production Place?

SHA-397 XXX-70*
Olbia, Sector E6, square 247, 436, room with walls 54, 45, 41, grey clay layer, O-E6-57-262, Kiev, Institute of Archaeology storeroom. Rim fr. H 3.8 × W 4.1, WT 0.6

SHA-398
Delphi. Fr. of body and rim. Large vessel. H 11 × W 14.5. Solid black coat. Subject unidentified.
– Perdrizet 1908, 176–177 cat. 433, fig. 741; Siebert 1978, 400 cat. Del.95.

SHA-399
Olympia.
– Schiering 1981, 171–191 figs. 70–72, pl. 20.

SHA-400
South Russia, Antikensammlung, Staatliche Museen zu Berlin. Complete. Main decoration: Greek warriors over horsemen alternating with Hathor's crown.
– Rostovcev 1967, pl. LXIV.3.

SUPPLEMENTARY SHAPES

SHA-401
Monte Sannace. Body fr. with part of handle. Main decoration: wreath (type?), figural.
– Puppo 1995, 100–101 cat. TA24.f, fig. 9.

SHA-402
Delos. Body fr. with horizontal ear-shaped handle. Calyx.
– Laumonier vol. 2, cat. 6028, pl. 6.

SHA-403
Delos. Fr. of rim, neck, shoulder and body. Reduced. Calyx: imbricate, large petals with central veins.
– Laumonier vol. 2, cat. 6085, pl. 1.

SHA-404
Delos. Several joining body frs. Calyx: imbricate, large rounded with central vein.
– Laumonier vol. 2, cat. 6202, pl. 4.

SHA-405
Delos. Fr. of lower body and part of foot. Main decoration: plastic long petals.
– Laumonier vol. 2, cat. 6193.

SHA-406
Delos. Complete profile joined from many frs., lacking only foot. Horizontal ear-shaped handle. Reduced. Main decoration: plastic long petals separated by dots.
– Laumonier vol. 2, cat. 6006, pl. 3.

SHA-407
Delos. Two joining body frs., non-joining body fr. Horizontal rope handle. Reduced. Main decoration: plastic long petals separated by circles.
– Laumonier vol. 2, cat. 6095, 6096, pl. 2.

SHA-408
Delos. Large body fr. Reduced. Main decoration: stylized long petals.
– Laumonier vol. 2, cat. 6009.

SHA-409
Delos. Fr. of rim, neck, shoulder and part of finely detailed handle. Reduced. Main decoration: stylized long petals.
– Laumonier vol. 2, cat. 6029, pl. 1.

SHA-410
Delos. Fr. of neck and body. Reduced. Main decoration: stylized long petals.
– Laumonier vol. 2, cat. 6034, pl. 3.

SHA-411
Delos. Fr. of upper body and horizontal ear-shaped handle.
– Laumonier vol. 2, cat. 6024, pl. 9.

KRATER WITH APPLIED FEET

Corinth

SHA-412
Corinth, Deposits 109 and 110, C-36-499 a-e, C-48-62. Numerous joining and non-joining frs. of body, medallion and two applied feet in the form of comic masks. Reduced. Main decoration: hunting scene(?) over frontal Erotes with outspread wings as space-filler amongst tall acanthus leaves.
– Edwards 1975, 172 cat. 873, pls. 38, 76; Siebert 1978, pl. 46.

SHA-413
Art market, inv. 756, Bonn, Akademisches Kunstmuseum. Fr. of base and lower body. Two applied feet in the form of human faces. Reduced. Main decoration: Hera as space-filler in calyx of tall acanthus leaves (Judgement of Paris).
– Siebert 1978, pl. 46; Zimmer 2005, 98–99 cat. A7, fig. 5.

Argos

SHA-414
Corinth, Manhole N: 20, C-47-796 a-c. Fr. of base and lower body. Two applied feet in the form of comic masks. Reduced. Main decoration: Hera and Athena as space-filler in calyx of tall acanthus leaves (Judgement of Paris).
– Weinberg 1949, 149, pl. 14.4; Edwards 1975, 166, 172 n. 26; Siebert 1978, 78, 167; Edwards 1981, 202 ns. 64 and 66 (identified as Argive); Romano 1994, 67 cat. 10, pl. 15 (identified as Argive).

Aiolis B

SHA-415   AIB-115*
Olbia, Sector NGS, O-НГС-86-689, Parutine, Olbia National Preserve storeroom. Fr. of base and lower body; applied feet in the shape of shells. H 6.3 × W 6.2, WT 0.4.

Production Place?

SHA-416 XXX-71*
Olbia, Sector NGS, O-НГС-91-185, Parutine, Olbia National Preserve storeroom. Applied foot in the shape of bald Silenos. H 5.4 × W 4.9, WT 0.5–0.7.

SHA-417 XXX-72*
Pantikapaion, palace foundation trench, M-85-45[f], 47, Moscow, Puškin Museum of Fine Arts. Fr. of base and lower body, non-joining body fr. Applied feet in the form of astragals. H 6.5 × W 6, WT 0.4.

KALATHOS

Production Place?

SHA-418
Kozani, Tomb 5. Complete. Vessel H 20.4. Main decoration: labours of Herakles?
– Batalis 2004, 226 pl. 79.

LARGE OPEN VESSEL, PROBABLY KRATER

Ephesos

SHA-419 EPH-1332*
Olbia, Sector NGS, House III-3 C 331/128, O-НГС-91-676, Parutine, Olbia National Preserve storeroom. Fr. of upper body. H 6.1 × W 3.8, WT 0.52–0.61. Menemachos.
– Guldager Bilde 2010, 284 cat. F-97, pl. 189.

SHA-420 EPH-1333*
Istros, His-B 503, Bucharest, Institute of Archaeology storeroom. Body fr. H 4.5 × W 4.5, WT 0.66.

SHA-421
Myrmekion, farmhouse, Room И, M-53-348. Numerous non-joining body fragments. Rim frieze: rosette. Main decoration: Eros musicians. Menemachos.
– Gajdukevič 1981, fig. 10.

SHA-422
Miletos. Fr. of mid- and lower body and part of wide, profiled base. Reduced. Main decoration: acanthus-vine scroll right. Calyx: straight acanthus alternating with acanthus with curved tip.
– Kossatz 1990, 11 cat. M 5, pl. 20.

SHA-423 EPH-1334
Pantikapaion, palace foundation trench, M-85-40, Moscow, Puškin Museum of Fine Arts. Fr. of shoulder and upper body. H 7.1 × W 7.2, WT 0.5.

Lousoi

SHA-424
Lousoi. Body fr. close to rim. Reduced. Rim frieze: guilloche right. Main decoration: dancing maenad alternating with lotus petal.
– Rogl 2008a, 153 cat. 346, pls. 43, 46.

SHA-425
Lousoi. Body fr. Oxidized. Main decoration: standing warrior alternating with lotus petals; rosette as space filler.
– Rogl 2008a, 153 cat. 344, pl. 25.

SHA-426
Lousoi. Body fr. Oxidized. Main decoration: male leaning; rosettes as space fillers.
– Rogl 2008a, 153 cat. 345, pls. 25, 43, 46.

SHA-427
Lousoi. Fr. of profiled foot.
– Mitsopoulos-Leon 1996, 187 K49/1984, figs. 6–7.

Achaia

SHA-428
Lousoi. Several non-joining frs. of rim and body. Oxidized. Multiple rim friezes: Ionian kyma; astragal. Calyx: bent acanthus leaves. I am not convinced of Rogl's identification of the shape.
– Rogl 2008a, 108 cat. 59, pls. 6, 32.

SHA-429
Lousoi. Several non-joining frs. of rim and body. Oxidized. Multiple rim friezes: Ionian kyma; astragal. Main decoration: stylized long petals.
– Rogl 2008a, 108–109 cat. 60, pls. 6, 32.

SHA-430
Lousoi. Several non-joining frs. of rim and body. Oxidized. Rim frieze: grooves. Main decoration: symplegma; stylized long petals.
– Rogl 2008a, 109 cat. 61, pls. 7, 32.

Production Place?

SHA-431
Athens, Agora, Area D 17, P 20358. Body fr. Reduced. Main decoration: stylized long petals.
– Rotroff 1997a, 404 cat. 1627 pl. 127.

SHA-432
Delos. Body fr. Reduced. Main decoration: stylized long petals separated by circles.
– Laumonier vol. 2, cat. 6056, pl. 2.

SHA-433
Miletos. Fr. of rim and upper body. Rim frieze: palmettes.
– Kossatz 1990, 42 cat. M 285, fig. 15, pl. 48.

SHA-434
Athens, Agora, Area C 16–17, P 18452. Fr. of body with handle. Reduced.
– Rotroff 1997a, 404–405 cat. 1628, pl. 127.

DINOS

Aiolis

SHA-435
Corinth, inv. 588, Bonn, Akademisches Kunstmuseum. Complete except for minor fragment of foot. ⌀ body 18; vessel H 14.2. Rim frieze: Ionian kyma. Main decoration: mantled dancing women. Calyx: straight acanthus; bent sepals. Frieze separators: astragal.
– Zimmer 2005, 114–115 cat. A61, fig. 38.

Ephesos

SHA-436   EPH-1335*
Olbia, V.I. 5002, Antikensammlung, Staatliche Museen zu Berlin (formerly Mavrogordato collection, 1909). Complete. ⌀ rim 11, ⌀ base 11.1; vessel H 14.5.

PLATE OR LID?

Lousoi?

SHA-437
Lousoi. Rim and part of wall. Reduced. Multiple rim friezes: Ionian kyma; guilloche.
– Mitsopoulos-Leon 1996, 187, 190, K27/1994.

LENTOID GUTTUS

Ephesos

SHA-438   EPH-1336*
Olbia, Sector NGS, O-НГС-05-914, Parutine, Olbia National Preserve storeroom. Shoulder fr. with attachment of ring handle. H 3.8 × W 4.8, WT 0.15, ⌀ neck 3.

SHA-439
Myrmekion, farmhouse, Room Γ. Shoulder fr. with part of handle and part of neck. Main decoration: Erotes around krater. Medallion: surrounded by jewellery droplets. Belles Méduses?
– Gajdukevič 1981, fig. 2.

SHA-440
Delos. Complete except for part of neck, rim and part of handle. ⌀ rim 11.2. Rim frieze: Ionian kyma. Main decoration: Amazons, Eros with thyrsos over shoulder, comic figure, symplegma on *kline*.
– Laumonier vol. 2, cat. 6111, pl. 22.

SHA-441
Delos. Complete except for rim and part of handle. ⌀ rim 11.5, ⌀ base 7; vessel H 11.3. Multiple rim friezes: small rosettes; Ionian kyma. Main decoration: dogs chasing rabbits left.
– Courby 1922, pl. XIV.3; Laumonier vol. 2, cat. 6093, pl. 22.

SHA-442
Delos. Body fr. Reduced. Main decoration: rabbit jumping left; dog.
– Laumonier 1977, 166 cat. 9361, pl. 37 (Monogram PAR).

SHA-443
Delos. Complete apart from minor abrasions of lip. Plastic attachments of theatre masks of slaves and old woman on shoulder. ⌀ rim 11.4, ⌀ base 6.8; vessel H 14. Rim frieze: Ionian kyma. Main decoration: Amazons hunting.
– Courby 1922, pl. XIV.4; Laumonier vol. 2, cat. 6092, pl. 22.

SHA-444
Paphos. Fragmentary; lacks lower part. Main decoration: griffins around stylized flower. WC1.
– Neuru 1991, 17 cat. 27, fig. 9, pl. 26.16.

Ephesos?

SHA-445
Delos. Shoulder fr. Rim frieze: astragal. Main decoration: bird and acanthus flower. Frieze separators: box meander, cw; dots.
– Laumonier vol. 2, cat. 3502, pl. 22.

SHA-446
Delos. Complete except for part of neck, rim and part of handle. ⌀ rim 11.2. Rim frieze: five-rayed sun wheel alternating with suspended wreath. Main decoration: heraldic winged griffins.
– Laumonier vol. 2, cat. 6110, pl. 22.

SHA-447   EPH-1337
Kepoi, Moscow, State Historical Museum? Fr. of foot and lower body.
– Usačeva 1978, fig. 1.29.

Production Place?

SHA-448   XXX-73*
Pantikapaion, 1905-109.1, present whereabouts unknown. Complete.
– St Petersburg, IIMK RAN photo archive neg. III 9925.

SHA-449
Delos. Fr. of shoulder and part of neck. Rim frieze: wave meander.
– Laumonier 1977, mentioned p. 81 as lagynos (cat. 3501); Laumonier vol. 2.

TEA-POT GUTTUS

Kyme?

SHA-450
Myrina(?), inv. S 4368, Paris, Louvre. Complete except for part of neck. ⌀ rim 5.8, ⌀ base 6.2; vessel H 15.6. Rim frieze: Ionian kyma. Calyx: straight acanthus; kantharoi as spacers.
– Jentel 1968, 13, pls. 11.4, 16.4. If, as Jentel suggests, this is the vessel described in the unpublished *Journal de fouilles* of excavations at Myrina, it originally had a lid.

SHA-451
Myrina(?), inv. S 4367, Paris, Louvre. Fragmentary, lacking handles. ⌀ rim 6.5, ⌀ base 7.7; vessel H 15. Rim frieze: Ionian kyma. Main decoration: bound garlands carried by boukrania. Calyx: acanthus.
– Jentel 1968, 13, pls. 11.3, 16.6.

GUTTUS?

Production Place?

SHA-452
Argos. Complete profile including tall twisted horseshoe-shaped handle; lacking part of rim and shoulder. No rim frieze. Main decoration: plastic long petals.
– Siebert 1978, 16 n. 3, pl. 41 (kiln waster; not attributed to workshop).

HYDRIA

SHA-453
Art market, inv. I 1154, Erlangen, Sammlung des Archäologisches Instituts. Complete. Vessel H 24. No rim frieze. Calyx: straight acanthus alternating with buds on wavy stems; signed MENISKOU.
– Parlasca 1982, 176, figs. a-b, 1–2.

FILTER JUG WITH FOOT

Athens

SHA-454
Athens, Agora, Area E 15, P 6050. Almost complete; lacking part of rim and part of foot. Main decoration: stylized long petals.
– Rotroff 1997a, 357 cat. 1191, fig. 73, pl. 87.

SHA-455
Athens, Agora, E 10: 1, P 25536. Fr. of base and lower body. Main decoration: stylized long petals separated by dots.
– Rotroff 1997a, 357–358 cat. 1193, fig. 73, pl. 87.

SUPPLEMENTARY SHAPES

Athens?

SHA-456
Delos. Complete except for part of rim and part of handle. Satyr head as handle attachment. Rim frieze: Ionian kyma. Calyx: ovoid petals with central decorated rib; between petals, small, pointed imbricate leaves. Ariston (signed).
– Courby 1922, 329, 332, 365, pl. IX.e; Laumonier vol. 2, cat. 2753, pl. 15.

SHA-457
Delos. Fr. of lower part. Calyx: imbricate, pointed petals with central and side veins.
– Laumonier vol. 2, cat. 2826, pl. 15.

SHA-458
Delos. Almost complete; lacking spout and rim. Calyx: imbricate palmettes.
– Laumonier vol. 2, cat. 2755, pl. 15.

SHA-459
Delos. Almost complete; lacking spout and rim. Calyx: imbricate palmettes.
– Laumonier vol. 2, cat. 2756, pl. 15.

SHA-460
Delos. Almost complete; lacking spout and rim. ⌀ base 6; vessel H 9.9. Main decoration: stylized long petals.
– Laumonier vol. 2, cat. 2775, pl. 17.

SHA-461
Delos. Almost complete; lacking part of rim. ⌀ base 10; vessel H 11. Main decoration: stylized long petals.
– Laumonier vol. 2, cat. 2779, pl. 18.

SHA-462
Delos. Almost complete; lacking spout. ⌀ base 8.9; vessel H 13. Main decoration: stylized long petals.
– Laumonier vol. 2, cat. 2780, pl. 18.

SHA-463
Delos. Almost complete; lacking part of rim. ⌀ base 8.8; vessel H 12.5. Main decoration: stylized long petals.
– Laumonier vol. 2, cat. 2822, pl. 18.

SHA-464
Delos. Almost complete; lacking part of rim and spout. ⌀ rim 18, ⌀ base 10.5; vessel H 17.4. Rim frieze: Ionian kyma. Main decoration: stylized long petals separated by circles.
– Laumonier vol. 2, cat. 2778, pl. 16.

SHA-465
Delos. Complete except for part of spout. ⌀ base 10; vessel H 12.5. Rim frieze: dots. Main decoration: stylized long petals separated by circles.
– Courby 1922, pl. XIV.6; Laumonier vol. 2, cat. 2760, pl. 16.

SHA-466
Delos. Complete except for part of rim and spout. ⌀ base 8.8; vessel H 13.5. Main decoration: stylized long petals.
– Laumonier vol. 2, cat. 2761, pl. 18.

SHA-467
Delos. Complete except for part of lip. ⌀ base 8.1; vessel H 13. No rim frieze. Main decoration: stylized long petals separated by circles.
Courby 1922, pl. XIV.5; Laumonier vol. 2, cat. 2762, pl. 16.

SHA-468
Delos. Almost complete; lacking part of rim and spout. ⌀ base 9.2; vessel H 12.5. Rim frieze: Ionian kyma. Main decoration: stylized long petals separated by circles.
– Laumonier vol. 2, cat. 2808, pl. 16.

Pergamon

SHA-469
Delos. Almost complete; lacking part of rim and spout. Main decoration: bundled ivy wreath with ivy-berry clusters. Calyx: imbricate, small pointed petals combined with incised scroll.
– Laumonier vol. 2, cat. 2812, pl. 20.

Production Place?

SHA-470
Delos. Almost complete; lacking part of rim and spout. Vessel H 11. Reduced. Main decoration: scroll (type?).
– Laumonier vol. 2, cat. 2788, pl. 20.

SHA-471
Athens, Agora, Area C18, P 18497. Complete. Rim frieze: circles. Calyx: imbricate ferns.
– Rotroff 1997a, 426 cat. 1789, fig. 105, pl. 140.

SHA-472
Athens, Agora, C 20: 3, P 17407. Complete profile; fragmentary. Reduced. Rim frieze: circles. Calyx: imbricate, pointed petals with central and side veins.
– Rotroff 1997a, 405 cat. 1629, fig. 97, pl. 127.

SHA-473
Athens, Agora, F 19:6, P 15027. Complete profile, lacking tip of spout and part of rim. Vessel H 14.5. No rim frieze. Main decoration: pendent-semicircle design with leaf in centre; in between, imbricate small pointed petals. Calyx: tall ovoid petals alternating with small curved acanthus. Ariston (signed).
– Rotroff 1982a, 93 cat. 410, pls. 69, 97.

SHA-474
Athens, inv. 2148, Athens, National Museum. Complete except for rim, handle and part of spout; vessel H 14. No rim frieze. Main decoration: pendent-semicircle design. Calyx: pointed petals inscribed ΑΙΟΝΟΣ (almost certainly Aristonos).
– Watzinger 1901, 69, fig. without number.

SHA-475
Delos. Complete except for neck and rim; joined from numerous fragments. Rim frieze: astragal. Main decoration: pendent-semicircle design with rosette with eight broad petals in the centre; semicircles separated by a wide field of dots.
– Laumonier vol. 2, cat. 3534, pl. 22.

SHA-476
Miletos. Large part of body and wide ring foot. Main decoration: plastic long petals separated by dots. Kossatz is of the opinion that it is a lamp.
– Kossatz 1990, 66 cat. M 459, pl. 20.

SHA-477
Delos. Complete. Main decoration: stylized long petals.
– Laumonier vol. 2, cat. 2704, pl. 16.

SHA-478
Delos. Almost complete; lacking spout and rim. Main decoration: stylized long petals separated by dots.
– Laumonier vol. 2, cat. 2705, pl. 16.

SHA-479
Delos. Several non-joining frs. of body, base, and spout. Main decoration: stylized long petals separated by dots.
– Laumonier vol. 2, cat. 2819, pl. 17.

FOOTLESS FILTER JUG

Ephesos?

SHA-480
Delos. Almost complete; lacking part of rim. Vessel H 10.4. Reduced. Main decoration: stylized myrtle wreath. Calyx: straight acanthus and columns of dots.
– Laumonier vol. 2, cat. 2809, pl. 20.

SHA-481
Delos, Almost complete; lacking rim, handle and spout. Vessel H 7.5. Reduced. Rim frieze: Ionian kyma. Calyx: straight acanthus.
– Laumonier vol. 2, cat. 2806, pl. 20.

SHA-482
Delos. Fr. of lower part. ⌀ base 8.5; vessel H 13. Reduced. Rim frieze: Ionian kyma. Calyx: lotus petals.
– Laumonier vol. 2, cat. 2810, pl. 20.

SHA-483
Delos. Complete. Vessel H 9.5. Reduced. Rim frieze: Ionian kyma. Calyx: isolated plastic long petal alternating with palmette on twisted stem.
– Laumonier 1977, 384 cat. 2785, pls. 92, 133 (unassigned, Series 3.2).

SHA-484
Delos. Fr. of lower part. Reduced. Rim frieze: Ionian kyma. Main decoration: stylized long petals.
– Laumonier vol. 2, cat. 2803, pl. 18.

SHA-485
Delos. Almost complete; lacking part of rim. Reduced. Main decoration: stylized long petals.
– Laumonier vol. 2, cat. 2811, pl. 19.

SHA-486
Delos. Fr. of lower part. Reduced. Main decoration: figural? Calyx: imbricate, large plastic petals.
– Laumonier vol. 2, cat. 2791, pl. 20.

SHA-487
Delos. Fr. of lower part. Reduced. Rim frieze: astragal. Main decoration: figural?
– Laumonier vol. 2, cat. 2792, pl. 20.

SHA-488
Delos. Almost complete; lacking part of rim and spout. Vessel H 9.4. Reduced. Main decoration: figural. Calyx: small acanthus.
– Laumonier vol. 2, cat. 2790, pl. 20.

SHA-489
Athens, Agora, Area K 11, P 6057. Body fr. Rim frieze: Ionian kyma. Calyx: imbricate, pointed petals with double outline.
– Rotroff 1997a, 426 cat. 1790, fig. 105, pl. 140.

SHA-490
Athens(?), inv. 1913–208, Stoddard Collection, Yale University. Complete except for handle and spout. Rim frieze: rosettes with 11 petals. Main decoration: pendent-semicircle design.
– Baur 1941, 241 cat. 208, fig. 11, pl. XI.

SUPPLEMENTARY SHAPES

SHA-491
Delos. Fr. of lower part. Main decoration: stylized long petals.
– Laumonier vol. 2, cat. 2806[a], pl. 16.

SHA-492
Delos. Almost complete profile, lacking part of rim, spout and handle. Rim frieze: stylized scroll. Main decoration: stylized long petals.
– Laumonier vol. 2, cat. 2871, pl. 19.

SHA-493
Delos. Fr. of lower part including spout. Reduced. Multiple rim friezes: astragal; dots. Main decoration: stylized long petals with row of circles inside petals.
– Laumonier vol. 2, cat. 2844, pl. 19.

FILTER JUG, TYPE?

Athens

SHA-494
Athens, Agora, Area C-G 13-16, P 4196. Upper body. Calyx: imbricate ferns.
– Rotroff 1997a, 357 cat. 1192, fig. 73, pl. 87.

Athens?

SHA-495
Delos. Body fr. Reduced. Calyx: ovoid petals with central decorated rib; between petals, small, pointed imbricate leaves. Ariston (signed).
– Laumonier vol. 2, cat. 2754, pl. 15.

SHA-496
Delos. Two non-joining frs. of spout and body. Rim frieze indistinct. Calyx: large petals and leaves.
– Laumonier vol. 2, cat. 2807, pl. 15.

SHA-497
Delos. Non-joining frs. of upper and lower part. Calyx: imbricate, pointed petals with central and side veins.
– Laumonier vol. 2, cat. 2824, pl. 15.

SHA-498
Delos. Complete upper part. Calyx: imbricate, pointed petals with double outline.
– Laumonier vol. 2, cat. 2757, pl. 15.

SHA-499
Delos. Fr. of upper part. Calyx: imbricate palmettes.
– Laumonier vol. 2, cat. 2758, pl. 15.

SHA-500
Delos. Fr. of upper part. Calyx: imbricate palmettes.
– Laumonier vol. 2, cat. 2759, pl. 15.

SHA-501
Delos. Body fr. Calyx: imbricate, pointed palmettes.
– Laumonier vol. 2, cat. 2841, pl. 15.

SHA-502
Delos. Fr. of upper part. Main decoration: pendent-semicircle design combined with field of imbrication.
– Laumonier vol. 2, cat. 2827, pl. 15.

SHA-503
Delos. Fr. of upper part. Main decoration: plastic long petals.
– Laumonier vol. 2, cat. 2782, pl. 17.

SHA-504
Delos. Fr. of upper part. Main decoration: stylized long petals.
– Laumonier vol. 2, cat. 2763, pl. 18.

SHA-505
Delos. Fr. of upper part. Main decoration: stylized long petals.
– Laumonier vol. 2, cat. 2768, pl. 18.

SHA-506
Delos. Fr. of upper part. Main decoration: stylized long petals.
– Laumonier vol. 2, cat. 2769, pl. 18.

SHA-507
Delos. Fr. of upper part with handle. Main decoration: stylized long petals.
– Laumonier vol. 2, cat. 2781, pl. 18.

SHA-508
Delos. Fr. of upper part with handle. Main decoration: stylized long petals.
– Laumonier vol. 2, cat. 2801, pl. 18.

SHA-509
Delos. Almost complete; lacking part of rim (and lower part?). Vessel H 10.5. Main decoration: stylized long petals.
– Laumonier vol. 2, cat. 2817, pl. 18.

SHA-510
Delos. Fr. of upper part. Main decoration: stylized long petals.
– Laumonier vol. 2, cat. 2825, pl. 18.

SHA-511
Delos. Fr. of lower part. Main decoration: stylized long petals.
– Laumonier vol. 2, cat. 2840, pl. 19.

SHA-512
Delos. Body fr. Main decoration: stylized long petals separated by dots.
– Laumonier vol. 2, cat. 2800, pl. 16.

SHA-513
Delos. Fr. of upper part. Main decoration: swirling stylized long petals separated by dots.
– Laumonier vol. 2, cat. 2776, pl. 17.

SHA-514
Delos. Fr. of upper part with part of neck. Main decoration: swirling stylized long petals separated by dots.
– Laumonier vol. 2, cat. 2802, pl. 17.

Ephesos

SHA-515
Delos. Four body frs., two join; attachment of handle. Rim frieze: Ionian kyma. Main decoration: stylized acanthus scroll with three-dot groups, left.
– Laumonier vol. 2, cat. 68 E 3336, 3340, 3360, 3380.

SHA-516
Delos. Fr. of upper part. Reduced. Calyx.
– Laumonier vol. 2, cat. 2818, pl. 20.

SHA-517
Delos. Fr. of lower part. Reduced. Calyx: vegetal?
– Laumonier vol. 2, cat. 2829, pl. 20.

SHA-518
Delos. Shoulder fr. Main decoration: pendent-semicircle design separated by dotted field. Medallion: surrounded by ivy-berry clusters.
– Laumonier vol. 2, cat. 3503, pl. 22.

Ephesos?

SHA-519
Delos. Fr. of upper part with spout. Reduced. Main decoration: stylized long petals.
– Laumonier vol. 2, cat. 2786, pl. 17.

SHA-520
Delos. Fr. of shoulder with handle attachment. Reduced. Main decoration: stylized long petals separated by dots.
– Laumonier vol. 2, cat. 2751, pl. 17.

SHA-521
Delos. Fr. of lower body. Reduced. Rim frieze: stylized scroll. Main decoration: vertical fluting.
– Laumonier vol. 2, cat. 2820, pl. 19.

SHA-522
Delos. Fr. of upper part. Reduced.
– Laumonier vol. 2, cat. 2830, pl. 20.

Production Place?

SHA-523
Delos. Body fr. with handle. Reduced. Rim frieze: Ionian kyma. Calyx?
– Laumonier vol. 2, cat. 6030, pl. 7.

SHA-524
Delos. Fr. of lower body. Rim frieze: Ionian kyma. Calyx: straight acanthus.
– Laumonier vol. 2, cat. 2751[a], pl. 20.

SHA-525
Delos. Almost complete; lacking part of rim and spout. Vessel H 10.4. Reduced. Calyx.
– Laumonier vol. 2, cat. 2789, pl. 20.

SHA-526
Athens. Large part preserved, lacks spout. Vessel H 15. Rim: dots. Main decoration: pendent-semicircle design. Calyx: pointed petals.
– Watzinger 1901, 69 cat. 5.

SHA-527
Delos. Three joining frs. of upper part. Main decoration: stylized long petals.
– Laumonier vol. 2, cat. 2771bis, pl. 18.

SHA-528
Delos. Fr. of upper part with spout. Main decoration: stylized long petals.
– Laumonier vol. 2, cat. 2774, pl. 18.

SHA-529
Delos. Fr. of upper part with handle. Main decoration: stylized long petals.

SUPPLEMENTARY SHAPES

– Laumonier vol. 2, cat. 2787, pl. 18.

SHA-530
Delos. Fr. of lower part. Main decoration: stylized long petals.
– Laumonier vol. 2, cat. 2842, pl. 18.

SHA-531
Delos. Two joining frs. of upper part. Main decoration: stylized long petals separated by dots.
– Laumonier vol. 2, cat. 2766, pl. 17.

SHA-532
Delos. Almost complete; lacking spout and rim. Main decoration: stylized long petals separated by dots.
– Laumonier vol. 2, cat. 2767, pl. 17.

SHA-533
Delos. Four body frs., two join; attachment of handle. Main decoration: stylized long petals separated by circles.
– Laumonier vol. 2, cat. C 62 C 2052(?), pl. 16.

SHA-534
Delos. Fr. of upper part with neck. Main decoration: stylized long petals separated by circles.
– Laumonier vol. 2, cat. 2805[a], pl. 18.

SHA-535
Delos. Fr. of upper part. Main decoration: stylized long petals separated by circles.
– Laumonier vol. 2, cat. 2831, pl. 16.

SHA-536
Delos. Three body frs., two join. Reduced. Main decoration: stylized long petals separated by circles.
– Laumonier vol. 2, cat. 2843, pl. 19.

SHA-537
Delos. Fr. of upper part. Main decoration: swirling stylized long petals separated by dots.
– Laumonier vol. 2, cat. 2777, pl. 17.

FILTER JUG?

Athens?

SHA-538
Athens, Agora, Area C 20, P 17563. Body fr. Calyx: lotus petals; part of signature (S) inside petal. Ariston? [PGB].
– Rotroff 1997a, 308 cat. 622 fig. 45, pl. 59.

Production Place?

SHA-539
Athens, Agora, Area D 17, P 11268. Body fr. Calyx: lotus petals with imbricate field in between.
– Rotroff 1997a, 425 cat. 1786, fig. 105, pl. 139.

SHA-540
Kyme. Fr. of base and lower body. Rim frieze: Ionian kyma. Main decoration: plastic long petals.
– Bouzek & Jansová 1974, 74 cat. MB 135, fig. 16, pl. 14.

LID?

Ephesos

SHA-541
Delos. Fragmentary; complete profile. Vessel H 6.8. Rim frieze: astragal. Main decoration: hunt (upside-down). Frieze separators: dots.
– Laumonier 1977, 415 cat. 9015, pl. 97 (unassigned).

FUNERARY URN WITH LID

Sardis?

SHA-542
Sardis, Tomb of the Lintel, inv. 2186, Manisa Museum inv. 2186. Complete. Covered with white slip. ⌀ rim 16, ⌀ base 18; vessel H 33.6. Rim frieze: Ionian kyma. Main decoration: Erotes, wreaths, columns, loutrophoroi; Amazons, animal, loutrophoroi; suspended garlands between loutrophoroi, masks over garlands. Calyx: acanthus.
– Rotroff 2003, 79–80, cat. 306, pl. 50 with references to earlier literature.

Production Place?

SHA-543
Sardis, Tomb 535, P1117, lost. Complete profile. WSl decoration. Vessel H 17.8. Main decoration: Erotes. Calyx: acanthus with Erotes as spacers. Medallion: rosette with eight petals.
– Rotroff 2003, 198–199, pl. 144 centre.

FUNERARY URN?

Ephesos

SHA-544
Delos. Fr. of shoulder and upper body. Reduced. Rim frieze: guilloche left. Main decoration: plastic pine cone.
– Laumonier 1977, 406 cat. 6016, pls. 95, 134 (Dionysios [B]).

Production Place?

SHA-545
Delos. Complete profile; fragmentary, lacking much of body and almost all of neck. Rim frieze: rosettes with eight petals. Main decoration: plastic long petals separated by dots.
– Courby 1922, pl. XIV.1; Laumonier vol. 2, cat. 6001, pl. 3.

LARGE CLOSED VESSEL WITH LION-HEAD SPOUT

Production Place?

SHA-546
Delos. Body fr. with perforated lion head appliqué over applied acanthus leaf. Reduced. Main decoration: stylized long petals separated by circles.
– Laumonier vol. 2, cat. 6169, pl. 2.

LARGE CLOSED VESSEL

Kyme

SHA-547   KYB-328
Olbia, Sector R25, O-P25-98-86, Parutine, Olbia National Preserve storeroom. Fr. of upper body. H 3.1 × W 2.8, WT 0.35. Kirbeis.

Aiolis

SHA-548   AIX-35*
Myrmekion, M-56-1893, St Petersburg, State Hermitage Museum. Fr. of mid- and lower body. H 8, WT 0.5.
– Gajdukevič 1959, 80 fig. 88; Petrova 2014, 227, fig. 15.4 (identified as Mesambrian).

Ephesos

SHA-549   EPH-1338
Istros, His-260, Bucharest, Institute of Archaeology storeroom. Body fr. H 2 × W 3, WT 0.58.
– Domăneanțu 2000, 92 cat. 441, pl. 30.

SHA-550   EPH-1341*
Olbia, Sector E2, square 55, Cistern Л, O-E2-49-623, Kiev, Institute of Archaeology storeroom. Body fr. H 4.5 × W 4.3, WT 0.32.

SHA-551   EPH-1342*
Pantikapaion, palace foundation trench, M-84-63, Moscow, Puškin Museum of Fine Arts. Fr. of mid-body. H 5 × W 5.5, WT 0.52.

SHA-552   EPH-1343*
Olbia, Sector R25, O-P25-06-647, Parutine, Olbia National Preserve storeroom. Fr. of upper body. H 2.8 × W 3.4, WT 0.38.

SHA-553   EPH-1344*
Olbia, Sector NGS, O-НГС-86-287, Parutine, Olbia National Preserve storeroom. Shoulder fr. H 2.7 × W 5.9, WT 0.23–0.4, ⌀ shoulder 16.5.

SHA-554
Delos. Fr. of shoulder and upper part of vessel. Multiple rim friezes: rosette 2/7; horizontal S-spirals. Menemachos?
– Laumonier vol. 2, cat. 3504, pl. 28.

SHA-555   EPH-1345
Olbia, Sector R25, O-P25-00-1707, Parutine, Olbia National Preserve storeroom. Fr. of upper body.

SHA-556   EPH-1346
Olbia, Sector NGS, O-НГС-91-592, Parutine, Olbia National Preserve storeroom. Fr. of lower body. Menemachos.

SHA-557   EPH-1347
Olbia, Sector R25, O-P25-04-3268, Parutine, Olbia National Preserve storeroom. Body fr.

SHA-558   EPH-1348*
Olbia, O-52-2431, Kiev, Institute of Archaeology storeroom. Body fr.

SHA-559   EPH-1349*
Olbia, Sector E6-7, square 474, grey clay layer, O-E6-7-62-264, Kiev, Institute of Archaeology storeroom. Body fr. H 3.7 × W 6.3, WT 0.35.

Knidos

SHA-560   KNI-75*
Istros, His-V 19367 B, Bucharest, Institute of Archaeology storeroom. Body fr. H 4.7 × W 4.5, WT 0.2.
– Domăneanțu 2000, 138 cat. 688, pl. 50.

Sardis

SHA-561
Sardis. Fr. of shoulder; lower part of vessel moulded. No rim frieze. Main decoration: ivy scroll.
– Rotroff 2003, 115 cat. 474, pl. 82.

Production Place?

SHA-562   XXX-74*
Istros, His-A 313, Bucharest, Institute of Archaeology storeroom. Fr. of shoulder and upper body. H 6.7 × W 7.1, WT 0.4.

SHA-563   XXX-75
Olbia, Sector NGCentre, squares 33se, 34s, 35s, 53ne, 54n, 55n, humus, О-НГЦ-67-180, 180[A], Kiev, Institute of Archaeology storeroom. Two joining body frs. H 6.6 × W 5.7, WT 0.4.

SHA-564   XXX-76*
Olbia, Sector E6, square 400, grey clay layer, O-E6-56-595, Kiev, Institute of Archaeology storeroom. Two joining frs. of mid- and lower body with tiny part of base. H 5 × W 5.5, WT 0.35.

SHA-565
Kyme. Lower part of bowl. ⌀ base 8.5. Main decoration: boar. Calyx: low small straight acanthus leaves and floral scrolls.
Bouzek & Jansová 1974, 62 cat. MB 74, fig. 12, pl. 10.

SHA-566
Delos. Two joining body frs. Reduced. Main decoration: figural.
– Laumonier vol. 2, cat. 6080, fig. 6.

SHA-567
Delos. Shoulder fr. Multiple rim friezes.
– Laumonier vol. 2, cat. 6198, pl. 9.

SHA-568   XXX-77*
Olbia, Sector NGS, О-НГС-04-439, House III-1 B 734/144, Parutine, Olbia National Preserve storeroom. Fr. of mid-body. H 3.5 × W 5.8, WT 0.35.

LARGE VESSEL, TYPE?

Athens?

SHA-569
Delos. Body fr. Main decoration: altar figs. A1, C2.
– Laumonier vol. 2, cat. 3300, pl. 6.

Ephesos

SHA-570   EPH-1350*
Olbia, O-63-1834, Kiev, Institute of Archaeology storeroom. Body fr. H 3.8 × W 5.3, WT 0.5.

SHA-571
Delos. Body fr. Reduced. Main decoration: Eros.
– Laumonier vol. 2, cat. 6068, pl. 8.

SHA-572   EPH-1351*
Olbia, O-61-no no., present whereabouts unknown. Two joining frs. of upper and mid-body. Menemachos.
– St Petersburg, IIMK RAN, photo archive neg. II 73210.

SHA-573
Miletos. Fr. of mid-body. Reduced. Rim frieze: Ionian kyma. Main decoration: huntsman with gorytos rides right.
Kossatz 1990, 70 cat. M 509 fig. 33, pl. 18.

SHA-574
Kara-Tobe, K-93-320, present whereabouts unknown. Body fr. Rim frieze: Ionian kyma. Main decoration: hunter right confronts boar and dog; repeated. Calyx: imbricate petals with central vein. Frieze separators: dots.
– Vnukov & Kovalenko 1998, fig. 3.1.

SHA-575
Delos. Body fr. Reduced. Main decoration: frontal woman holding skirt.
– Laumonier 1977, 101 cat. 6091, pl. 23 (Vases gris).

SHA-576
Delos. Body fr. Reduced. Main decoration: satyr playing aulos.
– Laumonier 1977, 101 cat. 6067, pl. 23 (Vases gris).

SHA-577
Delos. Body fr. Reduced. Main decoration: Herakles.
– Laumonier vol. 2, cat. 6073, pl. 8.

SHA-578
Delos. Body fr. Reduced. Main decoration: Judgement of Paris. Menemachos.
– Laumonier vol. 2, cat. 6179, pl. 7.

SHA-579
Delos. Body fr. Reduced. Main decoration: Greek warrior.
– Laumonier vol. 2, cat. 6074, pl. 8.

SHA-580
Delos. Body fr. Reduced. Rim frieze: Ionian kyma. Main decoration: figural (only heads preserved). Frieze separators: dots.
– Laumonier 1977, 103 cat. 6075, pl. 23 (Vases gris).

SHA-581
Delos. Body fr. Main decoration: plastic pine cone.
– Laumonier 1977, 482 cat. 6081, pl. 112 (unassigned).

SHA-582
Delos. Body fr. H 7.5 × W 10. Reduced. Rim frieze: two incised grooves. Calyx: filled 'nelumbo' with amorous couple on *kline* surrounded by S-curved acanthus with bent tip and hatched central vein; small Erotes as space fillers. VG Workshop?
– Laumonier vol. 2, cat. 8622.

Production Place?

SHA-583
Miletos. Fr. of mid-body. Reduced. Rim frieze: astragal. Main decoration: saluting Pan.
– Kossatz 1990, 79 cat. M 660 fig. 37.

SHA-584
Delos. Body fr. Reduced. Main decoration: Altar fig. A1, standing female, legs of male.
– Laumonier vol. 2, cat. 6078, pl. 7.

SHA-585
Delos. Numerous non-joining frs. Main decoration: dancing maenads and satyrs.
– Laumonier vol. 2, cat. 3492, pl. 6.

SHA-586
Delos. Body fr. Reduced. Rim frieze: Ionian kyma. Main decoration: mantled dancing women.
– Laumonier vol. 2, cat. 6155, pl. 7.

SHA-587
Delos. Body fr. Main decoration: figural. Calyx: lotus and acanthus.
– Laumonier vol. 2, cat. 6015, pl. 6.

SHA-588
Delos. Two joining body frs. Main decoration: figural.
– Laumonier vol. 2, cat. 6042, pl. 7.

SHA-589
Delos. Body fr. Reduced. Main decoration: figural. Calyx.
– Laumonier vol. 2, cat. 6047, pl. 6.

SHA-590
Delos. Body fr. Reduced. Main decoration: figural. Calyx: palmettes.
– Laumonier vol. 2, cat. 6069, pl. 6.

SHA-591
Delos. Body fr. Main decoration: bull running left.
– Laumonier vol. 2, cat. 6070, pl. 7.

SHA-592
Delos. Body fr. Reduced. Main decoration: mask, confronted Erotes, amphora.
– Laumonier vol. 2, cat. 6077, pl. 7.

SHA-593
Delos. Body fr. Reduced. Main decoration: figural. Calyx: stylized acanthus.
– Laumonier vol. 2, cat. 6079, pl. 7.

SHA-594
Delos. Body fr. Vessel H 10.5. Main decoration: warrior and maenad(?) below myrtle wreath.
– Laumonier vol. 2, cat. 6104, pl. 6.

SHA-595
Delos. Body fr. Main decoration: figural: column.
– Laumonier vol. 2, cat. 6157, pl. 7.

SHA-596
Delos. Body fr. Reduced. Main decoration: figural?
– Laumonier vol. 2, cat. 6199, pl. 6.

SHA-597
Delos. Body fr. Calyx: lotus and stylized acanthus.
– Laumonier vol. 2, cat. 6044, pl. 6.

SHA-598
Delos. Body fr. Calyx: lotus and stylized acanthus.
– Laumonier vol. 2, cat. 6048, pl. 6.

SHA-599
Delos. Two body frs. Reduced. Calyx.
– Laumonier vol. 2, cat. 6173, pl. 6.

SHA-600
Delos. Body fr. Reduced. Calyx: 'nelumbo'.
– Laumonier vol. 2, cat. 6178, pl. 6.

SHA-601
Delos. Two joining frs. of rim and body. Reduced. Main decoration: plastic long petals separated by circles.
– Laumonier vol. 2, cat. 6046, pl. 2.

SHA-602
Delos. Fr. of body and part of base. Reduced. Main decoration: stylized long petals.
– Laumonier vol. 2, cat. 6050, pl. 1.

SHA-603
Delos. Body fr. Main decoration: stylized long petals.
– Laumonier vol. 2, cat. 6149, pl. 3.

SHA-604
Delos. Body fr. Main decoration: stylized long petals.
– Laumonier vol. 2, cat. 6180, pl. 3.

SHA-605
Delos. Numerous body frs. Main decoration: stylized long petals.
– Laumonier vol. 2, cat. 6181, pl. 3.

SHA-606
Delos. Two non-joining body frs. Main decoration: stylized long petals separated by circles topped by bow.
– Laumonier vol. 2, cat. 4928, pl. 2.

SHA-607
Delos. Body fr. Reduced. Main decoration: stylized long petals separated by circles topped by bud.
– Laumonier vol. 2, cat. 6033, pl. 2.

SHA-608
Delos. Body fr. Reduced. Main decoration: stylized long petals separated by circles topped by bud.
– Laumonier vol. 2, cat. 6056, pl. 2.

SHA-609
Delos. Body fr. Main decoration: stylized long petals separated by circles.
– Laumonier vol. 2, cat. 6086, pl. 2.

SHA-610
Delos. Body fr. Reduced. Main decoration: stylized long petals separated by circles.
– Laumonier vol. 2, cat. 6134, pl. 2.

SHA-611
Delos. Body fr. Reduced. Main decoration: stylized long petals separated by circles topped by bud.
– Laumonier vol. 2, cat. 6177, pl. 2.

CHAPTER 6

Iconography and Interpretation

Whereas in the preceding chapter we discussed the shape of the MMB, in this chapter we will consider its decoration. This occupies three main zones: the rim, the body, and the base. The most important decoration is on the body, where a motif may occupy the full height of the zone, or the area be divided into friezes. The main decoration can be classified in one of the following eight overall categories:

(1) Purely vegetal
(2) Purely figural
(3) Vegetal with figural elements
(4) Decoration with a wreath
(5) Decoration with a scroll
(6) Linear decoration
(7) Multiple rim friezes
(8) Any mixture of the above

Each type of decoration can be further subdivided. The choice of composition and decoration depends on the time and place of the individual vessel's production, and, in general, decoration followed local trajectories. In Chapter 3, we have already discussed how the origin and early development of the MMB most likely can be connected with the movement of diplomatic gifts in the form of precious metal vessels from the Ptolemaic court in Alexandria to the Greek and Roman world, and how this came about in several successive impulses or waves, first in the 220s under Ptolemy III Euergetes, then later in the 160s under Ptolemy VI Philometor. In the same chapter, we also discussed particular elements of the iconography which powerfully invoke Ptolemaic and Egyptian imagery. In the first part of the current chapter we shall consider the terminology of vegetal elements, which can also be best understood in the light of Egyptian iconography, as well as a few particular elements with a clear Egyptian ancestry.

In the second part of the chapter we shall examine some of the decorations and motifs which transcended local preferences. It should be noted that the discussion includes only those types of decoration which are attested in the Pontic assemblages. Decoration which can be found on vessels of a single production place is discussed in the chapter on the production in question.

Terminology of Vegetal Elements

From the very beginning, vegetal elements feature significantly as decoration of the MMB. In general, scepticism reigns as to whether the ancient mould makers attempted to represent floral elements of the real world. I am inclined to believe that, at least in the early part of the production, there was a relationship between what was represented and real vegetation. In addition to the acanthus, the MMB feature all elements of the lotus flower: isolated petals, the entire corolla (the collective term for the petals), sepals, calyx (the collective term for the sepals), and perianth (the collective term for both the calyx and corolla). Lotus is the ordinary name used for two different families of water lilies that grow in the shallows of lakes and rivers, the *Nelumbonaceae* and the *Nymphaeaceae*. In antiquity as well as today, the two plant families have been confused due to their superficial similarities. The *Nelumbo nucifera* (lit. 'nut-bearing'; Figs. 34, 35), also called the sacred lotus of India, differs in a number of respects from the blue lotus, *Nymphaea caerulea*, and the white lotuses, *Nymphaea alba* and *Nymphaea lotus* (Figs. 36, 37), but all four species were cultivated in Egypt in antiquity.

The two plant families can be distinguished by the form and posture of their leaves: the leaves of the *Nelumbo* are fully circular and are held clear of the water, while those of the *Nymphaea* have a single notch from the edge to the centre of the lily pad and they float on the water. The flower of the *Nelumbo* has large, rounded and fleshy petals and tiny sepals, whereas the *Nymphaea* flower has many smaller and spikier petals and characteristically ribbed sepals; moreover, the *Nelumbo* ripens with a characteristic central seed pod held high above the water, which contains a number of small fleshy seeds. It is evident that the floral element called 'nelumbo' in the common terminology of the MMB is, in fact, the sepal of the *Nymphaea lotus*.

On the vessels of the 'baroque' style discussed in Chapter 3, where a 'nelumbo' with a low acanthus leaf in front alternates with acanthus leaves with a low 'nelumbo' in front, the leaves form a calyx, so that the bowl itself becomes the flower (the corolla). The mixing of different plant species, a terrestrial and an aquatic one, provides

© PIA GULDAGER BILDE AND SUSAN I. ROTROFF, 2024 | DOI:10.1163/9789004680463_007

FIGURE 34
Nelumbo nucifera. A. Dupuis & O. Réveil, *Flore médicale usuelle et industrielle du XIXe siècle* (Paris 1870)

FIGURE 35
Nelumbo nucifera.
PHOTO BY AND ©2007 DEREK RAMSEY (RAM-MAN), CC BY-SA 2.5; <HTTPS://CREATIVECOMMONS.ORG/LICENSES/BY-SA/2.5>, VIA WIKIMEDIA COMMONS

FIGURE 36
Nymphaea lotus. Curtis's Botanical Magazine 21 (London 1805) no. 797.
https://www.biodiversitylibrary.org/item/14313#page/2/mode/1up

FIGURE 37
Nymphaea lotus.
https://commons.wikimedia.org/wiki/File:Nymphaea_lotus3.JPG

the calyx with an almost 'cosmic' meaning – at least hypothetically. I will not stress this, because it may have been unintended. The mixing of the two may also show Greek influence, because the acanthus leaf had been a symbol of fertility and immortality in Greek culture for centuries. Bowls which feature the sepals of the *Nymphaea lotus* should in my opinion be called calyx bowls. However, I accept the retention of 'nelumbo' with inverted commas as the term for the *Nymphaea lotus* sepals, even though this is incorrect from a botanical point of view. I do so in order to avoid further confusion, because the term is so deeply imbedded in the terminology of the MMB.

I believe that the so-called imbricate bowls, where many layers of petals cover the entire bowl, were inspired by the lotus corolla in general, the rounded petals perhaps of the *Nelumbo nucifera* and the pointed ones of the *Nymphaea lotus* (unless this was just a matter of stylization). Bowls with this pattern also turn the entire bowl into a flower.

Wherever the lotus grows, then and now, the seeds, stems, and rhizomes have served as food, and all types of lotuses have numerous medicinal properties, of which the blue lotus's mildly narcotic effect should perhaps be mentioned in particular. The flower of the lotus, be it the *Nymphaea* or the *Nelumbo*, has been and still is imbued with deep religious significance in the societies of all the places where it grows, because it is connected with myths of fertility, creation and resurrection, no less in the traditions of ancient Egypt than in modern Hinduism or Buddhism.

Mouldmade Bowls: Ancient *Kiboria*?

Various suggestions have been put forward as to the ancient name of our bowls (see Chapter 2). Because of the iconography of the early MMB and their Egyptian predecessors, which, as we have just seen, was based on the rendering of various parts of the lotus, I should like to propose another ancient name for the mouldmade bowl: *kiborion*, or 'lotus bowl'. Athenaios (3.72b), citing Theophrastos and Nikander, makes it clear that *kiborion* is both a synonym for 'Egyptian bean' (*aiguptios kuamos*, i.e., the 'lotus' or 'melilotus', 3.73a) and the designation of a kind of drinking vessel (cf. 477e–f). This *kiborion* is mentioned as a drinking vessel of precious metal in a number of ancient sources. We learn from Athenaios, in his catalogue of drinking bowls in Book 11 of the *Deipnosophistai*, that at least some *kiboria* were 'luxuriously fashioned'

(*Deipn.* 11.477 f). The source for this information is Hegesander of Delphi, writing in the mid-2nd century BCE and thus contemporary with our bowls. Athenaios continues, referring to the Alexandrian writer Didymos of the second half of the 1st century, that the *kiborion* is a sort of drinking cup, commenting that 'perhaps the so-called *skyphia* are the same, because they are contracted to a narrow point at the bottom, like Egyptian beans'.[1] We acquire more information on these 'beans' in Athenaios' third book, and it becomes clear that the term applied to all parts of the lotus (3.72 b-d). According to Athenaios' sources, Nikander and Theophrastos, these plants grow in swamps and marshes, and all parts of them were used during banquets: the flowers were woven into garlands and the seeds (the 'beans' proper) and tubers were eaten 'boiled, raw, or baked'.[2]

From Athenaios' phrasing it seems clear that the vessel known as the *kiborion* did not exist in his own day (late 2nd–early 3rd century CE) and that he did not really understand the form of the vase. Let us therefore turn to an author who is closer in time to the circulation of the MMB: Strabo.[3] He provides a vivid description of Egyptian sympotic practices involving 'lotus cups':

"The byblus grows in the Egyptian marshes and lakes, as also the Egyptian bean, from which comes the *kiborion*; and they have stalks approximately equal in height, about ten feet. … the bean produces leaves and flowers in many parts, and also a fruit like our bean, differing only in size and taste. Accordingly, the bean-fields afford a pleasant sight, and also enjoyment to those who wish to hold feasts therein. They hold feasts in cabin-boats, in which they enter the thick of the beans and the shade of the leaves; for the leaves are so very large that they are used both for drinking-cups and for bowls, for these even have a kind of concavity suited to this purpose; and in fact Alexandria is full of these in the workshops [*ergasteria*], where they are also used as vessels …" Strabo, *Geogr.* 17.1.15.1 (H.L. Jones, Loeb 1982, adapted).

---

1 Stemmed silver skyphoi resembling the metal prototype of MMB are known: e.g., from the Bulgarian Sâcrăieni treasure (on tall stem: Slej 2004, 164 cat. 74, 1st century BCE/CE) and the Artjuchov kurgan in the Taman' (Strong 1966, pl. 31b).
2 A plant with the same characteristics and properties as Athenaios' Egyptian bean is mentioned by Herodotos in his description of Egyptian plants in connection with other lotuses (2.92) as 'lilies resembling roses'.
3 His contemporary, Horace, also once uses the term (*ciborium*) for a wine cup (*Carmina* 2.7.22).

FIGURE 38 Detail of the Nilotic mosaic from the grotto-nymphaeum in the Forum of Praeneste (Berlin, Antikensammlung, inv. Mos. 3). https://commons.wikimedia.org/w/index.php?title=File:Mosaic_of_of _banquet_during_Nile_flooding,_Praeneste_(Italy),_around_80_BC_8824.jpg&oldid=616434282

Even though the description was written in the Augustan age, it still refers to the late Hellenistic period. In fact, we find a precise illustration of the scene described by Strabo in the large late Republican Nilotic mosaic from the grotto-nymphaeum in the Forum of Praeneste, beneath the Sanctuary of Fortuna, a fragment of which is now the Altes Museum in Berlin (Fig. 38: Inv. Mos. 3: Kriseleit 1985, 38–41, 71 cat. 11; Meyboom 1995, 33–34). We can recognize the lotus swamp and the cabin built in the water, under the shade of which a symposium is in progress. Three of the reclining symposiasts hold drinking bowls, hemispherical vessels which they support on the palms of their hands. The bowls are rendered in light grey, probably intended as silver. Some of the tesserae of the bowls are rounded and of a darker shade, perhaps indicating decoration. Even though the evidence is circumstantial, I believe that we can connect the representation of hemispherical bowls in a setting fully corresponding to what was described by Strabo with the *kiborion*.

Lotus bowls of various types had a long history in Pharaonic Egypt. Even if we leave aside the religious and ceremonial importance of the lotus, the *kiborion's* close connection with Egypt and Egyptian banqueting practices is well attested. The precious metal bowls featuring various types of lotus calyces and corollas on the exterior that were later adapted to the MMB fit so closely with contemporary descriptions of the *kiborion* that naming this class of pottery 'lotus bowls' or *kiboria* should be taken into serious consideration.

Individual Elements of Egyptian Inspiration

In addition to the pervasive Egyptian connotations mentioned above, isolated elements of Egyptian inspiration may also appear on the vessels (see also the discussion of the thunderbolt below). On a limited number of vessels we find the Egyptian sun disc framed by cobras. The motif is

FIGURE 39
Hathor's crown: straight cow's horn flanking the sun disc topped by a pair of ostrich feathers (PER-15, from Myrmekion)
PHOTO BY THE AUTHOR

normally very stylized, and perhaps the mould maker was not aware of what he depicted. In the literature on MMB, this symbol is commonly called an Isis crown or 'naja'. Naja is Sanskrit for 'snake'; but in zoology, it applies to a particular genus of venomous elapid snakes, the cobra. In combination with the sun disc, this is the symbol of the ancient Egyptian goddess Wadjet, the patron goddess and protectress of Lower Egypt and, as the uraeus, the symbol of the Pharaoh and his power. It should not be confused with the very similar Hathor's crown, where straight cow horns surround the sun disc. A beautiful and very detailed representation this crown, with the sun disc also topped by a pair of ostrich feathers, is preserved on a fragment of a MMB from Myrmekion, probably of Pergamene manufacture (PER-15, Fig. 39). The Wadjet symbol represents the downwards curving heads of intertwined snakes, and frequently, the entire body of the snake is cross-hatched, probably to represent the snake's scales (EPH-33, Fig. 40).

After having considered the Egyptian connections to the decoration of the MMB, we shall now turn to other decorative elements.

Figural Decoration

Erotes
Erotes were popular at many production places. They come in many sizes, from the miniature *aidolon*-like Erotes of Athenian production (Chapter 7) to the medium-sized Erotes common in, for example, Ephesian production (Chapter 14), to the large-scale Erotes employed in the Kymean Meter Medallion Workshop (Chapter 11). Erotes perform various tasks, such as playing music, venerating drinking vessels and kraters, carrying garlands, riding dolphins and racing chariots. They normally occur in numbers, not as isolated figures, and, with one exception, never in the company of Aphrodite.[4] Eros may be depicted as a chubby child, an adolescent, or as a young man, corresponding to the three ages of man's youth.

Eros with Dolphin
Erotes are associated with dolphins in Greek and Roman art from the 5th century until the late Roman period, either riding them or using them to draw a cart (Ridgway 1970; de Decker 2007–2008, 89–94, 96–98). The dolphin-rider appears occasionally on MMB at Athens (Rotroff 1982a, 61, 64 cats. 147, 171, pls. 27, 31, 78, 79) and at Ephesos (EPH-22*), as well as on one of the relief rhyta from Athribis (Myśliwiec 2000a, pls. 128, 129). Erotes use dolphins as a team on a bowl produced in Pitane(?) and unearthed in Mesambria (AIB-1*).

Nike/Eros Racing a Two-Horse Chariot
The theme of a Nike or an Eros racing a two-horse chariot was a popular one on the MMB of many production places. In Athens we find it in the Workshop of Bion (Rotroff 1982a, 69 cat. 206, pl. 40, with Herakles and Auge; Rotroff 1982a, 62 cat. 152, pl. 78), and it occurs in other productions of the Greek mainland as well, perhaps under the influence of Athenian bowls.[5] At Ephesos, four different representations are known: a standard version and three unique variants (Chapter 14). In the standard depiction, the race evolves towards the right; the charioteer leans energetically forward and thrusts a short stick, evidently his whip, towards the horses with his right hand. The two horses are in full gallop. The frieze continues all around the widest part of the bowl and it is never mixed with other motifs, so the race continues perpetually in a

---

4 The only exception I know of is the representation of the Judgement of Paris, where a single Eros accompanies Aphrodite; see pp. 118–119.
5 Thebes, Kabirion: production place unknown, charioteer racing two-horse chariot left, clearly inspired by Athenian vessels but, judging from the description of the fabric, surely not Attic (Heimberg 1982, 103 cat. 817, pls. 57, 66); Nike/Eros racing two-horse chariot right (Heimberg 1982, 105 cat. 843, pls. 58, 66, suggesting a Boeotian origin for the sherd). Lousoi, local production (racing left; Rogl 2008a, 118–119 cats. 109, 111, pl. 11; 135 cat. 231, pl. 16).

ICONOGRAPHY AND INTERPRETATION

FIGURE 40 Wadjet symbol in the calyx of EPH-33, from Olbia
PHOTO FROM AUTHOR'S ARCHIVE

circular motion. At Sardis four vessels of local production feature a winged charioteer driving a two-horse chariot left as a base medallion (Rotroff 2003, 113, 130 cats. 456, 553–555, pls. 78, 97). Two different stamps are represented; the charioteers are termed Nikai by Rotroff (Rotroff 2003, 131).[6] Two clearly Sardian bowls with the same charioteer group have been published by Tuluk (2001, 61–62 cat. 1 and 5, pls. 28, 29, from Lydia).

It is also worth mentioning a fragment of the lower body of a vessel found at Olbia but documented solely by a drawing (XXX-3; Fig. 41). Below an unidentified frieze, an Eros driving his two-horse chariot towards the right functions as a space-filler between the leaves of the calyx. Though the horses are galloping, they do not overlap in the same way they do in the Ephesian decoration; moreover, the reins with which Eros guides them are clearly visible, and the six-spoked wheel of the chariot is enormous. It is difficult to form an opinion about where this piece was made.

FIGURE 41 Charioteer on a bowl from Olbia, from an unknown production place (XXX-3) SCALE 1:1
DRAWING IIMK RAN ARCHIVE

---

6 An Ephesian vessel with our motif was also unearthed at Sardis, with an Ionian kyma above and calyx B below (Rotroff 2003, 150 cat. 638, pl. 111).

The racing scene occurs in so many productions that it is difficult to maintain that it had no meaning for the mould makers and the users of the vessels. Rogl suggests that the scene had mythological associations, but she is not able to be more specific (2008a, 71). I am not so certain that mythology was its source, and I suggest that we look elsewhere in order to discover the meaning of the scene.

It is well-known that in his dialogue, *Phaidros*, Plato likened the endeavour of the human soul to maintain a righteous path to the efforts of a winged charioteer racing with a noble and an ignoble horse, each of which pulls the chariot in a different direction (Plat. *Phaedr.* 248a–b). The Platonic race evolves in an eternal circular motion, and many souls, because they are bad charioteers, bump into one other and therefore break their wings. Plato's image of the race of the souls is striking, and this could very well have been the background for the popularity of the charioteer on the vases. The same scene quite often appears on the sarcophagi of Roman children (e.g., Huskinson 1996, 42, 46; Schauenburg 1996), and even though the interpretation of the motif in that context is hotly debated, the parallel is striking. We shall return to the argument in the conclusion of this chapter.

Saluting Pan
Identical stamps of a saluting Pan are found in several productions, and there can be no doubt that they have a single origin. The motif exists in two mirror-image versions. On the right-facing stamp, Pan – clearly identified by goat legs, tail, and horns – has a lowered right arm, he lifts his left arm in front of him with the palm open (not holding a vessel as many describe it), and turns his horned head in the same direction. The left-facing stamp reverses the position, with a lifted right arm and a lowered left; Pan gazes in the direction of his raised arm. It is likely that the Pan stamps were invented in the Kymean workshops. On Kymean vessels we find the two stamps placed heraldically around the Dionysiac trio (altar scene D; see below) (**KYX-99**).[7] This representation was emulated at Sardis (Rotroff 2003, 102 cat. 402, pl. 67). On a fragment found at Thessaloniki we also find the two stamps flanking an ithyphallic satyr (Adam Veleni et al. 2000, 286 cat. 40, pl. 139).

Among Ephesian bowls the two stamps flank altar scene D, as in Kyme, in a single instance (Laumonier 1977, 92 cat. 3247, pls. 20, 131), but the Pan occurs most commonly in a frieze alternating with walking Erotes[8] or flanking a vase.[9] On several Ephesian vessels, the fragment featuring the Pan is so small that it is not possible to reconstruct the composition.[10] The saluting Pan appears on two further vessels of unknown production: heraldically flanking altar scene D on a bowl fragment found in Alexandria[11] and on a body fragment of a large vessel from Miletos (Kossatz 1990, 79 cat. M 660, fig. 37); both stamps are located under a rim frieze of astragals.

At least three of the bowls featuring saluting Pans heraldically around altar scene D are small ones. They were all found in tombs (**KYX-99** at Pantikapaion, **SHA-18** at Mesambria, and **SHA-19** at Torbali-Metropolis), and it is likely that they were made for funerary purposes. As we shall see below, this would be very much in keeping with the overall interpretation of altar scene D.

Altar Figures
The following four scenes[12] appear widely on MMB, but they are also found on the four sides of the small, mould-made terracotta altars generally nicknamed 'Tarentine', on the basis of early conclusions about their place of manufacture.[13] The altars have now been found throughout the Mediterranean and the Black Sea region, and moulds provide evidence of manufacture at sites other than Taranto (Fig. 42).[14] With few exceptions, the decoration is the same from one altar to the next. It draws on

---

7   Similar representation can be found on bowls from Campania(?) in Capua, Museo Campano: Patroni 1897–1898, 124 cat. 1015, pl. XIX; Wuilleumier 1929, 64 cat. h; Schwabacher 1941, 186 no. 8; Pochmarski 1990, 285 RK 87; from Mesambria in Nessebar, Archaeological Museum inv. 2008-38 (unpublished); and from Torbali-Metropolis in the Ephesos Museum inv. inv. 34/15/74 (Erdemgil et al. 1989, 111; Tuluk 2001, 61–62 cat. 3, pl. 30 and perhaps Siebert 1978, 245 note 3).

8   EPH-1303*; Laumonier 1977, 164 cat. 3272, pl. 36; 167 cat. 3242, pl. 37; 168 cat. 3243, pl. 37.

9   EPH-55; Laumonier 1977, 98 cat. 8537, pl. 21 (Delos); Kovalenko 2007, fig. 16.11; Popova 2007, figs. 74–75 (Čaika).

10 Laumonier 1977, 92 cat. 3247, pl. 20 (Belles Méduses); 168 cats. 3252, 8579, pl. 37; 375 cat. 3084, pl. 90; 419 cat. 3254, pl. 98.

11 Pagenstecher 1913, fig. 97c; Wuilleumier 1929, 65 cat. j; Schwabacher 1941, 186 no. 1; Pochmarski 1990, 285 RK 84.

12 [Ed. PGB originally included a separate chapter on these figures, with an exploration of the 'Tarentine' altars, their relationship to the bowls, and an extensive exploration of the iconography of these four scenes. This summary, along with Guldager Bilde 2005, an analysis of the Olbia situla, provides the gist of this chapter, which we plan to publish elsewhere.]

13 For earlier discussions of the altars, see Deonna 1907; Wuilleumier 1929; 1939; D.B. Thompson 1962, 258–260; Vermeule 1966, 111–113; Vafopoulo-Richardson 1982; Willers 1986, 143; Pochmarski 1990, 280–282; Ševčenko 1995; Rădulescu et al. 1995–1996. The scenes as they appear on MMB have been collected and discussed in the context of MMB by Schwabacher 1941, 185–193, Siebert 1978, 240–246, and Rotroff 1982a, 20–21.

14 E.g., Samos, Syracuse (Pochmarski 1990, 281 cat. RK 12, RK 19.)

ICONOGRAPHY AND INTERPRETATION   111

	Black Sea	Italy			Mainland Greece			Islands and Asia Minor			Levant	Provenance?	
	Altar		Altar	Mould		Altar	Mould		Altar	Mould		Altar	Altar	Mould
W, NW coast														
Kallatis	5	Cumae	1		Asine	1		Delos	1	1	Marisa	ca. 10	4	1
Albeşti	7	Syracuse		1	Athens	7		Samos		1				
Tyras	1	Tarentum	5	2	Corinth	4	1	Elaia		1				
Olbia	5	Tarentum?	1		Delphi?	1		Pergamon	3					
Chersonesos +home chora	20	Italy?		2	Eretria?	1		Troy	2					
Černomorskoe	5?				Mycenae	1								
Bosporan Kingdom					Maroneia		1							
Pantikapaion	4-5													
Myrmekion	1													
Nymphaion	1													
E Coast														
Vani	1													
S coast														
Amisos	1													
Total	52		9	3		15	2		6	3		10	4	1

FIGURE 42   Geographical distribution of the altars

the ornamentation of the Ionian architectural order: a top moulding ('sima') with an astragal above a band of pairs of horizontal S-spirals of alternating direction topped by a central palmette and flanked by two rosettes; it is identical in form and style to rim motifs on some Athenian bowls and underlines the relationship between the two classes. The main block of the altar is decorated with a figural frieze which makes use of a fixed iconography, with one moulded figural scene on each of the four sides: three two-figure groups (scenes A–C) and one three-figure group (scene D), almost always appearing in the same sequence. I take for granted that there must have been an inner coherence among these vignettes; the task is to see if we can provide a holistic and economical interpretation of the four scenes.

W. Deonna, who first published on the altars, concluded that they and the MMB were produced in the same workshops (1907, 254). Since then it has often been assumed, to the contrary, that the bowls precede the altars,[15] but a revue of the contextual and stylistic evidence convinces me that the altars take precedence.[16] The earliest bowls (the Athenian ones) incorporate the architectural crowning element of the altars, and, except for the Olbia situla (PER-91*), not a single mouldmade vessel depicts all four altar scenes. The clear implication is that the altars inspired the bowls and not vice versa. The altars, thus, provide the source for the scenes as they appear on mouldmade bowls, and it is to them that we must turn in deciphering the shared iconography.

Scholars have been struggling with the puzzle of the altar scenes for over a century, and two different 'sets' of interpretations have emerged: an Eastern one going back to von Stern and his analysis of the Olbia situla (1902; PER-91*), and a Western one harking back to Deonna's article on an altar found on Delos (1907). Here I summarize their views and present a new interpretation which I believe makes sense of the scenes as a coherent whole.

Scene A: woman and trophy (Fig. 43.A)
A standing female (A1) with a pony-tail faces right. She wears a chiton and a himation. In her lowered left hand she holds a rolled *tainia*, one end of which is hanging down, and with her right hand she extends a wreath towards a *tropaion* (A2). The *tropaion* is erected on a wooden pole supported by a heap of boulders. It consists of a Corinthian helmet, a round shield, a cuirass over a short chiton, and a spear.

Although some have seen the woman as a Nike *apteros*, there is no reason to mythologize her; a trophy can be a

---
15   E.g., Vafopoulou-Richardson 1982, 229, 231; Schürmann 1989, 188; Flashar 1992, 175. Braun (1970, 176), like Deonna, sees bowls and altars emerging contemporaneously from the same workshops.

16   Most telling is the discovery of seven altars at a fortified farm at Albeşti, in the chora of Kallatis, a site where no MMB have come to light (pers. comm. of the excavator, L. Buzoianu), and which is thought have been abandoned ca. 240/230 (Rădulescu et al. 1995–1996, 44–46 cat. 34–40, pls. 8–11).

grave marker as well as a victory monument,[17] and she may simply be a human visiting the tomb to adorn it with the wreath and *tainia* which she holds. I find it likely that scene A represents the turning point between life (the woman) and death (the trophy-tombstone).

Scene B: Poseidon and Amymone (Fig. 43.B)
A standing female (B1) clad in a peplos with a high-belted *apoptygma* carries a vessel in her lowered right hand. She raises her left hand to her shoulder in a gesture of female modesty. She is depicted almost frontally but with a slight movement towards a man standing at the right (B2). His torso is naked, but his lower body and left shoulder are wrapped in a himation with a triangular overfold. He places his right hand on the woman's left shoulder and supports a trident in the crook of his left arm.

Deonna's interpretation of scene B as Poseidon and Amymone has been almost universally accepted in the West, though Z. Kotitsa has recently identified these figures as Zeus and Semele.[18] In the East, von Stern's interpretation of the couple as Zeus and Hebe has had some followers (von Stern 1902; Belov 1962, 170; Ševčenko 1995), and other Black Sea researchers have suggested that the woman is Amphitrite (e.g., Farmakovskij 1909, 128; Levi 1959, 16; 1970, 46; Rădulescu et al. 1995–1996, passim).

The main reason for these differences is that the attribute of the male figure varies on the mouldmade vases: sometimes a short-shafted trident, sometimes a sceptre. On the altars, however, it can be recognised exclusively as a trident whenever it is preserved. I therefore follow Deonna's identification of this figure as Poseidon. If he is Poseidon, the woman must be Amymone – the 'Blameless one' – one of King Danaos' 50 daughters, who gained notoriety when they killed their husbands on their wedding night. For this deed they were condemned to eternal punishment in Tartaros, where they were obliged to pour water into a bottomless container. Amymone escaped this fate when she became Poseidon's *paramour*.

Amymone commonly occurs in a Dionysiac context, but, more importantly, she was also the namesake of a stream which emptied into the marshes of Lerna (Paus. 2. 36.1). This was one of the ancient world's passages to the Underworld, and the scene thus continues the theme of transition from life to death that we met in scene A.

Scene C: Orpheus and Persephone (Fig. 43.C)
A young male (C1) sits on a rock, his left thigh covered by a mantle, which is further draped over the rock. On his head he wears a wreath. He is playing a kithara and is facing right towards a standing female (C2). She is dressed in a peplos with a long *kolpos* and a himation worn short and drawn up over a low *polos* on her head. The mantle is gathered in a bundle at her left hip. With her left hand she grips part of the mantle, which forms a small pouch behind her left thigh. She holds a long-shafted object in her right hand.

Western scholars follow Deonna almost slavishly in seeing the couple as Apollo and Leto;[19] Black Sea scholars agree that the musician is Apollo but follow von Stern in identifying his companion as Artemis.[20] If one imagines scenes B and C as taking place in the Underworld, however, a reading of C1 as Orpheus becomes appealing. The figure fits nicely within the standard iconography of Orpheus, which borrows from Apolline imagery.[21] If he is indeed Orpheus rather than Apollo, there is no reason why his companion should be either Leto or Artemis. A matronly deity with polos and veil and with torch or sceptre in this milieu is more likely to be Persephone.

Scene D: Dionysos, Ariadne, and satyr ('the Dionysiac Trio') (Fig. 43.D)
In the centre stands a male (D2) wearing boots and a garland across the chest. His left shoulder is covered by a cloak. He turns to his right to receive a kiss from a standing female (D1), clad in a high-belted chiton slipping down and exposing her right shoulder. Over her left shoulder and lower body hangs a himation, which is also in the act of slipping down. She extends her arms to embrace the standing male. At the right, a smaller standing naked youth with wiry hair (D3) supports the central figure with both hands from behind.

There is general scholarly agreement that scene D shows Dionysos supported by a satyr[22] and kissed by Ariadne, a maenad, or a nymph. It transforms an older, much loved scene showing Dionysos supported by a satyr (Willers 1986; Pochmarski 1990) by the addition of an

---

17 As, e.g., Archaeological Museum of Rhodes, inv. 1224, from the Makristeno necropolis (Maiuri 1932, 57–61). Cf. also an Archaizing relief from Athens (Janssen 1957, 85, fig. 41).
18 On a black-gloss hydria with relief appliqués in Würzburg (Kotitsa 1998, 114). R. Zahn's earliest reading of the scene as Kalchas and Iphigeneia was immediately withdrawn by Zahn himself (Zahn in Conze 1903, 20; cf. Conze et al. 1913, 276; Schwabacher 1941, 189).
19 With the exception of Vermeule, who identifies C2 as Demeter or Tyche (1966, 111–113).
20 von Stern 1902; Farmakovskij 1909, 128; Levi 1959, 16; Rădulescu et al. 1995–1996; Ševčenko 1995.
21 Garezou 1994; according to Apollodoros (1.3.3) he is even considered the son of Apollo.
22 Vermeule suggests identifying this satyr as Ampelos (1966, 113).

ICONOGRAPHY AND INTERPRETATION

FIGURES 43.A–D   'Tarentine' altar in the Ashmolean Museum, Oxford. Oldfield collection inv. 51
REPRODUCED WITH PERMISSION OF THE ASHMOLEAN MUSEUM, OXFORD

			Corpus	Bowls/fragments/moulds with one or more altar figures	Date	%
Mainland Greece						
Athens	Kerameikos		Schwabacher 1941	219	21	broad date range	9.6
	Agora		Rotroff 1982	404	22	broad date range, 3rd-1st century	5.4
	Dipylon, well B1, layers VII and IX		Braun 1975	26	3	last quarter of 3rd-second quarter of 2nd century	11.5
Piraeus	Cistern		Metzger 1971	41	2	last quarter of 3rd-second quarter of 2nd century	4.9
Argos			Siebert 1978	1,024	27	broad date range	2.6
			(of these: Workshop of Monogramist)	(103)	(23)	first third of 2nd century	(22.3)
Corinth			Edwards 1975	164	26	before 146	15.9
	1926 Reservoir		Edwards 1986	46	4	filled between 175 and 165	8.7
	Southeast building, manhole at N:20		Romano 1994	15	2	second half of 2nd-first half of 1st century	13.3
Greek Islands						
Lemnos			Massa 1992	205[a] bowl frs.	32	late 3rd-first half of 2nd century	15.6
				215[a] mould frs.	36		16.7
Delos			Laumonier 1977	6,495	8	166-88/67	0.1
Asia Minor						
Miletos			Kossatz 1990	753	0	broad date range	
Sardis			Rotroff 2003	293	1	broad date range	0.3

FIGURE 44   The main corpora of MMB that include altar scenes in their decoration, with their dates
Note: a. Rim and base fragments of moulds and bowls from Lemnos are not included in the tallies

embrace and the exchange of a kiss between Dionysos and a female acolyte. I follow Pochmarski's argument in favour of D1 as Ariadne rather than a maenad due to the general intimacy of the scene (1990, 48).

With the aid of the interpretations developed above, we can now reconstruct a coherent 'narrative' sequence of the altar scenes: the transition from life to death (scene A), through the gates to the Nether World marked by Amymone and Poseidon alluding to the marshes of Lerna (scene B), to the halls of Persephone, where Orpheus is sitting on a rock playing the kithara, and, finally, the return to the light and the heavenly bliss promised by Dionysos to his followers, of which Ariadne, elevated by Dionysos to god-like status, is the paradigm (scene D). The union is

ICONOGRAPHY AND INTERPRETATION

Scene	As depicted or preserved	Athens	Lemnos	Argos	Corinth	Pergamon	Kyme	Ephesos	Other	Total
A	A	10-12	13	2	5	1		1	3	37
	A1	8-10	4	5	10			1	3	33
	A2	3-4	8	9	2-3	1			2	27
B	B	15-17	5	4	6	2				34
	B1	15	8	7	3			1	3	37
	B2	5	13-14	4	6				2	31
C	C	7	1	2	3	1			1	15
	C1	10	7	6	9		1		3	36
	C2	3-4	6	3	5					18
D		30-32	24	5-6	3	2	4	6	5	82
E	E	1	1			1				3
	E1	3								3
	E2	2								2

FIGURE 45 Frequency of individual altar stamps

symbolized by the kiss, a rare gesture in Greek art, and one redolent with meaning. Thus, the altar scenes provide us with a road map to salvation not unlike the gold tablets found in tombs in Magna Graecia, Thessaly, and Crete with instructions to the deceased on how to navigate the landscape of the Nether World (Edmonds 2011). If this interpretation can be accepted, I believe that we have the answer to the question of why the altars became so popular all over the Greek world. And although the details of this story may have been lost to some degree with the transfer of these scenes to the MMB and their isolation from one another, their original connection with the Dionysiac religion may explain their enduring popularity on the bowls.

That popularity is clear from Fig. 44, summarizing a corpus of almost 250 MMB and moulds for producing bowls with altar scenes or figures. It is possible to distinguish two interrelated groups among them. One is Attic and Atticizing moulds and bowls of the Greek Mainland (Corinth, Argos) and of Lemnos of the last quarter of the 3rd and the first half of the 2nd century; the second is Atticizing bowls (and moulds) produced in Asia Minor (Pergamon, Kyme, and Ephesos) in the second quarter of 2nd century. Admittedly this table includes many biases, because some deposits are too small to have statistical significance and some publications are of selected material. It is nevertheless clear that altar scenes are primarily a feature of the time between the introduction of the MMB around 225 and the mid-2nd century, when the classical Ephesian workshops took over the market. The scenes thus serve as a chronological marker: few bowls (if any) with altar scenes were produced after the mid-2nd century. Fig. 45 shows further that the four different stamps were about equally popular. Only scene C (Orpheus and Persephone) appears to be slightly underrepresented, whereas scene D (the Dionysiac trio) was by far the most popular stamp.

Hunt

Hunting was a popular theme in many workshops. The hunt may be either on horseback or on foot. The hunter is usually a non-mythological figure, but hunting Erotes and Amazons are also encountered.[23] The prey can be lions, boars, stags, and rabbits but also mythological creatures, such as griffins (e.g., KYB-38). Hunting scenes were particularly popular at Athens (ATH-3*–ATH-6; Schwabacher 1941, 207–212; Rotroff 1982a, 19 cats. 238–272). We find this theme sporadically in Peloponnesian workshops (Siebert 1978, 114–116; Rogl 2008a, 110 cat. 63, pls. 7, 27, 32–33, 44). We also encounter hunting in a number of Aiolian workshops: e.g., at Pergamon (PER-93) and Kyme (KYA-1*, KYA-52, KYB-21–22, KYB-38, KYX-30*), and at Ephesos (EPH-57*–EPH-71, EPH-1265*). In the latter case, hunting features mostly in the early phase of production (EE); in the subsequent classical phase (EC), the theme occasionally occurs in the form of hunting Amazons (Laumonier 1977, 76 cat. 5377, pl. 16). We also find 'abbreviated' versions of the hunt there, namely friezes with alternations of rabbits and dogs,[24] rabbits and eagles,[25] and eagles and dogs (Laumonier 1977, 323 cats. 3044–3045, pl. 76; 324 cat. 3473, pl. 77); even friezes of identical jumping rabbits can be considered an abbreviated version of the hunt.[26]

---

23 Erotes hunting: SHA-204, SHA-229, SHA-412; Amazons hunting: SHA-443; Laumonier 1977, 38 cat. 3382, pl. 5; 76 cat. 5377, pl. 16; 77 cats. 3063, 3440, pl. 16; 416 cat. 3340, pl. 97.

24 EPH-74*; EPH-75*; EPH-1307*; SHA-441–442; Laumonier 1977, 63 cat. 2203, pl. 13; 151 cat. 3053, pl. 34; 153 cat. 3058, pl. 34; 156 cat. 3050, pl. 35; 166 cat. 8580, pl. 37; Arsen'eva et al. 2001, cat. 250, pl. 16.

25 EPH-76; Laumonier 1977, 185 cats. 3049, 9318, pl. 40; 306 cat. 3482, pl. 72; 396 cat. 3042, pl. 93; Grzegrzółka 2010, 126–127 cat. 174.

26 SHA-238; Loseva 1962, fig. 1.2; Laumonier 1977, 99 cat. 9725, pl. 21; 151 cat. 9348, pl. 34; 153 cat. 8887, pl. 34; 166 cats. 1620, 3052, 3055, pl. 37; 167 cat. 3209, pl. 37; 329 cats. 3328, 3491 pl. 78; 368 cat. 8295, pl. 89; 414 cats. 3068, 8490 pl. 97.

Hunting scenes are also known from Knidos (Kögler 2010, 520 cat. F.132, pl. 29) as well as from Samos (Tsakos 1994, pl. 230.a–b).

Hunting scenes probably had a multitude of meanings. It is obvious that especially the mounted hunt for lion connoted the topos of the *Herrscherjagd* (Rogl 2008a, 71), and many other hunting scenes are probably to taken at face-value. However, the combination in Ephesos of rabbit and eagle, which occurs as a parallel to friezes of rabbit and dog, not to speak of the even more common representations of rabbits alone, may have had additional undertones of human vulnerability vis-à-vis greater powers.

Mantled Dancing Women
A frieze of heavily draped females dancing in a circle around the vase is known from a number of vessels, primarily of Aiolian origin.[27] In the most common version of this theme, the women move solemnly towards the right; each holds her lowered right arm in front of her body and with her left hand she grips the trailing end of the cloak of the dancer in front of her; while moving forwards, she gazes backwards and down (Fig. 46). This scene was also emulated at Ephesos.[28]

On EPH-1305*, we find a dancing woman holding a hemispherical bowl, in a frieze which also contained altar scene D, a centaur, and an Eros playing a musical instrument(?). Another type of dancing woman is positioned frontally and wears a peplos with overfold, which she lifts up (Fig. 47).[29] Depictions of mantled dancing women in the Greek Mainland are not so common, even though they occur from time to time (e.g., Sinn 1979, 146 cat. MB 114, pl. 31 [Volos]). At Athens there is a single candidate (Rotroff 1982a, 71 cat. 221 pl. 43, tentatively identified there as a maenad).

The theme of the mantled dancing woman was popular in many media in the Hellenistic period. A very good parallel is the frieze of a heroon in Sagalassos dating to the third quarter of the 2nd century, and thus closely contemporary with the MMB (Fleischer 1972–1973; Fleischer 1984; Webb 1996, 127–129, figs. 100–103). Both divine figures (nymphs, Horai and the like) and their human counterparts were portrayed in this guise (Friesländer 2001). It is difficult to decide how we should interpret the figures on the MMB. I am inclined to identify them as mortal women performing a dance which, given its solemn appearance, could very well have taken place in a ritual context, perhaps in emulation of the round dance of the nymphs.

Amazonomachy
The Amazonomachy was a popular theme on MMB. We find it, for example, at Athens (ATH-10*, ATH-11*), at Pergamon (PER-91*) and frequently in the Kymean Meter Medallion Workshop (KYB-1*–KYB-10*, KYB-321; see also KYX-57*), and it was also popular in the early Ephesian workshops, especially the *Vases gris* (VG) and Monogram PAR workshops.[30]

Labours of Herakles
The occurrence of this mythological cycle on MMB has been discussed by U. Hausmann (1959, esp. 94–99). We find it in a number of different productions, but never in profusion. Amongst others, it is known from Athenian,[31] Pergamene (SHA-143 [Hydra]), Kymean (KYB-347* [Hydra]), and Ephesian workshops,[32] as well as in the Peloponnesos (Siebert 1978, 238), Macedonia (SHA-418), and Liburnia (SHA-382). These depictions seem to have been influenced by the metopes of the Hephaisteion in Athens, and on several Ephesian vessels we even find a 'metopal' division of the scenes by means of columns.[33] At Ephesos, it was chiefly Menemachos who was behind the depictions of Herakles' *athla*, with the hero confronting the Nemean lion (EPH-106*; Laumonier 1977, 43 cat. 3423, pl. 8; 73 cat. 6088, pl. 16; 416 cat. 3306, pl. 97), the Hydra (Greifenhagen 1963, figs. 57–58; Laumonier 1977, 165; 174

---

27 AIB-8*–AIB-10; PER-2, PER-93; XXX-6; SHA-435; Conze et al. 1913, 274 no. 3; Courby 1922, fig. 87.12; Künzl 2002, 43 cat. 86, pls. 187–189; 44–45 cat. 92, pls. 204–206.
28 EPH-79*, EPH-80*, EPH-1266*, EPH-1267; Laumonier 1977, 92 cat. 3472, pl. 20; 97 cats. 2345, 3284, pl. 21; 98 cats. 2562, 9037, pl. 21; 101 cats. 3285, 3289, pl. 23; 116 cat. 3286 pl. 26; 234 cat. 3257, pl. 53; 398 cat. 9075, pl. 94; 403 cat. 3499, pl. 95.
29 KYX-9, KYX-10; Laumonier 1977, 101 cat. 6091, pl. 23 (Vases gris); the frontal woman can also be combined with the mantle-dancing woman (Laumonier 1977, 116 cat. 3286, pl. 26).

30 EPH-60(?), EPH-81*– EPH-92; Laumonier 1977, 65 cat. 3371, pl. 14; 66 cats. 3381, 9745, pl. 14; 96 cat. 3350, pl. 21; 97 cat. 3376, pl. 21; 101 cat. 3318, pl. 23; 102 cats. 3362, 3374, 3389, pl. 23; 102 cat. 9731, pl. 23; 106 cats. 3370, 8543, pl. 24; 133 cats. 2002, 3356, pl. 30; 139 cats. 526, 3343, pl. 31; 140 cat. 3441, pl. 31; 143 cats. 3352, 3396, pl. 32; 143 cat. 9252, pl. 32; 156 cats. 3343, 9485, pl. 35; 159 cat. 3347, 36; 168 cats. 3308, 3358–3360, 3380, pl. 37; 169 cats. 3433, 3460, 9195, 9289, 9483, pl. 37; 217 cat. 3246, pl. 48; 304 cats. 2426–2427, pl. 71; 370 cat. 8535, pl. 89; 375 cat. 3353, pl. 90; 376 cat. 3355, pl. 90; 388 cats. 3375, 3392, pl. 88; 416 cats. 3357, 3372–3373, pl. 97.
31 ATH-14*; Schwabacher 1941, 199–200; Rotroff 1982a, 23.
32 EPH-104*– EPH-106*; Laumonier 1977, 43 cat. 3423, pl. 8; 174 cat. 3311, pl. 38; 177 cats. 3312–3313, pl. 39; 414 cat. 3345, pl. 97; 416 cat. 3306, pl. 97; 417 cat. 3445, pl. 97.
33 Greifenhagen 1963, figs. 57, 58; Laumonier 1977, 165; 174 cat. 3311, pl. 38; 177 cats. 3312–3313 pl. 39; 414 cat. 3345, pl. 97; 417 cat. 3445, pl. 97; Košelenko 1992, fig. 23.

ICONOGRAPHY AND INTERPRETATION

FIGURE 46 Mantled dancing women on a Pergamene bowl from Olbia (PER-2)
PHOTO FROM AUTHOR'S ARCHIVE

FIGURE 47 Frontal dancing women on an unattributed Kymean bowl found at Olbia (KYX-10)
PHOTO FROM AUTHOR'S ARCHIVE

cat. 3311, pl. 38; 177 cats. 3312–3313, pl. 39), Kerberos, (EPH-104*, EPH-105*), and the Kerynian hind (EPH-104*).

Skylla

Depictions of Skylla are rare but nevertheless turn up from time to time in various workshops. She appears not just in a mythological context with Odysseus and his ship,[34] but also as an isolated figure without any connection to the main decoration.[35] We even find her as medallion decoration on Pergamene MMB.[36] The representation on a series of Ephesian bowls of the classical phase[37] has featured prominently in the discussion of the original behind the Sperlonga sculptural group. Following A. Greifenhagen, B. Andreae has argued that the bowls were Rhodian, because one of them was found on Rhodes and because the Skylla resembles the Sperlonga sculpture, which he believed to be Rhodian[!].[38] This attribution is erroneous: we know absolutely nothing about a Rhodian production of MMB, and the bowls brought forward by Greifenhagen and Andreae are products of the early Ephesian VG and Menemachos workshops.

Judgement of Paris

A series of identical large, detailed, and ambitious stamps representing the Judgement of Paris was employed in at least three different productions, namely the Argive workshops of Kleagoras[39] and the Monogram potter,[40] the Corinthian workshop making large mouldmade vessels (probably kraters) with applied feet (SHA-413, SHA-414), and the Ephesian workshop of Menemachos.[41] The original composition seems to have encompassed six figures. Three of these are goddesses. Aphrodite sits on a rock, turned towards the right. One thigh is placed over the other, and her folded hands are placed under her chin in a gesture of amazement or admiration. She is heavily draped, and a small Eros leans against her lap. Athena is clad in a dress with a long overfold; she is moving to the right but turns her helmeted head to face the spectator. With her lowered left arm she holds a round shield, the grip of which is clearly indicated; her right arm is crossed in front of her body and with her right hand she holds the upper rim of the shield. A spear leans across the front of her body and rests on her left shoulder. Hera, turned to the left, is dressed in a heavy peplos, the folds

---

34 As ATH-8*; EPH-1326 and perhaps EPH-107*; Greifenhagen 1963, 53–59, figs. 46, 48, 50–52, 55; Andreae 1996, cat. 2.63; Grzegrzółka 2010, 87 cat. 86.
35 As Rotroff 2003, 128 cat. 539, pl. 94 alternating with *agyieus*; as frieze with Herakles' athla: Greifenhagen 1963, 62, figs. 57–58; Laumonier 1977, 174 cat. 3311, pls. 38, 125; 177 cat. 3313, pl. 39.
36 Conze et al. 1913, Beibl. 42.8; de Luca 1975, pl. 45.1; 1997, 367, pl. 270.a; 1999, 114 cat. 568, pl. 20.
37 EPH-1326; Greifenhagen 1963, figs. 46, 48, 50–52, 55, 57–58; Andreae 1996, cat. 2.63; Grzegrzółka 2010, 87 cat. 86; Samojlova 1994, fig. 1.2 Samojlova & Batizat 1994, fig. 1; Laumonier 1977, 174 cat. 3311, pls. 38, 125; 177 cats. 3312–3313, pl. 39.
38 Greifenhagen 1963, 52–65; Andreae 1996, 150–151 cat. 2.63; see also the discussion in de Grummond 2000, 266.

---

39 Siebert 1978, 345–347 cats. K.321–344, pls. 38–39.
40 Siebert 1977, 133–134 cat. 96, fig. 19.a; Siebert 1978, 353 cat. M.34, pl. 25; Rogl 2008a, 102 cat. 25, pls. 3, 30.
41 EPH-101* (see also EPH-102 and EPH-1327); Pagenstecher 1913, pl. XX; Laumonier 1977, 42 cat. 3420, pl. 8, Puppo 1995, 164–165 cat. X39, pls. LXXIV–LXXV. Perhaps Ephesian: Puppo 1995 121–122 cat. M20, pl. LII.

of which render her almost as a column. Her left arm is held akimbo and with the right she holds a sceptre. The mainland and Ephesian depictions differ in small details: on the former, the overfold of Hera's peplos is pulled up at the back to cover a low polos,[42] whereas in the Ephesian representation, Hera wears a tall polos and the overfold is not drawn up. On another rock, but turned to the left, sits Paris dressed in Phrygian attire and holding a *lagobolon* in his lowered left hand; beneath him lies a dog. The final two figures are standing and turned to the right. One is a male in a short garment and with a cloak over his shoulder, leaning forward on a long stick; his traveller's attire identifies him as Hermes. The sixth person is clad in a short cloak and is clearly male; he supports his raised left foot on a rock and his right elbow on his knee. This figure, which does not feature on the pieces signed by Menemachos, is difficult to identify – perhaps he is Hermes too? Pagenstecher long ago identified the scene as the Judgement of Paris (Pagenstecher 1913, 65), and I see no reason to dispute this.

Each of the figures stands on a plinth, and they are evidently copied from something else. In terms of style, they seem to hark back to a variety of prototypes. The three goddess probably had different sculptural predecessors, because their poses are complicated and detailed and seemingly unrelated to the narrative of the scene. The Hera is Classical in style, while the Aphrodite reflects the same iconography as the Tyche of Antiocheia, both seated on rocky outcrops, a frequent trope of the 2nd century.[43] The vessels on which these figures appear can be dated to the first half (probably second quarter) of the 2nd century, whereas the sculptural predecessors are of various dates. Nevertheless, even if the figures are based on an eclectic selection of models, they must once have formed an ensemble. Pagenstecher offered a terracotta altar from the Sinadino Collection in Alexandria as an analogy for the Menemachos bowl he published (Pagenstecher 1913, 65, fig. 78). The altar is round but rests on a square base; the top is of the Near-Eastern horned altar type. The round body is decorated with five figures: all of the above with the exception of the seated Aphrodite. Obviously it was difficult to wrap the wide Aphrodite stamp around the side of a round altar, and this is probably the reason why it was omitted. The Hera on the altar is the same as the figure on Corinthian and Argive bowls of the Greek Mainland, which are most likely earlier than the Menemachos representations. Most interestingly, the horns of the altar are decorated with various Egyptian symbols: the crown of Hathor with ostrich feathers and several versions of the Wadjet symbol. So even though the Alexandrian terracotta altar in itself represents an elaboration of an original model, it probably contextualizes this model in Ptolemaic Egypt. And since the more or less simultaneous occurrence of the same scene in Argos, Corinth, and Ephesos in the second quarter of the 2nd century seems to correspond to the pattern already discussed concerning the contemporary spread of the 'baroque style', it is worth contemplating whether it could have been small Ptolemaic altars in precious metal that served as models for the Greek potters, perhaps part of the diplomatic gifts of the 160s which gave rise to the second wave of Egyptian inspiration.

Actors
Actors appear from time to time on the bowls of various production centres, e.g., at Pergamon (PER-2; de Luca 1997, pl. 271) and Ephesos,[44] and at Kyme we find a stamp of a phlyax Eros (KYB-57*, KYB-109*; see also AIX-1*), but in general, representations of actors were never common (Siebert 1978, 117 n. 2). To my knowledge, this subject is not found at Athens.

Symplegmata
With the 'second wave' of Ptolemaic inspiration (Chapter 3), representations of symplegmata were added to the repertoire of the MMB (see also SHA-202, a rhyton from Athribis). We have already discussed the depictions of these scenes inside 'nelumbos', and we have seen that a number of different workshops in Greece, Asia Minor, and Italy adopted them in the second quarter of the 2nd century. Menemachos elaborated further on the representation of the symplegma, and on a series of bowls, he rendered a number of different configurations of amorous couples on klinai (EPH-108*, EPH-109; SHA-440). Especially in the late 2nd and early 1st century, symplegmata once again became very popular, probably following the success of the *Applikenkeramik* made in Pergamon and imitated elsewhere (Hübner 1993a, pls. 25–32), where amorous couples on klinai were a common theme. In the same period, we find the theme on vessels of the Aiolis B production (AIB-11–AIB-14) and elsewhere in the Mediterranean, for example on the contemporary Pella moulds.[45]

---

42 See also a very fine and detailed positive stamp in a private collection (Siebert 1978, 71 n. 1, pl. 46).
43 See Pagenstecher 1913, 194; Züchner 1950–1951, 193–194; and Siebert 1978, 257–258 for discussion of possible sculptural prototypes of the goddesses.

44 EPH-1268* and perhaps EPH-136*; Laumonier 1977, 115–116 cats. 3215, 3256, pl. 26; 164 cat. 1305, pl. 36; 307 cat. 3480, pl. 72; Gajdukevič 1981, fig. 4; Grzegrzółka 2010, 38 cat. 5.
45 Akamatis 1993, 139–140 cats. 322–323; 214–215 cat. M-82; pls. 14, 28–29, 255–260. Macedonian(?): Schmid 2004, 495 cat. 1, pl. 237.1 (Eretria); SHA-394 (Olympia); Achaian: SHA-430 (Lousoi).

FIGURE 48 Silver tetradrachm of Ptolemy IV Philopator, r. 222–205 BCE. Obverse: Serapis and Iris; Reverse: eagle on winged thunderbolt (Svoronos [1904–1908] 1124)
SCAN OF SNG COP VIII PL. VIII NO. 197, COURTESY OF THE ROYAL COLLECTION OF COINS AND MEDALS, NATIONAL MUSEUM OF DENMARK

This scene may have had religious and perhaps even political connotations in Egypt (SHA-202), but it is difficult to know exactly how symplegmata were perceived in a Greek context. One possibility – and probably the most likely – is that they were understood in the context of sympotic practice, which could also involve sexual intercourse with *hetairai*, something which had a long tradition in the iconography of Greek painted pottery. However, it is of note that, to my knowledge, symplegma scenes were never rendered on Athenian MMB. The Athenians were hardly more prudish than their contemporaries elsewhere in the Mediterranean, so it is possible that the original connotations in Egypt made the Athenians shut their eyes to this representation.

Animals
Dolphins
On MMB, as elsewhere, dolphins are frequently included in Dionysiac iconography. In antiquity, the dolphin was regarded as a friend of mankind and was thought to have numerous human traits (e.g., Plin. NH 9.7). Dolphins symbolized a calm sea and a safe passage (Leroux 1913, 94), and, consequently, rescue of humans at sea by dolphins is a common mythological theme. When Dionysos turned the pirates into dolphins, it was a humorous way of turning bad guys into good guys.

Dolphins, and heraldic dolphins in particular, were very popular in the Kymean Meter Medallion Workshop (Chapter 11). However, the dolphins are normally quite small and frequently function as filling ornament. In this respect the workshop may be inspired by Athenian bowls, where dolphins feature prominently, but similarly in a secondary position. Heraldic dolphins also occur on Ephesian bowls, but as the main decoration. They normally frame a rosette, a palmette, or a krater (EPH-113–EPH-117*, EPH-120*); at Pergamon, heraldic dolphins flank an *agyieus* (de Luca 1975, cat. 112, pl. 48; 1999, 109 cat. 467, pl. 15). See also above, Erotes and dolphins.

Heraldic Rampant Goats
Rampant, heraldic goats constitute a timeless Egyptian and Near Eastern motif (also Courby 1922, 351). It was extremely popular in the Athenian workshops, the goats either confronting one another directly or flanking a krater (ATH-1, ATH-20*, ATH-21* with references). The latter configuration on Atticizing moulds from Myrina attests to the production of this motif on Lemnos as well (Archontidou-Argyri 1994, 233–234 pl. 180.b); it also occurs at Laurion, within the Attic sphere (Salliora-Oikonomakou 1979, 169 pl. 74c). As discussed in Chapter 3, we also find it as fill inside a 'nelumbo' in a number of different productions. It is likely that this representation was inspired by contemporary metalwork.

Objects
Thunderbolt
Various workshops from time to time depicted a thunderbolt as the decoration of the main zone. It is relatively common in the Early and Classical Ephesian production (see Chapter 14), and we also find it amongst the Italo-Megarian vessels (Jones 1958, 22 (chart) cats. 7, 9,[46] 4, 21, 22, 30). It occurs sporadically in the Greek mainland as well, e.g., at the Theban Kabirion (Heimberg 1982, 113 cat. 947a–b, pl. 64).

One may wonder what Zeus's symbol of power is doing in a Dionysiac context. There are several possible explanations:

(a) It was part and parcel of the Ptolemaic iconography which inspired the creation of the MMB. The winged thunderbolt, normally with an eagle standing on it, was part of the 'coat of arms' of the Ptolemies and was featured on the coins of all the Ptolemies (e.g., Fig. 48). One

---

46 The bowl signed by Popilius, which was discussed above, pp. 32–33.

of them, Ptolemy Keraunos, son of King Ptolemy I Soter and briefly king of Macedonia (281–279 BCE), was even called 'thunderbolt' (*keraunos*).

(b) It was an element of Dionysiac iconography. In some 'Orphic' myths, Dionysos as Zagreus was the offspring of Zeus and Persephone. Zeus set him upon his throne and gave him his own thunderbolts to rule the world. However, the child was seized by the Titans and killed. Zeus or Athena saved his heart, which was given in a drink to Zeus's mortal love, Theban Semele. This made her pregnant with Dionysos. While pregnant, tricked by jealous Hera, Semele asked Zeus to come to her in his divine attire. This he did as a thunderbolt, which burnt her to death. Hermes rescued the unborn child and sewed him into Zeus's thigh, whence 'twice-born' Dionysos was born again. Later, Dionysos descended to the Underworld to bring back Semele. She was made immortal under the name of Thyone and taken to heaven. This strand in Dionysiac mythology has to do with the chthonic or underworldly Dionysos, who has the power to bring humans back to life and even make them immortal. The thunderbolt is Zeus's, but also Zagreus's symbol of power. In antiquity, to be killed by a divine thunderbolt was a means of obtaining immortality (as also Asklepios).

Agyieus Set in Vegetation

A curious ornament, consisting of a phallus-like column growing out of an acanthus and with palmette-like sickle-'wings', can be found on vessels from several Aiolian production centres, especially Pergamon,[47] but also Kyme (**KYX-9**, where it is flanked by frontal dancing women) and Aiolis(?) (Laumonier vol. 2, cat. 3505, pl. 28), as well as their emulations at Sardis (Rotroff 2003, 128 cat. 539, pl. 94, flanked by Skylla), and elsewhere (**XXX-10**; Aydin 2007, 19–20 cat. 22, pls. 9, 13).

The ornament is most likely to be identified as Dionysos in an aniconic form as an *agyieus* (Fehrentz 1993) and the vegetal paraphernalia alludes to his power in the sphere of fertility. On vessels from Pergamon, the ornament is flanked by animals closely coupled with this god, namely bulls and dolphins, and in frieze three of the Olbia situla (**PER-91***), the *agyieus* is flanked by two Erotes, one with a thyrsus over his shoulder, the other performing the *aposkopein* gesture in front of the *agyieus*, thus underlining

FIGURE 49
Cake stamp from Alexandria (Pagenstecher 1913, pl. XLIX.3)

the sacred character of the object. Perhaps the ornament had an Egyptian connection. We find exactly the same rendering on a stamp from Alexandria used for stamping sacred cakes (Fig. 49; Pagenstecher 1913, pl. XLIX.3). Also of Alexandrian origin is the iconography of heraldic rampant goats flanking an *agyieus* set in a floral calyx, which we find inside a 'nelumbo' in a number of different productions (see Chapter 3).

Scroll Decoration

Scrolls were normally acanthus scrolls, which could be furnished with vine leaves, bunches of grapes, and occasionally ivy leaves, and they could also be decorated with buds, flowers and spiral tendrils. A scroll may run in a horizontal frieze or it may cover the entire wall, and it could be either stamped or incised free-hand with stamped details. In terms of meaning, the scrolls provide a picture of abundance and the vegetative power of Dionysos.

Garlands and Wreaths

Garlands and wreaths were popular motifs on the MMB of Asia Minor, whereas they are more or less unknown in the Greek Mainland, including at Athens. Both types of decoration constituted the vessels' main decoration. The wreaths, which would encircling the vessel, were either of myrtle or ivy, and not infrequently the stamps were

---

47 Conze et al. 1913, Beibl. 43.16 = Courby 1922, fig. 87.23 (flanked by bulls); Kraus 1951, 11 cat. 13, fig. 4.2, pl. 3.5; de Luca 1975, pl. 48.4 and 7 (flanked by heraldic dolphins); 1999, 109 cat. 467 pl. 15 (flanked by heraldic dolphins); Pinkwart 1984, pl. 27.K65–66; cf. also the magnificent *Applikenkeramik* fragment, Schäfer 1968, pl. 23.

applied so that they rendered a wreath realistically, running in two directions; occasionally its ends were even tied in a bow. Whereas the myrtle wreath was associated with several deities (see below), the ivy wreath was exclusively connected with Dionysos. Garlands also encircled the vessel. They could be suspended from columns, altars and/or boukrania/boukephalia, and they could be carried by Erotes. Often (at least in the first half of the 2nd century) they were furnished with a *tainia*, regularly tied in a bow, and even the garland itself was often bound and thus encircled at several places by a *tainia*.

Myrtle Wreath

A wreath with slender, spikey leaves and small, pomegranate-like fruits frequently occurs in Greek vase painting, from at least the late 5th century onwards (Kunze-Götte 2006, 53). This iconographic tradition continued on the MMB of a number of production centres. The plant which formed the wreath is frequently misidentified in the scholarly literature as laurel or olive. However, the presence of a small berry with (in the best representations) the remains of the flower at its outer end makes the identification as myrtle secure (Kunze-Götte 2006, 7, 10, 12).

The myrtle, *Myrtus communis*, is an evergreen shrub with long, slender branches and mostly white, star-shaped flowers with a fragrant smell (Fig. 50). It was the wreath most commonly worn by the Greeks at symposia and celebrations of marriage and similarly played a significant role in (mystery) cults, at funerals, and in the Underworld (Dickie 1995). In Greek religion, it was a well-known symbol connected with Aphrodite and other Oriental/Semitic deities, and in the Eleusinian cult, the myrtle branch and the myrtle bundle (the *bakchos*, an aniconic representation of Dionysos) were carried by initiands.[48] A stunning myrtle wreath is depicted on the Olbia situla, which was most likely fabricated as a funerary urn (PER-91*; see Guldager Bilde 2005).

The myrtle leaves on wreaths on MMB either run around the vessel in one direction or are rendered as a true wreath, with leaves running in two directions and, in the best specimens, the ends are even tied with a bow. A very fine example can be found on a mould in the Römisch-Germanische Zentralmuseum, Mainz (Künzl 2002, 43 cat. 82, pl. 177–179; production place unknown, probably Aiolian), and the same can be found on a bowl fragment from Pergamon of local production (de Luca 1968, 153 cat. 360, pl. 55). In general, the artisan took care

---

48   Blech 1982, 282–283; Cremer 1991, 33–35; Kunze-Götte 2006, 90–91; Palinkas 2008, 12, 200.

FIGURE 50   Myrtle, *Myrtus communis*, O.W. Thomé, *Flora von Deutschland, Österreich und der Schweiz* 1885 (Gera)

to show that the wreath was bound. Occasionally, and apparently mostly at Pergamon, myrtle bunches occur in a vertical position (e.g., PER-35*). Of note is a vessel from Olbia, documented only by a photograph, where the vertical myrtle bunch is furnished with a handle, probably representing a *bakchos* (PER-34).

The chronology of the trefoil-style myrtle wreath (*Dreiblattsträuschen*) has been intensively discussed (Callaghan 1980, esp. p. 43; Pfrommer 1993, 37; Hübner 1994; de Luca 1999, 102–107). However, different types of wreaths from different sites have been grouped together; this does not further the understanding of the occurrence of this motif.

At Pergamon, myrtle wreaths are normally represented with three bunched leaves, often with berries on dotted or incised stems. Myrtle wreaths are well represented amongst the fragments unearthed in the fill of the Great Altar,[49] whereas just a single fragment was unearthed in *Bauphase* 12 of the Asklepieion (de Luca 1968, 153 cat. 360, pl. 55). However, they are also represented on the weaponry frieze of the balustrade of the Athena Sanctuary in Pergamon, constructed by Eumenes II and finished by his brother Attalos II, as documented by the dedicatory inscriptions on the monument (Pfrommer 1993, fig. 36; Webb 1996, 57 with references), and we also find it on a Hellenistic marble base for a sun dial (Grüßinger et al. 2011, 446–447 cat. 3.8). So, with a lowered date for the Pergamon Altar (see below and Chapter 9), we may conclude that the myrtle wreath remained in vogue at Pergamon for a large part of the first half of the 2nd century.

We can also document Pergamene MMB with myrtle decoration in the Pontic assemblages (PER-30*–PER-33*, PER-35*). The same decoration occurs in other Aiolian productions (AIA-6*–AIA-8*, AIB-62*–AIB-66*, AIB-125*, AIB-136*; KYA-19*–KYB-21, KYA-24*–KYA-27*, KYB-172*–KYB-176*), and it is also known from Knidos (KNI-16*, KNI-17*, KNI-75*) as well as from a number of unidentified productions (XXX-15*–XXX-19*, XXX-62). However, it was in the classical workshops of Ephesos that the myrtle decoration became most popular (WC1 and WC2), and this pattern is known from two moulds found at the Magnesia Gate (Rogl 2001c, 109 cat. RB 16, pls. 63, 68; 111 cat. RB 23, pls. 65, 69).[50]

At Ephesos, the bundled myrtle leaves, which can be either three or five in number, are always depicted as bound. The berries are now completely stylized in the form of three dots grouped in a triangle. The myrtle wreath there is normally combined with a single rim frieze and with calyx B (Chapter 14). This decoration was very common in the entire third quarter of the 2nd century, thus, later than at Pergamon. Five vessels with this decoration came to light in the Pantikapaion palace foundation trench (EPH-356*, EPH-365*, EPH-367*, EPH-1342*, and a small uncatalogued fragment), which accumulated just before 125 (Chapter 24), and one such bowl (Kropotov & Leskov 2006, 33, fig. 7.5) was even found in the funerary meal offering of the Krinički burial, together with numerous vessels of Demetrios (Chapter 18).

Ivy Wreath
The ivy wreath can be found in many different productions, but before the MMB came under the influence of Pergamene *Applikenkeramik* in the late 2nd and early 1st century, this motif was far less common than the myrtle wreath. As with the myrtle wreath, the finest specimens represent a true wreath, where the ivy is running in two directions, as we can observe on a Pergamene bowl in Würzburg (Kotitsa 1998, 125–127 cat. 94, pl. 54). The ivy wreath is normally rendered in the form of three bundled leaves, which may be supplemented with a cluster of ivy berries and (in the Ephesian production) with the same group of three dots in a triangular formation that we found with the myrtles. In addition to Pergamon (PER-36*), an ivy wreath can also be found in the Aiolis B production (AIB-61). It is primarily in Ephesos, however, that this motif proliferates.[51] It is combined with the same rim and calyx motifs as the Ephesian myrtle wreath, and the two are probably contemporary, even though the ivy wreath seems to have gone out of use at Ephesos earlier than the myrtle wreath. It is striking, at least, that Ephesian bowls with ivy wreaths have not been found at all at Istros; the myrtle wreath is better represented there, though not to the same degree as at Olbia.

Garland
Suspended garlands were a very popular motif, especially in Aiolian MMB. They could be hung from columns, altars and/or boukrania/boukephalia or they could be carried by Erotes, and they were often furnished with a

---

49 Schäfer 1968, 154 cats. Z 109, Z 123, fig. 19; de Luca 1999, 109, 115–116 cats. 469, 474A, 487, 599–605, 609–613, pls. 15, 16, 23, Beil. 7, 15, 16.
50 SHA-153; Oxé 1933, pl. 11.3; Laumonier 1977, 60 cat. 2053, pl. 12; 62 cat. 1723, pl. 13; 63 cat. 2380, pl. 13; 64 cat. 9301, pl. 13; 67 cat. 1394, pl. 14; 74 cat. 1745, pl. 16; 85 cat. 1741, pl. 18; 88 cat. 5301, pl. 19; 90 cat. 1746, pl. 20; 91 cats. 1150, 1747, 9481, pl. 20; 121 cat. 4182, pl. 28; 123 cat. 395, pl. 28; 124 cat. 1079, pl. 28; 125 cat. 9517, pl. 28; 127 cats. 1520, 3033, pl. 29; 134 cat. 375, pl. 30; 136 cat. 376, pl. 30; 146 cat. 1432, pl. 33; 147 cat. 478, pl. 33; 156 cat. 385, pl. 35; 158 cat. 942, pl. 36; 163 cat. 1143, pl. 36; 165 cat. 1381, pl. 36; 183 cat. 359, pl. 40; 187 cat. 109, pl. 41; 202 cat. 2071, pl. 45; 203 cats. 1764, 8461, pl. 45; 206 cat. 9254, pl. 46; 220 cats. 1731, 1875, pl. 49; 222 cat. 9280, pl. 49; 225 cat. 1361, pl. 50; 227 cat. 2066, pl. 51; 228 cat. 1771, pl. 51; 233 cat. 1331, pl. 52; 236 cat. 8886, pl. 53; 321 cat. 1245, pl. 76; 322 cat. 1301, pl. 76; 323 cat. 1277, pl. 76; 324 cats. 1298, 2258, pl. 77; 332 cat. 9103, pl. 80; 358 cat. 1726, pl. 86; 363 cat. 916, pl. 87; 385 cat. 643, pl. 92; 394 cat. 9548, pl. 93; 397 cat. 1732, pl. 94; 402 cat. 1744, pl. 94; 409 cat. 5477, pl. 96; 438 cats. 1538, 1555, 1754, pl. 101; 444 cats. 1160, 1718, 1927, 9179, 9449, pl. 102; Puppo 1995, 154 cat. X13, pl. LXX; Kropotov & Leskov 2006, 33, fig. 7.5.
51 EPH-383*–EPH-388*, EPH-1316; Laumonier 1977, 72 cat. 2117, pl. 15; 84 cat. 8472, pl. 18; 124 cat. 470, pl. 28; 125 cat. 4680, pl. 29; 128 cat. 1532, pl. 29; 148 cats. 862, 9187, pl. 33; 149 cat. 471, pl. 33; 160 cat. 1281, pl. 36; 182 cats. 1518–1519, 1521, 1862, pl. 39; 186 cats. 463, 629, 940, pl. 40; 266 cat. 4435, pl. 61; 267 cats. 458, 870–871, pl. 61; 328 cat. 1930, pl. 78; 374 cat. 1534, pl. 90; 426 cat. 1344, pl. 99; 430 cat. 846, pl. 100.

ICONOGRAPHY AND INTERPRETATION

FIGURE 51   Mosaic in cella of temple dedicated to Hera Basileia at Pergamon (Schazmann 1923, pl. 35); the dedicatory inscription is dated to the reign of Attalos II (r. 159–138 BCE)

tainia tied in a bow. G. de Luca has already pointed out the close relationship between garlands in Pergamene MMB and in other media in Pergamon, where they were also very popular (de Luca 1990, 158–160). The parallels to, for example, the floor mosaics in the cella of the temple dedicated to Hera Basileia (Fig. 51),[52] which is dated by the dedicatory inscription to the reign of Attalos II (159–138), and in the contemporary so-called altar room in Palace V[53] are indeed striking (Fig. 52).[54] Not least the

presence of a solid, almost three-dimensional *tainia* tied in a bow is of note, because such *tainiai* came to play a major role on the MMB. It is not surprising that the motif of suspended garlands was taken up in other Aiolian productions, because the garland seems to have constituted part of the Aiolian koine of decorative types. In the Pontic assemblages, suspended garlands are documented a few times on Pergamene MMB (PER-19*, PER-20*, PER-92*), but this decoration was especially favoured on Kymean bowls (KYA-28*–KYA-35*, KYA-37–KYA-42*, KYA-57; KYB-40*, KYB-129*–KYB-171*, KYB-316, KYB-323–KYB-325*, KYB-361, KYB-362*, KYB-413*, KYB-414; KYX-20*, KYX-54*–KYX-66*). We also find it in the Aiolis B production (AIB-55–AIB-60*) and other unidentified Aiolian productions (AIX-8*, AIX-9*).

This Aiolian motif was also employed further south along the coast of Asia Minor. At Ephesos it was primarily rendered on bowls of WC1, mostly suspended between

---

52   Schazmann 1923, pl. 35; Grüßinger et al. 2011, 430–431 cats. 1.19–20.

53   Kawerau & Wiegand 1930, pls. 12–14; Grüßinger et al. 2011, 103, fig. 4; 519–520 cat. 5.42; 522 cat. 5.48. See also the more recently discovered mosaic at Tel Dor, probably of the late 2nd century, with a fine garland (Wootton 2012).

54   Since this 'palace' incorporates unused slabs from the Great Altar, the altar predates this building (Grüßinger et al. 2011, 24; 146 and n. 14).

FIGURE 52   Mosaic in the Altar Room, Palace V, Pergamon
PHOTO BY CAROLE RADDATO; HTTPS://TWITTER.COM/TICIAVERVEER/STATUS/1142432199242846213/PHOTO/4

kraters but also between boukrania.[55] We also find it on Knidian bowls (KNI-18*–KNI-25*; KNI-49*; Kögler 2010, 429 cat. B.52, pl. 3; 519 cat. F.118, pl. 27; 594 cat. Kn.350, pl. 60).

Suspended Wreath

A suspended wreath, often tied with a *tainia*, occurs chiefly in the Aiolian productions, for example, at Pergamon,[56] at Kyme (KYB-43*), and elsewhere in Aiolis (AIX-5). This motif was very rare at Ephesos (EPH-404*–EPH-406*). It is also rare in the productions of Mainland Greece, though it appears occasionally as a filling device at, e.g., Athens (Rotroff 1982a, 56 cats. 103–105, pls. 18, 75).

Vegetal Decoration

Pine Cone

Decoration of the entire vessel with plastic or stylized knobs imitating the scales of a pine cone is amongst the most wide-spread types, though it is never particularly common. Amongst the 414 Athenian bowls and moulds from the Agora, Rotroff records 12 bowls with pine-cone decoration and two further bowls on which pine-cone scales constitute part of the decoration, in total 2.9%.

---

55   EPH-389*– EPH-403. E.g., Laumonier 1977, 43 cat. 3115, pl. 8; 115 cats. 1111–1112, pl. 26; 149 cat. 3111, pl. 33; 178 cats. 1167, 2030, 3114, 3119, 8463, 8747–8748, pl. 39; 212 cats. 3112–3113, pl. 17; 305 cat. 3481, pl. 72; 306 cats. 3116, 3118, 3477, 9357, pl. 72.

56   Conze et al. 1913, Beibl. 43.11; de Luca 1968, 139 cat. 260, pl. 49; 1975, pl. 46.3; 1999, 111 cat. 509, pl. 17; 116 cat. II, pl. 24; Laumonier vol. 2, cat. 273, pl. VI; Grüßinger et al. 2011, 475 cat. 3.90 (cf. also cats. 3.85 and 3.89: white-ground lagynoi).

Similarly, on Delos, 165 (2.7%) of the Ephesian bowls feature pine-cone decoration (Laumonier 1977). Almost the same figure is encountered again at Sardis, where less than 2% carry pine-cone decoration (Rotroff 2003, 106; 177). According to Rotroff, this type of decoration was introduced in the 3rd century (2003, 106) and it continued at least throughout the 2nd century. Obviously, the Dionysiac connection to bowls with pine-cone decoration cannot be overlooked.

Filled 'Nelumbo'
This element is discussed in Chapter 3.

Linear Decoration

Three types of linear decoration[57] were introduced sometime in the second quarter of the 2nd century and were soon employed by many productions. In all three, the decoration was largely incised rather than stamped into the mould (Edwards 1975, 9, 175–176). Most popular and probably also most long-lived was the long-petal bowl, whereas the other two, the pendent-semicircle bowl and the net-pattern bowl, were relatively rare at any site (see Fig. 57 below).

Pendent-Semicircle Design (PSC)
The pendent-semicircle design, a name coined by Edwards (1975, 182–184) and here abbreviated PSC, has been the subject of considerable discussion. It consists of a frieze of grouped concentric semicircles on the wall; the base is encircled with concentric circles. Sun wheels, stars, and rosettes are common in the centre of the (semi) circles and as space-fillers between them. The (semi) circles can be jewelled, and a field of dots commonly fills the space between them. This decoration is also known as 'Macedonian (shield) decoration', because it features prominently on Macedonian shields and shield representations (see below).

R. Zahn was the first scholar to deal with PSC decoration. At first he was of the opinion that the scheme was inspired by the painted suspended garlands of West Slope pottery (Zahn 1904, 406–407 cat. 35). Later he argued instead that it was related to the design of the Macedonian shield (Zahn 1940); this connection has not since been disputed (e.g., Baur 1941, 241; Callaghan 1978; Edwards 1986, 395).[58]

The discovery of moulds attests to the production of vessels with PSC design at a number of different places, such as Ephesos,[59] Knidos,[60] Pergamon (Parlasca 1955, 132, fig. 1), and Sardis (Rotroff 2003, 103 cat. 411, pl. 69). The most varied use of this design is found at Ephesos and especially at Pergamon. As I shall argue below, it is likely that it was at Pergamon that this pattern was first employed on MMB.

The PSC design was employed as a shield device on actual[61] and depicted Macedonian shields (Fig. 53),[62] on jewellery (Segall 1938, 76–77 cat. 90, pl. 24), and, most prominently, as the main device of the obverse on a long series of Macedonian coins (Figs. 54–56). According to M.M. Markle, the earliest representation is found on a coin dated to the early reign of Alexander the Great, ca. 336/5-ca. 329/8 (1999, 247, fig. 48). Alexander's successors in particular employed this device, which was closely connected with Macedonian identity, and there is an unbroken series until and immediately after the fall of the kingdom, when it was still in use as the emblem on coins of the *koinon* of the Macedonians.[63]

This long series of representations cannot help in dating the introduction of this design on MMB. The comparanda do show, however, that the use of the five-rayed device in the centre of the concentric circles perhaps first appears in the time of Philip V (221–179)[64] whereas it is particularly common on the coins of King Perseus.[65] Callaghan points to a coin of that monarch from Amphaxis (Callaghan 1978, fig. 2D), and the same motif can be found on the shields carried by the defeated Macedonians in the Aemilius Paullus monument at Delphi, which was erected

---

57 The term was coined by G.R. Edwards (1975, 175).
58 Callaghan believes that their proper name should be 'shield bowls' (1978, 54).
59 Rogl 2001b, 108 cat. RB 11, pls. 62, 67; 111 cat. RB 24, pls. 65, 69; Seiterle 1981, 28; 1982, fig. 3.
60 Kögler 2010, 522 cat. F.154, pl. 31; 594 cat. Kn.352, pl. 60.
61 Dakaris 1968, 58–59, fig. 2, pl. 42c (Dodone); Adam Veleni 1993 (Vegoras, Northern Greece); http://antique-macedonia.blogspot.com/2008/11/antique-macedonian-shields-from.html [accessed 5/2020] (Bonče). It is also found on a limestone matrix for producing metal shields: Zahn 1940, pl. 3 (Allard Pierson Museum, Amsterdam, from Memphis). The latter, like the actual shield from Bonče, is furnished with a personal name (Ptolemaiou) around the central medallion.
62 Tomb of Lyson and Kallikles, entrance (south) wall of burial chamber (S.G. Miller 1993, 55–58, pls. 9, 13, II, III).
63 SNG Great Britain III, The Lockett Collection Part 3: Macedonia-Aegina. London 1942, nos. 1536–1539; SNG Great Britain VII, Manchester University Museum: The Raby and Güterbock Collections. London 1986, nos. 748–752.
64 SNG Great Britain III.3, The Lockett Collection, London 1942, no. 1303 (dated too early?).
65 SNG, Great Britain, V.3, Ashmolean Museum, Oxford, Macedonia. London 1976, nos. 3282–3284, 3288–3289.

FIGURE 53
Tomb of Lyson and Kallikles, south wall; late 3rd to early 2nd century
PHOTO COURTESY OF STELLA MILLER-COLLETT

FIGURE 54
Coin of Demetrios II, r. 239–229 BCE, with Macedonian shield on obverse. Scan of SNG Cop II pl. 31 no. 1223
PHOTO RASMUS HOLST NIELSEN, THE ROYAL COLLECTION OF COINS AND MEDALS, NATIONAL MUSEUM OF DENMARK

FIGURE 55
Silver tetradrachm of Antigonos Gonatas, r. 277–239 BCE, with head of Pan at centre of Macedonian shield on obverse (Mathisen 1981, pl. 21.36). SNG Cop II pl. 31 no. 1200.
PHOTO RASMUS HOLST NIELSEN, THE ROYAL COLLECTION OF COINS AND MEDALS, NATIONAL MUSEUM OF DENMARK

FIGURE 56
Silver tetradrachm probably struck in Thessaloniki, 183/2–174 BCE, with Macedonian shield on obverse (SNG Great Britain III.3, The Lockett Collection inv. 1539), after http://www.sylloge-nummorum-graecorum.org/

to commemorate his victory over Perseus at Pydna in 168 (Kähler 1965, pls. 4, 7, 20–21).

In his 1978 article, Callaghan suggested that the shield bowls constitute a fixed point in Hellenistic chronology. In his opinion, the PSC design was first introduced on MMB at Corinth in 150, earlier than at Athens (and elsewhere). Indeed, Callaghan argued that that their source of inspiration was the Macedonian shields captured by the Achaean League in the battle against Andriskos in 150 (1978, 60; 1982, 63). This chronology has not stood the test of time. C.M. Edwards has proposed that this decoration appeared in Corinth as early as the first quarter of the 2nd century (Edwards 1986, 395); there is, though, no evidence to support this supposition. The best contextual evidence comes from the so-called 1926-Reservoir (Edwards 1986), in which, out of 152 bowls, six PSC bowls and only two long-petal bowls were present, but there is no independent evidence for the date of this deposit. In Pergamon, the PSC decoration is connected with the Asklepieion's *Bauphasen* 10 and 11, both of which probably have an end date in the late 170s or immediately thereafter (see Chapter 9), and at least one fragment was found in *Bauphase* 12, dated to ca. 157–125 (de Luca 1968, 153 cat. 356 and perhaps cat. 357, pl. 54). In Ephesos, this decoration is found in a larger group in the classical (EC) production of the Monogram PAR Workshop (EPH-955*, EPH-1281*). This date is slightly later than the Pergamene date.

On the basis of the available evidence, I will suggest that emulation of Macedonian shields on MMB was first undertaken at Pergamon (see also Hübner 1994, 286). This is the place where not only the earliest but also the most varied and experimental renderings of the design can be found. The event that most likely lies behind its introduction is the defeat of the last Macedonian King, Perseus, at Pydna in 168. This battle concluded the Third Macedonian War, in which Pergamon and Rome fought side by side. The date 168 is sufficiently close to the date of the Pergamene deposits in which PSC decoration first occurs to make this reconstruction credible. It is likely that the decoration was emulated soon after in Ephesos, and in the 2nd half of the same century it occurred sporadically in other workshops and production places as well. If this reconstruction can be accepted, the PSC decoration on the MMB is to be understood as a reference to victory over the Macedonians: their main symbol was simply appropriated.

As mentioned above, PSC design was employed in a number of productions, but to date it has not been possible to assess how common it was. No more than 68 vessels featuring PSC decoration have been found in the Pontic assemblages (Fig. 57). It is surprising that, amongst the almost 400 fragments from Pantikapaion, not a single vessel featuring PSC decoration has been recorded; I can offer no explanation for this strange fact. The table shows that this decoration counts as one of the rarer designs, so it surfaces only in larger assemblages. If we compare the occurrence of the PSC decoration with that of the long petals, it is easy to see that the latter crops up four times as frequently. Moreover, there seems to be a reversed proportional relationship between the two designs. In the two largest assemblages, Olbia and Istros, the percentage of PSC design is highest at Olbia (Tyritake is the same, but since the assemblage is small, there can be uncertainty of

	PSC		Net pattern		Long petal		Total
	Sum	%	Sum	%	Sum	%	
Bol'šoj Kastel'			2	6.9	2	6.9	29
Chersonesos	2	2.1	1	1.1	5	5.2	96
Istros	18	1.1	16	1.0	115	7.4	1,558
Kepoi			1	2.3	1	2.3	43
Myrmekion	2	0.7	1	0.4	25	9.0	279
Olbia	42	2.3	22	1.2	83	4.5	1,830
Pantikapaion			12	3.1	25	6.4	388
Porthmion	2	0.7			21	7.7	272
Ruminskoe					1	9.1	11
Tyritake	2	2.3	1	1.1	5	5.7	87
Volna 1					1	2.7	37
Average	68	1.5	56	1.2	284	6.1	4,630

FIGURE 57   Comparison of the occurrence of PSC, net-pattern, and long-petal decoration in the Pontic assemblages. The production place is not taken into account

its interpretation), while Olbia has the smallest percentage of long-petal bowls of any large assemblage. At Istros, the proportions are reversed. I believe this has to do with chronology: PSC decoration was introduced earlier than long-petal decoration (contra: Callaghan 1978, 58) and so is better represented in the Olbian assemblage, which, overall, is decisively earlier than the Istrian one.

The same pattern, namely that PSC decoration is relatively rare at any given site, also holds true in the Mediterranean. The largest percentage can be found at Sardis, where, according to Rotroff, 15 vessels of a total of 919 (1.6%) had this decoration (Rotroff 2003, 177). On Delos, PSC decoration constitutes 0.8% of the entire assemblage (54 of 6,495 vessels) and similarly at the Athenian Agora, 4 vessels of 418 (slightly less than 1%) were thus decorated. At Argos, no more than three fragments of 1,024 (0.3%) were decorated with the PSC design (Siebert 1978, 318 cat. DI.124, DI.125, pl. 20; 361 cat. M.99, pl. 30).

Net Pattern
Net pattern is a geometric decoration in which pentagons cover the entire body zone of the vessel. The net could be incised in the mould with one or more lines, or it could be rendered with a dotted line. The field within the pentagons is normally plain, but occasionally it contains figures, such as various types of vessels (EPH-998*; Laumonier 1977, 69 cat. 4050, pl. 15; 309 cat. 4052, pl. 73), skeletons (EPH-995*; Laumonier 1977, 308 cat. 3270, pl. 73), Medusa heads (AIX-22*), or animals (rabbit and boukrania: PER-74). Rotroff has suggested that the pentagonal decoration imitates the pattern of the tortoise shell (1982a, 39; 1997a, 108).

Net-pattern decoration occurs earliest on metal vases (e.g., Zolotarev 2005, fig. 3, Velikoploskoe kurgan); it was imitated in West Slope pottery, where the pentagons were incised. Whether the metal bowls themselves or the West Slope bowls formed the source of inspiration for the MMB is difficult to say.[66]

The net pattern found its way into many MMB productions. In the Black Sea assemblages, net pattern is recorded chiefly on Ephesian vessels (and imitations of Ephesian vessels) from several workshops, but a few Aiolian specimens with this pattern are also found, such as bowls of Aiolis A (AIA-12*), the MMW (KYB-255*, KYB-256, KYB-382* and perhaps KYB-425), and it is also recorded in the Knidian production (KNI-59*; cf. Kögler 2010, 430 cat. B.54–55, pl. 3; 593 cat. Kn.335, pl. 59). Net pattern always

occurs in small numbers. In the Black Sea assemblages, the average percentage is 1.2% (Fig. 57), whereas on Delos, only 0.6% (41 of 6,495 vessels) were decorated in this way.

The chronology of net-pattern bowls has been discussed by several scholars (Edwards 1975, 180; Callaghan 1978, 58; Edwards 1986, 395; Zolotarev 2005 and others). Edwards was of the opinion that net-pattern bowls were introduced at Corinth around 160 and were produced there until the destruction of the city in 146 (Edwards 1975, 180), whereas Callaghan argued that they were invented at Pergamon shortly before 165 (1982, 66–67). Callaghan's only evidence, however, was fragments of West Slope bowls with an incised net pattern, which were also found in the fill of the Great Altar. Bowls like this appear in Athens as early as the second half of the 3rd century (lower fill of the Satyr Cistern: Rotroff 1997a, 275 no. 318, fig. 20, pl. 32) or even earlier (Rotroff 1997a, 109 with n. 106) and have no direct bearing on the introduction of the design in relief ware. Published mouldmade net-pattern bowls from Pergamon are scarce, so I do not find it likely that they originated there. From our available evidence we can conclude only that this decoration was in use on MMB before the sack of Corinth in 146, but precisely how early it was made there and elsewhere must remain an open question. It is, though, of note that there seems to be a chronological gap of more than half a century between the introduction of West Slope bowls with this decoration on the one hand and the MMB on the other. It is certain, however, that this decoration was in use over a considerable period of time. In the Athenian Agora, bowls with this decoration can still be found in contexts of the 1st century (Rotroff 1982a, 39).

Long-Petal (LP) Design
Long-petal design, a term coined by H.A. Thompson (1934, 456, 'long-petalled bowls'), consists of vertical fluting which normally covers the entire body zone. It comes in a number of variations and was employed at many different production places. The flutes (or petals) have a rounded top, and they can be either plastic (with a convex interior) or stylized (rendered purely in outline). Both types were normally engraved or incised directly in the mould rather than stamped. The petals can be contiguous or independent and spaced out. Often a vertical line of dots separates the petals, and the individual petal may be completely surrounded by a dotted line. In rare instances, contiguous or separated petals with or without dotted line undulate around the bowl (a variant not represented in the Pontic assemblages). In Eastern Mediterranean and Pontic workshops, isolated long petals are occasionally inserted into a vegetal calyx (e.g., AIB-128, KYB-387*, KYB-413*, KYB-414,

---

66 Mahler (1924, 36) and Zolotarev (2005, 58) favour the emulation of metal vessels.

KYX-56*, PER-34, EPH-595*–EPH-597*, EPH-601*, Pontic Demetrios decoration 2). In a few cases, long petals serve as a 'calyx' under a figural frieze.[67] This is not encountered in the Pontic assemblages.

The absolute chronology of the origin and development of the long-petal design has been intensively debated. Before the early 1980s, based on H.A. Thompson's pottery groups from the Athenian Agora, it was commonly accepted that bowls with this design were produced from around 150 (e.g., Thompson 1934, 370; Edwards 1956, 91; Weinberg 1961, 382; Edwards 1975, 176). This was challenged in the early 1980s. Based on new deposits, C.M. Edwards made it clear that long-petal bowls were more common at Corinth than previously assumed; this led him to propose that they must have been produced in the city for some time prior to its destruction in 146. He therefore suggested a date of ca. 165 for their first appearance in Corinth, albeit without any firm support (1981, 191–193; 1986, 392; Callaghan 1982, 65) and he entertained the idea that Corinth was the place where this type of decoration was invented (Edwards 1981, 193).

The main battle over the long-petal bowl, however, has been fought in Pergamon – without the problem having been solved. P.J. Callaghan (1981; 1982) was the first to notice the significance of three fragments with long-petal decoration amongst the no more than eight fragments of MMB unearthed in 1961 in the foundations of the Great Altar at Pergamon and published by J. Schäfer (1968, 154 cats. Z 108, Z 126, Z-127, fig. 19). Based on speculations about how long it would have taken to finish the superstructure of the altar before Eumenes' death in 159, he proposed that the foundation was filled prior to ca. 165; the material found inside was obviously earlier. This down-dating of the altar spurred further excavations in the fill of the foundation, undertaken in 1994 by W. Radt, and further long-petal fragments turned up (de Luca 1999, 107–110, 113 cats. 480, 544–550, pls. 12, 20, 24). Because scholars working at Pergamon believed that there was synchronicity between the layers of *Bauphasen* 10–11 in the Asklepieion (which contained no long-petal bowls) and the altar,[68] the presence of long-petal bowls in the altar foundation came as a surprise. The first phase at the Asklepieion with long-petal bowls was *Bauphase* 12, which de Luca dated to the period between 157 and the end of the 3rd quarter of the 2nd century (de Luca 1968, 152 cats. 343–344, pl. 54).

Even though they do not agree about the date, both Callaghan (1982, 66) and de Luca (1999, 107–109) surmise that it is conceivable that long-petal decoration was first employed at Pergamon. This is certainly a possibility. However, Callaghan cannot really prove that this form of decoration occurs earlier in Pergamon than in the Greek mainland, and the date given by de Luca follows her high date for the altar in the late 170s. Nevertheless, the Pergamene deposits seem to support my proposition that long-petal decoration was introduced later than PSC design. If the PSC decoration was first employed following the victory at Pydna in 168, we can probably place the inception of the long-petal bowl slightly later than that date, and since the date of the altar should follow that of the pottery rather than the opposite, it follows that Callaghan's suggestion for the down-dating of the altar is to be accepted. Thus, it is most likely that the construction of the altar was initiated only after 166, following the victory over the Gauls.[69] This makes it likely that the long-petal bowl first appeared in Pergamon around 165. This date corresponds well with the Corinthian evidence, even though it does not answer the question of where long-petal bowls were first made. Rotroff favours Pergamon over Corinth, because the same motif was also employed on Pergamene capitals (2003, 123). However, we need more well-dated find complexes in order to answer this question.

The long-petal design came to dominate the decoration of MMB in the second half of the 2nd century, lasting until production was abandoned sometime in the first half of the 1st century.[70] Overall, there seems to be a development from plastic to stylized petals (so also Edwards 1975, 174–175). This is also evident when we consider the relative representation of the two at Olbia and Istros, respectively. At Olbia, where, as we saw above (Fig. 57), the long-petal design accounts for only 4.5% of the vessels, the ratio between plastic and stylized long petals is 1:1.6, whereas at Istros, where 7.4% of the vessels were decorated with long-petal design, the same ratio is 1:2.6. So, long-petal bowls grew more common with time – and the simple stylized version became more frequent than the plastic one.

---

67 Adam Veleni 1997, 142 pl. 114.b; Rogl 2008a, 109 cat. 61, pls. 7, 32; two Italo-Megarian Lapius vessels: Marabini Moevs 1980, 206, 208 pl. 19.3 and 6; Puppo 1995, 37 cat. L7 and L8, pl. V.

68 Schäfer (1968, 26) even believed that the synchronicity was with 'Hellenistisch II'=*Bauphasen* 7–9.

69 It is beyond the scope of this publication to enter into the general discussion of the altar's date based on elements other than the pottery; a recent and balanced overview of current research positions is given by Stewart (2000).

70 For example, in a deposit in Eretria dated to 86, no less than 72% of the MMB were long-petal bowls (Schmid 2004).

Stamps of the Base Medallion

Some stamps were so simple that they were employed in multiple workshops, without one shop necessarily emulating the designs of another. A good example is the rosette with rounded petals, sometimes divided by tongues (Rosette A), which we find primarily at Ephesos but also elsewhere. The more complex rosette C, on the other hand, seems to be one that was probably either copied or emulated.

Rosette A

The commonest type of rosette is also the simplest: it has a varying number of slender, rounded petals, which may be divided by tongues. This rosette is employed in various workshops, but most commonly at Ephesos.

Rosette C

This rosette features six broad, lobed petals with finely ribbed interiors; the flower pistil is rendered with a stamp for an ivy-berry cluster. It was in use in several Aiolian workshops, especially at Kyme,[71] but also at Pergamon (PER-10*, PER-70*) and in Aiolis B (AIB-77*), and it was soon copied at other production centres as well, such as Sardis (Rotroff 2003, 128 cat. 539, pl. 94), and Ephesos (EPH-257, EPH-679*, EPH-1007*).

Iconography and Meaning: Summing Up

By and large, the decoration of the MMB followed four different trajectories, depending on where and when they were produced. One broad trend is represented by mythological and literary themes. These subjects seem to have been in particular vogue in Macedonia (e.g., Sinn 1979), but also in Athens and in areas inspired by Athenian vessels. A widespread (but relatively uncommon) trend is represented by motifs referring to the world of the elite, especially hunting scenes. A third, and pervasive development is the occurrence of linear decoration, which became progressively more and more common. Even though a design such as the PSC may originally have referred to a victory over the Macedonians, such connotations were probably lost over time. The last trend, which I find the most important, involves the world of Dionysos. Under this heading can be grouped a multitude of different depictions, not just figural, but also vegetal, scrolls, and wreaths.

Considering the fact that the vessels were intended for elegant drinking and dining, the prominence of Dionysiac imagery on the MMB is hardly surprising. As we have seen, however, there may be deeper reasons behind this, reflecting the spiritual climate of the late Hellenistic period. In Chapter 3, we discussed how the lush vegetation rendered on the bowls from the very beginning promulgated Ptolemaic ideas of a *paradeisos tes tryphes* which were deeply imbued with an understanding of Dionysos as the source of exuberance and fertility, and I have already quoted Laumonier, who called such decoration *paradisiaque* (Laumonier 1977, 32–33). Grape vine, myrtle, ivy, lotus, and acanthus occur as main and as secondary decoration, in friezes and scrolls.

Dionysos is celebrated on many bowls, and if he is not present himself, his symbols are. Thus, we find aniconic representations in the form of an *agyieus* or ubiquitous renderings of vases, chiefly kraters and drinking vessels, which are celebrated by Erotes and Pans performing the *aposkopein* gesture in front of them. Dolphins also figure prominently in many productions, again connoting Dionysos. Especially in the Aiolian workshops, masks, columns, boukrania, garlands, and *tainiai* are depicted as what Kossatz suggests is *verkürtzte Darstellungen ländlich-dionysischer Heiligtümern* … (Kossatz 1990, 112; see also Rogl 2008a, 70). I completely agree.

Of special note is the prominence of Erotes in many productions, where they perform various tasks, such as riding dolphins, driving chariots, carrying garlands, playing music, and enhancing Dionysiac symbols. In many ways, the best iconographic parallels for their multiple activities are found on the much later Roman sarcophagi. The significance of Erotes on sarcophagi is a much-discussed subject which we cannot engage in here.[72] However, I tend to follow J. Huskinson, who stresses their allegorical value as symbols of mankind (Plato would say, the soul) and their ability to transcend boundaries of human experience, such as time, gender, and social behaviour, and she also focuses on the self-irony in many representations of Erotes (1996, 105). I believe that we can extend this interpretation to the MMB without difficulty.

Dionysos played a major role in Hellenistic society. Several Ptolemaic kings were celebrated as Neos Dionysos

---

71 Bouzek & Jansová 1974, 51 cat. MB 3, pl. 2 (mould); bowl from Torbali in Ephesos Museum inv. 34/15/74, cf. Erdemgil et al. 1989, 111, Tuluk 2001, 61–62, fig. 3a, and perhaps Siebert 1978, 245 n. 3; and an unpublished bowl from Mesambria's necropolis in Nessebar, Archaeological Museum inv. 2008-38.

72 E.g., Bielefeld 1995; Huskinson 1996; Schauenburg 1996; Bielefeld 1997; Kranz 1999.

(Ptolemy IV, XII and XIII), and the same epithet designated the Seleucid kings Antiochos VI and Antiochos XII, and later the Bithynian King Mithridates VI and the Roman Antonius. In the spiritual climate of the late Hellenistic period, many people put their faith in Dionysos when it came to securing a better afterlife. I am sure this resulted in the popularity not just of the so-called Tarentine altars, but also of the altar sequence rendered in other media, chiefly the MMB. Even though we should not overstress this aspect, I believe that such an interpretation represents an undercurrent in the message of many of the pictures, and, thus, can be said to reflect (at least partially) the spiritual climate of late Hellenistic society. Preoccupation with death is unmistakeably spelled out in the case of the bowls, which even feature skeletons (EPH-995*). Surely, as was the case with the Erotes, the *memento mori* of the skeletons was crafted with a twinkle of the eye, but this does not detract from the seriousness of the matter.

PART 2

Mediterranean Productions

∴

CHAPTER 7

Athens

It is an established fact that the invention of the MMB took place in Athens in the last quarter of the 3rd century. Sometime in the 220s, an innovative potter let himself be inspired by precious metal vessels of the Ptolemaic court (discussion in Chapter 3 with references) – and some of the earliest vessels were even direct copies of metal vases (Rotroff 1982b, 332; Rotroff 2006b, 368–369).

The chronology of Athenian MMB has been gradually lowered during the 20th century.[1] F. Courby dated their invention to the end of the 4th century (1922, 360–361). This was revised when, in 1934, H.A. Thompson analysed deposits of the Athenian Agora and laid a firmer foundation for their dating. According to him, the bowls were introduced at the end of the first quarter of the 3rd century (1934, 457). This chronology was later lowered by G.R. Edwards, who dated their inception to ca. 250 (1956, 90; 1975, 152). In 1982, S. Rotroff re-examined the finds from the Agora and, based primarily on a number of wells and cisterns, she down-dated their beginning even further, to between 240 and 220, and, as mentioned elsewhere (Chapter 3), she proposed a connection between the initial production of the bowls and the first celebration of the Ptolemaia in Athens, in 224/3. Recently, she has 'recalibrated' her dates, following G. Finkielsztejn's lowered dates for the Rhodian stamped amphorae, so that the first occurrence of Athenian MMB should fall in the period between ca. 226 and 211 (Rotroff 2005, 22–24; 2006b, 360–361). The new type of vessel took time to catch the attention of the market (Rotroff 2006b), so for several decades production was apparently limited.

A considerable number of moulds have been found in Athens, around the Agora, on the Pnyx, in the Kerameikos, and at Syntagma Square (Chapter 4 and Appendix 4). Three workshops dominated the first half-century of the production – perhaps even longer – the Workshop of Bion, Workshop A, and Hausmann's Workshop. All three produced vegetal and figural bowls. The Workshop of Bion was destroyed at the end of the first quarter of the 2nd century (Rotroff 1982a, 27); Workshop A is contemporary with Bion, whereas Hausmann's Workshop started slightly later but ended at approximately the same time.[2] Contemporary with the demise of the Workshop of Bion, some Athenian potters moved to Lemnos (Rotroff 2013, 20–22), where in two different cities, Myrina (Archontidou-Argyri 1994) and Hephaistia (Massa 1992; 1997), MMB were produced in locally made moulds but of clearly Athenian extraction (discussion of Lemnian production in Chapter 4). Two Athenian(?) moulds have been found on Delos,[3] and an Atticizing mould has also been found at Laurion clearly imitating the Workshop of Bion (Salliora-Oikonomákou 1979, 169 pl. 74c). An equally Atticizing fragment recently came to light in the Boiotian Koroneia survey.[4]

The three Athenian workshops mentioned above were followed by a number of smaller workshops which after the middle of the 2nd century mostly produced long-petal bowls. It is generally believed that production did not continue beyond the destruction by Sulla in 86 (Rotroff 1982a, 36).

Athenian workshops primarily made relatively deep bowls with an everted lip. The height is generally between 7.5 and 9 cm and the rim diameter between 14 and 15 cm (see also Fig. 6). In general, the H:⌀ ratio is very standardized, at 1:1.7, with ratios of 1:1.8 and 1.9 significantly less common.[5] The bowls were covered with a black gloss of varying quality.

Athenian workshops also experimented with a few other shapes, mostly of small sizes, such as the small bowl (ATH-72*, ATH-73; SHA-2–SHA-7) and the juglet (ATH-74*–ATH-76*; SHA-79–SHA-82), which are also represented amongst our other sites. Apart from these very small shapes, we find a few vessels with the addition of West Slope decoration in Workshop A (a krater: SHA-333 and an amphora: SHA-207) as well as a kantharos also with West Slope decoration (SHA-136), and another krater (SHA-387). A stemmed bowl published by Edwards as Athenian (SHA-157) is most likely Ephesian.

---

1 A recent overview can be found in Rotroff 2006b, 358–359.
2 [Ed. For Hausmann's Workshop, see now Rotroff 2016; 2018, 578–585.]
3 Courby 1922, 392–393 cat. 159, pl. IX.d; Laumonier 1973, 254; Laumonier 1977, 2; Chatzidakis 1997, 302, pl. 223.a.
4 Oral paper by Ph. Bes and J. Poblome given 9 March 2012 at the Round table *Late Hellenistic and Roman Tableware in the Black Sea, Eastern Mediterranean and in the West (150 BC–250 AD)*, Berlin.
5 Data for this calculation derives from the present catalogue as well as from the catalogue of Rotroff 1982a.

Athenian Vessels in the Pontic Assemblages

Athenian vessels are found widely in the Pontic region, but their numbers are small. Of the more than 4,600 individual vessels from our Black Sea sites, at most 76 are of Athenian manufacture (1.6%). A similar picture is well known from the Mediterranean: outside the place of production and its immediate environs, Athenian vessels are widespread, but always present only in limited numbers (Guldager Bilde 1993, 197). However, a closer look shows some internal variation. First of all, it is striking that two-thirds of the Athenian vessels at our Pontic sites derive from Olbia, where the Athenian vessels constitute ca. 2.8% of all the MMB which I inventoried. This is in contrast to Istros, where considerably less than 1% of the vessels were produced at Athens. This difference in the relative numbers at these two sites is hardly fortuitous: it is most likely an indicator of a chronological difference between the assemblages, the Olbian one being the earlier of the two (see p. 512). In addition, the figures probably indicate that more Athenian vessels were in circulation in the years before Ephesian products flooded the market. It is worth noting that in the palace foundation trench at Pantikapaion, which is a closed assemblage characterized by nothing but Ephesian vessels of the classical phase, not a single scrap of an Athenian vessel was found. The same picture is provided by the funerary offering trench at the Krinički kurgan, where exclusively Ephesian vessels and local Bosporan vessels of the Demetrios workshop were unearthed (Kropotov & Leskov 2006, fig. 7).

Small numbers of Athenian bowls have been found at Pantikapaion, Chersonesos, Myrmekion, and Porthmion. Apparently, it takes relatively large assemblages for Athenian vessels to be manifest. Most of the Athenian vessels attested in our assemblage are quite small fragments, and, with only a fraction of the original vessel preserved, it is difficult to form a satisfactory opinion about the overall decorative pattern. By and large, however, vessels with figural designs clearly predominate over those with a purely vegetal decoration. It is remarkable that I have not been able to identify a single candidate for an Athenian long-petal bowl. Seemingly, there were no exports of Athenian MMB to the Pontic region after, say, 150. The same surprising conclusion was reached concerning Delos, where, even though after 166 the island came under Athenian control, next to no Athenian MMB have been found (see Fig. 4).[6]

Interestingly, all five of the Athenian vessels of supplementary shapes found in the region were excavated at Olbia: two small bowls (ATH-72*, ATH-73) and three juglets (ATH-74*–ATH-76*) (6.6% of the Athenian vessels in the Black Sea and 10% of the Athenian vessels from Olbia). Considering how uncommon supplementary shapes are at Athens, this number is of note; it corresponds well with the overall conclusion in Chapter 5 that in the Black Sea region, especially at Olbia, there was a predilection for a much broader range of vessels than was current in the Mediterranean.

The Workshop of Bion (ATH-1, ATH-12*, ATH-24, ATH-25[?], ATH-26*, ATH-34*[?], ATH-35*[?], ATH-37*, ATH-48*, ATH-50*, ATH-51*[?], ATH-52*[?], ATH-53*–ATH-59, ATH-60*[?], ATH-63, ATH-65*, ATH-66, ATH-73) and Workshop A (ATH-7, ATH-11*, ATH-15*, ATH-27*, ATH-47, ATH-61*, ATH-62, ATH-64*) are both well represented in the Pontic assemblages.

---

6 [Ed. Recent publication of Athenian mouldmade bowls from the French excavations has revealed, to the contrary and as PGB could not have known, that considerable numbers of Athenian bowls have been found on Delos, including many long-petal bowls; cf. Rotroff 2018, 573].

CATALOGUE TO CHAPTER 7

BOWLS

A Figural Decoration

Altar Figures

Occur in combination with other mythological scenes (see Chapter 6 for a thorough discussion).

ATH-1
Olbia, München, Antikensammlung (formerly Vogell collection). Complete. Groove below lip filled with miltos. ø rim 14; vessel H 8; H:ø 1:1.7. Dark brown coat ext., int. black. Multiple rim friezes: pairs of horizontal S-spirals with palmette above; Ionian kyma. Main decoration: abduction of Ganymede, altar scene D, Herakles and Auge; long-bearded masks as space-fillers. Calyx: tall, straight palmette alternating with tall, jewelled petal; low palmettes in between. Medallion: Medusa head. Frieze separators: dots. The Medusa head medallion is employed mostly by the Workshop of Bion (e.g., Rotroff 1982a, cats. 101, 121, 124, 152, 171, 295, pls. 24, 56, 75, 76, 78, 79) but also very occasionally by Classes 1 and 2 (e.g., Rotroff 1982a, cats. 73, 144, pls. 13, 27), and Workshop A (e.g., Rotroff 1982a, cat. 218, pl. 43). Workshop of Bion.
– Zahn 1908, 45–48 cat. 1, fig. 1a–b; Boehlau 1908, 30 no. 272; Wuilleumier 1929, 65 cat. k; Schwabacher 1941, 195 no. 6; Pochmarski 1990, 285 RK 86.

ATH-2
Olbia, Kassel Antikensammlung (formerly Vogell collection), inv. T 478. Complete. Groove below lip. ø rim 17.4; vessel H 10.6, H:ø 1:1.6. Brown coat. Rim friezes: effaced pattern(?); Ionian kyma. Main decoration: rampant goats flanking krater with small flying Eros and comic mask over krater, abduction of Ganymede, altar fig. C2; lower frieze of dolphins left. Calyx: alternating rows of rounded petals with central vein, palmettes, and rounded petals. Medallion: rosette with eight tongue-shaped petals.
– Zahn 1908, 48 cat. 2; Boehlau 1908, 30 no. 271; Schwabacher 1941, 195 no. 5; CVA Kassel 2 [Germany 38], 65, figs. 42–43, pl. 88.1–2.

Hunt

Hunting scenes were very popular in Athens (Schwabacher 1941, 207–212; Rotroff 1982a, 19 cats. 238–272). Represented amongst the Pontic fragments is the mounted hunter (ATH-3*) and an Eros as hunter (ATH-4*).

ATH-3*
Pantikapaion, M-57-1026(?), Moscow, Puškin Museum of Fine Arts. Fr. of upper body. H 6 × W 4.8. Dull black coat. Rim frieze: debased chevron pattern between lines of fine dots. Main decoration: horseman with raised spear on rearing horse left. Calyx: tip of single fern visible. For chevron of rim, cf. Rotroff 1982a, 52 cat. 70, pl. 13) and ATH-25.
– Zabelina 1984, 165, fig. 12b; AGSP 1984, pl. CLXIII.1.

ATH-4*
Olbia, Sector NGS, O-НГС-93-635, Parutine, Olbia National Preserve storeroom. Fr. of upper body. H 4.1 × W 3.7, WT 0.38–0.42. Fabric: fine, no visible inclusions, 7.5YR 6/4. Thin firm slightly lustrous coat, 5Y 2.5/1. Medium hard fired. Main decoration: hunting Eros moving right with (not preserved) spear. Identical(?): Rotroff 1982a, 76 cats. 256, 257, pl. 52; cat. 259 is related, but not from the same stamp (not attributed).

ATH-5*
Olbia, Sector R25, O-P25-93-1459, Parutine, Olbia National Preserve storeroom. Body fr. H 3.9 × W 4.2, WT 0.22. Fabric: very fine, 7.5YR 6/6. Slightly lustrous coat, Gley 1 2.5/N. Hard fired. Main decoration: opposing animals: at left, hind legs of dog(?) jumping right; at right, hare/rabbit jumping left. Calyx: small ferns.

ATH-6
Pantikapaion, Cistern N 179, 96-no.(?), Kerč Archaeological Museum. Fr. of lower body. Main decoration: dog or feline right, feet of man. Calyx: several rows of imbricate fern.
– Tolstikov & Zhuravlev 2004, pl. 101.3.

ATH-7
Porthmion, П-79-107, Kerč History and Culture Reserve inv. KMAK 9512. Fr. of upper body. Multiple rim friezes: pairs of horizontal S-spirals with rosette above; heart guilloche left. Main decoration: dog attacking deer from behind; in front of deer, another animal running left. Workshop A.
– Grzegrzółka 2010, 126 cat. 173.

Naval Scene

A few images of ships occur at Athens. Two (Rotroff 1982a, 64 cats. 165, 166, pl. 31) are less detailed than ours, and because the fragments are so small, it is impossible to tell whether the scene is mythological or shows a war ship. The third is on an amphora (Rotroff 1982a, 92 cat. 407, pls. 70 and 89), the ship alternating with Erotes riding goats. On the fourth, a bowl, Odysseus is tied to the mast of his ship, which is flanked by female marine monsters (Rotroff 1982a, 67 cat. 190, pl. 80). On the two Olbian fragments, which were made in two different moulds, the ship is very detailed. On both ships there is an aulos-player, and a Nike stands on the stern of the more detailed ship. Both probably represent battleships rather than a mythological scene.

ATH-8*
Olbia, O-1925-486, present whereabouts unknown. Fr. of upper body. Rim frieze: heart guilloche left. Main decoration: very detailed ship moving right; aulos-player and Nike in ship; perhaps Skylla behind ship.
– St Petersburg, IIMK RAN, photo archive neg. II 19399.

ATH-9*
Olbia, Sector R25, O-P25-96-1348, Parutine, Olbia National Preserve storeroom. Fr. of upper body. H 2.6 × W 2.6, WT 0.3. Fabric: very fine, 7.5YR 7/4. Slightly lustrous coat, Gley 1 2.5/N. Hard fired. Main decoration: stern of oared battleship moving right; in the front sits an aulos-player.

Amazonomachy

Seemingly, Amazonomachies were not as common in Athens as in Ephesos (see Chapter 14), but they do occur (Rotroff 1982a, 73 cats. 233–236). Perhaps the two Black Sea sherds point to a Pontic predilection for this subject?

ATH-10*
Pantikapaion, П-1877-79, St Petersburg, State Hermitage Museum. Four rim frs., four body frs., partially joining. Groove below rim. H 9, ⌀ rim 16. Multiple rim friezes: pairs of horizontal S-spirals with small palmettes above; Ionian kyma. Main decoration: Amazons with raised spear in right hand and shield held in left hand seen from the inside; Amazon wears short chiton and twists in spiral movement with legs turned left, frontal torso, and spear and head turned right. Low imbricate calyx of alternating rounded petals with central vein and small ferns. For Amazon, cf. Rotroff 1982a, 73 cats. 235–236, pl. 45 (neither attributed, 175–150), but the stamp at Athens seems to be smaller and more compressed, hence probably later.

ATH-11*
Olbia, Square Б5, O-Б5-76-22, Kiev, Institute of Archaeology storeroom. Two joining frs. of mid- and upper body. H 5.1 × W 8.8, WT 0.35. Fabric: fine, no visible inclusions, 10YR 7/6. Coat with slight bluish metallic sheen, 10YR 2/1. Hard fired. Rim frieze: Ionian kyma. Main decoration: Amazon with lifted battle axe riding left on horse turning its head back right; Greek mounted warrior with spear riding right. Frieze separators: small circles. Rim pattern common on vases attributed to Workshop A (e.g., Rotroff 1982a, 67 cat. 193, pl. 36). Workshop A.

Abduction of Ganymede

The abduction of Ganymede was a popular theme in Athenian MMB, apparently employed by several workshops (Schwabacher 1941, 195–196; Rotroff 1982a, 22); see also **ATH-1**. It was also reproduced in the Atticizing workshop of Lemnian Myrina, as attested by a mould fragment (Archontidou-Argyri 1994, 233 cat. BE 11244, pl. 179.β).

ATH-12*
Chersonesos, X-1903-92, St Petersburg, State Hermitage Museum. Five joining frs. of rim and upper body. H 7.5, WT 0.4, ⌀ rim 13, 23%, RH 0.55. Fabric: fine, slightly layered, no visible inclusions, 5YR 5/6. Thick dull coat, 10YR 2/1. Multiple rim friezes: pairs of horizontal S-spirals with palmette above; heart guilloche. Main decoration: abduction of Ganymede, frontal Nike with outspread wings; small flying Erotes, long-bearded mask, flying bird, round-headed mask in field. Frieze separators: dots. The long-bearded (Dionysos?) mask is typical of the Workshop of Bion (e.g., Rotroff 1982a, 55–56 cats. 99, 101, 105, pl. 75), as are the rim friezes (e.g., Rotroff 1982a, 55–56 cats. 99, 101, 103, 105 et al.; 225–175). For Nike, cf. Rotroff 1982a, 70 cat. 209, pl. 41. Workshop of Bion.
– IAK 1903, 33 fig. 36.

ATH-13
Chersonesos, Quarter VIII, present whereabouts unknown. Body fr. Main decoration: abduction of Ganymede.
– Chlystun 1996, 154, fig. 1.

Other Mythological Scenes

ATH-14*
Olbia, Sector E6, square 428, O-E6-57-990, Kiev, Institute of Archaeology storeroom. Body fr. H 5.5 × W 4.6, WT 0.32. Fabric: fine, no visible inclusions. Coat with dull lustre. Relatively hard fired. Main decoration: Herakles and Auge (Schwabacher 1941, 193–195; Rotroff 1982a, 21–22), lower part of female in peplos with long *apoptygma* (Athena?). Calyx: low, of imbricate ferns. The subject of Herakles and Auge was employed by several Athenian workshops (Rotroff 1982a, 69 cats. 203–207, pls. 39–40, 81).

ATH-15*
Olbia, Sector E6, square 428, O-E6-57-991, Kiev, Institute of Archaeology storeroom. Body fr. close to rim. H 5.4 × W 5.8,

WT 0.45. Fabric: fine, no visible inclusions, 10YR 6/2. Coat with slight metallic lustre, ext. Gley 1 4/N, int. Gley 1 3/N. Relatively hard fired. Multiple rim friezes: horizontal pairs of S-spirals with palmette above; heart guilloche right. Main decoration: Prokne? (Rotroff 1982a, 24); further decoration cannot be identified. The rim friezes are typical of Workshop A. Workshop A.

ATH-16*
Olbia, Antikensammlung, Staatliche Museen zu Berlin (formerly Becker collection), V.I. 7754.65. Body fr. H 3.1 × W 4.5, WT 0.5. Fabric: fine, a few light-reflecting particles, 5YR 6/6. Coat with dull lustre, 10YR 3/1. Main decoration: standing deities: Hera(?) with sceptre and Zeus(?) with sceptre.

ATH-17*
Olbia, Sector NGS, O-НГС-93-169g, Parutine, Olbia National Preserve storeroom. Fr. of upper body. Main decoration: Athena with round shield and spear, left.

ATH-18*
Olbia, Sector R25, O-P25-92-324, Parutine, Olbia National Preserve storeroom. Fr. of upper body. H 2.25 × W 1.9, WT 0.25. Fabric: very fine, 7.5YR 7/6. Lustrous coat, 10YR 2/1. Hard fired. Main decoration: Palladion right with shield lifted above head of Cassandra.

ATH-19*
Pantikapaion, inv. 21949, Odessa, Historical Museum. Complete. Vessel H 6. Multiple rim friezes: ivy leaf; short vertical strokes; heart guilloche left. Main decoration: Nike, Erotes around krater, standing male with mantle around lower body. Calyx: imbricate small ferns. Medallion: frontal Athena Parthenos head within two ridges. Athena Parthenos medallion occurs mostly on vessels attributed to the Workshop of Bion (good images: Rotroff 1982a, 56, 74 cats. 104, 240, pls. 18, 46, 98) and, later, Class 1 (69 cat. 208). Crude work, late or perhaps Atticizing rather than Attic, but if so imitating Workshop of Bion.
– Bodzek (ed.) 2006, 265 cat. 66 (considered to be from Asia Minor).

ATH-20*
Olbia, Sector Sever-Zapad, O-СЗ-68-1837, Parutine, Olbia National Preserve storeroom. Fr. of lower body. H 3.3 × W 4.8, WT 0.25. Fabric: fine, a few light-reflecting particles, 7.5YR 7/6. Thin glossy coat, worn, 5Y 2.5/1. Hard fired. Main decoration: confronted Erotes with crossed legs, between them a stick(?), bird flying, Eros striding right. Calyx: imbricate pointed petals with central vein.

Heraldic Rampant Goats Flanking Krater

This scene appears mostly in mixed representations (see also ATH-2). Rampant heraldic goats were extremely popular in the Athenian workshops, either on their own or flanking a krater (Schwabacher 1941, 200–202; Rotroff 1982a, cats. 104–118, 120–123, 145–146, 163, 186, 201, 211, 260, 311).

ATH-21*
Olbia, Sector D, semi-squares 6–7, О-Д-46-3154, Kiev, Institute of Archaeology storeroom. Body fr. H 3 × W 5, WT 0.25. Fabric: fine, 5YR 7/6. Slightly lustrous coat, Gley 1 2.5/N. Hard fired. Main decoration: rampant goat(s) flanking krater, Eros with torch, hind legs of animal leaping right. Low calyx of small ferns. Probably from same vessel as ATH-22*.

ATH-22*
Olbia, Sector D9, О-Д9-47-2191, Kiev, Institute of Archaeology storeroom. Body fr. Main decoration: rampant goats flanking krater. Probably from same vessel as ATH-21*.

Unidentified Scenes with Mythological Figures

ATH-23*
Olbia, Sector JuzA, О-ЮзА-74-150, Parutine, Olbia National Preserve storeroom. Fr. of lower body. H 4 × W 4, WT 0.35. Fabric: fine, no visible inclusions, 7.5YR 6/6. Thin dull coat, very pitted on int., 10YR 2/1. Relatively hard fired. Main decoration: lower part of rampant goat(?); below, volute krater with ribbed body and unidentified objects to either side.

ATH-24
Pantikapaion, area of 51 Armii Str., П-76-no.(?), Kerč History and Culture Reserve inv. KMAK 6285. Two joining frs. of rim and upper body. Multiple rim friezes: horizontal S-spirals with palmettes above; heart guilloche left. Main decoration: calyx of palm fronds with hatched veins; rampant goat and small flying Eros as space-fillers. Workshop of Bion.
– Grzegrzółka 2010, 54–55 cat. 25.

ATH-25
Pantikapaion, M-74-312, Moscow, Puškin Museum of Fine Arts. Fr. of rim and upper body. Scraped groove with miltos below lip. H 6 × W 4.5. Slightly lustrous black coat. Multiple rim friezes: sitting birds flanking column of dots, bird flying left; debased chevron pattern right between friezes of fine circles. Main decoration: Eros flying right over animal(?), boukranion over krater. Frieze separators: small circles. For chevron of rim, see ATH-14*. Workshop of Bion?
– Zabelina 1984, 165, fig. 12d.

ATH-26*
Olbia, Sector R25, O-P25-04-2805, Parutine, Olbia National Preserve storeroom. Fr. of upper body. H 1.35 × W 2.3, WT 0.35. Fabric: fine, dense and non-micaceous, 10YR 6/6. Lustrous coat, 5Y 2.5/1. Hard fired. Main decoration: long-bearded mask, wing of small flying Eros. The long-bearded (Dionysos?) mask is typical of the Workshop of Bion (e.g., Rotroff 1982a, 55–56 cats. 99, 101, 105, pl. 75). Workshop of Bion.

ATH-27*
Olbia, Sector NGS, O-НГС-05-148, 319, Parutine, Olbia National Preserve storeroom. Rim fr. and non-joining body fr. Scraped groove with miltos below lip. H 3.5 × W 4.6, WT 0.25, ⌀ rim 15, 10%, RH 1.2. Hard fired. Fabric: fine, non-micaceous, 7.5YR 6/6. Coat with dull lustre, Gley 1 2.5/N. Multiple rim friezes: rosettes alternating with palmette over pairs of horizontal S-spirals; rope pattern. Main decoration: bird with branch or rope in claws left, Eros right facing vegetal element. Frieze separators: dots. The rim frieze is typical of Workshop A (e.g., Rotroff 1982a, 75–76 cat. 252, pls. 50, 98). Workshop A.

ATH-28
Olbia, Sector Sever-Zapad, O-СЗ-68-1329, Parutine, Olbia National Preserve storeroom. Fr. of mid-body. H 3.7 × W 2.6, WT 0.4. Fabric: fine, a few light-reflecting particles, some voids, 10YR 6/4. Thin dull coat ext., glossier int., 10YR 2/1. Relatively hard fired. Main decoration: small Eros flying left.

ATH-29*
Istros, His-B 508 A, Bucharest, Institute of Archaeology storeroom. Fr. of upper body. H 2.5 × W 3. Main decoration: birds flying left. Calyx: pointed imbricate leaves.
– Domăneanțu 2000, 126 cat. 615, pl. 43.

ATH-30
Myrmekion, 1957-D d I 103, Warsaw, National Museum. Fr. of rim and upper body. Thin scraped groove on rim. Rim frieze: horizontal S-spirals; heart guilloche left. Main decoration: heads of two figures flanking column? Frieze separators: dots.
– Bernhard 1959, 43 cat. 171; Sztetyłło 1976, fig. 82.f.

Calyx and Lower Part of Unidentified Figural Decoration

ATH-31*
Istros, His-1927-1942-V 8570 J, Bucharest, Institute of Archaeology storeroom. Fr. of base and lower body. H 3.5 × W 3.7, WT 0.25, ⌀ base 2.5. Fabric: fine, crumbling, 7.5YR 7/6. Dull coat, 10YR 3/1. Not too hard fired. Main decoration: unidentified traces. Calyx: two rows of small ferns. Medallion: frontal Athena Parthenos head within two ridges. Parthenos from a different stamp from that on vessels attributed to the Workshop of Bion (see **ATH-19***). Possibly Atticizing rather than Attic.
– Domăneanțu 2000, 125 cat. 608, pl. 43.

ATH-32*
Olbia, Sector E6, square 428, O-E6-57-992, Kiev, Institute of Archaeology storeroom. Fr. of body and tiny part of base. Scraped groove with miltos around medallion. Calyx: small imbricate ferns.

B *Vegetal Decoration*

Pine Cone

Only a single fragment with plastic pine-cone design has been identified.

ATH-33*
Olbia, Antikensammlung, Staatliche Museen zu Berlin (formerly Becker collection), V.I. 7754.71. Fr. of lower body and base. Two mouldmade satyr masks (a third is missing) function as feet. H 11 × W 6.5, WT 0.6. Fabric: fine, non-micaceous, 7.5YR 7/6. Coat with dull lustre, 10YR 2/1. Main decoration: somewhat tired plastic pine cone. Identical: Rotroff 1982a, 45 cat. 1, pl. 1; https://agora.ascsa.net/id/agora/image/2000.02.0022; according to Rotroff, ca. 225–200.

Calyx of Vine Alternating with Slender Petals

ATH-34*
Olbia, Sector NGS, O-НГС-08-154, Parutine, Olbia National Preserve storeroom. Body fr. H 5.6 × W 4.4, WT 0.26. Fabric: fine, non-micaceous, 10YR 7/6. Coat with dull lustre, ext. 10YR 2/1 int. 10YR 2/1. Hard fired. Main decoration: slender petals alternating with vertical vine with looped tendrils and bunches of grapes. Identical(?): Schwabacher 1941, pl. VIII.B.11; very close: Rotroff 1982a, 51 cat. 61, pls. 10, 74 (figure on pl. 74 is wrongly labelled as cat. 72). Workshop of Bion?

ATH-35*
Olbia, Sector NGS, O-НГС-01-130, Parutine, Olbia National Preserve storeroom. Fr. of lower body, worn. H 3.5 × W 4 0.6. Fabric: fine, some light-reflecting particles, 7.5YR 7/4. Thin splintering semi-lustrous coat, 5Y 2.5/1. Medium hard fired. Calyx: slender petals alternating with vertical vine with looped tendrils and bunches of grapes. Comparanda as **ATH-34***. Workshop of Bion?

ATH-36
Olbia, O-70-2761, present whereabouts unknown. Fr. of rim and body. Scraped groove below lip. Main decoration: tall pointed petal and vertical floral stem.
– St Petersburg, IIMK RAN, photo archive neg. I 73750.

ATH-37*
Olbia, Sector R25, O-P25-96-1301, Parutine, Olbia National Preserve storeroom. Fr. of rim and upper body. Scraped groove with miltos below lip. H 4.8 × W 4.8, WT 0.38, ⌀ rim 15, 8%. Fabric: fine, non-micaceous, 7.5YR 7/6. Lustrous coat ext., duller int., 10YR 3/1. Hard fired. Multiple rim friezes: pairs of horizontal S-spirals with palmettes above; heart guilloche left. Main decoration: pointed leaf, vine(?) leaf at left; rosette(?) at right. Rim frieze typical of Workshop of Bion (e.g., Rotroff 1982a, 55–56 cats. 99, 101, 103, 105 et al., pls. 17, 18, 75, 98; 225–175 BCE). Workshop of Bion.

Calyx of slender Branches Alternating with Slender Petals and Vertical Scrolls

ATH-38*
Olbia, O-47(?)-5270, Kiev, Institute of Archaeology storeroom. Fr. of base and lower body. H 9.1 × W 6.5, WT 0.32, ⌀ base 1.8. Fabric: fine, some minute light-reflecting particles, 7.5YR 7/6. Slightly lustrous coat, 7.5YR 2.5/1. Relatively hard fired. Calyx: slender lotus petals alternating with vertical acanthus scroll and very slender acanthus leaves; small ferns around medallion. Medallion: small rosette with eight rounded petals surrounded by frieze of dots. Identical: Rotroff 1982a, 50 cat. 49, pls. 8, 73, not attributed; ca. 225–200.

Calyx of Acanthus Leaf Alternating with Palmette

ATH-39*
Olbia, Sector NGS, House III-3 B 368/107, O-НГС-93-1100, Parutine, Olbia National Preserve storeroom. Fr. of base and lower body. H 4.6 × W 4.4, WT 0.32–0.38, ⌀ base 1. Fabric: fine, a few light-reflecting particles, 10YR 5/4. Thin firm coat with bluish metallic sheen, 10YR 2/1. Medium hard fired. Main decoration: alternating acanthus leaves and palm fronds both with jewelled central vein. Medallion: small rosette with concave petals. Cf. Edwards 1956, 93 cat. 5, pl. 35.
– Guldager Bilde 2010, 275 cat. F-3, pl. 168.

Calyx of 'Nelumbo' With Internal Scales Alternating with Palmette and Wavy Incised Tendril

The occurrence of 'nelumbo' with internal scales demonstrates inspiration from contemporary metalware (see pp. 28–29). The ascription to Attica is tentative, however, since the 'nelumbo' is not otherwise documented among Athenian products.

ATH-40*
Olbia, Sector E2, square 55, Cistern Л, O-E2-49-199, Kiev, Institute of Archaeology storeroom. Body fr. H 5.1 × W 4.9, WT 0.4. Fabric: fine, no visible inclusions, 7.5YR 6/4. Coat with slight metallic lustre, worn, 7.5YR 2.5/1. Medium hard fired. Calyx: 'nelumbo' filled with scales, wavy stem, tall palmette.

ATH-41*
Istros, His-1014, Bucharest, Institute of Archaeology storeroom. Fr. of lower body. H 1.8 × W 3, WT 0.4. Fabric: relatively fine, no visible inclusions, some small voids, 7.5YR 7/6. Slightly lustrous coat, 10YR 3/1. Relatively hard fired. Calyx: tall 'nelumbo' with central vein and filled with scales; incised wavy stem.

Calyx of Acanthus Alternating with Palmette and Wavy Incised Tendril

ATH-42*
Olbia, Cliff "B-VIII", square 285, O-70-383+386, Parutine, Olbia National Preserve storeroom. Two joining frs. of mid- and lower body. H 7 × W 5, WT 0.36. Fabric: fine, slightly micaceous, sparse small lime particles, 2.5YR 6/8. Coat with dull lustre, 7.5YR 2.5/1. Relatively hard fired. Rim frieze: heart guilloche? Calyx: tall straight naturalistic acanthus leaf alternating with wavy stem and palmette.

ATH-43*
Istros, His-667, Bucharest, Institute of Archaeology storeroom. Fr. of lower body. H 2.8 × W 3.3, WT 0.28. Fabric: relatively fine, no visible inclusions, 5YR 6/8. Dull coat, 10YR 3/1. Relatively hard fired. Calyx: palmette; ivy leaf on stem.

Calyx of Lotus Petal Alternating with Wavy Incised Tendril

ATH-44*
Istros, His-B 435/V 8577 A-E, Bucharest, Institute of Archaeology storeroom. Five joining frs. of rim and body. H 7.5 × W 9.5, WT 0.4, ⌀ rim 14, 19%, RH 1.1. Fabric: fine, no visible inclusions, 7.5YR 7/6. Dull coat ext., int. with slight lustre, ext. 2.5Y 3/1, int. 2.5YR 4/6. Relatively hard fired. Multiple rim friezes: dolphins left; astragal. Calyx: tall, pointed lotus petals separated by thin

incised scroll work. Frieze separators: dots. The astragal does not occur in Rotroff 1982a as an element of the Athenian bowls, and the absence of a scraped groove below the lip is highly unusual; however, I feel confident that this is an Athenian vessel (fabric, shape).
– Domăneanțu 2000, 126 cat. 617, pl. 43.

Lower Part of Vessel Featuring Calyx of Imbricate Petals

ATH-45
Olbia(?), inv. 54791 [a], Moscow, State Historical Museum (Uvarov collection). Body fr. Calyx: pointed lotus petal and vertical, incised scroll.
– Uvarov 1851, pl. XIX.13.

ATH-46*
Olbia, Sector E6, square 475n, 476n, 477ne, O-E6-59-1122, Kiev, Institute of Archaeology storeroom. Four joining frs. of body with tiny part of base. H 4.3 × W 4.8, WT 0.5. Fabric: fine, no visible inclusions, 7.5YR 7/8. Coat with metallic lustre ext., dull int., Gley 1 3/N. Relatively hard fired. Calyx: low calyx of pointed imbricate ferns, from which grow rhomboidal petals with volutes. On body, slender lotus petals. One repair hole.

ATH-47
Pantikapaion, M-62-253, Moscow, Puškin Museum of Fine Arts. Fr. of base and lower body. Scraped groove around medallion. Calyx: small imbricate ferns. Medallion: double rosette. Rosette typical of Workshop A (Rotroff 1982a, pl. 98). Workshop A.
– Zabelina 1984, 165, fig. 12e.

ATH-48*
Istros, His-708, Bucharest, Institute of Archaeology storeroom. Fr. of base and lower body. H 4.3 × W 4.8, WT 0.4, ⌀ base 4. Fabric: fine, no visible inclusions, 5YR 7/8. Very worn shiny coat, ext. 10YR 2/1. Not too hard fired. Calyx: concentric, rhomboidal petals and small pointed petals with central and side veins. Medallion: small rosette with rounded petals surrounded by tiny leaves and small palmettes, and by ridge and beading with scraped groove between them. For medallion, cf. Rotroff 1982a, 70 cat. 212, pl. 82. Workshop of Bion.
– Domăneanțu 2000, 125 cat. 609, pl. 43.

ATH-49*
Olbia, Sector NGS, O-НГС-04-246, III-2 P 731/184, Parutine, Olbia National Preserve storeroom. Fr. of base and lower body. H 4 × W 3, WT 0.5, ⌀ base 5. Fabric: fine, non-micaceous, 7.5YR 6/6. Glossy coat, 7.5YR 2.5/1. Hard fired. Calyx: imbricate small ferns. Medallion: rosette surrounded by small ferns and by two ridges with miltosed groove between them. One repair hole.

ATH-50*
Olbia, Sector E6-7, square 580, Room 7, O-E6-7-63-407, Kiev, Institute of Archaeology storeroom. Body fr. Calyx: imbricate pointed ferns with central and side veins. Cf. Rotroff 1982a, 47 cat. 25, pl. 5; 55–56 cat. 99, pl. 17. Workshop of Bion.

C   Rim Fragments

ATH-51*
Olbia, Sector NGS, House III-3 B 368/106, O-НГС-93-914, Parutine, Olbia National Preserve storeroom. Fr. of rim and upper body; very worn. Thin groove below lip. H 4.25 × W 5.8, WT 0.31–0.33, ⌀ rim 14, 13%, RH 0.6. Fabric: fine, no visible inclusions, some larger and smaller voids, 7.5YR 6/6. Thin firm coat with slight bluish metallic sheen, 2.5Y 2/0. Hard fired. Multiple rim friezes: pairs of horizontal S-spirals with palmettes above; heart guilloche left; horizontal S-spirals. Main decoration: remains of small rosettes. Rim frieze typical of Workshop of Bion (e.g., Rotroff 1982a, cats. 99, 101, 103, 105 et al., pls. 18, 98, but usually with beading and without lowest frieze of horizontal S-spirals, which is uncommon; 225–175). Workshop of Bion?
– Guldager Bilde 2010, 275 cat. F-1, pl. 168.

ATH-52*
Olbia, Sector NR, square 2–3, inv. A 3597 (1930) Nikolaev, Historical Museum. Rim fr. Scraped groove below lip. H 4.1 × W 4, WT 0.4, ⌀? Dull black coat. Multiple rim friezes: pairs of horizontal S-spirals with small triangular leaf above; heart guilloche left; pairs of double spirals. For comparanda, see **ATH-51***. Workshop of Bion?

ATH-53*
Istros, His-B 459/V 19476, Bucharest, Institute of Archaeology storeroom. Rim fr. Scraped groove below lip. H 3.3 × W 3.3, WT 0.3. Fabric: fine, no visible inclusions, 7.5YR 7/6. Coat with dull lustre, 10YR 2/1. Hard fired. Multiple rim friezes: pairs of horizontal S-spirals with palmette above; heart guilloche left. For comparanda, see **ATH-51***. Workshop of Bion.
– Domăneanțu 2000, 125 cat. 611, pl. 43.

ATH-54*
Istros, His-807, Bucharest, Institute of Archaeology storeroom. Rim fr. Scraped groove below lip. H 3.2 × W 4, WT 0.2. Fabric: fine, no visible inclusions, 7.5YR 7/6. Very worn shiny coat, 10YR 2/1. Relatively hard fired. Multiple rim friezes: pairs of horizontal S-spirals; heart guilloche left. For comparanda, see **ATH-51***. Workshop of Bion.
– Domăneanțu 2000, 125 cat. 612, pl. 43.

ATH-55*
Pantikapaion, M-57-1034, Moscow, Puškin Museum of Fine Arts. Rim fr. Scraped groove with miltos below lip. H 3.5 × W 4.5. Multiple rim friezes: pairs of horizontal S-spirals with palmettes above; heart guilloche left. For comparanda, see ATH-51*. Workshop of Bion.
– Zabelina 1984, 165, fig. 12a.

ATH-56
Istros, His-1174, Bucharest, Institute of Archaeology storeroom. Rim fr. Scraped groove below lip. H 3.6 × W 3.6, WT 0.3, Fabric: relatively fine, no visible inclusions, 7.5YR 7/6. Coat with dull lustre, 10YR 3/1. Hard fired. Multiple rim friezes: pairs of horizontal S-spirals with palmettes above; heart guilloche left. Main decoration: rosette. Frieze separators: dots. For comparanda, see ATH-51*. Workshop of Bion.
– Domăneanțu 2000, 125 cat. 610, pl. 43.

ATH-57*
Istros, His-V 8574 F, Bucharest, Institute of Archaeology storeroom. Fr. of upper body close to rim. Multiple rim friezes: pairs of horizontal S-spirals with palmette above; heart guilloche left. For comparanda, see ATH-51*. Workshop of Bion.
– Domăneanțu 2000, 126 cat. 613, pl. 43.

ATH-58*
Olbia, Sector R25, O-P25-99-831, Parutine, Olbia National Preserve storeroom. Fr. of upper body. H 2.6 × W 4.5, WT 0.4. Fabric: very fine, 7.5YR 7/6. Slightly lustrous coat, Gley 1 2.5/N. Hard fired. Multiple rim friezes: pairs of horizontal S-spirals with palmette above; heart guilloche left. Frieze separators: dots. For comparanda, see ATH-51*. Workshop of Bion.

ATH-59
Olbia, Sector NGS, O-НГС-87-61, Parutine, Olbia National Preserve storeroom. Rim fr., rather worn. Scraped groove with traces of miltos below lip. H 3.5 × W 7.1, WT 0.3, ⌀ rim 15, 15%, RH 2.75. Fabric: fine, no visible inclusions, 7.5YR 6/6. Thin firm semi-lustrous coat, 7.5YR 2/0. Hard fired. Multiple rim friezes: small vertical leaves with incised side veins over two low ridges; horizontal diamonds filled with small dots, with vertical leaves where their points meet. The dotted diamond is used by the Workshop of Bion (e.g., Rotroff 1982a, 56 cat. 101, pl. 17, 225–175). Workshop of Bion.

ATH-60*
Olbia, Sector JuzA, O-ЮзА-74-25, Parutine, Olbia National Preserve storeroom. Rim fr. Scraped groove with miltos below lip. H 4.3 × W 5.1, WT 0.2, ⌀ rim 12, 14%, RH 1.6. Fabric: fine, compact, no visible inclusions, 7.5YR 6/6. Coat with dull lustre, 7.5YR 2.5/1. Hard fired. Rim frieze: horizontal S-spirals with palmette above. Very worn mould. Three repair holes. Workshop of Bion?

ATH-61*
Olbia, Sector NGS, O-НГС-05-189, Parutine, Olbia National Preserve storeroom. Rim fr. Scraped groove with miltos below lip and below rim frieze. H 3.1 × W 3.3, WT 0.28, ⌀?, RH 1.1. Fabric: fine, non-micaceous, 7.5YR 6/6. Coat with dull lustre, 7.5YR 2.5/1. Hard fired. Rim friezes: palmette and heraldic dolphins over pairs of horizontal S-spirals. Rim pattern typical of Workshop A (e.g., Rotroff 1982a, 68, 75 cats. 194, 247, pls. 37, 49, 98). Workshop A.

ATH-62
Olbia, Sector NGS, O-НГС-96-45a, Parutine, Olbia National Preserve storeroom. Rim fr. Scraped groove below lip. H 3.6 × W 4.4, WT 0.25–0.28, ⌀ rim 14, 10%, RH 1.3. Fabric: fine, few voids, 7.5YR 6/6. Thin firm semi-lustrous coat, 7.5YR 2/0. Hard fired. Multiple rim friezes: pairs of horizontal S-spirals with minute heraldic dolphins above; Ionian kyma. For comparanda, see ATH-61*. Workshop A.

ATH-63
Istros, His-1927-1942-V 8577 K, Bucharest, Institute of Archaeology storeroom. Rim fr. Scraped groove below lip. H 2.8 × W 4.3, WT 0.3. Fabric: fine, with some light-reflecting particles, 5YR 6/8. Very worn coat with slight lustre, 10YR 3/1. Relatively hard fired. Multiple rim friezes: pairs of horizontal S-spirals with palmette above; heart guilloche right. For comparanda, see ATH-51*. Workshop of Bion (Rotroff 1982a, pl. 98).
– Domăneanțu 2000, 126 cat. 614, pl. 43.

ATH-64*
Olbia, Sector E6, square 425, ash pit in Room, O-E6-57-1262, Kiev, Institute of Archaeology storeroom. Rim fr. Scraped groove with miltos below lip. H 4.8 × W 6.2, WT 0.33, ⌀ rim 18, 8%, RH 2.5. Fabric: fine, no visible inclusions, 7.5YR 7/6. Coat with dull lustre, 7.5YR 2.5/1. Relatively hard fired. Multiple rim friezes: pairs of horizontal S-spirals with palmette above; heart guilloche right. The rim frieze is typical of Workshop A. Workshop A.

ATH-65*
Olbia, Sector R25, O-P25-92-534, Parutine, Olbia National Preserve storeroom. Rim fr. Scraped groove with miltos below lip. H 3.2 × W 4.9, WT 0.28, ⌀ rim 15, 10%. Fabric: very fine, 7.5YR 7/6. Slightly lustrous coat, ext. 2.5YR 2.5/1, int. 5Y 2.5/1. Hard fired. Multiple rim friezes: pairs of horizontal S-spirals with palmette above; Ionian kyma. Frieze separators: dots. For palmette, cf. Rotroff 1982a, 49 cat. 43, pl. 7; for Ionian kyma, with small vertical lines at top, cf. 67 cat. 191, pl. 35. Workshop of Bion.

ATH-66
Olbia, Sector NGS, House III-2 R 164/76, O-НГС-88-293, Parutine, Olbia National Preserve storeroom. Rim fr. Groove below lip. H 2.4 × W 3, WT 0.3, ⌀ rim 14, 6%. Fabric: fine, no inclusions, 5YR 6/4. Lustrous coat, 5Y 2.5/1. Medium hard fired. Rim frieze: pairs of horizontal S-spirals with palmettes above. Palmettes as Rotroff 1982a, 49 cat. 43, pl. 7. Workshop of Bion.
– Guldager Bilde 2010, 275 cat. F-2, pl. 168.

ATH-67*
Olbia, Sector NGS, O-НГС-05-188, Parutine, Olbia National Preserve storeroom. Fr. of rim and upper body. Scraped groove below lip. H 4.3 × W 5.3, WT 0.2, ⌀ rim 13, 12%, RH 1.2. Fabric: fine, non-micaceous, 7.5YR 7/6. Shiny coat, 5Y 2.5/1. Medium hard fired. Multiple rim friezes: six-petalled rosettes; another type of six-petalled rosette. Main decoration: traces, with six-petalled rosette as space-filler. One repair hole.

ATH-68
Olbia, Sector NGS, O-НГС-87-201a, Parutine, Olbia National Preserve storeroom. Fr. of upper body. Scraped groove with miltos below lip. H 4.3 × W 5.85, WT 0.3–0.35, ⌀ rim 15, 13%, RH 1.45. Fabric: fine, few voids, 7.5YR 6/6. Thin firm semi-lustrous coat, 7.5YR 2/0. Hard fired. Multiple rim friezes: Ionian kyma, upside down; heart guilloche left. Main decoration: unidentified traces.

ATH-69*
Olbia, Sector R25, O-P25-00-1108, Parutine, Olbia National Preserve storeroom. Body fr. close to rim. H 5.8 × W 4.9, WT 0.32–0.36. Fabric: very fine, 7.5YR 7/6. Slightly lustrous coat, 7.5YR 2.5/1. Hard fired. Multiple rim friezes: pairs of horizontal S-spirals with rhomboidal element above; Lesbian kyma. The Lesbian kyma is rare on Athenian bowls, but identification of this fragment as Athenian is certain from fabric and coat.

ATH-70*
Olbia, Sector R25, O-P25-96-643, Parutine, Olbia National Preserve storeroom. Fr. of upper body. H 3.2 × W 3.5, WT 0.35. Fabric: fine, non-micaceous, 7.5YR 6/4. Slightly lustrous coat, 7.5YR 2.5/1. Hard fired. Rim frieze: heart guilloche right. Main decoration: imbricate with rounded petals and veined leaves. Ascription to Athens is tentative.

ATH-71
Pantikapaion, Cistern N 179, 96-no.(?), Kerč Archaeological Museum. Fr. of body close to rim. Rim frieze: grooves; palmettes(?) over pairs of horizontal S-spirals.
– Tolstikov & Zhuravlev 2004, pl. 101.12.

SUPPLEMENTARY SHAPES

Small Bowl

Figural Decoration

ATH-72*
Olbia, O-63-106, 106[A], Kiev, Institute of Archaeology storeroom. Two non-joining frs. of base and lower body. H 4.6 × W 4.6, WT 0.25. Fabric: relatively fine, slightly sandy, no visible inclusions, 7.5YR 7/6. Coat with slight metallic lustre, Gley 1 2.5/N. Relatively hard fired. Rim frieze: broad convex band between ridges. Main decoration: small flying Eros, boukranion, Eros walking right, flying birds. Calyx: small imbricate triangular fronds with miniature rosettes above as space-filler.

Calyx

ATH-73
Olbia, inv.(?), Frankfurt am Main, Kunst und Gewerbemuseum (formerly Vogell collection). Complete. Groove with miltos below lip. ⌀ rim 9.1, vessel H 4.6; H:⌀ 1:2. Rim frieze: chevron(?) left. Main decoration: tall, slender lotus petals alternating with vertical floral stems. Calyx: imbricate ferns surrounded by two ridges. Medallion: frontal Athena Parthenos head. For comparanda to Parthenos, see **ATH-19***. Workshop of Bion.
– Zahn 1908, 49 cat. 3; Boehlau 1908, 29 no. 264.

Juglet

Imbricate

Double rim frieze (Ionian kyma and astragal) as well as single rim frieze patterns (astragal) occur. Identification tentative since the astragal is not attested on Athenian bowls.

ATH-74*
Olbia, Sector Sever-Zapad, O-C3-77-43, Parutine, Olbia National Preserve storeroom. Fr. of shoulder and mid-body. H 4.3 × W 3.2, WT 0.47. Fabric: fine, non-micaceous, 2.5YR 6/8. Thin coat with slight metallic sheen ext., 5YR 2.5/1; uncoated int. Relatively hard fired. Multiple rim friezes: Ionian kyma; astragal. Calyx: imbricate ferns.

ATH-75*
Olbia, Sector E6, square 432w, foundation of Room "O", O-E6-59-2080, Kiev, Institute of Archaeology storeroom. Fr. of body with part of shoulder; almost half vessel. H 4.5 × W 6.5, WT 0.25,

ATHENS

maximum ⌀ 7.2. Fabric: fine, finely micaceous, 5YR 6/6. Coat with metallic sheen ext. Gley 1 3/N; uncoated int. Medium hard fired. Rim frieze: astragal. Main decoration: imbricate pointed petals with central and side veins.

ATH-76*
Olbia, Sector NGS, O-НГС-02-352, Parutine, Olbia National Preserve storeroom. Fr. of base and body; very worn. H 4.3 × W 5.1, WT 0.29–0.45, ⌀ base 2. Fabric: fine, slightly micaceous, a few minute lime particles, 5YR 6/6. Thin coat with slight lustre, ext., 10YR 3/1, uncoated int. Medium hard fired. Multiple rim friezes: Ionian kyma; astragal. Calyx: imbricate small pointed petals with slight indication of central and side veins.

DISTRIBUTION

Chersonesos

ATH-12*, ATH-13

Istros

ATH-29*, ATH-31*, ATH-41*, ATH-43*, ATH-44*, ATH-48*, ATH-53*, ATH-54*, ATH-56, ATH-57*, ATH-63

Myrmekion

ATH-30

Olbia

ATH-1, ATH-2, ATH-4*, ATH-5*, ATH-8*, ATH-9*, ATH-11*, ATH-14*–ATH-18*, ATH-20*–ATH-23*, ATH-26*–ATH-28, ATH-32*–ATH-40*, ATH-42*, ATH-45(?), ATH-46*, ATH-49*–ATH-52*, ATH-58*–ATH-62, ATH-64*–ATH-70*, ATH-72*–ATH-76*

Pantikapaion

ATH-3*, ATH-6, ATH-10*, ATH-19*, ATH-24, ATH-25, ATH-47, ATH-55*, ATH-71

Porthmion

ATH-7

CHAPTER 8

Aiolis: Introduction

Aiolis was a region in northwestern Asia Minor, mostly along the coast, but also including several offshore islands, of which the most important was Lesbos (Fig. 58). Its borders were ill-defined, and the cities and towns included changed through time. At the period of its maximum expansion, it extended north to the southern parts of Troas and Mysia (encompassing cities such as Assos, Ilion, and even Pergamon), and it bounded Ionia to the south, including Smyrna, and parts of Lydia to the east (Rubinstein 2004, 1033–1036). In this and the following five chapters, we shall discuss a number of individual production sites and proposed production sites within this general area. It will become clear that the MMB produced in this region share a number of distinctive iconographic elements, revealing that they are part of a cultural koine.

Places of Production

The production of MMB in this area is not well known. To my knowledge, moulds have been unearthed only at Pergamon (Chapter 9) and at Kyme (Chapter 10). The remaining Aiolian productions discussed in this book have been attributed to this region on the basis of their physical and morphological properties as well as their iconography, and, as we shall see in the following chapters, this attribution has recently been confirmed by archaeometric analyses.

In addition, one should not fail to mention the important group of 114 moulds and mould fragments which was acquired at the end of the 1970s by a number of German collections and published by S. Künzl in 2002. The moulds were purchased on the art market and were furnished with various provenances by their sellers. Most had the generic provenance 'Asia Minor' or 'Western Asia Minor' (75 moulds in the Rheinisch-Germanisches Zentralmuseum, Mainz), but more specific sites were also mentioned, such as 'Ankara' (31 moulds acquired by the Archäologischen Staatssammlung in Munich), 'between Burdur and Gölhisar' (one further mould in Mainz), 'Knidos' and 'Pergamon' (two moulds in Frankfurt). Künzl has analysed all of these moulds and her convincing conclusion is that they derive from a single workshop, which she has dubbed the 'Mainzer Workshop'. Künzl's description of their fabric corresponds well with that of Pergamon and the Kaikos Valley workshops, being very fine and only in rare instances including light-reflecting particles (Künzl 2002, 3). In terms of their iconography, the moulds clearly belong to the Aiolian koine; thus far, however, not a single piece of a vessel produced in one of these moulds has been identified, so it is likely that the workshop was located in the interior of the region, off the main trade routes along the coast. It nevertheless fully demonstrates the strong identity of the regional style.

Fabrics

The geology of Aiolis varies significantly, as do the fabrics of the different production places. The fabrics of Aiolis A and B are non-micaceous, whereas the Pergamene fabrics contain some fine mica, though never in abundance. The fabric of the Kymean workshops, on the other hand, is quite micaceous.

Shape

The area shares the same bowl shape, a heavy, deep, hemispherical bowl with a high, slightly S-curved rim and a plain, slightly everted lip. This shape was employed chiefly by the early Pergamene workshops (profile drawings in Conze et al. 1913, Beibl. 40–43) and the workshops of Kyme. Development in the second half of the 2nd century can best be followed in the Aiolis A and B workshops, where the rim gradually obtains a stronger S-curve. The same development can be seen in contemporary Pergamene sigillata and *Applikenkeramik* (e.g., Hübner 1993a, forms 6, 7, and 10, figs. 10, 14).

Iconography

As already mentioned, there seems to have been a strong cultural koine in Aiolis, and a number of characteristic iconographic elements were developed here. Amongst the most important are garlands suspended from columns, altars, and/or boukrania/boukephalia and often tied with a bow, suspended wreaths, mantled dancing women, theatre masks, and symplegma scenes. These are all discussed in Chapter 6 and arguments shall not be repeated here. Amongst the Aiolian workshops, the use of

© PIA GULDAGER BILDE AND SUSAN I. ROTROFF, 2024 | DOI:10.1163/9789004680463_009

AIOLIS: INTRODUCTION 147

FIGURE 58   Detail of map of Western Asia Minor, showing the location of Aiolis (Aeolia) along the sea route to the Black Sea.
https://commons.wikimedia.org/w/index.php?curid=58363914

an architectural moulding as frieze divider is much commoner than elsewhere (see Fig. 59 below). Even small iconographic details, such as the bird (a duck?) turning its head back, can be found in a number of Aiolian productions, such as Pergamon (Conze et al. 1913, Beibl. 43.5), Kyme (Bouzek & Jansová 1974, 51 cat. MB 7, pl. 2; 57 cats. MB 37, 39, 41, pl. 6), and Aiolis B, and because the source of inspiration was the last-mentioned, it even features in the earliest decoration of Pontic Demetrios (see Chapter 18). It is likely that the MMB produced in the royal capital of Pergamon served as the main source of inspiration for the Aiolian workshops.

Distribution

If we consider the distribution of Aiolian MMB, we may note that they have been very sparingly identified outside the region of production. On Delos, for example, perhaps eight of the ca. 6,500 vessels found there are of Pergamene production[1] and more or less the same number can be identified as Kymean MMW (Fig. 4).[2] Nor have vessels of these productions been identified further south in Asia Minor, e.g., at Ephesos, Miletos, or Knidos, although Aiolian (or Pergamene) MMB served as a source of inspiration for the inland production at Sardis (Rotroff 2003, 94).

The pattern described above is in stark contrast to the picture we find in the Pontic region. Overall, more than 17% of all the MMB found at the sites analysed in this book were manufactured in Aiolian workshops. We shall discuss the distribution pattern in more detail in the chapters on the individual workshops. Here it suffices to say that the geographical location of this region along the main north-bound sailing route in all likelihood can explain why its products are found much more frequently in the Black Sea region than elsewhere.

The catalogue incorporated in the present chapter includes fragments which are evidently of Aiolian production but derive from a number of different sources, as demonstrated by differences in fabric and surface treatment.

---

1 Laumonier vol. 2, cats. 273, 309, 2812, 3434, 4113, 6032, 8458, 9168.

2 Courby 1922, 395, pl. XVj; Laumonier vol. 2, cats. 1372, 2206, 3281, 9546, one without no.; Bouzek 1990, 66 cat. 20.

CATALOGUE TO CHAPTER 8

BOWLS

A *Figural Decoration*

Eros

A1X-1*
Olbia, Sector NGCentre, Basement 1, grey clay layer, О-НГЦ-68-2328, Kiev, Institute of Archaeology storeroom. Fr. of rim and upper body. H 5.5 × W 7, WT 0.32, ⌀ rim 13, 17%, RH 2.3. Fabric: fine, non-micaceous, 2.5YR 6/4. Mottled coat with dull lustre, ext. 2.5YR 3/3, 7.5YR 3/1, 6/6, int. 2.5YR 4/8, 4/2. Relatively hard fired, oxidized. Stacked in firing. Rim frieze: Ionian kyma. Main decoration: frontal phlyax Eros with thick belly and drapery around lower part of body.

Altar Scenes

A1X-2*
Olbia, Sector NGS, House III-3 B 368/104, О-НГС-93-210, 211, 267, 268, 680, 684, Parutine, Olbia National Preserve storeroom. Almost complete profile; two rim frs., one base fr., and three body frs., two frs. joining; H 5.6 × W 8.3, WT 0.33–0.45; ⌀ rim 17, 23%, RH 2. Fabric: fine, micaceous, fine lime particles, a few small voids, 5Y 4/1. Thin firm coat 5Y 3/1. Medium hard fired, reduced. Rim frieze: Ionian kyma. Main decoration: altar figs. D, C1; A1; non-joining fr. with standing draped female; altar fig. C1; non-joining fr. C1, D. Calyx: ovoid petal, slender palm frond, broad palm frond; small busts(?) as space-filler. Medallion: rosette with spiky petals and hatched central vein. Frieze separators: frieze with large rosette with six rounded petals. Same workshop and shape as **A1X-11***, **A1X-12***, **A1X-20***, **A1X-30**.
– Guldager Bilde 2010, 283 cat. F-79, pl. 183 (erroneously identified as Ephesian).

Amazons

A1X-3*
Olbia, Sector E7, square 558w, yellow clay layer, O-E7-59-1151, Kiev, Institute of Archaeology storeroom. Body fr. H 3.7 × W 8, WT 0.3. Fabric: fine, compact, no visible inclusions, 5Y 5/1. Dull coat, ext. 10YR 3/1, int. 10YR 3/2. Hard fired, reduced. Rim frieze: Ionian kyma. Main decoration: mounted Amazons riding right with lifted right arm holding a spear.

Battle?

A1X-4*
Myrmekion, M-58-626, St Petersburg, IIMK RAN. Fr. of rim and large part of wall. H 6.2, WT 0.35, ⌀ rim 11, RH 2.3. Fabric: fine, soft, some light-reflecting particles, 5Y 5/1, 4/1 Thin black slightly lustrous coat, preserved only at rim, 5Y 3/1. Reduced. Rim friezes: grooves; horizontal S-spirals. Main decoration: male figure (with shield?) turned left; vine(?) leaves used as spacer. Calyx: faint traces of at least one tall petal.

Suspended Wreath

A1X-5
Pantikapaion, Kerč History and Culture Reserve inv. KMAK 10122. Fr. of base and lower body. Oxidized. Main decoration: suspended wreath with bow, large T-shaped element. Medallion: unidentified, surrounded by two ridges; remains of signature A.
– Grzegrzółka 2010, 78–79 cat. 70 (identified as Pergamene).

Animals

A1X-6*
Olbia, Sector E7, square 578n, 579nw, yellow clay layer, O-E7-59-1663, Kiev, Institute of Archaeology storeroom. Body fr. H 3 × W 3.7, WT 0.45. Fabric: fine, soft, non-micaceous, some minute light-reflecting particles, 10YR 6/2. Dull coat, flaking and almost completely worn off, ext. 7.5YR 3/4, int. 7.5YR 2.5/1. Relatively hard fired, reduced. Main decoration: minute birds alternating with dolphin right. Frieze separators: astragal. The miniature style points to a Pergamene origin, but the clay is much softer than the Pergamene clay.

B *Scroll Decoration*

Ivy Scroll

A1X-7
Tyritake, Kerč History and Culture Reserve inv. KMAK 10404. Fr. of upper body. Oxidized. Main decoration: ivy scroll, right; bird sitting left above scroll.
– Grzegrzółka 2010, 106 cat. 128 (identified as Pergamene).

C Suspended Garlands

AIX-8*
Olbia, Sector NGS, O-НГС-02-254, 255, 255a, 255b, Parutine, Olbia National Preserve storeroom. Two rim and three body frs, non-joining. H 3.5 × W 7.3, WT 0.28–0.35; ⌀ rim 12, 20%, RH 1.6. Fabric: fine, slightly micaceous, a few minute lime particles, 7.5YR 7/6. Thin firm dull coat, 2.5YR 5/6. Hard fired, oxidized. Rim frieze: Ionian kyma, rounded with double outline. Main decoration: suspended garlands hanging from boukephalia and carried by small Erotes turned right; nine-petalled rosettes over garlands, large 'Macedonian' star below boukephalia; long, thin undulating streamers hang from ends of *tainia*. Calyx: tip of acanthus leaf with bent tip is preserved. One repair hole. The bowl is perhaps Pergamene.

AIX-9*
Olbia, Sector NGS, O-НГС-no year-no no., Parutine, Olbia National Preserve storeroom. Joining frs. of rim and upper to mid-body. H 6.1 × W 8.6, WT 0.3, ⌀ rim 12, 14%, RH 3. Fabric: fine, dense, non-micaceous, Gley 1 5/N, 3/N, 10YR 6/2. Firm coat, at rim ext. and entire int. burnished to dull lustre and soapy feel, ext. 10YR 2/1, int. Gley 4/10Y, 3/N. Hard fired, reduced. Rim frieze: grooves. Main decoration: bound garlands suspended from *tainia* tied in bow; female(?) head right over garlands.

D Vegetal Decoration

Plastic Pine-cone Decoration

AIX-10*
Istros, His-Dup723, in the possession of P. Dupont. Body fr., reduced.

Calyx

AIX-11* OLB-495
Olbia, Sector NGS, House III-3 B 368/106, O-НГС-93-916+04-156, 93–913 (join across years), Parutine, Olbia National Preserve storeroom. Frs. of rim and three joining body frs. H 6.8 × W 8.7, WT 0.22–0.45; ⌀ rim 13.5, 25%, RH 1.9. Fabric: fine, micaceous, a few minute lime inclusions, 5Y 6/1. Thin firm slightly lustrous coat, black at lip int. and at rim and upper body ext., ext. 2.5Y 6/2; 3/0, int. 2.5Y 6/2. Medium hard fired, reduced. Stacked in firing. Rim frieze: Ionian kyma. Main decoration: frieze of rosettes with eight rounded petals alternating with palmettes. Calyx: pointed petals. Frieze separators: Ionian kyma. Same workshop and shape as AIX-2*, AIX-12*, AIX-20*, AIX-30.
– Guldager Bilde 2010, 283 cat. F-81, pl. 184 (erroneously identified as Ephesian).

AIX-12*
Olbia, Sector NGS, House III-3 B 368/107, O-НГС-93-1099, 04–153, Parutine, Olbia National Preserve storeroom. Two non-joining frs. of rim and upper body. H 6 × W 6.5, WT 0.4; ⌀ rim 13, 9%, RH 1.6. Fabric: relatively fine, micaceous, some small lime inclusions, 5Y 4/1. Coat with slight lustre, Gley 1 2.5/1. Medium hard fired, reduced. Multiple rim friezes: Ionian kyma; large Lesbian kyma separated by dots. Calyx: lotus petals. Frieze separators: Ionian kyma. Same workshop and shape as AIX-2*, AIX-11*, AIX-20*, AIX-30.
– Guldager Bilde 2010, 284 cat. F-89, pl. 186 (erroneously identified as Ephesian).

AIX-13
Istros, His-889, Bucharest, Institute of Archaeology storeroom. Fr. of lower body. Reduced. Calyx: straight acanthus with double stem, vegetal stem.

AIX-14*
Istros, His-B 615, Bucharest, Institute of Archaeology storeroom. Fr. of base and lower body. H 4 × W 5, WT 0.32, ⌀ base 4.4. Fabric: very fine, soft, non-micaceous, 7.5YR 7/2. Dull coat, very worn int., 2.5Y 3/1. Relatively hard fired, reduced. Calyx: bound palmettes alternating with vertical element. Medallion: rosette with rounded petals separated by tongues.
– Domăneanţu 2000, 100 cat. 493, pl. 32 (identified as Ephesian).

AIX-15*
Istros, His-V 8571 J, Bucharest, Institute of Archaeology storeroom. Fr. of base and lower body. H 4.3 × W 6.2, WT 0.45, ⌀ base 3. Fabric: fine, compact, non-micaceous, Gley 1 7/N. Coat with dull lustre, Gley 1 2.5/N. Relatively hard fired, reduced. Calyx: 'nelumbo'(?) with three ovoid petals in front. Medallion: rosette E surrounded by dots.
– Domăneanţu 2000, 101 cat. 504, pl. 33 (identified as Ephesian).

AIX-16*
Olbia, cliff, grey clay layer over Pavement 9, O-68-245, Kiev, Institute of Archaeology storeroom. Fr. of base and lower body. H 5.1 × W 6.7, WT 0.3, ⌀ base 7. Fabric: fine, compact, some very fine light-reflecting particles, 10YR 4/2 with light orange edges. Fine slightly lustrous coat, 5YR 3/2. Very hard fired, reduced. Calyx: acanthus with hatched central vein alternating with ovoid petals separated by wavy stems. Medallion: missing, two wide grooves around base.

AIX-17*
Olbia, Sector NGS, House III-3 B 368/107, O-НГС-93-1103, Parutine, Olbia National Preserve storeroom. Non-joining frs. of base and body. H 2.95 × W 3.5, WT 0.3–0.35; ⌀ base 4.5. Fabric: fine, micaceous, small lime inclusions, a few small voids, 5Y 4/1. Thin

firm slightly lustrous coat, 5Y 3/1. Hard fired, reduced. Calyx: long pointed(?) lotus sepals with central vein alternating with groups of small pointed lotus leaves with central vein. Medallion: rosette with rounded petals separated by tongues.
– Guldager Bilde 2010, 284 cat. F-82, pl. 184.

Imbricate Pointed Petals

AIX-18*
Istros, His-882+V 19405[a], Bucharest, Institute of Archaeology storeroom. Two joining body frs. close to rim. H 3.4 × W 3.8, WT 0.25. Fabric: relatively fine, some small lime particles, Gley 1 3/N. Coat with slight lustre, burnished on rim int., ext. Gley 1 3/10Y, 2.5/N, int. Gley 1 2.5/N. Medium hard fired, reduced. Rim frieze: ridges. Calyx: imbricate slightly pointed petals with central vein.

AIX-19*
Chersonesos, X-1965-82, St Petersburg, State Hermitage Museum. Rim fr. H 2.9, WT 0.35, RH 1.8. Fabric: fine, dense, non-micaceous, Gley 1 6/10Y. Shiny black coat, Gley 1 2.5/N. Reduced. No rim frieze. Calyx: imbricate pointed petals with central and side veins.

AIX-20*
Olbia, Sector NGS, House III-3 B 368/107, О-НГС-93-1102, Parutine, Olbia National Preserve storeroom. Body fr. H 6.65 × W 6.75, WT 0.22–0.45. Fabric: relatively fine, micaceous, small lime inclusions, some voids, 5Y 5/1. Thin firm coat, ext. bicolour, ext. 5Y 5/1, 4/2, 7.5YR 3/0, int. 2.5Y 4/4. Medium hard fired, reduced. Stacked in firing. Calyx: imbricate pointed petals with central and side veins. Same workshop and shape as AIX-2*, AIX-11*, AIX-12*, AIX-30.
– Guldager Bilde 2010, 284 cat. F-85, pl. 185 (erroneously identified as Ephesian).

Imbricate Palmettes

AIX-21*
Istros, His-256, Bucharest, Institute of Archaeology storeroom. Fr. of base and lower body. H 3.5 × W 5, WT 0.28, ⌀ base 4. Fabric: very fine, soft, non-micaceous, 7.5YR 7/1. Dull coat, very worn int., 2.5Y 3/1. Relatively hard fired, reduced. Calyx: imbricate bound palmettes. Medallion: rosette with rounded petals separated by tongues.
– Domăneanţu 2000, 87 cat. 414, pl. 28 (identified as Ephesian).

E *Linear Decoration*

Net Pattern

AIX-22*
Istros, His-B 560, Bucharest, Institute of Archaeology storeroom. Body fr. H 2.3 × W 3.4, WT 0.33. Fabric: fine, some light-reflecting particles, 5Y 6/1. Dull coat, ext. 5Y 4,1, 3/1, int. Gley 1 2.5/N. Relatively hard fired, reduced. Main decoration: net pattern made of dots; Medusa head inside pentagon. A Medusa head employed as decoration inside a dotted pentagon can also be found on PER-86*.
– Domăneanţu 2000, 16 cat. 62, pl. 4 (identified as Ephesian [Vases gris]).

AIX-23*
Olbia, Sector E6, square 254, grey clay layer, O-E6-56-49, Kiev, Institute of Archaeology storeroom. Fr. of base and lower body. H 6.9 × W 5.3, WT 0.36. Fabric: fine, compact, many minute lime inclusions, a few minute light-reflecting particles, Gley 1 4/N. Thin dull coat, Gley 1 4/N, 3/N. Relatively hard fired, reduced. Main decoration: net pattern made of dots with figural decoration (identification of figures uncertain). Medallion: four lotus petals surrounded by one-row calyx of small pointed petals with central vein.

Plastic Long Petals

AIX-24*
Olbia, Sector M, depression to the west of Room "A", O-M-51-1484, Kiev, Institute of Archaeology storeroom. Fr. of rim and body. H 3.8 × W 5.8, WT 0.32, ⌀ rim 12, 15%, RH 2.2. Fabric: fine, soft, non-micaceous, no visible inclusions, Gley 1 6/N. Thin dull coat, flaking, Gley 1 5/N. Hard fired, reduced. No rim frieze. Main decoration: broad plastic long petals surrounded by frieze of dots alternating with stylized flower (or head?) on stem.

AIX-25*
Myrmekion, M-58-603, St Petersburg, IIMK RAN. Fr. of base and most of body. H 5.2, WT 0.5, ⌀ base 2.5. Fabric: fine, soft, some light-reflecting particles, 5Y 6/1. Thin dull coat, 5Y 3/1. Reduced. Main decoration: plastic long petals. Medallion: faint traces of rosette.

AIX-26
Pantikapaion, M-47-76, Moscow, Puškin Museum of Fine Arts. Almost complete profile, lacking rim. Reduced. Main decoration: slightly plastic long petals. Medallion: rosette with six broad petals.
– Zabelina 1984, 162, fig. 9c (identified as Pergamene); Bouzek 1990, pl. 21.8; Petrova 2014, 222 n. 33.

Stylized Long Petals with Double Outline

AIX-27*
Olbia, Sector R25, O-P25-04-565, Parutine, Olbia National Preserve storeroom. Fr. of base and lower body. H 3.5 × W 5.8, WT 0.3, RH 3. Fabric: fine, dense, non-micaceous, Gley 1 6/10Y. Thin dull coat with soapy feel, Gley 1 5/10Y. Very hard fired, reduced. Main decoration: stylized(?) long petals with double outline separated by dotted line; around base ring, single row of very small straight acanthus leaves. Medallion: rosette A.

AIX-28
Porthmion, Vachtina: pavement outside western defensive wall near wicket; Grzegrzółka: room 50, NE corner, depth 0.55, П-75-402, Kerč History and Culture Reserve inv. KMAK 6085. Fr. of lower body. Reduced. Main decoration: long petals with double outline separated by column of dots.
– Grzegrzółka 2010, 150 cat. 223.

AIX-29
Myrmekion, M-51-44+197, St Petersburg, IIMK RAN. Six frs. of mid- and lower body, four joining and one non-joining, one joining M 51–197. H 4.5, WT 0.4. Fabric: fine, dense, non-micaceous, 5YR 6/6. Thin dense coat with slight lustre, 10R 4/2. Hard fired, oxidized. Main decoration: narrow long petals with double outline separated by column of fine dots.

F *Rim Fragments*

Multiple Rim Friezes

AIX-30
Olbia, Sector NGS, O-НГС-90-255, Parutine, Olbia National Preserve storeroom. Rim fr. H 3.7 × W 3.8, WT 0.4; RH 1.5. Fabric: fine, dense, micaceous, Gley 1 4/10Y. Thin dull coat, Gley 1 2.5/N. Hard fired, reduced. Multiple rim friezes: small Ionian kyma; Lesbian kyma. Same workshop and shape as **AIX-2***, **AIX-11***, **AIX-12***, **AIX-20***.

AIX-31*
Istros, His-1927-1942-V 8572 J, Bucharest, Institute of Archaeology storeroom. Fr. of rim and upper body. H 4.5 × W 4.9, WT 0.35, RH 2.5. Fabric: fine, compact, non-micaceous, many small voids. Thin dull coat. Reduced. Multiple rim friezes: dots; heart ornament. Secondarily burnt.

AIX-32*
Istros, His-750, Bucharest, Institute of Archaeology storeroom. Rim fr. H 3.6 × W 4.6, WT 0.32, ⌀ rim 14, 10%, RH 1.8. Fabric: fine, compact, non-micaceous, no visible inclusions, 7.5YR 7/6. Slightly lustrous coat, ext. 7.5YR 3/1, int. 2.5YR 4/8. Relatively hard fired, reduced. Multiple rim friezes: fleur de lys alternating with rosette; astragal. The fleur de lys in the upper frieze resembles, but is not identical to, the one on **KYA-2*** and **KYA-26***.
– Domăneanțu 2000, 127 cat. 618, pl. 43 (identified as Athenian).

Single Rim Frieze

AIX-33*
Istros, His-198, Bucharest, Institute of Archaeology storeroom. Rim fr. H 3. Oxidized. Rim frieze: very debased rosettes?
– Domăneanțu 2000, 111 cat. 562.

SUPPLEMENTARY SHAPES

Small Bowl

AIX-34*
Pantikapaion, tomb, П-1908-82, St Petersburg, State Hermitage Museum. Complete. ⌀ rim 7.6; vessel H 5; H:⌀ 1:1.5. Reduced. Rim frieze: vine leaves, left. Calyx: lotus petals alternating with straight floral element. Medallion: feline walking left with head turned back.
– St Petersburg, IIMK RAN photo archive neg. III 12089.

Large Closed Vessel

AIX-35*
Myrmekion, M-56-1893, St Petersburg, State Hermitage Museum. Fr. of mid- and lower body. H 8, WT 0.5. Fabric: fine, soft, some light-reflecting particles (no fresh break). Dull black coat, ext. Gley 1 3/N. Reduced. Main decoration: large vine scroll left(?) incised in mould, with vine leaves, bunches of grapes and groups of three dots; lower frieze: large ivy scroll or wreath left with ivy-berry clusters.
– Gajdukevič 1959, 80, fig. 88; Petrova 2014, fig. 15.4 (identified as Mesambrian).

CHAPTER 9

Pergamon

Pergamon is an inland city located around 25 km from the sea. In the Hellenistic period, it flourished as the capital of the Pergamene Kingdom. Prior to this, the city was of no greater regional importance, and its ethnic composition is uncertain (Radt 1999, 25; Rubinstein 2004, 1048). It was chosen as a base by Lysimachos because of its qualities as an easily defendable stronghold. His governor, Philetairos, ruled the city on his behalf until 281. When Lysimachos was killed at Kouroupedion by Seleukos I Nikator, who had invaded Asia Minor, Philetairos and his successor, Eumenes I, took advantage of the power vacuum and established a small kingdom, which was consolidated when Attalos I took the title of king in 241. The acme of the kingdom was in the first half of the 2nd century, when Eumenes II, in alliance with the Romans, defeated the Seleucid army in the battle of Magnesia in 190. By the terms of the subsequent peace treaty of Apameia in 188, Pergamon received a large part of the territory earlier ruled by the Seleucids. Thus, Pergamon rose from a petty kingdom to a small empire which ruled a large part of Asia Minor (Radt 1999, fig. 6). In 133, King Attalos III bequeathed the kingdom to Rome.

One production site for MMB has been discovered in Pergamon itself, immediately southeast of Philetairos' city wall and northeast of the Gymnasium,[1] and another in the Ketios valley immediately east of the city (Özyiğit 1990, 95–96). The latter is of special importance. Between 1977 and 1980, and again in 1985–1988, the Turkish antiquities authority under the direction of S. Erdemgil carried out salvage excavations in the valley, which was destined to be inundated as a consequence of the construction of a dam. A number of pottery installations and kilns came to light during these excavations, but, regrettably, they have been only summarily published.[2] Today the zone is under water, and no further archaeological work can take place in this industrial zone of the ancient city.

Despite more than a century of excavation at Pergamon, we still lack a monographic treatment of Pergamene MMB. MMB were not included in J. Schäfer's monograph on Hellenistic pottery (1968), as might have been expected, because it was planned that U. Hausmann should publish this group of Pergamene pottery (Schäfer 1968, 2 n. 2). This task was later taken over by G. de Luca, who for decades has promised this publication (de Luca 1990, 158 n.), but, unfortunately, it has not yet appeared.[3] In the absence of a thorough analysis of the MMB found at Pergamon, one has to piece together a picture of Pergamene production from various publications, especially Conze et al. 1913, de Luca 1968; 1975; 1990; 1997; 1999.

It has always been assumed that Pergamon was one of the major centres of production and export of MMB,[4] even though the proportions of the industry have probably been exaggerated (e.g., Raeder 1986, 205). Certainly, the presence of a royal court led to significant production of various types of fine wares, including MMB. The best known are the Pergamene Sigillata, made between the middle of the 2nd century BCE and the middle of the 2nd century CE (Meyer-Schlichtmann 1988) and the so-called *Applikenkeramik* (Hübner 1993a).[5] The latter in particular is easily recognizable. It was exported in restricted numbers and imitated as well, and it also made its way to the Pontic region, albeit in restricted numbers.[6] It probably inspired the iconography of the Aiolis B production, especially in the rendering of symplegmata and bundled ivy leaves (Chapter 13).

---

1 Hepding 1952, pl. 4; Parlasca 1955, 132, fig. 1; de Luca 1968, 163 cat. 421, pl. 57; 1999, 96; Künzl 2002, 78 cat. 40. A mould deriving from the art market has been attributed to Pergamon (Kleiner 1975, pl. 44c, 45; CVA Frankfurt am Main 4 [Germany 66], 52 pl. 24.1–3 (inv. 155); Künzl is of the opinion that it belongs to the 'Mainzer Werkstatt' (2002, 1).

2 Erdemgil 1980; Erdemgil 1981; Özyiğit 1990; de Luca 1999, 96; Radt 1999, 111–112; Özyiğit 2000; Bounegru 2003.

3 [Ed. See now de Luca 2021.]

4 E.g., Byvanck-Quarles van Ufford 1953, 6; Šurgaja 1965; Zabelina 1984; Bouzek 1990.

5 Hübner places the beginning of this production in 170, following the 'high' Pergamene chronology; the date should probably be lowered by about half a century (so also Rotroff 1996), because no fragments were unearthed in the foundations of the Great Altar, and the earliest context in the Asklepieion where this pottery was found is *Bauphase* 13, dating in the 1st third of the 1st century. This corresponds to the down-dating of the Spargi shipwreck. This wreck, which sank off the coast of Sardinia, is normally dated to the last decades of the 2nd century (Parker 1992, 409–411 with references). Hübner, however, dates it in the 130s without arguments (1993, 48), whereas E.L. Will has down-dated it on the basis of the Dressel 1B/Will 4b amphorae, which, according to her, were not produced until 85–75 (Will 1984). A date in the mid-3rd century for the beginning of the Applikenkeramik, proposed by Özyiğit (2000) based on the Kestel excavations, is unrealistic.

6 E.g., Zabelina 1968; Žuravlev 1995; Zhuravlev 1998; 2000; see also Hübner 1993a, 50–57.

Fabric and Surface Treatment

J. Schäfer has briefly discussed the character of Pergamene clay (1968, 28). He writes that it is not as fine as Attic fabric, but can occasionally contain inclusions of lime and small stones; the content of 'Glimmer' is not very high, but nevertheless it is usually present (same description concerning the Pergamene sigillata: Meyer-Schlichtmann 1988, 14). de Luca (1999, 92) provides another brief description: an orange-brown to orange-yellow, medium fine to fine fabric with a varying amount of golden mica. The coat is thin and of a relatively poor quality. Its colour can vary on the individual sherd; normally it is black to brownish black, red-brown or yellowish red and often peeling (a fine colour picture is published in Radt 1999, fig. 221).

Most of vessels I have included in the present chapter correspond best to Schäfer's description. They are generally of a fine, compact fabric with some light-reflecting particles, occasionally a few small lime particles, and from time to time with some voids. All of the vessels are oxidized and mostly fired to the hue 6/6 in the colour 5YR, but also in the colours 10R, 10YR, and 7.5YR as well as to 5/6 and 6/8 in the colours 2.5YR, 5YR, and 7.5YR and 7/6 in the colours 5YR and 7.5YR. The coat is normally thin and has a dull lustre. It varies significantly in colour, from 10R 4/8-5/8, 6/6; 10YR 3/1-3/2; 2.5YR 4/6-4/8; 5/6; 5YR 3/3, 4/3-4/4, 4/6 to 7.5YR 3/1.

A few vessels are slightly coarser, with a medium fine, slightly sandy fabric with some light-reflecting particles and a few small lime inclusions (PER-8*, PER-13*, PER-19*, PER-21*, PER-36*, PER-48*). Two further groups of fragments are tentatively ascribed to Pergamon. One is of a fine, compact, non-micaceous fabric with some voids (PER-30*, PER-52*, PER-63*, PER-64*); the second group is of the same relatively fine fabric with fine mica, and with a characteristic dull brown coat (PER-49*, PER-50*, PER-56*, PER-57*, PER-60*, PER-61*, PER-66*). Both groups are found only in Istros.

Shape

The commonest shape is a heavy, deep, hemispherical bowl with a tall, slightly S-curved rim and a plain, slightly everted lip. Other shapes represented in the Pontic assemblages are a small bowl (PER-86*), a chalice (PER-87*), three juglets (PER-88*–PER-90*), and at least three situlae (PER-91*–PER-93). In Chapter 5, I discuss the attribution of further shapes to the Pergamene production, in particular amphorae.

Decoration

The Pergamene production of MMB, which must include several different independent workshops, shares a number of overall characteristics. According to de Luca, who knows this pottery intimately, vegetal decoration is the most common (1997, 367). This is also the case with the fragments from the Pontic assemblages which I have ascribed to a Pergamene production. The style is, first of all, miniaturistic: stamps are often very detailed and small in size. Therefore, several superposed friezes of figural decoration are often employed, something which is quite uncommon in other productions. Another important aspect is the way in which the bowls are given impact through rendering elements connoting sacred space, such as columns (PER-21*),[7] altars,[8] thymiateria,[9] a torch,[10] a tripod (PER-14*), boukrania/boukephalia,[11] garlands (PER-18*, PER-19*),[12] and wreaths.[13] Frequently, the garlands and wreaths are furnished with a *tainia* tied in a bow (PER-19*). As noted by de Luca, these elements mirror the public imagery of Pergamon (1990). The Pergamene iconography was emulated in other Aiolian production centres (see Chapter 8) and occasionally even in the early and classical production of Ephesos (e.g., EPH-397*, EPH-404*). Belonging to the sacred sphere, too, are the mantled dancing women (PER-2–PER-4, PER-93), and the numerous vessels depicted on the MMB contextualize the representations in a Dionysiac setting.

As already mentioned, vegetal decoration was preferred, and calyx bowls are common (PER-24*–PER-27*, PER-38*–PER-68*). They frequently incorporate buds and flowers on wavy stems, and often figural decoration is included as space-filler (PER-24*–PER-27*). A double rosette of several 'layers' appears to be very popular. Such a rosette is employed as a device in the base medallion

---

7   de Luca 1990, pl. 25.2; 1999, 109–111 cats. 471, 473, 479, 514, pls. 15, 18, Beilage 7; 116 cat. III, pl. 24.
8   Conze et al. 1913, Beibl. 43.4; de Luca 1968, 165 cat. 436, pl. 59; 1990, pls. 24.3; 28; 1999, 111 cat. 516, pl. 18, Beilage 10.
9   de Luca 1999, 111 cats. 511–512, pl. 17, Beilage 10.
10 de Luca 1997, pl. 272; a very fine piece found in Delos but evidently of Pergamene production combines torch, thymiaterion, and suspended wreath with *tainia* (Laumonier vol. 2, cat. 273, pl. VI).
11 de Luca 1990, pl. 24.1–2, 6.
12 de Luca 1968, 165 cats. 436–437, pl. 59; 1975, pl. 45.7; 1990, pl. 24.1–3, 6; pl. 25.2–6; pl. 28.1–2, 5; 1999, 109 cat. 473, pl. 15, Beilage 7; 111 cats. 514, 516, pl. 18, Beilage 10.
13 Suspended wreath with *tainia* tied in bow: Conze et al. 1913, Beibl. 43.11; de Luca 1968, 139 cat. 260, pl. 49; 1997, pl. 272; with *tainia*: de Luca 1975, pl. 46.3; 1999, 111 cat. 509, pl. 17, Beilage 9; 116 cat. II, pl. 24.

(PER-53*)[14] and it also occurs as an element in the main decoration (e.g., PER-16, PER-17*).[15] Another type of rosette, probably invented at Pergamon, was copied in other productions as well: termed rosette C, it consists of six broad, lobed petals with finely ribbed interiors; the flower pistil is rendered with a stamp for an ivy-berry cluster (PER-10*, PER-70*; see also Chapter 6). Base medallions featuring figural representations are known from several vessels: the head of Medusa (PER-21*, PER-50*),[16] Skylla,[17] a lion (PER-63*), and a theatre mask (PER-74).[18]

Because of her early dating of the layers mentioned below, de Luca, who is the main authority on Pergamene MMB, entertains the idea that two key designs perhaps first appeared in Pergamon: pendent-semicircle and long-petal decoration (de Luca 1999, 100–102, 107–109). Especially in the case of the PSC, we find much more experimentation at Pergamon than we do elsewhere (e.g., PER-72*); we even find depictions which include elements from the sacred sphere, such as altars (Conze et al. 1913, Beibl. 43.4). In the case of the long-petal bowls as well, we find representations that seems to be local to Pergamon,[19] especially the plastic long petals surrounded by a line of fine dots, a type of decoration which was imitated elsewhere in Aiolis (see Chapter 8). In Chapter 6, I argued that the PSC design was indeed first produced at Pergamon, whereas Pergamon's priority cannot be established with certainty in the case of the long-petal decoration. In addition, P.J. Callaghan has suggested that even the net-pattern bowl was a Pergamene invention (1982, 66); this, however, cannot be maintained – at least on the basis of the published evidence, because to my knowledge, next to no vessels thus decorated have been documented at Pergamon (see de Luca 1999, 114 cat. 561, pl. 19, Beilage 12, dotted). Nevertheless, I attribute four net-pattern bowls with dotted pentagons to Pergamon (PER-74–PER-77*).

14 Cf. Conze et al. 1913, Beibl. 42.2; Kraus 1951, 11 cat. 13, fig. 4.2, pl. 3.5; de Luca 1968, 143 cat. 285, pl. 51; 152 cat. 342, pl. 54.; 152 cat. 340, pl. 55; 166 cat. 439, pl. 59; 1975, pl. 47.2; Pinkwart 1984, pl. 27.K45; de Luca 1990, pl. 26.2, 7–8; 1999, 113–114 cats. 549, 564, pl. 20, Beilage 13.
15 Cf. de Luca 1968, 152 cat. 348, pl. 54; 165 cat. 436, pl. 59; 1990, pl. 24.3.
16 Cf. Conze et al. 1913, Beibl. 42.5, 7; Schäfer 1968, 154 cat. Z 129, fig. 20.; de Luca 1999, 114 cat. 567, pl. 20, Beilage 13.
17 Conze et al. 1913, Beibl. 42.8; de Luca 1975, pl. 45.1; 1997, pl. 270.a; 1999, 114 cat. 568, pl. 20.
18 Cf. Conze et al. 1913, Beibl. 42.6.
19 E.g., Conze et al. 1913, Beibl. 42.12; Schäfer 1968, 115 cat. F 62, pl. 46; de Luca 1975, pl. 47.1; Pinkwart 1984, pl. 26.K73; Özyiğit 1990, fig. 59a.1–2; de Luca 1968, 152 cat. 343–344, pl. 54 (Asklepieion *Bauphase* 12, mid-2nd century to around 125).

Chronology

Source of Inspiration and Relative Chronology

As we have just seen, Pergamene mould makers were inventive, and they were little influenced from the outside. The shape of Pergamene MMB is clearly related to that of the Athenian workshops; in terms of decoration, however, there is little resemblance between the two productions, and, by and large, the Pergamene industry features its own style. To my knowledge, there are no examples of filled 'nelumbo' decoration, and even though there are plenty of calyx bowls with 'nelumbo', acanthus leaves with wavy outline and bent tip, and buds and/or flowers on wavy (more often than looped) stems, the 'baroque' type, with a small 'nelumbo' in front of the acanthus and a small acanthus in front of the 'nelumbo', has not been found there. This suggests that the Pergamene industry was not directly impacted by what I have called the second wave of influence from Alexandria, in the second quarter of the 2nd century (see Chapter 3). Alexandrian inspiration in Pergamene MMB may rather have been at second hand. The best evidence for Alexandrian influence may be found in the double rosettes commonly employed as a base medallion or even as part of the main decoration on Pergamene bowls, and which may reflect the double-rosette medallions of Alexandrian bowls made of silver and glass.

Absolute Chronology

Pergamene chronology is a thorny issue. First of all, the stratigraphic situation is considered difficult by the site's excavators. Moreover, there have been and still are a number of different 'chronologies' in circulation, largely tied to the construction date of the Great Altar. Below I outline the main contexts taken into account by most researchers (e.g., Kossatz 1990, 115–120; Hübner 1993a; Rotroff 2003, 6–9) dealing with Pergamene pottery chronology.

The Foundation of the Great Altar

When the altar was excavated, between 1879 and 1904, the pottery could not be dated, because at that time no chronological sequence of Hellenistic pottery had been established. Further pottery turned up during an excavation in 1961 (Schäfer 1968, 153–154, figs. 17–20), but the fragments were few: in addition to other fine-ware pottery, only eight MMB were found. Twenty years later, the time was ripe for a reassessment of those eight sherds. P.J. Callaghan pointed out the importance of the three fragments of long-petal bowls, and, based on the chronology established at Corinth, he used these to down-date the altar (Callaghan 1981; Callaghan 1982).

In order to test this hypothesis, in 1994 new soundings in the foundations of the altar were conducted by W. Radt (de Luca & Radt 1999). On that occasion, significant amounts of ancient pottery were excavated, including 256 fragments of MMB, of which 163 came from undisturbed layers (de Luca 1999, 92). It should be noted that not a single fragment of Pergamene *Applikenkeramik* was found, and only one sherd with PSC decoration (de Luca 1999, 113–114 cat. 560, pl. 19, Beilage 12), whereas eight further fragments with long petals came to light. Moreover, two or three fragments of white-ground pottery were also found.

Even though there is no historical testimony on the matter, it is generally assumed that Eumenes II was the altar's patron. However, he reigned during most of the first half of the 2nd century (197–158), so this does not provide us with a precise date. Scholars have tried to couple various historical milestones with the altar's construction, but with little success. Accordingly, the pottery found in the foundation has been floating, with the result that the same fragments are dated within a period of almost half a century. Thus, at least three different chronologies for the construction of the altar have been adduced:

High: 200–180 (e.g., Schäfer 1968, 26, 153–154; Hübner 1993a, 40–41; Hübner 1994)
Middle: 180–159[20] (e.g., Callaghan 1980, 43; de Luca 1999, 124)
Low: 166–156[21] (e.g., Callaghan 1980, esp. 43; Callaghan 1981; Callaghan 1982; Rotroff 2003, 9).

Clearly, circular argumentation is immanent (see also Rotroff 2003, 123).

In Chapter 6, on iconography, I argued that the low chronology is the most likely, not least because of the discovery of several well-used long petal bowls, which I would date around 165 at the earliest. In fact, as also noted by Rotroff (2001, 130), the finds in the altar foundation best correspond to those from the Asklepieion's *Bauphase* 12 (dated by de Luca from 157 to ca. 125, see below), the earliest layer in which long-petal bowls were found (de Luca 1968, 152 cats. 343–344, pl. 54).

The Stratigraphy of the Asklepieion
The Asklepieion, which is located outside the city wall, was excavated between 1958 and 1963 (*AvP* XI 1–4, 1968–1984), and MMB were found throughout the stratigraphy of its *Bauphasen* 8–16. The dating of these layers as proposed by de Luca runs from the late 3rd century BCE to the late 1st century CE (de Luca 1968). However, no more than 57 MMB in total were inventoried, and it is obvious that old MMB occur in more recent layers, so the stratigraphy is not all that useful (de Luca 1999, 96). One should note that a well-worn fragment of a bowl with PSC decoration was apparently found in *Bauphase* 10 (de Luca 1968, 138–139 cat. 256, pl. 49); this is surprisingly early, because the date of this layer according to de Luca is 190–175 (1968, 134–135).[22] de Luca herself notes that fragments of the same bowl were found in both *Bauphase* 10 and 11,[23] and similarly, stamped amphora handles of the same fabricant (Damokrateus) were also found in both layers.[24] The latest date of the latter is in the late 170s, according to Finkielsztejn (2001, 192 table 19). Accordingly, both layers must have had an end date in the second quarter of the 2nd century (also Rotroff 2003, 8).

Cisterns
Six cisterns located above the Demeter terrace have been published by Meyer-Schlichtmann (1988, 18–59; Hübner 1993a). Material from these cisterns has been adduced by de Luca, but none of them were filled before ca. 75 at the earliest, and therefore they are not useful for establishing a relative chronology of material dated prior to this date (Rotroff 1996, 359; Özyiğit 2000, 195).

Ketios Valley
The date of the production in the Ketios Valley has been the subject of discussion. It was already in operation in the mid-4th century, but, according to Özyiğit, the pottery workshops were abandoned in the early (1990, 94) or first half of the 2nd century (2000, 195), when the area was given over to funerary purposes. However, he dates the finds far too early. He is of the opinion that production of MMB started much earlier at Pergamon than at Athens (1990, 96), and he dates a complete(?) bowl evidently with a decoration of pendent semicircles under a rim with box meander more than 100 years too early, in the beginning of the 3rd century (2000, pl. 58c).

---

20   First Nikephorion to death of Eumenes II.
21   Celebration of victory over Galatians (168–166 BCE) to before the assault of Prusian II on Pergamon in 156 BCE.
22   In her 1994 article, Hübner dates the layer even earlier: 191–180 BCE (Hübner 1994, 286).
23   de Luca 1968, 139 cat. 261 (*Bauphase* 10), 143–144 cat. 291 (*Bauphase* 11), pl. 49: an Attic bowl of Workshop A; see Rotroff 2003, 8.
24   de Luca 1968, 137 cat. 242 (*Bauphase* 10) and p. 142 cat. 279 (*Bauphase* 11), pl. 63; see Rotroff 2003, 8.

Pergamene Mouldmade Bowls in the Pontic Assemblages

Pergamene MMB arrived at the Pontic shores in limited numbers and occur only in the largest assemblages. I have been able to identify them at only six Black Sea sites. A few scraps have been found at Chersonesos, Myrmekion, Porthmion, and Pantikapaion (constituting +/– 1%). Only in Istros and Olbia are more than a handful of Pergamene MMB documented, in Istros up to 38 vessels (2.5%), and in Olbia up to 44 (2.4%). The most likely explanation for this pattern of distribution is Pergamon's inland location, 25 km from the coast. It was thus off the main sea route, and consequently its pottery apparently did not circulate to any great extent beyond Aiolis.

CATALOGUE TO CHAPTER 9

BOWLS

A   *Figural Decoration*

Erotes

PER-1*
Olbia, Sector NGS, House III-3 B 368/106, O-НГС-93-909, 1098, Parutine, Olbia National Preserve storeroom. Two non-joining frs. of rim and upper body. H 4.4 × W 5.9, WT 0.36; ⌀ rim 14, 25%, RH 2.2. Fabric: relatively fine, some mica, many roundish voids, 7.5YR 6/6. Thin slightly lustrous coat, 7.5YR 2/0. Medium hard fired, oxidized. Multiple rim friezes: astragal; Ionian kyma. Main decoration: lyre-playing Erotes right.
– Guldager Bilde 2010, 276 cat. F-4, pl. 168 (erroneously identified as Ephesian).

Mantled Dancing Women

PER-2 (see Fig. 46)
Olbia, Sector NGS, O-НГС-01-570, Parutine, Olbia National Preserve storeroom. Body fr. H 6 × W 4, WT 0.28. Fabric: fine, some light-reflecting particles, small lime inclusions, 10YR 6/6. Thick peeling coat with dull lustre ext., int. adhering better and duller, ext. 2.5YR 4/6, int. 7.5YR 3/1. Medium hard fired, oxidized. Main decoration: maenad or Amazon with sword, stamped upside-down; mantled dancing women moving right, holding end of cloak of woman in front. For mantled dancers at Pergamon, see Conze et al. 1913, 274, no. 3; Boehringer & Krauss. 1937, pl. 58.a.

PER-3*
Istros, His-1130, Bucharest, Institute of Archaeology storeroom. Body fr. H 2.8 × W 3.4, WT 0.55. Fabric: fine, some light-reflecting particles, 7.5YR 7/6. Thin dull coat, almost completely worn off, ext. 5YR 4/4, int. 5YR 3/1. Medium hard fired, oxidized. Stacked in firing. Main decoration: mantled dancing woman moving right.

PER-4
Porthmion, П-76-82, Kerč History and Culture Reserve inv. KMAK 6447. Fr. of upper body. Reduced. Rim frieze: Ionian kyma. Main decoration: mantled dancing woman moving right; frontal male aulos player. A fine and well-preserved specimen with the same aulos-player over a calyx of acanthus separated by collared buds was found on Delos (Laumonier vol. 2, cat. 3434).
– Grzegrzółka 2010, 129 cat. 180 (identified as Ephesian).

Battle and Trophies

PER-5*
Chersonesos, X-1951-36, St Petersburg, State Hermitage Museum. One rim fr., eight body frs., joining two and two. H 7, WT 0.3, RH 2.9. Fabric: fine, some light-reflecting particles, 2.5YR 5/6. Thin dull coat ext., slight lustre int., ext. 2.5YR 4/6, 3/1, int. 2.5YR 3/1. Oxidized. Stacked in firing. Rim friezes: ridges; palmette wreath with oblong clusters of berries. Main decoration: prancing horse left with rider behind round shield with Macedonian star; Greek warrior with cuirass and helmet crouching in ambush behind shield; lower frieze: birds (ducks?) flying right. No calyx. Four very small repair holes.

PER-6*
Myrmekion, M-59-7, St Petersburg, IIMK RAN. Fr. of lower body. H 2.5, WT 0.32. Fabric: very fine, compact, sparse minute inclusions of silvery mica, 10R 6/6. Thin dull coat, 10R 5/8. Oxidized. Main decoration: frieze with oval shields (trophies). Calyx: top of petal? Frieze separators: dots.

PER-7*
Istros, His-254, Bucharest, Institute of Archaeology storeroom. Fr. of upper body. H 2.5 × W 3. Glossy coat int. Hard fired, oxidized. Stacked in firing. Main decoration: part of oval shield with thunderbolt(?) device (battle or trophy?).
– Domăneanţu 2000, 19 cat. 70, pl. 5 (identified as Ephesian [Comique à la canne]).

Mythological Scenes?

PER-8*
Istros, His-B 618/V 19460, Bucharest, Institute of Archaeology storeroom. Fr. of base and lower body. H 6 × W 6.6, WT 0.45, ⌀ base 3. Fabric: medium fine, sandy, some light-reflecting particles, a few specks of golden mica, 7.5YR 7/6. Thin dull coat, 2.5YR 5/6. Hard fired, oxidized. Main decoration: oared ships left, dolphins right. Medallion: small rosette with eight rounded petals surrounded by three low ridges.
– Domăneanţu 2000, 110 cat. 556, pl. 37.

PER-9
Istros, His-B 440/V 19463, Bucharest, Institute of Archaeology storeroom. Body fr. H 3 × W 2.1, WT 0.3. Fabric: fine, slightly micaceous, much fine lime, 7.5YR 7/4. Dull mottled coat, ext. 5YR 5/6, 3/1, int. 5YR 3/1. Medium hard fired, oxidized. Main decoration: frontal, naked Aphrodite Diadoumene in contrapposto. The Aphrodite Diadoumene was apparently popular on Pergamene

vessels, cf. the lagynos SHA-287; cf. also Rotroff 2003, 121 cat. 504, pl. 87 (Sardis).
– Casan-Franga 1967, fig. 4.3; Domăneanţu 2000, 91 cat. 436, pl. 30 (identified as Ephesian).

Actors

PER-10*
Pantikapaion, tomb(?), M-48-205, XIV/17-1360, Moscow, Puškin Museum of Fine Arts. Four joining frs. of rim, body and base; complete profile. WT 0.45; vessel H 8. Fabric: fine, slightly micaceous. Dull red coat. Oxidized. Stacked in firing. Rim frieze: simple guilloche. Main decoration: comic actor sitting on altar alternating with frontal female. Calyx: acanthus with hatched central vein and bent tip alternating with twisted stem topped by stylized flower. Medallion: rosette C. The frontal female appears on a bowl found at Pergamon, in the company of male actors standing between columns (de Luca 1997, pl. 271.b).
– AGSP 1984, pl. CLXIII.10.

Symplegma?

PER-11*
Istros, His-1076, Bucharest, Institute of Archaeology storeroom. Body fr. H 1.8 × W 2.6, WT 0.3. Fabric: fine, compact, non-micaceous, no visible inclusions, 2.5YR 6/8. Coat with dull lustre, 2.5YR 4/8. Relatively hard fired, oxidized. Main decoration: left arm, shoulder, and chest of naked male reclining on *kline* with pillow, most likely part of symplegma scene.

Animals

PER-12*
Istros, His-V 19413, Bucharest, Institute of Archaeology storeroom. Body fr. Oxidized. Main decoration: snake hunting bird right. Calyx: small rounded petal with central vein.
– Domăneanţu 2000, 94 cat. 453, pl. 30 (identified as Ephesian).

PER-13*
Istros, His-V 19414, Bucharest, Institute of Archaeology storeroom. Fr. of lower body. H 3.7 × W 3.5, WT 0.35. Fabric: medium fine, sandy, some light-reflecting particles, 5YR 6/8. Thin dull coat, 2.5YR 5/6. Hard fired, oxidized. Main decoration: animal running right, vase on tall foot, bird sitting right. Medallion: surrounded by at least two low ridges; frieze of fine dots between the ridges.
– Domăneanţu 2000, 111 cat. 557, pl. 37.

Objects

PER-14*
Istros, His-67, Bucharest, Institute of Archaeology storeroom. Fr. of lower body. H 3 × W 3.2, WT 0.5. Fabric: fine, compact, non-micaceous, no visible inclusions. Coat with dull lustre. Relatively hard fired, oxidized. Main decoration: tripod, unidentified object. Frieze separators: dots. Secondarily burnt.

PER-15 (see Fig. 39)
Myrmekion, M-58-211, St Petersburg, IIMK RAN. Fr. of lower body. H 3, WT 0.35. Fabric: very fine, compact, sparse minute inclusions of silvery mica, 10R 6/6. Thick even, sigillata-like coat with dull lustre, partly darkened, slight metallic sheen, ext. 10R 4/8, 10R 2.5/1, int. 10R 5/8. Oxidized. Stacked in firing. Main decoration: Hathor's crown (straight cow's horns flanking sun disc topped by pair of ostrich feathers).

PER-16
Olbia, O-1928-1011, 2158, present whereabouts unknown. Two non-joining frs. of rim and upper body. No rim frieze. Main decoration: double rosette alternating with palmettes, upper part of stylized long petal with double outline. For rosettes and palmettes in this position, cf. Conze et al. 1913, Beibl. 43.14,
– St Petersburg, IIMK RAN, photo archive neg. I 5173.

PER-17*
Istros, His-1123, Bucharest, Institute of Archaeology storeroom. Body fr. H 3.4 × W 2.1, WT 0.32. Fabric: fine, some light-reflecting particles, 5YR 7/6. Coat with dull lustre, ext. 5YR 3/3, int. 5YR 3/1. Relatively hard fired, oxidized. Main decoration: triple rosette. Frieze separators: dots.

Garlands Carried by Erotes

PER-18*
Olbia, Sector NGS, House III-3 B 368/106, O-НГС-93-918, Parutine, Olbia National Preserve storeroom. Fr. of mid- and lower body. H 6.4 × W 6.7, WT 0.3–0.42. Fabric: fine, dense, slightly micaceous, no visible inclusions, few voids, 10YR 5/4. Thin firm lustrous coat with metallic sheen int., ext. 2.5Y 2/0, int. 2.5Y 3/0. Hard fired, oxidized. Rim frieze: Ionian kyma. Main decoration: Erotes carrying thick bound garlands right. Calyx: acanthus leaf with hatched vein and palm frond with hatched vein separated by seven-petalled flame palmette.
– Guldager Bilde 2010, 276 cat. F-5, pl. 168 (erroneously identified as Ephesian).

Garlands Suspended from Theatre Masks

PER-19*
Olbia, Sector NGS, House II-2 B 248/8, O-НГС-89-763, Parutine, Olbia National Preserve storeroom. Fr. of upper body. H 5.25 × W 6.9, WT 0.33–0.45. Fabric: medium fine, slightly sandy, some light-reflecting particles, a few small lime inclusions, 7.5YR 5/6. Thin, almost dull coat, bicolour, blotchy int. and ext., ext. 10YR 3/2, 2.5YR 5/6, int. 5Y 3/1, 4/2. Hard fired, oxidized. Stacked in firing. Rim frieze: Ionian kyma (very faint). Main decoration: comic mask between thick bows with double-outlined edges.
– Guldager Bilde 2010, 281 cat. F-64, pl. 180.

PER-20*
Olbia, Sector NGS, O-НГС-92-214, Parutine, Olbia National Preserve storeroom. Body fr. close to rim. H 5.4 × W 4.5, WT 0.35. Fabric: relatively fine, slightly micaceous, small lime inclusions, 10YR 6/4. Thin slightly lustrous coat, ext. 10YR 3/1, int. 2.5YR 4/8. Medium hard fired, oxidized. Stacked in firing. Rim frieze: Ionian kyma. Main decoration: garlands suspended between comic masks. One repair hole.

Unidentified Figural Decoration

PER-21*
Olbia, O-62-13, Kiev, Institute of Archaeology storeroom. Fr. of base and lower body. H 4.9 × W 2.7, WT 0.4, ⌀ base 3.5. Fabric: medium fine, soft, non-micaceous, minute light-reflecting inclusions, many small voids, 5YR 7/6. Dull worn coat, 5YR 3/1. Medium hard fired, oxidized. Main decoration: upper frieze: column, human figure walking right; lower frieze: feline left, rosette with eight rounded petals. Medallion: frontal Medusa head surrounded by minute triangular palmettes. Ascription to Pergamon is tentative, based mostly on fabric and the character of the decoration.

PER-22*
Olbia, Sector NGS, O-НГС-92-131, 131a, Parutine, Olbia National Preserve storeroom. Two non-joining body frs. Oxidized. Rim frieze: two ridges. Main decoration: palmettes alternating with bunches of grapes(?) (stamp faint). Calyx: acanthus leaves, groups of five dots; all widely spaced.

PER-23*
Istros, His-1093, Bucharest, Institute of Archaeology storeroom. Body fr. H 3 × W 3. Oxidized. Main decoration unidentified. Calyx: 'nelumbo' with segmented central vein filled with looping stems, palmette.
– Domăneanțu 2000, 95 cat. 460, pl. 31 (identified as Ephesian).

B *Calyx With Figural Elements*

PER-24*
Olbia, Sector NGS, House III-3 B 368/104, O-НГС-93-682, Parutine, Olbia National Preserve storeroom. Fr. of lower body. H 5.4 × W 5.8, WT 0.28–0.34. Fabric: relatively fine, some light-reflecting particles, many small lime inclusions, many voids, 7.5YR 6/6. Thin firm coat with slight lustre, ext. 2.5YR 5/4, int. 5YR 4/2. Medium hard fired, oxidized. Main decoration: lotus sepal with hatched central vein and edges, collared buds and frontal naked youth. Calyx: low, rounded lotus petals. Identical petal on **PER-45***.
– Guldager Bilde 2010, 281 cat. F-63, pl. 180.

PER-25
Olbia, Sector NGS, O-НГС-88-95, Parutine, Olbia National Preserve storeroom. Body fr. Oxidized. Main decoration: feline(?) left. Calyx: small 'nelumbo' with cabled edge and ribbed interior.

PER-26*
Olbia, Sector NGS, O-НГС-89-733, Parutine, Olbia National Preserve storeroom. Fr. of lower body. Oxidized. Calyx: triangular groups of small plastic leaves; dog jumping left as space-filler.

PER-27*
Olbia, Sector NGS, O-НГС-88-135+135a, 135b, Parutine, Olbia National Preserve storeroom. Three joining body frs., one non-joining body fr. H 6.8 × W 7.9, WT 0.3. Fabric: fine, rather micaceous, 10YR 6/3. Thin coat with dull lustre, pitted on int., ext. 10YR 3/1, 2.5YR 6/6, 5/6, int. 10YR 3/1. Medium hard fired, oxidized. Stacked in firing. Rim frieze: astragal. Calyx: vertical acanthus scrolls with looped tendrils with buds, rosettes on wavy stems in between; large rosettes above scrolls; small Erotes as space-fillers. Similar floral stem on **PER-41*** and **PER-42***.

C *Scroll Decoration*

PER-28*
Olbia, Sector R25, O-P25-95-1100, Parutine, Olbia National Preserve storeroom. Body fr. H 4 × W 4, WT 0.31. Fabric: fine, non-micaceous, 7.5YR 5/4. Slightly glossy coat, 7.5YR 2.5/1. Hard fired, oxidized. Main decoration: acanthus scroll right. Calyx: vertical trefoil myrtle bundle alternating with acanthus or frond.

PER-29
Pantikapaion, M-49-195, Moscow, Puškin Museum of Fine Arts. Main decoration: 'scroll' of incised tendrils; rosettes with eight rounded petals below. Calyx: straight acanthus with hatched central vein; vertical acanthus scroll. Frieze separators: astragal.
– Zabelina 1984, 164, fig. 11c; Kovalenko 1989, 374 cat. 20.

D Wreath Decoration

Myrtle Wreath

PER-30*
Istros, His-V 19367 F, Bucharest, Institute of Archaeology storeroom. Three joining frs. of lower body. H 5.5 × W 6.8, WT 0.25. Fabric: fine, non-micaceous, 7.5YR 7/6. Coat with dull lustre, 5YR 3/1. Relatively hard fired, oxidized. Main decoration: myrtle wreath with three leaves and berries on stems left. Calyx: narrow palmette alternating with jewelled leaves. Frieze separators: dots. Ascription to Pergamon is tentative.
– Domăneanțu 2000, 137 cat. 680, pl. 49.

PER-31*
Olbia, Sector E2, square 55, Cistern Л, O-E2-49-436, Kiev, Institute of Archaeology storeroom. Body fr. H 3.6 × W 3.7, WT 0.3. Fabric: fine, non-micaceous; no visible inclusions, 5YR 6/6. Lustrous coat ext., dull int., Gley 1 2.5/N. Hard fired, oxidized. Multiple rim friezes: wave meander right; astragal. Main decoration: myrtle wreath with large berries and dotted stems left.

PER-32*
Olbia, Sector NGS, House III-3 B 368/104, O-НГС-93-678+679 +683, Parutine, Olbia National Preserve storeroom. Two rim frs. and one body fr., two joining. H 4.84 × W 6.1, WT 0.41–0.55; ⌀ rim 14, 27%, RH 2.2. Fabric: slightly gritty and sandy, many small lime inclusions, much mica, many large and small voids, 7.5YR 6/6. Thin firm coat, dull bluish metallic sheen at lip int. and entire preserved ext., ext. 7.5YR 4/0, int. 2.5YR 5/6. Medium hard fired, oxidized. Rim frieze: Ionian kyma. Main decoration: myrtle wreath with three leaves and berries on hatched stems left. Secondarily burnt.
– Guldager Bilde 2010, 276 cat. F-8, pl. 169 (erroneously identified as Ephesian).

PER-33*
Istros, His-V 19343, Bucharest, Institute of Archaeology storeroom. Body fr. Oxidized. Rim frieze: heart guilloche left. Main decoration: myrtle wreath left.

PER-34
Olbia, O-1924-257a, present whereabouts unknown. Fr. of body and part of base. Shiny black coat. Rim frieze: Ionian kyma. Main decoration: isolated finely jewelled plastic long petals alternate with vertical *bakchoi* with handle and wrapped in acanthus leaves. Medallion: undecorated base with low ring foot of large diameter.
– St Petersburg, IIMK RAN, photo archive neg. II 19333.

PER-35*
Istros, His-522, Bucharest, Institute of Archaeology storeroom. Body fr. H 1.7 × W 2.8. Oxidized. Main decoration: vertical bunches of myrtle(?) with three leaves.
– Domăneanțu 2000, 111 cat. 563, pl. 37.

Ivy Wreath

PER-36*
Istros, His-575, Bucharest, Institute of Archaeology storeroom. Fr. of upper body. H 3.3 × W 2.3. Fabric: medium fine, slightly micaceous, many silvery particles, some small lime inclusions, 5YR 6/8. Coat with dull lustre, ext. 2.5YR 4/6, int. 5YR 5/6. Relatively hard fired, oxidized. Main decoration: ivy wreath with central cluster of ivy berries left.
– Domăneanțu 2000, 139 cat. 693, pl. 50.

Oak Wreath?

PER-37*
Myrmekion, M-56-1213, St Petersburg, IIMK RAN. Fr. of lower body. H 2.2, WT 0.38. Fabric: very fine, some light-reflecting particles, 7.5YR 6/6. Thick coat ext. with dull sheen, int. with slight metallic sheen, ext. 10R 5/8, 3/1, int. 2.5YR 4/4. Oxidized. Stacked in firing. Main decoration: oak wreath(?) with acorn. Identical: Conze et al. 1913, Beibl. 43.22 (Pergamon).

E Vegetal Decoration

Calyx

PER-38*
Olbia, V.I. 7754.58, Antikensammlung, Staatliche Museen zu Berlin (formerly Becker collection). Body fr. H 8 × W 7.5, WT 0.5. Fabric: fine, some light-reflecting particles, 5YR 5/8. Mottled coat, ext. 5YR 4/3, 7.5YR 2.5/1, int. 7.5YR 3/3. Oxidized. Stacked in firing. Rim frieze: miniature scroll. Calyx: lush vegetation: alternating straight acanthus and ovoid lotus petals, both with segmented central veins; two low lotus sepals in front of lotus petal; flowers on wavy acanthus stems in between. Same design: **PER-39***, **PER-40***.

PER-39*
Olbia, O-НГС-04-158, Parutine, Olbia National Preserve storeroom. Fr. of lower body. Fabric: fine, some light-reflecting particles. Oxidized. Calyx: alternating acanthus leaf and tall lotus petal, both with segmented central vein, two low lotus sepals in front. Same design: **PER-38***, **PER-40***.

PER-40*
Olbia, Sector NGS, House III-3 B 368/106, O-НГС-93-919, Parutine, Olbia National Preserve storeroom. Fr. of lower body and part of base. H 4 × W 3.5, WT 0.32–0.52. Fabric: fine, small light-reflecting particles, some small voids, 5YR 5/6. Thin firm uniform, semi-lustrous coat, 2.5YR 5/6. Medium hard fired, oxidized. Calyx: tall lotus petal with hatched central vein, with two low, narrow lotus sepals in front; acanthus at right. Medallion: traces of plastic rosette with lobed petals. Same design: PER-38* and PER-39*.
– Guldager Bilde 2010, 281 cat. F-65, pl. 180.

PER-41*
Olbia, Sector AGD, О-АГД-69-1256, Kiev, Institute of Archaeology storeroom. Fr. of base and lower body. H 5.8 × W 7.3, WT 0.28–0.4, ⌀ base 3. Fabric: fine, rather micaceous, 7.5YR 6/6. Coat with slight dull lustre, 10YR 3/1. Relatively hard fired, oxidized. Calyx: vertical acanthus-flower scroll alternating with twisted stem topped by floral element. Medallion: rosette with broad lobed petals. Similar floral stems on PER-27* and PER-42*.

PER-42*
Istros, His-V 19345, Bucharest, Institute of Archaeology storeroom. Fr. of lower body. H 2.8 × W 3.3, WT 0.2. Fabric: fine, no visible inclusions, 7.5YR 6/4. Slightly lustrous coat, 5Y 2.5/1. Hard fired, oxidized. Calyx: vertical acanthus-flower scroll. One repair hole. Similar floral stem on PER-27* and PER-41*.
– Domăneanțu 2000, 126 cat. 616, pl. 43.

PER-43
Olbia, O-1936-948, present whereabouts unknown. Fr. of mid- and lower body. Main decoration: full body frieze with lush vegetation including palm, straight acanthus with segmented central vein, collared buds on wavy stems. Medallion: edge of low base ring preserved. Same collared bud on wavy stem on PER-44*.
– Levi 1940, 125, pl. XXV.6; St Petersburg, IIMK RAN, photo archive neg. II 13807.

PER-44*
Olbia, Sector NGS, O-НГС-04-155, Parutine, Olbia National Preserve storeroom. Fr. of upper body. H 4 × W 3.3, WT 0.3. Fabric: fine, somewhat micaceous. Flaking coat. Medium hard fired, oxidized. Rim frieze: Ionian kyma? Calyx: acanthus scroll and collared bud on wavy stem, very fine and detailed. Secondarily burnt. Same collared bud on wavy stem on PER-43.

PER-45*
Olbia, Sector NGS, O-НГС-08-55, Parutine, Olbia National Preserve storeroom. Fr. of lower body. H 1.8 × W 3.5, WT 0.33. Fabric: relatively fine, some light-reflecting particles, 5YR 5/8. Fine dense coat, 2.5YR 4/8. Medium hard fired, oxidized. Calyx: ovoid petal with hatched central vein and edges alternating with curved petal. Identical petal on PER-24*.

PER-46*
Olbia, Sector NGS, O-НГС-04-159, Parutine, Olbia National Preserve storeroom. Body fr. H 3.8 × W 3.8, WT 0.38. Fabric: fine, some light-reflecting particles, 2.5YR 6/8. Slightly lustrous coat, ext. 2.5YR 4/6, 2.5/1, int. 2.5YR 4/6. Medium hard fired, oxidized. Stacked in firing. Calyx: 'nelumbo' with ribbed interior, acanthus with bent tip; bird sitting right on 'nelumbo'.

PER-47*
Istros, His-Dup720, in the possession of P. Dupont. Body fr. with tiny part of base. Oxidized. Calyx: straight acanthus leaves with hatched central vein alternating with 'nelumbo' with ribbed interior and cabled edges; above these, eight-petalled rosette and unidentified element. Ascription to Pergamon is tentative; it could also be from Kyme.

PER-48*
Istros, His-685, Bucharest, Institute of Archaeology storeroom. Body fr. H 3.3 × W 3.5, WT 0.4. Fabric: medium fine, some light-reflecting particles, abundant small voids, 5YR 7/6. Coat with dull lustre ext. where stacked, ext. 2.5YR 4/6, 3/1, int. 7.5YR 3/2. Relatively hard fired, oxidized. Stacked in firing. Calyx: 'nelumbo' filled with tiny triangular scales, flanked by looped tendrils with acanthus flowers. The 'nelumbo' on PER-49* is probably identical.
– Domăneanțu 2000, 18 cat. 66, pl. 5 (identified as Ionian [Comique à la canne]).

PER-49*
Istros, His-544, Bucharest, Institute of Archaeology storeroom. Fr. of lower body. H 2.3 × W 2, WT 0.3. Fabric: relatively fine, fine mica, abundant small lime particles, 5YR 6/8. Dull coat, ext. 5YR 4/2, int. 10YR 5/3. Relatively hard fired, oxidized. Calyx: slightly wavy acanthus leaves with low 'nelumbo' filled with scales in front. Ascription to Pergamon is tentative. The 'nelumbo' on PER-48* is probably identical.

PER-50*
Istros, Sector "Pescărie", His-63–83, Bucharest, Institute of Archaeology storeroom. Fr. of base and lower body. H 5.8 × W 5.8, WT 0.35, ⌀ base 4. Fabric: relatively fine, fine mica, 7.5YR 6/4. Coat with dull lustre, 7.5YR 3/1. Relatively hard fired, oxidized. Calyx: straight acanthus leaves with hatched central vein alternating with tall ovoid lotus petals, flowers on wavy stems as space-filler; around medallion, one row of low leaves.

PERGAMON

Medallion: frowning brow and wild hair of Medusa surrounded by two rows of small leaves. Ascription to Pergamon is tentative. Probably close: Conze et al. 1913, Beibl. 42.5 (Pergamon).
– Domăneanţu 2000, 135 cat. 667, pl. 48.

PER-51*
Pantikapaion, palace foundation trench, M-84-57, Moscow, Puškin Museum of Fine Arts. Fr. of mid- and lower body. H 3.3 × W 4.4, WT 0.4. Fabric: very fine, dense, non-micaceous. Thin dull coat with soapy feel. Oxidized. Traces of main decoration. Calyx: ovoid lotus petal alternating with straight(?) acanthus with segmented central vein, separated by column of crude dots.

PER-52*
Istros, Plateau, His-1175, Bucharest, Institute of Archaeology storeroom. Fr. of base and lower body. H 4.9 × W 5.2, WT 0.28. Fabric: fine, compact, non-micaceous, some voids, 5YR 7/6. Dull coat, 5YR 3/1. Relatively hard fired, oxidized. Calyx: Floral stem flanked by tall acanthus leaves with tips bent towards it. Medallion: rosette with petals separated by tongues. Ascription to Pergamon is tentative.
– Domăneanţu 2000, 136 cat. 670, pl. 48.

PER-53*
Olbia, Sector R25, O-P25-05-1209, Parutine, Olbia National Preserve storeroom. Fr. of base and lower body. H 6.6 × W 3.3, WT 0.2–0.3, Ø base 2.8. Fabric: relatively fine, slightly micaceous, 5YR 5/6. Dull coat, mottled int., ext. 2.5YR 5/6, int. 10R 5/6, 7/6. Medium hard fired, oxidized. Calyx: acanthus leaves with segmented central vein alternating with slender rhomboidal(?) petals. Medallion: double rosette (seven petals outside, eight inside). Ascription to Pergamon is tentative, based on fabric and the double rosette.

PER-54*
Olbia, Sector R25, O-P25-02-1858, Parutine, Olbia National Preserve storeroom. Fr. of lower body close to base. H 4.5 × W 3.8, WT 0.3. Fabric: fine, compact, a few light-reflecting particles, 2.5YR 6/8. Firm slightly lustrous coat, 10R 5/8. Hard fired, oxidized. Calyx: naturalistic acanthus alternating with slender petal, wavy stem in between.

PER-55*
Istros, His-692, Bucharest, Institute of Archaeology storeroom. Fr. of lower body. H 3.3 × W 2.7. Oxidized. Calyx: acanthus leaves.
– Domăneanţu 2000, 95 cat. 465, pl. 31 (identified as Ephesian).

PER-56*
Istros, His-950, Bucharest, Institute of Archaeology storeroom. Fr. of lower body and tiny part of base. H 3.7 × W 3.6, WT 0.5. Fabric: relatively fine, fine mica, 5YR 6/8. Dull coat, ext. 5YR 3/3, int. 5YR 4/6. Medium hard fired, oxidized. Calyx: tall ovoid lotus petals alternating with 'Knidian' palmette. Ascription to Pergamon is tentative.
– Domăneanţu 2000, 97 cat. 475, pl. 31 (identified as Ephesian).

PER-57
Istros, His-465, Bucharest, Institute of Archaeology storeroom. Fr. of lower body. Oxidized. Calyx: tip of straight acanthus leaf. Ascription to Pergamon is tentative.

PER-58*
Olbia, O-1938-5137, Kiev, Institute of Archaeology storeroom. Fr. of mid- and lower body. Fabric: fine, non-micaceous, no visible inclusions. Oxidized. Main decoration: unidentified traces. Calyx: rounded petal alternating with incised vertical tendrils. Frieze separators: dots.

PER-59*
Istros, His-707, Bucharest, Institute of Archaeology storeroom. Fr. of base and lower body. Oxidized. Calyx: lotus petals with one row of small acanthus leaves in front. Medallion: rosette with many narrow petals.

PER-60*
Istros, His-V 19412, Bucharest, Institute of Archaeology storeroom. Fr. of base and lower body. H 3.6 × W 5.3, WT 0.4. Fabric: relatively fine, fine mica, 5YR 6/6. Dull coat, 5YR 3/1. Medium hard fired, oxidized. Calyx: acanthus leaves. Medallion: rosette with nine or ten rounded petals. Ascription to Pergamon is tentative.

PER-61*
Istros, His-497, 683, Bucharest, Institute of Archaeology storeroom. Two non-joining frs. of rim, base and lower body, WT 0.3, Ø rim 12.5, 12%, RH 1.5, Ø base 4. Fabric: relatively fine, fine mica, 7.5YR 6/6. Coat with dull lustre, 7.5YR 3/1. Relatively hard fired, oxidized. Rim frieze: Ionian kyma. Calyx: tall ovoid petals separated by flower buds on wavy stems; low row of petals around medallion. Medallion: rosette. Ascription to Pergamon is tentative.
– Domăneanţu 2000, 135 cat. 668, pl. 48.

PER-62*
Olbia, Sector NGS, House III-3 B 368/106, O-НГС-93-917, Parutine, Olbia National Preserve storeroom. Body fr. H 5.7 × W 8, WT 0.25–0.46. Fabric: fine, porous, some light-reflecting particles, abundant larger and smaller voids, 7.5YR 6/6, 10YR 6/4; bicolour. Coat of varying thickness, adhering badly, 2.5YR 5/6. Medium hard fired, oxidized. Stacked in firing. Rim frieze: torus between two ridges. Calyx: long narrow lotus sepals with

grooved central vein and tip bent forward alternating with dotted stem topped with small palmettes.
– Guldager Bilde 2010, 281 cat. F-66, pl. 180.

PER-63*
Istros, His-B 620/V 8570 R, Bucharest, Institute of Archaeology storeroom. Fr. of base and lower body. H 3.3 × W 4.8. Fabric: relatively fine, non-micaceous, 5YR 6/6. Coat with dull lustre, ext. 5YR 3/1, int. surface not preserved. Relatively hard fired, oxidized. Calyx: vegetal (type?). Medallion: feline right surrounded by two ridges. Ascription to Pergamon is tentative.
– Domăneanțu 2000, 134 cat. 662, pl. 47.

PER-64*
Istros, His-1927-1942-B 622, Bucharest, Institute of Archaeology storeroom. Fr. of base and lower body. H 3.5 × W 4.5, WT 0.4. Fabric: fine, compact, non-micaceous, some voids, 5YR 7/6. Coat with dull lustre, ext. 7.5YR 2.5/1, int. 7.5YR 3/1. Relatively hard fired, oxidized. Calyx: lotus petals; in front, two low rows of lotus petals with segmented central vein. Medallion: small rosette (almost completely worn off). Ascription to Pergamon is tentative.
– Domăneanțu 2000, 135 cat. 669, pl. 48.

PER-65*
Istros, His-no no. 29, Bucharest, Institute of Archaeology storeroom. Fr. of base and lower body. Oxidized. Calyx: small acanthus and palmettes. Medallion: rosette?

PER-66*
Istros, His-B 607/V 19319, Bucharest, Institute of Archaeology storeroom. Fr. of base and lower body. H 3.5 × W 5.7, WT 0.45. Fabric: relatively fine, fine mica, 5YR 7/6. Dull coat, 5YR 3/1. Relatively hard fired, oxidized. Calyx: two rows of palmettes upside-down. Ascription to Pergamon is tentative.

PER-67*
Istros, His-B 585 A/V 19367, Bucharest, Institute of Archaeology storeroom. Fr. of base and lower body. H 3.7 × W 3.7, WT 0.3, ⌀ base 3. Fabric: fine, compact, no visible inclusions, 7.5YR 7/6. Coat with dull lustre, 7.5YR 3/1. Relatively hard fired, oxidized. Calyx: small acanthus (or vine?) leaves upside-down around base, detailed rosettes as space-filler. Medallion: plain base with thin ridge as low foot. Rosette: cf. de Luca 1990, pl. 24.2.
– Domăneanțu 2000, 136 cat. 671, pl. 48.

PER-68*
Istros, His-702, Bucharest, Institute of Archaeology storeroom. Fr. of lower body. Oxidized. Calyx: part of acanthus, rosette below.

PER-69*
Istros, His-676, Bucharest, Institute of Archaeology storeroom. Fr. of lower body, oxidized. Calyx: widely spaced small palmettes.

Imbricate

PER-70*
Olbia, Sector AGD, О-АГД-71-1590, Kiev, Institute of Archaeology storeroom. Fr. of lower body with part of base. H 7.4 × W 9.7, WT 0.3–0.4, ⌀ base 4. Fabric: fine, slightly micaceous, 7.5YR 5/5. Thin coat with grey metallic lustre, 7.5YR 4/1. Hard fired, oxidized. Calyx: imbricate small ferns. Medallion: rosette C.

PER-71*
Olbia, Sector NGS, House III-1 Stove 329/74, О-НГС-92-916, Parutine, Olbia National Preserve storeroom. Fr. of base and body. H 6.7 × W 5.2, WT 0.19–0.31, ⌀ base 4. Fabric: fine, compact, some light-reflecting particles, a few small lime particles, 5YR 5/8. Thick uniform and faintly lustrous coat, ext. 2.5YR 4/4, int. 2.5YR 4/6. Hard fired, oxidized. Rim frieze: astragal below torus. Calyx: imbricate small ferns. Medallion: traces of rosette.
– Guldager Bilde 2010, 281 cat. F-67, pl. 180.

F *Linear Decoration*

Pendent-Semicircle Design

PER-72*
Olbia, Sector AGD, Bothros 11, О-АГД-87-1000, 88–198, Kiev, Institute of Archaeology storeroom. Two joining frs. of upper body; non-joining fr. of base and lower body. WT 0.4, ⌀ base 2.7. Fabric: fine, compact, some fine light-reflecting particles, 5YR 5/6. Slightly soapy coat, int. almost completely worn off, 2.5YR 5/6. Relatively hard fired, oxidized. Multiple rim friezes: Ionian kyma; astragal. Main decoration: pendent semicircle outlined with small circles; in centre, rosette made of precursor to heart buds; above semicircle, row of small X's continuing below rim pattern with small circles. Between semicircles, small Eros with torch left surrounded by vertical S-spirals. Calyx: low 'Knidian' palmette. Medallion: pointed petals forming double star; around the medallion, two ridges with frieze of small circles between them. Same torch-bearing Eros on **KYX-6***.
– Rusjaeva & Nazarčuk 2006, pl. 193.21.

PER-73*
Istros, His-619, B 637, Bucharest, Institute of Archaeology storeroom. Two non-joining body frs. H 2.3 × W 2.6. Fabric: fine, compact, non-micaceous, 5YR 6/6. Coat with dull lustre, ext. 2.5YR 5/6, int. surface not preserved. Relatively hard fired, oxidized.

Main decoration: pendent-semicircle pattern; four-rayed sun wheel in centre; dots in field between semicircles.

Net Pattern Outlined with Dots

PER-74
Olbia, Giessen (formerly Vogell collection). Complete. ⌀ rim 11; vessel H 5.8; H:⌀ 1:1.9. Fabric: some light-reflecting particles, reddish. Brownish coat ext., int. and over top of relief reddish. Oxidized. No rim frieze. Inside pentagons, alternating rabbits and boukrania. Medallion: slave mask.
– Zahn 1908, 67 cat. 25; Boehlau 1908, 29 no. 267.

PER-75*
Olbia, Sector NGS, O-НГС-02-682, Parutine, Olbia National Preserve storeroom. Joining frs. of base and body; very worn. H 8.5 × W 7.5, WT 0.35–0.6. Fabric: relatively fine, slightly micaceous, abundant minute lime particles, many voids, 5YR 6/6. Thin firm slightly lustrous coat, 5YR 3/1. Medium hard fired, oxidized. Medallion: surrounded by three ridges; rosette with eight(?) lobed petals separated by tongues.

PER-76*
Istros, His-991, Bucharest, Institute of Archaeology storeroom. Fr. of base and lower body, oxidized. Medallion: edge of rosette with rounded petals preserved.

PER-77*
Olbia, Sector R25, O-P25-96-268, Parutine, Olbia National Preserve storeroom. Fr. of upper body. H 2.6 × W 3.2, WT 0.28. Fabric: relatively fine, slightly micaceous, 5YR 6/6. Dull mottled coat, ext. 2.5YR 4/8, 2.5/1, int. 2.5YR 3/6. Medium hard fired, oxidized. Stacked in firing. Large S-spiral(?) over pentagons.

Plastic Long Petals Combined With Figural Decoration

PER-78*
Istros, Sector Z1, His-51-V 17595, Bucharest, Institute of Archaeology storeroom. Body fr. H 3 × W 3.7, WT 0.3. Fabric: fine, compact, non-micaceous, no visible inclusions, 5YR 6/6. Coat with dull lustre, 2.5YR 5/6. Hard fired, oxidized. Main decoration: plastic long petal alternating with twisted stem topped by duck sitting left.
– Domăneanțu 2000, 141 cat. 704, pl. 51.

Plastic Long Petals

PER-79*
Istros, His-V 19366[a], Bucharest, Institute of Archaeology storeroom. Body fr. Oxidized. Main decoration: plastic long petals with fine dots inside edges.
– Domăneanțu 2000, 104 cat. 525, pl. 34 (identified as Ephesian).

PER-80*   OLB-87
Olbia, Sector R25, O-P25-04-1506, Parutine, Olbia National Preserve storeroom. Body fr. close to base. H 2.8 × W 5.1, WT 0.47. Fabric: fine, some light-reflecting particles, 5YR 6/6. Thin coat with pinkish metallic sheen, ext. 10R 6/6, int. 10R 5/4. Very hard fired, oxidized. Main decoration: plastic long petals surrounded by fine dots. Calyx: single row of small leaves. The surface is reminiscent of some vessels of the Aiolis B production.

Stylized Long Petals Alternating with Vegetation

PER-81*
Olbia, O-1939-1453, Kiev, Institute of Archaeology storeroom. Fr. of mid-body. Oxidized. Main decoration: isolated stylized long petals alternating with straight acanthus with segmented central vein. Identical: **PER-82**.

PER-82
Pantikapaion, M-63-684, Moscow, Puškin Museum of Fine Arts? Body fr. Main decoration: isolated stylized long petals alternating with straight acanthus with segmented central vein. Identical: **PER-81***.
– Zabelina 1984, 163, fig. 10c.

Stylized Long Petals

PER-83*
Istros, His-B 300a, Bucharest, Institute of Archaeology storeroom. Body fr. H 4.1 × W 3.8, WT 0.4. Fabric: fine, compact, non-micaceous, 5YR 6/8. Coat with dull lustre, 2.5YR 5/8. Relatively hard fired, oxidized. Rim frieze: heart guilloche left. Main decoration: stylized long petals.
– Domăneanțu 2000, 103 cat. 513, pl. 34 (identified as Ephesian).

G   *Rim Fragments*

PER-84*
Olbia, Sector E6, square 252w, below heap of tiles, O-E6-56-119, Kiev, Institute of Archaeology storeroom. Body fr. H 3.3 × W 5,

WT 0.4. Fabric: fine, non-micaceous, 5YR 6/8. Lustrous mottled coat, ext. 2.5YR 4/8, 3/4, int. 2.5YR 3/1. Relatively hard fired, oxidized. Multiple rim friezes: Ionian kyma; pendent drops ending in bud. Frieze separators: dots.

PER-85
Olbia, Sector NGS, O-НГС-00-1295, Parutine, Olbia National Preserve storeroom. Rim fr. Oxidized. Rim frieze: rosettes with eight petals.

SUPPLEMENTARY SHAPES

Small Bowl

PER-86*
Pantikapaion, П-1867-7, St Petersburg, State Hermitage Museum. Complete. H 5, ⌀ rim 8.5. Fabric: fine. Oxidized. Stacked in firing. Rim frieze: groove. Main decoration: net pattern made with dots; frontal Medusa heads in pentagons, flower over pentagons. Medallion: surrounded by ridge, which in turn is surrounded by triangular elements; frontal Eros with arms and legs outspread, Eros as Ixion on the wheel of fire. A Medusa head inside a dotted pentagon also occurs on an Aiolian vessel of unknown production: **AIX-22***.

Chalice

PER-87*
Olbia, Odessa, Historical Museum. Complete. Oxidized. Multiple rim friezes: circular motif (very faint); box meander ccw. Main decoration: plastic pine-cone decoration.

Juglet

PER-88*
Olbia, V.I. 4857, Antikensammlung, Staatliche Museen zu Berlin (formerly Vogell collection). Complete. Clay ring around handle. ⌀ rim 5.5; vessel H 7.5. Fabric: no break for observation. Dull blackish coat below, reddish-brown over shoulder. Oxidized. Rim frieze: astragal. Main decoration: net pattern made of dots; rosettes with five petals inside upper pentagons. Medallion: rosette with eight broad petals separated by tongues.

PER-89*
Olbia, Sector AGD, O-АГД-86-334, Kiev, Institute of Archaeology storeroom. Almost complete profile, lacking rim and part of handle, ca. 60% of the vessel preserved. H 4, WT 0.3. Fabric: relatively fine, non-micaceous, some minute lime inclusions, 5YR 6/6. Thin very worn coat ext., in places with metallic sheen, int. covered only at neck, ext. 5YR 4/6, 2.5.1, int. 2.5YR 4/8. Relatively hard fired, oxidized. Stacked in firing. No rim frieze. Calyx: four ovoid petals alternating with wavy floral stem. Medallion: surrounded by broad ridge; pattern completely worn off.

PER-90*
Istros, His-1147, Bucharest, Institute of Archaeology storeroom. Fr. of shoulder and upper body. H 4.3 × W 3.2, WT 0.35. Fabric: fine, fine mica, some flakes of golden mica, 7.5YR 7/4. Brownish coat with metallic sheen ext., ext. 2.5Y 3/1, 2.5YR 5/6, uncoated int. Hard fired, oxidized. Stacked in firing. Rim frieze: Ionian kyma. Main decoration: vine scroll.

Situla

PER-91*
Olbia, inv. Б.3274, St Petersburg, State Hermitage Museum (1899). Complete. ⌀ rim 21; vessel H 22.5. Fabric: fine, slightly micaceous, some lime inclusions, orange brown. Thin slightly lustrous black coat, mottled. Relatively hard fired, oxidized. Multiple rim friezes: Ionian kyma; astragal. Main frieze 1: 21 figural scenes in a continuous frieze, repeated three times. 15 of the stamps are identical to the four altar scenes; scene D is framed by an antithetical and mirror-image group of a half-naked Nymph seated on a rock facing a Silenos leaning cross-legged against a three. This frieze is the highest and the one with the most conspicuous location (interpretation and parallels are discussed in Guldager Bilde 2005). Main frieze 2: myrtle wreath with berries on stem right. Main frieze 3: two alternating scenes, (i) two Erotes placed heraldically around an *agyieus* in an acanthus calyx, and (ii) Dionysos-Eros holding a thyrsos and riding a feline side-saddle towards left. The scenes are repeated five times; the sixth time, where the sequence of stamping ends, the arrangement is Dionysos-Eros / Eros turned right / Dionysos-Eros. The joint of the stamping is located below one of the handles. Main frieze 4: continuous battle scenes showing Greeks fighting mounted Amazons. Main frieze 5: pair of Erotes placed heraldically around a krater, repeated six times. No calyx or medallion. I have had difficulties placing the situla correctly in a workshop. First I suggested that it was of Pontic production (Guldager Bilde 2005), then attributed it to Ephesian production. Even though we do find parallels for most of the stamps in Ephesos, I believe that those motifs emulated Pergamene stamps. The fabric of the situla, the close similarity to **PER-93**, which is easier to classify as Pergamene, and also the presence of the *agyieus* in the third frieze makes me inclined to believe in a Pergamene origin (as Finoguenova).

– von Stern 1899, 123–125, fig. 235; von Stern 1902; Bobrinskij 1904, 7 and 8, fig. 7; Wuilleumier 1929, 65 cat. s; Schwabacher 1941, 186, no. 15; 189, no. 10; 191, no. 4; 192, no. 9; Pochmarski 1990, 285 RK 89; Finoguenova 1991, 132–133 (identified as Pergamene); Samojlova 1994, 90, fig. 2.1; Guldager Bilde 2005.

PER-92*
Olbia, Sector NGS, O-НГС-05-149, Parutine, Olbia National Preserve storeroom. Body fr. H 5.8 × W 9.4, WT 0.5, ⌀ max. 20. Fabric: fine, slightly micaceous, 5YR 6/8. Thin lustrous coat, 7.5YR 2.5/1. Medium hard fired, oxidized. Multiple rim friezes(?): astragal (probably not top pattern). Main decoration: upper frieze: Eros right between suspended garlands with rings; lower frieze: standing figures (only heads preserved). Frieze separators: dots; broad astragal. Identical or closely related: de Luca 1990, pl. 25.4 (Pergamon); Mitsopoulos-Leon 1991, 71 cat. D23, pl. 80 (Ephesos).

PER-93
Olbia, O-1912-556, present whereabouts unknown. Lower half of vessel on wide, slightly profiled foot. Main decoration: upper frieze: mantled dancing women right; middle frieze: hunting scene with tree, male hunter with spear right, dog right attacking boar left, tree, lion left; lower frieze: small Erotes running right. Calyx of sepals bending toward ovoid petal. Medallion cannot be identified from photo.
– St Petersburg, IIMK RAN, photo archive neg. III 3428.

DISTRIBUTION

Chersonesos

PER-5*

Istros

PER-3*, **PER-7*–PER-9**, **PER-11*–PER-14***, **PER-17***, **PER-23***, **PER-30***, **PER-33***, **PER-35***, **PER-36***, **PER-42***, **PER-47*–PER-50***, **PER-52***, **PER-55*–PER-57**, **PER-59*–PER-61***, **PER-63*–PER-69***, **PER-73***, **PER-76***, **PER-78***, **PER-79***, **PER-83***, **PER-90***

Myrmekion

PER-6*, **PER-15**, **PER-37***

Olbia

PER-1*, **PER-2**, **PER-16**, **PER-18*–PER-22***, **PER-24*–PER-28***, **PER-31***, **PER-32***, **PER-34**, **PER-39*–PER-41***, **PER-43–PER-46***, **PER-53***, **PER-54***, **PER-58***, **PER-62***, **PER-70*–PER-72***, **PER-74**, **PER-75***, **PER-77***, **PER-80***, **PER-81***, **PER-84***, **PER-85**, **PER-87*–PER-89***, **PER-91*–PER-93**

Pantikapaion

PER-10*, **PER-29**, **PER-51***, **PER-82**, **PER-86***

Porthmion

PER-4

CHAPTER 10

Kyme (i)

Kyme was considered the most important of the Aiolian cities (Strab. 13.3.6). The city was founded sometime in the Iron Age by Greek settlers from Central Greece. It boasted a fine natural harbour, which was the key to the city's commercial success (Lagona 1993, 250). A 190 m long pier constructed of squared blocks can still be seen under water; in fact, the harbour of Kyme is one of the best-preserved ancient harbours of the Mediterranean (Lagona 1993, 284–289).

In 1881, S. Reinach and E. Pottier excavated in the city's necropolis (e.g., Reinach 1889). However, the first systematic excavations in the city itself were undertaken in 1925, by a Bohemian expedition directed by A. Salač. Amongst other features, he uncovered what was believed to be a 'potter's house'. After Salač's untimely death, work was suspended until 1953, when E. Akurgal briefly revived field work at the site (1953–1955). Between 1979 and 1981, the Izmir Museum conducted further excavations. Between 1982 and 1984, a joint Turco-Italian expedition was formed, directed by V. Idil and S. Lagona of the University of Catania. The latter directed archaeological field work in the city from 1986 until her retirement in 2008, when the direction of the expedition was taken over by A. la Marca (University of Calabria). The work of the Italian expedition continues to date.

There can be absolutely no doubt that MMB were produced at Kyme. In Salač's 1925 excavation, a number of moulds and MMB came to light in the 'potter's house'. Later, in 1972, J. Schäfer found another mould fragment not far from that building, and the Italian expedition uncovered a further mould fragment in 1993 (Lagona 1993, fig. 5b). Thus, in total, 19 moulds and mould fragments have been unearthed at Kyme.[1]

Salač's finds of the 1920s were donated to the Charles University in Prague. This collection was the point of departure for J. Bouzek and L. Jansová, who treated it in a small monograph published in 1974. This publication included a group of 17 complete and fragmentary moulds, as well as a number of vase fragments: in total, 140 objects. Of these, they considered only slightly over half of the moulds and bowls to be of Kymean or probable Kymean production. The remainder, according to Bouzek and Jansová, were products of the regional workshops of Pergamon and Myrina, one or two were Attic, whereas the largest batch, around one-fourth, were not attributed to a production place.

The two scholars subdivided the Kymean moulds and bowls into at least five different workshops and their circles: the Paniskos Workshop, the Little Eagles Workshop, the Erotes Workshop, the Birds and Imbrications Workshop, and the Smyrna Workshop. Because only a few pieces are attributed to each workshop, it is difficult to form an opinion about their characters (see also Chapter 3); moreover, Bouzek & Jansová believed that production was spread over most of the 2nd century, so the differences between 'workshops' could also indicate differences in date, as they themselves admit. Unfortunately, since the publication of Bouzek & Jansová 1974, little attention has been paid to Kymean MMB. Only two minute rim fragments of bowls and a mould fragment have been published since then (Lagona 1994, 36, fig. 5b [mould]; Landi 2007, 180–181 cats. 15–16), so our knowledge of this production has not increased significantly since 1974.

In this chapter, we shall discuss the MMB of Kymean production as defined by Bouzek and Jansová (1974). We also include fragments which correspond to the Kymean production in broad terms, even though their decoration has not necessarily been documented previously. I have not found it possible to classify the fragments according to Bouzek & Jansová's 'workshops', because the boundaries between the different sub-groups of this production seem to be quite vague (see also Fig. 63). For example, the stamp of Eros-Paniskos, which Bouzek and Jansová took as diagnostic for the Paniskos Workshop, can also be found on vessels attributed to Kirbeis (KYB-19*, KYB-20, KYB-70*, KYB-125). Moreover, I am in general inclined to follow Siebert's methodology, which requires at least 100 vessels as a basis for identifying a workshop (see Chapter 3). In the current state of our knowledge, too few Kymean MMB have been published to allow us to paint a true picture of the Kymean workshops. Thus, it is of note that none of the stamps on the mould fragment unearthed in 1994 are documented in the corpus published by Bouzek and Jansová, nor do they occur on any of the vessels in the current book.

I have been able to isolate one particular group of vessels, which I have termed Workshop A, despite the fact that

---

[1] See also Horáková-Jansová 1931 (note that fig. 4 was not included in the 1974 publication); Künzl 2002, 77 cat. 22.

	Kyme, unattributed	Workshop A	Meter Medallion Workshop
Astragal	**KYX-9**, **KYX-21**, **KYX-27**		**KYB-2**, **KYB-178**, **KYB-414**
Bird A	**KYX-8**		
Bird A, rosette B	**KYX-57**		
Rosette B	**KYX-54**		
Dots	**KYX-20**, **KYX-41**, **KYX-42**	**KYA-29**, **KYA-37**, **KYA-52**, **KYA-54**	**KYB-13**, **KYB-123**, **KYB-135**, **KYB-149**–**KYB-151**, **KYB-423**, **KYB-433**
Fleur de lys A left		**KYA-2**, **KYA-26**	
Fleur de lys B	**KYX-14**		
Heart guilloche left	**KYX-50**	**KYA-17**, **KYA-39**	**KYB-44**
Heart guilloche right	**KYX-98**		**KYB-38**, **KYB-152**
Ionian kyma	**KYX-51**, **KYX-63**[a]	**KYA-23**, **KYA-57**	**KYB-153**?
Ionian kyma, upside-down	**KYX-26**		
Small double-heart ornaments		**KYA-52**	
Small palmettes	**KYX-10**		

FIGURE 59   Frieze dividers on Kymean vessels; the patterns are set between single ridges
Note: a. Another with Ionian kyma but not in the present catalogue, Adam Veleni et al. 2000, 286 cat. 40, pl. 139.st, from Thessaloniki.

its numbers are too small to qualify as a workshop in the proper sense of the word. It is, nonetheless quite distinctive, though interwoven with the other Kymean groups of MMB and especially with the bowls of Kirbeis, with which it shares a significant number of stamps (Fig. 63).

The following Chapter 11 on the Meter Medallion Workshop continues the discussion of Kymean products, because, as we shall see, this workshop was also located in Kyme. However, since it has not previously been connected with Kyme, it warrants a separate discussion. Together, Chapters 10 and 11 portray an inventive and active production place with several independent workshops which functioned as a nucleated group, the stamps of which were interconnected in an intricate pattern (Fig. 63).

The Kymean workshops share a number of characteristics, first of all physical and morphological properties. A specialty of the Kymean workshops seems to have been the use of a frieze with an architectural moulding as separator between the friezes (Fig. 59).

This usage is found sparingly in other productions as well, e.g., in Pergamon (astragal),[2] Aiolis unassigned (astragal: **AIX-4***, rosette: **AIX-2***, Ionian kyma: **AIX-11***, **AIX-12***),

Ephesos (astragal;[3] Ionian kyma: Laumonier 1977, 77 cat. 3440, pl. 16; palmettes: **EPH-691***; Laumonier 1977, 417 cat. 3445, pl. 97), and Knidos (Ionian kyma: **KNI-18***, **KNI-19***; astragal: **KNI-75***).

It is obvious that Kyme was part of the Aiolian koine of decorative motifs. As part of this koine, we find the Ionian kyma with double outline, sometimes placed upside-down, and we frequently find suspended garlands and wreaths as the main decoration (**KYX-54***–**KYX-66***). We also find the female mantled dancer (albeit of a variant type; **KYX-9**, **KYX-10** [Fig. 47], **KYX-54***; Bouzek & Jansová 1974, 54 MB 29, fig. 1, pl. 5), and a Pergamene stamp such as an *agyieus* set in vegetation is found too (**KYX-9**, **KYX-27**). But at the same time, the production was highly original. It had a rustic charm which is in contrast to the finer Aiolian productions further north (Pergamon and Aiolia A and B).

It is possible that some Myrinaean MMB have been (erroneously) included in this chapter. Myrina is located 10 km northeast of Kyme. Very little has been published and we therefore know next to nothing about MMB from the site. It has been claimed that, in terms of decoration and style, its bowls are very like Kymean products (Courby 1922, 402–403; Bouzek & Jansová 1974, 50), but

---

2 **PER-29**; de Luca 1968, 163 cat. 421, pl. 57 (mould); Künzl 2002, 9, fig. 4.

3 Laumonier 1977, 158 cat. 1291, pl. 37; p. 360 cat. 562, pl. 86.

the fabric should be pinker; the amphoriskos with pointed base (KYX-101) is a possible example. However, since this group has never been studied in detail, it is currently not possible to distinguish between the two.

Unassigned Workshops

We shall first consider vessels which are clearly of Kymean production but cannot be attributed to a particular workshop. Chronology and distribution will be discussed in Chapter 11, after we have considered all of the Kymean workshops represented in the Pontic assemblages.

Fabric and Surface Treatment
According Bouzek & Jansová (1974, 16–17), the clay is soft and relatively fine with some mica, but only rarely in greater quantity. They describe it as usually pink, though more brownish than Attic, and sometimes yellower. They also call it reddish brown. Unintentionally reduced sherds occur, as do sherds with a grey core. The coat varies to a great extent, from black to brown to red and grey; it can be thicker or thinner and with more or less gloss.

By and large, the clay of the fragments attributed to the unassigned workshops corresponds to Bouzek and Jansová's description. Thus, the fabric ranges from fine to medium fine, more or less micaceous, and often with small lime inclusions. All vessels are oxidized in firing. The colour of the fabric is mostly 5YR 6/6, but it ranges from 2.5YR 6/6, 5YR 5/6 and 7/6 to 7.5YR 6/6. The coat varies enormously; it is usually dull or slightly lustrous. It is mostly of the hues 3/1 and 4/1 in the colours 10YR, 2.5YR, 5YR, and 7.5YR, but much variation can be found on the individual vessel, and a fair number of them give evidence of stacking during firing.

Shape
The most common shape is a deep, heavy, hemispherical bowl with a high, slightly S-curved rim and a plain, slightly everted lip. The Pontic assemblages confirm Bouzek & Jansová's observation that the rim diameter is normally relatively large, 13–15 cm (see also Bouzek & Jansová 1974, 17).

Decoration
Syntax
According to Bouzek and Jansová (1974), decoration is almost exclusively rendered in several superposed friezes (if not of linear or imbricate design). As already mentioned, the friezes are separated by single or double ridges, the space between which may or may not be decorated (Fig. 59). Our assemblage also documents full-body figural decoration (as KYX-12* and others) and calyx with figural decoration (KYX-31–KYX-46*).

Rim
Kymean bowls of all workshops characteristically have two or more deep grooves at the transition between the moulded part of the vase and the rim, rather crudely incised in the vessel before firing (Bouzek & Jansová 1974, 49), and often this is the only rim decoration (see also Fig. 62). By far the most common rim pattern is an Ionian kyma; in a number of cases, it comes in a version with rounded eggs with a double outline. We also find the heart guilloche, mostly turned towards left.

Calyx
A 'nelumbo' with cabled edges was popular in the unattributed Kymean workshops. It can be filled with vegetation (KYX-67*, KYX-68, as at Ephesos, EPH-584*, EPH-585*), furnished with scales (KYX-8*, KYX-69, as also in the MMW, KYB-123, KYB-177*–KYB-179*, KYB-350*, KYB-363*–KYB-366), or have a ribbed interior (KYX-71*).

Base
The base is normally surrounded by two ridges. Two bases feature rosette C, with six broad, lobed petals and a cluster of ivy berries in the centre (KYX-40, KYX-99), a motif also found on a mould unearthed at Kyme (Bouzek & Jansová 1974, 51 cat. MB 3, pl. 2). On three other bases we find various types of double rosette (KYX-22*, KYX-77*, KYX-80*). The base medallion of KYX-22* is the same one found on vessels attributed to the Paniskos Workshop (Bouzek & Jansová 1974, 52, 54 cats. MB 14 [mould], MB 19, MB 25, fig. 1, pls. 2, 4, 5). One vessel features a comic mask (KYX-31) which matches a mask on a mould unearthed at Kyme also attributed to the Paniskos Workshop (Bouzek & Jansová 1974, 51 cat. MB 1, pl. 1).

Body Decoration
One group of vessels is of particular note. In the fullest version, they render a scene of ritual preparation (Fig. 60). The centre of veneration is the Dionysiac trio, which is emphasized by the two saluting Pans that frame it (see also Chapter 6). As we can gather from, e.g., KYX-99, the scene also includes an Eros pouring wine from a pointed transport amphora into a tall-stemmed kantharos (*Pokalkantharos*), as well as an Eros with a torch leading Dionysos(?) with a cornucopia.

Production	Reference	Preservation	Saluting Pan right	Altar scene D	Saluting Pan left	Eros pouring wine	Eros with torch left	Dionysos(?) w/ cornucopia left	Dionysos-Eros side-saddle	Male with thyrsus left	Female with wreath	Ithyphallic Satyr right	Pokalkantharos
Kyme	**KYX-99**	Complete	X	X	X	X	X	X					
Kyme	**KYX-47**	Fr.					X	X		X			
Kyme	**KYX-4**	Fr.				X	X	X					
Kyme	**KYX-32**	Fr.				X	X						
Kyme	**KYX-3**	Fr.				X							
Kyme	**KYX-5**	Fr.				X							
Kyme	**KYX-6**	Fr.					X				X		
Kyme	**KYX-7**	Fr.					X				X		
Kyme	**KYX-31**	Fr.										X	
Kyme	Mesambria[a]	Complete	X	X	X	X	X	X	X				
Kyme	Campania?[b]	Complete	X	X	X	X	X	X					
Kyme	Torbali-Metropolis[c]	Complete	X	X	X								
Kyme	Thessaloniki[d]	Fr.	X		X							X	X
Unknown	Alexandria[e]	Fr.	X	X	X								
Ephesos?	Delos[f]	Fr.	X	X	X								
Sardis	Sardis[g]	Mould fr.	X	X									

FIGURE 60 Kymean vessels showing a scene of ritual preparation
Notes:
a. Nessebar, Archaeological Museum inv. 2008-38
b. Patroni 1897–1898, 124 cat. 1015, pl. XIX; Wuilleumier 1929, 64 cat. h; Schwabacher 1941, 186 no. 8; 189 no. 11; Pochmarski 1990, RK 87
c. Erdemgil et al. 1989, 111; Tuluk 2001, 61–62 cat. 3, pl. 30; and perhaps Siebert 1978, 245 n. 3: a small bowl like **KYX-99** and with the same base medallion
d. Adam Veleni et al. 2000, 286 cat. 40, pl. 139
e. Pagenstecher 1913, 67, fig. 79c
f. Laumonier 1977, 92 cat. 3247, pl. 20
g. Rotroff 2003, 102 cat. 402, pl. 67

Recurring Stamps
Many stamps occur just once; they are not included in the list below but are described under the particular vessel on which they appear. Amongst the minor stamps, some were used a number of times. This is true of the small palmette, which is used as a rim pattern (**KYX-59***, **KYX-95***) as well as a frieze divider (**KYX-10**, Fig. 47) and as space-filler in figural decoration (**KYX-9**). We also find a straight acanthus leaf with a double vein and hatched side veins (acanthus Z) more than once (**KYX-32**, **KYX-58**).

Stamps are often shared with other Kymean workshops (Fig. 63). This is especially the case with Workshop A, with which these unassigned bowls share a boukephalion (**KYX-22***, **KYX-61**, **KYX-63***; **KYA-40***), bird M, a dove(?) with a fan-shaped tail sitting left (**KYX-47***; **KYA-13***, **KYA-19***–**KYA-21***, **KYA-28***, **KYA-35***), a *Pokalkantharos* with a very slender neck (**KYX-17***; **KYA-35***), a miniature kantharos (**KYX-37***, **KYX-38***, **KYX-56***; **KYA-54***), a straight, naturalistic acanthus leaf (acanthus X) (**KYX-44***; **KYA-52**), a straight palm frond with fine veins (palm F) (**KYX-37***, **KYX-38***, **KYX-46***; **KYA-10***, **KYA-39**), and a rosette (rosette K) (**KYX-34**, **KYA-57**).

Workshop A

On the basis of a number of shared characteristics, I have classified the vessels in this section as products of the same workshop, termed Workshop A, even though it was hardly an isolated, independent workshop. The group consists of no more than 58 pieces and thus does not meet Siebert's criteria for establishing a workshop proper, but there can be no doubt that they were made by the same hand. In contrast to all other potters in Kyme, notable for their rather bold style, the person behind Workshop A is a miniaturist, making small shapes with a delicate appearance.

Fabric and Surface Treatment
The fabric in Workshop A ranges from fine to medium fine, is more or less micaceous, and often has small lime inclusions. Most vessels are oxidized in firing, but some reduced vessels can be found as well. The colour is mostly 5YR 6/6 and 7.5YR 6/6, but it can also be slightly lighter (5YR 7/6 and 7.5YR 7/6). Reduced vessels are of the hues 6/2 and 5/2 in the colours 7.5YR, 10YR, and 2.5Y. The coat is mostly dull or slightly lustrous and quite dark, mostly of the hues 3/1 and 2.5/1 in the colours 10YR, 5YR, and 7.5YR. Few vessels show signs of having been stacked during firing.

Shape
Bowls are overall of the usual Kymean shape, but the rim diameter is normally much smaller, usually 10.5 to 12 cm, and the walls are correspondingly thinner than the heavy-walled standard employed in Kyme in general. Apart from hemispherical bowls, Workshop A also produced skyphoi with ring handles and a low stemmed foot (KYA-52–KYA-56*), a small bowl (KYA-51), a jug (KYA-57), and a juglet (KYA-58*).

Decoration
Syntax
Superposed friezes are most popular in this workshop. They are for the most part separated by two ridges located ca. 0.5 cm apart. The space between the ridges is usually, but not always, undecorated (Fig. 59).

Rim
As in the case of the unassigned Kymean workshops, the most common rim patterns in Workshop A are grooves and the Ionian kyma. There are also small double-heart ornaments, which are found only in this workshop, both as a rim pattern (KYA-18*, KYA-44–KYA-46*) and as a frieze divider (KYA-2*). Often we find two grooves incised before firing immediately below the lip (KYA-1*, KYA-44–KYA-46*, KYA-48, KYA-52, KYA-53*, KYA-55) and on three vessels, the grooves are scraped after firing (KYA-43*, KYA-54*, KYA-56*). It is likely that the rendering of these grooves emulates Attic MMB.

Base
The most common base encountered in Workshop A is a small eight-petalled rosette. It can be over-stamped by a small comic mask (KYA-2*, KYA-49*, KYA-51, KYA-58*), a small-scale version of the mask used in the Paniskos Workshop (Bouzek & Jansová 1974, 51 cat. MB 1, pl. 1) and the Meter Medallion Workshop (KYB-320*, KYB-348*, KYB-350*, KYB-363*, KYB-364*). Sometimes the rosette is surrounded by a frieze of dots (KYA-19*–KYA-21*). We also find a rosette with broad, lobed petals and an ivy-berry cluster in the centre (KYA-28*), which is clearly related to rosette C also known from a Kymean mould (Bouzek & Jansová 1974, 51 cat. MB 3, pl. 2). The base is normally surrounded by two ridges.

Recurring Stamps
I have already mentioned that there is considerable overlap between Workshop A and the unassigned Kymean workshops. This is also the case with Workshop A and, in particular, the Workshop of Kirbeis. In fact, the only Kymean fragment with a rim frieze with heart buds which I have *not* attributed to Kirbeis most likely belongs to Workshop A, because it features not just the grooves below the lip but also the horseman C stamp (KYA-1*). Also the pointed Ionian kyma with a double outline, otherwise known only on vessels attributed to Kirbeis, appears on two vessels of Workshop A (KYA-34*, KYA-51). It would be interesting to have a clearer understanding of the relationship between the two potters. In the following are listed recurring stamps which are employed only in Workshop A.

Fleur de lys A
This simple but decorative stylized floral stamp is used as a rim pattern (KYA-38, KYA-40*), as a frieze separator (KYA-2*, KYA-26*), and as a figural element below a frieze of suspended wreaths (KYA-29*). The first four are stamped horizontally, turned left, whereas the last is upside-down.

Bird L
Dove(?) with fan-shaped tail sitting right.
KYA-12*, KYA-58*

Boar C
Boar with dotted body leaping left.
KYA-1*, KYA-52

Myrtle
Small, stylized, compressed bound myrtle wreath with three leaves.
KYA-19*–KYA-21*, KYA-24*–KYA-27*

Palmette G
Small palmette with double central vein, which is hatched.
KYA-12*, KYA-17*

Palmette H
Large palmette with two volutes. The same palmette can be found in Pergamon (Conze et al. 1913, Beibl. 43.21).
KYA-14*–KYA-16*, KYA-42*

Palmette I
Stylized and smaller version of palmette H; the top is triangular and inside is an incised branch with fine veins.
KYA-12*, KYA-13*, KYA-19*–KYA-21*, KYA-28*, KYA-29*, KYA-37

Palmette K
Small palmette; the stamp is incomplete.
KYA-42*, KYA-54*, KYA-58*

Small, slender lotus petal
KYA-24*, KYA-25*, KYA-51

CATALOGUE TO CHAPTER 10

WORKSHOP A

Note that, in the catalogue descriptions, a small Roman numeral in parentheses – (i), (ii), or (iii) – following the description of a motif indicates the stamp generation, as determined by the motif's relative size.

BOWLS

A   *Figural Decoration*

Hunt

KYA-1*
Istros, Plateau, His-Constanta E, year and no. unknown, Constanta Museum. Fr. of rim and upper body. Two grooves below lip. Oxidized. Rim frieze: heart buds. Main decoration: horseman C right, dog D left, boar C left, Greek warrior C with sword in left hand. Calyx: tip of vegetal element. Frieze separators: two ridges.

KYA-2*
Olbia, Sector R25, O-P25-93-178, Parutine, Olbia National Preserve storeroom. Fr. of base and body. H 7 × W 6.1, WT 0.32–0.42, ⌀ base 4. Fabric: relatively fine, micaceous, lime inclusions, 2.5YR 6/6. Thin dull coat, ext. 2.5YR 3/1, 3/2, 3/3, int. 2.5YR 3/4. Medium hard fired, oxidized. Main decoration: upper frieze: foot of vase(?) alternating with small theatre mask; lower frieze: repeated horseman C with spear right. Medallion: rosette with veined petals, small slave mask at centre (only mouth preserved; identical: **KYA-49***, **KYA-51**, **KYA-58***) surrounded by three ridges. Frieze separators: fleur de lys A left.

KYA-3*
Olbia, Sector R25, O-P25-95-739, Parutine, Olbia National Preserve storeroom. Fr. of base and lower body. H 3.8 × W 4.6, WT 0.35. Fabric: relatively fine and micaceous, 7.5YR 6/6. Dull coat, 7.5YR 2.5/1. Medium hard fired, oxidized. Main decoration: upper frieze not preserved; lower frieze: repeated horseman C with spear right. Medallion: surrounded by two crude ridges.

Chariot Race

KYA-4*
Olbia, Sector R25, O-P25-96-1311, Parutine, Olbia National Preserve storeroom. Fr. of upper body. H 4.4 × W 4.6, WT 0.4. Fabric: relatively fine and micaceous, 7.5YR 6/6. Thin dull mottled coat, ext. 2.5YR 4/6, 3/2, int. 2.5YR 3/3. Hard fired, oxidized. Stacked in firing. Rim frieze: miniature theatre masks. Main decoration: Eros(?) racing two-horse chariot right (stamp blurred). Ascription to Workshop A is tentative, based on the minute theatre mask in the rim frieze.

(Heraldic) Dolphins

KYA-5*
Istros, His-978, Bucharest, Institute of Archaeology storeroom. Fr. of rim and upper body. H 6 × W 4.5, WT 0.36, 10%, RH 2.1. Fabric: relatively fine and micaceous, many small lime inclusions, many voids, 7.5YR 6/6. Dull coat, almost completely worn off ext., int. much pitted, 10YR 3/2. Medium hard fired, oxidized. Rim frieze: grooves. Main decoration: antithetical dolphins (A and B); above these, rosette C, tip of unidentified vegetal element below. Frieze separators: two ridges.
– Domăneanțu 2000, 133 cat. 658, pl. 47.

KYA-6*
Pantikapaion, M-45-13, Moscow, Puškin Museum of Fine Arts. Fr. of rim and upper body. H 6 × W 4.2, RH 2.5. Oxidized. No rim frieze. Main decoration: heraldic dolphins (A and B) between palmette L (ii); rosette A above dolphins. Calyx: tip of acanthus or palmette. Frieze separators: three ridges.

KYA-7*
Istros, His-1135, Bucharest, Institute of Archaeology storeroom. Fr. of upper body. H 2.5 × W 3.2. Oxidized. Main decoration: dolphin A, palmette L. Calyx: unidentified traces. Frieze separators: two ridges.
– Domăneanțu 2000, 21 cat. 83, pl. 6 (identified as Ephesian [Comique à la canne]).

KYA-8*
Istros, Tumular necropolis, Tomb XXVI, His-58-958/V 19665+V 19665 A–F, H, K, Bucharest, Institute of Archaeology storeroom. Three rim sections with four, two, and two joining frs., and one fr. of rim and upper body. H 3.4, WT 0.35, ⌀ rim 10.5, 26%, RH 1.7. Fabric: fine, micaceous. Dull coat. Medium hard fired, oxidized. Rim frieze: grooves. Main decoration: dolphin A. Secondarily burnt.
– Alexandrescu 1966, 190 cat. XXVI.3; Domăneanțu 2000, 134 cat. 659, pl. 47.

Griffins

KYA-9*
Istros, Plateau, His-Constanta F, year and no. unknown, Constanta Museum. Body fr. Oxidized. Main decoration: eagle griffin left, eagle griffin right. Calyx: slender, pointed palm frond B, bunch of grapes as space-filler. Frieze separators: two ridges.

B Calyx with Figural Decoration (Free Style)

KYA-10*
Olbia, Sector R25, O-P25-96-1492, Parutine, Olbia National Preserve storeroom. Fr. of rim and upper body; mould and surface very worn. H 7 × W 6.9, WT 0.4–0.52, ⌀ rim 13, 17%, RH 2.7. Fabric: relatively fine, non-micaceous, much very fine lime, 7.5YR 7/6. Thin coat with slight lustre ext., int. dull and adhering badly, painted on (part is reserved), mottled, ext. 7.5YR 3/1, int. 7.5YR 2.5/1, 10R 4/6. Medium hard fired, oxidized. Stacked in firing. Rim frieze: miniature comic masks alternating with bird K flying left (both very blurred). Main decoration: feline (panther?) leaping right alternating with Eros Q placed over but not separated from calyx with small pointed palm F. Ascription to Workshop A is tentative, based on the minute mask of the rim frieze.

KYA-11*
Istros, Plateau, His-Constanta D, year and no. unknown, Constanta Museum. Fr. of rim and upper body, ⌀ rim 12. Fabric: fine, highly micaceous, many lime inclusions, 7.5YR 7/4. Blotchy flaking coat, mostly dull ext., ext. 5YR 5/4, 4/2, int. 7.5YR 3/1. Oxidized. Rim friezes: grooves; miniature Ionian kyma. Main decoration: male with thyrsos right as space-filler between tall palmettes C.

KYA-12*
Istros, Tumular necropolis, Tomb XXVI, His-58-V 19664 [His-985 N], Bucharest, Institute of Archaeology storeroom. Seven rim and six body frs., all joining. H 5.5, WT 0.15, ⌀ rim 10, 80%, RH 1.6. Fabric: fine, micaceous, some small lime inclusions, 5YR 6/8. Dull coat, worn, inside pitted, 7.5YR 3/1. Medium hard fired, oxidized. Rim frieze: grooves, Ionian kyma, rounded with double outline. Calyx: palmette G and I alternating, bird L sitting right as space-filler.
– Alexandrescu 1966, 190 cat. XXVI.2, pl. 94; Domăneanţu 2000, 127 cat. 620, pl. 43 (tentatively identified as Athenian).

KYA-13*
Istros, His-769, Bucharest, Institute of Archaeology storeroom. Body fr. H 2.2 × W 2.4, WT 0.25. Fabric: fine, micaceous, 5YR 7/8. Dull coat, ext. 10YR 3/1, int. 2.5YR 5/6. Relatively hard fired, oxidized. Main decoration: palmette I with birds M left above.
– Domăneanţu 2000, 127 cat. 621, pl. 43 (tentatively identified as Athenian).

KYA-14*
Olbia, Cistern Л, O-E2-49-637, Parutine, Olbia Archaeological Museum. Complete profile; fragmentary bowl. Oxidized. Rim frieze: dots. Main decoration: palmettes H in two tiers (upside down in upper tier); on their tips stands kantharos B, mutilated stamp lacking one handle; in between, rosette D and man with thyrsos walking right as space-fillers. Medallion: small rosette surrounded by two ridges.
– Levi 1964b, 250, fig. 12.2.

KYA-15*
Olbia, Sector E7, squares 475, 495, 515, yellow clay layer, O-E7-62-155, Kiev, Institute of Archaeology storeroom. Three joining body frs. H 5 × W 4.8, WT 0.26. Fabric: fine, micaceous, a few minute lime inclusions, some small voids, 5YR 6/8. Dull coat, ext. 5YR 4/3, 3/1, int. 5YR 3/1. Medium hard fired, oxidized. Rim frieze: groove. Main decoration: kithara-playing male with cloak over lower body seated right, above palmette H; kantharos B (ii) at point where palmettes meet.

KYA-16*
Istros, His-V 19367 J, Bucharest, Institute of Archaeology storeroom. Fr. of lower body. H 3.2 × W 4, WT 0.55. Fabric: relatively fine and micaceous, many small lime inclusions, many voids, 5YR 6/6. Dull coat, ext. 2.5YR 4/6, int. 5YR 3/3. Medium hard fired, oxidized. Main decoration: palmettes H, one with added floral stem(?); where the palmettes meet is kantharos B (ii).
– Domăneanţu 2000, 134 cat. 665, pl. 47.

C Calyx with Figural Decoration (Friezes)

KYA-17*
Olbia, Sector AGD, О-АГД-86-71, Kiev, Institute of Archaeology storeroom. Body fr. H 4.5 × W 4.5, WT 0.37. Fabric: relatively fine and micaceous, many small lime inclusions, some voids, 5YR 6/8. Thin dull coat, 5YR 3/1. Hard fired, oxidized. Main decoration: upper frieze: kantharos B (ii) between palm fronds in negative relief, their tips curling left and right; lower frieze: kantharos B (ii) between palmettes G. Frieze separators: heart guilloche left.

D   *Calyx with Figural Decoration (Composition Unknown)*

KYA-18*
Olbia, Sector Sever-Zapad, O-C3-68-1900, Parutine, Olbia National Preserve storeroom. Fr. of rim and upper body. H 3.8 × W 5.5, WT 0.35, RH 2.3. Fabric: fine, micaceous, a few minute lime inclusions, some small voids, 5YR 5/6. Thin dull coat ext., glossier int., 7.5YR 2.5/1. Hard fired, oxidized. Rim frieze: small double-heart ornaments. Main decoration: tip of palm frond(?), top of kantharos A (iii).

E   *Scroll Decoration*

Vine Scroll and Myrtle Wreath

KYA-19*, **KYA-20***, and **KYA-21*** are identical, most likely from the same mould.

KYA-19*
Olbia, Tomb 10, inv. A 2192 (1927), Nikolaev, Historical Museum. Complete; fragmentary but lacking only minor fragments. ⌀ rim 10.5, RH 2.3, ⌀ base 2; vessel H 6.6; H:⌀ 1:1.6. Thin dull mottled brownish coat, a reddish band in the middle from stacking. Oxidized. Rim frieze: grooves. Main decoration: above, incised vine scroll with stamped bunch of grapes and vine leaf B right; below, bound myrtle wreath left. Calyx: palmette I; over branches, bird M sitting left. Medallion: eight-petalled rosette surrounded by frieze of dots. Frieze separators: two ridges.

KYA-20*
Olbia, Tomb 164 or 168 (inventory card in doubt), inv. A 2688 (1920), Nikolaev, Historical Museum. Complete; fragmentary but lacking only minor fragments. ⌀ rim 10.5, RH 2.3, ⌀ base 2; vessel H 6.6; H:⌀ 1:1.6. Thin dull mottled brownish coat, reddish in a band in the middle from stacking. Oxidized. Decoration as **KYA-19***.

KYA-21*
Olbia, inv. H 4027, Würzburg, Martin von Wagner Museum der Universität Würzburg (formerly Vogell collection). Complete. ⌀ rim 11; vessel H 6.6; H:⌀ 1:1.7. Fabric: 2.5YR 6/6. Dark brown coat, rim reddish brown. Oxidized. Decoration as **KYA-19***.
– Zahn 1908, 59 cat. 11; Boehlau 1908, 30 no. 270; Langlotz 1932, no. 921; Kotitsa 1998, 133–135 cat. 97, pl. 58 ("wohl Kirbei-Werkstatt"); Rotroff 2010, 69 cat. 43 (follows Kotitsa).

KYA-22
Olbia, Sector R25, O-P25-93-1308, 1308a, Parutine, Olbia National Preserve storeroom. Two non-joining body frs. probably from one vessel. H 2.8 × W 2.8, WT 0.35. Fabric: relatively fine and micaceous, many small and larger lime inclusions, 5YR 6/8. Dull coat, 5YR 2.5/1. Medium hard fired, oxidized. Rim frieze: grooves, dots. Main decoration: incised vine scroll with stamped vine leaves B right.

Ivy Scroll

KYA-23
Olbia, inv. 54791 Uvarov A12-7b [b], Moscow, State Historical Museum (Uvarov collection). Four joining frs. of rim and body. Oxidized. Rim frieze: Ionian kyma. Main decoration: incised ivy scroll right with stamped leaves and groups of three-dot berries above and below; palmette L upside-down; cock over garland(?). Frieze separators: Ionian kyma between ridges.
– Farmakovskij 1903a, 45, fig. 42 (O-1901-214).

F   *Garlands and Wreaths*

Myrtle Wreath

KYA-24* and **KYA-25*** are identical and may derive from the same mould.

KYA-24*
Olbia, Sector R25, O-P25-97-2152.1+2+2194.1+2+3, Parutine, Olbia National Preserve storeroom. Two rim and three body frs., all joining; complete profile except for base. H 8 × W 9.5, WT 0.25–0.45, ⌀ rim 14, 15%, RH 1.5. Fabric: relatively fine and micaceous, 7.5YR 6/4. Thin mottled coat, dull ext., slightly lustrous int., 5YR 4/4, 7.5YR 2.5/1. Medium hard fired, oxidized. Stacked in firing. Multiple rim friezes: miniature Ionian kyma; two ridges; miniature Ionian kyma. Main decoration: bound myrtle wreath with three leaves left. Calyx: palmette M alternating with slender lotus petal. Frieze separators: two ridges.

KYA-25*
Istros, His-B 602/V 19374, Bucharest, Institute of Archaeology storeroom. Fr. of lower body. H 3.1 × W 3.5, WT 0.25. Fabric: fine, micaceous, 5YR 6/6. Dull coat, 5YR 4/3, 4/4. Relatively hard fired, oxidized. Main decoration: bound myrtle wreath with three leaves left. Calyx: palmette M alternating with slender lotus petal. Frieze separators: two ridges.
– Domăneanțu 2000, 139 cat. 690, pl. 50.

KYA-26*
Istros, His-B 493/V 19371, Bucharest, Institute of Archaeology storeroom. Fr. of mid- and lower body. H 5 × W 4.7, WT 0.4. Fabric: fine, micaceous, 5YR 6/6. Dull coat, mottled, ext. 7.5YR 3/1, 5/6, int. 7.5YR 4/2. Relatively hard fired. Oxidized. Stacked in

firing. Rim frieze: Ionian kyma. Main decoration: bound myrtle wreath with three leaves left. Frieze separators: fleur de lys A left between ridges.
– Domăneanțu 2000, 139 cat. 691, pl. 50.

KYA-27*
Olbia, Sector R25, O-P25-99-2093, Parutine, Olbia National Preserve storeroom. Fr. of rim and upper body. H 4.6 × W 4.1, WT 0.36, ⌀ rim 14, 10%, RH 2. Fabric: relatively fine and micaceous, some small voids, 5YR 7/6. Thin slightly lustrous coat, 5YR 3/1. Medium hard fired, oxidized. Rim frieze: miniature Ionian kyma, four ridges. Main decoration: bound myrtle wreath with three leaves left. Frieze separators: ridges. Two repair holes.

Bound Miniature Garland Suspended from Boukranion B

KYA-28*
Olbia, Sector R25, O-P25-95-1720, Parutine, Olbia National Preserve storeroom. Fr. of base and body. H 7.3 × W 3.6, WT 0.3, ⌀ base 2.2. Fabric: relatively fine and micaceous, some small lime inclusions, 5YR 6/6. Thin slightly lustrous coat, 5YR 2.5/1. Medium hard fired, oxidized. Rim frieze: Ionian kyma. Main decoration: suspended bound garland H between small boukrania B; below, bird M left. Calyx: palmette I, bunch of grapes as space-filler. Medallion: rosette with six broad, lobed petals, ivy-berry cluster in the centre. Frieze separators: two ridges. Medallion is closely related, but not identical to that of a mould from Kyme (Bouzek & Jansová 1974, 51 cat. MB 3, pl. 2).

KYA-29*
Istros, Sector SG, His-73-1186 [His-973], Bucharest, Institute of Archaeology storeroom. Body fr. H 3.6 × W 5.2, WT 0.35. Fabric: fine, micaceous, 5YR 7/6. Slightly lustrous coat, 7.5YR 3/1. Relatively hard fired, oxidized. Main decoration: suspended bound garland H between small boukrania B; bird A right below boukrania, fleur de lys A upside-down below garland. Calyx: tip of palmette I. Frieze separators: dots between ridges.
– Domăneanțu 2000, 122 cat. 603, pl. 42 (identified as Pontic).

KYA-30*
Istros, His-B 463/V 8572 B, Bucharest, Institute of Archaeology storeroom. Fr. of rim and upper body. H 5.2 × W 4.8, WT 0.35, ⌀ rim 11, 14%, RH 1.7. Fabric: fine, micaceous, 5YR 6/6. Dull coat partly worn off ext., int. more lustrous, brown at rim, reddish below, ext. 10YR 3/1, int. 10YR 3/1, 2.5YR 4/6. Medium hard fired, oxidized. Rim frieze: miniature Ionian kyma. Main decoration: suspended bound garland H between small boukrania B. Frieze separators: two ridges.
– Domăneanțu 2000, 122 cat. 602, pl. 42 (identified as Pontic).

KYA-31*
Olbia, Sector NGS, O-НГС-05-318, Parutine, Olbia National Preserve storeroom. Fr. of rim and upper body. H 4.1 × W 4.9, WT 0.35, RH 2.1. Fabric: relatively fine and micaceous, some small lime inclusions, 5YR 6/6. Thin slightly lustrous coat, 5YR 2.5/1. Hard fired, oxidized. Rim frieze: miniature Ionian kyma. Main decoration: suspended bound garland H between small boukrania B.

KYA-32*
Olbia, Sector NGS, House III-3 B 368/107, O-НГС-93-1101, Parutine, Olbia National Preserve storeroom. Fr. of upper body. H 2.2 × W 2.7, WT 0.28–0.35. Fabric: fine, micaceous, minute voids, 7.5YR 6/6. Thin firm semi-lustrous coat, 10YR 3/1. Medium hard fired, oxidized. Rim frieze: grooves. Main decoration: suspended bound garland H between small boukrania B.
– Guldager Bilde 2010, 287 cat. F-122, pl. 195 (erroneously identified as Pontic).

KYA-33*
Olbia, Sector R25, O-P25-96-267, Parutine, Olbia National Preserve storeroom. Fr. of rim and upper body. H 3.5 × W 3.7, WT 0.35, ⌀ rim 12, 10%, RH 1.9. Fabric: relatively fine and micaceous, 7.5YR 7/6. Thin dull coat, mottled int., ext. 2.5YR 5/6, int. 2.5YR 4/6, 5YR 3/2. Medium hard fired, oxidized. Stacked in firing. No rim frieze. Main decoration: suspended bound garland H between small boukrania B. One repair hole.

Bound Miniature Garland, Other Compositions

KYA-34*
Olbia, Sector NGS, O-НГС-06-132, Parutine, Olbia National Preserve storeroom. Fr. of mid-body. H 3.3 × W 3, WT 0.4. Fabric: relatively fine and micaceous, 7.5YR 6/6. Thin dull coat, 10YR 3/2. Medium hard fired, oxidized. Rim frieze: Ionian kyma, pointed with double outline. Main decoration (free style): suspended bound garlands H over kantharos B (ii); in between, tip of palmette L. This rim frieze is normally encountered on moulds attributed to Kirbeis; see also **KYA-51**.

KYA-35*
Olbia, Sector R25, O-P25-99-662, Parutine, Olbia National Preserve storeroom. Fr. of mid- and lower body. H 3.5 × W 4.4, WT 0.3. Fabric: relatively fine and micaceous, 7.5YR 5/4. Thin coat with slight lustre, ext. 7.5YR 3/2, int. 7.5YR 2.5/1. Hard fired, oxidized. Main decoration: above, suspended bound garland H over birds A (ii) and M; below, kantharos C alternating with palmette M. Frieze separators: two ridges.

KYA-36*
Istros, His-706, Bucharest, Institute of Archaeology storeroom. Fr. of rim and upper body. H 4.7 × W 4, WT 0.4, RH 1.5. Fabric: fine, micaceous, 5YR 6/6. Dull coat, redder at rim ext., ext. 7.5YR 3/1, 5/6, int. 7.5YR 3/1. Medium hard fired, oxidized. Stacked in firing. Multiple rim friezes: miniature theatre masks; miniature Ionian kyma. Main decoration: bound garland H, with small rosette C or related above.

Garlands Suspended from Bows

KYA-37
Olbia, Cistern Л, O-E2-49-685, present whereabouts unknown. Large fr. of rim and most of body. Rim frieze: upside-down hearts or small double-heart ornaments. Main decoration: bound garland E suspended between thick bows, with bird H above. Calyx: palmette L, dolphins A right as space-filler. Frieze separators: dots between ridges. The vessel could also have been made by Kirbeis, but the presence of palmette L and the dots between ridges lead me to attribute it to Workshop A; moreover, the rim frieze is probably a misunderstood version of the small double-heart ornaments.
– Levi 1964b, 250, fig. 12.1; Rotroff 2010, 68 cat. 12.

Garlands Suspended from Columns

KYA-38
Porthmion, П-78-10, Kerč History and Culture Reserve inv. KMAK 9526. Fr. of rim and upper body. Oxidized. Rim frieze: fleur de lys A left. Main decoration: bound garland E suspended from column C; over garland, bird N flying left.
– Grzegrzółka 2010, 129–130 cat. 181 (identified as Pergamene).

KYA-39
Pantikapaion, Cistern N 179, 96-no.(?), Kerč History and Culture Reserve. Fr. of rim and body. Rim frieze: Ionian kyma. Main decoration: bound garlands (type?) suspended between column C; dolphin(?) over garlands. Calyx: palm frond F with kantharos B (ii) as space-filler. Frieze separators: heart guilloche left.
– Tolstikov & Zhuravlev 2004, pl. 101.13.

Other Types of Garland

KYA-40*
Istros, His-833, Bucharest, Institute of Archaeology storeroom. Body fr. H 2.6 × W 4.8, WT 0.32. Fabric: relatively fine, micaceous, 10YR 6/1. Dull coat, almost completely worn off, 7.5YR 3/1. Medium hard fired, oxidized. Rim frieze: fleur de lys A left. Main decoration: bound garland E(?) suspended from boukephalion A (stamp very blurred).

– Domăneanțu 2000, 18 cat. 68, pl. 5 (identified as Ephesian [Comique à la canne]).

KYA-41*
Olbia, Sector E6, square 475n, 476n, 477ne, yellow clay layer with ash inclusions, O-E6-59-1123, Kiev, Institute of Archaeology storeroom. Two joining frs. of base and lower body. H 6.3 × W 5.6, WT 0.45, ø base 3.8. Fabric: relatively coarse and micaceous, many voids, erupting lime inclusions, 5YR 6/8. Dull coat, 5YR 3/2. Medium hard fired, oxidized. Main decoration: suspended garland A, perhaps flying bird above. Calyx: palmette L, not separated from the main decoration. Medallion: surrounded by frieze of dots and rounded petals with central and side veins.

KYA-42*
Olbia, Sector NGS, O-НГС-05-320, Parutine, Olbia National Preserve storeroom. Fr. of mid- and lower body. H 4.4 × W 4.6, WT 0.45. Fabric: relatively fine and micaceous, 5YR 5/8, 6/8. Thin slightly lustrous coat, ext. 5YR 4/6, 2.5/1, int. 2.5YR 4/8. Medium hard fired, oxidized. Stacked in firing. Main decoration: suspended bound garland E with rosette B below and above. Calyx: palmette H alternating with palmette K. Frieze separators: three ridges.

G *Rim Fragments*

Small Double-Heart Ornaments

KYA-43*
Olbia, Sector R25, O-P25-98-2248, Parutine, Olbia National Preserve storeroom. Rim fr. Three scraped grooves. Between the upper grooves, two zigzags in dull white paint (almost vanished). H 3.3 × W 2.9, WT 0.5, RH 2. Fabric: relatively fine and micaceous, 5YR 7/6. Thin lustrous coat, 7.5YR 2.5/1. Medium hard fired, oxidized.

KYA-44
Olbia, Sector NGS, O-НГС-02-433, Parutine, Olbia National Preserve storeroom. Rim fr. Two grooves below lip. H 2.9 × W 4.2, WT 0.35–0.45, ø rim 12, 10%, RH 1.65. Fabric: fine, slightly micaceous, a few minute lime inclusions and small dark grey inclusions, 5YR 5/8. Thin firm coat with slight lustre, slight crazing at rim, 2.5YR 4/8. Medium hard fired, oxidized.

KYA-45
Olbia, Sector NGS, O-НГС-02-728, Parutine, Olbia National Preserve storeroom. Rim fr. Two grooves below lip. H 4.5 × W 4.5, WT 0.32–0.35, ø rim 11, 10%, RH 3.7. Fabric: fine, dense, slightly

micaceous, a few minute lime inclusions, some small rounded voids, 5YR 5/1, 4/1. Thin firm slightly lustrous coat, ext. 2.5Y 3/0, int. 10YR 3/1. Medium hard fired, reduced. Stacked in firing.

KYA-46*
Istros, His-204, Bucharest, Institute of Archaeology storeroom. Rim fr. Two grooves below lip. H 4.2 × W 5.9, WT 0.31, RH 2.4. Fabric: fine, micaceous, some voids, 5YR 6/8. Dull coat, ext. 5YR 5/6, 3/2, int. 5YR 4/4. Relatively hard fired, oxidized.

KYA-47*
Myrmekion, M-57-2360 or 2960, St Petersburg, IIMK RAN. Rim fr. H 4.5, WT 0.35, ⌀ rim 15, 12%, RH 2. Fabric: fine, highly micaceous, numerous small voids, 7.5YR 6/2. Thin dull coat, adhering badly, Gley 1 3/N. Low fired, reduced. Rim friezes: deep groove; small double-heart ornaments of alternating direction.

Heart Guilloche Left

KYA-48
Olbia, Sector NGS, House IV-3 B 343/202, O-НГС-92-416, Parutine, Olbia National Preserve storeroom. Rim fr. Two grooves below lip. H 4.2 × W 7.5, WT 0.35–0.4, ⌀ rim 12.5, 22%, RH 3.2. Fabric: fine, soft, micaceous, a few small lime inclusions, some voids, 2.5Y 5/2. Thin coat, adhering badly, 5Y 2.5/1. Medium hard fired, reduced.
– Guldager Bilde 2010, 284 cat. F-94, pl. 187 (erroneously identified as Ephesian).

H   Base Fragments

KYA-49*
Istros, His-646, Bucharest, Institute of Archaeology storeroom. Base fr. H 3.6 × W 2.1, WT 0.4, ⌀ base 3.5. Fabric: fine, micaceous, a few minute lime inclusions, some small voids, 5YR 6/6. Slightly lustrous coat, 5YR 3/1. Relatively hard fired, oxidized. Calyx: slender lotus petal alternating with another vegetal element? Medallion: slave mask at centre of small rosette with small ribbed petals. Identical base: **KYA-2***, **KYA-51**, **KYA-58***.
– Domăneanțu 2000, 122 cat. 605, pl. 42 (identified as Pontic).

KYA-50
Olbia, Sector R25, O-P25-95-905, Parutine, Olbia National Preserve storeroom. Base fr. H 3.3 × W 1.8, WT 0.55, ⌀ base 3.5. Fabric: relatively fine and micaceous, 5YR 6/6. Slightly lustrous coat, ext. 5YR 2.5/1, int. 5YR 2.5/2. Hard fired, oxidized. Calyx cannot be identified. Medallion: rosette with small incised petals surrounded by crude ridge.

SUPPLEMENTARY SHAPES

Small Bowl

KYA-51
Olbia, Bonn, Akademisches Kunstmuseum (formerly Vogell collection). Complete. ⌀ rim 8.8; vessel H 5.6; H:⌀ 1:1.6. Fabric: relatively fine and micaceous, some small lime inclusions. Reddish brown coat. Oxidized. Rim frieze: Ionian kyma, pointed with double outline. Calyx: straight acanthus Y with hatched central vein alternating with tall slender lotus petals; small boukranion B as space-filler. Medallion: surrounded by two ridges; slave mask at centre of rosette with small incised petals. Identical base: **KYA-2***, **KYA-49***, **KYA-58***. This rim frieze is normally encountered on moulds attributed to Kirbeis; see also **KYA-34***.
– Zahn 1908, 59 cat. 12; Boehlau 1908, 29 no. 265; Zimmer 2005, 110 cat. A49.

Skyphos with Vertical Ring Handles and High Foot

KYA-52
Olbia, inv. T 493, Kassel Antikensammlung (formerly Vogell collection). Complete. Two grooves below lip. ⌀ rim 12.6; vessel H 12.6; H:⌀ 1:1. Fabric: micaceous, yellowish red. Brownish coat, red at foot. Oxidized. No rim frieze. Main decoration: upper frieze: horsemen C right; lower frieze: hunt, with hunter B and dog E right, boar B and C left and right, deer right. Calyx: straight, fleshy acanthus X. Frieze separators: small double-heart ornaments; broad dots.
– Zahn 1908, 68 cat. 30; Boehlau 1908, 27 no. 252; CVA Kassel 2 [Germany 38], 63–64, figs. 39–40, pl. 87.3–4.

KYA-53*
Myrmekion, M-57-339, St Petersburg, IIMK RAN. Fr. of rim and upper body. Two grooves below lip. H 5.5, WT 0.32, ⌀ rim 10, 10%. Fabric: fine, highly micaceous, 10YR 6/2. Slightly lustrous coat with soapy surface, Gley 1 2.5/N. Reduced. No rim frieze. Main decoration: horseman C right below handle; perhaps another horseman with raised spear.

KYA-54*
Olbia, Bonn, Akademisches Kunstmuseum (formerly Vogell collection). Complete. Scraped groove below lip. On rim, shadow of white-painted horizontal Z's; two scraped grooves below them. ⌀ rim 10.5; vessel H 12. Fabric: highly micaceous, yellowish red. Brownish coat. Oxidized. No rim frieze. Main decoration: upper frieze: kantharos D; middle frieze: palmette K; lower frieze: large

rosettes alternating with palmettes. Calyx: large rosette(?) and part of palmette (type?). Frieze separators: dots between two faint ridges.
– Zahn 1908, 68 cat. 31; Boehlau 1908, 27 no. 253; Zimmer 2005, 111 cat. A51.

KYA-55
Pantikapaion, area of 2 Lenin Str., Kerč History and Culture Reserve inv. KMAK 2381 (1961). Two joining frs. of rim and body with remains of handle attachment. Two grooves below lip. Oxidized. No rim frieze. Main decoration: dolphins right alternating with rosette A. Calyx: palmette C alternating with ovoid lotus petal. Frieze separators: two ridges. All the stamps belong to the MMW, but the shape, the grooves below the lip and the two ridges separating the frieze from the calyx induce me to attribute the vessel to Workshop A.
– Grzegrzółka 2010, 68 cat. 51 (identified as Pergamene).

KYA-56*
Olbia, square 55, Room [Cistern] Л, western part, grey clay layer, O-48-119+4982, Kiev, Institute of Archaeology storeroom. Two joining frs. of rim and body; remains of handle attachment. Scraped groove below lip. On rim, shadow of white-painted zigzag line, with two scraped grooves below. H 6.5 × W 8.7, WT 0.25, ⌀ rim 10, 27%, RH 2.8. Fabric: fine, very fine mica, 5YR 6/6. Slightly lustrous coat, ext. 5YR 3/1, int. 5YR 3/2. Medium hard fired, oxidized. No rim frieze. Calyx: imbricate small palmettes.

Jug with Round Bottom

KYA-57
Crimea, Kerč History and Culture Reserve inv. KMAK 1605. Almost complete profile, lacking rim and part of handle. Rim frieze: Ionian kyma with hatched dart. Main decoration: bound garland E carried by small boukrania B; over the garland, rosette K. Calyx: palmette N with rosette K as space-filler. Frieze separators: Ionian kyma between ridges.
– Grzegrzółka 2010, 42 cat. 11.

Juglet

KYA-58*
Olbia, Sector AGD, O-АГД-91-202, Parutine, Olbia National Preserve storeroom. Two joining frs., complete except for rim and handle. H 5.5, WT 0.35. Fabric: fine, micaceous, some lime, soft and poorly preserved, 2.5Y 5/2. Thin dull coat almost completely worn off, ext. 5Y 3/1, uncoated int. Not too hard fired, reduced. Rim frieze: heart guilloche right. Calyx: palmette K(?) and unidentified vegetal element; bird L as space-filler. Medallion: small slave mask at centre of rosette with eight small petals. Identical base: **KYA-2***, **KYA-49***, **KYA-51**.

KYME (I) 181

UNATTRIBUTED

BOWLS

A Figural Decoration

Divinities

KYX-1*
Istros, Sector ZS7b, His-69-77, Bucharest, Institute of Archaeology storeroom. Fr. of rim and upper body. H 6.5 × W 7.5, WT 0.37, ⌀ rim 15, 19%, RH 2.3. Fabric: medium fine, slightly micaceous, abundant small voids, 5YR 6/6. Thin dull coat, int. 5YR 3/1. Oxidized. Rim frieze: Ionian kyma, widely spaced. Main decoration: winged Potnia Theron(?) with tall polos alternating with Eros-Paniskos. Workshop of Paniskos.
– Domăneanțu 2000, 112 cat. 564, pl. 38.

KYX-2*
Istros, His-1172, Bucharest, Institute of Archaeology storeroom. Body fr. H 2.5 × W 3, WT 0.25. Fabric: relatively fine and micaceous, many small lime inclusions, some voids, 2.5Y 7/6. Dull coat, 2.5Y 3/1. Relatively hard fired, reduced. Main decoration: frontal woman with very narrow waist, both arms held out to the sides; *Rankenfrau*? Cf. Bouzek & Jansová 1974, 62 cat. MB 71, fig. 4, pl. 9 (identified as Syrian); in general concerning *Rankenfrau* on MMB: de Luca 1990, 161–162; cf. also Bouzek & Jansová 1974, 61 cat. MB 65, pl. 9, which they classify as Pergamene.
– Domăneanțu 2000, 16 cat. 60, pl. 4 (identified as Ephesian [Vases gris]).

Ritual Preparation

For this decoration, see Fig. 60 and **AIB-1***–**AIB-7*** in Chapter 12.

KYX-3*
Istros, Plateau, His-Constanta A, year and no. unknown, Constanta Museum. Fr. of lower body. Oxidized. Main decoration: Eros pouring wine into *Pokalkantharos* right, Eros walking right, figure with cloak walking left. Calyx: low rounded imbricate petals with central vein, separated from main decoration by torus.

KYX-4*
Olbia, Sector NGS, O-НГС-00-1236, Parutine, Olbia National Preserve storeroom. Fr. of upper body. H 2.6 × W 3.8, WT 0.4. Fabric: fine, slightly micaceous, 5YR 6/8. Thin firm slightly lustrous coat, mottled ext., ext. 2.5YR 5/8, 3/1, int. 7.5YR 3/2. Medium hard fired, oxidized. Stacked in firing. Main decoration: Eros pouring wine into *Pokalkantharos* right, Dionysos with cornucopia(?) left, chubby Eros with torch left.

KYX-5*
Istros, His-921, Bucharest, Institute of Archaeology storeroom. Body fr. H 2.6 × W 3, WT 0.3. Fabric: fine, slightly micaceous, 5YR 6/6. Slightly lustrous coat, dark red int. and ext. below, brown ext. above, ext. 2.5YR 4/8, 10YR 3/1, int. 2.5YR 4/8. Relatively hard fired, oxidized. Stacked in firing. Main decoration: Eros pouring wine from amphora into *Pokalkantharos*.
– Domăneanțu 2000, 92 cat. 440, pl. 30 (identified as Ephesian).

KYX-6*
Olbia, O-x8-483, Kiev, Institute of Archaeology storeroom. Fr. of rim and body. H 6.6 × W 6.9, WT 0.32, ⌀ rim 13, 16%, RH 2.8. Fabric: relatively fine and micaceous, some small lime inclusions, 5YR 6/6. Coat with dull lustre, 5YR 3/1. Medium hard fired, oxidized. Rim frieze: Ionian kyma, rounded with double outline. Main decoration: female extending wreath towards two Erotes with torches(?) moving left. The torch-bearing Eros is also found on **KYX-7***; though the female appears to be related to altar figure 1A, it is a different stamp and, if identical to the stamp on **KYX-7***, it is a Nike, because that figure is winged.

KYX-7*
Myrmekion, M-57-305, St Petersburg, State Hermitage Museum. Fr. of rim and upper body. H 4.5, WT 0.25, ⌀ rim 13, 10%, RH 1.8. Fabric: relatively fine and micaceous, many small lime inclusions, some voids, 2.5YR 6/6. Thin dull mottled coat, ext. 10R 5/6, 3/4, int. 10R 5/6. Oxidized. Rim frieze: Ionian kyma. Main decoration: winged female extending wreath towards an Eros with a torch moving left. See also **KYX-6***.

Eros

KYX-8*
Olbia, Sector R25, O-P25-97-1112, Parutine, Olbia National Preserve storeroom. Two joining frs. of mid- and lower body. H 5.6 × W 4.3, WT 0.3–0.4. Fabric: relatively fine and micaceous, some small lime inclusions, 5YR 6/6. Thin dull coat, mottled int., ext. 10R 4/6, 2.5YR 3/1, int. 2.5YR 3/1. Medium hard fired, oxidized. Stacked in firing. Main decoration: remains of small Eros flying left. Calyx: straight acanthus alternating with 'nelumbo' filled with scales; rosette A as space-filler. Frieze separators: bird A between ridges. The stamp of bird A is in pristine condition.

Mantled Dancing Women

KYX-9
Olbia, O-4183. Mainz, Römisch-Germanisches Zentralmuseum (formerly Vogell collection). Complete, ⌀ rim 12.5; vessel H 7.6; H:⌀ 1:1.6. Fabric: reddish. Black coat. Oxidized. Rim frieze: rosette with eight rounded petals. Main decoration: upper frieze: wide krater flanked by heraldic dolphins alternating with Medusa head; lower frieze: frontal dancing females holding out skirt alternating with *agyieus* furnished with palmette, small palmettes as space-fillers. Medallion unclear (worn?). Frieze separators: astragal between ridges. Probably the same krater as on **KYX-14*** and **KYX-27**.
– Zahn 1908, 66 cat. 23; Boehlau 1908, 31 no. 278; Kraus 1951, 7–8 cat. 6, fig. 2.1, pl. 2.3.

KYX-10 (see Fig. 47)
Olbia, Sector NGS, O-НГС-06-271, Parutine, Olbia National Preserve storeroom. Fr. of mid- and lower body. H 6.8 × W 9.8, WT 0.26. Fabric: relatively fine and micaceous, 5YR 6/8. Dull coat adhering badly, 2.5YR 4/8. Medium hard fired. Oxidized. Main decoration: upper frieze missing; lower frieze: frontal female dancers holding out skirt, between slender curving palm fronds and rhomboidal petals with volutes; above dancers, birds sitting left and right. Medallion: missing, surrounded by dots. Frieze separators: small palmettes between ridges. Two repair holes and a third with lead clamp in place.

Mythological (Odysseus and Skylla)

KYX-11*
Olbia, Sector NGS, House III-3 R 359/115, O-НГС-92-811. Fr. of rim and upper body. Oxidized. Rim frieze: heart guilloche left. Main decoration: Scylla attacking oared ship sailing right.
– Samojlova & Batizat 1994, fig. 2; Guldager Bilde 2010, 282 cat. F-72, pl. 182.

Mythological (Herakles and Telephos)

KYX-12*
Olbia, Sector NGS, House III-2 R 255/83, O-НГС-89-82+90-372 (join across years), Parutine, Olbia National Preserve storeroom. Rim and two joining body frs. H 7.5 × W 8.8, WT 0.5–0.6, ⌀ rim 15, 25%, RH 2.9. Fabric: medium fine, slightly micaceous, lumps of amorphous lime, many larger and smaller voids, 7.5YR 6/4. Thin firm coat with bluish metallic sheen, 7.5YR 4/0. Medium hard fired, oxidized. Rim frieze: Ionian kyma, rounded with double outline. Main decoration: four fighting males in cuirasses; standing Herakles with left hand on club, watching Telephos being suckled by she-wolf; Paniskos (alternative stamp); warrior (mould worn, image blurred).
– Guldager Bilde 2010, 282 cat. F-70, pl. 181.

Battle

KYX-13*
Olbia, Sector NGS, House IV-2 P 285/196, O-НГС-91-487, Parutine, Olbia National Preserve storeroom. Fr. of rim and upper body. Oxidized. Rim friezes: two deep grooves; Ionian kyma, rounded with double outline, upside-down. Main decoration: battle scene.
– Guldager Bilde 2010, 282 cat. F-71, pl. 182

Vases

KYX-14*
Olbia, Sector NGS, O-НГС-05-278, Parutine, Olbia National Preserve storeroom. Fr. of mid- and lower body. H 4.1 × W 5.3, WT 0.35. Fabric: relatively fine, some light-reflecting inclusions, 7.5YR 6/8. Thin dull coat, 7.5YR 3/1. Medium hard fired, oxidized. Main decoration: dog(s) flanking large krater (very dull stamp). Frieze separators: fleur de lys B probably between ridges. Probably the same krater as on **KYX-9** and **KYX-27**.

KYX-15*
Kepoi, Ke-66-183, Moscow, State Historical Museum. Three non-joining rim frs. and one body fr., ⌀ rim 13. Oxidized. Rim frieze: heart guilloche left. Main decoration: tops of loutrophoroi with lid. The same loutrophoroi can be found on Kymean moulds and bowls: Bouzek & Jansová 1974, 51 cat. MB 5, pls. 2–3 (mould of Erotes Workshop) and 54 cats. MB 21, MB 22, fig. 1, pl. 4 (bowls attributed to Paniskos Workshop). Workshop of Paniskos.
– Usačeva 1978, fig. 1.10.

Heraldic Animals

KYX-16*
Olbia, Sector NGS, O-НГС-02-432, Parutine, Olbia National Preserve storeroom. Fr. of rim and upper body. H 6 × W 6.8, WT 0.4–0.47, ⌀ rim 13, 15%, RH 3. Fabric: relatively fine, highly micaceous, a few lime inclusions, some small voids, 5YR 6/8. Thin slightly lustrous coat, adhering badly, int. worn off in patches, darkened at rim ext., ext. 2.5YR 4/8, 10YR 4/1, int. 2.5YR 4/8. Medium hard fired, oxidized. Stacked in firing. Rim frieze: heart guilloche right. Main decoration: heraldic dolphins between five-petalled rosettes. One repair hole.

KYX-17*
Olbia, Sector NGS, O-НГС-87-382, Parutine, Olbia National Preserve storeroom. Fr. of upper body close to rim. H 5.6 × W 4.4, WT 0.36. Fabric: relatively fine and micaceous, 2.5YR 6/6. Thin dull coat, 5YR 4/3. Hard fired, oxidized. Stacked in firing. Rim frieze: heart guilloche left. Main decoration: heraldic(?) goat(s) around kantharos, heraldic(?) dolphin(s) over kantharos C;

below the figures but not separated from them, slender palm frond with tip curving to right.

KYX-18*
Istros, His-912, Bucharest, Institute of Archaeology storeroom. Fr. of upper body. Oxidized. Main decoration: long-horned rampant goat left. The same goat can be found on **KYX-33**.
– Domăneanţu 2000, 4 cat. 8, pl. 1 (identified as Ephesian [Menemachos]).

KYX-19*
Olbia, Sector R25, O-P25-96-1622, Parutine, Olbia National Preserve storeroom. Fr. of upper body. H 3.4 × W 2.5, WT 0.48. Fabric: relatively fine and micaceous, small lime inclusions, 7.5YR 6/6. Slightly lustrous coat, 5YR 4/6. Medium hard fired, oxidized. Stacked in firing. Rim frieze: miniature theatre masks, double-stamped. Main decoration: rampant long-horned goat.

Objects (Columns and Vases)

KYX-20*
Olbia, Sector NGS, House IV-2 B 280/165, O-НГС-91-3, Parutine, Olbia National Preserve storeroom. Fr. of rim and upper body. H 5 × W 6.3, WT 0.38–0.52, ⌀ rim 13, 13%, RH 3.15. Fabric: fine and slightly micaceous, occasional orange lime inclusions, many small and a few larger voids, 5YR 6/6. Fine firm semi-lustrous coat with surface slightly pitted, ext. 10YR 2/1, int. 10YR 2/1, 2.5Y 3/2. Relatively hard fired, oxidized. Rim frieze: two deep grooves. Main decoration: small Ionian column between suspended wreaths with *tainia*. Frieze separators: dots.
– Guldager Bilde 2010, 282 cat. F-69, pl. 181.

KYX-21*
Istros, His-489, Bucharest, Institute of Archaeology storeroom. Fr. of upper body. H 2.8 × W 3.1, WT 0.24. Fabric: fine, slightly micaceous, 5YR 6/6. Dull coat ext., int. with slight lustre, ext. 7.5YR 3/2, int. 10YR 3/1. Relatively hard fired, oxidized. Main decoration: kantharos B (i) between columns on high bases. Frieze separators: astragal.
– Domăneanţu 2000, 35 cat. 144, pl. 10 (identified as Ephesian [Monogram PAR]).

Boukephalia and Rosettes

KYX-22*
Olbia, Sector AGD, O-АГД-85-191, Kiev, Institute of Archaeology storeroom. Fr. of base and lower body, WT 0.25–0.5, ⌀ base 3.5. Fabric: fine, slightly micaceous, some small voids, 7.5YR 7/4. Thin dull coat, ext. 7.5YR 6/6, 5/4, int. 5YR 5/4 (mottled). Hard fired, oxidized. No calyx; small boukephalia A alternating with rosette A. Medallion: double rosette with outer pointed petals, inner rounded ones; medallion surrounded by two ridges. Either misfired or secondarily burnt. The same medallion is found on vessels attributed to the Paniskos Workshop (Bouzek & Jansová 1974, 52, 54 cats. MB 1, [mould], MB 19, MB 25, fig. 1, pls. 2, 4, 5). Small boukranion alternates with small rosette on rims of the Athenian 'Hausmann's Workshop' (see Rotroff 1982a, 27–28, pl. 98).

Identification?

KYX-23*
Olbia, Sector E6-7, squares 618w, 628sw, grey clay layer, O-E6-7-63-334, Kiev, Institute of Archaeology storeroom. Fr. of rim and upper body. H 5.5 × W 5, WT 0.5. Fabric: fine, highly micaceous, some voids, 2.5YR 6/6. Dull coat, flaking, 10R 4/8. Relatively hard fired, oxidized. Rim frieze: grooves. Main decoration: altar with altar screen against which an object (thyrsos?) with bow(?) is leaning.

Animals

KYX-24
Olbia, Sector NGS, O-НГС-06-540, Parutine, Olbia National Preserve storeroom. Fr. of upper body close to rim. H 4.8 × W 4.6, WT 0.45. Fabric: relatively fine and micaceous, some small lime inclusions, 5YR 6/6. Thin dull coat, 5YR 3/1. Medium hard fired, oxidized. No rim frieze. Main decoration: several birds (hens?) right, one standing on a thin branch. One repair hole.

KYX-25*
Olbia, Sector NGS, O-НГС-93-88, Parutine, Olbia National Preserve storeroom. Fr. of rim and upper body; worn. H 4.7 × W 4.7, WT 0.3–0.45, ⌀ rim 12, 12%, RH 2.25. Fabric: fine, micaceous, a few minute lime inclusions, some small voids, 5YR 6/6. Thin firm semi-lustrous coat, darkened at rim int., ext. 5YR 3/1, 3/4, int. 5YR 3/4, 2.5YR 2.5/0. Medium hard fired, oxidized. Stacked in firing. Rim frieze: heart guilloche left. Main decoration: vegetal(?) (or garland?) with bird sitting right. Perhaps Possis because of the character of the rim pattern.

KYX-26*
Olbia, Sector E7, square 578n, 579nw, yellow clay layer, O-E7-59-1662, Kiev, Institute of Archaeology storeroom. Body fr. Oxidized. Stacked in firing. Main decoration: winged animal? Frieze separators: upside-down Ionian kyma between ridges.

Hunt

KYX-27
Olbia, Stettin (formerly Vogell collection). Complete. ø rim 13.5; vessel H 7.8; H:ø 1:1.7. Brown coat. Oxidized. Rim friezes: grooves; small palmettes. Main decoration: upper frieze: deer and panther flanking palmette; lower frieze: wide krater alternating with *agyieus* with vegetal elements, rosette between two palmettes above krater. Medallion: rosette with eight petals surrounded by frieze of dots. Frieze separators: astragal between ridges. Probably the same krater as on **KYX-9** and **KYX-14***.
– Zahn 1908, 65–66 cat. 22; Boehlau 1908, 31 no. 277.

KYX-28*
Istros, His-V 8566 D, Bucharest, Institute of Archaeology storeroom. Fr. of mid- and lower body. H 6.3 × W 8.2, WT 0.42. Fabric: medium fine, slightly micaceous, abundant minute shell, 2.5YR 6/8. Coat almost completely worn off together with large part of surface, 10YR 3/1. Not too hard fired, oxidized. Rim frieze: Ionian kyma. Main decoration: Eros with torch left alternating with animal (dog?) leaping left. Calyx: acanthus with tip folded right alternating with straight palmette C; single row of small pointed petals with central vein around the missing base.
– Domăneanţu 2000, 121 cat. 601, pl. 42 (identified as Pontic).

KYX-29*
Istros, Sector Z, His-57-403/V 17644, Bucharest, Institute of Archaeology storeroom. Body fr. H 4.8 × W 5, WT 0.4. Fabric: medium fine, slightly micaceous, 7.5YR 7/6. Dull mottled coat ext., int. with metallic lustre, 7.5YR 3/1, 4/4. Not too hard fired, oxidized. Rim frieze: Ionian kyma. Main decoration: upper frieze: animals running left (mould very worn and stamps blurred, animals cannot be identified); lower frieze: Eros-Paniskos sitting frontal with crossed legs. Workshop of Paniskos.
– Domăneanţu 2000, 110 cat. 555.

KYX-30*
Olbia, Sector NGS, O-НГС-08-148, Parutine, Olbia National Preserve storeroom. Fr. of upper body. H 4 × W 4.5, WT 0.45. Fabric: relatively fine and micaceous, some small lime inclusions, 5YR 6/6. Thin dull coat, ext. 2.5YR 5/6, 3/1, int. 2.5YR 5/6. Medium hard fired, oxidized. Stacked in firing. Rim frieze: heart guilloche left. Main decoration: stag left, turning head back; unidentified motif at right.

B   *Calyx with Figural Decoration (Free Style)*

KYX-31
Olbia, O-1926-no no., present whereabouts unknown. Complete profile; half bowl preserved. Multiple rim friezes: Ionian kyma; heart guilloche left. Main decoration: large Nike left offering wreath(?), ithyphallic satyr standing on pyramidal group of minute leaves, Eros-Paniskos sitting cross-legged as spacer. Calyx: pyramidal group of minute leaves repeated four times. Medallion: surrounded by two ridges; slave mask surrounded by small pointed petals. Workshop of Paniskos. The same base decoration can be found on a mould unearthed at Kyme (Bouzek & Jansová 1974, 51 cat. MB 1, pls. 1, 3), also attributed to the Workshop of Paniskos.
– Pharmakowskyi 1929, 53, fig. 46.

KYX-32
Olbia, O-1928-19142, present whereabouts unknown. Body fr. Rim frieze: Ionian kyma, rounded with double outline. Main decoration: Eros standing on tip of acanthus Z pouring wine from amphora into *Pokalkantharos*, Eros with torch left. The same acanthus can be found on **KYX-58**.
– St Petersburg, IIMK RAN, photo archive neg. I 75373.

KYX-33
Olbia, O-1925-242, present whereabouts unknown. Fr. of rim and upper body Rim frieze: Ionian kyma. Main decoration: calyx of straight acanthus flanked by rampant goats; on tip of acanthus sits satyr turned to the left, holding his right hand over his head; over the goats, small boukrania with up-turned horns and *tainia*. Same goat on **KYX-18***.
– St Petersburg, IIMK RAN, photo archive neg. II 19397.

KYX-34
Olbia, O-1925-207, present whereabouts unknown. Fr. preserving large part of bowl with base. Main decoration: slender acanthus leaves with tips bent to left alternating with slender straight acanthus leaves; on tips of the latter, birds sit left; in between, rosette K as filler and over the rosettes are rabbits jumping left. Medallion: rosette with lobed petals, surrounded by frieze of dots. The medallion rosette is deliberately perforated in the centre, probably for libation.
– Semenov-Zuser 1931, fig. 17; St Petersburg, IIMK RAN, photo archive neg. II 19420.

KYX-35*
Istros, His-1098, Bucharest, Institute of Archaeology storeroom. Body fr., surface very worn. H 3.2 × W 3, WT 0.3. Fabric: medium fine, abundant minute lime inclusions, very fine light-reflecting inclusions, 2.5YR 6/6. Dull wash almost completely worn off, 5YR 3/1. Relatively hard fired, oxidized. Main decoration: dolphin(?), kantharos A (ii), hind part of animal (stag? horse?) leaping or rampant right, over vegetal element, probably ovoid petal. Calyx: palmette, tip of pointed petal.
– Domăneanţu 2000, 119 cat. 593, pl. 40 (attributed to Kirbeis); Rotroff 2010, 69 cat. 23.

KYX-36*
Istros, His-B 438/V 19398, Bucharest, Institute of Archaeology storeroom. Fr. of lower body. H 3.7 × W 4.2, WT 0.7. Fabric: relatively fine and micaceous, many small lime inclusions, many voids, 5YR 6/6. Dull coat, 2.5YR 5/6. Medium hard fired, oxidized. Main decoration: kantharos A (ii) between palmettes.

KYX-37*
Istros, His-839, Bucharest, Institute of Archaeology storeroom. Body fr. H 2.3 × W 4.2, WT 0.35. Fabric: relatively fine and micaceous, many small lime inclusions, some voids, 5YR 6/6. Dull coat, worn, 7.5YR 3/1. Medium hard fired, oxidized. Main decoration: palm fronds F with kantharos D (iii) as space-filler.
– Domăneanțu 2000, 137 cat. 679, pl. 49.

KYX-38*
Olbia, Sector NGS, House I-1 R 36/2, O-НГС-85-231, Parutine, Olbia National Preserve storeroom. Fr. of rim and upper body. H 4.2 × W 5.3, WT 0.3, ⌀ rim 15, 11%, RH 2.3. Fabric: fine, micaceous, 5YR 5/8. Slightly lustrous mottled coat, ext. 10R 4/8, 2.5YR 4/6, 2.5/1, int. 10R 4/8, 2.5YR 2.5/1. Medium hard fired, oxidized. Stacked in firing. Rim frieze: deep grooves. Main decoration: palm fronds F(?) with kantharos D (iii) as space-filler. One repair hole. The stamps are completely blurred.
– Guldager Bilde 2010, 286 cat. F-108, pl. 192 (erroneously identified as Pontic).

KYX-39*
Istros, His-1011, Bucharest, Institute of Archaeology storeroom. Fr. of upper body. H 3.1 × W 3.7, WT 0.45. Fabric: medium fine, micaceous, abundant minute lime inclusions, 5YR 6/4. Dull wash, ext. 7.5YR 5/4, int. 7.5YR 5/3. Relatively hard fired, oxidized. Main decoration: kantharos B (i) standing on tip of palm frond B, vegetal scroll(?) left of kantharos.
– Domăneanțu 2000, 94 cat. 455, pl. 30.

C *Calyx with Figural Decoration (Friezes)*

KYX-40
Olbia, inv. 198564, Warsaw, National Museum (formerly Vogell collection). Complete. ⌀ rim 11.5; vessel H 6; H:⌀ 1:1.9. Fabric: orange-brown. Light brown to black coat with metallic sheen. Oxidized. No rim frieze. Main decoration: one dolphin right and two dolphins left heraldic around krater A. Calyx: palmette N alternating with tall lotus petals. Medallion: rosette with six broad, lobed petals, ivy-berry cluster in centre; surrounded by frieze of dots. Frieze separators: two ridges.
– Zahn 1908, 61 cat. 16; Boehlau 1908, 30 no. 269; Grzegrzółka 2001, cat. 4, fig. 4.

KYX-41*
Olbia, Sector NGS, O-НГС-90-190, Parutine, Olbia National Preserve storeroom. Fr. of rim and upper body; rather worn. H 5.5 × W 6.6, WT 0.3–0.45, ⌀ rim 12, 20%, RH 2.6. Fabric: relatively fine and micaceous, abundant small lime inclusions, 5YR 5/6. Thin slightly lustrous coat partially splintering off, 10YR 3/1. Medium hard fired, oxidized. No rim frieze. Main decoration: upper frieze: bell krater with tall fluted stem alternating with kantharos A (ii); in between, palmette N; lower frieze: tip of foliage? Frieze separators: dots between ridges. Very close to **KYX-42**.

KYX-42
Pantikapaion, Mithridates Hill, Kerč History and Culture Reserve inv. KMAK 8297 (1958). Fr. of upper body. Oxidized. Main decoration: bell krater with tall fluted stem alternating with palmette N. Frieze separators: broad dots between ridges. Very close to **KYX-41***.
– Grzegrzółka 2010, 75–76 cat. 65 (identified as Pergamene).

KYX-43*
Istros, His-B 604, Bucharest, Institute of Archaeology storeroom. Fr. of lower body. H 3.8 × W 3.8, WT 0.35. Fabric: fine, micaceous, many lime inclusions, some small voids, 7.5YR 6/6. Dull and very worn coat, 7.5YR 3/1. Medium hard fired, oxidized. Main decoration: kantharos A (ii) between palmettes. Frieze separators: two ridges.
– Domăneanțu 2000, 133 cat. 654, pl. 46.

KYX-44*
Olbia, Sector R25, O-P25-95-903.1+2+3+5, Parutine, Olbia National Preserve storeroom. Four joining frs. of base and lower body. H 7.6 × W 7.6, WT 0.35, ⌀ base 2.6. Fabric: relatively fine and micaceous, small lime inclusions, 2.5YR 5/8. Slightly lustrous coat, 5YR 2.5/1. Medium hard fired, oxidized. Main decoration: various stemmed vases (krater?) with fluted lower body. Calyx: alternating lotus petal and straight acanthus X. Medallion: rosette with long, rounded petals in high relief. Frieze separator: thin ridge.

KYX-45*
Olbia, Sector R25, O-P25-95-1220, Parutine, Olbia National Preserve storeroom. Fr. of mid- and lower body. H 6.5 × W 6.5, WT 0.4. Fabric: relatively fine and micaceous, small lime inclusions, many voids, 7.5YR 6/6. Thin coat with metallic sheen, ext. 5YR 4/1, int. 5YR 5/2. Medium hard fired, oxidized. Rim frieze: Ionian kyma. Main decoration: palmette alternating with unidentified object. Calyx: S-curved acanthus with bent tip; small boukrania related to boukrania B but with up-turned horns and stylized *tainia* hanging from horns as space-fillers. Frieze separators: thin ridge. Reminiscent of **KYX-18***.

KYX-46*
Myrmekion, M-58-84, St Petersburg, IIMK RAN. Fr. of lower body and part of base. H 4.3, WT 0.3. Fabric: relatively fine, very micaceous, many voids, 7.5YR 5/3. Thin slightly lustrous coat, 2.5YR 2.5/1. Oxidized. Main decoration: upper frieze missing; lower frieze: Eros-Paniskos sitting on low pillar alternating with palm frond F. Medallion surrounded by two ridges. Frieze separators: two ridges set close together. Workshop of Paniskos.

D   *Scroll Decoration*

Ivy-Vine Scroll

KYX-47*
Olbia, Sector R25, O-P25-97-2521.1+2+2522+2524, Parutine, Olbia National Preserve storeroom. One rim and three body frs., all joining; complete profile except for base. H 7.7 × W 7, WT 0.2–0.41, ⌀ rim 12, 13%, RH 1.8. Fabric: relatively fine and micaceous, small lime inclusions, 5YR 5/6. Dull mottled coat, 5YR 3/2, 3/3. Medium hard fired, oxidized. No rim frieze. Main decoration in three friezes: upper frieze: incised acanthus-vine-ivy scroll left with bunches of grapes, vine- and ivy leaves stamped, with bird A and M sitting above; middle frieze: procession of Eros(?), man with thyrsos right, Dionysos(?) with cornucopia(?) left, Eros with torch left, repeated; lower frieze: lyre alternating with transport amphora. Frieze separators: two ridges. One repair hole.

KYX-48
Olbia, Sector NGS, O-НГС-92-31, Parutine, Olbia National Preserve storeroom. Fr. of rim and upper body; very worn. H 5.25 × W 5, WT 0.35–0.75, ⌀ rim 12, 8%, RH 2.65. Fabric: fine, micaceous, a few minute lime inclusions, some small voids, 7.5YR 6/6. Thin firm slightly lustrous coat, darkened and mottled, ext. 7.5YR 2/0, 10YR 3/2, 2.5YR 4/6, int. 5YR 4/4. Medium hard fired, oxidized. Stacked in firing. Rim frieze: Ionian kyma. Main decoration: incised ivy-vine(?) scroll left with stamped ivy and vine(?) leaves.

Ivy Scroll

KYX-49*
Olbia, O-39-2057, Kiev, Institute of Archaeology storeroom. Fr. of mid-body. H 5.5 × W 5.5, WT 0.48. Fabric: medium fine, micaceous, lime inclusions, many minute rounded grey stones, 5YR 5/6. Dull coat, 5YR 3/2. Relatively hard fired, oxidized. Rim frieze: Ionian kyma. Main decoration: upper frieze: incised ivy scroll left with stamped ivy leaves and ivy-berry clusters; lower frieze: frontal lyre player, bird flying left.

KYX-50*
Olbia, Sector E6, squares 678, 644n, SW of house "B", central block, grey clay layer, O-E6-66-793, Kiev, Institute of Archaeology storeroom. Body fr. H 3.5 × W 4, WT 0.4. Fabric: fine, micaceous, a few minute lime inclusions, some small voids, 5YR 7/4. Slightly lustrous coat, 5YR 3/1. Relatively hard fired, oxidized. Main decoration: incised ivy scroll right with stamped ivy leaves and groups of three-dot berries. Calyx: imbricate pointed petals with double outline, upside-down. Frieze separators: heart guilloche left between ridges.

Vine Scroll?

KYX-51*
Olbia, Sector E6, square 247, room north of Wall 49, grey clay layer, O-E6-57-793, 1229, Kiev, Institute of Archaeology storeroom. Two non-joining frs. of rim and upper body. H 5.8 × W 5, WT 0.35. Fabric: relatively fine and micaceous, many small lime inclusions, some voids, 5YR 7/6. Dull coat, 5YR 4/2. Relatively hard fired, oxidized. Rim frieze: fine dots. Main decoration: incised vine(?) scroll right with stamped leaves (stamps very blurred). Frieze separators: Ionian kyma or astragal.

Scroll, Unidentified Type

KYX-52*
Istros, His-A 316/V 19458, B 451/V 19421, Bucharest, Institute of Archaeology storeroom. Three non-joining frs. of rim and upper body. H 4.8 × W 6.5, WT 0.25, ⌀ rim 14, 10%, RH 2.2. Fabric: fine, micaceous, 5YR 7/8. Thin dull mottled coat, 5YR 5/4, 4/4, 3/1. Relatively hard fired, oxidized. Rim frieze: two ridges. Main decoration: incised ivy(?) scroll with stamped ivy-berry clusters on short stems, birds flying left and right between berries.
– Domăneanţu 2000, 133 cats. 655 and 656, pl. 46.

KYX-53
Olbia, Sector NGS, O-НГС-86-280, Parutine, Olbia National Preserve storeroom. Rim fr., worn. H 4 × W 4.7, WT 0.36–0.36, ⌀ rim 13, 10%, RH 3.4. Fabric: relatively fine and micaceous, a few minute lime inclusions, some small voids, 5YR 6/6. Thin firm slightly lustrous coat, ext. 7.5YR 2/0, int. 10YR 3/1. Medium hard fired, oxidized. No rim frieze. Main decoration: scroll right?

E   *Garlands and Wreaths*

Bound, Medium-Sized Garland

KYX-54*
Olbia, Agora, Room "B", yellow clay layer, O-66-1114+1131+1649, 1115, 1650, Kiev, Institute of Archaeology storeroom. Four joining rim frs., joining body fr., and non-joining rim fr. H 6.8 × W 11.2, WT 0.3, ⌀ rim 14, 25%, RH 2.2. Fabric: fine and micaceous, a few minute lime inclusions, some small voids, 5YR 7/6. Dull mottled coat, 2.5YR 4/8, 3/1. Relatively hard fired, oxidized. Rim frieze: Ionian kyma. Main decoration: bound garland D suspended between frontal females lifting out their long *apoptygma*; over garland, large bird sitting right. Frieze separators: rosette B set between two(?) ridges. Two repair holes.

KYX-55*
Istros, His-V 8566 A-C, E, F, Bucharest, Institute of Archaeology storeroom. Rim fr. and three joining body frs., two non-joining body frs. ⌀ rim 11, 18%, RH 3. Fabric: micaceous, abundant minute lime inclusions, large voids, 5YR 6/8. Dull coat almost completely worn off, ext. 5YR 5/4, int. 5YR 4/4. Medium hard fired, oxidized. No rim frieze. Main decoration: columns supporting bound garland D, with kantharos A (iii) above. Calyx: acanthus with hatched central vein alternating with lotus petals pointed at both ends; boar, flying bird, dogs, heraldic goats lying down, and tree as space-fillers. The same acanthus appears on **KYX-63***.
– Domăneanțu 2000, 121 cat. 600, pl. 41 (identified as Pontic).

KYX-56*
Olbia, Sector E2, square 55, Cistern Л, O-E2-49-117, 119, Kiev, Institute of Archaeology storeroom. Lower half of bowl and part of body close to rim; today only two minor frs. are preserved. H 5.1 × W 6.1, WT 0.3. Fabric: relatively fine and micaceous, 5YR 6/6. Coat with dull lustre, 5YR 3/1. Medium hard fired, oxidized. Rim frieze: astragal. Main decoration: garlands with hanging cones or fruits suspended from kantharos D (i). Calyx: stylized acanthus, S-curved palm fronds, vertical floral elements, and isolated lightly plastic long petals; above the vegetation, heraldic dolphins and further suspended garlands with cones. No base decoration? Frieze separators: two ridges.
– St Petersburg, IIMK RAN, photo archive neg. I 43053.

KYX-57*
Olbia, Sector АГД, О-АГД-85-190, Kiev, Institute of Archaeology storeroom. Body fr. WT 0.25–0.5. Fabric: fine, slightly micaceous, some small voids, 7.5YR 7/4. Thin dull coat, ext. 7.5YR 6/6, 5/4, int. 5YR 5/4 (mottled). Hard fired, oxidized. Main decoration: upper frieze: suspended bound garland with *tainia* with tassel; lower frieze: warrior with shield and raised sword left. Frieze separators: bird A, rosette B between ridges. Either misfired or secondarily burnt. The stamp of bird A is in pristine condition.

KYX-58
Istros, His-437, Bucharest, Institute of Archaeology storeroom. Body fr. Oxidized. Main decoration: suspended garland (too little preserved to identify type). Calyx: acanthus Z. Frieze separators: two ridges. The same acanthus can be found on **KYX-32**.

KYX-59*
Olbia, Cliff, grey clay layer, fill in room, O-68-2600, Kiev, Institute of Archaeology storeroom. Fr. of rim and upper body. H 3.9 × W 7.1, WT 0.25, ⌀ rim 13, 17%, RH 1.3. Fabric: fine, micaceous, 5YR 6/6. Thick dull coat, 5YR 4/2. Relatively hard fired, oxidized. Rim frieze: small palmettes. Main decoration: garlands suspended from slender bows. The same palmette is employed as rim pattern on **KYX-95***.

KYX-60*
Olbia, Sector NGS, O-НГС-02-44, Parutine, Olbia National Preserve storeroom. Joining frs. of rim and body. H 6.5 × W 9.2, WT 0.33–0.46, ⌀ rim 12, 17%, RH 3. Fabric: medium fine, micaceous, many small lime inclusions, larger inclusions rendering surface very pimply, small and large voids, 5YR 6/8, 6/4, 7.5YR 6/6. Thin firm coat with slight lustre int. and at rim ext., mottled ext., ext. 10YR 3/1, 2.5YR 5/6, int. 10YR 3/1. Medium hard fired, oxidized. Stacked in firing. No rim frieze. Main decoration: bound garlands suspended from bows with undulating ends; above the garlands, incised circles, probably intended as phialai. Calyx: top of vegetal element. Ascription to Kyme is tentative.

KYX-61
Pantikapaion, Mithridates Hill, Kerč History and Culture Reserve inv. KMAK 2145 (1964). Fr. of rim and upper body. Oxidized. Rim frieze: Ionian kyma with hatched tongues. Main decoration: garlands suspended from boukephalion A; above garland, cross-legged syrinx-playing Eros-Paniskos. Workshop of Paniskos.
– Grzegrzółka 2010, 72–73 cat. 59.

Bound Miniature Garland

KYX-62
Olbia, Hamburg, Museum für Kunst und Gewerbe (formerly Vogell collection). Complete. ⌀ rim 11.5; vessel H 6; H:⌀ 1:1.9. Fabric: yellowish red, slightly micaceous. Brownish coat, reddish at rim ext. Oxidized. Rim frieze: Ionian kyma. Main decoration: suspended, bound garland H with rosette above. Calyx: palmette N alternating with tall lotus petals, with palm frond B in between. Medallion unclear in photograph; according to Zahn, effaced. Frieze separators: two ridges.

– Zahn 1908, 61 cat. 15; Boehlau 1908, 29 no. 268.

KYX-63*
Olbia, Sector I, square 318, clay layer, О-И-48-1841, Kiev, Institute of Archaeology storeroom. Fr. of rim and large part of body. H 7.2 × W 7.3, WT 0.28, ⌀ rim 14, 15%, RH 2. Fabric: relatively fine and micaceous, many small lime inclusions, some voids, 7.5YR 6/6. Dull coat, 7.5YR 3/1. Medium hard fired, oxidized. Main decoration: bound miniature garland suspended between boukephalia A, rosette G over garlands. Calyx: acanthus with hatched central vein alternating with ovoid petals. Frieze separators: Ionian kyma with finely hatched tongues between ridges. Same Ionian kyma on **KYX-66*** and **KYX-89***; same acanthus on **KYX-55***.

KYX-64*
Pantikapaion, palace foundation trench, M-89-illegible-11, Moscow, Puškin Museum of Fine Arts. Fr. of mid-body. H 4.6 × W 5, WT 0.3. Fabric: relatively fine and micaceous, small lime inclusions. Thick dull dark red coat blackened at rim ext. Oxidized. Stacked in firing. Rim frieze: Ionian kyma. Calyx: straight acanthus on the tips of which birds sit right; in between, small bound garland. Same stamp of garland and bird on **KYX-65***.

KYX-65*
Istros, His-V 19463 A, Bucharest, Institute of Archaeology storeroom. Fr. of upper body. H 3.5 × W 3.7, WT 0.22. Fabric: relatively fine, micaceous, small lime inclusions, 5YR 7/6. Dull coat, ext. 10YR 3/1, 2.5YR 4/6, int. 2.5YR 5/6. Medium hard fired, oxidized. Stacked in firing. Rim frieze: Ionian kyma. Main decoration: suspended small bound garland, with bird right above; rosette with eight petals between garlands. Same garland and bird on **KYX-64***.
– Casan-Franga 1967, fig. 3.1; Domăneanțu 2000, 93 cat. 448, pl. 30 (identified as Ephesian).

KYX-66*
Olbia, Sector E6, square 433w, Room "O", yellow clay layer, O-E6-59-824, Kiev, Institute of Archaeology storeroom. Fr. of rim and upper body. H 6.3 × W 4.8, WT 0.35, RH 2.6. Fabric: relatively fine and micaceous, many small lime inclusions, some voids, 5YR 6/6. Slightly lustrous int., ext. with slight metallic sheen, ext. 5YR 2.5/1, int. 2.5YR 4/6, 5YR 2.5/1. Medium hard fired, oxidized. Stacked in firing. Rim frieze: Ionian kyma with finely hatched tongues. Main decoration: small bound garland suspended from *tainia*; the garland is floating in the air. Same Ionian kyma on **KYX-63*** and **KYX-89***.

F   *Vegetal Decoration*

Calyx with 'Nelumbo'

KYX-67*
Olbia, Square B5, O-Б5-76-206, Kiev, Institute of Archaeology storeroom. Complete profile; one large fr. from rim to base. RH 1.8, ⌀ base 4; vessel H 7. Fabric: medium fine, abundant minute lime inclusions, some mica. Thin dull coat. Not too hard fired, oxidized. Rim frieze: Ionian kyma. Calyx: 'nelumbo' with cabled edges filled with vegetation, small acanthus leaf in front, all flanked by flowers on incised wavy stems; copy from Menemachos? (e.g., **EPH-584***, **EPH-585***). Medallion: surrounded by two ridges. Two repair holes. Secondarily burnt. Same 'nelumbo' on **KYX-68**.

KYX-68
Istros, His-809, Bucharest, Institute of Archaeology storeroom. Fr. of lower body. H 2.5 × W 1.7, WT 0.35. Fabric: medium fine, abundant minute lime inclusions, very fine light-reflecting inclusions, 5YR 6/6. Dull wash, 5YR 3/1. Relatively hard fired, oxidized. Calyx: 'nelumbo' with cabled edge filled with vegetation; acanthus leaf. Same 'nelumbo' on **KYX-67***.

KYX-69
Istros, His-908 or 806, Bucharest, Institute of Archaeology storeroom. Fr. of base and lower body. H 2.2 × W 2.8, WT 0.4. Fabric: relatively fine, fine mica, 5YR 7/6. Dull coat, 5YR 3/1. Relatively hard fired, oxidized. Calyx: 'nelumbo' with twisted central vein and internal scales, surrounded by acanthus leaves. Medallion: surrounded by two ridges.

KYX-70
Istros, His-834, Bucharest, Institute of Archaeology storeroom. Fr. of lower body. Fabric: relatively fine, fine mica. Oxidized. Calyx: 'nelumbo' with cabled edge alternating with acanthus leaf.

KYX-71*
Istros, His-B 578/V 19384, Bucharest, Institute of Archaeology storeroom. Fr. of lower body. H 2.8 × W 4.7, WT 0.5. Fabric: medium fine, abundant minute lime inclusions, very fine light-reflecting inclusions, 5YR 5/6. Dull wash, 5YR 4/1. Relatively hard fired, oxidized. Calyx: 'nelumbo' with cabled edges and ribbed interior, small rosettes in negative relief as space-filler. Frieze separators: ridge(s).
– Casan-Franga 1967, fig. 1.1; Domăneanțu 2000, 94 cat. 458, pl. 31 (identified as Ephesian).

Other Types of Calyx

KYX-72*
Olbia, Sector R25, O-P25-95-1118, Parutine, Olbia National Preserve storeroom. Fr. of rim and upper body. H 5.1 × W 7, WT 0.4, ⌀ rim 14, 15%, RH 2.3. Fabric: relatively fine and micaceous, many small lime inclusions, many voids, 5YR 5/6. Thin firm coat with slight metallic lustre, 10YR 3/2. Hard fired, oxidized. Rim frieze: heart guilloche left. Main decoration: top of palmette and funnel-shaped flower.

KYX-73
Olbia, Sector NGS, O-НГС-06-366, Parutine, Olbia National Preserve storeroom. Fr. of rim and upper body. H 5 × W 7.6, WT 0.2, ⌀ rim 16, 11%, RH 2.5. Fabric: very fine, slightly micaceous, Gley 1 4/10Y. Mottled flaking coat with slight lustre, Gley 1 2.5/1, 4/10Y. Medium hard fired, reduced. Rim frieze: large dots alternating with small busts(?). Calyx: tip of pointed petal, funnel-shaped flower.

KYX-74*
Istros, His-168, 729, Bucharest, Institute of Archaeology storeroom. Two non-joining body frs. H 3.6 × W 4.3, WT 0.36. Fabric: medium fine, micaceous, some small lime or shell inclusions, 7.5YR 6/4. Dull wash, 7.5YR 4/2, 4/3. Relatively hard fired, oxidized. Calyx: straight acanthus with double stem, flower on stem; large rosettes as space-filler.
– Domăneanțu 2000, 140 cat. 695, pl. 50.

KYX-75
Istros, His-455, Bucharest, Institute of Archaeology storeroom. Fr. of lower body. Oxidized. Calyx: straight acanthus with double stem.

KYX-76
Istros, His-722, Bucharest, Institute of Archaeology storeroom. Fr. of lower body. Oxidized. Calyx: acanthus (type?) with tips of low acanthus with segmented central vein; in front of these, two rows of low, slightly pointed lotus petals with central vein.

Calyx with Bud or Flower on Stem

KYX-77*
Olbia, inv. A 697, Nikolaev, Historical Museum (new inventory card in 1974). Complete; partly cracked in two. ⌀ rim 13.6, RH 2.5, ⌀ base 4; vessel H 8.1; H:⌀ 1:1.7. Dull wash, brownish above, reddish brown below. Oxidized. No rim frieze. Calyx: tall lotus petals alternating with buds on incised wavy stem. Medallion: surrounded by two ridges; double rosette.

KYX-78*
Olbia, Sector NGS, O-НГС-04-208, Parutine, Olbia National Preserve storeroom. Fr. of base and body. H 8.8 × W 8.8, WT 0.35, ⌀ base 3.6. Fabric: relatively fine and micaceous, 5YR 6/6. Thin dull coat, 5YR 3/1. Medium hard fired, oxidized. Rim frieze: Ionian kyma. Calyx: tall pointed lotus petals alternating with thin incised wavy line. Medallion: plain, strongly concave base with false ring foot.

KYX-79*
Olbia, inv. A 3587, Nikolaev, Historical Museum. Fr. of rim and upper body. H 5 × W 9, WT 0.45, ⌀ rim 12.5, 17%, RH 1.9. Fabric: micaceous, reddish brown. Slightly lustrous brownish coat. Oxidized. Rim friezes: grooves; large dots. Calyx: tall pointed lotus petals alternating with blurred rosettes on dotted stems.

Calyx with Palmette

KYX-80*
Olbia, Sector NG-40/41, square 14, grey clay layer, O-НГ-63-1395, 68-193, Kiev, Institute of Archaeology storeroom. One fourth of bowl, lacking rim; non-joining body fr. H 10.1 × W 6.3, WT 0.4, ⌀ base 3.5. Fabric: fine, slightly micaceous, abundant lime, 5YR 6/6. Dull wash, ext. 5YR 4/3, 3/2, int. 5YR 3/2. Medium hard fired, oxidized. Rim frieze: heart guilloche right. Calyx: palmettes alternately upside-down separated by fields of imbricate pointed petals with hatched central vein. Medallion: surrounded by two ridges; double rosette. Large palmette upside-down: cf. de Luca 1975, pl. 45.6; 1999, 113 cat. 543, pl. 19, Beil. 11; see also de Luca 1975, pl. 45.2 (Pergamon).

KYX-81*
Olbia, Sector E, square 66, grey clay layer, O-E-49-2496, Kiev, Institute of Archaeology storeroom. Fr. of lower body and tiny part of base. H 2.3 × W 5.2, WT 0.21, ⌀ base 4. Fabric: relatively fine and micaceous, some small lime inclusions, 5YR 6/6. Thin dull coat, 5YR 2.5/1. Medium hard fired, oxidized. Calyx: palmettes with acanthus stem in between. Medallion: surrounded by ridge.

Unidentified

KYX-82
Istros, His-374, Bucharest, Institute of Archaeology storeroom. Body fr. close to rim. Oxidized. Stacked in firing. Rim frieze: Ionian kyma. Calyx: top of ovoid petal.

KYX-83
Istros, His-1031, Bucharest, Institute of Archaeology storeroom. Fr. of lower body. Oxidized. Calyx: vegetal (type?). Attribution is tentative, based on fragment's physical properties.

Various Imbricate Patterns

KYX-84*
Olbia, V.I. 7754.70, Antikensammlung, Staatliche Museen zu Berlin (formerly Becker collection). Fr. of rim and most of body. H 7 × W 7, WT 0.4, ⌀ rim 14, RH 2. Fabric: very coarse, highly micaceous, many lime inclusions, 5YR 6/6. Dull mottled coat, 7.5YR 3/1, 2.5/1. Oxidized. Rim frieze: heart guilloche left. Calyx: imbricate broad pointed petals with hatched central vein. One repair hole.

KYX-85*
Olbia, Sector NGS, House III-3 C 332/131, O-НГС-91-712, Parutine, Olbia National Preserve storeroom. Fr. of rim and upper body. H 5 × W 3.6, WT 0.25–0.5, ⌀ rim 13, 8%, RH 2.3. Fabric: relatively fine and micaceous, a few lime dots, some oblong voids, 5YR 6/6. Thin slightly lustrous flaking coat, slightly mottled, 2.5YR 4/4. Hard fired, oxidized. Rim frieze: grooves. Calyx: imbricate small leaves with central and side veins.
– Guldager Bilde 2010, 279 cat. F-42, pl. 176 (erroneously identified as Ephesian).

KYX-86
Olbia, Sector R25, O-P25-95-903.4, Parutine, Olbia National Preserve storeroom. Fr. of upper body. H 3 × W 3, WT 0.32. Fabric: relatively fine and micaceous, 5YR 6/8. Thin coat with slight lustre ext., dull int., 7.5YR 3/2. Hard fired, oxidized. Calyx: imbricate slightly pointed petals with central vein. Frieze separators: two ridges. Lower body with imbricate petals separated from main decoration by ridges can also be found on KYX-3*.

KYX-87
Olbia, Sector Sever-Zapad, O-СЗ-68-1926, Parutine, Olbia National Preserve storeroom. Fr. of lower body. H 3 × W 3.5, WT 0.45. Fabric: relatively fine and micaceous, many small lime inclusions, some voids, 5YR 5/8. Thin dull coat, 5YR 2.5/1. Relatively hard fired, oxidized. Calyx: imbricate ferns. Ascription to Kyme is tentative, based on fabric and surface treatment.

G   *Linear Decoration*

Pendent-Semicircle Design

This decoration is not unknown at Kyme: Bouzek & Jansová 1974, 68 cats. MB 99–101, figs. 5, 8, pl. 14. See also KYB-380* attributed to Possis(?).

KYX-88*
Istros, His-287, Bucharest, Institute of Archaeology storeroom. Body fr. H 4.3 × W 3.2, WT 0.35. Fabric: relatively fine, slightly micaceous, 5YR 6/6. Dull coat, 5YR 3/1. Relatively hard fired, oxidized. No rim frieze. Main decoration: sun wheel at centre of semicircle, field of well-spaced dots and a rosette between semicircles.
– Domăneanțu 2000, 106 cat. 537, pl. 35 (identified as Ephesian).

Stylized Long Petals

KYX-89*
Olbia, Sector AGD, ashy grey clay layer, О-АГД-69-1246, Kiev, Institute of Archaeology storeroom. Two joining frs. of rim and upper body. H 5.3 × W 7.8, WT 0.35, ⌀ rim 13, 13%, RH 2.2. Fabric: relatively fine and micaceous, many small lime inclusions, some voids, 5YR 6/6. Dull mottled coat, ext. 5YR 6/6, 5/4, int. 7.5YR 3/1. Low fired, oxidized. Stacked in firing. Rim frieze: Ionian kyma with finely hatched tongues. Main decoration: stylized long petals. Same Ionian kyma on KYX-63* and KYX-66*.

H   *Rim Fragments*

Ionian Kyma

KYX-90*
Olbia, Sector AGD, Bothros 11, О-АГД-88-211, Kiev, Institute of Archaeology storeroom. Rim fr. H 4.3 × W 5, WT 0.3, RH 2. Fabric: relatively fine and micaceous, some small lime inclusions. Thin dull coat. Relatively hard fired, oxidized. Rim frieze: Ionian kyma, rounded with double outline.

KYX-91
Olbia, Sector E6, square 476s, 477se, yellow clay layer with ash inclusions, O-E6-59-1403, Kiev, Institute of Archaeology storeroom. Rim fr. Oxidized.

KYX-92
Olbia, O-52-2959, Kiev, Institute of Archaeology storeroom. Fr. of body close to rim. Oxidized.

KYX-93
Olbia, Sector NGS, O-НГС-08-363, Parutine, Olbia National Preserve storeroom. Fr. of upper body. H 3.3 × W 3.6, WT 0.32. Fabric: relatively fine and micaceous, some small lime inclusions, 5YR 6/8. Thin dull coat, 2.5YR 4/6. Medium hard fired, oxidized. Rim frieze: Ionian kyma with hatched tongues. One repair hole.

Other Rim Patterns

KYX-94*
Olbia, Sector R25, O-P25-98-2138, Parutine, Olbia National Preserve storeroom. Rim fr. H 4 × W 5.2, WT 0.3, ⌀ rim 14, 12%, RH 2.8. Fabric: relatively fine and micaceous, 2.5YR 6/8. Thin dull coat, mottled ext., ext. 10R 5/8, 3/1, 5YR 6/6, int. 10R 5/8, 3/1. Medium hard fired, oxidized. Stacked in firing. Rim frieze: fleur de lys B alternating with rosette B.

KYX-95*
Olbia, Sector NGS, House III-3 B 368/106, O-НГС-93-912, Parutine, Olbia National Preserve storeroom. Fr. of rim and upper body. H 4.42 × W 5.3, WT 0.3–0.5, ⌀ rim 14, 10%, RH 3.25. Fabric: fine, rather dense, micaceous, a few small lime inclusions, no voids, 7.5YR 6/6. Thin firm coat with fair lustre especially ext., 10YR 3/1. Medium hard fired, oxidized. Rim frieze: grooves, palmettes. Same palmette in rim pattern on **KYX-59***.
– Guldager Bilde 2010, 282 cat. F-74, pl. 182.

KYX-96*
Istros, His-589[a], Bucharest, Institute of Archaeology storeroom. Rim fr. H 4 × W 4.5, WT 0.35, RH 2.3. Fabric: fine, micaceous, a few minute lime inclusions, some small voids. Reddish brown coat with soapy feel. Medium hard fired, oxidized. Rim frieze: grooves, miniature myrtle wreath left with single-dot berries.

I   Body Fragments, Unidentifiable

KYX-97
Istros, His-474, Bucharest, Institute of Archaeology storeroom. Fr. of lower body and base. Oxidized. Calyx: unidentified traces. Medallion: surrounded by two ridges.

KYX-98
Olbia, O-1910-670, present whereabouts unknown. Body fr. Calyx: tip of slender petal. Frieze separators: heart guilloche right between ridges One repair hole.
– St Petersburg, IIMK RAN, archive inv. 4058.519.6 (pl. III).

SUPPLEMENTARY SHAPES

Small Bowl

KYX-99
Pantikapaion, tomb N 14/60-27/IV-1960, Kerč History and Culture Reserve inv. KMAK 1895 (1960). Complete, ⌀ rim 9.5, ⌀ base 3.7; vessel H 7. Oxidized. Rim frieze: Ionian kyma. Main decoration: altar scene D flanked by saluting Pans, Eros pouring wine from amphora into *Pokalkantharos*, Eros with torch left, Dionysos(?) with cornucopia. Medallion: rosette with six broad, lobed petals and ivy-berry cluster at centre.
– Grzegrzółka 2010, 49–50 cat. 18.

KYX-100*
Istros, His-V 19429, Bucharest, Institute of Archaeology storeroom. Fr. of rim and upper body. H 5.2 × W 4.2, WT 0.3, ⌀ rim 9, 14%, RH 2.5. Fabric: fine, soft, abundant fine mica, 7.5YR 7/6. Coat with dull lustre, 7.5YR 3/1. Medium hard fired, oxidized. No rim frieze. Calyx: isolated palmette.
– Domăneanțu 2000, 138 cat. 687, pl. 49.

Amphoriskos with Pointed Toe

KYX-101
Olbia, inv. T 462, Kassel Antikensammlung (formerly Vogell collection). Complete. Vessel H 17.4. Fabric: orange. Light brown to brownish black coat. Rim frieze: Ionian kyma. Main decoration: columns alternating with four types of masks (male and female) repeated twice. The vessel could also be from near-by Myrina, where the shape is also attested (Chapter 5, **SHA-132**).
– CVA Kassel 2 [Germany 38], 64–65, fig. 41, pl. 87.5.

CHAPTER 11

Kyme (ii): The Meter Medallion Workshop

The evidence for the Meter Medallion Workshop (MMW) consists of a large group of complete and fragmentary vessels. If we include vessels of evidence category C, which are listed in the literature but not illustrated, no less than 552 vessels can be documented. In the current analysis, however, we consider only items of evidence groups A and B, which I have either dealt with personally or seen an illustration of; this group totals 456 vessels (Fig. 61).

Vessels of the MMW share the same iconographic element, namely a turreted female, as a stamp in the base medallion. Different medallion stamps were in use by four different mould makers, whose names we know from their signatures: Kirbeis, Possis, Zenodotos, and Zenodoules. Kirbeis was in all likelihood the main person behind the workshop: he was the most prolific (Fig. 61), and he also employed the largest number of individual stamps, 124 of the 163 documented for the shop (Fig. 63). The first three craftsmen signed around the medallion stamp, the fourth in a rectangular box on the body. These four artisans have not previously been gathered in a single workshop.[1] However, the analysis of the vessels' physical and morphological properties and of the stamps employed for the decoration of the bowls fully document that they had access to the same clay sources, firing facilities, shape repertoire, and tool box and, thus, were members of the same workshop, which I have termed the Meter Medallion Workshop.[2]

Evidence category A+B	Signed	Attributed
Kirbeis	97	232
Possis	23	59
Zenodotos	7	4
Zenodoules	1	
Unassigned		33
Total	128	328

FIGURE 61   Extent of the Meter Medallion Workshop and distribution of its products amongst the artisans of the workshop

The MMW is prominently represented in the Black Sea region, and at many sites the characteristic bowls of this workshop constituted from 6 to 13% of the finds (Fig. 64). Before we look in more detail at the products of this workshop and the individual potters, we shall briefly sketch the history of research on this group, which is closely connected with the battle over its provenance.

History of Research and Discussion of the Production Place

Vessels signed by Kirbeis have been repeatedly discussed in previous research.[3] The same attention has not been directed towards Possis, probably because vases with his signature are much rarer. The provenance of the Kirbeis vases in particular has been debated intensively in past – and current – research. Were they Mediterranean or Pontic? No moulds have ever been found which could establish the production place beyond doubt. V.V. Latyšev long ago drew attention to the formation of the name Kirbeis, with a genitive in –ei, as characteristic of Hellenised 'barbarian' names of the Black Sea region (Latyšev 1902; repeated in Zahn 1908, 49 and Zgusta 1956, 412–413), and because vessels signed by Kirbeis have been unearthed in considerable quantities in the northern Black Sea region, particularly in the northwestern part, they were first attributed to this area.[4] Later, the general tendency has been for Black Sea scholars to locate the production in Asia Minor, primarily because of the vessels' micaceous fabric,[5] whereas most scholars working in the Mediterranean are still of the opinion that they were produced in the Black Sea region.[6] A middle ground was proposed by U. Hausmann and J. Bouzek based on aesthetic arguments: Hausmann found the bowls too poor to be from Asia Minor, whereas Bouzek found the same bowls

---

1   Apart from Guldager Bilde 2006; Guldager Bilde 2010; Rotroff 2010.
2   When I first wrote about this group, I called it the Tyche Medallion Group (Guldager Bilde 2006), but, as I argue on p. 198, the female of the medallion is Meter rather than Tyche.

3   E.g., Latyšev 1902; Zahn 1908; Courby 1922; Mahler 1924; Blavatskij 1953, 279–289; Jentel 1964; Bouzek 1990, 65–66; Kovalenko 1987b; Kovalenko 1989; Domăneanţu 2000, 117–120; Rotroff 2010.
4   Zahn 1908, 49–50 n. 6; Courby 1922, 411–412; Mahler 1924, 27; Blavatskij 1953, 279–289; Levi 1964b, 252; Rostovcev 1967, 600; Gajdukevič 1971, 157 n. 108.
5   For example, Loseva 1962, 201–203; Šurgaja 1962; Ocheşeanu 1969, 233–236; Usačeva 1978, 101; Samojlova 1984, 123; Kovalenko 1987b; Kovalenko 1989; Vnukov & Kovalenko 1998, 71.
6   Simon (ed.) 1975, 187; Kossatz 1990, 136; Rogl 2001a, 140; Rotroff 2010, 67.

too fine to be products of the northern Pontic region; both, therefore, suggested the south coast of the Black Sea, a region which is a blank spot on the map as concerns finds in general, not to speak of MMB (Hausmann 1977–1978, 223 n. 40; Bouzek 1990, 65).[7] Until recently, I too was of the opinion that they were produced in the northwestern Black Sea region, probably at Olbia, because the vessels have been found predominantly in that city (Guldager Bilde 2010, 285).

Now, however, the riddle of the provenance of this pottery has been solved, because two independent archaeometric analyses locate its production place in southern Aiolis. According to the Lyon laboratory of P. Dupont, **KYB-416*** "seems to originate from the Kyme area" together with **KYA-29***.[8] The same general location has been given by the Bonn laboratory of H. Mommsen as a result of the analysis of a bowl found in Golubickoe in 2010 (**KYB-140***). According to the Bonn laboratory, the vessel belongs to their chemical group G = Aiolis, the region around Kyme or Larisa on the Hermos, mid-way between Kyme and Smyrna.[9] As already discussed in Chapter 10, the production of Kyme is well known due to the discovery of moulds and bowl fragments. Several scholars have already pointed to a certain relationship between the MMW and the Kymean production in terms of morphology and style.[10] It is therefore welcome that the recent archaeometric analyses now confirm this suspicion.

Base Medallion: The Signatures and the Persons behind Them

As already mentioned, we know of four individuals who proudly signed their moulds: Kirbeis, Possis, Zenodotos, and Zenodoules. The handwriting differs considerably from one person to the next. Kirbeis uses very elongated and rather awkward letters, as if he was not completely sure of his Greek. Kirbeis' inscription was part of the stamp, so the letters are always located in exactly the same position. The two syllables KIR-BEI on the standard stamp, which is the dominant one, are placed at either side of the head, with KIR- vertically behind the back of the head and -BEI vertically in front of the forehead. However, two bowls deviate from this pattern. On one the -BEI is located over the crown (**KYB-266***) and on the other the signature reads KIRBEIDOS (**KYB-267**)!

In contrast, Possis signs with a self-conscious Π, small round o's touching the preceding letter, and three lunate sigmas. Possis added his signature *after* stamping the central medallion figure into the mould. For this reason, the location of the inscription and the way the individual syllables are separated or joined differ from vessel to vessel. Zenodoules, in turn, signed around the previously stamped image, as Possis did, but wrote his name boustrophedon, with the last part reading backwards. Zenodoules, whom we know from a single vessel only, signed in a square field on the body of the vessel. With the exception of Zenodoules (signing ΖΗΝΟΔΟΥΛΗΣ), all the other names are given in the genitive: ΚΙΡΒΕΙ, ΠΟΣΣΙΔΟΣ, and ΖΗΝΟΔΟΤΟΥ.

Later in the present chapter, we shall return to the iconography of the medallion stamps. But first we shall briefly consider the persons behind the signatures.

Kirbeis

Kirbeis is a *hapax* among Greek personal names. As has already been mentioned, V.V. Latyšev discussed the particular formation of the name, with genitive in -ei, as characteristic of Hellenised names of the Black Sea region (Latyšev 1902; repeated by Zahn 1908, 49). With the search machine of *LGPN* available on-line (https://www.lgpn.ox.ac.uk/), this can easily be checked today – and we can base our search on a much larger corpus of Black Sea as well as comparative Mediterranean material than what was available to Latyšev and Zahn. A search made 3 October 2006 and repeated 7 July 2011 fully confirms their conclusion, revealing the existence of more than 50 Hellenized personal male names ending in -eis, in addition to that of Kirbeis, none of which is known from the Mediterranean. Both *LGPN* IIIB (Central Greece: From the Megarid to Thessaly) and *LGPN* VA (Coastal Asia Minor, Pontos to Ionia) also list other similarly Hellenized names (and *Lalnamen*) ending in -eis, for example, Biotteis, Boukatteis, Dusareis, Oxateis, Samulleis, Skeibeis, Sokaleis, Troxeis in the first mentioned volume; Babeis, Kakoleis, Kireis, Tateis in the latter. At any rate, Kirbeis is a non-Greek name, either Thracian or Anatolian; this individual's non-Greek ethnicity can also be recognized from the letters he used to sign his bowls, as well as from the somewhat crude depiction of Meter, with her long, drooping nose, which also has a somewhat 'barbarian' look. The existence of an alternative spelling of the genitive Kirbeidos (**KYB-267**) points in the same direction.

---

7   Apparently, Bouzek changed his mind; at least in a recent contribution, he quotes the NW Pontic region as their place of production (Bouzek 2008, without page numbers).
8   Pers. comm., 3 February 2011.
9   U. Schlotzhauer, pers. comm. 22 February 2011; Žuravlev & Schlotzhauer 2011. See Kerschner 2006 for Group G.
10 Bouzek 1990, 66; Kotitsa 1998, 135; Guldager Bilde 2006, 345–346; Guldager Bilde 2010, 285.

Possis

Recovery of the name of the person signing Possis has proven a challenge. Over the years, scholars have provided a number of different readings of incomplete inscriptions, as well as erroneous readings and citations, which have later been cited by other scholars as proven names. The first to contribute to the confusion was E. von Stern, who mentioned a bowl in the museum in Odessa deriving from P.A. Mavrogordato's collection of finds from Olbia. According to von Stern, this bowl featured a "male head" and the inscription PASIDEOS, with the sigmas transcribed as lunate (ΠΑϹΙΔΕΟϹ; von Stern 1902, 98 and n. 3). Laumonier later cited this reference, substituting an omicron for the alpha (Posideos rather than Pasideos), and including the name in the workshop of Posidos [sic!], in his view a single shop signing variously as Posidos, Possidos, Poseidos, and Posideos (Laumonier 1977, 407 n. 1, also with incorrect reference to the number of von Stern's note).

Meanwhile, Loseva had reconstructed an inscription on a bowl from Phanagoreia reading PO[...] as Posideos (Loseva 1962, 204, later repeated by Kotitsa 1998, 135; KYB-361). In 1984, Samojlova published a larger number of MMB from Tyras. The drawings are unfortunately very sketchy, and one includes a bowl medallion inscribed POSEIDOS (ΠΟϹΕΙΔΟϹ) (Samojlova 1984, 125, fig. 3.7; KYB-388). Of course the name may have been Pos(e)is, as she read it, assuming that the second of the double lunate sigmas that actually appear on the bowl is an epsilon that is lacking its horizontal stroke. I feel certain, however, that this is an erroneous reading inspired by Laumonier's Posei[...] mentioned above.

A major confusion entered the discussion with Bouzek, who quoted von Stern's PASIDEOS (ΠΑΣΙΔΕΟΣ) as POSILEOU (ΠΟΣΙΛΕΟΥ) (Bouzek 1990, 85 n. 100, also with incorrect reference to year of von Stern's article). POSILEOU (ΠΟΣΙΛΕΟΥ) now occurs in Rogl's list of potter signatures as a completely fictitious potter by the name of Posiles (Rogl 2001a, 143; see also Rogl 1999, without pagination).

It is evident that our Possis was not the only potter who signed with a name starting with Pos-. Two bowl fragments found on Delos carry the inscription Posei[...] and Posid[...] (Laumonier 1977, 404, fig. 1; 407 cats. 1987, 1990, pl. 95) under their plain bases. The bowls are Ephesian and probably belong to Menemachos' workshop. Therefore, Laumonier is right when he distinguishes between the bowls with a turreted female signed by Possis and the two bowls on Delos. They are, accordingly, excluded from the workshop dealt with here. On one further Ephesian bowl from Myrmekion (EPH-731*), we find the signature Posei[...] incised in the mould, but on the body rather than under the base. So it appears that several potters with the same or a closely similar name worked in Ephesos. A further bowl should also be mentioned, a body fragment in the Louvre (inv. CA 1106[b]), which also preserves part of a signature starting with Po[...]. The signature very much resembles that of our Possis, but its location on the body of the vase is unusual. The bowl's decoration shows an imprint of a coin or a coin-like device with a helmeted bust facing right and surrounded by a dotted frieze; the coin is placed over a finely detailed kithara resembling but not identical to a stamp on KYB-431*. The Louvre piece cannot readily be attributed to a workshop or a production place. The conclusion is, thus, that there were several potters of several production places who had names beginning with Pos-. Such names were very common: *LPGN* gives 56 different names occurring over 1,000 times. They should not be combined. To the MMW belongs only the potter signing Possis (with the genitive Possidos).

In general, names beginning Poss- are very unusual. In *LGPN* we find one reference to a Possikrates and one to a Possitos, both in *LGPN* IIIA. Possis is recorded only in *LGPN* IV (Macedonia, Thrace, Northern Shores of the Black Sea) and *LGPN* VA (Coastal Asia Minor: Pontos to Ionia) five and three times, respectively. Possis is probably a later formation of the more commonly occurring name with single sigma, Posis, which we find no less than 117 times in *LGPN* IV and 17 times in *LGPN* VA as well as two times in *LGPN* I and once each in *LGPN* IIA and *LGPN* IIIA. Both variants are in all likelihood a hypocoristic form of a longer name, e.g., Poseidonios or Poseidippos, but this need not concern us here.[11]

Zenodotos

Zenodotos occurs in the *LPGN* 150 times. It is most frequent in *LGPN* VA (Coastal Asia Minor: Pontos to Ionia), where it occurs 81 times. It is documented 46 times in *LGPN* I (The Aegean Islands, Cyprus, Cyrenaica), whereas it is rarer in *LGPN* IIA (Attica: 13 times), *LGPN* IIIA (The Peloponnese, Western Greece, Sicily, Magna Graecia: once), *LGPN* IIIB (Central Greece: From the Megarid to Thessaly: twice), and *LGPN* IV (Macedonia, Thrace, Northern Shores of the Black Sea: seven times).

Zenodoules

Zenodoules, the 'slave of Zenon', is also a *hapax* amongst Greek personal names, occurring only once in the *LPGN*.

The persons behind the two names starting with Zeno- must have been related. Perhaps they were both

---

11   I thank G. Hinge for this suggestion.

slaves of the same Zenon? If indeed so, what was his relationship to the Meter Medallion Workshop? Was he the owner?

Fabric and Surface Treatment

The fabric used in the MMW is relatively fine and micaceous with some inclusions of lime. With few exceptions, the vessels were fired in an oxidizing atmosphere. It is characteristic that the colour of fabric and coat varies enormously – even on the same vessel. The majority of Kirbeis' vessels were fired to 5YR 6/6, 7.5YR 6/6, 5YR 6/8 and 7/6, whereas Possis' vessels were fired to 5YR 6/8 and 6/6. The fabric of Zenodotos is slightly darker and not so coarse: 7.5YR 6/4, 6/6, 10YR 6/3. The coat, which is intended as black, comes in various qualities. With the exception of the rim, which can have a good lustre, on most vessels the coat is uniformly dull. Occasionally there is a deep lilac band where the vessel was stacked during firing. The coat is normally so thin that the uppermost surface of the relief is barely covered, and it characteristically fires reddish. The standard hue of the external coat is 3/1 (10YR, 7.5YR, and 5YR), but it can vary considerably even on the same sherd.

Shapes

The shape employed by all four members of the workshop is invariably a deep bowl with a plain, tall, straight, or slightly out-turned rim with a plain, rounded lip. Basically, it emulates the Athenian shape. On average, the rim diameter is slightly smaller than the Athenian one, but larger than the Ephesian (see the comparison in Fig. 6). The majority of the MMW bowls have a diameter of between 12 and 14 cm, with 13 cm occurring most commonly. The height of the plain rim over the moulded part is normally as much as 2.5–3 cm; this is in contrast to the Ephesian vessels, where the rim height is normally 1.5–2.5 cm. Also in terms of height and proportions, the vessels of the MMW fall between the Athenian and the Ephesian, though closer to the former (Fig. 6). The height of the Kymean vessels varies from 7.1 to 8.8 cm, with 7.8–8.5 cm being the most common. The proportions range from 1:1.5 to 1:1.9, with 1:1.7 being the most common. In general, the walls of the MMW bowls are quite thick, 0.35–0.4 cm.

In addition to the bowls, Kirbeis and Possis both made small bowls: Kirbeis four, of which one is signed (KYB-316–KYB-319*), and Possis one (KYB-411*). To Kirbeis can also be attributed a juglet (KYB-320*) and a closed vessel of unknown shape (KYB-328). He was also the creator of at least seven amphorae, five of which are signed (KYB-321–KYB-327*). One preserves only the lower part and even the separately applied foot has been lost (KYB-327*). Four are relatively similar, with a projecting rim, strap handles with rotellae, and a profiled foot, conforming to the Pergamene type of Hellenistic amphora (KYB-321, KYB-322*, KYB-324, KYB-325*), whereas two more are hybrids mixing Pergamene elements with the moulded rim of Athenian amphorae (KYB-323 and KYB-236).[12] According to Rotroff, the latter belong to the third quarter of the 2nd century.

The Decoration of the Meter Medallion Workshop

Syntax

Whereas in the preceding chapter we were able to demonstrate that Kymean vessels in general are quite frequently divided into superposed friezes, this is the case only to a limited extent in the Meter Medallion Workshop. We never find this composition on Possis' vases, and only infrequently on vessels by Kirbeis (KYB-2*, KYB-13*, KYB-21, KYB-36*, KYB-38–KYB-40*, KYB-43*, KYB-44*, KYB-90*, KYB-123, KYB-134*, KYB-135, KYB-149–KYB-153*, KYB-170*, KYB-178*, KYB-207*, KYB-414) and Zenodotos (KYB-423, KYB-433*). Not surprisingly, it is primarily designs with garlands and wreaths which were employed on vessels divided into friezes.

Full-body figural decoration is rare. We find it on bowls with an Amazonomachy (KYB-1* and possibly further bowls), on a single bowl where a large garland is combined with figural decoration (KYB-129*), as well as on bowls with a vegetal scroll (KYB-128*, KYB-353*, KYB-355*–KYB-358). The absolutely most common decoration is a calyx, normally in combination with figural elements.

Rim Decoration

The decoration of the rim is a simple affair with relatively few variations. Normally, only a single rim frieze – if any – is employed. The different types and their frequency are given in Fig. 62. Kirbeis mostly employs an Ionian kyma or a heart guilloche, which may be turned either left or right. In addition, we find a frieze of heart buds, a pattern which, with one exception (KYA-1*), is unique to Kirbeis. It is based on a heart ornament furnished with a bud growing out of a more or less well-defined vegetal element. It also comes in a negative version, where the stamp

---

12 As discussed by Rotroff (2010, 69).

	Kirbeis		Possis		Zenodotos		Zenodoules
	Signed	Attr.	Signed	Attr.	Signed	Attr.	Signed
No rim frieze	3	7			1		
Astragal	2	1	1	1			
Ionian kyma	7	20		2	1		
Ionian kyma, rounded with double outline			4	1			
Ionian kyma, pointed with double outline		19					
Heart guilloche left	2	18	4	37			
Heart guilloche right	7	20		2		1	
Dots	2	1	1	1	1		
Heart buds	2	25					
Heart buds in negative relief		1					
Grooves	7	14		1		1	
Rosette A alternating with boukranion B	1						
Small horizontal petal, left		1					
Spirals							1

FIGURE 62 The occurrence of various rim patterns in the MMW; only fragments with a single rim pattern are included

is mechanically copied from an image on an existing vase (**KYB-183***, **KYB-209***, **KYB-210***, **KYB-290***). The fact that it was copied, and accordingly is later, tells us that this pattern had a value as part of the potter's identity.

This ornament is extremely rare in other workshops. In nearby Pergamon we find a related ornament (e.g., employed in the PSC design on **PER-72***).[13] Amongst the almost 6,500 MMB on Delos published by Laumonier, the heart bud occurs on only eight vessels: on two vessels attributed to the Vases gris[14] and on two vessels which Laumonier considered as annexed to that workshop (1977, 107 cats. 877, 3268, pl. 24 [placed horizontally]). It is also found on three vessels attributed to CI[15] and on one vessel of the workshop of the *Rosette échancrée*.[16] The rarity of this ornament amongst vessels of Ephesian production and its secondary use as filler or in secondary positions shows that it is not at home in this production. In fact, it is only in the Levant that we find it used to the same degree as in the MMW.[17] The parallels are striking, but I find it hard to believe that there was a direct connection between the Meter Medallion Workshop and the Levantine ones; accordingly, there must have been a common source of inspiration for both of them. Perhaps Pergamon was the intermediary.

Possis almost exclusively employed a heart guilloche turned left as a rim pattern. The style of the heart (or simplified) guilloche used by Kirbeis and Possis respectively differs considerably. Kirbeis' stamp is made with a bold hand, resulting in an almost organic motif which was popular from the very beginning of his production, whereas Possis' stamp is more compressed and, in the most-used stamp, the lower rounding of the heart protrudes beyond the upper one. The heart guilloche was typical of the Athenian workshops, and it is likely that its use in Kyme was influenced by Athenian bowls. On Ephesian bowls the heart guilloche is rare (e.g., **EPH-479***, **EPH-1305***).

Multiple rim friezes are not particularly common in the MMW. Thus, 28 of Kirbeis' vessels, of which five are signed, employ a double rim pattern. The majority, 13 in all, feature heart buds as the upper frieze. This is in contrast to Possis, where we find only one attributed fragment with a double rim pattern (**KYB-391***).

Base Medallion: Iconography

The base medallion is normally surrounded by one, two, or even three broad ridges, giving the base a diameter of between 3 and 5 cm. As mentioned, the very large majority

---

13 See also Conze et al. 1913, Beibl. 43.10, 17, 23; de Luca 1968, 153 cat. 359, pl. 54; 1999, 115 cat. 590, pl. 21, Beil. 14.

14 Laumonier 1977, 106 cat. 2140, pl. 24 as second rim frieze below a Ionian kyma; cat. 2252, pl. 24 as second rim frieze below a box meander.

15 Laumonier 1977, 345 cat. 2107, pl. 82 as second rim frieze; 343 cat. 2442, pl. 82 employed as filler in body design; 350 cat. 9208, pl. 83 as rim frieze.

16 Laumonier 1977, 368 cat. 1407, pl. 89 placed upside-down as isolated body decoration (as **KYB-138**, **KYB-142***, **KYB-284***, **KYB-315***).

17 E.g., Antioch: Waagé 1948, fig. 9.28, 32, 51; fig. 10.1, 3, 4, 6, 11, 25, 27–29; fig. 11.10; fig. 12.4, 17; fig. 14.12, 20; fig. 15.20; Tell Dor: Rosenthal-Heginbottom 1995, pl. 12.6, pl. 13.3, pl. 15.6, pl. 19.1, 2, 5; Tel Anafa: Cornell 1997, 409 cats. MB 2, MB 3, pl. 1.

of the vases featured a turreted female on the medallion. However, the different potters did not employ the same stamp for this figure.

Kirbeis

The dominant stamp of Kirbeis renders a female bust turned towards the right. She has a long, drooping nose and a very large eye. The hair seems to be gathered in a small bun at the back of her head and, from this, one long straight lock hangs over her shoulder. She wears a tall mural crown with three sharp-angled, slightly trapezoidal crenellations or towers. Though it is not visible, she must have worn a wreath or *tainia* over the crown, because the fluttering end of a ribbon is always shown behind her neck. She is dressed in a high-belted, sleeveless chiton with a cloak over her left shoulder. Her left hand is lifted up in front of the body and curves around a round object which is partially obscured by her body. It may seem as though she is pulling a veil or a cloak forward, and this is how drawings frequently represent the gesture. But she is definitely not furnished with a veil. Several of the better-preserved stamps, such as **KYB-258***, for example, show beyond doubt that she is supporting a tympanon from underneath; on **KYB-232*** the upper curvature of the tympanon is very clear. A variant of the stamp (**KYB-267**) also clearly renders a large, round tympanon.

As just mentioned, **KYB-267** as well as **KYB-266*** are variants of the standard stamp: the former features a completely different Meter, with a tall polos instead of the crenellated one; the latter depicts the standard Meter, but the placement of the letters differs. On **KYB-255*** the Meter stamp is smaller than usual, so the original stamp must have been mechanically copied; it is even retouched, so that a wreath is clearly indicated.

Apart from the ubiquitous Meter bust, three further medallion stamps can be attributed to Kirbeis: a comic mask, a wreath, and a rosette. A comic mask is employed on **KYB-320***. The same mask medallion was also used by Possis (see below) and in the Kymean Workshop A in a miniature version (**KYA-2***, **KYA-49***, **KYA-51**, **KYA-58***). The mask medallion is also known from a mould found at Kyme attributed to the Paniskos Workshop (Bouzek & Jansová 1974, 51 cat. MB 1, fig. 6, pl. 1; cf. **KYX-31**) and from two moulds found at Sardis (Rotroff 2003, 104 cats. 420, 421, pl. 70), neither inscribed with a mould maker's signature. It is also common on Sardian bowls (Rotroff 2003, cats. 427, 428, 449, 470, 547–551, 604–605, mostly of Sardian production), on Kymean bowls (Bouzek & Jansová 1974, 54 cat. MB 23, fig. 8), and is attested at Pergamon as well (Conze et al. 1913, Beibl. 42.6). The use of a theatre mask in the medallion seems to be characteristic of the Aiolian koine.

In the medallions of two vessels, **KYB-268*** and **KYB-324**, the latter an amphora, Kirbeis employed a wreath with *tainia*, a stamp which was normally used in the decoration of the body. Three bowls, two of them small, have a rosette in this position (**KYB-123**, **KYB-317***, **KYB-318***).

The fact that one and the same medallion stamp (which was not even particularly worn) was employed on almost every single one of Kirbeis' moulds tells us that the production must have been relatively short-lived and that the output was not very large.

Possis

Possis employs a stamp with a turreted female bust turned towards the right. In contrast to the image on Kirbeis' bowls, the bust is much smaller and terminates above the shoulders. The face is much more 'classical' than that of Kirbeis' goddess, with a straight brow and nose and a rather heavy chin. Her hair is drawn back but without the bun of the Kirbeis Meter, and one loose wavy lock hangs by the side of the neck. The crown features three crenellations or towers with rounded tops, with ample space between them. Each individual tower is doubly outlined. The goddess wears a wreath over the crown; this is accurately rendered, as is one straight end of a fluttering ribbon. **KYB-376*** bears a variant stamp, a very crude version of the Possis Meter stamp.

Apart from the Meter bust, Possis also sparingly employed a comic mask. In one case he signed the mould around the mask (**KYB-350***), but on three further bowls which without doubt can be attributed to Possis, he employed the mask without signature (**KYB-348***, **KYB-363***, **KYB-364***).

Zenodotos

I know of no more than seven medallions signed by Zenodotos (**KYB-412***, **KYB-413***, **KYB-415–KYB-419**). They all display the same female head turned towards the left. She has a big nose and a pronounced double chin. Her hair is gathered at the neck in a bun and, below this bun, three spiral locks hang down the neck. She wears a low mural crown where only slight incisions indicate the crenellations (four or more). Domăneanțu erroneously considered the figure a male (Domăneanțu 2000, 123 cat. 606).

Zenodoules

Only one vessel stamped by Zenodoules is known to me (**KYB-423**). It shows a very debased version of a turreted female turned towards the right. The published image is difficult to make out.

Base Medallion: Conclusions

As we have seen, the female rendered on least the Kirbeis medallions can be identified as Meter Theon (Kybele), not just because of the mural crown, which could also have indicated a city Tyche, but because of the tympanon which she clearly supports from below with her left hand. Though this feature does not appear on the vessels of the other members of the workshop, I believe that we may infer by analogy that the turreted deity depicted by Possis, Zenodotos, and Zenodoules is Meter too. At the end of the chapter, we shall briefly consider why Meter was chosen as the workshop's logo (pp. 214–215).

The medallion was from time to time surrounded by an additional pattern, either immediately around the Meter stamp or between the two inner ridges: a frieze of dots (Kirbeis: KYB-37*, KYB-73, KYB-96, KYB-130*, KYB-185, KYB-186, KYB-196, KYB-224, KYB-231*, KYB-256; Possis: KYB-344*) or of astragals (Kirbeis: KYB-4*, KYB-96, KYB-258*, KYB-264; Possis: KYB-367*, KYB-376*) used both by Kirbeis and Possis; a frieze of small, dart-shaped petals, which Possis and Zenodoules employed (Possis: KYB-349, KYB-351*, KYB-354*, KYB-363*, KYB-388; Zenodoules: KYB-423). The reason for this extra ornamentation is not clear. Perhaps it was just a whim of the day.

The Stamps

At least 163 stamps were certainly or very probably used in the MMW, in addition to the stamps employed for the rim patterns and for the medallion. Many stamps are documented only once or a few times, and it is a rarity to find two vessels which we can postulate come from the same mould. This can probably tell us that the majority of the vessels once produced in the Kymean workshops are yet to be discovered!

When we consider internal workshop organization, Fig. 63 illustrates very well the extent to which stamps of the individual mould makers of the MMW were interwoven on the workshop's moulds, and how this workshop to a lesser extent shared stamps with other contemporary workshop(s) at the same site. It makes it clear that the Kymean workshops can probably be classified as nucleated workshops (Chapter 4). One of these was the MMW. It is obvious that craftsmen must have moved between the

Individual stamps	Kirbeis	Signed	57
		Attributed	10
	Possis	Signed	15
		Attributed	18
Shared stamps	Kirbeis, Possis		25
	Kirbeis, Possis, Zenodotos		3
	Kirbeis, Possis, Zenodotos, Workshop A		1
	Kirbeis, Possis, Zenodotos, other Kymean workshops		1
	Kirbeis, Possis, Workshop A		3
	Kirbeis, Possis, other Kymean workshops		1
	Kirbeis, Possis, Workshop A, other Kymean workshops		3
	Kirbeis, Zenodotos		3
	Kirbeis, Workshop A		8
	Kirbeis, Workshop A, other Kymean workshops		7
	Kirbeis, other Kymean workshops		2
	Possis, Zenodotos		1
	Possis, Workshop A		3
	Possis, Workshop A, other Kymean workshops		1
	Zenodotos, Workshop A		1
Grand total			163

FIGURE 63 Numbers of individual and shared stamps in the MMW; only body decoration is included.
Zenodotos: no unique stamps (apart from base medallion)

workshops, since this is the only explanation which can account for the appearance of the same stamps on the moulds of several workshops within the nucleated group. Nevertheless, to a large degree, the individual mould makers retain their own individual character, as do the individual workshops. It is striking, for example, that the heart bud, so common on Kirbeis' vessels, is virtually never found on other Kymean vessels (KYA-1* is a rare exception), even within the MMW, and in the rare instances when it is, it is in a secondary position (KYB-433*, unattributed).

The following is a list of the individual stamps which can be found on vessels of the MMW, including both signed and attributed fragments. Because a number of stamps are shared by several mould makers, the Meter Medallion Workshop is considered in its totality. (i), (ii), and (iii) indicate the mould generation, with (i) being the earliest.

Figural Elements
Erotes
At least 16 different Eros stamps were used in the MMW. Eight are at a large scale, three at medium scale, and four are small in scale. The large Erotes are almost exclusively employed by Kirbeis. Of these, three (Erotes A, B, C) were introduced on what must be one of the earliest bowls (KYB-129*). None of them seems to have been created for this context. At least, their movement does not look particularly motivated by the action of the scene, and they were probably copied from elsewhere. The most popular Eros is Eros D, which often appears in a narrative composition. The medium-sized Erotes were also mostly employed by Kirbeis, whereas the small Erotes were chiefly used by Possis.

Eros A (Large)
Frontal Eros with outspread wings; he is looking to his right but turns his body back towards the left and holds a torch in his lowered right hand. His left leg turns towards his left and in his lowered left hand he holds an oblong object, perhaps a piece of cloth, e.g., a handkerchief. It is likely that this is, in fact, a corrupt stamp of Eros burning Psyche in the shape of a butterfly, of which only the wing is preserved (e.g., Sichtermann 1969; Burn & Higgins 2001, 123 [terracotta from Myrina]). H: 3.2 cm. Occurs together with acanthus K, O, S.
– Kirbeis, signed: KYB-47*, KYB-129*
– Kirbeis, attributed: KYB-84*, KYB-113(?)

Eros B (Large)
Eros wearing a loin cloth, walking left with his left leg forward; his left arm is held up and backwards, and in the hand he holds a round wreath. H: 3.8 cm. With acanthus A, D, E, S.
– Kirbeis, signed: KYB-129*
– Kirbeis, attributed: KYB-79, KYB-108*
– Possis, signed: KYB-331*

Eros C (Large)
Chubby Eros moving slowly right while playing a kithara. This Eros has been erroneously reconstructed as carrying a cornucopia (Rostovcev 1967, 600, pl. LXVIII.2). H: 4.2 cm. With acanthus P, S.
– Kirbeis, signed: KYB-47*, KYB-129*
– Kirbeis, attributed: KYB-13*, KYB-48*, KYB-49, KYB-51, KYB-60*, KYB-80

Eros D (Large)
Eros with small outspread wings moving left; he holds his left arm akimbo and the left leg is trailing; his right arm is held forward. This was a very popular stamp. Frequently it is combined with bird A or B in a scene where the Eros is freeing the bird from a leash. The best-preserved specimens show a ribbon in his hand from which the bird is released. In one variant, the Eros wears a nebris across his chest. The motif of the tied and freed bird seems to belong to a narrative or at least to have had a meaning which escapes us today. The liberator is always Eros D, the stamp of which shows the hanging ribbon of the leash. It is of note that the nebris contextualizes the liberator in a Dionysiac setting. I find it likely that the freeing of the bird alludes to the role of Dionysos as Lysios, the liberator. The stamp occurs in at least three stamp generations of decreasing height: (i): 3.5, (ii): 2.5, (iii): 1.9 cm.

With nebris, acanthus N, S:
– Kirbeis, signed: KYB-131
– Kirbeis, attributed: KYB-80, KYB-81*, KYB-328
Without nebris, acanthus K, M, P, Q, R, S, V:
– Kirbeis, signed: KYB-50, KYB-55, KYB-64, KYB-66, KYB-68*, KYB-69*, KYB-322*
– Kirbeis, attributed: KYB-14*–KYB-18*, KYB-36*, KYB-37*, KYB-46*, KYB-65, KYB-67*, KYB-82, KYB-83*, KYB-91*, KYB-92*, KYB-112, KYB-150, KYB-323
– Unattributed: KYB-427*

Eros E (Large)
Eros with outspread wings moving left in a sweeping motion; both arms are held up and forwards; left leg is trailing.
– Kirbeis, signed: KYB-149

Eros F (Large)
Mirror image of Eros E; perhaps the two were originally conceived as a pair.
– Possis, signed: KYB-335

Eros G (Large)
Phlyax Eros moving right; the Eros is dressed in short trousers and wrapped in a cloak(?), and from KYB-109* it appears that he wears a comic mask. H: 2.8 cm. With acanthus K, L.
– Kirbeis, signed: KYB-57*
– Kirbeis, attributed: KYB-109*

Eros H (Large)
Eros moving right; the Eros wears a loin cloth(?); only half a stamp is preserved and the identification as an Eros is tentative.
– Kirbeis, attributed: KYB-71*

Eros I (Medium-Sized)
Eros moving left; left arm akimbo; in his right hand he holds a long stick – sceptre? thyrsos? walking-stick? H: 2.2 cm. Acanthus P.
– Kirbeis, signed: KYB-61*, KYB-140*, KYB-141

Eros K (Medium-Sized)
Kithara-playing Eros moving right with right leg trailing; the head of the Eros is frontal. H: 2.5 cm.
– Kirbeis, signed: KYB-58
– Kirbeis, attributed: KYB-59*

Eros L (Medium-Sized)
Frontal syrinx-playing Eros-Paniskos with horns; he is sitting cross-legged; the arms rest on the knees. H: 1.5 cm. Acanthus R.
– Kirbeis, attributed: KYB-19*, KYB-20, KYB-70*, KYB-125
– Other Kymean workshops: KYX-1*, KYX-29*, KYX-31, KYX-46*, KYX-61

Eros M (Small)
Eros moving right; both arms are held up and forwards; right foot is trailing. H: 1.8 cm. Acanthus I.
– Kirbeis, signed: KYB-68*, KYB-140*, KYB-141
– Kirbeis, attributed: KYB-105, KYB-110, KYB-170*
– Possis, signed: KYB-344*, KYB-361
– Possis, attributed: KYB-345*, KYB-346*

Eros N (Small)
Frontal Eros with outspread wings; legs are spread and the arms are lowered. H: 1.6 cm.
– Possis, signed: KYB-344*

Eros O (Small)
Eros with legs held closely together, flying right; both arms are held forwards. H: 1.6 cm.
– Possis, signed: KYB-331*

Eros P (Small)
Eros flying left; both arms are held forward. H: 1 cm.
– Possis, signed: KYB-342*, KYB-353*
– Possis, attributed: KYB-384

The miniature Eros O and P are most likely influenced by the small flying Erotes of the Attic production (e.g., ATH-12*).

Amazons
Fighting Amazon A
Amazon in short chiton striding right; left leg bent at the knee is set far forward, right leg is behind and turned left. Behind the shoulder of the Amazon is a short, flying cloak. She holds up an oblong shield with indented upper part in front of her; the shield, including the grip, is seen from the inside. In the lowered right hand she holds a sword upwards and slightly forward. H (i): 3.2, (ii): 2.8 cm.
– Kirbeis, signed: KYB-1*, KYB-2*
– Kirbeis, attributed: KYB-10*(?)
– Possis, signed: KYB-330*

Fighting Amazon B
Amazon in short chiton moving left but looking right. In her lowered right hand she holds a double axe; with her outstretched left arm she holds an oblong shield with indented upper part out in front of her; the shield, including the grip, is seen from the inside. H: 3.2 cm.
– Kirbeis, signed: KYB-2*, KYB-5, KYB-321
– Possis, signed: KYB-330*

Fighting Amazon C
Amazon in short chiton turned left but stepping back. With her right arm she holds an oblong shield with indented upper part forward; in her lowered left hand she holds a double axe. H: 3 cm. A closely similar Amazon can be found on an Ephesian vessel probably by Menemachos (EPH-81*).
– Kirbeis, signed: KYB-1*, KYB-2*, KYB-5, KYB-321
– Kirbeis, attributed: KYB-6

Fighting Amazon D
Amazon in short chiton striding right; left leg bent at the knee and set forward, right leg is behind and turned left. Behind the shoulder of the Amazon is a short, flying cloak. She holds an oblong shield with indented upper part up in front of her; the shield, including the grip, is seen from the

inside. With her right hand, which is held high, she swings a double axe, which is rendered behind her head. H (i): 3.2, (ii): 2.8 cm.
– Kirbeis, signed: KYB-2*
– Kirbeis, attributed: KYB-10*(?)
– Possis, signed: KYB-330*

Fighting Amazon E
Amazon in short chiton turned left but stepping back and looking back to the right. With her lowered left arm she holds forward an oblong shield with indented upper part. The shield, including the grip, is seen from the inside. Her right arm is lowered and held forward; over it is an animal skin(?). H: 2.8 cm.
– Kirbeis, signed: KYB-1*, KYB-2*

Dying Amazon A
Amazon in short chiton lying on the ground, left; she supports herself with her elbows, which are placed behind her. Can also be used upside-down curving around base medallion.
– Kirbeis, signed: KYB-1*–KYB-4*
– Kirbeis, attributed: KYB-6, KYB-10*

Dying Amazon B
Amazon in short chiton lying on the ground, left. Can be upside-down curving around base medallion.
– Kirbeis, signed: KYB-2*, KYB-3, KYB-9
– Kirbeis, attributed: KYB-10*

Dying Amazon C
Amazon in short chiton sitting on the ground, left, but turning her head towards right. She is sitting on her right, bent leg; the left leg is stretched out behind her. She supports herself with her right arm.
– Kirbeis, signed: KYB-1*

Dying Amazon D
Amazon lying on the ground(?) turned left; her right hand is placed on her forehead in a gesture of grief or pain.
– Kirbeis, signed: KYB-2*

Dying Amazon E
Amazon lying on the ground(?) turned left. An arm is held forward.
– Kirbeis, signed: KYB-1*

Fighting Greeks
Greek A
Large Greek in short chiton and cuirass striding right, with left leg forward and bent at the knee, and right leg trailing. In his lowered right hand, he holds a spear horizontally across his body. He holds up a round shield in front of him; the shield, including the grip, is seen from the inside. H: 3.2 cm.
– Kirbeis, signed: KYB-1*, KYB-2*, KYB-5
– Kirbeis, attributed: KYB-6, KYB-8*

Greek B
Large Greek in short chiton and cuirass(?) striding right, his left leg forward and bent at the knee, his right leg trailing. He holds a sword in his right hand, which is held over his head in a striking pose. With his lowered left arm he holds a round shield; the shield, including the grip, is seen from the inside. H: 3.2 cm.
– Kirbeis, signed: KYB-2*
– Kirbeis, attributed: KYB-103*

Hunter
Male hunter with naked upper body and a loin cloth, striding right, holding a spear across his body. The stamp is not completely preserved.
– Kirbeis, attributed: KYB-38

Horsemen
Horseman A
Large horseman on horse in flying gallop, right. The rider wears a short chiton and boots and perhaps a cuirass; behind his shoulder is a small, fluttering cloak. In his raised right hand he holds a spear. H: 3.2 cm.
– Kirbeis, signed: KYB-1*, KYB-321
– Kirbeis, attributed: KYB-7*, KYB-11, KYX-12*

Horseman B
Large horseman wearing boots, on horse galloping left but turning its head back. H: 3 cm.
– Kirbeis, signed: KYB-1*, KYB-3
– Kirbeis, attributed: KYB-7*

Horseman C
Large horseman on a horse prancing to right; the horse bends its head strongly inwards; the rider holds a spear in his lowered right hand. H: 3.5 cm. This stamp is employed chiefly in Workshop A, but also occurs in the MMW on vessels signed by and attributed to Possis.
– Possis, signed: KYB-330*
– Workshop A: KYA-1*–KYA-3*, KYA-52, KYA-53*

Horse Turning Its Head Back
Horse moving left and turning its head back. H: 2.5 cm. A similar stamp occurs in the Ephesian production (e.g., EPH-1307*).
– Kirbeis, signed: KYB-2*

Mythological Figures

Dancing Satyr
Satyr with small tail, dancing with lifted left leg and moving left. Both arms are held upward in order to balance the figure. H: 2.2 cm.
– Possis, attributed: KYB-339*

Priapos
Frontal Priapos lifting long garment revealing erect penis. The stamp is partially preserved. Attributed to Possis because it occurs in combination with acanthus T and Eros P, which are predominantly used by this mould maker.
– Possis, attributed: KYB-340*

Herakles Fighting the Hydra
Herakles grips the Hydra with his extended left hand; with the right, he swings his club over his head ready to strike the monster. The stamp is partially preserved. This stamp is most likely inspired by an early Ephesian stamp (Laumonier 1977, 177 cats. 3311, 3312, pls. 39, 125).
– Possis, attributed: KYB-347*

Ship
The lower part of a partially preserved stamp with an oared ship and the legs of a male (Odysseus?) standing in the ship. It may depict a mythological scene. A ship is also rendered on KYX-11*, which clearly shows Skylla attacking Odysseus' ship; a ship representation is also known from another fragment of Kymean production (Bouzek & Jansová 1974, 54 cat. MB 20, fig. 1, pl. 4).
– Kirbeis, attributed: KYB-23*

Pan Mask
Long-bearded mask probably of Pan.
– Possis, attributed: KYB-337*

Comic Mask
A comic mask employed as body decoration.
– Possis, attributed: KYB-349

Other Male Representations

Aulos-Playing Herdsman
Naked male walking towards the right while playing an aulos; he wears a long cloak which flutters behind him.
– Possis, signed: KYB-331*
– Possis, attributed: KYB-332*, KYB-333*

Thyrsos-Bearer
Small male wearing loin cloth(?) walking right; his right arm is bent and held in front of his body; with the left hand he holds a long-shafted object over his left shoulder, probably a thyrsos. H: 1.8 cm.
– Kirbeis, signed: KYB-55, KYB-68*
– Workshop A: KYA-11*, KYA-14*
– Other Kymean workshops: KYX-47*

Male
Medium-sized male wearing loin cloth, moving left but looking back; left arm is bent and held upwards; right arm is lowered.
– Kirbeis, attributed: KYB-24*

Female Representations

Draped Frontal Female
A large female(?) in long chiton and completely wrapped in a himation is rendered frontally. Her lowered right arm is completely wrapped in the mantle; her left arm is bent and held in front of her body, and also completely wrapped in the mantle. In her left hand she holds a hemispherical bowl. This stamp can be placed above the altar stamp to form the image of a statue on a high base (KYB-56*, KYB-129*). It is possible that this particular combination hints at the identification of the figure as Dionysos rather than a female. In the catalogue, it is nevertheless classified as female. H: 3.3 cm. Acanthus L, N, O, P, S, V.
– Kirbeis, signed: KYB-50, KYB-54*, KYB-57*, KYB-93*, KYB-129*
– Kirbeis, attributed: KYB-48*, KYB-51, KYB-56*, KYB-67*, KYB-85*, KYB-94*, KYB-104*, KYB-105

Mantled Dancing Woman
Large frontal woman with a long chiton and a mantle draped across her body. She dances holding her arms stretched out to each side. A similar though not identical stamp can be found on a fragment from Kyme of unknown production (Bouzek & Jansová 1974, 64–65 cat. MB 82, fig. 4, pl. 11). H (i): 2.9, (ii): ca. 1.7 cm.
– Kirbeis, signed: KYB-58
– Kirbeis, attributed: KYB-71*, KYB-336*

Naked Woman
Naked woman walking right. She holds her bent right arm in front of her breast. Together with the following stamp, part of toilet scene.
– Possis, attributed: KYB-346*

Woman Pouring Water
Naked woman pouring water from jar into basin on tall conical foot, right. Together with the preceding stamp, part of toilet scene. The closest parallel is the scene on an early Aiolis B bowl (AIB-1*).

– Possis, attributed: KYB-346*

Woman with wreath
Woman in long chiton walking (or flying?) left. Both of her arms are stretched forwards and upwards holding a round wreath. Perhaps Nike *apteros*; see also KYX-6*.
– Possis, attributed: KYB-346*

Dolphins
Dolphin with tail turned upwards. Dolphins are common on the vessels of the MMW. They normally occur in mirror-image pairs of the same size, mostly placed heraldically, often around rosette A, but they can also be employed as a space-filler. There seem to be two standard sizes: medium and large. The first was employed by Kirbeis, the second mostly by Possis and Zenodotos.

Dolphin A
Medium-sized dolphin swimming right. L 1.5–1.6 cm.
– Kirbeis, signed: KYB-72, KYB-86*, KYB-97*–KYB-99*, KYB-118, KYB-128*, KYB-129*, KYB-131, KYB-149, KYB-152*, KYB-316, KYB-325*
– Kirbeis, attributed: KYB-23*, KYB-30*–KYB-34*, KYB-76*, KYB-83*, KYB-89*, KYB-102*, KYB-117*, KYB-133*, KYB-143*, KYB-163*–KYB-165*
– Possis, attributed: KYB-411*
– Workshop A: KYA-5*–KYB-8*, KYA-37, KYA-55

Dolphin B
Medium-sized dolphin swimming left. L 1.5–1.6 cm.
– Kirbeis, signed: KYB-72, KYB-97*–KYB-99*, KYB-118, KYB-128*, KYB-129*, KYB-131, KYB-149, KYB-152*, KYB-316, KYB-325*
– Kirbeis, attributed: KYB-30*, KYB-32*, KYB-33, KYB-76*, KYB-89*, KYB-117*, KYB-121, KYB-133*, KYB-163*–KYB-165*
– Possis, attributed: KYB-411*
– Workshop A: KYA-5*, KYA-6

Dolphin C
Large dolphin swimming right. L 2.3 cm.
– Kirbeis, signed: KYB-255*
– Possis, signed: KYB-361
– Possis, attributed: KYB-337*, KYB-338*, KYB-386*

Dolphin D
Large dolphin swimming left. L 2.3 cm.
– Kirbeis, signed: KYB-255*
– Possis, signed: KYB-361
– Possis, attributed: KYB-337*, KYB-338*, KYB-348*, KYB-386*

Dogs
Dog A
Long-haired dog with open mouth and long tail held upwards moving right. The dog wears a collar. The stamp is partially preserved.
– Possis, attributed: KYB-347*

Dog B
Dog turned right. The stamp is partially preserved.
– Kirbeis, attributed: KYB-38

Dog C
Dog turned left. The stamp is partially preserved.
– Kirbeis, attributed: KYB-38
– Possis, attributed: KYB-345*

Birds
Birds were the single most popular motif in the MMW. This is in tune with the Kyme workshops in general, as was noted by Bouzek & Jansová, who mentioned birds as a trademark of the Kymean workshops (1974, 44–45). It is likely that the ubiquitous representation of birds was ultimately inspired by Athenian bowls, where they figure equally prominently. At least nine different birds were rendered in the MMW. Of these, birds A–D are by far the most common.

Bird A
Slender bird, perhaps a dove, sitting right. The long tail and slender wings are turned slightly upwards. On KYX-8* and KYX-57* the bird is employed as a frieze divider, and in both cases, the stamp seems to be in pristine condition. It is particularly popular with Kirbeis, where it is used as a space-filler but also as part of a narrative, when it is combined with Eros D. Strangely enough, it is never used by the other members of the MMW. L: 1.5 cm. A closely related stamp is employed in another Kymean workshop (Bouzek & Jansová 1974, 55, 57 cats. MB 35, MB 38, fig. 2).
– Kirbeis, signed: KYB-62, KYB-64, KYB-68*, KYB-96, KYB-100*, KYB-106, KYB-107, KYB-129*, KYB-132*, KYB-149, KYB-316, KYB-322*, KYB-326*, KYB-327*
– Kirbeis, attributed: KYB-7*, KYB-25*–KYB-29, KYB-37*, KYB-52, KYB-65, KYB-75*, KYB-80, KYB-102*, KYB-104*, KYB-117*–KYB-121, KYB-122, KYB-133*, KYB-139, KYB-143*, KYB-163*, KYB-164, KYB-166, KYB-170*, KYB-317*, KYB-318*, KYB-324
– Workshop A: KYA-29*, KYA-35*
– Other Kymean workshops: KYX-8*, KYX-47*, KYX-57*

Bird B
Bird, a dove(?), flying left. One sickle-shaped wing is held high above the body. This bird was seemingly created for the composition of 'Eros freeing bird' together with Eros D; for this reason, a small end of the leash with which it was tied is hanging below its tail. L: 1.4 cm.
- Kirbeis, signed: KYB-1*, KYB-50, KYB-69*, KYB-96, KYB-124*, KYB-149, KYB-327*
- Kirbeis, attributed: KYB-25*, KYB-26*, KYB-92*, KYB-133*, KYB-142*, KYB-150, KYB-323

Bird C
Mirror image of Bird B.
- Kirbeis, signed: KYB-1*, KYB-54*, KYB-149, KYB-326*
- Kirbeis, attributed: KYB-49, KYB-92*, KYB-117*, KYB-158*, KYB-317*

Bird D
Bird with outspread wings seen almost frontally, flying left.
- Kirbeis, signed: KYB-1*, KYB-50, KYB-62, KYB-69*, KYB-132*
- Kirbeis, attributed: KYB-115, KYB-157*, KYB-170*
- Possis, signed: KYB-351*
- Possis, attributed: KYB-383*, KYB-384

Bird E
Slightly long-necked bird (a goose?) sitting right. The feathers of the wings are dotted. L (i): 1.1, (ii): 0.8 cm.
- Kirbeis, attributed: KYB-123, KYB-126
- Possis, signed: KYB-354*
- Possis, attributed: KYB-383*, KYB-385*

Bird F
Mirror image of bird E. L (i): 1.2, (ii): 1 cm.
- Kirbeis, signed: KYB-73(?)
- Kirbeis, attributed: KYB-74*, KYB-123, KYB-127*
- Possis, attributed: KYB-334*, KYB-385*

Bird G
Long-necked bird (a goose?) sitting left. The feathers of the wings are dotted. H (i): 1.3, (ii): 1.1 cm.
- Kirbeis, signed: KYB-73(?)
- Kirbeis, attributed: KYB-127*
- Possis, signed: KYB-342*, KYB-354*

Bird H
Dove sitting right. L (i): 2.0, (ii): 1.4 cm.
- Kirbeis, attributed: KYB-35*
- Workshop A: KYA-37

Bird I
Long-necked bird (heron?) flying left. The animal has very long wings. L: 3.7 cm.
- Kirbeis, signed: KYB-64, KYB-149
- Kirbeis, attributed: KYB-101*

Other Animals
Small Feline
Small feline walking left. H: 1.1 cm.
- Kirbeis, signed: KYB-326*
- Kirbeis, attributed: KYB-170*

Boar
Boar(?) with dotted pelt leaping right. The stamp is rather blurred. H: 1.4 cm.
- Kirbeis, signed: KYB-2*, KYB-21

Stag Leaping Right
- Kirbeis, signed: KYB-21
- Kirbeis, attributed: KYB-22*
- Workshop A: KYA-52

Mythological Animals
Eagle Griffin A
Eagle griffin with tall sickle wing, curled tail held high. The griffin is walking right but turns its head backwards. H: 2.1 cm.
- Kirbeis, attributed: KYB-36*, KYB-39*, KYB-40*
- Workshop A: KYA-9*

Eagle griffin B
Mirror image of eagle griffin A. H: 2.1 cm.
- Kirbeis, attributed: KYB-37*, KYB-39*, KYB-41, KYB-42
- Workshop A: KYA-9*

Ketos?
Animal with a long snout and a looped hind body, left. The stamp is partially preserved.
- Kirbeis, attributed: KYB-36*

Boukrania
Boukranion A
Large boukranion with long, straight horns, double ridge around eyes and single ridge over nose. On rare occasions the stamp is furnished with a dotted line as a *tainia* hanging down (KYB-151*).
- Kirbeis, signed: KYB-130*, KYB-151*, KYB-152*
- Kirbeis, attributed: KYB-39*, KYB-43*, KYB-46*, KYB-154–KYB-156, KYB-324

Boukranion B
Small boukranion with small, down-turned horns (perhaps a goat rather than a bull?). The skull is always furnished with a *tainia* of un-spun wool. H: 1.0 cm.
– Kirbeis, attributed: KYB-120*, KYB-153*
– Workshop A: KYA-28*–KYA-33*, KYA-51, KYA-57

Vases
Krater A
Calyx krater with plain, conical neck, ribbed body, and tall, ribbed pedestal foot. H (i): ca. 2.7, (ii): 1.9 cm.
– Kirbeis, signed: KYB-129*
– Possis, attributed: KYB-341*
– Other Kymean workshops: KYX-40

Krater B
Volute krater with high-swung handles attached to the rim, ribbed body and tall, profiled foot. H: 2.5 cm.
– Kirbeis, signed: KYB-86*, KYB-129*, KYB-151*, KYB-322*
– Kirbeis, attributed: KYB-87*, KYB-117*, KYB-323
– Possis, signed: KYB-361

Kantharos A
Pokalkantharos with high-swung handles attached to the rim, a ribbed body, and a tall stem. H (i): 2.5, (ii): 2.0, (iii): 1.3 cm.
– Kirbeis, signed: KYB-50, KYB-88*, KYB-129*, KYB-326*
– Kirbeis, attributed: KYB-52, KYB-116, KYB-119
– Workshop A: KYA-18*
– Other Kymean workshops: KYX-35*, KYX-36*, KYX-42, KYX-43*, KYX-55*

Kantharos B
Cup-kantharos with high-swung handles shown two-dimensionally, a ribbed body, and a low, profiled foot. H (i): 2.5, (ii): 1.7 cm.
– Kirbeis, signed: KYB-99*
– Kirbeis, attributed: KYB-35*, KYB-53*, KYB-87*, KYB-103*, KYB-328
– Possis, attributed: KYB-343*
– Workshop A: KYA-14*–KYA-17*, KYA-34*, KYB-39*
– Other Kymean workshops: KYX-21*, KYX-39*

One-Handled Jug
Tall jug with one handle. H: 2.0 cm.
– Possis, attributed: KYB-383*, KYB-384

Other Objects
Altar
Tall altar decorated with a bound garland. H: 2.7 cm. The altar could also function as a pedestal for the representation of a frontal female (KYB-56*, KYB-129*) as well as for Amazon D (KYB-46*). The occurrence of an altar is probably influenced by Pergamon (see Chapter 9).
– Kirbeis, signed: KYB-129*, KYB-152*
– Kirbeis, attributed: KYB-46*, KYB-56*

Column A
Corinthian(?) column with decorated torus. H: 2.7 cm.
– Kirbeis, attributed: KYB-40*, KYB-46*

Column B
Plain column. H: 2.2 cm.
– Kirbeis, signed: KYB-326*

Kithara A
Large kithara; only the upper right-hand corner is preserved.
– Unattributed: KYB-431*

Kithara B
Large kithara, a finely detailed stamp. H: 2.8 cm.
– Kirbeis, signed: KYB-128*
– Kirbeis, attributed: KYB-95, KYB-162*

Gorytos
A very detailed stamp of a gorytos, including the bow and the strap for carrying or fastening it. The bow-case is finely decorated. H: 3.7 cm.
– Kirbeis, signed: KYB-54*, KYB-55

Medusa Head
Frontal female head with short locks and wings: a beautiful Medusa. On three vessels a garland is suspended between the heads (KYB-138, KYB-140*, KYB-142*), on two the head is located over the garland (KYB-143*, KYB-144), and on the remainder the head is used as a space-filler. H: 1.3 cm.
– Kirbeis, signed: KYB-61*, KYB-62, KYB-138, KYB-140*, KYB-326*
– Kirbeis, attributed: KYB-17*, KYB-142*–KYB-144

Bow
Tainia tied in a bow with ends hanging down. Stamps of various sizes rather than different mould generations exist. The *tainia* tied in a bow is a common motif on Aiolian MMB (see Chapter 10). H: 1.3, 1.7, 2.0 cm.
– Kirbeis, signed: KYB-132*, KYB-316, KYB-325*
– Kirbeis, attributed: KYB-45, KYB-78, KYB-143*, KYB-157*–KYB-161, KYB-174
– Possis, attributed: KYB-362*
– Workshop A: KYA-37

Plaque with Standing Figure
Small plaque with standing female(?) figure dressed in a long garment. She is turned slightly to the right with her right leg trailing; her right arm is bent and held in front of her breast.
– Kirbeis, signed: KYB-326*

Garlands and Wreaths
Wreaths
Wreath
Suspended wreath with a *tainia* tied in a bow, its fringed ends hanging down. This stamp was also used as a base medallion stamp (KYB-268*, KYB-324). H 2.5 cm.
– Kirbeis, signed: KYB-54*, KYB-152*, KYB-327*
– Kirbeis, attributed: KYB-19*, KYB-43*, KYB-70*, KYB-136*, KYB-137*, KYB-268*, KYB-323, KYB-324

Myrtle Wreath
Myrtle wreath with three petals and separate stamps of rounded berries with decorated ends.
– Kirbeis, signed: KYB-172*
– Kirbeis, attributed: KYB-173–KYB-176*
– Possis, signed: KYB-361

Garlands
Strangely enough, suspended garlands are very rare on the bowls of Possis, occurring on only one signed and one attributed vessel (KYB-361 and KYB-362*, respectively). This is in stark contrast to Kirbeis, who used a suspended garland on no less than 48 vessels (almost 15%). The garlands come in a number of different versions: a large garland with individually stamped leaves, and a smaller, bound garland, which is stamped as a whole. Both types are found in a number of variants. Garlands could be suspended between columns (KYB-40*), from boukranion A (KYB-130*, KYB-151*, KYB-152*, KYB-155*, KYB-156, KYB-324), a kithara (KYB-149, KYB-162*), Medusa heads (KYB-138, KYB-140*, KYB-142*), or a frontal draped female (KYB-129*), as well as from a *tainia* tied in a bow (KYB-132*, KYB-143*, KYB-157*–KYB-161, KYB-316, KYB-325*).

Garland A
Large garland with oblong leaves and berries (myrtle?).
– Kirbeis, signed: KYB-129*, KYB-131, KYB-132*, KYB-134*
– Kirbeis, attributed: KYB-133*, KYB-135–KYB-137*
– Workshop A: KYA-41*

Garland B
Large garland with oak leaves and acorns.
– Kirbeis, signed: KYB-130*

Garland C
Large garland with bunches of grapes and vine leaves.
– Kirbeis, signed: KYB-130*, KYB-132*

Garland D
Large bound garland. H: ca. 2.3 cm.
– Kirbeis, signed: KYB-138, KYB-140*, KYB-141, KYB-145*, KYB-147*–KYB-149, KYB-151*, KYB-152*, KYB-171*, KYB-316
– Kirbeis, attributed: KYB-142*–KYB-144, KYB-146*, KYB-150, KYB-153*–KYB-155*, KYB-157*, KYB-158*, KYB-160–KYB-165*, KYB-167*–KYB-169, KYB-324
– Other Kymean workshops: KYX-54*

Garland E
Large bound garland. H: 2.3 cm.
– Kirbeis, signed: KYB-325*
– Workshop A: KYA-37, KYA-38, KYA-40*, KYA-42*, KYA-57

Garland F
Medium-sized bound garland. H: 1.7 cm.
– Kirbeis, attributed: KYB-40*, KYB-159*

Garland G
Medium-sized bound garland. H: 1.7 cm.
– Zenodotos, signed: KYB-413*
– Zenodotos, attributed: KYB-414
– Workshop A: KYA-36*

Garland H
Small bound garland. H: 1.3 cm.
– Kirbeis, attributed: KYB-170*
– Workshop A: KYA-28*–KYA-35*
– Other Kymean workshops: KYX-62

Vegetal Elements
Acanthus Leaves
Acanthus A
A tall, naturalistic acanthus leaf with hatched central vein and the tip bent elegantly towards left. H: ca. 6 cm.
– Kirbeis, signed: KYB-177*, KYB-325*
– Kirbeis, attributed: KYB-79, KYB-183*(?), KYB-187*

Acanthus B
As acanthus A but with lower half covered with ovoid petal with segmented central vein. H: ca. 6 cm.
– Kirbeis, signed: KYB-96

Acanthus C
Naturalistic leaf with single stem and the tip turned towards left. H: 4.3 cm.
– Kirbeis, signed: KYB-145*
– Kirbeis, attributed: KYB-121, KYB-180*

Acanthus D
Naturalistic leaf with single stem and the tip turned towards right. Very close to acanthus C, but not same stamp.
– Possis, signed: KYB-331*, KYB-335

Acanthus E
Mirror image of acanthus D.
– Possis, signed: KYB-331*

Acanthus F
Slender leaf with segmented central vein and tip bent towards right. In front of its lower half, an ovoid petal. The stamp is partially preserved.
– Possis, attributed: KYB-336*, KYB-339*

Acanthus G
Slender, straight acanthus leaf.
– Kirbeis, attributed: KYB-320*
– Possis, signed: KYB-331*

Acanthus H
Slender, straight acanthus leaf in negative relief. The stamp is partially preserved.
– Unattributed: KYB-433*

Acanthus I
Straight, naturalistic leaf; in front of the lower part of the acanthus is a small stamped palmette with segmented central vein. H: 6 cm. The stamp can be reconstructed on the basis of KYB-351* and KYB-370*.
– Possis, signed: KYB-344*, KYB-349, KYB-351*, KYB-367*–KYB-369
– Possis, attributed: KYB-337*, KYB-370*, KYB-383*
– Zenodotos, signed: KYB-416*
– Unattributed: KYB-434*, KYB-437*

Acanthus K
Low, straight naturalistic acanthus.
– Kirbeis, signed: KYB-185, KYB-215
– Kirbeis, attributed: KYB-109*, KYB-111–KYB-115
– Possis, attributed: KYB-334*

Acanthus L
Straight, naturalistic leaf with segmented central vein. H: 5 cm.
– Kirbeis, signed: KYB-57*, KYB-58, KYB-151*
– Kirbeis, attributed: KYB-123, KYB-184*, KYB-188*–KYB-190, KYB-207*
– Possis, attributed: KYB-348*, KYB-365*
– Unattributed: KYB-435

Acanthus M
As acanthus L, with lower half covered with ovoid petal with segmented central vein. H: 4.3 cm.
– Kirbeis, signed: KYB-2*, KYB-21, KYB-88*, KYB-93*, KYB-96–KYB-100*, KYB-130*, KYB-134*, KYB-148*, KYB-151*, KYB-221*, KYB-222*, KYB-224, KYB-229, KYB-236
– Kirbeis, attributed: KYB-80, KYB-87*, KYB-91*, KYB-92*, KYB-95, KYB-174, KYB-223*, KYB-225*–KYB-228*, KYB-230*

Acanthus N
As acanthus L, with upper half in form of ovoid petal with concentric veins.
– Kirbeis, signed: KYB-21, KYB-68*, KYB-96–KYB-98, KYB-134*, KYB-224, KYB-229
– Kirbeis, attributed: KYB-81*, KYB-91*, KYB-94*, KYB-228*

Acanthus O
Almost straight leaf with slightly curved stem and a crude outline. H: 3.8 cm.
– Kirbeis, signed: KYB-47*, KYB-72, KYB-124*, KYB-172*, KYB-235*
– Kirbeis, attributed: KYB-48*, KYB-119, KYB-173, KYB-206*, KYB-208*, KYB-209*, KYB-238*

The following three acanthus leaves all have a double central vein. The leaf is very bold, and it has a certain baroque character. The feature of the double stem is also known from other Kymean workshops (Bouzek & Jansová 1974, 51, 52 cats. MB 1, MB 10, pls. 1, 2), but as far as I am aware, it was never used at other production places. With one exception, a bowl signed by Zenodotos (KYB-416*), the three leaves were exclusively used by Kirbeis. Whereas the first two are not particularly common, though both documented on signed bowls, the straight acanthus R is the most common of all the acanthus leaves, occurring on no less than 36 bowls, 13 of which are signed. Most likely, the three leaves represent an advanced stage in the development of Kirbeis' mouldmaking, with P and Q probably being the earlier of the three. Acanthus R is never combined with the large Erotes, and on the two vessels where Eros D freeing a bird is rendered, it is of stamp generation (ii) (KYB-68*, KYB-69*). On one vessel (KYB-210*), acanthus R is combined with a rim frieze with heart buds in negative relief, something which also points to a later stage in his production.

Acanthus P
Stylized leaf with double central vein and tip curled towards right. H: 3.8 cm.
– Kirbeis, signed: KYB-61*–KYB-64, KYB-66
– Kirbeis, attributed: KYB-60*, KYB-65, KYB-67*, KYB-181

Acanthus Q
Stylized leaf with double central vein and tip curled towards left. This stamp is only partially preserved and the identification not secure.
– Kirbeis, signed: KYB-69*
– Kirbeis, attributed: KYB-182*

Acanthus R
Stylized, straight leaf with double central vein. H: 4.8 cm.
– Kirbeis, signed: KYB-68*, KYB-69*, KYB-72, KYB-73, KYB-124*, KYB-185, KYB-186, KYB-194–KYB-196, KYB-198*, KYB-211
– Kirbeis, attributed: KYB-70*, KYB-71*, KYB-75*–KYB-78, KYB-125, KYB-126, KYB-180*, KYB-193*, KYB-197, KYB-199*, KYB-200*, KYB-201*, KYB-204*, KYB-206*, KYB-210*, KYB-212, KYB-216–KYB-220
– Zenodotos, signed: KYB-416*

Acanthus S
Stylized acanthus with double central vein; every other side vein is also segmented; the entire leaf grows out of a low acanthus calyx. H: 5.4 cm.
– Kirbeis, signed: KYB-55, KYB-86*, KYB-88*, KYB-90*, KYB-107, KYB-185, KYB-196, KYB-231*, KYB-322*
– Kirbeis, attributed: KYB-76*, KYB-79–KYB-85*, KYB-87*, KYB-89*, KYB-117*, KYB-146*, KYB-213*, KYB-214*, KYB-241*, KYB-243*, KYB-323
– Possis, attributed: KYB-386*, KYB-387*

Acanthus T
Slender, stylized acanthus with segmented central vein; every other side vein is also segmented. This leaf is almost identical to acanthus S and probably inspired by it.
– Kirbeis, attributed: KYB-89*, KYB-103*
– Possis, signed: KYB-342*, KYB-349, KYB-368, KYB-372, KYB-373*
– Possis, attributed: KYB-339*–KYB-341*, KYB-343*
– Zenodotos, signed: KYB-413*

Acanthus U
Straight, stylized leaf with triangular top.
– Kirbeis, attributed: KYB-318*
– Zenodotos, attributed: KYB-414
– Unattributed: KYB-429*

Acanthus V
Tree-like leaf with segmented leaves or 'branches'; as is clear from KYB-237* and KYB-322*, the tip curves to the right.
– Kirbeis, signed: KYB-55, KYB-236, KYB-322*
– Kirbeis, attributed: KYB-56*, KYB-82, KYB-104*, KYB-237*, KYB-238*, KYB-244, KYB-323

Palmettes
Palmette A
Simple palmette.
– Kirbeis, signed: KYB-54*, KYB-93*, KYB-106, KYB-118, KYB-149, KYB-196, KYB-316

Palmette B
Tall palmette with sickle-shaped branches curving inward. The palmette is furnished with a small 'foot' below. H: 5.0 cm.
– Kirbeis, signed: KYB-88*, KYB-198*, KYB-232*, KYB-233*
– Kirbeis, attributed: KYB-84*, KYB-101*, KYB-102*, KYB-191–KYB-193*, KYB-234*
– Possis, attributed: KYB-337*
– Zenodotos, signed: KYB-415

Palmette C
Slender 'Knidian' palmette, with 'branches' curling in opposite directions on the same side of the stem. H: 4.7 cm.
– Kirbeis, signed: KYB-21, KYB-134*, KYB-265
– Kirbeis, attributed: KYB-234*
– Possis, signed: KYB-371*
– Unattributed: KYB-436*, KYB-437*
– Workshop A: KYA-11*, KYA-55
– Other Kymean workshops: KYX-28*

Palmette D
Large 'Knidian' palmette, with large, sloppy 'branches' curling in opposite directions on the same side of the stem. H: ca. 5.5 cm.
– Possis, signed: KYB-344*, KYB-367*

Palmette E
Low 'Knidian' palmette, with large, sloppy 'branches' curling in opposite directions on the same side of the stem. H: ca. 2.7 cm.
– Possis, attributed: KYB-411*

Palmette F
Miniature palmette with a triangular top and jewelled central vein. The stamp is also used to adorn the lower part of acanthus I, which is also a stamp employed predominantly by Possis. H: ca. 2.8 cm.
– Possis, attributed: **KYB-411***

Palm Fronds
Palm A
Stylized, slender frond curving either left or right.
– Kirbeis, signed: **KYB-50**, **KYB-326***
– Kirbeis, attributed: **KYB-51–KYB-53***, **KYB-245***

Palm B
Straight, slender palm frond with a 'handle'
– Kirbeis, signed: **KYB-239***
– Workshop A: **KYA-9***
– Other Kymean workshops: **KYX-39***, **KYX-62**

Palm C
Small stylized palm fronds. H: 1.4 cm.
– Kirbeis, signed: **KYB-64**, **KYB-147***, **KYB-254**
– Kirbeis, attributed: **KYB-238***

Lotus Petals
Lotus Petal A
Ovoid lotus petal; on the best-preserved specimens it is clear that it grows out of a low calyx with curled ends. Most likely more stamps for making the lotus petal were in use. The lotus petal was employed with all types of leaves. This is a stock element used in many workshops, not just at Kyme.
– Kirbeis, signed: **KYB-54***, **KYB-57***, **KYB-61***, **KYB-63**, **KYB-66**, **KYB-68***, **KYB-69***, **KYB-90***, **KYB-93***, **KYB-106**, **KYB-118**, **KYB-149**, **KYB-172***, **KYB-240***, **KYB-249**
– Kirbeis, attributed: **KYB-46***, **KYB-70***, **KYB-74***, **KYB-75**, **KYB-108***, **KYB-117***, **KYB-121**, **KYB-122**, **KYB-126**, **KYB-147***, **KYB-173**, **KYB-174**, **KYB-202***–**KYB-204***, **KYB-206***, **KYB-208***–**KYB-210***, **KYB-213***, **KYB-226**, **KYB-227***, **KYB-230***, **KYB-237***, **KYB-241***, **KYB-250***, **KYB-318***
– Possis, signed: **KYB-324**, **KYB-344***, **KYB-367***, **KYB-374**
– Possis, attributed: **KYB-345***, **KYB-370***
– Zenodotos, signed: **KYB-415**, **KYB-419**
– Zenodotos, attributed: **KYB-420***–**KYB-422***
– Unattributed: **KYB-427**, **KYB-433***, **KYB-439***, **KYB-440***
– Workshop A: **KYA-55**

Lotus Petal B
Ovoid lotus petal with hatched central vein.
– Kirbeis, signed: **KYB-62**, **KYB-145***, **KYB-148***, **KYB-235***, **KYB-327***
– Kirbeis, attributed: **KYB-49**, **KYB-51**, **KYB-67***, **KYB-110**, **KYB-164**, **KYB-180***, **KYB-212**, **KYB-251***, **KYB-252**
– Possis, signed: **KYB-330***

Lotus Petal C
Rhomboidal lotus petal.
– Possis, signed: **KYB-350***, **KYB-372**

Lotus Petal D
Lotus petal with pointed top and concentric veins.
– Kirbeis, signed: **KYB-100***
– Kirbeis, attributed: **KYB-223***

Lotus Petal E
Strongly rhomboidal lotus petal with concentric indentations.
– Possis, signed: **KYB-330***

Lotus Petal F
Small pointed petal with central vein; can be used as fill around a base medallion or placed in a pyramidal group.
– Kirbeis, signed: **KYB-130***, **KYB-132***, **KYB-253***
– Kirbeis, attributed: **KYB-103***

'Nelumbo'
'Nelumbo' A
'Nelumbo' with cabled edges, central vein, and internal scales. H: 6.0 cm.
– Kirbeis, attributed: **KYB-123**, **KYB-179***
– Possis, attributed: **KYB-363***, **KYB-364***

'Nelumbo' B
'Nelumbo' with cabled edges, central vein, and internal scales. H: 5.0 cm.
– Kirbeis, attributed: **KYB-123**, **KYB-178***, **KYB-179***
– Possis, signed: **KYB-350***
– Possis, attributed: **KYB-365***, **KYB-366**

'Nelumbo' C
'Nelumbo' with central vein and small internal scales. The stamp is only partially preserved.
– Kirbeis, signed: **KYB-177***
– Kirbeis, attributed: **KYB-123**, **KYB-179***
– Zenodotos, signed: **KYB-412***

'Nelumbo' D
'Nelumbo' with central jewelled vein and ribbed interior. H: 5.8 cm.
– Possis, attributed: KYB-363*, KYB-364*

'Nelumbo' E
Bulky 'nelumbo' with double outline and jewelled central vein. H: 3.5 cm.
– Possis, attributed: KYB-383*, KYB-384

'Nelumbo' F
'Nelumbo' with hatched concentric veins.
– Possis, attributed: KYB-346*

Rosettes
Rosette A
Rosette with five rounded petals. H: 1.0 cm. This is the standard rosette of Kirbeis; it is quite strange that it was never used by the other members of the workshop.
– Kirbeis, signed: KYB-55, KYB-86*, KYB-98, KYB-100*, KYB-118, KYB-128*, KYB-129*, KYB-131, KYB-140*, KYB-148*, KYB-149, KYB-151*, KYB-316, KYB-322*
– Kirbeis, attributed: KYB-28*, KYB-30*, KYB-31, KYB-56*, KYB-70*, KYB-84*, KYB-85*, KYB-89*, KYB-104*, KYB-133*, KYB-135, KYB-146*, KYB-165*, KYB-166, KYB-168, KYB-225*, KYB-323, KYB-324
– Workshop A: KYA-6*, KYA-55
– Other Kymean workshops: KYX-8*, KYX-22*

Rosette B
Rosette with eight rounded petals.
– Kirbeis, attributed: KYB-208*
– Workshop A: KYA-42*
– Other Kymean workshops: KYX-54*, KYX-57*, KYX-94*

Rosette C
Miniature rosette with seven rounded petals.
– Possis, attributed: KYB-386*
– Workshop A: KYA-5*, KYA-36*

Rosette D
Rosette with six petals, the tips of which curl forward. H: 1.2 cm.
– Kirbeis, signed: KYB-62, KYB-64, KYB-132*, KYB-326*
– Kirbeis, attributed: KYB-34*, KYB-76*, KYB-102*, KYB-108*, KYB-142*, KYB-163*, KYB-164, KYB-199*
– Workshop A: KYA-14*

Rosette E
Rosette in negative relief.
– Kirbeis, attributed: KYB-159*, KYB-167*, KYB-201*

– Possis, signed: KYB-331*
– Possis, attributed: KYB-343*, KYB-347*

Rosette F
Rosette with four petals separated by tongues.
– Kirbeis, signed: KYB-255*, KYB-325*
– Unattributed: KYB-430*

Rosette G
Rosette with five petals separated by tongues.
– Kirbeis, attributed: KYB-206*
– Possis, attributed: KYB-348*
– Zenodotos, signed: KYB-413*
– Other Kymean workshops: KYX-63*

Rosette H
Rosette with eight bow-like petals. The stamp, which is not entirely preserved, is reminiscent of the Menemachos rosette (see Chapter 14, rosette 1).
– Kirbeis, attributed: KYB-158*, KYB-159*

Rosette 'Shield'
Large rosette 'shield' with eight tongue-shaped petals set inside a circle. H: 2.3 cm. The stamp may originally have been made for a base medallion. Such a medallion occurs on other Kymean bowls (Bouzek & Jansová 1974, 51 cat. MB 4, pls. 2, 3), but not on the bowls of the MMW.
– Kirbeis, signed: KYB-130*, KYB-152*
– Kirbeis, attributed: KYB-133*, KYB-154, KYB-324

Flowers and Buds
Funnel-Shaped Flower
A related flower (though with two layers of petals) was employed in another Kymean workshop (Bouzek & Jansová 1974, 57–58 cats. MB 44 and MB 47, fig. 2, pl. 7).
– Kirbeis, attributed: KYB-44*, KYB-317*

Lily
This stamp can be found in three mould generations. On the earliest, it can be seen that a bud with three small 'spikes' is placed in the middle. The lily can be free-floating or combined with a wavy stem. H (i): 1.5, (ii): 1.2, (iii): 1.0 cm.
– Kirbeis, signed: KYB-198*
– Kirbeis, attributed: KYB-101*, KYB-179*, KYB-202*–KYB-205, KYB-207*, KYB-319*
– Possis, attributed: KYB-334*, KYB-370*

Collared Bud
– Kirbeis, signed: KYB-73

- Kirbeis, attributed: KYB-74*
- Possis, signed: KYB-349

Looped Acanthus Stem with Bud
This stem occurs in two versions, turned left and turned right. The bud has three small 'spikes'.
- Kirbeis, signed: KYB-58, KYB-124*, KYB-194–KYB-196
- Kirbeis, attributed: KYB-123, KYB-125, KYB-126, KYB-187*, KYB-189, KYB-190, KYB-193*, KYB-197
- Possis, signed: KYB-349

Looped Acanthus Stem with Flower
This stem occurs in two versions, turned left and turned right.
- Kirbeis, signed: KYB-194
- Kirbeis, attributed: KYB-127*, KYB-188*, KYB-319*
- Possis, attributed: KYB-364*
- Zenodotos, signed: KYB-412*
- Unattributed: KYB-436*

Twisted Stem
A twisted stem topped by a heart bud and two heart stamps, which function as a 'flower', is rendered on KYB-433*. The twisted stem appears in other productions as well, e.g., PER-41*, Laumonier 1977, 31 cat. 1036, pls. 2, 114.
- Unattributed: KYB-433*

Other Vegetal Elements
Tree A
Palm-like tree.
- Possis, signed: KYB-331*, KYB-335
- Possis, attributed: KYB-332*, KYB-334*

Tree B
'Fir' tree.
- Possis, signed: KYB-371*

Tree C
Fantasy tree.
- Possis, signed: KYB-351*

Volutes
Pair of heraldic volutes.
- Kirbeis, signed: KYB-138
- Kirbeis, attributed: KYB-139, KYB-246*

Oak Leaf
- Kirbeis, signed: KYB-130*

Vine Leaf A
- Kirbeis, signed: KYB-128*

Vine Leaf B
- Possis, signed: KYB-354*
- Possis, attributed: KYB-356–KYB-359*
- Workshop A: KYA-19*–KYB-22*

Ivy Leaf
- Possis, signed: KYB-353*
- Workshop A: KYA-23
- Other Kymean workshops: KYX-47*–KYX-50*

Ivy-Berry Cluster A
Group of three dots.
- Kirbeis, signed: KYB-128*
- Kirbeis, attributed: KYB-174, KYB-176*
- Possis, attributed: KYB-359*
- Workshop A: KYA-23

Ivy-Berry Cluster B
Group of five dots.
- Possis, signed: KYB-353*

Bunch of Grapes
It is possible that more stamps are involved.
- Kirbeis, signed: KYB-21, KYB-90*, KYB-128*
- Possis, signed: KYB-354*
- Possis, attributed: KYB-355*–KYB-360
- Workshop A: KYA-9*, KYA-19*–KYA-21*, KYA-28*
- Other Kymean workshops: KYX-47*

Pendent Drop with Bud A
Pendent drops ending in a bud with a spiky end and furnished with 'wings'. The same bud can be found on Pergamene MMB (Conze et al. 1913, Beibl. 40:1; de Luca 1968, 153 cat. 352, pl. 55).
- Possis, signed: KYB-351*
- Possis, attributed: KYB-343*

Pendent Drop with Bud B
Pendent drops ending in bud with a spiky end and furnished with a 'skirt'. The drop is identical to A.
- Possis, attributed: KYB-336*

Stylized Pendent Drop with Bud
Stylized version of A?
- Possis, attributed: KYB-352*

Bud with 'Wings'
– Kirbeis, signed: KYB-325*

Sun Wheel
– Possis, attributed: KYB-380*, KYB-381*

Chronology

Relative Chronology
As we have already seen, Kirbeis was by far the most prolific of the four potters; this is clear not just from the number of signed pieces but also from the equal proportion of unsigned fragments (Fig. 61). He is also the one who used the largest number of different stamps, 124 to be precise. An attentive study of the stamps used together on the same vessel, as well as of the stamp generations, which can in particular be studied on stamps of Eros D, can help us to understand the development of his production, and, with the help of such a framework, we can place the other three artisans of the workshop in a relative sequence.

In the early part of the production, the number and variety of stamps employed is much higher than it becomes later. Large figural stamps are common then, whereas the size of figural stamps becomes progressively smaller with time. The style of the acanthus is developed from organic and quasi-naturalistic to completely stylised; thus, the stylized acanthus with double stem (P, Q, and R) seems to be the latest development, with acanthus R being the latest of these three.[18] The large Erotes A, B, C, and E do not occur on the same vessels as acanthus R. Purely vegetal bowls with or without looped stems and with or without 'nelumbo' seem to be late in the development. If the looped stems and the 'nelumbo' were first introduced into the Mediterranean MMB repertoire after ca. 168 (Chapter 3), this date marks an advanced stage of the MMW. To a certain extent, Possis' production is parallel to that of Kirbeis, even though we also find new stamps and new stamp combinations there. Zenodotos and Zenodoules are known from few vessels, but they seem to be contemporary with the middle or late part of the workshop's production.

Forms of decoration like PSC and long-petal designs, which are normally good pointers for chronology, are extremely rare in the MMW. Only two examples of the former can be cited, both attributed to Possis (KYB-380*,

---

[18] However, acanthus K, a low, naturalistic acanthus is also late, because it occurs together with Eros D in stamp generation (ii) and (iii).

KYB-381*). The long petal too was chiefly used by Possis, in all cases as an isolated motif in a vegetal calyx combined with figural decoration (KYB-383*–KYB-387*). Zenodotos also signed two bowls where he employed isolated plastic long petals (KYB-413*, KYB-414). Kirbeis made only a single bowl which is exclusively based on a long-petal design (KYB-257). It is difficult to decide whether the absence of these types of decoration is a sign of chronology (indicating that the workshop dates early, that is, largely before ca. 168, see Chapter 6), or whether it is a matter of the mould maker's personal taste. It is probably a mixture of the two: thus, it is hardly fortuitous that it is primarily Possis and Zenodotos, the members of the workshop who were not part of it from the beginning, who were the exponents for decorations which we can probably date after 168.

Absolute Chronology
Few scholars have touched on the question of this workshop's chronology. One of them is Bouzek, who is of the opinion that it is late, that is, of the late 2nd and early 1st century (2008, without page numbers). As we shall see, this is far too late. I have already mentioned the relationship of the MMW to the Athenian workshops. These must have been directly or indirectly seminal for its establishment, for the Kymean vessels emulate the shape, size, and proportions as well as the black coat of the Athenian ones. This observation, however, does not provide us with an absolute chronology.

Olbia, Cistern Л
Rotroff has recently drawn attention to the evidence of Cistern Л in Olbia for the date of this workshop (2010, 69). The cistern and its contents and date are further discussed in Chapter 20, and the arguments shall not be repeated here. However, it can be briefly mentioned that 90% of the Rhodian amphorae found in the cistern can be dated to a short interval of no more than 20 years, between 181/179 and 161; this is probably also the date of the majority of the MMB found in the reservoir. The latest Rhodian amphora in the cistern is dated to 144 (eponym Astymedes II). This is most likely close to the date when the material was deposited.

This cistern contained not only the single Kirbeis fragment mentioned by Rotroff (KYB-88*), but a further 12 vessels of Kymean production: six more vessels made by Kirbeis (KYB-14*, KYB-28*, KYB-81*, KYB-233*, KYB-243*, KYB-301*), two by Possis (KYB-352*, KYB-359*), three from Workshop A (KYA-14*, KYA-37, KYA-56*), and one unattributed Kymean vessel (KYX-56*).

Olbia, Bothros 11
I should like also to point to another closed Olbian context which can help us to date the MMW: Bothros 11, excavated in the Western Temenos (see discussion in Chapter 20). Vessels of the MMW were found in this pit as well (Kirbeis: KYB-206* [with acanthus R]; Possis: KYB-383*; Zenodotos: KYB-412*; MMW unattributed: KYB-448*), along with a fragment of an unattributed Kymean vessel (KYX-90*). The deposit is dominated, however, by a very homogeneous group of Ephesian vessels; this is not true of the cistern, but fragments with an imbricate pattern of the Monogram PAR Workshop found in both contexts are so alike that it is conceivable that they were even made in the same mould (EPH-773* from the cistern and EPH-771* from the bothros). This suggests that the overlap in time between the two deposits was probably greater than the distance. No amphorae were found in the bothros, so it cannot be dated as precisely as the cistern. However, not least the predominance of vessels with PSC design in the bothros and the character of the Ephesian vessels, which belong to the early part of the Monogram PAR Workshop, show us that the bothros was most likely filled in contemporaneously with the cistern, that is in the late 140s.

Olbia, Fill Layers in Sector NGS
If we turn to Sector NGS, the story of deposition is very much the same as we have just seen was the case in the upper city. The latest Rhodian amphora in the 'closed deposits' in the lower city's Sector NGS is dated to 146 (eponym Autokrateus; Lawall et al. 2010, 388 cat. L-166), followed by a gap of almost 30 years in the amphora sequence (see Chapter 20).[19] A total of 73 vessels of the MMW were found in Sector NGS, 23 of which were unearthed in the 'closed contexts' of the sector. Most of the fragments come from rather mixed contexts, which are the evidence of clean-up operations in the late 2nd century. However, one basement in House III-3 (Basement 368) is of interest for the discussion of the chronology. Fragments of 25 vessels were found in this basement. Five came from the upper fill, in which the only Ephesian vessel belonging to the classical phase was found (Guldager Bilde 2010, 279 cat. F-36, pl. 175), as well as a Knidian vessel (KNI-16*) and a fragment from an unidentified production place (XXX-21*). A fragment of a vessel attributed to Kirbeis (KYB-127*) and one confidently attributed to Zenodotos (KYB-421*) were also recovered here. The deposit date is probably in the late 140s or later. Beneath this layer was a fill which is very informative in terms not just of chronology but also of the predominance of the Aiolian workshops prior to the classical phase of the Ephesian workshops. In this fill were found two Athenian fragments (ATH-39*, ATH-51), fragments of six Pergamene vessels (PER-1*, PER-18*, PER-24*, PER-32*, PER-40*, PER-62*), and five vessels of other Aiolian provenance (AIX-2*, AIX-11*, AIX-12*, AIX-17*, AIX-20*). Just one Ephesian vessel was recovered: EPH-22*, which dates earlier than the classical phase. The Kymean workshops are documented by a fragment from Workshop A (KYA-32*) and two fragments each attributed to Kirbeis (KYB-32*, KYB-84*) and Possis (KYB-334*, KYB-340*). The assemblage in the lower fill is most likely contemporary with the majority of the finds in the cistern, that is, it dates between 181/179 and 161.

The contexts at Olbia make it clear that the MMW was active throughout the second quarter of the 2nd century, perhaps for as long as until immediately before the destructions in the upper city and in Sector NGS, which took place in the second half of the 140s. The date of Workshop A should match that of the MMW, and the other Kymean workshops were probably contemporary as well. This date corresponds very well to the date proposed by Bouzek and Jansová. According to them, the earliest of the Kyme workshops (Paniskos and Erotes) date to the second quarter of the 2nd century, and they believe that some of the 'workshops' continued to be active in the third quarter of the century (1974, 22).

Distribution

Kymean bowls, including those of the Meter Medallion Workshop, are very uncommon outside the Black Sea region (Fig. 64). A very thin scatter can be documented down the coast of Asia Minor from Kyme to Smyrna, Miletos, and Rhodes, and a few pieces were of course found on Delos. As mentioned, this is in stark contrast to the Pontic region, where no less than 97% of the vessels have been found. This is evidently due to the fact that Kyme was located on the main north-bound sailing route. Therefore, it is not so surprising that a few bowls of the MMW were found in the northernmost of the Greek islands, Samothrace and Thasos, as well as at Abdera in the Thasian peraia.

Mouldmade Bowls and the Cults of Kyme

The MMB of Kyme are very particular in their iconographic language, and it is therefore appropriate to

---

[19] See, however, also Lawall 2011, 42, fig. 2, which is based on all finds no matter the context; his graph places the gap exclusively in the 120s.

consider whether they can tell us anything about preferences in local cults. We know relatively little about the cults of Kyme. In 1925, A. Salač uncovered the remains of a temple dedicated to Isis (*BCH* 49, 1925, 477–478; Schäfer 1974, 211), and the Isis hymn on a stone inscription found nearby is famous (IG XII.5.739; IG XII Suppl. 14; Engelmann 1976, no. 41). The temple may go back to the 4th century (İdil 1939, 527), and was originally dedicated to a different deity, perhaps Meter or Artemis. In the 2nd century there was a Dionysos sanctuary at Kyme (a *hieron* called the Bakchaion) as well as a thiasos devoted to his cult (Engelmann 1976, cat. 30).

Meter
There is ample evidence for the early cult of Meter in Kyme. A cache of Archaic stone sculptures was found in 1881,

	Evidence groups A+B	Kirbeis Signed	Attr.	Possis Signed	Attr.	Zenodotos Signed	Attr.	Zenodoules Signed	MMW un-attrib.	Sum	% of assemblage (A+B)	Evidence group C[a]
Mediterranean	Abdera	2								2		
	Delos	2	2							4		1[b]
	Kyme	1								1		
	Miletos											1[c]
	Samothrace	1								1		
	Rhodes											1[d]
	Smyrna?	1		1		1				3		
	Vicinity of Smyrna			1						1		
	Thasos		1	1						2		
Black Sea	Beljaus		1							1		
	Chersonesos	4	6	1						11	11.5	22
	Golubickoe	1								1		
	Istros	7	52	2	16	1			17	95	6.1	
	Kepoi	2	1							3	7	
	Mesambria	2		2						4		
	Myrmekion	2	5		1					8	2.9	3
	Nymphaion	1								1		
	Olbia	44	130	9	37	1	4		13	238	13	14
	Olbia or Pantikapaion	4								4		
	Olbia?	1	2		1					4		
	Pantikapaion	7	18	1	2	1			1	30	7.8	24
	Pantikapaion?	1								1		
	Petuchovka (Gute Maritzyn)					1				1		
	Phanagoreia			1						1		4
	Phanagoreia (Vinogradnoe 7)			1						1		
	Porthmion			1						1	0.4	
	South Russia	3				1				4		
	Tanais				1					1		
	Theodosia				1					1		
	Tomis	3						1		4		
	Tyras	5	7	2		1			2	17		23
	Tyritake		3							3	3.4	
?	Provenance?	1	2	2						5		

FIGURE 64   Geographical distribution of vessels of the Meter Medallion Workshop
Notes:
a. Primarily von Stern 1902, 98 n. 3; Samojlova 1984, 123; Kovalenko 1989. They may partly overlap with vessels of evidence category A and B; this cannot be verified, because they are not illustrated
b. Laumonier 1977, 7; Bouzek 1990, 66 cat. 20
c. Kossatz 1990, 136 n. 468 (not illustrated)
d. Mentioned in Kossatz 1990, 136 n. 648; no information concerning decoration

FIGURE 65
Bronze coin of Kyme, 3rd century CE, SNG Cop V pl. 3 no. 136.
PHOTO RASMUS HOLST NIELSEN, THE ROYAL COLLECTION OF COINS AND MEDALS, NATIONAL MUSEUM OF DENMARK

one in the round and five *naiskoi*, all made of local stone (Reinach 1889), and a number of terracottas representing the goddess have been found as well. Some provide an interesting syncretistic example of Meter as *kourotrophos* (Hadzisteliou Price 1978, 158, 193; Lagona 2007; Taliano Grasso 2008).

Even though Meter clearly played a significant role from an early time in the city's history, she is not portrayed on Kyme's coins, which, instead, mostly feature the bare head of a female supposed to be the mythological foundress, the Amazon Kyme. It is not until the Roman period that we find a turreted female head, and nothing indicates that she is Meter rather than a city personification or Tyche (e.g., Wroth 1894, 117, 119, 120, pl. XXIII.3–5; Fig. 65).

Pan
Bouzek & Jansová (1974) have already discussed the importance of Pan in the Kymean production: they defined a particular workshop, the one of Paniskos, on the basis of the occurrence of a Pan sitting cross-legged and playing a syrinx (Bouzek & Jansová 1974, 19–21; 51–52 cats. MB 1, MB 16, Smyrna A, fig. 1, pls. 1, 3, 4, 19). It should be noted that this stamp shows a syncretistic deity, because he is furnished with wings. In addition to this Eros-Paniskos there is also a closely similar but more detailed stamp of a cross-legged Paniskos without wings (KYX-12*). A saluting Pan also features prominently on a group of bowls which were created in Kyme and emulated elsewhere (KYX-99; see also Chapters 6 and 10 for references to other productions).

Pan is rarely found in other productions of MMB, and one may therefore wonder whether the presence of several Pan stamps at Kyme indicates that he was particularly venerated in the city. Pan's theriomorphism and association with madness (*panic*) brought him into connection with other ecstatic forms of worship, such as the cults of Dionysos and Meter (Borgeaud 1979, 157), and he is frequently invoked or rendered as a follower of the two. In the Hellenistic period, Pan is made cognate with Phanes/Protogonos, Zeus, Dionysos, and Eros (West 1983, 205). Therefore, there is good reason to emphasise not just Meter but also Pan, who could have been venerated in a single religious complex in the city.

CATALOGUE TO CHAPTER 11

KIRBEIS: SIGNED AND ATTRIBUTED

BOWLS

A *Figural Decoration*

Amazonomachy

KYB-1*
Olbia or Pantikapaion, Buračkov A 22/75, Moscow, State Historical Museum (Buračkov collection). Complete; consists of a number of joining frs. ⌀ rim 14, RH 2.5, ⌀ base 3.5; vessel H 7.4; H:⌀ 1:1.9. Reduced. Rim frieze: heart buds. Main decoration: very tightly packed with figures in two registers and every gap filled with birds B, C, and D; upper register: horseman A, Greek A, horseman B, Amazon A, horseman A, Greek A; lower register: Amazon C, dying Amazons C and A, Amazon E, dying Amazon A, Greek A, dying Amazon E. Medallion: surrounded by a ridge; Meter bust, right; signed KIRBEI.

KYB-2*
South Russia, Olbia(?), inv. AI 16, Köln, University Collection, formerly collection of G. Windscheid (German consul in Odessa; to Köln in 1931). Complete. ⌀ rim 13.8, RH 2.5, ⌀ base 4.2; vessel H 8.3; H:⌀ 1:1.7. Fabric: fine, micaceous. Blackish brown coat, dark red at rim int. and partly ext. Stacked in firing. Rim frieze: miniature astragal. Main decoration: upper frieze: boar(?) right alternating with tip of acanthus M, repeated 10 times; lower frieze: horse turning head back, Greek A, Amazon D, Amazon A, Amazon C, Amazon B, Amazon A, Amazon E, Amazon B, Greek B; around the medallion dying Amazons A, B, and E. Medallion: two ridges; signed KIRBEI. Frieze separators: miniature astragal. Restored with treatment leaving the surface shiny
– Berger 1993, 272–273, fig. 75.a–c.

KYB-3
Olbia, Sector E, House E14, over pavement 704, O-E14-71-1550, present whereabouts unknown. Fr. of base and lower body. Oxidized. Main decoration: dying Amazon A, Amazon D, horseman B, dying Amazon B (remaining decoration cannot be identified from photograph in report). Medallion: surrounded by three ridges; signed KIRBEI.
– L.M. Slavin & A.S. Rusjaeva, Report of work in Olbia 1971 (Kiev archive inv. 7032), pl. 16.

KYB-4*
Chersonesos, X-1901-36, St Petersburg, State Hermitage Museum. Fr. of base and lower body. ⌀ base 4.5. Fabric: fine, micaceous, many voids, grey core (no fresh break). Slightly lustrous coat ext., more lustrous int., 10R 2.5/1. Oxidized. Main decoration: lower part of Amazonomachy: only dying Amazons A curling around the base are preserved; above these, feet of battling figures. Medallion: fine astragal between ridges; signed KIRBEI; small pointed leaves around Kirbeis stamp. One repair hole.
– Kocjuško-Valjužinič 1902, 85; Bouzek 1990, 66 cat. 17; Rotroff 2010, 69 cat. 35.

KYB-5
Olbia(?), inv. 54791 [i], Moscow, State Historical Museum (Uvarov collection) (not found December 2009). Fr. of base and lower body. Oxidized. Main decoration: Greek A, Amazon C, Amazon B. Medallion: surrounded by three ridges; Meter bust, right; signed KIRBEI.
– Uvarov 1851, pl. XIX.14; Bouzek 1990, 66 cat. 1; Rotroff 2010, 68 cat. 6.

KYB-6
Olbia, Sector E6-7, squares 412e, 417e, yellow clay layer, O-E6-7-61-121, Kiev, Institute of Archaeology storeroom. Body fr. H 5.4 × W 6.1, WT 0.24. Fabric: relatively fine and micaceous, many small lime inclusions, some voids, 5YR 5/8. Dull coat, 5YR 3/1. Relatively hard fired, oxidized. Rim frieze: Ionian kyma, pointed with double outline. Main decoration: Greek A, Amazon C; underneath, dying Amazon A.

KYB-7*
Olbia, Sector R25, O-P25-93-176, Parutine, Olbia National Preserve storeroom. Fr. of rim and upper body. H 6.2 × W 5.2, WT 0.25. Fabric: relatively fine and micaceous, 5YR 6/8. Thin dull coat, 10YR 3/2. Hard fired, oxidized. Rim frieze: heart guilloche left (blurred). Main decoration: horseman A and B; bird A as space-filler.

KYB-8*
Olbia, Sector AGD, О-АГД-71-1945, Kiev, Institute of Archaeology storeroom. Fr. of mid-body. H 3.5 × W 4.3, WT 0.4. Fabric: fine, micaceous, a few minute lime inclusions, some small voids, 5YR 6/6. Dull coat, 10YR 3/1. Relatively hard fired, oxidized. Rim frieze: heart guilloche right. Main decoration: Greek A.

KYB-9
Tyras, present whereabouts unknown, Belgorod? Joining frs. of base and lower body, ⌀ rim 12. Dark brown coat. Main decoration: dying Amazons B surrounding medallion. Medallion: surrounded by two ridges; Meter bust, right; signed KIRBEI (stamp very worn).
– Nicorescu 1924, 399–401 cat. 13, figs. 19b, 21; Rotroff 2010, 69 cat. 25.

KYB-10*
Istros, His-B 619, Bucharest, Institute of Archaeology storeroom. Fr. of lower body close to base. H 3.3 × W 4.1, WT 0.5. Fabric: relatively fine and micaceous, many small lime inclusions, many voids, 7.5YR 5/4. Dull dark brown coat, 10YR 3/1. Medium hard fired, oxidized. Main decoration: Amazon A or D; below, dying Amazons A and B. Medallion: surrounded by frieze of dots.
– Domăneanțu 2000, 132 cat. 650, pl. 46.

KYB-11
Olbia, Sector R25, O-P25-97-2157, Parutine, Olbia National Preserve storeroom. Fr. of upper body. H 2.2 × W 2.6, WT 0.45. Fabric: relatively fine and micaceous, 2.5YR 6/6. Dull coat, almost completely worn off ext., 5YR 2.5/1. Medium hard fired, oxidized. Main decoration: horseman A.

KYB-12*
Istros, His-423, Bucharest, Institute of Archaeology storeroom. Fr. of upper body. Oxidized. Rim frieze: Ionian kyma, pointed with double outline. Main decoration: horseman A with raised spear right.

Erotes

KYB-13*
Olbia, Square B5, O-Б5-76-88, Kiev, Institute of Archaeology storeroom. Fr. of rim and upper body. H 6.2 × W 4.8, WT 0.35, RH 2.3. Fabric: relatively fine and micaceous, many small lime inclusions, some voids, 5YR 6/8. Dull mottled coat, ext. 10YR 3/1, 2.5YR 4/8, int. 10YR 3/1. Relatively hard fired, oxidized. Stacked in firing. Rim frieze: heart guilloche left. Main decoration: Eros C. Frieze separators: dots.

KYB-14*
Olbia, Sector E2, square 55, Cistern Л, O-E2-49-437, Kiev, Institute of Archaeology storeroom. Fr. of rim and body. H 6 × W 5.2, WT 0.25, ⌀ rim 13, 10%, RH 2.8. Fabric: relatively fine and micaceous, many small lime inclusions, some voids, 5YR 6/6. Slightly lustrous mottled coat, 5YR 4/3, 3/1, 2.5YR 4/8. Relatively hard fired, oxidized. Stacked in firing. Multiple rim friezes: heart buds; dots. Main decoration: Eros D (i).

KYB-15
Olbia, Sector NGS, House IV-2 B 280/160, O-НГС-90-217, Parutine, Olbia National Preserve storeroom. Fr. of rim and body. H 6 × W 5.7, WT 0.3–0.6, ⌀ rim 13, 13%, RH 3.05. Fabric: fine, soft, highly micaceous, many voids, 7.5YR 6/6. Thin slightly lustrous coat, flaking off in large patches, blotchy black/red, colours altered by burning, ext. 5Y 2.5/1, 2.5YR 3/6, int. 5YR 3/2, 4/4. Medium hard fired, oxidized. Stacked in firing. Rim frieze: heart guilloche right. Main decoration: Eros D (i). Three repair holes. Secondarily burnt.
– Guldager Bilde 2010, 286 cat. F-105, pl. 192 (erroneously identified as Pontic).

KYB-16
Istros, His-V 19463 C, Bucharest, Institute of Archaeology storeroom. Fr. of upper body. H 3.5 × W 3.8, WT 0.47. Fabric: relatively fine and micaceous, many small lime inclusions, many voids, 5YR 6/8. Dull coat, 5YR 3/2, 3/3. Oxidized. Rim frieze: Ionian kyma. Main decoration: Eros D (ii).
– Domăneanțu 2000, 14 cat. 56, pl. 4 (attributed to Belle Méduses).

KYB-17*
Olbia, Sector E6, square 436, ash layer north of Wall 43, O-E6-56-4417, Kiev, Institute of Archaeology storeroom. Three joining frs. of rim and upper body. H 5.3 × W 10.2, WT 0.25, ⌀ rim 14, 26%, RH 2.3. Fabric: fine and micaceous, a few minute lime inclusions, some small voids, 2.5YR 6/6. Dull mottled coat, ext. 2.5YR 3/1, 4/6, int. 2.5YR 3/1. Medium hard fired, oxidized. Rim frieze: heart guilloche right. Main decoration: frontal Medusa head, Eros D (i).
– Kovalenko 1989, 374 cat. 38.

KYB-18*
Olbia, Sector R25, O-P25-92-3224, Parutine, Olbia National Preserve storeroom. Fr. of rim and upper body. H 4.4 × W 5.6, WT 0.41, ⌀ rim 12, 12%, RH 1.9. Fabric: relatively fine and micaceous, many small lime inclusions, laminated, 2.5YR 5/4, core 7.5YR 5/2. Thin coat with metallic sheen, 7.5YR 4/1. Medium hard fired, oxidized. Rim frieze: two grooves. Main decoration: Eros D (ii) between suspended garlands(?). One repair hole.

KYB-19*
Olbia, Sector NGS, O-НГС-92-980, Parutine, Olbia National Preserve storeroom. Fr. of rim and upper body. H 4.85 × W 5.3, WT 0.4–0.5, ⌀ rim 13, 12%, RH 3. Fabric: relatively fine and micaceous, small and larger lime inclusions, larger grey particles, many small voids, 5YR 6/8. Thin firm semi-lustrous coat, ext. mainly dark but slightly mottled, ext. 5YR 3/3, 2.5YR 5/6, int. 5YR 3/3. Medium hard fired, oxidized. Stacked in firing. Rim

frieze: minute Ionian kyma. Main decoration: Eros-Paniskos sitting next to suspended wreath tied with *tainia*.

KYB-20
Istros, His-1927-1942-V 8572 N, Bucharest, Institute of Archaeology storeroom. Fr. of rim and upper body. Oxidized. Rim frieze: Ionian kyma, pointed with double outline. Main decoration: upper right part of Eros-Paniskos.

Hunt

KYB-21
Art market, inv. 248, Eichenzell, Schloss Fasanerie. Complete. ⌀ rim 13.5, RH 2.7; vessel H 7.8; H:⌀ 1:1.7. Fabric: reddish brown. Mottled red, black, and brown coat. Oxidized. Rim frieze: Ionian kyma, pointed with double outline. Main decoration: stag alternating with boar A. Calyx: acanthus M and N alternating with palmette C; bunch of grapes as space-filler. Medallion: surrounded by two ridges; Meter bust right; signed KIRBEI. Frieze separators: two ridges. The same stag can also be found on another Kymean fragment (Bouzek & Jansová 1974, cat. MB 45A, pl. 7).
– CVA Schloss Fasanerie 2 [Germany 16], 55–56, pl. 95.1–2.

KYB-22*
Olbia, Sector I, Pit E(?) ash clay layer, O-И-48-2086, Kiev, Institute of Archaeology storeroom. Fr. of rim and upper body. Oxidized. Stacked in firing. Rim frieze: Ionian kyma, pointed with double outline. Main decoration: hind part of stag leaping right.

Mythological (Skylla and the Ship of Odysseus?)

KYB-23*
Olbia, Sector R25, O-P25-00-642, Parutine, Olbia National Preserve storeroom. Fr. of upper body. H 3.3 × W 2.5, WT 0.35. Fabric: relatively fine and micaceous, 7.5YR 6/6. Thin slightly lustrous coat, ext. 5YR 3/3, int. 5YR 3/2. Medium hard fired, oxidized. Main decoration: stern of battleship left; on board, legs of standing person; below ship, dolphin A.

Unidentifiable

KYB-24*
Provenance unknown, year and number unknown [b], Moscow, State Historical Museum. Fr. of rim and upper body. H 6 × W 4.5, WT 0.5, RH 2.7. Rim frieze: heart guilloche left. Main decoration: male figure with lifted left arm moving left. Attribution is tentative and based on the character of the rim pattern.

Animals

KYB-25*
Olbia, O-64-801, Kiev, Institute of Archaeology storeroom. Fr. of rim and upper body. H 3.5 × W 4.7, WT 0.34, RH 1.8. Fabric: relatively fine and micaceous, some small lime inclusions. Medium hard fired, oxidized. No rim frieze. Main decoration: bird A, bird B, bird A. Secondarily burnt. Blurred stamps, late?

KYB-26*
Olbia, Sector NGS, O-НГС-02-35, Parutine, Olbia National Preserve storeroom. Fr. of rim and upper body. H 5.8 × W 7.1, WT 0.21–0.4, ⌀ rim 14, 10%, RH 4.3. Fabric: relatively fine and micaceous, small and larger lime inclusions up to 3 mm, 5YR 6/6. Thin firm semi-lustrous coat, darkened at rim, mottled lower down, 2.5YR 5/6, 10YR 3/2. Medium hard fired, oxidized. Stacked in firing. Rim frieze: grooves. Main decoration: bird B, two birds A. One repair hole.

KYB-27
Olbia, Sector NGS, House II-2 B 248/8, O-НГС-89-762, Parutine, Olbia National Preserve storeroom. Fr. of rim and upper body. H 5.6 × W 9.5, WT 0.25–0.5, ⌀ rim 13.5, RH 2.6. Fabric: relatively fine and micaceous, small inclusions of lime, small round voids, 7.5YR 6/6. Slightly lustrous diluted coat, sloppily applied, leaving areas uncoated and others blotched, 10YR 3/1. Hard fired, oxidized. Rim frieze: heart buds. Main decoration: bird A.
– Guldager Bilde 2010, 286 cat. F-100, pl. 189 (erroneously identified as Pontic).

KYB-28*
Olbia, Sector E2, square 55, Cistern Л, O-E2-49-430, 431, Kiev, Institute of Archaeology storeroom. Two non-joining frs. of rim and upper body. H 5.3 × W 8.3, WT 0.32, ⌀ rim 13, 23%, RH 2.6. Fabric: fine, micaceous, a few minute lime inclusions, some small voids, 5YR 6/6. Coat with slight dull lustre, 5YR 3/1, 3/2. Medium hard fired, oxidized. Rim frieze: heart buds. Calyx: bird A, rosette A; on fr. 49–431, ovoid petal D with concentric veins.

KYB-29
Olbia, Sector E6-7, squares 512, 513, 492, 493, Basement 8, grey clay layer, O-E6-7-63-494, Kiev, Institute of Archaeology storeroom. Body fr. close to rim. Oxidized. Rim frieze: heart buds. Main decoration: bird A and indistinguishable object.

KYB-30*
Olbia, Sector NGS, O-НГС-87-108, Parutine, Olbia National Preserve storeroom. Fr. of rim and upper body. H 5.2 × W 4.5, WT 0.2–0.48, ⌀ rim 13, 7%, RH 2.7. Fabric: fine, micaceous, many voids, 7.5YR 6/6. Thin firm slightly lustrous coat, slightly diluted on top of relief, 5YR 3/1. Medium hard fired,

oxidized. Multiple rim friezes: dots; heart buds. Main decoration: heraldic dolphins (A and B) swimming away from rosette A.

KYB-31
Istros, His-1190, Bucharest, Institute of Archaeology storeroom. Fr. of upper body. Oxidized. Main decoration: dolphin A (probably heraldic) flanking rosette A.
– Domăneanțu 2000, 21 cat. 84, pl. 6 (identified as Ephesian [Comique à la canne]).

KYB-32*
Olbia, Sector NGS, House III-3 B 368/106, O-НГС-93-911, Parutine, Olbia National Preserve storeroom. Fr. of rim and upper body; rather abraded. H 5.8 × W 5.15, WT 0.4–0.49, ⌀ rim 13, 12%, RH 2.9. Fabric: relatively fine and micaceous, some small lime inclusions, many voids, 7.5YR 6/6. Thin firm coat with slight lustre int. and on rim ext., body dark ext. with slight bluish metallic sheen, mottled int., ext. 10YR 3/1, int. 2.5YR 5/6, 10YR 3/1. Medium hard fired, oxidized. Stacked in firing. Multiple rim friezes: heart buds; dots. Calyx: large pointed petal(?) or *tainia*(?); heraldic dolphins A and B above.
– Guldager Bilde 2010, 286 cat. F-101, pl. 190 (erroneously identified as Pontic).

KYB-33
Pantikapaion, area of 51 Armii Str., П-76-no.(?), Kerč History and Culture Reserve inv. КМАК 6315. Fr. of upper body. Oxidized. Rim frieze: heart buds. Main decoration: dolphins A and B.
– Grzegrzółka 2010, 56 cat. 27 (identified as Pergamene).

KYB-34*
Olbia, Sector E6-7, squares 475, 494, 495, 515, yellow clay layer, O-E6-7-62-38, 153, Kiev, Institute of Archaeology storeroom. Two non-joining frs. of rim and upper body. H 5.8 × W 5.6, WT 0.38, ⌀ rim 13, 10%, RH 3. Fabric: relatively fine and micaceous, many small lime inclusions, some voids, 5YR 7/6. Slightly lustrous coat, 5YR 3/2, 2.5/1, 2.5YR 4/6. Relatively hard fired, oxidized. Stacked in firing. Rim frieze: Ionian kyma. Main decoration: heraldic(?) dolphins A around rosette D; chain of small heart guilloche stamps to left.

KYB-35*
Olbia, Sector R25, O-P25-96-1303, Parutine, Olbia National Preserve storeroom. Fr. of rim and upper body. H 6.4 × W 4, WT 0.47, RH 2.9. Fabric: relatively fine and micaceous, 5YR 7/6. Thin dull mottled coat, adhering badly, ext. 10R 5/8, 2.5/2, int. 2.5YR 5/8. Hard fired, oxidized. Stacked in firing. Rim frieze: Ionian kyma, pointed with double outline. Main decoration: bird H, kantharos B.

Eagle Griffins

A small group of vessels (**KYB-36***–**KYB-42**) feature one or more eagle griffins with a tall sickle wing, turning its head back. The griffin comes in two variants, A and B, turned right and left, respectively, and frequently both occur on the same vessel as a heraldic pair. Unfortunately, not a single one of the seven vessels preserves the signature. Nevertheless, I feel confident in ascribing them to Kirbeis, because on one vessel they are rendered together with Eros D (ii) and bird A (**KYB-37***) and on another with boukranion A (**KYB-39***). All three of these stamps are connected primarily with Kirbeis, even though they can also be found in Workshop A, as can the griffins (**KYA-9***). Both of those workshops also share the pointed Ionian kyma with double outline as a rim frieze, which is also found on two vessels with eagle griffins (**KYB-41**, **KYB-42**).

KYB-36*
Olbia, Sector AGD, ashy grey clay layer, O-АГД-69-1248, 1258, Kiev, Institute of Archaeology storeroom. Two non-joining frs. of rim and upper body. H 5.7 × W 4.3, WT 0.25, RH 3.5. Fabric: relatively fine and micaceous, many small lime inclusions, some voids, 5YR 6/6. Dull coat, 2.5YR 4/6, 4/4. Relatively hard fired, oxidized. Rim frieze: grooves. Main decoration: Eros D (iii), Ketos left, eagle griffin A. Frieze separators: single ridge.

KYB-37*
Olbia, Sector E6-7, squares 475, 494, 495, 515, yellow clay layer, O-E6-7-62-40, Kiev, Institute of Archaeology storeroom. Two joining frs. of base and lower body. H 4.3 × W 5.7, WT 0.4, ⌀ base 4. Fabric: fine and micaceous, a few minute lime inclusions, some small voids, 5YR 6/6. Thin dull coat, int. flaking, ext. 5YR 4/3, int. 2.5YR 4/8. Not too hard fired, oxidized. Main decoration: eagle griffins B with Eros D (ii) in between; bird over griffin A. Medallion: surrounded by three ridges and an inner frieze of dots; motif blurred and partly missing.

KYB-38
Olbia, O-1910-287, present whereabouts unknown. Body fr. No rim frieze (or grooves?). Main decoration: hunter A with spear and dog right, hunting eagle griffin B; another dog behind griffin. Frieze separators: heart guilloche right.
– St Petersburg, IIMK RAN, archive inv. 4060.519.8 (pl. I).

KYB-39*
Olbia, Sector NGS, O-НГС-02-132, 301, Parutine, Olbia National Preserve storeroom. Two non-joining rim frs. H 5.8 × W 10.9, WT 0.34–0.5, ⌀ rim 12, 55%, RH 2.7. Fabric: medium fine, slightly micaceous, abundant larger (up to 3 mm) and smaller lime inclusions, some grey particles and large voids, 5YR 5/6.

Thin firm coat with dull pink sheen, pinkish metallic lustre at rim ext. and lip int., ext. 10R 5/2, 5Y 3/1, int. 10R 5/2. Hard fired, oxidized. Stacked in firing. Rim frieze: heart guilloche left. Main decoration: upper frieze: heraldic eagle griffins (A and B) flanking boukranion A; lower frieze: unidentified traces (tips of foliage?). Frieze separators: single ridge.

KYB-40*
Olbia, Sector NGS, House IV-2 B 302/183, О-НГС-94-339+397, 02-400, Parutine, Olbia National Preserve storeroom. Rim and joining body fr., non-joining rim fr. H 7.2 × W 6.6, WT 0.25–0.55, ⌀ rim 14, 14%, RH 3.05. Fabric: medium fine, micaceous, abundant small lime inclusions, some large lime inclusions up to 4 mm popping off, relatively few voids, 2.5YR 5/8, 5YR 5/3, 5/6, bicolour from stacking. Thin firm dull coat, diluted on tops of relief, bluish metallic sheen on lip int. and rim ext., ext. 5YR 3/2, int. 5YR 4/3. Medium hard fired, oxidized. Stacked in firing. Rim frieze: grooves. Main decoration: upper frieze: garland F with long, thick-ended *tainia* suspended from Corinthian(?) column A with scored torus; small birds(?) over garlands; lower frieze: eagle griffin A. Frieze separators: single ridge. Bouzek & Jansová 1974, cat. MB A, pl. 19 is identical, though smaller (and accordingly later?).
– Guldager Bilde 2010, 282 cat. F-73, pl. 182.

KYB-41
Olbia, Sector E6-7, squares 58on, 56o, fill in basement III, SE building of agora, O-E6-7-62-516, Kiev, Institute of Archaeology storeroom. Fr. of rim and body. H 5.1 × W 4.9, WT 0.4, RH 3.2. Fabric: relatively fine and micaceous, many small lime inclusions, some voids, 5YR 6/6. Dull worn coat, 5YR 3/1. Medium hard fired, oxidized. Rim frieze: Ionian kyma, pointed with double outline. Main decoration: eagle griffin B.
– Kovalenko 1989, 375 cat. 59.

KYB-42
Olbia, Sector R25, O-P25-99-660, Parutine, Olbia National Preserve storeroom. Fr. of rim and upper body. H 4.5 × W 4.3, WT 0.4, RH 2.8. Fabric: relatively fine and micaceous, many voids, 5YR 6/6. Dull mottled coat, ext. 2.5YR 4/4, int. 2.5YR 4/6, 3/1. Medium hard fired, oxidized. Rim frieze: Ionian kyma, pointed with double outline. Main decoration: wing of eagle griffin B.

Boukranion/Wreath

KYB-43*
Olbia, Sector NGS, O-НГС-05-752, Parutine, Olbia National Preserve storeroom. Fr. of upper body. H 3.5 × W 3.8, WT 0.31. Fabric: relatively fine, a few light-reflecting inclusions, 5YR 6/6. Thin coat with slight pinkish metallic sheen, 5YR 4/2. Hard fired, oxidized. Main decoration: suspended wreath with *tainia*, boukranion A. Frieze separators: single ridge.

Funnel-Shaped Flowers

KYB-44*
Olbia, Sector AGD, О-АГД-71-1943, Kiev, Institute of Archaeology storeroom. Fr. of rim and upper body. H 4.8 × W 4.6, WT 0.35, RH 2. Fabric: relatively fine and micaceous, many small lime inclusions, some voids, 5YR 5/8. Slightly lustrous coat, 10YR 3/1. Relatively hard fired, oxidized. Rim frieze: heart guilloche left. Main decoration: vertical funnel-shaped flowers right. Frieze separators: heart guilloche left.

Bow

KYB-45
Istros, His-V 8573 J, Bucharest, Institute of Archaeology storeroom. Body fr. close to rim. Oxidized. Rim frieze: Ionian kyma. Main decoration: *tainia* tied in a bow.
– Domăneanțu 2000, 134 cat. 664, pl. 47.

B   *Calyx with Figural Decoration*

KYB-46*
Chersonesos, Quarter XVIII, room абвд, X-1947-83, St Petersburg, State Hermitage Museum. Quarter of bowl preserved; almost complete profile. H 9.5, ⌀ rim 14. Fabric: fine, finely micaceous, 7.5YR 6/3. Thin slightly lustrous coat with soapy surface ext., ext. 10YR 4/3, int. 7.5YR 3/3. Oxidized. Multiple rim friezes: heart buds; astragal; Ionian kyma. Main decoration: Eros D (i) standing on Corinthian column, Amazon D on garlanded altar functioning as statue base, boukranion A over ovoid petal A between them; unidentifiable element right of Amazon. Two repair holes.
– Belov, Streželeckij & Jakobson 1953, pl. VII 3; attribution PGB.

KYB-47*
Pantikapaion, M-47-140, Moscow, Puškin Museum of Fine Arts. Fr. of base and lower part of vessel. H 9.2 × W 9, WT 0.6, ⌀ base 3.5. Fabric: micaceous, greyish brown (no fresh break). Dull black-brown coat. Reduced. Calyx: acanthus O with Eros A, C, and C in between; bird A over tip of acanthus. Medallion: surrounded by three ridges; signed KIRBEI.
– Loseva 1962, 202, fig. 4.2; Zabelina 1984, 164, fig. 11a; AGSP 1984, pl. CLXIII.8; Rotroff 2010, 69 cat. 29.

KYB-48*
Chersonesos, Quarter XVIII, room абвд, X-1947-84, St Petersburg, State Hermitage Museum. Fr. of rim and upper body. H 7.7,

⌀ rim 14. Fabric: relatively fine, highly micaceous, 5YR 7/6. Thin slightly lustrous coat, ext. Gley 1 3/N, int. 2.5YR 2.5/2. Oxidized. Rim frieze: grooves. Main decoration: frontal draped female alternating with Eros C, acanthus O between them; over tip of acanthus, Eros M, repeated.
– Belov, Streželeckij & Jakobson 1953, pl. VII3; attribution PGB.

KYB-49
Pantikapaion, M-45-4688, Moscow, Puškin Museum of Fine Arts. Body fr. H 3.6 × W 4. Oxidized. Main decoration: Eros C, tip of ovoid petal B, bird C as space-filler.
– Kovalenko 1987b, fig. 2.1.

KYB-50
Olbia, O-1928-92, present whereabouts unknown. Fr. of base and lower body. Main decoration: Eros D (i), frontal draped female and kantharos A alternating with slender palm frond A, the tip of which curves right; birds B and D as space-filler. Medallion: surrounded by two ridges; Meter bust, right; signed KIRBEI.
– St Petersburg, IIMK RAN, photo archive neg. II 13908.

KYB-51
Olbia, O-1925-330, present whereabouts unknown. Body fr. Main decoration: Eros C, draped frontal female over ovoid lotus petal B, slender palm fronds A in between.
– St Petersburg, IIMK RAN, photo archive neg. II 19397.

KYB-52
Olbia, O-1928-255, present whereabouts unknown. Fr. of upper body. Main decoration: draped frontal female, kantharos A, slender palm frond A on the tip of which sits bird A.
– St Petersburg, IIMK RAN, photo archive neg. II 13930.

KYB-53*
Olbia, Sector R25, O-P25-97-2416, Parutine, Olbia National Preserve storeroom. Fr. of upper body. H 2.7 × W 3, WT 0.35. Fabric: relatively fine and micaceous, 5YR 6/8. Thin firm coat, dull ext., slightly lustrous int., ext. 2.5YR 4/6, int. 5YR 2.5/1. Medium hard fired, oxidized. Main decoration: two kantharoi B separated by slender palm frond.

KYB-54*
Olbia, V.I. 5004, Antikensammlung, Staatliche Museen zu Berlin (formerly Mavrogordato collection, 1909). Complete. ⌀ rim 12; vessel H 7.2; H:⌀ 1:1.7. Fabric: highly micaceous, 5YR 6/6. Black, brown, to red coat ext., int. brown, 5YR 3/1, 2.5YR 5/8. Oxidized. Stacked in firing. Rim frieze: rosette A alternating with boukranion B. Main decoration: over low calyx consisting of palmette A and petal A, not separated from main frieze, are repeated four times: gorytos, suspended wreath, and frontal draped female; birds A and C as space-filler. Medallion: surrounded by three ridges; Meter bust right; signed KIRBEI. The gorytos is extremely detailed; the stamp is unique, as is the rim frieze
– *Flower of Pergamon*, 95, fig. 94, 165; Grüßinger et al. 2011, 476 cat. 3.95.

KYB-55
Olbia, O-59-no no. [C], present whereabouts unknown. Three non-joining frs. of rim, body and base. Rim frieze: heart guilloche left between grooves. Main decoration: over calyx of acanthus S and V but not separated from it, Eros D in front of rosette A, gorytos, lower part of male with thyrsos. Medallion: surrounded by two ridges; signed […]BEI.
– St Petersburg, IIMK RAN, photo archive neg. II 68191.

KYB-56*
Olbia, Sector NGS, O-НГС-92-637, Parutine, Olbia National Preserve storeroom. Body fr. H 5.5 × W 4.9, WT 0.3–0.5. Fabric: fine, dense, micaceous, a few minute lime inclusions, 5YR 6/6. Thin firm slightly lustrous coat, diluted so leaving tops of relief decoration a lighter colour, 5YR 3/1. Hard fired, oxidized. Calyx: acanthus V out of which grow tendrils with rosette A, frontal draped female as statue on garlanded altar acting as statue base.

KYB-57*
Olbia, Sector NGS, O-НГС-02-353+401, 374, Parutine, Olbia National Preserve storeroom. Two joining frs. of body and part of base; one non-joining body fr. H 9.5 × W 6.3, WT 0.25–0.52. Fabric: medium fine, micaceous, many small lime inclusions, some large voids, 5YR 6/6, 6/8, bicolour from stacking. Thin lustrous coat with slight crazing, mottled, 5YR 3/1, 2.5/1. Medium hard fired, oxidized. Stacked in firing. Rim frieze: grooves. Calyx: acanthus L with petal A in between; amongst the vegetation, phlyax Eros and dancing frontal female. Medallion: surrounded by two ridges; traces of the letters KIR[…]. Most likely from the same mould as **KYB-58**.

KYB-58
Olbia, V.I. 4953, Antikensammlung, Staatliche Museen zu Berlin (formerly Vogell collection), lost in WW II. Complete. ⌀ rim 14; vessel H 7.5; H:⌀ 1:1.9. Brown coat. Oxidized. Rim frieze: three deep grooves. Calyx: acanthus L separated by buds on looped tendrils; on the loops, alternating Eros K and mantled dancing woman. Medallion: surrounded by two ridges; Meter bust right; signed KIRBEI. Most likely from the same mould as **KYB-57***.
– von Stern 1902, 113 additional note; Zahn 1908, 59 cat. 13; Boehlau 1908, 28 no. 276; Neugebauer 1932, 191; Verluste 2005, 205; Rotroff 2010, 69 cat. 36. Note the diverging heights: Zahn gives H 7.5, whereas the original registration records H 9.75.

KYB-59*
Olbia, Sector NGS, O-НГС-08-186, Parutine, Olbia National Preserve storeroom. Fr. of rim and upper body. H 6 × W 6, WT 0.45. Fabric: coarse, micaceous, many voids. Thin dull coat. Medium hard fired, oxidized. Rim frieze: Ionian kyma. Main decoration: kithara-playing Eros K, tip of acanthus (type?).

KYB-60*
Olbia, Square Б5, O-Б5-76-24, Kiev, Institute of Archaeology storeroom. Fr. of mid- and lower body. H 5 × W 5.8, WT 0.3. Fabric: relatively fine and micaceous, many small lime inclusions, some voids, 2.5YR 6/6. Thin dull coat with slight bluish sheen where thicker, 10YR 4/2. Relatively hard fired, oxidized. Calyx: acanthus P with Eros C as space-filler.

KYB-61*
Olbia, Sector E6, square 430, 247, yellow clay layer, O-E6-57-688+690+750+1161, 1161[A], Kiev, Institute of Archaeology storeroom. Complete profile; four joining frs. of rim, body, and base; non-joining body fr. WT 0.25, ⌀ rim 13, 14%, RH 2.3, ⌀ base 4; vessel H 7.8; H:⌀ 1:1.7. Fabric: relatively fine and micaceous, many small lime inclusions, some voids, 2.5YR 7/6. 'Lacquer'-like coat with dull sheen, 5YR 2.5/1. Medium hard fired, oxidized. Rim frieze: heart guilloche right. Calyx: acanthus P with petal A in between; over vegetation but not separated from it, alternating Medusa head and Eros I. Medallion: surrounded by two ridges; head of Meter partially preserved; signed [...]ΒΕΙ.
– Kovalenko 1989, 375 cat. 47.

KYB-62
Olbia, Bonn, Akademisches Kunstmuseum (formerly Vogell collection). Complete. ⌀ rim 12.3; vessel H 8.2; H:⌀ 1:1.5. Brown coat. Oxidized. Rim frieze: heart guilloche right. Calyx: acanthus P alternating with petal B and triangular, imbricate group of the same petals; over the vegetation but not separated from it, Medusa heads alternating with rosette D; birds A and C as space-filler. Medallion: surrounded by two ridges; Meter bust right; signed ΚΙΡΒΕΙ. 16 repair holes.
– von Stern 1902, 113 additional note; Zahn 1908, 60–61 cat. 14; Boehlau 1908, 30–31 no. 275; Zimmer 2005, 110–111 cat. A50; Rotroff 2010, 69 cat. 37.

KYB-63
Olbia, O-1936-no.(?), present whereabouts unknown. Lower part of bowl. Calyx: acanthus P alternating with lotus petal A. Medallion: surrounded by two ridges; Meter bust right; signed ΚΙΡΒΕΙ. The piece was already lost when Levi wrote the text of her 1940 publication.
– Levi 1940, 124, pl. XXV.3 and n. 5; Bouzek 1990, 65 cat. 10; Rotroff 2010, 68 cat. 1.

KYB-64
Olbia, necropolis, O-1909-no no., present whereabouts unknown. Complete. Rim frieze: heart guilloche right. Main decoration: over calyx of acanthus P alternating with triangular group of small palm frond E but not separated from it are Eros D, bird A and K(?) and rosette D. Medallion: surrounded by three ridges; Meter bust, right; signed ΚΙΡΒΕΙ.
– Pharmakowsky 1910, 240–241, fig. 34; Farmakovskij 1913, fig. 131; Rotroff 2010, 68 cat. 5.

KYB-65
Tyras, present whereabouts unknown, Belgorod? Fr. of upper body. Rim frieze: grooves? Calyx: on the curled tip of acanthus P sits bird A; to right, bird B being freed by Eros D. The hand of the Eros and the ribbon are just distinguishable.
– Batizat 2002, fig. 7.23; attribution PGB.

KYB-66
Olbia, Sector NGS, O-НГС-06-912, Parutine, Olbia National Preserve storeroom. Fr. of base and two joining body frs. H 5.8 × W 3.8, WT 0.35, ⌀ base 3. Fabric: relatively fine and micaceous, some small lime inclusions, 2.5YR 6/8. Thin dull coat, 2.5YR 5/6. Medium hard fired, oxidized. Calyx: acanthus P, petal A, Eros D (ii). Medallion: surrounded by ridge; lower part of bust; signed ΚΙΡ[...].

KYB-67*
Chersonesos, X-1952-153, St Petersburg, State Hermitage Museum. Fr. of lower body. H 3.4. Fabric: fine, micaceous, 10YR 5/2. Thin dull coat, 10YR 2/1. Oxidized. Calyx: acanthus P alternating with lotus petal B; between the vegetation, Eros D (iii) and frontal draped female statue (ii). Second mould generation: figures much smaller than normal.

KYB-68*
Pantikapaion, inv. N 7604, Köln, Römisch-Germanisches Museum (formerly collection of C.A. Niessen). Complete. ⌀ rim 14.2, RH 3.5; vessel H 8.8; H:⌀ 1:1.6. Fabric: relatively fine and micaceous. Firm blackish brown coat. Hard fired, oxidized. Rim frieze: heart guilloche right. Calyx: acanthus R alternating with acanthus N and separated by petal A; over the vegetation but not separated from it, male with thyrsos over shoulder, Eros D (ii) freeing bird A, Eros M; repeated four times, with frontal draped woman once. Medallion: surrounded by three ridges; Meter bust right; signed ΚΙΡΒΕΙ.
– Berger 1995a, 56–57 cat. 59, figs. 100–101.

KYB-69*
Olbia, Sector NGS, House IV-3 B 343/205, O-НГС-92-665, Parutine, Olbia National Preserve storeroom. Complete profile, ca.

one-third of bowl: two rim frs., two base frs., four body frs., all joining. Extremely worn, almost no coat in lower part, upper part much pitted. WT 0.33–0.5, ⌀ rim 13, 25%, RH 3, ⌀ base 5; vessel H 8.2; H:⌀ 1:1.6. Fabric: medium fine, micaceous, many small lime inclusions, 7.5YR 5/6. Thin firm coat, intended dark but with some mottling, rim ext. rather shiny, int. and lower part ext. slightly lustrous, ext. 10YR 2/1, int. 5YR 2.5/1. Medium hard fired, oxidized. No rim frieze. Calyx: acanthus Q with petal A as filler; in between the vegetation, Eros H(?) and Eros D (ii) freeing bird B flying towards bird D. Medallion: surrounded by two ridges; single row of small triangular leaves encircles Meter bust right (⌀ 2.5); signed KIRBEI. Two repair holes.
– Guldager Bilde 2010, 286 cat. F-104, pl. 191 (erroneously identified as Pontic).

KYB-70*
Olbia, Sector NGS, O-НГС-94-499, 500, Parutine, Olbia National Preserve storeroom. Two non-joining body frs.; very worn. H 5.6 × W 6.4, WT 0.28–0.35. Fabric: coarse, micaceous, many large lime inclusions up to 2 mm, 2.5YR 6/4. Thin dull coat, 5YR 3/1. Hard fired, crisp, oxidized. Calyx: acanthus R alternating with triangular groups of ovoid petals; over the vegetation hangs a wreath tied with a bow; below the wreath, rosette A; on tip of acanthus leaf and on triangular group of petals sits small winged Eros-Paniskos with crossed legs playing syrinx. One repair hole.

KYB-71*
Olbia, Sector NGS, House IV-2 B 302/180, O-НГС-94-47, Parutine, Olbia National Preserve storeroom. Fr. of mid body. H 5.25 × W 5.2, WT 0.28–0.49. Fabric: relatively coarse and micaceous, brittle, abundant small lime inclusions, larger and smaller voids, 2.5YR 5/6. Thin firm slightly diluted coat, slightly lustrous and with dark 'oily' appearance, 10YR 3/1. Medium hard fired, oxidized. Rim frieze: heart buds. Calyx: acanthus R separating figures, to the left a mantled dancing woman (i), to the right Eros H with flying cloak.
– Guldager Bilde 2010, 286 cat. F-106, pl. 192 (erroneously identified as Pontic).

KYB-72
Smyrna(?), inv. CA 1102[b], Paris, Louvre, donated by P. Gaudin. Fr. of base and lower body. Calyx: acanthus O alternating with acanthus R, with dolphins in between (tails visible). Medallion: surrounded by two ridges; signed KIRBEI.
– Courby 1922, 408 n. 3; Rotroff 2010, 70 cat. 45.

KYB-73
Crimea(?), inv. КП 783, Yalta Museum. Complete. Rim frieze: Ionian kyma. Calyx: acanthus R separated by bird F or G tied to stick; over the birds, flying collared bud; over these and tips of acanthus, bird D. Medallion: surrounded by two ridges, around the medallion stamp a frieze of dots; Meter bust right; signed KIRBEI.
– Turova & Kovalenko 2005, 341–342, fig. 2 (attributed to Smyrna).

KYB-74*
Olbia, Sector NGS, House IV-2 B 302/182, O-НГС-94-334, 94–336, 94–505, 94–625, Parutine, Olbia National Preserve storeroom. Two rim frs. and two body frs., all joining; almost complete profile. The outline of the ridge encircling the base can just be seen. H 7.9 × W 12.1, WT 0.42–0.52, ⌀ rim 14, RH 2.5; vessel H 7.9; H:⌀ 1:1.8. Fabric: relatively coarse and micaceous, numerous small lime inclusions, some quite large up to 3 mm, many smaller voids, 5YR 6/6. Thin, uneven and mostly dull, dark 'oily' coat, lighter brownish and with slight lustre at rim, 10YR 3/1, 4/2. Medium hard fired, oxidized. Stacked in firing. Multiple rim friezes: Ionian kyma; heart guilloche left. Calyx: ovoid lotus petals A with birds F tied to sticks; above these, flying collared buds.
– Guldager Bilde 2010, 286 cat. F-102, pl. 190 (erroneously identified as Pontic).

KYB-75*
Olbia, Sector R25, O-P25-95-1099, Parutine, Olbia National Preserve storeroom. Fr. of lower body. H 3.6 × W 4.5, WT 0.47. Fabric: relatively fine and micaceous, some small lime inclusions, 5YR 7/6. Thin dull coat, 10YR 3/1. Medium hard fired, oxidized. Calyx: acanthus R alternating with lotus petal A; bird A over vegetation as space-filler.

KYB-76*
Pantikapaion, M-49-45, Moscow, Puškin Museum of Fine Arts. Body fr. H 4.5 × W 5.5. Dull reddish brown coat. Oxidized. Rim friezes: grooves; Ionian kyma. Calyx: acanthus R or S with heraldic dolphins around rosette D as space-filler.
– Kovalenko 1989, 374 cat. 29.

KYB-77
Istros, His-274, Bucharest, Institute of Archaeology storeroom. Body fr. H 3 × W 4, WT 0.5. Fabric: relatively fine and micaceous, some small lime inclusions. Dull red-brown coat. Oxidized. Rim frieze: groove. Calyx: acanthus R with badly stamped bird D as space-filler.

KYB-78
Delos, present whereabouts unknown. Body fr. Calyx: acanthus R with *tainia* (ii) tied in bow as space-filler.
– Laumonier vol. 2, cat. 3281 (identified as Athenian); attribution PGB.

KYB-79
Tyras, present whereabouts unknown, Belgorod? Six non-joining body frs. Rim frieze: grooves? Calyx: acanthus A alternating with acanthus S, between them Eros B rendered three times.
– Batizat 2002, fig. 1.13; attribution PGB.

KYB-80
Pantikapaion, area of 2 Lenin Str., Kerč History and Culture Reserve inv. KMAK 2152 (1961). Fr. of rim and upper body. Oxidized. Rim frieze: astragal. Calyx: acanthus S and M with Eros C and Eros D var. with nebris freeing bird A, which sits on the tip of acanthus S.
– Grzegrzółka 2010, 67–68 cat. 50.

KYB-81*
Olbia, Sector E2, square 55, Cistern Л, O-E2-49-122[A], Kiev, Institute of Archaeology storeroom. Body fr. H 5.3 × W 5.8, WT 0.28. Fabric: fine, micaceous, a few minute lime inclusions, some small voids, 5YR 7/4. Dull worn coat, 5YR 3/2. Medium hard fired, oxidized. Main decoration: Eros D var. with nebris between acanthus N and S. Two repair holes.

KYB-82
Olbia, Sector AGD, O-АГД-74-474, Kiev, Institute of Archaeology storeroom. Fr. of mid-body. H 4.9 × W 5.4, WT 0.3. Fabric: relatively fine and micaceous, some small lime inclusions, 7.5YR 6/6. Coat with slight dull lustre, 2.5YR 5/6. Not too hard fired, oxidized. Calyx: acanthus S and V with Eros D (iii) as space-filler.

KYB-83*
Olbia, Sector R25, O-P25-95-904, Parutine, Olbia National Preserve storeroom. Fr. of upper body. H 4 × W 3.6, WT 0.33–0.4. Fabric: relatively fine and micaceous, 5YR 5/4. Thin slightly lustrous coat, 7.5YR 2.5/1. Medium hard fired, oxidized. Calyx: acanthus S, Eros D (ii), dolphin A.

KYB-84*
Olbia, Sector NGS, House III-3 B 368/106, O-НГС-93-915, Parutine, Olbia National Preserve storeroom. Fr. of lower body; coat very pitted inside. H 7 × W 5.5, WT 0.25–0.45. Fabric: fine, micaceous, a few small lime inclusions, many small voids, 5YR 6/6. Thin firm mottled coat, 2.5YR 4/4, 10YR 3/1. Medium hard fired, oxidized. Stacked in firing. Calyx: acanthus S alternating with palmette B, rosette A, Eros A and leg of one further figure walking left.
– Guldager Bilde 2010, 286 cat. F-103, pl. 190 (erroneously identified as Pontic).

KYB-85*
Olbia, Agora, squares 644nw, 678ne, Room "B", Southwest house, yellow clay layer, O-66-1132, Kiev, Institute of Archaeology storeroom. Body fr. H 3.5 × W 3.7, WT 0.35. Fabric: relatively fine, 5YR 6/6. Slightly lustrous coat, ext. 2.5YR 4/8, int. 2.5YR 4/8, 3/2. Relatively hard fired, oxidized. Calyx: acanthus S with draped frontal female over rosette A.
– Kovalenko 1989, 375 cat. 42.

KYB-86*
Olbia, Sector R25, O-P25-99-661, Parutine, Olbia National Preserve storeroom. Fr. of base and lower body. H 4.7 × W 3.1, WT 0.4–0.85, ⌀ base 5. Fabric: relatively fine and micaceous, 7.5YR 5/4. Thin dull coat, ext. 7.5YR 3/2, int. 7.5YR 3/1. Hard fired, oxidized. Calyx: acanthus S with rosette A, krater B flanked probably by heraldic dolphins (A). Medallion: surrounded by two ridges; signed KIR[...].

KYB-87*
Olbia, Sector E6, square 405, grey clay layer, O-E6-56-207, Kiev, Institute of Archaeology storeroom. Fr. of base and lower body. H 6 × W 6, WT 0.4, ⌀ base 4. Fabric: fine, micaceous, a few minute lime inclusions, some small voids, 7.5YR 6/4. Coat with dull lustre, 7.5YR 3/1. Hard fired, reduced. Calyx: acanthus M and acanthus S alternating; between them, kantharos B and krater B. Medallion: surrounded by two ridges.
– Kovalenko 1989, 374 cat. 39.

KYB-88*
Olbia, Sector E2, square 55, Cistern Л, O-E2-49-326, Kiev, Institute of Archaeology storeroom. Fr. of base and lower body. H 5.3 × W 5.3, WT 0.25. Fabric: fine, micaceous, a few minute lime inclusions, some small voids, 5YR 6/6. Thin coat with slight dull lustre, ext. 5YR 4/3, int. 5YR 3/2. Relatively hard fired, oxidized. Calyx: acanthus S alternating with palmette B and acanthus M; above the vegetation, foot of vase, probably kantharos A (ii). Medallion: surrounded by two ridges; signed [...]EI. Stamps in pristine condition.
– Levi 1964b, 252, fig. 13.3 (probably northern Black Sea region); St Petersburg, IIMK RAN, photo archive neg. I 43058; Kovalenko 1989, 375 cat. 58; Bouzek 1990, 65 cat. 12; Rotroff 2010, 68 cat. 4.

KYB-89*
Olbia, Sector R25, O-P25-98-2450, Parutine, Olbia National Preserve storeroom. Body fr. H 3.6 × W 5.8, WT 0.35–0.55. Fabric: relatively fine and micaceous, some small lime inclusions and shell, 5YR 7/6. Thin dull coat, ext. 5YR 2.5/2, int. 5YR 2.5/1. Hard fired, oxidized. Calyx: acanthus S alternating with acanthus T; dotted stems with rosette A in between; over rosettes, heraldic dolphin A and B.

KYB-90*
Kepoi, Ке-63-135, Moscow, State Historical Museum. Fr. of base and large part of body. Dull dark brown coat fully covering surface. Oxidized. Main decoration: not preserved. Calyx: acanthus S alternating with ovoid petals A with bunches of grapes as space-fillers. Medallion: Meter bust right; signed [...]BEI. Frieze separators: two ridges.
– Usačeva 1978, fig. 1.20 ('probably Asia Minor').

KYB-91*
Istros, His-58-inv. V 21147, Istros Archaeological Museum. Complete apart from base. Oxidized. Rim frieze: Ionian kyma. Calyx: acanthus M alternating with acanthus N, Eros D (i) in between.

KYB-92*
Istros, His-B 540/V 19389, Bucharest, Institute of Archaeology storeroom. Fr. of mid-body. H 3.8 × W 5, WT 0.5. Fabric: fine, micaceous, a few minute lime inclusions, some small voids, 5YR 7/6. Dull worn coat, ext. 5YR 2.5/1, int. 5YR 3/2. Medium hard fired, oxidized. Rim frieze: heart guilloche? Main decoration: Eros D (i) freeing bird C, acanthus M, bird B as space-filler.
– Domăneanțu 2000, 132 cat. 649, pl. 46.

KYB-93*
Olbia, Sector R25, O-P25-00-139, Parutine, Olbia National Preserve storeroom. Fr. of base and lower body. H 4.3 × W 6.9, WT 0.3–0.5, ⌀ base 4. Fabric: relatively fine and micaceous, 5YR 7/4, core 7.5YR 7/2. Thin dull coat ext., slightly lustrous int., ext. 2.5Y 4/2, 3/2, int. 2.5Y 4/2. Hard fired, oxidized. Calyx: over low calyx of palmette A are acanthus M alternating with petal A; in between, frontal draped female separated from vegetation by column of dots. Medallion: surrounded by two ridges; remains of slightly double-stamped signature KIR[...].

KYB-94*
Pantikapaion, M-58-312, Moscow, Puškin Museum of Fine Arts. Body fr. H 3.5 × W 3.5. Good reddish brown coat ext. with slight lustre, int. lustrous red. Oxidized. Main decoration: frontal draped female, acanthus N.
– Kovalenko 1989, 373 cat. 8.

KYB-95
Phanagoreia, Vinogradnoe 7, kurgan 2 2006, present whereabouts unknown. Fr. of base and lower body. Rim frieze: grooves. Calyx: acanthus M with kithara B as space-filler.
– N.J. Lemberis & I.I. Marčenko, poster presented at the Bosporskij Fenomen conference, St Petersburg 2007.

KYB-96
Olbia, inv. I 1909/2.5, Leiden, Rijksmuseum van Oudheden. Complete. Multiple rim friezes: heart buds; astragal; Ionian kyma with double outline. Calyx: acanthus B, M, and N alternating; on the tips of the vegetation sit bird A and B. Medallion: Meter bust right; signed KIRBEI; the stamp is surrounded by an inner frieze of astragals (same as second rim frieze) and an outer frieze of dots.
– Rogl 2008b, 525, fig. 3.

KYB-97*
Olbia, Sector E6, squares 412e, 417e, yellow clay layer, O-E6-61-93, Kiev, Institute of Archaeology storeroom. Fr. of base and body. H 8 × W 5.8, WT 0.4, ⌀ base 4. Fabric: relatively fine and micaceous, many small lime inclusions, some voids, 5YR 6/6. Dull worn coat, ext. 5YR 3/1, 5/6, int. 5YR 3/2, 2.5YR 4/6. Relatively hard fired, oxidized. Rim frieze: dots. Calyx: acanthus M alternating with acanthus N with heraldic dolphins (A and B) over the vegetation. Medallion: surrounded by two ridges; partially preserved Meter bust; signed [...]BEI.
– Kovalenko 1989, 375 cat. 49.

KYB-98
Olbia, O-1900-3252, present whereabouts unknown. Complete profile, joined from a number of frs. Multiple rim friezes: heart buds; heart guilloche left. Main decoration: heraldic dolphins (A and B) around rosette A over but not separated from acanthus M alternating with acanthus N. Medallion: surrounded by two ridges; Meter bust right; signed KIRBEI.
– St Petersburg, IIMK RAN, photo archive neg. II 18555.

KYB-99*
Olbia, Sector R25, O-P25-00-1148, Parutine, Olbia National Preserve storeroom. Fr. of lower body with part of base. H 3.9 × W 3.8, WT 0.3, ⌀ base 5.5. Fabric: relatively fine and micaceous, 7.5YR 6/4. Thin firm slightly lustrous coat, ext. 10YR 3/1, int. 10YR 2/1. Hard fired, oxidized. Calyx: acanthus M flanked by heraldic dolphins (A and B) oriented vertically, and kantharos B. Medallion: surrounded by a ridge; remains of signature KI[...].

KYB-100*
Olbia, Sector NGS, O-НГС-92-527, Parutine, Olbia National Preserve storeroom. Fr. of base and lower body. H 5.9 × W 6.3, WT 0.25–0.42. Fabric: relatively fine and micaceous, small and larger lime inclusions up to 2 mm, some larger voids, 7.5YR 6/6, 10YR 6/4, bicolour from firing. Thin firm slightly lustrous coat, diluted and lighter on tops of relief, ext. slightly 'oily', ext. 10YR 3/2, int. 5Y 3/2. Hard fired, oxidized. Calyx: acanthus M alternating with petal D; over and in between the vegetation, rosette A and bird A. Medallion: surrounded by two thin ridges; Meter bust right encircled by inscription KIR[...]. Fine, crisp design in rather high relief.

KYB-101*
Olbia, O-52-1205+1211, 1206+1209+1209[A]+1213, Kiev, Institute of Archaeology storeroom. Two groups of joining frs.: two rim and two body frs. and a rim and a body fr. H 7.4 × W 8.4, WT 0.28, ⌀ rim 14, 13%, RH 2.7. Fabric: relatively fine and micaceous, many small lime inclusions, 5YR 5/6. Dull coat, 5YR 3/1. Relatively hard fired, oxidized. Rim frieze: heart guilloche left. Calyx: heron flying left over palmette B alternating with acanthus or palmette, (type?) separated by lily (i) with bud on wavy stem.

KYB-102*
Olbia, Sector E6, square 429s, north of Wall 49, yellow clay layer, O-E6-57-607, Kiev, Institute of Archaeology storeroom. Fr. of rim and body. H 5.1 × W 5.3, WT 0.35. Fabric: fine, micaceous, a few minute lime inclusions, some small voids, 2.5YR 5/8. Dull coat, mottled int., ext. 2.5YR 4/6, 3/1, int. 2.5YR 4/6, 3/2. Relatively hard fired, oxidized. Stacked in firing. Rim frieze: heart guilloche right. Calyx: palmette B(?), with rosette D, dolphin A, and bird A above.
– Kovalenko 1989, 375 cat. 52.

KYB-103*
Pantikapaion, M-47-3684, Moscow, Puškin Museum of Fine Arts. Fr. of lower body. H 5.2 × W 5.5. Fabric: dark red, micaceous. Dull, dark brown coat. Oxidized. Main decoration: kantharos B (ii), Greek warrior B right, shield lying on ground, acanthus U alternating with pyramidal group of small pointed petals with central vein. Medallion: part of ridge.
– Loseva 1962, fig. 2.7 (identified as Pergamene); Zabelina 1984, 164, fig. 11e.

KYB-104*
Olbia, Sector NGS, O-НГС-01-129, Parutine, Olbia National Preserve storeroom. Body fr., worn. H 3.8 × W 4, WT 0.3–0.4. Fabric: relatively fine and micaceous, a few minute lime inclusions, some small voids, 7.5YR 6/4. Thin firm slightly lustrous coat, slightly mottled, 10YR 3/2. Medium hard fired, oxidized. Main decoration: frontal female wrapped in cloak, tip of acanthus V, edge of rosette A probably growing out of the acanthus; bird A above.

KYB-105
Olbia(?), inv. 54791 Uvarov 79/60, Moscow, State Historical Museum (Uvarov collection). Three non-joining body frs., oxidized. Main decoration: draped frontal female, Eros H over acanthus (type?).

KYB-106
Delos, present whereabouts unknown. Fr. of base and large part of body. Rim frieze: heart guilloche right. Calyx: superposed palmette A alternating with lotus petal A; bird A on tip of palmette. Medallion: surrounded by one ridge; Meter bust right; signed KIRBEI.
– Courby 1922, 395, pl. XVj; Laumonier vol. 2, cat. 2206, pl. III; Rotroff 2010, 70 cat. 46.

KYB-107
Olbia, O-1928-no no. [C], present whereabouts unknown. Body fr. Calyx: acanthus S on the tip of which sits bird A.
– St Petersburg, IIMK RAN, photo archive neg. II 13934.

KYB-108*
Olbia, Sector NGS, O-НГС-86-906, Parutine, Olbia National Preserve storeroom. Fr. of lower body. H 2.9 × W 4, WT 0.46. Fabric: fine, soft, micaceous, 7.5YR 7/4. Thin dull coat, partly worn off, ext. 5YR 4/3, int. 2.5YR 4/8. Medium hard fired, oxidized. Main decoration: Eros B, pointed lotus petal A, rosette D.

KYB-109*
Olbia, Square B5, O-Б5-76-162, Kiev, Institute of Archaeology storeroom. Fr. of mid body. H 4.1 × W 4.7, WT 0.45. Fabric: relatively fine and micaceous, many small lime inclusions, some voids, 7.5YR 6/6. Thin dull coat, 7.5YR 2.5/1. Relatively hard fired, oxidized. Calyx: acanthus K, phlyax Eros as space-filler.

KYB-110
Olbia, Sector NGS, O-НГС-05-960, Parutine, Olbia National Preserve storeroom. Fr. of mid-body. H 3.6 × W 3.3, WT 0.5. Fabric: relatively fine and micaceous, some small lime inclusions, 5YR 7/6. Thin dull coat, completely lost int., 5YR 3/1. Medium hard fired, oxidized. Calyx: acanthus (type?) and ovoid lotus petal B, Eros M above.

KYB-111
Olbia, Sector R25, O-P25-97-2474, Parutine, Olbia National Preserve storeroom. Fr. of base and lower body. H 4 × W 4.3, WT 0.6–0.73, ⌀ base 5. Fabric: relatively fine and micaceous, 7.5YR 7/6. Thin slightly lustrous coat, almost completely worn off, ext. 7.5YR 3/1, int. 2.5YR 4/8. Medium hard fired, oxidized. Calyx: acanthus K with Eros walking left (type?).

KYB-112
Istros, His-405, Bucharest, Institute of Archaeology storeroom. Fr. of upper body. Oxidized. Calyx: acanthus K; above, lower legs of Eros D (iii).

KYB-113
Istros, Sector "Pescărie", His-63-34, Bucharest, Institute of Archaeology storeroom. Fr. of lower body. H 3.2 × W 3.4, WT 0.5. Fabric: relatively fine and micaceous, some small lime inclusions. Dull red-brown coat. Oxidized. Calyx: acanthus K, Eros A(?).

KYB-114
Myrmekion, M-58-1158, St Petersburg, IIMK RAN. Fr. of lower body. H 2.8, WT 0.4. Fabric: fine, finely micaceous, 7.5YR 6/4. Thin coat, adhering badly, ext. mottled, ext. 5YR 4/6, 2.5/1, int. 5YR 3/1. Not too hard fired, oxidized. Stacked in firing. Calyx: acanthus K, indistinguishable figure as space-filler.

KYB-115
Porthmion, П-73-378, Kerč History and Culture Reserve inv. KMAK 6199/92. Body fr. Oxidized. Multiple rim friezes: heart buds; Ionian kyma with hatched tongue. Calyx: acanthus K with bird D as space-filler.
– Grzegrzółka 2010, 152–153 cat. 228.

KYB-116
Beljaus, Square 92, Bel-1997-1. Fr. of base and lower body. Rim frieze: groove(s?). Calyx: two types of acanthus and either slender pointed branch or twisted stem with kantharos A as space-filler. Medallion: surrounded by two ridges; around the stamp a row of small pointed petals; lower part of Meter bust?
– S. Lancov, annual report (2000), unpublished.

KYB-117*
Olbia, Sector R25, O-P25-96-1117, Parutine, Olbia National Preserve storeroom. Fr. of lower body with part of base. H 4.6 × W 4.4, WT 0.26–0.5. Fabric: relatively fine and micaceous, 7.5YR 7/2. Thin slightly lustrous coat, ext. 10YR 3/2, int. 10YR 3/1. Medium hard fired, oxidized. Calyx: tip of acanthus S alternating with jewelled lotus petal; in between, krater B flanked by probably four heraldic dolphins (A and B) with bird A and C as space-fillers.

KYB-118
Olbia, Sector E8, O-E8-70-2771, present whereabouts unknown. Fr. of base and large part of body. Oxidized. Multiple rim friezes: not preserved; heart buds. Main decoration: heraldic dolphins (A and B) around rosette A placed above but not separated from a low calyx of palmette A with tips of lotus petal A as space-filler. Medallion: surrounded by two ridges; signed [...]IR[...].
– St Petersburg, IIMK RAN, photo archive neg. I 73750.

KYB-119
Tyras, present whereabouts unknown, Belgorod? Fr. of rim and upper body. Rim frieze: heart buds. Calyx: acanthus O(?) with kantharos A (ii) as space-filler.
– Klejman 2001–2002, 410, fig. 5.33; attribution PGB.

KYB-120*
Olbia, Sector R25, O-P25-93-177, Parutine, Olbia National Preserve storeroom. Fr. of rim and upper body. H 5.9 × W 7.9, WT 0.35–0.65, ⌀ rim 14, 18%, RH 2.4. Fabric: relatively fine and micaceous, 5YR 6/6. Thin dull coat, partly blackened at lip, ext. 10R 5/6, int. 10R 5/8. Medium hard fired, oxidized. Multiple rim friezes: heart buds; dots. Main decoration: small boukrania B as spacer between vegetation.

KYB-121
Olbia, Sector NGS, O-НГС-90-257, Parutine, Olbia National Preserve storeroom. Fr. of lower body. H 3.2 × W 3.7, WT 0.23–0.28. Fabric: fine, dense, slightly micaceous, many small voids, 5YR 6/6. Thin firm slightly lustrous coat, slightly diluted on top of relief, 10YR 3/1. Hard fired, oxidized. Calyx: acanthus C and pointed lotus petal A, heraldic(?) dolphin(s) B facing acanthus, bird A over petal.

KYB-122
Chersonesos, no. 4349, National Preserve "Tauric Chersonesos". One fourth of bowl, base to rim. ⌀ rim 14. Rim frieze: heart guilloche right. Calyx: slender lotus petals alternating with dotted stem; birds A sit on the petals.
– Kovalenko 1989, 376 cat. 67, fig. 19.2.

KYB-123
Istros, Tumular necropolis, Tomb XXXVII, His-61-V 19866, present whereabouts unknown. Complete profile; fragmentary, lacking ca. one-fourth. Rim frieze: Ionian kyma. Calyx: acanthus L and 'nelumbo' (type?) separated by looped stems with bud; over the vegetation, birds E and F (i). Medallion: rosette with lobed petals; no signature. Frieze separators: dots.
– Alexandrescu 1966, 196, cat. XXXVII.27, pl. 97.

KYB-124*
Tomis, necropolis, inv. 5025, Constanta Museum. Complete profile; partially preserved. Rim frieze: Ionian kyma. Calyx: acanthus O and R alternating with buds on looped stems, birds B and D on tips of vegetation. Medallion: two ridges; signed [...]ΒΕΙ.
– Bucovală 1967, 122, fig. 79b; Ocheșeanu 1969, 233–234 cat. 18, figs. 29–31; Bouzek 1990, 66 cat. 19; Rotroff 2010, 69 cat. 24.

KYB-125
Pantikapaion, M-47-675(?), Moscow, Puškin Museum of Fine Arts. Body fr. H 4.5 × W 4. Oxidized. Rim frieze: Ionian kyma. Calyx: acanthus R alternating with bud on looped stem; Eros-Paniskos sits cross-legged on tip of acanthus.

KYB-126
Tyras, present whereabouts unknown, Belgorod? Complete side of bowl, lacking medallion. Rim frieze: Ionian kyma. Calyx: acanthus R alternating with triangular group of small ovoid lotus petals, with looped stems with buds and bird E(?) above.
– Samojlova 1984, fig. 4.5 (composite drawing); Samojlova 1988, pl. 23.8, 9; attribution PGB.

KYB-127*
Olbia, Sector NGS, House III-3 B 368/102, O-НГС-93-105+353, Parutine, Olbia National Preserve storeroom. Two joining frs. of mid-body. H 3.2 × W 2.7, WT 0.3–0.52. Fabric: relatively coarse, slightly micaceous, lime inclusions of varying size (up to 6 mm), many larger and smaller voids, 7.5YR 6/6. Thin fairly firm coat, int. slightly lustrous, ext. dull in patches, more lustrous in patches, ext. 5Y 3/1, int. 5Y 2.5/1. Medium hard fired, oxidized. Rim frieze: heart buds. Calyx: bird F or G(?), flower on looped acanthus stem.
– Guldager Bilde 2010, 287 cat. F-112, pl. 193 (erroneously identified as Pontic).

C   Scroll

Vine Scroll

KYB-128*
Olbia, O-1903-5143, St Petersburg, State Hermitage Museum. Complete. ⌀ rim 13.5; vessel H 7.9; H:⌀ 1:1.7. Oxidized. No rim frieze. Main decoration: incised full-body vine scroll combined with stamps of vine leaves, bunches of grapes and groups of three-dot berries. On the scroll sit numerous birds K; in the lower part of the bowl are three kitharai alternating with heraldic dolphins (A and B) around rosette A. Medallion: surrounded by two ridges; Meter bust right; signed KIRBEI.

D   Garlands and Wreaths

Suspended Garlands

KYB-129*
Olbia, bought from local, inv. Ол-4246, St Petersburg, State Hermitage Museum. Complete. Oxidized. Rim frieze: heart buds. Main decoration: garland A suspended from frontal female standing on garlanded altar functioning as statue base; over garland, heraldic dolphins (A and B) around rosette A; between statue bases, Erotes A, B, and C repeated two times; in between, kraters A and B and kantharos A; six birds A fill the space between garlands and vases. Medallion: Meter bust right; signed KIRBEI.
– Rostovcev 1967, 600, pl. LXVIII.2; Rotroff 2010, 69 cat. 42.

KYB-130*
Chersonesos, pit 2 (1877), X-1908-13, St Petersburg, State Hermitage Museum. Fr. of base, mid- and lower body. H 6.8, ⌀ base 4.4. Fabric: fine, micaceous, many voids, 5YR 6/6. Slightly lustrous coat, 10R 5/6, 3/1. Oxidized. Stacked in firing. Rim frieze: five shallow grooves. Main decoration: four large garlands suspended from boukrania A, alternating oak with acorn (garland B) and vine with bunches of grapes (garland C); between oak garlands, rosette 'shield'; decoration above vine garlands not preserved. Calyx of four acanthus M separated by small pointed petals. Medallion: surrounded by two ridges and a frieze of dots; Meter bust, right; signed KIRBEI. Four repair holes.

KYB-131
Chersonesos, no. 711.9, National Preserve "Tauric Chersonesos". Two joining frs. of base and lower body. Main decoration: large myrtle garland; below this, Eros D var. with nebris standing on ridge surrounding medallion; between Erotes, heraldic dolphins (A and B) flanking rosette A. Medallion: surrounded by two ridges; Meter bust right; signed KIRBEI.
– Kovalenko 1989, 376 cat. 71, fig. 19.4.

KYB-132*
Mesambria, necropolis, inv. 2000, Nessebar, Archaeological Museum. Complete. Rim frieze: heart guilloche right. Main decoration: four large garlands, alternating myrtle (garland A) and vine (garland C), suspended from bows; above garlands, rosette D with spiral tendrils; bird A perches on tendrils; bird D above rosette. Calyx: triangular groups of small, loosely imbricate triangular petals filling space below garlands. Medallion: two ridges; Meter bust right; signed KIRBEI.
– Čimbuléva 2005, 112, fig. 31.

KYB-133*
Olbia, Sector Sever-Zapad, O-СЗ-68-1961, Parutine, Olbia National Preserve storeroom. Fr. of mid-body. H 4 × W 5, WT 0.28. Fabric: fine, micaceous, a few minute lime inclusions, some small voids, 5YR 5/6. Thin dull coat, 10YR 3/2. Not too hard fired, oxidized. Main decoration: garland A with rosette 'shield' and rosette A above; bird A sits on rosette A; below garland, heraldic dolphins A and B, bird B.

KYB-134*
Pantikapaion, Tomb 106.VII, inv. 49469, Moscow, State Historical Museum (Zabelina collection). Fr. of base and large part of body; joined from two halves. ⌀ base 3.3. Fabric: micaceous, some lime inclusions, reddish brown. Dull black coat, lacking on large part of ext., pitted on int. Oxidized. Main decoration: garland A. Calyx: acanthus M and N alternating, separated by slender palmette C. Medallion: surrounded by ridge; Meter bust right; signed KIRBEI. Frieze separators: two thin ridges.

KYB-135
Istros, His-V 8574 E, Bucharest, Institute of Archaeology storeroom. Fr. of upper body. Oxidized. Main decoration: garland A with rosette A above. Frieze separators: dots between ridges.

KYB-136*
Olbia, Sector E6, squares 644, 645, SW of House "B", heaps of rocks nos. 543 and 545, O-E6-66-469, Kiev, Institute of Archaeology storeroom. Body fr. H 3.7 × W 3.5, WT 0.3. Fabric: fine, micaceous, 5YR 6/8. Coat with dull lustre, 5YR 3/1. Medium hard fired, oxidized. Rim frieze: Ionian kyma, pointed with double outline. Main decoration: garland A; above, suspended wreath with *tainia* tied in bow.

KYB-137*
Olbia, Sector A, square 110–113, north of wall 107, O-A-46-1324 (or 2324?), Kiev, Institute of Archaeology storeroom. Body fr. H 4.5 × W 4, WT 0.25. Fabric: fine, micaceous, a few minute lime inclusions, some small voids, 5YR 6/8. Thin dull coat, ext. 2.5YR 4/7, 4/8, int. 2.5YR 4/7. Relatively hard fired, oxidized. Main decoration: garland A, with suspended wreath with *tainia* tied in bow above.

KYB-138
Olbia, Sector E9, O-E9-61-no no. [B], present whereabouts unknown. Two groups of joining frs., three rim frs. and a body fr.; base and body fr. Rim frieze: heart guilloche right. Main decoration: garland D suspended between Medusa heads; above, rosette D flanked by two heart stamps, upside-down; below garland but not separated from it, heraldic volutes. Medallion: surrounded by two ridges; Meter bust right; signed KIRBEI.
– St Petersburg, IIMK RAN, photo archive neg. II 73233.

KYB-139
Tyras, present whereabouts unknown, Belgorod? Fr. of mid-body. Main decoration: garland D with rosette above; garland is placed over 'calyx' of volute elements; on the volutes sits bird A and a rosette separates the birds.
– Batizat 2002, fig. 9.33; attribution PGB.

KYB-140*
Golubickoe (2010), БАЭ-10-495, present whereabouts unknown. Complete profile; one fourth of bowl joined from numerous frs. Rim friezes: astragal; ridges. Main decoration: garland D suspended between Medusa heads; over garland, rosette A; below Medusa head, Eros H; below garland, Eros M. Medallion: surrounded by two ridges; Meter bust right; signed KIRBEI.

KYB-141
Provenance and present whereabouts unknown. Two joining frs. of base and lower body. Main decoration: lower part of garland D, with Eros I and Eros M below. Medallion: surrounded by two ridges; Meter bust right; signed KIRBEI. Documentation lost.

KYB-142*
Olbia, O-87-999, Parutine, Olbia National Preserve storeroom. Two joining frs. of rim and body. H 6.5 × W 5.6, WT 0.4, RH 2.8. Fabric: relatively fine and micaceous, many small lime inclusions, some voids, 5YR 6/6. Thin dull coat, mottled int., 7.5YR 3/1. Relatively hard fired, oxidized. Rim frieze: heart guilloche right. Main decoration: garland D suspended between Medusa heads; over garland, rosette D and isolated heart stamps upside-down; below Medusa head, bird B.

KYB-143*
Olbia, Sector NGS, O-НГС-06-602, Parutine, Olbia National Preserve storeroom. Body fr. H 5.4 × W 6.9, WT 0.25. Fabric: relatively fine and micaceous, some small lime inclusions, 2.5YR 6/8. Thin dull coat, ext. 2.5YR 5/6, 3/1, int. 2.5YR 5/6. Medium hard fired, oxidized. Stacked in firing. Rim frieze: heart guilloche right. Main decoration: garland D suspended by bows; frontal Medusa head; below head, bird A; below garland, dolphin A.

KYB-144
Tyras, present whereabouts unknown, Belgorod? Fr. of rim and upper body. Rim frieze: heart guilloche left. Main decoration: garland D suspended from unidentified object, with Medusa head above.
– Samojlova 1984, 124, 125, fig. 3.4 (identified as Samian).

KYB-145*
Olbia or Pantikapaion, Buračkov 91.3, Moscow, State Historical Museum (Buračkov collection). Fr. of base and lower body. H 8 × W 9, WT 0.6, ⌀ base 3.5. Oxidized. Main decoration: garland D over a calyx of acanthus C alternating with lotus petal B. Medallion: surrounded by two ridges; Meter bust right; signed KIRBEI.
– Žuravlev & Žuravleva 2014, 258, figs. 4.3, 5.2.

KYB-146*
Pantikapaion, M-57-1060+1089, Moscow, Puškin Museum of Fine Arts. Three joining frs. of rim and body. ⌀ rim 13, 24%, RH 2.5. Lustrous brown coat ext., dull int. Oxidized. No rim frieze. Main decoration: garland D with rosette A above. Calyx: acanthus S alternating with ovoid lotus petal A.
– AGSP 1984, pl. CLXIII.7 (erroneously depicted as if complete).

KYB-147*
Olbia, Sector R25, O-P25-96-1309, 1310, Parutine, Olbia National Preserve storeroom. Two non-joining frs. of base and body. H 3 × W 3.6, WT 0.25, ⌀ base 4. Fabric: relatively fine and micaceous, many small lime inclusions, 5YR 6/6. Thin dull coat ext., int. slightly lustrous, ext. 2.5YR 4/6, int. 5YR 4/3 and 4/4. Hard fired, oxidized. Main decoration: garland D suspended over low calyx

of small palm fronds E. Medallion: surrounded by two ridges; remains of inscription KI[...].

KYB-148*
Istros, Plateau, His-Constanta B, year and no. unknown, Constanta Museum. Fr. of base and lower body. Oxidized. Main decoration: garland D with rosette A above. Calyx: tip of acanthus M alternating with tip of lotus petal B, not separated from decoration. Medallion: surrounded by two ridges; Meter bust right; signed [...]BEI.

KYB-149
Olbia, Heidelberg (formerly Vogell collection). Complete. ⌀ rim 14; vessel H 8.1; H:⌀ 1:1.7. Brown coat. Oxidized. Rim frieze: groove. Main decoration: upper frieze: garland D suspended from kithara; above garland, rosette A flanked by heraldic dolphins (A and B); below garland, birds A, B, and C; lower frieze: over low calyx of lotus and palmette but not separated from it, Eros E alternating with bird K, dolphins left and right, and rosette A. Medallion: one ridge; Meter bust right; signed KIRBEI. Frieze separators: dots.
– von Stern 1902, 113 additional note; Zahn 1908, 62–63 cat. 20; Boehlau 1908, 30 no. 273; Rotroff 2010, 69 cat. 38.

KYB-150
Chersonesos, no. 234, National Preserve "Tauric Chersonesos". Two joining frs. from base to rim. ⌀ rim 13. No rim frieze. Main decoration: upper frieze: garland D (unclear from what they are suspended); lower frieze: Eros D freeing bird B. Frieze separators: dots between ridges.
– Kovalenko 1989, 375 cat. 65, fig. 19.1.

KYB-151*
Olbia, inv. Б 6657 (1928), Kiev, Historical Museum. Complete. ⌀ rim 12.9, RH 2.3, ⌀ base 3.8; vessel H 8.5; H:⌀ 1:1.5. Slightly lustrous black coat. Oxidized. Rim frieze: dots. Main decoration: garland D suspended between boukrania A with dotted *tainia*, repeated seven times; rosette A over garland. Calyx: acanthus H and I alternating, with krater B and boukranion A alternating as space-filler. Medallion: surrounded by two ridges; Meter bust right; signed KIRBEI. Frieze separators: dots. The find place was not known to the museum, but it can be identified on the basis of the negative in the Petersburg photo archive.
– St Petersburg, IIMK RAN, photo archive neg. II 13907.

KYB-152*
Mesambria, Tomb 2/1971, to left of head., inv. 1418, Nessebar, Archaeological Museum. Complete. Rim frieze: Ionian kyma, pointed with double outline. Main decoration: upper frieze: garlands D suspended from alternating boukranion A and rosette 'shield'; dolphins of alternating directions (A and B) over garlands; lower frieze: garlanded altar alternating with wreath tied with bow. Medallion: surrounded by two ridges; Meter bust right; signed KIRBEI. Frieze separators: heart guilloche right.
– Čimbuléva 2005, 102–103, fig. 15.1.

KYB-153*
Olbia, Sector AGD, О-АГД-87-154, Kiev, Institute of Archaeology storeroom. Fr. of rim and upper body. H 5.4 × W 4.8, WT 0.25, ⌀ rim 15, 10%, RH 1.8. Fabric: relatively fine and micaceous, many small lime inclusions, some voids, 7.5YR 6/4. Coat with dull lustre, ext. 7.5YR 3/1, 2.5YR 4/8, int. 7.5YR 3/1. Very hard fired, oxidized. Stacked in firing. Rim frieze: Ionian kyma, pointed with double outline. Main decoration: garland D with small boukranion B above. Frieze separators: Ionian kyma? One repair hole attempted.

KYB-154
Thasos, Herakleion, present whereabouts unknown. Fr. of rim and upper body; surface very worn. Rim frieze: grooves. Main decoration: garland D suspended from boukranion A; rosette 'shield' over garland.
– Ghali-Kahil 1960, 133 cat. 13, pl. LIX.13.

KYB-155*
Olbia, Sector E6-7, squares 475, 494, 495, 515, yellow clay layer, О-Е6-7-62-39, Kiev, Institute of Archaeology storeroom. Fr. of rim and body. H 6 × W 5.3, WT 0.26, ⌀ rim 13, 12%, RH 2.8. Fabric: fine, micaceous, a few minute lime inclusions, some small voids, 10YR 7/3. Dull coat ext., int. slightly lustrous, 10YR 2/1. Relatively hard fired, oxidized. Rim frieze: Ionian kyma, pointed with double outline. Main decoration: garland D suspended from boukrania A with *tainia* hanging from horns.

KYB-156
Olbia, Sector NGS, О-НГС-02-484, Parutine, Olbia National Preserve storeroom. Fr. of rim and upper body; rather worn. H 4.3 × W 3.4, WT 0.31–0.41, ⌀ rim 13, 6%, RH 2.2. Fabric: fine, soft, highly micaceous, 5YR 6/6. Relatively thin slightly lustrous coat, adhering badly, slightly darkened at lip int. and at lower body ext., ext. 2.5YR 4/6, 5YR 3/2, int. 2.5YR 4/6. Medium hard fired, oxidized. Stacked in firing. Rim frieze: Ionian kyma, pointed with double outline. Main decoration: boukranion A between suspended garlands.

KYB-157*
Istros, His-B 564/V 19373, Bucharest, Institute of Archaeology storeroom. Body fr. close to rim. H 4.2 × W 4.6, WT 0.45. Fabric: relatively fine and micaceous, many small lime inclusions, many voids, 7.5YR 7/6. Dull flaking coat, 2.5YR 4/6. Medium hard fired, oxidized. Rim frieze: Ionian kyma. Main decoration: garland(s) suspended from bows, bird D above.

– Domăneanţu 2000, 109 cat. 547, pl. 36 (identified as Pergamene).

KYB-158***
Olbia, Sector NGS, House IV-2 B 302/182, O-НГС-94-166, Parutine, Olbia National Preserve storeroom. Fr. of rim and upper body. H 4.8 × W 9.9, WT 0.25–0.45, ∅ rim 12.5, 25%, RH 2.25. Fabric: relatively fine and micaceous, small lime inclusions, 5YR 6/6. Thin firm coat, diluted and leaving top of reliefs lighter, ext. 7.5YR 2/0, int. 10YR 3/1. Medium hard fired, oxidized. Rim frieze: heart guilloche left. Main decoration: garland D suspended from bow, with rosette H and bird C above.
– Guldager Bilde 2010, 286 cat. F-99, pl. 189 (erroneously identified as Pontic).

KYB-159***
Olbia, Sector NGS, House III-3 R 278/96, O-НГС-93-19, Parutine, Olbia National Preserve storeroom. Fr. of rim and upper body. H 5.7 × W 5.8, WT 0.37–0.55, ∅ rim 13.5, 8%, RH 2.65. Fabric: relatively coarse, many lime inclusions, many small and large voids, 2.5YR 5/6. Diluted coat partly covering the vessel ext., leaving top of reliefs lighter, ext. slightly lustrous, int. semi-lustrous, 5YR 3/1. Hard fired, oxidized. Rim frieze: Ionian kyma. Main decoration: slender suspended garland F separated by *tainia* tied in bow, rosette E and H.
– Guldager Bilde 2010, 286 cat. F-98, pl. 189 (erroneously identified as Pontic).

KYB-160
Istros, His-V 19364 A, Bucharest, Institute of Archaeology storeroom. Fr. of upper body. Oxidized. Rim frieze: Ionian kyma. Main decoration: garland D suspended from *tainia* tied in bow.
– Domăneanţu 2000, 92 cat. 444, pl. 30 (identified as Ephesian); Rotroff 2010, 68 cat. 20.

KYB-161
Istros, His-176, Bucharest, Institute of Archaeology storeroom. Fr. of upper body. Oxidized. Main decoration: garland D suspended from bow.

KYB-162***
Olbia, Sector NGS, O-НГС-05-196, Parutine, Olbia National Preserve storeroom. Fr. of rim and upper body. H 3.4 × W 3.1, WT 0.3, RH 1.4. Fabric: relatively fine and micaceous, 5YR 6/6. Thin dull coat, ext. 5YR 5/8, 2.5/1, int. 5YR 2.5/1. Medium hard fired, oxidized. Stacked in firing. Rim frieze: Ionian kyma. Main decoration: garland D suspended from kithara B.

KYB-163***
Olbia, Sector NGS, O-НГС-02-426, Parutine, Olbia National Preserve storeroom. Fr. of rim and upper body. H 7.1 × W 7.4, WT 0.23–0.54, ∅ rim 14, 16%, RH 3.3. Fabric: relatively fine, slightly micaceous, a few small lime inclusions, some large voids, 5YR 5/6. Thin firm slightly lustrous coat, 10YR 3/1. Medium hard fired, oxidized. Rim frieze: heart guilloche right. Main decoration: garland D; above, rosette D flanked by two miniature dolphins (A and B, ii) and bird A. Identical: **KYB-164**.

KYB-164
Myrmekion, M-58-421, St Petersburg, IIMK RAN. Two joining frs. of mid-body. H 5.3, WT 0.45. Fabric: relatively fine and micaceous, slightly sandy, 5YR 6/6. Thin black coat with dull sheen, 5YR 3/1. Oxidized. Stacked in firing. Rim frieze: heart guilloche right. Main decoration: garland D; above, rosette D flanked by two miniature dolphins (A and B, ii) and bird A. Calyx: lotus petal B. Identical: **KYB-163***.

KYB-165***
Istros, His-1110, Bucharest, Institute of Archaeology storeroom. Fr. of upper body. H 4.1 × W 4.5, WT 0.5. Fabric: relatively fine and micaceous, many small lime inclusions, some voids, 5YR 6/6. Slightly lustrous ext., dull int., ext. 10YR 3/1, int. 5YR 3/3. Medium hard fired, oxidized. Rim frieze: dots. Main decoration: garland D with heraldic dolphins (A and B) above; over these, rosette A.
– Domăneanţu 2000, 93 cat. 447, pl. 30 (identified as Ephesian); Rotroff 2010, 68 cat. 18.

KYB-166
Istros, His-V 19417, Bucharest, Institute of Archaeology storeroom. Fr. of rim and upper body. H 5.4 × W 4.6, WT 0.4, ∅ rim 12, 12%, RH 2.7. Fabric: relatively fine and micaceous, many small lime inclusions, some voids, 7.5YR 6/6. Dull coat, 7.5YR 3/2. Medium hard fired, oxidized. Rim frieze: heart buds. Main decoration: suspended garlands(?), bird A, rosette A.
– Domăneanţu 2000, 130 cat. 638, pl. 45.

KYB-167***
Olbia, Sector E6-7, squares 475, 494, 495, 515, yellow clay layer, O-E6-7-62-12, Kiev, Institute of Archaeology storeroom. Fr. of rim and body. H 7.4 × W 8, WT 0.35, ∅ rim 12.5, 23%, RH 3. Fabric: fine and micaceous, a few minute lime inclusions, some small voids, 5YR 7/6. Dull coat, int. flaking, ext. 2.5YR 3/1, 2.5/1, 4/6, int. 2.5YR 4/8. Relatively hard fired, oxidized. Stacked in firing. Rim frieze: heart guilloche right. Main decoration: bound garland with rosette E above.

KYB-168
Istros, His-512, Bucharest, Institute of Archaeology storeroom? (not found March 2010). Fr. of upper body. H 2.7 × W 3.2. Oxidized. Main decoration: garland D with rosette A above.

– Dománeanțu 2000, 93 cat. 446, pl. 30 (identified as Ephesian); Rotroff 2010, 68 cat. 19.

KYB-169
Istros, His-400, Bucharest, Institute of Archaeology storeroom. Fr. of upper body. Oxidized. Main decoration: lower part of bound garland D.

KYB-170*
Olbia, Sector R25, O-P25-96-1440, Parutine, Olbia National Preserve storeroom. Body fr. H 5 × W 5.8, WT 0.35–0.4. Fabric: relatively fine and micaceous, many small lime inclusions, many voids, 5YR 5/6. Thin firm coat with slight metallic lustre, 7.5YR 2.5/1. Medium hard fired, oxidized. Main decoration: upper frieze: feline flanking rosette (type?); lower frieze: suspended bound miniature garlands H, below these but not separated from them, Eros M and birds D and A over small lotus petals. Frieze separators: thin ridge.

KYB-171*
Istros, His-276, Bucharest, Institute of Archaeology storeroom. Fr. of base and lower body. H 3.6 × W 2, WT 0.4, ⌀ base 3. Fabric: fine, non-micaceous, a few large silvery inclusions, 2.5Y 5/1. Dull coat, 2.5Y 3/1. Not too hard fired, oxidized. Main decoration: garland D with *tainia* placed upside-down around medallion. Medallion: signature retrograde and in negative relief [...]EI, clearly mechanically copied, as the small base diameter confirms.

Myrtle Wreath

KYB-172* to **KYB-175** all employ the same myrtle wreath with very fine and detailed berries on short, straight stems. It is characteristic that the depiction of the wreath is as a wreath proper, where the bundled leaves run in two directions, meeting in the back and front. **KYB-172*** and **KYB-173** also have the same calyx, separated from the wreath, and they most likely derive from the same mould. **KYB-176***, with groups of three-dot berries, is probably later than **KYB-172*** to **KYB-175**.

KYB-172*
Tomis, inv. 996, Constanta Museum. Complete profile, half of bowl missing. No rim frieze. Main decoration: bound myrtle wreath with three leaves and decorated berries on stems; proper wreath, with leaves running in two directions. Calyx: straight acanthus O alternating with lotus petal A as space-filler. Medallion: surrounded by two ridges; signed [...]BEI.
– Ocheșeanu 1969, 219–220 cat. 8, figs. 9–10.

KYB-173
Olbia, Sector A, square 12, inv. A 3592 (1926), Nikolaev, Historical Museum. Fr. of mid- and lower body. H 4.5 × W 6.6, WT 0.4. Fabric: relatively fine and micaceous, some small lime inclusions. Dull blackish brown coat. Oxidized. Main decoration: myrtle wreath left with single decorated berries. Calyx: straight acanthus O alternating with ovoid lotus petals A.

KYB-174
Tyras, present whereabouts unknown, Belgorod? Three joining frs. of rim, upper and lower body. Rim frieze: heart guilloche left. Main decoration: bound myrtle wreath with three leaves and groups of three-dot berries. Leaves run in two directions and wreath is tied with a bow. Calyx: acanthus M alternating with ovoid lotus petal A.
– Batizat 2002, fig. 8.2; attribution PGB.

KYB-175
Istros, His-309, Bucharest, Institute of Archaeology storeroom. Fr. of upper body. H 3.2 × W 3.2, WT 0.42. Fabric: relatively fine and micaceous, many small lime inclusions, some voids, 5YR 5/6. Dull coat, ext. 10YR 4/2, int. 5YR 3/2. Medium hard fired, oxidized. Main decoration: bound myrtle wreath with three leaves and decorated berries on stems; proper wreath, with leaves running in two directions.

KYB-176*
Istros, Sector "Pescărie", His-63–16, Bucharest, Institute of Archaeology storeroom. Fr. of upper body. Oxidized. Main decoration: bound myrtle wreath left, with three bundled leaves and groups of three-dot berries.

E   *Vegetal Decoration*

Calyx

KYB-177*
Olbia, Sector NGS, O-НГС-02-387, 392, Parutine, Olbia National Preserve storeroom. Two non-joining frs. of base and body; extremely worn, very little of medallion can be made out. H 8.8 × W 9, WT 0.39–0.8, ⌀ base 3. Fabric: relatively fine and micaceous, some small lime inclusions, some small voids, 5YR 6/6, 7.5YR 6/4. Thin firm coat with slight lustre ext. where fired reddish, black apart from upper part of vessel, 7.5YR 2/0, 2.5YR 3/6. Medium hard fired, oxidized. Stacked in firing. Rim frieze: grooves. Calyx: acanthus A alternating with 'nelumbo' C. Medallion: surrounded by two ridges; Meter bust right; very worn inscription KI[...]BEI. One repair hole.

KYB-178*
Olbia, Square B5, О-Б5-76-54+87, 56, Kiev, Institute of Archaeology storeroom. Two joining rim frs. and one non-joining fr. of upper and mid-body. WT 0.5, ⌀ rim 14, 30%, RH 2.2. Fabric: relatively fine and micaceous, many small lime inclusions, some voids, 7.5YR 6/6. Dull coat, 2.5YR 5/6. Not too hard fired, oxidized. Rim frieze: small horizontal petals with central vein, left. Calyx: 'nelumbo' B(?) with scales and floral elements? Frieze separators: astragal between ridges. Secondarily burnt.

KYB-179*
Olbia, Sector NGS, House III-1 Stove 329/74, О-НГС-92-915, Parutine, Olbia National Preserve storeroom. Fr. of rim and upper body. H 5 × W 5.9, WT 0.35–0.42, ⌀ rim 15, 12%, RH 2.95. Fabric: micaceous, abundant small round voids, traces of burnt-out vegetal material, 7.5YR 6/4. Thin dull coat, blotchy, ext. 5YR 3/1, int. 7.5YR 4/2. Medium hard fired, oxidized. Rim frieze: heart guilloche left. Calyx: 'nelumbo's with lily (iii) on stem(?) between them. Probably Kirbeis because of the character of the rim pattern.
– Guldager Bilde 2010, 286 cat. F-111, pl. 193 (erroneously identified as Pontic).

KYB-180*
Pantikapaion, M-75-119(?), Moscow, Puškin Museum of Fine Arts. Fr. of base and lower body. H 6 × W 6. Very fine shiny black coat ext., dull brown int. Oxidized. Calyx: acanthus C alternating with acanthus R; in between, ovoid petal B also used as space-filler. Medallion: surrounded by ridges.
– Zabelina 1984, 164, fig. 11b.

KYB-181
Olbia, O-1928-542, present whereabouts unknown. Body fr. Calyx: acanthus P.
– St Petersburg, IIMK RAN, photo archive neg. II 13922.

KYB-182*
Olbia, Sector NGS, О-НГС-05-137, Parutine, Olbia National Preserve storeroom. Fr. of upper body close to rim. H 3.3 × W 2.7, WT 0.3. Fabric: relatively fine and micaceous, 5YR 6/8. Thin dull coat, 7.5YR 3/2. Medium hard fired, oxidized. Rim frieze: Ionian kyma, pointed with double outline. Calyx: acanthus Q(?).

KYB-183*
Olbia, Sector R25, O-P25-96-1561+97-2415 (join across years), Parutine, Olbia National Preserve storeroom. Two joining frs. of rim and upper body. H 6.5 × W 12, WT 0.5, ⌀ rim 13.5, 27%, RH 3.4. Fabric: relatively fine and micaceous, many small lime inclusions, 5YR 6/6. Thin mottled coat, adhering badly, slightly lustrous int. and rim ext., dull below, 5YR 2.5/2, 2.5YR 5/8. Medium hard fired, oxidized. Stacked in firing. Multiple rim friezes: heart buds in negative relief; astragal. Calyx: top of acanthus A(?).

KYB-184*
Istros, His-B 599/V 19376, Bucharest, Institute of Archaeology storeroom. Fr. of lower body. H 3.5 × W 2.5. Oxidized. Stacked in firing. Calyx: acanthus L.
– Domăneanţu 2000, 73 cat. 343, pl. 22 (identified as Ionian [Heraios]).

KYB-185
Tyras, present whereabouts unknown, Belgorod? Fr. of base and large part of body. Calyx: acanthus K, R, and S alternating. Medallion: two ridges, around the medallion stamp a frieze of dots; Meter bust right; signed KIRBEI.
– Samojlova 1988, pl. 23.1.

KYB-186
Kyme, inv. M 780, Bruxelles, Musées Royaux (Cinquantenaire, ex-collection Misthos). Fr. of base and lower body. Calyx: acanthus R. Medallion: surrounded by two ridges, around the stamp a frieze of dots; Meter bust right; signed KIRBEI.
– CVA Brussels, Musées Royaux (Cinquantenaire) 3 [Belgium 3], III N, pl. 4 (142).25; Rotroff 2010, 69 cat. 44.

KYB-187*
Istros, His-1927-1942-V 8574 K, Bucharest, Institute of Archaeology storeroom. Fr. of upper body. H 3.2 × W 4.3, WT 0.5. Fabric: fine, micaceous, a few minute lime inclusions, some small voids. Dull coat. Medium hard fired, oxidized. Calyx: acanthus A with tip bent towards left, bud or flower on looped stem. Secondarily burnt.

KYB-188*
Olbia, Sector R25, O-P25-93-2908[a], Parutine, Olbia National Preserve storeroom. Large fr., almost complete profile, lacking base, broken and reassembled. H 7.5 × W 8, WT 0.35–0.4, ⌀ rim 16, 12%, RH 2.2. Fabric: fairly coarse and micaceous, many small lime inclusions, 5YR 5/8. Thin dull coat, slight lustre at rim ext., ext. 5YR 3/1, int. 5YR 3/2. Medium hard fired, oxidized. Rim frieze: heart guilloche left. Calyx: acanthus L alternating with flower on looped acanthus stem.

KYB-189
Olbia, Sector NGS, О-НГС-03-397, Parutine, Olbia National Preserve storeroom. Fr. of base and lower body. H 6 × W 3.3, WT 0.5. Fabric: relatively fine and micaceous, 10YR 6/4. Dull coat, ext. 10YR 2/1, int. 10YR 3/1. Medium hard fired, oxidized. Calyx: acanthus L, looped stem with bud.

KYB-190
Olbia, O-40-2447, Kiev, Institute of Archaeology storeroom. Body fr. H 4.1 × W 4.4, WT 0.35. Fabric: relatively fine and micaceous, many small lime inclusions, some voids, 7.5YR 6/6. Dull coat, ext. lacquer-like, ext. 7.5YR 2.5/1, int. 2.5YR 4/8. Relatively hard fired, oxidized. Stacked in firing. Calyx: acanthus L(?), looped stem with bud.

KYB-191
Istros, His-V 19372, Bucharest, Institute of Archaeology storeroom. Body fr. close to rim H 4.5 × W 6, WT 0.5. Fabric: relatively fine and micaceous, many small lime inclusions, many voids, 7.5YR 6/6. Dull coat, redder at rim ext., ext. 10YR 4/2, 2.5YR 5/6, int. 10YR 4/2. Medium hard fired, oxidized. Stacked in firing. Rim frieze: grooves. Calyx: acanthus (type?) and palmette B with bud on looped tendril in between.
– Domăneanțu 2000, 137 cat. 681, pl. 49.

KYB-192
Delos, present whereabouts unknown. Small body fr. Calyx: palmette B, acanthus stem.
– Laumonier vol. 2, cat. 1372, pl. III.

KYB-193*
Olbia, Sector E6-7, squares 412w, 417w, ash layer, O-E6-7-61-406[A], Kiev, Institute of Archaeology storeroom. Body fr. H 3.8 × W 3.8, WT 0.3. Fabric: relatively fine and micaceous, many small lime inclusions, some voids, 5YR 6/8. Dull coat, ext. 2.5YR 4/6, int. 2.5YR 3/1. Medium hard fired, oxidized. Stacked in firing. Calyx: acanthus R and palmette B with bud on looped stem in between.

KYB-194
Myrmekion, year and no. unknown, present whereabouts unknown, Warsaw? Complete profile; almost half preserved, joined from several frs. Rim frieze: heart guilloche left. Calyx: acanthus R alternating with buds and flower on looped stems. Medallion: surrounded by two ridges; Meter bust right; signed KIRBEI.
– Gajdukevič 1959, 79, fig. 87; Bouzek 1990, 66 cat. 18; Rotroff 2010, 69 cat. 34.

KYB-195
Tomis, inv. 19473, Constanta Museum. Complete. Rim frieze: Ionian kyma. Calyx: acanthus R alternating with buds on looped stems. Medallion: surrounded by two ridges; signed KIRBEI.
– Ocheșeanu 1969, 235–236 cat. 19, figs. 32–34; Rotroff 2010, 69 cat. 26.

KYB-196
Tyras, present whereabouts unknown, Belgorod? Fr. of base and large part of body. Calyx: acanthus R alternating with acanthus S and palmette A; in between, buds on looped stems, left and right. Medallion: surrounded by two ridges, around the stamp a frieze of dots; Meter bust right; signed KIRBEI.
– Samojlova 1984, 123, fig. 2.5 (attributed to Asia Minor).

KYB-197
Pantikapaion, M-62-14, Moscow, Puškin Museum of Fine Arts. Body fr. H 4.8 × W 4.5. Dull cracking red-brown coat. Oxidized. Rim frieze: heart guilloche left. Calyx: acanthus R alternating with bud on looped stem.
– Kovalenko 1989, 373 cat. 10.

KYB-198*
Istros, Sector Z2, His-57-V 17439 A, B, C [His-957], Bucharest, Institute of Archaeology storeroom. Fr. of base and mid-body; non-joining body fr. H 7.7 × W 5, WT 0.42, Ø base 4. Fabric: relatively fine and micaceous, many small lime inclusions, many voids, 5YR 6/6. Dull coat almost completely worn off, 5YR 3/2. Medium hard fired, oxidized. Rim frieze: grooves. Calyx: acanthus R alternating with palmette B; in between, lily (ii) on wavy stem. Medallion: surrounded by two ridges; face of Meter right preserved; signed [...]BEI.
– Domăneanțu 2000, 118 cat. 587, pl. 40; Rotroff 2010, 68 cat. 14.

KYB-199*
Olbia, Sector R25, O-P25-99-2275, Parutine, Olbia National Preserve storeroom. Large fr., almost complete profile, lacking base. H 8.5 × W 10, WT 0.28–0.45, Ø rim 12, 30%, RH 3.2. Fabric: relatively fine and micaceous, laminated, 5YR 6/6. Thin coat with slight lustre, ext. 5YR 3/1, int. 7.5YR 5/4, at rim mottled 3/2. Medium hard fired, oxidized. Rim frieze: heart guilloche right. Calyx: acanthus R alternating with rosette D on incised wavy stem.

KYB-200*
Myrmekion, M-56-942, St Petersburg, IIMK RAN. Fr. of mid-body. H 2.8, WT 0.48. Fabric: relatively fine, non-micaceous, a few minute lime inclusions, 2.5YR 6/6. Thin dull black coat ext., brownish and almost completely worn off int. Oxidized. Calyx: acanthus R, incised wavy stem.

KYB-201*
Myrmekion, M-54-10 II, St Petersburg, IIMK RAN. Fr. of mid-body. H 2.8, WT 0.53. Fabric: relatively fine and micaceous, slightly sandy, some small lime inclusions, 2.5YR 5/6. Thin dull coat, ext. 2.5YR 3/1, int. 7.5YR 4/3. Oxidized. Calyx: acanthus R, rosette E probably on wavy stem.
– Kovalenko 1989, 374 cat. 35.

KYB-202*
Olbia, Sector NGS, O-НГС-02-37, 43, 79, Parutine, Olbia National Preserve storeroom. Four rim and body frs., two joining. H 8.2 × W 7.6, WT 0.31–0.5, ⌀ rim 13, 52%, RH 2.8. Fabric: medium fine, micaceous, abundant small lime inclusions, small rounded black and brown stones, many voids, 2.5YR 5/8. Thin firm coat, dull black, slightly lustrous at rim ext. and at lip int. and both places have a violet stripe, 2.5Y 3/0. Medium hard fired to a particular crispness, oxidized. Stacked in firing. Multiple rim friezes: heart buds; Ionian kyma. Calyx: ovoid lotus petals A growing out of vegetal calyx alternating with lily (ii) on incised wavy stems.

KYB-203
Istros, His-210, Bucharest, Institute of Archaeology storeroom. Fr. of mid- and lower body. H 4.1 × W 5.3, WT 0.5. Fabric: relatively fine and micaceous, many small lime inclusions, some voids, 7.5YR 6/4. Dull coat almost completely worn off, 10YR 4/2. Medium hard fired, oxidized. Calyx: ovoid lotus petals A alternating with lily (iii) on incised wavy stems.
– Domăneanțu 2000, 118 cat. 588, pl. 40; Rotroff 2010, 68 cat. 15.

KYB-204*
Olbia, Sector NGS, O-НГС-02-41, 113, 137, Parutine, Olbia National Preserve storeroom. Three non-joining rim frs. and one body fr. H 7.2 × W 9.3, WT 0.3–0.5, ⌀ rim 13, 54%, RH 2.8. Fabric: medium fine, micaceous, abundant small and some large lime inclusions up to 2 mm, small rounded black and brown stones, many voids, 5YR 6/6. Thin firm coat, dull 'oily' black, slightly lustrous at rim ext. and at lip int., and both places have a violet stripe, 10YR 3/1. Medium hard fired, oxidized. Rim frieze: Ionian kyma. Calyx: acanthus R alternating with ovoid lotus petal, lily in between.
– Guldager Bilde 2010, 287 cat. F-113, pl. 193 (erroneously identified as Pontic).

KYB-205
Olbia, Sector R25, O-P25-05-463, Parutine, Olbia National Preserve storeroom. Body fr. H 4 × W 4, WT 0.4. Fabric: relatively fine and micaceous, 5YR 6/6. Thin dull coat, 7.5YR 2.5/1. Medium hard fired, oxidized. Multiple rim friezes: very compressed Ionian kyma; heart buds. Calyx: tip of acanthus (type?) or petal alternating with lily.

KYB-206*
Olbia, Sector AGD, Bothros 11, O-АГД-88-201, Kiev, Institute of Archaeology storeroom. Six rim frs., two body frs., and one body fr. with part of base, all joining; almost complete profile. WT 0.4, ⌀ rim 14, 60%, RH 2.1, ⌀ base 4; vessel H 7.4; H:⌀ 1:1.9. Fabric: relatively fine and micaceous, many small lime inclusions, 5YR 5/6. Thin dull coat, slight purplish sheen at rim, 10YR 3/1. Not too hard fired, oxidized. Stacked in firing. Multiple rim friezes: heart buds; Ionian kyma. Calyx: acanthus O alternating with acanthus R with tip of lotus petal A, rosette G as space-filler. Medallion: surrounded by two ridges.
– Rusjaeva & Nazarčuk 2006, pl. 193.13.

KYB-207*
Istros, His-836, Bucharest, Institute of Archaeology storeroom. Fr. of lower body. Oxidized. Calyx: acanthus L and upper part of lily (i). Frieze separators: ridge(s).
– Domăneanțu 2000, 73 cat. 344, pl. 22 (identified as Ephesian [Heraios]).

KYB-208*
Istros, His-1097, Bucharest, Institute of Archaeology storeroom. Fr. of lower body. H 3.2 × W 3.2, WT 0.35. Fabric: relatively fine and micaceous, many small lime inclusions, some voids, 5YR 6/6. Dull coat, ext. 5YR 4/2, int. 5YR 2.5/1. Medium hard fired, oxidized. Calyx: acanthus O and ovoid lotus petals A, rosette B as space-filler.
– Domăneanțu 2000, 95 cat. 464, pl. 31 (identified as Ephesian).

KYB-209*
Olbia, Agora, square 645, Room "D", Southwest House, Area 22, yellow clay layer, O-66-1148, Kiev, Institute of Archaeology storeroom. Two joining body frs. H 8 × W 9, WT 0.35–0.4. Fabric: relatively fine and micaceous, many small lime inclusions, some voids, 5YR 6/8. Dull coat, very worn, 7.5YR 3/1. Not too hard fired, oxidized. Multiple rim friezes: heart buds in negative relief; heart guilloche right. Calyx: acanthus O alternating with groups of lotus petal A.

KYB-210*
Olbia, Sector NGS, O-НГС-92-636, Parutine, Olbia National Preserve storeroom. Fr. of rim and upper to mid-body. H 7.1 × W 8, WT 0.33–0.4, ⌀ rim 13, 15%, RH 3.05. Fabric: relatively fine and micaceous, a few small lime inclusions, some small round voids, 5YR 6/6. Thin firm slightly lustrous coat, diluted, leaving tops of relief a different colour, ext. 2.5Y 3/2, 5YR 3/2, int. 5YR 3/1. Medium hard fired, oxidized. Rim frieze: heart buds in negative relief. Calyx: acanthus R alternating with groups of pointed lotus petals A.

KYB-211
Pantikapaion, M-48-1964, present whereabouts unknown. Fr. of base and lower body. Calyx: acanthus R, pyramidal group of small pointed petals; further decoration cannot be distinguished from photograph. Medallion: surrounded by two ridges; signed […]ΕΙ.
– Loseva 1962, 202, fig. 4.1; Rotroff 2010, 69 cat. 28.

KYB-212
Istros, His-892, Bucharest, Institute of Archaeology storeroom. Fr. of lower body. Oxidized. Calyx: acanthus R with pyramidal group of imbricate lotus petals B below.
– Domăneanțu 2000, 140 cat. 700, pl. 51.

KYB-213*
Olbia, Sector AGD, О-АГД-74-473, Kiev, Institute of Archaeology storeroom. Fr. of mid-body. H 3.8 × W 5.3, WT 0.4. Fabric: relatively fine and micaceous, many small lime inclusions, some voids, 7.5YR 4/6, 6/6. Dull coat, ext. 10YR 3/2, 2.5YR 5/6, int. 10YR 3/2. Relatively hard fired, oxidized. Stacked in firing. Multiple rim friezes: heart buds; Ionian kyma, pointed with double outline. Calyx: acanthus S alternating with broad pointed lotus petal. Identical: **KYB-241***.

KYB-214*
Istros, His-776, Bucharest, Institute of Archaeology storeroom. Fr. of lower body. Oxidized. Calyx: acanthus S.

KYB-215
Delos, 67 E 478, present whereabouts unknown. Fr. of base and lower body. Calyx: acanthus K. Medallion: upper part of Meter bust right; signed KIRBE[…].
– Laumonier vol. 2, cat. 9546.

KYB-216
Istros, His-716, Bucharest, Institute of Archaeology storeroom. Fr. of base and lower body. H 3.4 × W 4, WT 0.55. Fabric: relatively fine and micaceous, many small lime inclusions, many voids, 5YR 7/8. Dull coat, ext. 7.5YR 3/1, int. 5YR 2.5/1. Medium hard fired, oxidized. Calyx: acanthus R. Medallion: surrounded by two ridges; traces of lower part of Meter bust.
– Domăneanțu 2000, 136 cat. 674, pl. 49.

KYB-217
Istros, His-363, Bucharest, Institute of Archaeology storeroom. Body fr. H 4 × W 2.8, WT 0.7. Fabric: relatively fine and micaceous, some small lime inclusions. Dull brown coat. Oxidized. Calyx: acanthus R.

KYB-218
Istros, His-842, Bucharest, Institute of Archaeology storeroom. Body fr. H 1.8 × W 2.5, WT 0.35. Fabric: relatively fine and micaceous, some small lime inclusions. Dull brown coat. Oxidized. Calyx: acanthus R.

KYB-219
Istros, His-639, Bucharest, Institute of Archaeology storeroom. Fr. of lower body. Oxidized. Calyx: acanthus R.

KYB-220
Olbia, Sector NGS, О-НГС-05-899, Parutine, Olbia National Preserve storeroom. Fr. of rim and upper body. Oxidized. No rim frieze. Calyx: acanthus R.

KYB-221*
Olbia, O-64-802, Kiev, Institute of Archaeology storeroom. Fr. of base and lower body. H 4.7 × W 2.5, WT 0.4, ⌀ base 3. Fabric: fine and micaceous, a few minute lime inclusions, some small voids, 10YR 5/2. Coat with dull lustre, ext. 10YR 5/1, 3/1, int. 10YR 3/1. Hard fired, reduced. Stacked in firing. Calyx: acanthus M. Medallion: surrounded by two ridges; head of Meter right preserved; signed […]BEI. Stamp in pristine condition.
– Kovalenko 1989, 375 cat. 53.

KYB-222*
Olbia, Sector E6-7, squares 332sw, 352sw, 372nw, humus, O-E6-7-63-1664, Kiev, Institute of Archaeology storeroom. Fr. of base and lower body. H 3.7 × W 4.3, WT 0.38, ⌀ base 4. Fabric: relatively fine and micaceous, many small lime inclusions, some voids, 7.5YR 6/6. Dull coat, 7.5YR 2.5/1. Relatively hard fired, oxidized. Calyx: acanthus M. Medallion: surrounded by single ridge: signed […]EI; the pattern inside the medallion is worn off.
– Kovalenko 1989, 375 cat. 55.

KYB-223*
Olbia, Sector NGS, House III-3 R 278/96, О-НГС-93-22, Parutine, Olbia National Preserve storeroom. Joining frs. of rim and body; almost complete profile. H 7.5 × W 10, WT 0.4–0.55, ⌀ rim 12, 35%, RH 2.6. Fabric: relatively fine and micaceous, some small lime inclusions and oblong voids, 7.5YR 6/6. Rather thick coat with slight metallic lustre int. and at rim and upper body ext., top of relief lighter in colour, ext. 2.5YR 4/4, 3/0, int. 5YR 2.5/1. Medium hard fired, oxidized. Stacked in firing. Multiple rim friezes: dots; heart guilloche right; Ionian kyma. Calyx: acanthus M alternating with groups of pointed petals D with concentric veins. One repair hole.
– Guldager Bilde 2010, 286 cat. F-110, pl. 192 (erroneously identified as Pontic).

KYB-224
Istros, His-V 10063, present whereabouts unknown. Fr. of base and lower body. Calyx: acanthus M alternating with acanthus N. Medallion: surrounded by two ridges, around the stamp a frieze of dots; Meter bust right; signed KIRBEI.
– Domăneanțu 2000, 118 cat. 586, pl. 40; Rotroff 2010, 68 cat. 13.

KYB-225*
Olbia, Sector R25, O-P25-97-2523, Parutine, Olbia National Preserve storeroom. Fr. of lower body. H 3.5 × W 2.9, WT 0.4. Fabric: relatively fine and micaceous, 7.5YR 7/6. Thin slightly lustrous

coat, ext. 7.5YR 3/2, int. 7.5YR 3/1. Medium hard fired, oxidized. Calyx: acanthus M, rosette A on incised stem.

KYB-226
Istros, His-225, Bucharest, Institute of Archaeology storeroom. Body fr. H 3.3 × W 3.6, WT 0.5. Fabric: relatively fine and micaceous with some small lime inclusions. Dull reddish coat. Oxidized. Calyx: acanthus M with ovoid lotus petal A above.

KYB-227*
Istros, Sector "Pescărie", His-63-?[a], Bucharest, Institute of Archaeology storeroom. Body fr. H 2 × W 2.8, WT 0.35. Fabric: relatively fine and micaceous, some small lime inclusions. Dull red-brown coat. Oxidized. Calyx: acanthus M with ovoid lotus petal A.

KYB-228*
Chersonesos, X-1961-60[d], St Petersburg, State Hermitage Museum. Fr. of lower body. H 2.7, WT 0.45. Fabric: relatively fine and micaceous, many small lime inclusions, some voids, 2.5YR 6/6. Slightly lustrous coat, 2.5YR 3/1. Oxidized. Calyx: acanthus M alternating with acanthus N, heart bud as space-filler.

KYB-229
Chersonesos, no. 384.9, National Preserve "Tauric Chersonesos". Fr. of base and lower body. Calyx: alternating acanthus M and N. Medallion: surrounded by two ridges; Meter bust right; signed KIRBEI.
– Kovalenko 1989, 376 cat. 73, fig. 19.3.

KYB-230*
Tyritake, Sector A, A-55-128, St Petersburg, IIMK RAN. Fr. of lower body. Reduced. Calyx: acanthus M, ovoid lotus petal A.

KYB-231*
Olbia, Sector NGS, House II-2 B 248/8, O-НГС-89-764, Parutine, Olbia National Preserve storeroom. Fr. of most of medallion and part of lower body. H 5.9 × W 6.5, WT 0.28–0.42, ⌀ base 4. Fabric: relatively fine and micaceous, small voids, 7.5YR 6/2–6/4. Slightly lustrous coat, diluted, leaving top of relief partially coated, 10YR 3/1. Very hard fired, oxidized. Calyx: acanthus S. Medallion: surrounded by thin ridge and frieze of large dots; Meter bust right; signed KIRBEI.
– Guldager Bilde 2010, 286 cat. F-109, pl. 192 (erroneously identified as Pontic).

KYB-232*
Istros, His-V 8570 D [His-987-42], Bucharest, Institute of Archaeology storeroom. Fr. of base and lower body. H 4.1 × W 4, WT 0.5, ⌀ base 3.5. Fabric: relatively fine and micaceous, many small lime inclusions, many voids, 7.5YR 6/6. Coat with metallic sheen int., 7.5YR 3/2. Relatively hard fired, oxidized. Calyx: palmette B. Medallion: surrounded by one ridge; Meter bust right; signed KIRBEI.
– Domăneanțu 2000, 119 cat. 591, pl. 40; Rotroff 2010, 68 cat. 16.

KYB-233*
Olbia, Sector E2, square 55, Cistern Л, O-E2-49-120, Kiev, Institute of Archaeology storeroom. Fr. of base and lower body. H 4.4 × W 4.4, WT 0.65, ⌀ base 3.6. Fabric: relatively fine and micaceous, many small lime inclusions, some voids, 5YR 6/6. Dull, very worn ext., int. with slight lustre, ext. 5YR 4/1, int. 5YR 5/6. Relatively hard fired, oxidized. Stacked in firing. Calyx: palmette B. Medallion: surrounded by two ridges; remains of Meter bust right; signed [...]EI.

KYB-234*
Tyritake, Sector A, A-55-155, St Petersburg, IIMK RAN. Body fr. H 3.6, WT 0.42. Fabric: fine, soft, micaceous, slightly sandy, 5YR 7/6. Dull flaking coat, 5YR 3/1. Not too hard fired, oxidized. Stacked in firing. Rim frieze: heart guilloche right. Calyx: palmette B alternating with palmette C(?) with isolated stamp of heart bud as space-filler.

KYB-235*
Olbia, Sector E6, square 425, southwest corner, west of Drain 99, grey clay layer, O-E6-57-1243, Kiev, Institute of Archaeology storeroom. Fr. of base and lower body. H 5.3 × W 5.3, WT 0.3, ⌀ base 4. Fabric: fine, micaceous, a few minute lime inclusions, some small voids, 5YR 7/6. Dull coat, ext. 5YR 4/1, int. 5YR 4/2. Relatively hard fired, oxidized. Calyx: acanthus O alternating with lotus petal B. Medallion: surrounded by two ridges; lower part of Meter bust; signed [...]EI.
– Kovalenko 1989, 375 cat. 51.

KYB-236
Olbia, Sector E9 or 10, O-E9 or E10-62-no no., present whereabouts unknown. Fr. of base and part of lower body. Calyx: acanthus V alternating with tip of acanthus M stamped many times almost on top of one other. Medallion: surrounded by two ridges; face of Meter right; signed [...]BEI.
– St Petersburg, IIMK RAN, photo archive neg. I 43837.

KYB-237*
Olbia, Sector R25, O-P25-97-2155, Parutine, Olbia National Preserve storeroom. Fr. of lower body. H 3.9 × W 3.2, WT 0.51. Fabric: relatively fine and micaceous, some small lime inclusions, 7.5YR 6/6. Thin dull coat, 7.5YR 3/1. Medium hard fired, oxidized. Calyx: acanthus V alternating with lotus petal A growing out of vegetal calyx.

KYB-238*
Olbia, V.I. 7754.66, Antikensammlung, Staatliche Museen zu Berlin (former Becker collection). Fr. of base and lower body. W 4.8, WT 0.43; vessel H 4.7. Fabric: fine and slightly micaceous, 5YR 6/6. Dark coat, ext. 7.5YR 3/1, int. 7.5YR 4/1. Oxidized. Calyx: acanthus V and acanthus O with palm frond E as space-filler. Medallion: surrounded by one ridge; *tainia* and lock of Meter preserved.

KYB-239*
Istros, Plateau, His-Constanta C, year and no. unknown, Constanta Museum. Fr. of base and lower body. Oxidized. Calyx: tall spiky palm frond B growing out of calyx; every second palm frond upside-down. Medallion: surrounded by thin ridge; Meter bust right; signed KIRBEI.

KYB-240*
Samothrace, inv. 2000.6. Fr. of base and lower body. Calyx: ovoid lotus petal A emerging from calyx. Medallion: surrounded by two ridges; Meter bust right; signed KIRBEI.
– Rotroff 2010, 62, figs. 5.4.2, 5.5.3.

KYB-241*
Olbia, Sector E6, square 476s, 477se, yellow clay layer with ash inclusions, O-E6-59-1417, Kiev, Institute of Archaeology storeroom. Fr. of base and lower body. H 4.3 × W 3.7, WT 0.35, ⌀ base 4. Fabric: fine, micaceous, a few minute lime inclusions, some small voids, 5YR 5/6. Lustrous coat, 5YR 2.5/2. Relatively hard fired, oxidized. Calyx: columns of superposed tips of acanthus S; in between, lotus petal. Medallion: surrounded by two ridges: lower part of Meter bust and one of the fingers of her left hand holding tympanon. Identical: **KYB-213***.

KYB-242*
Istros, His-107, Bucharest, Institute of Archaeology storeroom. Fr. of base and lower body. H 3.8 × W 4, WT 0.4, ⌀ base 4.2. Fabric: relatively fine and micaceous, many small lime inclusions and voids, 7.5YR 6/6. Dull coat almost completely worn off, 7.5YR 2.5/1. Medium hard fired, oxidized. Calyx: lower part of vegetal calyx of uncertain type. Medallion: surrounded by three ridges; Meter bust almost completely worn off; signed KI[...]I.
– Domăneanțu 2000, 119 cat. 592, pl. 40; Rotroff 2010, 68 cat. 17.

KYB-243*
Olbia, Sector E2, square 55, Cistern Л, O-E2-49-122, Kiev, Institute of Archaeology storeroom. Fr. of rim and body. H 5.3 × W 5.9, WT 0.32, ⌀ rim 13, 14%, RH 2.2. Fabric: relatively fine and micaceous, many small lime inclusions, some voids, 5YR 6/4. Dull coat, worn, 5YR 3/2. Medium hard fired, oxidized. Rim frieze: heart buds. Calyx: tip of acanthus S(?). One repair hole.

KYB-244
Istros, His-295, Bucharest, Institute of Archaeology storeroom. Fr. of lower body. Oxidized. Calyx: tip of acanthus V(?). Attributed to Kirbeis because acanthus V is employed only by him.

KYB-245*
Olbia, Sector AGD, О-АГД-74-475, Kiev, Institute of Archaeology storeroom. Fr. of mid-body. H 4.8 × W 4.6, WT 0.2–0.4. Fabric: relatively fine and micaceous, many small lime inclusions, some voids, 10YR 6/4. Dull coat, ext. 10YR 3/2, int. 2.5YR 5/6. Not too hard fired, oxidized. Stacked in firing. Calyx: palm frond A.

KYB-246*
Olbia, Sector AGD, grey ashy clay layer, О-АГД-69-1259, Kiev, Institute of Archaeology storeroom. Body fr. WT 0.35. Fabric: relatively fine and micaceous, many small lime inclusions, some voids, 5YR 6/6. Dull mottled coat, ext. 2.5YR 3/1, 5/6, int. 2.5YR 4/2. Medium hard fired, oxidized. Calyx: heraldic volutes with jewelled central vein.
– Kovalenko 1989, 375 cat. 46.

KYB-247
Ukrainian part of Black Sea region(?), S. Platonov collection, Kiev. Complete profile, partially preserved. Rim frieze: Ionian kyma. Calyx: type cannot be identified. Medallion: signed [...]BEI.
– exhibited in the Tobi Ukraino exhibition (2003), S. Sofia, Kiev.

Imbricate

KYB-248*
Pantikapaion, year and number unknown, Kerč History and Culture Reserve inv.(?). Fr. of base and lower body. Calyx: imbricate pointed petals with central vein. Medallion: surrounded by two ridges; Meter bust right; signed KIRBEI.
– Žuravlev & Žuravleva 2014, figs. 2.5, 3.6, 4.1.

KYB-249
Abdera, year and no. unknown, present whereabouts unknown. Fr. of base and lower body. Calyx: imbricate, tip of pointed petals with central vein. Medallion: two ridges; Meter bust almost completely worn off; signed [...]E[...].
– Kranioti 1997, 795–796, 806, fig. 9.d.

KYB-250*
Olbia, Sector E7, square 537s, grey clay layer, O-E7-57-495, Kiev, Institute of Archaeology storeroom. Body fr. close to rim. H 5 × W 5, WT 0.35. Fabric: relatively fine and micaceous, many small lime inclusions, many voids, 5YR 6/6. Dull coat, 5YR 4/1.

Relatively hard fired, oxidized. Multiple rim friezes: heart buds; wave meander. Calyx: tip of pointed lotus petal A.

KYB-251*
Olbia, Sector E6-7, squares 475, 494, 495, 515, yellow clay layer, O-E6-7-62-14, Kiev, Institute of Archaeology storeroom. Fr. of base and lower body. H 4.6 × W 6.6, WT 0.4, ⌀ base 4. Fabric: relatively fine and micaceous, many small lime inclusions, some voids, 5YR 7/6. Slightly lustrous coat, ext. 5YR 5/4, 4/1, int. 5YR 3/1. Relatively hard fired, oxidized. Calyx: imbricate, tips of lotus petals B with jewelled central vein closely set. Medallion: surrounded by three ridges. Identical: KYB-252.

KYB-252
Olbia, O-1929-1584, present whereabouts unknown. Fr. of base and lower body. Calyx: imbricate, tips of lotus petals B with jewelled central vein closely set. Medallion: surrounded by three ridges. Identical: KYB-251*.
– St Petersburg, IIMK RAN, photo archive neg. II 4840.

KYB-253*
Pantikapaion, M-49-162, Moscow, Puškin Museum of Fine Arts. Fr. of base and lower body. H 4.2 × W 4.5. Dull reddish brown coat. Oxidized. Calyx: imbricate pointed petals with central vein. Medallion: surrounded by two ridges; signed KIR[…].
– Kovalenko 1989, 374 cat. 22.

KYB-254
Olbia, Sector R25, O-P25-96-1310, Parutine, Olbia National Preserve storeroom. Fr. of base and lower body. H 3.7 × W 3.5, WT 0.3, ⌀ base 4. Fabric: relatively fine and micaceous, many small lime and shell inclusions, 5YR 5/6. Thin dull coat ext., int. slightly lustrous, ext. 2.5YR 4/6, int. 5YR 3/2. Hard fired, oxidized. Calyx: imbricate palm fronds E. Medallion: surrounded by two ridges; signed KI[…].

F *Linear Decoration*

Net Pattern

KYB-255*
Olbia, Square Б5, O-Б5-76-57, Kiev, Institute of Archaeology storeroom. Complete profile, two thirds of bowl preserved. WT 0.3–0.5, RH 2.2; vessel H 7.1. Fabric: relatively fine and micaceous, many small lime inclusions, 2.5YR 6/8. Dull coat, pitted inside, 7.5YR 2.5/1. Relatively hard fired, oxidized. Rim frieze: Ionian kyma. Main decoration: net pattern made with dots; inside pentagons, rosette F; above pentagons, dolphins C and D alternate. Medallion: surrounded by two ridges; signed KIRBEI. The Meter medallion stamp is smaller than usual but features the same error; retouched with addition of wreath as Possis; the original stamp was clearly mechanically copied. Also the dolphins in the pentagons are the large version (C and D), used by Possis and Zenodotos, but not by Kirbeis.

KYB-256
Abdera, year and no. unknown, present whereabouts unknown. Fr. of base and lower body. Main decoration: net pattern made with dots. Medallion: surrounded by two ridges, around the stamp a frieze of dots; Meter bust right; signed […]BEI.
– Kranioti 1997, 795–796, 806, fig. 9.g.

Long Petal

KYB-257
Tyras, present whereabouts unknown, Belgorod? Fr. of base and lower body. Calyx: long petals of uncertain type separated by dots. Medallion: surrounded by two ridges; Meter bust right; signed KIRBEI.
– Samojlova 1984, 123, fig. 2.4.

G *Base Fragments*

KYB-258*
South Russia, V.I. 4982.90, Antikensammlung, Staatliche Museen zu Berlin (Sammlung de Massonneau). Base fr. W 3.3, WT 0.45. Fabric: medium fine, micaceous (no fresh break). Dull coat, 10YR 3/1. Medallion: surrounded by two ridges with astragal between them; Meter bust right; signed KIRBEI. Stamp in pristine condition; the tympanon can be seen clearly.

KYB-259*
Olbia, Sector R25, O-P25-98-87, Parutine, Olbia National Preserve storeroom. Base fr. H 3.7 × W 2.7, WT 0.31, ⌀ base 5. Fabric: relatively fine and micaceous, 7.5YR 6/4. Thin shiny coat, 2.5Y 2.5/1. Hard fired, oxidized. Medallion: surrounded by two ridges; Meter bust right; signed KIRBEI.

KYB-260*
Kepoi, Ke-61-536, Moscow, State Historical Museum. Base fr. ⌀ base 3.5. Fabric: abundant lime inclusions, reddish. Dull dark brown coat. Oxidized. Medallion: surrounded by one ridge; Meter bust right; signed KIRBEI.
– Usačeva 1978, fig. 1.21 ('probably Asia Minor'); Bouzek 1990, fig. 32.9; Rotroff 2010, 69 cat. 27.

KYB-261*
Olbia or Pantikapaion, Buračkov 146, Moscow, State Historical Museum (Buračkov collection). Base fr. H 3.5 × W 5, ⌀ base 4.5. Slightly lustrous black coat, covering the surface well. Oxidized.

Calyx: tiny part of calyx(?), cannot be identified. Medallion: surrounded by two ridges; Meter bust right; signed KIRBEI.
– Latyšev 1890, 131; Latyšev 1892, 383 with fig.; Bouzek 1990, 65 cat. 2; Rotroff 2010, 68 cat. 7/8.

KYB-262
Pantikapaion(?), present whereabouts unknown. Base fr. Medallion: turreted female bust right; signed KIRBEI.
– AGSP 1984, pl. CLXIII.8; Kovalenko 1987b, fig. 2.5.

KYB-263
Tyras, present whereabouts unknown, Belgorod? Fr. of base and lower body. Calyx: tiny part of calyx preserved (type cannot be identified from published drawing). Medallion: surrounded by one ridge; Meter bust right, partially preserved; signed KIR[...].
– Batizat 2002, fig. 9.4.

KYB-264
Olbia, O-1925-85, present whereabouts unknown. Base fr. Medallion: surrounded by two thin ridges with astragal between them; part of Meter bust right; signed K[...].
– St Petersburg, IIMK RAN, photo archive neg. II 19396.

KYB-265
Nymphaion, St Petersburg, State Hermitage Museum. Fr. of medallion and lower body. Calyx: palmette C(?). Medallion: signed KIRBEI.
– Grzegzółka 2001, 120 and n. 38 (mentioned as an unpublished fragment).

KYB-266*
Myrmekion, M-58-1609, St Petersburg, IIMK RAN. Fr. of base and lower body. H 5.2, WT 0.78, ⌀ base 3.5. Fabric: relatively fine and micaceous, slightly sandy, 5YR 5/6. Thin black coat with slight metallic sheen, 7.5YR 2.5/1. Oxidized. Stacked in firing. Calyx: vegetal, of uncertain type. Medallion: surrounded by two ridges; stamp very abraded, but the B of KIRBEI can be distinguished. The letter is placed horizontally in front of the right side of the crown. This is the only example of the stamp I know of; it differs from the normal stamp and also from the stamp known from Pantikapaion signed Kirbeidos.

KYB-267
Pantikapaion, M-47-1115, present whereabouts unknown. Base fr. Medallion: surrounded by a single ridge; Meter bust right; a large tympanon held with her left hand is easily distinguishable behind the head; signed KIRBEIDOS. The signature is unique; it is not divided by the head, as in the standard stamp, but written in one line arching over the head.
– Loseva 1962, 203, fig. 4.4; Kovalenko 1987b, fig. 2.6; Kovalenko 1989, 374 cat. 24, fig. 18.3; Rotroff 2010, 69 cat. 30.

KYB-268*
Olbia, Sector AGD, grey ashy clay layer, О-АГД-69-1260, Kiev, Institute of Archaeology storeroom. Base fr. H 3.9 × W 6.2, WT 0.35, ⌀ base 3.8. Fabric: relatively fine and micaceous, many small lime inclusions, some voids, 5YR 6/6. Dull mottled coat, ext. 2.5YR 3/1, 5/6, int. 2.5YR 4/2. Medium hard fired, oxidized. Calyx cannot be identified. Medallion: surrounded by two ridges; wreath tied with bow; no signature.
– Kovalenko 1989, 375 cat. 46.

H *Rim Fragments*

Multiple Rim Friezes

KYB-269
Olbia, O-1925-485, present whereabouts unknown. Fr. of rim and upper body. Multiple rim friezes: Ionian kyma; heart buds.
– St Petersburg, IIMK RAN, photo archive neg. II 19399.

KYB-270
Olbia, Sector I, Pit E(?) ash clay layer, О-И-48-2087, Kiev, Institute of Archaeology storeroom. Rim fr. Oxidized. Multiple rim friezes: dots; Ionian kyma, pointed with double outline.

KYB-271*
Istros, His-B 532/V 8573 K, Bucharest, Institute of Archaeology storeroom. Rim fr. H 4.3 × W 2.6, WT 0.35, RH 2.1. Fabric: fine, micaceous, a few minute lime inclusions, some small voids, 5YR 6/8. Dull coat, 7.5YR 3/1. Medium hard fired, oxidized. Multiple rim friezes: heart buds; fine dots.
– Domăneanțu 2000, 130 cat. 640, pl. 45.

KYB-272*
Myrmekion, M-58-1779, St Petersburg, IIMK RAN. Fr. of upper body. H 2.3, WT 0.2. Fabric: fine, slightly micaceous, ext. 5YR 5/4, int. Gley 1 6/N. Thin dull coat, Gley 1 3/N. Hard fired, oxidized. Multiple rim friezes: heart guilloche right; Ionian kyma.

Single Rim Friezes

Heart Buds

KYB-273
Olbia, Sector JuzA, О-ЮзА-74-1440, Parutine, Olbia National Preserve storeroom. Rim fr. H 3.7 × W 8.3, WT 0.37, ⌀ rim 14, 21%, RH 2.3. Fabric: relatively fine, micaceous, small rounded inclusions, 5YR 6/6. Thin dull coat, 5YR 2.5/1. Relatively hard fired, oxidized.

KYB-274*
Olbia, O-64-1068, Kiev, Institute of Archaeology storeroom. Fr. of rim and upper body. H 5.3 × W 6.3, WT 0.35, ⌀ rim 13, 15%, RH 3.5. Fabric: relatively coarse and micaceous, many large voids, 5YR 6/6. Mottled coat with dull lustre ext., more lustrous int., ext. 2.5YR 4/8, 3/1, int. 2.5YR 4/6, 4/8, 3/1. Not too hard fired, oxidized.

KYB-275
Olbia, Sector NGS, O-НГС-08-49, Parutine, Olbia National Preserve storeroom. Rim fr. H 4.1 × W 5.8, WT 0.4, ⌀ rim 14, 13%, RH 2.7. Fabric: relatively fine and micaceous, some small lime inclusions, 5YR 6/8. Thin dull coat, ext. 5YR 5/4, int. 2.5YR 5/6, 5YR 4/4. Medium hard fired, oxidized. Stacked in firing.

KYB-276
Olbia, Sector NGS, O-НГС-02-34, Parutine, Olbia National Preserve storeroom. Rim fr. H 4.3 × W 3.6, WT 0.28–0.4, RH 1.9. Fabric: relatively fine and micaceous, a few small dark stones, 5YR 5/8. Thin firm slightly lustrous coat, mottled at rim, darkened below, 2.5YR 4/6, 10YR 3/2. Medium hard fired, oxidized. Stacked in firing.

KYB-277*
Olbia, Sector NGS, House IV-2 B 302/189, O-НГС-94-595, Parutine, Olbia National Preserve storeroom. Rim fr. H 4.45 × W 5.8, WT 0.48–0.64, ⌀ rim 16, 6%, RH 3. Fabric: rather sloppily made, micaceous, some small lime and larger inclusions of lighter colour, large voids, 5YR 6/6. Thin diluted coat with crazing and bluish metallic sheen, ext. 5YR 3/1, int. 5YR 3/1, 2.5YR 4/4. Medium hard fired, oxidized. Stacked in firing. One repair hole (not drilled through).
– Guldager Bilde 2010, 287 cat. F-116, pl. 194 (erroneously identified as Pontic).

KYB-278*
Olbia, Sector R25, O-P25-93-175, Parutine, Olbia National Preserve storeroom. Rim fr. H 4.9 × W 3.5, WT 0.45, ⌀ rim 12, 9%, RH 3.1. Fabric: relatively fine and micaceous, 7.5YR 5/4. Thick glossy coat, 7.5YR 2.5/1. Hard fired, oxidized.

KYB-279
Pantikapaion, M-62-609, Moscow, Puškin Museum of Fine Arts. Rim fr. H 4 × W 5, ⌀ rim 13, RH 2. Dull worn reddish-brown coat. Oxidized.
– Kovalenko 1989, 374 cat. 27.

KYB-280
Pantikapaion, M-58-360, Moscow, Puškin Museum of Fine Arts. Rim fr. H 4 × W 4.5, RH 1.8. Oxidized. Rim friezes: grooves; heart buds.

KYB-281
Pantikapaion, M-47-1146, Moscow, Puškin Museum of Fine Arts. Rim fr. H 4 × W 3.5, RH 2.4. Oxidized.

KYB-282
Pantikapaion, M-46-308, Moscow, Puškin Museum of Fine Arts. Rim fr. H 3.5 × W 3.5, RH 1.6. Dull brownish coat. Oxidized.

KYB-283
Olbia, O-1928-113, present whereabouts unknown. Body fr. Main decoration uncertain, perhaps tail of dolphin.
– St Petersburg, IIMK RAN, photo archive neg. II 13908.

KYB-284*
Istros, His-438[a], Bucharest, Institute of Archaeology storeroom. Body fr. close to rim H 3.8 × W 3.4, WT 0.38. Fabric: fine, micaceous, a few minute lime inclusions, some small voids, 5YR 6/8. Dull coat, ext. 5YR 2.5/1, int. 5YR 4/4. Relatively hard fired, oxidized. Rim friezes: grooves; heart buds. Main decoration: heart bud upside-down as space-filler.
– Domăneanţu 2000, 130 cat. 639, pl. 45.

KYB-285
Olbia, Sector R25, O-P25-99-2337, Parutine, Olbia National Preserve storeroom. Body fr. Oxidized. Main decoration cannot be identified from drawing.

KYB-286
Istros, Sector SZ, His-89(?)1, Bucharest, Institute of Archaeology storeroom. Rim fr. Oxidized.

KYB-287
Istros, His-V 8569 N, Bucharest, Institute of Archaeology storeroom. Body fr. close to rim. Oxidized.

KYB-288
Istros, His-891(?), Bucharest, Institute of Archaeology storeroom. Rim fr. Oxidized.

KYB-289
Olbia, Square B5, O-Б5-76-86, Kiev, Institute of Archaeology storeroom. Rim fr. H 3.8. Oxidized.

Heart Buds in Negative Relief

This strange pattern, which we also find on two vessels with multiple rim friezes (**KYB-183*** and **KYB-209***) as well as on one with a calyx decoration and a single rim frieze (**KYB-210***), is created by mechanical copying from a vessel with the heart bud pattern. Accordingly, it post-dates the true heart buds.

KYB-290*
Olbia, Sector NGS, О-НГС-92-136, Parutine, Olbia National Preserve storeroom. Body fr., worn. H 3.3 × W 3.7, WT 0.32-0.38. Fabric: fine, dense, micaceous, a few small voids, 7.5YR 6/6. Thin firm slightly lustrous coat, slightly diluted on top of relief, ext. 5YR 3/1, 2.5YR 4/8, int. 5YR 3/1. Medium hard fired, oxidized. Stacked in firing. Rim friezes: grooves; heart buds in negative relief.

Heart Guilloche, Left

KYB-291*
Istros, His-84, Bucharest, Institute of Archaeology storeroom. Rim fr. H 3.5 × W 3.5, WT 0.35, RH 1.9. Fabric: relatively fine and micaceous, some small lime inclusions. Dull red-brown coat. Oxidized.

KYB-292
Olbia, Sector NGS, О-НГС-02-140, Parutine, Olbia National Preserve storeroom. Rim fr. H 4 × W 5.4, WT 0.5–0.58, ⌀ rim 13, 10%, RH 2.5. Fabric: medium fine, micaceous, abundant small lime inclusions, many voids, 5YR 6/8, 7.5YR 6/6 (bicolour from stacking). Thin firm coat, ext. dull, int. slightly lustrous, ext. 7.5YR 3/0, int. 5Y 3/1. Medium hard fired, oxidized. Stacked in firing.

KYB-293*
Olbia, Sector R25, O-P25-95-1219, Parutine, Olbia National Preserve storeroom. Rim fr. Oxidized.

KYB-294
Istros, His-no no. 3, Bucharest, Institute of Archaeology storeroom. Body fr. close to rim. Oxidized.

KYB-295
Istros, His-no no. 4, Bucharest, Institute of Archaeology storeroom. Body fr. close to rim. Oxidized.

Heart Guilloche, Right

KYB-296*
Pantikapaion, M-46-534, Moscow, Puškin Museum of Fine Arts. Rim fr. ⌀ rim 13, 14%. Reddish brown coat with a fair lustre. Oxidized.
– Kovalenko 1989, 373 cat. 1.

KYB-297
Istros, His-803, Bucharest, Institute of Archaeology storeroom. Rim fr. H 4 × W 4.5, WT 0.4, RH 2.3. Fabric: relatively fine and micaceous, some small lime inclusions. Dull red-brown coat. Oxidized. Calyx: ovoid lotus petal.

KYB-298
Istros, His-V 19422, Bucharest, Institute of Archaeology storeroom. Rim fr. H 4 × W 5, WT 0.4, RH 2.1. Fabric: relatively fine and micaceous, some small lime inclusions. Dull reddish to red-brown coat, worn, int. pitted. Oxidized.

KYB-299*
Tyritake, Sector L, Л-51-36, St Petersburg, IIMK RAN. Rim fr. H 4.2, WT 0.35, ⌀ rim 14, 13%, RH 2.4. Fabric: relatively fine and micaceous, slightly sandy, 5YR 7/6. Slightly lustrous coat, ext. 5YR 3/1, int. 5YR 3/2. Oxidized. Stacked in firing.

KYB-300
Istros, His-1141, Bucharest, Institute of Archaeology storeroom. Body fr. H 3.2 × W 4.5, WT 0.58. Fabric: relatively fine and micaceous, some small lime inclusions. Dull red-brown coat. Oxidized. Calyx: ovoid lotus petal.

KYB-301*
Olbia, Sector E2, square 55, Room Л, western part, grey clay layer, O-E2-48-4983, Kiev, Institute of Archaeology storeroom. Fr. of rim and upper body. Oxidized. Main decoration: unidentified traces.

KYB-302
Olbia, Sector NGS, О-НГС-02-507, Parutine, Olbia National Preserve storeroom. Rim fr., very worn. H 3.8 × W 3.1, WT 0.45, ⌀ rim 13, 7%, RH 2.5. Fabric: relatively fine and micaceous, abundant minute lime inclusions, some small voids, 7.5YR 6/4. Thin dull coat, 10YR 3/1. Medium hard fired, oxidized.

KYB-303
Istros, His-800, Bucharest, Institute of Archaeology storeroom. Body fr. close to rim. Oxidized.

Ionian Kyma

KYB-304
Pantikapaion, M-69-no no., Moscow, Puškin Museum of Fine Arts. Body fr. close to rim. H 4 × W 3.5. Dark shiny coat with purple band over Ionian kyma. Oxidized. Stacked in firing. Main decoration: unidentified traces.
– Kovalenko 1989, 373 cat. 3.

KYB-305*
Olbia, Sector NGS, House IV-3 B 343/202, О-НГС-92-417, Parutine, Olbia National Preserve storeroom. Rim fr. H 3.9 × W 4.4, WT 0.28–0.4, ⌀ rim 12, 12%, RH 2.9. Fabric: relatively fine and micaceous, many small and some up to 2 mm lime inclusions, 7.5YR 6/6. Thin firm coat with slight metallic sheen ext., 10YR 3/1. Medium hard fired, oxidized.

– Guldager Bilde 2010, 287 cat. F-118, pl. 194 (erroneously identified as Pontic).

KYB-306
Olbia, Sector NGS, O-НГС-92-525, Parutine, Olbia National Preserve storeroom. Rim fr. Oxidized.

KYB-307
Olbia, Sector NGS, O-НГС-02-371, Parutine, Olbia National Preserve storeroom. Rim fr. H 3.5 × W 6.6, WT 0.5, ø rim 12.5, 18%, RH 2.6. Fabric: Medium fine and micaceous, many lime inclusions up to 2 mm, many voids, 7.5YR 6/6. Thin firm slightly lustrous coat, ext. 10YR 3/1, int. 5YR 3/1. Medium hard fired, oxidized.

KYB-308*
Olbia, Sector NGS, O-НГС-04-237, Parutine, Olbia National Preserve storeroom. Two joining rim frs. H 4.6 × W 9.3, WT 0.32, ø rim 13.5, 25%, RH 2.6. Fabric: relatively fine and micaceous, some small lime inclusions, 5YR 6/8. Thin coat with slight metallic sheen, 2.5YR 5/4, 3/2. Medium hard fired, oxidized. Stacked in firing.

Ionian Kyma, Pointed with Double Outline

KYB-309
Pantikapaion, M-67-131(?), Moscow, Puškin Museum of Fine Arts. Rim fr. H 4.5 × W 5.5, ø rim 12, 12%, RH 2.2. Dull brown coat. Oxidized. Rim friezes: grooves; Ionian kyma, pointed with double outline. Main decoration: unidentified traces.

KYB-310*
Istros, His-1164, Bucharest, Institute of Archaeology storeroom. Rim fr. Oxidized.

KYB-311*
Olbia, Sector Sever-Zapad, O-СЗ-68-1952, Parutine, Olbia National Preserve storeroom. Rim fr. H 4.4 × W 3, WT 0.41, RH 3.3. Fabric: fine, micaceous, a few minute lime inclusions, some small voids, 5YR 5/6. Thin rather soapy coat, 7.5YR 2.5/1. Relatively hard fired, oxidized

KYB-312*
Olbia, Sector R25, O-P25-95-1172, Parutine, Olbia National Preserve storeroom. Rim fr. H 3.2 × W 1.8, WT 0.3, RH 2.1. Fabric: relatively fine and micaceous, 5YR 6/6. Slightly glossy coat ext., int. dull, ext. 5YR 3/1, int. 5YR 3/2. Medium hard fired, oxidized.

KYB-313
Olbia, Sector R25, O-P25-92-837, Parutine, Olbia National Preserve storeroom. Rim fr. H 4 × W 2.5, WT 0.4, RH 2.7. Fabric: relatively fine and micaceous, 7.5YR 5/4, core 7.5YR 5/1. Dull coat, 2.5Y 2.5/1. Medium hard fired, oxidized.

KYB-314*
Istros, His-655, Bucharest, Institute of Archaeology storeroom. Rim fr. H 3.5 × W 4.2. Oxidized.
– Domăneanțu 2000, 81 cat. 388, pl. 26 (identified as Ephesian [Si]).

Grooves

KYB-315*
Istros, His-1085, Bucharest, Institute of Archaeology storeroom. Fr. of rim and upper body. H 4.2 × W 5.2, WT 0.3, RH 2.5. Fabric: relatively fine and micaceous, some small lime inclusions. Dull reddish brown coat. Oxidized. Main decoration: only heart bud upside-down as space-filler preserved.

SUPPLEMENTARY SHAPES

Small Bowl

KYB-316
Olbia, Göttingen (formerly Vogell collection). Complete. ø rim 8.5. Rim frieze: grooves. Main decoration: garland D separated by bows and suspended wreaths; over garlands, isolated dolphin alternating left and right (A and B); below the garlands but not separated from them, low calyx of palmette A on the tip of which sits a row of birds A. Medallion: surrounded by three ridges; Meter bust right; signed KIRBEI.
– von Stern 1902, 113 additional note; Boehlau 1908, 30 no. 274; Zahn 1908, 64–65 cat. 21; Rotroff 2010, 69 cat. 39.

KYB-317*
Olbia(?), inv. 54791 Uvarov 643, Moscow, State Historical Museum (Uvarov collection). Complete. WT 0.4, ø rim 7.6, RH 3, ø base 3.3; vessel H 5; H:ø 1:1.5. Fabric: relatively fine and micaceous. Dull red coat. Oxidized. Stacked in firing. No rim frieze. Calyx: bird A and C sitting on funnel-shaped flower calyxes; isolated stamp of egg as space-filler below; repeated 15 times. Medallion: surrounded by two ridges; rosette with nine rounded petals; no signature.

KYB-318*
Pantikapaion, П-1868-254, St Petersburg, State Hermitage Museum. Complete. H 5.2, ø rim 7.5. Reduced. No rim frieze. Calyx: straight acanthus U with ovoid lotus petals as spacer; over tip of acanthus, bird A. Medallion: surrounded by one ridge; rosette with eight rounded petals; no signature.
– Kovalenko 1989, 374 cat. 26.

KYB-319*
Olbia, Sector E, square 250, O-E-49-2895, Kiev, Institute of Archaeology storeroom. One-third of bowl, lacking base; interior covered with lime. WT 0.35, ⌀ rim 8.5, 12%, RH 2; vessel H 4.5; H:⌀ 1:1.9. Fabric: relatively fine and micaceous, many small lime inclusions, some voids, 5YR 6/8. Dull coat, worn 5YR 3/1. Relatively hard fired, oxidized. Rim frieze: Ionian kyma with hatched tongues. Calyx: looped tendril with flower flanked by lily (ii) on wavy stem, separated by acanthus. Very small base, perhaps no decoration.

Juglet without Handle

KYB-320*
Kepoi, Tomb 43, Ke-60-43/14, Moscow, State Historical Museum, inv. 97173. Complete except for part of rim; surface very worn. ⌀ rim 5.7; vessel H 7.3. Fabric: micaceous, light greyish brown. Thin brownish grey coat, almost completely worn off. Not too hard fired, oxidized. Rim frieze: heart buds. Calyx: closely set straight, slender acanthus G. Medallion: slave mask.
– Usačeva 1978, fig. 2.22.

Amphora

KYB-321
Olbia, V.I. 5862, Antikensammlung, Staatliche Museen zu Berlin (formerly Mavrogordato collection, 1909), lost in WW II. Complete. Vessel H 19.5. Brownish coat. Rim frieze: Ionian kyma(?). Main decoration: Amazon B, horseman A, Amazon C. Medallion: signed KIRBEI. Known only from small drawing in the inventory book of the museum.
– Neugebauer 1932, 188; Verluste 2005, 205.

KYB-322*
Olbia, V.I. 4952, Antikensammlung, Staatliche Museen zu Berlin (formerly Vogell collection). Complete. ⌀ rim 13.9, ⌀ base 12.8; vessel H 17.2. Fabric: medium fine, micaceous, 2.5Y 5/1.5. Mottled coat, 10YR 4/1-2/1. Reduced. Multiple rim friezes: heart buds; grooves. Calyx: widely spaced acanthus S alternating with arched acanthus V; between the vegetal elements, Eros D (ii) alternating with krater B repeated five times; on the tip of the vegetation sits bird A; rosette A as space-filler. Medallion: surrounded by two ridges; Meter bust right; signed KIRBEI. The relief is very high.
– von Stern 1902, 113 additional note; Zahn 1908, 68 cat. 28; Boehlau 1908, 26–27 no. 249; Neugebauer 1932, 188–189; Rotroff 2010, 69 cat. 40.

KYB-323
Olbia, inv. 2122, Tübingen, Antikensammlung (formerly Vogell collection). Complete. Vessel H 16. Fabric: light red to greyish. Brownish coat. Oxidized. Main decoration: acanthus S and V alternating with krater B and Eros D (i) as space-fillers; over the krater, suspended wreath with *tainia*; bird B and rosette A as space-fillers in upper part of frieze. The amphora is a hybrid, with the moulded rim of Attic amphorae and the strap handles with rotellae and the heavy foot of Pergamene vessels (Rotroff 2010, 67). Same shape as **KYB-326***.
– Zahn 1908, 68 cat. 29 (attributed to Kerbeis); Boehlau 1908, 27 no. 250; Watzinger 1924, 70 cat. G 30, pl. 49; Watzinger 1926, 205 cat. 30; Raeder 1986, 204 cat. 15, pl. 37.3; Rotroff 2010, 69 cat. 41. According to Zahn (1908, 77), the vessel was bought by a museum in Kassel, but the curator of the Antikensammlung in Kassel, Dr. R. Splitter, informs me (1 Nov. 2007) that the vessel is not and never has been in the collection.

KYB-324
Olbia, Odessa, Historical Museum. Complete. On the neck, applied clay blobs (leaves of a painted garland). Vessel H 18. Oxidized. Rim frieze: grooves. Main decoration: garland D suspended from boukrania A with *tainia* hanging from horns; above and below garlands, large rosette 'shields', bird A; rosette A as space-filler. Medallion: wreath with small bow and hanging ends of *tainia* (mistaken for torches by Samojlova); no signature.
– Samojlova 1994, fig. 3.1 (identified as Pergamene).

KYB-325*
Olbia, Sector E6-7, squares 493, 473, grey clay layer, O-E-6-7-63-762, Kiev, Institute of Archaeology storeroom. Complete profile, lacking edge of rim, one handle and part of foot. WSl decoration on neck (astragal) and shoulder (necklace) painted in slip paint and painted over with white (reels in white only and therefore preserved only as shadows). WT 0.4, ⌀ ca. 12 (reconstructed); vessel H at least 17 cm. Fabric: relatively fine and micaceous, many small lime inclusions, some voids, 5YR 6/6. Thin dull coat, 7.5YR 3/1. Not too hard fired, oxidized. Rim frieze: Ionian kyma. Main decoration: acanthus A repeated four times; in between the acanthus, garland E suspended from *tainia* tied in a bow; over the garland, rosette F; below the garland, heraldic dolphins (A and B) flanking tip of lotus petal; between acanthus and garland, winged 'bud'. Medallion: surrounded by two ridges; Meter bust right; signed KIRBEI.
– Samojlova 1984, fig. 4.7.

KYB-326*
Olbia, necropolis, O-1901-3070/inv. Ол-519, St Petersburg, State Hermitage Museum. Complete profile, lacking some fragments;

separately applied foot lost but documented by faint line across decoration. ⌀ rim 12.3, ⌀ base 3.8; vessel H 14.5. Fabric: relatively fine and micaceous, many small lime inclusions, some voids, Gley 1 5/N, core 5Y 8/1. Dull coat, 2.5Y 4/1, 10YR 4/2. Medium hard fired, oxidized. Stacked in firing. Multiple rim friezes: stylized myrtle(?) wreath left; astragal. Calyx: slender palm frond A alternating with column B, above which stand a feline and square plaques with draped human figure; above these, kantharos A (ii) alternating with rosette D and Medusa heads and with birds A and C as space-fillers. Medallion: surrounded by three ridges; Meter bust right; signed [...]BE[...]. The amphora is a hybrid, with the moulded rim of Attic amphorae and the strap handles with rotellae (and presumably the foot) of Pergamene vessels. Same shape as KYB-323.
– Farmakovskij 1903a, 58, fig. 64; Farmakovskij 1903b, 18, fig. 35; IIMK RAN photo archive neg. II 17935.

KYB-327*
Olbia or Pantikapaion, Buračkov 173b, Moscow, State Historical Museum (Buračkov collection). Fr. of base and lower body. Separately applied foot has been lost but its location is revealed by discolouration of lower part of vessel. ⌀ base 3.5. Oxidized. Calyx: tall ovoid lotus petal B; between petals, birds A and B; over calyx, suspended wreath tied with *tainia*. Medallion: surrounded by two ridges; Meter bust right; signed KIRBEI.
– Žuravlev & Žuravleva 2014, 258, figs. 4.2, 5.1.

Closed Vessel

KYB-328
Olbia, Sector R25, O-P25-98-86, Parutine, Olbia National Preserve storeroom. Fr. of upper body. H 3.1 × W 2.8, WT 0.35. Fabric: relatively fine and micaceous, 5YR 5/8. Thin pitted coat with slight metallic lustre, ext. 7.5YR 2.5/1, uncoated int. Hard fired, oxidized. Main decoration: Eros D var. with nebris, kantharos B, wing of another Eros. Secondarily burnt.

KYB-329
Erlangen, Antikensammlung der Friedrich-Alexander-Universität.
– Parlasca & Boss 2000, 27 cat. 35; Zimmer 2005, 90 n. 60.

POSSIS: SIGNED AND ATTRIBUTED

BOWLS

A   *Calyx with Figural Decoration*

Amazonomachy

KYB-330*
Olbia, V.I. 4942, Antikensammlung, Staatliche Museen zu Berlin (formerly Vogell collection). Complete. ⌀ rim 13; vessel H 8; H:⌀ 1:1.6. Fabric: medium fine, micaceous, 5YR 6/8. Dull coat, mottled, ext. 7.5YR 4/2, 3/1, int. 2.5YR 4/6. Oxidized. Rim frieze: dots. Main decoration: over low calyx of alternating rhomboidal and ovoid petals (B and E) but not separated from it, Amazonomachy with Amazon A, Amazon D, Amazon A, horseman C, Amazon B, Amazon D, Amazon A, Amazon B, Amazon D, horseman C, Amazon D; all the Amazons are of stamp generation (ii). Medallion: surrounded by two ridges; Meter bust right; signed POSSIDOS. Very sloppily made transition from moulded part to handmade rim.
– Zahn 1908, 68 n. 24; Neugebauer 1932, 190.

Aulos-Playing Herdsman and Tree

KYB-331*
Mesambria, necropolis, 2008 Tomb 54, Nessebar, Archaeological Museum. Complete. Rim frieze: Ionian kyma, rounded with double outline. Calyx: two pairs of slender, curved acanthus leaves (D and E); between these, Eros B; outside these, tree A set between tip of acanthus G; over the latter, alternating aulos-playing herdsman and Eros K; over the scenes, flying Eros O alternating with rosette E. Medallion: surrounded by single broad ridge; very crude Meter bust right; signed POSSIDOS.

KYB-332*
Olbia, Sector NGS, O-НГС-92-8, Parutine, Olbia National Preserve storeroom. Fr. of upper body. H 4.3 × W 5.3, WT 0.4. Fabric: relatively fine and micaceous, 7.5YR 6/4. Dull coat, 2.5YR 4/3. Medium hard fired, oxidized. Main decoration: aulos-playing herdsman, tree A.

KYB-333*
Istros, His-B 447/V 19463, Bucharest, Institute of Archaeology storeroom. Body fr. H 2.5 × W 2.5. Fabric: very micaceous, 5YR 6/8. Slightly lustrous, 5YR 4/4. Medium hard fired, oxidized. Main decoration: aulos-playing herdsman with fluttering mantle, part of acanthus leaf (type?).

– Casan-Franga 1967, fig. 4.5; Domăneanţu 2000, 92 cat. 439, pl. 30.

KYB-334*
Olbia, Sector NGS, House III-3 B 368/104, O-НГС-93-681, Parutine, Olbia National Preserve storeroom. Fr. of lower body. H 5.2 × W 5.2, WT 0.35–0.58. Fabric: relatively fine and micaceous, many small lime inclusions, many voids, 5YR 6/6. Thin firm coat with slight lustre, 10YR 3/1, 2.5YR 5/4. Medium hard fired, oxidized. Stacked in firing. Calyx: acanthus K, lily (iii) on thin undulating stem, tree A with flower, bird F (ii) sits in tree. Cf. Rotroff 2003, 113–114 cats. 460, 461, pl. 79 and p. 94 with discussion of the bud and its relationship to Pergamene production.
– Guldager Bilde 2010, 281 cat. F-62, pl. 179 (erroneously identified as Pergamene).

KYB-335
Thasos, present whereabouts unknown. Fr. of base and mid-body. Main decoration: tree A, acanthus D, Eros F. Medallion: surrounded by one ridge; signed [...]SIDOS.
– Ghali-Kahil 1960, 133 cat. 11, pl. LIX.11; Laumonier 1977, 407 n. 1.

Mantled Dancing Women

KYB-336*
Olbia, Sector E6, square 410, grey clay layer, O-E6-56-1232, Kiev, Institute of Archaeology storeroom. Body fr. H 4.3 × W 5, WT 0.4. Fabric: relatively fine and micaceous, many small lime inclusions, some voids, 5YR 6/8. Coat with slight metallic sheen, ext. 2.5YR 4/6, 3/1, int. 2.5YR 4/6. Relatively hard fired, oxidized. Stacked in firing. Calyx: acanthus F, over which stands mantled dancing woman (ii); pendent bud with 'collar' as space-filler.

Dolphins

KYB-337*
Olbia, Sector E6, square 250, 251w, Depression "O", O-E6-56-619, Kiev, Institute of Archaeology storeroom. Two large joining frs. of rim and body. H 8.5 × W 10.2, WT 0.25, ⌀ rim 14, 23%, RH 2.4. Fabric: relatively coarse, large lime inclusions, 5YR 6/6. Thin dull coat, ext. 5YR 4/1, 3/1, int. 5YR 4/1, 3/1, 4/4. Medium hard fired, oxidized. Rim frieze: minute Ionian kyma. Main decoration: dolphins C and D heraldic around palmette B, alternating with acanthus I; below dolphins, Pan mask with long beard.
– Kovalenko 1989, 374 cat. 37.

KYB-338*
Olbia, Sector AGD, O-АГД-82-195, Parutine, Olbia National Preserve storeroom. Fr. of rim and upper body. H 5.6 × W 6.3, WT 0.35–0.4, ⌀ rim 12, 12%, RH 3. Fabric: relatively fine, minute

lime inclusions, small mica flecks. Thin dull coat. Oxidized. Stacked in firing. Rim friezes: grooves; Ionian kyma, rounded with double outline. Main decoration: heraldic dolphins (A and B). Secondarily burnt.

Dancing Silenos

KYB-339*
Istros, His-1136, Bucharest, Institute of Archaeology storeroom. Body fr. H 4.7 × W 5.3, WT 0.43. Fabric: relatively fine and micaceous, many small lime inclusions, many voids, 7.5YR 7/6. Dull coat, 7.5YR 3/2. Medium hard fired, oxidized. Rim frieze: fine dots. Main decoration: dancing Silenoi left (the stamp background can be seen) separated by rosette (type?) over acanthus F and T.
– Domăneanţu 2000, 132 cat. 648, pl. 46.

Priapos

KYB-340*
Olbia, Sector NGS, House III-3 B 368/106, O-НГС-93-920, Parutine, Olbia National Preserve storeroom. Fr. of lower body. H 4.3 × W 3.5, WT 0.41–0.51. Fabric: relatively fine, some minute light-reflecting inclusions, many voids, 2.5YR 6/6. Thin firm dark coat, slightly lustrous int., ext. with slight bluish metallic sheen, ext. 7.5YR 3/0, int. 10YR 3/1. Medium hard fired, oxidized. Calyx: acanthus T; Priapos with long beard standing frontally and lifting up his garment to show his erect penis; above to the left a small flying Eros (P).
– Guldager Bilde 2010, 286 cat. F-107, pl. 192 (erroneously identified as Pontic).

Vases

KYB-341*
Olbia, Sector NGS, O-НГС-90-256, Parutine, Olbia National Preserve storeroom. Body fr., worn. H 2.9 × W 3.7, WT 0.39–0.52. Fabric: relatively fine and micaceous, voids, 7.5YR 6/6. Thin firm slightly lustrous coat, diluted on top of relief, ext. 5YR 3/1, int. 5YR 3/3. Medium hard fired, oxidized. Calyx: acanthus T, krater A.

Animals

KYB-342*
Olbia, Sector NGS, House IV-2 B 302/180, O-НГС-94-46, 48, Parutine, Olbia National Preserve storeroom. Joining frs. of base and body. H 7.3 × W 6, WT 0.1–0.35, ⌀ base 4. Fabric: highly micaceous, brittle, many small lime inclusions, 5YR 6/6. Thin firm diluted coat with slight lustre, mottled, top of reliefs light, ext. 5YR 3/1, 5/6, int. 5YR 4/5, 3/1. Very hard fired, oxidized. Calyx:

tall pointed lotus petals with central vein alternating with acanthus U; bird G sits on tip of acanthus; small flying Eros P as space-filler. Medallion: surrounded by two ridges; remains of Meter bust right; signed POSSI[...]. One repair hole.
– Guldager Bilde 2010, 287 cat. F-120, pl. 194 (erroneously identified as Pontic).

Drooping Buds

KYB-343*
Istros, His-Dup-[2], in the possession of P. Dupont. Body fr. Oxidized. Calyx: acanthus T surrounded by kantharos B, winged drooping bud and rosette E.

KYB-344*
Olbia, Sector E6, square 425, ash pit in Room Sector E, O-E6-57-1259+1259[a]+1259[b–d], 1261, Kiev, Institute of Archaeology storeroom. Complete profile; three joining frs. of rim and body; two non-joining body frs. and a base. WT 0.35, ⌀ rim 13, 50%, RH 1.7, ⌀ base 4; vessel H 7.8; H:⌀ 1:1.7. Fabric: relatively fine and micaceous, many small lime inclusions, some voids, 5YR 7/6. Mottled coat, partly worn off, partly with dull lustre, ext. 2.5YR 3/4, 3/1, int. 2.5YR 3/1. Medium hard fired, oxidized. Rim frieze: heart guilloche left. Calyx: tall pointed lotus petal A alternating with palmette D and acanthus I; Eros M and N alternating as space-fillers. Medallion: surrounded by frieze of large dots outside a ridge; lower part of Meter bust right; signed POSSID[...]. Two repair holes. **KYB-367*** is very similar, though without the Erotes.

Eros/Dog

KYB-345*
Olbia, Sector NGS, O-НГС-02-300, Parutine, Olbia National Preserve storeroom. Fr. of rim and upper body. H 5.3 × W 6.6, WT 0.2–0.4, ⌀ rim 12, 14%, RH 2.4. Fabric: coarse and micaceous, many small lime inclusions and stones thicker than the wall itself, up to 0.44–0.6 cm, 5YR 6/6. Thin firm dull coat, mottled, ext. 2.5YR 4/6, 3/0, int. 2.5YR 4/4, 5YR 3/1. Medium hard fired, oxidized. Stacked in firing. Rim frieze: heart guilloche left. Calyx: ovoid lotus petal A, Eros M, dog C.

Female Toilette

KYB-346*
Olbia, Sector E6, square 415n, 410s, grey clay layer, O-E6-57-115, Kiev, Institute of Archaeology storeroom. One third of bowl; very worn. WT 0.5, ⌀ rim 13, 14%, RH 2.4. Fabric: rather coarse, micaceous, large and small lime inclusions, 5YR 7/4. Dull coat, very worn, 5YR 3/1. Low fired, oxidized. Rim frieze: astragal. Calyx: double petal with ornamented edges, over which an

'acroterion' of two large vertical double S-spirals topped with a bud, repeated four times; in between, low palmettes (difficult to distinguish) on which the following figures are placed: Eros M, naked female moving right but turning left and holding right arm to her breast, female extending a wreath with her lifted hands left; naked female pouring water into basin. Medallion: effaced. Secondarily burnt.
– Kovalenko 1989, 375 cat. 48 (attributed to Kirbeis).

Mythological (Herakles and Hydra)

KYB-347*
Olbia, Sector NGS, O-НГС-92-981, Parutine, Olbia National Preserve storeroom. Fr. of upper body, worn. H 5.1 × W 5.7, WT 0.3–0.5. Fabric: relatively fine, some small lime inclusions, many small voids, 7.5YR 6/6. Thin firm slightly lustrous coat, slightly diluted on top of relief, mottled ext., ext. 5YR 3/2, 4/6, int. 5YR 3/1. Medium hard fired, oxidized. Rim frieze: heart guilloche left. Main decoration: Herakles wearing *exomis* with club in raised right hand attacking Hydra; in between, rosettes E; above, fluttering drapery of missing figures and dog A with long tail and collar leaping right after an animal whose hind legs are preserved.

Dolphins

KYB-348*
Olbia?, inv. 54791 Uvarov 225/15, Moscow, State Historical Museum (Uvarov collection). Complete. ⌀ rim 13.6, RH 1.8, ⌀ base 3.5; vessel H 8; H:⌀ 1:1.7. Fabric: light brown (no fresh break). Coat with pinkish metallic sheen. Not too hard fired, oxidized. Rim frieze: Ionian kyma. Calyx: straight acanthus L with rosettes G (i) as space-fillers and, above these, dolphins D. Medallion: surrounded by two thin ridges; comic mask; no signature.

Masks

KYB-349
Mesambria, Tomb 4/1975, inv. 1800, Nessebar, Archaeological Museum. Complete. Calyx: acanthus I alternating with acanthus T separated by collared bud on looped stem; over the acanthus leaves, slave mask. Medallion: surrounded by one broad ridge; small pointed petals inside ridge; crude Meter bust right; signed POSSIDOS.
– Čimbuléva 2005, 106, fig. 21.

Birds

KYB-350*
Chersonesos, pit 2 (1877), X-1908-12, St Petersburg, State Hermitage Museum. Fr. of base and large part of body. H 5.3, ⌀ base 4.5. Fabric: highly micaceous, 2.5YR 5/6. Thin coat with soapy surface ext. and slight lustre, 2.5YR 4/6, 5YR 2.5/1. Oxidized. Stacked in firing. Calyx: alternating tall 'nelumbo' B filled with pine scales, tall rhomboidal leaf, and undulating stems with flower (poorly preserved), birds(?) over vegetation (upper frieze is in very low relief). Medallion: surrounded by two ridges; slave mask; signed POSSIDOS.

KYB-351*
Olbia, Tomb 5 (1928), O-1928-95+96/inv. A 2443, Nikolaev, Historical Museum. Complete; joined from many fragments. ⌀ rim 14.4, RH 2, ⌀ base 4; vessel H 8.3; H:⌀ 1:1.8. Thin brown coat. Oxidized. Rim frieze: heart guilloche left. Calyx: acanthus I alternating with tree C; over the vegetation, winged bud alternating with bird D. Medallion: surrounded by two ridges, small dart-shaped petals around the stamp; Meter bust right; signed POSSIDOS.
– St Petersburg, IIMK RAN, photo archive neg. II 13957; Zajceva 1973, pl. 53.21 (part of vessel).

KYB-352*
Olbia, Sector E2, square 55, Cistern Л, O-E2-49-121, Kiev, Institute of Archaeology storeroom. Body fr. H 5.5 × W 5.3, WT 0.3. Fabric: relatively fine and micaceous, many small lime inclusions, some voids, 5YR 6/6. Dull coat, 5YR 3/1. Relatively hard fired, oxidized. Rim frieze: heart guilloche left. Main decoration: winged drooping bud A and C over vegetation (type?).

B *Scroll*

Ivy Scroll

KYB-353*
Istros, Sector SG, His-73-76, Bucharest, Institute of Archaeology storeroom. Fr. of base and lower body. H 4.6 × W 5.8, WT 0.44, ⌀ base 5. Fabric: relatively fine and micaceous, many small lime inclusions, 2.5YR 6/8. Dull coat, ext. 5YR 4/3, int. 7.5YR 3/2. Relatively hard fired, oxidized. Main decoration: full-body ivy scroll left; scroll incised directly in the mould; ivy leaves and ivy-berry cluster B stamped; Eros P as space-filler. Medallion: surrounded by two ridges; Meter bust right; signed PO[...]; very fresh stamp.
– Dománeanțu 2000, 120, 122 cat. 604, pl. 42 (identified as Pontic).

Acanthus-Vine Scroll

KYB-354*

V.I. 30837, Antikensammlung, Staatliche Museen zu Berlin. Complete. ⌀ rim 13.8; vessel H 7.8; H:⌀ 1:1.8. Rim frieze: heart guilloche left. Main decoration: vine scroll incised directly into mould with stamped vine leaves (B) and bunches of grapes as well as birds E (ii) and G (ii). Medallion: surrounded by one ridge; outside the ridge a single row of small pointed petals with central vein; Meter bust right; signed POSSIDOS.

KYB-355*
Olbia, Sector NGS, О-НГС-90-371, 91-484, Parutine, Olbia National Preserve storeroom. Two non-joining frs. of rim and body. H 7 × W 7, WT 0.32. Fabric: relatively fine and micaceous, some small lime inclusions, 5YR 6/8. Dull coat, 5YR 3/1. Medium hard fired, oxidized. Rim frieze: heart guilloche left. Main decoration: full-body incised acanthus-vine scroll left with bunches of grapes.

KYB-356
Tanais, Tomb 65-III-131, Tanais archaeological museum. Two joining frs. of rim and upper body. Rim frieze: heart guilloche left. Main decoration: incised full-body acanthus-vine scroll with stamped bunches of grapes and vine leaves B.
– Šelov 1969, cat. 59, pl. V.59.

KYB-357*
Olbia, Sector NGS, О-НГС-04-241, Parutine, Olbia National Preserve storeroom. Body fr. H 5.3 × W 3.7, WT 0.35. Fabric: relatively fine and micaceous, 5YR 6/8. Firm slightly lustrous coat, 5YR 2.5/1. Medium hard fired, oxidized. Rim frieze: heart guilloche left. Main decoration: full-body incised acanthus-vine scroll with stamped bunch of grapes, vine leaf B, and bird D.

KYB-358
Olbia, Cliff, grey clay layer, O-68-1384, Kiev, Institute of Archaeology storeroom. Body fr. H 4.8 × W 5.3, WT 0.43. Fabric: relatively fine and micaceous, many small lime inclusions, some voids, 5YR 6/8. Thin dull coat, ext. 5YR 3/1, 5/6, int. 5YR 3/1. Medium hard fired, oxidized. Rim frieze: heart guilloche left. Main decoration: full-body incised vine scroll right with looped tendrils and stamped vine leaves B and bunch of grapes.

KYB-359*
Olbia, Sector E2, square 55, Cistern Л, O-E2-49-265, Kiev, Institute of Archaeology storeroom. Body fr. Oxidized. Main decoration: incised vine scroll left, with stamped bunch of grapes, vine leaf B, and group of three dots.

KYB-360
Olbia, Sector R25, O-P25-97-2272, Parutine, Olbia National Preserve storeroom. Fr. of rim and upper body. H 4.2 × W 4.7, WT 0.6, RH 2.1. Fabric: relatively fine and micaceous, 5YR 6/6. Thin slightly lustrous coat, almost completely worn off ext., mottled int., ext. 2.5YR 4/6, int. 2.5YR 4/6, 5YR 2.5/1. Not too hard fired, oxidized. Stacked in firing. Rim frieze: heart guilloche left, very compressed. Main decoration: bunch of grapes.

C   *Garlands and Wreaths*

Suspended Garlands

KYB-361
Phanagoreia, Tomb 66 (1950) (child burial), present whereabouts unknown. Complete. Rim frieze: heart guilloche left. Main decoration: groups of three bundled myrtle leaves placed as suspended garland; over this, Eros M repeated; below, krater B surrounded by heraldic dolphins (C and D). Medallion: surrounded by one ridge; Meter bust right; signed PO[...]. The restoration of the signature varies: Possidos or Pasideos (Marčenko 1956, 112), Posideos (Loseva 1962, 204), Posideou (Kotitsa 1998, 135); there can be no doubt that the reading should be POSSIDOS.
– Marčenko 1956, 112 (no ill.); Loseva 1962, 203, fig. 4.3, 204; Kotitsa 1998, 135.

KYB-362*
Olbia, Sector Sever-Zapad, O-C3-77-21, Parutine, Olbia National Preserve storeroom. Fr. of upper body close to rim. H 3.3 × W 3.5, WT 0.45. Fabric: relatively fine, slightly micaceous, abundant small lime inclusions, 5YR 6/8. Thin dull coat ext., int. with slight lustre, ext. 7.5YR 2.5/1, int. 7.5YR 2.5/2. Not too hard fired, oxidized. Rim frieze: heart guilloche left. Main decoration: two bows, possibly tip of garland suspended from them.

D   *Vegetal Decoration*

Calyx

KYB-363*
Olbia, Tomb 95, O-1901-3066/inv. Ол-17718, St Petersburg, State Hermitage Museum. Complete. WT 0.4, ⌀ rim 13, ⌀ base 3.8; vessel H 8.5; H:⌀ 1:1.5. Fabric: fine, highly micaceous, a few minute lime inclusions, some small voids, 5YR 7/4. Dull coat, 5YR 5/4, 5/6, 3/1. Medium hard fired, oxidized. Rim frieze: Ionian kyma, pointed with double outline. Calyx: 'nelumbo' A and D alternating. Medallion: surrounded by single row of small pointed petals outside two ridges; comic mask; no signature. Very similar: **KYB-364***, though without looped stems
– Farmakovskij 1903a, 47, fig. 46; St Petersburg, IIMK RAN, photo archive neg. II 17932.

KYB-364*
Pantikapaion, M-65-122, Moscow, Puškin Museum of Fine Arts, inv. KP 294447. Three joining frs. of base and lower body. H 8.7, WT 0.4, ⌀ base 3.5. Fabric: micaceous, reddish-brown. Thin dull red-brown coat. Hard fired, oxidized. Stacked in firing. Calyx: 'nelumbo' A and D alternating, separated by flower on looped stem. Medallion: surrounded by two ridges; comic mask; no signature. Very similar: KYB-363*, though with looped stems

KYB-365*
Olbia, Sector E6-7, squares 412w, 417w, ash layer, O-E6-7-61-407, Kiev, Institute of Archaeology storeroom. Body fr. H 5.4 × W 4.5, WT 0.48. Fabric: coarse, very large lime inclusions erupting, 10YR 7/6. Dull coat, ext. 2.5YR 4/8, 3/1, int. 2.5YR 4/8. Medium hard fired, oxidized. Stacked in firing. Calyx: 'nelumbo' B alternating with acanthus L separated by wavy stem.

KYB-366
Olbia, O-1901-no no. [D], present whereabouts unknown. Fr. of rim and upper body. Rim frieze: heart guilloche right. Calyx: tip of 'nelumbo' B.
– St Petersburg, IIMK RAN, photo archive neg. III 3052.

KYB-367*
Olbia, Sector NGS, O-НГС-03-291, Kiev, Institute of Archaeology storeroom. Complete; joined from several frs.; lacking a few minor sherds. Rim frieze: astragal. Calyx: tall pointed lotus petal A alternating with palmette D and acanthus I. Medallion: surrounded by low ridge, around the stamp an astragal frieze; Meter bust right; signed POSSIDOS. Many repair holes. KYB-344* is very similar, but with Erotes.

KYB-368
Smyrna(?), inv. CA 1102[a], Paris, Louvre, donation by P. Gaudin. Fr. of base and lower body. Calyx: acanthus I alternating with acanthus T. Medallion: surrounded by two ridges; Meter bust right; signed [...]DOS.
– Laumonier 1977, 407 n. 1.

KYB-369
Tyras, present whereabouts unknown, Belgorod? Fr. of base and lower body. Calyx: acanthus I. Medallion: surrounded by two ridges; top of Meter's crown; signed [...]SI[...].
– Batizat 2002, fig. 10.1.

KYB-370*
Olbia, Sector R25, O-P25-95-1165, Parutine, Olbia National Preserve storeroom. Fr. of lower body. H 4.7 × W 6.2, WT 0.42. Fabric: medium coarse, micaceous, small lime inclusions, small stones, many voids, 5YR 5/6. Thin dull coat, 5YR 3/1. Medium hard fired, oxidized. Calyx: acanthus I alternating with lotus petals A; in between, dotted stem with lily (ii).

KYB-371*
Olbia, O-1909-4397, St Petersburg, State Hermitage Museum. Complete. ⌀ rim 13.2, ⌀ base 3.5; vessel H 8; H:⌀ 1:1.7. Fabric: coarse, very large lime inclusions erupting, 5YR 6/6. Dull coat, ext. 5YR 4/1, int. 5YR 3/2. Relatively hard fired, oxidized. Rim frieze: Ionian kyma, rounded with double outline. Calyx: palmette C alternating with tree B. Medallion: surrounded by low frieze of lotus petal B; Meter Bust right; signed POSSIDOS. Nine repair holes; the clamp is still present in one hole.

KYB-372
Istros, His-A 316, Bucharest, Institute of Archaeology storeroom. Fr. of base and lower body. H 3.5 × W 6, WT 0.35. Fabric: relatively fine and micaceous, many small lime inclusions, many voids, 5YR 6/6. Dull coat, almost completely worn off, 5YR 3/1. Medium hard fired, oxidized. Calyx: acanthus T alternating probably with lotus petal C. Medallion: surrounded by one ridge; signed [...]DOS.
– Domăneanțu 2000, 136 cat. 672, pl. 48.

KYB-373*
Olbia, Sector NGS, House II-1 R 156/7, O-НГС-87-817, Parutine, Olbia National Preserve storeroom. Fr. of base and lower body. H 4.2 × W 4.1, WT 0.2–0.45, ⌀ base 5. Fabric: relatively fine, some mica and small lime inclusions, small voids, 7.5YR 6/4. Thin diluted coat leaving top of relief decoration a lighter colour, 10YR 3/1. Hard fired, oxidized. Calyx: acanthus T alternating with two vegetal(?) elements. Medallion: surrounded by two ridges; tiny part of Meter bust; signed POS[...].
– Guldager Bilde 2010, 287 cat. F-119, pl. 194 (erroneously identified as Pontic).

KYB-374
Provenance unknown, inv. M 582, Bruxelles, Musées Royaux (Cinquantenaire, ex-collection Misthos). Fr. of base and large part of body. Calyx: tall lotus petal A separated by incised wavy stem; bud/flower not preserved. Medallion: two ridges; Meter bust right; signed POSSIDOS.
– CVA Brussels, Musées Royaux (Cinquantenaire) 3 [Belgium 3], III N, pl. 4 (142).33.

KYB-375
Vicinity of Smyrna, inv. CA 1108, Paris, Louvre. Base fr. and tiny part of lower body. Calyx: remains of small triangular petal around medallion. Medallion: surrounded by two ridges; Meter bust right; signed POSSIDOS.
– Laumonier 1977, 407 n. 1.

KYB-376*
Olbia, Sector NGS, O-НГС-92-91, Parutine, Olbia National Preserve storeroom. Fr. of base and lower body. H 5.7 × W 6, WT 0.4, ⌀ base 3. Fabric: relatively fine and micaceous, abundant small lime inclusions, 5YR 7/6. Thin dull coat, 2.5YR 4/3. Low fired, oxidized. Calyx: tips of petals and leaves. Medallion: surrounded by two ridges; between the ridges a crude astragal; crude Meter bust right; signed POSSIDOS.

KYB-377
Myrmekion, M-57-218, St Petersburg, IIMK RAN. Fr. of rim and upper body. H 5.8, WT 0.55, ⌀ rim 13. Fabric: relatively fine and micaceous, slightly sandy, 5YR 6/8. Thin coat with slight metallic sheen, 5YR 2.5/1. Oxidized. Rim frieze: heart guilloche left between shallow grooves. Calyx: small ovoid petals alternating with acanthus (type?).

KYB-378
Olbia, Sector NGS, House IV-2 B 280/160, O-НГС-90-218, Parutine, Olbia National Preserve storeroom. Fr. of rim and upper body. H 4.6 × W 6, WT 0.5–0.52, ⌀ rim 13, 13%, RH 3. Fabric: relatively coarse and micaceous, numerous minute line inclusions as well as some large ones, up to more than 4 mm, popping off and giving a pitted surface, many large and small voids, 7.5YR 7/4. Relatively thick, firm coat, slightly blotchy ext. with bluish silvery sheen, ext. mostly 10YR 3/1. Medium hard fired, oxidized. Rim frieze: heart guilloche left. Main decoration: lily?
– Guldager Bilde 2010, 287 cat. F-117, pl. 194 (erroneously identified as Pontic).

KYB-379
Olbia, Sector R25, O-P25-98-84, Parutine, Olbia National Preserve storeroom. Rim fr. H 4.1 × W 4.5, WT 0.4. Fabric: relatively fine and micaceous, many small lime inclusions, some voids, 5YR 6/8. Thin dull coat, mottled, ext. 2.5YR 5/6, 5/8, 3/1, int. 2.5YR 4/4, 3/1. Medium hard fired, oxidized. Stacked in firing. Rim frieze: heart guilloche left. Calyx: tip of slender palm frond.

E   *Linear Decoration*

Pendent-Semicircle Design

KYB-380*
Istros, His-85, Bucharest, Institute of Archaeology storeroom. Fr. of rim and body. H 6 × W 6.3, WT 0.45, ⌀ rim 14, 14%, RH 1.9. Fabric: relatively fine and micaceous, many small lime inclusions, some voids, 5YR 6/6. Dull coat, mottled, 2.5YR 4/4, 3/1. Relatively hard fired, oxidized. Stacked in firing. Rim frieze: heart guilloche left. Main decoration: PSC pattern; sun wheel at centre of semicircles; field surrounding semicircles filled with crude dots. Probably Possis because of the character of the rim pattern.
– Domăneanțu 2000, 106 cat. 535, pl. 35.

KYB-381*
Olbia, Sector NGS, House IV-2 B 302/180, O-НГС-94-45, Parutine, Olbia National Preserve storeroom. Fr. of upper body. Oxidized. Rim frieze: grooves. Main decoration: sun wheel, probably fill inside PSC.
– Guldager Bilde 2010, 287 cat. F-115, pl. 193 (erroneously identified as Pontic).

Net pattern

KYB-382*
Olbia, Sector E6–7, squares 597e, 607e, humus, O-E6-7-63-1487, Kiev, Institute of Archaeology storeroom. Body fr. H 5 × W 6.2, WT 0.3. Fabric: relatively fine and micaceous, abundant lime, 7.5YR 7/6. Dull coat, 7.5YR 2.5/1. Relatively hard fired, oxidized. Rim frieze: heart guilloche left. Main decoration: net pattern made with dots.

Isolated Plastic Long Petals in Calyx with Figural Decoration

KYB-383*
Olbia, Sector AGD, Bothros 11, O-АГД-88-204+205, Kiev, Institute of Archaeology storeroom. Three joining frs. of rim and body, one non-joining body fr. and one large non-joining rim fr. H 9 × W 7.3, WT 0.4, ⌀ rim 13, 13%, RH 2.5. Fabric: relatively fine and micaceous, many small lime inclusions, some voids, 5YR 6/6. Dull coat, 2.5YR 4/4, 7.5YR 3/1. Relatively hard fired, oxidized. Stacked in firing. Rim frieze: heart guilloche left. Main decoration: isolated plastic long petals alternating with acanthus I and broad 'nelumbo' E with segmented central vein; small pointed petals as space-filler; above these, bird D and bird E; on 'nelumbo' stands a one-handled jug. Secondarily burnt. Identical in decoration and shape: **KYB-384**.
– Rusjaeva & Nazarčuk 2006, pl. 193.12, 16.

KYB-384
Theodosia, inv. 32733, Moscow, State Historical Museum (Berthier de la Garde collection). Fr. of rim and upper body. H 6.3 × W 6, WT 0.6, RH 2.2. Fabric: no fresh break for observation. Coat with metallic sheen. Rim frieze: heart guilloche left. Main decoration: isolated plastic long petals alternating with acanthus(?) and broad 'nelumbo' E with segmented central vein; small pointed petals as space-filler; above these, bird D and Eros P; on 'nelumbo' stands a one-handled jug. Identical in decoration and shape: **KYB-383***.

KYB-385*
Olbia, Sector I, grey clay layer, О-И-48-2057, Kiev, Institute of Archaeology storeroom. Fr. of rim and body. H 5.2 × W 4, WT 0.42, RH 2.8. Fabric: relatively fine and micaceous, many small lime inclusions, some voids, 5YR 5/8. Dull coat ext., int. slightly lustrous, 2.5YR 4/8, 4/4. Relatively hard fired, oxidized. Stacked in firing. Rim frieze: heart guilloche left. Main decoration: sitting birds E and F heraldic around isolated plastic long petal. Probably from a bowl with the same pattern as KYB-383* and KYB-384.

Isolated Stylized Long Petals in Calyx of Acanthus S

KYB-386*
Olbia, Sector E6, square 405, grey clay layer, O-E6-56-270, 617, Kiev, Institute of Archaeology storeroom. Large fr. of rim and body, non-joining body fr. H 6.5 × W 7.5, WT 0.35, ⌀ rim 14, 13%, RH 2.8. Fabric: relatively fine and micaceous, many small lime inclusions, some voids, 5YR 6/6. Dull mottled coat, ext. 2.5YR 4/6, 8/6, 4/2, int. 2.5YR 4/6, 8/6. Relatively hard fired, oxidized. Stacked in firing. Rim frieze: heart guilloche left. Main decoration: isolated stylized long petal alternating with acanthus S; dolphins C and D flank the long petals heraldically; between tails of dolphins, rosette C. Even though acanthus S is employed, which is normally used by Kirbeis, the decoration of this vessel, including the rim pattern, has more the character of Possis' hand.
– Kovalenko 1989, 375 cat. 40.

KYB-387*
Olbia, Sector NGS, О-НГС-00-48, Parutine, Olbia National Preserve storeroom. Fr. of lower body. H 3.7 × W 4.1, WT 0.35–0.38. Fabric: relatively fine and micaceous, a few minute lime inclusions, some small voids, 5YR 6/4. Thin firm slightly lustrous coat, ext. 10YR 3/1, int. 10YR 3/2. Hard fired, oxidized. Calyx: acanthus S alternating with plastic long petal(?). Attributed to Possis because KYB-386* features the same combination of acanthus S and a stylized long petal.

F *Base Fragments*

KYB-388
Tyras, present whereabouts unknown, Belgorod? Base fr. Medallion: surrounded by two ridges, around the stamp a single row of small pointed petals with central vein; Meter bust right; signed POSSIDOS. Samojlova's reading as Poseidos, turning the second lunate sigma into an epsilon, is probably mistaken.
– Samojlova 1984, 124, 125, fig. 3.7 (identified as Samian).

KYB-389
Olbia, O-1929-898, present whereabouts unknown. Fr. of base and lower body. Calyx: base of unidentified vegetation. Medallion: surrounded by two ridges; signed POSSID[...].
– St Petersburg, IIMK RAN, photo archive neg. II 4829.

KYB-390*
Pantikapaion, M-70-672, Moscow, Puškin Museum of Fine Arts. Fr. of base and lower body. H 3 × W 4. Oxidized. Calyx: unidentified traces. Medallion: surrounded by two ridges; signed POS[...].
– Laumonier 1977, 407 n. 1; AGSP 1984, pl. CLXIII.8a.

G *Rim Fragments*

Multiple Rim Friezes

KYB-391*
Istros, His-1927-1942-V 8574 X, Bucharest, Institute of Archaeology storeroom. Body fr. close to rim. Oxidized. Multiple rim friezes: heart guilloche left; horizontal S-spirals. Attributed to Possis because of the character of the heart guilloche, but this is the only fragment with multiple rim friezes which can be coupled with him.

Single Rim Frieze: Heart Guilloche, Left

KYB-392
Olbia, Sector NGS, О-НГС-86-914, Parutine, Olbia National Preserve storeroom. Rim fr. Oxidized.

KYB-393*
Olbia, Sector Sever-Zapad, О-СЗ-68-1889, Parutine, Olbia National Preserve storeroom. Rim fr. H 4.8 × W 6, WT 0.55, ⌀ rim 13, 9%, RH 3.4. Fabric: relatively coarse and micaceous, some lime, 10YR 6/4. Thin coat with slight metallic sheen ext., duller int., 10YR 3/1. Relatively hard fired, oxidized.

KYB-394*
Olbia, Sector AGD, О-АГД-87-1028a, Kiev, Institute of Archaeology storeroom. Rim fr. H 3.6 × W 5.8, WT 0.38, ⌀ rim 14, 14%, RH 2.4. Fabric: relatively fine and micaceous, many small lime inclusions, some voids, 5YR 5/6. Thin dull coat, 7.5YR 2.5/1, 5YR 4/6. Relatively hard fired, oxidized. Stacked in firing.

KYB-395*
Istros, His-V 19336, Bucharest, Institute of Archaeology storeroom. Rim fr. H 3.6 × W 3, WT 0.4, RH 2.3. Fabric: relatively fine and micaceous, many small lime inclusions, some voids, 5YR 6/6. Coat with slight lustre, very worn, 7.5YR 3/1. Medium hard fired, oxidized.

KYB-396
Pantikapaion, M-56-1413, Moscow, Puškin Museum of Fine Arts. Rim fr. H 4.5 × W 3.5, RH 2. Oxidized.
– Kovalenko 1989, 374 cat. 30.

KYB-397
Olbia, Sector NGS, O-НГС-08-185, Parutine, Olbia National Preserve storeroom. Rim fr. Oxidized.

KYB-398
Olbia, Sector NGS, O-НГС-06-598, Parutine, Olbia National Preserve storeroom. Rim fr. Oxidized.

KYB-399*
Istros, His-1927-1942-V 8569 L, Bucharest, Institute of Archaeology storeroom. Rim fr. Oxidized.

KYB-400
Istros, His-1927-1942-V 8573 G, Bucharest, Institute of Archaeology storeroom. Rim fr. Oxidized.

KYB-401
Istros, His-816, Bucharest, Institute of Archaeology storeroom. Rim fr. Oxidized.

KYB-402
Istros, Sector "Pescărie", His-63-39, Bucharest, Institute of Archaeology storeroom. Body fr. close to rim. Oxidized.

KYB-403
Istros, His-177, Bucharest, Institute of Archaeology storeroom. Body fr. close to rim. Oxidized.

KYB-404
Istros, His-V 19313[a], Bucharest, Institute of Archaeology storeroom. Rim fr. Oxidized.

KYB-405*
Istros, His-220, Bucharest, Institute of Archaeology storeroom. Rim fr. Oxidized.

KYB-406
Istros, His-297, Bucharest, Institute of Archaeology storeroom. Body fr. close to rim. Oxidized.

KYB-407
Istros, His-1057, Bucharest, Institute of Archaeology storeroom. Body fr. close to rim. Oxidized.

KYB-408
Istros, His-438, Bucharest, Institute of Archaeology storeroom. Body fr. close to rim. Oxidized.

KYB-409
Olbia, Sector E, square 66 (119?), grey clay layer, O-E-49-3115, Kiev, Institute of Archaeology storeroom. Rim fr. Oxidized.

KYB-410
Olbia, Cliff, O-68-1281, Kiev, Institute of Archaeology storeroom. Rim fr. Oxidized.

SUPPLEMENTARY SHAPES

Small Bowl

KYB-411*
Olbia, Sector E6, square 415e, yellow clay layer, O-E6-56-993, Kiev, Institute of Archaeology storeroom. Two large joining frs. of rim and bowl; almost half preserved. H 6.2 × W 8, WT 0.4, ⌀ rim 8, 37%, RH 1.7. Fabric: relatively fine and micaceous, many small lime inclusions, some voids, 5YR 6/8. Coat with dull shine, 5YR 4/1. Medium hard fired, oxidized. Rim frieze: heart guilloche right. Calyx: palmette E, dolphins (iii) heraldic around palmette F. Medallion: tiny part of ridge surrounding base preserved.

ZENODOTOS: SIGNED AND ATTRIBUTED

BOWLS

A   *Figural Decoration*

Calyx with Figural Decoration

KYB-412*
Olbia, Sector AGD, О-АГД-87-925+926, Kiev, Institute of Archaeology storeroom. Complete profile, lacking one-fourth of bowl; consists of three large rim frs., a body and a base fr., all joining. ⌀ rim 12.9, 75%, RH 2.7; vessel H 7.6; H:⌀ 1:1.7. Fabric: no break for observation (vessel is reconstructed). Thin dull cracking coat, ext. 5YR 4/2, 3/1, int. 5YR 4/2. Not too hard fired, oxidized. Stacked in firing. Rim frieze: ridges. Calyx: 'nelumbo' C alternating with lily (iii) on looped stems; over these, dolphins D. Medallion: surrounded by two ridges; crowned female, left; signed [...]E[...]O[...].
– Rusjaeva & Nazarčuk 2006, pl. 193.10, 11; pl. 194.1.

B   *Suspended Garlands*

KYB-413*
South Russia (Olbia?), inv. AI 15, Köln, University Collection (formerly collection of G. Windscheid, German consul in Odessa to Köln in 1931). Complete. ⌀ rim 12.6, ⌀ base 4.2; vessel H 8.3; H:⌀ 1:1.5. Fabric: micaceous, some lime inclusions. Thin pinkish red wash, slightly brown at rim ext. and on int. Oxidized. Rim frieze: large dots. Main decoration: garland G alternating with rosette G (i) repeated eight times. Calyx: straight acanthus T alternating with isolated plastic long petals repeated six times; calyx not separated from frieze. Medallion: surrounded by two ridges; crowned female head left; signed [...]ODO[...]O[...]. Identical acanthus and garland stamps on **KYB-414**.
– Berger 1993, 271–272, inv. AI 15, fig. 74.

KYB-414
Olbia, Tomb 2, O-1900-3247, present whereabouts unknown. Complete. Rim frieze: groove. Main decoration: bound garland G; bow made with punch of plastic long petal upside-down. Calyx: straight acanthus U. Medallion: rosette with eight petals surrounded by two ridges. Frieze separators: astragal. Identical acanthus and garland stamps on **KYB-413***.
– Farmakovskij 1902, 12, fig. 24; St Petersburg, IIMK RAN, photo archive neg. II 18586.

C   *Vegetal Decoration*

Calyx

KYB-415
Tyras, present whereabouts unknown, Belgorod? Complete. Rim friezes: ridges; Ionian kyma. Calyx: palmette B(?) alternating with lotus petal A; lily or bud free-floating as space-filler. Medallion: surrounded by two ridges; crowned female bust left; signed ZE[...]ODO[...].
– Samojlova 1984, 124–125, fig. 3.8 (identified as Samian); attribution PGB.

KYB-416*
Istros, His-178, Bucharest, Institute of Archaeology storeroom. Fr. of base and lower body. H 6 × W 6.7, WT 0.48, ⌀ base 3.5. Fabric: micaceous, abundant small lime inclusions, 7.5YR 6/6. Dull coat, mottled, ext. 7.5YR 3/1, int. 7.5YR 4/3. Hard fired, oxidized. Calyx: acanthus Q alternating with acanthus I. Medallion: surrounded by two ridges; female bust with low crown left; signed ZENODOTOU (TOU retrograde).
– Domăneanțu 2000, 123 cat. 606, pl. 42 (identified as Pontic).

KYB-417
Smyrna(?), inv. CA 1106[a], Paris, Louvre. Base fr. with tiny part of lower body. Calyx: end of incised, wavy stem. Medallion: surrounded by one ridge; female head with low crown left; signed [...]DO[...].

KYB-418*
Pantikapaion, year and number unknown, Kerč History and Culture Reserve inv.(?). Fr. of base and lower body. Calyx: type cannot be identified. Medallion: surrounded by ridge; crowned female head left; signed ZENO[...]O[...].
– Žuravlev & Žuravleva 2014, 258, figs. 2.4, 3.4.

KYB-419
Petuchovka (Gute Maritzyn), Olbia's chora, Tomb 2S, present whereabouts unknown. Complete. ⌀ rim 13. Rim frieze cannot be identified from photograph. Calyx: upper frieze with ovoid petal A growing out of vegetal calyx; lower frieze: calyx of imbricate lotus petal A. Medallion: surrounded by two ridges; female bust with low crown left; signed ZENODO[...]O[...]. Repair holes mentioned in publication.
– Ebert 1913, 60, fig. 62; 62, fig. 65; Zajceva 1973, pl. 53.21.

KYB-420*
Olbia, Sector NGS, O-НГС-96-13, Parutine, Olbia National Preserve storeroom. Fr. of lower body; worn and pitted inside.

H 4.5 × W 4.7, WT 0.35–0.72. Fabric: fine, dense, micaceous, a few minute lime inclusions, some small voids, 7.5YR 6/4. Thin firm slightly lustrous coat, diluted on top of reliefs, mottled ext., ext. 10YR 3/1, 5YR 3/4, int. 10YR 3/2. Medium hard fired, oxidized. Stacked in firing. Calyx: imbricate lotus petal A. Identical to **KYB-419**, which is signed, and therefore attributed to Zenodotos

KYB-421*
Olbia, Sector NGS, House III-3 B 368/102, O-НГС-93-123, Parutine, Olbia National Preserve storeroom. Body fr., very worn. H 4.1 × W 4.3, WT 0.35–0.42. Fabric: relatively fine, slightly micaceous, small lime inclusions, small voids, bicolour from stacking. Thin dull coat, ext. 5Y 3/5, int. 2.5YR 4/4. Medium hard fired, oxidized. Stacked in firing. Rim frieze: heart guilloche right. Calyx: lotus petal A growing out of calyx; palmette? Identical to **KYB-419**, which is signed, and therefore attributed to Zenodotos.
– Guldager Bilde 2010, 287 cat. F-121, pl. 195 (erroneously identified as Pontic).

KYB-422*
Olbia, Sector NGS, O-НГС-92-982, Parutine, Olbia National Preserve storeroom. Fr. of lower body; very worn, completely pitted. H 3.5 × W 5.35, WT 0.25–0.4. Fabric: fine, slightly micaceous, a few minute lime inclusions, many small voids, 10YR 6/3. Thin slightly lustrous coat, almost completely worn off, 5Y 2.5/1. Hard fired, oxidized. Main decoration: rosette with concave petals? Calyx: pointed lotus petals. Resembles **KYB-419**, which is signed, and therefore attributed to Zenodotos

ZENODOULES: SIGNED

BOWL

KYB-423
Tomis, Tomb 41, inv. 498, ex-Constanta Museum; according to Livia Buzioanu, in Bucharest, Institute of Archaeology storeroom (not found).
Complete. Rim frieze: spirals. Main decoration: cannot be identified from published photograph; around the base, dolphins D. Medallion: surrounded by two ridges; crude Meter bust right; stamp surrounded by small pointed petals; signed ZENOD/OULES in square stamp on body of vessel. Frieze separators: dots.
– Bucovală 1967, 65 cat. C, 122, fig. 79c; Ocheşeanu 1969, 228–232 cat. 16, figs. 23–27.

PROBABLY METER MEDALLION WORKSHOP: UNATTRIBUTED

BOWLS

A Bases with Meter Bust but No Signature

A small group of four vessels have a Meter bust surrounded by one or two ridges with a very wide diameter and apparently no signature

KYB-424*
Olbia, Sector E6-7, square 580, room, grey clay layer, O-E6-7-63-69, Kiev, Institute of Archaeology storeroom. Fr. of base and lower body. H 7.8 × W 7.5, WT 0.3, ⌀ base 4. Fabric: relatively fine and micaceous, some small lime inclusions, 2.5YR 6/6. Dull wash, ext. 2.5YR 5/4, 3/1, int. 2.5YR 4/2. Relatively hard fired, oxidized. Stacked in firing. Main decoration: slender lotus petals separated by incised wavy stems. Medallion: large base surrounded by two ridges; top of Meter bust (crown and hair) preserved; no signature.

KYB-425
Tyras, present whereabouts unknown, Belgorod? Fr. of base and lower body. Main decoration: net pattern? Medallion: surrounded by two ridges; Meter bust with crenellated crown and tympanon; no signature.
– Batizat 2002, fig. 9.6; attribution PGB.

KYB-426
Tyras, present whereabouts unknown, Belgorod? Fr. of base and lower body. Main decoration cannot be identified from published drawing. Medallion: two ridges; top of crenellated crown; no signature (preserved).
– Batizat 2002, fig. 17.3; attribution PGB.

KYB-427*
Olbia, O-87-1028, Parutine, Olbia National Preserve storeroom. Fr. of base and lower body. H 5.1 × W 6.2, WT 0.2–0.5, ⌀ base 4.5. Fabric: relatively fine and micaceous, many small lime inclusions, many voids, 2.5YR 5/6. Thin dull coat, ext. 2.5YR 3/1, int. 10YR 5/3. Relatively hard fired, oxidized. Main decoration: small figures walking left, probably Eros D (iii). Calyx: imbricate pointed lotus petals. Medallion: remains of figure surrounded by two ridges (top of crown of Meter?); no signature (preserved?).

B   *Figural Decoration*

KYB-428*
Olbia, Square B5, O-Б5-76-113, Kiev, Institute of Archaeology storeroom. Fr. of rim and upper body. H 4.8 × W 4.8, WT 0.35, RH 2.1. Fabric: relatively coarse, 7.5YR 7/6. Dull coat, 7.5YR 2.5/1. Relatively hard fired, oxidized. Rim frieze: grooves. Main decoration: tail of dolphin(?), Eros(?). One repair hole.

KYB-429*
Istros, His-326, Bucharest, Institute of Archaeology storeroom. Fr. of lower body. Oxidized. Calyx: straight acanthus U with figure(?) as space-filler?

KYB-430*
Istros, His-992, Bucharest, Institute of Archaeology storeroom. Fr. of rim and upper body. H 5.3 × W 7.7, WT 0.45, ⌀ rim 14, 10%, RH 2.9. Fabric: relatively fine and micaceous, many small lime inclusions, many voids. Dull coat. Medium hard fired, oxidized. Rim frieze: Ionian kyma. Main decoration: rosette F. Secondarily burnt.

KYB-431*
Istros, His-1113, Bucharest, Institute of Archaeology storeroom. Fr. of rim and upper body. H 3.8 × W 4, WT 0.36, RH 2. Fabric: fine and micaceous, a few minute lime inclusions, some small voids, 5YR 6/8. Reddish brown coat with soapy lustre, red at rim ext. and int. from stacking, ext. 5YR 4/6, 7.5YR 3/2, int. 5YR 5/8. Medium hard fired, oxidized. Rim frieze: grooves. Main decoration: large kithara, very detailed, with only the upper right-hand part preserved.

C   *Scroll Decoration*

KYB-432*
Istros, His-V 19427, Bucharest, Institute of Archaeology storeroom. Fr. of rim and upper body. H 6.7 × W 5.7, WT 0.35, RH 2.8. Fabric: relatively fine and micaceous, some small lime inclusions. Dull brownish coat, partly worn off ext., int. much pitted. Oxidized. Rim frieze: heart guilloche left. Main decoration: fine tendrils. Perhaps Kirbeis, based on the character of the rim pattern, but the decoration has no parallel.

D   *Vegetal Decoration*

Calyx

KYB-433*
Olbia, Sector NGS, O-НГС-02-373, Parutine, Olbia National Preserve storeroom. Fr. of base and body. H 5.3 × W 5.2, WT 0.32–0.45, ⌀ base 2.5. Fabric: relatively fine, slightly micaceous, many minute lime inclusions, many small round voids, 5YR 6/6. Thin firm dull coat, 10R 5/8. Medium hard fired, oxidized. Rim frieze: rosettes? Calyx: straight acanthus H in negative relief alternating with lotus petals pointed at both ends; twisted stem topped by heart bud placed upside-down and two worn stamps of a heart guilloche. Medallion: trace only, bordered by dotted line. Frieze separators: dots. The attribution to the MMW is based primarily on the presence of the heart-bud stamp.

KYB-434*
Istros, His-V 19367, Bucharest, Institute of Archaeology storeroom. Fr. of lower body. Oxidized. Calyx: acanthus I(?) closely stamped.

KYB-435
Olbia, Sector R25, O-P25-99-955, Parutine, Olbia National Preserve storeroom. Fr. of base and lower body. H 3.5 × W 3.5, WT 0.55, ⌀ base 4. Fabric: relatively fine and micaceous, some small lime inclusions, 5YR 5/6. Thin slightly lustrous coat, 5YR 3/1. Hard fired, oxidized. Calyx: lower part of acanthus L(?) with lightly segmented central vein. Medallion: surrounded by ridge.

KYB-436*
Pantikapaion, M-73-339, Moscow, Puškin Museum of Fine Arts. Body fr. H 4 × W 5. Dull brown coat. Oxidized. Calyx: flower on looped acanthus stems, right and left, alternating with palmette C.
– Zabelina 1984, 164, fig. 11d; Kovalenko 1989, 373 cat. 5.

KYB-437*
Istros, His-300, Bucharest, Institute of Archaeology storeroom. Fr. of lower body. H 3.5 × W 4.3, WT 0.45. Fabric: relatively fine and micaceous, many small lime inclusions, many voids, 7.5YR 6/6. Dull coat, ext. 7.5YR 3/1, 2.5YR 5/6, int. 7.5YR 3/1. Medium hard fired, oxidized. Stacked in firing. Calyx: acanthus I(?) alternating with palmette C; in between, lily (iii) on incised wavy stem.
– Domăneanțu 2000, 138 cat. 685, pl. 49.

KYB-438*
Olbia, Cliff "B-VIII", square 285, O-70-199, Parutine, Olbia National Preserve storeroom. Two joining frs. of rim and body. H 5.6 × W 9.7, WT 0.55, ⌀, 22%, RH 2.9. Fabric: medium fine, not very micaceous, abundant lime, small voids, 7.5YR 6/4. Thin coat with metallic sheen ext., int. duller, 7.5YR 2.5/1. Not too hard fired, oxidized. Rim frieze: heart guilloche left. Calyx: imbricate small pointed petals.

KYB-439*
Istros, His-230, Bucharest, Institute of Archaeology storeroom. Body fr. H 2.7 × W 3.5, WT 0.55. Fabric: relatively fine and micaceous, some small lime inclusions. Dull brown coat. Oxidized. Calyx: ovoid lotus petal A.

KYB-440*
Istros, His-935, Bucharest, Institute of Archaeology storeroom. Body fr. H 3.5 × W 2.7, WT 0.6. Fabric: relatively fine and micaceous, some small lime inclusions. Dull red-brown coat. Oxidized. Calyx: ovoid lotus petal A.

KYB-441
Istros, His-661, Bucharest, Institute of Archaeology storeroom. Body fr. close to rim. Oxidized. Stacked in firing. Rim frieze: Ionian kyma. Calyx: tip of acanthus leaf (type?).

E   *Rim Fragments*

Multiple Rim Friezes

KYB-442*
Olbia, O-year(?)-27, Kiev, Institute of Archaeology storeroom. Fr. of rim and upper body. H 4.8 × W 8.1, WT 0.38, ⌀ rim 14, 12%, RH 2.3. Fabric: relatively fine and micaceous, many small lime inclusions, some voids, 5YR 7/6. Dull coat, 5YR 3/1. Medium hard fired, oxidized. Multiple rim friezes: heart guilloche left; Ionian kyma with scored tongues.

Single Rim Friezes

Horizontal S-spirals

KYB-443*
Istros, His-898, Bucharest, Institute of Archaeology storeroom. Rim fr. H 4 × W 3.6, WT 0.25, RH 2.3. Fabric: relatively fine and micaceous, some small lime inclusions. Dull reddish brown coat. Oxidized.

Ionian Kyma

KYB-444*
Istros, His-307, Bucharest, Institute of Archaeology storeroom. Rim fr. H 3.6 × W 4.5, WT 0.35, RH 2. Dull reddish-brown coat. Oxidized.

KYB-445
Olbia, Sector NGS, O-НГС-08-182, Parutine, Olbia National Preserve storeroom. Rim fr. Oxidized.

KYB-446
Olbia, Sector R25, O-P25-93-2913, Parutine, Olbia National Preserve storeroom. Fr. of upper body close to rim. H 4.5 × W 5.8, WT 0.55, RH 2.7. Fabric: relatively fine and micaceous, small lime inclusions, 7.5YR 5/4. Dull coat, 7.5YR 3/1. Medium hard fired, oxidized.

KYB-447
Olbia, Sector NGS, O-НГС-06-144, Parutine, Olbia National Preserve storeroom. Fr. of upper body close to rim. Oxidized.

KYB-448*
Olbia, Sector AGD, Bothros 11, O-АГД-88-215, Kiev, Institute of Archaeology storeroom. Rim fr. H 4.2 × W 4.4, RH 2.1. Fabric: relatively fine and micaceous, some small lime inclusions. Dull red coat ext., blackish int. Low fired, oxidized. Stacked in firing.

KYB-449
Istros, His-315, Bucharest, Institute of Archaeology storeroom. Body fr. close to rim. Oxidized.

KYB-450*
Istros, His-1182, Bucharest, Institute of Archaeology storeroom. Body fr. close to rim. Oxidized.
– Domăneanțu 2000, 58 cat. 270, pl. 17 (identified as Ephesian).

KYB-451
Istros, His-154, Bucharest, Institute of Archaeology storeroom. Body fr. close to rim. Oxidized.

KYB-452*
Olbia, Square B5, O-Б5-76-50, Kiev, Institute of Archaeology storeroom. Rim fr. H 3.4. Oxidized.

KYB-453
Olbia, Square B5, O-Б5-76-89, Kiev, Institute of Archaeology storeroom. Body fr. close to rim. H 3.5. Oxidized.

KYB-454
Istros, His-162[a], Bucharest, Institute of Archaeology storeroom. Rim fr. Oxidized.

KYB-455*
Istros, His-B 162/V 19486, Bucharest, Institute of Archaeology storeroom. Rim fr. Oxidized.

Design Not Preserved

KYB-456
Istros, His-383, Bucharest, Institute of Archaeology storeroom. Rim fr. Oxidized.

DISTRIBUTION: ALL KYMEAN WORKSHOPS

Abdera

KYB-249, KYB-256

Art Market

KYB-21

Beljaus

KYB-116

Chersonesos

KYB-4*, KYB-46*, KYB-48, KYB-67*, KYB-122, KYB-130*, KYB-131, KYB-150, KYB-228*, KYB-229, KYB-350*

Crimea

KYA-57

Crimea?

KYB-73

Delos

KYB-78, KYB-106, KYB-192, KYB-215

Golubickoe

KYB-140*

Istros

KYA-1*, KYA-5*, KYA-7*–KYB-9, KYA-11*–KYB-13*, KYA-16*, KYA-25*, KYB-26*, KYA-29*, KYB-30*, KYA-36*, KYA-40*, KYA-46*, KYA-49*
KYB-10*, KYB-12*, KYB-16, KYB-20, KYB-31, KYB-45, KYB-77, KYB-91*, KYB-92*, KYB-112, KYB-113, KYB-123, KYB-135, KYB-148*, KYB-157*, KYB-160, KYB-161, KYB-165*, KYB-166, KYB-168, KYB-169, KYB-171*, KYB-175, KYB-176*, KYB-184*, KYB-187*, KYB-191, KYB-198*, KYB-203, KYB-207*, KYB-208*, KYB-212, KYB-214*, KYB-216–KYB-219, KYB-224, KYB-226, KYB-227*, KYB-232*, KYB-239*, KYB-242*, KYB-244, KYB-271*, KYB-284*, KYB-286–KYB-288, KYB-291*, KYB-294, KYB-295, KYB-297, KYB-298, KYB-300, KYB-303, KYB-310*, KYB-314*, KYB-315*, KYB-333*, KYB-339*, KYB-343*, KYB-353*, KYB-372, KYB-380*, KYB-391*, KYB-395*, KYB-399*–KYB-403, KYB-404–KYB-408, KYB-416*, KYB-429*–KYB-432*, KYB-434*, KYB-437*, KYB-439*–KYB-441, KYB-443*, KYB-444*, KYB-449–KYB-451, KYB-454–KYB-456
KYX-1*–KYX-3*, KYX-5, KYX-18*, KYX-21*, KYX-28*, KYX-29*, KYX-35*–KYX-37*, KYX-39*, KYX-43*, KYX-52*, KYX-55*, KYX-58, KYX-65*, KYX-68–KYX-71*, KYX-74*–KYX-76, KYX-82, KYX-83, KYX-88*, KYX-96*, KYX-97, KYX-100*

Kepoi

KYB-90*, KYB-260*, KYB-320*
KYX-15*

Kyme (Excluding Bouzek & Jansová 1974 et al.)

KYB-186

Mesambria

KYB-132*, KYB-152*, KYB-331*, KYB-349

Myrmekion

KYA-47*, KYA-53*
KYB-114, KYB-164, KYB-194, KYB-200*, KYB-201*, KYB-266*, KYB-272*, KYB-377
KYX-7*, KYX-46*

Nymphaion

KYB-265

Olbia

KYA-2*–KYA-4*, KYA-10*, KYA-14*, KYA-15*, KYA-17*–KYA-24*, KYA-27*, KYA-28*, KYA-31–KYA-35*, KYA-37, KYA-41*–KYA-45, KYA-48, KYA-50–KYA-52, KYA-54*, KYA-56*, KYA-58*

KYME (II): THE METER MEDALLION WORKSHOP

KYB-3, KYB-6–KYB-8*, KYB-11, KYB-13*–KYB-15*, KYB-17*–KYB-19*, KYB-22*, KYB-23*, KYB-25*–KYB-30*, KYB-32*, KYB-34*–KYB-44*, KYB-50–KYB-64, KYB-66, KYB-69*–KYB-71*, KYB-74*, KYB-75*, KYB-81*–KYB-89*, KYB-93*, KYB-96–KYB-102*, KYB-104*, KYB-107–KYB-111, KYB-117*, KYB-118, KYB-120*, KYB-121, KYB-127*–KYB-129*, KYB-133*, KYB-136*–KYB-138, KYB-142*, KYB-143*, KYB-147*, KYB-149, KYB-151*, KYB-153*, KYB-155*, KYB-156, KYB-158*, KYB-159*, KYB-162*, KYB-163*, KYB-167*, KYB-170*, KYB-173, KYB-177*–KYB-179*, KYB-181–KYB-183*, KYB-188*–KYB-190, KYB-193*, KYB-199*, KYB-202*, KYB-204*–KYB-206*, KYB-209*, KYB-210*, KYB-213*, KYB-220–KYB-223*, KYB-225*, KYB-231*, KYB-233*, KYB-235*–KYB-238*, KYB-241*, KYB-243*, KYB-245*, KYB-246*, KYB-250*–KYB-252, KYB-254, KYB-255*, KYB-259*, KYB-264, KYB-268*–KYB-270, KYB-273–KYB-278*, KYB-283, KYB-285, KYB-289, KYB-290*, KYB-292, KYB-293*, KYB-301*, KYB-302, KYB-305*–KYB-308*, KYB-311*–KYB-313, KYB-316, KYB-319*, KYB-321–KYB-326*, KYB-328, KYB-330*, KYB-332*, KYB-334*, KYB-336*–KYB-338*, KYB-340*–KYB-342*, KYB-344*–KYB-347*, KYB-351*, KYB-352*, KYB-355*, KYB-357*–KYB-360, KYB-362*, KYB-363*, KYB-365*–KYB-367*, KYB-370*, KYB-371*, KYB-373*, KYB-376*, KYB-378, KYB-379, KYB-381*–KYB-383*, KYB-385*–KYB-387*, KYB-389, KYB-392–KYB-394*, KYB-397, KYB-398, KYB-409–KYB-412*, KYB-414, KYB-420*–KYB-422*, KYB-424*, KYB-427*, KYB-428*, KYB-433*, KYB-435*, KYB-438*, KYB-442*, KYB-445–KYB-448*, KYB-452*, KYB-453
KYX-4*, KYX-6*, KYX-8*–KYX-14*, KYX-16*, KYX-17*, KYX-19*, KYX-20*, KYX-22*–KYX-27, KYX-30*–KYX-34, KYX-38*, KYX-40, KYX-41*, KYX-44*, KYX-45*, KYX-47*–KYX-51*, KYX-53, KYX-54*, KYX-56*, KYX-57*, KYX-59*, KYX-60*, KYX-62, KYX-63*, KYX-66*, KYX-67*, KYX-72*, KYX-73, KYX-77*–KYX-81*, KYX-84*–KYX-87, KYX-89*–KYX-95*, KYX-98, KYX-101

Olbia?

KYB-5, KYB-105, KYB-317*, KYB-348*

Olbia or Pantikapaion

KYB-1*, KYB-145*, KYB-261*, KYB-327*

Pantikapaion

KYA-6*, KYA-39, KYA-55
KYB-33, KYB-47*, KYB-49, KYB-68*, KYB-76*, KYB-80, KYB-94*, KYB-103*, KYB-125, KYB-134*, KYB-146*, KYB-180*, KYB-197, KYB-211, KYB-248*, KYB-253*, KYB-267, KYB-279–KYB-282, KYB-296*, KYB-304, KYB-309, KYB-318*, KYB-364*, KYB-390*, KYB-396, KYB-418*, KYB-436*
KYX-42, KYX-61, KYX-64*, KYX-99

Pantikapaion?

KYB-262

Petuchovka (Gute Maritzyn)

KYB-419

Phanagoreia

KYB-361

Phanagoreia, Vinogradnoe 7

KYB-95

Porthmion

KYA-38
KYB-115

Samothrace

KYB-240*

Vicinity of Smyrna

KYB-375

Smyrna?

KYB-72, KYB-368, KYB-417

South Russia

KYB-2*, KYB-258*, KYB-413*

Tanais

KYB-356

Thasos

KYB-154, KYB-335

Theodosia

KYB-384

Tomis

KYB-124*, KYB-172*, KYB-195, KYB-423

Tyras

KYB-9, KYB-65, KYB-79, KYB-119, KYB-126, KYB-139, KYB-144, KYB-174, KYB-185, KYB-196, KYB-257, KYB-263, KYB-369, KYB-388, KYB-415, KYB-425, KYB-426

Tyritake

KYB-230*, KYB-234*, KYB-299*

Ukrainian Part of Black Sea Region?

KYB-247

Provenance?

KYB-24*, KYB-141, KYB-329, KYB-354*, KYB-374

CHAPTER 12

Aiolis A: Elaia or Pitane?

In this chapter we bring together the fragments of a small, yet distinct group of vessels which undoubtedly were produced at the same location. The assemblage consists mostly of rim fragments, but some body fragments are also included; I have not been able to identify any bases belonging to this production. The fragments are ascribed to Aiolis because of their close connection with Aiolis B, which it seems to precede. Furthermore, an Aiolian origin is supported by archaeometric analysis (see below).

Fabric and Surface Treatment

The fabric is invariably fine, compact, and non-micaceous, with no visible inclusions and occasionally some small voids. It is almost always hard fired. It comes in two finishes. The most common is the reduced version, fired mostly to either 2.5Y 7/2 or Gley 1 5/N, with a dull blackish coat in the colour range of 2.5Y 3/1-4/1 and Gley 1 3/1-4/1. The oxidized version is fired to 5YR 6/6, 7/4 and 7/6, and the coat varies from 5YR 4/2, 4/4, 5/4 and 5/6.

Shape

Only bowls are encountered in the small assemblage ascribed to this production. They all have relatively thin walls (0.25–0.4 cm) and a tall rim (1.8–2.6 cm) over the moulded part with an out-turned lip, which can be more or less accentuated. The rim diameter is normally relatively large, mostly 13–15 cm.

Decoration

The fact that we are dealing only with fragments severely hampers our understanding of this group. In most cases we are able to distinguish only the vessels' rim pattern and only to a limited extent their main decoration. It is unknown whether they had a calyx and whether their walls were divided into more than a single frieze. And as mentioned, their bases have not been identified.

Chronology

Because the assemblage is so small, it is difficult to form an opinion about its date. The bowls have been found predominantly at Istros, which suggests that they could be relatively late. AIA-4* was unearthed in the palace foundation trench at Pantikapaion; as will be discussed in Chapter 24, this trench was perhaps dug around 125, which would, then, be the terminus ante quem for this piece. It was found together with Ephesian MMB predominantly of the classical phase, as well as with four non-joining fragments probably of the same Knidian bowl with rouletting (M-89-no no. 1). The latter is typologically of a stage that belongs to the 2nd century, prior to its end (Kögler 2010, fig. 71.a, middle group). Not a single fragment of Demetrios' production was found in this trench. As we shall see in Chapter 18, the earliest absolutely dated fragments of Demetrios' production are from the years around 126–125 BCE, and their main source of inspiration seems to have been Aiolis B vessels. Since the production of Aiolis B must have been initiated before around 125 BCE, perhaps immediately before, accordingly, Aiolis A must be immediately before this date.

Place of Production

AIA-15 has been analysed by the Lyon laboratory of P. Dupont. The fragment was characterized as Dupont's Group E, which, according to Dupont, is Aiolian of the lower Kaikos Valley, that is Pitane or Elaia. Both of these cities, the territories of which were separated by the Kaikos river, served as Pergamon's harbour in the Hellenistic period.

Elaia

Elaia is located in the interior of Çandarlı Gulf. Since 2006, the German Archaeological Institute has been carrying out archaeological investigations in and around the city, which before this date was virtually unexplored.[1]

---

1 Lang 2003, 281–288; Grüßinger et al. 2011, 62–65. An overview of the recent investigations is available at: http://www.poliskultur.de/elaia [accessed 28 Oct. 2023].

© PIA GULDAGER BILDE AND SUSAN I. ROTROFF, 2024 | DOI:10.1163/9789004680463_013

According to the recent investigations, the city expanded significantly in the Hellenistic period, when it became Pergamon's maritime satellite. Its urban lay-out was in the form of orthogonal streets, and the harbour was enlarged with mighty fortifications, detected with geomagnetic measurements. Currently, we know nothing about a pottery production in Elaia, but the Germans have initiated archaeometric investigations, which, in due course, will allow us to attribute pottery to Elaian production with confidence.

Pitane

Pitane is located west of Elaia and today lies under the modern city of Çandarlı (Lang 2003, 322–325). In the Roman period, Pitane was the home of a fine red-slipped table ware production, which at the outset drew on Hellenistic traditions. It has been termed Eastern Sigillata C (ESC) (Kenyon 1957) and Çandarli Ware (Loeschcke 1912; see also Hayes 1972, 316–322; 1985, 71–78, pls. 16–18). The production was initiated at least as early as the end of the 1st century BCE and continued perhaps as late as the 4th century CE. However, according to Loeschcke, that ware contains considerable amounts of mica (Loeschcke 1912, 351; see also Hayes 1972, 316–317), so Pitane is perhaps less likely than Elaia as a provenance for Aiolis A.

Distribution

I have not been able to identify a single specimen of this production in the Mediterranean. Vessels of this group are almost exclusively encountered at Istros. Up to four vessels were found at Olbia (Sector E and Sector NGS), but the ascription of three of them is tentative, and only one, **AIA-31***, certainly belongs to this production. As already mentioned, one fragment, **AIA-4***, was found in the palace foundation trench in Pantikapaion.

CATALOGUE TO CHAPTER 12

BOWLS

A   *Figural Decoration*

Fish

Two vessels feature a long, slender fish, perhaps a tuna. Fish are common emblems on coins of cities located by the sea. On MMB, marine life is normally limited to dolphins as creatures connected with Dionysos. I know of no further fish representations on MMB.

AIA-1*
Istros, His-970, Bucharest, Institute of Archaeology storeroom. Fr. of upper body. H 4.7 × W 4.5, WT 0.3. Fabric: fine, compact, non-micaceous, no visible inclusions, some small voids, Gley 1 5/N. Slightly lustrous flaking coat, Gley 1 3/N. Hard fired, reduced. Rim frieze: Ionian kyma, double-outlined. Main decoration: fish jumping left.
– Domăneanțu 2000, 134 cat. 660, pl. 47.

AIA-2*
Istros, His-V 19482, Bucharest, Institute of Archaeology storeroom. Fr. of upper body. H 3.6 × W 2.3, WT 0.35. Fabric: fine, compact, non-micaceous, no visible inclusions, some small voids, Gley 1 5/N. Wash with slight dull lustre, 2.5Y 3/1. Hard fired, reduced. Rim frieze: Ionian kyma, double-outlined. Main decoration: fish jumping or swimming right.
– Domăneanțu 2000, 134 cat. 661, pl. 47.

Thunderbolts

AIA-3*
Istros, His-1005+V 8572 P, Bucharest, Institute of Archaeology storeroom. Two joining frs. of rim and upper body. H 4.5 × W 4.8, WT 0.2, RH 2.4. Fabric: fine, compact, non-micaceous, no visible inclusions, some small voids, 2.5Y 6/2. Wash with slight dull lustre, Gley 1 3/N. Hard fired, reduced. No rim frieze. Main decoration: horizontal thunderbolts, top of small long petal(?) below.
– Domăneanțu 2000, 130 cat. 637, pl. 45.

B   *Scroll Decoration*

AIA-4*
Pantikapaion, palace foundation trench, M-84–34, 84–34[a], Moscow, Puškin Museum of Fine Arts. Fr. of rim and upper body, fr. of lower body, non-joining. H 6 × W 9.3, WT 0.2, ⌀ rim 10, 15%. Fabric: very fine, dense. Thin coat, burnished to a soapy feel on int. and ext. of rim. Reduced. Rim friezes: grooves; dots. Main decoration: ivy-acanthus scroll left, with flowers with eight rhomboidal petals enclosed by tendrils and buds. The ascription to Aiolis A is tentative; this fragment probably bridges AIA and AIB. The fabric and shape correspond to AIA, whereas we find much the same (though slightly debased) decoration on AIB-39*, which also features an AIB shape. The context of AIA-4* (the Pantikapaion palace foundation trench) can probably be dated to around 125.

AIA-5*
Istros, His-V 19424, Bucharest, Institute of Archaeology storeroom. Fr. of rim and upper body. H 4.4 × W 5.8, WT 0.3, ⌀ rim 14, 13%, RH 1.8. Fabric: fine, compact, non-micaceous, no visible inclusions, some small voids, Gley 1 5/N. Wash with slight dull lustre, 2.5Y 4/1. Hard fired, reduced. Rim frieze: horizontal eggs left. Main decoration: acanthus scroll. One repair hole.
– Domăneanțu 2000, 128 cat. 627, pl. 44.

C   *Wreath Decoration*

Myrtle

In the orbit of Pergamon, the myrtle bundle with three leaves, also placed vertically, is much more common than other versions of the myrtle, as encountered at Ephesos, for example (see also Chapter 6).

AIA-6*
Olbia, Sector E6, square 247, Pit 53, O-E6-57-186, 186[A], Kiev, Institute of Archaeology storeroom. Two non-joining frs. of rim and body. H 5 × W 9, WT 0.25, ⌀ rim 15, 18%, RH 2.6. Fabric: fine, compact, abundant fine lime, some fine light-reflecting particles, 5YR 5/4. Thin dull coat, 5YR 4/1, 2.5YR 3/1. Hard fired, reduced. Stacked in firing. Rim frieze: Ionian kyma. Main decoration: myrtle wreath with berries left. Ascription to Aiolis A is tentative.
– Kovalenko 1989, 375 cat. 60 (attributed to Kirbeis).

AIA-7
Istros, His-510, Bucharest, Institute of Archaeology storeroom. Rim fr. Reduced. Rim frieze: Ionian kyma. Main decoration: myrtle.

AIA-8*
Istros, His-V 19367 C, Bucharest, Institute of Archaeology storeroom. Fr. of upper body. H 3.1 × W 3.4, WT 0.35. Fabric: fine, compact, non-micaceous, no visible inclusions, some small voids, Gley 1 4/N. Wash with slight dull lustre, 2.5Y 4/1. Hard fired, reduced. Rim frieze: horizontal eggs left. Main decoration: vertical bundle of three bound myrtle leaves.
– Domăneanțu 2000, 129 cat. 630, pl. 44.

D   *Multiple Rim Friezes*

This type of decoration seems to be quite uncommon. Apart from **AIA-9***, **AIA-13*** probably also features multiple rim friezes, there over a main frieze of small long petals.

AIA-9*
Istros, His-1125, Bucharest, Institute of Archaeology storeroom. Rim fr. H 3.8 × W 4.2, WT 0.3, RH 2. Fabric: fine, compact, non-micaceous, no visible inclusions and some small voids, 2.5Y 7/2. Dull wash, ext. 2.5Y 5/1, 4/1, int. 2.5Y 4/1. Hard fired, reduced. Multiple rim friezes: Ionian kyma, upside-down; horizontal eggs left.
– Domăneanțu 2000, 129 cat. 631, pl. 44.

E   *Vegetal Decoration*

Pine-Cone Decoration?

AIA-10*
Istros, His-V 19377, Bucharest, Institute of Archaeology storeroom. Fr. of rim and upper body. H 3.8 × W 4.1, WT 0.32, RH 2.5. Fabric: fine, compact, non-micaceous, no visible inclusions, 2.5Y 7/2. Wash with slight dull lustre, 2.5Y 3/1. Hard fired, reduced. No rim frieze. Main decoration: tall, rhomboidal, plastic pine-cone scales.

Calyx?

AIA-11*
Istros, His-200, 799, V 19336[a], Bucharest, Institute of Archaeology storeroom. Three non-joining body frs. H 3.3 × W 3.3, WT 0.4. Fabric: fine, compact, non-micaceous, no visible inclusions, some small voids, 5YR 6/6. Dull coat, ext. 5YR 4/2, int. 5YR 5/4. Hard fired, oxidized. No rim frieze. Calyx: imbricate rounded petals. Frieze separators: dots.
– Domăneanțu 2000, 86 cat. 409, pl. 28 (identified as Ephesian).

F   *Linear Decoration*

Net Pattern

AIA-12*
Istros, His-B 527, V 19327, Bucharest, Institute of Archaeology storeroom. Two non-joining frs. of rim and upper body. H 4.2 × W 5.7, WT 0.26, ⌀ rim 14, 14%, RH 2. Fabric: fine, compact, non-micaceous, no visible inclusions, some small voids, 5YR 7/4. Coat with slight dull lustre, ext. 10YR 3/1, int. 7.5YR 3/2. Hard fired, oxidized. Rim frieze: guilloche right. Main decoration: net pattern. Frieze separators: dots.
– Domăneanțu 2000, 7 cat. 26, pl. 2 (V 19327 only; identified as Ephesian [Menemachos]).

Long Petals

The long petals encountered are exclusively very small; one fragment definitely has plastic petals (**AIA-13***), whereas so little is preserved of the other two (**AIA-3***, **AIA-14***) that it is difficult to tell whether the petals are plastic or stylized.

AIA-13*
Istros, His-B 523, Bucharest, Institute of Archaeology storeroom. Fr. of rim and upper body. H 4.1 × W 4.2, WT 0.4, RH 1.9. Fabric: fine, compact, non-micaceous, no visible inclusions, some small voids, Gley 1 5/N. Wash with slight dull lustre, 2.5Y 3/1. Hard fired, reduced. Multiple rim friezes: astragal; unidentified element. Main decoration: small plastic long petals.
– Domăneanțu 2000, 87 cat. 413, pl. 28 (identified as Ionian).

AIA-14*
Istros, His-V 19430, Bucharest, Institute of Archaeology storeroom. Fr. of rim and upper body. H 4 × W 5.5. Reduced. Rim frieze: horizontal eggs left. Main decoration: probably small long petals (only tops preserved).
– Domăneanțu 2000, 129 cat. 629, pl. 44.

G   *Rim Fragments*

In general, only a single rim frieze is encountered. More than half of the fragments feature an Ionian kyma. This can also be placed upside down (**AIA-9***) and the eggs can be stamped individually lying on their sides and turned to the left (**AIA-5***,

AIA-8*, AIA-14*, AIA-29*). Palmettes stamped upside down are another common rim pattern (AIA-32*–AIA-36*).

Astragal

AIA-15
Istros, His-Dup744, in the possession of P. Dupont. Rim fr. Reduced.

AIA-16*
Istros, His-98, Bucharest, Institute of Archaeology storeroom. Body fr. close to rim. H 3 × W 2.7. Reduced.
– Domăneanțu 2000, 86 cat. 412, pl. 28 (identified as Ephesian).

Ionian Kyma

AIA-17*
Istros, His-115, Bucharest, Institute of Archaeology storeroom. Rim fr. H 4 × W 5.2, WT 0.3, ⌀ rim 14, 12%, RH 2.2. Fabric: fine, compact, non-micaceous, no visible inclusions, some small voids, Gley 1 5/N. Wash with slight dull lustre, 2.5Y 3/1. Hard fired, reduced.

AIA-18*
Olbia, Sector NGS, О-НГС-06-265, Parutine, Olbia National Preserve storeroom. Rim fr. H 4 × W 4.8, WT 0.25, RH 1.9. Fabric: relatively fine, some small lime inclusions, 5Y 4/1. Dull coat, 5Y 3/1. Medium hard fired, reduced. One repair hole. Ascription to Aiolis A is tentative.

AIA-19*
Olbia, Sector E6, square 454s, Room "И" (or "Н"?), yellow clay layer with grey clay inclusions, О-Е6-59-774, Kiev, Institute of Archaeology storeroom. Rim fr. H 4.5 × W 7.8, WT 0.3, ⌀ rim 17, 12%, RH 2.3. Fabric: fine, finely micaceous, 5Y 6/1. Thin dull flaking coat, 5Y 4/1. Medium hard fired, reduced. Ascription to Aiolis A is tentative.

AIA-20
Istros, His-no no. 1, Bucharest, Institute of Archaeology storeroom. Body fr. close to rim. Reduced.

AIA-21
Istros, His-303, Bucharest, Institute of Archaeology storeroom. Rim fr. Reduced.

AIA-22*
Istros, His-95, Bucharest, Institute of Archaeology storeroom. Rim fr. Reduced.

AIA-23
Istros, His-390, 591, Bucharest, Institute of Archaeology storeroom. Two non-joining frs. of rim and body close to rim. Reduced.

AIA-24*
Istros, His-1045, Bucharest, Institute of Archaeology storeroom. Body fr. close to rim. Reduced.

AIA-25
Istros, His-306, Bucharest, Institute of Archaeology storeroom. Body fr. close to rim. Reduced.

Ionian Kyma, Eggs with Double Outline

AIA-26
Istros, His-112, Bucharest, Institute of Archaeology storeroom. Rim fr. Reduced.

AIA-27
Istros, His-122, Bucharest, Institute of Archaeology storeroom. Rim fr. H 3.8 × W 2.8, WT 0.35, ⌀ rim 13, 9%, RH 2.1. Fabric: fine, compact, non-micaceous, no visible inclusions, some small voids, 2.5Y 7/2. Wash with slight dull lustre, ext. Gley 1 4/N, 2.5Y 4/2, int. Gley 1 4/N. Hard fired, reduced.

AIA-28*
Istros, His-846, Bucharest, Institute of Archaeology storeroom. Body fr. close to rim. Reduced.
– Domăneanțu 2000, 80 cat. 386, pl. 26.

Horizontal Eggs Left

AIA-29*
Istros, His-527, 766, 1150, Bucharest, Institute of Archaeology storeroom. Three non-joining frs. of rim and upper body. H 3.8 × W 4.3, WT 0.3, ⌀ rim 13, 10%, RH 1.8. Fabric: fine, compact, non-micaceous, no visible inclusions, some small voids, 5YR 7/6. Coat with slight dull lustre, ext. 5YR 5/6, 4/4, int. 5YR 3/2, 4/4. Hard fired, oxidized. Main decoration: top of frieze preserved, but pattern cannot be identified (figural or vegetal?). Frieze separators: dots.
– Domăneanțu 2000, 129 cat. 628, pl. 44.

Lesbian Kyma

AIA-30*
Istros, His-117, Bucharest, Institute of Archaeology storeroom. Rim fr. Reduced.

Dots

This decoration as well as the type and appearance of the coat of AIA-31* corresponds to Aiolis B (especially AIB-32*), but the shape belongs to this group, and it is in particular close to AIA-4*, which also features the frieze of dots, which becomes diagnostic of AIB. AIA-31* (along with AIA-4*) can most likely be taken as an indicator that AIA continues as AIB.

AIA-31*
Olbia, Sector NGS, O-НГС-05-904, Parutine, Olbia National Preserve storeroom. Rim fr. H 3.8 × W 4.9, WT 0.25, ⌀ rim 13, 12%, RH 2.3. Fabric: fine, compact, non-micaceous, no visible inclusions, 5YR 7/6. Slightly lustrous coat with some metallic sheen, ext. 5YR 5/4, int. 2.5YR 4/6. Hard fired, oxidized.

Palmettes, Upside-Down

AIA-32*
Istros, His-726, Bucharest, Institute of Archaeology storeroom. Rim fr. H 4.4 × W 4.1, WT 0.4. Fabric: fine, compact, non-micaceous, no visible inclusions, some small voids, Gley 1 5/N. Wash with slight dull lustre, 2.5Y 4/1. Hard fired, reduced.
– Domăneanţu 2000, 129 cat. 632, pl. 44.

AIA-33
Istros, His-1160, Bucharest, Institute of Archaeology storeroom. Rim fr. H 4 × W 5.5, WT 0.3, ⌀ rim 12, 15%, RH 2.5. Fabric: fine, compact, non-micaceous, no visible inclusions, some small voids, Gley 1 5/N. Wash with slight dull lustre, ext. Gley 1 4/N, 3/N, int. Gley 1 3/N. Hard fired, reduced.
– Domăneanţu 2000, 129 cat. 633, pl. 44.

AIA-34
Istros, His-815, Bucharest, Institute of Archaeology storeroom. Body fr. close to rim. Reduced.
– Domăneanţu 2000, 130 cat. 635, pl. 44.

AIA-35*
Istros, His-1927-1942-14/V 8572 H, Bucharest, Institute of Archaeology storeroom. Rim fr. Reduced.
– Domăneanţu 2000, 130 cat. 636, pl. 45.

AIA-36*
Istros, His-712, Bucharest, Institute of Archaeology storeroom. Body fr. close to rim. Reduced.
– Domăneanţu 2000, 129 cat. 634, pl. 44.

DISTRIBUTION

Istros

AIA-1*–AIA-5*, AIA-7–AIA-17*, AIA-20–AIA-30*, AIA-32*–AIA-36*

Olbia

AIA-6*, AIA-18*, AIA-19*, AIA-31*

Pantikapaion

AIA-4*

CHAPTER 13

Aiolis B: Elaia, Pitane, Gryneion or Pergamon?

Recently, A. Petrova has drawn attention to an assemblage of vessels from Mesambria, which she grouped on the basis of their fabric, shape, and decoration (Petrova 2014). All are reduced and have a characteristic S-shaped rim, mostly with a rim frieze of dots below one or more deep grooves. According to Petrova, vessels of this group are found throughout the Black Sea region, but only in small numbers at any one site – with the exception of Mesambria, where they constitute up to 30% of the MMB retrieved in one particular excavation sector. She therefore suggested that this group was manufactured at Mesambria.

Petrova included 48 vessels and fragments in her pioneering article. To this corpus I can now add almost 100 more. With a corpus of almost 150 vessels, we can form a general opinion of the workshop's production in terms of fabric and shape as well as its stylistic features, stamps, and stamp combinations, and there can be absolutely no doubt that Petrova was right in viewing this assemblage as coming from a single locality, albeit hardly from the same workshop. However, as we shall see in the following, her identification of Mesambria as their production place cannot be maintained.

Fabric and Surface Treatment

The vessels of this production are encountered in both reduced and oxidized versions (not just reduced, as Petrova believed). The fabric of the two is identical, namely a compact, very highly levigated, non-micaceous fabric, which may contain a few light-reflecting particles, and occasionally some silvery mica can be seen on the surface. The reduced vessels occur mainly in the colours Gley 1 4/N and 5/10Y. They are mostly covered with a thin blackish wash, Gley 1 5/10Y, 3/N; Gley 4/10Y, 3/N; 5Y 3/1, 2.5/1; 10YR 2/1, which may have a somewhat blotchy look. The oxidized vessels come in two variants with two different surface finishes. One is reddish, mostly 2.5YR 6/8 and 5YR 6/8. It is covered with a coat fired to a dull, silky sheen, occasionally with a soapy feel; sometimes it is completely dull. The colour of the coat is one tone darker than that of the main fabric: 10R 4/8; 2.5YR 4/8, 5/8, 6/6. The fabric of the second group is more orange (5YR 6/6 and 7/6); it has a thinner coat, 10R 4/6, 5/6, which in the firing obtains some metallic highlights. It too is somewhat blotchy, and,

in this, resembles the grey variant. The blotchy appearance of a number of the fragments may attest to difficulties in properly controlling the firing.

As can be seen from Fig. 66, the two types of finish were equally popular, but their geographical distribution is somewhat uneven. The preponderance of oxidized vessels in Istros and especially in Olbia is noticeable. The finds from one Olbian excavation sector, Sector R25, are of a particular interest. With the exception of AIB-53*, the remaining 16 vessels are all of the oxidized finish. Even though the tendency amongst the production of MMB in general goes from reduced to oxidized vessels (see Chapter 3), all types of decoration are encountered in both types of finish. This may attest to a relatively brief period of production.

Manufacture

The vessels are hard to very hard fired and always fired through. Wall thickness is normally 0.3–0.4 cm. The reduced vessels of this production are very characteristic, because the S-shaped rim is burnished on the exterior as well as on the interior, a procedure which was probably carried out when the vessel was still in the mould and on the wheel. As a result, the bowls have a dull lustre with a silky feel in their upper parts. This surface treatment has a long ancestry in the local grey-ware pottery of pre-Hellenistic and Hellenistic times (Schäfer 1968, 29). There is very little evidence for stacking of the vessels during firing, and not a single fragment carries traces of repair.

Shapes

Bowls

The shape is normally a more or less hemispherical bowl with a high, everted, S-curved rim and a plain lip. On the grey vessels, the lip is mostly slightly pointed, whereas on the oxidized vessels it is more rounded. In addition, on some of the oxidized vessels (e.g., AIB-4*, AIB-35, AIB-37*, AIB-100*), the S-curve of the rim is considerably less prominent than on, in particular, the reduced vessels. This morphological development is probably a chronological indicator. Two vessels differ typologically from the

	Total	% at site	Reduced	Oxidized	Firing unknown
Apollonia	5		2		3
Beljaus	1				1
Chersonesos	2	2.1		2	
Čaika	2		2		
Istros	17	1.2	7	11	
Kara Tobe	4				4
Kuban	1				1
Libknechtovka village	1			1	
Mesambria	28		28		
Myrmekion	7	2.5	3	4	
Odessos	1		1		
Olbia	44	2.4	7	34	3
Pantikapaion	7	1.8	3	3	1
Pergamon	1			1	
Porthmion	1	0.4	1		
Stranja region	7				7
Tomis	1		1		
Vani	5		2	2	1
'Köln'	1			1	
Total	136		57	59	21

FIGURE 66 Distribution of Aiolis B vessels according to firing, in total numbers and percentage of vessels found at the site in question

standard bowl, featuring an incurved lip and a slightly more accentuated transition from body to rim (AIB-86*, AIB-87*).

The rim diameter of the bowls varies considerably, from 10.5 to 15 cm, with 11–13 cm as the most common, and the rim height varies accordingly from 1.7 to 3.8 cm. The base diameter is normally 3–3.2 cm. The vessels are 6.5 to 7.8 cm high and the ratio between height and rim diameter either 1:1.8–1.9 (reduced vessels) or 1:1.5 (one oxidized vessel).

The high, strongly concave, S-curved rim can also be found on vessels of Pergamene production, not on the MMB, but on the contemporary *Applikenkeramik* (e.g., Hübner 1993a, forms 6, 7 and 10, figs. 10, 14).

Supplementary Shapes

In addition to the bowl, the Aiolis B production includes several shapes which have no parallels amongst the other productions of MMB. With the exception of the krater(?) on feet in the shape of shells (AIB-115), fired in a reducing atmosphere, all other vessels in shapes deviating from the standard bowl are oxidized.

The most common of these is a cup with a low, shallow body, high collared rim with in-turned lip, (ridged) band handle(s), and a wide, flat, undecorated base. Only one vessel which I have had access to preserves almost the entire profile (AIB-118*). Its height is 5.6 cm, the diameter of the rim is 11 cm, the height of the rim over the moulded part is 3 cm, and the diameter of the base 5 cm. Further specimens show that the base diameter of this shape ranges from 5 to 7 cm. There is a single, deep groove on the shoulder.

Several types of cups with one (or more?) band handles (AIB-133*–AIB-136*) are also found, as well as perhaps a beaker (AIB-137*), but they are so few that it is difficult to form an opinion about their typology.

More interesting are the chalices, of which I know of two (AIB-116*, AIB-117). They have a pronounced vertical hanging rim and a slightly profiled, hollow foot on a low, broad stem. They are almost the same height, 15.8 and 15 cm respectively, but whereas the former has a rim diameter of 14.1 cm, the rim of the latter is somewhat wider at 19 cm. The shape is also found at Pergamon (PER-87*), and it was still being made in the local or nearby Čandarli ware of the early Empire (though with a much shallower bowl; Loeschcke 1912, pl. 28.10). There can hardly be any doubt that this shape is the forerunner of the mid- to late Augustan chalices of terra sigillata, especially of the form *Conspectus* R 2 (*Conspectus*, 168, pl. 53) and Dragendorff Form 11 (Dragendorff 1895, pl. 1), and we also find it in contemporary lead-glazed pottery (Hochuli-Gysel 1977, 35–42).

Decoration

The decorative patterns of this workshop are relatively varied, and some of the vessels are rather ambitious. The wall is normally not divided into friezes (as Ephesian bowls are), even though this does occur occasionally (AIB-71). The decoration includes a number of figural elements. They can appear as full-body figural decoration showing mythological or ritual scenes (AIB-1*–AIB-7*, AIB-115*), mantled dancing women (AIB-8*–AIB-10*), symplegma scenes (AIB-11*–AIB-14), and animals (AIB-15–AIB-18*). Mythological figures can also be depicted in combination with vegetal elements (AIB-19–AIB-26, AIB-116*, AIB-117, AIB-119*). Various types of scrolls are very popular (AIB-27–AIB-54), and we find a number of vessels featuring suspended garlands (AIB-55–AIB-60*) or ivy (AIB-61) and myrtle (AIB-62*–AIB-66*, AIB-125*) wreaths. A significant number of vessels include plastic or, more commonly, stylized long petals in their design. In particular, the decoration combining a 'nelumbo' filled with a floral stem alternating with two stylized long petals is quite common and is found at a number of localities (AIB-73*–AIB-82). Most likely this decoration marks the heyday of this production. Three vessels feature crossing, stylized long petals, a design I know only from this production (AIB-128–AIB-130*). We also find vessels decorated exclusively with plastic (AIB-93*–AIB-96) or stylized (AIB-97–AIB-103) long petals.

With the exception of AIB-1* and AIB-116*, the acanthus leaves are bent at the tip, not folded. In general, the vessels are heavily grooved.

Rim Pattern

The most common rim pattern is a series of grooves on the shoulder of the vessel, a frieze of medium-sized dots above, then another one or more grooves.[1] Occasionally, one or more grooves occurs without dots,[2] and sometimes the dotted frieze is not enclosed by grooves.[3] This dotted frieze seems unconnected with the Athenian and Ephesian friezes of dots; it is likely that the inspiration came from metalwork.

In addition to the frieze of dots, there are also several types of Ionian kyma. One is large with double-outlined eggs below grooves and between friezes of dots (AIB-9, AIB-51, AIB-116*); others are smaller and without dots,[4] and a number of vessels feature the Ionian kyma placed upside-down between two grooves (AIB-43, AIB-44, AIB-108, AIB-118*).

Multiple rim friezes are very uncommon, even though they do occur. Thus, three vessels feature a Lesbian kyma below the standard frieze of grooves and dots (AIB-104–AIB-106) and two have a horizontal stem of stylized tendrils of alternating direction below the frieze of grooves and dots (AIB-99, AIB-107). With the exception of AIB-106, where we do not know the type of firing, the remaining four vessels are all of the reduced finish. Three oxidized vessels feature rouletting; they are probably late in the series (AIB-66*, AIB-133*, AIB-137*).

Base Medallion

We can distinguish only two main base medallion stamps, which are equally popular (rosette A and B). Both share the same feature of an ivy-berry cluster in the centre as a representation of the flower's pistil. Rosette C is a variant of rosette B, without the ivy-berry stamp and with only two layers of petals. The bowls with the high, collared rim have a wide, plain, undecorated base (AIB-118*, AIB-119*, AIB-122*, AIB-127*, AIB-130*).

Rosette A

Rounded relief petals alternating with relief tongues, with an ivy-berry cluster at the centre. With the exception of AIB-39*, which at any rate is a variant (over-stamped at the centre with a smaller, 10-petalled rosette), this rosette is exclusively found on reduced vessels (AIB-1*, AIB-19, AIB-41*, AIB-85, AIB-89, AIB-91*, AIB-95, and perhaps AIB-72).

Rosette B

Three layers of broad petals with an ivy-berry stamp at the centre. With one exception (AIB-28*), all bases with this

---

1 AIB-1*, AIB-6, AIB-7*, AIB-11*, AIB-15, AIB-16*, AIB-19, AIB-27, AIB-29*, AIB-40*–AIB-42, AIB-48, AIB-52, AIB-58, AIB-69, AIB-73*, AIB-76*, AIB-78*, AIB-82, AIB-85, AIB-88, AIB-90–AIB-93*, AIB-96, AIB-98–AIB-102*, AIB-104–AIB-107, AIB-111.

2 AIB-25*, AIB-34, AIB-37*, AIB-47, AIB-57, AIB-75, AIB-97, AIB-103, AIB-117, AIB-122*–AIB-124*, AIB-126*, AIB-131*, AIB-134*.

3 AIB-13, AIB-17*, AIB-18*, AIB-28*, AIB-31–AIB-33, AIB-35, AIB-36*, AIB-39*, AIB-49, AIB-56*, AIB-84, AIB-86*, AIB-87*, AIB-110.

4 AIB-45, AIB-61, AIB-64*, AIB-65*, AIB-120, AIB-121, AIB-137*.

rosette are reduced (AIB-23, AIB-24, AIB-28*, AIB-73*, AIB-97, AIB-98 and perhaps AIB-22). The double- or triple-layered rosette is a feature frequently encountered in the Pergamene production and it is likely that Pergamon was the source of inspiration (see also pp. 154–155).

Rosette C
Two layers of broad petals; plain centre. Closely related to Rosette B (only AIB-77* and perhaps AIB-22).

Recurring Stamps
Many stamps occur just once; they are not included in the list below but are described under the particular vessel on which they appear. Some stamps, however, were very popular, such as rosette A, ivy A, the palmette on looped stem, the duck turning its head back, and Eros A, in addition to the ubiquitous ivy berry cluster, which occurs on most vessels.

Figural Decoration
Eros A, an Eros walking towards right with his right leg and right arm held forward
AIB-1*, AIB-2, AIB-4*–AIB-6, AIB-20–AIB-22, AIB-55, AIB-116*, AIB-117

Syrinx-Player
Naked male (Pan?) sitting right, probably playing syrinx
AIB-19, AIB-27, AIB-28*, AIB-117, AIB-119*

Wine-Pourer
Female in long garment pouring wine from amphora into large krater
AIB-2*, AIB-3*

Duck
Sitting duck turning its head back. This stamp is shared with the Bosporan Workshop of Demetrios (see Demetrios decoration 1a, DEM-12, DEM-16–DEM-23, DEM-35*, DEM-36*, DEM-38). We also find it on a vessel of which the production place is unknown, but which nevertheless must have been inspired by Aiolis B, for it also features the acanthus scroll enclosing a flower (XXX-5*). Flying ducks turning their heads are recurrently found at Kyme, even on a mould fragment (Bouzek & Jansová 1974, 51, 55–57 cats. MB 7, MB 34, MB 35, MB 37, MB 39–MB 41, pls. 2, 6).
AIB-19, AIB-41*, AIB-43, AIB-44, AIB-73*–AIB-75, AIB-83*, AIB-84

Wadjet Symbol(?)
For a discussion of this element, see Chapter 6.
AIB-26, AIB-56*, AIB-92

Vegetal Decoration
Acanthus A
A relatively naturalistic leaf, the tip of which is turned to the left; the stem is usually beaded.
The same acanthus leaf can be found in the production of Demetrios (Decoration 1), see Chapter 18.
AIB-68*, AIB-85, AIB-86*, AIB-123, AIB-129*

'Nelumbo' A
Horizontally ribbed at top, field divided vertically and furnished with a straight acanthus leaf in front of its lower part
A discussion of this type of 'nelumbo' can be found in Chapter 3.
AIB-19, AIB-73*, perhaps AIB-67*, AIB-75, and AIB-82

'Nelumbo' B
Horizontally ribbed at top, filled with vertical acanthus-flower scroll with tendril enclosing rosette A
AIB-74, AIB-76*–AIB-79

Ivy A
Relatively large leaf with two shallow depressions in the widest part of the leaf
This type of ivy leaf is characteristic of Pergamene *Applikenkeramik* (Hübner 1993a, pls. 16–23).
AIB-27–AIB-30, AIB-32*, AIB-33, AIB-39*, AIB-43, AIB-44, AIB-117, AIB-137*; AIB-39* is furnished with an ivy-berry cluster over the ivy leaf

Ivy B
A smaller, flat ivy leaf without the depressions, but instead divided in the middle
AIB-35–AIB-38*, AIB-122*–AIB-124*

Rosette A
Rosette with four rounded petals and a circle in the centre
AIB-10*, AIB-20, AIB-26, AIB-39*, AIB-41*–AIB-43, AIB-60*, AIB-74–AIB-77*, AIB-84, AIB-117, AIB-123, AIB-126*, AIB-128

Rosette B
Rosette with eight or ten rhomboidal petals
AIB-10*, AIB-40*

Palmette on Looped Stem
AIB-60*, AIB-67*, AIB-71, AIB-72, AIB-80, AIB-81, AIB-117

Palmette with Rhomboidal Finial
AIB-23, AIB-24, AIB-71

Acanthus Stem with Hatched Leaf Sheaths
AIB-123, AIB-124*, AIB-134*, AIB-137* (only on oxidized vessels and on shapes other than the standard bowl)

Stem with Stylized Tendrils of Alternating Direction
This element occurs horizontally as a rim pattern (AIB-99, AIB-107) and vertically as part of the calyx (AIB-10*, AIB-22, AIB-80, AIB-88).

Linear Decoration
Three yoked stylized long petals
AIB-82, AIB-91*

Crossed Long Petals
AIB-128–AIB-130* (only on oxidized vessels and bowl with tall collared rim)

Double-Stamping

Many of the vessels share the feature of slight double-stamping, which leaves the figures with a double outline. It was hardly done on purpose, so, most likely, it attests to a particular workshop procedure: perhaps the bowl was removed from the mould before it was completely dry. Double-stamping occurs mostly on the reduced vessels,[5] but it can be found on a few oxidized vessels too.[6] This feature is not found in other workshops that I know of.

Source of Inspiration

In terms of motifs and style, it is evident that the production is much inspired by Pergamene vessels, not just the MMB but also the *Applikenkeramik* (Hübner 1993a). This is particularly clear in the case of the symplegma scenes (Hübner 1993a, pls. 25–32) and the very popular ivy leaf with two rounded depressions (ivy A) (Hübner 1993a, pls. 16–23). In both productions, we also find the mannerism of rendering figures with naked upper body (or entirely naked) from behind (AIB-1*, AIB-3*, AIB-25*; Hübner 1993a, figs. 35.247, 263.2; 36.153, 156; 38.235, 241; 40.182); indeed, AIB-25* seems to be a copy of a Pergamene stamp or at least closely inspired by it. We may also mention the dressed female pouring wine from an amphora into a krater (AIB-2*, AIB-3*; Hübner 1993a, pls. 22.126, 45.219a, 46.223, 224), a dancer in spiral torsion (AIB-11*, AIB-12 [playing aulos]; Hübner 1993a, fig. 35.269.3 [dancing with torch]) and Priapos lifting his garment to reveal an erect phallus (AIB-1*; Hübner 1993a, fig. 40.199). Other decorative elements, such as suspended garlands and wreaths, correspond to the Aiolian koine in general, probably also ultimately of Pergamene origin, as discussed in Chapters 6 and 9.

Chronology

We have no firm dating evidence for this group. Petrova argued that the Mesambrian workshop was short-lived, functioning in the second quarter of the 2nd century. She referred to a sherd found in a building context at Apollonia together with material dating to the end of the 3rd to the middle of the 2nd century. In the same context were found 45 fragments of MMB, approximately half of which were attributed to the Ephesian Monogram PAR Workshop (unpublished). Because she dates this workshop's activity to the second quarter of the 2nd century, she arrives at the same date for her Mesambrian workshop (Petrova 2014, 225). This is probably too early for the Monogram PAR Workshop (see Chapter 14) and accordingly, also for the date of the Aiolis B production.

At Olbia, one fragment (AIB-37*) comes from a context (Cistern Л) which was probably closed in the second half of the 140s (see Chapter 20). Furthermore, a proportionally large number of fragments were found in Olbia's Sector R25, to which the city contracted in the second half of the 2nd century BCE (see Chapter 20). AIB-72 was found at Porthmion, together with several fragments of Demetrios' production (DEM-40, DEM-205, DEM-238, DEM-249), but the find designation is rather broad (Sector V), so perhaps we should not put too much weight on this. We are therefore obliged to resort to style in order to narrow down the chronology of this workshop.

As I suggested in Chapter 12, the production of Aiolis A probably preceded Aiolis B. This is especially evident in the case of the closely related AIA-4* and AIB-40*, which bridge the two groups. Because the earliest of Demetrios' production seems to derive directly from the heyday of the Aiolis B production, we can probably date the inception of the latter sometime before ca. 125, when Demetrios' first bowls were made. By and large, however, the two productions seem to have developed simultaneously. Accordingly, the production of Aiolis B can be tentatively dated to the (later part of the) third quarter of the 2nd century, most likely continuing to the end of the century and perhaps even beyond, if we are to bridge the gap

---

5 AIB-1*, AIB-3*, AIB-6, AIB-15, AIB-21–AIB-24, AIB-30, AIB-55, AIB-59*, AIB-71, AIB-90, AIB-91*, AIB-115*.
6 AIB-60*, AIB-84, AIB-118*, AIB-135*.

between the chalices of this production and the earliest Arretine sigillata inspired by it.

Distribution

Vessels attributed to the Aiolis B production have been found throughout the Pontic region (Fig. 66). Most come from the west coast, from Stranja at the south to Istros at the north (Agathopolis, Mesambria, Apollonia, Odessos, Tomis, Istros). As already mentioned, according to Petrova, they were most frequent in Mesambria, where they constituted up to 30% of the MMB in one excavation sector. At Istros, the percentage is no more than 1.2. On the north coast, the largest number was unearthed at Olbia, where Aiolis B vessels constitute 2.4%. Few were found at Chersonesos and within its chora (Beljaus, Čaika, and Kara Tobe), whereas in the Bosporan Kingdom, finds have been made at Pantikapaion (1.8%), Myrmekion (2.5%), Porthmion, and Libknechtovka village near Kerč, and a single instance is mentioned from the Kuban area. From the east coast are several fragments from Vani, where they seem to be quite common. Petrova refers to two fragments from Daskyleion (Petrova 2014, 224, fig. 8.3, 4), but I am not convinced that they belong to this group – at least neither shape nor decoration matches – and I have therefore left them out. From the Mediterranean, I have been able to identify only one vessel, the chalice AIB-116*, which, according to the Berlin museum's inventory, comes from Pergamon.

Place of Production

In previous research, vessels belonging to this group, such as AIB-20, AIB-76*, AIB-101, AIB-104, AIB-105, and AIB-123 from Pantikapaion, were attributed by V.S. Zabelina to Pergamon (1984, 162–163) and the same opinion has been expressed by S.A. Kovalenko (1987, 9), J. Bouzek (1990, 108, fig. 32.5), and S.Ju. Vnukov & S.A. Kovalenko (1998, figs. 4.6 and 6.1). However, as already mentioned, I have identified only one vessel of this production at Pergamon (AIB-116*), and if we compare our group with the Pergamene MMB published, for example, by de Luca (see also Chapter 9), it is clear that there is very little overlap in shape or in stamp motifs. Nevertheless, as mentioned above, Aiolis B seems to be much inspired by the Pergamene *Applikenkeramik*. So there is surely a connection.

As stated above, based on the proportions of the finds at Mesambria, Petrova suggested a Mesambrian origin for this group. This is indirectly supported by the finds from a survey in the Stranja region, located 50–100 km south of Mesambria. According to the illustrations in the brief report of this survey, 50% of the fragments of MMB can, in fact, be ascribed to Aiolis B (Gauvin 1997, pl. 6). One must assume that the sherds are illustrated because they were thought to be representative. They are unfortunately not commented upon in the publication. At any rate, they were published before a localization in southeast Bulgaria was proposed for the workshop, so this cannot be the reason for their inclusion in Gauvin's publication. Nevertheless, the situation is similar to the one we saw in Chapter 11 concerning the Meter Medallion Workshop: patterns of distribution do not necessarily reveal the place of production.

In 2010, AIB-29* was analysed archaeometrically by the Lyon laboratory of P. Dupont. The result of this analysis was that the clay is Aiolian and very close to that of Gryneion or Pergamon. This is a relatively broad characterization, and I should like to mention that, since there most likely was continuity from Aiolis A to Aiolis B, it is probable that they were produced the same place. AIA-15 has also been analysed by the Lyon laboratory and identified as Aiolian of the lower Kaikos Valley, that is, in the neighbourhood of Elaia or Pitane. As I have argued in Chapter 12, Elaia, located mid-way between Pergamon and Gryneion and less than 10 km from Gryneion, is the more likely of the two, because the fabric of Pitane is seemingly much more micaceous than the fabric of Aiolis A and B (and Pergamon).

CATALOGUE TO CHAPTER 13

BOWLS

A *Figural Decoration*

Dionysiaca and Erotes

AIB-1*

Mesambria, Tomb 119/2008, inv. 3954, Nessebar, Archaeological Museum. Fragmentary bowl, ca. two-thirds preserved; almost complete shape. ⌀ rim 14.5; vessel H 7.8; H:⌀ 1:1.9. Fabric: very fine, a few light-reflecting particles, some silvery mica on surface. Hard fired, reduced. Rim friezes: grooves; dots. Main decoration: two friezes, not separated. In upper frieze, Eros A with two dolphins on leashes; below, Dionysiac procession, Priapos lifting a long garment revealing his erect phallus, Papposilenos with thyrsos pointing at his genitalia, figures with lanterns and torches, women bathing, couple embracing. Calyx: small 'nelumbo' alternating with small acanthus folded at tip. Medallion: rosette A. Double-stamped.

AIB-2*

Vani, year and number unknown, Vani, Archaeological Museum. Upper half of bowl, joined from numerous frs. Dull red coat. Oxidized. No rim frieze. Main decoration: female right pouring wine from amphora into krater, kithara-playing Eros right; Eros A as space-filler.

AIB-3*

Olbia, Sector E7, square 578n, 579nw, yellow clay layer, O-E7-59-1664, Kiev, Institute of Archaeology storeroom. Body fr. H 3 × W 4.8, WT 0.45. Fabric: fine, compact, with light grey core and black margins, 7.5YR 3/1, core 4/2. Thin worn coat, slightly lustrous ext., int. glossy burnish with soapy feel, ext. 5YR 5/6, int. 10YR 4/3. Hard fired, reduced. Main decoration: figure with naked upper body and cloak wrapped around legs viewed from behind, extending left arm to left; draped female right pouring wine into krater on a high foot; leg of naked figure moving right. Double-stamped.

AIB-4*

Olbia, Sector NG, square 63, 64e, grey clay layer, O-НГ-46-3340, Kiev, Institute of Archaeology storeroom. Fr. of rim and upper body. H 5.6 × W 7, WT 0.32, ⌀ rim 12, 22%, RH 3.8. Fabric: fine, dense, 5YR 7/8. Dull coat, 10R 5/8. Hard fired, oxidized. No rim frieze. Main decoration: Eros A venerating cornucopia right.

AIB-5*

Istros, His-B 563, Bucharest, Institute of Archaeology storeroom. Fr. of upper body. H 2 × W 4.5, WT 0.4. Fabric: fine, compact, some very fine light-reflecting particles, 2.5YR 6/8. Dull coat, 2.5YR 5/8. Relatively hard fired, oxidized. Main decoration: Eros A venerating cornucopia right.
– Casan-Franga 1967, fig. 4.1; Domăneanțu 2000, 91 cat. 433, pl. 30.

AIB-6

Mesambria, Nessebar? Body fr. Reduced. Rim friezes: grooves; dots. Main decoration: Eros A(?). Double-stamped.
– Petrova 2014, 218, 225, figs. 2.2, 10.1.

AIB-7*

Olbia, O-39-1150, Kiev, Institute of Archaeology storeroom. Fr. of mid-body. H 4.1 × W 8.5, WT 0.32. Fabric: fine, compact, 5YR 6/8. Coat with slight lustre ext., int. with metallic sheen, 5YR 6/6. Very hard fired, oxidized. Rim friezes: grooves; dots. Main decoration: male dressed in fur and with a tall cap carrying *kanoun* piled with abundant rounded fruit to left.

Mantled Dancing Women

AIB-8*

Olbia, Sector NGS, O-НГС-08-287, Parutine, Olbia National Preserve storeroom. Fr. of rim and upper body. H 5.1 × W 5.5, WT 0.2, ⌀ rim 14, 10%, RH 2.3. Fabric: fine, dense, non-micaceous, 5YR 6/6. Thin slightly lustrous coat, ext. 5YR 4/6, 3/3, int. 2.5YR 4/6. Hard fired, oxidized. No rim frieze. Main decoration: female dancers moving right, each holding the end of the cloak of the woman in front of her.

AIB-9

Mesambria, Nessebar? Almost complete profile, lacking base. Reduced. Rim friezes: grooves; large Ionian kyma between friezes of dots. Main decoration: female dancers moving right, each holding the end of the cloak of the woman in front of her.
– Petrova 2014, 217, 225, figs. 1.1, 9.1.

AIB-10*

Istros, Sector MC1 Sa, His-56-55 [His-956], Bucharest, Institute of Archaeology storeroom. Fr. of upper body. H 5 × W 6, WT 0.45. Fabric: fine, compact. Thin slip. Relatively hard fired, oxidized. Rim frieze: ten-petalled rosette B alternating with leaf of Lesbian kyma. Main decoration: frontal female dancer between

tendrils with rosette A and vertical stem with stylized tendrils of alternating direction, ten-petalled rosette B as space-filler. Frieze separators: dots. Secondarily burnt.
– Domăneanţu 2000, 109 cat. 546, pl. 36 (identified as Pergamene).

Symplegma

AIB-11*
Istros, His-1064+B 433, Bucharest, Institute of Archaeology storeroom. Two joining body frs. H 7 × W 4.6, WT 0.39. Fabric: fine, compact. Self slip, burnished int. to a soapy feel. Very hard fired, reduced. Rim friezes: grooves; dots. Main decoration: male relining on *kline* (symplegma?), aulos-player in spiral motion; small wreath suspended above. Secondarily burnt. **AIB-11*** and **AIB-12*** could very well derive from the same (or related) mould(s); since they were found in different excavation sectors, they probably do not belong to the same bowl.
– Casan-Franga 1967, fig. 4.4; Domăneanţu 2000, 109 cat. 549, pl. 36 (identified as Pergamene).

AIB-12*
Istros, Sector Z2. His-57-957, Bucharest, Institute of Archaeology storeroom. Body fr. H 5.2 × W 5.2, WT 0.35. Fabric: fine, compact. Self slip, burnished at rim ext. and on int. to a soapy feel. Hard fired, reduced. Main decoration: aulos-player in spiral motion, symplegma; suspended wreath above. Secondarily burnt. Perhaps from same or related mould as **AIB-11**.
– Domăneanţu 2000, 109 cat. 548, pl. 36 (identified as Pergamene).

AIB-13
Istros, His-379, Bucharest, Institute of Archaeology storeroom. Body fr. H 4 × W 4.2, WT 0.35. Fabric: fine, compact. Int. burnished to a soapy feel. Hard fired, reduced. Rim frieze: dots. Main decoration: largely lost; part of bed (symplegma?). Secondarily burnt.
– Domăneanţu 2000, 108 cat. 545, pl. 36 (identified as Pergamene).

AIB-14
Apollonia, present whereabouts unknown. Fr. of lower body. Reduced. Main decoration: symplegma scene with *coitus a tergo*: couple on *kline* with profiled legs right.
– Petrova 2014, 217, 225, figs. 1.2, 9.2.

Animals

AIB-15
Mesambria, Nessebar? Body fr. Reduced. Rim friezes: grooves; dots. Main decoration: feline left; unidentified figure. Double-stamped.
– Petrova 2014, 219, 225, figs. 3.1, 9.5.

AIB-16*
Olbia, Sector E7, squares 624, 625, 626, House 14, O-E7-69-277, Kiev, Institute of Archaeology storeroom. Body fr. H 3.3 × W 4.3, WT 0.38. Fabric: fine, compact, no visible inclusions, 2.5Y 4/1. Thin coat with slight lustre ext., int. burnished to soapy feel, ext. 7.5YR 5/2, 10YR 2/1, int. 7.5YR 5/2. Relatively hard fired, reduced. Stacked in firing. Rim friezes: grooves; dots. Main decoration: two cranes flanking trident-like object, perhaps a Wadjet symbol on a sceptre?

AIB-17*
Olbia, Sector NGS, O-НГС-01-380, Parutine, Olbia National Preserve storeroom. Body fr. Oxidized. Rim frieze: dots. Main decoration: dolphin right; female with naked upper body right.

AIB-18*
Olbia, O-39-1454, Kiev, Institute of Archaeology storeroom. Fr. of mid-body. Fabric: finely micaceous, oxidized. Rim frieze: dots. Main decoration: dolphin left.

B   Calyx with Figural Decoration

AIB-19
Mesambria, Tomb 4/1964; found together with kantharos with pinched handles, Nessebar? Complete. Fabric: grey. Black coat. Reduced. Rim friezes: grooves; dots. Calyx: 'nelumbo' A alternating with straight acanthus leaves with double segmented vein; naked male seated right playing syrinx and bird turning head as space-fillers. Medallion: rosette A.
– Čimbuléva 2005, 95–96, fig. 5.1; Petrova 2014, 226, fig. 13.1.

AIB-20
Pantikapaion, M-63-315, Moscow, Puškin Museum of Fine Arts. Fr. of base and body. Oxidized. Calyx: straight acanthus leaves with double stem alternating with acanthus leaf with S-curved stem and tip bent towards left and acanthus stems with tendrils enclosing rosette A; above bent acanthus leaf, Eros A as space-filler. Medallion: missing, surrounded by ridge.
– Zabelina 1984, 163, fig. 10b (identified as Pergamene); Bouzek 1990, pl. 19.9; Petrova 2014, 220 n. 17.

AIB-21
Mesambria, Nessebar? Body fr. Reduced. Main decoration: Eros A alternating with bird right. Calyx: acanthus leaf with segmented vein and tip bent right alternating with lotus petal and acanthus flower with ivy-berry cluster. Double-stamped.
– Petrova 2014, 218, 225, figs. 2.3, 10.2.

AIB-22
Mesambria, Nessebar? Fr. of base and lower body. Reduced. Calyx: horizontal stem with stylized tendrils of alternating direction, Eros A, 'nelumbo' with ribbed interior. Medallion: rosette B or C. Double-stamped.
– Petrova 2014, 218, 225, figs. 2.1, 9.4.

AIB-23
Mesambria, Nessebar? Fr. of base and lower body. Reduced. Main decoration: Erotes(?) and an unidentified object. Calyx: palmettes with rhomboidal finial. Medallion: rosette B. Double-stamped. AIB-23 and AIB-24 may come from the same vessel.
– Petrova 2014, 223, 226, figs. 7.2, 13.2a.

AIB-24
Mesambria, Nessebar? Fr. of base and lower body. Reduced. Decoration as AIB-23, perhaps from the same vessel.
– Petrova 2014, 226, fig. 13.2b.

AIB-25*
Olbia, O-64-174, Kiev, Institute of Archaeology storeroom. Large body fr. H 7.2 × W 9.5, WT 0.35 14. Fabric: fine, compact, Gley 1 4/N. Thin dull coat, mottled ext.; int. highly burnished to a soapy feel with burnishing marks clearly showing, ext. Gley 1 5/N, 4/N, 2.5Y 6/3, int. Gley 1 3/N. Not too hard fired, reduced. Stacked in firing. Rim frieze: grooves. Main decoration: tall, straight acanthus leaf alternating with double-outlined plastic long petal and female with naked upper body and cloak around legs seen from behind; she holds a tortoise lyre in her left hand; between the above, 10-petalled rosettes on wavy stems. The figure on AIB-25* is so close to an applied relief figure on a fragment of a vessel from Pergamon (Hübner 1993a, 202 cat. 241, pl. 51) that it is conceivable that it was copied from the Pergamene vessel. The Pergamene figure wears an ivy wreath on her head and thus is most likely a maenad.

AIB-26
Vani, year and number unknown, Vani, Archaeological Museum. Body fr. Reduced. Calyx: acanthus stem with tendril enclosing rosette A, vertical stem with tendrils of opposite direction, Wadjet symbol.

C Scroll Decoration

Acanthus-Ivy Scroll with Figures as Space-Fillers

AIB-27
Beljaus, present whereabouts unknown. Complete. Firing unknown. Rim friezes: grooves; dots. Main decoration: acanthus-ivy scroll left with ivy A and ivy-berry clusters on wavy stems; naked male seated right playing syrinx as space-filler. Medallion: cannot be identified from photograph.
– Daševskaja et al. 1976, 321; Bouzek 1990, pl. 23.1 (identified as Pergamene); Petrova 2014, 220.

AIB-28*
Istros, Sector MC1 Sa. His-56-1184, Bucharest, Institute of Archaeology storeroom. Four joining frs. of base and lower body. H 4.5 × W 10, WT 0.4, ⌀ base 3.2. Self slip. Medium hard fired, oxidized. Rim frieze: dots. Main decoration: acanthus-ivy scroll right with ivy A. Above and below scroll, Eros right, naked male seated right playing syrinx, bird. Medallion: rosette B. Secondarily burnt.
– Domăneanțu 2000, 108 cat. 544, pl. 36 (identified as Pergamene); Petrova 2014, 220 n. 19.

Acanthus-Ivy Scroll

AIB-29*
Istros, His-485, Bucharest, Institute of Archaeology storeroom. Fr. of mid-body. H 3 × W 4.1, WT 0.35. Fabric: fine, compact. Burnished at rim ext. and on int. to a soapy feel. Hard fired, reduced. Rim friezes: grooves; dots. Main decoration: ivy scroll left with ivy A on wavy stems. Secondarily burnt. Sample analysed by P. Dupont/Lyon.
– Domăneanțu 2000, 111 cat. 560 (identified as Pergamene).

AIB-30
Mesambria, Nessebar? Body fr. Reduced. Main decoration: ivy scroll left with ivy A and ivy-berry cluster on wavy stems. Double-stamped.
– Petrova 2014, 220, 225, figs. 4.5, 10.8.

AIB-31
Stranja region, Akhtopol Museum. Body fr. Firing unknown. Rim frieze: dots. Main decoration: ivy scroll left with ivy-berry cluster on stem.
– Gauvin 1997, pl. 6, fourth fragment in lower row.

AIB-32*
Olbia, Sector NGS, O-НГС-05-615, Parutine, Olbia National Preserve storeroom. Fr. of rim and upper body. H 5.1 × W 5.3, WT 0.25, ⌀ rim 11, 15%, RH 2.2. Fabric: fine, dense, non-micaceous, 5YR 6/8. Thin slightly soapy coat, 2.5YR 5/8. Hard fired, oxidized. Rim frieze: dots. Main decoration: ivy A.

AIB-33
Stranja region, Akhtopol Museum. Body fr. Firing unknown. Rim frieze: dots. Main decoration: ivy A on stem, ivy-berry cluster.
– Gauvin 1997, pl. 6 last fragment in lower row.

AIB-34
Olbia, Sector R25, O-P25-09-3545, Parutine, Olbia National Preserve storeroom. Nine fragments of mid- and upper body, two joining. WT 0.2. Fabric: fine, a few light-reflecting particles, 2.5YR 6/8. Thin slightly soapy coat, ext. 2.5YR 4/8, uncoated int. Hard fired, oxidized. Rim frieze: grooves. Main decoration: large, simple ivy scroll left.

AIB-35
Olbia, Sector R25, O-P25-93-174, Parutine, Olbia National Preserve storeroom. Fr. of rim and upper body. H 3.6 × W 5.8, WT 0.35, ⌀ rim 12, 13%, RH 1.4. Fabric: relatively fine, micaceous, 2.5Y 6/3. Dull coat, 2.5Y 2.5/1. Medium hard fired, oxidized. Rim frieze: dots. Main decoration: ivy scroll with ivy B.

AIB-36*
Istros, His-993, Bucharest, Institute of Archaeology storeroom. Body fr. Oxidized. Rim frieze: dots. Main decoration: ivy scroll with ivy B and ivy-berry cluster.

AIB-37*
Olbia, O-E2-49-435, Kiev, Institute of Archaeology storeroom. Rim fr. H 4.3 × W 5.2, WT 0.4, ⌀ rim 13, 14%, RH 2.1. Fabric: fine, compact, 2.5YR 7/4, core 2.5YR 7/1. Coat with dull lustre, Gley 1 3/N. Hard fired, oxidized. Rim frieze: grooves. Main decoration: ivy scroll with ivy B right, with minute group of three-dot berries.
– Levi 1964b, 251, fig. 13.1; Petrova 2014, 227, fig. 15.3; St Petersburg, IIMK RAN, photo archive neg. I 43058.

AIB-38*
Myrmekion, M-57-1001, St Petersburg, IIMK RAN. Fr. of rim and upper body. H 5, WT 0.32, ⌀ rim 15, 8%, RH 3. Fabric: fine, highly micaceous, small lime inclusions, 2.5Y 5/2. Thin slightly lustrous coat with soapy surface, 5Y 3/1. Low fired, reduced. No rim frieze. Main decoration: ivy scroll with ivy B right.

Acanthus-Ivy-Flower Scroll

AIB-39*
According to museum inventory from "Köln", inv. 67,33, Köln, Römisch-Germanisches Museum (formerly collection of Joseph Max). Complete. ⌀ rim 10.6, RH 3; vessel H 7.3; H:⌀ 1:1.5. Fabric: very fine, non-micaceous. Dull slightly flaking orangish coat, slightly shiny on rim ext. from stacking. Relatively hard fired, oxidized. Rim frieze: dots. Main decoration: acanthus-ivy scroll with ivy A over-stamped with ivy-berry cluster on looped stems and tendrils enclosing rosette A and flowers with nine petals as well as bell-shaped flower; repeated three times. Medallion: rosette A over-stamped in the centre with ten-petalled rosette. The Cologne provenience is theoretically possible, though highly unlikely. The town was first settled in 38 BCE by the Ubii, a Germanic tribe.
– Berger 1995b, 135 cat. 10, figs. 30–31.

Acanthus-Flower Scroll

AIB-40*
Pantikapaion, M-63-289, Moscow, Puškin Museum of Fine Arts. Fr. of rim and upper body. H 4 × W 4, RH 1.7. Reduced. Rim friezes: grooves; dots. Main decoration: acanthus-flower scroll left, tendril enclosing rosette B.

Acanthus-Vine-Flower Scroll

AIB-41*
Olbia, Odessa, Historical Museum. Complete. Reduced. Rim friezes: grooves; dots. Main decoration: full body acanthus-vine-flower scroll left; tendrils enclosing various types of rosettes, palmettes on looped stems, bunches of grapes, birds turning head. Medallion: rosette A.

AIB-42
Mesambria, Nessebar? Two non-joining frs. of rim and body. Reduced. Rim friezes: grooves; dots. Main decoration: vine scroll with tendrils enclosing rosette A, bunch of grapes, bird.
– Petrova 2014, 220, 226, figs. 4.2a, 2b, 11.1.

Acanthus-Vine-Ivy Scroll

AIB-43
Čaika, present whereabouts unknown. Complete. Reduced. Rim frieze: Ionian kyma, upside-down between two grooves. Main decoration: full body acanthus-vine-ivy scroll left with bunches of grapes, tendrils enclosing rosette A; bird turning head back.
– Kovalenko 1987a, fig. 2.1; Petrova 2014, 224, fig. 8.7.

AIB-44

Čaika, present whereabouts unknown. Body fr. Reduced. Rim frieze: Ionian kyma, upside-down between two grooves. Main decoration: full body acanthus-vine-ivy scroll right with bunches of grapes; bird turning head back.
– Kovalenko 1987a, fig. 2.2; Petrova 2014, 224, fig. 8.6.

AIB-45

Myrmekion, Kerč History and Culture Reserve inv. KMAK 7882 (1960). Two joining body frs. Oxidized. Rim frieze: Ionian kyma. Main decoration: acanthus-ivy-vine scroll left.
– Grzegrzółka 2010, 101 cat. 117 (identified as Pergamene).

Vine Scroll

AIB-46

Mesambria, Nessebar? Body fr. Reduced. Rim frieze: Ionian kyma? Main decoration: vine scroll, bird flying right.
– Petrova 2014, 220, 225, figs. 4.3, 10.6.

AIB-47

Apollonia, present whereabouts unknown. Fr. of body close to rim. Reduced. Rim frieze: grooves. Main decoration: vine scroll.
– Petrova 2014, 220, 225, figs. 4.4, 10.7.

AIB-48

Vani, VII-225, present whereabouts unknown. Almost complete profile, lacking base. Firing unknown. Rim friezes: grooves; dots. Main decoration: vine(?) scroll, ivy-berry clusters on stems.
– Bouzek 1990, 120, fig. 36.5 (attributed to Asia Minor).

AIB-49

Istros, His-1927-1942-V 8575 R, Bucharest, Institute of Archaeology storeroom. Body fr. Oxidized. Rim frieze: dots. Main decoration: vine scroll(?) (top of vine leaf preserved).

Acanthus Scroll

AIB-50*

Olbia, Sector R25, O-P25-98-2449, Parutine, Olbia National Preserve storeroom. Fr. of lower body. H 3.3 × W 4.3, WT 0.3. Fabric: fine, non-micaceous, 7.5YR 6/4. Coat with pink metallic sheen ext., slightly duller int., 10R 4/3. Very hard fired, oxidized. Main decoration: acanthus scroll. Calyx: straight acanthus leaf below scroll as space-filler.

Scroll, type?

AIB-51

Vani, year and number unknown, Vani, Archaeological Museum. Fr. of rim and upper body. Reduced. Rim friezes: grooves; Ionian kyma with broad, double-outlined eggs separated by vertical astragal. Main decoration: part of scroll and buds (type?).

AIB-52

Mesambria, Nessebar? Three non-joining body frs. Reduced. Rim friezes: grooves; dots. Main decoration: scroll right (type?).
– Petrova 2014, 226, fig. 11.3.

AIB-53*

Olbia, Sector R25, O-P25-04-1906, Parutine, Olbia National Preserve storeroom. Rim fr. H 3.1 × W 5.3, WT 0.27. Fabric: fine, some light-reflecting particles, Gley 1 6/N. Dull coat, ext. 5Y 2.5/1, int. 5Y 4/1. Medium hard fired, reduced. No rim frieze. Main decoration: scroll (type?).

AIB-54

Kuban area, tomb, Armavir Museum. Firing unknown. Main decoration: scroll (type?).
– Lopatin & Malyšev 2002, pl. 6 (not seen).

D Garlands and Wreaths

Suspended Garlands

AIB-55

Mesambria, Nessebar? Fr. of lower body. Reduced. Main decoration: suspended garland(?) with *tainia*, the end of which hangs down; Eros A; birds right; several unidentified elements. Double-stamped.
– Petrova 2014, figs. 217, 225, 1.3, 9.3.

AIB-56*

Olbia, Sector NGS, O-НГС-06-768, Parutine, Olbia National Preserve storeroom. Fr. of mid-body. H 5 × W 4.1, WT 0.3. Fabric: fine, dense, a few light-reflecting particles, 2.5YR 6/8. Thin wash, 2.5YR 6/6. Hard fired, oxidized. Rim frieze: dots. Main decoration: bound garland suspended from *tainia* tied in knot; over garland, probably Wadjet symbol.

AIB-57

Olbia, O-1912-68, present whereabouts unknown. Fr. of rim and upper body. Firing unknown. Rim frieze: grooves. Main decoration: garlands suspended from *tainia* tied in bow; bird left over garland.
– St Petersburg, IIMK RAN, photo archive neg. II 19421.

AIB-58

Mesambria, Nessebar? Body fr. Reduced. Rim friezes: grooves; dots. Main decoration: bound garland; above it, rosette with four

petals and ivy-berry cluster at centre. Calyx: tip of palmette visible.
– Petrova 2014, 219, 225, figs. 3.2, 10.3.

AIB-59*
Myrmekion, M-58-470, St Petersburg, IIMK RAN. Fr. of mid body. H 3.8, WT 0.45. Fabric: very fine, dense, few light-reflecting particles, smooth on surface, Gley 2 7/5PB. Self slip, mottled ext. Hard fired, reduced. Main decoration: bound garlands suspended from *tainia* tied in bow, over horizontal floral elements; below this, remains of cross-hatched object. Double-stamped.

AIB-60*
Chersonesos, X-1965-78, St Petersburg, State Hermitage Museum. Body fr. H 4.4, WT 0.37. Fabric: fine, many very fine light-reflecting particles, 2.5YR 6/6. Dull coat, 2.5YR 5/8. Oxidized. Main decoration: bound garland suspended from *tainia*(?). Calyx: palmette on looped stem alternating with vertical acanthus stem with rosette A. Double-stamped.

Ivy Wreath

AIB-61
Mesambria, Nessebar? Almost complete profile, lacking base. Reduced. Rim friezes: grooves; Ionian kyma between friezes of dots. Main decoration: ivy wreath left.
– Petrova 2014, 220, 225, figs. 4.1, 10.5.

Myrtle Wreath

AIB-62*
Olbia, Sector NGS, House III-2 R 255/85, O-НГС-89-497+397a, Parutine, Olbia National Preserve storeroom. Two non-joining rim frs. H 5 × W 8.4, WT 0.23–0.41, ⌀ rim 13.5, 38%, RH 2.5. Fabric: fine, slightly micaceous, small voids, 5YR 5/6. Thin flaking coat with very slight lustre, 2.5YR 5/6. Hard fired, oxidized. No rim frieze. Main decoration: myrtle wreath right with three slender leaves and ivy-berry clusters. Attribution to Aiolis B is tentative.
– Guldager Bilde 2010, 281 cat. F-68, pl. 181 (identified as Pergamene).

AIB-63*
Olbia, Sector R25, O-P25-09-442, Parutine, Olbia National Preserve storeroom. Fr. of mid-body. H 3.8 × W 3.1, WT 0.25. Fabric: fine, compact, no visible inclusions, 5YR 6/6. Thin coat with bluish metallic sheen, ext. 10R 4/8, uncoated int. Hard fired, oxidized. Main decoration: above, myrtle wreath with three bound petals and berries left; below, ivy-acanthus scroll left.

AIB-64*
Olbia, Sector R25, O-P25-09-3546, Parutine, Olbia National Preserve storeroom. Fr. of mid-body. H 4.1 × W 2.8, WT 0.3. Fabric: fine, a few light-reflecting particles, 2.5YR 6/8. Thin slightly soapy coat, 10R 4/8. Hard fired, oxidized. Rim frieze: groove; Ionian kyma with double outline. Main decoration: simple myrtle wreath with dotted stem left.

AIB-65*
Olbia, Sector R25, O-P25-09-61[?], Parutine, Olbia National Preserve storeroom. Fr. of upper body close to rim. H 4.6 × W 3.5, WT 0.25. Fabric: fine, compact, no visible inclusions, 5YR 6/6. Thin dull coat, 10R 5/8. Hard fired, oxidized. Rim friezes: groove; Ionian kyma. Main decoration: myrtle wreath with three bound leaves left.

AIB-66*
Olbia, Sector R25, O-P25-93-555, Parutine, Olbia National Preserve storeroom. Fr. of upper body. H 3.2, WT 0.32. Fabric: fine, some light-reflecting particles, 5YR 6/6. Thin coat ext. with pinkish metallic sheen, 10R 5/6. Hard fired, oxidized. Rim frieze: rouletting. Main decoration: bound myrtle wreath left with three leaves and berries on stems.

E   *Vegetal Decoration*

Calyx

AIB-67*
Olbia, Sector R25, O-P25-06-818, Parutine, Olbia National Preserve storeroom. Fr. of upper body. H 3.3, WT 0.4. Fabric: fine, some light-reflecting particles, some voids, 5YR 7/6. Thin coat ext. with pinkish metallic sheen, ext. 10R 4/6, int. 2.5YR 4/8. Hard fired, oxidized. Calyx: palmette on looped stem, 'nelumbo' A or B.

AIB-68*
Olbia, Sector R25, O-P25-00-1947, Parutine, Olbia National Preserve storeroom. Fr. of lower body. H 3.2, WT 0.3. Fabric: fine, some light-reflecting particles, 5YR 6/6. Thin coat with pinkish metallic sheen, ext. 10R 5/6, int. 10R 4/6. Hard fired, oxidized. Calyx: acanthus A alternating with lotus petal and naturalistic acanthus leaf with curved stem.

AIB-69
Mesambria, Nessebar? Fr. of rim and upper body. Reduced. Rim friezes: grooves; dots. Calyx: lotus petal flanked by acanthus flowers(?) on vertical stems.
– Petrova 2014, 223, 226, figs. 7.1, 12.7.

AIB-70
Mesambria, Nessebar? Body fr. Reduced. Calyx: slender, pointed lotus petals.
– Petrova 2014, 224, 226, figs. 8.2, 11.2.

AIB-71
Mesambria, Nessebar? Fr. of lower body. Reduced. Main decoration: palmettes with rhomboidal finial. Calyx: palmettes on looped stems. Double-stamped.
– Petrova 2014, 219, 225, figs. 3.3, 10.4.

AIB-72
Porthmion, Sector V, П-77-116, Kerč History and Culture Reserve inv. KMAK 9514. Fr. of base and lower body. Reduced. Calyx: palmettes on looped stems; around base, a single row of very small straight acanthus leaves. Medallion: rosette A?
– Grzegrzółka 2010, 154 cat. 231 (attributed to Asia Minor).

Calyx with 'Nelumbo' and Isolated Long Petals

AIB-73*
Myrmekion, Sector И, M-49-798, St Petersburg, State Hermitage Museum. Complete profile; all of rim, part of wall and complete medallion. H 8.2, WT 0.25, ⌀ rim 12, RH 3.2, ⌀ base 3.1. Fabric: fine, dense. Thin dull black coat, burnished at rim. Reduced. Rim friezes: grooves; dots. Main decoration: plastic long petals alternating with 'nelumbo' A and straight acanthus leaf; in between, small Corinthian(?) columns upon which sits bird turning head back. Medallion: rosette B.
– Gajdukevič 1958, fig. 64.1; Petrova 2014, 224, fig. 8.5

AIB-74
Stranja region, Akhtopol Museum. Fr. of mid-body. Firing unknown. Calyx: 'nelumbo' B, bird turning head back, long petals not preserved because fragment is small.
– Gauvin 1997, pl. 6, first fragment in lower row (oriented incorrectly).

AIB-75
Stranja region, Akhtopol Museum. Fr. of rim and body. Firing unknown. Rim frieze: grooves. Calyx: 'nelumbo' A or B alternating with tendrils which enclose rosette A, probably bird turning head, long petals not preserved because fragment is small.
– Gauvin 1997, pl. 6, first fragment in middle row; Petrova 2014, 218 n. 7.

AIB-76*
Pantikapaion, M-63-458, Moscow, Puškin Museum of Fine Arts, inv. KP 280574. Three joining frs. of mid- and lower body. H 7.4, WT 0.45. Fabric: very fine buff, a few light-reflecting particles (no fresh break). Dull orange coat, glossy at rim ext. Oxidized. Rim friezes: grooves; dots. Main decoration: two stylized long petals alternating with 'nelumbo' B.
– Zabelina 1984, 163, fig. 10a; AGSP 1984, pl. CLXIII.4; Bouzek 1990, fig. 32.5, pl. 19.7 (identified as Pergamene).

AIB-77*
Olbia, Sector R25, O-P25-02-1829, Parutine, Olbia National Preserve storeroom. Two joining frs. of base and lower body. H 4.2 × W 5.8, WT 0.22, ⌀ base 3. Fabric: fine, slightly micaceous, 7.5YR 7/4. Thin dull coat, ext. 10R 6/6, int. 10R 5/6. Medium hard fired, oxidized. Main decoration: three stylized long petals alternating with 'nelumbo' B; calyx of small leaves around medallion. Medallion: rosette C.

AIB-78*
Myrmekion, M-58-650+1156+1265, St Petersburg, IIMK RAN. Three joining frs., one close to rim, mid- and lower body. WT 0.33. Fabric: very fine, compact, sparse minute inclusions of silvery mica, 10R 6/6. Thick uniform sigillata-like coat with dull lustre, 10R 4/8. Oxidized. Rim friezes: grooves; dots. Main decoration: two stylized long petals alternating with 'nelumbo' B.

AIB-79
Istros, His-736, Bucharest, Institute of Archaeology storeroom. Fr. of upper body. H 2.3 × W 3.4, WT 0.25. Fabric: fine, compact, some very fine light-reflecting particles, 5YR 6/8. Dull coat ext., slightly glossy int., 2.5YR 5/6. Relatively hard fired, oxidized. Main decoration: two stylized long petals alternating with 'nelumbo' B.
– Domăneanțu 2000, 95 cat. 461, pl. 31 (identified as Ephesian).

AIB-80
Stranja region, Akhtopol Museum. Fr. of base and lower body. Firing unknown. Main decoration: palmette on looped stem, vertical stem with stylized tendrils of alternating direction, stylized long petals. Medallion: cannot be identified from photograph.
– Gauvin 1997, pl. 6 second fragment in middle row; Petrova 2014, 206 n. 5.

AIB-81
Stranja region, Akhtopol Museum. Body fr. Firing unknown. Main decoration: palmette on looped tendril alternating with stylized long petals.
– Gauvin 1997, pl. 6 last fragment in upper row.

AIB-82
Olbia, Sector NGS, O-НГС-00-49, Parutine, Olbia National Preserve storeroom. Fr. of upper body. H 4 × W 7.1, WT 0.3 10. Fabric: fine, dense, non-micaceous, 5YR 7/8. Firm dull coat with

soapy feel, 2.5YR 4/8. Hard fired, oxidized. Rim friezes: grooves; dots. Main decoration: groups of three stylized long petals alternating with 'nelumbo' A or B.

Calyx with Isolated Long Petals, No 'Nelumbo'

AIB-83* (see also Fig. 86)
Olbia, O-64-2609, Parutine, Olbia National Preserve storeroom. Three body frs., two joining. H 4.8 × W 5.8, WT 0.4–0.55. Max. ⌀ 10. Fabric: fine, dense, non-micaceous, 5YR 6/8. Thin slightly soapy coat, ext. 10R 6/8 int. 10R 5/8. Oxidized. Rim friezes: groove; dots. Main decoration: two stylized long petals alternating with straight acanthus leaf on tip of which sits bird turning its head back; leaf is flanked by rosettes A on floral stems.

AIB-84
Olbia, Sector NGS, O-НГС-04-242, Parutine, Olbia National Preserve storeroom. Fr. of mid-body. H 2.9 × W 4.3, WT 0.32. Fabric: fine, dense, a few light-reflecting particles, 2.5YR 6/8. Thin wash, 2.5YR 6/6. Hard fired, oxidized. Rim frieze: dots. Main decoration: two stylized long petals alternating with straight acanthus leaf on tip of which sits bird turning its head back; leaf is flanked by rosettes A on floral stems. Double-stamped.

AIB-85
Kara Tobe, K-85-92, 124, present whereabouts unknown. Almost complete shape, lacking rim. Firing unknown. Rim friezes: grooves; dots. Main decoration: two long petals alternating with acanthus A. Medallion: rosette A.
– Vnukov & Kovalenko 1998, fig. 6.2 (identified as Pergamene).

AIB-86*
Istros, His-V 8573 O, Bucharest, Institute of Archaeology storeroom. Fr. of rim and upper body. H 5.8 × W 4.4, WT 0.41, RH 2.4. Fabric: fine, slightly micaceous. Red-brown coat with metallic sheen. Relatively hard fired, oxidized. Rim frieze: dots. Main decoration: double-outlined long petals alternating with acanthus A. Secondarily burnt.
– Domăneanțu 2000, 130 cat. 641, pl. 45.

AIB-87*
Istros, His-B 457/V 19426, Bucharest, Institute of Archaeology storeroom. Fr. of rim and upper body. H 4 × W 8, WT 0.38, ⌀ rim 10.5, 8%, RH 2.5. Fabric: fine, dense, non-micaceous with some voids, 5YR 7/6. Coat with metallic sheen ext. at rim and int., 5YR 5/4. Relatively hard fired, oxidized. Rim frieze: dots. Main decoration: double-outlined long petals alternating with acanthus (type?).
– Domăneanțu 2000, 131 cat. 642, pl. 45.

AIB-88
Mesambria, Nessebar? Body fr. Reduced. Rim friezes: grooves; dots. Main decoration: two stylized long petals alternating with acanthus leaf bent to right and vertical stem with stylized tendrils of alternating direction.
– Petrova 2014, 222, 226, figs. 6.1, 11.5.

AIB-89
Mesambria, Nessebar? Fr. of base and lower body. Reduced. Main decoration: isolated stylized long petal alternating with acanthus leaves with segmented mid rib. Medallion: rosette A.
– Petrova 2014, 224, 226, figs. 8.1, 12.6.

AIB-90
Mesambria, Nessebar? Fr. of rim and upper body. Reduced. Rim friezes: grooves; dots. Main decoration: two stylized long petals alternating with elements of vine (bunch of grapes) and rosette (type?). Double-stamped.
– Petrova 2014, 221, 226, figs. 5.1, 12.4.

AIB-91*
Tomis, Tomb II/1962, inv. 3807, Constanta Museum. Complete. ⌀ rim 11.5; vessel H 6.5; H:⌀ 1:1.8. Fabric: fine, a few small lime inclusions. Thin slip of the same clay as the main fabric. Hard fired, reduced. Rim friezes: grooves; dots. Main decoration: groups of three yoked stylized long petals alternating with column of small vine leaves placed on top of one another. Medallion: rosette A. Double-stamped.
– Bucovală 1967, 93; Ocheșeanu 1969, cat. 20; Petrova 2014, 226, fig. 14.

AIB-92
Mesambria, Nessebar? Fr. of rim and upper body. Reduced. Rim friezes: grooves; dots. Main decoration: stylized long petal with double outline alternating with Wadjet symbol(?).
– Petrova 2014, 221, 226, figs. 5.2, 12.2.

F   *Linear Decoration*

Plastic Long Petals

AIB-93*
Istros, His-V 19352, Bucharest, Institute of Archaeology storeroom. Body fr. H 3.4 × W 2.9, WT 0.4. Fabric: fine, compact. Self slip, burnished at rim ext. and on int. to a soapy feel. Hard fired, reduced. Rim friezes: grooves; dots. Secondarily burnt.

AIB-94
Istros, His-995, Bucharest, Institute of Archaeology storeroom. Fr. of upper body. Reduced.

AIB-95
Mesambria, Nessebar? Fr. of base and lower body. Reduced. Around base ring probably single row of very small straight acanthus leaves. Medallion: rosette A.
– Petrova 2014, 223, 226, figs. 7.3, 12.8.

AIB-96
Mesambria, Nessebar? Fr. of rim and upper body. Reduced. Rim friezes: grooves; dots.
– Petrova 2014, 221, 226, figs. 5.4, 12.5.

Stylized Long Petals

AIB-97
Olbia, Tomb 56, O-1901-3069/inv. Ол-522, St Petersburg, State Hermitage Museum. Complete. Firing unknown. Rim frieze: grooves. Medallion: rosette B.
– Farmakovskij 1903a, 46, fig. 43; Parovič-Pešikan 1974, fig. 86.5; Petrova 2014, 222 n. 34; St Petersburg, IIMK RAN, photo archive neg. II 17934.

AIB-98
Odessos, present whereabouts unknown. Complete. Reduced. Rim friezes: grooves; dots. Medallion: rosette B.
– Tončeva 1953, 38, fig. 65; Petrova 2014, 227, fig. 15.1.

AIB-99
Mesambria, Nessebar? Two non-joining frs. of rim and large part of body. Reduced. Multiple rim friezes: grooves; dots; horizontal stem of stylized tendrils of alternating direction.
– Petrova 2014, 222, 226, figs. 6.3, 11.4.

AIB-100*
Istros, His-1187, Bucharest, Institute of Archaeology storeroom. Fr. of rim and upper body. H 6.3 × W 10, WT 0.31, ⌀ rim 13, 27%, RH 2.8. Fabric: fine, compact, fine light-reflecting particles, some voids, 2.5YR 6/6. Thin dull coat with slight lustre at rim ext. and int., ext. 2.5YR 5/6, int. 2.5YR 5/8. Hard fired, oxidized. Rim friezes: grooves; dots.
– Domăneanțu 2000, 141 cat. 703, pl. 51.

AIB-101
Pantikapaion, M-48-86, Moscow, Puškin Museum of Fine Arts. Fr. of rim and upper body. Reduced. Rim friezes: grooves; dots.
– Zabelina 1984, 162, fig. 9b (identified as Pergamene); Bouzek 1990, pl. 21.7; Petrova 2014, 222 n. 33.

AIB-102*
Olbia, cliff, humus layer, O-68-393, Kiev, Institute of Archaeology storeroom. Body fr. H 2.6 × W 4.3, WT 0.3. Fabric: standard, Gley 1 4/N. Dull ext. except for rim, where burnished, burnished to soapy feel int., Gley 1 2.5/N. Hard fired, reduced. Rim friezes: grooves; dots.

AIB-103
Mesambria, Nessebar? Fr. of rim and upper body. Reduced. Rim frieze: grooves. Main decoration: stylized long petals with double outline.
– Petrova 2004, 221, 226, figs. 5.3, 12.3.

G Rim Fragments

Multiple Rim Friezes

AIB-104
Pantikapaion, M-62-615, Moscow, Puškin Museum of Fine Arts. Two joining rim frs. Reduced. Multiple rim friezes: grooves; dots; Lesbian kyma.
– Zabelina 1984, 162, fig. 9a (identified as Pergamene); Bouzek 1990, pl. 21.6; Petrova 2014, 222 n. 33.

AIB-105
Pantikapaion, M-58-938, Moscow, Puškin Museum of Fine Arts. Rim fr. Reduced. Multiple rim friezes: grooves; dots; Lesbian kyma.
– Zabelina 1984, 162, fig. 9d (identified as Pergamene); Bouzek 1990, pl. 21.9; Petrova 2014, 222 n. 33; 227, fig. 15.2

AIB-106
Stranja region, Akhtopol Museum. Rim fr. Firing unknown. Multiple rim friezes: grooves; dots; Lesbian kyma.
– Gauvin 1997, pl. 6 third fragment in upper row.

AIB-107
Mesambria, Nessebar? Fr. of rim and upper body. Reduced. Multiple rim friezes: grooves; dots; horizontal stem of stylized tendrils of alternating direction.
– Petrova 2014, 222, 226, figs. 6.2, 12.1.

Single Rim Friezes

AIB-108
Kara Tobe, K-94-183, present whereabouts unknown. Rim fr. Firing unknown. Rim frieze: Ionian kyma, upside-down between two grooves.
– Vnukov & Kovalenko 1998, fig. 7.1 (identified as Pergamene).

AIB-109*
Istros, His-507, Bucharest, Institute of Archaeology storeroom. Fr. of upper body. Oxidized. Rim friezes: groove; dots. Main decoration: unidentified traces.

AIB-110
Istros, His-823, Bucharest, Institute of Archaeology storeroom. Body fr. close to rim. Reduced. Rim frieze: dots. Main decoration: unidentified traces.

AIB-111
Vani, year and number unknown, Vani, Archaeological Museum. Body fr. close to rim. Blotchy reddish-brown coat. Oxidized. Rim friezes: grooves; dots. Main decoration: unidentified traces.

H   Decoration Unknown

AIB-112
Apollonia, present whereabouts unknown.
– Nedev & Draževa 2007, 357 (not seen); Petrova 2014, 222 n. 30.

AIB-113
Apollonia, present whereabouts unknown.
– Gjuzelev 2007, 274 (not seen); Petrova 2014, 222 n. 30.

AIB-114
Apollonia, present whereabouts unknown.
– Nedev & Gospodinov 2007, 353–354 (not seen); Petrova 2014, 222 n. 31.

SUPPLEMENTARY SHAPES

Bowl or Krater with Feet in the Form of Shells

AIB-115*
Olbia, Sector NGS, O-НГС-86-689, Parutine, Olbia National Preserve storeroom. Fr. of base and lower body. H 6.3 × W 6.2, WT 0.4. Fabric: fine, non-micaceous, Gley 1 5/10Y. Thin dull wash, int. with soapy feel, 5Y 2.5/1, 3/1. Medium hard fired, reduced. Main decoration: kithara player seated on rock, unidentified figure, Eros left in between. Medallion: frieze of large astragals surrounds missing medallion. Double-stamped. Secondarily burnt.

Chalice

AIB-116*
Pergamon, V.I. 5863, Berlin, Antikensammlung (formerly Mavrogordato collection, 1910). Complete. ⌀ rim 14.1, ⌀ base 9.6; vessel H 15.8. Fabric: fine, dense. Dull blotchy reddish-brown coat. Very hard fired, oxidized. Rim frieze: large double-outlined Ionian kyma. Main decoration: Eros A repeated 22 times. Calyx: acanthus with folded tip alternating with broad lotus petals; in between, stem with stylized tendrils of alternating direction. Medallion: covered by foot. Frieze separators: dots.
– Grüßinger et al. 2011, 476 cat. 3.96.

AIB-117
Libknechtovka village near Kerč, present whereabouts unknown. Fragmentary vessel; complete profile. ⌀ rim 19; vessel H 15. Oxidized. Rim frieze: grooves. Main decoration: ivy scroll left with ivy A and ivy-berry clusters on looped stems. Calyx: palmettes on looped stems alternating with acanthus stem with tendril enclosing rosette A, left and right; below rosettes, Eros A repeated five times and naked male seated right playing syrinx represented once.
– Smirnova 1967, figs. 55, 56 (fig. 55 reversed); Petrova 2014, 220 n. 20.

Bowl with Shallow Body, High Collared Rim, and (Ridged) Band Handle(s)

AIB-118*
Olbia, Sector E3, square 63, pit, O-E3-54-2851, Kiev, Institute of Archaeology storeroom. Complete profile; three frs. of rim and neck and two frs. of base and body, all joining; attachment of vertical band handle, width 1.7. H 7 × W 11.5, WT 0.3, vessel H 5.6, ⌀ rim 11, 26%, ⌀ base 5. Fabric: fine, compact, no visible inclusions, 2.5YR 7/6. Mottled coat with slight lustre ext., dull int., ext. 10R 5/4, 5/6, 4/1, int. 10R 4/4, 4/6, 4/1. Hard fired, oxidized. Rim frieze: Ionian kyma, upside-down (very blurred). Calyx: double-stamped palmettes with egg as space-filler. Wide, flat base.

AIB-119*
Myrmekion, M-57-97, St Petersburg, State Hermitage Museum. Two joining frs. of base and lower body. H 12, WT 0.35, ⌀ base 5.6. Fabric: no fresh break for observation. Thin coat with metallic sheen. Oxidized. Main decoration: above, acanthus scroll with ivy-berry cluster; below, short long petals with double outline alternating with male seated right and probably playing syrinx (stamp mutilated). Plain flat base.

AIB-120
Kara Tobe, K-97-187, present whereabouts unknown. Fr. of body and shoulder. Firing unknown. Rim frieze: small Ionian kyma. Main decoration: scroll left; rosette with six petals. AIB-120 and AIB-121 probably belong to the same vessel.
– Vnukov & Kovalenko 1998, fig. 6.1 (identified as Pergamene); Petrova 2014, 222 n. 36.

AIB-121
Kara Tobe, K-91-102, present whereabouts unknown. Large fr. of rim and body with attachments of handle. Firing unknown. Decoration as AIB-120, probably from the same vessel.
– Vnukov & Kovalenko 1998, fig. 4.6 (identified as Pergamene); Petrova 2014, 222 n. 36.

AIB-122*
Olbia, O-64-1686, 1689(?), Kiev, Institute of Archaeology storeroom. Fr. of neck and body with part of base, non-joining fr. of base and lower body. H 5.4 × W 6, WT 0.35, ⌀ base 7. Fabric: fine, compact, non-micaceous, 2.5YR 6/8. Dull coat, 10R 6/8. Hard fired, oxidized. Rim frieze: groove. Main decoration: ivy-acanthus scroll with ivy B left. Calyx: acanthus with bent tip alternating with lotus petal. Wide, profiled base.

AIB-123
Pantikapaion, M-63-392, Moscow, Puškin Museum of Fine Arts. Body fr. Oxidized. Rim frieze: deep groove. Main decoration: ivy-acanthus scroll with ivy B left; acanthus stem has hatched leaf sheaths. Calyx: acanthus A alternating with rosette A on incised stems with tendrils.
– Zabelina 1984, 163, fig. 10d (identified as Pergamene); Bouzek 1990, pl. 19.10.

AIB-124*
Olbia, Sector R25, O-P25-93-554, Parutine, Olbia National Preserve storeroom. Fr. of lower body. H 3, WT 0.3. Fabric: fine, some light-reflecting particles, 5YR 6/6. Thin coat ext. with pinkish metallic sheen, 10R 5/6. Hard fired, oxidized. Rim frieze: groove. Main decoration: ivy-acanthus scroll with ivy B left; acanthus stem has hatched leaf sheaths.

AIB-125*
Olbia, Sector E, "B", Pit 3, O-E-51-1906, Kiev, Institute of Archaeology storeroom. Fr. of neck, shoulder and body. H 3.4 × W 6.5, WT 0.25, max. ⌀ 11.6. Fabric: fine, soft, non-micaceous, no visible inclusions, 2.5YR 7/4. Thin dull rather worn coat, 2.5YR 5/8. Relatively hard fired, oxidized. No rim frieze. Main decoration: alternating buds and pointed petals left, probably myrtle wreath.

AIB-126*
Chersonesos, X-1959-20, St Petersburg, State Hermitage Museum. Body fr. H 4.2, WT 0.26. Fabric: very fine, compact (no fresh break). Coat with metallic sheen, especially int., 2.5YR 3/1. Oxidized. Rim frieze: groove. Calyx: acanthus with bent tip, ovoid petal, rosette A on incised wavy stem between them.

AIB-127*
Istros, His-B 512/V 19332406, Bucharest, Institute of Archaeology storeroom. Fr. of base and lower body. H 4.3 × W 6, WT 0.35, ⌀ base 6. Fabric: fine, compact, no visible inclusions, 5YR 7/8. Dull coat, 2.5YR 5/8. Hard fired, oxidized. Calyx: tall lotus petals alternating with other straight vegetal elements with finely dotted outline.
– Domăneanțu 2000, 137 cat. 676, pl. 49.

AIB-128
Olbia, O-1909-1582, present whereabouts unknown. Fragmentary; complete profile except for base; one ridged band handle preserved. Firing unknown. Rim friezes: groove; spool-like element (stylized astragal?). Main decoration: crossed stylized long petals, rosette A.
– St Petersburg, IIMK RAN, photo archive neg. III 3430.

AIB-129*
Olbia, Sector R25, O-P25-02-1421, 1422, Parutine, Olbia National Preserve storeroom. Two non-joining body frs.; tiny part of handle attachment. H 3.2, WT 0.4. Fabric: fine, some light-reflecting particles, 5YR 6/6. Thin coat with pinkish metallic sheen, 10R 5/6. Hard fired, oxidized. Main decoration: crossed stylized long petals alternating with acanthus A.

AIB-130*
Olbia, Sector R25, O-P25-99-2321+2321a, Parutine, Olbia National Preserve storeroom. Two joining frs. of base and lower body, one non-joining body fr. H 6 × W 8.8, WT 0.27, ⌀ base 7. Fabric: fine, micaceous, 5YR 7/6. Thin coat with pinkish metallic sheen, 10R 5/4. Hard fired, oxidized. Main decoration: three stylized long petals alternating with two crossed ones, with vertical wavy line between them. Plain disc base.

AIB-131*
Myrmekion, M-57-1391, St Petersburg, IIMK RAN. Fr. of shoulder and body. H 4.6, WT 0.4. Fabric: very fine, compact, sparse minute inclusions of silvery mica, 10R 6/8. Thin dull coat, ext. 10R 5/8, uncoated int. Oxidized. Rim frieze: deep groove. Main decoration: two slender long petals separated by dotted line alternating with partly stamped, partly incised vertical acanthus-floral scroll. No calyx.

AIB-132*
Olbia, Sector R25, O-P25-99-2072, Parutine, Olbia National Preserve storeroom. Fr. of lower body with tiny part of base. Oxidized. Main decoration: stylized long petals.

Cup with Band Handle(s)

AIB-133*
Olbia, Sector R25, O-P25-93-1706+1708, Parutine, Olbia National Preserve storeroom. Two joining frs. of mid- and lower body; attachment of flat handle at base. H 5.3, WT 0.3. Fabric: fine, some light-reflecting particles, 5YR 6/6. Thin coat ext. with pinkish metallic sheen, 10R 5/6. Medium hard fired, oxidized. Rim frieze: rouletting. Calyx: widely distanced acanthus leaf, lotus petal, and incised vertical floral stem.

AIB-134*
Olbia, Sector R25, O-P25-03-1913, Parutine, Olbia National Preserve storeroom. Fr. of rim and upper body with handle attachment at rim. H 4.5, WT 0.15. Fabric: fine, some light-reflecting particles, 5YR 6/6. Thin coat with pinkish metallic sheen, ext. 10R 5/6, int. 10R 4/6. Hard fired, oxidized. Rim frieze: groove. Main decoration: acanthus scroll(?) left; the acanthus stem has hatched leaf sheaths.

AIB-135*
Olbia, Sector E6-7, squares 598e, 608e, grey clay layer, O-E6-7-61-256, Kiev, Institute of Archaeology storeroom. Fr. of rim and body; attachment of band handle below rim, 2.3 cm wide. H 6 × W 7.3, WT 0.3, ⌀ rim 9, 32%, RH 3.8. Fabric: fine, compact, no visible inclusions, 5YR 7/6. Thin slip, dull ext., with dull lustre int., 2.5YR 5/8. Hard fired, oxidized. No rim frieze. Main decoration: stylized long petals alternating with rosette on incised stem. Double-stamped.

Cup?

AIB-136*
Olbia, Sector R25, O-P25-09-3548, Parutine, Olbia National Preserve storeroom. Fr. of base and lower body. H 3.1 × W 3.5, WT 0.2. Fabric: fine, compact, no visible inclusions, 5YR 6/6. Thin dull coat, 10R 5/8. Hard fired, oxidized. Main decoration: vertical myrtle leaves between pairs of stylized long petals(?) enclosing vertical column of upside-down veined petals.

Beaker

AIB-137*
Olbia, Sector Sever-Zapad, O-C3-81-14, Parutine, Olbia National Preserve storeroom. Fr. of rim and body. H 5.7 × W 4.7, WT 0.35, ⌀ rim 7, 13%, RH 3.5. Fabric: fine, compact, non-micaceous, 5YR 6/6. Thin dull coat with a few lustrous highlights ext., int. coated only at rim, 10R 5/6. Hard fired, oxidized. Rim frieze: rouletting; Ionian kyma (partly effaced by rouletting). Main decoration: ivy scroll with ivy A left; the stem has hatched leaf sheaths (small, worn stamp).

DISTRIBUTION

Apollonia

AIB-14, AIB-47, AIB-112–AIB-114

Beljaus

AIB-27

Čaika

AIB-43, AIB-44

Chersonesos

AIB-60*, AIB-126*

Istros

AIB-5*, AIB-10*–AIB-13, AIB-28*, AIB-29*, AIB-36*, AIB-49, AIB-79, AIB-86*, AIB-87*, AIB-93*, AIB-94, AIB-100*, AIB-109*, AIB-110, AIB-127*

Kara Tobe

AIB-85, AIB-108, AIB-120, AIB-121

Kuban Area

AIB-54

Libknechtovka Village Near Kerč

AIB-117

Mesambria

AIB-1*, AIB-6, AIB-9, AIB-15, AIB-19, AIB-21–AIB-24, AIB-30, AIB-42, AIB-46, AIB-52, AIB-55, AIB-58, AIB-61, AIB-69–AIB-71, AIB-88–AIB-90, AIB-92, AIB-95, AIB-96, AIB-99, AIB-103, AIB-107

Myrmekion

AIB-38*, AIB-45, AIB-59*, AIB-73*, AIB-78*, AIB-119*, AIB-131*

Odessos

AIB-98

Olbia

AIB-3*, AIB-4*, AIB-7*, AIB-8*, AIB-16*–AIB-18*, AIB-25*, AIB-32*, AIB-34, AIB-35, AIB-37*, AIB-41*, AIB-50*, AIB-53*, AIB-56*, AIB-57, AIB-62*–AIB-68*, AIB-77*, AIB-82–AIB-84, AIB-97, AIB-102*, AIB-115*, AIB-117, AIB-118*, AIB-122*, AIB-124*, AIB-125*, AIB-128–AIB-130*, AIB-132*–AIB-137*

Pantikapaion

AIB-20, AIB-40*, AIB-76*, AIB-101, AIB-104, AIB-105, AIB-123

Pergamon

AIB-116*

Porthmion

AIB-72

Stranja Region

AIB-31, AIB-33, AIB-74, AIB-75, AIB-80, AIB-81, AIB-106

Tomis

AIB-91*

Vani

AIB-2*, AIB-26, AIB-48, AIB-51, AIB-111

"Köln"

AIB-39*

CHAPTER 14

Ephesos

As repeatedly mentioned, Ephesos was beyond dispute the main manufacturing centre of MMB, from at least the middle of the 2nd century, throughout the second half of the century, and into the first part of the 1st century. It was thus also one of the most long-lived productions, perhaps rivalled only by Athens. Ephesos had a decisively larger output than the Athenian workshops, however, and, as we have already discussed (Chapter 4), Ephesian production – at least in its classical and later phases – can be classified as a manufactory, while Athenian production consisted instead of a series of nucleated workshops.

Ephesian MMB excavated at Ephesos have been published in a number of articles and anthologies,[1] but none of these contributions provides us with a systematic analysis of the overall patterns of this production site. An assessment of the Ephesian workshops as found at Ephesos was undertaken by C. Rogl. Unfortunately, it has not been published, but Rogl 2014a provides an overview of some of her conclusions.[2]

The largest corpus of Ephesian vessels from any site is Laumonier's publication of ca. 6,000 so-called 'Ionian' bowls from Delos (Laumonier 1977). The no less than 108 complete or fragmentary moulds (Rogl 2014a, 116) which have been found at various localities in Ephesos make it clear that Laumonier's 'Ionian' bowls were manufactured there (see p. 288 and Appendix 4). His publication is the only general classification of the Ephesian workshops we have, but, as already discussed in Chapter 2, its built-in methodological weaknesses present a number of challenges. In Chapter 4, we saw that a considerable number of potters were active at Ephesos, many of whom we know from their signatures. Laumonier was of the opinion that each individual potter constituted a 'workshop' proper (Chapter 2), a belief that has ultimately been a stumbling block rather than an aid to the better understanding of Ephesian production. In the Pontic assemblages, we can count over 3,000 individual Ephesian bowls (more than 65% of the finds). The scale of this assemblage allows us to discuss Ephesian production in more general terms, even though it will not enable us to clarify all issues concerning this industry. In the following discussion, we will employ a tripartite chronological scheme: Early (EE: establishment of the industry and earliest, small-scale production, before the middle of the 2nd century); Classical (EC: expansion and industrialization of the manufacturing process and the development of a vigorous export trade); Late (EL: until the end of production in the 1st century).

Fabric and Surface Treatment

The fabric of the Ephesian bowls is not particularly fine. It is micaceous and somewhat grainy, with lime inclusions, and it is always relatively hard fired (see also Gassner 1997, 71). Oxidized and reduced vessels occur, and both types of firing were intentional. The oxidized vessels are normally fired brownish, mainly in the range of 2.5YR 6/8, 5/8, 5YR 6/6, 6/8, and 7.5YR 6/6. The coat normally covers the vessel fully, and it fires to a dull or slightly lustrous sheen, occasionally with metallic highlights. On many vessels of the Classical phase, the coat is somewhat grainy. Frequently the vessels were stacked during firing, resulting in a bicolour coat with a slightly lustrous red-brown body (2.5YR 5/6, 4/6, 4/8) and with the exterior rim frequently fired to a more metallic lustrous grey (5YR 3/1, 7.5YR 3/1, 2.5/1, 10YR 3/1). The reduced vessels come in a number of varieties. The fabric is most commonly fired to 5Y 5/1, but also 4/1 and 6/1, and a group is clustered around Gley 1 5/10Y, 4/N, 5/N and 6/10Y. The coat of the reduced vessels is not really black, but dark grey or brownish-grey, mostly Gley 1 3/N and 2.5/N as well as 5Y 3/1 and 2.5/1 (also Mitsopoulos-Leon 1991, 67).

Decoration

In contrast to other production centres, such as the mainland workshops and (most of) the production of the MMW, Ephesian decoration almost exclusively took the form of superposed, horizontal registers (part of Menemachos' production is an exception). The friezes were normally laid out by the potter before stamping the mould; as a rule,

---

[1] Most important are: Seiterle 1981; Seiterle 1982; Mitsopoulos-Leon 1985; Mitsopoulos-Leon 1991; Gassner 1997; Krinzinger (ed.) 2001; Rogl 2001b; Giuliani & Rogl 2002; Kerschner et al. 2002; Ladstätter et al. 2003.
[2] [Ed.: It has now appeared as Rogl 2021; 2022.]

thin, wheel-run lines were incised in the mould in order to configure the balance between the individual zones of decoration, even before the first stamp was sunk into the mould. In the early and classical phases of Ephesian production, a frieze of tiny dots sometimes separates the friezes. It was normally stamped (with a rouletting tool?) on top of the separating line. In all likelihood, this was inspired by Athenian vases. On the Magnesia Gate moulds, which mark the heyday of the classical production of the Monogram PAR Workshop, beading had all but disappeared. It can be found on only two mould fragments, evidently from the same mould (Seiterle 1981, 28, fig; 1982, 148 pl. 26.3). Rogl has suggested that the mould fragments are Samian (2001b, 105, note 38), but archaeometric investigation affirms that they are Ephesian, despite their unusual decoration (Kerschner et al. 2002, 195). In the late phase of Ephesian production, beading is no longer found.

The four main zones carrying decoration are:
a) The rim zone
b) The upper body zone
c) The lower body zone
d) The base zone

In general, the four zones can be analysed individually, but the overall assessment of the vessel's decoration is to be viewed as a combination of the four. It is important to distinguish between larger shapes and bowls, because the former have room for more frieze zones. With these overall compositional principles outlined, let us break down the individual decoration zones into further sub-groups.

Each of these zones will be discussed in greater detail below, but a few general orienting remarks are appropriate here. In contrast to other productions, the rim zone often takes greater priority. Vessels may be ornamented with two, three, or in rare instances even four or five rim friezes, with the result that the rim zone may constitute the main decoration of a bowl. The base zone shows a sharp division into two types: one with the rounded base and medallion familiar from other productions, the other with a flat, undecorated base. These two variants correspond in general to the overall workshop organization of the industry.

Between these two zones, decoration may fall into one or two registers. The lower part of the bowl usually hosts a vegetal calyx. This is often highly developed and may occupy the whole height of the body. In other cases, the calyx is limited to the lower part of the body, and the upper area is devoted to a horizontal vegetal design, such as a wreath or scroll, or, less commonly, figured decoration.

Shapes

Bowl profiles develop over the life of the industry, but in its classic phase, Ephesian potters produced a relatively shallow bowl with an inwardly inclined rim. Ephesos was also a vigorous producer of supplementary shapes, especially in the earliest phase of the industry, including both small vessels, such as small bowls and gutti, and large symposium equipment, like kraters, amphorae, and situlae.

Early Production: The Südtor Workhsop

Ephesian production at its height can be divided into broad groups embracing a number of individual workshops, as I will explain below. This pattern emerged over time, however, and during the earliest days of production, several small workshops can be distinguished. They were to a certain extent interrelated and they can probably be classified as nucleated workshops.

The only one of these earliest workshops that can be defined with any clarity is represented by a small group of vessels found in a drainage ditch near the south tower of the Tetragonos Agora at Ephesos (Gassner 1997, 71–88, pls. 14–20, 84–86). Twelve largely complete vessels and 50 fragments have been published from the deposit, the contents of which appear to date largely in the second quarter of the 2nd century (though it was deposited later),[3] thus at about the time the Ephesian industry was first developing. It includes some early products of the Monogram PAR Workshop, along with others that follow different conventions of shape and decoration. Christine Rogl has christened this the "Südtor-Atelier", characterizing it as follows.[4] The workshop was following the model of the earlier industries at Athens or Pergamon in both shape and decoration. The bowls tend to be deep, with a thickened or a slightly outturned rim, and there is sometimes a groove below the rim, a common Attic detail. Calyxes of rather plain vegetal elements sometimes fill the entire wall, figured zones are located above a low calyx, rim zones and medallions are small, and beading often separates the registers. Very few examples of this early phase have been found, even at Ephesos, and it was probably

---

3 See Hayes 1999 for this date, a revision to the published date of the last third of the 2nd century (Gassner 1997, 39); see also Rotroff 1999, 614 on the wide range of date of the pottery in the deposit.
4 [Ed. This brief description of earliest production, left uncompleted by PGB, is supplied from Rogl 2014a, 132 with n. 26.]

little exported. Rogl has identified a few possible early Ephesian bowls at Pantikapaion, Pergamon, and Tel Dor, but Laumonier publishes none from Delos.[5] This deposit was apparently laid down before the great burst of expansion that saw the rapid development of the Ephesian manufactory and its export network.

Workshop Circles

In Chapter 4, we discussed workshop organization at Ephesos, and we saw that a considerable number of potters were active. We know some of them from their signatures, but, considering the enormous output of the Ephesian workshops, there must have been many more active in the various ateliers; they remain, however, anonymous.

Concentrations of moulds suggest the locations of various workshops. The largest batch, which we can ascribe to the workshop of the Monogram PAR potter (see pp. 298–301), even though they are not signed, was found in the fill of the towers of the Magnesia Gate, the main entrance to the city from southeast (see Fig. 26). It is likely that this workshop was located somewhere in the vicinity – and probably outside the wall, a common location for a pottery workshop. The second (though much smaller) batch was found at three different locations in the Agora, so most likely there was also a workshop in the vicinity of the Agora. However, it is difficult to distinguish a particular workshop style based on these fragments.

In the following, I will argue that there were two main workshop circles operating in Ephesos, dominated by the workshop of Menemachos and the workshop of Monogram PAR potter respectively (Fig. 67).[6] Laumonier's *Vases gris* is probably to be recognized as the forerunner of the Menemachos Workshop, whereas the Workshop of the Belles Méduses is the forerunner of the Monogram PAR Workshop. These two workshops and their circles probably account for 80–90% (perhaps even more) of the output of the Ephesian workshops.

Workshop Circle 1: *Vases gris* (VG Workshop)

Laumonier named this workshop for a particular group of grey-fired vessels found on Delos (1977, 95–107). The workshop also produced oxidized vessels, however, and it

	Early (EE) Second quarter of 2nd century	**Classical (EC)** Third quarter of 2nd century	**Late (EL)** Fourth quarter of 2nd century
	Südtor Workshop		
Workshop Circle 1	VG (Vases gris) → → →	My(...) Pan mask medallion Menemachos Arkesilaos/Arkesialos Ap(...)/Pa(...) Gorgias Moiragenes/Moragenes Ni(...)	
			Athenaios, Philon/Philonnios
Workshop Circle 2	Belle Méduses →	Monogram PAR	

FIGURE 67   Some of the Ephesian workshops documented in the Black Sea region and their relationships. Grey indicates workshops that produced bowls with a plain, undecorated base

---

5   Rogl 2014a, 12. Pantikapaion: EPH-482, EPH-676. Pergamon: de Luca, 2004. Tel Dor: Rosenthal-Heginbottom 1995, pls. 6.2, 9.2. [Ed. PGB did not identify any examples in her examination of the plates of Laumonier's unpublished manuscript, making it likely that they are not present on Delos.]

6   [Ed. PGB appended a note to the effect that this table is incomplete, but without any indication of what further information she intended to include. Even as it is, it provides a graphic illustration of her concept of the relationships amongst the workshops.]

seems to me misleading to name it after a physical property which was not shared by all vessels of the production. However, since the name *Vases gris* has made its way into the terminology of the MMB, I retain it, though shortening it to the VG Workshop to create a more neutral term.[7]

The corpus is a small one (121 in Laumonier's publication) but large enough to define the workshop with confidence. A number of features place it among the earliest shops, as Laumonier pointed out (Laumonier 1977, 11). The percentage of fragments with figured decoration in the Delian corpus is high (about a third), and the number with long-petals in any configuration is very low (only four, Laumonier 1977, 95 cats. 564, 1309, pl. 21; 104, 106 cats. 9002, 2090, pl. 24). Net pattern and PSC design are absent. The shop produced many supplementary shapes, mostly large ones and of high quality (amphorae and kraters: EPH-1304, EPH-1306*, EPH-1311*, EPH-1312*, EPH-1318; cf. Laumonier 1977, 98 cat. 6010, pl. 21; 100 cat. 6201, pls. 22, 131).

The following motifs appear among the 18–21 products of the workshop in our corpus:

Rim. A single rim frieze was preferred, though multiple friezes occasionally appear.

- By far the most common motif is the Ionian kyma (EPH-6*, EPH-7*, EPH-98*, EPH-694, EPH-1304); sometimes the tongue is twisted or hatched (e.g., Laumonier 1977, 99 cat. 9725, pl. 21), and the egg is sometimes ornamented (e.g., 102 cat. 3374, pls. 23, 119).
- An unusual ultra-stylized scroll is unique to a small group of bowls made either in this workshop or in that of Menemachos (EPH-1217*, EPH-1218*).
- Astragal (EPH-5), box meander (EPH-694), crossed dotted lines (EPH-112*), flower (EPH-1311*, EPH-1312*), guilloche right (EPH-1301*), jewellery pendants (EPH-1304), rosette 2 (EPH-1306*), and the unusual and distinctive pattern of H's in alternating orientation (EPH-1244*), all associated solely with the VG Workshop, appear on vessels in the Black Sea assemblage.

Body
- A large number and variety of figural scenes, in one or two registers. The most common subjects are Erotes playing music, dancing, or walking (EPH-5–EPH-7*, EPH-112*; cf. Laumonier 1977, 97 cat. 3331, pls. 21, 120) and hunts and animal friezes (EPH-68*, EPH-69*, EPH-71, EPH-1306*).
- Less common figured subjects that appear in the Black Sea are Dionysos-Eros on a panther (EPH-97*, EPH-98*) and perhaps a feline phallus and grotesques (EPH-112*), and labours of Herakles (EPH-104*) (the latter two possibly produced by Menemachos instead).
- Thunderbolts: EPH-1304, EPH-1311*, EPH-1312*; cf. Laumonier 1977, 98 cat. 9031, pl. 21.
- The rim and body friezes are usually separated by beading.

Calyx
- Acanthus X: a tall, slender, frilly acanthus with deeply indented sides: EPH-6*, EPH-69*, EPH-677*, EPH-694, EPH-1318; cf. Laumonier 1977, 97–98 cats. 2375, 3331, 6010, pls. 21, 120 (his acanthus c)
- Possibly a filled 'nelumbo' occupied by a kissing couple (EPH-1301*)
- The calyx rarely extends far up the wall (Laumonier 1977, 105 cat. 366, pls. 24, 120 is an exception); more commonly it is confined to a small zone just above the base.

The base medallion is always a rosette, sometimes in one of the forms commonly used by the Monogram PAR Workshop.
- Rosette A or a variant of it: EPH-677*, EPH-694, EPH-1304; cf. Laumonier 1977, 100 cat. 3326, pl. 22; 150 cat. 366, pls. 24, 120; 164 cat. 3272, pl. 36
- More unusual is a five-rayed sun-wheel, surrounded by hearts (EPH-1306*).

Three workshops continued the tradition of the VG Workshop: Menemachos, the Pan mask medallion 'workshop'[8] and My(...). Even though the products of the three differ in shape and size, they are, nevertheless, interwoven in terms of their decoration. We shall first consider the workshop of Menemachos and his followers, which was large and long-lived, then we will briefly discuss the workshop of My(...), which was probably short-lived and produced bowls with large rim diameters, perhaps a special-purpose shape.

Workshop Circle 1: Workshop of Menemachos

The earliest of the two large Ephesian workshops is that of Menemachos. A significant number of vessels, more than 50, preserve a signature encircling the bottom in bold

---

7 [Ed. I have supplied the description of the VG Workshop using information from PGB's data base.]

8 [Ed: PGB identified a small group of vessels on which the medallion is a striking frontal male face with wild hair, the basis for the reconstruction of a small workshop: EPH-1308; Greifenhagen 1963, 58 fig. 55; Hellström 1965, 62 no. 114, pl. 9; Laumonier 1977, 76 cat. 5377, pls. 16, 118; 185–186 cats. 463, 772, 1297, pls. 40, 126; 233–234 cats. 773, 1406, pls. 52, 127; 414 cat. 3072, pl. 97. One piece shares acanthus X with the VG Workshop (Greifenhagen, op. cit.), suggesting a position in WC1 and early in its history. She clearly intended to discuss it further, but did not leave notes on how she might have done so. She identified only 14 pieces as belonging to this group in her data base, not enough to reconstruct a feasible production group.]

letters with his name in the genitive. A few vessels employ an abbreviated form of the signature (ME in ligature). The popularity and wide distribution of these products made this workshop into a *brand*. Thus, the Pontic Workshop of Demetrios, active in the last quarter of the 2nd century (see Chapter 18), emulated not just the Menemachean shape, but also the way the signature was made. Menemachos' enterprise was very long-lived, perhaps in operation for more than half a century. Menemachos himself can hardly have lived as long as his production; in all likelihood, many of the late 'workshops' of Laumonier are to be understood as mid- and late 'Menemachos' rather than true, individual workshops proper.

Shapes

Menemachos' main form is a cup-like bowl ca. 6.5–7 cm high with a simple, inturned rim with a diameter of 11–12 cm; completely preserved vessels have a H:Ø ratio of between 1:1.6 and 1:1.7. The base is always concave and undecorated, occasionally furnished with a low, false ring foot. The workshop also produces other shapes, such as a small bowl and a number of larger shapes, such as krater, situla, and a large kantharos (see below, pp. 323–324).

Decoration

In contrast to the workshop of Monogram PAR, Menemachos sometimes produced vessels with decoration in a single zone. Occasionally, a low calyx of one or two rows of imbricate petals occurs, perhaps inspired by Athenian vessels; this is not separated from the high main frieze of decoration.

The signed bowls give us a good idea about his preferences in terms of decoration. At least 15 bowls are completely preserved and further 38 partially so. If we take them as our point of departure, Menemachos's decoration may be described as follows.

Signed Vessels

Rim Decoration

Single and multiple rim friezes are equally common. Common rim motifs are: rosette 1, a rosette with eight bow-like petals, alternately large and small (appearing as if set in a box) (EPH-580*; Laumonier 1977, 23 cat. 1971, pls. 1, 113); astragal with decorated reels (Laumonier 1977, 23, 26 cats. 1981, 1260, pls. 1, 113); horizontal S-spirals (EPH-870*; Laumonier 1977, 23, 26, 34 cats. 1260, 1980, 1981, pls. 1, 3, 113, 116); and a miniature acanthus scroll running left (EPH-870*; Laumonier 1977, 36 cat. 2264, pls. 4, 116). These patterns are largely confined to his workshop. To a lesser degree we find the Ionian kyma (EPH-785; Laumonier 1977, 45 cat. 117, pl. 9), large dots (Laumonier 1977, 31 cat. 682, pls. 2, 114), horizontal flower left (Laumonier 1977, 34 cat. 1980, pls. 3, 116), and rosette 2/7 (M) (Laumonier 1977, 31, 45 cats. 117, 682, pls. 2, 9, 114; M designates the particularly Menemachean version of the rosette, see p. 304). Occurring once is a box meander, cw (Laumonier 1977, 50 cat. 9134, pl. 10), a guilloche right (EPH-101*), and crossed dotted lines with box (EPH-595*).

Main Decoration

Erotes playing musical instruments (Chatzidakis 2000, pl. 64b).[9]

Dionysiac scenes with several of the following stamps: Erotes playing musical instruments, Dionysos, maenads, centaur, dancing satyr, satyr pulling a vine down toward a krater (Laumonier 1977, 42 cat. 3421, pls. 7, 118; Chatzidakis 2000, pl. 64b)

Hunt (Laumonier 1977, 43 cat. 3422, pl. 8)

Mythological scenes: Herakles and the Nemean lion (EPH-106*; Laumonier 1977, 43 cat. 3423, pl. 8); judgement of Paris (EPH-101*; Laumonier 1977, 42 cat. 3420, pl. 8)

Multiple rim friezes with vegetal calyx (Laumonier 1977, 31 cat. 682, pls. 2, 114; 23 cat. 1260, pl. 1; 26 cat. 1981, pls. 1, 113)

Multiple rim friezes with imbricate rounded petals with central vein (Laumonier 1977, 45 cat. 117, pl. 9)

Multiple rim friezes with imbricate pointed petals with central and side veins (EPH-870*)

Plastic pine cone (Laumonier 1977, 57 cat. 4150–4153, pl. 12)

Filled 'nelumbo' with symplegma scene, surrounded by acanthus leaves (EPH-580*, EPH-582*; Laumonier 1977, 34 cat. 1980, pls. 3, 116), occasionally with vegetal tendril, once with vertical fluting (Laumonier 1977, 36 cat. 2264, pl. 4, 116)

Imbricate rounded petals with central and side veins (EPH-783–EPH-785)

Imbricate pointed petals with central and side veins (EPH-895*, EPH-896*)[10]

Stylized long petals separated by dots (Dereboylu 2001, 36 cat. 2, pls. 18.131, 25.3.)

Long petal and 'nelumbo' (EPH-595*)

Vertical fluting (Pierobon 1985, figs. 5–6)

---

9 [Ed. PGB left a partial list of motifs on signed vases, which I augmented on the basis of information in her data base.]

10 Laumonier 1977, 26 cat. 186, pl. 1; 37 cat. 5049, pl. 5; 47–48 cats. 5017, 5019, 5022, 5028, 5034, 5040, 5040bis, 8275, pl. 9; 48, 50, 52 cats. 5041, 5045, 5353, 5354, 9134, pl. 10.

Base
All of the signed bases are undecorated.

Unsigned Vessels
It is interesting to note the types of decoration *not* represented on the signed vessels: all types of scroll and wreath decoration, net pattern, and PSC design. This may be a matter of chance, as we can see from the motif of the Eros racing a two-horse chariot to the right. This pattern is not recorded on the signed vessels, but since we find it in combination with three certain Menemachean rim patterns (rosette 1, the miniature acanthus scroll left, and the crossed dotted lines with box; Laumonier 1977, 39 cats. 3141, 3429, 9394, pl. 5; EPH-27*), it is quite clear that this motif was (also) used in Menemachos' workshop. Nevertheless, the decorative patterns mentioned remain rare even on the unsigned, attributed vessels.

With the above skeleton of decorative elements which we can connect with Menemachos with certainty through the signed specimens, a number of unsigned vessels of the same shape and with the same and related decoration can easily be attributed to his workshop. From these we obtain further decorative elements which must have been part of Menemachos' repertoire:[11]

Main Decoration
A   *Figural Decoration*
Eros racing a chariot to the right: EPH-27*; cf. Laumonier 1977, 39 cats. 3141, 3429, 9394, pl. 5 (linked to Menemachos by rim patterns: rosette 1, miniature acanthus scroll, crossed dotted lines with box)
Nike racing a chariot to the right: Laumonier 1977, 65 cat. 3163, pls. 14, 118 (with rosette 1)
A wider variety of hunting scenes, mostly in the early phase of the industry: EPH-67*, EPH-1332*; cf. Laumonier 1977, 37–38 cats. 3079+3336, 3087, pls. 5, 117 (with miniature acanthus scroll, horizontal S-spirals, and flower)
Dogs: Laumonier 1977, 179 cat. 3059, pl. 39 (with crossed dotted lines)
Freestanding symplegma scenes with or without music-playing Erotes and/or Dionysiac elements: EPH-108*, EPH-109; Laumonier 1977, 40 cat. 3323, pls. 6, 117; 40–41 cat. 9709, pl. 7; 348 cat. 3436, pl. 83 (with horizontal S-spirals, rosette 2/7[M], crossed dotted lines with box, astragal with decorated reel)
Satyr mask: Laumonier 1977, 42 cat. 3275, pls. 7, 118 (with rosette 1)
Sceptre: Laumonier 1977, 31 cat. 477, pls. 2, 114 (with box meander, horizontal S spirals)
Thunderbolt: EPH-127*, EPH-128; Laumonier 1977, 60 cat. 9316, pl. 12; 439 cat. 1206, pl. 101 (with rosette 2/7, miniature acanthus frieze, horizontal S-spirals, rosette 1)
Caduceus: Laumonier 1977, 28 cat. 627, pl. 2; 32 cat. 1328, pls. 3, 115; 33 cat. 1238, pls. 3, 115; 36 cat. 1947, pl. 4; 42, cat. 3275, pls. 7, 118 (with rosette 1, rosette 2/7[M], horizontal S spirals, crossed dotted lines with box)

B   *Scroll*
Ultra-stylized acanthus scroll: Laumonier 1977, 61 cat. 9476, pl. 13 (with miniature acanthus scroll left)

C   *Garlands and Wreaths*
Myrtle wreath: EPH-354* (with rosette 1)

D   *Multiple Rim friezes*
With imbricate rounded petals with central and side veins: EPH-753*, EPH-754*; Laumonier 1977, 78 cat. 3, pl. 17 (with astragal with decorated reel, rosette 1, miniature acanthus scroll)

E   *Vegetal Decoration*
Stylized pine-cone decoration: Laumonier 1977, 58 cat. 4000, pl. 12; 307 cat. 4001, pl. 72 (with rosette 1)
Calyx A (acanthus alternating with nelumbo in various arrangements, see below, pp. 316–318): Laumonier 1977, 23 cat. 1260, pl. 1 (with astragal with decorated reels, horizontal S-spirals)
Calyx B2 (lotus petals flanked by acanthus with bent or folded top): EPH-635*; Laumonier 1977, 24 cat. 377, pl. 1 (with miniature acanthus scroll, crossed dotted lines with box)
Menemachean bud, a large bud with a tall, plump, and vertically ribbed body, topped by a knob formed of short horizontal ridges: EPH-572, EPH-573*; Laumonier 1977, 317 cat. 9667, pl. 74; 325 cat. 1155, pl. 77 (with rosette 2, thunderbolt)
Sistrum bud, a lotus bud sitting in a stylized calyx which resembles a sistrum: EPH-684*, EPH-685*, EPH-700*, EPH-713*, EPH-1272*, EPH-1275*; Laumonier 1977, 328 cat. 1402, pl. 78, alternating with rosette 2/8 (M)

---

11   [Ed: The remainder of the description of the stamps of Menemachos, up to bases, has been supplied from the data base. The attributions cited are those of PGB, also extracted from the data base. In many cases, they differ from those of Laumonier; these instances are listed in Appendix 3.]

F   *Linear Decoration*
Plastic long petals separated by dots: Laumonier 1977, 55–56 cats. 4797, 4800, 303, pl. 11 (with crossed dotted lines, miniature acanthus scroll, crossed dotted lines with box)
Net pattern: EPH-991* (with miniature acanthus scroll)

Base
On a few unsigned bowls, Menemachos adopts the rosette typical of the Monogram PAR Workshop (e.g., Laumonier 1977, 33 cat. 1356, pls. 3, 115; 36 cat. 737, pl. 4).

In the late phase, various rim patterns of Menemachos are further developed (mostly in a debased form). Rosette 1 becomes much smaller and occasionally is stylized as the 'sunburst' rosette (Laumonier 1977, 57 cat. 4151, pl. 12). Crossed dotted lines continue, but oblique boxes emerge as a sole motif, not just combined with crossed dotted lines (Laumonier 1977, 168 cat. 8579, pl. 37). Large dots are retained as a second rim frieze.

I would argue that 'workshops' such as Laumonier's Plagiaire and Comique à la canne are not independent entities, but rather constitute the late phase of the Menemachos Workshop.[12]

Workshop Circle 1: Collaborators and/or Followers of Menemachos

Laumonier was right, I am sure, in connecting a number of signed vessels with the Menemachos Workshop. However, many of his particular ascriptions are completely without foundation. The following will be based exclusively on the signed pieces, because they are obviously the only solid point of departure.

Signatures
In total, of 565 bases of the Menemachean shape which I have recorded, 217 (38%) were signed. Of these, as already mentioned, 52 were signed by Menemachos,[13] so almost three fourths of the signed vessels were made by his associates rather than by Menemachos himself. The vessels signed by artisans other than Menemachos employed the same shape, even though the proportions gradually evolve from Menemachos' standard H:⌀ ratio of 1:1.6–1:1.7 to a shallower bowl with the ratio H:⌀ 1:1.7–1:1.9. This is a development which appears to take place over time, as already discussed in Chapter 3.

As we have already discussed in Chapter 4, the mould-maker's/potter's signature can take a number of different forms with the name being spelled out, being abbreviated to a few letters or a single letter, or appearing as a monogram; and the signature could be incised in the mould or directly in the vessel before firing. The following signatures are documented on Menemachean bases. (This information is laid out in tabular form in Fig. 24; see also Laumonier 1977, 404 fig. 1 and 408 fig. 2.)

Signature Proper, Incised in the Mould before Firing
Apollonios   *Delos*: Laumonier 1977, 224 cat. 1994, pl. 50
Arkesilaos   *Berenike*: Kenrick 1985, 113 cat. B168, fig. 22, pl. IX (Arkesialos, a misspelling of the nominative). *Pantikapaion*: EPH-900*, EPH-901. *Vieille-Toulouse*: Laumonier 1967, 32 cats. 33 (Arkesialos), and 34 (Arkesil), pl. 6.
also signing as Arkesilas – *Melos*: Zahn 1908, 72–73, Berlin inv. 4828; Laumonier 1967, 32 under cat. 33
Damokles   *Čaika*: Kovalenko 1996, fig. 1.3 (erroneously considered to be Bosporan)
Gorgias   *Berenike*: Kenrick 1985, 113 cat. B169, fig. 22, pl. IX. *Čaika*: Vnukov & Kovalenko 1998, 69. *Delos*: Laumonier 1977, 403 cats. 1312, 1986, 1988, 1989, 3499, 4155, 4156, pl. 95; 405 cat. 4586, pl. 95; 405 cat. 4157; Zapheiropoulou & Chatzidakis 1994, 240 cat. 14737, pl. 184.a. *Kara Tobe*: Vnukov & Kovalenko 1998, fig.

---

12   [Ed. PGB left no information about the precise ways in which these 'workshops' are related to the larger production of Menemachos. Several bowls in the Catalogue from Istros were previously published by C. Domăneanțu (2000) with attributions to the Comique à la canne (EPH-9*, EPH-523*, EPH-816, EPH-993*, EPH-1023*, EPH-1101*, EPH-1225*, EPH-1241*) and the Plagiaire (EPH-426, EPH-430*, EPH-516*, EPH-947*, EPH-1174*). At least for the former, most of the Delian comparanda Domăneanțu cites are compelling; the Istrian fragments clearly belong to the groups that Laumonier had so defined. Yet PGB declined to attribute them to any workshop, perhaps because she was still developing her ideas about the relationships amongst these late groups.]

13   *Alexandria*: Pagenstecher 1913, pl. XX. *Chersonesos*: EPH-142*, EPH-582*, EPH-895*; *Delos*: Laumonier 1977, 23, 26 cats. 186, 1260, 1971, 1981, 1982, pls. 1, 113; 34 cats. 1980, 1983, 1984, pls. 3, 116; 36 cat. 2264, pls. 4, 116; 37 cats. 3086, 5049, pl. 5; 42 cat. 3421, pls. 7, 118; 42–44 cats. 3420, 3422, 3423, 8423, pl. 8; 45, 47–48 cats. 117, 8275, 5017, 5019, 5022, 5028, 5034, 5040, 5040bis, pl. 9; 48, 50 cats. 5041, 5045, 9134, pl. 10; 57 cats. 4150–4153, pl. 12; Chatzidakis 2000, pl. 64b. *Ephesos*: Dereboylu 2001, 36 cat. 2, pls. 18.130, 25.3. *Iasos*: Pierobon 1985, figs. 5, 6. *Istros*: EPH-896*. *Mesambria*: Mesambria Archaeological Museum inv. 3002 (unpublished). *Olbia*: EPH-870*. *Pantikapaion*: EPH-99*, EPH-101*, EPH-106*, EPH-580*, EPH-595*, EPH-783–EPH-785, EPH-1246*. *Rome*: Paris, Cabinet des Medailles inv. 1667, Puppo 1995, 164–165 cat. X39, pl. LXXIV–LXXV. *Samos*: Isler 1978, cat. 311, pl. 59.

5.1. *Kenkreai*: Adamsheck 1979, 18 pl. 3 cat. 41b (erroneously read as LO). *Samos*: Tsakos 1990, 143 inv. 1630, pl. 78.b, c

Moiragenes *Chersonesos*: EPH-786*. *Pantikapaion*: EPH-1247
also signing as Moragenes – *Olbia*: EPH-693*

Posei[...] *Delos*: Laumonier 1977, 407 cat. 1987, pl. 95
Posid[...] *Delos*: Laumonier 1977, 407 cat. 1990, pl. 95
Posi[...] *Porthmion*: EPH-745

Signature Proper, Incised in the Vessel before Firing

Athenaios *Chersonesos*: EPH-815*. *Delos*: Laumonier 1977, 232–233 cats. 1991, 1992, pl. 52; 235–236 cats. 3431, 4154, pl. 53. *Didyma*: Tuchelt 1971, pl. 11.174. *Istros*: EPH-1037*. *Miletos*: Kossatz 1990, 64 cat. M 451, pl. 28. *Pantikapaion*: EPH-863. *Porthmion*: EPH-539, EPH-714

Dias *Delos*: Laumonier 1977, 406 cat. 4160, pl. 95
Dionysios *Delos*: Laumonier 1977, 406 cat. 4351, pl. 95. *S. Sabina shipwreck*: Siebert 1977, 113 cat. 1, fig. 2a
Melidon *Ephesos*: Rogl 2001a, 141
Philon *Corinth*: Edwards 1981, 199 cat. C 1980–82, pl. 46. *Crimea*: Grzegrzółka 2010, 38 cat. 5. *Delos*: Laumonier 1977, 251–253 cats. 5004, 5014, 5016, pl. 56; 254–255 cats. 5002, 5007, 5533, 5576, pl. 57; 257–259 cats. 4962, 8696, 8834, pls. 58, 133; 261–262 cat. 4534, 4619–4621, pl. 59. *Ephesos*: Meriç 2002, 34 cat. K45, pl. 6. *Iasos*: Pierobon 1987, figs. 5, 6. *Knidos*: Kögler 2010, 493 cats. E.386–E.388, pl. 19. *Olbia*: EPH-1065, EPH-1069. *Pantikapaion*: Loseva 1962, 197; EPH-1066, EPH-1278(?). *S. Sabina shipwreck*: Siebert 1977, 113 cat. 2, fig. 2b. *Shapla Dere*: Kazarow 1918, 27 fig. 31. *Starokorsunsk 2*: Limberis & Marčenko 2000, figs. 1.8, 2.
also signing Philonnios! – *Olbia*: EPH-802, EPH-803, EPH-805*. *Pantikapaion*: EPH-804
too little preserved to distinguish between the two forms – *Chersonesos*: EPH-808*. *Delos*: Laumonier 1977, 256 cat. 5006, pl. 57; 259 cat. 9340, pl. 58. *Istros*: EPH-807*, EPH-809, EPH-899*, EPH-1067*, EPH-1068*. *Pantikapaion*: EPH-806, EPH-1248

Zoilos Ex-Ovilis, cf. Rogl 2001a, 153–154. *Delos*: Laumonier 1977, 406 cats. 4760, 4960, 8977, pl. 95. *South Russia*: Zahn 1908, 73–74; Puppo 1995, pl. XXXIV; Rogl 2001a, 153–154

[...]onu[...] or [...]ont[...] *Istros*: EPH-1249*
[...]rinos *Delos*: Laumonier 1977, 263 cat. 3476, pl. 60
[...]on *Olbia*: EPH-1072

Name Abbreviation, Incised in the Mould before Firing

Anti(...) *Akko*: Dothan 1976, 34, fig. 31
Ad(...) or Da(...) *Delos*: Laumonier 1977, 309 cats. 4052, 4266, pl. 73. *Bosporos*: Šurgaja 1962, 118, fig. 4.4; Kovalenko 1996, fig. 1.2 (erroneously considered to be Bosporan)
An(...) or Na(...) (lig.) *Delos*: Laumonier 1977, 407 cat. 1, pl. 95
Di(...) *Delos*: Laumonier 1977, 406 cat. 4160, pl. 95
Ei(...) *Delos*: Laumonier 1977, 335, 338 cats. 339, 5210, pl. 81
Me(...) (lig.) *Delos*: Laumonier 1977, 31 cat. 682, pls. 2, 114; 48, 52 cats. 5353, 5354, pl. 10
Ni(...) *Delos*: Laumonier 1977, 69–70 cats. 3210, 4050, 4633, 8441, pls. 15, 131. *Istros*: EPH-1071*. *Pantikapaion*: EPH-1070
Pe(...) (lig.) *Delos*: Laumonier 1977, 405, 407, 409 cats. 291, 292, 4158, pl. 95; 409 cat. 293. *Istros*: EPH-1038*.
Ph(...) *Istros*: EPH-897*. *Olbia*: EPH-898*.
Si(...) *Delos*: Laumonier 1977, 342 cats. 4327, 8967, 9311, 9347, pls. 82, 133

Name Monogram, Incised in the Mould before Firing

Ad(...) or Da(...) *Delos*: Laumonier 1977, 113 cat. 1999, pl. 25
Ap(...) or Pa(...) *Beljaus*: Bel-00-124, S. Lancov, Annual report 2000 (unpublished). *Delos*: Laumonier 1977, 224–225, 227 cats. 338, 1995, 2081, 9275, pl. 50; 227–228 cats. 5356, 5357, 5538, 8854, pl. 51. *Minoa (Amorgos)*: Pappa 2000, 111 pls. 55.d2, 59.a1. *Findspot unknown*: Firenze, Museo Archeologico inv. 4765, Oxé 1933, pl. 11.3; Puppo 1995, 154 cat. X13, pl. LXX
Ly(...); can also contain letter M and A or D instead of L! *Vieille-Toulouse*: Laumonier 1967, 35–38, pl. 7

Name Monogram, Incised in the Vessel before Firing

Hera(...) *Delos*: Laumonier 1977, 281, 282 cats. 5152, 5356, pl. 65; 297 cat. 4845, pls. 69, 133. *Labraunda*: Hellström 1965, 63 cat. 129, pls. 10, 34.

Single Letter, Incised in the Mould before Firing

A *Crimea*: Grzegrzółka 2010, 37–38 cat. 4. *Delos*: Laumonier 1977, 409–410 cats. 294, 1997, 4584, 9294, pl. 96. *General'skoe*: Maslennikov 2007, fig. 72.1. *Pantikapaion*: EPH-386*
D *Delos*: Laumonier 1977, 110 cat. 358, pl. 25. *Istros*: EPH-816*

K   *Delos*: Laumonier 1977, 410 cats. 5539, 5579, pl. 96
L   *Delos*: Laumonier 1977, 114 cat. 369, pl. 25; 114–115 cats. 1003, 1122, 3215, pl. 26
M   *Delos*: Laumonier 1977, 410 cats. 4159, 4867, pl. 96
N   *Delos*: Laumonier 1977, 411 cats. 4361, 4380, pl. 96
X [Greek Ξ]   *Delos*: Laumonier 1977, 411 cat. 3427, pl. 96
Ch [Greek Χ] *Delos*: Laumonier 1977, 256–257 cats. 5350, 5352, pl. 57; 257, 259 cats. 4482, 5351, pl. 58; 262 cat. 4957, pl. 60. *Porthmion*: EPH-787

Vessels signed with one of the above signatures almost exclusively employ a single rim frieze, normally an Ionian kyma. Often, and this appears to be a speciality of Menemachos and in particular of his followers, the tongue is hatched. Interestingly enough, with the exception of Menemachos and My(...), there is not a single example of rosette 1 on the signed vessels, so I feel confident in ascribing this rim pattern to Menemachos and My(...), and, most likely, it belongs to the early part of this workshop circle's existence.

Gorgias

Gorgias is known from 15 signed bases (see Rogl 2001a, 138 for a list), some with enough of the wall preserved to comment on the design. The signature is incised in the mould, mostly in one line (GORGI), but also in a circle around the edge (GORGIOU), appearing in retrograde on the finished bowl. Signed bowls show that he employed Menemachos' acanthus with a small 'nelumbo' in front (Laumonier 1977, 403 cats. 1312, 1986, pl. 95; related, 403 cat. 1988, pl. 95; Tsakos 1990, 143, pl. 78,b; Zapheiropoulou & Chatzidakis 1994, 240, pl. 184.a), the 'Knidian' palmette with its alternately curling fronds (Adamsheck 1979, 18 cat. Gr41b, pl. 3), plastic pine cone (Laumonier 1977, 403 cats. 4155, 4156, pl. 95), and the frieze of female dancers common in WC1 (Laumonier 1977, 403 cat. 3499, pl. 95). Unfortunately, poor preservation and the limited number of examples make it impossible to draw a satisfactory portrait of his production and he remains a shadowy figure.

Workshop of My(...)

This workshop is known from four signed bases on Delos, where the signature is incised in the mould over the base medallion in the form of MY in ligature.[14] Strangely enough, this was overlooked as a proper workshop by Laumonier, even though the vessels which I propose to ascribe to this workshop share a number of very characteristic features. Laumonier attributed bowls with these features to no less than seven different workshops plus two non-assigned groups: mostly to Philon, Plagiaire, and Hera(...), but also Menemachos, Si(...), Comique à la canne, and Doubles filets épais. This is due to the fact that Laumonier considered only single elements, especially the rim pattern (and did not consider the characteristic bases at all). Therefore, he was of the opinion that My(...) was part of Philon's workshop (1977, 247–251). It is true that one large bowl (Laumonier 1977, 266 cat. 1214, pls. 61, 128) does display rosette 8, which is very characteristic of Philon(nios) (see p. 305), but this only underlines the fact that My(...) was most likely part of WC1, not of WC2. The following description is based on the 112 pieces that I can attribute to the shop without question.

My(...) produced chiefly oxidized vessels, but reduced vessels also occur, two of them with a signature (Laumonier 1977, 270–271 cats. 4578, 8675, pl. 63). This workshop shows an independent and creative mixture of styles, which are related both to the workshop of Menemachos and to that of Monogram PAR – in fact, it is the only one of the Ephesian workshops which we could almost call a hybrid between the two workshop circles. The main shape is a bowl which corresponds well to that of Monogram PAR, with a H:Ø ratio normally between 1:2 and 1:2.2, thus relatively shallow, but the rim diameter is much larger than that of Monogram PAR: 14.5–17 cm, with an average of 16 cm.

This craftsman employed a number of stamps which are unique amongst the Ephesian production.

Rim Decoration

Single rim friezes are the most common, but multiple rim friezes also occur. Common stamps are the Ionian kyma and the distinctive rosette 6, with seven or eight rhomboidal petals (EPH-90*, EPH-514*, EPH-1191*, EPH-1192; e.g., Laumonier 1977, 319, 321 cats. 874, 454, pl. 75), which is unique to My(...). He also employs a rim pattern in which only the left half of rosette 1 is stamped (e.g., Laumonier 1977, 269 cat. 1859, pl. 62), a pattern which is later further stylized into a 'paw' motif by Philon(nios).

---

14   *Delos*: Laumonier 1977, 266–267 cat. 634, pl. 61; 270–271 cats. 2004, 4578, 8675, pl. 63. The signature was overlooked by Laumonier on cats. 2004 and 8675. Rogl (2001a, 150 no. 10) mentions a bowl signed by My(...) at Heraklaia Minoa (Falco 2000, 384 cat. RB5, fig. 3.5 [not seen]).

Main Decoration

The most common type of main decoration in this workshop, occurring on almost 25% of the vessels, is a tiny acanthus scroll with a tendril ending with a small rosette evolving towards left (EPH-265*).[15] A myrtle wreath with five thick and sloppy leaves occurs on five vessels, evidently imitating the Monogram PAR Workshop.[16] Net pattern can be found on four vases.[17] Figural decoration is scarce, but there is one instance of Eros racing a two-horse chariot to the right, over a low 'calyx' of stylized long petals separated by dots (Laumonier 1977, 305 cat. 3330, pl. 71) and one example of an Amazonomachy (EPH-90). On several vessels we find the reduced hunt motif of alternating eagle and dog (apparently unique to this workshop; Laumonier 1977, 323 cats. 3044, 3045, pl. 76; 324 cat. 3473, pl. 77), the dog alone alternating with a krater (Laumonier 1977, 324 cat. 8959, pl. 77), or another type of hunting scene (Laumonier 1977, 304 cat. 3096, pl. 71). Two vessels feature a winged thunderbolt.[18]

Calyx

The lower decoration of the vessel is either a calyx, often with 'nelumbo' with acanthus leaf in front or even stylized long petals. Occasionally, isolated stylized long petals occur in between the acanthus leaves. A calyx with vegetal elements and one or more of the following figural elements is also very common: a trident furnished with a *tainia* tied in a bow, 'sceptres' with twisted shaft and finished with a palmette-like finial (two types; EPH-145*), and a winged caduceus also furnished with a *tainia* tied in a bow. The trident appears only on My(...)'s vessels,[19] whereas the 'sceptre' can also be found on Menemachos' vessels,[20] and Menemachos and Si(...) equally employed the winged caduceus.[21] On My(...)'s vessels, the elements mentioned above occur in combination with all three types of his base medallion. From time to time, My(...) makes use of a straight twisted stem with a small 'hook' at the top.[22] I do not know this detail from other mould makers; on Delos, it is combined with all three of the base rosettes employed by My(...).

Base Medallion

In contrast to his contemporary Menemachos, My(...) employs three different base medallion rosettes. The use of a rosette continues the tradition of the VG Workshop and is parallel to what we find in the Monogram PAR Workshop.

Rosette B, var. A variation of Monogram PAR's rosette B, with 12 overlapping, veined petals (EPH-145*).[23]

Rosette G. A rosette with eight broad, ribbed petals, between and behind which the tips of eight more petals can be seen; in the centre is a small rosette, also with eight petals. This medallion finds no parallels elsewhere in the Ephesian repertoire.[24]

Rosette H. A rosette with ten tongue-shaped petals.[25]

My(...) was even copied by other members of WC1. On a bowl found on Delos with a plain, concave base without a rosette and a more Menemachean shape, with a H:⌀ ratio of 1:1.9 (Laumonier 1977, 359 cat. 360+1688, pl. 86),

---

15 Delos: Laumonier 1977, 266–267 cats. 568, 634, 1967, 2260, 2367, 4429, pl. 61; 267–269 cats. 670, 1117, 1229, 1278, 1679, 1681–1683, 1859, 2039, 2055, 2321, pl. 62; 322–323 cats. 1249, 1253, 2007, 9106, pl. 76; 324 cat. 1271, pl. 77; 333 cat. 1684, pl. 80; 336 cat. 5555, pl. 81; Miletos: Kossatz 1990, 37 cat. M 241a, pl. 30.

16 Laumonier 1977, 321, 323 cats. 1245, 1277, pl. 76; 324 cats. 1298, 2258, pl. 77; 332 cat. 9103, pl. 80 (with net pattern on the lower part of the vessel!).

17 Laumonier 1977, 266 cat. 761, pl. 61; 332 cats. 4070, 4091, 4126, pl. 80.

18 Laumonier 1977, 329, 331 cats. 619, 4405, pl. 79.

19 Laumonier 1977, 267 cat. 875, pl. 61; 268 cats. 1117, 2038, pl. 62; 271 cats. 8675, 8676 [signed], pl. 63; 318–319 cats. 874, 1019, 2259, pl. 75; 323–325 cats. 1116, 1159, 1326, pl. 77; 327 cat. 1147, pl. 78.

20 Menemachos: Laumonier 1977, 25 cat. 2366, pl. 1; 31 cat. 477, pl. 2; 346 cats. 2011, 3123, pl. 82; 350 cat. 3276, pl. 84. My(...): Laumonier 1977, 268 cats. 2038, 2039, pl. 62; 304 cat. 3096, pl. 71; 317 cat. 9009, pl. 74; 318–319 cats. 874, 1014, 1019, 2259, 9346, 9769, pl. 75; 323–326 cats. 1113, 1115, 1116, 1159, 1250, 2060, pl. 77; 327 cat. 1215, pl. 78; 329–330 cats. 351, 619, pl. 79. My(...)?: Laumonier 1977, 318 cat. 572, pl. 74; 318 cat. 955, pl. 75; 325 cat. 732, pl. 77.

21 Menemachos: Delos: Laumonier 1977, 28 cat. 627, pl. 2; 32–33, 35 cats. 1238, 1240, 1328, 2266, pl. 3; 36 cat. 1947, pl. 4; 42 cat. 3275, pl. 7; 195 cat. 4666, pl. 43; 327 cats. 1119, 1204, pl. 78; 343 cat. 2368, pl. 82; Ephesos: Meriç 2002, 34 cat. K42, pl. 6; Menemachos or My(...): Laumonier 1977, 35 cat. 1343, pl. 3; My(...): Laumonier 1977, 268 cat. 1117, pl. 62; 271 cat. 8675 [signed], pl. 63; 300 cat. 1130, pl. 70; 346 cat. 3121, pl. 83; Si(...): Laumonier 1977, 342 cat. 9311 [signed], pl. 82.

22 Laumonier 1977, 323 cat. 3044, pl. 76; 324–325 cats. 1113, 1115, 1233, 1250, 1298, 2221, 2258, 3473, pl. 77.

23 Laumonier 1977, 31 cat. 9303, pl. 2; 44 cat. 736, pl. 8; 299–302 cats. 638, 733, 1130, 1977, 2429, pl. 70; 302 and 305 cats. 738, 3330, pl. 71; 316 and 318 cats. 641, 1131, pl. 74; 319–320 cats. 1218, 8953, 9769, pl. 75; 322 cats. 1252, 8957, pl. 76; 325–326 cats. 1115, 1116, 2060, pl. 77; 346 cat. 3121, pl. 83.

24 Laumonier 1977, 391 cat. 4793, pl. 55; 265 cats. 760, 795, 4955, 9758, pl. 60; 265–267 cats. 634 [signed], 761, 875, 1967, 2260, 4435, pl. 61; 267–268 cats. 670, 1117, 1300, 2037, 2038, 2039, pl. 62; 319–320 cats. 2259, 8952, 9346, pl. 75; 321–323 cats. 1245, 1253, 2304, 8453, 8958, 9106, 9753, pl. 76; 324 cats. 1250, 1298, 3473, pl. 77; 329, 331 and 332 cats. 619, 4572, 4577, 9335, pl. 79; 332 cats. 4070, 4126, 9103, pl. 80.

25 Laumonier 1977, 26 cat. 371, pl. 1; 27–28 cats. 667, 801, pl. 2; 44 cat. 2449, pl. 8; 270–271 cats. 4578, 8675, 2004, pl. 63; 316 cat. 559, pl. 74; 325 cat. 2221, pl. 77; 326 cat. 2268, pl. 78; 330 cat. 351, pl. 79.

we can observe how the rosettes of the rim frieze, as well as the rosette in the tendril of the main decoration, occur in negative relief – evidently mechanically copied – over a calyx of very crude acanthus. Similarly, it is conceivable that even the bowls with medallion rosette B in negative relief also found on Delos could be either late products of My(…) or of a follower.[26]

There is no contextual evidence that can pin down the dates of My(…)'s activity, but his stamp repertoire suggests he was a contemporary of Menemachos and the height of the Monogram PAR Workshop, probably working in the third quarter of the 2nd century.[27]

Late Members of Workshop Circle 1

Potters active in the later years of Workshop Circle 1[28] can be identified by the combination of the flat, Menemachean base with the designs most typical of the later 2nd century: long-petal and imbricate decoration. The best represented of these in the Black Sea area is Philon(nios), who identified himself by the genitive of his name (PHILONOS or PHILONNIOU, presumably the same man).[29] He may also lie behind the isolated letter phi that identifies several bowls (e.g., EPH-809, EPH-897*, EPH-898*). The signature was incised into the vessel (not the mould) before firing. The 19 signed bowls in our assemblage include 12 of imbricate and five of long-petal design.[30] Three of these bear the distinctive 'paw' rim motif, which occurs on many more imbricate and long-petal bowls that can thereby be attributed to this artisan. In all, he can be credited with about 40 bowls in our assemblage, to add to the hundreds present on Delos. The 'paw' is the dominant rim pattern, but others occur sporadically: Ionian kyma (EPH-1066, EPH-1067*, EPH-1278), rosette 7 alternating with jewellery pendants (EPH-1242*, EPH-1243), astragal (once, as the second frieze of the only bowl with more than one, EPH-1065), and rosette 9 (EPH-1089). Rosette 8 occurs commonly on his products at Delos (e.g., Laumonier 1977, 263 cats. 3171, 5653, pl. 60); rim fragments with this motif (EPH-890*, EPH-1198*) may also come from his workshop, but not enough is preserved to make a secure attribution. Where the wall decoration survives, it consists either of imbricate pointed petals (19 examples) or long petals (7 examples). Decoration appears on the base only once: a tiny rosette at the centre of a floor signed with the letter phi (EPH-897*).

Also in this late group is Athenaios, of whom we have five signatures, also incised into a plain base before firing.[31] Two have pointed imbricate petals (EPH-815*, EPH-863), one is long-petal (EPH-1037*), the other two preserve traces of pine-cone scales (EPH-539) and a vegetal calyx (EPH-714). It has not been possible to assign any other fragments to this modest workshop. All of these patterns appear on bowls on Delos attributed to Athenaios by Laumonier. The Delos bowls also include five with a 'nelumbo' populated by floral tendrils,[32] a favourite Menemachean pattern that supports a connection between the workshops. Some of these, however, have rosette medallions, so the constitution of this workshop still remains to be worked out.

Workshop Circle 2: Belles Méduses Workshop

This workshop was identified by Laumonier on the basis of a few vessels which employ a frontal Medusa head with long tresses in the base medallion.[33] It is characteristic that in a number of cases, the medallion is surrounded by a rim-frieze pattern,[34] something which is very uncommon in Ephesian production.

The evidence for this workshop is slight. Laumonier assembled 151 vessels under this name, but[35] they are not a

---

26 Laumonier 1977, 280 cat. 9282, pl. 64; 283–284 cats. 5179, 5387, pl. 65; 285 cat. 5581, pl. 66; 290–291 cats. 153, 8492, pl. 67; 294 cat. 789, pl. 68; 300 cat. 1126, pl. 70; 309 cat. 9682, pl. 73 (all considered to be of Hera(…)'s workshop).

27 [Ed. This paragraph has been added at a point where PGB indicated that she planned comments on the chronology of My(…).]

28 [Ed. This section is my addition, based primarily on information in PGB's data base.]

29 See p. 293 above for a complete list of his signatures. Those in the present catalogue are: EPH-802–EPH-808*, EPH-899*, EPH-1065–EPH-1069, EPH-1248, EPH-1278, including the complete signatures Philonniou and Philonos, as well as parts of the same. For Laumonier's account of this workshop, see Laumonier 1977, 247–273.

30 Other signed bowls known from the region: Loseva 1962, 197; Grzegrzółka 2010, 38 cat. 5 (figures of actors and Erotes); Limberis & Marčenko 2000, figs. 1.8, 2 (long petal).

31 See p. 293 above for other known signatures. For the workshop on Delos, to which Laumonier attributed about 90 bowls, see Laumonier 1997, 231–238, pls. 52, 53.

32 Laumonier 1977, 232–234 cats. 1329–1331, 1992, 8861, pl. 52. Laumonier mentions other Menemachean connections as well (231); the thunderbolt of WC1 also appears on a signed bowl (cat. 1991).

33 Laumonier 1977, 81–83 cats. 632, 769, 770, 1941, 2068, pl. 18; see also Ladstätter et al. 2003, 27.

34 EPH-170*, surrounded by ivy-berry clusters; EPH-403 and Gajdukevič 1981, fig. 2 by jewellery pendants; Laumonier 1977, cat. 769 and 2068 by a wave meander; cat. 1941 by an Ionian kyma.

35 [Ed. PGB's text ended here; she did not complete her discussion of the Belles Méduses. I have supplied a few comments on

closely knit or even clearly defensible group, as Laumonier himself pointed out (1977, 81). The first five series of his Group A (constituting 46 pieces) clearly belong together, but the sixth is essentially unconnected; the only link is through an Ionian kyma that is similar but not rigorously identical (Laumonier 1977, 85). Since the sixth series provides the link to Group B (amounting to about two-thirds of the attributed pieces), those float rather far from the coherent centre of the workshop. Taking the restrictive view of including only the first the five series of Group A, the repertoire of the Belles Méduses is as follows. (Those in Laumonier 1977 are all illustrated on his pl. 18.)

In the rim zone, in addition to the ubiquitous Ionian kyma (Laumonier 1977, 81–82, 84 cats. 1448, 1463, 8100), the workshop makes most frequent use of a distinctive wave meander drawn with a single line;[36] although wave meanders appear in other workshops, the linear style of this version seems to be unique to the Belles Méduses. Other patterns are a miniature stylized acanthus scroll (Laumonier 1977, 83–84 cats. 367, 997, 1191, 1516), and single instances of a guilloche and a large star rosette (Laumonier 1977, 83 cat. 383 [guilloche]; Kotitsa 1998, 121–123 cat. 90, pl. 53 [rosette]). Multiple rim friezes are rare, with only one in the narrow definition of the workshop espoused here (Laumonier 1977, 84 cat. 8100).

The limited evidence suggests that the shop had a preference for full-body decoration. The most striking instance is a bold acanthus or acanthus-vine scroll filling the wall from medallion to rim pattern.[37] Lower horizontal friezes are not common, but those that exist host figured decoration: feline phalli (Laumonier 1977, 83 cat. 3274; Puppo 1995, 152 cat. X9, pl. LXVIII), wreaths (Laumonier 1977, cats. 8472, 1746), a row of suspended wreaths (Kotitsa 1998, 121–123 cat. 90, pl. 53), or, most unusually, a series of large, eight-petalled rosettes (Puppo 1995, 152 cat. X9, pl. LXVIII). Stylized long-petal decoration occurs (Laumonier 1977, 83 cat. 770), but it is uncertain whether it filled the wall or functioned as a lower calyx.

Calyx decoration of the lower wall of two bowls consists of plastic long petals alternating with an ovoid petal and a wavy line in one case and acanthus leaves with tips uniformly bent to the left on the other.[38] Full-body calyces occur more frequently, in keeping with the shop's preference for this larger field. The more elaborate examples include tall, slender overlapping lotus petals (Laumonier 1977, 83 cat. 308; Tsakos 1990, 140–141 inv. 3204, pl. 77.a) or acanthus leaves (Laumonier 1977, 83 cats. 367, 383) separated by dot columns. Simpler compositions present alternations of various simple forms (lotus petal, long petal, straight acanthus), again separated by dot columns or wavy lines (Laumonier 1977, 83–84 cat. 868, 997, 1068, 1191, 1192).

The namesake Medusa is the most commonly attested, and unmistakable, medallion design.[39] Other motifs, each appearing only once, are: a distinctive eight-petalled rosette with puffy petals and a large centre with a small dot (Laumonier 1977, 85 cat. 768), a motif which also appears once in a lower wall frieze (Puppo 1995, 152 cat. X9, pl. LXVIII); an eight-pointed star (Laumonier 1977, 83 cat. 3274); and a rosette-like motif of radiating rhomboidal petals and acanthus leaves (Laumonier 1977, 82 cat. 1438, pls. 18, 119). Only a small part of another rosette is preserved (Laumonier 1977, 84 cat. 746), but it may be the rosette A favoured by the Monogram PAR Workshop.

Two features in particular attest to a close relationship between the Belles Méduses and Monogram PAR workshops. The first is the band of decoration surrounding the Medusa medallion, which has already been mentioned above. This rare practice finds its best parallel in the Monogram PAR Workshop, where the monogram itself is surrounded by a decorated band (as discussed below). The second link between the two shops is the full-body scrolls, another rare feature that is shared by these two workshops alone.[40] Laumonier placed the Belles Méduses near the beginning of production, as the naturalistic treatment of some of the vegetal elements and the near absence of long petals from the decoration suggest. One detail that may further support this dating is the Medusa medallion. The subject is not found in other Ionian workshops, but it was a favourite on the Athenian bowls that may have provided some of the early models for Ionian production.[41] Even though the style of the two gorgoneia

---

the workshop, based on Laumonier's catalogue and PGB's data base.]

36 Laumonier 1977, 82 cats. 988, 2006, pl. 18; 83 cats. 308, 868, 1068, 3274, pl. 18; 84 cats. 1192, 5619, 5621, 5713, 8472, 9452, pl. 18; Puppo 1995, 152 cat. X9, pl. LXVIII.

37 EPH-170*; Laumonier 1977, 81–82 cats. 632, 1448, 1449, 2006, 9675, pls. 18, 119 (acanthus); 82 cats. 769, 865, 1941, 1463, 1463 bis, 1953, pl. 18 (acanthus-vine). Several examples of both have been found in the Black Sea region, but, for most, not enough is preserved for an attribution (EPH-161*–EPH-177*).

38 EPH-403 = Kotitsa 1998, 121–123 cat. 90, pl. 53 (long petals); Laumonier 1977, 83 cat. 3274, pl. 18 (acanthus).

39 EPH-170*, EPH-403; Laumonier 1977, 81–83 cat. 632, 769, 770, 1941, 2068, pls. 18, 119; Tsakos 1990, 140–141 inv. 3204, pl. 77.a; Puppo 1995, 152 cat. X9, pl. LXVIII.

40 Compare Laumonier 1977, Series XV of the PAR Workshop, 169–171, pls. 35, 124; EPH-164*.

41 Common in the Workshop of Bion, e.g., Rotroff 1982a, 26; for good illustrations, see cats. 101, 121, 152, 171, pls. 75, 76, 78, 79, 98.

is very different, the idea of a Medusa medallion might have come from Athens.

Workshop Circle 2: Workshop of Monogram PAR and His Associates

This workshop is closely related to (and probably in its early phase identical with) the Belle Méduses Workshop. The Monogram PAR potter takes over (or continues) the band of rim pattern surrounding the base medallion, as we can see from the extremely few signed vessels in existence.

To my knowledge, ten signed vessels have been found. Four of them are amongst the finds from Delos published by Laumonier (1977, 133 cat. 2000–2003, pl. 30; Fig. 68); one was unearthed in Entremont and therefore must date before 125, when the city was destroyed (Benoit 1947, 82–83, fig. 2; Fig. 69). The remainder were all found in the Black Sea region.[42] With the exception of the vessel in the Ashmolean Museum, where the medallion is surrounded by three concentric ridges (unless the middle ridge is a fine astragal), all the vessels feature an Ionian kyma around the monogram stamp.

The monogram contains (at least) the letters ΑΔΠΡ as well as an I or T (or both) and perhaps an M and/or an N, so the possible reconstructions of the potter's name are many. Courby (1922, 393), followed by Benoit, suggested Parios; Laumonier, in turn, advocated Paris or Pindaros (1977, 131).

Shapes

The main shape is a hemispherical bowl with an inturned rim, the lip of which is finished in a number of different ways. The base always features a medallion with a rosette, the design of which varies (see below, 321–323). The rim diameter is normally between 12 and 13 cm, and the height mostly 6–7 cm; completely preserved vessels have a H:⌀ ratio of between 1:1.7 and 1:2.3, thus a significantly lower ratio than bowls of Menemachos, i.e., a shallower shape. In addition to the bowls, the Monogram PAR potter also experimented with a few other shapes, but he never made large vessels, as Menemachos did. The workshop predominantly produced oxidized vessels, but some grey-ware vessels occur, mainly in the early part of the workshop's existence.

Decoration

From time to time, the workshops of Menemachos and Monogram PAR exchanged stamps and ideas. Occasionally, Menemachos borrowed rim patterns (e.g., the box meander) and calyx B from the workshop of Monogram PAR, and the latter also occasionally borrowed rim patterns (e.g., rosette 1, horizontal S-spirals) from Menemachos (e.g., Laumonier 1977, 150, 151 cats. 372, 8594, pl. 34). Some stamps were shared, for example, Eros racing a chariot to the right. By and large, however, the two workshops kept their own style in terms of shape and decoration.[43]

Syntax
The Monogram PAR Workshop adhered to the Ephesian model of superposed, horizontal registers, bordered by one or more rim friezes above and by a calyx bounded by a ridge below. The underside was universally occupied by a rosette. Friezes were divided by a ridge, except perhaps in the shop's very earliest days, documented by two mould fragments from the Magnesia Gate, where beading played this role (Seiterle 1981, 28, fig.).

Rim
C. Rogl has collected and illustrated the rim motifs of the workshop (Rogl 2014a, 128, fig. 13); patterns that are particularly characteristic and are present in our Black Sea assemblage are:

Astragal with decorated beads: EPH-748*, EPH-750*; cf. Laumonier 1977, 142–143 cats. 427, 431, 451 (centre of pl. 32, not labelled), 1054, pls. 32, 123; 157 cat. 438, pl. 35

Box meander: EPH-202, EPH-220, EPH-221, EPH-750*, EPH-1302*; cf. Laumonier 1977, 207 cats. 1923, 2146, et al., pl. 47; Rogl 2014a, fig. 13.8

Guilloche: EPH-636; cf. Laumonier 1977, 141 cats. 392, 396, pl. 32; Rogl 2014a, fig. 13.9

Triple guilloche, a pattern restricted to this workshop: EPH-188, EPH-778*, EPH-858, EPH-859*, EPH-1167*; cf. Laumonier 1977, 204 cats. 1920, 1489, pl. 46, 126; Rogl 2014a, fig. 13.9, middle

Wave meander with double outline: EPH-518*; cf. Laumonier 1977, 143 cat. 451, pls. 32 (centre of plate, not labelled), 123; Rogl 2014a, fig. 13.10

---

42 Istros: EPH-1251 (Fig. 70). Myrmekion: EPH-613. Čaika: Ч-64-215, 224, Vnukov & Kovalenko 1998, 66. Kara Tobe: K-91-246, Vnukov & Kovalenko 1998, figs. 1, 2.1. South Russia: Ashmolean Museum, Beazley's Gifts 1967, 116 cat. 445, pl. XLII (Fig. 71).

43 [Ed. Aside from some comments scattered throughout the text, PGB did not leave a discussion of the PAR Monogram Workshop. The following description of the products of the workshop, from decoration through discussion of supplementary shapes, is almost completely constructed from her data base.]

FIGURE 68
Monogram PAR signature from Delos (Laumonier 1977, cat. 2000, pl. 30)

FIGURE 69
Monogram PAR signature from Entremont (Benoit 1947, fig. 2). Published with the permission of *Gallia*

FIGURE 70
Monogram PAR signature from Istros (**EPH-1251**)
PHOTO BY THE AUTHOR

FIGURE 71
Monogram PAR signature from South Russia (Ashmolean Museum, i.n. 1966.268). Beazley's Gifts 1967, 116 cat. 445, pl. LXII
REPRODUCED WITH PERMISSION OF THE ASHMOLEAN MUSEUM, OXFORD

Rosette 2/7: EPH-420, EPH-497*(?), EPH-612*, EPH-650*, EPH-1046*, EPH-1303*; cf. Laumonier 1977, 170 cats. 1176, 1450, pl. 35; Rogl 2014a, fig. 13.4. Occasionally the rosette alternates with jewellery pendants, which are otherwise not found in this shop (cf. Laumonier 1977, 172–173 cats. 878, 4220, and others on pl. 38)

Rosette 4 (star rosette): EPH-420, EPH-421; cf. Laumonier 1977, 170, 171 cats. 1439, 1457, 1458, pls. 35, 124; Rogl 2014a, fig. 13.3

Miniature acanthus-flower scroll, another pattern restricted to this workshop: EPH-29*, EPH-161*, EPH-192*, EPH-262*, EPH-306*, EPH-362*, EPH-420, EPH-421, EPH-517, EPH-518*, EPH-636, EPH-650*, EPH-681, EPH-756, EPH-992, EPH-1046*, EPH-1202–EPH-1204, EPH-1281*, EPH-1303*, cf. Laumonier 1977, 160 cat. 1281, pls. 36, 125

Main Decoration

A   *Figural Decoration*

Erotes walking, playing musical instruments: EPH-1303*; cf. Laumonier 1977, 146 cat. 3179, pl. 33; 167 cats. 3209, 3242, 3243, pl. 37

Eros racing two-horse chariot to the right: EPH-29*; cf. Laumonier 1977, 167 cat. 3151 et al., pl. 37

Saluting Pan: EPH-1303*; cf. Laumonier 1977, 167, 168 cats. 3242, 3252, pl. 37

Rabbit and dog: cf. Laumonier 1977, 151 cats. 3053, 3054, pl. 34

Rabbit and eagle (and eagle alone): cf. Laumonier 1997, 185 cat. 3049, 9318, pl. 40

Amazonomachy: cf. Laumonier 1977, 139 cats. 526, 3343, pl. 31. Some of the stamps in the Black Sea assemblage are close to those of the Monogram PAR Workshop (e.g., EPH-88*, cf. Laumonier cat. 3347, pl. 36)

Actors: cf. Laumonier 1977, 164 cat. 1305, pl. 36

Dolphins: cf. Laumonier 1977, 165, pl. 37, top two rows

B   *Scroll Decoration*

Full-body scroll: EPH-161*; cf. Laumonier 1977, 170–171, pl. 35

Acanthus-vine scroll: EPH-186, EPH-192*, EPH-202, EPH-205 (running left); EPH-180, EPH-181, EPH-188, EPH-226, EPH-227, EPH-238, EPH-247 (running right); cf. Laumonier 1977, 204 cats. 1469, 1489, et al., pls. 46, 126

Acanthus-vine-ivy scroll, left: EPH-249*, EPH-251(?); cf. Laumonier 1977, 154 cat. 408, pl. 34; 205 cat. 1502, pl. 46

Stylized acanthus scroll: EPH-280*(?), EPH-306*, EPH-518*(?); cf. Laumonier 1977, 158 cat. 1291, pls. 36, 124; 203–204 cat. 1423 and many others on pl. 45

C   *Wreath Decoration*

Myrtle wreath: EPH-186, EPH-362*, EPH-518*(?); cf. Laumonier 1977, 134, 136 cats. 375, 376, pl. 30

Ivy wreath: cf. Laumonier 1977, 182 cat. 1518, 1521, 1862, pl. 39

D   *Multiple Rim Friezes*

Three friezes: EPH-420, EPH-421, EPH-612*, EPH-650*, EPH-748*(?), EPH-750*(?)

Two friezes: EPH-449*(?), EPH-473*(?), EPH-497*(?), EPH-517, EPH-518*, EPH-636, EPH-756, EPH-1046*, EPH-1302*, EPH-1303*

E   *Vegetal Decoration*

Pine-Cone Decoration

Plastic pine-cone decoration: cf. Laumonier 1977, 200, pl. 44, lowest two rows

Stylized pine-cone decoration. It is uncertain whether this form of decoration occurs in the workshop. The following are tentatively attributed on the basis of their rosette medallions (rosettes A and B): Laumonier 1977, 200 cats. 4020, 4021, pl. 44; 477 cat. 4016, pl. 111

Calyx

Calyx A1 (rare): cf. Laumonier 1977, 159, 160 cats. 1231, 1281, 1282, pls. 36, 125

Calyx A2 (rare): cf. Laumonier 1977, 158 cats. 1284, 1291, pls. 36, 124

Calyx B1 (common): EPH-180, EPH-181, EPH-1303*; cf. Laumonier 1997, 149 cat. 1097, pl. 33.

Calyx B2 (common): EPH-186, EPH-188, EPH-612*, EPH-613, EPH-624*(?), EPH-636; cf. Laumonier 1977, 139 cats. 884, pl. 31; 143 cat. 451, pls. 32, 123

Calyx C: EPH-92(?); cf. Laumonier 1977, 155–157 cat. 403 and others at the top of pl. 35

Imbricate Decoration

Imbricate petals with rounded tip: EPH-202, EPH-205, EPH-748*(?), EPH-750*(?), EPH-756, EPH-766*, EPH-770*(?), EPH-771*, EPH-773*, EPH-778*, EPH-795*(?), EPH-797*(?); cf. Laumonier 1977, pls. 41, 42, upper rows.

Imbricate petals with pointed tip: EPH-858, EPH-859*; cf. Laumonier 1977, pl. 42, lower rows.

F   *Linear Decoration*
   Pendent-semicircle design: EPH-955*, EPH-1281*; cf. Laumonier 1977, pl. 45, top two rows
   Net pattern: EPH-992; cf. Laumonier 1977, 199 cat. 4056 and others on pl. 44
   Plastic long petals: EPH-1251(?); cf. Laumonier 1977, 181 cat. 4769, pl. 39; 196 cats. 4683, 4684, et al., pl. 43
   Stylized long petals: EPH-1046*; cf. Laumonier 1977, 181 cats. 4439, 4556, 4576, pl. 39

Base
   Rosette A: EPH-92(?), EPH-161*, EPH-186, EPH-202, EPH-250*, EPH-612*, EPH-624*(?), EPH-795*(?); cf. Laumonier 1977, 134 cat. 597, pl. 30; 141 cat. 903, pl. 32
   Rosette B: EPH-180, EPH-181, EPH-188, EPH-636; cf. Laumonier 1977, 184 cat. 669, pl. 40
   Rosette E: cf. Laumonier 1977, 136 cat. 715, pl. 30; 139 cat. 714, pl. 31

Supplementary Shapes
   Small bowl: EPH-1281*; cf. Laumonier 1977, 213 cat. 5394, pls. 17, 132; 202 cat. 2071, pls. 45, 132
   Skyphos with pinched handle: EPH-1302*; cf. Laumonier 1977, 201 cat. 4336, pls. 45, 132
   Amphora, Pergamene type: EPH-1303*
   Krater: Laumonier vol. 2, cats. 6019+6041, 1516, pl. 7

Decorative Motifs of the Ephesian Industry

This section provides an overview of the decoration of the Ephesian industry, with emphasis on the ways it is represented in the Black Sea assemblage.

Rim
Ephesian rim decoration comes in three variants, and its conventions are shared by all workshops:
– no rim pattern above the main decoration
– a single rim frieze
– multiple rim friezes (two or more)
The first is rare. It is difficult to be sure how common the single rim frieze is in comparison to the multiple rim frieze; the ratio in my catalogue is approximately 5:1, but since this figure includes fragments where additional rim friezes may once have existed but are now lost, the single rim frieze is overrepresented. Nevertheless, it is likely that single rim friezes are significantly more common than multiple rim friezes.

Multiple rim friezes tend to appear as a decoration proper; bowls with such a pattern in the upper part of the vessel are therefore discussed below under main decoration. Every pattern that appears in the lower rim friezes can also be found in the uppermost frieze (even though the frequency of a pattern is different in the different positions), so the review of rim patterns below is relevant to multiple rim friezes as well as single ones. The ornaments used in this zone draw almost exclusively on the repertoire of architectural detail. Fig. 72 provides an overview of the relative frequency of the individual rim patterns of Ephesian bowls in the Black Sea assemblage.

From Fig. 72, we can easily see that the larger the sample, the more likely it is that a high number of rim patterns will be represented at any single site. Nevertheless, not all decorative patterns are equally common. By far the most common is the Ionian kyma (38.3%); it has hardly any rivals, but next in number are the box meander (all types, 9.9%), Lesbian kyma (6.8%), the star rosettes (5.3%), and rosette 2 with seven petals (4.7%). When it comes to representativity, only four rim patterns are present at almost all of our Black Sea sites: the Ionian kyma, the Lesbian kyma, the box meander, and the guilloche. The others are found on a more limited number of sites.

When considering the overall pattern, I should like to mention two observations: one is the predominance of the box-meander pattern at Olbia (more on this below), the other is the generally diverging pattern represented by Istros, where the Ionian kyma constitutes no less than 41.3% of all the single-rim-pattern rims; also the star rosettes, rosettes 5 and 7, and large dots are over-represented there compared with the other sites. Both of these phenomena can in all likelihood be explained chronologically, and result from the fact that the assemblage at Olbia is *earlier* and that at Istros *later* than the site average (more on this pp. 503 and 512).

In the following, we shall discuss the individual rim patterns, where possible, with a reference to Rogl's illustration of the motif and to examples published by Laumonier, ideally illustrated by a drawing.

Astragal
Rogl 2014a, fig. 13.11; e.g., Laumonier 1977, 35 cat. 1343, pls. 3, 116
The astragal comes in a number of different stamps. Characteristic of Menemachos is an astragal with decorated reels (EPH-432, EPH-433, EPH-409, EPH-753*; cf. Laumonier 1977, 26 cat. 1981, pls. 1, 113; 41 cat. 9709, pl. 7), whereas in the Monogram PAR Workshop we encounter an astragal with decorated beads (EPH-748*; cf. Laumonier 1977, 142–143 cats. 427, 431, 451, pls. 32 [in the middle of the plate, not labelled], 123; 157 cat. 438, pl. 35). The most common astragal, however, is undecorated, and a number of such plain stamps are employed by workshops

	Average % (1,577=100%)	Bol'šoj Kastel'	Chersonesos	Istros	Kepoi	Myrmekion	Olbia	Pantikapaion	Porthmion	Ruminskoe	Tyritake	Volna 1
No rim pattern	1.3	1	1	7	1	2	7	1				
Astragal	3.2	1		27	4	1	14	2		2		
Box meander, ccw	2.2		1			1	31	2				
Box meander, cw	6.5	1	4	16	2	4	63	6	2	1	1	2
Box meander, type?	1.2		1	1		1	14	2				
Ionian kyma	37.8	2	8	256	4	23	253	24	12	1	5	8
Lesbian kyma	6.9	1	1	39		8	47	6	2			5
Hanging leaf				1			1					
Heart-shaped leaf				1								
S-spirals, horizontal	1.4			12		2	5	2				1
S-spirals, vertical				4			7				1	
Simple guilloche				1				1				
Heart guilloche right				2			2	1				
Heart guilloche left				1			1	1				
Guilloche right	3.0	3	3	11	1	2	22	3	1			
Guilloche left	3.0		1	9		2	29	2	2			
Triple guilloche				2	1		1	1				
Wave meander	0.8			1		1	10	1				
Rosette 1 (Menemachos rosette)	2.3		1	17		2	11	5	1			
Rosette 2/7	4.6		2	27		6	31	5			1	
Rosette 2, other	1.1		1	10			3	4				
Rosette 3				7			1					
Rosette 4 (star rosette)	5.2	1	1	37		3	32	8				
Rosette 5	3.0			8	3	5	24	5	2			
Rosette 6 (My(…))				2								
Rosette 7	3.6			47			6	3				
Rosette 8 (Philon(nios))				12			1	1				
Rosette 9				1			2	1				
Rosette, type?	1.0		1	13				1				
Miniature acanthus-flower scroll			1	2		1	6				1	
Miniature acanthus scroll left				6		3	3	1				
Miniature acanthus scroll right				2			1	1				
Miniature stylized acanthus scroll				2		1		1				
Miniature ultra-stylized scroll				1				1				
Miniature myrtle wreath				1		1						
Large dots	1.5	2		14			5	1			1	
Crossed dotted lines with box				7	1	1	1	4				
Crossed dotted lines with rosette						1						
Crossed dotted lines				4			2		1			
Oblique boxes				3			1					
Concentric boxes							1					
'Paw'	1.3			7	1		9	2				1

FIGURE 72 Relative and absolute frequency of Ephesian rim patterns in single rim friezes (as preserved); ECA+ECB

of the early and classical phases. The astragal most commonly occurs as the second rim frieze (Fig. 76).[44]

Box Meander
Rogl 2014a, fig. 13.8; e.g., Laumonier 1977, 31 cat. 477, pls. 2, 114
The box meander almost always runs in a counter-clockwise direction and is spaced with small rectangles containing four-pointed starbursts. It is especially favoured by the Monogram PAR Workshop but occurs repeatedly throughout Ephesian production. It is an earmark of the early and classic phase of production, a fact that is reflected in the high numbers of the motif at Olbia in comparison to its representation in the generally later material at Istros (see Fig. 72).

Ionian kyma
Rogl 2014a, figs. 13.2, 14.89; e.g., Laumonier 1977, 26 cat. 1981, pls. 1, 113; 233 cats. 1209+1406, pls. 52, 127
This is the commonest Ephesian rim pattern in all periods, shared across workshops and workshop circles. It is usually plain, but the tongue can be hatched and the egg can be ornamented.

Lesbian kyma
Rogl 2014a, figs. 13.1, 14.88; e.g., Laumonier 1977, 156, 165 cats. 9620, 3050, pls. 35, 37, 125
Much less common than the Ionian kyma, but also represented throughout Ephesian production. Various parts of the pattern can be hatched.

Hanging Leaf
Rogl 2014a, fig. 14.100
A rare motif consisting of a rounded leaf ornamented with vertical lines.
EPH-159*, EPH-857

Heart-Shaped Leaf
A hanging heart-shaped or ivy leaf, occurring only once.
EPH-470*

S-Spirals
E.g., Laumonier 1997, 26 cat. 636, pls. 1, 113; 210 cat. 5567, pl. 17
An S-shaped spiral or double spiral occurs with some regularity. It may be positioned either horizontally (the preferred orientation) or vertically. The Delian material suggests that the pattern is spread throughout the industry, but the bulk of the examples are on bowls of Workshop Circle 1, especially Menemachos and Ni(…).
Horizontal S-spirals: EPH-55, EPH-61*, EPH-67*, EPH-109, EPH-337*, EPH-386*, EPH-416*, EPH-426, EPH-432, EPH-439*, EPH-471–EPH-474*, EPH-479*, EPH-559, EPH-601*, EPH-617, EPH-648, EPH-690*, EPH-735, EPH-736*, EPH-869, EPH-870*, EPH-882*, EPH-1024*, EPH-1045*, EPH-1274*, EPH-1284*, EPH-1285*, EPH-1293, EPH-1294, EPH-1324*
Vertical S-spirals: EPH-116, EPH-159*, EPH-252*, EPH-427*, EPH-450*, EPH-473*, EPH-475*–EPH-477*, EPH-601*, EPH-610*, EPH-935*, EPH-954*, EPH-968, EPH-1011*, EPH-1050*, EPH-1159*

Guilloche
Rogl 2014a, fig. 13.9; e.g., Laumonier 1977, 24 cat. 1216, pls. 1, 113; 141 cat. 396, pl. 32
At its best, this is the tightly braided pattern familiar from architectural ornamentation, though it is often considerably debased. The wider end can be either to the right or to the left (guilloche right or guilloche left, respectively). It is most common in the Monogram PAR Workshop but used occasionally by workshops across the industry. There are about 60 in the present catalogue.

Heart Guilloche
A simplified, linear version of the guilloche, consisting of two spirals joining in a rough heart pattern. Rare in Ephesian production, but very common in the workshops of Kyme and Athens.
Heart guilloche right: EPH-343*, EPH-596*
Heart guilloche left: EPH-238, EPH-479*, EPH-1298, EPH-1305*

Triple Guilloche
Rogl 2014a, fig. 13.9, middle; e.g., Laumonier 1977, 204 cat. 1489, pls. 46, 126.
An expansion of the elaborate braid to three instead of two levels; exclusive to the Monogram PAR Workshop.
EPH-188, EPH-778*, EPH-858, EPH-859*, EPH-1167*

Wave Meander
Rogl 2014a, fig. 13.10; e.g., Laumonier 1977, 83–84 cats. 1068, 1192, pl. 18; 200 cats. 4010, 4222, pl. 44
A wave meander with a single or, more usually, a double outline and usually oriented upside down. It is most common in Workshop Circle 2, especially the Belles Méduses and Monogram PAR workshops.
EPH-121*, EPH-353*, EPH-382*, EPH-383*, EPH-441*, EPH-454*, EPH-488*–EPH-491*, EPH-518*, EPH-559,

---

44 [Ed. After this point, PGB left only a list of rim motifs, which has been filled out with descriptions and references from her database.]

EPH-611*, EPH-617, EPH-856*, EPH-1051*, EPH-1086, EPH-1168*–EPH-1171*, EPH-1315*, EPH-1344*

Rosette 1 (Menemachos Rosette)
Rogl 2014a, fig. 14.96; e.g., Laumonier 1977, 23 cat. 1971, pls. 1, 113; 42 cat. 3275, pl. 7; 65 cats. 3163, 3371, pl. 14; 76 cats. 5377, pl. 16, the last four also on pl. 118
A rosette with an even number of petals (most commonly eight, occasionally six), alternately long and short, fitting within a square field. The petals are usually hollow (drawn in outline) and pointed, sometimes diamond shaped. This motif is characteristic of Menemachos, to the degree that it can be nicknamed the 'Menemachos rosette', though it is occasionally borrowed by the Monogram PAR potter.
EPH-28, EPH-129, EPH-130, EPH-288*, EPH-289*, EPH-354*, EPH-455*, EPH-466*, EPH-493*, EPH-531*, EPH-532, EPH-580*, EPH-737*, EPH-779*, EPH-780*, EPH-852*, EPH-860*, EPH-884–EPH-886, EPH-995*, EPH-1045*, EPH-1052*, EPH-1172–EPH-1174*

Rosette 2
Rogl 2014a, fig. 13.4; e.g., Laumonier 1977, 31 cats. 682, pls. 2, 114 (rosette 2 [M]); 155–156 cats. 424, 2185, pl. 35
A simple rosette with hollow, rounded petals within a circular perimeter. By far the commonest scheme is with seven petals (rosette 2/7), though other numbers occur occasionally (4, 6, 8, 10). The workshops of both Menemachos and the Monogram PAR employed rosette 2/7, but the rosettes differ stylistically: in the Menemachean version, the petals are larger and more boldly incised. In order to distinguish the two, rosette 2 (M) is used for the Menemachean variant.
EPH-43*–EPH-46*, EPH-54*, EPH-62, EPH-96*, EPH-115, EPH-127*, EPH-182*, EPH-189*, EPH-242*, EPH-307*, EPH-308*, EPH-328*, EPH-344*, EPH-355*, EPH-361*, EPH-378*, EPH-414, EPH-415, EPH-419*, EPH-420, EPH-423*, EPH-429*, EPH-430*, EPH-456*–EPH-459*, EPH-467*, EPH-477*, EPH-488*, EPH-494*–EPH-504*, EPH-509*, EPH-533*, EPH-534*, EPH-550*, EPH-551, EPH-561*, EPH-572, EPH-579*, EPH-609, EPH-612*, EPH-638, EPH-639, EPH-643*, EPH-650*, EPH-651*, EPH-702, EPH-706*, EPH-727*, EPH-729, EPH-755*, EPH-758*, EPH-853*, EPH-854*, EPH-887, EPH-888, EPH-971*, EPH-1024*, EPH-1027*, EPH-1046*, EPH-1063*, EPH-1113*, EPH-1175*–EPH-1183*, EPH-1273*, EPH-1280, EPH-1303*, EPH-1306*

Rosette 3
Rogl 2014a, fig. 13.5; e.g., Laumonier 1977, 264 cat. 4179, pl. 60

Broad, roughly triangular, hollow petals alternating with narrower, teardrop-shaped rays. A variant has solid petals, in negative relief.
EPH-861*, EPH-1184*, EPH-1185*

Rosette 4 (Star Rosette)
Rogl 2014a, fig. 13.3; e.g., Laumonier 1977, 170 cat. 1457, pls. 35, 124
A starburst consisting of eight solid, pointed rays, filling a square field. This very common pattern is typical of the Monogram PAR Workshop but is occasionally borrowed by Menemachos and others.
EPH-12, EPH-48*, EPH-49*, EPH-52*, EPH-53*, EPH-59*, EPH-95*, EPH-110*, EPH-168*, EPH-239*–EPH-241, EPH-261*, EPH-309*, EPH-320*, EPH-324*, EPH-345, EPH-346*, EPH-393, EPH-410*, EPH-418–EPH-421, EPH-460*, EPH-489*, EPH-490*, EPH-494*, EPH-501*, EPH-505*–EPH-509*, EPH-535*, EPH-548*, EPH-611*, EPH-614–EPH-618*, EPH-639, EPH-662*, EPH-680, EPH-705, EPH-726*, EPH-738, EPH-739*, EPH-759*, EPH-781*, EPH-816*, EPH-817, EPH-866*, EPH-930*, EPH-1013*, EPH-1016*, EPH-1062*, EPH-1078*, EPH-1186*–EPH-1189*, EPH-1288*, EPH-1309, EPH-1342*

Rosette 5
E.g., Laumonier 1977, 126–127 cats. 9495, 1733, 1931, pl. 29
Eight solid petals, alternately shorter and longer and so fitting within an approximately square field. Present in both workshop circles.
EPH-30, EPH-131*, EPH-276, EPH-310*, EPH-311*, EPH-356*, EPH-357, EPH-360*, EPH-373, EPH-461*, EPH-487*, EPH-502*, EPH-510*–EPH-512, EPH-536, EPH-560*, EPH-670*, EPH-730*, EPH-824*, EPH-869, EPH-889*, EPH-936*, EPH-952*, EPH-1017*, EPH-1053, EPH-1079, EPH-1087, EPH-1088, EPH-1105*, EPH-1190*, EPH-1330*

Rosette 6
E.g., Laumonier 1977, 304 cat. 3096, pls. 71, 129; 323 cats. 3044, 3045, pl. 76
Seven- or (less commonly) eight solid, diamond-shaped petals in a round field. The motif is characteristic of My(...). It does not occur on bowls of Menemachos or Monogram PAR.
EPH-90*, EPH-514*, EPH-1191*, EPH-1192

Rosette 7
E.g., Laumonier 1977, 305 cat. 9739, pl. 71; 478 cat. 4219, pl. 111
Seven (rarely six) solid, pointed or rhomboidal petals, loosely constructed around a button centre.

EPH-123*, EPH-132, EPH-300, EPH-318*, EPH-319*, EPH-323, EPH-367*, EPH-1193–EPH-1197

Rosette 8
E.g., Laumonier 1977, 261 cat. 4534, pl. 59; 263 cats. 3171, 5653, pl. 60; 268 cat. 1300 pls. 62, 128
Eight solid petals with deeply notched ends, sometimes nearly V-shaped. Frequently found in the Workshop of Philon(nios).
EPH-890*, EPH-1198*, EPH-1329*

Rosette 9
E.g., Laumonier 1977, 236 cat. 4350, pl. 53
A daisy-like motif, with a large number of long, thin, solid petals, widening at the end. A common space-filler on the walls of PSC bowls (e.g., EPH-955*–EPH-960, EPH-970*) and occasionally elsewhere (e.g., EPH-114, EPH-115, EPH-127*), but rare as a rim motif. In that role it occurs in the shop of Athenaios (Laumonier 1977, 233 cat. 1336, pl. 52), and on a bowl attributed to Menemachos (Laumonier 1977 61 cat. 2121, pl. 13).
EPH-56, EPH-462*, EPH-515*, EPH-537*, EPH-598*, EPH-931*, EPH-1089, EPH-1199*

Rosette 10
E.g., Laumonier 1977, 252 cat. 5527, pl. 56
Many petals consisting of straight, stick-like rays with no further definition, like a child's drawing of the sun. It is also used as a wall motif (EPH-154*, EPH-974).
EPH-153*, EPH-600*, EPH-1200*

Rosette 11
For convenience we may mention here another small rosette which appears only as a wall motif: eight well-formed, rounded petals with a dot within each petal.
EPH-113, EPH-155*, EPH-962*, EPH-969*, EPH-970*

Miniature Acanthus-Flower Scroll
E.g., Laumonier 1977, 160 cat. 1281, pls. 36, 125
A sketchy miniature scroll running to the left, with tendrils and poorly defined flower forms. Limited to the Monogram PAR Workshop.
EPH-29*, EPH-161*, EPH-192*, EPH-262*, EPH-306*, EPH-362*, EPH-420, EPH-421, EPH-517, EPH-518*, EPH-636, EPH-650*, EPH-681, EPH-756, EPH-992, EPH-1046*, EPH-1202–EPH-1204, EPH-1281*, EPH-1303*

Miniature Acanthus Scroll
E.g., Laumonier 1977, 24 cat. 1425, pl. 1; 36 cat. 2264, pls. 4, 116 (left); 74 cat. 188, pl. 16 (right)

A miniature acanthus scroll, without flowers, occurs in a left-running and a right-running version, the former far more common. The motif belongs to WC1, almost exclusively to the Menemachos Workshop, with a few examples found on bowls of Ni(…).
EPH-67*, EPH-158*, EPH-422–EPH-424*, EPH-519*–EPH-521, EPH-635*, EPH-711, EPH-712, EPH-870*, EPH-891*, EPH-1054, EPH-1205*–EPH-1214 (left); EPH-128, EPH-991*, EPH-1080*, EPH-1215*, EPH-1216* (right)

Miniature Stylized Acanthus Scroll
Rogl 2014a, fig. 13.15; e.g., Laumonier 1977, 118, 120 cats. 4656, 1114+1134, pls. 27, 122.
In a stylized version of this same motif, the tendrils are lacking elaboration but still resemble a vegetal scroll. It is never a common pattern but is shared by both workshop circles. It is most frequently found on bowls of the Comique à la canne (e.g., Laumonier 1955, 116 cats. 3240, 3256, pls. 26, 122), to be regarded as the later phase of Menemachos, with a few instances in the workshop of the Belles Méduses (84 cats. 1191, 1516a, pl. 18) and of Menemachos (119 cat. 1836, pl. 27).
EPH-122, EPH-379, EPH-522, EPH-523

Miniature Ultra-stylized scroll
Rogl 2014a, fig. 13.14; e.g., Laumonier 1977, 177 cat. 3313, pl. 39
In this rare form, the scroll is reduced to little more than an elaborate running spiral. It is found on a series of vases that can be attributed either to Menemachos or the VG Workshop,[45] thus clearly the preserve of Workshop Circle 1.
EPH-1217*, EPH-1218*

Miniature Myrtle Wreath
E.g., Laumonier 1977, 224 cat. 373, pl. 50
This very rare rim pattern is a miniature version of the bound myrtle wreath which forms a common wall pattern. It appears on only a handful of bowls on Delos.[46]
EPH-516*, EPH-1219*

Large Dots
E.g., Laumonier 1977, 31 cat. 682, pls. 2, 114
A simple and widely shared rim pattern. These large and generally widely spaced dots are to be distinguished from

---

45 [Ed. These attributions differ from those of Laumonier, who assigned them to the Monogram PAR Workshop (Laumonier 1977, 177–178 cats. 3312, 3313, 8747, 1674, 1861, 1860, pl. 39).]
46 Laumonier 1977, 203 cat. 1423, pl. 45; 227 cat. 2066, pl. 51; 233 cat. 1331, pl. 52; 237 cats. 1759, 8886, pl. 53.

Crossed Dotted Lines

E.g., Laumonier 1977, 45 cat. 116, pl. 9; 57 cats. 4202–4204, pl. 12

Continuous dotted lines forming a series of low, broad diamonds. The point at which the lines cross is emphasized by three short radiating lines above, or both above and below. This and the two similar patterns described below are almost completely limited to the workshop of Menemachos.[47]

EPH-112*, EPH-932*, EPH-1029*, EPH-1030, EPH-1056, EPH-1057, EPH-1223*, EPH-1224

Crossed Dotted Lines with Box

E.g., Laumonier 1977, 33 cats. 1238, 2318, pls. 3, 115

Here the wide dotted crosses alternate with an oblique box with a double outline and containing a small cross.

EPH-27*, EPH-525*, EPH-526, EPH-584*, EPH-586, EPH-595*, EPH-1055*, EPH-1220–EPH-1222*

Crossed Dotted Lines Alternating with Rosette

E.g., Laumonier 1977, 26 cat. 371, pl. 1

In this rare variant, rosette 2/7 replaces the oblique box.

EPH-1107*

Oblique Boxes

Rogl 2014a, fig. 14.104 ('Rautenfisch'); e.g., Laumonier 1977, 115 cats. 1111, 1112, pls. 26, 121

Boxes set at an oblique angle, sometimes with a vertical line between them so that the image resembles a stylized fish. It occurs on bowls of the Comique à la canne, the late phase of Menemachos.

EPH-523*, EPH-527, EPH-993*, EPH-1225*, EPH-1226*

Concentric Boxes

E.g., Laumonier 1977, 106–107 cats. 4027, 4028, pl. 24

Three small, nested, concentric boxes with a dot at the centre occur as a rim motif very rarely. The design is the same as stamps used for the stylized pine-cone design (e.g., Laumonier 1977, 200 cat. 4010, pl. 44, possibly a late product of Menemachos).

EPH-424*, EPH-994*

'Paw'

E.g., Laumonier 1977, 263 cats. 2147, 3483, pl. 60

A pattern that appears to have originated as the left half of a rosette (usually rosette 1), stamped close together, with three petals forming the toes of the 'paw,' facing left. Characteristic of Philon(nios).

EPH-802*–EPH-804, EPH-810*–EPH-814, EPH-1081*, EPH-1227*–EPH-1237

Flower

E.g., Laumonier 1977, 121–122 cats. 4178, 8751, pl. 28; 229 cat. 4654, pl. 51

In its finer versions (EPH-1323*), a horizontally-oriented palmette, but most stamps resemble a loosely associated bunch of thin, splaying petals, or nested chevrons, oriented horizontally, either to left or to right.

EPH-1311*, EPH-1312*, EPH-1323*, EPH-1332*, EPH-1350*, EPH-1351*

Ivy-Berry Cluster

E.g., Laumonier 1977, 272 cat. 8668, pl. 63

A circular stamp of closely packed dots representing ivy berries, perhaps in some cases debased rosettes.

EPH-826, EPH-892*, EPH-1238*, EPH-1239

Sun Wheel

A wheel with varying numbers of curved rays (most commonly five) occurs only rarely as a rim pattern; more commonly it forms the centre of semicircles on PSC bowls (e.g., EPH-970*, EPH-971*).

EPH-1240*

Jewellery Pendants

E.g., Laumonier 1977, 122 cat. 1872 et al., pl. 28

A closely-packed row of motifs consisting of a dot above a long, tapering element, a pattern familiar from West Slope painting, where it reproduces the pendants common on Hellenistic 'spearhead' necklaces (Rotroff 1997, 58–59).

EPH-416*, EPH-463*, EPH-1241*, EPH-1304

Isolated Jewellery Pendants Alternating with Rosette

E.g., Laumonier 1977, 173 cat. 4352 et al., pl. 38

Single pendants may alternate with a rosette, most commonly rosette 2/7.

EPH-491*, EPH-1242*, EPH-1243

---

47 [Ed. Laumonier assigned a few pieces with such rims to the Monogram PAR Workshop (Laumonier 1977, 175–176 cat. 357, pl. 38; 176 cat. 3176, pls. 38, 125; 179 cats. 3059, 9046, pl. 39; 180 cat. 5065, pl. 39; 183 cat. 2166, pls. 39, 125). PGB, however, attributes them to Menemachos.]

Combing
A practically unique pattern consisting of closely spaced triangles along an irregular line, as though impressed by a small, toothed tool; on a single figural bowl probably of Menemachos.
EPH-81*

X's
Carefully stamped X's.
EPH-137, EPH-671*

H's in Alternating Orientation
Cf. Laumonier 1977, 106 cats. 640, 1939, pl. 24
Hatched motifs resembling the letter eta, alternately upright and on their sides, constitute a rare pattern known only from a few bowls attributed to the VG Workshop.
EPH-1244*

Eyed Chevron
E.g., Laumonier 1977, 286 cat. 8801, pl. 66
Horizontally oriented chevrons with dotted circles or eyes at the ends. Rare.
EPH-1031*

Main Decoration
A   *Figural Decoration*
In general, figural decoration[48] is much less common than it is, for example, in Athens. It is found most regularly in early production but declines in frequency with the passing of time. It is rare in the Classical phase, consisting of friezes with walking and gesticulating Erotes, Erotes racing a two-horse chariot, as well as simple friezes of an Amazonomachy. Actors, heraldic dolphins, and a winged thunderbolt also occur. In the late phase, imbricate and long-petal bowls have largely pushed figural decoration aside. The following figures appear on Ephesian bowls in our Black Sea assemblage.

Erotes
Erotes play several roles in addition to the charioteer described below. They are commonly portrayed playing a musical instrument; the kithara, harp, aulos, syrinx, and krotala can all be identified (EPH-1*–EPH-3*, EPH-5, EPH-6*, EPH-8*, EPH-9*, EPH-14*, EPH-112*, EPH-406*, EPH-1305*, EPH-1330*, EPH-1351*).[49] Usually they are in movement, perhaps participating in a procession or a dance, and in one early instance they play their instruments while riding on the backs of dolphins and hippocamps (EPH-22*). On one bowl, however, the musicians alternate with symplegmata and so contribute to the private erotic character of the composition (EPH-109; cf. Laumonier 1977, 40 cat. 3424, pl. 6). A characteristic pose shows Eros walking with one hand on his hip and the other extended before him and raised above shoulder level, a gesture of adoration, perhaps, or a dance (EPH-7*, EPH-10, EPH-11*, EPH-1303*; cf. Laumonier 1977, 127 cat. 3192, pl. 29; 167 cat. 3242, pl. 37; 305 cat. 3190, pls. 71, 129). Another shows him running with his arms flung aloft (EPH-15, EPH-16*; cf. Laumonier 1977, 116 cat. 3286, pls. 26, 122; 164 cat. 3181, pl. 36), a stamp that may have devolved from the krotala-playing figure (compare the stamp on EPH-5). These two stamps seem to be a pair, however, sometimes confronting one another or as flanking figures,[50] and the gestures may be ones of respect or adoration; see, for example, the pair that flank an *agyieus* on the Olbia situla, which is probably of Pergamene manufacture (PER-91*), illustrating, as well, that the origins of the pair may lie outside the Ephesian industry. Torch-bearing Erotes may be participating in a procession or possibly a stylized race (EPH-19–EPH-21). Sometimes Eros places a large crown on his head (EPH-13*, EPH-1303*); in some versions of the stamp he holds an object that has convincingly been called a sistrum in his raised left hand, but the object is depicted differently (and vaguely) in other versions.[51] Often, however, these little figures function simply as space-fillers, adding to the joyful and lush atmosphere in a larger composition (e.g., EPH-23*–EPH-26).
EPH-1*–EPH-26, EPH-97*, EPH-98*, EPH-109, EPH-112*, EPH-119*, EPH-404*–EPH-406*, EPH-1303*, EPH-1305*, EPH-1330*, EPH-1351*

---

48   [Ed. PGB completed discussions of Eros driving a biga, rabbit and eagle, trident, and thunderbolt. I have supplied the remainder of the text on figural decoration.]

49   Cf. (for example), Laumonier 1977, 41 cats. 3222, 3223, pl. 7 (harp); 39 cat. 3216 bis, pl. 6 (kithara); 42 cat. 3478, pls. 8, 118 (kithara); 71 cat. 3474, pl. 15 (aulos, syrinx); 87 cat. 9302, pls. 19, 119 (syrinx); 97 cat. 3331, pls. 21, 120 (aulos, syrinx, sistrum[?]); 100 cat. 6201, pl. 22 (aulos, syrinx, sistrum); 167 cat. 3209, pl. 37 (syrinx).

50   Cf. Laumonier 1977, 124 cat. 3174, pl. 28 (confronting); 125 cats. 3204 and 3206, pl. 29 (flanking a krater?); 176 cat. 3176, pls. 38, 125 (flanking a lotus petal).

51   Laumonier 1977, 100 cat. 6201, pl. 22, where the object is clearly a sistrum. Its shape and hence its identity is unclear in our stamps and in (for example) Laumonier 1977, 97 cat. 3331, pls. 21, 120; 101 cat. 3196, pl. 23; 167 cat. 3242, pl. 37.

FIGURE 73
Nike racing a two-horse chariot on an Ephesian fragment from Olbia or Pantikapaion (EPH-54) SCALE 1:1
PHOTO BY THE AUTHOR

Eros Racing Two-Horse Chariot to Right

Amongst the few figural decorations of the early classical Ephesian production is the frieze of a race with a two-horse chariot towards the right. The charioteer features a small triangular wing, the same which is normally seen on Erotes (see Chapter 6). In the best-preserved stamps, it is clear that the charioteer is wearing a garment which partly flows behind him/her. Therefore, there has been discussion as to whether the charioteer is a Nike or an Eros (Courby 1922, 385; Laumonier 1977, 12 n. 4). I prefer to identify the figures as Erotes (though dressed as a charioteer), since racing Erotes are well known in other media (see Chapter 6). There are only two (unique) Ephesian bowls where I would accept an identification of the charioteer as a Nike. One is EPH-54*, where a much larger figure with large wings, dressed in a peplos with overfold, is driving a two-horse chariot towards the left, not the right (Fig. 73). As indicated by its large size, this particular bowl is probably relatively early – perhaps even belonging to the earliest phase of production. The second one is Laumonier 1977, 65 cat. 3163, pls. 14, 118 with a much larger Nike(?) driving the chariot to the right. The chariot wheels of both these bowls have six spokes, not four as the normal type does. Apart from these two bowls and one other,[52] all the other pieces seem to derive from the same stamp, even though there may be several stamp generations. On all of them, the charioteer strains forward, urging the team on with the whip(?) in his right hand. The wheel of the chariot has four spokes, which are always in the same position (corresponding to 10, 14, 16, and 20 o'clock). The two horses are in full gallop; the harness of the fully visible horse is rendered by a band over its belly and back.

The frieze continues all around the widest part of the bowl and it is never mixed with other types of design. In the classical phase, it occurs almost exclusively with calyx B. The occurrence of calyx C on EPH-34* finds parallels on Delos (Laumonier 1977, 226 cat. 3168, pl. 50; 376 cat. 8934, pl. 90). Bowls with this decoration are normally furnished with a single rim frieze, usually an Ionian kyma or rosette 2/7.

The pattern is similar on Delos; the only rim pattern represented there which is not attested with the biga in the Black Sea region is the horizontal S-spirals (Laumonier 1977, 305 cat. 8705, pl. 71). Oddities are a bowl with no rim pattern (Laumonier 1977, 420 cat. 3164, pl. 98) and three bowls with multiple rim friezes (Laumonier 1977, 167 cat. 2191, pl. 37; 216 cat. 3162, pl. 48; 420 cat. 9325, pl. 98). None of these are represented amongst the Black Sea bowls.

This decoration mainly belongs to the Classical phase of Ephesian production, and primarily to the Monogram PAR Workshop. However, some of the rim patterns tend to suggest that it was also occasionally employed in the Menemachos Workshop: EPH-27* with crossed dotted lines with a box and EPH-28 with Menemachos rosettes; and, on Delos, Laumonier 1977, 39 cat. 3141, pl. 5; 65 cat.

---

52   Gassner 1997, 75 cat. 211, pls. 14, 84; Tuluk 2001, 61 cat. 2, pl. 29 (with absurd attribution to the Monogram PAR Workshop): a grey-ware bowl of the Südtor Workshop. The chariot and charioteer racing towards the right are undoubtedly related to the standard representation of the scene, but it is a different stamp. Too little is known about this workshop to clarify its relationship to the other Ephesian workshops, apart from the fact that it seems to be relatively early.

3163, pls. 14, 118. The only signed vessel (Athenaios) with this motif is found on Delos (Laumonier 1977, 235 cat. 3431, pl. 53). This example, together with some other odd pieces (Laumonier 1977, 226 cat. 3124, pls. 50, 127; 360 cat. 562, pl. 86), shows that it was also sparingly employed in the late phase. Note also the small size and effaced detail of the stamps on EPH-50*–EPH-53*, indicators of a late date.
EPH-27*–EPH-54*

Saluting Pan
The figure of Pan with one hand raised as if in a salute has been discussed in Chapter 6, where we argued that the motif originated at Kyme. Pan occurs in several Ephesian workshops of both circles, most commonly as a single figure intermingled with friezes of Erotes (EPH-1303*; cf. Laumonier 1977, 167–168 cats. 3242, 3243, pl. 37 of the Monogram PAR Workshop), or as antithetical figures flanking a krater (EPH-55; cf. Laumonier 98 cat. 8537, pl. 21 of the VG Workshop). In a highly unusual arrangement, Pans flank an acanthus leaf in the calyx of a PSC bowl (EPH-981*).
EPH-55, EPH-981*, EPH-1303*

Altar Figures
In Chapter 6 we discussed the iconography of the four vignettes derived from small altars. Some are represented wholly or in part in the Ephesian industry, but they are rare (see Fig. 44); the time of greatest interest in these figures had apparently passed by the time the Ephesian industry developed. Interestingly, more fragments bearing these scenes have been found in the Black Sea region than among the thousands of bowls on Delos,[53] underlining the regional interest in this iconography demonstrated by the many altars found there. Altar figures D (the Dionysiac trio: EPH-56, EPH-1305*, EPH-1338) and B1 (Amymone: EPH-1339) are represented on Ephesian products in our assemblage.

Hunt
A number of small fragments attest to the popularity of the hunting theme in the Black Sea region. A large grey-ware amphora of the VG Workshop found at Pantikapaion (EPH-1306*) preserves a hunting scene where two of the riders carry a *gorytos*, an indication that Ephesian potters were aware of and catered to local Black Sea tastes.

The same stamp appears on a fragment found at Miletos, from a large, grey-ware vessel (Kossatz 1990, 70 cat. M 509, fig. 33, pl. 18). More formal arrangements of predators (dog, panther: EPH-72*–EPH-74) also allude to the hunt.
EPH-57*–EPH-74*, EPH-1265*, EPH-1297*, EPH-1306*, EPH-1332*

Rabbit and Dog
In a distillation of the hunt, baying dogs flank a cowering rabbit on a small series of bowls of the Monogram PAR Workshop (e.g., Laumonier 1977, 156 cat. 3050, pls. 35, 125). A closely similar example occurs in our assemblage (EPH-75*).

Rabbit and Eagle (Eagle Alone)
Another series of bowls shows the rabbit again, this time alternating with an eagle with outspread wings (turned either left or right), as a representation of the predator and its prey (EPH-76). It is difficult to avoid recognizing a reference to the Ptolemaic 'coat of arms', where an eagle perches on a winged thunderbolt. We find the eagle alternating with a thunderbolt on fragments from Olbia (EPH-129; Fig. 74), from Delos (Laumonier 1977, 166 cat. 3043, pl. 37), and from Entremont (Benoit 1947, 82–83, fig. 2; see Fig. 11). At a deeper level, representations of the paired eagle and rabbit may refer to human vulnerability (see also Chapter 6).
EPH-76–EPH-78*, EPH-129

FIGURE 74   Eagle and winged thunderbolt on an Ephesian fragment from Olbia (EPH-129) SCALE 1:1
DRAWING IIMK RAN ARCHIVE

---

53   Laumonier 1977, 92 cats. 3247, 3295+3297, pl. 20; 421 cat. 3296, pl. 98, with altar figures A and D; cf. also Gassner 1997, 75 cat. 217, pls. 15, 84 from Ephesos, with figure A2.

Mantled Dancing Women

The frieze of heavily draped woman dancing, perhaps in a ritual context, is especially common in Aiolis, but occurs sporadically at Ephesos, mostly on bowls of the VG Workshop. For full discussion of the motif and a list of Ephesian examples found on Delos, see Chapter 6.

EPH-79*, EPH-80*, EPH-1266*, EPH-1267

Amazonomachy and Amazons Hunting

The Amazonomachy is a favourite among figured scenes, occurring throughout the industry. To judge from the Delos material, the subject is most common in the Monogram PAR Workshop but is also found in Workshop Circle 1: the VG Workshop, with a few examples of Menemachos and Hera(...).[54] Amazons also participate in hunts (e.g., Laumonier 1977, 416 cat. 3340, pl. 97, Amazon and griffin), and some of our very small fragments may represent hunts rather than battles. For a list of Amazonomachies on Ephesian bowls, see Chapter 6.

EPH-60(?), EPH-81–EPH-93, EPH-94*(?), EPH-95*, EPH-96*, EPH-1306*

Judgement of Paris

The judgement of Paris appears on bowls of Menemachos,[55] probably derivative from Argive workshops and ultimately traceable to Alexandrian prototypes (see Chapter 6 for a full discussion). Our assemblage includes a complete bowl from Pantikapaion in the Hermitage (EPH-101*), which preserves the full scene, with Paris, the three goddesses, and Hermes, as well as the complete signature of Menemachos on its base.

EPH-101*–EPH-103*, EPH-1327

Actors

Actors appear only rarely on Ephesian bowls,[56] but a few examples have been found in the Black Sea region (Gajdukevič 1981, fig. 4; Grzegrzółka 2010, 38 cat. 5).

EPH-1268*, perhaps EPH-136*

Erotic Symplagmata

Scenes depicting an amorous couple on a *kline* are found exclusively in Workshop Circle 1, and primarily on bowls of Menemachos. As argued in Chapter 6, their origins may lie in Ptolemaic iconography, but symplegmata were also a staple of the decoration of late Hellenistic Pergamene *Applikenkeramik* (Schäfer 1968, 79–80, pls. 27–32; Hübner 1993, 95–106, pls. 25–32), which may have enhanced demand for this imagery. Menemachos' bowls present two main arrangements; the couple may be situated simply on the wall of the bowl, or they may be framed by a 'nelumbo', making up part of a calyx that was part and parcel of the baroque style introduced from Egypt in the second quarter of the 2nd century (see Chapter 3). Within the 'nelumbo', Menemachos made use of three different symplegmata. In one, the woman reclines with her legs to the left, turning up her face to kiss the man, who is standing behind the *kline*, and encircling his head with her left arm (EPH-580*, EPH-582*, EPH-583, EPH-1301*).[57] In the second, the woman sits in the man's lap, both of them facing left. She lifts her right arm above her head and rests her left hand on the man's thigh (*coitus a tergo* A: Laumonier 1977, 35–36 cats. 1340, 1342, 2264, pls. 4, 116). In the third, both recline with their legs to the left, resting their weight on their left elbows (*coitus a tergo* B: Laumonier 1977, 35 cat. 1343, pls. 3, 116). In the other arrangement, with the scenes placed freely on the wall, the symplegmata are repeated around the bowl, alternating with Eros musicians or satyrs, or punctuated by small Erotes.[58]

EPH-580*, EPH-582*, EPH-583, EPH-1301* (in filled 'nelumbo'); EPH-108*, EPH-109

Feline Phallus

A large and perky phallus propelled by the vigorously striding hind legs of a feline with a long, looped tail is a clear symbol of masculinity and perhaps also a protective device. It makes an occasional appearance on bowls of the Belles Méduses, Menemachos, and the VG Workshop.[59]

---

54 Monogram PAR: Laumonier 1977, 139 cat. 3343, pl. 31; 133 cat. 3356 (signed), pls. 30, 37, and others on pl. 37; 156 cat. 3343 bis, pl. 35. VG: 96 cat. 3350, pl. 21; 101–102 cats. 3318, 3374, pls. 23, 119. Menemachos: 65 cat. 3371, pls. 14, 118. Hera(...): 304 cat. 2426, pls. 71, 128. The list is not exhaustive.

55 Pagenstecher 1913, pl. XX; Laumonier 1977, 42 cat. 3420, pl. 8; Puppo 1995, 164–165 cat. X39, pls. LXXIV–LXXV and perhaps 121–122 cat. M20, pl. LII.

56 Laumonier 1977, 78 cat. 3248, pl. 17; 101 cat. 8744, pl. 23; 164 cat. 1305, pl. 36; 234–235 cat. 3257, pl. 53; 307 cat. 3480, pl. 72; and the repeated figure of the Comique à la canne in the 'workshop' that bears his name (115–116, pls. 26, 122).

57 Laumonier 1977, 34 cats. 1345, 1980, pls. 3, 116. Details of this composition are clearer in the Italo-megarian bowl and Peloponnesian bowls that derive from it (or from the same prototypes): the man is winged (presumably Eros), and a drapery hangs behind the couple (e.g., Marabini Moevs 1980, pl. 18.2, upper left 'nelumbo'; Siebert 1978, pl. 90.5).

58 Laumonier 1977, 40 cat. 3323, 3424, pls. 6, 117 (alternating with musicians); 40 cat. 3479, pl. 7 (with small Erotes in foliage); 348 cat. 3436, pl. 83 (with satyr and vine); 344 cat. 3231, 3232, pl. 82 (a late version signed by Si(...)).

59 Laumonier 1977, 83 cat. 3274, pl. 18 and Puppo 1995, 152 cat. X9, pl. LXVIII (Belles Méduses); Laumonier 1977, 164 cat. 3272, pl. 36 (VG); Ladstätter 2003, 49 cat. K 56, pls. 6, 156 (Menemachos). In the Black Sea region, also Kovalenko 2007, fig. 16.11 = Popova 2007, figs. 74–75.

EPHESOS 311

FIGURES 75.A–B   Gold octadrachm issued by Ptolemy IV Philopator to honour his deified father, Ptolemy III Euergetes
(Svoronos [1904–1908] 1117)
COURTESY OF THE METROPOLITAN MUSEUM OF ART

There is a definite element of humour in some of the Black Sea fragments, as when a diminutive horseman confronts an enormous phallus on EPH-110*, and on EPH-111*, where a stream of semen spurts from the phallus. On EPH-112*, the phallus takes part a bawdy scene with grotesques, Eros musicians, and a racy inscription.
EPH-110*–EPH-112*.

Dolphins
Dolphins are usually heraldic; in the Delian corpus, they generally flank a palmette (as EPH-116) or a sunburst (rosette 9, as EPH-114 and EPH-115).[60] Most of our examples are very fragmentary, but the heraldic compositions were probably separated by repetitions of the palmette or sunburst. The Black Sea assemblage preserves other foci as well: a rosette (EPH-113), an acanthus flower (EPH-118), and a krater (EPH-120*). Dolphins also appear with Eros, though the complete composition is lost (EPH-119*). They may also play the role of mounts for Eros (EPH-22*). The Monogram PAR Workshop provides most of the examples, but heraldic dolphins also appear in the late production of Workshop Circle 1 (Comique à la canne).
EPH-22*, EPH-113–EPH-125, EPH-1300*

Thunderbolt
The thunderbolt from time to time occurs as decoration of the main zone. As we explained in Chapter 6, this may be another reference to Ptolemaic power, recalling the thunderbolt that serves as a perch for the Ptolemaic eagle on coins of the dynasty. Alternately, it could make reference to Dionysos, in whose Orphic biography the thunderbolt plays an important part. It is found only in WC1.[61]
EPH-126–EPH-133*, EPH-1304, EPH-1311*, EPH-1312*

Trident
A trident features on a series of bowls which Laumonier attributed to a variety of producers, but which were actually made by My(...).[62] Its presence is somewhat puzzling, but the fact that it is adorned with a *tainia* tied in a bow makes it likely that it is not just a random decorative element. I wonder whether it originates in Ptolemaic iconography, where it features as a symbol of power, cf. the gold octadrachm issued by Ptolemy IV Philopator to honour his deified father, Ptolemy III Euergetes (Fig. 75). The coin shows the bust of Euergetes with radiant diadem, trident, and aegis, demonstrating his cosmic power over heaven, land, and sea.

---

60   Palmette, e.g., Laumonier 1977, 146 cats. 2437, 3024, pl. 33; 165 cat. 3013, pls. 37, 125 (Monogram PAR); 127 cats. 3022, 3023, pl. 29 (late Menemachean Comique à la canne). Sunburst, e.g., 165 cats. 3009, 1118+3172, pls. 37, 125 (Monogram PAR).

61   This conclusion results from the reassignment of some bowls which Laumonier attributed to the Monogram PAR Workshop (Laumonier 1977, 134 cat. 1185, pl. 30; 166 cat. 3043, pl. 37; 185 cat. 8806, pls. 40, 126; 187 cat. 111, pl. 41; 209 cat. 496, pl. 17).

62   Laumonier 1977, 267 cat. 875, pl. 61; 268 cats. 1117, 2038, pls. 62, 127; 271 cats. 8675, 8676, pl. 63; 318–319 cats. 874, 1019, 2259, pl. 75; 323–325, cats. 1116, 1159, 1326, pl. 77; 327 cat. 1147, pl. 78; 343 cat. 2368, pl. 82, the last probably by Menemachos, the rest attributed to My(...).

B   Scroll Decoration[63]

Full-Body Scroll

Although scroll decoration is relatively common, the application of the motif to the full height of the body is unusual and limited to only two workshops: Belles Méduses and Monogram PAR (Laumonier 1977, 81–82, 169–171, pls. 18, 35, 119, 124). It is probably a feature of the early part of the Classical phase. There is considerable variety. The scrolls usually consist of thick, striated, undulating stems, punctuated by acanthus calyces from which further spiralling tendrils grow. They may be characterized as floral (with stamped flowers of different designs) or grape-vine (with grape leaves and bunches of fruit). Occasionally the stems are thinner and fully incised. Several of the bowls have the same version of medallion rosette A (with tongues between the petals) typical of the Monogram PAR Workshop (EPH-161*–EPH-163*, EPH-171, EPH-172*), one with an acanthus-flower scroll as a rim device that allows a definite attribution (EPH-161*).

EPH-161*–EPH-169* (floral); EPH-170*–EPH-172*, EPH-173*(?), EPH-174*–EPH-177* (vine)

Scrolls in Friezes

Other scrolls are smaller, designed to fit into a low, horizontal frieze, bordered by rim patterns above and a calyx below. The basic unifying pattern is the coiling acanthus stem, but the addition of different leaf, flower, and fruit stamps individualizes the scrolls as one of the following types.

Acanthus-Vine Scroll

The motif has the typical undulating, striated acanthus stem punctuated with leafy calyxes, from which grow bunches of grapes and grape leaves on thin stems. The scroll can run either way, but leftward is almost three times as common as rightward among the Black Sea examples. This is the standard scheme, known in hundreds of examples, mostly associated with the Monogram PAR Workshop (e.g., Laumonier 1977, 204–205 cats. 1475, 1489, pls. 46, 125, 126).

EPH-178–EPH-247, EPH-1310, EPH-1314(?), EPH-1315*

Acanthus-Vine-Ivy Scroll

Heart-shaped ivy leaves are added in this version of the scroll, sometimes together with round clusters of ivy berries, but the grape bunches are retained. The motif is present in only a few examples on Delos, also mostly attributed to the Monogram PAR Workshop,[64] but a total of eight appear in the Black Sea assemblage.

EPH-248*–EPH-255*

Acanthus-Flower Scroll

This scroll bears no fruit, only flowers of various forms. Only a handful appear in Laumonier's corpus,[65] but it is not uncommon in the Black Sea region, with 28 examples, over half of them at Olbia. Some distinctive types recur in our collection. One is characterized by a fat, pear-shaped bud with a crossed tip, which blooms as a collared flower – a crown of petals from which a long stamen protrudes (EPH-256*–EPH-262*). Another group is characterized by a flower with an even longer, wavy stamen (EPH-263*, EPH-264*; cf. Laumonier 1977, 90 cats. 1189+1690, 1558, pl. 20, attributed to the Belles Méduses Workshop). The alignment of stems, daisy-like flower, bud, and corkscrew tendril defines another (EPH-267*, EPH-268*). And a tiny fragment (EPH-265*) comes from a bowl with the distinctive flower encircled by a tendril that is typical of My(…).

EPH-256*–EPH-273*

Stylized Acanthus Scroll

Most of the detail has been eliminated from this scroll, which almost always runs to the left. A single spiral tendril springs from each calyx, and spaces are filled with three dots in place of the flowers or fruit of the more naturalistic scrolls (e.g., Laumonier 1977, 158 cat. 1291, pls. 36, 124, and many examples on pl. 45). The majority of the attributed examples on Delos belong to the Monogram PAR Workshop, which is also represented in the Black Sea area (EPH-280*, EPH-306*).

EPH-274*–EPH-314*, EPH-518*(?)

Stylized Acanthus-Vine Scroll

The same as the preceding, but with a bunch of grapes substituted for the three dots.

EPH-315*–EPH-317

Ultra-stylized Acanthus Scroll

In a further simplification, the motif is reduced to nothing but the undulating stem and spirals (e.g., Laumonier 1977, 113 cat. 984, pls. 25, 121).

EPH-318*–EPH-323

---

63   [Ed. Discussion of scrolls, garlands, and wreaths was supplied by the editor.]
64   Laumonier 1977, 94 cat. 1551, pl. 20; 154 cat. 408, pl. 34; 205 cats. 1502–1503, pl. 46; 211 cats. 1516j, 1554, pl. 17.
65   Laumonier 1977, 90 cat. 1189 et al., pl. 20, top row; 154 cat. 437, pl. 34; 394–395 cats. 1517, 5553, pl. 93.

EPHESOS

C   *Wreath Decoration*

For the history and iconography of the two main types of wreaths (myrtle and ivy), see Chapter 6. Our Black Sea assemblages preserve examples of both, with the myrtle much more common than the ivy.

Myrtle Wreath

Bound bunches of three or five slender, pointed leaves are strung together to represent a wreath. Single berries on stems may grow from the bunch, but are sometimes replaced by a stylized group of three dots as space-fillers above and below the wreath; many bowls combine both. Rare examples have larger numbers of leaves (EPH-368*), or only two (EPH-369*). As argued above (Chapter 6), the plant represented is myrtle, not laurel or olive, as it has frequently been described (e.g., Courby 1922, 381–382, fig. 77.8; Pfrommer 1993, 37). It is most commonly combined with calyx B and a single rim pattern, and it was very common in the third quarter of the 2nd century (see Chapter 6 for further discussion and a list of examples on Delos). In one unusual instance, on a particularly large bowl crafted by the Monogram PAR Workshop, it occurs as a second frieze, below an acanthus-vine scroll (EPH-186), and is designed as a naturalistic wreath, with leaves on either side running in opposing directions. The large size and extra care taken in its design makes one wonder if the bowl was destined for some special function.

EPH-186, EPH-324*–EPH-382*, EPH-518*(?), EPH-1323*, EPH-1333*, EPH-1342*

Ivy Wreath

The less common ivy wreath follows some of the same conventions, with bundles of three leaves, sometimes with ivy berries and/or the three dots familiar from the myrtle wreaths. The ivy wreath is found in several workshops, with the largest number attributed to the Monogram PAR Workshop; Menemachos does not appear to have used it. It is contemporary with the myrtle wreath but may go out of use earlier. For further discussion of the motif and a list of Ephesian examples on Delos, see Chapter 6.

EPH-383*–EPH-388*, EPH-1316

Garland

Thick garlands wrapped with fillets are a theme of limited interest to Ephesian potters, and mostly concentrated in WC1, but they found favour in the Black Sea region; about as many have been recovered there as on Delos. The swags often hang from kraters,[66] occasionally from rosettes (EPH-389*, EPH-390*, EPH-392*, EPH-393),[67] or boukrania/boukephalia (EPH-396*–EPH-398*).[68] Unusual variants in the assemblage show garlands supported by a female figure (EPH-399*)[69] or Eros (EPH-400*) or joining at a *tainia* (EPH-394*, EPH-395*).

EPH-389*–EPH-403

Suspended Wreath

A suspended wreath with a large bow, common in some industries (e.g., Athens, Pergamon), is very rare on Ephesian bowls. In all three of our examples, the wreaths are attended by Erotes.

EPH-404*–EPH-406*

D   *Multiple Rim Friezes*

It is debatable whether multiple rim friezes should be regarded as decoration proper or as 'just' more rim patterns added on top of one other. However, of 303 vessels from Black Sea sites with multiple rim friezes, 46 had not just two, but three or more friezes, covering most of the side of the vessel. In these cases, the multiple rim friezes obviously constitute the main decoration, supplemented by either a calyx or a lower body of imbricate petals. Vessels with multiple rim friezes over figural decoration, a scroll, or a wreath are relatively few (25 of 303 vessels); the same is the case with decorations such as pine cone, pendent semicircles, and long petals (in total 17 vessels). This contrasts with 51 vessels which combine a multiple rim frieze with a lower body with imbrications (mostly of rounded petals), whereas 58 vessels combine it with a calyx (mostly calyx B). The remainder are rim fragments where the decoration of the lower body is not preserved.

Fig. 76 tells us that a much narrower repertoire of patterns was used for the second rim frieze than for the first frieze. Moreover, some motifs occur more frequently there than in the first frieze; thus, the astragal is canonical in a lower frieze level (corresponding to the practice of architecture) and occurs on almost 20% of the vessels with multiple rim friezes. The astragal is closely followed by the Ionian kyma (19.1%), then by the Lesbian kyma (8.6%) and rosette 2 with seven petals (7.6%). But what is most interesting is the fact that the occurrence of multiple rim

---

66 Usačeva 1978, fig. 1:23, from Kepoi. Cf. Laumonier 1977, 178 cat. 8747 and others on pl. 39, VG Workshop or Menemachos (attribution of PGB).

67 Cf. Laumonier 1977, 212 cat. 3112, 3113, pl. 17.

68 Cf. Laumonier 1997, 115 cats. 1111, 1112, pls. 26, 121; 305 cat. 3481, pls. 72, 129.

69 Cf. a recurring Pergamene pattern, where altar figure B1 supports the garlands: e.g., Conze et al. 1913, 274; de Luca 1975, cat. 193, pl. 46.2; cat. 446, pl. 54.8.

	Average % (303=100%)	Bol'šoj Kastel'	Chersonesos	Istros	Kepoi	Myrmekion	Olbia	Pantikapaion	Porthmion	Ruminskoe	Tyritake	Volna 1
Astragal	19.8			13	1	5	27	9	3		1	
Box meander, ccw							1					
Box meander, cw	4.3			2			10		1			
Box meander, type?							1					
Ionian kyma	19.1	1		8		4	36	5	1			3
Lesbian kyma	8.6			3		4	15	2	1		1	
Hanging leaf				1								
S-spirals, horizontal	5.0		2	6			5	1	1			
S-spirals, vertical	3.0			2		1	4	1	1			
Guilloche right	2.3				1	1	5					
Guilloche left	3.6					2	8	1				
Wave meander	1.7						3	1				1
Rosette 1 (Menemachos rosette)	2.3			2			5					
Rosette 2/7	7.6		1	1	1	2	11	6	1			
Rosette 2, other	4.0		1	1			8		1		1	
Rosette 4 (star rosette)	5.6		1	1			10	4		1		
Rosette 5	2.3					1	5		1			
Rosette 6				1								
Rosette, type?	1.7			3				1			1	
Miniature acanthus-flower scroll	1.0			1			2					
Miniature acanthus scroll left						1						
Miniature myrtle wreath				1								
Large dots	4.3	1		7			3		1			1
Oblique boxes				1								
Jewellery pendants	1.7						5					
Isolated jewellery pendants and rosette				1								
Total				55			164					

FIGURE 76   Decorative patterns of the second frieze of multiple rim friezes

friezes seems to be a chronological feature. It is striking the degree to which Olbia deviates from all other sites, and especially Istros. At Istros, 55 (5%) of 1,094 Ephesian vessels are decorated with multiple rim friezes, whereas the figure for Olbia is significantly higher, namely 164 vessels (14%) of a total of 1,152 Ephesian vessels.

Multiple rim friezes also figure prominently amongst the moulds from the Magnesia Gate in Ephesos.[70] These moulds belong to the heyday of the Monogram PAR potter, they are quite uniform in style, and since they must have been in use more or less contemporaneously, it is evident that the occurrence of multiple rim friezes can be considered an element of chronology, and the developmental trend was towards single friezes as time went on.

Five friezes: EPH-601*
Four friezes: EPH-407*
Three friezes: EPH-56, EPH-159*, EPH-408*–EPH-424*, EPH-559, EPH-601*, EPH-611*, EPH-612*, EPH-614, EPH-615, EPH-617, EPH-643*, EPH-650*, EPH-670*, EPH-694, EPH-711, EPH-717*–EPH-720*, EPH-748*, EPH-750*, EPH-866*, EPH-1315*, EPH-1317*, EPH-1335*

---

70   Rogl 2001b, 106–108 cats. RB 1–RB 5, RB 7, RB 9, pls. 60, 61, 66, 67; Tuluk 2001, 68 cat. 30, pl. 45.

Pine cone decoration		Sum	% of all Ephesian at site
Plastic	Bol'šoj Kastel'	1	
	Istros	31	2.8
	Myrmekion	1	
	Olbia	7	0.6
	Pantikapaion	4	
Stylized	Istros	10	0.9
	Olbia	4	0.3
Total		58	2.0

FIGURE 77   Pine-cone decoration in the Pontic assemblages

Two friezes: EPH-67*, EPH-90*, EPH-109, EPH-116, EPH-118, EPH-121*, EPH-182*, EPH-239*, EPH-275, EPH-337*, EPH-357, EPH-425*–EPH-527, EPH-541, EPH-550*, EPH-551, EPH-553*, EPH-561*, EPH-572, EPH-576*, EPH-600*, EPH-605, EPH-609, EPH-610*, EPH-616, EPH-625*, EPH-636, EPH-638, EPH-639, EPH-641*, EPH-648, EPH-651*, EPH-671*, EPH-676, EPH-678*, EPH-705, EPH-721–EPH-732*, EPH-751*–EPH-759*, EPH-767*, EPH-799*, EPH-852*–EPH-870*, EPH-930*, EPH-1010*–EPH-1013*, EPH-1024*, EPH-1045*, EPH-1046*, EPH-1062*, EPH-1063*, EPH-1065, EPH-1070, EPH-1117, EPH-1206*, EPH-1273*, EPH-1303*, EPH-1304, EPH-1309, EPH-1313*, EPH-1314, EPH-1324*, EPH-1336*, EPH-1343*

E   *Vegetal Decoration*

We find the following types of vegetal decoration on Ephesian bowls:

   Pine-cone decoration (plastic and stylized)
   Calyx with filled 'nelumbo' and other Menemachean calyces
   Vegetal calyx
   Imbricate calyx

The pine-cone motif occurs almost exclusively as a full-body decoration, whereas the calyx designs can be found as main decoration in combination with single- and multiple-frieze rims as well as on the lower wall, below a number of other types of decoration.

Pine-Cone Decoration

Ephesian pine-cone decoration exists in two variants: with plastic and with stylized scales. The scales normally cover the entire body of the vessel,[71] usually below a single rim frieze. Almost all types of rim pattern occur in combination with pine-cone decoration, and in relative proportions corresponding to the overall pattern of types of rim decoration. Thus, the Ionian kyma is the most common, followed by box meander, Lesbian kyma, and most of the rosettes.

Pine-cone decoration was employed by both of the main workshop circles of Ephesos, but it was never particularly common. Overall, in the Black Sea assemblages only 58 Ephesian vessels (2%) bear pine-cone decoration. The only site where the frequency of pine-cone decoration is above the average is Istros, where almost 4% are thus decorated (Fig. 77). This figure is in contrast to the number at Olbia, where less than 1% feature pine-cone decoration. In fact, the figure from Istros finds its best parallel on Delos, where 165 vessels, 2.7% of all of the Ephesian bowls, feature pine-cone decoration. As was the case at Istros, also at Delos, plastic pine cone occurs three times as frequently as the stylized version.

The fact that pine-cone decoration is more common at Istros and on Delos than, for example, at Olbia, with its generally earlier assemblage, as well as the fact that many of the pine-cone vessels belong to WC1, Menemachos and his followers, tend to suggest that it became more frequent in the second half of the 2nd century.

Plastic Pine-Cone Decoration

In general, plastic pine-cone decoration is more common than the stylized version (Fig. 77). On Delos and elsewhere, a number of signed vessels attest to the use of this decoration in WC1. The following signatures are represented:

   Menemachos (Laumonier 1977, 57 cats. 4150–4153, pl. 12, from Delos; Isler 1978, cat. 311, pl. 59, from Samos)
   Gorgias (Laumonier 1977, 403 cats. 4155–4156, pl. 95, from Delos; Kenrick 1985, 112–113, fig. 22 cat. 169, from Berenike),
   Arkesilas (Kenrick 1985, 112–113 cat. B168, fig. 22, from Berenike)

---

71   I know only one vessel where (stylized) pine-cone decoration is combined with a calyx: Laumonier 1977, 175 cat. 357, pl. 38.

Athenaios (Laumonier 1977, 236 cat. 4154, pl. 53, from Delos)

Da(...)(Laumonier 1977, 309 cat. 4266, pl. 73, from Delos)

Di(...) (Laumonier 1977, 406 cat. 4160, pl. 95, from Delos)

M (Laumonier 1977, 410 cat. 4159, pl. 96, from Delos)

Pe(...) (Laumonier 1977, 409 cat. 4158, pl. 95, from Delos)

Overall, very few pine-cone bowls feature the rosette base typical of WC2: three on Delos, all with stylized scales (Laumonier 1977, 200 cats. 4020 and 4021, pl. 44 [rosette B]; 477 cat. 4016, pl. 111 [rosette A]) and not a single one in the Black Sea assemblages. There, as on Delos, vessels with pine-cone decoration normally have the undecorated, slightly concave base of WC1.

EPH-528*–540, EPH-1345

Stylized Pine-Cone Decoration

Stylized scales occur in several variants: as a box with a star in positive or (most commonly) in negative relief (the same stamp which was also employed in a positive version in the rim friezes with a box meander), and as concentric boxes, which may or may not feature a cross or a star in the middle. The same decoration is encountered on Delos, where 32 vessels are decorated with stylized scales (18 with box with star in negative relief, one with box with star, 13 with concentric boxes) (Laumonier 1977, pls. 12, 15, 44, 55, 72, 73, 111).

A single signed vessel with stylized pine-cone decoration was found on Delos. Its plain, undecorated base preserves a tiny part of a signature. Laumonier attributed the vessel to Heraios, but too little is preserved for a secure reading (Laumonier 1977, 308 cat. 4035, pl. 72).

EPH-541–EPH-549

Calyx (Fig. 78)

Calyx Type A

Characteristic of Calyx A is the inclusion of a broad 'nelumbo' with a rounded top and a vertically ribbed interior, with a small, straight acanthus leaf in front of it. The inspiration for the design comes from Ptolemaic silverware; see pp. 28–36 for a detailed discussion of the mechanism of its adoption. As explained in Chapter 3, I believe Menemachos should be credited with the introduction of this motif to Ephesian bowls, but other workshops, including the Monogram potter, subsequently adopted it as well. Calyx A can be divided into a number of subgroups according to the type of acanthus leaf that is combined with the 'nelumbo' and to the inclusion in the first type only of a sepal with a twisted top.

Calyx A is not very common amongst our vessels, and more than 50% of the known examples were found at Olbia.

Calyx A1

A full version of this type can be found on EPH-550*: it features four 'nelumbos' with rounded tops and interior vertical ribs and with a small acanthus leaf in front. The 'nelumbo' is framed by two slender sepals with interior vertical ribs and a finely scored central vein, their tips twisted toward the 'nelumbo'; they are in turn framed by two acanthus leaves with segmented central veins and tops again bent toward the 'nelumbo'. In between the 'nelumbo' and the sepal as a spacer we find a rosette 2 on a wavy stem. Calyx A1 is most likely the earliest type: it is very detailed and closely related to the metal prototypes.

In a few cases, calyx A1 functions as the main decoration in combination with a single rim frieze (Laumonier 1977, 160 cat. 1282, pl. 36), but it is more commonly found with multiple rim friezes. It also occurs beneath other main decorations, such as various figural schemes as well as with a stylized acanthus scroll.

EPH-88*, EPH-125, EPH-274*, EPH-550*–EPH-565

Calyx A2

This calyx is simpler than A1. It too features four 'nelumbos' with rounded top, interior ribbing, and a small acanthus leaf in front, but the upper edge of the 'nelumbo' sags slightly, as though the petal were drooping towards the viewer. The 'nelumbos' are separated by four acanthus leaves of a particular type: they are rather stylized with noticeable 'eyed' dentations, and their tops are not bent to the side but folded forwards. In terms of style, they correspond to a type of acanthus leaf which was current for a short period in the architecture of Asia Minor, for example in the acroterion of the bouleuterion of Miletos dated by epigraphical evidence to the span 175–164 (Robertson 1969, 161–162, fig. 162). This acanthus type is mostly found in combination with the acanthus-vine scroll (EPH-178, EPH-179), but it also occurs with multiple rim friezes (EPH-572, EPH-576*) and with a stylized acanthus scroll (EPH-275).

EPH-178, EPH-179, EPH-275, EPH-566*–EPH-572, EPH-576*, EPH-577*

Variants

On signed bowls of Menemachos on Delos, four 'nelumbos' with a v-shaped, dipping top, interior vertical ribs, and a small acanthus leaf in front are flanked by normal Ephesian folded acanthus leaves (the 'typical leaf' of calyx B, see below). A tall, pointed lotus petal appears between

A1	'Nelumbo' with small acanthus leaf in front, flanked by rosette on stem and by sepal and acanthus with nodding tips (EPH-551)	
A2	'Nelumbo' flanked by fleshy folded acanthus leaf; groups separated by another 'nelumbo' (EPH-179)	
B1	Folded acanthus leaf alternating with lotus petal (EPH-183)	
B2	Acanthus leaf with straight top folded forward and flanking lotus or rhomboidal petal, the groups separated by a petal of the opposite type (EPH-290)	
C	Straight, stylized acanthus leaf alternating with lotus petal (EPH-92)	

FIGURE 78   Ephesian calyces. Photos from the author's archive; drawing of EPH-551, IIMK RAN archives; drawing of EPH-179, CVA Kassel 2 [Germany 38], 66, fig. 45

each of the acanthus/'nelumbo' groups, all below single or multiple rim friezes (Laumonier 1977, 23 cats. 1260, 1971, pls. 1, 113; EPH-1335*). A number of simpler variants have been found in the Black Sea region. The 'nelumbo' occasionally stands alone (EPH-120*), or is combined with a simpler form of leaf (EPH-248*, EPH-605), long petals (EPH-595*–EPH-597*, EPH-601*), a column of dots like the one that often separates long petals (EPH-600*), or an ordinary lotus petal (EPH-598*). One early fragment includes a wadjet symbol (EPH-602*).

Filled 'Nelumbo'
The ribbing of the 'nelumbo' in calyx type A is sometimes replaced by more elaborate decoration, either figured (EPH-580*, EPH-582*, EPH-583, EPH-1301*; see above under symplegmata) or vegetal (EPH-584*, EPH-585*).[72] See Chapter 3 for further discussion of this motif and arguments that it was Menemachos or perhaps the proprietor of the VG Workshop who introduced it to the relief-bowl repertoire. It is found mostly in those workshops, with a few instances attributed to Athenaios, a later member of Workshop Circle 1 (Laumonier 1977, pl. 52).
EPH-580*–EPH-594, EPH-1301*

Calyx Type B
The earmark of calyx type B is a rather slender and simple leaf, folded forward and to the side, the *feuille typique* of Laumonier (1977, 129), which he attributed to the Monogram PAR Workshop – a decision supported by a signed fragment of a bowl with calyx B2 (Laumonier 1977, 133 cat. 2000, pl. 30; see Fig. 68). It is difficult to identify the leaf botanically, but we may loosely refer to it as an acanthus. It is combined with a variety of plain lotus petals. In the classic form of the design, the leaf folds alternately to left and right, highlighting a petal by the direction of its folds. The style of the acanthus and the floral elements that it flanks or alternates with varies. Two of the commonest schemes, well represented in the Black Sea assemblage are described below.

Calyx B1
A pair slender acanthus leaves, folded down softly in a languid flop, flank an ovoid lotus petal, and these groups are separated by ovoid petals.
EPH-87*, EPH-180–EPH-184, EPH-276, EPH-387, EPH-389*, EPH-390*, EPH-606*–EPH-610*, EPH-1303*

---

72   For drawings of well-preserved examples on Delos, see Laumonier 1977, pls. 115–117.

Calyx B2
The basic template is the same as that of B1, but there is much more variety. The acanthus leaves are stylistically more varied and are folded stiffly forward, sometimes straight across the top. The petal they flank may be either ovoid or rhomboidal; the spacing petal between the groups is almost always of the alternate type (e.g., EPH-187*, EPH-189*; Laumonier 1977, 134 cat. 1976, pl. 30; 143 cat. 451, pl. 123), but it is not unusual for rhomboidal petals to be used throughout (e.g., EPH-639–EPH-643*). The acanthus leaves are stiff, sometimes almost comb-like (e.g., EPH-618*, EPH-631*), but occasionally more naturalistic (e.g., EPH-633*–EPH-635*). They usually bend symmetrically around the petal, but sometimes all bend in the same direction (e.g., EPH-643*).
EPH-5, EPH-30, EPH-31, EPH-97*, EPH-185*–EPH-189*, EPH-256*, EPH-257, EPH-271*, EPH-277*, EPH-282*, EPH-288*, EPH-290, EPH-291, EPH-293*, EPH-327, EPH-333, EPH-363*, EPH-364*, EPH-385*, EPH-438*, EPH-611*–EPH-649*, EPH-660*, EPH-1273*

Calyx Type C
In this simpler design, a rigorously straight acanthus leaf alternates with an ovoid or, occasionally, rhomboidal lotus petal.
EPH-33(?), EPH-34*, EPH-92–EPH-94*, EPH-116, EPH-129, EPH-194, EPH-297, EPH-322*, EPH-324*, EPH-348*, EPH-365*, EPH-393, EPH-485*, EPH-662*–EPH-667

Other Calyces
Although they are in the minority, there is a considerable collection of other calyx patterns. Most involve the alternation of two or more vegetal forms (straight acanthus or frond and lotus petal, EPH-668*–EPH-675*; straight acanthus and floral tendril, EPH-676–EPH-681; or other combinations EPH-682–EPH-689*). A single leaf or petal form may also be repeated throughout (EPH-690*–EPH-707*).

Imbricate Decoration
Vessels decorated with imbricate (overlapping) petals are very common. This arrangement can fill the wall below a single or multiple rim friezes, or it may function as the lower decoration, most commonly under scrolls (EPH-199*–EPH-211*, EPH-261*, EPH-300, EPH-1315*), but in rare cases wreaths (EPH-329*, EPH-349*, EPH-371) or figures (EPH-8*, EPH-1313*). Frequently, when only smaller fragments are at hand, it is not possible to determine the type of the overall vessel decoration.

There are a number of stylistic variants, in two main groups: with rounded or pointed petals. Both can be found in a number of further variants, with a central vein or with both central and side veins, occasionally in negative relief; the pointed petals may also have a double outline. The pointed petals are normally smaller and more stylized than the rounded ones.

Imbricate Petals with Rounded Tip
This somewhat more naturalistic design is probably the earlier of the two. It was used by both workshop circles, though is more common with the plain underside of WC1. The petals are sometime quite large (W. at base over 1 cm), giving a more naturalistic impression (e.g., EPH-199*, EPH-200*). More commonly, however, they are smaller and the emphasis is rather on the texture of the overall pattern.
EPH-199*–EPH-211*, EPH-250*, EPH-261*, EPH-300, EPH-349*, EPH-371, EPH-481*, EPH-520*, EPH-717*–EPH-800*, EPH-1309, EPH-1321*, EPH-1347, EPH-1348*

Imbricate Petals with Pointed Tip
Imbricate petals with pointed tip are always small and seem to occur almost exclusively in WC1: only a single fragment combining pointed imbricate petals with the rosette base medallion indicative of WC2 has been found (Laumonier 1977, 88 cat. 5301, pl. 19). Instead, a number of vessels display the plain, slightly concave and undecorated base of WC1, and many are signed either by Menemachos or his followers, especially Philon(nios). The following signatures are also documented:

Menemachos (EPH-895*, from Chersonesos. EPH-896*, from Istros. Laumonier 1977, 26 cat. 186, pl. 1; 37 cat. 5049, pl. 5; 47–48 cats. 5017, 5019, 5022, 5028, 5034, 5040, 8275, pl. 9; 48, 50 cats. 5041, 5045, 5353, 5354, 9134, pl. 10 from Delos)

Philon(nios) (Signing as Philon: EPH-1278, from Pantikapaion? Laumonier 1977, 251–253 cats. 5004, 5014, 5016, pl. 56; 254–255 cats. 5002, 5007, 5533, 5576, pl. 57; 257 cat. 8696, pl. 58, from Delos; Pierobon 1985, figs. 5, 6, from Iasos. Signing as Philon[…]: EPH-808*, from Chersonesos. EPH-807*, EPH-809, EPH-897*, EPH-899*, from Istros. EPH-898*, from Olbia. EPH-806, from Pantikapeion. Laumonier 1977, 256 cat. 5006, pl. 57, from Delos. Signing as Philonnios: EPH-802, EPH-803, EPH-805*, from Olbia. EPH-804, from Pantikapeion)

A (Laumonier 1977, 409 cat. 9294, pl. 96, from Delos)
Anti(…) (Dothan 1976, 34, fig. 31, from Akko)
Ap(…)/Pa(…) (Bel-00-124, S. Lancov, Annual report 2000 [unpublished], from Beljaus; Laumonier 1977, 227–228 cats. 5356, 5357, 5538, 8854, pl. 51, from Delos)
Arkesilaos (EPH-900*, EPH-901, from Pantikapaion)

Athenaios (EPH-815*, from Chersonesos; Tuchelt 1971, pl. 11.174, from Didyma; Kossatz 1990, 64 cat. M 451, pl. 28, from Miletos)
Ch (Laumonier 1977, 256–257 cats. 5350, 5352, pl. 57; 257 cat. 5351, pl. 58, from Delos)
D (EPH-816*, from Istros)
Dias (Laumonier 1977, 405 cat. 5058, pl. 95, from Delos)
Ei(…) (Laumonier 1977, 335 cat. 5210, pl. 81, from Delos)
Hera(…) (Laumonier 1977, 281, 282 cats. 5152, 5356, pl. 65, from Delos)
K (Laumonier 1977, 410 cats. 5539, 5579, pl. 96, from Delos)

Thus, the imbricate design with pointed petals is most likely a development towards further stylization of the version with rounded petals.
EPH-329*, EPH-802–EPH-945, EPH-1277*–EPH-1280, EPH-1294, EPH-1328*

Other Imbricate Designs
Other small, leaf- or petal-like motifs are occasionally arranged in overlapping rows: acanthus (EPH-946*), palmettes (EPH-947*, EPH-948*, EPH-1313*), generic veined leaves (EPH-949*–EPH-951), 'paw' (EPH-952*), even egg motifs (EPH-953*) or tiny rosettes (EPH-954*).

F   *Linear Decoration*[73]
Pendent-Semicircle Design
The pendent-semicircle design is rare in Ephesian production. Laumonier (1977, 483–484) describes its distribution in the Delian corpus: none by Menemachos, 15 in the Monogram PAR Workshop, a few distributed among Belles Méduses, Heraios, Si(…), and Philon(nios), along with over 30 unattributable fragments. One may also perhaps be assigned to My(…).[74] In the Black Sea assemblage, it is the five-rayed sun wheel that most frequently appears at the middle of the semicircles, with four-, six-, or eight-rayed wheels or a rosette as rare alternatives; rosette 9 is the standard space-filler. For a full discussion of this design, see Chapter 6.
EPH-955*–EPH-981*, EPH-1281*–EPH-1287, EPH-1322*

Net Pattern
The net pattern comes in a number of variations. Networks can be drawn with solid or, more rarely, dotted

---

[73] [Ed. The descriptions of linear decoration and bases below are largely reconstructed from PGB's data base.]
[74] Laumonier 1977, 266 cat. 1214, pls. 61, 128, attributed there to Philon.

lines. The compartments may be empty or may host a variety of vignettes: concentric circles or rhomboids, a rosette, a skeleton, a dolphin(?), or a vessel.[75] They are found throughout the corpus on Delos, but only the Monogram PAR Workshop produced a significant number (Laumonier 1977, 482).
EPH-982–EPH-1009*, EPH-1288*

Long Petals
Long-petal design is placed in its own category, because it can be debated whether this is actually a stylised vegetal design or was in fact inspired by the vertical fluting known from other types of vessels. The petals in Ephesian production are always spaced out, never contiguous. They may alternate with columns of dots or circles topped with a stamped motif or a pair of dots. They may cover the entire wall or serve as a calyx below other decoration. Over 200 examples are included in our Black Sea assemblage. Although the motif was introduced in the course of the second quarter of the 2nd century, long-petal decoration is most typical of the latest Ephesian production. This accounts for its heavy representation on Delos, where destructions of the early 1st century are responsible for much of the material recovered.[76]

Plastic Long Petals
Petals with a convex interior, the less common of the two types, occur on about 70 vessels. On a third of them, the petals appear alone, but there is often some additional embellishment. This may be as simple as a group of three dots between the petal tops, but a column of dots is much more common, sometimes topped by a flower or bud (e.g., EPH-1036*, EPH-1042*). Occasionally the line of dots arches over the tops of the petals, completely surrounding them (EPH-1033*–EPH-1035*, EPH-1349*). This is usually full-body decoration, but two bowls from Olbia use it in combination with other floral elements as a calyx below a body frieze (EPH-299, EPH-403). Both plain and decorated bases appear on bowls with plastic long petals, two of the plain bases with partial signatures (EPH-1037*, EPH-1038*), the former of which can be restored as that of Athenaios. The rosettes of the medallion are quite varied (rosettes A, B, D, and E). It is clear, then, that products of both workshop circles reached the area.
EPH-299, EPH-403, EPH-601*, EPH-1010*–EPH-1043*, EPH-1251, EPH-1308, EPH-1343*, EPH-1349*

Stylized Long Petals
Long petals with flat interiors, simpler to make and perhaps for this reason more common, occur in over 140 examples. These petals too may appear alone, but two-thirds have separating elements, usually a column of dots, only rarely crowned by double dots or a bud (e.g., EPH-1082, EPH-1103*). More inventive separating elements include S-spirals, pointed petals, or a wavy stem (EPH-1111*–EPH-1113*). There are a few unusual variants, such as petals of varying heights (EPH-1109*, EPH-1110*), or with double outlines (EPH-1106*, EPH-1110*, EPH-1112*). All the preserved bases are the plain ones of WC1, but in a couple of instances a single row of small leaves created a low calyx at the base of the wall (EPH-1060*, EPH-1061*); this is a rare early feature in Athenian bowls (Rotroff 2011b, 641), but there is no evidence for its chronology among Ephesian bowls. The petals fill the whole wall below a single or, rarely, double rim frieze, but they may also function as a calyx below other wall decoration (EPH-42*, EPH-1114*).
EPH-42*, EPH-1045*–EPH-1115*

Long Petals with Vegetal Elements
Long petals of both types occasionally intrude into more naturalistic vegetal schemes, where they alternate with ferns, acanthus leaves, lotus petals, 'nelumbos', or floral elements.
EPH-299, EPH-595*, EPH-596*, EPH-601*, EPH-1041*, EPH-1044*, EPH-1105*, EPH-1107*, EPH-1116–EPH-1118

Vertical Fluting
A few bowls bear plain ridges which spread out to a triangle at the top, creating vertical flutes. This is a rare design, found in Workshop Circle 1 (Menemachos and the late Menemachean Comique à la canne). The bowls from the Black Sea use the flutes alone, but some examples on Delos show that they could also be combined effectively with other types of vegetal decoration.[77]
EPH-1119*–EPH-1121

---

75   For similar filling devices on Delos, cf. Laumonier 1977, 69 cat. 4050, pl. 15; 309 cats. 4052, 9682, pl. 73 (krater); 71 cat. 3475, pl. 15 (rosette, satyr mask); 182 cat. 4054, pl. 39 (rhomboid); 308 cats. 3270, 3271, pls. 73, 129 (skeleton).

76   Spread throughout all of the workshops, with also hundreds of unassigned fragments; e.g., Laumonier 1977, pls. 11, 39, 43, 55, 58–59, 68–69, 103–105.

77   Some examples on Delos: Laumonier 1977, 119 cats. 4851, 4852, pl. 27 (fluting alone); 36 cat. 2264, pls. 4, 116; 120 cat. 1114, pls. 27, 122 (fluting combined with vegetal calyx).

Bases (Fig. 79)

Rosette A

Rogl 2014a, 123–124, figs. 9–10, type 1a–c

Rosette with six to eight outlined petals with convex surfaces, separated by narrow, convex tongues. This is viewed as typical for the PAR potter, even though it has never been found associated with his signature.[78] It is well-represented on his products, appearing, for example, with the miniature acanthus-flower scroll rim exclusive to his workshop (EPH-161*), although it occasionally occurs in other workshops as well.[79] Variants on the pattern include the following:

1. eight larger petals, grouped in pairs, with a tongue between each pair (e.g., EPH-589*)
2. petals without intervening tongues (e.g., EPH-299, EPH-682)
3. petals with central veins (EPH-611*, EPH-1256*)
4. two different petal forms alternating (EPH-743, EPH-982).

EPH-92, EPH-94*, EPH-120*, EPH-161*–EPH-163*, EPH-171, EPH-172*, EPH-178, EPH-179, EPH-186, EPH-199*–EPH-202, EPH-204*, EPH-210, EPH-249*, EPH-275, EPH-348*, EPH-389*, EPH-550*, EPH-553*, EPH-554, EPH-557–EPH-559, EPH-570, EPH-571*, EPH-605, EPH-606*, EPH-612*, EPH-616, EPH-617, EPH-621*, EPH-622, EPH-624*, EPH-626*, EPH-639, EPH-640*, EPH-643*, EPH-657*, EPH-663*, EPH-664*, EPH-676, EPH-677*, EPH-687*–EPH-689*, EPH-695, EPH-716, EPH-718*–EPH-720, EPH-724*, EPH-727*, EPH-731*–EPH-733, EPH-739*–EPH-741, EPH-749*, EPH-752*, EPH-768, EPH-793*–EPH-796, EPH-840*, EPH-999, EPH-1005*, EPH-1021*, EPH-1253*–EPH-1255, EPH-1270*, EPH-1299*, EPH-1304, EPH-1309, EPH-1335*

Variants: EPH-299, EPH-327, EPH-589*, EPH-611*, EPH-628, EPH-678*, EPH-682, EPH-694, EPH-742*, EPH-743, EPH-982, EPH-1252*, EPH-1256*, EPH-1257, EPH-1310

Rosette B

Rogl 2014a, 124, fig. 10, type 2; e.g., Laumonier 1977, 299 cat. 733, pl. 70

A base rosette with many (usually 12) overlapping Nymphaea lotus sepals is found in the Monogram PAR Workshop (e.g., EPH-188, EPH-636) and in the Workshop of My(…) (EPH-145*) (cf. Laumonier 1977, 44 cat. 736, pl. 8; 300 cat. 1130, pl. 70).

EPH-93, EPH-145*, EPH-180, EPH-181, EPH-187*–EPH-189*, EPH-203, EPH-288*, EPH-290, EPH-291, EPH-324*, EPH-393, EPH-556*, EPH-564, EPH-587*, EPH-610*, EPH-629*, EPH-630*, EPH-633*, EPH-634*, EPH-636, EPH-637, EPH-665*, EPH-666, EPH-696*, EPH-744, EPH-986, EPH-1006*, EPH-1013*, EPH-1022, EPH-1258*–EPH-1261*, EPH-1273*

Rosette C

Rogl 2014a, 124, fig. 10, type 4c

Six broad, lobed petals with a finely ribbed interior and a cluster of ivy berries at the centre. This medallion rosette counts amongst the earliest ones and is rare in Ephesian production. A similar rosette was employed at Kyme (Bouzek & Jansová 1974, 51 cat. MB 3, pl. 2 [mould]) and at Sardis (Rotroff 2003, 128 cat. 539, pl. 94). Possibly Pergamene in origin (cf. PER-10*, PER-70*).

EPH-257, EPH-679*, EPH-1007*

Rosette D

E.g., Laumonier 1977, 112 cat. 466+612, pls. 25, 121

Four wide, heart-shaped petals with a scored or dotted central vein, with narrow tongues between them. The motif is rare on Delos, occurring on a few late Menemachean bowls attributed to the Comique à la canne.

EPH-396*, EPH-607*, EPH-661*, EPH-1008*, EPH-1023*

Rosette E

Rogl 2014a, 124, fig. 10, type 1d; e.g., Laumonier 1977, 139 cat. 714, pl. 31

Eight rather plain, heart-shaped petals with narrow tongues between them. Occasionally found in the Monogram PAR Workshop.

EPH-601*, EPH-675*, EPH-919*, EPH-1044*, EPH-1263

Rosette F

Eight heart-shaped petals with a small circle at the centre.

EPH-841*, EPH-1262*

---

[78] Some authors identify the Ionian kyma surrounding the PAR stamp on some of the vessels (e.g., Laumonier 1977, 133 cat. 2000–2003, pl. 30) as Rosette A. I do not agree with this.

[79] For example, VG Workshop (EPH-677*; Laumonier 1977, 105 cat. 366, pls. 24, 120); Belles Méduses(?) (85 cat. 2386, pl. 19), Athenaios (233–234 cats. 8860, 8861, pl. 52).

A	Six to eight outlined petals separated by narrow tongues (**EPH-796**)	
B	Many overlapping Nymphaea lotus sepals (**EPH-665**)	
C	Six broad, lobed petals or sepals with cluster of ivy berries at centre (**EPH-1007**)	
D	Four heart-shaped leaves separated by narrow tongues (**EPH-396**)	
E	Seven or eight heart-shaped leaves separated by narrow tongues (**EPH-601**)	
F	Eight heart-shaped leaves (**EPH-1262**)	

FIGURE 79
Rosettes of Ephesian base medallions
PHOTOS FROM THE AUTHOR'S ARCHIVE

Supplementary Shapes

The Ephesian workshops were amongst the most prolific when it came to producing supplementary shapes. This is a feature of, particularly, the early Ephesian phase, when workshops such as Menemachos, Belles Méduses, and Vases gris turned out a variety of shapes, including amphorae, kraters, and lentoid gutti. In the classical phase, Menemachos and the Monogram PAR potter introduced new shapes, mostly smaller ones, including the small bowl, funnel, and skyphos with pinched handles. In the late phase, exclusively bowls and cups were manufactured.

Small Bowl

Along with many other production places (see p. 56), Ephesian workshops, probably of Menemachos and Monogram PAR, produced a small bowl with a rim diameter of 7.5–9 cm. One group consists of a small series of bowls with a simple, more or less straight rim characterized by a thin, everted lip with two to three incised grooves below it (EPH-1284*, EPH-1285*, EPH-1289*, EPH-1293, EPH-1294). They are exclusively made in grey ware with a good, shiny, black coat.

Some bowls are decorated with figural motifs, such as mantled dancing women (EPH-1266*, EPH-1267), altar group D flanked by antithetical, saluting Pans,[80] hunters (EPH-1265*), or actors (EPH-1268*). Others use a vegetal pattern, such as a calyx with 'nelumbo' and/or lotus sepals with twisted top (EPH-1269–EPH-1271*); two feature the Menemachean bud (EPH-1272*, EPH-1275*). The PSC design is common (EPH-1281*–EPH-1287), one bowl has a net pattern (EPH-1288*), and a few late small bowls are decorated with pointed imbricate petals (EPH-1277*–EPH-1280).[81]

EPH-1265*–EPH-1295*

Juglet

Five very small jugs, all in grey fabric, come from Myrmekion, Pantikapaion, and Olbia; preserved decoration is figured and imbricate. A sixth example (EPH-1321*), its scale unclear from the illustration, may also belong here.

EPH-1296–EPH-1300*, EPH-1321*

---

80   Laumonier 1977, 92 cat. 3247, pl. 20. A bowl from Alexandria with the same decoration under a single rim frieze of astragal is probably also a miniature bowl (no measurements are given: Pagenstecher 1913, fig. 97c; Wuilleumier 1929, 65 cat. j; Schwabacher 1941, 186 no. 1; Pochmarski 1990, RK 84).

81   [Ed. The remainder of the discussion of supplementary shapes was completed by the editor.]

Kantharos

The unique kantharos EPH-1301 from Bothros 11 at Olbia has been discussed above (p. 32). The shape as preserved is not very different from a bowl, but with the rim straighter than usual. The handles had elaborately shaped thumb-plates with a spur below; nothing of a foot or stem survives, though there must once have been one. Despite its worn condition, the quality of the decoration, with a baroque calyx with a 'nelumbo' filled with a symplegma, suggests it was copied directly from a metal vessel, and it stands close to the origin of this iconography. It probably numbers among the earliest products of its maker (Menemachos or the VG Workshop), dating in the second quarter of the 2nd century.

EPH-1301*

Skyphos with Pinched Handles

The Black Sea assemblage preserves one example of this form, probably a product of the early Classical phase of the Monogram PAR Workshop and dating in the third quarter of the 2nd century. Unusually, it preserves a painted laurel wreath above the mouldmade rim pattern.

EPH-1302*

Amphora

With 18 examples, the Black Sea assemblage contains a remarkably large number of amphoras. Those that are well enough preserved for identification belong mostly to the Ephesian type, with a broad, heavy foot with an upturned edge balanced by a widely spreading, undercut rim, and strap handles. One amphora is a hybrid, combining features of the Athenian (a plain rim and foot) and the Pergamene and Ephesian types (strap handles) (EPH-1310). Several of these amphoras come from the VG Workshop (EPH-1304, EPH-1306*, EPH-1311*, EPH-1312*, EPH-1318), which seems to have specialized in large shapes; one example each can be attributed to the Monogram PAR Workshop (EPH-1303*) and the still poorly defined Pan mask medallion 'workshop' (EPH-1308). They probably date no later than the third quarter of the 2nd century.

EPH-1303*–EPH-1320

Lagynos?

Two fragments perhaps from a lagynos share the PSC decoration of the well-known complete lagynos in the Vogell Collection (XXX-68*), from an unidentified production center.

EPH-1322*

Situla

Reduced firing characterizes fragments of seven situlae, a rare early shape, dating in the second quarter of the 2nd century. Consistent with their early date, the quality of the decoration is high, and some of the compositions are unusual: the myrtle wreath and fine design of the palmettes of EPH-1323*, suggesting a close link with metalwork; the large and elaborate box meander of the rim of EPH-1324*; and both the rim and the elaborate figural decoration of EPH-1326.
EPH-1323*–EPH-1329*

Krater

There are fragments of four kraters, all of grey ware and two (EPH-1330*, EPH-1332*) featuring figured decoration, attributable to Menemachos. They probably date early in the series. One has unusual relief decoration on the inside of the rim (EPH-1331*).
EPH-1330*–EPH-1333*

Dinos

A single, completely preserved example of this rare shape presents some puzzles. To a large bowl form is added a sloping shoulder, a thick rim with a pair of lug handles, and an elaborately moulded foot. The form suggests mixing, but with a maximum diameter of only about 17 cm, the vessel seems small for that function. The frieze of horizontally oriented imbricate petals is particularly unusual. The decoration suggests a fairly early date, third or even second quarter of the 2nd century.
EPH-1335*

Guttus

Fragments of two small oil vessels, probably dating in the second quarter of the 2nd century.
EPH-1336*, EPH-1337

Unidentified Vessels

The remaining pieces are fragments of vessels, most of them large and closed (amphorae?), but all too small for identification.
EPH-1334, EPH-1338–EPH-1351*

Chronology

Relative Chronology

Because it is so monumental, we tend to regard the corpus of Laumonier as a complete representation of the Ephesian workshops. However, this is not a true picture. The bulk of the Delian material probably dates after 166; in fact, the Delian bowls belong mostly to the second half of the 2nd century and perhaps even the early 1st century (Chatzidakis 1997), harvested by the massive destructions of 88 and 69. As mentioned in Chapter 2, Laumonier proposed a summary relative chronology (1977, 11–12):

(1) Menemachos seems to represent the oldest current, and Belle Méduses and Vases gris are also among the early workshops;
(2) Monogram PAR dates to the middle of the production;
(3) Philon with long petals and Heraios with imbricate petals signal the end of the production;
(4) CI and the Plagiaire date to the 1st century, the Plagiaire between 88 and 69.

By and large, this relative sequence is correct, but it can be much refined. I propose to divide the Ephesian production into three broad stylistic groupings, which correspond to consecutive phases, each covering approximately one quarter of a century: Ephesos, early; Ephesos, classical, and Ephesos, late. Each of these phases shares a number of characteristics, regardless of which workshop we are dealing with.

Ephesos, Early (EE)

This is a phase of experimentation: most of the supplementary shapes are produced in this period, and the bowls are also larger than in the following phases. Decoration is bold and often narrative. Workshops of this period are Vases gris, Belles Méduses, early Menemachos, and the Südtor Workshop (Gassner 1997).[82] The output is probably relatively limited. Calyx A, full-body scrolls, large vases, large rim diameters, and bowls with tall, straight rims are typical in this phase.

Ephesos, Classical (EC)

During this phase, production and decoration are 'industrialized': bowls are stacked during firing, resulting in a bicolour exterior. The bowls become smaller, and they are now very standardized in size and shape. A few new shapes appear, e.g., the funnel and the skyphos with pinched handles (Chapter 5). There is still some figural decoration,

---

82 The Südtor deposit does not seem to include any fragments which we can ascribe to Menemachos' workshop. I wonder if this material is somehow refuse from a production place or shop in the vicinity, because it seems to include only material of the Südtor Workshop and early Monogram PAR. Were it a 'normal' fill, Menemachos would undoubtedly have been represented, because part of his production is contemporary with those workshops.

chiefly Erotes performing various tasks, including driving a two-horse chariot, but the decoration is increasingly based on linear patterns such as PSC and long petals, the former introduced in the repertoire of MMB around 168, the latter slightly later (see Chapter 6). This is the heyday of Ephesian production. The Menemachos Workshop continues, but the leading workshop seems to be that of Monogram PAR, who is a true classicist. Amongst his early patterns are the full body scrolls, Calyx B, the *feuille typique*, and fine rounded eggs in the rim. In general, however, vegetal patterns move towards significant stylization, not least with the numerous imbricate bowls. The rosette base medallion is characteristic for this phase.

Ephesos, Late (EL)
In this phase, only bowls are produced; vessels shrink further in size, and bases are mostly simple, slightly concave, perhaps with a low false ring foot, and normally undecorated. There is some lingering figural decoration, mostly ill-produced stamps, perhaps often mechanically copied from earlier vessels or stamps, but the most typical formulations of this period are the long-petal and imbricate schemes. A number of individuals start signing their bowls in this phase, many by incising their names directly on the bowl before firing (Athenaios, Philon(nios)). A significant part of the Delian corpus (Laumonier 1977) belongs to this phase.

Absolute Chronology
The chronology of the Ephesian workshops is, to put it mildly, very coarse. Laumonier concluded that the Delian excavations did not allow for a finer chronology than 166–69 (1977, 7), the span from the declaration of Delos as a free port under the control of Athens to the final destruction by the pirate raiders of Athenodoros. At Ephesos too, chronology is not very detailed, but a number of moulds and closed contexts have come to light there since Laumonier's book was published. A scrutiny of these can help us come to terms with at least some of the Ephesian workshops.

The Südtor deposit provides a good collection of vessels in the early stages of Ephesian production. Unfortunately, there is no external evidence for its date, but the other objects found there suggest that, whatever its actual deposit date, most of the material probably dates within the second quarter of the 2nd century.[83] The

moulds from the Magnesia Gate – purely vegetal and linear except for a single human figure – document the late part of the production of the Monogram PAR Workshop. Again, however, we are lacking evidence for an absolute date. A well in Hanghaus 1 contains a homogeneous collection of 15 mouldmade bowls, again of the Monogram PAR Workshop, preserved in large fragments (Ladstätter et al. 2003, 26–28, 46–49 cats. K 43–K 57, pls. 5–6, 155–156). They generally resemble the assemblage at Olbia which, we have argued, falls rather earlier than the average of the Black Sea material. But again, the well does not provide an absolute date; the excavators suggest that it was filled around 100 (Ladstätter et al. 2003, 40), a date which seems to me far too late.

We get some firmer assistance from Cistern Л at Olbia, which contained a small collection of relief bowls, two of them attributable to the Monogram PAR Workshop (EPH-766*, EPH-773*). The cistern was rich in stamped amphora handles, the bulk of which date between 181–161, and the latest to ca. 144 (see Chapter 20 for a full discussion). The material probably entered the cistern shortly thereafter. The number of Ephesian bowls there is limited, but a larger assemblage of bowls in Bothros 11 is closely similar – even including another imbricate bowl of the Monogram PAR shop (EPH-771*) that could come from the same mould as EPH-773* from the cistern. Together, these observations show that the Classical production of the Monogram PAR Workshop was already well established and exporting its wares vigorously to the Black Sea region shortly after the middle of the 2nd century.

As we saw in Chapter 3, a few pieces have been found elsewhere in well-dated contexts, e.g., at Entremont, destroyed in 125 (Benoit 1947, 82–83, fig. 2), and in the foundations of the Temple of Castor and Pollux in the Roman Forum, dedicated in 117 (Guldager Bilde 2008, 188 cat. R-1, fig. 178, pl. 81). Further fragments similar to the latter have come to light in an even earlier context, a cistern in Athens that, on the basis of the amphora handles and the Attic pottery it contains, was probably filled around 150.[84] These fragments belong to the Classical phase of the Monogram PAR Workshop and again confirm production and export in mid-century.

---

83   This is the date suggested by John Hayes (1999), in contrast to a terminal date in the last third of the 2nd century suggested in the primary publication (Gassner 1997, 39) and of ca. 130–120 by Rogl (Ladstätter et al. 2003, 28).

84   Rotroff 1982a, 89 cat. 377, pls. 66, 88 from cistern F 5:1 (for most recent discussion of the date, see Rotroff 2006a, 354–355). The bowl is noted by Rogl (2014a, 133), though assigned to the wrong deposit.

More deposits of the later 2nd century will be necessary to fix the date of the rise of the late phase of production that is so richly documented by the early 1st-century destruction deposits on Delos. P. Chatzidakis' discussion of a Delian wine shop is of importance for the date of the latest phase of the Ephesian MMB, especially of late WC1, because a significant number of complete or near-complete bowls of the late phase of the Menemachos Workshop have been found in the shop, which was in operation from ca. 110 until it was destroyed, probably in 88 (Chatzidakis 1997). But contextual evidence for the close tracking of developments throughout the second half of the 2nd century and the early 1st century is lacking.

CATALOGUE TO CHAPTER 14

[Ed. This catalogue is more selective than most of the others in this book; it encompasses less than half of the Ephesian fragments from the 11 sites under consideration. Almost all attributed vessels have been included, but many bowls previously published in Domăneanţu 2000 (Istros), Bernhard 1957, 1959 (Mirmekion), Grzegrzółka 2010 (Tyritake, Porthmion, Pantikapaion), and Guldager Bilde 2010 (Olbia) have been omitted, along with other items that duplicate catalogued items, or preserve minimal decoration, or about which PGB's data base provides minimal information.]

BOWLS

A   *Figural Decoration*

Erotes

EPH-1*
Pantikapaion, palace foundation trench, M-84-30, Moscow, Puškin Museum of Fine Arts. Fr. of base and lower body. H 6.5 × W 7.5, WT 0.4, ⌀ base 5. Fabric: fine. Blotchy pinkish red coat. Hard fired, oxidized. Main decoration: Eros playing harp walking left alternating with Erotes(?) walking right. Plain, concave base. Cf. Laumonier 1977, 41 cat. 3223, pl. 7. Menemachos.
– Košelenko 1992, fig. 23.

EPH-2*
Pantikapaion, M-46-4219, Moskow, Puškin Museum of Fine Arts. Fr. of base and lower body. ⌀ base 5. Slightly lustrous reddish-brown coat. Oxidized. Main decoration: Eros playing kithara walking left alternating with vertical vegetal scrolls. Plain, slightly concave base. Cf. Laumonier 1977, 40 cat. 3323, pl. 6. Menemachos.
– Zabelina 1984, 157 fig. 4c

EPH-3*
Olbia, Sector NGS, O-НГС-86-843, Parutine, Olbia National Preserve storeroom. Body fr. close to rim. H 3.6 × W 4, WT 0.32. Fabric: relatively fine and micaceous, many small lime inclusions, Gley 1 4/N. Thin firm slightly lustrous coat, Gley 1 2.5/N. Medium hard fired, reduced. Rim frieze: box meander. Main decoration: Unidentified figure right, Eros playing kithara right. One repair hole.

EPH-4
Olbia, Sector NGS, House II-5 B 390/25 O-НГС-93-240, Parutine, Olbia National Preserve storeroom. Fr. of lower body. H 3.8 × W 4.85, WT 0.2–0.3. Fabric: fine, micaceous, a few small lime particles, N4/. Thin dull coat, 7.5R 2.5/0. Very hard fired, reduced. Main decoration: Eros facing left, satyr facing right. Menemachos.
– Guldager Bilde 2010, 284 cat. F-96, pl. 189.

EPH-5
Pantikapaion, П-1864-46. Two joining frs. of rim and body. ⌀ rim 12.8. Oxidized. Rim frieze: astragal. Main decoration: Eros playing aulos right, alternating with Eros playing krotala left. Calyx B2. VG Workshop.

EPH-6*
Olbia, Sector E6, squares 644, 678, northern part, grey clay layer, O-E6-66-802, Kiev, Institute of Archaeology storeroom. Three joining frs. of rim and body. H 5.7 × W 9.8, WT 0.25, ⌀ rim 13, 26%, RH 1.6. Fabric: standard, 2.5YR 6/6. Dull coat, ext. 10R 5/6, 2.5YR 4/1, 3/1, int. 2.5YR 4/8. Not too hard fired, oxidized. Stacked in firing. Rim frieze: Ionian kyma. Main decoration: Eros playing aulos right, alternating with Eros playing krotala left. Calyx: two types of acanthus: folded and straight (acanthus X) with indentations. VG Workshop.

EPH-7*
Olbia, Sector D3, clay layer, ОД-3-46-713, Kiev, Institute of Archaeology storeroom. Body fr. H 5.5 × W 4.8, WT 0.3. Fabric: standard, Gley 1 10Y/N. Dull coat, Gley 1 3/N. Relatively hard fired, reduced. Rim frieze: Ionian kyma. Main decoration: Eros walking right, hand on hip, between vertical bound myrtle bunches with three petals (*bachkoi?*); below, *agyieus* in palmette. Cf. Laumonier 1977, 167 cat. 3242, pl. 37. VG Workshop.

EPH-8*
Myrmekion, M-58-817, St Petersburg IIMK RAN. Two joining frs. of mid-body. H 3, WT 0.3. Fabric: standard, 2.5YR 6/6. Thin slightly lustrous coat, 2.5YR 4/8. Oxidized. Main decoration: Eros walking right playing aulos; at right, lower leg of figure walking left. Calyx: tip of pointed petal. Cf. Laumonier 1977, 146 no. 3179, pl. 33.

EPH-9*
Istros, His-B 516/V 19461, Bucharest, Institute of Archaeology storeroom. Fr. of rim and large part of wall. H 5.5 × W 6.7, WT 0.3, ⌀ rim 12, 17%, RH 1.5. Fabric: standard, 5Y 6/6. Dull coat, Gley 1 2.5/N. Relatively hard fired, reduced. Rim frieze: large dots. Main decoration: Eros walking right playing syrinx; wing and legs of two more Erotes(?) to left and right, widely distanced. Calyx: lotus petal between acanthus leaves. Late. Cf. Laumonier 1977, 124 cat. 3175, pl. 28.
– Domăneanţu 2000, 21 cat. 85, pl. 6 (attributed to Comique à la canne).

EPH-10
Istros, His-788, Bucharest, Institute of Archaeology storeroom. Fr. of rim and upper body. H 3.7 × W 3.7, WT 0.25, RH 1.6. Fabric: standard, 5Y 6/1. Coat with dull lustre, Gley 1 2.5/N. Relatively hard fired, reduced. Rim frieze: large dots. Main decoration: Eros facing right, hand on hip; trace of Eros facing left at left. Late. Cf. Laumonier 1977, 124 cat. 3174, pl. 28.
– Domăneanţu 2000, 22 cat. 86, pl. 6

EPH-11*
Myrmekion, Sector И, courtyard VII, M-56-10, M-49-675+56-10 (join across years), Saint Petersburg IIMK RAN. Two joining frs. of rim and upper body. H 4.8, WT 0.4, ⌀ rim 12.5, 30 %, RH 1.7. Fabric: standard, 7.5YR 6/6. Thin slightly lustrous coat, ext. 2.5YR 5/8, int. 2.5YR 5/6. Oxidized. Rim frieze: large dots. Main decoration: widely spaced Erotes dancing, hand on hip (mould-generation 2). Cf. Laumonier 1977, 124 cat. 3174, pl. 28.

EPH-12
Istros, His-B 569/V 19450, Bucharest, Institute of Archaeology storeroom. Fr. of rim and upper body. H 4.4 × W 4.5, WT 0.26, ⌀ rim 12, 10%, RH 1.8. Fabric: standard, 5YR 6/8. Dull coat, 2.5YR 5/6. Medium hard fired, oxidized. Rim frieze: star rosettes. Main decoration: Erotes facing right.
– Domăneanţu 2000, 91 cat. 432, pl. 30.

EPH-13*
Olbia, O-52-1991, Kiev, Institute of Archaeology storeroom. Fr. of rim and body. H 5.2 × W 4.3, WT 0.25. Fabric: standard, 5YR7/6. Dull coat, 2.5YR 4/6, 3/1. Relatively hard fired, oxidized. Stacked in firing. Rim frieze: Lesbian kyma. Main decoration: frontal Eros placing wreath on head and holding unidentified object in left hand; another Eros at right. Cf. Laumonier 1977, 97 cat. 6201, pl. 22, 120.

EPH-14*
Tyritake, Sector B, B-54-62, Saint Petersburg IIMK RAN. Fr. of mid-body. Oxidized. Main decoration: Eros walking right with hand on hip, holding musical instrument(?) in left arm.

EPH-15
Olbia, O-1936-643, present whereabouts unknown Fr. of rim and upper body. Rim frieze: Ionian kyma. Main decoration: Eros with raised arms running left; unidentified figure at right. Cf. Laumonier 1977, 116 cat. 3286, pls. 26, 122; 125 cat. 3204, pls. 29, 123.
– Levi 1940, 124, pl. XXV.2; St Petersburg, IIMK RAN, photo archive neg. II 13807.

EPH-16*
Olbia, Sector R25, O-P25-95-578, Parutine, Olbia National Preserve storeroom. Fr. of upper body. H 1.9 × W 2.9, WT 0.15. Fabric: relatively fine and micaceous, 2.5YR 6/8. Thin dull coat, 2.5YR 4/6. Hard fired, oxidized. Main decoration: Eros facing left with arms lifted. Cf. Laumonier 1977, 116 cat 3286, pls. 26, 122.

EPH-17
Olbia, Sector NGS, O-P25-08-192, Parutine, Olbia National Preserve storeroom. Body fr. H 2.6 × W 2.3, WT 0.2. Fabric: relatively fine and micaceous, 10YR 6/4. Thin dull coat, 10YR 3/1. Hard fired, oxidized. Main decoration: Erotes walking in opposite directions. Calyx B.

EPH-18*
Istros, His-B 610, Bucharest, Institute of Archaeology storeroom. Fr. of upper body. H 2.5 × W 2. Oxidized. Main decoration: Eros with raised right arm facing right.
– Domăneanţu 2000, 91 cat. 434, pl. 30.

EPH-19*
Istros, His-B 442/V 19463, Bucharest, Institute of Archaeology storeroom. Body fr. H 2.1 × W 3, WT 0.35. Fabric: standard, fine, 5Y 5/1. Dull coat, Gley 1 2.5/N. Relatively hard fired, reduced. Main decoration: Eros wrapped in short cloak moving left, carrying torch.
– Domăneanţu 2000, 4 cat. 9, pl. 1.

EPH-20*
Olbia, O-65-677+677[a, b], 66-392, Kiev, Institute of Archaeology storeroom. Four body frs., three joining. H 5.5 × W 5.7, WT 0.45. Fabric: standard, fine, 5YR 6/6. Thin coat with metallic lustre, 2.5Y 2.5/1. Relatively hard fired, oxidized. Rim frieze: Ionian kyma. Main decoration: torch-bearing(?) Erotes walking right. Calyx: acanthus leaves with bent tips.

EPH-21
Olbia, Sector AGD, О-АГД-73-276, Kiev, Institute of Archaeology storeroom. Fr. of mid-body. H 3.7 × W 5.3, WT 0.38. Fabric: standard, fine, 2.5YR 6/8. Coat with slight dull lustre, ext. 2.5YR 4/8, 2.5/1, int. 2.5YR 4/8, 2.5/1. Relatively hard fired, oxidized.

Stacked in firing. Main decoration: torch-bearing(?) Erotes walking right.

EPH-22*
Olbia, Sector NGS, House III-3 B 368/104, O-НГС-93-677+507, 667, 674, 675, 676, 910, Parutine, Olbia National Preserve storeroom. Three joining and three non-joining rim frs. H 5.5 × W 6.5, WT 0.23–0.45, ⌀ rim 13.5, RH 1.8. Fabric: relatively fine, micaceous, fine lime particles. Thin firm coat with slight lustre, more lustrous where darkened in firing, blotchy ext., perhaps due to secondary firing, ext. 2.5YR 4/6, 10YR 3/1, int. 2.5YR 4/6. Hard fired, oxidized. Stacked in firing. Rim frieze: Ionian kyma. Main decoration: Erotes riding dolphins and hippocamps, at least one Eros playing a lyre. The two mounts at left are hippocamps (their horse heads are clearly visible); second from right is probably a dolphin. Frieze separators: dots. Early.
– Guldager Bilde 2010, 277 cat. F-12, pl. 170.

EPH-23*
Istros, Sector SB, His-79-1145, Bucharest, Institute of Archaeology storeroom. Rim fr. H 4.4 × W 5.7, WT 0.4, ⌀ rim 13, 12%, RH 2. Fabric: standard, 5Y 6/1. Dull coat, Gley 1 2.5/N. Relatively hard fired, reduced. Rim frieze: Ionian kyma. Main decoration: Eros facing right, reaching arm toward frontal mask (mostly effaced).
– Domăneanțu 2000, 132 cat. 651, pl. 46.

EPH-24*
Istros, His-B 494/V 19401, Bucharest, Institute of Archaeology storeroom. Fr. of lower body. H 2.1 × W 2.7, WT 0.4. Fabric: standard, 5YR 6/8. Dull coat, 2.5YR 5/6. Medium hard fired, oxidized. Calyx: lotus petal; at left, small Eros flying right as space filler.
– Domăneanțu 2000, 91 cat. 435, pl. 30.

EPH-25*
Olbia, Sector NGS, O-НГС-06-127, Parutine, Olbia National Preserve storeroom. Fr. of base and lower body. H 5.3 × W 2.8, WT 0.2. Fabric: fine, micaceous, 5YR 6/8. Thin dull coat, 2.5YR 4/8. Medium hard fired, oxidized. Calyx: tall rhomboidal petal and acanthus; Eros walking right as space filler. Medallion: rosette (type?).

EPH-26
Porthmion, square 42–43c, depth 1.7 m, П-75-59. Fr. of lower body. Calyx: Small Eros as space filler walks right between ovoid petal and rhomboidal petal with segmented central vein.

Eros Racing a Two-Horse Chariot

EPH-27*
Pantikapaion, M-46-1542, Moscow, Puškin Museum of Fine Arts. Fr. of rim and upper body. H 4.5 × W 5, RH 1.9. Dull red coat. Oxidized. Rim frieze: crossed dotted lines with box. Menemachos.

EPH-28
Pantikapaion, year and no. unknown, present whereabouts unknown. Fr. of rim and upper body. Rim frieze: rosette 1. Menemachos?
– Loseva 1962, fig. 1.4.

EPH-29*
Myrmekion, M-58-2966, St Petersburg IIMK RAN. Body fr. H 3.7, WT 0.35. Fabric: standard, 5YR 6/6. Thin coat with slight lustre ext., 5YR 4/6. Oxidized. Rim frieze: miniature acanthus-flower scroll left. Monogram PAR.

EPH-30
Olbia, O-59-1918, present whereabouts unknown. Complete, lacks a few minor frs. Rim frieze: rosette 5. Calyx B2. Medallion not visible in photograph. Similar: Guldager Bilde 2010, 277 cat. F-15, pl. 171.
– Levi 1964a, fig. 7.2; St Petersburg, IIMK RAN, photo archive neg. II 68177.

EPH-31
Olbia, Sector E6–7, squares 598e, 608e, yellow clay layer, O-E6-7-63-1434[a], Kiev, Institute of Archaeology storeroom. Body fr. Oxidized. Calyx B2.

EPH-32
Olbia, Sector R25, O-P25-98-1726, Parutine, Olbia National Preserve storeroom. Body fr. Oxidized. Calyx: top of folded acanthus of calyx B.

EPH-33 (see Fig. 40)
Olbia, Sector NGS, O-НГС-02-633a+679+739+840, Parutine, Olbia National Preserve storeroom. Three rim frs. and two body frs.; ca. one fourth of vessel preserved; very worn. WT 0.2–0.5, ⌀ rim 13, RH 2.2; vessel H 7; H:⌀ 1:1.9. Fabric: fine, micaceous, many small lime particles, a few small brownish stones, 7.5YR 6/6. Thin firm slightly lustrous coat, very badly fired, mottled, very pitted, ext. 10YR 3/1, 5YR 4/6, int. 10YR 3/1, 5YR 4/6. Medium hard fired, oxidized. Stacked in firing. Rim frieze: Ionian kyma. Calyx C(?): straight(?) acanthus leaf, Wadjet symbol. Large rim diameter and Wadjet symbol suggest early date.

EPH-34*
Myrmekion, M-46-389, St Petersburg IIMK RAN. Fr. of mid- and lower body. H 4.4, WT 0.35. Fabric: standard, 5YR 6/6. Thin coat with slight lustre ext., 5YR 4/6. Oxidized. Calyx C? (straight acanthus leaf).

EPH-35*
Olbia, Sector E6, square 427e, 498w, 432w, grey clay layer over Room "O", O-E6-59-1709, Kiev, Institute of Archaeology storeroom. Fr. of rim and upper body. Oxidized. Rim frieze: box meander, cw.

EPH-36*
Myrmekion, M-47-545, St Petersburg IIMK RAN. Fr. of rim and upper body. H 3.8, WT 0.33, ∅ rim 13, RH 1.6. Fabric: standard, 2.5YR 5/8. Thin coat with metallic sheen, ext. 7.5YR 4/1, int. 2.5YR 4/6, 7.5YR 4/1. Oxidized. Stacked in firing. Rim frieze: Ionian kyma with hatched tongue.

EPH-37*
Myrmekion, M-57-258, St Petersburg IIMK RAN. Fr. of rim and upper body. H 3.7, WT 0.2, ∅ rim 12, 10%, RH 1.45. Fabric: standard, 5YR 6/6. Thin coat with slight metallic lustre, 10YR 4/1. Oxidized. Stacked in firing. Rim frieze: Ionian kyma.

EPH-38
Tyritake, Sector K, K-39-114, St Petersburg IIMK RAN. Fr. of rim and upper body. Oxidized. Rim frieze: Ionian kyma.

EPH-39
Istros, His-1927-1942-V 8569 A, Bucharest, Institute of Archaeology storeroom. Rim fr. H 4.2 × W 4.5, WT 0.2, RH 1.7. Fabric: standard, fine, 5YR 6/8. Dull coat, ext. 2.5YR 5/610YR 7/6, int. 2.5YR 5/6, 10YR 3/1. Relatively hard fired, oxidized. Stacked in firing. Rim frieze: Ionian kyma with hatched tongue.
– Domăneanțu 2000, 32 cat. 129, pl. 9 (attributed to Monogram PAR).

EPH-40
Pantikapaion, M-49-41, Moscow, Puškin Museum of Fine Arts. Fr. of rim and upper body. Rim frieze: Lesbian kyma.
– Zabelina 1984, 161 fig. 8d (identified as Pergamene)

EPH-41*
Chersonesos, behind church (1877), X-1908-9, St Petersburg, State Hermitage Museum. Fr. of rim and upper body. H 5.3, WT 0.25, ∅ rim 13, RH 1.4. Fabric: no fresh break for observation. Thin coat with slight lustre, 2.5YR 2.5/1. Oxidized. Rim frieze: guilloche left.

EPH-42*
Istros, His-1927-1942-V 8569 R, Bucharest, Institute of Archaeology storeroom. Fr. of rim and large part of wall. H 5.4 × W 8.3, ∅ rim 12, 20%, RH 1.6. Fabric: standard, 5YR 6/8. Thin, dull coat, 2.5YR 4/6. Medium hard fired, oxidized. Stacked in firing. Rim frieze: very sloppy guilloche left. Calyx: stylized long petals.
– Domăneanțu 2000, 33 cat. 130, pl. 9 (attributed to Monogram PAR).

EPH-43*
Myrmekion, Sector И, courtyard VII, M-49-690, St Petersburg IIMK RAN. Fr. of rim and upper body. H 4.4, WT 0.3, ∅ rim 13, 10%, RH 1.6. Fabric: standard, 2.5YR 5/8. Thin dull mottled coat, ext. 2.5YR 4/8, 5YR 2.5/1, int. 2.5YR 4/8. Oxidized. Stacked in firing. Rim frieze: rosette 2/7.

EPH-44*
Olbia, Sector E6, square 405, basement with walls 4, 15, 16, 18, O-E6-56-273, 273[A], 441, Kiev, Institute of Archaeology storeroom. Rim fr. and two non-joining body frs. Oxidized. Stacked in firing. Rim frieze: rosette 2/7.

EPH-45*
Olbia, Sector Sever-Zapad, O-C3-68-1923+1924, Parutine, Olbia National Preserve storeroom. Two joining frs. of rim and upper body. H 4.3 × W 7, WT 0.3, ∅ rim 12, 19%, RH 1.3. Fabric: standard, 5YR 6/8. Dull coat, much pitted on int., ext. 7.5YR 2.5/1, int. 7.5YR 3/3. Relatively hard fired, oxidized. Rim frieze: rosette 2/7.

EPH-46*
Olbia, Sector E6–7, squares 598e, 608e, yellow clay layer, O-E6-7-63-1434, Kiev, Institute of Archaeology storeroom. Fr. of rim and body. H 5.4 × W 5.4, WT 0.35, RH 1.2. Fabric: standard, 5YR 6/8. Dull coat, ext. 2.5YR 4/6, 3/1, int. 2.5YR 4/6. Relatively hard fired, oxidized. Stacked in firing. Rim frieze: rosette 2/7.

EPH-47
Olbia, Sector NGS, O-НГС 08-235, Parutine, Olbia National Preserve storeroom. Fr. of upper body. H 3.8, × W 3.5, WT 0.3. Fabric: relatively fine and micaceous, 5YR 6/6. Thin dull coat, ext. 2.5YR 4/6, 3/1, int. 2.5YR 4/6. Medium hard fired, oxidized. Stacked in firing.

EPH-48*
Olbia, Sector E6, square 405, basement with walls 4, 15, 16, 18, O-E6-56-442, Kiev, Institute of Archaeology storeroom. Fr. of rim and upper body. Oxidized. Rim frieze: star rosettes. Secondarily burnt.

EPHESOS

331

EPH-49*
Olbia, Sector NGS, O-НГС-92-134, 135, Parutine, Olbia National Preserve storeroom. Two non-joining frs. of rim and upper body probably from the same vessel. H 4.7 × W 4.5, WT 0.24–0.5, ⌀ rim 16, RH 1.7. Fabric: medium fine with some voids, 5YR 6/6. Thin firm semi-lustrous coat, partly darkened at rim ext., ext. 5YR 3/4, 3/1, int. 5YR 3/4. Medium hard fired, oxidized. Stacked in firing. Rim frieze: star rosettes. Heavier than the standard Ephesian vessels.

EPH-50*
Olbia, Sector AGD, O-АГД-69-946, Kiev, Institute of Archaeology storeroom. Fr. of rim and upper body. H 6.1 × W 7, WT 0.2, ⌀ rim 16, 12%, RH 1.8. Fabric: standard, 2.5YR 6/8. Dull coat, ext. slightly mottled, ext. 10R 5/8, 10YR 3/1, int. 2.5YR 5/8. Medium hard fired, oxidized. Stacked in firing. Rim frieze: Ionian kyma. Small stamp, late.

EPH-51*
Myrmekion, M-48-363, St Petersburg IIMK RAN. Fr. of rim and upper body. H 5, WT 0.3, ⌀ rim 15, 8%, RH 2.6. Fabric: standard, Gley 1 5/N. Thin dull coat, Gley 1 3/N. Not too hard fired, reduced. Rim frieze: Ionian kyma. Late.

EPH-52*
Olbia, Sector NGS, O-НГС-05-905, Parutine, Olbia National Preserve storeroom. Fr. of rim and upper body. H 5 × W 5.2, WT 0.25, RH 1.5. Fabric: relatively fine and micaceous, 10YR 6/6. Thin dull coat ext., slightly lustrous int., ext. 10YR 2/1, int. 2.5YR 4/6. Medium hard fired, oxidized. Stacked in firing. Rim frieze: star rosettes. Tired stamps.

EPH-53*
Olbia, Sector NGS, O-НГС-05-908, Parutine, Olbia National Preserve storeroom. Fr. of rim and upper body. H 4.8 × W 8.3, WT 0.3, ⌀ rim 12, 24%, RH 1.7. Fabric: relatively fine and micaceous, many small lime inclusions and voids, 5YR 6/8. Thin dull coat, ext. 5YR 4/3, int. 2.5YR 4/6. Medium hard fired, oxidized. Rim frieze: star rosettes. Tired stamps.

Nike Racing a Two-Horse Chariot

EPH-54* (see also Fig. 73)
Olbia or Pantikapaion, Buračkov 30/2.1, Moscow State Historical Museum, Buračkov collection. Fr. of rim and upper part of body. H 6.5 × W 8, WT 0.4, ⌀ rim 16, 18%, RH 1.8. Fabric: light brown (no fresh break). Slightly lustrous blackish brown coat. Oxidized. Rim frieze: rosette 2/7. Main decoration: Nike racing two-horse chariot left; larger than the standard representation.

Saluting Pan

EPH-55
Olbia, O-1928-281, present whereabouts unknown. Fr. of rim and upper body. Rim frieze: horizontal S-spirals. Main decoration: saluting Pans flanking krater. Frieze separators: dots. One repair hole. The motif is also reported on a fragment from Čaika (Kovalenko 2007, fig. 16.11; Popova 2007, figs. 74–75).
– St Petersburg, IIMK RAN, photo archive neg. II 13930

Altar Figures

EPH-56
Olbia, Sector AGD, ashy grey clay layer, O-АГД-69-1257, Kiev, Institute of Archaeology storeroom. Fr. of mid- and lower body. H 3.9 × W 4.9, WT 0.26. Fabric: standard, 5YR 6/8. Dull mottled coat, ext. 2.5YR 3/3, 3/1, int. 2.5YR 4/4. Hard fired, oxidized. Stacked in firing. Multiple rim friezes: not preserved; astragal; rosette 9/8. Main decoration: altar fig. D.

Hunt and Animal Friezes

EPH-57*
Olbia, O-64-1798, Kiev, Institute of Archaeology storeroom. Four joining frs. of rim and body. H 4.3 × W 9, WT 0.25, ⌀ rim 13, 24%, RH 1.5. Fabric: standard, 5Y 5/1. Coat with dull lustre, Gley 1 3/N. Relatively hard fired, reduced. Rim frieze: Ionian kyma. Main decoration: mounted hunter rides left towards deer facing right; repeated.

EPH-58*
Olbia, Sector R25, O-P25-96-1441, Parutine, Olbia National Preserve storeroom. Fr. of upper body. H 3.6 × W 4. WT 0.3–0.55. Fabric: relatively fine and micaceous, Gley 1 6/10Y. Slightly lustrous coat, 10YR 3/1. Hard fired, reduced. Main decoration: horseman riding right.

EPH-59*
Olbia, Sector R25, O-P25-05-259, Parutine, Olbia National Preserve storeroom. Fr. of rim and upper body. H 4.2 × W 4, WT 0.3, ⌀ rim 12, 10%, RH 1.8. Fabric: relatively fine and micaceous, small lime inclusions, 5YR 6/6. Coat with metallic lustre ext., int. dull, ext. 5YR 3/1, int. 2.5YR 4/8. Medium hard fired, oxidized. Stacked in firing. Rim frieze: star rosettes. Main decoration: hunter with raised spear facing right. One repair hole.

EPH-60
Istros, His-533, Bucharest, Institute of Archaeology storeroom. Fr. of rim and upper body. H 3.5 × W 3. Oxidized. Rim frieze:

Ionian kyma. Main decoration: two raised hands with spears (hunt or Amazonomachy).
– Domăneanţu 2000, 63 cat. 294, pl. 19.

EPH-61*
Pantikapaion, M-58-522, Moscow, Puškin Museum of Fine Arts. Two joining frs. of rim and body. H 6 × W 10, ⌀ rim 14, 10%, RH 1.5. Fine black coat with slight lustre. Reduced. Rim frieze: horizontal S-spirals. Main decoration: dog chases rabbit to left; warrior behind shield facing left; male facing right confronts animal. Calyx: fern-like acanthus alternating with slender rounded petal. Frieze separators: dots.
– Zabelina 1984, 161 fig. 8a (number wrongly given as M-62-532; identified as Pergamene).

EPH-62
Istros, His-1002, Bucharest, Institute of Archaeology storeroom. Body fr. Reduced. Rim frieze: rosette 2. Main decoration: hunter right with lowered spear.

EPH-63*
Olbia, Sector NGS, O-НГС-02-39, Parutine, Olbia National Preserve storeroom. Fr. of rim and upper body, worn. H 4.85 × W 7, WT 0.33–0.4, ⌀ rim 11, RH 2.45. Fabric: relatively fine, slightly micaceous, a few small lime particles, some larger voids, 5YR 6/4–6/6. Thin firm slightly lustrous coat, dark at lip, ext. 7.5YR 2/0, int. 2.5YR 3/4, 7.5YR 2/0. Medium hard fired, oxidized. Stacked in firing. Rim frieze: astragal. Main decoration: animal jumping left, man (or Eros) walking right. Two repair holes.

EPH-64*
Olbia, O-52-2019, Kiev, Institute of Archaeology storeroom. Fr. of rim and upper body. Oxidized. Rim frieze: astragal. Main decoration: dog jumping left. Frieze separators: dots

EPH-65*
Olbia, Square Б5, O-Б5-76-148a, Kiev, Institute of Archaeology storeroom. Fr. of mid body. H 3.5 × W 5.3, WT 0.3. Fabric: standard, fine, 5YR 6/6. Fine, rather soapy coat, 2.5YR 5/8. Hard fired, oxidized. Main decoration: two dogs leap left, attacking feline(?) leaping right.

EPH-66*
Chersonesos, X-1965-85, St Petersburg, State Hermitage Museum. Fr. of rim and upper body. H 4.1, WT 0.35, RH 1.4. Reduced. Rim frieze: flower right. Main decoration: dog confronting boar. Frieze separators: dots.

EPH-67*
Istros, His-B 483/V 19410, Bucharest, Institute of Archaeology storeroom. Fr. of rim and body. H 5.7 × W 7.3. WT 0.35, ⌀ rim 11, 20%, RH 1.8. Fabric: standard, 5YR 6/8. Slightly lustrous coat, almost completely worn off ext. rim, 5YR 3/1. Relatively hard fired, oxidized. Multiple rim friezes: miniature acanthus scroll left; horizontal S-spirals. Main decoration: boar facing left. Menemachos.
– Domăneanţu 2000, 3 cat. 4, pl. 1 (attributed to Menemachos).

EPH-68*
Olbia, Sector NGS, O-НГС-04-352, Parutine, Olbia National Preserve storeroom. Fr. of mid-body. H 3.1 × W 3.8, WT 0.3. Fabric: relatively fine, micaceous, some small lime inclusions, 5Y 4/1. Dull coat, Gley 1 2.5/1. Hard fired, reduced. Main decoration: lion confronting boar. Cf. Laumonier 1977, 100 cat. 8425, pl. 22. VG Workshop.

EPH-69*
Istros, His-B 452/V 19373, Bucharest Institute of Archaeology storeroom. Body fr. H 3 × W 6, WT 0.35. Fabric: standard, fine, 5Y 7/1. Slightly lustrous coat, 5Y 2.5/1. Relatively hard fired, reduced. Main decoration: deer walking left, back foot of lion moving right? Calyx: acanthus X with slightly bent tip, wavy stem in between. Frieze separators: dots. VG Workshop
– Domăneanţu 2000, 15 cat. 57, pl. 4

EPH-70
Istros, His-416+1121, Bucharest, Institute of Archaeology storeroom. Two joining body frs. close to rim. H 3.5 × W 6.5, WT 0.4. Fabric: standard, fine, 5Y 7/1. Dull coat, 5Y 3/1. Relatively hard fired, reduced. Rim frieze: Ionian kyma with hatched tongue. Main decoration: deer facing left with head turned back. Frieze separators: dots
– Domăneanţu 2000, 3 cat. 5, pl. 1 (attributed to Menemachos).

EPH-71
Olbia, Sector E, House E14, over pavement 704, O-E14-71-1553, Kiev, Institute of Archaeology storeroom. Body fr. Reduced. Main decoration: dog chases large feline(?) left. Below, winged thunderbolt alternating with gorgoneia. Calyx: tip of straight acanthus. Frieze separators: dots. VG Workshop.
– L.M. Slavin & A.S. Rusjaeva, Očet 1971 (Kiev archive inv. 7032), pl. 16; Samojlova 1994, fig. 1.4; Rusjaeva & Nazarčuk, pl. 194.8.

EPH-72*
Istros, His-B 579/V 19480+V 8573 U, Bucharest Institute of Archaeology storeroom. Two joining frs. of rim and upper body. H 4 × W 8.3, WT 0.33, ⌀ rim 12, 20%, RH 1.2. Fabric: standard, 5Y 7/2. Dull coat, very worn, 5Y 3/1. Relatively hard fired, reduced. Rim frieze: Ionian kyma. Main decoration: dogs moving left.
– Domăneanţu 2000, 63 cat. 293, pl. 19.

EPH-73*
Olbia, Sector Sever-Zapad, O-СЗ-68-1844, Parutine, Olbia National Preserve storeroom. Fr. of rim and upper body. H 4.2 × W 4.8, WT 0.3, ⌀ rim 12, 11%, RH 1.4. Fabric: standard, fine, 7.5 6/6. Thin dull coat with slight lustre at ext. rim, 7.5YR 2.5/1. Relatively hard fired, oxidized. Rim frieze: Ionian kyma. Main decoration: feline (probably heraldic) around large eight-petalled rosette.

EPH-74*
Olbia, Sector NGS, О-НГС-91-211, Parutine, Olbia National Preserve storeroom. Body fr. H 5.3 × W 6.4, WT 0.3–0.4. Fabric: relatively fine and micaceous, small lime inclusions, 5Y 4/1. Thin firm slightly lustrous coat, Gley 1 2.5/N. Medium hard fired, reduced. Rim frieze: Ionian kyma. Main decoration: rabbit leaping left alternating with feline leaping right. Calyx A, with tall sepal with drooping tip.

EPH-75*
Ruminskoe/Za Rodinu, Рум-71-33, Moscow, State Historical Museum. Fr. of rim and body. ⌀ rim 11, 30%. Dull reddish coat, blackened at rim. Oxidized. Stacked in firing. Rim frieze: astragal. Main decoration: alternating rabbit and dog running left. Early.

Rabbit and Eagle

EPH-76
Porthmion, Sector G, sector 2, fill in rooms, П-87-109, St Petersburg IIMK RAN. Two joining frs. of rim and upper body. Rim frieze: box meander, cw. Main decoration: eagle and rabbit facing left. One repair hole. Another from Porthmion: Grzegrzółka 2010, 126–127 cat. 174.

EPH-77*
Olbia, Sector NGS, О-НГС-05-950, 983, 06-117, 263, Parutine, Olbia National Preserve storeroom. Four non-joining frs. of rim and body. H 6.5 × W 7.3, WT 0.28, ⌀ rim 14, 16%, RH 1.6. Fabric: relatively fine and micaceous, many small lime inclusions, 5YR 6/8. Thin coat with slight metallic sheen ext., int. dull, ext. 2.5YR 3/4, int. 2.5YR 4/8. Medium hard fired, oxidized. Stacked in firing. Rim frieze: guilloche left. Main decoration: eagle left; eight-petalled rosettes with petals separated by dots. Calyx: tip of slender rhomboidal petal. Incised anchor on ext. rim.

EPH-78*
Pantikapaion, palace foundation trench, M-84-62[d], Moscow, Puškin Museum of Fine Arts. Fr. of mid-body. H 2.1 × W 3.9, WT 0.25. Thin coat with pinkish metallic sheen. Oxidized. Main decoration: eagle left; eight-petalled rosette with petals separated by dots. Trace of calyx preserved.

Mantled Dancing Women

EPH-79*
Istros, His-506, Bucharest, Institute of Archaeology storeroom. Body fr. H 3.1 × W 2.2, WT 0.26. Fabric: standard, 5Y 6/1. Slightly lustrous coat, Gley 1 2.5/N. Relatively hard fired, reduced. Main decoration: lower bodies of two mantled dancers right. Woman completely wrapped in mantle, her right hand at her breast, wrapped in drapery; left hand grips edge of mantle of woman in front of her.

EPH-80*
Pantikapaion, M-57-2, Moscow, Puškin Museum of Fine Arts. Fr. of base and lower body. H 4 × W 4. Fabric: no fresh break for observation. Dull, reddish brown coat. Oxidized. Main decoration: lower bodies of two mantled dancers right. No calyx. Edge of base preserved.

Amazonomachy, Battle

EPH-81*
Pantikapaion, П-1914-8, St Petersburg, State Hermitage Museum. Complete. ⌀ rim 11, ⌀ base 4.2; vessel H 7.2; H:⌀ 1:1.5. Oxidized. Rim frieze: vertical combing. Main decoration: small horseman gallops right, alternating with two types of Amazons: Amazon with shield gesturing left; Amazon with battle axe striding right. Plain, concave base. Menemachos?

EPH-82*
Volna 1, СЗ-98-74, St Petersburg, State Hermitage Museum. Several joining frs. preserving large part of profile, lacking base. Oxidized. Rim frieze: Ionian kyma. Main decoration: alternating Greek and Amazon. Amazon with battle axe in left hand, shield on right arm, moving right. Greek with sword in right hand, shield on left arm, moving left. A second Greek, partially preserved, with shield on right arm. Calyx B.

EPH-83*
Olbia, Sector NGS, О-НГС-05-895, Parutine, Olbia National Preserve storeroom. Fr. of rim and upper body. H 5.1 × W 3.4, WT 0.3, RH 1.4. Fabric: relatively fine and micaceous, many small lime inclusions, 2.5YR 6/8. Coat with metallic sheen, 5YR 3/2. Medium hard fired, oxidized. Rim frieze: Lesbian kyma. Main decoration: Amazon with battle axe and shield left.

EPH-84*
Olbia, Sector R25, O-P25-93-990, Parutine, Olbia National Preserve storeroom. Fr. of rim and upper body. H 5.1 × W 6.4, WT 0.25, ⌀ rim 12, 16%, RH 1.4. Fabric: relatively fine and micaceous, 7.5YR 5/6. Dull coat, 7.5YR 3/1. Medium hard fired, oxidized. Rim frieze: Ionian kyma. Main decoration: three

Amazons. One moves right but looks left, axe in left hand; one moves left but looks right, axe in right hand; trace of a third, holding shield.

EPH-85*
Istros, His-B 430, Bucharest, Institute of Archaeology storeroom. Fr. of upper body. H 2.7 × W 3.5, WT 0.35. Fabric: standard, fine, 2.5YR 6/8. Dull coat, 2.5YR 4/3. Relatively hard fired, oxidized. Main decoration: Amazon striding left, shield on left arm, axe in right hand.
– Domăneanțu 2000, 73 cat. 346, pl. 22 (attributed to Heraios).

EPH-86*
Istros, His-1099, Bucharest Institute of Archaeology storeroom. Body fr. H 4 × W 3.5, WT 0.33. Fabric: fine, 7.5YR 6/6. Very worn shiny coat, 7.5YR 3/1. Medium hard fired, oxidized. Main decoration: Amazon striding left. Calyx B (tip of folded acanthus leaf visible).
– Domăneanțu 2000, 73 cat. 347, pl. 22 (attributed to Heraios).

EPH-87*
Myrmekion, M-58-830, St Petersburg, IIMK RAN. Fr. of mid- and lower body. H 4.4, WT 0.33. Fabric: standard, fine, 2.5YR 5/8. Thin, slightly lustrous coat, 2.5YR 4/8. Hard fired, oxidized. Main decoration: lower part of two Amazons. Calyx B1.

EPH-88*
Olbia, Sector E6–7, squares 581w, 561w, humus, O-E6-7-62-240, Parutine, Olbia National Preserve storeroom. Fr. of mid- and lower body. H 5.9 × W 6.8, WT 0.35. Fabric: relatively fine, micaceous, small lime inclusions, 7.5YR 6/4. Thin coat with slight lustre, 7.5YR 2.5/1. Hard fired, oxidized. Rim frieze: Ionian kyma? Main decoration: two Amazons with shields, one striding left, one right. Calyx A1.

EPH-89
Olbia, Sector NGS, О-НГС-05-400, Parutine, Olbia National Preserve storeroom. Fr. of rim and upper body. H 3.8 × W 4.3, WT 0.3, RH 1.3. Fabric: relatively fine and micaceous, many small lime inclusions, 5YR 6/8. Thin dull coat, lustrous at stack marks, ext. 2.5YR 4/8, 2.5/1, int. 2.5YR 4/8. Medium hard fired, oxidized. Stacked in firing. Rim frieze: Ionian kyma. Main decoration: two Amazons, one with axe, one with shield.

EPH-90*
Olbia, O-52-1978, Kiev, Institute of Archaeology storeroom. Fr. of rim and body. H 6.2 × W 8.8, WT 0.28, ⌀ rim 16, 18 %, RH 2. Fabric: standard, 7.5YR 6/3. Dull coat, 5YR 3/1. Hard fired, oxidized. Multiple rim friezes: Lesbian kyma; rosette 6. Main decoration: Amazonomachy (top of battle ax preserved). My(…).

EPH-91*
Olbia, Sector AGD, О-АГД-71-1588, Kiev, Institute of Archaeology storeroom. Fr. of rim and upper body. Oxidized. Stacked in firing. Rim frieze: box meander, cw. Main decoration: Amazonomachy (battle ax preserved). Frieze separators: dots.

EPH-92 (see Fig. 78)
Olbia, Sector NGS, House III-1 Stove 329/71, О-НГС-91-618, 92-735, Parutine, Olbia National Preserve storeroom. Complete profile; rim, base, and body, two joining frs.; one non-joining fr. H 5.9 × W 6.8, WT 0.3–0.4, ⌀ rim 13, ⌀ base 4.5. Fabric: relatively fine and micaceous, small lime inclusions, 2.5YR 5/8. Thin firm coat, blackened at lip int. and at rim and upper body ext., slightly lustrous, ext. 10R 5/6, 5YR 3/1, int. 10R 5/6. Medium hard fired, oxidized. Stacked in firing. Rim frieze: Ionian kyma. Main decoration: Amazonomachy (parts of five figures): with axe moving right, with spear and shield facing right, lower parts of three more. Calyx C. Medallion: rosette A. Monogram PAR?
– Guldager Bilde 2010, 277 cat. F-13, pl. 170.

EPH-93
Olbia, Sector NGS, О-НГС-06-425, Parutine, Olbia National Preserve storeroom. Fr. of base and lower body. H 4.4 × W 2.7, WT 0.3. Fabric: relatively fine and micaceous, some small lime inclusions, 5YR 6/6. Coat with metallic sheen ext., int. duller, ext. 7.5YR 3/2, int. 2.5YR 4/8. Medium hard fired, oxidized. Stacked in firing. Main decoration: leg and part of shield of warrior striding left. Calyx C. Medallion: rosette B.

EPH-94*
Olbia, Sector NGS, О-НГС-92-528, Parutine, Olbia National Preserve storeroom. Fr. of base and lower body. H 7.2 × W 8, WT 0.22–0.35, ⌀ base 4. Fabric: relatively fine and micaceous, a few lime particles and voids, 2.5YR 6/8. Dull coat int., ext. with a slight metallic sheen, ext. 2.5YR 4/6, 4/3, int. 2.5YR 5/8. Medium hard fired, oxidized. Main decoration: lower leg and foot of striding figure, probably warrior. Calyx C. Medallion: rosette A.

EPH-95*
Olbia, Sector NGS, О-НГС-86-14, Parutine, Olbia National Preserve storeroom? (not found in 2009). Fr. of rim and upper body. H 5.7 × W 5.85, WT 0.2–0.4, ⌀ rim 12, RH 1.95. Fabric: relatively fine and micaceous, some voids, 5YR 5/6, 10YR 5/3. Thick firm semi-lustrous coat, slightly darkened at rim, ext. 2.5YR 3/4, int. 2.5YR 3/6. Medium hard fired, oxidized. Rim frieze: star rosettes. Main decoration: Greek warrior striding left, his back to viewer, wearing anatomic cuirass over short chiton, helmet, round shield, spear in raised right hand. One repair hole.

EPH-96*
Olbia, Sector NGS, О-НГС-88-1, Parutine, Olbia National Preserve storeroom. Fr. of rim and upper body; worn. H 4.9 × W 4.8, WT 0.23–0.42, ⌀ rim 12, 9%, RH 2.1. Fabric: relatively fine and micaceous, some large voids, 2.5YR 5/8, 7.5YR 6/6. Thin firm slightly lustrous coat, darkened at rim, ext. 2.5YR 3/4, 5YR 3/2, 10YR 3/1, int. 2.5YR 3/4, 10YR 3/1. Medium hard fired, oxidized. Stacked in firing. Rim frieze: rosette 2/7. Main decoration: Greek warrior with anatomic cuirass holding round shield and sword, moving right. Frieze separators: dots.

Other Mythological Subjects

EPH-97*
Olbia, Sector R25, O-P25-92-3230, Parutine, Olbia National Preserve storeroom. Two non-joining frs. of upper body. H 4.5 × W 5.2, WT 0.3. Fabric: relatively fine and micaceous, 2.5YR 5/8. Dull coat, more lustrous at top, ext. 2.5YR 4/6, 3/1, int. 2.5YR 4/6. Medium hard fired, oxidized. Stacked in firing. Main decoration: Dionysos-Eros riding side saddle on panther left (twice); lower legs of Aphrodite Diadumene at right. Calyx B2. The iconography emulates Pergamene; see PER-91* (Dionysos-Eros) and PER-9 (Aphrodite Diadumene). VG Workshop.

EPH-98*
Istros, His-V 19485, Bucharest, Institute of Archaeology storeroom. Rim fr. H 3.5 × W 3, WT 0.28, RH 1.2. Fabric: standard, fine, 5YR 6/8. Dull coat, ext. 2.5YR 5/6, 2.5/1, int. 2.5YR 5/6. Relatively hard fired, oxidized. Stacked in firing. Rim frieze: Ionian kyma. Main decoration: Dionysos-Eros riding side saddle on panther left. VG Workshop.
– Domăneanțu 2000, 14 cat. 55, pl. 4 (attributed to Belles Méduses).

EPH-99*
Pantikapaion, M-46-5510, Moscow, Puškin Museum of Fine Arts. Fr. of base and lower body. H 6.5 × W 5.5, ⌀ base 4.6. Dull blotchy reddish brown coat. Oxidized. Main decoration: dancing Satyr? No calyx. Plain, concave base on low ring foot, signed MEN[...]. Menemachos.

EPH-100*
Pantikapaion, M-47-137, Moscow, Puškin Museum of Fine Arts. Fr. of upper body. H 6 × W 5, WT 0.3. Fabric: fine, micaceous, grey. Dull black coat. Reduced. Rim frieze: Ionian kyma. Main decoration: centaur walking left with branch of tree over left shoulder. Frieze separators: dots.

EPH-101*
Pantikapaion, П-1873-116, St Petersburg, State Hermitage Museum. Complete profile, lacking minor frs. ⌀ rim 11.4; vessel H 6.6; H:⌀ 1:1.7. Oxidized. Stacked in firing. Rim frieze: guilloche right. Main decoration: judgement of Paris. Paris seated with dog beneath, Hermes with caduceus, Athena with helmet, Aphrodite sitting on rock with Eros on her lap, Hera standing with tall polos and sceptre. Plain, concave base, signed MENEMACHOU. Menemachos. Surmoulage? The letters are rather small, and the stamps of the figures very tired.

EPH-102
Olbia, East Trade Building, Room 6, O-47-5053. Two joining frs. of rim and body. ⌀ rim 7. Rim frieze: Ionian kyma. Main decoration: judgement of Paris. Hera standing with spear, Aphrodite with Eros on lap (reversed verison), Athena standing with spear and round shield. Menemachos?
– Levi 1956, 80, fig. 49.2.

EPH-103*
Pantikapaion, M-45-1668, Moscow, Puškin Museum of Fine Arts. Body fr. H 3 × W 3. Dull black coat. Reduced. Main decoration: woman with tall polos and sceptre in right hand (Hera). Menemachos?

EPH-104*
Pantikapaion, palace foundation trench, M-84-31, Moscow, Puškin Museum of Fine Arts. Fr. of mid- and lower body with tiny part of base. H 5.5 × W 8, WT 0.4. Fabric: fine. Thin dull red-brownish coat covering well. Hard fired, oxidized. Main decoration: Herakles with Kerberos at right, Herakles with Keryniean hind at left; scenes separated by Ionic columns. Calyx: low calyx of alternating ovoid petals and small straight acanthus. Plain, concave base with large diameter. VG Workshop/Menemachos.
– Košelenko 1992, fig. 23.

EPH-105*
Olbia, Sector NGS, О-НГС-06-469, Parutine, Olbia National Preserve storeroom. Fr. of upper body. H 3.3 × W 4.3, WT 0.25. Fabric: fine, micaceous, 5YR 6/6. Coat with metallic sheen ext., int. duller, ext. 10YR 2/1, 2.5YR 4/6, int. 7.5YR 3/2. Hard fired, oxidized. Stacked in firing. Main decoration: Herakles in high relief with Kerberos right. Menemachos.

EPH-106*
Pantikapaion, M-47-183, Moskow, Puškin Museum of Fine Arts. Three joining frs. of base and lower body. H 11.5 × W 7.5, ⌀ base 5.5. Black coat with slight lustre. Reduced. Main decoration: Herakles and Nemean lion; feet of standing and walking figures preserved around base. No calyx. Plain, concave base on low ring foot, signed MENEMACHOU. Menemachos.
– Zabelina 1984, 157 fig. 4a.

EPH-107*
Istros, His-642, Bucharest Institute of Archaeology storeroom. Body fr. H 3.6 × W 3, WT 0.5. Fabric: standard, 5Y 6/1. Slightly lustrous coat, Gley 1 2.5/N. Relatively hard fired, reduced. Main decoration: frontal Skylla with vegetal skirt and naked upper body, her right hand at ship(?); below, person with arms over head (swimming?). Cf. Greifenhagen 1963, fig. 51; Grzegrzółka 2010, 87 cat. 86.

Symplegmata

EPH-108*
Kepoi. Ке-67-140, Moscow, State Historical Museum. Fr. of base and lower body. ⌀ base 5. Thin, blotchy coat, ext. with slight lustre. Reduced. Main decoration: symplegma, with parts of two couples preserved. Plain, slightly concave base; graffito ARCH. Menemachos.
– Usačeva 1978, fig. 1.28.

EPH-109
Pantikapaion(?), inv. CA 2285, Paris, Musée du Louvre. Complete. Multiple rim friezes: horizontal S-spirals; astragal. Main decoration: three symplegmata alternating with three Erotes playing music, with vegetal spacers. Eros with kithara; symplegma (man taking woman from behind, right); Eros playing aulos; vine; symplegma on *kline* left; vertical floral stem (with Eros?); Eros playing harp; symplegma with man taking woman from behind on *kline*, right; vertical floral stem. Plain, concave base with low false ring foot. Frieze separators: dots. Menemachos.
– Jentel 1964, 116 cat. 1, pl. XI.

Feline Phallus

EPH-110*
Pantikapaion, M-47-141 Moscow, Puškin Museum of Fine Arts. Fr. of rim and upper body. H 6.5 × W 6.5, WT 0.4. ⌀ rim 16, RH 2. Fabric: fine, micaceous, grey. Dull black coat. Reduced. Rim frieze: star rosettes. Main decoration: horseman with raised right arm on prancing horse, right, confronting feline phallus. Identical phallus: Popova 2007, figs. 74–75. The combination of the hunter with the feline phallus is probably intended to underline the potency(!) of the rider.

EPH-111*
Chersonesos, X-1952-155, St Petersburg, State Hermitage Museum. Fr. of rim and upper body. H 4.4, WT 0.3, ⌀ rim 13, RH 1.5. Fabric: standard, 2.5YR 6/8. Thin slightly lustrous coat, ext. 2.5YR 4/4, int. 10R 5/8. Oxidized. Stacked in firing. No rim frieze. Main decoration: feline phallus right, ejaculating. Frieze separators: dots. Secondarily burnt. One repair hole.

EPH-112*
Pantikapaion, no. unknown, St Petersburg, State Hermitage Museum. Complete. Rim frieze: crossed dotted lines. Main decoration divided into panels by four columns: two grotesques flank feline phallus (twice), grotesque Eros, Eros playing syrinx. Below, relief inscription (inscribed in the mould): *hedypoios kallipygos* (sweet-drinking, pretty bottom). Calyx: single row of small rounded petals with central vein. Plain, flat base with wide ring foot. VG Workshop/Menemachos. Single instance of crossed dotted lines not associated exclusively with Menemachos.
– Stephani 1879, pl. VI.11; Laumonier 1977, 174.

Dolphins

EPH-113
Pantikapaion, Cistern N 179, 96-no. unknown. Two joining frs. of mid- and lower body. Main decoration: heraldic dolphins flank rosette 11, three dots above and below. Calyx: traces of vegetation. Frieze separators: dots.
– Tolstikov & Zhuravlev 2004, pl. 101.6.

EPH-114
Olbia, O-1925-905, present whereabouts unknown. Fr. of rim and most of body. Rim frieze: Lesbian kyma. Main decoration: (probably heraldic) dolphin(s) around large rosette 9/12. Calyx B. One repair hole.
– Semenov-Zuser 1931, fig. 17; St Petersburg, IIMK RAN, photo archive neg. II 19420.

EPH-115
Olbia, O-1910-993+997, present whereabouts unknown. Two joining frs. of rim and upper body. Rim frieze: rosette 2/7. Main decoration: heraldic dolphins around rosette 9/11.
– St Petersburg, IIMK RAN, archive inv. 4060.519.8 (pl. I).

EPH-116
Olbia, O-87-996, Olbia Museum. Complete. Oxidized. Multiple rim friezes: Ionian kyma; vertical S-spirals. Main decoration: heraldic dolphins flank palmette. Calyx C. One repair hole.

EPH-117*
Chersonesos, X-1952-161, St Petersburg, State Hermitage Museum. Fr. of mid- and lower body. H 3, WT 0.3. Fabric: no fresh break for observation. Thin slightly lustrous coat, Gley 1 2.5/N. Reduced. Rim frieze: box meander, cw. Main decoration: heraldic(?) dolphin(s), palmette. Another bowl with dolphins from Chersonesos: Chlystun 1996, 155, fig. 1.

EPH-118
Olbia, Sector NGS O-НГС-02-179, Parutine, Olbia National Preserve storeroom. Fr. of rim and upper body; very worn. H 5.9 ×

W 7.5, WT 0.22–0.67, ⌀ rim 14, 15%, RH 2.4. Fabric: relatively fine and micaceous, some small lime particles, a few minute grey stones, small voids, 5YR 5/6, 6/8. Thin firm slightly lustrous coat, especially on upper body ext. and on lip int., ext. 10R 5/6, 2.5YR 4/4, 3/0, int. 2.5YR 4/6, 3/0. Medium hard fired, oxidized. Stacked in firing. Multiple rim friezes: Ionian kyma; guilloche left. Main decoration: probably heraldic dolphins flanking acanthus flower.

EPH-119*
Myrmekion. M-58-171(?), St Petersburg IIMK RAN. Body fr. H 5, WT 0.4. Fabric: standard, 2.5YR 5/8, core 5YR 6/6. Thin coat with slight lustre, ext. 2.5YR 4/8, 2.5/2, int. 2.5YR 4/8. Oxidized. Stacked in firing. Rim frieze: Ionian kyma. Main decoration: two dolphins right (two different stamps) and part of Eros with torch. Another Eros with dolphins, perhaps from Olbia: Uvarov 1851, pl. XIX.12.

EPH-120*
Olbia, inv. A 2440, Nikolaev, Historical Museum. Complete profile, lacking rim fr.; joined from a number of frs. ⌀ rim 13.3, RH 2.1, ⌀ base 2.4; vessel H 7; H:⌀ 1:1.9. Dull red coat, brown patch on upper part ext. Oxidized. Stacked in firing. Rim frieze: Ionian kyma. Main decoration: heraldic dolphins flanking krater. Calyx: 'nelumbo' with small acanthus leaf in front repeated eight times. Medallion: rosette A.

EPH-121*
Olbia, Sector NGS, О-НГС-02-302, Parutine, Olbia National Preserve storeroom. Fr. of rim and upper body. H 5.8 × W 8.4, WT 0.3–0.5, ⌀ rim 13, 22%, RH 1.85. Fabric: relatively fine and micaceous, some minute lime particles, a few grey stones, some voids, 5YR 5/6. Thin firm slightly lustrous coat, slightly mottled at rim ext., ext. 2.5YR 4/6, 10YR 3/2, int. 2.5YR 4/8. Medium hard fired, oxidized. Stacked in firing. Multiple rim friezes: wave meander, upside-down; Ionian kyma. Main decoration: dolphin right, probably one of a heraldic pair.

EPH-122
Myrmekion, M-52-311, 311a, St Petersburg IIMK RAN. Two non-joining frs. of rim and upper body. H 4.7, WT 0.23, ⌀ rim 11.5, RH 1.8. Fabric: standard, with lime, 7.5YR 5/3. Thin dull coat, ext. 7.5YR 4/2, 2.5/1, int. 7.5YR 4/2. Not too hard fired, oxidized. Stacked in firing. Rim frieze: miniature stylized acanthus scroll left. Main decoration: dolphins left.

EPH-123*
Istros, His-V 19454, Bucharest, Institute of Archaeology storeroom. Body fr. H 3 × W 3.8, WT 0.3. Fabric: standard, fine, 7.5YR 7/4. Dull coat, worn, 7.5YR 4/1. Medium hard fired, oxidized.

Rim frieze: rosette 7. Main decoration: dolphins left. Additional bowls with dolphins at Istros: Domăneanţu 2000, 31, 32 cats. 122, 127, pls. 8, 9.

EPH-124*
Olbia, Sector I, Pit N, ash layer, О-И-48-3830, Kiev, Institute of Archaeology storeroom. Fr. of rim and upper body. H 4.4 × W 6.7, WT 0.2, ⌀ rim 12, 17%, RH 1.6. Fabric: standard, 5YR 6/8. Dull coat, ext. 2.5YR 4/8, 4/3, 3/3, int. 2.5YR 4/8. Relatively hard fired, oxidized. Stacked in firing. Rim frieze: Ionian kyma. Main decoration: dolphin left.

EPH-125
Olbia, Sector NGS, О-НГС-92-263, Parutine, Olbia National Preserve storeroom. Body fr. H 5.4 × W 6.1, WT 0.3. Fabric: relatively fine and micaceous, 7.5YR 6/6. Dull coat, 7.5YR 3/1. Medium hard fired, oxidized. Main decoration: tail of dolphin, foot of Eros? Calyx A1.

Thunderbolt

EPH-126
Kepoi, no. unknown, Moscow, State Historical Museum. Three non-joining frs. of rim, body and base. Rim frieze: astragal. Main decoration: winged thunderbolt. Calyx: rhomboidal petal, palmette or acanthus leaf. Plain base with false ring foot. Menemachos.
– Usačeva 1978, fig. 1.15.

EPH-127*
Pantikapaion, palace foundation trench, M-85-56, Moscow, Puškin Museum of Fine Arts. Two joining frs. of rim and body. H 5.1 × W 7.6, WT 0.15, ⌀ rim 15, 15%, RH 1.5. Dull red coat. Oxidized. Stacked in firing. Rim frieze: rosette 2/7 (M). Main decoration: winged thunderbolt, large rosette 9/10. Calyx: tip of ovoid petal preserved. Menemachos.
– Košelenko 1992, fig. 23.

EPH-128
Porthmion, П-73-474, Kerč History and Culture Reserve. Fr. of upper body. Oxidized. Rim frieze: miniature acanthus scroll right. Main decoration: thunderbolt. Menemachos.
– Grzegrzółka 2010, 176–177 cat. 285.

EPH-129 (see Fig. 74)
Olbia, О-1910-998, present whereabouts unknown. Fr. of rim and large part of body. Rim frieze: rosette 1. Main decoration: eagle, winged thunderbolt. Calyx C. Menemachos?
– St Petersburg, IIMK RAN, archive inv. 4059.519.7 (pl. II).

EPH-130
Olbia, Sector R25, O-P25-96-978, Parutine, Olbia National Preserve storeroom. Two joining frs. of upper body close to rim. H 4.5 × W 5.7, WT 0.33. Fabric: relatively fine and micaceous, small lime inclusions, 5Y 5/2. Thin dull coat, Gley 1 2.5/N. Medium hard fired, reduced. Rim frieze: rosette 1, small. Main decoration: thunderbolt at left, rosette(?) at right. Menemachos?

EPH-131*
Myrmekion, M-58-307 or 397, St Petersburg IIMK RAN. Fr. of rim and upper body. H 4.4, WT 0.37, ⌀ rim 11.5, 20%, RH 1.85. Fabric: standard, slightly porous, 2.5YR 5/8. Thin dull coat, slightly blotchy, ext. 2.5YR 4/8, int. 2.5YR 5/8. Oxidized. Rim frieze: rosette 5. Main decoration: thunderbolt. Another bowl with thunderbolts at Myrmekion: Bernhard 1959, 58 cat. 256; Sztetyłło 1976, 87, fig. 81.a. Workshop Circle 1.

EPH-132
Istros, His-V 19437, Bucharest, Institute of Archaeology Storeroom. Fr. of rim and upper body. H 4.7 × W 3.4, WT 0.25, RH 1.7. Fabric: standard, fine, 5YR 7/6. Dull coat, mottled ext., ext. 2.5YR 5/8, 3/1, int. 5YR 6/4. Medium hard fired, oxidized. Stacked in firing. Rim frieze: rosette 7 (double-stamped). Main decoration: thunderbolt, rosette 10. Workshop Circle 1.
– Domăneanțu 2000, 76 cat. 367, pl. 24 (attributed to Heraios).

EPH-133*
Bol'šoj Kastel', БК-82-31, Černomorskoe Museum of Historical Lore. Rim fr. H 3.3, ⌀ rim 14, RH 2. Fabric: 7.5YR 6/6. Fine dull coat, ext. 2.5YR 4/4–4/6, int. 5YR 2.5/2, at rim 2.5YR 4/6. Oxidized. No rim frieze. Main decoration: thunderbolt with large wing. Workshop Circle 1.

Unidentified and Miscellaneous Figures

EPH-134*
Istros, His-644, Bucharest, Institute of Archaeology storeroom. Fr. of upper body. H 3 × W 3.1. Oxidized. Main decoration: figure clad in mantle walking right (same as on EPH-135*).
– Domăneanțu 2000, 91 cat. 437, pl. 30.

EPH-135*
Istros, His-1128, Bucharest, Institute of Archaeology storeroom. Fr. of lower body. H 2 × W 2, WT 0.3. Fabric: standard, fine, 5YR 7/6. Dull coat, ext. 5YR 4/6, int. 5YR 3/3. Relatively hard fired, oxidized. Calyx: tall lotus petal with figure clad in mantle walking right (same as on EPH-134).
– Domăneanțu 2000, 91 cat. 438, pl. 30.

EPH-136*
Istros, His-746, Bucharest, Institute of Archaeology storeroom. Body fr. Reduced. Rim frieze: Ionian kyma. Main decoration: frontal male head, possibly wearing comic mask, right arm bent.

EPH-137
Olbia, Sector NGS, House III-2 R 164/76, O-НГС-88-292, Parutine, Olbia National Preserve storeroom. Fr. of rim and upper body. H 3.6 × W 4.45, WT 0.25–0.3, ⌀ rim 10, RH 1.2. Fabric: relatively fine, many small lime particles, 10YR 4/1. Slightly lustrous coat, ext. 2.5Y 2/0, int. 10YR 3/1. Very hard fired, reduced. Rim frieze: X's. Main decoration: upper part of standing(?) figure; rosette with eight pointed petals.
– Guldager Bilde 2010, 283 cat. F-78, pl. 183.

EPH-138*
Olbia, Sector NGS, O-НГС-06-137, Parutine, Olbia National Preserve storeroom. Fr. of mid-body. H 2.7 × W 3, WT 0.3. Fabric: fine, micaceous, 5Y 5/1. Slightly lustrous coat, Gley 1 3/N. Medium hard fired, reduced. Rim frieze: box meander. Main decoration: frontal female, man with raised arm.

EPH-139*
Olbia, Sector NGS, O-НГС-05-753, Parutine, Olbia National Preserve storeroom. Fr. of upper body. H 2.4 × W 2.1, WT 0.35. Fabric: fine, micaceous, 5YR 7/6. Thin dull coat, ext. 5YR 3/1, int. 2.5YR 4/6. Medium hard fired, oxidized. Stacked in firing. Main decoration: woman in high relief, right, curving fingers around unidentified object; left arm reaches up. One repair hole.

EPH-140*
Istros, His-651, 1161, Bucharest, Institute of Archaeology storeroom. Two non-joining body frs. H 2.8 × W 1.9, WT 0.26. Fabric: standard, 5YR 6/8. Dull coat, 2.5YR 5/8. Medium hard fired, oxidized. Main decoration: frontal Silenos mask. Identical: Pappa 2000, pl. 58 (complete bowl with calyx B and rosette A, making the attribution secure). Monogram PAR.
– Domăneanțu 2000, 128 cats. 624, 625, pl. 44.

EPH-141
Pantikapaion, palace foundation trench, M-89-illegible 17, Moscow, Puškin Museum of Fine Arts. Fr. of base and lower body. H 4 × W 4, WT 0.25. Thin dull black coat, partially missing. Reduced. Main decoration: unidentified figures. Calyx: two rows of small pointed petals with central vein. Plain base.

EPH-142*
Chersonesos, X-1952-156, St Petersburg, State Hermitage Museum. Fr. of base and body. H 4.2, WT 0.2, ⌀ base 5.5.

Fabric: no fresh break for observation, Gley 1 5/N. Thin dull black coat, Gley 1 3/N. Reduced. Main decoration: feet of figures. No calyx. Plain concave base with low ring foot, signed M[...]. Menemachos.

EPH-143
Istros, His-1927-1942-V 8570 X, Z, Bucharest Institute of Archaeology storeroom. Two non-joining frs. of base and lower body. Reduced. Main decoration: unidentified. Plain, concave base. Menemachos?

EPH-144*
Olbia, Sector NGS, О-НГС-92-292, Parutine, Olbia National Preserve storeroom. Fr. of base and lower body. Reduced. Main decoration: feet of figures? Medallion: seven- or eight-petalled rosette separated by hatched tongues.

EPH-145*
Olbia, Sector Sever-Zapad, O-СЗ-68-1827+1828, Parutine, Olbia National Preserve storeroom. Two joining frs. of base and lower body. H 5.8 × W 6.3, WT 0.28, ⌀ base 3.5. Fabric: standard, 10YR6/3. Thin slightly lustrous coat, almost completely missing on ext., int. 10YR2/2. Relatively hard fired, reduced. Main decoration: feet of figure walking left. Calyx: straight acanthus alternating with sceptre with twisted stem and broad lotus petal with twisted central vein. Medallion: rosette B, var. My(...).

EPH-146*
Olbia, Sector R25, O-P25-93-1398, Parutine, Olbia National Preserve storeroom. Fr. of mid- and lower body. H 5.3 × W 3.5, WT 0.5. Fabric: relatively fine and micaceous, small lime inclusions, 5YR 6/8. Dull coat ext., int. slightly lustrous, ext. 2.5YR 4/6, int. 2.5YR 4/8. Medium hard fired, oxidized. Stacked in firing. Main decoration: figures standing or walking left. Calyx: slender petals.

EPH-147*
Olbia, Sector AGD, О-АГД-71-1724, Kiev, Institute of Archaeology storeroom. Fr. of mid- and lower body. H 4.3 × W 3.1, WT 0.25. Fabric: standard, fine, 5Y 5/1. Dull coat, 5Y 2.5/1. Relatively hard fired, reduced. Main decoration: legs of person walking right. Calyx: vertical floral element with bunch of grapes at top. Frieze separators: dots.

Inanimate Motifs

EPH-148*
Istros, His-441, Bucharest, Institute of Archaeology storeroom. Rim fr. H 3.7 × W 2.5, WT 0.2, RH 1.3. Fabric: standard, fine, some voids, 7.5YR 7/6. Dull lustre, ext. 5YR 4/6, 10YR 3/1, int. 5YR 4/6, 10YR 3/1. Relatively hard fired, oxidized. Stacked in firing. Rim frieze: large dots. Main decoration: volute kraters. Menemachos.
– Domăneanțu 2000, 35 cat. 146, pl. 10 (attributed to Monogram PAR).

EPH-149*
Istros, His-713, Bucharest, Institute of Archaeology storeroom. Fr. of lower body and edge of base. H 2.5 × W 3. Oxidized. Main decoration: lower part of krater with fluted body. Menemachos.
– Domăneanțu 2000, 94 cat. 454, pl. 30.

EPH-150*
Istros, His-647, 720s, Bucharest, Institute of Archaeology storeroom. Two non-joining frs. of rim and body. H 2.1 × W 4, WT 0.33. Fabric: standard, 5Y 5/1. Coat with dull lustre, Gley 1 2.5/N. Relatively hard fired, reduced. Rim frieze: Lesbian kyma. Main decoration: volute krater with ribbed body; vertical floral element.
– Domăneanțu 2000, 35 cat. 145, pl. 10.

EPH-151*
Myrmekion, Sector И, courtyard VII, M-49-139, St Petersburg IIMK RAN. Fr. of rim and upper body. H 5.7, WT 0.25, ⌀ rim 13, 5%, RH 2. Fabric: fine, a few light-reflecting particles, 7.5YR 6/4. Slightly lustrous coat, 7.5YR 2.5/1. Oxidized. Rim frieze: astragal. Main decoration: stemmed volute krater.

EPH-152*
Istros, His-B 473, V 8573 E, Bucharest, Institute of Archaeology storeroom. Two non-joining frs. of rim and body. H 3.7 × W 3.8, WT 0.23, RH 1.6. Fabric: standard, 5YR 6/8. Slightly lustrous coat, ext. 5YR 3/1, 4/6, int. 2.5YR 5/8. Relatively hard fired, oxidized. Stacked in firing. Rim frieze: Ionian kyma. Main decoration: amphora.

EPH-153*
Istros, His-969+V 19402, Bucharest, Institute of Archaeology storeroom. Two joining frs. of mid- and lower body. H 5 × W 6, WT 0.3. Fabric: standard, 5YR 6/6. Dull coat, pitted, 5YR 3/1. Relatively hard fired, oxidized. Main decoration: rosette 10/12. Calyx: rhomboidal petals alternating with vertical miniature acanthus-flower scroll.
– Domăneanțu 2000, 32 cat. 126, pl. 9 (attributed to Monogram PAR).

EPH-154*
Istros, His-B 487/V 8575 L, Bucharest, Institute of Archaeology storeroom. Body fr. Oxidized. Main decoration: rosette 10/12.

EPH-155*
Myrmekion, M-47-253, St Petersburg IIMK RAN. Fr. of rim and upper body. H 4.6, WT 0.4, ⌀ rim 13, 20%, RH 1.45. Fabric: standard, 2.5YR 5/8. Thin dull coat, ext. 2.5YR 4/8, 5YR 2.5/1, int. 2.5YR 4/8. Oxidized. Stacked in firing. Rim frieze: large dots. Main decoration: palmette alternates with complex double rosette. Outer rosette 11/8, inner rosette 10/16. Outer rosette also occurs on early PSC bowls (EPH-962*, EPH-969*, EPH-970*).

EPH-156
Istros, His-1106, Bucharest, Institute of Archaeology storeroom. Body fr. close to rim. H 4.5 × W 3, WT 0.23. Fabric: standard, fine, 2.5YR 6/8. Coat with slight lustre, ext. 5YR 3/1, int. 7.5YR 3/2, 2.5YR 3/4. Relatively hard fired, oxidized. Rim frieze: large dots. Main decoration: rosette and palmette.
– Domăneanțu 2000, 140 cat. 697, pl. 50.

EPH-157*
Istros, His-V 19315, Bucharest, Institute of Archaeology storeroom. Body fr. close to rim. Oxidized. Stacked in firing. Rim frieze: Ionian kyma. Main decoration: rosette 9/12, five-rayed sun wheel.
– Domăneanțu 2000, 106 cat. 538, pl. 35.

EPH-158*
Istros, His-V 19415, Bucharest, Institute of Archaeology storeroom. Fr. of rim and upper body. Oxidized. Rim frieze: miniature acanthus scroll left. Main decoration: floral element. Menemachos.
– Domăneanțu 2000, 32 cat. 125, pl. 9 (attributed to Monogram PAR).

EPH-159*
Istros, His-V 19403, Bucharest, Institute of Archaeology storeroom. Body fr.
H 3.2 × W 3.6. Oxidized. Multiple rim friezes: vertical S-spirals; hanging leaf. Wall: heart bud upside down.
– Domăneanțu 2000, 83 cat. 399, pl. 27.

EPH-160*
Olbia, Sector NGS, O-НГС-05-160, 910, Parutine, Olbia National Preserve storeroom. Two non-joining frs. of rim and body. H 5 × W 7.5, WT 0.25, ⌀ rim 12, 20%, RH 1.7. Fabric: relatively fine and micaceous, some small lime inclusions, 5YR 6/8. Thin dull coat, 2.5YR 4/8, 3/1. Medium hard fired, oxidized. Stacked in firing. Rim frieze: astragal. Main decoration: 'double axes', groups of three-dot berries above and below. For brief comment on the double-axe motif, see Laumonier 1977, 233 cat. 1209, pl. 52.

B *Scroll Decoration*

Full-Body Acanthus Scroll

EPH-161*
Chersonesos, pit И, X-1908-19, St Petersburg, State Hermitage Museum. Complete profile; three large non-joining fragments. H 7, ⌀ rim 12, ⌀ base 3.4. Fabric: standard. Oxidized. Stacked in firing. Rim frieze: miniature acanthus-flower scroll left. Main decoration: scroll left with rosette 2/7 and groups of three dot berries. Medallion: rosette A. Monogram PAR.

EPH-162*
Olbia, Agora, squares 646, 680, Room "E", Southwest house, yellow clay layer, O-66-1627, Kiev, Institute of Archaeology storeroom. Fr. of base and lower body. H 6.4 × W 7.7, WT 0.3. ⌀ base 4. Fabric: standard. Lustrous coat. Relatively hard fired, oxidized. Main decoration: scroll left with groups of three-dot berries. Medallion: rosette A. Secondarily burnt

EPH-163*
Olbia, O-52-1214, Kiev, Institute of Archaeology storeroom. Fr. of base and lower body. H 5.6 × W 4.4, WT 0.25, ⌀ base 4. Fabric: standard, fine, 5YR 6/8. Coat with dull lustre ext., int. lustrous, ext. 5YR 3/1, int. 2.5YR 2.5/2. Relatively hard fired, oxidized. Main decoration: scroll left. Medallion: rosette A.

EPH-164*
Olbia, Sector R25, O-P25-93-2910, Parutine, Olbia National Preserve storeroom. Fr. of rim and upper body. H 4.8 × W 5.9, WT 0.3, RH 1.6. Fabric: relatively fine and micaceous, 2.5YR 6/6. Thin dull coat, ext. 2.5YR 5/6, int. 2.5YR 4/6. Medium hard fired, oxidized. Rim frieze: Ionian kyma. Main decoration: scroll left.

EPH-164 bis*
Olbia, Sector E2, square 55, Room [Cistern] Л, western part, grey clay layer, O-E2-48-4973, Kiev, Institute of Archaeology storeroom. Fr. of rim and upper body. Oxidized. Rim frieze: Ionian kyma. Scroll left.

EPH-165*
Olbia, Sector R25, O-P25-06-1282, Parutine, Olbia National Preserve storeroom. Fr. of upper body. H 3.3 × W 3.5, WT 0.3. Fabric: fine, micaceous, 2.5YR 6/6. Dull coat, almost completely lost int., ext. 2.5YR 5/6, 3/1 int. 2.5YR 5/6. Hard fired, oxidized. Stacked in firing. Rim frieze: Ionian kyma. Main decoration: scroll left. Fine classicistic piece.

EPH-166*
Olbia, Sector R25, O-P25-99-1973, Parutine, Olbia National Preserve storeroom. Fr. of rim and upper body. H 4.4 × W 6.1, WT 0.32, ⌀ rim 13, 15%, RH 1.5. Fabric: relatively fine and micaceous, small voids, 7.5YR 7/6. Dull coat, ext. 7.5YR 3/1, int. 2.5YR 4/6, 7.5YR 3/1. Medium hard fired, oxidized. Stacked in firing. Rim frieze: box meander, cw. Main decoration: scroll left.

EPH-167*
Olbia, Sector NGF, room, ash, garbage layer, O-НГФ-47-782, Kiev, Institute of Archaeology storeroom. Fr. of rim and body. Oxidized. Rim frieze: Lesbian kyma. Main decoration: scroll left. One repair hole.

EPH-168*
Olbia, Sector AGD, O-АГД-71-1457, Kiev, Institute of Archaeology storeroom. Fr. of rim and upper body. H 5.2 × W 5.8, WT 0.45, ⌀ rim 13, 14%, RH 1.5. Fabric: standard, 10YR 6/4. Coat with slight dull lustre, ext. 10YR 4/2, int. 10YR 4/2. Relatively hard fired, oxidized. Rim frieze: star rosettes. Main decoration: scroll left.

EPH-169*
Olbia, O-39-188, Kiev, Institute of Archaeology storeroom. Fr. of rim and upper body. Oxidized. Stacked in firing. No rim frieze. Main decoration: scroll right.

Full-Body Acanthus-Vine Scroll

EPH-170*
Olbia, Sector E6, square 405, basement with walls 4, 15, 16, 18, O-E6-56-449, Kiev, Institute of Archaeology storeroom. Fr. of base and lower body. H 8.1 × W 7.1, WT 0.45, ⌀ base 3.3. Fabric: fine, non-micaceous, 5YR 7/6. Thin dull coat, worn int., 5YR 4/1. Hard fired, oxidized. Main decoration: scroll right. Medallion: Medusa head with long tresses surrounded by zone of large ivy-berry clusters between ridges. Cf. Laumonier 1977, 81 cat. 632, pls. 18, 119, identical, though lacking the frieze of ivy-berry clusters around the base medallion. Belles Méduses.

EPH-171
Olbia, Tomb 29, O-1901-no.?/inv. O-518 [17931?]. Complete. Oxidized. Rim frieze: Ionian kyma. Main decoration: scroll left with rosette 9/8 in tendril. Medallion: rosette A. Closely similar: Zahn 1908, 55 cat. 6.
– Farmakovskij 1903a, 46, fig. 44; Farmakovskij 1903b, 15 fig. 26; Parovič-Pešikan 1974, fig. 86.4; St Petersburg, IIMK RAN, photo archive neg. II 17934.

EPH-172*
Olbia, Cliff, Well 12, yellow clay layer, O-68-1366, Kiev, Institute of Archaeology storeroom. Fr. of base and lower body. H 3.5 × W 5.3, WT 0.3, ⌀ base 4. Fabric: standard, fine, 5YR 6/8. Dull mottled coat, 2.5YR 4/8, 4/2. Medium hard fired, oxidized. Main decoration: scroll right. Medallion: rosette A.

EPH-173*
Olbia, Cliff "B-VIII", square 285, Slope 1, Terrace I, O-70-382 Parutine, Olbia National Preserve storeroom. Fr. of rim and upper body. H 4 × W 5.2, WT 0.3, RH 1.3. Fabric: standard, fine, 2.5YR 6/8. Coat with dull lustre, ext. 2.5YR 4/8, int. 2.5YR 5/8. Relatively hard fired, oxidized. Rim frieze: Ionian kyma. Main decoration: full-body(?) vine scroll(?) (only bunch of grapes preserved).

EPH-174*
Olbia, O-61-5411+5412, Kiev, Institute of Archaeology storeroom. Two joining frs. of rim and upper body. H 4.7 × W 8.3, WT 0.2, ⌀ rim 13, 22%, RH 1.9. Fabric: standard, fine, 5YR 6/8. Coat with slight lustre, ext. 5YR 2.5/1, int. 5YR 3/1, 2.5YR 4/8. Relatively hard fired, oxidized. Rim frieze: box meander, cw. Main decoration: scroll left. Three repair holes.

EPH-175*
Olbia, Sector R25, O-P25-04-1769, Parutine, Olbia National Preserve storeroom. Fr. of rim and mid-body. H 5.7 × W 6.6, WT 0.33, ⌀ rim 12, 13%. RH 1.7. Fabric: fine and micaceous, 5YR 5/6. Thin firm dull coat, slightly metallic sheen on ext. at stacking marks, 2.5YR 4/6, 3/1. Hard fired, oxidized. Stacked in firing. Rim frieze: box meander, cw. Main decoration: scroll (direction?). Very fine and fresh mould.

EPH-176*
Olbia, Square B5, O- Б5-76-85, Kiev, Institute of Archaeology storeroom. Two joining frs. of rim and body. H 5.5 × W 9.2, WT 0.4, ⌀ rim 12.5, 25%, RH 2. Fabric: standard, fine, 5YR 6/6. Mottled coat with slight bluish sheen, ext. 2.5YR 4/6, 5YR 2.5/1, int. 2.5YR 4/6, 7.5YR 3/2. Hard fired, oxidized. Stacked in firing. Rim frieze: box meander, cw. Main decoration: scroll left.

EPH-177*
Olbia, Cliff, square 285, O-70-145, Parutine, Olbia National Preserve storeroom. Fr. of rim and body. H 5.8 × W 5.8, WT 0.35–0.4, ⌀ rim 12, 10%, RH 1.7. Fabric: standard, 5YR 6/6. Coat with slight lustre, mottled int., 2.5YR 4/6. Not too hard fired, oxidized. Stacked in firing. Rim frieze: box meander, cw. Main decoration: scroll left.

Acanthus-Vine Scroll

EPH-178
Olbia, O-1912-120a. Complete. Rim frieze: Ionian kyma. Main decoration: scroll left. Calyx A2 with rosette 9/8 as space filler. Medallion: rosette A.
– Slavin 1938, fig. 44; St Petersburg, IIMK RAN, photo archive neg. II 18317.

EPH-179 (see Fig. 78)
Olbia, inv. T 477, Kassel, Antikenabteilung des Staatlischen Kunstsammlungen. Complete. ⌀ rim 13; vessel H 7.2; H:⌀ 1:1.8. Reddish brown coat. Oxidized. Rim frieze: Ionian kyma. Main decoration: scroll left. Calyx A2. Medallion: rosette A.
– Zahn 1908, 51–54 cat. 4; Boehlau 1908, 31 no. 281; CVA Kassel 2 [Germany 38], 66, figs. 44–45, pl. 88.3–4 (identified as South Russian production).

EPH-180
Porthmion, cleaning of pavement 118 N of wall 127 and E of wall 126, П-75-182+185, Kerč History and Culture Reserve. Fr. of base and body. Oxidized. Main decoration: scroll right. Calyx B1. Medallion: rosette B. Monogram PAR.
– Grzegrzółka 2010, 134–135 cat. 191.

EPH-181
Porthmion, cleaning of pavement 118 N of wall 127 and E of wall 126, П-75-183+186, Kerč History and Culture Reserve. Fr. of base and body. Oxidized. Main decoration: scroll right. Calyx B1. Medallion: rosette B. Monogram PAR.
– Grzegrzółka 2010, 136 cat. 192.

EPH-182*
Olbia, Sector AGD, Bothros 11, О-АГД-88-200, Kiev, Institute of Archaeology storeroom. Almost half of bowl consisting of two groups of joining sherds: two rim frs. and a body fr.; one rim fr. and two body frs.; one rim fr. and one body fr. which do not join. WT 0.3–0.45, ⌀ rim 13, 22%, RH 1.8. Fabric: standard, fine, 7.5YR 7/6. Dull coat, 10YR 3/1. Relatively hard fired, oxidized. Multiple rim friezes: Ionian kyma; rosette 2/7. Main decoration: scroll left. Calyx B1.
– Rusjaeva & Nazarčuk 2006, pl. 193.7.

EPH-183* (see also Fig. 78)
Olbia, Sector NGS, О-НГС-02-520, Parutine, Olbia National Preserve storeroom. Body fr. H 4.4 × W 6.4, WT 0.16–0.3. Fabric: fine, micaceous, a few minute lime particles and very small voids, 5YR 5/6. Thin firm coat, darkened on both sides with a slight metallic sheen, ext. 10YR 3/1, int. 10YR 3/2. Hard fired, oxidized. Main decoration: scroll left. Calyx B1. Early in the series, the bent tips of the acanthus are still quite naturalistic.

EPH-184
Myrmekion, M-58-2943, St Petersburg IIMK RAN. Fr. of mid- and lower body. H 4, WT 0.4. Fabric: slightly finer than standard, 2.5YR 5/8. Thin mottled slightly lustrous coat, ext. 2.5YR 4/6, int. 2.5YR 4/6, 2.5/1. Oxidized. Main decoration: scroll left. Calyx B1. One repair hole.

EPH-185*
Olbia, Sector E6, square 410e–415e, grey clay layer, O-E6-56-918, Kiev, Institute of Archaeology storeroom. Three large frs. of rim and body, two joining. H 6.3 × W 12.8, WT 0.3, ⌀ rim 12.5, 42%, RH 1.4. Fabric: standard, 2.5YR 6/6. Dull coat, ext. 2.5YR 4/6, 2.5/1, int. 2.5YR 2.5/1. Relatively hard fired, oxidized. Stacked in firing. Rim frieze: Ionian kyma. Main decoration: scroll left. Calyx B2. Secondarily burnt.

EPH-186
Pantikapaion(?), inv. 50.365, Budapest, Musée Hongrois des Beaux-Arts. Complete; joined from two halves in antiquity, as attested by repair holes. ⌀ rim 17.2; vessel H 7.5, RH 1:2.3. Rim frieze: Lesbian kyma. Main decoration: above, scroll left.; below, bound myrtle wreath with five petals and groups of three-dot berries, left and right (true wreath). Calyx B2. Medallion: rosette A. Monogram PAR. Repaired.
– Falco 1999, 32 cat. 2, figs. 5, 6.

EPH-187*
Olbia, Sector NGS, О-НГС-97-482, Parutine, Olbia National Preserve storeroom. Fr. of base and large part of body. H 5.5 × W 9.5, WT 0.3, ⌀ base 4. Fabric: fine, micaceous, 5YR 6/8. Thin dull coat, 2.5YR 5/6. Medium hard fired, oxidized. Rim frieze: Lesbian kyma. Main decoration: scroll right. Calyx B2. Medallion: rosette B. Graffito A on lower body. One repair hole.

EPH-188
Kepoi, Tomb 43, with KYB-320*, Ke-60-number(?), Moscow, State Historical Museum. Complete. Rim frieze: triple guilloche left. Main decoration: scroll right. Calyx B2. Medallion: rosette B. Monogram PAR.
– Usačeva 1978, fig. 2.21.

EPH-189*
Pantikapaion, П-1904-4, St Petersburg, State Hermitage Museum. Complete. ⌀ rim 12.5, ⌀ base 3.8; vessel H 6.1; H:⌀ 1:2. Oxidized. Stacked in firing. Rim frieze: rosette 2/7. Main decoration: scroll right. Calyx B2. Medallion: rosette B.

EPH-190*
Kepoi, Ke-63-184(?), Moscow State Historical Museum. Fr. of rim and upper body. ⌀ rim 12, 18%. Thin black coat. Reduced. Rim frieze: box meander, cw. Main decoration: scroll left. Calyx B

(rounded petal and acanthus leaf with folded tip, illustrated in publication but no longer preserved).
– Usačeva 1978, fig. 1.12.

EPH-191*
Olbia, Sector NGS, O-НГС-98-189, Parutine, Olbia National Preserve storeroom. Fr. of rim and large part of body. H 5.8 × W 8.4, WT 0.3, ⌀ rim 13, 22%, RH 1.4. Fabric: relatively fine and micaceous, 5YR 6/8. Thin firm coat with slight pinkish metallic lustre, ext. 2.5YR 5/4, 5YR 4/2, int. 5YR 5/4, 4/2. Medium hard fired, oxidized. Stacked in firing. Rim frieze: Ionian kyma. Main decoration: scroll right. Calyx B.

EPH-192*
Olbia, Sector NGF, room, ash, garbage layer, O-НГФ-47-781 Kiev, Institute of Archaeology storeroom. Fr. of rim and body. H 6 × W 6.7, WT 0.25, ⌀ rim 13, 15%, RH 1.9. Fabric: standard, 5YR 6/6. Dull coat, 2.5YR 4/6. Relatively hard fired, oxidized. Rim frieze: miniature acanthus-flower scroll left. Main decoration: scroll left. Calyx B (tips of pointed petal and bent acanthus preserved). Monogram PAR.

EPH-193
Olbia, Sector NGS, O-НГС-86-213, Parutine, Olbia National Preserve storeroom. Body fr. Oxidized. Main decoration: scroll right. Calyx B.

EPH-194
Olbia, O-60-no no. Four joining fragments, half of bowl. Rim frieze: box meander, cw. Main decoration: scroll right. Calyx C.
– St Petersburg, IIMK RAN, photo archive neg. II 73319.

EPH-195*
Olbia, Sector E6, square 410, grey clay layer, O-E6-56-1238 Kiev, Institute of Archaeology storeroom. Two joining frs. of rim and body. H 7.3 × W 8.7, WT 0.26, ⌀ rim 13, 19%, RH 1.5. Fabric: standard, 2.5YR 6/6. Dull coat, 2.5YR 4/6, 2.5/1. Relatively hard fired, oxidized. Stacked in firing. Rim frieze: Ionian kyma. Main decoration: scroll left. Calyx: vertical acanthus scroll with flower alternating with ovoid lotus petal. Frieze separators: dots. One repair hole.

EPH-196*
Chersonesos, X-1952-146, St Petersburg, State Hermitage Museum. Fr. of mid- and lower body. H 5.1, WT 0.45. Fabric: standard, 2.5YR 5/8. Thin slightly lustrous coat, 2.5YR 5/6. Oxidized. Main decoration: scroll left. Calyx: looped tendrils with rosette alternating with straight acanthus(?).

EPH-197*
Olbia, Sector E6–7, squares 555sw, 554s, 553s, 552e, humus, O-E6-7-63-292, 292[A,] Kiev, Institute of Archaeology storeroom. Two non-joining frs. of rim and body. H 6.3 × W 6.5, WT 0.3, ⌀ rim 13, 15%, RH 1.8. Fabric: standard, 2.5YR 5/8. Dull coat, worn, 2.5YR 4/8. Relatively hard fired, oxidized. Rim frieze: Ionian kyma. Main decoration: scroll left. Calyx: broad lotus petal; bird, right as space filler.

EPH-198*
Olbia, Sector NGCentre, Basement 1, grey clay layer, O-НГЦ-68-2498, 2499, 2500, Kiev, Institute of Archaeology storeroom. Three non-joining frs. of rim and body. Oxidized. Rim frieze: Ionian kyma. Main decoration: scroll left. Calyx: ovoid lotus petals. Frieze separators: dots.

EPH-199*
Olbia, Sector NGS, House III-3 R 278/91, O-НГС-91-476, Parutine, Olbia National Preserve storeroom. Complete profile; four joining and one non-joining frs. WT 0.21–0.4, ⌀ rim 13, RH 1.9. ⌀ base 3; vessel H 7.3; H:⌀ 1:1.8. Fabric: relatively fine and micaceous, small lime inclusions, 5YR 5/6. Thin firm coat with slight lustre, partly blackened at rim, ext. 2.5YR 5/6, 5YR 3/1, int. 2.5YR 5/6. Hard fired, oxidized. Stacked in firing. Rim frieze: box meander, ccw. Main decoration: scroll left. Calyx: imbricate large rounded petals with central vein. Medallion: rosette A. Three repair holes. Monogram PAR.
– Guldager Bilde 2010, 278–279 cat. F-25, pl. 173.

EPH-200*
Olbia, Sector AGD, O-АГД-88-82+95, Kiev, Institute of Archaeology storeroom. Complete profile; five rim frs., four body frs., all joining. WT 0.3, ⌀ rim 12.5, 55%, RH 1.7; vessel H 6.2; H:⌀ 1:2. Fabric: standard, fine, 5YR 5/8. Thin dull coat, ext. 2.5YR 5/6, 5YR 2.5/1, int. 2.5YR 5/6. Relatively hard fired, oxidized. Stacked in firing. Rim frieze: box meander, ccw. Main decoration: scroll left. Calyx: imbricate, rounded petals with central vein. Medallion: rosette A. Repaired.
– Rusjaeva & Nazarčuk 2006, pl. 193.1, 4.

EPH-201
Pantikapaion, П-1883-4, St Petersburg, State Hermitage Museum. Complete. H 7.1, ⌀ rim 12.5. Oxidized. Stacked in firing. Rim frieze: box meander, ccw. Main decoration: scroll left. Calyx: imbricate large rounded petals with central vein. Medallion: rosette A.

EPH-202
Pantikapaion, Beliakov Str., no. unknown, Kerč History and Culture Reserve. Complete. ⌀ rim 13.2; vessel H 7.7. Oxidized. Rim

frieze: box meander, ccw. Main decoration: scroll left. Calyx: imbricate large rounded petals with central vein. Medallion: rosette A. Monogram PAR.
– Grzegrzółka 2010, 51 cat. 20,

EPH-203
Olbia, Sector B, square 1, inv. A 3611 (1926), Nikolaev, Historical Museum. Fr. of base and body. H 6.5 × W 4.5, WT 0.3–0.4. Red coat with slight shine. Oxidized. Main decoration: scroll left. Calyx: imbricate, large rounded petals with central vein. Medallion: rosette B.

EPH-204*
Olbia, Sector AGD and Bothros 11, О-АГД-87-207+997, 88-197, Kiev, Institute of Archaeology storeroom. Complete profile; joining frs. of rim, body, and base (1987); two joining rim frs. (1988); frs. from 1987 and 1988 do not join but are from the same vessel. WT 0.32, ⌀ rim 13.5, RH 1.4; vessel H 7.3; H:⌀ 1:1.8. Fabric: standard. Dull coat, 10YR 3/1. Relatively hard fired, oxidized. Rim frieze: guilloche right. Main decoration: scroll left. Calyx: imbricate rounded petals with two central veins. Medallion: rosette A surrounded by small triangular petals inside ridge. Frieze separators: dots. Secondarily burnt.
– Rusjaeva & Nazarčuk 2006, pl. 193.14, 18, pl. 194.2.

EPH-205
Porthmion, П-73-13, Kerč History and Culture Reserve. Body fr. Oxidized. Main decoration: scroll left. Calyx: imbricate rounded petals with central vein. Monogram PAR.
– Grzegrzółka 2010, 133–134 cat. 189.

EPH-206*
Olbia, Sector NGS, House IV-1 B 253/148 О-НГС-89-895, Parutine, Olbia National Preserve storeroom. Large fr. of rim and body. H 5.5 × W 11, WT 0.21–0.35, ⌀ rim 12.5, 30%, RH 1.85. Fabric: fine, micaceous, a few minute lime inclusions, small voids, 5YR 5/6. Thin firm coat, darkened at rim, semi-lustrous, with slight metallic sheen in darkened areas, ext. 2.5YR 4.5/6, 5YR 3/3, int. 2.5YR 4/6. Hard fired, oxidized. Stacked in firing. Rim frieze: box meander, ccw. Main decoration: scroll left. Calyx: imbricate rounded petals with central and side veins. Cf. Laumonier 1977, 469 cat. 9140, pl. 108 (unassigned). Very thin and delicate piece, beginning of series.
– Guldager Bilde 2010, 279 cat. F-26, pl. 174.

EPH-207*
Olbia, Sector AGD, Bothros 11, О-АГД-87-996, Kiev, Institute of Archaeology storeroom. One third of bowl; two rim frs. and fr. of mid- and lower body, all joining. WT 0.28–0.4. ⌀ rim 12.5, 32%, RH 1.8. Fabric: standard, fine, 2.5YR 6/8. Thin dull coat with slight lustre at rim ext., where blackened, ext. 2.5YR 4/8, 10YR 3/2, int. 2.5YR 4/6. Relatively hard fired, oxidized. Stacked in firing. Rim frieze: box meander, ccw. Main decoration: scroll left. Calyx: imbricate, rounded petals with central and side veins.
– Rusjaeva & Nazarčuk 2006, pl. 194.4.

EPH-208*
Olbia, Sector NGS, О-НГС-92-1071, 1071[A], Parutine, Olbia National Preserve storeroom. Two rim frs. and one body fr., all joining; joining rim and body fr. H 6.1 × W 8.3, WT 0.2–0.3, ⌀ rim 12, 18%, RH 1.8. Fabric: fine, micaceous, 5YR 6/8. Thin firm semi-lustrous coat, darkened at rim int., ext. 2.5YR 4/6, 7.5YR 3/2, int. 2.5YR 4/6. Hard fired, oxidized. Stacked in firing. Rim frieze: box meander, ccw. Main decoration: scroll left. Calyx: imbricate rounded petals with central and side veins.

EPH-209
Olbia, Sector E6, square 410e–415e, grey clay layer O-E6-56-971, Kiev, Institute of Archaeology storeroom. Body fr. Oxidized. Rim frieze: box meander, ccw. Main decoration: scroll left. Calyx: imbricate rounded petals with central and side veins.

EPH-210
Olbia, O-1901-3068. Slightly fragmentary, but complete profile. Rim frieze: guilloche left. Main decoration: scroll right. Calyx: imbricate rounded petals with central and side veins. Medallion: rosette A.
– St Petersburg, IIMK RAN, photo archive neg. II 17933,

EPH-211*
Olbia, Sector E6, square 410, 415, grey clay layer, O-E6-57-36, Kiev, Institute of Archaeology storeroom. Fr. of mid- and lower body. Oxidized. Main decoration: scroll left. Calyx: imbricate rounded petals with central and side veins. Secondarily burnt. One repair hole.

EPH-212*
Olbia, Sector NGS, О-НГС-02-258 Parutine, Olbia National Preserve storeroom. Two joining frs. of rim and upper body. H 4.4 × W 8.9, WT 0.19–0.41, ⌀ rim 13, RH 1.9. Fabric: relatively fine and micaceous, many large and small lime particles, 5YR 6/6. Thin firm coat with slight lustre, but partial bluish metallic sheen at rim, where blackened, ext. 10R 5/6; 2.5Y 3/0, int. 2.5YR 4/6. Medium hard fired, oxidized. Stacked in firing. Rim frieze: box meander, cw. Main decoration: scroll left.

EPH-213
Olbia, Sector R25, O-P25-00-1109+1614, Parutine, Olbia National Preserve storeroom. Two joining rim frs. and one non-joining body fr. H 4.4 × W 6.8, WT 0.28, ⌀ rim 13, 17%, RH 1.7. Fabric: relatively fine and micaceous, 5YR 6/8. Slightly lustrous coat, ext. 2.5YR 4/6, int. 2.5YR 4/8. Medium hard fired, oxidized. Stacked

in firing. Rim frieze: box meander, ccw. Main decoration: scroll left.

EPH-214*
Chersonesos, Х-1952-158, St Petersburg, State Hermitage Museum. Fr. of rim and upper body. H 4.5, WT 0.3, ⌀ rim 12, RH 2. Fabric: standard, fine, 2.5YR 6/6. Thin slightly lustrous coat, ext. 2.5YR 5/6, int. 10R 5/8. Oxidized. Rim frieze: box meander, cw. Main decoration: scroll (direction unknown).

EPH-215*
Chersonesos, X-1961–60[a], St Petersburg, State Hermitage Museum. Rim fr. ⌀ rim 13, 8%. Oxidized. Rim frieze: box meander, ccw. Main decoration: scroll (left?).

EPH-216*
Olbia, Sector R25, O-Р25-95-1098, Parutine, Olbia National Preserve storeroom. Fr. of upper body close to rim. H 5.3 × W 4.5, WT 0.22. Fabric: relatively fine and micaceous, some voids, 2.5YR 6/8. Slightly lustrous coat, 2.5YR 5/8. Hard fired, oxidized. Rim frieze: box meander, ccw. Main decoration: scroll left. Frieze separators: dots

EPH-217
Olbia, Sector AGD, О-АГД-76-199, Kiev, Institute of Archaeology storeroom. Fr. of mid-body. H 4 × W 5.8, WT 0.28–0.38. Fabric: standard, fine, 5YR 6/8. Coat with metallic sheen, 2.5Y 2.5/1. Relatively hard fired, oxidized. Rim frieze: box meander, cw. Main decoration: scroll left.

EPH-218*
Olbia, Sector NGS, О-НГС-06-601 Parutine, Olbia National Preserve storeroom. Fr. of upper body. H 2.6 × W 3.8, WT 0.3. Fabric: fine, micaceous, 5YR 6/6. Coat with slight lustre, ext. 2.5YR 4/6, 2.5/1, int. 2.5YR 4/6. Hard fired, oxidized. Stacked in firing. Rim frieze: box meander. Main decoration: scroll left.

EPH-219
Myrmekion, M-58-818. St Petersburg IIMK RAN. Body fr. H 3.5, WT 0.25. Fabric: standard, 5YR 5/8. Thin coat with metallic sheen ext., slight sheen int., ext. 5Y 3/1, int. 5Y 2.5/2. Oxidized. Rim frieze: box meander, ccw. Main decoration: scroll left.

EPH-220
Pantikapaion, area of 2 Lenin Str., Kerč History and Culture Reserve. Fr. of rim and upper body. Oxidized. Rim frieze: box meander, cw. Main decoration: scroll (direction unknown). Monogram PAR.
– Grzegrzółka 2010, 70 cat. 54.

EPH-221
Porthmion, П-73-50, Kerč History and Culture Reserve. Fr. of rim and upper body. Oxidized. Rim frieze: box meander, cw. Main decoration: scroll (direction unknown). Monogram PAR.
– Grzegrzółka 2010, 141 cat. 203.

EPH-222*
Olbia, Sector E6–7, squares 597w, 607w, yellow clay layer, O-E6-7-63-2149. Fr. of rim and body. Oxidized. Rim frieze: Ionian kyma. Main decoration: scroll left. Frieze separators: dots. One repair hole.

EPH-223*
Olbia, Sector AGD, О-АГД-74-70, Kiev, Institute of Archaeology storeroom. Fr. of rim and upper body. H 4.4 × W 4.2, WT 0.3, RH 1.5. Fabric: standard, 5YR 7/8. Thin dull coat with slight metallic sheen at rim ext., 7.5YR 3/1. Relatively hard fired, oxidized. Rim frieze: Ionian kyma. Main decoration: scroll right.

EPH-224*
Olbia, Cliff "B-VIII", square 285, Terrace I, yellow clay layer, O-70-951, Parutine, Olbia National Preserve storeroom. Fr. of rim and body. H 5.1 × W 4.5, WT 0.25, RH 2.3. Fabric: standard, fine, 2.5YR 6/8. Coat with slight lustre, metallic sheen ext., mottled int., ext. 2.5YR 2.5/1, 2.5/3, int. 2.5YR 4/6, 3/4. Relatively hard fired, oxidized. Rim frieze: Ionian kyma. Main decoration: scroll left.

EPH-225*
Tyritake, Sector L, Л-47-77, St Petersburg IIMK RAN. Fr. of upper body. H 5, WT 0.28. Fabric: relatively fine and micaceous, many small lime inclusions, 10YR 4/3. Slightly lustrous coat ext., dull int., ext. 10YR 4/3, 2/1, int. 10YR 4/3, 2/1. Oxidized. Stacked in firing. Rim frieze: Ionian kyma. Main decoration: scroll left. Early.

EPH-226
Porthmion, square 42–43c, depth 1.4 m, П-75-42, Kerč History and Culture Reserve. Fr. of rim and upper body. Reduced. Rim frieze: Ionian kyma. Main decoration: scroll right. Monogram PAR.
– Grzegrzółka 2010, 134 cat. 190.

EPH-227
Porthmion, cleaning of pavement 118 N of wall 127 and E of wall 126, П-75-176, Kerč History and Culture Reserve. Fr. of rim and upper body. Oxidized. Rim frieze: Ionian kyma. Main decoration: scroll right. Monogram PAR.
– Grzegrzółka 2010, 137 cat. 194.

EPH-228*
Olbia, Sector A, square 110–113, north of wall 107, O-A-46-1829, Kiev, Institute of Archaeology storeroom. Fr. of rim and upper body. Oxidized. Stacked in firing. Rim frieze: Lesbian kyma. Main decoration: scroll left.

EPH-229
Olbia, Sector NGS, О-НГС-08-362, Parutine, Olbia National Preserve storeroom. Fr. of upper body. Oxidized. Stacked in firing. Rim frieze: Lesbian kyma. Main decoration: scroll (direction unknown).

EPH-230
Volna 1, С3-00-129, St Petersburg, State Hermitage Museum. Fr. of rim and upper body. Oxidized. Stacked in firing. Rim frieze: Lesbian kyma. Main decoration: scroll left. Another small fr. preserving part of the rim pattern probably comes from the same bowl (С3-99-40A).

EPH-231*
Myrmekion, M-47-254, St Petersburg, State Hermitage Museum. Body fr. H 3.8, WT 0.42. Fabric: standard, slightly porous, 5YR 5/8. Thin slightly lustrous coat, ext. 2.5YR 4/6, 2.5/1, int. 2.5YR 4/6. Oxidized. Stacked in firing. Rim frieze: Lesbian kyma. Main decoration: scroll right.

EPH-232
Istros, UI 1913, His-V 7527 E, Bucharest, Institute of Archaeology storeroom. Fr. of upper body. H 2.5 × W 4, WT 0.25. Fabric: standard, 5Y 5/1. Dull coat, Gley 1 3/N. Relatively hard fired, reduced. Rim frieze: Lesbian kyma. Main decoration: scroll right.
– Domăneanţu 2000, 37 cat. 159, pl. 11 (upside-down) (attributed to Monogram PAR).

EPH-233*
Bol'šoj Kastel', БК-86-74[b]+87-31, Černomorskoe Museum of Historical Lore. Two joining body frs. close to rim. H 1.8. Fabric: 5YR 5/6. Dull coat sightly darkened at rim ext., 2.5YR 3/6–4/6. Oxidized. Stacked in firing. Rim frieze: Lesbian kyma. Main decoration: bunch of grapes of acanthus-vine scroll. One repair hole.

EPH-234*
Chersonesos, X-1952-157, St Petersburg, State Hermitage Museum. Fr. of rim and upper body. H 4.8, WT 0.35, ⌀ rim 12.5, RH 2. Fabric: standard, 2.5YR 6/6. Thin coat, slightly lustrous int., ext. 7.5YR 7/4, int. 2.5YR 4/4, mottled. Badly misfired, almost yellowish ext. Oxidized. Rim frieze: guilloche right. Main decoration: scroll left. One repair hole.

EPH-235*
Chersonesos, X-1952-154, St Petersburg, State Hermitage Museum. Fr. of rim and upper body. H 4.2, WT 0.3, ⌀ rim 13, RH 1.8. Fabric: fine, compact, slightly micaceous. Thin lustrous coat, Gley 1 2.5/N. Reduced. Rim frieze: guilloche right. Main decoration: scroll right.

EPH-236*
Porthmion, П-53-191, St Petersburg IIMK RAN. Fr. of rim and upper body. H 4.5, WT 0.22, ⌀ rim 14, RH 1.4. Fabric: standard, 5YR 6/4. Thin coat with slight lustre, 5YR 2.5/1. Oxidized. Rim frieze: guilloche left. Main decoration: scroll right.

EPH-237
Olbia, O-52-2958, Kiev, Institute of Archaeology storeroom. Fr. of rim and body. Oxidized. Stacked in firing. Rim frieze: guilloche left. Main decoration: scroll right.

EPH-238
Porthmion, П-68-86, Kerč History and Culture Reserve. Fr. of rim and upper body. Oxidized. Rim frieze: heart guilloche left. Main decoration: scroll right. Monogram PAR.
– Grzegrzółka 2010, 133 cat. 188.

EPH-239*
Olbia, Sector R25, O-P25-95-797, Parutine, Olbia National Preserve storeroom. Fr. of upper body. H 3.3 × W 4, WT 0.35. Fabric: relatively fine and micaceous, 5YR 5/6. Thin dull coat, 2.5YR 4/6. Hard fired, oxidized. Multiple rim friezes: Ionian or Lesbian kyma; star rosettes. Main decoration: scroll right.

EPH-240*
Myrmekion, M-58-2967, St Petersburg IIMK RAN. Body fr. H 4, WT 0.32. Fabric: standard, 7.5YR 5/4. Thin slightly lustrous coat, ext. 2.5YR 4/6, 2.5/1, int. 2.5YR 4/6. Oxidized. Stacked in firing. Rim frieze: star rosettes. Main decoration: scroll right.

EPH-241
Olbia, Sector R25, O-P25-02-1172, Parutine, Olbia National Preserve storeroom. Fr. of rim and upper body. Oxidized. Rim frieze: star rosettes. Main decoration: scroll (direction unknown). One repair hole with lead clamp still in place.

EPH-242*
Olbia, Sector NGS, О-НГС-92-7, Parutine, Olbia National Preserve storeroom. Fr. of rim and upper body. Oxidized. Stacked in firing. Rim frieze: rosette 2/7. Main decoration: scroll left. One repair hole.

EPH-243*
Istros, His-1116, Bucharest, Institute of Archaeology storeroom. Fr. of upper body. H 2.5 × W 2.5, WT 0.22. Fabric: standard, 2.5Y 5/2. Dull coat, 2.5Y 3/1. Medium hard fired, oxidized. Rim frieze: flower, right. Main decoration: scroll right.
– Domăneanțu 2000, 93 cat. 452, pl. 30.

EPH-244*
Olbia, Sector I, square 22oe, clay layer О-И-49-4064, Kiev, Institute of Archaeology storeroom. Fr. of rim and upper body. Oxidized. Stacked in firing. Rim frieze: large dots. Main decoration: scroll left.

EPH-245*
Chersonesos, X-1965-81, St Petersburg, State Hermitage Museum. Body fr. H 2.2, WT 0.21. Fabric: no fresh break for observation. Shiny coat, Gley 1 2.5/N. Reduced. Main decoration: scroll left.

EPH-246
Olbia, Sector NGS, О-НГС-06-298(?), Parutine, Olbia National Preserve storeroom. Fr. of mid-body. H 1.8 × W 2.6, WT 0.2. Fabric: fine, micaceous, 5Y 5/1. Dull coat, 5Y 2.5/1. Medium hard fired, reduced. Main decoration: scroll left.

EPH-247
Porthmion, П-75-92, Kerč History and Culture Reserve. Fr. of upper body. Oxidized. Main decoration: scroll right. Monogram PAR.
– Grzegrzółka 2010, 136–137 cat. 193.

Acanthus-Vine-Ivy Scroll

EPH-248*
Olbia, O-48-3866[A], year(?)-2085, Kiev, Institute of Archaeology storeroom. Two non-joining frs. of rim and body. H 6.8 × W 5.5, WT 0.35, ⌀ rim 12, 10%, RH 2. Fabric: standard, 2.5YR 6/8. Dull coat, ext. 2.5YR 4/8, 3/1, int. 2.5YR 4/8. Medium hard fired, oxidized. Rim frieze: Ionian kyma. Main decoration: scroll right with ivy-berry clusters. Calyx A, 'nelumbo' with small acanthus leaf in front alternating with slender palm branch.

EPH-249*
Kepoi, inv. 98170-160/7, Moscow, State Historical Museum. Complete. ⌀ rim 13, RH 2, ⌀ base 3.7; vessel H 6.3; H:⌀ 1:1.9. Fabric: 7.5YR 7/6. Dull black coat, 2.5Y 2.5/1. Oxidized. Rim frieze: Ionian kyma. Main decoration: scroll left. Calyx: acanthus with drooping tip alternating with rhomboidal petal and vertical miniature flower scroll. Medallion: rosette A. Monogram PAR.
– Usačeva 1978, fig. 1.1.

EPH-250*
Olbia, Sector D, square 13, yellow clay layer О-Д-47-3802, Kiev, Institute of Archaeology storeroom. Body fr. H 4.3 × W 4.5, WT 0.2. Fabric: standard, fine, 2.5YR 6/6. Dull coat, 2.5YR 4/6. Relatively hard fired, oxidized. Rim frieze: Ionian kyma. Main decoration: scroll left with ivy-berry clusters; rosette 2/8 alternating with small palmette. Calyx: imbricate, rounded petals with central vein.

EPH-251
Olbia, Sector NGS, О-НГС-05-216 Parutine, Olbia National Preserve storeroom. Fr. of rim and upper body. H 3.6 × W 6.2, WT 0.32, ⌀ rim 12.5, 15%, RH 1.5. Fabric: relatively fine and micaceous, 5YR 6/6. Thin coat with dull metallic sheen, Gley 1 3/N. Medium hard fired, oxidized. Rim frieze: Ionian kyma. Main decoration: scroll left. Monogram PAR?

EPH-252*
Olbia, Square B5, О-Б5-76-23, Kiev, Institute of Archaeology storeroom. Fr. of mid body. H 4.2 × W 4.5, WT 0.32. Fabric: standard, fine, 5YR 6/8. Dull coat, 10YR 3/1. Hard fired, oxidized. Rim frieze: vertical S-spirals. Main decoration: scroll right.

EPH-253*
Istros, His-1181, Bucharest, Institute of Archaeology storeroom. Fr. of rim and upper body. H 3.9 × W 5, WT 0.35, ⌀ rim 13, 13%, RH 1.6. Fabric: standard, fine, 5Y 6/1. Coat with slight lustre, Gley 1 3/N. Relatively hard fired, reduced. No rim frieze. Main decoration: scroll left. Frieze separators: dots.
– Domăneanțu 2000, 45 cat. 206, pl. 13 (attributed to Monogram PAR).

EPH-254*
Olbia, O-no no. M, Kiev, Institute of Archaeology storeroom. Body fr. H 3.6 × W 3, WT 0.3. Fabric: standard, 2.5YR 6/8. Slightly lustrous coat, ext. 2.5YR 4/8, Gley 1 3/N, int. 2.5YR 4/8. Relatively hard fired, oxidized. Stacked in firing. Main decoration: scroll right with ivy-berry clusters.

EPH-255*
Olbia, Sector R25, O-Р25-93-2908[b], Parutine, Olbia National Preserve storeroom. Fr. of upper body. H 3.5 × W 5.3, WT 0.35. Fabric: relatively fine and micaceous, 5YR 6/6. Dull coat, ext. 2.5YR 5/6, 3/1, int. 2.5YR 3/1. Medium hard fired, oxidized. Stacked in firing. Main decoration: scroll left.

Acanthus-Flower Scroll

EPH-256*
Olbia, O-1910-723, present whereabouts unknown. Complete profile consisting of a number of fragments. Rim frieze: Ionian

kyma. Main decoration: scroll left, with simple flowers, collared buds, and collared flowers. Calyx B2. Medallion: rosette with petals alternating with rhomboidal leaves. Frieze separators: dots.
– St Petersburg, IIMK RAN, archive inv. 4058.519.6 (pl. III).

EPH-257
Olbia, tomb(?), inv. 22522, Odessa Museum. Complete. Vessel H 6.5. Oxidized. Rim frieze: Ionian kyma. Main decoration: scroll left. Calyx B2. Medallion: rosette C. Same scroll type as EPH-256*.
– Bodzek (ed.) 2006, 264 fig. 62.

EPH-258*
Olbia, Sector NGS, O-НГС-92-211, Parutine, Olbia National Preserve storeroom. Fr. of rim and upper body. H 3.9 × W 4.3, WT 0.3, RH 1.5. Fabric: relatively fine and micaceous, 7.5YR 6/6. Thin slightly lustrous coat, ext. 7.5YR 2.5/1, int. 7.5YR 3/2. Medium hard fired, oxidized. Rim frieze: Ionian kyma. Main decoration: scroll left. Same scroll type as EPH-256*.

EPH-259*
Olbia, Sector Sever-Zapad O-СЗ-77-167, Parutine, Olbia National Preserve storeroom. Fr. of mid-body. H 4.4 × W 4.3, WT 0.3. Fabric: standard, fine, 2.5YR 6/8. Thin dull coat, 10R 5/8. Relatively hard fired, oxidized. Main decoration: scroll left. Calyx B. Same scroll type as EPH-256*.

EPH-260*
Olbia, Sector NGS, O-НГС-02-282, Parutine, Olbia National Preserve storeroom. Body fr. H 3.6 × W 3.5, WT 0.28–0.31. Fabric: relatively fine and micaceous, small lime inclusions, 5YR 5/8. Thin firm slightly lustrous coat, lightly pitted, 2.5YR 4/8. Medium hard fired, oxidized. Main decoration: scroll left. Calyx B (acanthus leaf with folded tip preserved). Same scroll type as EPH-256*.

EPH-261*
Olbia, Sector NGCentre, grey clay layer, О-НГЦ-68-611, Kiev, Institute of Archaeology storeroom. Large fr. of rim and body. H 6.5 × W 7.7, WT 0.28, ⌀ rim 13, 20%, RH 1.4. Fabric: standard, 2.5YR 6/6. Dull coat, slight metallic lustre where stacked, 2.5YR 4/6, 4/1. Medium hard fired, oxidized. Stacked in firing. Rim frieze: star rosettes. Main decoration: scroll left. Calyx: imbricate, rounded petals with central and side veins. Same scroll type as EPH-256*.

EPH-262*
Olbia, Sector NGS, O-НГС-05-802, Parutine, Olbia National Preserve storeroom. Fr. of rim and upper body. H 4.7 × W 3, WT 0.3, RH 1.4. Fabric: relatively fine and micaceous, 7.5YR 6/6. Thin dull coat, 7.5YR 2.5/1. Medium hard fired, oxidized. Rim frieze: miniature acanthus-flower scroll left. Main decoration: scroll left. Same scroll type as EPH-256*. Monogram PAR.

EPH-263*
Olbia, Sector AGD, yellow clay layer, О-АГД-69-1212, Kiev, Institute of Archaeology storeroom. Fr. of rim and upper body. H 5 × W 7, WT 0.35, ⌀ rim 13, 18%, RH 1.5. Fabric: standard, 2.5YR 6/8. Dull coat with slight metallic sheen at rim, ext. 10R 5/6, 10YR 3/1, int. 2.5YR 4/8. Relatively hard fired, oxidized. Stacked in firing. Rim frieze: Ionian kyma. Main decoration: scroll right. For type of scroll, cf. Laumonier 1977, 90 cat. 1558, pl. 20.

EPH-264*
Olbia, Sector NG, square 42ne, 32ne О-НГ-46-3121, Kiev, Institute of Archaeology storeroom. Fr. of rim and body. H 5 × W 7.1, WT 0.25, ⌀ rim 18, RH 1.8. Fabric: standard, 5YR 6/6. Dull coat, mottled ext., ext. 5YR 4/1, 4/4, int. 5YR 3/1. Relatively hard fired, oxidized. Rim frieze: Ionian kyma. Main decoration: scroll right. Same scroll as EPH-263*.

EPH-265*
Istros, His-B 542/V 19364, Bucharest, Institute of Archaeology storeroom. Body fr. H 3.6 × W 3.5, WT 0.3. Fabric: fine and soft with a few light-reflecting particles, 7.5YR 7/6. Dull coat, very worn, 7.5YR 3/2. Medium hard fired, oxidized. Main decoration: scroll left with flower in spiral tendril and groups of three-dot berries. Calyx B: pointed lotus petal, folded acanthus leaf. My(...).
– Domăneanţu 2000, 82 cat. 390, pl. 26.

EPH-266*
Olbia, O-40-2161, Kiev, Institute of Archaeology storeroom. Fr. of rim and upper body. H 4.6 × W 4, WT 0.23, RH 1.4. Fabric: standard, 5YR 6/8. Dull coat, 2.5YR 4/6. Relatively hard fired, oxidized. Stacked in firing. Rim frieze: Ionian kyma. Main decoration: scroll left.

EPH-267*
Porthmion, pavement of 2nd longitudinal street, with three bronze coins of Pantikapaion (first half of the 3rd century; mid-3rd century; 2nd century), П-77-275, St Petersburg IIMK RAN. Body fr. H 2, WT 0.3. Fabric: standard, fine, Gley 1 5/10Y. Thin slightly lustrous black coat, Gley 1 3/N. Hard fired, reduced. Main decoration: acanthus-flower scroll with tendrils left.

EPH-268*
Istros, His-B 505, Bucharest, Institute of ARchaeology storeroom. Fr. of upper body. H 2.7 × W 2, WT 0.25. Fabric: standard, fine,

Gley 1 5/10Y. Slightly lustrous coat, Gley 1 2.5/N. Relatively hard fired, reduced. Main decoration: same scroll type as EPH-267*.
– Domăneanţu 2000, 98 cat. 485, pl. 32.

EPH-269*
Porthmion, pavement of 2nd longitudinal street, with three bronze coins of Pantikapaion (first half of the 3rd century; mid-3rd century; 2nd century), П-77-268, St Petersburg IIMK RAN. Fr. of rim and upper body. H 4.7, WT 0.4, ⌀ rim 13, RH 1.5. Fabric: standard, Gley 1 5/10Y. Thin slightly lustrous black coat, Gley 1 3/N. Hard fired, reduced. Rim frieze: Ionian kyma. Main decoration: scroll left.

EPH-270*
Istros, His-V 19409, Bucharest, Institute of Archaeology storeroom. Two joining frs. of rim and upper body. H 5.1 × W 9.1, WT 0.22, ⌀ rim 12, RH 1.6. Fabric: standard, abundant small lime inclusions, 2.5Y 5/1. Coat with dull lustre ext. where stacked, ext. 2.5Y 4/2, 10YR 5/3, int. 10YR 5/3. Relatively hard fired, reduced. Stacked in firing. Rim frieze: Ionian kyma. Main decoration: scroll left.
– Domăneanţu 2000, 31 cat. 118, pl. 8 (attributed to Monogram PAR).

EPH-271*
Myrmekion, M-57-1078, St Petersburg IIMK RAN. Fr. of mid- and lower body. H 4, WT 0.38. Fabric: standard, 2.5YR 5/8. Thin dull coat, 2.5YR 4/6. Oxidized. Main decoration: scroll right. Calyx B2.

EPH-272*
Olbia, Sector E6, square 251w, grey clay layer, O-E6-56-529, 674, Kiev, Institute of Archaeology storeroom. Two non-joining frs. of rim and body. Oxidized. Stacked in firing. Rim frieze: Lesbian kyma. Main decoration: scroll right. Calyx B (tip of lotus petal preserved). One repair hole.

EPH-273*
Olbia, Sector R25, O-P25-98-85, Parutine, Olbia National Preserve storeroom. Fr. of upper body. H 3 × W 3.2, WT 0.25. Fabric: relatively fine and micaceous, 5Y 6/2. Thin coat, slightly lustrous ext., dull int., Gley 1 3/N. Medium hard fired, oxidized. Main decoration: vertical(?) acanthus scroll with flower and bud on looped tendril; acanthus leaf. Early.

Stylized Acanthus Scroll

EPH-274*
Olbia, Sector NGS, O-НГС-06-333, Parutine, Olbia National Preserve storeroom. Fr. of mid- and lower body. H 6 × W 4.7, WT 0.35. Fabric: relatively fine and micaceous, some small lime inclusions, 5YR 5/8. Thin dull coat, ext. 2.5YR 4/8, 3/1, int. 2.5YR 4/8. Medium hard fired, oxidized. Stacked in firing. Rim frieze: Ionian kyma. Main decoration: scroll left with groups of three-dot berries,. Calyx A1. Secondarily burnt. Two repair holes. Similar: Uvarov 1851, pl. XX.7.

EPH-275
Pantikapaion, Cistern N 179 96-no.? Fragmentary; complete profile. Multiple rim friezes: box meander, cw; Ionian kyma. Main decoration: scroll left with groups of three-dot berries. Calyx A2. Medallion: rosette A. Frieze separators: dots.
– Tolstikov & Zhuravlev 2004, pl. 101.1.

EPH-276
Kepoi, no. unknown, Moscow, State Historical Museum. Complete. Rim frieze: rosette 5. Main decoration: scroll left with groups of three-dot berries. Calyx B1. Medallion: rosette with many petals.
– Usačeva 1978, fig. 1.3.

EPH-277*
Olbia, Sector NGCentre, Hellenistic basement, O-НГЦ-68-1093[a], 1094, Kiev, Institute of Archaeology storeroom. Fr. of rim and body and non-joining body fr. H 6 × W 8, WT 0.35, ⌀ rim 13, 17%, RH 1.4. Fabric: standard, fine, 2.5YR 6/8. Dull coat, metallic lustre on ext. where stacked, ext. 2.5YR 4/6, 3/1, int. 5YR 4/2. Relatively hard fired, oxidized. Stacked in firing. Rim frieze: Ionian kyma. Main decoration: scroll left with groups of three dot berries. Calyx B2. Same combination of motifs occurs on fragment from Porthmion: Grzegrzółka 2010, 50–51 cat. 19.

EPH-278
Olbia, Square Б5, O-Б5-76-119, Kiev, Institute of Archaeology storeroom. Fr. of mid- and lower body. H 3.5 × W 3.1, WT 0.3. Fabric: standard, 5YR 6/8. Dull coat, 2.5YR 5/8. Relatively hard fired, oxidized. Main decoration: scroll left with groups of three-dot berries. Small rosette below.

EPH-279*
Myrmekion, M-47-242, St Petersburg IIMK RAN. Fr. of rim and upper body. H 4.1, WT 0.2, ⌀ rim 12, 10%, RH 1.3. Fabric: standard, relatively fine, 5YR 6/6. Slightly lustrous coat, ext. 10R 4/6, 2.5YR 2.5/1, int. 10R 4/6. Oxidized. Stacked in firing. Rim frieze: Ionian kyma. Main decoration: scroll left with groups of three-dot berries.

EPH-280*
Olbia, Sector NGS, O-НГС-05-298+06-95 (join across years), Parutine, Olbia National Preserve storeroom. Five joining frs. of rim and upper body; one joining fr. of body. H 5.8 × W 10, WT 0.35, ⌀ rim 12, RH 1.8. Fabric: relatively fine and micaceous,

5YR 6/6. Thin dull coat, slight lustre at stacking marks, 5YR 3/2. Medium hard fired, oxidized. Stacked in firing. Rim frieze: Ionian kyma. Main decoration: scroll left with groups of three dot berries. Crude dedication incised on ext. rim: AG[A]TYCHES. Monogram PAR?

EPH-281
Myrmekion, M-58-694, St Petersburg IIMK RAN. Fr. of mid-body. H 4.2, WT 0.25. Fabric: standard, 5YR 6/6. Slightly lustrous coat, ext. 5YR 3/3, 2.5YR 4/8, int. 5YR 3/2. Oxidized. Stacked in firing. Rim frieze: Ionian kyma. Main decoration: scroll left with groups of three-dot berries.

EPH-282*
Myrmekion, M-49-790, St Petersburg IIMK RAN. Two non-joining frs. of mid- and lower body with tiny part of base. H 6.5, WT 0.4. Fabric: standard, 2.5YR 5/8. Thin mottled coat, slightly lustrous, 2.5YR 3/3, 4/6. Oxidized. Rim frieze: Lesbian kyma. Main decoration: scroll left with group of three-dot berries. Calyx B2.

EPH-283*
Pantikapaion, M-47-139, Moscow, Puškin Museum of Fine Arts. Fr. of rim and body. H 6 × W 5, WT 0.3. Fabric: fine, micaceous, grey. Dull black coat. Oxidized. Rim frieze: Lesbian kyma. Main decoration: scroll left with groups of three-dot berries. Calyx: calyx B (tip of ovoid petal preserved). Frieze separators: dots.

EPH-284*
Olbia, Sector E6–7, squares 598, 608, yellow clay layer O-E6-7-63-1128+no no. AB, G+I, Kiev, Institute of Archaeology storeroom. Four frs. of rim and body, joining two and two. H 5.7 × W 11.6, WT 0.15, ⌀ rim 15, 28%, RH 2.2. Fabric: standard, 2.5YR 5/8. Slightly lustrous coat, pitted and worn, ext. 2.5YR 2.5/2, 2.5/1, int. 2.5YR 4/8, 2.5/1. Relatively hard fired, oxidized. Stacked in firing. Rim frieze: Lesbian kyma. Main decoration: scroll left with groups of three-dot berries.

EPH-285*
Olbia, Sector E6, square 400, ash layer O-E6-56-736 Kiev, Institute of Archaeology storeroom. Fr. of rim and upper body. Oxidized. Rim frieze: Lesbian kyma. Main decoration: scroll left, probably with three-dot berries.

EPH-286
Olbia, Sector I, square 268, 269, clay layer, O-И-48-3399, Kiev, Institute of Archaeology storeroom. Fr. of rim and upper body. Oxidized. Stacked in firing. Rim frieze: Lesbian kyma. Main decoration: scroll left with groups of three-dot berries.

EPH-287*
Olbia, Sector Sever-Zapad, O-СЗ-77-22, Parutine, Olbia National Preserve storeroom. Fr. of body close to rim. H 4.8 × W 4.2, WT 0.2. Fabric: standard, 5YR 6/8. Thin dull coat, ext. 2.5YR 4/6, 5YR3/1, int. 2.5YR 4/6. Relatively hard fired, oxidized. Stacked in firing. Rim frieze: Lesbian kyma. Main decoration: scroll left with groups of three-dot berries.

EPH-288*
Porthmion, square 6, depth 0.9 m, with material of 3rd–2nd century, П-53-212, 214, St Petersburg IIMK RAN. Two non-joining frs. of rim and upper body and base, lower- and mid-body; complete profile. WT 0.3, ⌀ rim 12, RH 1.8. Fabric: standard, 2.5YR 6/8. Thin slightly lustrous coat, ext. 2.5YR 5/6, 5YR 3/1, int. 10R 5/6. Oxidized. Stacked in firing. Rim frieze: rosette 1, var. Main decoration: scroll left. Calyx B2. Medallion: rosette B.

EPH-289*
Pantikapaion, palace foundation trench, M-89-no no. 12, Moscow, Puškin Museum of Fine Arts. Fr. of rim and upper body. H 5 × W 8.2, WT 0.32, ⌀ rim 16, 13%, RH 1.9. Dull red coat, at ext. rim brownish with slight metallic sheen. Oxidized. Stacked in firing. Rim frieze: rosette 1, var. Main decoration: scroll left with groups of three-dot berries.
– Košelenko 1992, fig. 23.

EPH-290 (see Fig. 78)
Myrmekion, M-57-727, St Petersburg IIMK RAN. Two joining frs. of base and part of body. H 10, WT 0.25, ⌀ base 4.1. Fabric: standard, relatively fine, 7.5YR 6/6. Thin slightly lustrous coat, 5YR 2.5/1. Oxidized. Main decoration: scroll left with group of three-dot berries. Calyx B2. Medallion: rosette B.

EPH-291
Olbia, O-1936-1654, present whereabouts unknown. Almost all of lower bowl, joined from a number of frs. Main decoration: scroll left with groups of three-dot berries. Calyx B2. Medallion: rosette B. Two repair holes, or perhaps intentionally perforated for libation.
– Levi 1940, 125, pl. XXV.5; St Petersburg, IIMK RAN, photo archive neg. II 42015.

EPH-292
Istros, His-144, Bucharest, Institute of Archaeology storeroom. Body fr. H 4.5 × W 4, WT 0.35. Fabric: standard, 7.5YR 7/6. Dull coat, 7.5YR 3/2. Medium hard fired, oxidized. Main decoration: scroll with groups of three-dot berries. Calyx B.
– Domăneanțu 2000, 27 cat. 99, pl. 7 (attributed to Monogram PAR).

EPH-293*
Olbia, Sector NGS, O-НГС-96-42a, Parutine, Olbia National Preserve storeroom. Fr. of mid- and lower body. H 4.2 × W 4.8, WT 0.25. Fabric: relatively fine and micaceous, some small lime inclusions, 5YR 6/8. Thin dull coat, ext. 2.5YR 4/6, int. 5YR 4/4.

Medium hard fired, oxidized. Main decoration: scroll left with groups of three-dot berries. Calyx B2.

EPH-294*
Olbia, Sector R25, O-P25-92-2483, Parutine, Olbia National Preserve storeroom. Fr. of mid- and lower body. H 4 × W 5.5, WT 0.3. Fabric: relatively fine and micaceous, 5YR 6/6. Thin dull coat, 2.5YR 5/6. Hard fired, oxidized. Main decoration: scroll left with groups of three-dot berries. Calyx B (top of folded acanthus leaf preserved).

EPH-295*
Olbia, Sector AGD, О-АГД-92-31, Parutine, Olbia National Preserve storeroom. Fr. of mid- and lower body. H 4.1 × W 5.2, WT 0.2–0.4. Fabric: standard, 10YR 5/4. Thin dull coat, worn int., 5Y 2.5/1. Relatively hard fired, oxidized. Main decoration: scroll left with groups of three-dot berries. Calyx B.

EPH-296*
Chersonesos, X-1957-17, St Petersburg, State Hermitage Museum. Fr. of mid-body. H 3.1, WT 0.35. Fabric: standard, 2.5YR 6/8. Dull coat, 2.5YR 4/8. Oxidized. Main decoration: scroll left with group of three-dot berries. Calyx B.

EPH-297
Porthmion, trench A, rooms 42 and 43, П-75-22, Kerč History and Culture Reserve. Body fr. Oxidized. Main decoration: scroll (direction unknown). Calyx C.
– Grzegrzółka 2010, 139 cat. 199.

EPH-298
Olbia, O-1925-259, present whereabouts unknown. Fr. of mid-body. Main decoration: finely detailed scroll left. Calyx: part of rhomboidal leaf and funnel-shaped flower preserved. Identical flower: EPH-690*, EPH-1036*.
– St Petersburg, IIMK RAN, photo archive neg. II 19397.

EPH-299
Olbia, inv. 22523, Odessa Museum. Complete. Vessel H 5.5. Oxidized. Rim frieze: ring-shaped star rosettes with seven branches. Main decoration: scroll left with groups of three-dot berries. Calyx: plastic long petals alternating with vertical floral stem. Medallion: rosette A, var. 2.
– Bodzek (ed.) 2006, 264, fig. 64.

EPH-300
Istros, Sector X, His-96-1176, Bucharest, Institute of Archaeology storeroom. Large part of bowl; in 2010, only one rim and one body fr. extant. Oxidized. Rim frieze: rosette 7. Main decoration: scroll left with groups of three-dot berries. Calyx: imbricate large rounded petals with central vein.
– Domăneanțu 2000, 35 cat. 147, pl. 10 (attributed to Monogram PAR).

EPH-301
Istros, Sector "Pescărie", His-74-86, Bucharest, Institute of Archaeology storeroom. Body fr. H 5.5 × W 4, WT 0.35. Fabric: standard, 5YR 6/6. Coat with slight lustre ext., 7.5YR 4/2. Medium hard fired, oxidized. Main decoration: scroll left with groups of three-dot berries. Calyx: alternating ovoid and rhomboidal petals.
– Domăneanțu 2000, 27 cat. 100, pl. 7 (attributed to Monogram PAR).

EPH-302
Olbia, Sector NGS, House IV-4 B 397/219, О-НГС-93-842, Parutine, Olbia National Preserve storeroom. Fr. of rim and upper body. H 4 × W 3.8, WT 0.23–0.42, ⌀ rim 14, RH 2.8. Fabric: relatively fine and micaceous, many small lime particles and voids, 5YR 6/6, 7.5YR 6/4. Thin firm coat with slight metallic sheen, 10YR 3/1. Medium hard fired, oxidized. Rim frieze: box meander, cw. Main decoration: scroll left. One repair hole.
– Guldager Bilde 2010, 279 cat. F-29, pl. 174.

EPH-303
Olbia, Sector NGS, О-НГС-08-361, Parutine, Olbia National Preserve storeroom. Fr. of rim and upper body. H 4.4 × W 6.9, WT 0.3, ⌀ rim 14, 15%, RH 2. Fabric: relatively fine and micaceous, 5Y 5/1. Coat with slight lustre, Gley 1 2.5/1. Hard fired, reduced. Rim frieze: box meander, cw. Main decoration: stylized acanthus scroll?

EPH-304*
Olbia, Sector NGS, О-НГС-06-24, Parutine, Olbia National Preserve storeroom. Two joining frs. of rim and mid-body. H 5.1 × W 6, WT 0.2, ⌀ rim 12, 16%, RH 1.6. Fabric: fine, micaceous, 2.5YR 6/8. Thin dull coat, almost completely lost int., 2.5YR 5/6. Medium hard fired, oxidized. Rim frieze: guilloche right. Main decoration: scroll left with groups of three-dot berries. One repair hole.

EPH-305
Porthmion, Sector G, sector 2, fill in rooms, П-87-111, St Petersburg IIMK RAN. Fr. of rim and upper body. Rim frieze: guilloche right. Main decoration: scroll left with group of three-dot berries.

EPH-306*
Olbia, Sector NGS, О-НГС-08-360, Parutine, Olbia National Preserve storeroom. Fr. of rim and upper body. H 4.3 × W 4.9, WT 0.35. Fabric: relatively fine and micaceous, 5Y 5/1. Slightly lustrous coat, Gley 1 2.5/N. Medium hard fired, reduced. Rim

frieze: miniature acanthus-flower scroll left. Main decoration: scroll left. Monogram PAR.

EPH-307*
Olbia, Sector NGS, O-НГС-06-113[a], Parutine, Olbia National Preserve storeroom. Fr. of rim and upper body. H 4 × W 5.7, WT 0.2, ⌀ rim 12, 15%, RH 1.6. Fabric: relatively fine and micaceous, some small lime inclusions, 5YR 6/6. Thin dull coat, 2.5YR 4/6. Medium hard fired, oxidized. Rim frieze: rosette 2/7. Main decoration: scroll left.

EPH-308*
Olbia, Sector NGS, O-НГС-88-202, Parutine, Olbia National Preserve storeroom. Fr. of rim and upper body. Mottled coat. Oxidized. Rim frieze: rosette 2/7. Main decoration: scroll left with groups of three-dot berries.

EPH-309*
Olbia, Sector R25, O-P25-05-2974, Parutine, Olbia National Preserve storeroom. Fr. of rim and upper body. H 4 × W 4, WT 0.22, RH 1.8. Fabric: relatively fine and micaceous, small lime inclusions, 10YR 5/4. Thin coat with slight metallic sheen ext., dull int., 10YR 3/1. Medium hard fired, oxidized. Rim frieze: star rosettes. Main decoration: scroll left.

EPH-310*
Olbia, Sector NGS, O-НГС-06-114, Parutine, Olbia National Preserve storeroom. Fr. of rim and upper body. H 4.7 × W 5.8, WT 0.32, ⌀ rim 12, 15%, RH 1.2. Fabric: relatively fine and micaceous, 5YR 6/6. Thin dull coat, 5YR 4/3. Medium hard fired, oxidized. Rim frieze: rosette 5. Main decoration: scroll left. Three repair holes.

EPH-311*
Olbia, Sector Sever-Zapad, O-СЗ-68-1820+1821+1825+1826, Parutine, Olbia National Preserve storeroom. Two rim frs. and two frs. of body, all joining. H 5.5 × W 11, WT 0.3–0.35, ⌀ rim 11, 26%, RH 1.4. Fabric: standard, some very large lime particles, 2.5YR 6/8. Dull coat, ext. 10R 5/8, 7.5YR 2.5/1, int. 10R 5/8. Relatively hard fired, oxidized. Stacked in firing. Rim frieze: rosette 5. Main decoration: scroll left with groups of three-dot berries.

EPH-312*
Olbia, Sector NGS, O-НГС-06-360, Parutine, Olbia National Preserve storeroom. Fr. of rim and upper body. H 5 × W 8.5, WT 0.3, ⌀ rim 12.5, 22%, RH 1.6. Fabric: relatively fine and micaceous, 10YR 6/4. Thin coat with slight metallic sheen, 10YR 3/1. Medium hard fired, oxidized. Rim frieze: Ionian kyma. Main decoration: scroll right, without berries. One repair hole.

EPH-313*
Olbia, Cliff "B-VIII", square 285, yellow clay layer, O-70-213, Parutine, Olbia National Preserve storeroom. Fr. of rim and body. H 6.2 × W 5.6, WT 0.31, RH 2.3. Fabric: standard, many small lime particles, 2.5Y 5/1. Coat with slight lustre, 5Y 2.5/1. Relatively hard fired, reduced. Rim frieze: Ionian kyma. Main decoration: scroll left, without berries.

EPH-314*
Pantikapaion, palace foundation trench, M-89-illegible 46, Moscow, Puškin Museum of Fine Arts. Fr. of mid-body. Oxidized. Main decoration: scroll left, without berries. Calyx B (top of folded acanthus leaf preserved).

Stylized Acanthus-Vine Scroll

EPH-315*
Olbia, Sector NGS, O-НГС-02-40, 40a, Parutine, Olbia National Preserve storeroom. Two non-joining frs. of rim and body. H 5.9 × W 7, WT 0.35–0.6, ⌀ rim 12.5, 15%, RH 2.15. Fabric: relatively fine and micaceous, many small lime particles, some voids of different sizes, 5YR 6/6, 7.5YR 6/4. Thin firm semi-lustrous coat, 10YR 3/1. Medium hard fired, oxidized. Stacked in firing. Rim frieze: Ionian kyma. Main decoration: scroll left with bunch of grapes.

EPH-316*
Olbia, Sector NGS, O-НГС-92-187, Parutine, Olbia National Preserve storeroom. Fr. of rim and upper body. H 5.2 × W 5.3, WT 0.32, RH 2. Fabric: relatively fine and micaceous, 5YR 6/8. Dull coat, 5YR 4/2. Medium hard fired, oxidized. Stacked in firing. Rim frieze: Ionian kyma. Main decoration: scroll left with bunch of grapes.

EPH-317
Olbia, Sector NGS, O-НГС-06-394, Parutine, Olbia National Preserve storeroom. Fr. of rim and upper body. H 5.3 × W 6.2, WT 0.4, RH 1.4. Fabric: relatively fine and micaceous, some small lime inclusions, 7.5YR 6/4. Thin coat with metallic sheen, 7.5YR 4/1. Medium hard fired, oxidized. Rim frieze: Ionian kyma. Main decoration: scroll left with bunch of grapes. Calyx: calyx or imbricate (only tip of pointed petal preserved).

Ultra-Stylized Acanthus Scroll

EPH-318*
Istros, His-B 479/V 8573 P+V 8573 X, Bucharest, Institute of Archaeology storeroom. Two joining frs. of rim and upper body. H 8.2 × W 5.1, WT 0.25, ⌀ rim 12, 20%, RH 2.3. Fabric: standard,

abundant small lime inclusions, large voids, 5YR 6/6. Mottled coat with slight lustre, ext. 5YR 3/1, 3/2 int. 5YR 3/1, 4/4. Relatively hard fired, oxidized. Rim frieze: rosette 7. Main decoration: scroll left.
– Domăneanțu 2000, 106 cat. 539, pl. 35.

EPH-319*
Istros, His-V 19434, Bucharest, Institute of Archaeology storeroom. Fr. of rim and body. H 6 × W 6.3, WT 0.3, ⌀ rim 13, RH 1.8. Fabric: standard, abundant small lime inclusions, 2.5YR 5/8. Mottled coat with slight lustre, ext. 10YR 3/1, 2.5YR 4/8, int. 10YR 3/1. Relatively hard fired, oxidized. Stacked in firing. Rim frieze: rosette 7. Main decoration: scroll left. Calyx: lotus petal, bud on stem?
– Domăneanțu 2000, 106 cat. 540, pl. 35.

EPH-320*
Olbia, Sector E6–7, squares 598e, 608e, yellow clay layer, O-E6-7-61-452+693, Kiev, Institute of Archaeology storeroom. Four rim frs., five body frs., all joining; two rim frs. and a body fr., joining. WT 0.35, ⌀ rim 13, 6%, RH 1.5. Fabric: standard, 5YR 6/8. Dull coat, ext. 2.5YR 5/6, 10YR 3/1, int. 2.5YR 5/6. Not too hard fired, oxidized. Stacked in firing. Rim frieze: small star rosettes. Main decoration: scroll right. Calyx: straight sloppy acanthus alternating with Menemachos bud. Menemachos?

EPH-321*
Istros, His-735, Bucharest, Institute of Archaeology storeroom. Body fr. Oxidized. Rim frieze: Ionian kyma. Main decoration: scroll with groups of three dot berries.

EPH-322*
Olbia, Sector NGS, O-НГС-05-226, 226a, Parutine, Olbia National Preserve storeroom. One third of bowl, almost complete profile, lacking base; non-joining body fr. H 7.4 × W 9.4, WT 0.35, ⌀ rim 12, 22%, RH 1.7; vessel H 6; H:⌀ 1:2. Fabric: relatively fine and micaceous, 5YR 6/6. Thin dull coat, ext. 2.5YR 4/6, 7.5YR 3/2, int. 2.5YR 4/6. Medium hard fired, oxidized. Stacked in firing. Rim frieze: Ionian kyma. Main decoration: scroll right. Calyx C, var. (acanthus with spear-head top alternating with rhomboidal petal). Two repair holes.

EPH-323
Istros, His-1102, Bucharest, Institute of Archaeology storeroom. Body fr. H 4.5. Oxidized. Rim frieze: rosette 7. Main decoration: scroll running in alternating directions.

C Garlands and Wreaths

Myrtle Wreath

EPH-324*
Pantikapaion, П-1906-34, St Petersburg, State Hermitage Museum. Complete. ⌀ rim 13, ⌀ base 3.3; vessel H 6.3; H:⌀ 1:1.9. Oxidized. Rim frieze: star rosettes. Main decoration: wreath left, berries on stems and groups of three-dot berries. Calyx: calyx C, var. (straight acanthus alternating with rhomboidal petal with hatched central vein). Medallion: rosette B. Frieze separators: dots.

EPH-325*
Olbia, Sector NGS, O-НГС-02-260 Parutine, Olbia National Preserve storeroom. Three joining frs. of rim and upper body. H 5.3 × W 11.6, WT 0.25–0.36, ⌀ rim 12.5, RH 2. Fabric: fine, highly micaceous, numerous minute lime inclusions, few voids, 2.5YR 5/8. Thin flaking coat with a slight lustre, slightly mottled ext., blackened at rim int., int worn off in large patches, ext. 2.5YR 4/6, 10YR 3/2, int. 2.5YR 4/6. Medium hard fired, oxidized. Stacked in firing. Rim frieze: box meander, cw. Main decoration: wreath left, berries on stems and three-dot berries.

EPH-326*
Volna 1, С3-00-179, St Petersburg, State Hermitage Museum. Fr. of mid- and lower body. Oxidized. Stacked in firing. Rim frieze: Lesbian kyma? Main decoration: wreath left, berries on stems and three-dot berries. Calyx B.

EPH-327
Pantikapaion, 1903–15. Complete. Rim frieze: Lesbian kyma. Main decoration: wreath left, berries on stems and single berries in field. Calyx B2, low. Medallion: rosette A, var. 2.
– St Petersburg, IIMK RAN photo archive neg. III 9672.

EPH-328*
Olbia, Sector NGS, House IV-4 B 351/218, O-НГС-93-559, 559a, Parutine, Olbia National Preserve storeroom. Two non-joining frs. of rim and upper body. H 4.2 × W 6.3, WT 0.15–.44, ⌀ rim 14, RH 1.85. Fabric: relatively fine and micaceous, many small lime particles, 5YR 5/6, 10YR 6/4. Thin firm slightly lustrous coat, darkened at lip, ext. 2.5YR 3/4, 3/0, int. 2.5YR 3/4. Medium hard fired, oxidized. Stacked in firing. Rim frieze: rosette 2/8, var. Main decoration: wreath left, berries on short stems and single berries in field.
– Guldager Bilde 2010, 278 cat. F-18, pl. 172.

EPH-329*
Myrmekion, M-57-219, St Petersburg IIMK RAN. Body fr. H 5.5, WT 0.42. Fabric: standard, 5YR 6/6. Slightly lustrous coat ext.

2.5YR 4/6, 10R 2.5/1, int. 2.5YR 4/1. Oxidized. Stacked in firing. Rim frieze: Ionian kyma. Main decoration: wreath left, dotted stems. Calyx: imbricate, small pointed petals with central vein.

EPH-330*
Istros, His-B 543 C, Bucharest, Institute of Archaeology storeroom. Fr. of upper body. H 3.5 × W 4.7. Oxidized. Stacked in firing. Rim frieze: Ionian kyma. Main decoration: wreath left, berries on stems,.
– Domăneanţu 2000, 47 cat. 214, pl. 14 (attributed to Petite rose spiralée).

EPH-331
Pantikapaion, M-64-375, Moscow, Puškin Museum of Fine Art. Fr. of rim and upper body. Rim frieze: box meander, cw. Main decoration: wreath left, berries on stems.
– Zabelina 1984, 161 fig. 8e (idenfitied as Pergamene).

EPH-332
Olbia, Sector NGS, House IV-3 B 343/200, О-НГС-92-74, Parutine, Olbia National Preserve storeroom. Body fr. H 2.8 × W 3.4, WT 0.33-0.5. Fabric: fine, dense, slightly micaceous, a few minute lime particles, some small voids, 5YR 6/6. Thin firm slightly lustrous coat, diluted on top of reliefs, mottled ext., ext. 10YR 3/1, 7.5YR 5/6, int. 2.5Y 4/2. Medium hard fired, oxidized. Stacked in firing. Main decoration: wreath left, berries on stems. Calyx: acanthus leaf alternating with nelumbo with parallel veins; monogram PA or AP between the leaves.
– Guldager Bilde 2010, 278 cat. F-22, pl. 173.

EPH-333
Bol'šoj Kastel', room 12, БК-85-inv. 3562/A-131, Černomorskoe Museum of Historical Lore. Almost complete bowl, lacking base. Bicolour coat. Oxidized. Stacked in firing. Rim frieze: Ionian kyma. Main decoration: wreath right, berries on stems and three-dot berries. Calyx B2.

EPH-334
Chersonesos, X-1952-148, St Petersburg, State Hermitage Museum. Fr. of mid- and lower body close to base. H 5.7, WT 0.35. Fabric: standard, 2.5YR 5/8. Thin slightly lustrous coat, ext. 10R 5/6, 3/,1 int. 2.5YR 5/6. Oxidized. Stacked in firing. Main decoration: wreath right, berries on stems and three-dot berries. Calyx B.

EPH-335*
Myrmekion, M-57-148(?), St Petersburg IIMK RAN. Fr. of mid- and lower body. H 4.4, WT 0.25. Fabric: standard, 5YR 6/6. Lustrous coat, 5YR 3/1. Oxidized. Main decoration: wreath right, berries on stems and three-dot berries. Calyx B.

EPH-336*
Istros, His-893, Bucharest, Institute of Archaeology storeroom. Fr. of upper body. H 3 × W 3.3, WT 0.25. Fabric: standard, fine, 5YR 6/8. Dull coat, 2.5YR 5/8. Medium hard fired, oxidized. Main decoration: wreath right, berries on short stems and three-dot berries. Rim frieze: rosette 2/7.
– Domăneanţu 2000, 41 cat. 180, pl. 12 (attributed to Monogram PAR).

EPH-337*
Chersonesos, X-1953-464, St Petersburg, State Hermitage Museum. Fr. of rim and upper body. H 4.8, WT 0.35, ⌀ rim 12, RH 1.8. Fabric: standard, fine, 10YR 7/2. Thin dull coat, Gley 1 2.5/N. Oxidized. Multiple rim friezes: Ionian kyma; horizontal S-spirals. Main decoration: wreath right.

EPH-338*
Olbia, Sector R25, O-P25-99-1024, Parutine, Olbia National Preserve storeroom. Fr. of rim and upper body. H 5.3 × W 5.8, WT 0.3–0.5, ⌀ rim 13, 15%, RH 1.5. Fabric: relatively fine and micaceous, small lime inclusions, 5YR 6/6. Slightly lustrous coat, ext. 2.5YR 4/6, 5YR 2.5/1, int. 5YR 3/3, mottled. Medium hard fired, oxidized. Stacked in firing. Rim frieze: Ionian kyma. Main decoration: wreath right, berries on stems and three-dot berries.

EPH-339
Istros, His-226, Bucharest, Institute of Archaeology storeroom. Fr. of rim and upper body. Reduced. Rim frieze: Ionian kyma. Main decoration: wreath right, three-dot berries.

EPH-340*
Olbia, Sector E7, squares 613e, 623ne, grey clay layer, O-E7-71-621, Kiev, Institute of Archaeology storeroom. Two joining frs. of rim and body. H 5.2 × W 6.8, WT 0.25, RH 1.3. Fabric: standard, 2.5YR 6/8. Dull coat, ext. 10R 5/6, 7.5YR 5/6, int. 10R 5/6, 3/1. Relatively hard fired, oxidized. Stacked in firing. Rim frieze: Lesbian kyma. Main decoration: wreath right, berries on stems and three-dot berries.

EPH-341
Myrmekion, M-57-307, St Petersburg IIMK RAN. Body fr. H 3.8, WT 0.25. Fabric: standard, 2.5YR 5/8. Slightly lustrous coat, ext. 2.5YR 4/6, 4/3, int. 2.5YR 4/6. Oxidized. Stacked in firing. Rim frieze: Lesbian kyma. Main decoration: wreath right, berries on stems and three-dot berries. May be from same bowl as EPH-342.

EPH-342
Myrmekion, M-58-2962, St Petersburg IIMK RAN. Fr. of rim and upper body. H 4, WT 0.35, RH 1.4. Fabric: standard, 2.5YR 5/8. Dull coat, slightly lustrous at rim ext., ext. 2.5YR 4/6, 4/3, int.

2.5YR 4/6. Oxidized. Stacked in firing. Rim frieze: Lesbian kyma. Main decoration: wreath right, three-dot berries. May be from same bowl as EPH-341.

EPH-343*
Istros, Plateau, His-88, Bucharest, Institute of Archaeology storeroom. Rim fr. H 5.5 × W 2.7, WT 0.2, RH 1.4. Fabric: standard, 2.5YR 6/8. Dull coat, 2.5YR 5/6. Relatively hard fired, oxidized. Rim frieze: heart guilloche right. Main decoration: wreath right, berries on stems and three-dot berries.
– Domăneanțu 2000, 41 cat. 181, pl. 12 (attributed to Monogram PAR).

EPH-344*
Myrmekion, M-47-209, St Petersburg IIMK RAN. Fr. of rim and upper body. H 4.1, WT 0.32, ⌀ rim 14, RH 1.6. Fabric: standard, 2.5YR 5/8. Thin dull coat int. with slight lustre ext., ext. 2.5YR 4/6, 4/3, int. 2.5YR 4/6. Oxidized. Stacked in firing. Rim frieze: rosette 2/7. Main decoration: wreath right, berry (on stem?) and three-dot berries.

EPH-345
Olbia, Sector R25, O-P25-93-1362, Parutine, Olbia National Preserve storeroom. Fr. of rim and upper body. H 3.7 × W 5.7, WT 0.4, ⌀ rim 14, 12%, RH 1.55. Fabric: relatively fine and micaceous, some small voids, 5YR 7/8. Dull coat, ext. 5YR 3/2, int. 5YR 3/1. Medium hard fired, oxidized. Rim frieze: star rosettes. Main decoration: wreath right, berries (on stems?) and three-dot berries.

EPH-346*
Chersonesos, X-1965-64, St Petersburg, State Hermitage Museum. Fr. of rim and upper body. H 3.5, WT 0.35, ⌀ rim 12, 11%, RH 2.35. Fabric: standard, 2.5YR 6/6. Lustrous coat ext., ext. 2.5YR 3/6, 2.5/1 int. 2.5YR 4/6. Oxidized. Stacked in firing. Rim frieze: star rosettes. Main decoration: wreath right.

EPH-347*
Istros, Sector MC1 Sa, His-56-60, Bucharest, Institute of Archaeology storeroom. Body fr. Oxidized. Main decoration: wreath left, three-dot berries. Calyx A (top of 'nelumbo' preserved).

EPH-348*
Chersonesos, pit 2 (1877)f, X-1908-10, St Petersburg, State Hermitage Museum. Complete profile; half of bowl, restored from fragments. H 5.3, ⌀ rim 12.2, RH 1.35, ⌀ base 3.9. Fabric: no fresh break for observation. Thin slightly lustrous coat, ext. 2.5YR 4/6, 2.5/1, int. 2.5YR 4/6. Oxidized. Stacked in firing. Rim frieze: Ionian kyma. Main decoration: wreath left, three-dot berries. Calyx C (tips of pointed lotus petal, straight acanthus). Medallion: rosette A.

EPH-349*
Olbia, Sector NGS, O-НГС-97-222+98-330+511+511a+511b (join across years), Parutine, Olbia National Preserve storeroom. Five rim frs. joining two and two and one joining body fr. H 6.15 × W 5.85, WT 0.38, ⌀ rim 13, RH 2. Fabric: relatively fine, micaceous, a few small lime particles, 10YR 6/3. Thin dark coat with metallic lustre, 2.5Y 3/0. Medium hard fired, oxidized. Rim frieze: Ionian kyma. Main decoration: wreath left, three-dot berries. Calyx: pointed lotus petal with central vein, probably imbricate. Graffito A on rim.
– Guldager Bilde 2010, 278 cat. F-20, pl. 172.

EPH-350
Pantikapaion, M-47-901, Moscow, Puškin Museum of Fine Arts. Fr. of rim and body. Rim frieze: astragal. Main decoration: wreath left, three-dot berries.
– Zabelina 1984, 156 fig. 3f.

EPH-351
Olbia, Sector Sever-Zapad, O-СЗ-68-1822, Parutine, Olbia National Preserve storeroom. Rim fr. H 3.3 × W 3.4, WT 0.35, RH 1.6. Fabric: standard, fine, 2.5YR 6/8. Thin coat with dull lustre, 10YR 3/1. Relatively hard fired, oxidized. Rim frieze: astragal with decorated beads. Main decoration: wreath left.

EPH-352*
Olbia, Sector E7, squares 628n, 629ne, humus O-E7-62-1240, Kiev, Institute of Archaeology storeroom. Fr. of rim and body. Oxidized. Rim frieze: box meander, cw. Main decoration: wreath left, three-dot berries. Frieze separators: dots

EPH-353*
Olbia, Sector E6, square 405, basement with walls 4, 15, 16, 18, O-E6-56-443, Kiev, Institute of Archaeology storeroom. Fr. of rim and upper body. Oxidized. Stacked in firing. Rim frieze: wave meander, upside-down. Main decoration: wreath left, three-dot berries. Secondarily burnt

EPH-354*
Myrmekion, M-56-1572, St Petersburg IIMK RAN. Body fr. close to rim. H 3.3, WT 0.4. Fabric: standard, 2.5YR 5/8. Thin dull coat, ext. 2.5YR 3/1, int. 10R 4/6. Oxidized. Stacked in firing. Rim frieze: rosette 1. Main decoration: wreath left, three-dot berries. Menemachos.

EPH-355*
Chersonesos, X-1965-67, St Petersburg, State Hermitage Museum. Fr. of rim and upper body. H 5.8, WT 0.32, ⌀ rim 12, 10%, RH 1.9. Fabric: standard, 2.5YR 6/6. Thin lustrous coat, 2.5YR 4/6, 3/1. Oxidized. Stacked in firing. Rim frieze: rosette 2/7. Main decoration: wreath left, three-dot berries. Only traces of calyx preserved.

EPH-356*
Pantikapaion, palace foundation trench, M-89-illegible 34, Moscow, Puškin Museum of Fine Arts. Fr. of upper body. H 4.3 × W 3.8, WT 0.35. Oxidized. Rim frieze: rosette 5. Main decoration: wreath left, three-dot berries. Secondarily burnt.

EPH-357
Porthmion, Sector G, sector 2, square 17–18, depth 0.42 m, П-87-84, St Petersburg IIMK RAN. Fr. of rim and upper body. Multiple rim friezes: rosette 5; Ionian kyma. Main decoration: wreath left.

EPH-358
Olbia, O-1910-280, present whearabouts unknown. Fr. of rim and body. Rim frieze: Lesbian kyma. Main decoration: wreath right, three-dot berries.
– St Petersburg, IIMK RAN, archive inv. 40…(?) (pl. XIII).

EPH-359*
Olbia, Sector NGS, O-НГС-06-98, 250, Parutine, Olbia National Preserve storeroom. Two non-joining frs. of rim and upper body. H 4.3 × W 6.9, WT 0.3, ⌀ rim 12, 19%, RH 1.6. Fabric: relatively fine and micaceous, some small lime inclusions, 5YR 6/8. Thin dull coat, ext. 2.5YR 4/8, 4/3, int. 2.5YR 4/8. Medium hard fired, oxidized. Stacked in firing. Rim frieze: Lesbian kyma. Main decoration: wreath right, three-dot berries.

EPH-360*
Olbia, Sector NGS, House IV-2 B 280/160, O-НГС-90-216+301, Parutine, Olbia National Preserve storeroom. Two joining frs. of rim and upper body and non-joining rim fr. H 5.1 × W 8.6, WT 0.42–0.63, ⌀ rim 16.5, RH 1.8. Fabric: relatively fine and slightly micaceous, a few small lime inclusions, 7.5YR 7/6, 10YR 6/4. Thin firm coat, darkened at rim, slight lustre, ext. 10YR 3/2, 2.5YR 3/4, int. 5Y 2.5/1, 5YR 3/3. Medium hard fired, oxidized. Stacked in firing. Rim frieze: rosette 5. Main decoration: wreath right, three-dot berries. Cf. Laumonier 1977, 134 cat. 375, pl. 30 (Monogram PAR).
– Guldager Bilde 2010, 278 cat. F-21, pl. 172.

EPH-361*
Olbia, Sector NGS, O-НГС-02-261, Parutine, Olbia National Preserve storeroom. Two joining frs. of rim and upper body. H 2.8 × W 11.5, WT 0.17–0.35, ⌀ rim 14, RH 2.2. Fabric: fine, some lime particles, small black particles, 7.5YR 7/6. Thin firm coat with bluish metallic sheen, dull ext. beneath frieze of rosettes, ext. 5Y 4/1, int. N4/. Medium hard fired, oxidized. Stacked in firing. Rim frieze: rosette 2/7. Main decoration: wreath right, three-dot berries.

EPH-362*
Olbia, Sector AGD, O-АГД-71-1152, Kiev, Institute of Archaeology storeroom. Fr. of rim and upper body. Oxidized. Stacked in firing. Rim frieze: miniature acanthus-flower scroll left. Main decoration: wreath right, three-dot berries,. Monogram PAR.

EPH-363*
Olbia, Sector Sever-Zapad, O-СЗ-68-1824+1846, Parutine, Olbia National Preserve storeroom. Two joining frs. of body. H 7 × W 7, WT 0.3. Fabric: standard, 2.5YR 6/8. Thin dull coat, 2.5YR 4/6. Relatively hard fired, oxidized. Main decoration: wreath with five(?) leaves right, three-dot berries. Calyx B2.

EPH-364*
Olbia, Cliff "B-VIII", square 285, yellow clay layer, O-70-209, Parutine, Olbia National Preserve storeroom. Fr. of mid- and lower body. H 4.3 × W 6.6, WT 0.36. Fabric: standard, fine, 7.5YR 6/6. Coat with slight lustre, 7.5YR 2.5/1. Relatively hard fired, oxidized. Main decoration: wreath right, three-dot berries. Calyx B2.

EPH-365*
Pantikapaion, palace foundation trench, M-84-61, Moscow, Puškin Museum of Fine Arts. Fr. of mid- and lower body. H 4 × W 7.5, WT 0.5. Dull coat. Oxidized. Main decoration: wreath right, three-dot berries. Calyx C. Secondarily burnt.
– Košelenko 1992, fig. 23.

EPH-366
Volna 1, С3-00-26, St Petersburg, State Hermitage Museum. Fr. of rim and upper body. Oxidized. Rim frieze: Ionian kyma. Main decoration: wreath left. Frieze separators: dots.

EPH-367*
Pantikapaion, palace foundation trench, M-89-illegible no., M-89-no no. 20, Moscow, Puškin Museum of Fine Arts. Rim fr. and non-joining body fr. Oxidized. Stacked in firing. Rim frieze: rosette 7. Main decoration: wreath left, three-dot berries. Secondarily burnt.

EPH-368*
Olbia, Sector NGS, O-НГС-08-149, Parutine, Olbia National Preserve storeroom. Fr. of upper body. H 3.2 × W 3.6, WT 0.31. Fabric: relatively fine and micaceous, Gley 1 6/N. Slightly lustrous coat, Gley 1 3/N. Hard fired, reduced. Main decoration: wreath with seven(?) leaves, left, three-dot berries.

EPH-369*
Olbia, Sector NGS, O-НГС-04-154 Parutine, Olbia National Preserve storeroom. Fr. of upper body. H 3.6 × W 4.4, WT 0.3. Fabric: relatively fine and micaceous, 5Y 4/1. Dull coat, Gley 1 2.5/1.

Medium hard fired, reduced. Rim frieze: Ionian kyma. Main decoration: wreath with two leaves, left, berries on stems.

EPH-370*
Olbia, Sector NGS, House IV-2 B 302/182, О-НГС-94-165, 596, 96-14, Parutine, Olbia National Preserve storeroom. Two joining body frs. and one non-joining rim fr. H 4.3 × W 8.7, WT 0.33–0.36, ⌀ rim 13, RH 2.2. Fabric: fine and micaceous, some minute lime inclusions, few voids, 2.5YR 5/8. Thin firm semi-lustrous coat, darkened at rim and part of bowl, ext. 2.5YR 4/6, 10YR 3/3, int. 2.5YR 3/4–3/6. Hard fired, oxidized. Stacked in firing. Rim frieze: Ionian kyma. Main decoration: wreath with three leaves, left, berries on stems. One repair hole.
– Guldager Bilde 2010, 278 cat. F-16, pl. 171.

EPH-371
Olbia, V.I. 7754.64, Antikensammlung, Staatliche Museen zu Berlin. Fr. of mid-body. H 4 × W 4.7, WT 0.5. Fabric: very fine, 2.5YR 5/6. Dull coat ext., slight lustre int., ext. 2.5YR 3/4, int. 2.5YR 4/8. Oxidized. Rim frieze: Ionian kyma. Main decoration: wreath with three leaves, left, berries on stems. Calyx: imbricate rounded petals with central vein. One repair hole.

EPH-372*
Olbia, Sector NGS, House III-3 R 359/115, О-НГС-92-810, Parutine, Olbia National Preserve storeroom. Three rim frs. and two body frs., joining. Oxidized. Stacked in firing. Rim frieze: Ionian kyma. Main decoration: wreath with three leaves, left, berries on stems.
– Guldager Bilde 2010, 278 cat. F-17, pl. 171.

EPH-373
Myrmekion, M-57-618, St Petersburg IIMK RAN. Fr. of rim and upper body. H 3.9, WT 0.25, RH 1.6. Fabric: standard, 2.5YR 5/8. Coat with pink metallic sheen, ext. 2.5YR 3/1, int. 2.5YR 3/2. Oxidized. Stacked in firing. Rim frieze: rosette 5. Main decoration: wreath with three(?) rounded leaves and three(?) dot berries, left.

EPH-374*
Chersonesos, X-1953-463, St Petersburg, State Hermitage Museum. Fr. of rim and upper body. H 5.1, WT 0.3, ⌀ rim 13, RH 1.7. Fabric: no fresh break for observation. Thin dull coat, ext. 10R 6/6, 2.5YR 4/2, int. 10R 5/6. Oxidized. Stacked in firing. Rim frieze: Ionian kyma. Main decoration: wreath left; some of the leaves are made with same punch used for imbricate leaves with central and side veins.

EPH-375*
Olbia, Sector R25, O-P25-98-2807, Parutine, Olbia National Preserve storeroom. Body fr. H 4.3 × W 6.3, WT 0.2–0.35. Fabric: relatively fine and micaceous, 7.5YR 6/6. Dull coat, ext. 10R 4/6, 3/1, int. 10R 4/8. Medium hard fired, oxidized. Stacked in firing. Rim frieze: vertical astragal. Main decoration: wreath with three leaves, left, berries on stems. Calyx: tip of vertical palm branch. Frieze separators: horizontal S-spirals. Early.

EPH-376*
Olbia, Sector R25, O-P25-99-1943, Parutine, Olbia National Preserve storeroom. Fr. of rim and upper body. H 4.1 × W 3.3, WT 0.35, RH 1.5. Fabric: relatively fine and micaceous, 2.5YR 5/8. Slightly lustrous coat, ext. 2.5YR 4/3, int. 2.5YR 4/6. Medium hard fired, oxidized. Stacked in firing. Rim frieze: Ionian kyma. Main decoration: wreath left, three-dot berries.

EPH-377
Olbia, Sector AGD, О-АГД-71-1389, Kiev, Institute of Archaeology storeroom. Fr. of upper body close to rim. Oxidized. Rim frieze: Ionian kyma. Main decoration: wreath left, three-dot berries.

EPH-378*
Chersonesos, X-1965-68, St Petersburg, State Hermitage Museum. Fr. of rim and upper body. H 4.1, WT 0.2, ⌀ rim 13, 10%, RH 1.8. Fabric: standard, Gley 1 5/10Y. Thin dull coat, Gley 1 3/N. Reduced. Rim frieze: rosette 2/8 (M). Main decoration: wreath with three leaves, left, single dot berries. Menemachos?

EPH-379
Pantikapaion, M-46-4447, Moscow, Puškin Museum of Fine Arts. Fr. of rim and body. Rim frieze: miniature stylized acanthus scroll left. Main decoration: wreath with three leaves, left, three-dot berries. Frieze separators: large dots.
– Zabelina 1984, 156 fig. 3b.

EPH-380*
Olbia, Sector E, square 250, Pit "A", NW corner, O-E-49-2937, Kiev, Institute of Archaeology storeroom. Fr. of rim and upper body. H 3.4 × W 5.5, WT 0.2, ⌀ rim 12, 15%, RH 1.9. Fabric: standard, 5Y 6/1. Thin dull coat, ext. Gley 1 3/N, int. Gley 1 5/N. Relatively hard fired, reduced. Rim frieze: pointed petal with double outline left. Main decoration: wreath with dot berries left. Frieze separators: dots. Menemachos?

EPH-381
Olbia, Sector AGD, О-АГД-74-472, Kiev, Institute of Archaeology storeroom. Fr. of rim and upper body. Dull coat. Oxidized. Stacked in firing. Rim frieze: Ionian kyma. Main decoration: wreath right.

EPH-382*
Myrmekion, M-56-981, St Petersburg IIMK RAN. Fr. of rim and upper body. H 3.6, WT 0.25, ⌀ rim 12, 17%, RH 1.6. Fabric: standard, 5YR 6/6. Dull coat, slightly lustrous at rim ext., 2.5YR 4/6, 10R 2.5/1. Oxidized. Stacked in firing. Rim frieze: wave meander, upside-down. Main decoration: wreath with three-dot berries right.

Ivy Wreath

EPH-383*
Olbia, Sector NGS, House IV-2 B 302/180, O-НГС-94-42+115, 335, Parutine, Olbia National Preserve storeroom. Two joining and one non-joining rim frs. H 5.25 × W 9.8. WT 0.25–0.4, ⌀ rim 13, RH 1.85. Fabric: highly micaceous, a few small lime inclusions, some small reddish and brownish stones, 7.5YR 6/4. Thin firm slightly lustrous coat, darkened at lip int. and blotched at rim ext. with slight metallic sheen where darkened, ext. 2.5YR 4/6, int. 2.5YR 5/6. Hard fired, oxidized. Stacked in firing. Rim frieze: wave meander, upside-down. Main decoration: ivy wreath with three leaves around ivy-berry cluster left, three-dot berries above and below. Two repair holes.
– Guldager Bilde 2010, 278 cat. F-23, pl. 173.

EPH-384*
Tyritake, Sector L, Л-47-152, St Petersburg IIMK RAN. Fr. of rim and upper body. H 4.6, WT 0.31, ⌀ rim 15, RH 1.6. Fabric: standard, 5YR 5/8. Coat with bluish metallic sheen ext., int. slightly lustrous, ext. 5YR 3/2, int. 5YR 4/3. Oxidized. Stacked in firing. Rim frieze: large dots. Main decoration: ivy wreath with three leaves around ivy-berry cluster left, three-dot berries above and below.

EPH-385*
Olbia, Sector AGD, O-АГД-87-313, Kiev, Institute of Archaeology storeroom. Fr. of mid- and lower body. H 4.3 × W 4.5, WT 0.4. Fabric: standard, Gley 1 5/10Y. Thin dull coat, slightly shiny where thicker, Gley 1 2.5/N. Relatively hard fired, reduced. Main decoration: ivy wreath with three leaves around ivy-berry cluster left, three-dot berries and additional ivy-berry cluster below. Calyx B2.

EPH-386*
Pantikapaion, П-1867-6, St Petersburg, State Hermitage Museum. Complete. H 7, ⌀ rim 11.5. Oxidized. Stacked in firing. Rim frieze: horizontal S-spirals. Main decoration: bound ivy wreath left, with ivy-berry clusters above and below. Calyx: ovoid lotus petals. Base: plain and slightly concave; A incised in mould before firing.

EPH-387
Pantikapaion, M-65-598, Moscow, Puškin Museum of Fine Art. Fr. of mid- and lower body. Rim frieze: box meander. Main decoration: ivy wreath with three leaves left, ivy-berry clusters above and below. Calyx B1.
– Zabelina 1984, 158 fig. 5d.

EPH-388*
Olbia, Sector R25, O-P25-92-3236+93–1361, 92-3225, 3228, 3231, (join across years), Parutine, Olbia National Preserve storeroom. Rim fr. and joining fr. of lower body (93–1861+92–3236) and three non-joining body frs. H 4.5 × W 4.3, WT 0.28, ⌀ rim 12, 9%, RH 1.5. Fabric: relatively fine and micaceous, many long voids, 10YR 6/4. Dull coat, 10YR 3/1. Medium hard fired, oxidized. Rim frieze: Ionian kyma. Main decoration: ivy wreath with three leaves around ivy-berry clusters right.

Suspended Garlands

EPH-389*
Olbia, Square B5, O-Б5-76-84+90+91, 207, Kiev, Institute of Archaeology storeroom. Complete profile; two rim frs., two body frs. and large fr. of base and lower body, all joining; one non-joining fr. of rim and upper body. WT 0.3–0.8, ⌀ rim 12, RH 1.6; vessel H 6.5; H:⌀ 1:1.9. Fabric: standard, abundant lime, 7.5YR 6/6. Dull coat, slight metallic sheen at rim ext. where blackened, ext. 10R 5/8, 7.5YR 3/1, int. 2.5YR 5/6, 7.5YR 4/2, 3/1. Relatively hard fired, oxidized. Stacked in firing. Rim frieze: Ionian kyma. Main decoration: bound garlands suspended from rosette 2/4; rosette 2/7 over garland. Calyx B1. Medallion: rosette A.

EPH-390*
Olbia, Sector AGD, Bothros 11, O-АГД-88-203, 87-999, Kiev, Institute of Archaeology storeroom. Two large frs. of rim and body; sherds from 1987 and 1988 do not join but are from the same vessel. H 7 × W 7, WT 0.2–0.3, ⌀ rim 12.5, RH 1.8. Fabric: standard, 10YR 6/4. Coat with dull lustre, 10YR 3/1. Hard fired, oxidized. Rim frieze: Ionian kyma. Main decoration: bound garlands suspended from rosette 2/7; rosette 2/7 over garland. Calyx: calyx B1.

EPH-391*
Istros, His-V 19382, Bucharest, Institute of Archaeology storeroom. Fr. of lower body. H 3.7 × W 5, WT 0.5. Fabric: standard, fine, 2.5YR 7/6. Dull mottled coat, ext. 10YR 4/3, int. 10R 5/8, 10YR 4/1. Medium hard fired, oxidized. Main decoration: bound garland. Calyx B.
– Domăneanțu 2000, 30 cat. 117, pl. 8 (attributed to Monogram PAR).

EPH-392*
Volna 1, C3-00-121, St Petersburg, State Hermitage Museum. Fr. of upper body. Oxidized. Stacked in firing. Rim frieze: Ionian kyma. Main decoration: bound garlands suspended from rosette 2/4; rosette 2/7 over garland.

EPH-393
Pantikapaion, Mt Mithridates, chance find, M-year(?)-30. Complete. Oxidized. Stacked in firing. Rim frieze: star rosettes. Main decoration: bound garland suspended from small rosette 2/6; rosette 2/7 over garlands. Calyx C. Medallion: rosette B.
– Loseva 1962, 197, fig. 1.9; AGSP 1984, pl. CLXIV.5.

EPH-394*
Istros, Sector ZS7, His-65-237/V 25358 F, Bucharest, Institute of Archaeology storeroom. Fr. of rim and upper body. H 5 × W 5, WT 0.25, ⌀ rim 12, 10%, RH 1.3. Fabric: standard, fine, 5YR 7/8. Dull coat, ext. 2.5YR 5/4, 10YR 3/1, int. 2.5YR 6/4. Relatively hard fired, oxidized. Stacked in firing. Rim frieze: Ionian kyma. Main decoration: bound garlands suspended from *tainia*; rosette 2 var. over garland.
– Domăneanțu 2000, 98 cat. 482, pl. 32.

EPH-395*
Istros, His-670, Bucharest, Institute of Archaeology storeroom. Fr. of upper body. H 3.7 × W 5.3, WT 0.25. Fabric: standard, 5YR 6/8. Dull mottled coat, ext. 5YR 3/2, 2.5/1, int. 2.5YR 4/6, 3/4. Medium hard fired, oxidized. Stacked in firing. Rim frieze: Ionian kyma. Main decoration: garland suspended from *tainia*, the ends of which hang down; rosette 2, var. over garland.
– Domăneanțu 2000, 92 cat. 445, pl. 30.

EPH-396* (see also Fig. 79)
Olbia(?), inv. 54791 Uvarov 311/60, Moscow, State Historical Museum (Uvarov Collection). Complete profile; half preserved. ⌀ rim 12.5, RH 3, ⌀ base 3; vessel H 6.5; H:⌀ 1:1.9. Fabric: standard, with much lime. Thin coat, very blotchy in colour. Oxidized. Rim frieze: Lesbian kyma. Main decoration: bound garlands suspended from boukephalia; five-petalled rosettes over garlands. Calyx: ovoid lotus petals alternating with vertical miniature acanthus-flower scroll. Medallion: rosette D.
– Uvarov 1851, pl. XX.8.

EPH-397*
Olbia, Sector NGS, О-НГС-06-369, 485, Parutine, Olbia National Preserve storeroom. Two non-joining frs. of upper body. H 3.3 × W 3.9, WT 0.31. Fabric: relatively fine and micaceous, some small lime inclusions, 5YR 6/6. Slightly lustrous coat, ext. 2.5YR 4/8, Gley 1 2.5/N, int. 2.5YR 4/8. Hard fired, oxidized. Stacked in firing. Rim frieze: Ionian kyma. Main decoration: garlands suspended from boukrania, their ends tied by *tainia*; groups of three dots over garlands. Frieze separators: dots.

EPH-398*
Istros, His-B 500, Bucharest, Institute of Archaeology storeroom. Fr. of upper body. H 2.1 × W 2.4, WT 0.3. Fabric: standard, fine, 5YR 6/8. Dull coat, 2.5YR 5/8. Relatively hard fired, oxidized. Main decoration: garlands suspended from boukranion.
– Casan-Franga 1967, fig. 3.2; Domăneanțu 2000, 92 cat. 442, pl. 30.

EPH-399*
Myrmekion, M-57-619, St Petersburg IIMK RAN. Fr. of rim and upper body. H 4.8, WT 0.3, ⌀ rim 13, 12%, RH 2.4. Fabric: standard, fine, 5YR 6/6. Coat with metallic sheen, 5YR 3/1. Oxidized. Stacked in firing. Rim frieze: Ionian kyma. Main decoration: frontal female between two garlands, which she probably holds. Frieze separators: dots.

EPH-400*
Olbia, Sector NGS, О-НГС-05-462, Parutine, Olbia National Preserve storeroom. Fr. of rim and upper body. H 4.6 × W 4, WT 0.3, RH 1.3. Fabric: relatively fine and micaceous, many small lime inclusions, 5YR 6/6. Thin lustrous coat, ext. 2.5YR 4/8, 2.5/1, int. 5YR 3/1, 2.5YR 4/6. Medium hard fired, oxidized. Stacked in firing. Rim frieze: Ionian kyma. Main decoration: bound garland, Eros with raised arms running left. Pristine, sharp stamp.

EPH-401*
Istros, His-1071 Bucharest, Institute of Archaeology storeroom. Body fr. H 2.1 × W 2.3, WT 0.2. Fabric: standard, fine, 5Y 4/2. Dull coat, ext. 5Y 4/1, int. 5Y 3/1. Relatively hard fired, reduced. Rim frieze: traces. Main decoration: prancing horse right, bound garland with round motif above it. For the round motif, cf. Usačeva 1978, fig. 1.13.

EPH-402
Istros, His-V 19404, Bucharest, Institute of Archaeology storeroom. Fr. of lower body. H 2.5 × W 4.5. Oxidized. Main decoration: lower part of garland(?). Calyx A.
– Domăneanțu 2000, 31 cat. 123, pl. 9 (attributed to Monogram PAR).

EPH-403
Olbia, inv. H 4028, Würzburg, Martin von Wagner Museum der Universität Würzburg. Complete. ⌀ rim 13.7; vessel H 8.2; H:⌀ 1:1.7. Fabric: reddish, micaceous. Brown coat. Oxidized. Rim frieze: large star rosette with eight rays. Main decoration: suspended wreaths. Calyx: plastic long petals alternating with ovoid petals, with incised wavy line between them. Medallion: Medusa head with long tresses surrounded by frieze of jewellery pendants. Belles Méduses.
– Zahn 1908, 62 cat. 19; Boehlau 1908, 31 no. 279; Langlotz 1932, no. 922; Kotitsa 1998, 121–123 cat. 90, pl. 53.

Suspended Wreath

EPH-404*
Olbia, Sector R25, O-P25-95-1115a+b+1123, Parutine, Olbia National Preserve storeroom. Three joining frs. of rim and upper body. H 5.6 × W 6.4, WT 0.28. Fabric: relatively fine and micaceous, 2.5YR 5/8. Dull coat with slight metallic lustre where stacked, ext. 2.5YR 4/6, Gley 1 3/N, int. 2.5YR 4/6. Hard fired, oxidized. Stacked in firing. Rim frieze: guilloche left. Main decoration: Eros (with *kanoun*?) approaching suspended wreath with bow, suspended *tainia*, Eros repeated.

EPH-405*
Olbia, Square B5, basement 1, O-Б5-76-188, Kiev, Institute of Archaeology storeroom. Body fr. H 2.5 × W 2.5, WT 0.4. Oxidized. Main decoration: Eros left, holding *tainia*, next to suspended wreath.

EPH-406*
Olbia, Sector NGS, О-НГС-02-521, Parutine, Olbia National Preserve storeroom. Joining frs. of rim and body. H 5.4 × W 5.5, WT 0.35–0.5, ⌀ rim 12, RH 2. Fabric: relatively fine and micaceous, small lime particles, some voids, 2.5YR 5.5/8, 7.5YR 6/4. Thin firm coat, darkened with silvery lustrous sheen on lip, slight lustre int. where oxydised, ext. 2.5Y 3/0, int. 2.5YR 4/6, 5YR 3/4. Medium hard fired, oxidized. Stacked in firing. Rim frieze: Ionian kyma. Main decoration: Erotes playing syrinx flank suspended wreath with *tainia*.

D   *Multiple Rim Friezes*

Four Rim Friezes

EPH-407*
Olbia, Sector E6, squares 408s, 413n, grey clay layer, O-E6-61-53, Kiev, Institute of Archaeology storeroom. Fr. of rim and body. H 6 × W 8.2, WT 0.25, ⌀ rim 18, 14%, RH 2.2. Fabric: standard, fine, 2.5YR 6/8. Dull lustre, ext. 2.5YR 4/8, 3/3, int. 2.5YR 4/8, 3/1. Medium hard fired, oxidized. Stacked in firing. Rim friezes: Ionian kyma with hatched tongue; astragal; box meander, cw; guilloche left.

Three Rim Friezes

EPH-408*
Olbia, Sector NGS, House IV-4 B 397/219, О-НГС-93-840, Parutine, Olbia National Preserve storeroom. Fr. of rim and upper body. H 4 × W 3.5, WT 0.27–0.54, ⌀ rim 13, RH 1.5. Fabric: relatively fine and micaceous, abundant minute lime particles, 5YR 5/6, 10YR 6/6. Thin firm dull coat, semi-lustrous and darkened on lip int. and part of ext., ext. 5Y 3/1, 7.5YR 4/2, int. 2.5YR 4/6. Medium hard fired, oxidized. Stacked in firing. Rim friezes: astragal; crude Ionian kyma with hatched tongues; crude astragal.
– Guldager Bilde 2010, 280 cat. F-51, pl. 178.

EPH-409
Porthmion, П-73-253[a]+337, Kerč History and Culture Reserve. Two joining frs. of rim and upper body. Reduced. Rim friezes: astragal with decorated reels; Ionian kyma; astragal with decorated reels. Menemachos.
– Grzegrzółka 2010, 179 cat. 291.

EPH-410*
Ruminskoe/Za Rodinu. Рум-72-195, Moscow state historical museum. Fr. of rim and upper body. ⌀ rim 13, 15%. Oxidized. Rim friezes: astragal; star rosettes; Lesbian kyma.

EPH-411*
Olbia, Sector E6, square 250, 251w, grey clay layer, O-E6-56-673, Kiev, Institute of Archaeology storeroom. Two large joining frs. of rim and body. H 5.2 × W 12.4, WT 0.25, ⌀ rim 13, 38%, RH 1.6. Fabric: standard, 2.5YR 6/6. Coat with slight metallic sheen, ext. 10R 5/4, 2.5YR 3/1, int. 2.5YR 4/4. Hard fired, oxidized. Stacked in firing. Rim friezes: box meander; cw astragal; Lesbian kyma. Frieze separators: dots.

EPH-412*
Olbia, Sector R25, O-P25-00-1211, Parutine, Olbia National Preserve storeroom. Fr. of rim and upper body. ⌀ rim 16, 13%. Oxidized. Rim friezes: box meander, ccw; Ionian kyma; astragal with decorated beads.

EPH-413
Olbia, O-1910-1636, present whereabouts unknown. Fr. of rim and upper body. Rim friezes: Ionian kyma; astragal; guilloche right. Frieze separators: dots.
– St Petersburg, IIMK RAN, archive inv. 4058.519.6 (pl. III).

EPH-414
Olbia, Sector NGS, House IV-3 B 343/202, О-НГС-92-418, 419, 420, 423, Parutine, Olbia National Preserve storeroom. Four non-joining frs. of rim and body. H 4.1 × W 5, WT 0.25–0.5, ⌀ rim 13, RH 1.5. Fabric: relatively fine and micaceous, abundant small lime particles, a few small voids, 5YR 6/8. Thin firm coat, slightly lustrous. Medium hard fired, oxidized. Rim friezes: Ionian kyma; Lesbian kyma; rosette 2.
– Guldager Bilde 2010, 280 cat. F-50, pl. 177.

EPH-415
Olbia, Sector NGS, House IV-2 B 302/177, O-НГС-91-208+210, 208a, 209, 307, Parutine, Olbia National Preserve storeroom. Almost complete profile; two thirds of bowl consisting of two halves. WT 0.18–0.35, ⌀ rim 13, RH 2.3; vessel H 6.7; H:⌀ 1:1.9. Fabric: relatively fine, slightly micaceous, a few small lime inclusions and voids, 5YR 6/6. Thin mottled coat, black with bluish metallic sheen, mottled red in spots, ext. 7.5YR 3/0, 2.5YR 4/6, int. 10YR 3/2. Medium hard fired, oxidized. Stacked in firing. Rim friezes: Ionian kyma; rosette 2/7; birds sitting left alternating with palmettes. Calyx: low calyx of acanthus leaf with bent tip and jewelled central vein alternating with lotus petal with jewelled central vein. Edge of medallion only. Two repair holes. Cf. Laumonier 1977, 127 cats. 1063, 3033–3034, 3192, pl. 29 (bird alternating with palmette as secondary frieze, Comique á la canne, Annexe); Zahn 1908, 58 cat. 10.
– Guldager Bilde 2010, 280 cat. F-48, pl. 177.

EPH-416*
Olbia, Sector E6, square 247, room north of Wall 49, grey clay layer, O-E6-57-792, Kiev, Institute of Archaeology storeroom. Fr. of rim and upper body. H 5 × W 6.7, WT 0.35, ⌀ rim 15, 13%, RH 2. Fabric: standard, fine, but with some large lumps of lime, 2.5YR 6/8. Coat with dull lustre, ext. 2.5YR 4/8, 3/1, int. 2.5YR 3/1. Medium hard fired, oxidized. Stacked in firing. Rim friezes: Ionian kyma; jewellery pendants; horizontal S-spirals.

EPH-417*
Istros, His-310+B 467, Bucharest, Institute of Archaeology storeroom. Two joining frs. of rim and upper body. H 4.5 × W 8, WT 0.31, ⌀ rim 12, 18%, RH 2. Fabric: standard, 5YR 6/8. Dull coat, ext. 2.5YR 5/6, 7.5YR 3/2, int. 2.5YR 5/6. Medium hard fired, oxidized. Stacked in firing. Rim friezes: Ionian kyma; small palmettes; small palmettes? Lowest element could be top of calyx.
– Domăneanțu 2000, 98 cat. 483, pl. 32.

EPH-418
Olbia, O-1910-255, present whereabouts unknown. Fr. of rim and upper body. Rim friezes: star rosettes; astragal; guilloche right.
– St Petersburg, IIMK RAN, archive inv. 40...(?) (pl. XIII).

EPH-419*
Olbia, Sector NGS, O-НГС-92-526, Parutine, Olbia National Preserve storeroom. Fr. of rim and large part of body. H 5.3 × W 6.6, WT 0.3, ⌀ rim 12, 9%, RH 1.4. Fabric: relatively fine and micaceous with a few lime particles, 5YR 6/6. Thin firm coat with a slight lustre, ext. 2.5YR 4/6, 3/1, int. 2.5YR 4/6. Medium hard fired, oxidized. Stacked in firing. Rim friezes: star rosettes; rosette 2/7; Ionian kyma. Calyx: tip of pointed petal.

EPH-420
Porthmion, П-73-476, Kerč History and Culture Reserve. Body fr. Oxidized. Rim friezes: star rosettes; rosette 2/7; miniature acanthus-flower scroll left. Monogram PAR.
– Grzegrzółka 2010, 184 cat. 303.

EPH-421
Porthmion, П-76-37+43, Kerč History and Culture Reserve. Fr. of rim and upper body. Oxidized. Rim friezes: star rosettes; miniature acanthus-flower scroll left; Ionian kyma. Monogram PAR.
– Grzegrzółka 2010, 174–175 cat. 281.

EPH-422
Porthmion, Sector G, sector 2, fill in rooms, П-87-117, Kerč History and Culture Reserve. Fr. of rim and upper body. Rim friezes: miniature acanthus scroll left; astragal; box meander, cw. Menemachos.

EPH-423*
Olbia, Sector Sever-Zapad, O-СЗ-68-1943[?], Parutine, Olbia National Preserve storeroom. Fr. of mid-body. H 3.6 × W 2.4, WT 0.25. Fabric: standard, 10YR 4/1. Thin dull coat, 10YR 2/1. Relatively hard fired, reduced. Rim friezes: miniature acanthus scroll left; rosette 2/7; Ionian kyma with hatched tongue. One repair hole. Menemachos.

EPH-424*
Myrmekion, M-54-106, St Petersburg IIMK RAN. Fr. of rim and upper body. H 4.1, WT 0.3, ⌀ rim 12, 15%, RH 1.6. Fabric: standard, 10YR 5/1. Thin dull flaking coat, ext. 10YR 4/3, int. 10YR 4/2. Not too hard fired, reduced. Rim friezes: large dots; miniature acanthus scroll left; concentric boxes. Menemachos.

Two Rim Friezes

EPH-425*
Istros, His-V 19337, Bucharest, Institute of Archaeology storeroom. Rim fr. H 4.2 × W 4.2, WT 0.25, ⌀ rim 11, 10%, RH 1.7. Fabric: standard, 5YR 6/8. Dull coat with slight metallic lustre where stacked, ext. 2.5YR 4/6, 7.5YR 4/2, int. 2.5YR 5/8. Relatively hard fired, oxidized. Stacked in firing. Rim friezes: astragal; box meander, cw.

EPH-426
Istros, His-125, Bucharest, Institute of Archaeology storeroom. Rim fr. Oxidized. Rim friezes: astragal; horizontal S-spirals.
– Domăneanțu 2000, 78 cat. 376, pl. 24 (attributed to Plagiaire).

EPH-427*
Istros, His-1096, Bucharest, Institute of Archaeology storeroom. Fr. of rim and upper body. H 3.3 × W 5, WT 0.33, ⌀ rim 10, 12%,

RH 1.7. Fabric: standard, 5YR 6/8. Dull coat, ext. 2.5YR 4/4, 5/4, int. 2.5YR 5/6. Relatively hard fired, oxidized. Rim friezes: astragal; vertical S-spirals.
– Domăneanţu 2000, 9 cat. 33, pl. 2 (attributed to Menemachos).

EPH-428*
Myrmekion, M-57-291, St Petersburg IIMK RAN. Fr. of rim and upper body. H 3.65, WT 2.3, ⌀ rim 11, 10%, RH 1.4. Fabric: standard, 2.5YR 5/8. Thin dull coat, ext. 2.5YR 6/6, 4/3, int. 2.5YR 4/6. Oxidized. Stacked in firing. Rim friezes: astragal; guilloche left.

EPH-429*
Tyritake, Sector L, Л-46-9, St Petersburg IIMK RAN. Fr. of rim and upper body. H 3.4, WT 0.28, ⌀ rim 13, RH 1.8. Fabric: standard, 2.5YR 5/6. Dull coat, 2.5YR 5/6. Oxidized. Rim friezes: astragal; rosette 2.

EPH-430*
Istros, His-V 19443, Bucharest, Institute of Archaeology storeroom. Rim fr. Oxidized. Rim friezes: astragal; rosette 2, var.
– Domăneanţu 2000, 80 cat. 383, pl. 25 (attributed to Plagiaire).

EPH-431*
Istros, His-1122, Bucharest, Institute of Archaeology storeroom. Rim fr. Oxidized. Rim friezes: astragal with decorated reel; Ionian kyma with hatched tongue. Frieze separators: dots.
– Domăneanţu 2000, 8 cat. 27, pl. 2 (attributed to Menemachos).

EPH-432
Porthmion, П-75-89, Kerč History and Culture Reserve. Fr. of rim and upper body. Oxidized. Rim friezes: astragal with decorated reel; horizontal S-spirals. Menemachos.
– Grzegrzółka 2010, 179–180 cat. 292.

EPH-433
Porthmion, П-78-62, Kerč History and Culture Reserve. Rim fr. Oxidized. Rim friezes: astragal with decorated reel; large dots. Menemachos.
– Grzegrzółka 2010, 181 cat. 296 (attributed to Asia Minor).

EPH-434
Olbia, O-1910-346, present whereabouts unknown. Fr. of rim and upper body. Rim friezes: box meander, cw; astragal.
– St Petersburg, IIMK RAN, archive inv. 4059.519.7 (pl. II).

EPH-435*
Myrmekion, M-58-232, St Petersburg IIMK RAN. Fr. of rim and upper body. H 4.1, WT 0.27, ⌀ rim 13, 16%, RH 1.1. Fabric: standard, 2.6YR 6/6. Thin slightly lustrous coat, ext. 2.5YR 4/8, int. 2.5YR 5/6. Oxidized. Stacked in firing. Rim friezes: box meander, cw; Ionian kyma.

EPH-436*
Volna 1, C3-00-120, St Petersburg, State Hermitage Museum. Body fr. close to rim. Oxidized. Rim friezes: box meander, cw; Ionian kyma.

EPH-437*
Myrmekion, M-57-586 or 1586, St Petersburg IIMK RAN. Fr. of rim and upper body. H 4.3, WT 0.25, ⌀ rim 13, 8%, RH 1.2. Fabric: standard, 2.5YR 6/6. Thin dull coat, metallic where blackened, ext. 2.5YR 4/8, 7.5YR 3/2, int. 2.5YR 4/8, 7.5YR 3/2. Oxidized. Stacked in firing. Rim friezes: box meander, cw; Lesbian kyma.

EPH-438*
Olbia, Sector AGD, О-АГД-71-866-2 and 3, Kiev, Institute of Archaeology storeroom. Two non-joining frs. of rim and upper body. H 5, WT 0.2, ⌀ rim 14, 10%, RH 1.6. Fabric: standard, fine, 2.5YR 6/8. Dull coat, 5YR 3/1. Relatively hard fired, oxidized. Rim friezes: box meander, cw; Lesbian kyma. Calyx B2 (tip of folded acanthus preserved).

EPH-439*
Olbia, Sector R25, O-P25-04-2909, Parutine, Olbia National Preserve storeroom. Fr. of rim and upper body. H 3.8 × W 2.4, WT 0.22, RH 1.5. Fabric: fine, micaceous, many minute lime particles, 5Y 5/1. Dull coat, Gley 1 2.5/N. Hard fired, reduced. Rim friezes: box meander, cw; horizontal S-spirals.

EPH-440*
Olbia, Sector E7, squares 783, 782s, 764s, 710s, House 12, O-E7-69-485+486+487+488, Kiev, Institute of Archaeology storeroom. Four joining frs. of rim and upper body. Oxidized. Rim frieze: box meander, cw; guilloche right.

EPH-441*
Olbia, Sector A, square 23, inv. A 3594 (1928), Nikolaev, Historical Museum. Fr. of rim and upper body. H 5.5 × W 5.2, WT 0.3, RH 1.8. Dull red coat. Oxidized. Rim friezes: box meander, cw; wave meander. Calyx: tip of acanthus leaf preserved.

EPH-442*
Pantikapaion, palace foundation trench, M-84-41[a], Moscow, Puškin Museum of Fine Arts. Rim fr. H 4.4 × W 3.4, WT 0.3, RH 2.1. Oxidized. Rim friezes: Ionian kyma; astragal. Secondarily burnt.

EPH-443*
Olbia, Sector R25, O-P25-04-no no.[3], Parutine, Olbia National Preserve storeroom. Fr. of upper body. Oxidized. Rim friezes: Ionian kyma; astragal.

EPH-444*
Tyritake, Sector K, К-39-17, St Petersburg IIMK RAN. Rim fr. Oxidized. Rim friezes: Ionian kyma; astragal.

EPH-445*
Olbia, Sector Sever-Zapad, O-C3-77-20, Parutine, Olbia National Preserve storeroom. Fr. of rim and upper body. H 4.2 × W 6.7, WT 0.4, ⌀ rim 14, 10%, RH 2. Fabric: standard, fine, 2.5YR 6/8. Thin slightly lustrous coat, ext. 2.5YR 4/8, 7.5YR 2.5/1, int. 2.5YR 4/8. Hard fired, oxidized. Stacked in firing. Rim friezes: Ionian kyma; astragal.

EPH-446*
Pantikapaion, palace foundation trench, M-89-illegible 19, Moscow, Puškin Museum of Fine Arts. Rim fr. Reduced. Rim friezes: Ionian kyma with hatched tongue; astragal.

EPH-447*
Porthmion, square 1, depth 1 m, П-53-41, Kerč History and Culture Reserve. Fr. of rim and upper body. H 4.2, WT 0.18, ⌀ rim 12, RH 1.85. Fabric: standard, with much fine lime, 10YR 4/1. Thin dull coat, 2.5Y 3/1. Reduced. Rim friezes: Ionian kyma; box meander, cw.

EPH-448*
Olbia, Sector NGS, О-НГС-97-507, Parutine, Olbia National Preserve storeroom. Fr. of rim and upper body. H 4.2 × W 5.6, WT 0.3, ⌀ rim 12, 15%, RH 1.6. Fabric: relatively fine, micaceous, a few small lime particles, 5YR 6/8. Thin firm coat with slight metallic lustre ext., ext. 10R 5/6, 5YR 3/1, int. 10R 5/6, 5YR 3/1. Medium hard fired, oxidized. Stacked in firing. Rim friezes: Ionian kyma; box meander, cw.

EPH-449*
Olbia, Sector NGS, О-НГС-06-249, Parutine, Olbia National Preserve storeroom. Fr. of rim and upper body. H 4.6 × W 5.7, WT 0.25, ⌀ rim 11, 12%, RH 1.7. Fabric: relatively fine and micaceous, 5YR 5/8. Thin dull coat, 2.5YR 4/6. Medium hard fired, oxidized. Rim friezes: Ionian kyma; Lesbian kyma. Monogram PAR?

EPH-450*
Istros, His-1124, Bucharest, Institute of Archaeology storeroom. Body fr. close to rim. Oxidized. Rim friezes: Ionian kyma; vertical S-spirals with alternating orientations.

EPH-451*
Olbia, Sector E6, square 405, basement with walls 4, 15, 16, 18, O-E6-56-440+735, Kiev, Institute of Archaeology storeroom. Two joining frs. of rim and upper body. Oxidized. Rim friezes: Ionian kyma; guilloche left.

EPH-452
Olbia, Sector NGS, House IV-2 B 302/182 О-НГС-94-338, Parutine, Olbia National Preserve storeroom. Fr. of rim and upper body. H 4.58 × W 5.05, WT 0.42–0.57, ⌀ rim 14, RH 2.4. Fabric: relatively fine and micaceous, some small lime particles, a few small voids, 2.5YR 5/8. Thin firm slightly lustrous coat, mottled at rim and darkened below ext., int. darkened at rim, ext. 2.5YR 4/8, 10YR 3/1, int. 10YR 3/1, 2.5YR 4/6. Medium hard fired, oxidized. Stacked in firing. Rim friezes: Ionian kyma; guilloche left.
– Guldager Bilde 2010, 280 cat. F-54, pl. 178.

EPH-453
Olbia, Sector Sever-Zapad, O-C3-68-1905, Parutine, Olbia National Preserve storeroom. Fr. of rim and upper body. H 4.7 × W 3.3, WT 0.4, RH 2.3. Fabric: standard, 2.5YR 6/8. Thin dull coat, ext. 2.5YR 4/6, 7.5YR 3/2, int. 2.5YR 4/6. Relatively hard fired, oxidized. Stacked in firing. Rim friezes: Ionian kyma; guilloche left.

EPH-454*
Volna 1, C3-97-79, St Petersburg, State Hermitage Museum. Fr. of rim and upper body. Oxidized. Rim friezes: Ionian kyma; wave meander, right.

EPH-455*
Olbia, Sector R25, O-P25-92-1486, Parutine, Olbia National Preserve storeroom. Fr. of upper body close to rim. H 4.2 × W 4.4, WT 0.5. Fabric: relatively fine and micaceous, 5YR 5/8. Dull coat, ext. 2.5YR 4/4, 3/1, int. 2.5YR 4/4. Hard fired, oxidized. Stacked in firing. Rim friezes: Ionian kyma; rosette 1.

EPH-456*
Olbia, Sector NGS, О-НГС-02-45, Parutine, Olbia National Preserve storeroom. Fr. of upper body. H 2.9 × W 3.8. WT 0.27–0.36. Fabric: relatively fine and micaceous, a few small lime particles, 5YR 5/6, 7.5YR 6/6. Thin firm slightly lustrous coat, darkened at rim ext., ext. 2.5YR 4/6, 10YR 3/2, int. 2.5YR 4/6. Medium hard fired, oxidized. Stacked in firing. Rim friezes: Ionian kyma; rosette 2/6.

EPH-457*
Olbia, Sector NGS, О-НГС-02-42, Parutine, Olbia National Preserve storeroom. Fr. of rim and upper body. H 4.3 × W 4.8, WT 0.29–0.45, ⌀ rim 12.5, RH 2.05. Fabric: relatively fine and micaceous, some small lime particles, many voids, 5YR 5/8. Thin firm slightly lustrous coat, blackened with metallic bluish sheen at rim, ext. 2.5YR 4/8, 2.5Y 3/0, int. 2.5YR 4/8, 2.5Y 3/0. Medium hard fired, oxidized. Stacked in firing. Rim friezes: Ionian kyma; rosette 2/7.

EPH-458*
Porthmion, square 11, depth 0.4 m, П-53-421, Kerč History and Culture Reserve. Two non-joining frs. of rim and upper body. H 4.1, WT 0.2, ⌀ rim 12, RH 1.9. Fabric: standard, 5YR 5/8. Thin dull coat, 2.5YR 4/6. Oxidized. Rim friezes: Ionian kyma; rosette 2/8. Indistinct trace of main decoration below. One repair hole.

EPH-459*
Olbia, Sector NGCentre, squares 33s, 34s, 35s, 53ne, 54n, 55n, humus, О-НГЦ-67-179. Kiev, Institute of Archaeology storeroom. Fr. of rim and upper body. Oxidized. Stacked in firing. Rim friezes: Ionian kyma; rosette 2 var. Two repair holes.

EPH-460*
Olbia, Sector NGS, О-НГС-05-744, Parutine, Olbia National Preserve storeroom. Fr. of rim and upper body. Oxidized. Rim friezes: Ionian kyma; star rosettes.

EPH-461*
Porthmion, square 15, depth 0.85 beneath pavement, with material of the 3rd–2nd century, П-53-711, Kerč History and Culture Reserve. Fr. of rim and upper body. H 3.8, WT 0.35, ⌀ rim 18, RH 2.1. Fabric: standard, 2.5YR 6/8. Thin dull flaking coat, 10R 5/6. Oxidized. Rim friezes: Ionian kyma; rosette 5.

EPH-462*
Olbia, Sector NGS, О-НГС-08-195, Parutine, Olbia National Preserve storeroom. Fr. of mid-body. H 2.3 × W 2.8, WT 0.3. Fabric: relatively fine and micaceous, 5YR 6/8. Thin dull coat, ext. 5YR 4/3, int. 5YR 4/4. Medium hard fired, oxidized. Rim frieze: Ionian kyma(?); rosette 9/12. Traces below.

EPH-463*
Olbia, Sector E6, square 476s, 477se, yellow clay layer with ash inclusions, O-E6-59-1404, Kiev, Institute of Archaeology storeroom. Fr. of rim and upper body. ⌀ rim 12, 10%. Oxidized. Rim friezes: Ionian kyma; jewellery pendants.

EPH-464*
Istros, His-795, Bucharest, Institute of Archaeology storeroom. Rim fr. Oxidized. Stacked in firing. Rim friezes: Lesbian kyma; astragal.
– Domăneanţu 2000, 65 cat. 303, pl. 20.

EPH-465*
Istros, Sector SG, -0.6, His-973, Bucharest, Institute of Archaeology storeroom. Rim fr. H 3.3 × W 4.3, WT 0.3, ⌀ rim 11, 9%, RH 1.2. Fabric: standard, 5YR 6/8. Dull coat, ext. 5YR 3/1, int. 5YR 3/2. Relatively hard fired, oxidized. Rim friezes: Lesbian kyma; Ionian kyma.

– Domăneanţu 2000, 40 cat. 174, pl. 12 (attributed to Monogram PAR).

EPH-466*
Istros, Sector SG, His-73-92, Bucharest, Institute of Archaeology storeroom. Body fr. close to rim. Oxidized. Rim friezes: Lesbian kyma; rosette 1, small.
– Domăneanţu 2000, 48 cat. 221, pl. 14 (atttributed to Petite rose spiralée).

EPH-467*
Myrmekion. M-49-765+58-2941 (join across years), St Petersburg IIMK RAN. Two joining frs. of rim and upper body. H 4.6, WT 0.25, ⌀ rim 16, 10%, RH 1.5. Fabric: standard, 2.5YR 5/8. Thin coat with metallic sheen, ext. 2.5YR 4/8, 3/3, 2.5/1, int. 2.5YR 4/4, 7.5YR 2.5/1. Oxidized. Stacked in firing. Rim friezes: Lesbian kyma; rosette 2/7.

EPH-468*
Olbia, Sector NGS, О-НГС-08-359, Parutine, Olbia National Preserve storeroom. Rim fr. H 3.8 × W 2.6, WT 0.2, RH 1.4. Fabric: relatively fine and micaceous, some small lime inclusions, 2.5YR 6/8. Thin dull coat, 2.5YR 5/6. Medium hard fired, oxidized. Rim friezes: Lesbian kyma; large dots.

EPH-469*
Olbia, Sector R25, O-P25-04-1029, Parutine, Olbia National Preserve storeroom. Body fr. close to rim. H 3.8 × W 4.3, WT 0.15–0.4. Fabric: fine, micaceous, 5Y 4/1. Dull coat, ext. 5Y 4/1, 3/1, int. 5Y 4/1. Hard fired, reduced. Stacked in firing. Rim frieze: Lesbian kyma; acanthus flowers.

EPH-470*
Istros, His-B 525/V 19313, Bucharest, Institute of Archaeology storeroom. Body fr. close to rim. Oxidized. Rim friezes: heart-shaped leaf; large dots.
– Domăneanţu 2000, 16 cat. 65, pl. 4 (attributed to Vases gris).

EPH-471
Olbia, Sector NG, square 65e, north of defense wall, О-НГ-46-3327, Kiev, Institute of Archaelogy storeroom. Fr. of rim and upper body. Oxidized. Stacked in firing. Rim friezes: horizontal S-spirals; astragal.

EPH-472*
Olbia, Sector E6, squares 408s, 413n, grey clay layer, O-E6-61-51, Kiev, Institute of Archaeology storeroom. Fr. of rim and upper body. Oxidized. Rim friezes: horizontal S-spirals; Ionian kyma.

EPH-473*
Olbia, Sector NGS, O-НГС-08-288, Parutine, Olbia National Preserve storeroom. Rim fr. H 3.7 × W 4.3, WT 0.4, RH 2.1. Fabric: relatively fine and micaceous, some small lime inclusions, 5YR 6/8. Slightly lustrous coat, 2.5YR 4/6, 2.5/1. Medium hard fired, oxidized. Stacked in firing. Rim friezes: horizontal S-spirals; vertical S-spirals.

EPH-474*
Olbia, Sector NGS, O-НГС-08-184, Parutine, Olbia National Preserve storeroom. Fr. of rim and upper body. H 3.5 × W 3.8, WT 0.25, RH 1.8. Fabric: relatively fine and micaceous, some small lime inclusions, 5Y 4/1. Dull coat, 5Y 3/1. Medium hard fired, reduced. Rim friezes: horizontal S-spirals; large dots.

EPH-475*
Istros, His-66-10, Bucharest, Institute of Archaeology storeroom. Two joining frs. of rim and upper body. Oxidized. Rim friezes: vertical S-spirals; astragal.
– Domăneanțu 2000, 9 cat. 34, pl. 2.

EPH-476*
Myrmekion, M-56-367, St Petersburg IIMK RAN. Fr. of rim and upper body. H 3.6, WT 0.32, ∅ rim 10, 8%, RH 1.4. Fabric: standard, 5YR 6/6. Thin dull coat, mottled, 2.5YR 4/6, 3/1. Oxidized. Stacked in firing. Rim friezes: vertical S-spirals; astragal.

EPH-477*
Olbia, Sector A, square 114–117, clay layer, O-A-46-163, Kiev, Institute of Archaeology storeroom. Fr. of rim and upper body. H 4.3 × W 7, WT 0.2, ∅ rim 13, 15%, RH 1.8. Fabric: standard, 5YR 7/8. Dull coat, mottled, ext. 5YR 3/1, 3/3, 4/6, int. 5YR 3/1, 3/3, 4/6. Relatively hard fired, oxidized. Stacked in firing. Rim friezes: vertical S-spirals; rosette 2/6. One repair hole.

EPH-478*
Olbia, Sector NGS, O-НГС-05-245, Parutine, Olbia National Preserve storeroom. Fr. of rim and upper body. H 3.8 × W 3.2, WT 0.37, RH 1.4. Fabric: relatively fine and micaceous, 7.5YR 6/6. Coat with metallic sheen ext., int. duller, 7.5YR 2.5/1. Medium hard fired, oxidized. Rim friezes: oblique S-spirals; box meander, cw. Frieze separators: dots.

EPH-479*
Istros, His-V 19328, Bucharest Institute of Archaeology storeroom. Rim fr. Oxidized. Rim friezes: heart guilloche left; horizontal S-spirals.

EPH-480*
Olbia, Sector NGS, O-НГС-93-70, Parutine, Olbia National Preserve storeroom. Fr. of rim and upper body. H 4.1 × W 4.6, WT 0.15–0.47, ∅ rim 12.5, RH 1.65. Fabric: relatively fine, many small lime inclusions, 5YR 5/6. Thin slightly lustrous coat, partly blackened and with slight metallic sheen at lip, int. blotchy, ext. 10YR 3/1, int. 2.5YR 5/6, 10YR 4/2. Hard fired, oxidized. Stacked in firing. Rim friezes: guilloche right; astragal. Frieze separators: dots.

EPH-481*
Olbia, Sector M, square 15n, ash clay layer, O-M-51-4053, 4953[a], 4079, Kiev, Institute of Archaeology storeroom. Two joining frs. of rim and upper body, one non-joining rim fr. Oxidized. Stacked in firing. Rim friezes: guilloche right; box meander, cw. Calyx: perhaps small rounded imbricate petals. Frieze separators: dots.

EPH-482
Pantikapaion, Cistern N, 179 96-no.? Fr. of rim and body. Rim friezes: guilloche left; box meander, cw, with rosettes instead of box with star. Two thin grooves below rim. Early. Südtor Workshop?
– Tolstikov & Zhuravlev 2004, pl. 101.14.

EPH-483*
Olbia, Sector E7, square 537n, yellow clay layer, O-E7-60-349, Kiev, Institute of Archaeology storeroom. Two non-joining frs. of rim and upper body. Oxidized. Stacked in firing. Rim friezes: guilloche left; box meander, cw. One repair hole.

EPH-484*
Olbia, Sector E6, square 405, basement with walls 4, 15, 16, 18, O-E6-56-445, Kiev, Institute of Archaeology storeroom. Fr. of rim and upper body. Oxidized. Stacked in firing. Rim friezes: guilloche left; Ionian kyma.

EPH-485*
Olbia, Sector NGS, O-НГС-98-329+502+503, 415, Parutine, Olbia National Preserve storeroom. Two joining frs. and two non-joining frs. of rim and body. H 4 × W 6.9, WT 0.29–0.4, ∅ rim 12, RH 1.5. Fabric: fine, micaceous, small dots of lime, some small voids, 7.5YR 6/6. Thin firm coat with slight lustre, 2.5YR 4/4. Medium hard fired, oxidized. Rim friezes: guilloche left; Lesbian kyma. Calyx C (tip of straight acanthus leaf preserved).
– Guldager Bilde 2010, 280 cat. F-53, pl. 178.

EPH-486*
Tyritake, Sector A, A-55-183, St Petersburg IIMK RAN. Fr. of upper body. Oxidized. Stacked in firing. Rim friezes: guilloche left; Lesbian kyma.

EPH-487*
Olbia, Sector E6, square 405, grey clay layer, O-E6-56-268, Kiev, Institute of Archaeology storeroom. Rim fr. Oxidized. Rim friezes: guilloche left; rosette 5.

EPH-488*
Pantikapaion, palace foundation trench, M-85-45[g], Moscow, Puškin Museum of Fine Arts. Fr. of rim and upper body. H 3 × W 4.3, WT 0.2, RH 1.3. Oxidized. Rim friezes: wave meander, upside-down; rosette 2/7. Secondarily burnt.

EPH-489*
Olbia, Sector A, square 22, inv. A 4290 (1930), Nikolaev, Historical Museum. Rim fr. H 3.6 × W 5.5, WT 0.28, RH 1. Fabric: standard. Dull red coat, brownish at rim ext. Oxidized. Stacked in firing. Rim frieze: wave meander, upside-down; star rosettes.

EPH-490*
Pantikapaion, palace foundation trench M-85-45 Moscow, Puškin Museum of Fine Arts. Fr. of rim and upper body. H 3.7 × W 5.1, WT 0.35, RH 1.7. Dull reddish coat, light brown at rim ext. Oxidized. Stacked in firing. Rim friezes: wave meander, upside-down; star rosettes.

EPH-491*
Istros, His-B 580/V 19452, Bucharest, Institute of Archaeology storeroom. Fr. of body close to rim. Oxidized. Rim friezes: wave meander, upside-down; rosette 2/7 alternating with jewellery pendants.
– Domăneanţu 2000, 33 cat. 133, pl. 9 (attributed to Monogram PAR).

EPH-492*
Chersonesos, X-1952-150, St Petersburg, State Hermitage Museum. Fr. of rim and upper body. H 3.2, WT 0.36, ⌀ rim 13, RH 1.35. Fabric: standard, 2.5YR 6/6. Thin dull coat ext., slightly lustrous int., ext. 2.5YR 3/1, int. 2.5YR 6/6. Oxidized. Rim friezes: spiral meander, left; box meander. Frieze separators: dots. Two thin grooves below rim.

EPH-493*
Olbia, Sector R25, O-P25-03-134, Parutine, Olbia National Preserve storeroom. Fr. of rim and upper body. Oxidized. Stacked in firing. Rim friezes: rosette 1; Lesbian kyma.

EPH-494*
Olbia, Sector NGS, O-НГС-05-227, Parutine, Olbia National Preserve storeroom. Large fr. of rim and upper body. H 4.8 × W 9.2, WT 0.4, ⌀ rim 12, 17%, RH 1.45. Fabric: relatively fine and micaceous, 5YR 6/6. Thin dull coat, ext. 2.5YR 5/6, 4/6, int. 2.5YR 5/6. Medium hard fired, oxidized. Stacked in firing. Rim friezes: rosette 2/4; star rosettes. Late: very widely spaced and tired stamps.

EPH-495*
Istros, His-V 19444, Bucharest, Institute of Archaeology storeroom. Two joining frs. of rim and upper body. Reduced. Rim friezes: rosette 2/7; box meander, cw.
– Domăneanţu 2000, 31 cat. 121, pl. 8 (attributed to Monogram PAR).

EPH-496*
Olbia, Cliff, grey clay layer, O-68-1388, Kiev, Institute of Archaeology storeroom. Body fr. Reduced. Rim friezes: rosette 2/7; Ionian kyma with hatched tongue.

EPH-497*
Olbia, Sector NGS, O-НГС-05-801, Parutine, Olbia National Preserve storeroom. Two joining frs. of rim and upper body. H 5 × W 9.3, WT 0.25, ⌀ rim 14, 16%, RH 1.8. Fabric: relatively fine and micaceous, 5YR 6/8. Thin coat with dull metallic sheen, ext. 5YR 3/1, int. 5YR 3/1, 2.5YR 4/8. Medium hard fired, oxidized. Stacked in firing. Rim friezes: rosette 2/7; Lesbian kyma. One repair hole. Monogram PAR?

EPH-498
Myrmekion, M-49-789, St Petersburg IIMK RAN. Two joining frs. of rim and upper body. H 3.8, WT 0.2, ⌀ rim 12.5, RH 1.8. Fabric: standard, slightly soft, 7.5YR 6/4. Thin coat with slight lustre, ext. 2.5YR 4/8, 3/3, int. 2.5YR 4/8. Oxidized. Stacked in firing. Rim friezes: rosette 2/7; Lesbian kyma.

EPH-499*
Olbia, Sector NGS, O-НГС-06-99, Parutine, Olbia National Preserve storeroom. Fr. of rim and upper body. H 3.8 × W 4.9, WT 0.25, ⌀ rim 12, 12%, RH 1.5. Fabric: relatively fine and micaceous, some small lime inclusions, 7.5YR 7/6. Slightly lustrous coat int., ext. duller, ext. 5YR 5/3, int. 2.5YR 4/6. Medium hard fired, oxidized. Stacked in firing. Rim friezes: rosette 2/7; guilloche left.

EPH-500
Myrmekion, M-49-234, St Petersburg IIMK RAN. Fr. of rim and upper body. H 3.55, WT 0.27, ⌀ rim 12, RH 1.4. Fabric: standard, 5YR 6/6. Thin slightly lustrous coat, ext. 2.5YR 4/8, 5YR 2.1/1, int. 2.5YR 4/8, 5YR 2.1/1. Oxidized. Stacked in firing. Rim friezes: rosette 2/7; guilloche left.

EPH-501*
Chersonesos, X-1959-21, St Petersburg, State Hermitage Museum. Fr. of rim and upper body. H 3.6, WT 0.31, ⌀ rim 12, 12%, RH 2. Fabric: no fresh break for observation. Dull coat, mottled ext., 2.5YR 4/6, 2.5/1. Oxidized. Stacked in firing. Rim friezes: rosette 2/7; star rosettes.

EPH-502*
Olbia, Sector AGD, О-АГД-69-864, Kiev, Institute of Archaeology storeroom. Fr. of rim and upper body. H 4.1 × W 3.7, WT 0.25, RH 1.4. Fabric: standard, 10YR 5/2. Dull coat, 10YR 3/1. Relatively hard fired, reduced. Rim friezes: rosette 2/7 in negative relief; rosette 5.

EPH-503*
Volna 1, С3-98-143, St Petersburg, State Hermitage Museum. Rim fr. Oxidized. Rim friezes: rosette 2/8; Ionian kyma.

EPH-504*
Olbia, Sector R25, O-P25-02-2108, Parutine, Olbia National Preserve storeroom. Fr. of rim and upper body. H 4.5 × W 4.3, WT 0.4, RH 1.9. Fabric: fine and micaceous, many minute lime particles, Gley 1 3/5GY. Slightly lustrous coat, 5Y 2.5/1. Medium hard fired, reduced. Rim frieze: rosette 2/9 between vertical line; box meander, ccw. Frieze separators: dots

EPH-505*
Olbia, Sector NGS, О-НГС-04-55, Parutine, Olbia National Preserve storeroom. Fr. of rim and upper body. H 3.1 × W 4.8, WT 0.3, ⌀ rim 11, 13%, RH 1.1. Fabric: relatively fine and micaceous, many small lime inclusions, 10YR 5/3. Thin dull coat, Gley 1 3/N. Medium hard fired, reduced. Rim friezes: star rosettes; astragal.

EPH-506*
Olbia, Cliff "B-VIII", square 285, Slope 1, Terrace I, O-70-377, Parutine, Olbia National Preserve storeroom. Rim fr. Oxidized. Rim friezes: star rosettes; box meander.

EPH-507*
Olbia, Sector NGS, О-НГС-06-103, Parutine, Olbia National Preserve storeroom. Fr. of rim and upper body. H 3.4 × W 4.3, WT 0.35, RH 1.5. Fabric: relatively fine and micaceous, 5YR 6/8. Thin coat, slightly lustrous ext., dull int., ext. 2.5YR 5/4, 5/8, 3/1, int. 2.5YR 4/6. Medium hard fired, oxidized. Stacked in firing. Rim friezes: star rosettes; Ionian kyma.

EPH-508
Olbia, Cliff "B-VIII", square 285, low terrace, O-70-224, Parutine, Olbia National Preserve storeroom. Fr. of rim and upper body. Oxidized. Stacked in firing. Rim friezes: star rosettes; Lesbian kyma.

EPH-509*
Olbia, Sector NGS, О-НГС-08-147, Parutine, Olbia National Preserve storeroom. Two non-joining frs. of rim and upper body. H 3.5 × W 4.3, WT 0.25, ⌀ rim 10, 13%, RH 1.6. Fabric: relatively fine and micaceous, some small lime inclusions, 5YR 7/8. Thin slightly lustrous coat, ext. 5YR 3/1, int. 2.5YR 4/8. Medium hard fired, oxidized. Stacked in firing. Rim friezes: star rosettes; rosette 2/7.

EPH-510*
Porthmion, square 21, depth 0.75 m, 1st longitudinal street, with material of the 3rd–2nd century, П-53-972, Kerč History and Culture Reserve. Fr. of rim and upper body. H 4.6, WT 0.2, ⌀ rim 12, RH 2.3. Fabric: standard, fine, Gley 1 4/N. Thin dull coat, Gley 1 3/N. Hard fired, reduced. Rim friezes: rosette 5; large astragal. Calyx: imbricate (tips of pointed petals).

EPH-511*
Olbia, V.I. 7754.61, Antikensammlung, Staatliche Museen zu Berlin (former Becker collection). Fr. of rim and upper body. H 5.3 × W 10.7, ⌀ rim 17.5, RH 2.2. Fabric: standard. Dull coat, mottled ext. and slightly lustrous at rim, blackened at lip int., ext. 7.5YR 4/2, 2.5YR 4/4, int. 2.5YR 5/6. Oxidized. Stacked in firing. Rim friezes: rosette 5; Ionian kyma with hatched tongue.

EPH-512
Porthmion, square 42–43c, depth 1.7 m, П-75-57, Kerč History and Culture Reserve. Fr. of rim and upper body. Reduced. Rim friezes: rosette 5; Lesbian kyma.
– Grzegrzółka 2010, 185–186 cat. 306.

EPH-513*
Bol'šoj Kastel', БК-84-24[c], 53, 86-11, Černomorskoe Museum of Historical Lore. Three non-joining rim frs. H 3.6, ⌀ rim 13, RH 1.8. Fabric: highly micaceous, 7.5YR 6/6. Dull flaking coat, 2.5YR 4/6. Oxidized. Rim friezes: rosette 5/6, var.; Ionian kyma.

EPH-514*
Istros, His-182, Bucharest, Institute of Archaeology storeroom. Body fr. close to rim. Oxidized. Rim friezes: rosette 6; astragal. My(…).

EPH-515*
Olbia, Sector NGS, О-НГС-03-535, Parutine, Olbia National Preserve storeroom. Body fr. close to rim. Reduced. Rim friezes: rosette 9/8; guilloche left.

EPH-516*
Istros, His-B 475/V 8575 Y, Bucharest, Institute of Archaeology storeroom. Rim fr. H 3.5 × W 4. Reduced. Rim friezes: rosette (type?); miniature bound myrtle wreath left.
– Domăneanțu 2000, 80 cat. 384, pl. 25 (attributed to Plagiaire).

EPH-517
Porthmion, П-73-372, Kerč History and Culture Reserve. Fr. of rim and upper body. Oxidized. Rim friezes: miniature acanthus-flower scroll left; Ionian kyma. Monogram PAR.
– Grzegrzółka 2010, 175 cat. 282.

EPH-518*
Olbia, Sector R25, O-P25-95-1097, Parutine, Olbia National Preserve storeroom. Fr. of rim and upper body. H 4.3 × W 4.4, WT 0.3–0.48, RH 1.8. Fabric: relatively fine and micaceous, some small voids, 10YR 6/4. Thin slightly lustrous coat, ext. 7.5YR 3/1, 2.5YR 5/6, int. 10R 5/6. Medium hard fired, oxidized. Stacked in firing. Rim friezes: miniature acanthus-flower scroll left; wave meander, upside-down. Main decoration: remains of group of three-dot berries (myrtle or stylized acanthus scroll). Monogram PAR.

EPH-519*
Olbia, Sector NGS, O-НГС-98-397, Parutine, Olbia National Preserve storeroom. Fr. of lower body. Oxidized. Rim friezes: miniature acanthus scroll left; astragal. Calyx: tip of leaf preserved. Menemachos.

EPH-520*
Olbia, Sector NGS, O-НГС-06-105, 254, Parutine, Olbia National Preserve storeroom. Two joining(?) frs. of rim and upper body. H 4.9 × W 3.5, WT 0.5, RH 1.4. Fabric: relatively fine and micaceous, some small lime inclusions, 5YR 6/8. Thin dull coat, ext. 5YR 4/4, 2.5/1, int. 5YR 4/4, 2.5/1. Medium hard fired, oxidized. Stacked in firing. Rim friezes: miniature acanthus scroll left; rosette 1. Calyx: imbricate (tops of rounded petals preserved). Menemachos.

EPH-521
Porthmion, no. unknown, Kerč History and Culture Reserve. Rim fr. Reduced. Miniature acanthus scroll left; large dots. One repair hole. Menemachos.
– Grzegrzółka 2010, 178 cat. 288.s

EPH-522
Volna 1, П-99-15, St Petersburg, State Hermitage Museum. Rim fr. Reduced. Rim friezes: miniature stylized acanthus scroll left; large dots.

EPH-523*
Istros, His-B 491/V 8574 N, Bucharest, Institute of Archaeology storeroom. Body fr. close to rim. Reduced. Rim friezes: miniature stylized acanthus scroll left; oblique boxes.
– Domăneanţu 2000, 20 cat. 77, pl. 6 (attributed to Comique à la canne).

EPH-524
Tyritake, Sector A, A-55-114, St Petersburg IIMK RAN. Body fr. Reduced. Rim friezes: large dots; rosettes (type?).

EPH-525*
Istros, His-B 521, Bucharest, Institute of Archaeology storeroom. Rim fr. Oxidized. Rim friezes: crossed dotted lines with box; astragal.
– Domăneanţu 2000, 9 cat. 36, pl. 2 (attributed to Menemachos).

EPH-526
Porthmion, П-73-475, Kerč History and Culture Reserve. Fr. of upper body. Oxidized. Rim friezes: crossed dotted lines with box; Lesbian kyma. Menemachos.
– Grzegrzółka 2010, 201 cat. 346.

EPH-527
Porthmion, Sector G, sector 2, fill in rooms, П-87-113, Kerč History and Culture Reserve. Rim fr. Rim friezes: oblique boxes; large dots. Traces of main decoration below: ivy-berry cluster? Frieze separators: dots.

E *Vegetal Decoration*

Plastic Pine-Cone Decoration

EPH-528*
Istros, His-666 or 999, Bucharest, Institute of Archaeology storeroom. Body fr. close to rim. Reduced. Rim frieze: astragal.

EPH-529*
Istros, Sector Z2, –1.60, His-56-960/V 20461, Bucharest, Institute of Archaeology storeroom. Body fr. H 7.8 × W 5.8, WT 0.35. Fabric: standard, 5Y 4/1. Dull coat, 5Y 3/1. Relatively hard fired, reduced. Rim frieze: Ionian kyma.
– Domăneanţu 2000, 49 cat. 228, pl. 14 (attributed to Petite rose spiralée).

EPH-530*
Olbia, Sector R25, O-P25-06-748, Parutine, Olbia National Preserve storeroom. Fr. of rim and upper body. H 4.2 × W 4.1, WT 0.26, ⌀ rim 12, 10%, RH 1.9. Fabric: relatively fine and micaceous with some small voids, Gley 1 6/N. Thin dull coat, Gley 1 3/N. Medium hard fired, reduced. Rim frieze: Ionian kyma.

EPH-531*
Istros, His-1927-1942-V 8569 G, Bucharest, Institute of Archaeology storeroom. Fr. of rim and upper body. H 4.1 × W 5.8, WT 0.2, ⌀ rim 12, 12%, RH 2.1. Fabric: standard, 7.5YR 7/4. Dull coat, ext.

2.5YR 5/6, 10YR 4/2, int. 2.5YR 5/6. Relatively hard fired, oxidized. Stacked in firing. Rim frieze: rosette 1.
– Domăneanțu 2000, 74 cat. 352, pl. 23 (attributed to Heraios).

EPH-532
Istros, His-V 19314 A, Bucharest, Institute of Archaeology storeroom. Body fr. close to rim. Oxidized. Rim frieze: rosette 1.
– Domăneanțu 2000, 55 cat. 253, pl. 16 (attributed to Athenaios).

EPH-533*
Istros, His-589+960[a], Bucharest, Institute of Archaeology storeroom. Two joining body frs. close to rim. H 3.7 × W 4.3, WT 0.38. Fabric: standard, fine, 5Y 6/1. Dull coat, ext. 5Y 3/1, 4/1, int. 5Y 3/1. Relatively hard fired, reduced. Rim frieze: rosette 2/4
– Domăneanțu 2000, 38 cat. 162, pl. 11 (attributed to Monogram PAR).

EPH-534*
Myrmekion, M-52-158, Saint Petersburg IIMK RAN. Two joining frs. of rim and upper body. H 5.3, WT 0.25, ⌀ rim 12, 14%, RH 1.8. Fabric: fine, soft, micaceous, 7.5YR 7/6. Thin dull coat, 7.5YR 3/1. Oxidized. Stacked in firing. Rim frieze: rosette 2/7.

EPH-535*
Olbia, Sector NGCentre, 36s, 56n, humus layer under heap of rocks and wall, О-НГЦ-66-442, Kiev, Institute of Archaeology storeroom. Fr. of rim and body. H 4.2 × W 6.7, WT 0.2, ⌀ rim 11, 20%, RH 1.5. Fabric: standard, fine, Gley 1 6/10Y. Slightly lustrous coat, Gley 1 2.5/N. Relatively hard fired, reduced. Rim frieze: star rosettes. Frieze separators: dots.

EPH-536
Pantikapaion, M-46-5041, Moscow, Puškin Museum of Fine Arts. Fr. of rim and body. Rim frieze: rosette 5.
– Zabelina 1984, 156, fig. 3e; AGSP 1984, pl. CLXIV.13 (erroneously illustrated as a complete vessel).

EPH-537*
Istros, His-561, Bucharest, Institute of Archaeology storeroom. Body fr. close to rim. H 2.7 × W 3.8, WT 0.35. Fabric: standard, 5Y 5/1. Coat with dull lustre, Gley 1 3/N. Relatively hard fired, reduced. Rim frieze: rosette 9.
– Domăneanțu 2000, 105 cat. 532, pl. 35.

EPH-538
Olbia, Sector R25, O-P25–98–2531.1, 2, Parutine, Olbia National Preserve storeroom. Two non-joining body frs. H 5.3 × W 5, WT 0.32. Fabric: relatively fine and micaceous, 5YR 6/8. Slightly lustrous coat, ext. 5YR 2.1/1, int. 5YR 2.1/1. Hard fired, oxidized.

EPH-539
Porthmion, П-78-no.(?), Kerč History and Culture Reserve. Fr. of base and lower body. Reduced. Base: signed ATHEN[...], incised in bowl before firing. Athenaios.
– Grzegrzółka 2010, 173–174 cat. 278.

EPH-540*
Bol'šoj Kastel', БК-87-22, Černomorskoe Museum of Historical Lore. Lower body fr.; secondarily used, large part of relief rubbed off. H 3.1. Fabric: very fine and micaceous, 10YR 5/6. Dull coat, 5YR 4/4. Oxidized.

Stylized Pine-Cone Decoration

EPH-541
Olbia, O-1928-112, present whereabouts unknown. Fr. of rim and upper body. Multiple rim friezes: astragal; horizontal buds left. Main decoration: stylized pine-cone (concentric boxes with central star).
– St Petersburg, IIMK RAN, photo archive neg. II 13908.

EPH-542
Istros, Sector SC, His-69-96, Bucharest, Institute of Archaeology storeroom. Body fr. H 5 × W 6. Oxidized. Main decoration: stylized pine-cone (concentric boxes with central star in negative relief).
– Domăneanțu 2000, 74 cat. 350, pl. 23 (attributed to Heraios).

EPH-543*
Istros, His-491/B 584, B 584/V 19xxx, Bucharest, Institute of Archaeology storeroom. Fr. of rim and upper body. H 4.1 × W 4.9, WT 0.3, ⌀ rim 11, 10%, RH 1.7. Fabric: standard, 5Y 4/1. Dull coat, Gley 1 4/N. Relatively hard fired, reduced. Rim frieze: star rosettes or rosette 5. Main decoration: stylized pine-cone (concentric boxes with central star in negative relief).
– Domăneanțu 2000, 105 cat. 530, pl. 35.

EPH-544*
Olbia, Sector R25, O-P25-97-2154.1,2,3,4, 2193.1,2, Parutine, Olbia National Preserve storeroom. Two non-joining rim frs. and four non-joining body frs. H 3.8 × W 5.4, WT 0.41, ⌀ rim 13, 9%, RH 2.1. Fabric: relatively fine and micaceous, 5Y 5/1. Dull coat, Gley 1 2.5/N. Medium hard fired, reduced. No rim frieze. Main decoration: stylized pine-cone (concentric boxes with central star).

EPH-545*
Istros, His-B 584[a]/V 19431 H, Bucharest, Institute of Archaeology storeroom. Fr. of base and lower body. H 3.5 × W 6.3, WT 0.3,

⌀ base 5. Fabric: standard, 5Y 5/1. Dull coat ext., with slight lustre int., Gley 1 3/N. Relatively hard fired, reduced. Main decoration: stylized pine-cone (concentric boxes with central star in negative relief). Plain concave base.
– Domăneanţu 2000, 74 cat. 351, pl. 23 (attributed to Heraios).

EPH-546*
Istros, His-844, Bucharest, Institute of Archaeology storeroom. Fr. of lower body and base. Oxidized. Main decoration: stylized pine-cone (concentric boxes with central star in negative relief). Plain concave base. .

EPH-547
Istros, His-V 8576 F, Bucharest Institute of Archaeology storeroom. Fr. of lower body and edge of base. Oxidized. Main decoration: stylized pine-cone (concentric boxes with central star in normal relief). Base type uncertain.

EPH-548*
Istros, His-B 520/V 19441+V 19447, Bucharest, Institute of Archaeology storeroom. Two joining frs. of rim and upper body. H 4.2 × W 5.9, WT 0.28, ⌀ rim 10, 13%, RH 1.9. Fabric: standard, 5YR 6/8. Dull coat, ext. 2.5YR 5/6, 7.5YR 4/2, int. 2.5YR 5/6. Relatively hard fired, oxidized. Stacked in firing. Rim frieze: star rosettes. Main decoration: stylized pine-cone (concentric boxes).
– Domăneanţu 2000, 105 cat. 528, pl. 35.

EPH-549
Olbia O-1928-502, present whereabouts unknown. Fr. of lower body. Main decoration: stylized pine-cone (concentric boxes). Medallion: rosette A, var.
– St Petersburg, IIMK RAN, photo archive neg. II 13922.

Calyx A1

EPH-550*
Olbia, inv. A 2442, Nikolaev, Historical Museum. Complete; joined from a number of frs. ⌀ rim 12.8, RH 1.4, ⌀ base 3.8; vessel H 6.5; H:⌀ 1:1.8. Dull reddish coat, brownish on upper part ext. Oxidized. Stacked in firing. Multiple rim friezes: rosette 2/7; Ionian kyma. Calyx A1 with seven-petalled rosettes on wavy stems. Medallion: rosette A. Frieze separators: dots.

EPH-551 (see Fig. 78)
Olbia O-1910-935, 935a, present whereabouts unknown. Two non-joining body frs. Multiple rim friezes: rosette 2/7; Ionian kyma. Calyx A1 with seven-petalled rosette on incised wavy stem. Frieze separators: dots.
– St Petersburg, IIMK RAN, archive inv. 4060.519.8 (pl. I); 40…(?) (pl. XIII).

EPH-552*
Olbia. Sector NGS O-НГС-92-264, Parutine, Olbia National Preserve storeroom. Fr. of lower body. Oxidized.

EPH-553*
Myrmekion, M-49-61, St Petersburg, State Hermitage Museum. Fr. of base and lower body. H 7.3, WT 0.25, ⌀ base 4. Fabric: standard, 2.5YR 6/8. Thin coat with slight metallic sheen ext., slightly lustrous int., ext. 10R 5/6, 3/2, int. 10R 2.5/1. Oxidized. Stacked in firing. Multiple rim friezes: Ionian kyma; astragal with decorated bead. Medallion: rosette A. Frieze separators: dots.

EPH-554
Olbia, Sector R25, O-P25-97-2274.1+2, Parutine, Olbia National Preserve storeroom. Two joining frs. of base and lower body. H 7.3 × W 5.3, WT 0.4–0.5, ⌀ base 2.8. Fabric: relatively fine and micaceous, small lime inclusions, 7.5YR 6/6. Coat with metallic sheen ext., lustrous int., 7.5YR 4/1. Medium hard fired, oxidized. Medallion: rosette A.

EPH-555*
Olbia, Sector NGS, O-НГС-02-471, Parutine, Olbia National Preserve storeroom. Fr. of base and lower body. H 4.8 × W 5.7, WT 0.2–0.35, ⌀ base 4. Fabric: fine, slightly micaceous, a few minute lime particles, 5YR 6/8. Thin firm slightly lustrous coat, 2.5YR 4/8. Hard fired, oxidized. Medallion encircled by ridge, only tip of narrow petal preserved (rosette A?). Very fine, naturalistic piece, extremely thin wall.

EPH-556*
Myrmekion, M-58-827, St Petersburg IIMK RAN. Fr. of base and lower body. H 5.3, WT 0.27, ⌀ base 4. Fabric: standard, 2.5YR 5/8. Dull coat, 2.5YR 4/8. Oxidized. Calyx A1? Medallion: rosette B.

EPH-557
Olbia, Sector R25, O-P25-98-3085, Parutine, Olbia National Preserve storeroom. Fr. of base and lower body. H 6.5 × W 6.8, WT 0.3–0.4, ⌀ base 3.6. Fabric: relatively fine and micaceous, small lime inclusions, 7.5YR 6/6. Thin slightly lustrous coat, 7.5YR 2.5/1. Medium hard fired, oxidized. Medallion: rosette A.

EPH-558*
Porthmion, square 3, pit n. 3, with material of the 3rd–2nd century, П-53-190, Kerč History and Culture Reserve. Fr. of base and lower body. H 5.8, WT 0.3, ⌀ base 4.5. Fabric: standard, fine, 10YR 6/3. Thin slightly lustrous coat, 10YR 3/1. Oxidized. Medallion: rosette A.

EPH-559
Olbia, O-72-717, present whereabouts unknown. Complete profile, one quarter of bowl preserved. Multiple rim friezes: wave

meander, upside-down; astragal with decorated beads; horizontal S-spirals. Medallion: rosette A. Frieze separators: dots.
– St Petersburg, IIMK RAN, photo archive neg. I 80697.

EPH-560*
Istros. His-1105, Bucharest, Institute of Archaeology storeroom. Body fr. Oxidized. Rim frieze: rosette 5.

EPH-561*
Porthmion, П-53-192, Kerč History and Culture Reserve. Fr. of rim and large part of body. H 4.3, WT 0.25, ⌀ rim 11, RH 1.15. Fabric: standard, fine, 10YR 5/3. Thin slightly lustrous coat, 10YR 2/1. Oxidized. Multiple rim friezes: astragal; rosette 2/7. Calyx A1 var., 'nelumbo' replaced by lotus petal.

EPH-562
Olbia, Sector R25, O-P25-95-1116.2, Parutine, Olbia National Preserve storeroom. Fr. of lower body. H 2.8 × W 3.6, WT 0.21. Fabric: relatively fine and micaceous, small lime inclusions, 10YR 4/2. Slightly lustrous coat, Gley 1 2.5/N. Hard fired, reduced. Calyx A1 var, 'nelumbo' replaced by lotus petal.

EPH-563
Olbia, Sector NGS, O-НГС-96-41 Parutine, Olbia National Preserve storeroom. Fr. of lower body. Oxidized.

EPH-564
Olbia, Sector NGS, O-НГС-06-1156, Parutine, Olbia National Preserve storeroom. Fr. of base and lower body. H 4.4 × W 2.9, WT 0.4, ⌀ base 3. Fabric: relatively fine and micaceous, 5YR 6/8. Thin dull coat, 2.5YR 5/6. Medium hard fired, oxidized. Medallion: rosette B.

EPH-565
Volna 1, C3-98-44, St Petersburg, State Hermitage Museum. Fr. of mid-body. Reduced. Main decoration: lower legs of man or animal. Frieze separators: astragal.

Calyx A2

EPH-566*
Olbia, Sector NGS, House IV-3 B 343/200, O-НГС-92-100, Parutine, Olbia National Preserve storeroom. Fr. of lower body close to base. H 3.6 × W 3.5. WT 0.3. ⌀ base 5. Fabric: fine, micaceous, 5YR 6/8. Thin slightly lustrous coat, ext. 2.5YR 5/6, int. 2.5YR 5/6, 4/3. Medium hard fired, oxidized.
– Guldager Bilde 2010, 279 cat. F-31, pl. 175.

EPH-567*
Olbia, Sector E7, square 517, grey clay layer, O-E7-60-553, Kiev, Institute of Archaeology storeroom. Fr. of lower body. H 3.2 × W 4.5, WT 0.3. Fabric: standard, fine, 2.5YR 6/6. Thin coat, int. almost completely worn off, 2.5YR 4/8. Relatively hard fired, oxidized. Same acanthus as EPH-566*.

EPH-568*
Olbia, Sector NGS, O-НГС-08-365, Parutine, Olbia National Preserve storeroom. Fr. of lower body. H 2.9 × W 2.6, WT 0.3. Fabric: relatively fine and micaceous, some small lime inclusions, 2.5YR 6/8. Thin firm coat with a slight metallic lustre ext., ext. 2.5YR 4/3, int. 2.5YR 4/8. Medium hard fired, oxidized. Stacked in firing. Same acanthus as EPH-566*.

EPH-569*
Istros, His-1029, Bucharest, Institute of Archaeology storeroom. Fr. of lower body. H 2.5 × W 2.2, WT 0.2. Fabric: standard, 2.5YR 6/6. Dull coat, 2.5YR 5/8. Relatively hard fired, oxidized. Same acanthus as EPH-566*.
– Domăneanţu 2000, 95 cat. 462, pl. 31.

EPH-570
Pantikapaion, M-48-1124, Moscow, Puškin Museum of Fine Arts. Three joining frs. of base and lower body. Medallion: rosette A. Same acanthus as EPH-566*.
– Loseva 1962, fig. 2.1 (part of vessel); Zabelina 1984, 158 fig. 5e.

EPH-571*
Olbia, Sector NGS, O-НГС-04-245, Parutine, Olbia National Preserve storeroom. Fr. of base and lower body. H 3.8 × W 3.6, WT 0.35, ⌀ base 4.5. Fabric: relatively fine and micaceous, some small lime inclusions, 5Y 3/1. Slightly lustrous coat, 5Y 2.5/1. Medium hard fired, reduced. Calyx A2; rosette 9 as space filler. Medallion: rosette A.

EPH-572
Pantikapaion, П-1867-29, St Petersburg, State Hermitage Museum. Complete. H 6.7, ⌀ rim 11.7. Oxidized. Multiple rim friezes: rosette 2/7; astragal. Calyx A2 with Menemachos bud. Plain, concave base. Menemachos?

EPH-573*
Chersonesos, X-1965-84, St Petersburg, State Hermitage Museum. Fr. of rim and upper body. H 3.6, WT 0.3, RH 1.7. Fabric: standard, 2.5YR 6/6. Dull coat, 2.5YR 4/6, 3/1. Oxidized. Stacked in firing. Rim frieze: Ionian kyma. Calyx A2(?): top of Menemachos bud. Cf. Laumonier 1977, 30 cat. 1893, pl. 2. Menemachos.

EPH-574*
Pantikapaion, M-47-881, Moscow, Puškin Museum of Fine Arts. Fr. of rim and upper body. H 5.2 × W 5.5, ⌀ rim 12, 12%, RH 1.7. Oxidized. Rim frieze: guilloche right. Secondarily burnt. Menemachos.

EPH-575
Porthmion, Sector G, sector 2, fill in rooms, П-87-126, Kerč History and Culture Reserve. Fr. of lower body and tiny part of base. Base surrounded by low ridge.

EPH-576*
Volna 1, C3-98-143a, St Petersburg, State Hermitage Museum. Fr. of mid-body. Oxidized. Multiple rim friezes: missing; Ionian kyma.

EPH-577*
Volna 1, C3-98-157a, St Petersburg, State Hermitage Museum. Fr. of lower body. Oxidized. Calyx A2 (part of 'nelumbo' and bent acanthus leaf).

EPH-578*
Olbia, Sector R2,5 O-P25-00-1107, Parutine, Olbia National Preserve storeroom. Fr. of lower body close to base. H 4.2 × W 2.5, WT 0.3. Fabric: relatively fine and micaceous, small lime inclusions, 2.5YR 5/8. Thin slightly lustrous coat, ext. 2.5YR 5/6, int. 2.5YR 4/8. Hard fired, oxidized. Stacked in firing. Calyx A?

EPH-579*
Olbia, Sector NGS, О-НГС-05-228, Parutine, Olbia National Preserve storeroom. Fr. of rim and upper body. H 4.4 × W 5.1, WT 0.32, RH 1.5. Fabric: relatively fine and micaceous, 5YR 6/8. Thin dull coat, 2.5YR 5/6. Medium hard fired, oxidized. Rim frieze: rosette 2/7. Calyx A: upper part of large drooping acanthus leaf.

Calyx A with Filled 'Nelumbo'

EPH-580*
Pantikapaion, П-1873-115, St Petersburg, State Hermitage Museum. Complete profile, lacking minor frs. ⌀ rim 11.8; vessel H 7.3; H:⌀ 1:1.6. Reduced. Rim frieze: rosette 1. Calyx: four filled 'nelumbos' with cabled edges, surrounded by buds on looped stems and alternating with curving acanthus with ornamented central vein, with small Eros in foliage. Two 'nelumbos' contain kissing couple (*coitus a tergo* A), with flowers below; the others contain vegetation and a sitting duck, with small acanthus leaf below. Plain, concave base, signed MENEMACHOU. Menemachos. For floral fill of 'nelumbo', with duck, cf. Laumonier 1977, 427 cat. 1325, pl. 99.
– AGSP 1984, pl. CLXIII.16, 17a (but the drawing, especially of the rosettes, is misleading).

EPH-581*
Istros, His-540, Bucharest, Institute of Archaeology storeroom. Fr. of lower body. H 4 × W 2.5. Oxidized. Calyx: acanthus with drooping tip, with small 'nelumbo' in front. Menemachos?
– Domăneanțu 2000, 3 cat. 3, pl. 1 (attributed to Menemachos).

EPH-582*
Chersonesos, X-1900-31, St Petersburg, State Hermitage Museum. Two joining frs. of most of base and part of lower wall. H 8, WT 0.3, ⌀ base 4.7. Fabric: standard, Gley 1 3/N. Thin dull coat, Gley 1 2.5/N. Hard fired, reduced. Calyx: 'nelumbo' with cabled edges enclosing couple on mattress (*coitus a tergo* A) with flowers below, alternating with acanthus with small 'nelumbo' in front. Plain, concave base, signed MENEMACHOU. Menemachos.

EPH-583
Pantikapaion, M-46-5103, Moscow, Puškin Museum of Fine Arts. Fr. of base and lower body. H 4.5 × W 6, ⌀ base 5. Dull black coat. Reduced. Calyx: 'nelumbo' with cabled edge enclosing kissing couple (*coitus a tergo* A) with flowers below, alternating with acanthus leaves with segmented central vein and small 'nelumbo' in front. Plain, concave base on low ring foot, no trace of signature preserved. Possibly from same bowl as EPH-584*. Menemachos.

EPH-584*
Pantikapaion, M-46-6063, Moscow, Puškin Museum of Fine Arts. Body fr. H 4 × W 4. Dull black coat. Reduced. Rim frieze: crossed dotted lines with box. Calyx: 'nelumbo' with cabled edge and floral filling, surrounded by buds on looped stems. Frieze separators: dots. Possibly from same bowl as EPH-583. Menemachos.

EPH-585*
Istros, His-770, Bucharest, Institute of Archaeology storeroom. Body fr. H 4 × W 4, WT 0.35. Fabric: very fine, compact, non-micaceous. Dull coat, int. almost completely worn off. Relatively hard fired, oxidized. Calyx: 'nelumbo' with cabled edge and floral filling. Secondarily burnt. Menemachos.

EPH-586
Porthmion, П-73-365, Kerč History and Culture Reserve. Fr. of rim and upper body. Oxidized. Rim frieze: crossed dotted lines with box. Calyx: top of filled(?) 'nelumbo' surrounded by buds. Menemachos.
– Grzegrzółka 2010, 130–131 cat. 183.

EPH-587*
Pantikapaion, palace foundation trench, M-89-illegible 12. Moscow, Puškin Museum of Fine Arts. Fr. of base and lower body. H 4 × W 3, WT 0.3. Slightly lustrous reddish brown coat. Oxidized. Calyx: naturalistic acanthus leaf, cabled edge perhaps of filled 'nelumbo'. Medallion: rosette B with small star rosette in centre. Menemachos?

EPH-588*
Olbia, Sector R25, O-P25-04-3393, Parutine, Olbia National Preserve storeroom. Body fr. H 2.3 × W 3.3, WT 0.28. Fabric: relatively fine and micaceous, small lime inclusions, 5Y 3/1. Thin lustrous coat, Gley 1 2.5/N. Medium hard fired, reduced. Calyx: thick vegetation (of calyx?), surrounding man playing aulos (shepherd?), standing right with drapery over head and upper body. Twisted line at right may be edge of 'nelumbo'.

EPH-589*
Myrmekion, M-58-558, St Petersburg IIMK RAN. Four joining base frs. H 5.65, WT 0.4, ø base 3.8. Fabric: standard, 2.5YR 5/8. Thin dull coat, 2.5YR 5/8. Oxidized. Calyx: filled 'nelumbo' alternating with twisted stems. Medallion: rosette A, var. 1. Menemachos?

EPH-590
Olbia, O-1910-1008, present whereabouts unknown. Fr. of lower body. Calyx: twisted edge of filled 'nelumbo'; lotus bud on wavy stem; acanthus leaf with segmented central vein and small 'nelumbo' in front; palmette on twisted stem. Menemachos.
– St Petersburg, IIMK RAN, archive inv. 4057.519.5 (pl. XII)

EPH-591
Porthmion, П-73-364, Kerč History and Culture Reserve. Body fr. Oxidized. Calyx: filled 'nelumbo' with cabled edge alternating with acanthus leaf with 'nelumbo' in front. Menemachos.
– Grzegrzółka 2010, 131 cat. 184.

EPH-592
Porthmion, trench A, SE corner of rooms 42 and 43, depth 1.4 m, П-75-41, Kerč History and Culture Reserve. Fr. of lower body. Oxidized. Calyx as the preceding. Menemachos.
– Grzegrzółka 2010, 131–132 cat. 185.

EPH-593
Istros, His-Dup729, in the possession of P. Dupont. Fr. of lower body and base. Oxidized. Calyx: 'nelumbo' with tall, slender acanthus leaf in front of lower part. Plain base.

EPH-594
Istros, His-151, Bucharest, Institute of Archaeology storeroom. Fr. of lower body. Oxidized. Calyx A (part of 'nelumbo' and acanthus leaf).
– Domăneanțu 2000, 13 cat. 54, pl. 4.

Other Calyces with 'Nelumbo'

EPH-595*
Pantikapaion, M-74-345, 345[a], Moscow, Puškin Museum of Fine Arts. Non-joining frs. of rim, body and base; complete profile. RH 1.5, ø base 4.5. Thin dull red coat. Oxidized. Rim frieze: crossed dotted lines with box. Calyx: 'nelumbo' with small, straight acanthus in front, alternating with groups of at least two stylized long petals. Plain slightly concave base, signed MENEMACHOU. Menemachos.

EPH-596*
Olbia, Sector NGS, O-НГС-92-243, Parutine, Olbia National Preserve storeroom. Body fr. Oxidized. Rim frieze: heart guilloche right. Calyx: plastic long petal between acanthus and 'nelumbo'.

EPH-597*
Ruminskoe/Za Rodinu, Рум-72-221, Moscow, State Historical Museum. Fr. of rim and body. ø rim ca. 11. Slightly metallic black coat. Reduced. Rim frieze: Ionian kyma. Calyx: stylized long petals delimited by column of dots alternating with jewelled 'nelumbo'. Menemachos.

EPH-598*
Olbia, Sector E6, square 432w, grey clay layer over Room "O", O-E6-59-2209, 2209[a], Kiev, Institute of Archaeology storeroom. Two non-joining body frs. H 6.7 × W 6.5, WT 0.25. Fabric: standard, 5Y 5/1. Dull coat, 5Y 2.5/1. Relatively hard fired, reduced. Rim frieze: rosette 9/11. Calyx: ovoid lotus petal alternating with 'nelumbo' with dotted central vein; in between, column of dots topped by two dots. Low ridge around base.

EPH-599
Tyritake, no. unknown, Kerč History and Culture Reserve. Fr. of lower body. Oxidized. Calyx: 'nelumbo' with tall acanthus in front alternating with column of dots topped by two dots.
– Grzegrzółka 2010, 102–103 cat. 121.

EPH-600*
Myrmekion, M-57-381, St Petersburg IIMK RAN. Three joining frs. of base and lower wall. H 3.9, WT 0.25, ø base 4.7. Fabric: standard, slightly brittle, 2.5YR 5/2. Thin dull coat, 2.5Y 4/1. Hard fired, reduced. Multiple rim friezes: rosette 10; astragal. Calyx: 'nelumbo' with small acanthus leaf in front alternating with column of dots. Base: plain and concave. Cf. Domăneanțu 2000, 94 cat. 456, pl. 31.

EPH-601* (see also Fig. 79)
Olbia, Sector NGS, O-НГС-02-283, Parutine, Olbia National Preserve storeroom. Three body frs. and one base fr., all joining. Almost complete profile. WT 0.31–0.6, ø base 4.9; vessel H 6.5. Fabric: fine, micaceous, many minute and some larger lime particles, 5YR 6/6–5/6. Thin firm coat with slight lustre except on ext. rim, where blackened to metallic blue sheen, ext. 2.5YR 4/6, 3/0, int. 2.5YR 4/6. Medium hard fired, oxidized. Stacked in firing. Multiple rim friezes: Ionian kyma; vertical S-spirals;

horizontal S-spirals; astragal; Ionian kyma. Calyx: plastic long petals alternating with 'nelumbo' with small acanthus in front and lily(?) atop stem of small circles. Medallion: rosette E. Frieze separators: dots. Four repair holes.

EPH-602*
Istros, His-881, Bucharest, Institute of Archaeology storeroom. Body fr. H 3.2 × W 2.7, WT 0.35. Fabric: standard, fine, 5YR 6/8. Dull coat, ext. 2.5YR 4/6, 3/1, int. 2.5YR 4/6. Relatively hard fired, oxidized. Stacked in firing. Rim frieze: Ionian kyma. Calyx: 'nelumbo'(?) with Wadjet symbol as space filler. Monogram PAR.
– Domăneanţu 2000, 32 cat. 124, pl. 9 (attributed to Monogram PAR).

EPH-603*
Bol'šoj Kastel', БК-84-32, Černomorskoe Museum of Historical Lore. Fr. of rim and upper body. H 3.3, ⌀ rim 13, RH 1.2. Fabric: 5YR 5/6, 10YR 5/3. Slightly metallic coat, ext. 5YR 2.5/1, int. 5YR 3/4. Oxidized. Rim frieze: box meander, cw. Calyx: 'nelumbo' with crab as space filler. For crab, cf. Laumonier 1977, 106 cat. 8542, pl. 24.

EPH-604*
Porthmion, square 18, depth 0.45 m, with material of the 2nd century, П-53-850, Kerč History and Culture Reserve. Fr. of rim and upper body. H 3.8, WT 0.25, ⌀ rim 13, RH 1.8. Fabric: standard, 2.5Y 4/1. Thin dull coat, Gley 1 3/N. Reduced. Rim frieze: Ionian kyma. Calyx: top of 'nelumbo'.

EPH-605
Pantikapaion, 1903-18. Complete. Multiple rim friezes: box meander, cw; astragal. Calyx: straight acanthus alternating with slender, stylized 'nelumbo'; bird right as space filler. Medallion: rosette A.
– St Petersburg, IIMK RAN photo archive neg. III 9672.

Calyx B1

EPH-606*
Istros, His-V 8579 H, Bucharest Institute of Archaeology storeroom. Fr. of base and lower body. H 5 × W 7.5, WT 0.3, ⌀ base 4. Fabric: standard, Gley 1 5/N. Coat with dull lustre, Gley 1 2.5/N. Relatively hard fired, reduced. Medallion: rosette A.
– Domăneanţu 2000, 30 cat. 113, pl. 8 (attributed to Monogram PAR).

EPH-607*
Myrmekion, M-58-153, St Petersburg IIMK RAN. Four joining frs. of base and lower body. H 5.8, WT 0.37, ⌀ base 4. Fabric: standard, slightly denser than normal, 7.5YR 7/4. Thin coat with slight metallic sheen, 7.5YR 3/1. Oxidized. Stacked in firing. Medallion: rosette D. Two repair holes.

EPH-608
Kepoi, necropolis, square 59A, funerary meal, no. unknown, Moscow, State Historical Museum. Fr. of rim and body. Rim frieze: astragal.
– Usačeva 1978, fig. 3.7.

EPH-609
Kepoi, Kurgan 14, funerary meal, no. unknown, Moscow, State Historical Museum. Fr. of rim and upper body. Multiple rim friezes: astragal; rosette 2/7(?).
– Usačeva 1978, fig. 2.15.

EPH-610*
Myrmekion, M-57-616, St Petersburg IIMK RAN. Two joining frs. of base and mid-body. H 5.6, WT 0.3, ⌀ base 4. Fabric: standard, 5YR 5/8. Lustrous coat ext., int. with slight metallic lustre, 5YR 3/1. Oxidized. Stacked in firing. Multiple rim friezes: missing; vertical S-spirals. Medallion: rosette B.

Calyx B2

EPH-611*
Olbia, inv. A 1026, Nikolaev, Historical Museum. Complete; joined from a number of frs. in antiquity. ⌀ rim 12.5, RH 1.1, ⌀ base 4.4; vessel H 5.6; H:⌀ 1:2.2. Dull reddish coat, darkened at rim ext. Oxidized. Stacked in firing. Multiple rim friezes: Ionian kyma; star rosettes; wave meander, upside-down. Medallion: rosette A, var. 3. 15 repair holes.

EPH-612*
Olbia, Sector NGS, O-НГС-06-94, 251, Parutine, Olbia National Preserve storeroom. Complete profile; though fragmentary, large part of bowl preserved. H 4.7 × W 7.3, WT 0.32, ⌀ rim 14, 12%, RH 1.8. Fabric: relatively fine and micaceous, some small lime inclusions, 5YR 6/8. Thin dull coat, ext. 2.5YR 4/6, 3/1, int. 2.5YR 4/6. Medium hard fired, oxidized. Stacked in firing. Multiple rim friezes: rosette 2/7; Ionian kyma; astragal. Medallion: rosette A. Secondarily burnt. Three repair holes. Monogram PAR.

EPH-613
Myrmekion, no. unknown, Kerč History and Culture Reserve. Fr. of base and lower body. Oxidized. Medallion: Monogram PAR surrounded by three ridges. Monogram PAR.
– Grzegrzółka 2010, 99–100 cat. 114

EPH-614
Olbia, Sector NGS, O-НГС-90-300, Parutine, Olbia National Preserve storeroom. Fr. of rim and body. Oxidized. Stacked in firing. Multiple rim friezes: star rosettes; Ionian kyma; astragal.

EPH-615
Pantikapaion, M-73-154, Moscow, Puškin Museum of Fine Arts? Fr. of rim and body. Multiple rim friezes: star rosettes; Lesbian kyma; astragal with decorated beads. Similar: Zabelina 1984, fig. 7c, also from Pantikapaion.
– Zabelina 1984, 160 fig. 7b.

EPH-616
Olbia, O-1929-1350, present whereabouts unknown. Fr. of base and large part of body. Multiple rim friezes: star rosettes; astragal with decorated beads. Medallion: rosette A.
– St Petersburg, IIMK RAN, photo archive neg. II 4833.

EPH-617
Pantikapaion, П-1847-22, St Petersburg, State Hermitage Museum. Complete. H 5.5, ⌀ rim 13. Oxidized. Multiple rim friezes: horizontal S-spirals; wave meander; upside-down; star rosettes. Medallion: rosette A.

EPH-618*
Olbia, Sector E6, squares 678, 644n, SW of house "B", central block, grey clay layer, O-E6-66-792, Kiev, Institute of Archaeology storeroom. Fr. of lower body. Oxidized. Rim frieze: star rosettes.

EPH-619*
Olbia, Sector E6, square 250, 251w, grey clay layer, O-E6-56-675, Kiev, Institute of Archaeology storeroom. Body fr. Oxidized.

EPH-620*
Volna 1, C3-98-45, St Petersburg, State Hermitage Museum. Fr. of lower body. Oxidized.

EPH-621*
Olbia, Sector R25, O-P25-98-200, Parutine, Olbia National Preserve storeroom. Fr. of base and lower body. H 5.5 × W 7.6, WT 0.28–0.6, ⌀ base 2.6. Fabric: relatively fine and micaceous, 5YR 5/8. Dull coat, mottled ext., ext. 2.5YR 4/6, 5YR 2.5/1, int. 2.5YR 4/8. Medium hard fired, oxidized. Stacked in firing. Medallion: rosette A.

EPH-622
Olbia, Sector R25, O-P25-93-990c, Parutine, Olbia National Preserve storeroom. Fr. of base and lower body. H 5.5 × W 6.7 WT 0.25–0.35, ⌀ base 3. Fabric: relatively fine and micaceous, small lime inclusions, 10YR 5/3. Thin slightly lustrous coat, 10YR 3/1. Medium hard fired, oxidized. Medallion: rosette A (tongues rather crude).

EPH-623*
Olbia, Sector R25, O-P25-95-16, Parutine, Olbia National Preserve storeroom. Fr. of lower body. H 4 × W 7.3, WT 0.3–0.5. Fabric: relatively fine and micaceous, small lime inclusions, 2.5YR 6/8. Dull coat, ext. 2.5YR 3/1, int. 10R 5/8. Medium hard fired, oxidized. Stacked in firing.

EPH-624*
Olbia, Sector NGS, O-НГС-05-805+06-324 (join across years), Parutine, Olbia National Preserve storeroom. Two joining frs. of base and lower body. H 7.9 × W 6.2, WT 0.4, ⌀ base 3.6. Fabric: relatively fine and micaceous. Medium hard fired, oxidized. Medallion: rosette A. Secondarily burnt? Monogram PAR?

EPH-625*
Myrmekion, M-58-1157, St Petersburg IIMK RAN. Fr. of mid- and lower body. H 3.5, WT 0.35. Fabric: standard, 2.5YR 5/8. Dull coat, 2.5YR 4/8. Oxidized. Multiple rim friezes: missing; guilloche right. Frieze separators: dots

EPH-626*
Olbia, Sector I, square 318, Pit E(?), yellow clay layer, O-И-48-2089 Kiev, Institute of Archaeology storeroom. Fr. of base and lower body. Oxidized. Medallion: rosette A.

EPH-627*
Myrmekion, M-58-691, St Petersburg IIMK RAN. Fr. of lower body. H 3.7, WT 0.2. Fabric: standard, 5YR 6/6. Slightly lustrous coat, ext. 5YR 3/2, int. 2.5YR 4/6. Oxidized. Stacked in firing.

EPH-628
Myrmekion, M-58-2965, St Petersburg IIMK RAN. Fr. of base and lower body. H 4.8, WT 0.25, ⌀ base 4. Fabric: standard, 5YR 6/6. Lustrous coat, 5YR 4/3. Oxidized. Medallion: rosette A, var. 1.

EPH-629*
Porthmion, square 21, depth 0.75 m, 1st longitudinal street, with material of the 3rd–2nd century, П-53-970, Kerč History and Culture Reserve. Fr. of base and lower body. H 4.3, WT 0.25, ⌀ base 4. Fabric: standard, fine, 7.5YR 6/4. Thin slightly lustrous coat, mottled ext., 7.5YR 3/1. Oxidized. Medallion: rosette B.

EPH-630*
Olbia, O-52-68, Kiev, Institute of Archaeology storeroom. Fr. of base and lower body. Oxidized. Rim frieze: Lesbian kyma. Medallion: rosette B.

EPH-631*
Olbia, Sector NGS, O-НГС-06-125, Parutine, Olbia National Preserve storeroom. Fr. of lower body. Oxidized.

EPH-632*
Myrmekion, M-47-241, St Petersburg IIMK RAN. Fr. of lower body. H 3.5, WT 0.25. Fabric: standard, 2.5YR 5/8. Dull coat ext., slightly lustrous int., ext. 2.5YR 4/8, int. 2.5YR 4/6. Oxidized.

EPH-633*
Olbia, Sector E6, square 252w, below heap of tiles, O-E6-56-120+276, Kiev, Institute of Archaeology storeroom. Two joining frs. of base and lower body. Oxidized. Medallion: rosette B. Secondarily burnt.

EPH-634*
Olbia, O-4x-3760, Kiev, Institute of Archaeology storeroom. Fr. of base and lower body. Oxidized. Medallion: rosette B.

EPH-635*
Myrmekion, M-47-195, St Petersburg IIMK RAN. Fr. of mid- and lower body. H 4.2, WT 0.28. Fabric: standard, 5YR 6/8. Slightly lustrous coat ext., int. dull, 2.5YR 3/6. Oxidized. Rim frieze: miniature acanthus scroll left. Menemachos.

EPH-636
Kepoi, necropolis, square 59A, funerary meal, no. unknown, Moscow, State Historical Museum. Complete. Multiple rim friezes: miniature acanthus-flower scroll left; guilloche right. Medallion: rosette B. Monogram PAR.
– Usačeva 1978, fig. 3.6.

EPH-637
Myrmekion, M-58-2942, St Petersburg IIMK RAN. Fr. of base and lower body. H 6, WT 0.3, ⌀ base 4. Fabric: standard, 2.5YR 6/6. Lustrous coat, 2.5YR 4/4. Oxidized. Medallion: rosette B.

EPH-638
Pantikapaion, M-61-656, Moscow, Puškin Museum of Fine Arts. Fr. of rim and body. Multiple rim friezes: dots, large rosette 2/7.
– Zabelina 1984, 160 fig. 7a.

EPH-639
Chersonesos, pit 2 (1877), X-1908-11, St Petersburg, State Hermitage Museum. Restored, almost complete. H 5.9, ⌀ rim 12.8, RH 1.2, ⌀ base 4.4. Fabric: no fresh break for observation. Thin dull coat, ext. 2.5YR 4/8, 2.5/1, int. 2.5YR 4/8. Oxidized. Stacked in firing. Multiple rim friezes: star rosettes; rosette 2/7. Calyx B2 var. (all petals rhomboidal). Medallion: rosette A surrounded by broad low raised dots. Stamps are somewhat tired.

EPH-640*
Istros, His-203, 790+911, Bucharest, Institute of Archaeology storeroom. Two joining frs. of lower body and non-joining base fr. H 4 × W 5.6, WT 0.33, ⌀ base 3.5. Fabric: standard, fine with many small voids, 5YR 6/8. Dull coat, 2.5YR 5/8. Relatively hard fired, oxidized. Calyx B2 var. (all petals rhomboidal). Medallion: rosette A.
– Domăneanțu 2000, 27 cat. 102, pl. 7 (attributed to Monogram PAR).

EPH-641*
Pantikapaion, palace foundation trench, M-85-45[b], Moscow, Puškin Museum of Fine Arts. Three joining frs. of mid- and lower body. H 4.1 × W 8.8, WT 0.3. Blackish coat with dull metallic sheen. Oxidized. Multiple rim friezes: missing; Ionian kyma. Calyx B2 var. (all petals rhomboidal). Frieze separators: dots. One repair hole.

EPH-642
Istros, His-B 598/V 19450, Bucharest, Institute of Archaeology storeroom. Fr. of lower body. H 3.5 × W 4. Oxidized. Calyx B2 var. (all petals rhomboidal).
– Domăneanțu 2000, 30 cat. 116, pl. 8 (attributed to Monogram PAR).

EPH-643*
Olbia, O-75-no no., present whereabouts unknown. Complete profile, one quarter of bowl preserved. Multiple rim friezes: rosette 2/8; rosette 1; vertical astragal. Calyx B2 var. (all acanthus leaves folded in the same direction). Medallion: rosette A. Menemachos?
– St Petersburg, IIMK RAN, photo archive neg. I 93695.

EPH-644
Istros, His-V 19373 C, Bucharest, Institute of Archaeology storeroom. Fr. of lower body. H 7 × W 3.5. Reduced. Calyx B2, rhomboidal petal with hatched vein.
– Domăneanțu 2000, 25 cat. 90, pl. 7 (attributed to Monogram PAR).

EPH-645*
Volna 1, C3-00-29, St Petersburg, State Hermitage Museum. Fr. of lower body. Oxidized.

EPH-646*
Myrmekion, M-56-1877, St Petersburg IIMK RAN. Fr. of mid-body. H 2.4, WT 0.22. Fabric: standard, fine, 5YR 5/8. Thin dull coat, 2.5YR 5/6. Oxidized. Calyx B2, rhomboidal petal with hatched border and cross-bar.

EPH-647
Myrmekion, M-58-2940, St Petersburg IIMK RAN. Fr. of upper and mid-body. H 4.9, WT 0.35. Fabric: standard, 7.5YR 5/6. Slightly lustrous coat, ext. 7.5YR 3/1, int. 2.5YR 4/6, 7.5YR 3/2. Oxidized. Stacked in firing. Rim frieze: box meander, cw. Calyx B2?

EPH-648
Olbia, Sector R25, O-P25-06-648, Parutine, Olbia National Preserve storeroom. Fr. of mid- and lower body. H 4 × W 2.7, WT 0.28. Fabric: relatively fine and micaceous. Thin dull coat. Medium hard fired, oxidized. Multiple rim friezes: Ionian kyma(?); horizontal S-spirals. Calyx B2(?) with very slender rhomboidal petal.

EPH-649*
Bol'šoj Kastel', БК-86-74[c], Černomorskoe Museum of Historical Lore. Lower body fr. H 2. Fabric: 2.5YR 5/6. Slightly lustrous coat, 2.5YR 4/6. Oxidized. Calyx B2?

Calyx B, Type Unknown

EPH-650*
Olbia, Sector NGS, O-НГС-06-106+107+126+130+139, 106a, 108, Parutine, Olbia National Preserve storeroom. Eight frs. of rim and body joining in pairs, two joining body frs., one non-joining body fr. H 5.3 × W 11, WT 0.4, ⌀ rim 16, 24%, RH 1.7. Fabric: relatively fine and micaceous, 7.5YR 6/6. Thin dull coat, ext. 5YR 4/4, 7.5YR 3/1, int. 5YR 4/4. Medium hard fired, oxidized. Stacked in firing. Multiple rim friezes: rosette 2/7; miniature acanthus-flower scroll left; astragal. Calyx B. One repair hole, with lead clamp still in place. Monogram PAR.

EPH-651*
Pantikapaion, palace foundation trench, M-84-155, Moscow, Puškin Museum of Fine Arts. Fr. of rim and body. H 5.9 × W 6.7, WT 0.4, ⌀ rim 11.5, 12%, RH 1.8. Dull red coat. Oxidized. Stacked in firing. Multiple rim friezes: box meander, cw; rosette 2/7. Calyx B.
– Košelenko 1992, fig. 23.

EPH-652*
Volna 1, C3-98-43, St Petersburg, State Hermitage Museum. Fr. of lower body. Oxidized. Calyx B.

EPH-653*
Tyritake, Sector A, A-55-163, St Petersburg IIMK RAN. Fr. of lower body. Oxidized. Calyx B.

EPH-654*
Olbia, Sector R25, O-P25-92-3226, Parutine, Olbia National Preserve storeroom. Fr. of lower body. H 5.3 × W 5, WT 0.26. Fabric: relatively fine and micaceous, small lime inclusions, 2.5YR 5/8. Thin dull coat, 2.5YR 5/6. Hard fired, oxidized. Calyx B, with tall, thin lotus petal with segmented vein.

EPH-655* (see also Fig. 79)
Volna 1, C3-99-40[b], St Petersburg, State Hermitage Museum. Fr. of lower body and tiny part of base. Oxidized. Calyx B. Base surrounded by ridge.

EPH-656*
Bol'šoj Kastel', БК-82-32, Černomorskoe Museum of Historical Lore. Body fr. H 3. Fabric: 2.5YR 5/8. Slightly shiny coat, 2.5YR 4/6. Oxidized. Calyx B.

Other Calyces with Folded or Swaying Acanthus Leaf

EPH-657*
Istros, His-673, Bucharest, Institute of Archaeology storeroom. Fr. of base and lower body. H 4.1 × W 4.8, WT 0.3, ⌀ base 3. Fabric: standard, Gley 1 5/N. Dull coat, Gley 1 3/N. Relatively hard fired, reduced. Calyx: fine, naturalistic acanthus leaf, bent at top, alternating with slender, pointed lotus petal. Medallion: rosette A.

EPH-658
Istros, His-V 19167 E, Bucharest, Institute of Archaeology storeroom. Fr. of lower body. H 3.4 × W 4.6, WT 0.35. Fabric: standard but with large lump of lime (4 mm), 5Y 5/2. Dull coat, 5Y 3/1. Relatively hard fired, reduced. Calyx: acanthus flower flanked by acanthus leaf with bent tip.
– Domăneanţu 2000, 140 cat. 696, pl. 50.

EPH-659*
Myrmekion, M-58-1267, St Petersburg IIMK RAN. Fr. of lower body. H 2.3, WT 0.35. Fabric: standard, 5YR 5/8. Thin dull coat, 2.5YR 5/6. Oxidized. Calyx: folded acanthus leaf, looped stem with bud.

EPH-660*
Olbia, Cliff, square 285, O-70-150, location? Fr. of lower body. Dull red coat. Oxidized. Folded acanthus leaf, thin rhomboidal petal, partial floral element. Medallion: rosette A?

EPH-661*
Olbia, Sector NGS, O-НГС-08-188, Parutine, Olbia National Preserve storeroom. Fr. of lower body and base. H 4 × W 5, WT 0.2,

⌀ base 3. Fabric: fine, micaceous, 2.5YR 6/8. Thin dull mottled coat, ext. 2.5YR 4/3, 4/4, int. 2.5YR 4/3, 4/4. Hard fired, oxidized. Calyx: curved acanthus leaf alternating with slender rhomboidal petal. Medallion: rosette D.

Calyx C

EPH-662*
Olbia, Sector R25, O-P25-04-2809+3724+3745+3747+05-1208 (join across years), Parutine, Olbia National Preserve storeroom. Two joining frs. of base and lower body, two joining body frs. H 5.4 × W 8.3, WT 0.3–0.5, ⌀ base 4. Fabric: relatively fine and micaceous, 2.5Y 4/1. Thin dull coat, Gley 1 2.5/N. Medium hard fired, reduced. Rim frieze: star rosettes. Plain base with small false ring foot.

EPH-663*
Myrmekion, M-47-244, St Petersburg IIMK RAN. Fr. of base and lower body. H 7.8, WT 0.4, ⌀ base 4.5. Fabric: standard, 7.5YR 6/6. Coat with slight metallic sheen, 7.5YR 3/3. Oxidized. Medallion: rosette A. Secondarily burnt.

EPH-664*
Olbia, Sector NGS, House IV-3 B 343/204 O-НГС-92-619, Parutine, Olbia National Preserve storeroom. Fr. of base and lower body. H 5 × W 5.2, WT 0.22–0.4, ⌀ base 3.5. Fabric: fine and micaceous, a few small voids, 5Y 4/1. Thin firm slightly lustrous coat, 5Y 2.5/1. Hard fired, oxidized. Medallion: rosette A.
– Guldager Bilde 2010, 279 cat. F-34, pl. 175.

EPH-665*
Olbia, Sector NGS, O-НГС-96-45, Parutine, Olbia National Preserve storeroom. Fr. of base and body. H 9.2 × W 7.3, WT 0.3, ⌀ base 3. Fabric: relatively fine and micaceous, many small lime particles, 5YR 6/8. Thin dull coat, ext. 10R 5/6, int. 2.5YR 5/8. Medium hard fired, oxidized. Rim frieze: astragal. Medallion: rosette B.

EPH-666
Olbia, Sector NGS, O-НГС-06-128, 129, Parutine, Olbia National Preserve storeroom. Two non-joining frs. of base and lower body. H 3.7 × W 4.7, WT 0.25. Fabric: relatively fine and micaceous, some small lime inclusions, 5YR 6/6. Thin dull coat, 5YR 4/3. Medium hard fired, oxidized. Medallion: rosette B.

EPH-667
Porthmion, Sector G, sector 2, square 17–18, depth 0.42 m, П-87-106, Kerč History and Culture Reserve. Fr. of rim and upper body. Rim frieze: Ionian kyma. Calyx C with three dots as space filler.

Other Calyces with Alternating Acanthus Leaf/Frond and Lotus Petal

EPH-668*
Olbia, Sector NGS, O-НГС-06-151, Parutine, Olbia National Preserve storeroom. Fr. of base and lower body. H 7.1 × W 7.3, WT 0.25, ⌀ base 4.8. Fabric: relatively fine and micaceous, some small lime inclusions, 5Y 5/1. Dull coat, Gley 1 3/N. Medium hard fired, reduced. Calyx: acanthus leaf alternating with lotus petal. Plain base with false ring foot.

EPH-669*
Pantikapaion, palace foundation trench, M-89-illegible 6+no no. 22, Moscow, Puškin Museum of Fine Arts. Joining frs. of rim and body. H 5.1 × W 8.4, WT 0.28, ⌀ rim 12, 18%, RH 1.5. Blackish coat with slight metallic lustre, almost completely worn off at rim ext. Oxidized. Rim frieze: large dots. Calyx: straight acanthus leaf alternating with slender pointed petal.

EPH-670*
Myrmekion, M-49-592, St Petersburg, State Hermitage Museum. Fr. of rim and large part of body. H 6, WT 0.25. ⌀ rim 12, RH 1.3. Fabric: standard, 2.5YR 6/6. Dull coat with slight metallic lustre at rim, ext. 10R 5/5, 5/4, int. 10R 5/6. Oxidized. Stacked in firing. Multiple rim friezes: rosette 5; Ionian kyma; rosette 5. Calyx: palm frond alternating with ovoid petal.

EPH-671*
Pantikapaion, П-1902-130, St Petersburg, State Hermitage Museum. Complete. H 5.5, ⌀ rim 13.2. Oxidized. Stacked in firing. Multiple rim friezes: widely spaced X's; tiny lotus petal, pointed at both ends, alternating with tiny palmette. Calyx: acanthus leaf alternating with petal pointed at both ends. Medallion: seven-rayed sun wheel. Graffito PA on rim.
– Škorpil 1904, fig. 52.

EPH-672*
Istros, Sector SG, 0.11-0.8, His-973[a], Bucharest, Institute of Archaeology storeroom. Fr. of lower body. H 3.1 × W 3.6, WT 0.45. Fabric: standard, 5Y 5/1. Dull coat, Gley 1 2.5/N. Medium hard fired, reduced. Calyx: slender palm frond alternating with petal.

EPH-673*
Olbia, Sector NGS, O-НГС-05-746, 06-133, Parutine, Olbia National Preserve storeroom. Two joining frs. of lower body. H 4.1 × W 5.1, WT 0.3. Fabric: relatively fine and micaceous, some small lime inclusions, 5YR 5/8. Thin dull coat, ext. 2.5YR 4/8, 3/1, int. 2.5YR 4/8. Medium hard fired, oxidized. Stacked in firing. Rim frieze: sunburst rosette. Calyx: palm frond alternating with ovoid petal. One repair hole. Cf. Laumonier 1977, 110 cat. 358, pl. 25. Late Menemachean.

EPH-674*
Myrmekion, M-58-1760, St Petersburg IIMK RAN. Fr. of base and lower body. H 7.8, WT 0.2, ⌀ base 4.2. Fabric: standard, slightly brittle, 2.5Y 4/1. Thin lustrous black coat, Gley 1 3/N. Hard fired, reduced. Calyx: acanthus leaf, alternating rhomboidal and ovoid petals. Plain base with low foot. Graffito: X.

EPH-675*
Olbia, O-no no. X, Kiev, Institute of Archaeology storeroom. Fr. of base and lower body. H 8.1 × W 7.5, WT 0.3, ⌀ base 2.8. Fabric: standard, fine, Gley 1 4/N. Slightly lustrous coat, Gley 1 3/N. Relatively hard fired, reduced. Calyx: fine acanthus leaf alternating with rhomboidal petal. Medallion: rosette E.

Calyces with Alternating Acanthus Leaf and Floral Tendril

EPH-676
Pantikapaion, Cistern N 179 96-no.(?). Fragmentary, ca. two-thirds preserved, with complete profile. Multiple rim friezes: Ionian kyma; astragal. Calyx: acanthus leaf alternating with flower stem with looped tendrils. Medallion: rosette A. Early. Tolstikov & Žuravlev 2004, pl. 101.5 is from the same mould, or perhaps the same bowl. Südtor Workshop.
– Tolstikov & Zhuravlev 2004, pl. 100.9.

EPH-677*
Olbia, Sector AGD, O-АГД-71-620, Kiev, Institute of Archaeology storeroom. Two joining frs. of base and body. H 8.2 × W 5.3, WT 0.15–0.25, ⌀ base 2.5. Fabric: standard, fine, Gley 1 6/10Y. Coat with slight dull lustre, Gley 1 2.5/N. Relatively hard fired, reduced. Calyx: Acanthus X and frond-like acanthus leaf alternating with twisted stem with ivy-berry cluster and unidentified element. Medallion: rosette A var. with ribbed krater at center. VG Workshop.

EPH-678*
Olbia(?), inv. 54791 Uvarov 311/61, Moscow, State Historical Museum (Uvaroc Collection). Complete. ⌀ rim 12, RH 2, ⌀ base 2.7; vessel H 7; H:⌀ 1:1.7. Fabric: light brown (no fresh break for observation). Dull black coat. Oxidized. Multiple rim friezes: astragal; box meander, alternating cw and ccw. Calyx: acanthus leaf with tip bent forward (incorrectly rendered in drawing), with small petal and sepals at base, alternating with vertical acanthus scroll; in between, acanthus flower on looped stem growing out of bud. Medallion: rosette A, var. 2. Early.

EPH-679*
Olbia, Sector E7, Room(?), grey clay layer, O-E7-59-2139, Kiev, Institute of Archaeology storeroom. Fr. of base and lower body. H 3.6 × W 6.5, WT 0.35, ⌀ base 3. Fabric: standard, 2.5YR 6/8.

Dull coat, 10R 4/8. Relatively hard fired, oxidized. Calyx: acanthus leaf alternating with vertical acanthus scroll. Medallion: rosette C.

EPH-680
Olbia, O-no no. L, Kiev, Institute of Archaeology storeroom? Fr. of rim and upper body. Oxidized. Rim frieze: star rosettes. Calyx: edge of acanthus leaf, top of Menemachos bud. Menemachos.

EPH-681
Tyritake, number unknown, Kerč History and Culture Reserve. Fr. of rim and upper body. Oxidized. Rim frieze: miniature acanthus-flower scroll left. Calyx: straight acanthus leaf alternating with palmette on twisted stem. Monogram PAR?
– Grzegrzółka 2010, 107 cat. 131 (attributed to Asia Minor).

Calyces with Other Alternating Elements

EPH-682
Olbia, Sector Sever-Zapad, O-C3-77-(no. effaced), Parutine, Olbia National Preserve storeroom. Fr. of base and lower body. H 4 × W 4.8, WT 0.35, ⌀ base 3. Fabric: standard with much lime, 2.5YR 5/8. Thin slightly lustrous coat, 2.5YR 4/6. Hard fired, oxidized. Calyx: vertical miniature floral scroll alternating with tall sepals(?) with segmented mid-vein. Medallion: rosette A, var. 2.

EPH-683*
Olbia, Sector AGD O-АГД-87-664, Kiev, Institute of Archaeology storeroom. Fr. of rim and upper body. H 4.3 × W 5, WT 0.25, ⌀ rim 12, 11%, RH 1.3. Fabric: standard with abundant lime, 5YR 6/6. Dull coat, ext. 2.5YR 5/6, 7.5YR 6/6, int. 2.5YR 5/6. Relatively hard fired, oxidized. Stacked in firing. Rim frieze: Ionian kyma with hatched tongue. Calyx: vertical miniature floral scroll. Misfired or secondarily burnt.

EPH-684*
Olbia, Sector R25, O-P25-96-1332, Parutine, Olbia National Preserve storeroom. Fr. of upper body. H 4.5 × W 4.4, WT 0.3. Fabric: relatively fine and micaceous, 7.5YR 6/6. Slightly lustrous mottled coat, ext. has patches of metallic sheen, ext. 7.5YR 2.5/1, 5YR 5/6, int. 7.5YR 2.5/1. Hard fired, oxidized. Stacked in firing. Rim frieze: Ionian kyma. Calyx: broad petal ('nelumbo'?) alternating with sistrum bud. Identical: Mitsopoulos-Leon 1991, 72 cat. D 37, pl. 82. Early? Menemachos.

EPH-685*
Porthmion, pavement of 2nd longitudinal street, with three bronze coins of Pantikapaion (first half of the 3rd century; mid-3rd century; 2nd century), П-77-262, Kerč History and Culture Reserve. Fr. of body close to rim. H 3.5, WT 0.2. Fabric: standard, 2.5YR 5/8. Thin slightly lustrous coat, ext. 2.5YR

2.5/1, int. 2.5YR 5/6. Oxidized. Stacked in firing. Rim frieze: Ionian kyma. Calyx: broad petal ('nelumbo'?), with sistrum bud. Menemachos.

EPH-686
Olbia, O-1910-1132, present whereabouts unknown. Fr. of lower body and tiny part of base. Calyx: sequence of acanthus leaf, vertical scroll, rhomboidal petal, floral element. Medallion: surrounded by low ridge.
– St Petersburg, IIMK RAN, archive inv. 40...(?) (pl. XIII).

EPH-687*
Olbia, Sector R25, O-P25-02-257, Parutine, Olbia National Preserve storeroom. Fr. of base and lower body. H 4.2 × W 4.4, WT 0.3. Fabric: relatively fine and micaceous, small lime inclusions, 5Y 4/1. Firm dull coat, 5Y 2.5/1. Hard fired, reduced. Calyx: vertical floral scrolls. Medallion: rosette A.

EPH-688*
Olbia, Sector R25, O-P25-03-2425, Parutine, Olbia National Preserve storeroom. Fr. of base and lower body. H 3 × W 4.5, WT 0.4, ⌀ base 3.5. Fabric: relatively fine and micaceous, small lime inclusions, 5YR 6/6. Thin slightly lustrous coat, ext. 7.5YR 2.5/1, int. 2.5YR 4/8. Medium hard fired, oxidized. Stacked in firing. Calyx: acanthus leaves. Medallion: rosette A.

EPH-689*
Olbia, O-37-806, Kiev, Institute of Archaeology storeroom. Fr. of base and lower body. Oxidized. Calyx: alternating ovoid and rhomboidal petals. Medallion: rosette A.

Calyces with Repeated Single Floral Elements

EPH-690*
Volna 1, C3-98-47, St Petersburg, State Hermitage Museum. Fr. of rim and upper body. Oxidized. Rim frieze: horizontal S-spirals. Calyx: funnel-shaped flowers. Same flower: EPH-298, EPH-1036*.

EPH-691*
Olbia, O-69-2222, Kiev, Institute of Archaeology storeroom. Body fr. H 5 × W 4.3, WT 0.55. Fabric: standard, fine, 5Y 4/1. Coat with slight lustre ext., lustrous int., Gley 1 2.5/N. Relatively hard fired, reduced. Calyx: broad acanthus leaves. Frieze separators: small horizontal palmettes.

EPH-692*
Olbia, O-no no. Z, Kiev, Institute of Archaeology storeroom. Fr. of rim and upper body. H 4.8 × W 7.3, WT 0.25, ⌀ rim 13, 15%,

RH 1.5. Fabric: standard, fine, Gley 1 4/N. Dull coat, Gley 1 3/N. Relatively hard fired, reduced. Rim frieze: Ionian kyma. Calyx: slender acanthus leaves. Frieze separators: dots.

EPH-693*
Olbia, O-40-714, Kiev, Institute of Archaeology storeroom. Fr. of base and lower body. H 4.1 × W 5.3, WT 0.3, ⌀ base 3.6. Fabric: standard but with abundant minute lime, 5Y 7/1. Coat with dull lustre, Gley 1 4/N. Relatively hard fired, reduced. Calyx: acanthus leaves. Plain, concave base, signed MORAG/ENO, incised in mould before firing. Same maker as Moiragenes (EPH-786*, EPH-1247).

EPH-694
Purchased in the environs of Tyras, 32/23/95, Ephesos Museum. Complete. Fabric: fine, 5Y 6/1. Metallic coat, N3/. Hard fired, reduced. Multiple rim friezes: Ionian kyma; box meander, cw; hatched H's. Calyx: Acanthus X. Medallion: rosette A var. (7 petals). VG Workshop.
– Tuluk 2001, 64 cat. 11, pl. 34.

EPH-695
Olbia, Sector R25, O-P25-03-2473, Parutine, Olbia National Preserve storeroom. Fr. of base and lower body. H 3.8 × W 4.6, WT 0.4, ⌀ base 3. Fabric: relatively fine and micaceous, small lime inclusions, 2.5YR 6/8. Dull coat, 2.5YR 5/6. Medium hard fired, oxidized. Calyx: crude acanthus leaves. Medallion: rosette A.

EPH-696*
Pantikapaion, palace foundation trench, M-89-illegible 3, Moscow, Puškin Museum of Fine Arts. Fr. of base and lower body. H 3.1 × W 4.4, WT 0.25. Dull red coat. Oxidized. Calyx: acanthus leaves. Medallion: rosette B.

EPH-697*
Olbia, Sector NGS, O-НГС-06-153, Parutine, Olbia National Preserve storeroom. Fr. of lower body and base. H 3.6 × W 5.5, WT 0.2, ⌀ base 4. Fabric: relatively fine and micaceous, some small lime inclusions, 5Y 6/1. Dull coat, 5Y 3/1. Medium hard fired, reduced. Calyx: acanthus leaves. Medallion: rosette with alternating overlapping ovate and pointed petals.

EPH-698
Olbia, Cliff, square 285, O-70-151, Parutine, Olbia National Preserve storeroom. Fr. of base and lower body. H 4 × W 4.5, WT 0.35, ⌀ base 4. Fabric: standard, fine, 10YR 6/3. Slightly lustrous coat, 10YR 2/1. Relatively hard fired, reduced. Calyx: acanthus leaves. Medallion: rosette of broad petals with sun wheel at center, surrounded by two ridges.

EPH-699*
Olbia, Sector R25, O-P25-03-2424, Parutine, Olbia National Preserve storeroom. Fr. of lower body. H 3.4 × W 3, WT 0.3. Fabric: relatively fine and micaceous. Slightly lustrous coat, ext. partly lacking. Oxidized. Calyx: acanthus leaves, row of small rounded petals with central and side veins. Secondarily burnt.

EPH-700*
Olbia, Sector NGS, O-НГС-96-200, Parutine, Olbia National Preserve storeroom. Fr. of lower body. H 4 × W 7.1, WT 0.3. Fabric: fine, micaceous, 5YR 6/8. Thin dull coat, 2.5YR 5/6. Medium hard fired, oxidized. Calyx: acanthus with sistrum bud as space filler. Menemachos.

EPH-701*
Porthmion, pavement of 2nd longitudinal street, with three bronze coins of Pantikapaion (first half of 3rd century; mid-3rd century; 2nd century), П-77-271[a], Kerč History and Culture Reserve. Fr. of lower body. H 3, WT 0.38. Fabric: standard, fine, Gley 1 4/10Y. Thin dull coat, Gley 1 3/N. Hard fired, reduced. Calyx: acanthus leaves with group of three dots as space fillers. Cf. Laumonier 1977, 232 cat. 1991, pl. 52 (signed Athenaios). Menemachos?

EPH-702
Pantikapaion, M-47-904, Puškin Museum of Fine Arts. Several joining frs. of rim, body, and base; complete profile. Rim frieze: rosette 2/7. Calyx: ferns. Plain, concave base with wide, low ring foot
– Loseva 1962, fig. 1.7; Zabelina 1984, 154 fig. 1b; AGSP 1984, pl. CLXIV.12.

EPH-703*
Istros, His-V 19331, Bucharest, Institute of Archaeology storeroom. Two joining frs. of rim and upper body. H 4.9 × W 6.2, WT 0.25, ⌀ rim 11, 13%, RH 1.8. Fabric: relatively coarse, abundant lime, many small voids, 5YR 6/8. Dull coat, ext. 7.5YR 3/1, int. 2.5YR 5/6. Medium hard fired, oxidized. Rim frieze: Lesbian kyma. Calyx: columns of guilloche creating tall ferns.
– Domăneanțu 2000, 98 cat. 479, pl. 32.

EPH-704*
Olbia, Sector NGCentre, square 57sw, yellow clay layer, O-НГЦ-66-1680, Kiev, Institute of Archaeology storeroom. Two joining frs. of rim and body. H 5.5 × W 5.5, WT 0.3, ⌀ rim 12, 10%, RH 1.8. Fabric: standard, 5YR 6/6. Slightly lustrous coat especially int., ext. 2.5YR 4/8, 4/3, int. 2.5YR 4/8. Medium hard fired, oxidized. Stacked in firing. Rim frieze: Ionian kyma. Calyx: large lotus petals.

EPH-705
Bol'šoj Kastel', БК-86-99, Černomorskoe Museum of Historical Lore. Fragmentary bowl, lacking base. Fabric: grey. Black coat. Reduced. Multiple rim friezes: star rosettes; large dots. Calyx: broad lotus petals.

EPH-706*
Pantikapaion, palace foundation trench M-84-42, Moscow, Puškin Museum of Fine Arts. Fr. preserving complete profile. H 8 × W 4.5, WT 0.5, ⌀ 13(?), RH 1.4, ⌀ base 3; vessel H 5.2. Thin, black coat with slight lustre. Reduced. Rim frieze: rosette 2/7. Calyx: ovoid petal alternating with column of large dots. Medallion: rosette.
– Košelenko 1992, fig. 23.

EPH-707*
Olbia, Sector E6–7, square 580, O-E6-7-63-116, Kiev, Institute of Archaeology storeroom. Fr. of lower body. Oxidized. Calyx: tall lotus petals separated by dots.

EPH-708*
Olbia, Sector E6–7, squares 494s, 514ne, 515nw, grey clay layer, O-E6-7-61-795, Kiev, Institute of Archaeology storeroom. Fr. of base and body. H 6.5 × W 5.7, WT 0.25, ⌀ base 3. Fabric: standard, coarse, Gley 1 6/N. Thin dull coat, ext. Gley 1 5/N, int. Gley 1 4/N. Relatively hard fired, reduced. Calyx: alternating pointed and rhomboidal lotus petals separated by dotted stem topped by rosette. Medallion: double-layered rosette(?) surrounded by two ridges.

Unclassified Calyx Fragments

EPH-709
Istros, His-1062, Bucharest, Institute of Archaeology storeroom. Fr. of lower body. Oxidized. Calyx: acanthus leaf. Menemachos?

EPH-710
Porthmion, 1st longitudinal street, pavement in rooms 27, 29, 30–31, depth 0.9 m, П-75-356, Kerč History and Culture Reserve. Fr. of lower body. Oxidized. Calyx: wavy acanthus leaf with segmented vein. Menemachos.
– Grzegrzółka 2010, 132 cat. 186.

EPH-711
Porthmion, П-68-87+88+93+94, Kerč History and Culture Reserve. Four non-joining frs. of rim and body. Oxidized. Multiple rim friezes: guilloche left; miniature acanthus scroll left; Ionian kyma. Calyx: ovoid lotus petal. Menemachos.
– Grzegrzółka 2010, 176 cat. 284.

EPH-712
Pantikapaion, palace foundation trench M-84-54, Moscow, Puškin Museum of Fine Arts. Fr. of rim and upper body. H 4 × W 6.8, WT 0.3, ⌀ rim 13, 12%, RH 1.3. Dull coat. Oxidized. Rim frieze: miniature acanthus scroll left. Calyx: tip of ovoid lotus petal. Secondarily burnt. Menemachos.
– Košelenko 1992, fig. 23.

EPH-713*
Istros, His-556, Bucharest, Institute of Archaeology storeroom. Body fr. Oxidized. Calyx: sistrum bud on dotted stem. Menemachos.

EPH-714
Porthmion, Sector G, sector 2, square 17–18; depth 0.42 m, П-87-90, Kerč History and Culture Reserve. Fr. of base and lower body. Calyx: acanthus alternating with lotus sepal(?). Plain, concave base, signed ATHEN[...] (retrograde), incised in vessel before firing. Athenaios.

EPH-715
Olbia, Sector NGS, O-НГС-06-131, Parutine, Olbia National Preserve storeroom. Body fr. H 4 × W 3.4, WT 0.3. Fabric: fine, micaceous, some voids, 5YR 7/6. Thin lustrous coat, ext. 2.5YR 6/6, 3/1, int. 2.5YR 5/6. Hard fired, oxidized. Stacked in firing. Calyx: lotus petal with rosette 6 as space filler. Frieze separators: dots.

EPH-716
Olbia, Sector AGD, ashy grey clay layer, O-АГД-69-1262, Kiev, Institute of Archaeology storeroom. Fr. of base and lower body. H 3.8 × W 2.3, WT 0.65, ⌀ base 2.5. Fabric: standard, Gley 1 6/10Y. Dull coat ext., int. shiny, Gley 1 2.5/N. Medium hard fired, reduced. Calyx: vertical element with rosette as space filler. Medallion: rosette A.

Imbricate Rounded Petals with Central Vein

EPH-717*
Olbia, Sector AGD, Bothros 11, O-АГД-87-995+88-199 (join across years), Kiev, Institute of Archaeology storeroom. Two joining frs. of rim and body; two rim frs. and two body frs., four last frs. join; almost half of bowl preserved. WT 0.18–0.3, ⌀ rim 13.5, RH 1.9. Fabric: standard, fine, 5YR 5/8. Thin dull coat, ext. 2.5YR 4/8, 10YR 3/2, int. 2.5YR 4/6. Relatively hard fired, oxidized. Stacked in firing. Multiple rim friezes: box meander, ccw; Ionian kyma; astragal with decorated beads.
– Rusjaeva & Nazarčuk 2006, pl. 193.3, pl. 194.3.

EPH-718*
Olbia, Sector A, inv. A 5501, Nikolaev, Historical Museum. Complete; broken into many fragments but lacking only minor parts. ⌀ rim 12.7, RH 1.5, ⌀ base 3.5; vessel H 7; H:⌀ 1:1.8. Dull dark brown coat. Oxidized. Multiple rim friezes: box meander, cw; guilloche right; astragal. Medallion: rosette A (7 petals). Frieze separators: dots.

EPH-719*
Olbia, Sector NGS, O-НГС-02-481+518, 519, Parutine, Olbia National Preserve storeroom. Joining fr. of rim, body and base, non-joining body fr.; complete profile; ca. 20% of vessel preserved. WT 0.22–0.48, ⌀ rim 13, RH 1.9 ⌀ base 3; vessel H 7.5; H:⌀ 1:1.7. Fabric: relatively fine and micaceous, a few small lime particles, 5YR 5/8, 10YR 5/4. Thin firm coat, slightly lustrous, darkened in firing in upper part, ext. 2.5YR 4/8, 5YR 3/1, int. 2.5YR 4/6, 10YR 2/2. Medium hard fired, oxidized. Stacked in firing. Multiple rim friezes: guilloche right; astragal; guilloche right. Medallion: rosette A. Frieze separators: dots.

EPH-720
Pantikapaion, П-1902-97, St Petersburg, State Hermitage Museum. Complete. Oxidized. Multiple rim friezes: guilloche right; astragal; guilloche right. Medallion: rosette A (7 petals). Frieze separators: dots. Secondarily burnt. Closely similar: Domăneanţu 2000, 143 cat. 711, pl. 53.
– Škorpil 1904, fig. 36.

EPH-721
Olbia, Sector R25, O-P25-97-2156.1, Parutine, Olbia National Preserve storeroom. Fr. of mid- and lower body. H 4.2 × W 4.9, WT 0.4. Fabric: relatively fine and micaceous, 2.5YR 5/8. Thin dull coat, ext. 2.5YR 5/6, 5YR 3/1, int. 2.5YR 5/6. Medium hard fired, oxidized. Stacked in firing. Multiple rim friezes: astragal; Ionian kyma. Frieze separators: dots.

EPH-722*
Olbia, Sector NGS, O-НГС-02-259, Parutine, Olbia National Preserve storeroom. Two joining frs. of rim and body. H 5.3 × W 10, WT 0.22–0.46, ⌀ rim 12, RH 1.72. Fabric: relatively fine and micaceous, some minute lime particles, small dark grey and red-brown particles, 5YR 5/67, 5YR 6/6. Thin firm slightly lustrous coat, pitted inside on one fr., 5YR 3/1. Medium hard fired, oxidized. Stacked in firing. Multiple rim friezes: box meander, cw; astragal. Frieze separators: dots. Two repair holes.

EPH-723
Olbia, O-46-239(?), Kiev, Institute of Archaeology storeroom. Body fr. Oxidized. Multiple rim friezes: box meander; guilloche right. Frieze separators: dots.

EPH-724*
Olbia, Sector NGF, room, ash, garbage layer, O-НГФ-47-2354, 2354[a], Kiev, Institute of Archaeology storeroom. Two joining

frs. of base and body. H 12.3 × W 8.5, WT 0.3, ⌀ base 3. Fabric: standard. Dull coat. Relatively hard fired, oxidized. Stacked in firing. Multiple rim friezes: Ionian kyma; astragal with decorated beads (weak stamp). Medallion: rosette A. Secondarily burnt. Three repair holes.

EPH-725*
Pantikapaion, palace foundation trench, M-84-60+85-34 (join across years), Moscow, Puškin Museum of Fine Arts. Joining frs. of rim and body. H 6.6 × W 9.8, WT 0.35, ⌀ rim 12, 17%, RH 1.4. Dull red coat. Oxidized. Stacked in firing. Multiple rim friezes: Ionian kyma; oblique S-spirals.

EPH-726*
Olbia, Cliff "B-VIII", square 285, Slope 1, Terrace I, O-70-375, Parutine, Olbia National Preserve storeroom. Fr. of rim and upper body. Oxidized. Stacked in firing. Multiple rim friezes: Ionian kyma; star rosettes.

EPH-727*
Pantikapaion, inv. 22742 (Zabelina 497), Moscow, State Historical Museum (Zabelina collection). Complete profile, ca. half of bowl preserved, mended from a few frs; almost completely covered with lime. ⌀ rim 14.5, RH 1.9, ⌀ base 3.8; vessel H 6.7; H:⌀ 1:2.2. Red coat. Oxidized. Multiple rim friezes: Lesbian kyma; rosette 2/7. Medallion: rosette A (8 petals).

EPH-728
Olbia, Sector NGS, O-НГС-02-370, Parutine, Olbia National Preserve storeroom. Fr. of rim and body. H 5.5 × W 6.6, WT 0.3–0.5, ⌀ rim 12, RH 2.1. Fabric: relatively fine and micaceous, some minute lime particles, larger red-brown inclusions, 5YR 5/6, 7.5YR 6/4. Thin firm slightly lustrous coat, ext. 5YR 3/3, 10YR 3/1, int. 5YR 3/2. Medium hard fired, oxidized. Stacked in firing. Multiple rim friezes: guilloche right; astragal. Frieze separators: dots.

EPH-729
Olbia, O-1910-740, present whereabouts unknown. Body fr. Multiple rim friezes: rosette 2/7; Lesbian kyma.
– St Petersburg, IIMK RAN, archive inv. 4057.519.5 (pl. XII).

EPH-730*
Olbia, Sector NGS, House IV-4 B 353/227, O-НГС-93-991, Parutine, Olbia National Preserve storeroom. Three rim frs. and three lower body frs., all joining. H 4.7 × W 11, WT 0.23–0.32, ⌀ rim 13, RH 1.7. Fabric: relatively fine and micaceous, fine lime particles, 5YR 6/8. Thin firm dull coat, slightly lustrous and darkened at rim ext., ext. 2.5YR 5/6, 5YR 4/2, int. 2.5YR 5/6. Medium hard fired, oxidized. Stacked in firing. Multiple rim friezes: rosette 5; box meander, cw.
– Guldager Bilde 2010, 280 cat. F-52, pl. 178.

EPH-731*
Myrmekion, M-57-216[a], St Petersburg IIMK RAN. Fr. of base and body. H 5.4, WT 0.45, ⌀ base 4.75. Fabric: standard, 2.5YR 5/8. Dull coat, 5YR 3/2. Oxidized. Stacked in firing. Multiple rim friezes: unidentified; Ionian kyma. Over petals the letters [...]OSEI[...], retrograde, incised in mould, perhaps signature. Medallion: rosette A. The signature Posei[...] is known from Delos (Laumonier 1977, 407 cat. 1987, pl. 95; cf. also Rogl 2001a, 142).

EPH-732*
Olbia, Sector AGD, Bothros 11, О-АГД-88-206, Kiev, Institute of Archaeology storeroom. Fr. of base and body. H 8.3 × W 9.5, WT 0.28–0.4, ⌀ base 3.8. Fabric: standard, with much lime, 2.5YR 5/8. Coat with slight lustre, blackened at rim ext., 2.5YR 5/6. Relatively hard fired, oxidized. Stacked in firing. Multiple(?) rim friezes: missing; Lesbian kyma. Medallion: rosette A (6 petals). Two repair holes.
– Rusjaeva & Nazarčuk 2006, pl. 193.19.

EPH-733
Olbia, Sector E9, O-E9-61-no no. [a], Kiev, Institute of Archaeology storeroom. Complete profile, one quarter of bowl preserved. Rim frieze: box meander, cw. Medallion: rosette A. Also with meander rim, but plain base: CVA Kassel 2 [Germany 38], 68, figs. 48–49, pl. 89.3–4.
– St Petersburg, IIMK RAN, photo archive neg. II 73233.

EPH-734*
Olbia, Sector AGD, Bothros 11, О-АГД-87-994, 994[a], 594, Kiev, Institute of Archaeology storeroom. Fr. of rim and upper body and non-joining body fr.; sherds from inside and outside the bothros do not join but are from the same vessel. H 4.7 × W 8.5, WT 0.2–0.3, ⌀ rim 11.5, 25%, RH 1.4. Fabric: standard, fine, 2.5YR 6/8. Coat with dull lustre, ext. 2.5YR 4/6, 10YR 2/1, int. 10YR 3/1 (mottled). Hard fired, oxidized. Stacked in firing. Rim frieze: Ionian kyma. Calyx: petals in high relief.
– Rusjaeva & Nazarčuk 2006, pl. 194.10.

EPH-735
Myrmekion, M-58-693, St Petersburg IIMK RAN. Fr. of rim and upper body. H 4.1, WT 0.3, ⌀ rim 12, 9%, RH 1.9. Fabric: standard, Gley 1 4/N. Slightly lustrous black coat, Gley 1 2.5/N. Reduced. Rim frieze: horizontal S-spirals.

EPH-736*
Istros, His-V 8575 T, Bucharest Institute of Archaeology storeroom. Body fr. Reduced. Rim frieze: horizontal S-spirals with palmette above (Attic imitation, but very worn and crude stamp).

EPH-737*
Olbia, Cliff "B-VIII", square 285, yellow clay layer, O-70-211, Parutine, Olbia National Preserve storeroom. Fr. of rim and body. H 5.5 × W 6, WT 0.3, RH 1.8. Fabric: standard, fine, 2.5YR 6/8. Coat with dull lustre, bluish metallic sheen at rim where stacked, ext. 2.5YR 4/6, 2.5/1, int. 2.5YR 4/6. Relatively hard fired, oxidized. Stacked in firing. Rim frieze: rosette 1. Menemachos.

EPH-738
Olbia, Sector NGS, О-НГС-05-747, Parutine, Olbia National Preserve storeroom. Fr. of upper body. H 2.8 × W 4, WT 0.3. Fabric: relatively fine and micaceous, some small lime inclusions, 5Y 6/1. Dull coat, 5Y 3/1. Medium hard fired, reduced. Rim frieze: star rosettes.

EPH-739*
Olbia, Sector NGS, О-НГС-06-272, Parutine, Olbia National Preserve storeroom. Fr. of mid- and lower body with part of base. H 7 × W 6.5, WT 0.25, ø base 4. Fabric: relatively fine and micaceous. Slightly shiny brown coat. Medium hard fired, oxidized. Rim frieze: star rosettes. Medallion: rosette A. Secondarily burnt.

EPH-740*
Olbia, Sector AGD, Bothros 11, О-АГД-88-207, Kiev, Institute of Archaeology storeroom. Fr. of base and body. H 5.3 × W 6.8, WT 0.32–0.35, ø base 3. Fabric: standard, fine, 2.5YR 6/8. Thin slightly lustrous coat, 2.5YR 5/8. Relatively hard fired, oxidized. Medallion: rosette A (7 petals).
– Rusjaeva & Nazarčuk 2006, pl. 193.23

EPH-741
Olbia, Sector NGS, О-НГС-92-460, Parutine, Olbia National Preserve storeroom. Fr. of base and lower body. ø base 3.5. Oxidized. Medallion: rosette A (8 petals?).

EPH-742*
Olbia, Sector E6, square 410e–415e, grey clay layer, O-E6-56-972, Kiev, Institute of Archaeology storeroom. Fr. of base and lower body. Oxidized. Medallion: rosette A, var. 1.

EPH-743
Porthmion, Sector G, sector 2, square 17–18, depth 0.42 m, П-87-87, Kerč History and Culture Reserve. Fr. of base and lower body. Medallion: rosette A, var. 4 (alternating rounded and pointed petals).

EPH-744
Istros, His-V 8570 O, Bucharest Institute of Archaeology storeroom. Fr. of base and lower body. H 3 × W 3.5. Reduced. Medallion: rosette B. One repair hole.
– Domăneanțu 2000, 36 cat. 152, pl. 10 (attributed to Monogram PAR).

EPH-745
Porthmion, П-75-429, Kerč History and Culture Reserve. Fr. of base and lower body. Reduced. Plain base, signed [...]OSI[...], incised in bowl before firing; Posi[...]?
– Grzegrzółka 2010, 171 cat. 270 (signature not read).

EPH-746*
Pantikapaion, palace foundation trench, M-84-43, Moscow, Puškin Museum of Fine Arts. Fr. of base and lower body. H 4.2 × W 5.3, WT 0.25, ø base 5. Black coat with slight sheen. Reduced. Flat base with false ring foot.

EPH-747*
Chersonesos, X-1965-76, St Petersburg, State Hermitage Museum. Fr. of base and lower body. H 3.3, WT 0.25, ø base 5. Fabric: standard, 5Y 6/1. Dull coat, 5Y 2.5/1. Reduced. Plain, concave base.

Imbricate Rounded Petals with Central and Side Veins

EPH-748*
Olbia, Sector NGS, О-НГС-02-281+281a, Parutine, Olbia National Preserve storeroom. Two groups of joining frs. of rim and body, more than half of vessel preserved. WT 0.25–0.35, ø rim 12.5, RH 2.2. Fabric: relatively fine and micaceous, a few minute lime particles, 5YR 6/6. Thin firm coat with slight lustre, mottled, 2.5YR 4/6, 10YR 3/1. Medium hard fired, oxidized. Stacked in firing. Multiple rim friezes: box meander, ccw; Ionian kyma; astragal with decorated beads. One repair hole. EPH-749* could be from the same bowl. Monogram PAR?

EPH-749*
Olbia, Sector NGS, О-НГС-02-85, Parutine, Olbia National Preserve storeroom. Fr. of base and lower body, rather worn on ext. H 4.7 × W 6.3, WT 0.36–0.5, ø base 3.3. Fabric: relatively fine and micaceous, a few lime particles, many oblong voids, 5YR 5/6, 7.5YR 6/6, sandwiched due to stacking. Thin firm slightly lustrous coat, slightly mottled ext., ext. 2.5YR 4/6, 10YR 3/2, int. 2.5YR 4/6. Medium hard fired, oxidized. Stacked in firing. Medallion: rosette A. May be from same bowl as EPH-748*. Monogram PAR?

EPH-750*
Olbia, Sector NGS, О-НГС-06-543, Parutine, Olbia National Preserve storeroom. Fr. of mid- and lower body. H 4.7 × W 5, WT 0.4. Fabric: relatively fine and micaceous, some small lime inclusions, 5YR 6/8. Dull coat with metallic sheen at stacking marks ext., ext. 2.5YR 4/6, 2.5/1, int. 2.5YR 4/6. Hard fired, oxidized. Stacked in firing. Multiple rim friezes: box meander; Ionian kyma; astragal with decorated beads. Monogram PAR?

EPH-751*
Olbia, Sector NGS, O-НГС-02-236, Parutine, Olbia National Preserve storeroom. Fr. of rim and large part of body. H 6.7 × W 7.8, WT 0.28–0.36, ⌀ rim 12, RH 1.85. Fabric: relatively fine, some small lime inclusions and long voids, 5YR 5/8, 7.5YR 6/6. Thin firm coat with slight lustre, darkened and with a slight metallic lustre at rim and upper body, ext. 2.5YR 4/6, 5YR 3/1, int. 2.5YR 4/8, 5YR 3/1. Medium hard fired, oxidized. Stacked in firing. Multiple rim friezes: astragal; box meander, cw. Frieze separators: dots. Two repair holes.

EPH-752*
Olbia, inv. A 2454, Nikolaev, Historical Museum. Complete; mended from a number of frs. ⌀ rim 13, RH 1.3, ⌀ base 3.5; vessel H 5.6; H:⌀ 1:2.3. Dull red coat, darkened at rim ext. Oxidized. Stacked in firing. Multiple rim friezes: astragal; Ionian kyma. Medallion: rosette A (6 petals).

EPH-753*
Pantikapaion, palace foundation trench, M-89-no no. 19, Moscow, Puškin Museum of Fine Arts. Body fr. Reduced. Multiple rim friezes: Ionian kyma; astragal with decorated reels. Menemachos?

EPH-754*
Olbia, Sector NGS, O-НГС-05-912, Parutine, Olbia National Preserve storeroom. Body fr. H 4.7 × W 4.5, WT 0.32. Fabric: relatively fine and micaceous, some small brownish inclusions, 7.5YR 6/6. Thin coat with dull metallic sheen, 5YR 3/1. Medium hard fired, oxidized. Multiple rim friezes: Ionian kyma; rosette 1. Menemachos.

EPH-755*
Olbia, Sector NGS, O-НГС-02-420, Parutine, Olbia National Preserve storeroom. Two joining frs. of rim and body. H 5.45 × W 7.7, WT 0.22–0.51, ⌀ rim 13, RH 1.95. Fabric: relatively fine and micaceous, larger and smaller lime particles, some voids, 5YR 5/8. Thin firm slightly lustrous coat, slightly mottled at rim ext., 2.5YR 4/8. Medium hard fired, oxidized. Multiple rim friezes: Ionian kyma; rosette 2/7.

EPH-756
Olbia(?), inv. 54791 Uvarov 185, Moscow, State Historical Museum (Uvarov Collection). Fr. of rim and body. Oxidized. Multiple rim friezes: Lesbian kyma; miniature acanthus-flower scroll left. Monogram PAR.

EPH-757*
Olbia, Sector R25, O-P25-92-3220+3221, Parutine, Olbia National Preserve storeroom. Fr. of rim and upper body and joining fr. of lower body; one non-joining rim fr. H 6.2 × W 10.5, WT 0.28, ⌀ rim 12, 20%, RH 1.1. Fabric: relatively fine and micaceous, small and large (up to 0.9 cm) lime inclusions, 5YR 6/6. Thin slightly lustrous coat, ext. 2.5YR 4/3, 7.5YR 3/1, int. 2.5YR 4/3, 7.5YR 3/1. Medium hard fired, oxidized. Stacked in firing. Multiple rim friezes: oblique S-spirals; box meander, cw. Frieze separators: dots. Secondarily burnt.

EPH-758*
Olbia, Sector NGS, O-НГС-91-566+92-594+914 (join across years), Parutine, Olbia National Preserve storeroom. Three joining frs. of rim and upper body. H 3.8 × W 9, WT 0.28–0.5, ⌀ rim 12.5, RH 1.74. Fabric: relatively fine, some small lime inclusions, 5YR 5/6. Thin firm coat with bluish metallic sheen ext. and int. at rim, where blackened due to stacking, ext. 5Y 4/2, int. 2.5YR 4/4–4/6. Hard fired, oxidized. Stacked in firing. Multiple rim friezes: rosette 2/7; Ionian kyma. Frieze separators: dots.
– Guldager Bilde 2010, 280 cat. F-49, pl. 177.

EPH-759*
Olbia, Sector E6, square 410e–415e, grey clay layer, O-E6-56-969, Kiev, Institute of Archaeology storeroom. Large fr. of rim and body. H 5.4 × W 6.6, WT 0.38, ⌀ rim 13, 16%, RH 1.7. Fabric: standard, 2.5YR 6/8. Dull coat with slight metallic sheen ext. where stacked, 2.5YR 4/6, 3/1. Relatively hard fired, oxidized. Stacked in firing. Multiple rim friezes: star rosettes; Ionian kyma. Graffito HP (lig.) on rim ext., name of owner(?) starting with Hera-.

EPH-760*
Istros, His-B 481/V 19474, Bucharest, Institute of Archaeology storeroom. Fr. of rim and upper body. H 4.8 × W 4.5, WT 0.35, RH 1.7. Fabric: standard, fine, 5YR 6/8. Coat with dull lustre, ext. 7.5YR 3/1, 4/6, int. 5YR 5/8, 7.5YR 3/1. Relatively hard fired, oxidized. Stacked in firing. Rim frieze: astragal. One repair hole.
– Domăneanțu 2000, 36 cat. 153, pl. 10 (attributed to Monogram PAR).

EPH-761
Olbia, Sector NGS, O-НГС-05-398, Parutine, Olbia National Preserve storeroom. Fr. of rim and upper body. H 3.2 × W 3.3, WT 0.2, small diameter, RH 1.4. Fabric: fine and micaceous, 5YR 6/6. Slightly lustrous coat, mottled ext., ext. 2.5YR 4/6, 2.5/1, int. 2.5YR 2.5/1. Hard fired, oxidized. Rim frieze: astragal.

EPH-762*
Olbia, Sector NGS, O-НГС-04-152+239, 240, Parutine, Olbia National Preserve storeroom. Three rim frs., two joining. H 3.5 × W 4.5, WT 0.3, ⌀ rim 12, 11%, RH 1.4. Fabric: fine and micaceous but with large lump of lime (0.5 cm), which has exploded, 7.5YR 6/6. Coat with metallic sheen ext., int. duller, 7.5YR 3/1. Medium hard fired, oxidized. Rim frieze: box meander, cw. Calyx: only one petal tip preserved. Frieze separators: dots.

EPH-763*
Olbia, Sector R25, O-P25-03-1502, Parutine, Olbia National Preserve storeroom. Fr. of upper body. H 2.6 × W 4.2, WT 0.37. Fabric: relatively fine and micaceous, some small voids, Gley 1 5/10Y. Slightly lustrous coat, Gley 1 2.5/N. Hard fired, reduced. Rim frieze: box meander, cw. Frieze separators: dots.

EPH-764*
Olbia, O-62-811, Kiev, Institute of Archaeology storeroom. Body fr. close to rim. Oxidized. Rim frieze: box meander, cw. Frieze separators: dots.

EPH-765*
Olbia, Sector NGS, O-НГС-02-483+485, 38, Parutine, Olbia National Preserve storeroom. Two joining frs. of rim and upper body and two non-joining rim frs. probably from the same vessel. H 4.7 × W 7.4, WT 0.3–0.5, ⌀ rim 13, RH 1.75. Fabric: relatively fine and micaceous, some small lime inclusions and small voids, 5YR 5/6, 7.5YR 5/6. Thin firm semi-lustrous coat, darkened except on rim ext., where mottled, ext. 2.5YR 4/8, 5YR 3/2, int. 5YR 3/2. Medium hard fired, oxidized. Stacked in firing. Rim frieze: Ionian kyma. Frieze separators: dots. One repair hole.

EPH-766*
Olbia, Sector E2, square 55, Room [Cistern] Л, western part, grey clay layer, O-E2-48-4981, Kiev, Institute of Archaeology storeroom. Fr. of rim and body. Oxidized. Stacked in firing. Rim frieze: Ionian kyma. Frieze separators: dots. Monogram PAR.

EPH-767*
Olbia, Sector NGS, O-НГС-88-188, 189, Parutine, Olbia National Preserve storeroom. Fr. of rim and upper body, non-joining body fr. Reduced. Multiple rim friezes: large dots; Ionian kyma.

EPH-768
Olbia. O-1928-no no. [a], present whereabouts unknown. Complete. Rim frieze: Ionian kyma. Medallion: rosette A?
– St Petersburg, IIMK RAN, photo archive neg. II 13900a.

EPH-769*
Olbia, Sector NGS, O-НГС-06-97, Parutine, Olbia National Preserve storeroom. Two joining frs. of rim and upper body. H 5.2 × W 8.5, WT 0.23, ⌀ rim 12, 25%, RH 1.3. Fabric: relatively fine and micaceous, some small lime inclusions, 5YR 6/8. Coat with pinkish metallic sheen, 5YR 4/2. Medium hard fired, oxidized. Rim frieze: Ionian kyma.

EPH-770*
Olbia, Sector NGS, O-НГС-08-122, Parutine, Olbia National Preserve storeroom. Fr. of rim and upper body. H 4.3 × W 7.1, WT 0.21, ⌀ rim 13, 14%, RH 1.4. Fabric: relatively fine and micaceous, 7.5YR 6/6. Coat with pinkish metallic sheen, 5YR 4/2. Hard fired, oxidized. Rim frieze: Ionian kyma. Monogram PAR?

EPH-771*
Olbia, Sector AGD, Bothros 11, О-АГД-88-210, Kiev, Institute of Archaeology storeroom. Two joining frs. of rim and body. H 4.8 × W 6, WT 0.4, ⌀ rim 12, 16%, RH 2.1. Fabric: standard, 7.5YR 6/6. Slightly lustrous coat, ext. 10YR 3/2, int. 2.5YR 4/6. Relatively hard fired, oxidized. Stacked in firing. Rim frieze: Ionian kyma. Monogram PAR.

EPH-772*
Olbia, Sector R25, O-P25-93-2914, Parutine, Olbia National Preserve storeroom. Fr. of upper body. H 4 × W 4.8, WT 0.26. Fabric: relatively fine and micaceous, 5YR 6/8. Slightly lustrous coat, ext. 5YR 3/1, int. 5YR 4/4, 2.5YR 4/6. Medium hard fired, oxidized. Stacked in firing. Rim frieze: Ionian kyma.

EPH-773*
Olbia, Sector E2, square 55, Cistern Л, O-2-49-118, Kiev, Institute of Archaeology storeroom. Fr. of rim and body. Oxidized. Stacked in firing. Rim frieze: Ionian kyma. Monogram PAR.
– Levi 1964b, 251, fig. 13.4; St Petersburg, IIMK RAN, photo archive neg. I 43058.

EPH-774*
Olbia, Sector R25, O-P25-98-2809, Parutine, Olbia National Preserve storeroom. Fr. of mid- and lower body. H 3.4 × W 2.9, WT 0.25. Fabric: relatively fine and micaceous, 5YR 6/8. Thin dull coat, ext. 5YR 3/2, int. 5YR 4/3. Hard fired, oxidized. Rim frieze: Lesbian kyma.

EPH-775*
Istros, Sector MC1 Sa, His-56-45, Bucharest, Institute of Archaeology storeroom. Complete profile; 11 rim frs., 10 body frs. and two base frs., all joining.; very worn. H 5.5, ⌀ rim 12.5, RH 1.7, ⌀ base 3.8. Fabric: no break for observation, vessel restored in plaster. Thin dull coat, 10YR 3/1. Not too hard fired, reduced. Rim frieze: Lesbian kyma, very worn. Plain, slightly concave base with false ring foot
– Domăneanţu 2000, 71 cat. 331, pl. 21 (attributed to Heraios).

EPH-776*
Olbia, Sector E6, square 193, pavement, second layer, O-E6-56-1018, Kiev, Institute of Archaeology storeroom. Fr. of rim and body. Oxidized. Rim frieze: guilloche right. Frieze separators: dots. Two repair holes.

EPH-777
Pantikapaion, palace foundation trench, M-89-illegible 1, Moscow, Puškin Museum of Fine Arts. Fr. of rim and upper body. H 4.7 × W 7.1, WT 0.35, ⌀ rim 12, 18% RH 1.5. Dull dark red coat, black with slight metallic sheen at rim. Oxidized. Stacked in firing. Rim frieze: guilloche right.

EPH-778*
Olbia, Sector I, square 219w, part semi-square 269w, cleaning of staircase, О-И-49-3975, Kiev, Institute of Archaeology storeroom. Fr. of rim and upper body. Oxidized. Stacked in firing. Rim frieze: triple guilloche right. Monogram PAR.

EPH-779*
Olbia, Sector NGS, О-НГС-06-115, 122, Parutine, Olbia National Preserve storeroom. Fr. of rim and upper body, non-joining body fr. H 4.3 × W 2.9, WT 0.3, RH 1.5. Fabric: relatively fine and micaceous, some voids, 7.5YR 6/6. Coat with pinkish metallic sheen, 7.5YR 4/2. Medium hard fired, oxidized. Rim frieze: rosette 1. Menemachos.

EPH-780*
Olbia, Sector NGS, О-НГС-05-218+989 + 06-113, Parutine, Olbia National Preserve storeroom. Fr. of rim and upper body and two further joining rim frs. H 4.3 × W 4.6, WT 0.26, ⌀ rim 12, 10%, RH 1.4. Fabric: relatively fine and micaceous, some small lime inclusions, 5Y 5/1. Slightly lustrous coat, Gley 1 2.5/1. Medium hard fired, reduced. Rim frieze: rosette 1, small.

EPH-781*
Olbia, Sector NGS, О-НГС-06-101, Parutine, Olbia National Preserve storeroom. Fr. of rim and upper body. H 4.3 × W 4.6, WT 0.3, ⌀ rim 13, 10%, RH 1.4. Fabric: relatively fine and micaceous, some small lime inclusions, 5Y 4/1. Dull coat, ext. 5Y 3/1, int. 5Y 2.5/1. Medium hard fired, reduced. Rim frieze: star rosettes.

EPH-782
Kepoi, Kurgan 14, funerary meal, no. unknown, Moscow, State Historical Museum? Fr. of rim and upper body. No rim frieze.
– Usačeva 1978, fig. 2.16.

EPH-783
Pantikapaion, M-46-2887, Moscow, Puškin Museum of Fine Art. Fr. of base and lower body. Plain, concave base, signed MENEMACHOU. Menemachos.
– Zabelina 1984, 157 fig. 4.b.

EPH-784
Pantikapaion, M-46-3887, 7175, Moscow, Puškin Museum of Fine Art. Fr. of base and lower body. Plain concave base with low ring foot, signed MENEMACHOU. Menemachos.
– Loseva 1962, 197 n. 10, fig. 1.5.

EPH-785
Pantikapaion, year and no. unknown. Complete? Ionian kyma. Plain, concave base with low ring foot, signed MENEMACHOU. Menemachos.
– AGSP 1984, pl. CLXIII.17, 17b.

EPH-786*
Chersonesos, X-1901-35, St Petersburg, State Hermitage Museum. Two joining frs. of base and lower body. H 7.1, WT 0.2, ⌀ base 3.5. Fabric: standard, 2.5YR 5/6. Very thin dull coat, 2.5YR 4/6. Hard fired, oxidized. Plain, slightly concave base, signed MOIRA/GEN[...], incised in mould before firing. For signature, cf. EPH-693*, EPH-1247.
– Košjuško-Valjužinič 1902, 85–86, fig. 35; Bouzek 1990, 75.

EPH-787
Porthmion, П-68-85, Kerč History and Culture Reserve. Complete. ⌀ rim 12.3, ⌀ base 5.5; vessel H 7.9. Oxidized. Rim frieze: box meander, cw. Plain base, signed CH in mould before firing.
– Grzegrzółka 2010, 167 cat. 261.

EPH-788*
Olbia, Sector NGS, О-НГС-06-138, 150, 154, Parutine, Olbia National Preserve storeroom. Lower half of bowl; non-joining body and base frs. H 9.5 × W 8.3, WT 0.32, ⌀ base 5.4. Fabric: relatively fine and micaceous, 10YR 6/6. Thin dull coat, 7.5YR 4/2. Medium hard fired, oxidized. Plain base with wide stand ring.

EPH-789*
Myrmekion, M-58-21 St Petersburg IIMK RAN. Fr. of base and lower body. H 4.1, WT 0.35, ⌀ base 4. Fabric: standard, 5 YR 5/8. Thin dull coat, 2.5YR 4/8. Oxidized. Calyx: petals in negative relief. Plain, concave base with false ring foot.

EPH-790*
Istros, Sector X His-96-1177, Bucharest, Institute of Archaeology storeroom. Fr. of upper body. H 2.5 × W 3. Oxidized. Calyx: petals in negative relief.
– Domăneanțu 2000, 37 cat. 154, pl. 11 (attributed to Monogram PAR).

EPH-791*
Pantikapaion, palace foundation trench, M-84-55, Moscow, Puškin Museum of Fine Arts. Fr. of base and part of lower body.

H 3.8 × W 3.5, WT 0.25, ⌀ base 3. Dull red coat. Oxidized. Plain, almost flat base.

EPH-792*
Olbia, Sector E6–7, squares 598e, 608e, grey clay layer, O-E6-7-61-438+451, Kiev, Institute of Archaeology storeroom. Five joining frs. of base and body. Oxidized. Rim frieze: Ionian kyma. Plain, concave base.

EPH-793*
Olbia, Sector NGCentre, Basement 1, grey clay layer, О-НГЦ-68-2501, Kiev, Institute of Archaeology storeroom. Fr. of base and lower body. Oxidized. Medallion: rosette A (7 petals).

EPH-794*
Olbia, Sector R25, O-P25-98-2885, Parutine, Olbia National Preserve storeroom. Fr. of base and lower body. H 5.3 × W 6.8, WT 0.25–0.3, ⌀ base 3.4. Fabric: relatively fine and micaceous, 5YR 6/8. Thin slightly lustrous coat, 2.5YR 4/6. Hard fired, oxidized. Medallion: rosette A (6 petals).

EPH-795*
Olbia, Sector NGS, O-НГС-06-526, 527, Parutine, Olbia National Preserve storeroom. Fr. of lower body and base and joining(?) body fr. H 4.5 × W 4.5. WT 0.3. ⌀ base 3.5. Fabric: relatively fine and micaceous, 5YR 6/8. Thin dull coat, 2.5YR 5/6. Medium hard fired, oxidized. Medallion: rosette A. Monogram PAR?

EPH-796 (see Fig. 79)
Olbia, O-52-2962, Kiev, Institute of Archaeology storeroom. Fr. of base and lower body. Oxidized. Medallion: rosette A (7 petals) with no surrounding ridge.

EPH-797*
Olbia, Sector NGS, House III-3 R 278/96 O-НГС-93-20, Parutine, Olbia National Preserve storeroom. Fr. of lower body. H 4.5 × W 4.8, WT 0.45–0.5. Fabric: relatively fine, highly micaceous, some small lime inclusions, many small voids, 5YR 5/6, 10 YR 5/4. Thin slightly lustrous coat, flaking off in large areas, 2.5YR 5/4. Medium hard fired, oxidized. Stacked in firing. Secondarily burnt. Monogram PAR.
– Guldager Bilde 2010, 279 cat. F-40, pl. 175.

EPH-798*
Istros, His-583, Bucharest, Institute of Archaeology storeroom. Fr. of lower body. Oxidized. Calyx: petals in negative relief, no outline.

EPH-799*
Olbia, Sector E6, square 250, 251w, Depression "O", O-6-56-618+1235, 1237+1237[a+b, c], Kiev, Institute of Archaeology storeroom. Two joining rim frs., three joining body frs., one non-joining body fr. H 5.6 × W 11.2, WT 0.25, ⌀ rim 13, 31%, RH 1.9. Fabric: standard, 2.5YR 6/8. Coat with dull lustre, ext. 2.5YR 4/8, Gley 1 3/N, int. 2.5YR 4/8. Relatively hard fired, oxidized. Stacked in firing. Multiple rim friezes: box meander, cw; Ionian kyma. Calyx: petals in negative relief.

Imbricate Designs with Different Petal Combinations

EPH-800*
Porthmion, pavement of 2nd longitudinal street, with three bronze coins of Pantikapaion (first half of 3rd century; mid-3rd century; 2nd century), П-77-261, 264, 265, Kerč History and Culture Reserve. Fr. of base and lower body and two non-joining body frs. H 2.8, WT 0.35. Fabric: standard, 2.5YR 5/8. Thin dull coat, ext. 2.5YR 5/6, 5YR 3/1, int. 2.5YR 5/6. Oxidized. Stacked in firing. Rim frieze: Lesbian kyma. Calyx: rows of imbricate rounded petals with central and side veins in negative relief, alternating with rows of petals without side veins. Plain, concave base.

EPH-801*
Istros, His-366, Bucharest, Institute of Archaeology storeroom. Fr. of lower body. H 3 × W 2. Reduced. Calyx with uniform rows of different types of rounded petals in imbricate pattern: with central vein; with central and side veins, alternating; with central and side veins, upside-down.

Imbricate Pointed Petals with Central Vein

EPH-802
Olbia, Sector NGS, House IV-3 B 343/202, O-НГС-92-415, 459, Parutine, Olbia National Preserve storeroom. Complete profile; fragmentary bowl. Reduced. Rim frieze: 'paw' left. Plain concave base, signed PHILON/NIOU (boustrophedon), incised in vessel before firing. Philonnios.
– Guldager Bilde 2010, 284 cat. F-83.

EPH-803
Olbia, O-1912-120b, present whereabouts unknown. Complete. Rim frieze: 'paw' left. Plain concave base, signed PHILON/NIOU (boustrophedon), incised in vessel before firing. Philonnios.
– St Petersburg, IIMK RAN, photo archive neg. II 18395.

EPH-804
Pantikapaion, 1908-no.? Complete. Rim frieze: 'paw' left. Plain concave base, signed PHILON/NIOU, boustrophedon, incised in vessel before firing. Philonnios.
– St Petersburg, IIMK RAN photo archive neg. III 12089.

EPH-805*
Olbia, Sector R25, O-P25-04-2803b, Parutine, Olbia National Preserve storeroom. Two joining frs. of base and lower body. H 7.8 × W 8, WT 0.18–0.4, ⌀ base 4. Fabric: relatively fine and micaceous, small lime inclusions, 5Y 4/1. Thin dull coat, ext. 10YR 4/1, 4/2, int. 10YR 5/1. Medium hard fired, reduced. Plain concave base, signed [...]ILON/NI[...] (boustrophedon), incised in vessel before firing. Philonnios.

EPH-806
Pantikapaion, M-46-3853, Moscow, Puškin Museum of Fine Arts. Fr. of base and lower body. Plain concave base, signed PHILO[...], incised in vessel before firing. Philon(nios)
– Zabelina 1984, 156, fig. 3d; AGSP 1984, pl. CLXIII.17b.

EPH-807*
Istros, His-108, Bucharest, Institute of Archaeology storeroom. Fr. of base and lower body. H 2.7 × W 2.5, WT 0.35. Fabric: standard, 5Y 6/1. Thin coat with slight lustre, 5Y 3/1. Medium hard fired, reduced. Plain concave base, signed PHI[...], incised in vessel before firing. Philon(ios).
– Domăneanţu 2000, 62 cat. 284, pl. 18.

EPH-808*
Chersonesos, X-1961-60[g], St Petersburg, State Hermitage Museum. Fr. of base and lower body. ⌀ base 5. Reduced. Plain concave base, signed PH[...], incised in vessel before firing. Philon(nios).

EPH-809
Istros, His-V10080[a], Bucharest, Institute of Archaeology storeroom. Fr. of lower body and part of base. Reduced. Plain slightly concave base, surrounded by low ridge; remains of letter, perhaps PH, incised in vessel before firing. Philon(nios)?

EPH-810*
Kepoi, Tomb 373/3 no. 21, Ke-66-373/3 no. 21, Moscow, State Historical Museum. Complete. ⌀ rim 11.6, RH 1.4, ⌀ base 4.4; vessel H 6.6; H:⌀ 1:1.7. Fabric: orange. Dull orange coat almost completely worn off. Oxidized. Rim frieze: 'paw' left. Plain concave base. Philon(nios)?
– Usačeva 1978, fig. 2.1.

EPH-811*
Olbia, O-70-200[?]+210+212, Parutine, Olbia National Preserve storeroom. Three joining frs. of base and body. H 8 × W 8, WT 0.2–0.4, ⌀ base 5. Fabric: standard, 10YR 5/1. Thin dull coat, 10YR 3/1. Not too hard fired, reduced. Rim frieze: 'paw', left. Plain concave base. Philon(nios)?

EPH-812*
Istros, Plateau, surface, His-74-100, 457, Bucharest, Institute of Archaeology storeroom. Rim fr. and non-joining body fr. H 4.3 × W 5, WT 0.25, ⌀ rim 12, 10%, RH 1.6. Fabric: standard with much fine lime, Gley 1 5/10Y. Dull coat, 5Y 3/1. Medium hard fired, reduced. Rim frieze: 'paw' left. Philon(nios)
– Domăneanţu 2000, 60 cat. 273, pl. 18.

EPH-813*
Olbia, Sector R25, O-R25-05-741, 1206, Parutine, Olbia National Preserve storeroom. Two non-joining body frs. H 2.4 × W 2.9, WT 0.3. Fabric: relatively fine and micaceous, small lime inclusions, 5Y 4/2. Dull coat, Gley 1 2.5/N. Hard fired, reduced. Rim frieze: 'paw' left. Philon(nios)?

EPH-814
Olbia, Sector R25, O-P25-06-751, Parutine, Olbia National Preserve storeroom. Fr. of upper body. H 2.1 × W 2.7, WT 0.23. Fabric: relatively fine and micaceous, small lime inclusions, 5Y 4/1. Thin slightly lustrous coat, Gley 1 2.5/N. Hard fired, reduced. Rim frieze: 'paw' left. Philon(nios)?

EPH-815*
Chersonesos, X-1904-4, St Petersburg, State Hermitage Museum. Fr. of base and part of body. H 5.5, WT 0.35. ⌀ base 4. Fabric: standard, layered, 2.5Y 4/1. Dull self slip, ext. 2,5Y 4/1, int. 2,5Y 4/1. Reduced. Plain slightly concave base, signed ATHENAI/OU (retrograde), incised in vessel before firing. Athenaios.
– IAK 20, pp. 64–65.

EPH-816*
Istros, Sector MC1, His-56-44, 47, 69, Bucharest, Institute of Archaeology storeroom. Complete profile; four rim frs., two of which join four body frs.; five non-joining body frs., three non-joining base frs.; very worn. WT 0.35, ⌀ rim 12, 23%, RH 1.6, ⌀ base 5. Fabric: standard, 5YR 6/8. Dull coat, very worn, 2.5YR 5/6. Not too hard fired, oxidized. Stacked in firing. Rim frieze: star rosettes. Plain slightly concave base with false ring foot, signed D in the mould before firing.
– Domăneanţu 2000, 19 cat. 69, pl. 5 (attributed to Comique à la canne).

EPH-817
Olbia, Sector NGS, O-НГС-05-159, Parutine, Olbia National Preserve storeroom. Two joining rim frs. Oxidized. Rim frieze: star rosettes.

EPH-818
Olbia O-1910–1607, present whereabouts unknown. Fr. of rim and upper body. Rim frieze: astragal. Calyx: petals very closely spaced.
– St Petersburg, IIMK RAN, archive inv. 4060.519.8 (pl. I).

EPH-819
Volna 1, C3-98-73, 99-40, St Petersburg, State Hermitage Museum. Six frs. of rim and upper body, two body frs., partially joining. Oxidized. Rim frieze: Ionian kyma.

EPH-820*
Istros, His-B 518/V 19470, Bucharest, Institute of Archaeology storeroom. Fr. of rim and body. H 6.3 × W 5.8, WT 0.25, RH 1.7. Fabric: relatively coarse, abundant small lime inclusions, 5YR 6/8. Dull coat, int. very worn, ext. 2.5YR 6/6, 7.5YR 7/6, int. 2.5YR 6/6. Not too hard fired, oxidized. Stacked in firing. Rim frieze: Ionian kyma.
– Domăneanțu 2000, 100 cat. 495, pl. 33

EPH-821*
Olbia, Sector NGS, О-НГС-08-183, Parutine, Olbia National Preserve storeroom. Fr. of rim and upper body. H 4.2 × W 4, WT 0.3, RH 1.6. Fabric: relatively fine and micaceous, some small lime inclusions, 5Y 4/1. Dull coat, Gley 1 2.5/1. Medium hard fired, reduced. Rim frieze: Ionian kyma with hatched tongue.

EPH-822*
Olbia, Sector R25, О-25-09-1318, Parutine, Olbia National Preserve storeroom. Fr. of rim and upper body. Reduced. Stacked in firing. Rim frieze: crude Lesbian kyma.

EPH-823*
Istros, His-B 526/V 19333D, Bucharest, Institute of Archaeology storeroom. Two joining frs. of rim and upper body. H 4.5 × W 8.7, WT 0.3, ⌀ rim 12, 22%, RH 1.8. Fabric: standard, 7.5YR 6/6. Dull coat, worn off in places ext., 10YR 3/1. Medium hard fired, oxidized. Rim frieze: guilloche left.
– Domăneanțu 2000, 48 cat. 222, pl. 14 (attributed to Petite rose spiralée).

EPH-824*
Olbia, Sector NGS, О-НГС-05-161, 161a, Parutine, Olbia National Preserve storeroom. Four joining body frs. and one non-joining body fr. H 6.3 × W 5.3, WT 0.3. Fabric: relatively fine and micaceous, some small lime inclusions, 5Y 5/1. Dull coat, 5Y 2.5/1. Medium hard fired, reduced. Rim frieze: rosette 5.

EPH-825*
Volna 1, C3-00-6 St Petersburg, State Hermitage Museum. Fr. of upper body. Oxidized. Rim frieze: rosette.

EPH-826
Olbia, inv. 198563, Warsaw, National Museum (former Vogell collection). Complete. ⌀ rim 12.5; vessel H 8; H:⌀ 1:1.6. Fabric: reddish, with fine mica. Light reddish brown coat with metallic sheen. Oxidized. Rim frieze: ivy-berry clusters. Plain base with false ring foot.
– Zahn 1908, 72 cat. 36; Boehlau 1908, 32 no. 285; Grzegrzółka 2001, cat. 3, fig. 3.

EPH-827*
Istros, His-V 8570 N, Bucharest, Institute of Archaeology storeroom. Fr. of base and lower body. H 7 × W 7, WT 0.3, ⌀ base 3.8. Fabric: standard, 5Y 5/1. Thin dull coat ext., with slight lustre int., 5Y 2.5/1. Relatively hard fired, reduced. Plain concave base with false ring foot.
– Domăneanțu 2000, 60 cat. 274, pl. 18.

EPH-828
Olbia, Sector R25, O-P25-00-2108, Parutine, Olbia National Preserve storeroom. Fr. of base and lower body. Reduced. Plain concave base.

EPH-829*
Porthmion, square 14, depth 0.4 m, П-53-603, Kerč History and Culture Reserve. Small fr. of base and lower body. H 2.7, WT 0.2, ⌀ base 5. Fabric: standard, 5YR 5/8. Thin dull coat, 5YR 3/2. Oxidized. Stacked in firing. Plain concave base.

EPH-830*
Porthmion, square 14, depth 0.2 m, П-53-665, Kerč History and Culture Reserve. Fr. of base and lower body. H 4.4, WT 0.3, ⌀ base 4.5. Fabric: standard, but with many very large lime inclusions (up to 0.6 cm), 2.5YR 5/8. Thin dull coat, ext. 2.5YR 5/6, int. 2.5YR 4/6. Oxidized. Plain concave base.

EPH-831*
Volna 1, C3-00-166, St Petersburg, State Hermitage Museum. Fr. of lower body and tiny part of base. Reduced.

EPH-832*
Bol'šoj Kastel', БК-84-39, Černomorskoe Museum of Historical Lore. Fr. of base and part of lower body. ⌀ base 5. Fabric: 2.5YR 5/8. Dull coat, 2.5YR 5/6. Oxidized. Plain concave base with ring foot.

EPH-833
Olbia, Sector E6, squares 598e, 608e, grey clay layer, O-E6-61-138 Kiev, Institute of Archaeology storeroom. Two joining frs. of base and body. Oxidized. Plain slightly concave base with low false ring foot.

EPH-834*
Chersonesos, X-1963-57, St Petersburg, State Hermitage Museum. Fr. of base and body. H 4.7, WT 0.33, ⌀ base 5. Fabric: standard, 2.5YR 6/6. Dull coat, 2.5YR 5/6. Oxidized. Plain concave base.

EPH-835
Olbia, Sector NGS, O-НГС-05-152, Parutine, Olbia National Preserve storeroom. Fr. of base and lower body. H 5.2 × W 5.8, WT 0.4, ⌀ base 5. Fabric: relatively fine and micaceous, 7.5YR 6/6. Thin dull coat, 7.5YR 5/4. Medium hard fired, oxidized. Plain base with ring foot.

EPH-836
Istros, His-922[a], Bucharest, Institute of Archaeology storeroom. Fr. of base and lower body. Reduced. Plain concave base.

EPH-837*
Olbia, Sector NGS, O-НГС-08-236, Parutine, Olbia National Preserve storeroom. Fr. of lower body and base. H 3 × W 5.1, WT 0.3, ⌀ base 5. Fabric: relatively fine and micaceous, 5YR 6/8. Thin dull coat, 2.5YR 5/6. Medium hard fired, oxidized. Calyx: imbricate petals bounded by ridge above. Low ring base.

EPH-838
Porthmion, П-74-58(?), Kerč History and Culture Reserve. Fr. of base and lower body. Reduced. Plain concave base.
– Grzegrzółka 2010, 173 cat. 275.

EPH-839
Porthmion, П-75-401, Kerč History and Culture Reserve. Fr. of base and lower body. Oxidized. Plain concave, base.
– Grzegrzółka 2010, 171 cat. 271.

EPH-840*
Istros, His-761, Bucharest, Institute of Archaeology storeroom. Fr. of base and lower body. H 3 × W 3.3. Oxidized. Medallion: rosette A.
– Domăneanţu 2000, 102 cat. 507, pl. 33.

EPH-841*
Istros, His-1134, Bucharest, Institute of Archaeology storeroom. Fr. of base and lower body. H 4.5 × W 3. Reduced. Medallion: rosette F.
– Domăneanţu 2000, 101 cat. 503, pl. 33.

EPH-842*
Istros, His-398, Bucharest, Institute of Archaeology storeroom. Fr. of base and lower body. H 3.3 × W 2. Reduced. Medallion: rosette with six pointed petals with large dots between them, surrounded by dots.
– Domăneanţu 2000, 102 cat. 506, pl. 33.

EPH-843*
Istros, His-634, Bucharest, Institute of Archaeology storeroom. Fr. of lower body. H 2 × W 2.8. Oxidized.
– Domăneanţu 2000, 69 cat. 323, pl. 21 (attributed to Heraios).

EPH-844*
Porthmion, П-53-22, Kerč History and Culture Reserve. Fr. of lower body. Oxidized. Secondarily burnt.

EPH-845*
Pantikapaion, palace foundation trench, M-84-36[a], Moscow, Puškin Museum of Fine Arts. Fr. of mid-body. H 3.8 × W 3.4, WT 0.3. Dull coat. Reduced.

EPH-846
Istros, His-B 506, Bucharest, Institute of Archaeology storeroom. Fr. of lower body. H 2 × W 2.5. Reduced.
– Domăneanţu 2000, 12 cat. 49, pl. 3 (tentatively attributed to NI).

EPH-847
Istros, His-476, Bucharest, Institute of Archaeology storeroom. Fr. of upper body. H 1.5 × W 2.5, WT 0.3. Reduced. Trace of rim frieze.

EPH-848
Istros, His-599, Bucharest, Institute of Archaeology storeroom. Fr. of upper body. H 2 × W 2.4, WT 0.25. Reduced.

EPH-849
Istros, His-827, Bucharest, Institute of Archaeology storeroom. Body fr. H 1.7 × W 2.3, WT 0.4. Reduced.

EPH-850
Olbia, Sector R25, O-P25-96-538, Parutine, Olbia National Preserve storeroom. Fr. of lower body. H 4.5 × W 4.3, WT 0.39. Fabric: relatively fine and micaceous, some small voids, 10YR 4/2. Dull coat, Gley 1 2.5/N. Medium hard fired, reduced.

EPH-851
Olbia, Sector NGS, O-НГС-05-750, Parutine, Olbia National Preserve storeroom. Fr. of lower body. Reduced.

Imbricate Pointed Petals with Double Outline

EPH-852*
Istros, His-V 8567 A+B, Bucharest, Institute of Archaeology storeroom. Two joining frs. of rim and body. H 2.8 × W 2, WT 0.25, ⌀ rim 11, 23%, RH 1.8. Fabric: standard with much lime, 5YR 6/8. Dull coat, red below, brown above. Medium hard fired, oxidized. Stacked in firing. Multiple rim friezes: rosette 1; Lesbian kyma. Calyx: imbricate pointed petals with double outline and central vein.
– Domăneanţu 2000, 71 cat. 333, pl. 21 (attributed to Heraios).

EPH-853*
Myrmekion, M-56-2264, St Petersburg IIMK RAN. Fr. of rim and upper body. H 4.7, WT 0.35, ⌀ rim 12.5, RH 1.7. Fabric: standard, 5YR 6/6. Thin coat with slight metallic lustre, mottled ext., ext. 2.5YR 4/6, 5YR 3/3, 3/1, int. 5YR 3/2–3/3. Oxidized. Stacked in firing. Multiple rim friezes: rosette 2/7; broad astragal. Calyx: imbricate pointed petals with double outline (details missing).

EPH-854*
Chersonesos, X-1959-24, St Petersburg, State Hermitage Museum. Fr. of rim and upper body. H 4.3, WT 0.3, RH 1.8. Fabric: standard, 2.5YR 6/6. Slightly lustrous coat, ext. 2.5YR 4/6, 3/1, int. 2.5YR 4/6. Oxidized. Stacked in firing. Multiple rim friezes: rosette 2/7 (very tired stamp); small rosette 2/9. Calyx: imbricate pointed petals with double outline and central vein.

EPH-855*
Olbia, Sector NGS, House IV-4 B 397/219, О-НГС-93-843+843а, Parutine, Olbia National Preserve storeroom. Two body frs. and one base fr., all joining; complete profile with only the lip missing. WT 0.28–0.4, ⌀ base 4.5; vessel H 6. Fabric: relatively fine and micaceous, some small lime particles, a few voids, 7.5YR 6/6. Thin firm coat with dull metallic sheen, mottled ext., ext. 2.5YR 5/4, 2.5YR 3/0, int. 5YR 4/1. Medium hard fired, oxidized. Stacked in firing. Multiple rim friezes: sunburst rosette; large dots. Calyx: imbricate small pointed petals with double outline. Concave base with low ring foot, small circle at center.
– Guldager Bilde 2010, 279 cat. F-44, pl. 176.

EPH-856*
Olbia, Sector NGS, О-НГС-06-102, Parutine, Olbia National Preserve storeroom. Fr. of rim and upper body. H 3.8 × W 4.9, WT 0.2, RH 1.5. Fabric: relatively fine and micaceous, 5Y 5/1. Dull coat, Gley 1 2.5/N. Medium hard fired, reduced. Multiple rim friezes: large dots; wave meander, upside-down. Calyx: imbricate pointed petals with double outline.

EPH-857 (see Fig. 81)
Olbia, Sector NGS, О-НГС-97-506, Parutine, Olbia National Preserve storeroom. Fr. of rim and upper body. H 4.3 × W 6.6, WT 0.3, ⌀ rim 12, 15%, RH 2.1. Fabric: relatively fine, micaceous, a few small lime particles, 5YR 6/8. Thin dull mottled coat, ext. 10R 5/6, 5YR 3/2, int. 10R 5/6. Medium hard fired, oxidized. Stacked in firing. Rim frieze: hanging leaf. Calyx: imbricate, pointed petals with double outline. Two repair holes, with lead clamp in one of them.

EPH-858
Istros, Sector A, His-88-1158, Bucharest, Institute of Archaeology storeroom. Body fr. close to rim. H 4.5 × W 2.5. Oxidized. Rim frieze: triple guilloche left. Calyx: imbricate pointed petals with double outline. Monogram PAR.
– Domăneanţu 2000, 37 cat. 158, pl. 11 (attributed to Monogram PAR).

EPH-859*
Istros, His-V 8575 K, Bucharest Institute of Archaeology storeroom. Body fr. Oxidized. Rim frieze: very crude triple guilloche left. Calyx: imbricate pointed petals with double outline. Monogram PAR.
– Domăneanţu 2000, 37 cat. 157, pl. 11.

EPH-860*
Istros, Sector MC1 Sa, His-56-51, Bucharest, Institute of Archaeology storeroom. Six joining body frs., from rim to tiny part of base. H 6 × W 9.3, WT 0.28. Fabric: standard, relatively coarse, 7.5YR 7/8. Dull coat, 7.5YR 3/2. Medium hard fired, oxidized. Rim frieze: rosette 1 var. Calyx: imbricate pointed petals with double outline.
– Domăneanţu 2000, 61 cat. 277, pl. 18.

EPH-861*
Istros, His-V 19390+V 19469, Bucharest, Institute of Archaeology storeroom. Two joining frs. of rim and upper body. H 4.1. Oxidized. Rim frieze: rosette 3 var., in negative relief. Calyx: imbricate pointed petals with double outline and central vein.
– Domăneanţu 2000, 54 cat. 245, pl. 16 (attributed to Athenaios).

EPH-862*
Olbia, Sector NGS, О-НГС-06-147+270, 136, Parutine, Olbia National Preserve storeroom. Two joining body frs.; non-joining body fr. H 3.4 × W 3.6, WT 0.34. Fabric: relatively fine and micaceous, Gley 1 6/10Y. Dull coat, Gley 1 2.5/1. Medium hard fired, reduced. Rim frieze: rosette 2/7 alternating with box with star in negative relief. Calyx: imbricate pointed petals with double outline and central vein. Frieze separators: dots.

EPH-863
Pantikapaion, Mithridates Hill. Fr. of base and lower body. Reduced. Calyx: imbricate, pointed petals with double outline; in between single row of rosette 3. Plain concave base, signed ATHE[...]//AI, incised in vessel before firing. Athenaios.
– Grzegrzółka 2010, 76 cat. 66.

EPH-864*
Myrmekion, M-56-1237, St Petersburg IIMK RAN. Fr. of base and lower body. H 6.9, WT 0.15, ⌀ base 4. Fabric: standard, 2.5YR 5/8. Thin slightly lustrous coat, 10R 5/6. Oxidized. Calyx: imbricate tall pointed petals with double outline and central vein. Plain concave base with false ring foot.

EPH-865
Istros, His-54, Bucharest, Institute of Archaeology storeroom. Body fr. H 4.5 × W 2.7. Oxidized. Rim frieze: Ionian kyma? Calyx: imbricate pointed petals with double outline.
– Domăneanţu 2000, 71 cat. 334, pl. 22 (attributed to Heraios).

Imbricate Pointed Petals with Central and Side Veins

EPH-866*
Pantikapaion, palace foundation trench, M-84-48, Moscow, Puškin Museum of Fine Arts. Fr. of rim and upper body. H 4.5 × W 7.7, WT 0.25, Ø rim 12, 20%, RH 1. Dull coat. Hard fired, oxidized. Stacked in firing. Multiple rim friezes: large dots; star rosettes; box meander, cw. Calyx: imbricate (tips of pointed petals preserved).
– Košelenko 1992, fig. 23.

EPH-867
Porthmion, П-75-431, Kerč History and Culture Reserve. Fr. of rim and upper body. Oxidized. Multiple rim friezes: box meander, cw; large dots.
– Grzegrzółka 2010, 169–170 cat. 267.

EPH-868*
Olbia, Sector R25, O-P25-05-1204, Parutine, Olbia National Preserve storeroom. Body fr. H 4.8 × W 4.2, WT 0.25. Fabric: relatively fine and micaceous, small lime inclusions, 5YR 6/6. Thin slightly lustrous coat, ext. 5YR 4/2, 3/1, int. 5YR 4/2, 3/1. Hard fired, oxidized. Stacked in firing. Multiple rim friezes: Lesbian kyma; astragal alternating with pairs of crossed boxes.

EPH-869
Porthmion, pavement outside western defensive wall near wicket, П-75-81[a], Kerč History and Culture Reserve. Two non-joining frs. of rim and upper body. Multiple rim friezes: rosette 5; horizontal S-spirals.

EPH-870*
Olbia, Sector R25, O-P25-04-1880+2801+2807b+3750+2807a, Parutine, Olbia National Preserve storeroom. Two joining base frs., two rim frs., one of which joins lower body, non-joining body fr. WT 0.18–0.22, Ø rim 13, 18%, RH 2, Ø base 5. Fabric: fine, micaceous, many minute lime particles, 5Y 5/1. Dull coat, ext. Gley 1 2.5/N, 7.5YR 2.5/1, int. Gley 1 2.5/N. Hard fired, reduced. Multiple rim friezes: miniature acanthus scroll left; horizontal S-spirals. Plain concave base, signed MENEMACHOU. Menemachos.

EPH-871
Kepoi, Tomb 38, Ке-63-38, Moscow, State Historical Museum. Complete. Ø rim 11.5, Ø base 4.5; vessel H 6.7; H:Ø 1:1.7. Fabric: fine grey. Dull black coat almost completely worn off. Reduced. Rim frieze: astragal. Plain slightly concave base.
– Usačeva 1978, fig. 1.2.

EPH-872
Istros, His-184+378, Bucharest, Institute of Archaeology storeroom. Two joining frs. of rim and body. H 4.6 × W 7.1, WT 0.2, Ø rim 11, 15%, RH 1.9. Fabric: standard with some small lime particles, Gley 1 3/5GY. Thin dull coat, Gley 1 3/N. Medium hard fired, reduced. Rim frieze: box meander, cw.
– Domăneanţu 2000, 5 cat. 13, pl. 1 (attributed to Menemachos).

EPH-873*
Pantikapaion, palace foundation trench, M-89-illegible 52, M-89-no no. 2, Moscow, Puškin Museum of Fine Arts. Frs. of rim and upper body. Oxidized. Rim frieze: box meander, cw. Calyx: tips of imbricate pointed petal with central (and side?) veins.

EPH-874
Olbia, Sector NGS, О-НГС-02-372+427, Parutine, Olbia National Preserve storeroom. Two joining frs. of rim and upper body; very worn. H 5.3 × W 8.1, WT 0.26–0.56, Ø rim 13, 20%, RH 2.05. Fabric: relatively fine and micaceous, abundant minute lime particles, many voids of varying size, 7.5YR 6/4. Thin firm slightly lustrous coat, darkened at rim, ext. 2.5YR 4/4, 10YR 3/2, int. 2.5YR 4/4, 10YR 3/1. Medium hard fired, oxidized. Stacked in firing. Rim frieze: Ionian kyma.

EPH-875*
Pantikapaion, palace foundation trench, M-84-36, Moscow, Puškin Museum of Fine Arts. Fr. of rim and large part of body. H 6 × W 10, WT 0.3, Ø rim 11, 25%, RH 2.2. Dull coat, very worn int. Oxidized. Rim frieze: Ionian kyma. Secondarily burnt.
– Košelenko 1992, fig. 23.

EPH-876*
Olbia, Sector R25, O-P25-03-2031, Parutine, Olbia National Preserve storeroom. Fr. of rim and upper body. H 4.4 × W 4.3, WT 0.23. Fabric: fine, micaceous, Gley 1 5/10Y. Dull coat, Gley 1 3/N. Medium hard fired, reduced. Rim frieze: Ionian kyma.

EPH-877*
Olbia, Sector R25, O-P25-05-1198, Parutine, Olbia National Preserve storeroom. Fr. of rim and upper body. H 4.75 × W 4.5, WT 0.3, Ø rim 13, 11%, RH 2.1. Fabric: relatively fine and micaceous, Gley 1 6/10Y. Thin dull coat, Gley 1 2.5/N. Medium hard fired, reduced. Rim frieze: Ionian kyma.

EPH-878
Olbia, Sector R25, O-P25-96-979, Parutine, Olbia National Preserve storeroom. Fr. of rim and upper body. H 4 × W 4.2,

WT 0.45, ⌀ rim 12, 11%, RH 1.5. Fabric: relatively fine and micaceous, small lime inclusions, 5YR 5/8. Dull coat, 2.5YR 5/6. Hard fired, oxidized. Rim frieze: Ionian kyma.

EPH-879
Myrmekion, M-53-562 or 569, St Petersburg IIMK RAN. Fr. of rim and upper body. ⌀ rim 11, 18%. Thin dull black coat. Reduced. Rim frieze: Ionian kyma. Calyx: imbricate, top of pointed petals preserved.

EPH-880
Pantikapaion, M-48-1479, Moscow, Puškin Museum of Fine Arts. Several joining frs. of rim, body, and base; complete profile. Rim frieze: Lesbian kyma. Wide plain slightly concave base.
– Zabelina 1984, 155 fig. 2.

EPH-881*
Istros, His-V 10080 A, Bucharest, Institute of Archaeology storeroom. Body fr. close to rim. H 3.5 × W 3. Reduced. Rim frieze: Lesbian kyma.
– Domăneanţu 2000, 4 cat. 11, pl. 1 (attributed to Menemachos).

EPH-882*
Olbia, Sector NGCentre, square 57sw, yellow clay layer, О-НГЦ-66-1678, Kiev, Institute of Archaeology storeroom. Fr. of rim and body. H 5.6 × W 4.7, WT 0.2, RH 1.6. Fabric: standard, 10YR 4/1. Thin dull coat, ext. 10YR 3/1, int. 10YR 3/2. Relatively hard fired, reduced. Rim frieze: horizontal S-spirals.

EPH-883*
Olbia, Cliff, grey clay layer, O-68-1380, Kiev, Institute of Archaeology storeroom. Fr. of rim and body. Oxidized. Rim frieze: guilloche left.

EPH-884
Olbia(?), inv. 54791 Uvarov 312, Moscow, State Historical Collection (Uvarov collection). Two joining frs. of rim and body. Oxidized. Stacked in firing. Rim frieze: rosette 1. Menemachos.

EPH-885
Istros, His-901, Bucharest, Institute of Archaeology storeroom. Fr. of upper body. H 2.2 × W 2.2. Oxidized. Rim frieze: small rosette 1.
– Domăneanţu 2000, 70 cat. 326, pl. 21 (attributed to Heraios).

EPH-886
Olbia, O-1910-1156, present whereabouts unknown. Two joining frs. of rim and body. Rim frieze: rosette 1.
– St Petersburg, IIMK RAN, archive inv. 4057.519.5 (pl. XII).

EPH-887
Istros, His-553, 632, Bucharest, Institute of Archaeology storeroom. Two non-joining body frs. close to rim. H 2.4 × W 3.3, WT 0.25. Fabric: standard, not too fine, small lime particles, sand, 2.5Y 6/1. Dull coat, ext. 2.5Y 4/1, 5Y 2.5/1, int. 2.5Y 3/1. Medium hard fired, reduced. Stacked in firing. Rim frieze: rosette 2/4.
– Domăneanţu 2000, 37 cat. 156, pl. 11.

EPH-888
Porthmion, П-75-430, Kerč History and Culture Reserve. Fr. of rim and upper body. Reduced. Rim frieze: rosette 2/10 (M). Menemachos?
– Grzegrzółka 2010, 169 cat. 266.

EPH-889*
Olbia, O-no no. F, Kiev, Institute of Archaeology storeroom. Fr. of rim and upper body. Oxidized. Rim frieze: rosette 5.

EPH-890*
Istros, Sector Z2I, His-57-957[a]/V 17590 B, Bucharest, Institute of Archaeology storeroom. Fr. of rim and upper body. H 4.8 × W 4.1, WT 0.25, RH 2.1. Fabric: standard, 5Y 7/1. Dull mottled coat, Gley 1 3/N, 5Y 4/1. Relatively hard fired, reduced. Rim frieze: rosette 8.
– Domăneanţu 2000, 67 cat. 314, pl. 20.

EPH-891*
Olbia, Sector NGS, О-НГС-08-194, Parutine, Olbia National Preserve storeroom. Body fr. H 2 × W 2.6, WT 0.25. Fabric: relatively fine and micaceous, 7.5YR 6/6. Thin dull coat, ext. 7.5YR 3/1, int. 5YR 4/3. Medium hard fired, oxidized. Rim frieze: miniature acanthus scroll left. Menemachos.

EPH-892*
Istros, His-V 10080[b], Bucharest, Institute of Archaeology storeroom. Fr. of rim and upper body. Oxidized. Rim frieze: ivy-berry clusters.

EPH-893
Istros, His-709, Bucharest, Institute of Archaeology storeroom. Rim fr. Reduced. No rim frieze.

EPH-894*
Olbia, O-year(?)-3615, Kiev, Institute of Archaeology storeroom? Fr. of rim and upper body. Reduced. No rim frieze.

EPH-895*
Chersonesos, X-1889-6, St Petersburg, State Hermitage Museum. Four joining frs. of base and body. H 5.6, WT 0.35, ⌀ base 4.7.

Fabric: standard, with much lime, 5YR 4/4. Thin dull coat ext, slight lustre int., 5YR 4/2. Oxidized. Plain concave base, signed MENEMACHOU. Menemachos.
– Mal'mberg 1892, 27 cat. 30; Bouzek 1990, 75.

EPH-896*
Istros, His-106, Bucharest, Institute of Archaeology storeroom. Fr. of base and lower body. H 4 × W 3, WT 0.2, ⌀ base 4. Fabric: standard, with some voids, 5YR 6/8. Dull coat, 2.5YR 5/8. Relatively hard fired, oxidized. Plain concave base, signed MEN[...] by mechanical copying of Menemachos stamp. Menemachos.
– Domăneanțu 2000, 53 cat. 244, pl. 16 (attributed to Athenaios).

EPH-897*
Istros, His-V 8570 M, Bucharest, Institute of Archaeology storeroom. Fr. of base and lower body. H 4 × W 3.5, WT 0.4, ⌀ base 5. Fabric: standard, with much lime, 5Y 5/1. Thin coat with slight lustre, 5Y 2.5/1. Medium hard fired, reduced. Concave base with rosette 2/7 at center, signed PH, incised in vessel before firing. Philon(nios).
– Domăneanțu 2000, 90 cat. 428, pl. 29.

EPH-898*
Olbia, Sector Sever-Zapad, O-C3-68-1962, Parutine, Olbia National Preserve storeroom. Fr. of base and lower body. H 6 × W 6.7, WT 0.2–0.4, ⌀ base 6.5. Fabric: standard, 10YR5/1. Thin dull coat, 10YR 2/1. Not too hard fired, reduced. Plain concave base, signed PH, incised in vessel before firing. Philon(nios).

EPH-899*
Istros, His-140, Bucharest, Institute of Archaeology storeroom. Fr. of base and lower body. H 2.7 × W 3, WT 0.25, ⌀ base 5. Fabric: standard, with much lime, 5Y 5/1. Dull coat ext., slight lustre int., 5Y 2.5/1. Medium hard fired, reduced. Plain concave base, faint traces of letter incised in vessel before firing, probably PH. Philon(nios).
– Domăneanțu 2000, 90 cat. 429, pl. 29.

EPH-900*
Pantikapaion, palace foundation trench, M-84-39, Moscow, Puškin Museum of Fine Arts. Base fr. H 4.3 × W 4.5, WT 0.28, ⌀ base 5. Dull black coat. Reduced. Plain concave base, signed [...]KESIL[...] in negative relief on lunate stamp (mechanically copied). Arkesilaos.

EPH-901
Pantikapaion, M-57-766, Moscow, Puškin Museum of Fine Arts. Fragmentary bowl; complete profile. H 4.3 × W 4.5, WT 0.28, ⌀ base 5. Reduced. Rim frieze: Ionian kyma. Plain concave base, signed ARKESILAOU in negative relief on lunate stamp (mechanically copied). Arkesilaos.
– Loseva 1962, fig. 1.8; AGSP 1984, pl. CLXIII.1b.

EPH-902
Beljaus, Bel-00-124. Fr. of base and lower body. Plain concave base with low ring foot, signed with AP or PA monogram incised in mould before firing.
– S. Lancov, Annual report 2000 (unpublished).

EPH-903*
Istros, His-150, Bucharest, Institute of Archaeology storeroom. Fr. of base and lower body. H 2 × W 2.6. Reduced. Base surrounded by low ridge.
– Domăneanțu 2000, 121 cat. 597, pl. 41 (identified as Pontic).

EPH-904
Istros, His-557, Bucharest, Institute of Archaeology storeroom. Fr. of lower body and part of base. H 2 × W 2.5. Reduced. Plain concave base.
– Domăneanțu 2000, 5 cat. 12, pl. 1 (attributed to Menemachos).

EPH-905
Porthmion, Sector G, sector 2, square 17–18, depth 0.42 m, П-87-89, Kerč History and Culture Reserve. Fr. of base and lower body. Plain concave base.

EPH-906
Istros, His-285, Bucharest, Institute of Archaeology storeroom. Fr. of base and lower body. Reduced. Plain concave base with false ring foot.

EPH-907*
Ruminskoe/Za Rodinu, Рум-72-13, Moscow, State Historical Museum. Base fr. ⌀ base 5. Dull black coat. Reduced.

EPH-908*
Myrmekion, M-58-696, St Petersburg IIMK RAN. Fr. of base and body. H 3, WT 0.35, ⌀ base 4. Fabric: standard, slightly coarse, 5YR 4/1. Thin dull coat, misfired, ext. 5YR 5/3, int. 5YR 5/4. Oxidized. Plain base, faint traces of signature running parallel to the foot; at least the letter H (eta) can be distinguished. Secondarily burnt.

EPH-909
Olbia, Sector R25, O-P25-99-663, Parutine, Olbia National Preserve storeroom. Fr. of base and lower body. H 4.4 × W 5, WT 0.55, ⌀ base 3.6. Fabric: relatively fine and micaceous, 2.5Y 6/1. Thin dull coat, 2.5Y 4/1. Medium hard fired, reduced. Plain concave base with low false ring foot.

EPH-910*
Olbia, Sector E6, square 425, ash layer O-E6-57-1042, Kiev, Institute of Archaeology storeroom. Fr. of base and lower body. Oxidized. Plain concave base with false ring foot.

EPH-911*
Olbia, Sector E6–7, squares 598e, 608e, grey clay layer, O-E6-7-61-437 Kiev, Institute of Archaeology storeroom. Fr. of base and body. Reduced. Plain concave base.

EPH-912
Istros, His-564, Bucharest, Institute of Archaeology storeroom. Fr. of base and lower body. H 2.4 × W 3.5. Reduced. Plain concave base.
– Domăneanţu 2000, 121 cat. 598, pl. 41 (identified as Pontic).

EPH-913*
Olbia, Sector R25, O-P25-04-3873, Parutine, Olbia National Preserve storeroom. Fr. of base and lower body. Oxidized. Plain concave base.

EPH-914
Porthmion, Sector G, sector 2, fill in rooms, П-87-130, Kerč History and Culture Reserve. Fr. of base and lower body. Plain concave base.

EPH-915
Istros, His-478, Bucharest, Institute of Archaeology storeroom. Fr. of base and lower body. H 3.2 × W 3. Reduced. Plain concave base with false ring foot.
– Domăneanţu 2000, 70 cat. 330, pl. 21 (attributed to Heraios).

EPH-916
Porthmion, П-75-355, Kerč History and Culture Reserve. Fr. of base and lower body. Oxidized. Plain concave base.
– Grzegrzółka 2010, 172 cat. 274 (attributed to Asia Minor).

EPH-917
Porthmion, П-73-no.(?), Kerč History and Culture Reserve. Fr. of base and lower body. Oxidized. Plain concave base.
– Grzegrzółka 2010, 172 cat. 273.

EPH-918
Porthmion, П-73-27, Kerč History and Culture Reserve. Fr. of base and lower body. Oxidized. Plain concave base.
– Grzegrzółka 2010, 171–172 cat. 272.

EPH-919*
Olbia, Sector E6, fill in Cistern 128, O-E6-59-2268, Kiev, Institute of Archaeology storeroom. Fr. of base and lower body. H 5.6 × W 7.5, WT 0.4, ⌀ base 5. Fabric: standard, fine, 2.5YR 6/6. Slightly lustrous coat, flaking, 2.5YR 4/6. Hard fired, oxidized. Medallion: rosette E.

EPH-920
Olbia, Sector R25, O-P25-04-no no.[12], Parutine, Olbia National Preserve storeroom. Body fr. Oxidized.

EPH-921
Olbia, Sector NGS, O-НГС-05-280, Parutine, Olbia National Preserve storeroom. Fr. of upper body. Reduced. Calyx: central vein of petals hatched.

EPH-922*
Istros, His-186, Bucharest, Institute of Archaeology storeroom. Fr. of lower body. H 3.5 × W 3. Reduced.
– Domăneanţu 2000, 70 cat. 325, pl. 21 (attributed to Heraios).

EPH-923
Istros, His-678, Bucharest, Institute of Archaeology storeroom. Fr. of lower body. Oxidized.

EPH-924
Istros, His-614, Bucharest, Institute of Archaeology storeroom. Fr. of lower body. Reduced. Calyx: imbricate petals bounded at top by ridge.

EPH-925*
Istros, His-772, Bucharest, Institute of Archaeology storeroom. Body fr. Reduced.

EPH-926
Olbia, Sector NGS, O-НГС-05-748, Parutine, Olbia National Preserve storeroom. Fr. of upper body. Reduced.

EPH-927*
Istros, His-V 17589 B, Bucharest, Institute of Archaeology storeroom. Fr. of lower body. Reduced. Calyx: petals barely overlapping.

EPH-928
Porthmion, П-73-33(?), Kerč History and Culture Reserve. Fr. of lower body. Reduced.
– Grzegrzółka 2010, 173 cat. 276.

EPH-929
Porthmion, П-77-276, Kerč History and Culture Reserve. Fr. of lower body. Reduced.
– Grzegrzółka 2010, 173 cat. 277 (considered to be from an unidentified production place).

EPH-930*
Olbia, Sector E6, square 252w, below heap of tiles O-6-56-118, 274[a, b] Kiev, Institute of Archaeology storeroom. Three non-joining frs. of rim, body, and base. Reduced. Multiple rim friezes: large dots; star rosettes. Calyx: petals in negative relief. Plain concave base.

EPH-931*
Pantikapaion, palace foundation trench, M-84-35, 35[a], 51, Moscow, Puškin Museum of Fine Arts. Fr. of rim and upper body, frs. of base and lower body, not joining but probably from same vessel. H 4.5 × W 4, WT 0.4, RH 1.6. Dull black coat. Reduced. Rim frieze: rosette 9/11. Calyx: petals in negative relief. Plain concave base.
– Košelenko 1992, fig. 23.

EPH-932*
Olbia, Cliff, O-68-1299, Kiev, Institute of Archaeology storeroom. Fr. of rim and upper body. H 4.5 × W 5.7, WT 0.25, ⌀ rim 12, 15%, RH 1.7. Fabric: standard, 2.5YR 6/8. Dull coat, ext. 2.5YR 5/6, int. 2.5YR 5/8. Medium hard fired, oxidized. Rim frieze: crossed dotted lines. Calyx: petals in negative relief.

EPH-933
Istros, His-629, Bucharest, Institute of Archaeology storeroom. Fr. of lower body. Oxidized. Calyx: petals in negative relief, not overlapping.

Imbricate Pointed Petals with Central and Side Veins, Double Outline

EPH-934*
Istros, His-V 19466, Bucharest, Institute of Archaeology storeroom. Body fr. H 5 × W 5.5. Oxidized. Stacked in firing. Rim frieze: astragal.
– Domăneanțu 2000, 37 cat. 155, pl. 11 (attributed to Monogram PAR).

EPH-935*
Tyritake, Sector L, Л-37-316, St Petersburg IIMK RAN. Body fr. H 3.2, WT 0.32. Fabric: standard, 5Y 4/2. Thin dull coat, 5Y 4/2. Reduced. Rim frieze: vertical S-spirals.

EPH-936*
Myrmekion, M-57-217, St Petersburg IIMK RAN. Fr. of rim and upper body. H 6.1, WT 0.3, ⌀ rim 12, 9%, RH 2.3. Fabric: standard, fine, 7.5YR 4/3. Thin coat, Gley 1 3/. Hard fired, reduced. Rim frieze: rosette 5.

EPH-937*
Olbia, Sector R25, O-P25-04-3017, Parutine, Olbia National Preserve storeroom. Fr. of base and lower body. Reduced. Plain concave base.

EPH-938
Istros, His-320, Bucharest, Institute of Archaeology storeroom. Fr. of lower body. H 2 × W 3. Reduced.
– Domăneanțu 2000, 61 cat. 282, pl. 18.

EPH-939*
Olbia, Sector NGS, O-НГС-00-328, Parutine, Olbia National Preserve storeroom. Fr. of lower body. Reduced.

EPH-940
Istros, His-739, Bucharest, Institute of Archaeology storeroom. Fr. of lower body. H 2.8 × W 2. Reduced.
– Domăneanțu 2000, 71 cat. 332, pl. 21 (attributed to Heraios).

EPH-941
Olbia, Cliff, grey clay layer, O-68-1989, Kiev, Institute of Archaeology storeroom. Body fr. Reduced.

Other Imbricate Pointed Petal Patterns

EPH-942*
Pantikapaion, palace foundation trench, M-89-no no. 8, Moscow, Puškin Museum of Fine Arts. Base fr. Oxidized. Calyx: imbricate pointed petals with triple outline. Plain flat base with false ring foot.

EPH-943*
Pantikapaion, palace foundation trench, M-89-illegible 23, Moscow, Puškin Museum of Fine Arts. Body fr. Reduced. Calyx: imbricate pointed petals with triple outline.

EPH-944*
Olbia, Cliff, O-68-1300, Kiev, Institute of Archaeology storeroom. Fr. of rim and body. H 4.4 × W 5.3, WT 0.36, ⌀ rim 13, RH 1.8. Fabric: fine and micaceous, 10YR 7/3. Dull coat ext., slight lustre int., 5Y 2.5/1. Medium hard fired, oxidized. Rim frieze: Ionian kyma with hatched tongue. Calyx: imbricate pointed petals with hatched central vein.

EPH-945
Istros, His-905, Bucharest, Institute of Archaeology storeroom. Fr. of upper body. H 1.5 × W 2.5, WT 0.3. Reduced. Calyx: imbricate pointed petals with dotted central vein.

Imbricate Designs Using Other Elements

EPH-946*
Istros, His-1927-1942-V 8569 H, Bucharest Institute of Archaeology storeroom. Fr. of rim and upper body. Oxidized. Stacked in firing. Rim frieze: Ionian kyma. Calyx: closely set straight acanthus leaves.
– Domăneanțu 2000, 98 cat. 481, pl. 32.

EPH-947*
Istros, His-977, Bucharest, Institute of Archaeology storeroom. Fr. of rim and upper body. H 4.7 × W 5.4, WT 0.25, ⌀ rim 12, 10%, RH 1.6. Fabric: standard, with abundant small lime particles, 2.5Y 5/1. Dull coat, ext. 2.5Y 4/2, 2.5/1, int. 10YR 4/3. Medium hard fired, reduced. Stacked in firing. Rim frieze: Ionian kyma. Calyx: imbricate palmettes.
– Domăneanțu 2000, 79 cat. 382, pl. 25 (attributed to Plagiaire).

EPH-948*
Olbia, Sector NGS, O-НГС-06-25+120+617, Parutine, Olbia National Preserve storeroom. Three joining body frs., one close to rim, two non-joining body frs. H 6.1 × W 5.8, WT 0.28. Fabric: relatively fine and micaceous, 7.5YR 6/6. Thin dull coat, 7.5YR 2.5/1. Low fired, oxidized. Rim frieze: Ionian kyma. Calyx: imbricate palmettes.

EPH-949*
Olbia, Sector AGD, O-АГД-71-1944, Kiev, Institute of Archaeology storeroom. Fr. of rim and upper body. H 4.4 × W 8.7, WT 0.4, ⌀ rim 13, 16%, RH 1.6. Fabric: standard, 2.5YR 6/8. Slightly lustrous coat ext., duller int., ext. 10YR 2/1, int. 2.5YR 4/8. Relatively hard fired, oxidized. Rim frieze: Ionian kyma. Calyx: imbricate small leaves.

EPH-950*
Olbia, Sector E, square 66, grey clay layer, O-E-49-2495 Kiev, Institute of Archaeology storeroom. Fr. of rim and upper body. H 4.1 × W 6.3, WT 0.22, ⌀ rim 13, 16%, RH 2. Fabric: standard, fine, Gley 1 4/N. Dull, not completely covering ext., Gley 1 3/N. Relatively hard fired, reduced. Rim frieze: Ionian kyma. Calyx: imbricate small leaves. Frieze separators: dots.

EPH-951
Olbia, O-46-3156(?), no no. [a], Kiev, Institute of Archaeology storeroom. Two non-joining frs. of rim and body close to rim. H 4.4 × W 3.4, WT 0.45. Fabric: standard, fine, 5Y 6/1. Slightly lustrous coat, Gley 1 3/N. Relatively hard fired, reduced. Rim frieze: Ionian kyma with hatched tongue. Calyx: imbricate small leaves. Frieze separators: dots.

EPH-952*
Myrmekion, M-58-556, St Petersburg IIMK RAN. Fr. of mid-body. H 4.4, WT 0.45. Fabric: standard, 5Y 6/1. Thin coat, slightly lustrous ext., Gley 1 2.5/N. Hard fired, reduced. Rim frieze: rosette 5. Calyx: imbricate half rosette or 'paw'.

EPH-953*
Istros, His-264, Bucharest, Institute of Archaeology storeroom. Body fr. Reduced. Rim frieze: Ionian kyma. Calyx: imbricate pattern of upside-down eggs. Frieze separators: dots.

EPH-954*
Olbia, Sector R25, O-P25-04-2803a, Parutine, Olbia National Preserve storeroom. Fr. of rim and upper body. H 4.3 × W 3.5, WT 0.35, RH 1.6. Fabric: fine, micaceous, some small lime inclusions, 5Y 5/1. Dull coat, ext. 5Y 5/1, 4/1, 2.5/1, int. 5Y 3/1. Medium hard fired, reduced. Stacked in firing. Rim frieze: vertical S-spirals. Main decoration: rows of rosette 2/4.

F   *Linear Decoration*

Pendent-Semicircle Design

EPH-955*
Olbia, Sector AGD, Bothros 11, O-АГД-87-998[b], Parutine, Olbia National Preserve storeroom. Four joining frs. preserving complete profile. WT 0.4, ⌀ rim 12.5, 62%, RH 1.7; vessel H 6.4; H:⌀ 1:2. Fabric: standard, with large voids, 5YR 6/8. Thin dull coat with some dark metallic patches at rim, ext. 2.5YR 4/6, 5YR 4/4, int. 2.5YR 4/6. Relatively hard fired, oxidized. Stacked in firing. Rim frieze: Ionian kyma. Main decoration: pendent semicircles outlined by dots; five-rayed sun wheel at centre, rosette 9/8 as space filler. Medallion: three concentric circles with sun-wheel at centre; outer circle surrounded by dots. Probably from same bowl as **EPH-956**. Monogram PAR.
– A.S. Rusjaeva, Očet 1987, pl. XXVII.2.

EPH-956
Olbia, Sector AGD, Bothros 11, O-АГД-87-998, Kiev, Institute of Archaeology storeroom. Fr. of lower body. H 2.5 × W 2.7, WT 0.38. Fabric: standard, 5YR 6/6. Dull coat, 5YR 4/4. Relatively hard fired, oxidized. Main decoration: pendent semicircles outlined by dots; rosette 9/8 as space filler. Probably from the same bowl as **EPH-955***. Monogram PAR?
– Rusjaeva & Nazarčuk 2006, pl. 193.5.

EPH-957*
Olbia, Cliff, square 285, O-70-146+1128, 1137, Parutine, Olbia National Preserve storeroom. Two joining frs. of rim and upper body; one non-joining fr. H 4.1, WT 0.2, ⌀ rim 13, 22%, RH 1.6.

Fabric: standard, 2.5YR 5/8. Slightly lustrous coat, blackened at rim int., ext. 2.5YR 5/6, 7.5YR 4/3, int. 2.5YR 4/8, 2.5/1. Relatively hard fired, oxidized. Stacked in firing. Rim frieze: Ionian kyma. Main decoration: pendent semicircles outlined by dots; five-rayed sun wheel at centre, rosette 9/8 as space-filler.

EPH-958
Olbia, Sector NGS, О-НГС-02-680, Parutine, Olbia National Preserve storeroom. Two joining frs. of rim and upper body. H 4.4 × W 6.2, WT 0.25–0.43, ⌀ rim 13, RH 2. Fabric: relatively fine and micaceous, small lime particles, some small voids, 7.5YR 6/6. Thin firm slightly lustrous coat, black ext. and int. at lip, ext. 7.5YR 2/0, int. 2.5YR 5/6. Medium hard fired, oxidized. Rim frieze: Ionian kyma. Main decoration: pendent semicircles outlined by dots; rosette 9 as space filler.

EPH-959*
Olbia, O-64-53, Kiev, Institute of Archaeology storeroom. Fr. of base and lower body. H 6.7 × W 6.7, WT 0.4, ⌀ base 4. Fabric: standard, fine, 5YR 6/8. Coat with slight metallic shine ext., dull lustre int., ext. 5YR 3/1, 2.5YR 4/6, int. 2.5YR 4/8. Hard fired, oxidized. Stacked in firing. Main decoration: pendent semicircles outlined by dots; rosette 9/8 as space filler. Medallion: three concentric circles with five-rayed sun wheel. One repair hole.

EPH-960
Olbia, Sector NGS, О-НГС-92-132, Parutine, Olbia National Preserve storeroom. Fr. of base and lower body. H 6.2 × W 9, WT 0.22–0.45, ⌀ base 4.5. Fabric: relatively fine and micaceous, small lime inclusions, 2.5YR 6/8. Thin slightly lustrous coat, 5YR 3/2. Medium hard fired, oxidized. Main decoration: pendent semicircles outlined by dots; five-rayed sun wheel at centre, rosette 9/8 as space fillers. Medallion: three concentric circles with circle of large dots within.

EPH-961*
Olbia, Sector AGD, О-АГД-71-1765, Kiev, Institute of Archaeology storeroom. Fr. of lower body with tiny part of base. H 5.8 × W 6.8, WT 0.25–0.35. Fabric: standard, fine, 2.5YR 6/8. Thin mottled coat with dull lustre ext., ext. 2.5YR 4/8, 10YR 3/1, int. 2.5YR 4/8. Relatively hard fired, oxidized. Stacked in firing. Main decoration: widely spaced pendent semicircles in field of relatively crude dots; eight-rayed sun wheel at center and as space filler.

EPH-962*
Olbia, Sector JuzA, О-ЮзА-74-149, Parutine, Olbia National Preserve storeroom. Fr. of rim and body. H 5.9 × W 4.8, WT 0.4, RH 1.9. Fabric: standard, 2.5YR 6/8. Dull coat, mottled, ext. 2.5YR 2.5/1, 4/6, int. 2.5Y 3/1. Relatively hard fired, oxidized. Stacked in firing. Rim frieze: astragal. Main decoration: pendent semicircles outlined by dots; rosette 11 as space filler. Frieze separators: dots.

EPH-963*
Chersonesos, X-1953-406, St Petersburg, State Hermitage Museum. Two joining rim frs., two non-joining frs. of upper body. H 4.1, WT 0.2, ⌀ rim 12, 12%, RH 1.9. Fabric: standard, Gley 1 5/N. Dull coat, Gley 1 3/N. Reduced. Rim frieze: Ionian kyma. Main decoration: pendent semicircles outlined by widely spaced dots; five-rayed sun wheel at centre and 10-petalled rosette as space filler. Frieze separators: dots. Early.

EPH-964
Istros, His-B 504/V 19344, Bucharest, Institute of Archaeology storeroom. Body fr. H 4.6 × W 3.2, WT 0.41. Fabric: standard, fine, 5Y 5/1. Dull coat, ext. Gley 1 3/N, 5YR 4/1, int. Gley 1 3/N. Relatively hard fired, reduced. Rim frieze: box meander, cw. Main decoration: pendent semicircles; five-rayed sun wheel at center, rosette as space filler. Frieze separators: dots
– Domăneanțu 2000, 38 cat. 164, pl. 11 (attributed to Monogram PAR).

EPH-965*
Olbia, Sector NGS, О-НГС-87-200, Parutine, Olbia National Preserve storeroom. Fr. of rim and upper body. H 5.4 × W 5.5, WT 0.25, ⌀ rim 13, 11%, RH 1.8. Fabric: fine, micaceous, 5YR 6/8. Thin dull coat, ext. 7.5YR 3/2, 2.5/1, int. 2.5YR 4/8, 7.5YR 2.5/1. Medium hard fired, oxidized. Stacked in firing. Rim frieze: box meander, cw. Main decoration: pendent semicircles; five-rayed sun wheel at centre. Frieze separators: dots. One repair hole.

EPH-966
Olbia, Sector NGS, О-НГС-02-299, Parutine, Olbia National Preserve storeroom. Fr. of rim and upper body. H 4.5 × W 6.85, WT 0.3–0.5, ⌀ rim 13, RH 1.9. Fabric: fine, micaceous, a few minute lime particles, 5YR 5/6. Thin firm slightly lustrous coat, mottled ext., mostly dark ext. and at lip int., 5Y 2.5/1, 2.5YR 4/8. Medium hard fired, oxidized. Stacked in firing. Rim frieze: box meander, cw. Main decoration: pendent semicircles outlined by dots. Frieze separators: dots.

EPH-967
Olbia, Sector R25, O-P25-00-679, Parutine, Olbia National Preserve storeroom. Fr. of rim and upper body. H 4.1 × W 4, WT 0.25, RH 1.8. Fabric: relatively fine and micaceous, 5YR 6/6, 6/8. Thin firm coat with slight metallic lustre ext., int. duller, ext. 5YR 2.5/1, int. 5YR 4/4, 2.5/1. Medium hard fired, oxidized. Stacked in firing. Rim frieze: box meander, cw. Main decoration: pendent-semicircle pattern suggested by row of large dots below rim frieze. Frieze separators: dots.

EPH-968
Olbia, O-1909-975, present whereabouts unknown. Fr. of rim and body. Rim frieze: vertical S-spirals. Main decoration: pendent semicircles outlined by dots; rosette 2/6 as space filler.
– St Petersburg, IIMK RAN, archive inv. 4057.519.5 (pl. XII).

EPH-969*
Olbia, Sector NGS, O-НГС-02-114, 482, 650, 833, Parutine, Olbia National Preserve storeroom. Two large joining frs. of rim and body, three non-joining frs. of rim and body probably from the same vessel. H 3.9 × W 5.3, WT 0.25–0.35, ⌀ rim 13, RH 1.9. Fabric: relatively fine and micaceous, small lime particles, a few small voids, 5YR 5/6, 10YR 6/4. Thin firm slightly lustrous coat, mottled ext., mostly dark, ext. 5Y 2.5/1, 5YR 4/6, int. 2.5YR 4/8. Medium hard fired, oxidized. Stacked in firing. Rim frieze: guilloche right. Main decoration: pendent semicircles outlined by dots; five-rayed sun wheel at center, rosette 11 and 9/8 as space fillers. Frieze separators: dots.
– Guldager Bilde 2010, 280 cat. F-45, pl. 176.

EPH-970*
Olbia, V.I. 7754.59, 60 (Becker), Antikensammlung, Staatliche Museen zu Berlin. Two non-joining frs. of lower body and base. H 6.5 × W 7.5, WT 0.5. Fabric: standard, 5YR 5/6. Coat with metallic lustre ext., ext. 10YR 2/1, int. 7.5YR 4/2. Oxidized. Main decoration: pendent semicircles; five-rayed sun wheel at center, rosette 9/8 and rosette 11 as space fillers. Medallion: three concentric circles.

EPH-971*
Olbia, Sector E7, square 537n, yellow clay layer, O-E7-60-350+350[d], 350[b], Kiev, Institute of Archaeology storeroom. Two joining frs. of rim and body; one non-joining body fr. H 5.5 × W 12, WT 0.45, ⌀ rim 12, 37%, RH 1.4. Fabric: standard, 10YR 7/4. Dull coat, Gley 1 3/N. Relatively hard fired, oxidized. Rim frieze: rosette 2/7. Main decoration: pendent semicircles within tightly-packed field of dots; six-rayed sun wheel at centre of semicircle. Two repair holes.

EPH-972*
Olbia, Sector NGS, O-НГС-02-238, Parutine, Olbia National Preserve storeroom. Fr. of base and lower body. H 5.9 × W 3.1, WT 0.27–0.7, ⌀ base 4.5. Fabric: relatively fine and micaceous, many minute lime particles, 10YR 6/4. Thin firm slightly lustrous coat, very pitted inside, 10YR 2/1. Medium hard fired, oxidized. Main decoration: pendent semicircles outlined by dots. Medallion: field of dots within three concentric circles.

EPH-973*
Olbia, Sector R25, O-P25-95-1166, Parutine, Olbia National Preserve storeroom. Fr. of upper body. H 3.3 × W 4, WT 0.45. Fabric: relatively fine and micaceous, small lime inclusions, 5YR 6/6. Dull coat, ext. 2.5YR 4/6, 3/1, int. 2.5YR 4/4. Medium hard fired, oxidized. Stacked in firing. Rim frieze: guilloche right. Main decoration: pendent semicircles outlined by dots; four-rayed sun wheel made of crossed S's at center.

EPH-974
Istros, Sector X, His-50-87 [His-950], Bucharest, Institute of Archaeology storeroom. Two joining body frs. H 2.3 × W 5.1, WT 0.3. Fabric: standard, 5YR 6/8. Dull coat, ext. 10YR 3/1, int. 7.5YR 4/2. Relatively hard fired, oxidized. Main decoration: pendent semicircles; rosette 10/6 at center.
– Domăneanțu 2000, 106 cat. 536, pl. 35.

EPH-975*
Olbia, O-52-1230, Kiev, Institute of Archaeology storeroom. Fr. of rim and upper body. Oxidized. Rim frieze: Lesbian kyma. Main decoration: pendent-semicircle pattern (only dots preserved).

EPH-976
Myrmekion, M-57-63, St Petersburg IIMK RAN. Fr. of mid-body. H 3.4, WT 0.2. Fabric: fine, slightly micaceous, 2.5YR 6/6. Lustrous coat, Gley 1 2.5/N. Hard fired, oxidized. Main decoration: pendent semicircles with five-rayed sun wheel at centre.

EPH-977*
Olbia, Sector Sever-Zapad, O-C3-68-1902, Parutine, Olbia National Preserve storeroom. Fr. of lower body. H 2.6 × W 4.7, WT 0.3. Fabric: standard, 2.5YR 6/8. Thin coat with dull lustre, 2.5YR 4/6. Relatively hard fired, oxidized. Main decoration: pendent semicircles outlined by dots; six-rayed sun wheel at centre.

EPH-978
Olbia, Sector R25, O-P25-93-179, Parutine, Olbia National Preserve storeroom. Fr. of upper body. H 4.2 × W 2.2, WT 0.4. Fabric: relatively fine, micaceous, 5YR 6/8. Slightly lustrous coat, mottled ext., ext. 2.5YR 5/6, 3/2, int. 2.5YR 4/6. Medium hard fired, oxidized. Stacked in firing. Main decoration: pendent semicircles outlined by dots; five-rayed sun wheel at centre.

EPH-979
Chersonesos, X-1965-86, St Petersburg, State Hermitage Museum. Fr. of lower body close to base. H 2.3, WT 0.2. Fabric: no fresh break for observation. Lustrous coat, Gley 1 2.5/N. Oxidized. Main decoration: pendent semicircles outlined by dots; rosette 9/8 as space filler.

EPH-980
Tyritake, no. unknown, Kerč History and Culture Reserve. Fr. of lower body. Oxidized. Main decoration: pendent semicircles surrounded by dots, with rosette as space filler.
– Grzegrzółka 2010, 117–118 cat. 154 (attributed to Asia Minor).

EPH-981*
Myrmekion, M-47-88, St Petersburg IIMK RAN. Fr. of lower body. H 3.7, WT 0.4. Fabric: standard, slightly porous, 5YR 5/6. Slightly lustrous coat, 5YR 3/4. Oxidized. Main decoration: pendent semicircles in field of dots. Calyx: saluting Pans flank straight acanthus leaf with segmented central vein. Pans same height as those on EPH-1303*.

Net Pattern

EPH-982
Kepoi, Kurgan 14, funerary meal, no. unknown, Moscow, State Historical Museum. Complete. Rim frieze: Ionian kyma. Medallion: rosette A. var. 4 (alternating rounded and pointed petals).
– Usačeva 1978, fig. 2.5.

EPH-983
Pantikapaion, M-64-741, Moscow, Puškin Museum of Fine Art. Fr. of rim and body. Rim frieze: Ionian kyma.
– Zabelina 1984, 156 fig. 3a; AGSP 1984, pl. CLXIV.15 (erroneously drawn as a complete vessel).

EPH-984
Olbia, V.I. 7754.62, Antikensammlung, Staatliche Museen zu Berlin (Becker). Fr. of rim and upper body. H 4 × W 5.5, WT 0.5, ⌀ rim 12, RH 1.5. Fabric: standard with some large grey stones, 5YR 4/6. Coat with dull lustre, 2.5YR 4/4. Oxidized. Rim frieze: Ionian kyma.

EPH-985*
Olbia, Sector E6, cleaning of room with north-west cistern, O-E6-60-1154, Kiev, Institute of Archaeology storeroom. Fr. of rim and upper body. H 4 × W 11, WT 0.35, ⌀ rim 13, 30%, RH 1.6. Fabric: standard, 2.5YR 6/8. Dull coat, worn, int. flaking, ext. 2.5YR 4/6, 4/4, 3/1, int. 2.5YR 4/6. Hard fired, oxidized. Stacked in firing. Rim frieze: Ionian kyma

EPH-986
Pantikapaion, П-1902-143, St Petersburg, State Hermitage Museum. Complete. H 6.7, ⌀ rim 13.3. Oxidized. Rim frieze: Lesbian kyma. Medallion: rosette B. Frieze separators: dots.

EPH-987
Olbia, Sector NGS, O-НГС-05-379, Parutine, Olbia National Preserve storeroom. Fr. of rim and upper body. H 5 × W 5.7, WT 0.35, ⌀ rim 12, 12%, RH 1.4. Fabric: relatively fine and micaceous, 2.5YR 6/8. Dull coat, mottled at rim ext., ext. 2.5YR 5/8, 7.5YR 4/4, int. 2.5YR 5/8. Medium hard fired, oxidized. Stacked in firing. Rim frieze: guilloche right. One repair hole.

EPH-988*
Olbia, Sector NGS, O-НГС-06-230(?), Parutine, Olbia National Preserve storeroom. Fr. of rim and upper body. H 3.8 × W 5.7, WT 0.25, ⌀ rim 14, 12%, RH 1.4. Fabric: relatively fine and micaceous, some small lime inclusions, 5Y 5/1. Dull coat, 5Y 3/1. Medium hard fired, reduced. Rim frieze: guilloche right

EPH-989*
Pantikapaion, palace foundation trench, M-85-45[c], 56[a] Moscow, Puškin Museum of Fine Arts. Two non-joining frs. of rim and upper body. H 4 × W 5.8, WT 0.2, ⌀ rim 11, 13%, RH 1.8. Reduced. Rim frieze: guilloche left. Secondarily burnt.

EPH-990*
Istros, UI 1913, His-V 7527 A, Bucharest, Institute of Archaeology storeroom. Fr. of rim and upper body. H 3.4 × W 4.7, WT 0.25, RH 1.1. Fabric: standard, 5YR 6/6. Slightly lustrous coat, pitted inside, 10YR 3/1. Relatively hard fired, oxidized. Rim frieze: guilloche left. Frieze separators: dots.
– Domăneanțu 2000, 49 cat. 225, pl. 14 (attributed to Petite rose spiralée).

EPH-991*
Istros, His-62+521/V 19411+His-393, Bucharest, Institute of Archaeology storeroom. Two rim frs. and a body fr., all joining; two non-joining body frs. H 5.4 × W 9.8, WT 0.25, ⌀ rim 11.5, 15%, RH 1.9. Fabric: standard, fine, 7.5YR 7/6. Dull coat, worn, 10YR 3/1. Relatively hard fired, oxidized. Rim frieze: miniature acanthus scroll right. Menemachos.
– Domăneanțu 2000, 11 cat. 45, pl. 3 (attributed to NI).*

EPH-992
Istros, His-1133, Bucharest, Institute of Archaeology storeroom. Fr. of rim and upper body. Oxidized. Rim frieze: miniature acanthus-flower scroll left. Monogram PAR.
– Domăneanțu 2000, 38 cat. 161, pl. 11 (attributed to Monogram PAR).

EPH-993*
Istros, His-B 489, Bucharest, Institute of Archaeology storeroom. Fr. of rim and upper body. H 4.9 × W 3.7, WT 0.45, RH 2.2. Fabric: medium fine and micaceous, many small voids, 2.5YR 6/6. Dull coat, ext. 5YR 5/6, 10YR 3/1, int. 10YR 3/1. Medium hard fired, oxidized. Stacked in firing. Rim frieze: oblique boxes.
– Domăneanțu 2000, 19 cat. 73, pl. 5 (attributed to Comique à la canne).

EPH-994*
Olbia, Sector NGS, House VI-3 Stove 561/308, O-НГС-93-841+ 98-254+512 (join across years), Parutine, Olbia National Preserve storeroom. Two joining rim frs. and one body fr. H 5.3 ×

W 12.5, WT 0.28–0.6, ⌀ rim 15, RH 2.8. Fabric: fine, relatively soft, highly micaceous, a few lime particles, some long voids, 10YR 4/1. Thin slightly lustrous coat ext, int. partly worn off, ext. 2.5Y 3/0–3/2, int. 10YR 3/1. Medium hard fired, reduced. Rim frieze: concentric boxes.
– Guldager Bilde 2010, 284 cat. F-88, pl. 186.

EPH-995*
Pantikapaion, palace foundation trench, M-84-32+illegible no., Moscow, Puškin Museum of Fine Arts. Two joining frs. of rim and upper body. H 5.5 × W 5.5, WT 0.5, ⌀ rim 10, 12%, RH 1.6. Reduced. Rim frieze: rosette 1. Main decoration: skeleton walking left inside pentagon of net pattern. Secondarily burnt.
– Košelenko 1992, fig. 23.

EPH-996*
Istros, His-V 19436, Bucharest, Institute of Archaeology storeroom. Body fr. H 4.1 × W 4.2, WT 0.3. Fabric: standard, fine, 5YR 7/6. Dull flaking coat, ext. 5YR 4/4, int. 5YR 5/3. Medium hard fired, oxidized. Rim frieze: Lesbian kyma. Main decoration: rosettes with eight broad petals below rim, within and overlapping net pattern. Menemachos?
– Domăneanțu 2000, 140 cat. 699, pl. 51.

EPH-997*
Istros, His-1927-1942-V 8571 P, Bucharest Institute of Archaeology storeroom. Fr. of base and lower body. H 2.8 × W 3. Reduced. Main decoration: rosette 2 inside pentagon of net pattern. Plain concave base.
– Domăneanțu 2000, 11 cat. 44, pl. 3 (attributed to N1).

EPH-998*
Pantikapaion, palace foundation trench, M-89-illegible 9, Moscow, Puškin Museum of Fine Arts. Fr. of base and lower body. H 4.2 × W 6.2, WT 0.35, ⌀ base 4.5. Dull reddish brown coat. Oxidized. Main decoration: vessel (krater?) in pentagon of net pattern. Plain concave base.

EPH-999
Pantikapaion, M-47-3672, Moscow, Puškin Museum of Fine Arts. Three joining frs. of base and lower body. Main decoration: concentric rhomboids in pentagon of net pattern. Medallion: rosette A.
– Zabelina 1984, 158 fig. 5c.

EPH-1000*
Olbia, Cliff, grey clay layer, O-68-1928, Kiev, Institute of Archaeology storeroom. Body fr. Reduced. Main decoration: net pattern made of dots, unidentified motif in pentagon (dolphin? frog?).

EPH-1001
Istros, Sector "Pescărie", His-63-3, Bucharest, Institute of Archaeology storeroom. Body fr. H 4 × W 6. Oxidized. Main decoration: net pattern made of dots.
– Domăneanțu 2000, 105 cat. 534, pl. 35.

EPH-1002*
Pantikapaion, palace foundation trench, M-89-no no. 9, Moscow, Puškin Museum of Fine Arts. Base fr. H 4.8 × W 5.1, WT 0.15, ⌀ base 3.5. Dull red coat. Hard fired, oxidized. Plain slightly concave base.

EPH-1003
Istros, His-B 581, Bucharest, Institute of Archaeology storeroom. Fr. of base and lower body. H 2.9 × W 3.1, WT 0.22, ⌀ base 3. Fabric: standard, 5YR 6/8. Dull coat, 5YR 4/3. Relatively hard fired, oxidized. Base surrounded by low ridge.
– Domăneanțu 2000, 105 cat. 533, pl. 35.

EPH-1004*
Bol'šoj Kastel', БК-84-no no.[b], Černomorskoe Museum of Historical Lore. Base with low ring foot. H 3.4, ⌀ base 4.5. Fabric: hard, sandy, some light-reflecting particles, 10YR 4/2. Dull coat, 5YR 4/4. Oxidized. Plain concave base with false ring foot.

EPH-1005*
Olbia, Sector E6, square 476s, 477se, yellow clay layer with ash inclusions, O-E6-59-1418, Kiev, Institute of Archaeology storeroom. Two joining frs. of base and lower body. H 6.5 × W 7.5, WT 0.3, ⌀ base 3. Fabric: standard, 2.5YR 5/8. Lustrous coat, mottled ext., ext. 2.5YR 4/6, 3/1, int. 2.5YR 3/2. Relatively hard fired, oxidized. Medallion: rosette A.

EPH-1006*
Myrmekion, M-58-31+171[a], St Petersburg IIMK RAN. Two joining base frs. H 6.3, WT 0.4, ⌀ base 4. Fabric: standard, 2.5YR 5/8. Thin coat with slight lustre, 2.5YR 4/8. Oxidized. Medallion: rosette B.

EPH-1007* (see also Fig. 79)
Olbia, Sector AGD, Bothros 11, О-АГД-88-196, Kiev, Institute of Archaeology storeroom. Joining frs. of base and lower body; non-joining body fr. H 5.3 × W 6.3, WT 0.2–0.26, ⌀ base 3. Fabric: standard, fine, 5YR 5/8. Thin dull coat, 2.5YR 5/6. Relatively hard fired, oxidized. Medallion: rosette C.
– Rusjaeva & Nazarčuk 2006, pl. 193.20.

EPH-1008*
Olbia, Sector R25, O-P25-98-485, Parutine, Olbia National Preserve storeroom. Fr. of base and lower body. H 4.1 × W 3,

WT 0.35, ⌀ base 4. Fabric: relatively fine and micaceous, small lime inclusions, 5YR 6/6. Thin dull coat, 5YR 6/6. Medium hard fired, oxidized. Main decoration: net pattern made of dots. Medallion: rosette D.

EPH-1009*
Bol'šoj Kastel', БК-86-74[a], Černomorskoe Museum of Historical Lore. Lower body fr. H 2.3. Fabric: highly micaceous, 7.5YR 6/4. Dull flaking coat, ext. 5YR 5/6, int. 2.5YR 4/6. Oxidized.

Plastic Long Petals

EPH-1010*
Myrmekion, M-57-2071, St Petersburg IIMK RAN. Fr. of rim and upper body. H 4.7, WT 0.35, ⌀ rim 13, RH 1.5. Fabric: standard, 2.5YR 5/8. Thin dull coat with slight metallic sheen where blackened, 2.5YR 4/6, 10R 2.5/1. Oxidized. Stacked in firing. Multiple rim friezes: Ionian kyma; broad astragal.

EPH-1011*
Olbia, Sector Sever-Zapad, O-C3-77-44, Parutine, Olbia National Preserve storeroom. Three rim frs. and a body fr., all joining. H 7 × W 12, WT 0.25–0.4, ⌀ rim 13.5, 25%, RH 2.1. Fabric: standard, fine, 7.5 6/6. Thin dull mottled coat, partially worn off, 2.5YR 4/6, 5YR3/1. Relatively hard fired, oxidized. Stacked in firing. Multiple rim friezes: vertical S-spirals; vertical S-spirals in alternating orientations. Main decoration: slightly plastic long petals.

EPH-1012*
Istros, His-988+V 19367 A, Bucharest, Institute of Archaeology storeroom. Two joining frs. of rim and upper body. H 4.3 × W 6.8, WT 0.32, ⌀ rim 12, 10%, RH 1.5. Fabric: standard, fine, 5YR 6/8. Dull coat, ext. 2.5YR 4/6, 7.5YR 4/1, int. 2.5YR 5/6. Relatively hard fired, oxidized. Stacked in firing. Multiple rim friezes: large dots; Ionian kyma.
– Domăneanțu 2000, 38 cat. 160, pl. 11 (attributed to Monogram PAR).

EPH-1013*
Olbia, Sector E6, square 405, grey clay layer, O-E6-56-260, 260[a–d], Kiev, Institute of Archaeology storeroom. Complete profile; frs. of base and lower body, rim fr., and two non-joining body frs. WT 0.35, ⌀ rim 14, 20%, RH 1.8, ⌀ base 3.3. Fabric: standard, 2.5YR 6/8. Dull mottled coat, ext. 2.5YR 4/4, 3/1, int. 2.5YR 5/6. Relatively hard fired, oxidized. Stacked in firing. Multiple rim friezes: large dots; star rosettes. Medallion: rosette B.

EPH-1014
Istros, His-B 574/V 19366, Bucharest, Institute of Archaeology storeroom. Fr. of lower body. Oxidized. Rim frieze: astragal.
– Domăneanțu 2000, 72 cat. 337, pl. 22 (attributed to Heraios).

EPH-1015*
Olbia, O-39-421, Kiev, Institute of Archaeology storeroom. Fr. of rim and upper body. Oxidized. Stacked in firing. Rim frieze: box meander, cw. One repair hole.

EPH-1016*
Olbia, Sector E6, square 405, grey clay layer, O-6-56-261, 118[a], Kiev, Institute of Archaeology storeroom. Two joining frs. of rim and body. Reduced. Rim frieze: star rosettes.

EPH-1017*
Myrmekion, M-58-404, St Petersburg IIMK RAN. Fr. of rim and upper body. H 3.8, WT 0.45, RH 2.2. Fabric: standard, 10YR 5/2. Thin dull coat, ext. 10YR 3/1, int. 10YR 5/3. Reduced. Stacked in firing. Rim frieze: rosette 5.

EPH-1018*
Istros, His-939, Bucharest, Institute of Archaeology storeroom. Body fr. close to rim. Oxidized. No rim frieze.

EPH-1019
Istros, UI 1913, His-V 7527 B, Bucharest, Institute of Archaeology storeroom. Fr. lower body and tiny part of base. Reduced. Base surrounded by low ridge.

EPH-1020*
Istros, His-165[a], Bucharest, Institute of Archaeology storeroom. Fr. of base and lower body. Reduced. Plain concave base.

EPH-1021*
Myrmekion, M-57-343. St Petersburg IIMK RAN. Fr. of base and lower body. H 3.3, WT 0.4, ⌀ base 3. Fabric: sandy, non-micaceous, 7.5YR 6/4. Dull coat ext., with slight metallic sheen int., ext. 2.5YR 5/4, 2.5/1, int. 10YR 3/1. Oxidized. Stacked in firing. Medallion: rosette A.

EPH-1022
Porthmion, П-75-90, Kerč History and Culture Reserve. Fr. of base and lower body. Oxidized. Medallion: rosette B.
– Grzegrzółka 2010, 157 cat. 239 (attributed to Asia Minor).

EPH-1023*
Istros, His-V 19364 D, Bucharest, Institute of Archaeology storeroom. Fr. of base and lower body. H 2.9 × W 2.9, WT 0.25, ⌀ base 3. Fabric: standard, 5YR 6/6. Dull coat, 2.5YR 5/6. Relatively hard fired, oxidized. Main decoration: plastic long petals combined with unidentified leaf bases. Medallion: rosette D.
– Domăneanțu 2000, 19 cat. 72, pl. 5 (attributed to Comique à la canne).

Plastic Long Petals with Three-Dot Spacers

EPH-1024*
Istros, His-959, Bucharest, Institute of Archaeology storeroom. Body fr. H 3.2 × W 3. Oxidized. Multiple rim friezes: rosette 2; horizontal S-spirals.
– Domăneanțu 2000, 7 cat. 24, pl. 2 (attributed to Menemachos).

EPH-1025*
Myrmekion, M-56-9[a], St Petersburg IIMK RAN. Fr. of rim and upper body. H 4.5, WT 0.3, ⌀ rim 13, RH 1.6. Fabric: standard, 2.5YR 6/6, 6/8. Thin dull coat with slight metallic sheen where blackened, 2.5YR 3/1, 3/3. Oxidized. Stacked in firing. Rim frieze: box meander, cw.

EPH-1026*
Olbia, Sector NGS, O-НГС-06-427, 248, Parutine, Olbia National Preserve storeroom. Fr. of rim and large part of bowl and one non-joining body fr. H 7.1 × W 6.1, WT 0.2, ⌀ rim 12, 7%, RH 1.3. Fabric: relatively fine and micaceous, 10YR 6/4. Thin coat with slight metallic sheen, 10YR 4/1. Medium hard fired, oxidized. Rim frieze: Lesbian kyma.

EPH-1027*
Olbia, Sector NGCentre, grey clay layer, O-НГЦ-68-646, Kiev, Institute of Archaeology storeroom. Body fr. Oxidized. Rim frieze: rosette 2/7. One repair hole.

Plastic Long Petals Separated by Columns of Dots

EPH-1028*
Olbia, Sector NGS, O-НГС-88-256, Parutine, Olbia National Preserve storeroom. Fr. of rim and body. H 6.1 × W 5.8, WT 0.3, RH 1.1. Fabric: relatively fine and micaceous, 5YR 7/6. Thin dull coat, ext. 2.5YR 4/4, 2.5/1, int. 2.5YR 4/4. Hard fired, oxidized. Stacked in firing. Rim frieze: guilloche left.

EPH-1029*
Istros, His-B 517 A, Bucharest, Institute of Archaeology storeroom. Fr. of rim and upper body. H 3.5 × W 3.1, WT 0.2, RH 1.5. Fabric: standard, 2.5Y 5/1. Dull coat, 2.5Y 3/1. Relatively hard fired, reduced. Rim frieze: crossed dotted lines.
– Domăneanțu 2000, 34 cat. 140, pl. 9 (attributed to Monogram PAR).

EPH-1030
Istros, His-1077, Bucharest, Institute of Archaeology storeroom. Fr. of upper body close to rim. Reduced. Rim frieze: crossed dotted lines.
– Domăneanțu 2000, 34 cat. 139, pl. 9 (attributed to Monogram PAR).

EPH-1031*
Myrmekion, M-52-205, 53–54, St Petersburg IIMK RAN. Two non-joining frs. of rim and upper body. H 4.84, WT 0.5, ⌀ rim 12, 12%, RH 1.9. Fabric: medium fine, abrasive, much mica, small grey and white inclusions, 5YR 5/6. Thin dull coat almost completely worn off, ext. 2.5YR 4/8, 5YR 3/1, int. 2.5YR 5/8. Oxidized. Stacked in firing. Rim frieze: eyed chevron. Late.

EPH-1032*
Myrmekion, M-56-9[b], St Petersburg IIMK RAN. Fr. of rim and upper body. H 4.3, WT 0.22, ⌀ rim 12, 9%, RH 1.4. Fabric: standard, 5YR 6/6. Thin slightly lustrous coat, ext. 7.5YR 3/1, int. 7.5YR 3/2. Oxidized. No rim frieze.

EPH-1033*
Myrmekion, M-47-97 St Petersburg IIMK RAN. Fr. of rim and upper body. H 5.3, WT 0.3, ⌀ rim 12.5, 17%, RH 1.1. Fabric: standard, 2.5YR 5/8. Thin dull coat with slight metallic sheen where blackened, 2.5YR 4/6, 10R 2.5/1. Oxidized. Stacked in firing. Rim frieze: box meander, cw. Main decoration: dots surround long petals. Frieze separators: dots

EPH-1034*
Myrmekion, M-58-811, St Petersburg IIMK RAN. Fr. of rim and upper body. H 5.3, WT 0.2, RH 2.3. Fabric: standard, 7.5YR 6/6. Coat with slight metallic sheen, 7.5YR 3/1. Oxidized. Stacked in firing. Rim frieze: large dots. Main decoration: dots surround long petals, with rosette 2/7 as space filler.

EPH-1035*
Olbia, Sector L, square 13sw, 14ne, cleaning of clay rammed area with ash spots, O-Л-55-247, Kiev, Institute of Archaeology storeroom. Body fr. Oxidized. Rim frieze: rosette 5 or 6. Dots surround long petals.

EPH-1036*
Olbia, Cliff, O-68-1285, Kiev, Institute of Archaeology storeroom. Body fr. H 4.7 × W 4.6, WT 0.32. Fabric: standard, Gley 1 6/N. Coat with dull lustre, Gley 1 4/N. Relatively hard fired, reduced. Rim frieze: box meander, cw. Main decoration: plastic long petals separated by dots topped by funnel-shaped flower. The same flower on **EPH-298**, **EPH-690***.

EPH-1037*
Istros, His-110, Bucharest, Institute of Archaeology storeroom. Fr. of base and lower body. H 2.6 × W 3.8, WT 0.4, ⌀ base 4. Fabric: standard, 5Y 7/1. Dull coat, Gley 1 4/N. Relatively hard fired,

reduced. Plain concave base; undecorated, signed [.]ENAI (retrograde), incised in vessel before firing. Athenaios.
– Domăneanțu 2000, 54 cat. 246, pl. 16 (attributed to Athenaios).

EPH-1038*
Istros, His-139, Bucharest, Institute of Archaeology storeroom. Fr. of base and lower body. H 3.4 × W 3.6, WT 0.45, ⌀ base 4. Fabric: standard, 5Y 6/1. Thin coat of the same clay as main fabric. 5Y 6/1. Medium hard fired, reduced. Plain concave base, signed PE (lig.) incised in mould before firing. Cf. Laumonier 1977, 407, 409, nos. 291–292, pl. 95.
– Domăneanțu 2000, 89 cat. 426, pl. 29.

EPH-1039
Myrmekion, M-56-1298 or 1228, St Petersburg IIMK RAN. Fr. of base and lower body. H 2.5, WT 0.3. Fabric: standard, 2.5YR 5/8. Thin dull coat, 2.5YR 4/6. Oxidized. Stacked in firing. Plain concave base with false ring foot.

EPH-1040
Porthmion, room 50, SE corner, depth 1.45 m, П-75-446, Kerč History and Culture Reserve. Four non-joining frs. of base and lower body. Reduced. Plain concave base.
– Grzegrzółka 2010, 162–163 cat. 251.

Plastic Long Petals with Other Spacing Devices

EPH-1041*
Bol'šoj Kastel', БК-87-33, Černomorskoe Museum of Historical Lore. Body fr. H 1.9. Fabric: 5YR 5/6. Dull coat, 2.5YR 5/4. Oxidized. Main decoration: plastic long petals alternating with floral element (stem not preserved).

EPH-1042*
Olbia, Sector R25, O-P25-98-2808+00-979 (join across years), Parutine, Olbia National Preserve storeroom. Two joining frs. of mid- and lower body. H 5.4 × W 6.6, WT 0.31–0.38. Fabric: relatively fine and micaceous, small lime inclusions, 5YR 6/6. Dull coat, 2.5YR 5/6. Medium hard fired, oxidized. Main decoration: long petals in slight relief separated by vertical lines of circles topped by lotus bud.

EPH-1043*
Olbia, Sector E7, square 578n, 579nw, yellow clay layer, O-E7-59-1665, 1666, 1666[a], Kiev, Institute of Archaeology storeroom. Two joining frs. of rim and body; two non-joining frs. of base and body. H 4.8 × W 10.3, WT 0.16, ⌀ rim 12, 22%, RH 1.8; vessel H 6.9; H:⌀ 1:1.7. Fabric: standard, 10YR 6/1. Thin dull coat, not completely covering surface, ext. Gley 1 3/N, int. 10YR 4/1. Relatively hard fired, reduced. Rim frieze: astragal. Main decoration: plastic long petals separated by floral element, upside-down. Medallion: rosette with broad, lobed petals. Same floral element occurs as rim motif on EPH-1332*.

EPH-1044*
Olbia, Sector NGS, O-НГС-02-419, Parutine, Olbia National Preserve storeroom. Fr. of base and lower body, worn underneath. H 4.7 × W 5.2, WT 0.35–0.62, ⌀ base 4.5. Fabric: relatively fine and micaceous, some small lime particles, up to very large voids, 7.5YR. Thin firm slightly lustrous coat, slightly mottled, 2.5YR 4/6, 10YR 2/1. Medium hard fired, oxidized. Stacked in firing. Main decoration: plastic long petals alternating with tall fern. Medallion: rosette E.

Stylized Long Petals

EPH-1045*
Istros, His-518, Bucharest, Institute of Archaeology storeroom. Body fr. H 4 × W 4.2, WT 0.38. Fabric: standard, 5YR 6/8. Dull coat, ext. 5YR 4/1, 4/2, int. 2.5YR 4/6. Relatively hard fired, oxidized. Multiple rim friezes: rosette 1; horizontal S-spirals.
– Domăneanțu 2000, 82 cat. 394, pl. 26.

EPH-1046*
Istros, His-V 19325, Bucharest, Institute of Archaeology storeroom. Body fr. H 2.5 × W 3, WT 0.3. Fabric: standard, fine, Gley 1 7/N. Dull coat, ext. Gley 1 3/N, int. Gley 1 4/N. Relatively hard fired, reduced. Multiple rim friezes: rosette 2/7; miniature acanthus-flower scroll left. Monogram PAR.
– Domăneanțu 2000, 33 cat. 135, pl. 9 (attributed to Monogram PAR).

EPH-1047*
Istros, His-523, Bucharest, Institute of Archaeology storeroom. Fr. of base and body. H 5 × W 4.1, WT 0.22, ⌀ base 4. Fabric: standard, 5YR 6/8. Dull coat, 2.5YR 5/6. Relatively hard fired, oxidized. Rim frieze: astragal. Base surrounded by low ridge.
– Domăneanțu 2000, 103 cat. 514, pl. 34.

EPH-1048*
Olbia, Sector R25, O-P25-97-1803, Parutine, Olbia National Preserve storeroom. Fr. of upper body. H 3 × W 2.4, WT 0.35. Fabric: relatively fine and micaceous, 5YR 6/8. Dull coat, 2.5YR 5/6. Medium hard fired, oxidized. Rim frieze: Ionian kyma. Early?

EPH-1049*
Olbia, Sector AGD, О-АГД-69-1255, Kiev, Institute of Archaeology storeroom. Two joining body frs. H 5.5 × W 7.8, WT 0.47. Fabric: standard with many small voids, 5YR 7/6. Dull coat,

mottled ext., ext. 5YR 5/6, 3/1, int. 5YR 3/1. Relatively hard fired, oxidized. Rim frieze: Ionian kyma, rather crude. Main decoration: relatively crude stylized long petals.

EPH-1050*
Olbia, Sector NGS, О-НГС-01-195, Parutine, Olbia National Preserve storeroom. Joining frs. of rim and body. Reduced. Rim frieze: vertical S-spirals.

EPH-1051*
Olbia, Sector NGS, О-НГС-05-909, Parutine, Olbia National Preserve storeroom. Fr. of rim and upper body. H 4.3 × W 5.6, WT 0.3, ⌀ rim 13, 11%, RH 1.4. Fabric: relatively fine and micaceous, Gley 1 6/N. Dull coat, Gley 1 2.5/1. Medium hard fired, reduced. Rim frieze: wave meander, upside-down.

EPH-1052*
Olbia, Sector R25, O-P25-04-3746+05-1203 (join across years), Parutine, Olbia National Preserve storeroom. Three joining body frs. H 5.8 × W 9.3, WT 0.3. Fabric: relatively fine and micaceous, small lime inclusions, 2.5YR 6/8. Dull wash, ext. 10R 5/6, int. 2.5YR 5/6. Medium hard fired, oxidized. Rim frieze: rosette 1. Early?

EPH-1053
Porthmion, Sector G, sector 2, fill in rooms, П-87-114, Kerč History and Culture Reserve. Fr. of rim and upper body. Rim frieze: rosette 5. Main decoration: stylized(?) long petals.

EPH-1054
Myrmekion, 1957-D 212. Large fr. of rim and body. Rim frieze: miniature acanthus scroll left. Menemachos.
– Bernhard 1959, 38–39 cat. 148; Sztetyłło 1976, fig. 81.c.

EPH-1055*
Istros, His-V 10313, Bucharest, Institute of Archaeology storeroom. Fr. of rim and upper body. Oxidized. Rim frieze: crossed dotted lines with box.
– Domăneanţu 2000, 35 cat. 143, pl. 10 (attributed to Monogram PAR).

EPH-1056
Porthmion, no. unknown, Kerč History and Culture Reserve. Fr. of rim and upper body. Oxidized. Rim frieze: crossed dotted lines. Menemachos.
– Grzegrzółka 2010, 159–160 cat. 245.

EPH-1057
Porthmion, П-73-32, Kerč History and Culture Reserve. Fr. of upper body. Oxidized. Rim frieze: crossed dotted lines. Menemachos.
– Grzegrzółka 2010, 160 cat. 246.

EPH-1058*
Istros, His-1927-1942-V 8572 R, Bucharest Institute of Archaeology storeroom. Rim fr. Oxidized. No rim frieze.
– Domăneanţu 2000, 103 cat. 515, pl. 34.

EPH-1059
Olbia, Sector E6–7, squares 598e, 608e, grey clay layer, O-E6-7-61-450, Kiev, Institute of Archaeology storeroom. Fr. of base and body. Oxidized. Plain flat base with slight ring foot.

EPH-1060*
Pantikapaion, palace foundation trench, M-89-illegible 10, Moscow, Puškin Museum of Fine Arts. Base fr. H 3.6 × W 5.5, WT 0.48, ⌀ base 3.3. Dull red coat. Oxidized. Main decoration: stylized long petals? Single row of pointed petals with central vein around base. Plain concave base.

EPH-1061*
Istros, His-V 19361[a]+V 19366, Bucharest, Institute of Archaeology storeroom. Two joining body frs. Oxidized. Main decoration: stylized long petals, with row of small palmettes at base of wall.
– Domăneanţu 2000, 141 cat. 706, pl. 51.

Stylized Long Petals Separated by Columns of Dots

EPH-1062*
Porthmion, square 11, depth 0.4 m, П-53-422+607, 479, Kerč History and Culture Reserve. Two joining frs. of rim and upper body; one non-joining body fr. H 4, WT 0.25, ⌀ rim 11.5, RH 1.8. Fabric: standard, 5YR 5/8. Thin dull coat, 2.5YR 5/6. Oxidized. Multiple rim friezes: star rosettes (blurred stamp); very large astragal.

EPH-1063*
Olbia, Sector NGS, О-НГС-99-497, Parutine, Olbia National Preserve storeroom. Fr. of rim and upper body. H 4.5 × W 3.9, WT 0.2–0.35, ⌀ rim 12.5, RH 1.5. Fabric: fine, a few small lime inclusions, 5Y 4/1. Thin firm coat with slight lustre, 7.5YR 3/0. Reduced. Multiple rim friezes: large dots; rosette 2/7. Frieze separators: dots.

EPH-1064*
Volna 1, C3-00-60, St Petersburg, State Hermitage Museum. Fr. of rim and upper body. Reduced. Rim frieze: box meander, cw.

EPH-1065
Olbia. Complete. ⌀ rim 12; vessel H 6.7; H:⌀ 1:1.8. Red coat, brown at rim; one side black. Oxidized. Multiple rim friezes:

Ionian kyma; astragal. Plain concave base, signed PHILONOS, incised in vessel before firing.
Philon(nios).
– Zahn 1908, 72 cat. 35; Boehlau 1908, 32 no. 287.

EPH-1066
Pantikapaion, inv.? [a], Odessa, Historical Museum. Complete. Vessel H 6. Oxidized. Stacked in firing. Rim frieze: Ionian kyma. Plain slightly concave base, signed PHILONOS, incised in vessel before firing. Philon(nios).

EPH-1067*
Istros, His-134, Bucharest, Institute of Archaeology storeroom. Fr. of base and lower body. H 3.1 × W 2.3, WT 0.35, ⌀ base 4. Fabric: standard, 2.5Y 7/1. Dull coat, 5Y 5/1. Relatively hard fired, reduced. Plain concave base, signed PH[…], incised in vessel before firing. Philon(nios).
– Domăneanțu 2000, 90 cat. 430, pl. 29.

EPH-1068*
Istros, His-137, Bucharest, Institute of Archaeology storeroom. Fr. of base and lower body. H 2.2 × W 2.8, WT 0.25. Fabric: standard, fine, 2.5Y 4/1. Coat with slight lustre, Gley 1 3/N. Relatively hard fired, reduced. Plain concave base, signed PH[…], incised in vessel before firing. Philon(nios).
– Domăneanțu 2000, 104 cat. 521, pl. 34.

EPH-1069
Olbia, O-1910-921, present whereabouts unknown. Fr. of base and lower body. Plain base, signed […]OS. Philon(nios).
– St Petersburg, IIMK RAN, archive inv. 4057.519.5 (pl. XII).

EPH-1070
Pantikapaion, 1903–16. Complete. Reduced. Multiple rim friezes: Ionian kyma; astragal. Plain, slightly concave base, signed NI, incised in mould. Ni(…).
– St Petersburg, IIMK RAN photo archive neg. III 9672.

EPH-1071*
Istros, His-1927-1942-V 8570 T, Bucharest, Institute of Archaeology storeroom. Fr. of base and lower body. H 3.6 × W 3.4, WT 0.55, ⌀ base 5. Fabric: standard, 5Y 7/1. Thin wash of the same clay as main fabric, 5Y 6/1. Medium hard fired, reduced. Plain, concave base, signed N[…], incised in mould. Ni(…).
– Domăneanțu 2000, 90 cat. 427, pl. 29.

EPH-1072
Olbia, Sector R25, O-P25-04-2811a, b, Parutine, Olbia National Preserve storeroom. Two non-joining frs. of base and lower body. H 4.1 × W 4.5, WT 0.25, ⌀ base 5. Fabric: fine, micaceous, many minute lime particles, 5Y 4/2. Dull coat, Gley 1 2.5/N. Hard fired, reduced. Plain slightly concave base, […]ON faintly incised on base.

EPH-1073*
Olbia, Sector R25, O-P25-05-1199+1210+1210a+b, Parutine, Olbia National Preserve storeroom. Complete profile, two rim frs., two base frs., and one body fr. joining two and two; complete profile. WT 0.23–0.4, ⌀ rim 12, 16%, RH 1.9, ⌀ base 5; vessel H 7; H:⌀ 1:1.7. Fabric: relatively fine and micaceous, many small lime inclusions, 5Y 3/1. Thin dull coat, Gley 1 2.5/N. Medium hard fired, reduced. Rim frieze: Ionian kyma with hatched tongue. Plain concave base.

EPH-1074
Istros, His-V 19487, Bucharest, Institute of Archaeology storeroom. Fr. of rim and upper body. H 4.2 × W 5.3, WT 0.25, ⌀ rim 12, 12%, RH 1.8. Fabric: standard, 5Y 5/1. Slightly lustrous coat, Gley 1 3/N. Relatively hard fired, reduced. Rim frieze: Ionian kyma.
– Domăneanțu 2000, 62 cat. 287, pl. 19.

EPH-1075
Tyritake, no. unknown, Kerč History and Culture Reserve. Fr. of rim and upper body. Reduced. Rim frieze: Ionian kyma.
– Grzegrzółka 2010, 113 cat. 144.

EPH-1076*
Myrmekion, M-53-485, St Petersburg IIMK RAN. Fr. of upper body. H 5.2, WT 0.3. Fabric: medium fine, gritty, much mica, small grey and white inclusions, 5YR 5/8. Thin dull coat almost completely worn off, ext. 2.5YR 4/8, 5YR 3/1, int. 2.5YR 5/8. Oxidized. Stacked in firing. Rim frieze: Lesbian kyma.

EPH-1077
Porthmion, П-76-71, Kerč History and Culture Reserve. Two non-joining frs. of rim and body. Reduced. Rim frieze: Lesbian kyma.
– Grzegrzółka 2010, 162 cat. 250.

EPH-1078*
Istros, His-610, Bucharest, Institute of Archaeology storeroom. Fr. of rim and upper body. H 3.6 × W 3.2, WT 0.35, RH 2.1. Fabric: standard, Gley 1 7/10Y. Dull coat, Gley 1 4/N. Relatively hard fired, reduced. Rim frieze: star rosettes.
– Domăneanțu 2000, 84 cat. 403, pl. 27.

EPH-1079
Porthmion, П-73-467, Kerč History and Culture Reserve. Fr. of rim and upper body. Oxidized. Rim frieze: rosette 5.
– Grzegrzółka 2010, 203 cat. 351.

EPH-1080*
Olbia, Sector NGS, O-НГС-08-146, Parutine, Olbia National Preserve storeroom. One third of bowl in joining fragments; complete profile. H 6.5 × W 10, WT 0.35, ⌀ rim 12, 22%, ⌀ base 5; vessel H 6.5; H:⌀ 1:1.9. Fabric: relatively fine and micaceous, 10YR 6/6. Thin dull coat, 10YR 3/1. Medium hard fired, oxidized. Rim frieze: miniature acanthus scroll right. Plain concave base with false ring foot. Menemachos.

EPH-1081*
Olbia, Sector NGS, O-НГС-08-46, Parutine, Olbia National Preserve storeroom. Fr. of rim and upper body. H 5 × W 6.1, WT 0.3, ⌀ rim 16, 9%, RH 1.9. Fabric: relatively fine and micaceous, some small lime inclusions, 5Y 5/1. Dull coat, Gley 1 3/1. Medium hard fired, reduced. Rim frieze: rosette 1/'paw'. Philon(nios).

EPH-1082
Pantikapaion, M-63-288, Moscow, Puškin Museum of Fine Art. Several joining frs. of rim and body and edge of base. Rim frieze: Ionian kyma with hatched tongue. Main decoration: stylized long petals, separated by dots with two dots at top.
– Zabelina 1984, 154 fig. 1a.

EPH-1083*
Myrmekion, M-57-382, St Petersburg IIMK RAN. Two joining frs. of rim and upper body. H 5, WT 0.3, ⌀ rim 14, 18%, RH 2.3. Fabric: standard, 10YR 6/1. Slightly lustrous coat, ext. 10YR 4/2, 2/1, int. 10YR 4/2. Reduced. Stacked in firing. Rim frieze: Ionian kyma with hatched tongue. Main decoration: stylized long petals, separated by dots with two dots at top.

EPH-1084*
Chersonesos, X-1965-70, St Petersburg, State Hermitage Museum. Fr. of upper body close to rim. H 3, WT 0.25. Fabric: no fresh break for observation. Dull coat, Gley 1 2.5/N. Reduced. Rim frieze: Ionian kyma. Main decoration: stylized long petals, separated by dots with two dots at top.

EPH-1085
Myrmekion, M-56-1355, St Petersburg IIMK RAN. Fr. of rim and upper body. H 3.7, WT 0.25 ⌀ rim 12, 12%, RH 1.8. Fabric: standard, slightly coarse, 2.5YR 5/8. Dull coat, 10R 5/6. Oxidized. Rim frieze: guilloche left. Main decoration: stylized long petals(?), separated by dots with two dots at top.

EPH-1086
Tyritake, no. unknown, Kerč History and Culture Reserve. Fr. of rim and upper body. Reduced. Rim frieze: wave meander. Main decoration: stylized long petals separated by three-dot group.
– Grzegrzółka 2010, 110 cat. 138.

EPH-1087
Porthmion, pavement outside western defensive wall near wicket, П-75-84, Kerč History and Culture Reserve. Fr. of mid-body. Rim frieze: rosette 5. Main decoration: stylized long petals, separated by widely spaced dots with two dots at top.

EPH-1088
Porthmion, П-75-83, Kerč History and Culture Reserve. Body fr. Reduced. Rim frieze: rosette 5. Main decoration: widely spaced stylized long petals, separated by column of widely spaced dots with two dots at top.
– Grzegrzółka 2010, 161–162 cat. 249.

EPH-1089
Porthmion, П-78-70, Kerč History and Culture Reserve. Fr. of rim and upper body. Reduced. Rim frieze: rosette 9. Main decoration: stylized long petals, separated by dots with two dots at top. Philon(nios).
– Grzegrzółka 2010, 158 cat. 241.

EPH-1090*
Istros, His-B 541/V 19354, Bucharest, Institute of Archaeology storeroom. Body fr. H 5 × W 5.2, WT 0.38. Fabric: standard, fine, 7.5YR 6/6. Dull coat, ext. 10YR 3/1, 5YR 3/3, int. 10YR 3/1. Medium hard fired, oxidized. Stacked in firing. Rim frieze: rosette. Main decoration: stylized long petals, separated by dots with two dots at top.
– Domăneanțu 2000, 104 cat. 527, pl. 34.

EPH-1091
Chersonesos, X-1965-77, St Petersburg, State Hermitage Museum. Fr. of upper body. H 1.6, WT 0.4. Fabric: standard, 5Y 4/1. Dull coat, Gley 1 2.5/N. Reduced. Main decoration: stylized long petals, separated by dots with two dots at top.

EPH-1092
Istros, His-A 316/V 19349, Bucharest, Institute of Archaeology storeroom. Fr. of base and lower body. H 3.4 × W 3.8, WT 0.3, ⌀ base 4. Fabric: standard, 5YR 6/8. Dull coat, 2.5YR 5/6. Relatively hard fired, oxidized. Plain concave base.
– Domăneanțu 2000, 104 cat. 524, pl. 34.

EPH-1093*
Olbia, Sector E6, square 249n, 420n, yellow clay layer over Wall 62, O-E6-57-218, Kiev, Institute of Archaeology storeroom. Fr. of base and lower body. H 3.2 × W 4.8, WT 0.2, ⌀ base 5. Fabric: standard, 5Y 6/1. Dull wash, ext. 10YR 5/1, int. 10YR 5/2. Relatively hard fired, reduced. Plain concave base.

EPH-1094
Pantikapaion, palace foundation trench, M-89-no no. 14, Moscow, Puškin Museum of Fine Arts. Base fr. Reduced. Plain concave base.
– Košelenko 1992, fig. 23.

EPH-1095
Chersonesos, X-1965-83, St Petersburg, State Hermitage Museum. Fr. of base and body. H 2.5, WT 0.34. Fabric: standard, fine, with much lime (no fresh break). Lustrous coat, Gley 1 2.5/N. Reduced. Plain concave base.

EPH-1096*
Chersonesos, X-1965-80, St Petersburg, State Hermitage Museum. Fr. of base and body. H 3.2, ⌀ base 2.8. Fabric: standard, 5Y 3/1. Dull coat, Gley 1 2.5/N. Reduced. Plain slightly concave base.

EPH-1097*
Olbia, Sector NGS, O-НГС-85-75, Parutine, Olbia National Preserve storeroom. Fr. of base and lower body. H 7 × W 7, WT 0.2, ⌀ base 4.4. Fabric: relatively fine and micaceous, a few minute lime particles, 2.5YR 6/8. Thin dull wash, ext. 2.5YR 3/1, int. 2.5YR 3/1, 4/6. Medium hard fired, oxidized. Medallion: plain slightly concave base with low ring foot.

EPH-1098
Olbia, Sector NGS, House III-2 R 52/73, O-НГС-86-549, Parutine, Olbia National Preserve storeroom. Fr. of base and lower body. H 4.4 × W 7.7, WT 0.2–0.45, ⌀ base 5. Fabric: fine, slightly micaceous, some relatively large lime inclusions and large stones, 0.15 cm, 5Y 5/1. Diluted, slightly lustrous coat, 5Y 4/1. Very hard fired, reduced. Plain concave base
– Guldager Bilde 2010, 284 cat. F-87, pl. 185.

EPH-1099
Olbia, O-1910-999, present whereabouts unknown. Fr. of base and lower body. Plain base?
– St Petersburg, IIMK RAN, archive inv. 4057.519.5 (pl. XII).

EPH-1100
Olbia, O-1910-824, present whereabouts unknown. Fr. of base and lower body. Plain base?
– St Petersburg, IIMK RAN, archive inv. 40...(?) (pl. XIII).

Stylized Long Petals Separated by Other Motifs

EPH-1101*
Istros, His-444 Bucharest, Institute of Archaeology storeroom. Fr. of upper body. Oxidized. Main decoration: stylized long petals separated by teardrops.
– Domăneanțu 2000, 19 cat. 71, pl. 5 (attributed to Comique à la canne).

EPH-1102*
Istros, His-891, Bucharest, Institute of Archaeology storeroom. Fr. of upper body. Reduced. Main decoration: stylized long petals separated by cabled line/stem.
– Domăneanțu 2000, 103 cat. 519, pl. 34.

EPH-1103*
Istros, His-B 577/V 19353, Bucharest, Institute of Archaeology storeroom. Fr. of upper body. H 3 × W 2.8, WT 0.35. Fabric: standard, 5Y 6/1. Dull coat, ext. 5Y 5/1, 3/1, int. 5Y 5/1. Relatively hard fired, oxidized. Stacked in firing. Main decoration: stylized long petals separated by column of small circles with bud at top.
– Domăneanțu 2000, 103 cat. 518, pl. 34.

EPH-1104
Istros, His-835, Bucharest, Institute of Archaeology storeroom. Fr. of base and lower body. Reduced. Main decoration: stylized long petals separated by small circles. Plain concave base.
– Domăneanțu 2000, 121 cat. 596, pl. 41 (idenfitied as Pontic).

EPH-1105*
Olbia, Cliff, "B-VIII", square 285, low terrace, O-70-223, Parutine, Olbia National Preserve storeroom. Fr. of rim and body. H 3.9 × W 5.3, WT 0.4, ⌀ rim 13, 10%, RH 1.2. Fabric: standard, with many small lime particles, 2.5YR 6/8. Thin dull coat, 2.5YR 5/6. Not too hard fired, oxidized. Rim frieze: rosette 5/8. Main decoration: broad stylized long petals outlined with dots alternating with floral element. Menemachos.

EPH-1106*
Istros, His-1043, Bucharest, Institute of Archaeology storeroom. Fr. of upper body. Reduced. Main decoration: stylized long petals with double outline, separated by dots.

EPH-1107*
Myrmekion, Sector И, courtyard VII M-49-720, St Petersburg IIMK RAN. Fr. of rim and body. H 5.5, WT 0.25, ⌀ rim 14, RH 1.75. Fabric: standard, 2.5YR 6/6. Thin coat with slight metallic lustre, ext. 2.5YR 4/2, int. 2.5YR 4/1. Oxidized. Rim frieze: crossed dotted lines alternating with rosette 2/7. Main decoration: two stylized long petals alternating with Menemachos bud on stem. Menemachos.

EPH-1108
Istros, His-931, Bucharest, Institute of Archaeology storeroom. Fr. of upper body. Oxidized. Main decoration: stylized long petal and unidentified motif.

EPH-1109*
Istros, His-V 19362, Bucharest, Institute of Archaeology storeroom. Two joining body frs. H 3.5 × W 4.7, WT 0.3. Fabric: standard, fine, 5Y 4/1. Dull coat, 5Y 3/1. Hard fired, reduced. Main decoration: stylized long petals with double outline and of alternating heights; a bud over the lower ones.
– Domăneanțu 2000, 103 cat. 517, pl. 34.

EPH-1110*
Istros, His-698, Bucharest, Institute of Archaeology storeroom. Fr. of upper body. Reduced. Main decoration: stylized long petals with double outline.
– Domăneanțu 2000, 57 cat. 263, pl. 17 (attributed to Doubles filets épais).

EPH-1111*
Olbia, Sector NGS, О-НГС-05-378, 382, 383, Parutine, Olbia National Preserve storeroom. Fr. of rim and large part of bowl and two non-joining body frs. H 6.4 × W 7.1, WT 0.3, ⌀ rim 12.5, 12%, RH 1.4. Fabric: relatively fine and micaceous, some small lime inclusions, 7.5YR 6/6. Thin dull coat, mottled, 5YR 4/6, 3/3. Medium hard fired, oxidized. Stacked in firing. Rim frieze: large dots. Main decoration: stylized long petals separated by wavy line.

EPH-1112*
Olbia, Sector R25, O-P25-04-no no.[18], Parutine, Olbia National Preserve storeroom. Fr. of upper body. Oxidized. Main decoration: stylized long petals with double outline separated by column of pointed petals with central vein.

EPH-1113*
Istros, His-609, Bucharest, Institute of Archaeology storeroom. Fr. of upper body. Oxidized. Rim frieze: rosette 2/7. Main decoration: stylized long petals separated by vertical S-spirals.

EPH-1114*
Olbia, Cliff, O-68-1277, Kiev, Institute of Archaeology storeroom. Body fr. Oxidized. Main decoration: rosette 9/11, with stylized long petals separated by dots below. Secondarily burnt.

Stylized Long Petals with Other Vegetal Motifs

EPH-1115*
Istros, His-B 573/V 19400, Bucharest, Institute of Archaeology storeroom. Fr. of base and lower body. Oxidized. Calyx: long petals with two rows of small pine-cone bosses between them? Or 'nelumbos' filled with pine-cone bosses? Menemachos.

EPH-1116
Pantikapaion, palace foundation trench M-89-illegible 27, 36, 37, 38, Moscow, Puškin Museum of Fine Arts. Four non-joining frs. of mid- and lower body. WT 0.3. Dull red coat. Oxidized. Main decoration: jewelled lotus petal alternating with stylized long petal. One fr. secondarily burnt. Menemachos.

EPH-1117
Porthmion, П-73-374+469, Kerč History and Culture Reserve. Two non-joining frs. of rim and body. Oxidized. Multiple rim friezes: Ionian kyma; large dots. Main decoration: three stylized long petals alternating with acanthus.
– Grzegrzółka 2010, 160–161 cat. 247.

EPH-1118
Pantikapaion, Mithridates Hill, Kerč History and Culture Reserve. Fr. of upper body. Oxidized. Main decoration: stylized long petals alternating with acanthus leaf with folded top.
Grzegrzółka 2010, 74 cat. 62.

Vertical Fluting

EPH-1119*
Istros, Sector MC1 Sa, His-56-52, 53, Bucharest, Institute of Archaeology storeroom. Two joining rim frs. and one non-joining rim fr. H 4.4 × W 9.8, WT 0.28, ⌀ rim 12, 22%, RH 1.9. Fabric: standard, 5YR 6/8. Dull coat, almost completely worn off, ext. 5YR 4/6, 3/1, int. 5YR 4/3. Not too hard fired, oxidized. Rim frieze: astragal. Menemachos.
– Domăneanțu 2000, 72 cat. 341, pl. 22 (attributed to Heraios).

EPH-1120*
Istros, His-B 507, Bucharest, Institute of Archaeology storeroom. Fr. of rim and upper body. H 4.5 × W 6.7, WT 0.3, ⌀ rim 12, 12%, RH 2.2. Fabric: standard, many small voids, 5Y 6/2. Dull coat, Gley 1 2.5/N. Relatively hard fired, reduced. Rim frieze: Ionian kyma. Menemachos.
– Domăneanțu 2000, 56 cat. 262, pl. 17.

EPH-1121
Porthmion, П-75-352, Kerč History and Culture Reserve. Fr. of rim and upper body. Oxidized. Rim frieze: large dots. Menemachos?
– Grzegrzółka 2010, 202–203 cat. 350.

G   Rim Fragments (Single Frieze)

Astragal

EPH-1122*
Bol'šoj Kastel', БК-84-no no.[a], Černomorskoe Museum of Historical Lore. Rim fr. H 3.8, ⌀ rim 13, RH 2.3. Fabric: 10YR 4/1. Slightly lustrous coat, Gley 1 2.5/N. Reduced.

EPH-1123
Istros, His-269, Bucharest, Institute of Archaeology storeroom. Rim fr. Oxidized.

EPH-1124*
Istros, His-133, Bucharest, Institute of Archaeology storeroom. Rim fr. Oxidized.

EPH-1125*
Istros, Sector MC1 Sa, His-56-956, Bucharest, Institute of Archaeology storeroom. Rim fr. Oxidized. Rim frieze: astragal with decorated beads.
– Domăneanţu 2000, 39 cat. 167, pl. 11.

Box Meander

EPH-1126
Olbia, Sector R25, O-P25-95-1117, Parutine, Olbia National Preserve storeroom. Rim fr. H 1.7 × W 7.2, WT 0.25, ⌀ rim 13, 20%, RH 2. Fabric: relatively fine and micaceous, small voids, 5YR 5/6. Thin firm coat with metallic lustre ext. and at rim int., ext. 5YR 3/1, int. 2.5YR 5/6, 5YR 3/1. Hard fired, oxidized. Stacked in firing. Rim frieze: meander ccw.

EPH-1127
Istros, His-44, Bucharest, Institute of Archaeology storeroom. Rim fr. H 3.2 × W 4.3, WT 0.45, RH 1.7. Fabric: standard, 5Y 4/1. Coat with dull lustre, Gley 1 3/N. Relatively hard fired, reduced. Frieze separators: dots.

EPH-1128*
Olbia, V.I. 7754.68+69, Antikensammlung, Staatliche Museen zu Berlin. Two joining rim frs. H 4.7, WT 0.4, ⌀ rim 12, RH 1.9. Fabric: standard, 7.5YR 5/6. Coat with slight lustre, 7.5YR 2.5/1. Oxidized. Rim frieze: meander cw. Frieze separators: dots.

EPH-1129*
Chersonesos, X-1965-71, St Petersburg, State Hermitage Museum. Rim fr. H 3.1, WT 0.25, RH 1.8. Fabric: standard, 2.5YR 6/8. Dull coat, 2.5YR 5/6. Oxidized. Rim frieze: meander cw.

EPH-1130
Istros, His-V 19340, Bucharest, Institute of Archaeology storeroom. Rim fr. Reduced. Rim frieze: meander cw.

EPH-1131
Olbia, Sector R25, O-P25-05-2506, Parutine, Olbia National Preserve storeroom. Rim fr. H 2.9 × W 4, WT 0.3, RH 1.3. Fabric: relatively fine and micaceous, 7.5YR 5/6. Thin dull coat, 7.5YR 2.5/1. Medium hard fired, oxidized. Rim frieze: meander cw. One repair hole.

EPH-1132*
Olbia, Cliff, square 285, O-70-147, Parutine, Olbia National Preserve storeroom. Rim fr. Oxidized. Rim frieze: meander cw.

EPH-1133*
Tyritake, Sector L, Л-52-354, St Petersburg IIMK RAN. Rim fr. H 3.4, WT 0.3, ⌀ rim 14, RH 1.9. Fabric: standard, fine, 5Y 5/1. Slightly lustrous coat, Gley 1 2.5/N. Hard fired, reduced. Rim frieze: meander cw.

Ionian kyma

EPH-1134*
Olbia, Sector R25, O-P25-92-533, Parutine, Olbia National Preserve storeroom. Rim fr. H 3.1 × W 4.9, WT 0.24, ⌀ rim 14, 6%, RH 1. Fabric: fine, micaceous, 5YR 6/6. Glossy coat, 5YR 3/1. Hard fired, oxidized. Rim frieze: tongue has trifurcated end, not shown in drawing. A fine early piece.

EPH-1135*
Olbia, Sector NGS, О-НГС-08-430, Parutine, Olbia National Preserve storeroom. Rim fr. Oxidized. Frieze separators: dots.

EPH-1136*
Porthmion, square 16, depth 1.05 m, with material of the 2nd–1st century, П-53-786, Kerč History and Culture Reserve. Rim fr. H 3.9, WT 0.18, ⌀ rim 15, RH 2. Fabric: standard, 2.5Y 5/1. Thin slightly lustrous coat, Gley 1 3/N. Hard fired, reduced. Frieze separators: dots.

EPH-1137
Olbia, Sector R25, O-P25-95-1115, Parutine, Olbia National Preserve storeroom. Fr. of upper body. H 2.2 × W 3.3, WT 0.27. Fabric: relatively fine and micaceous, Gley 1 6/10Y. Thin dull coat, Gley 1 2.5/N. Hard fired, reduced. Rim frieze: tongue is lightly hatched. Frieze separators: dots.

EPH-1138*
Istros, His-449, Bucharest, Institute of Archaeology storeroom. Body fr. close to rim. Reduced. Rim frieze: tongue is lightly hatched.

EPH-1139
Olbia, Sector R25, O-P25-06-1035, Parutine, Olbia National Preserve storeroom. Rim fr. H 4 × W 3, WT 0.35, RH 2.5. Fabric: relatively fine and micaceous, some small voids, 2.5Y 5/1. Dull coat, Gley 1 2.5/N. Medium hard fired, reduced. Rim frieze: tongue is hatched.

EPH-1140*
Olbia, Sector NGS, O-НГС-92-640, Parutine, Olbia National Preserve storeroom. Rim fr. Reduced. Rim frieze: tongue is hatched.

EPH-1141*
Porthmion, pavement of 2nd longitudinal street, with three bronze coins of Pantikapaion (first half of the 3rd century; mid-3rd century; 2nd century), П-77-267, Kerč History and Culture Reserve. Rim fr. H 3.3, WT 0.15, ø rim 11, RH 1.8. Fabric: standard, Gley 1 7/10Y. Thin dull coat, ext. 5Y 2.5/1, int. Gley 1 3/N. Reduced. Rim frieze: tongue is hatched.

EPH-1142
Istros, His-1927-1942-V 8573 D, Bucharest Institute of Archaeology storeroom. Rim fr. Oxidized. Stacked in firing.

EPH-1143
Myrmekion, M-56-1884, 1886, St Petersburg IIMK RAN. Two non-joining rim frs. H 3.3, WT 0.2, ø rim 12, 13%, RH 2. Fabric: standard, with lime inclusions, 10YR 4/1. Thin dull coat, slight lustre at rim ext., Gley 1 2.5/N. Hard fired, reduced. Stacked in firing.

EPH-1144
Olbia, Sector NGS, O-НГС-06-388, Parutine, Olbia National Preserve storeroom. Two joining rim frs. H 4.4 × W 5.9, WT 0.22, ø rim 15, 11%, RH 2.4. Fabric: relatively fine and micaceous, some small lime inclusions, 5Y 5/1. Dull coat, 5Y 2.5/1. Medium hard fired, reduced.

EPH-1145
Olbia, Sector R25, O-P25-06-750, Parutine, Olbia National Preserve storeroom. Rim fr. H 2.7 × W 3.2, WT 0.28, RH 1.6. Fabric: relatively fine and micaceous, small lime inclusions, 5Y 6/2. Dull coat, 5Y 2.5/1. Hard fired, reduced.

EPH-1146*
Olbia, Sector E2, square 55, Room [Cistern] Л, western part, grey clay layer, O-E2-48-4978, Kiev, Institute of Archaeology storeroom. Rim fr. Oxidized.

EPH-1147*
Porthmion, square 15, depth 1 m, 6 cm beneath pavement, with material of the 2nd century, П-53-721, Kerč History and Culture Reserve. Rim fr. H 4.6, WT 0.25, ø rim 18, RH 2.7. Fabric: standard, 2.5Y 5/1. Thin dull coat, 2.5Y 3/1. Reduced.

EPH-1148*
Porthmion, square 6, depth 0.75 m, with material of 3rd–2nd century, П-53-180, Kerč History and Culture Reserve. Rim fr. H 3.7, WT 0.25, ø rim 12, RH 2.1. Fabric: standard, Gley 1 4/10Y. Dull coat, mottled inside, Gley 1 3/N. Reduced.

EPH-1149*
Olbia, Sector NGS, O-НГС-90-370, Parutine, Olbia National Preserve storeroom. Rim fr. ø rim 13. Oxidized. Stacked in firing.

EPH-1150*
Tyritake, Sector L, Л-52-359, St Petersburg IIMK RAN. Rim fr. H 2.2, WT 0.3, ø rim 12, 8%, RH 1.3. Fabric: fine, much fine lime, some light-reflecting particles, 5YR 4/6, core 5Y 4/1. Uncoated. Oxidized.

EPH-1151
Myrmekion, M-58-17, St Petersburg IIMK RAN. Rim fr. H 3.2, WT 0.28, ø rim 14, 13%, RH 1.5. Fabric: standard, slightly denser than normal, 5YR 5/8. Thin coat with dull metallic sheen, 10YR 2/1. Oxidized.

EPH-1152*
Tyritake, Sector L, Л-52-358, St Petersburg IIMK RAN. Rim fr. H 3.2, WT 0.2, ø rim 10, 3%, RH 1.8. Fabric: standard, fine, Gley 1 6/N. Slightly lustrous coat, Gley 1 2.5/N. Hard fired, reduced.

Lesbian kyma

EPH-1153
Myrmekion, M-57-1442, St Petersburg IIMK RAN. Rim fr. H 3.5, WT 0.31, ø rim 14, 12%, RH 1.9. Fabric: standard, fine, 2.5Y 6/3. Thin coat with very slight lustre, 2.5Y 2.5/1. Oxidized.

EPH-1154
Myrmekion, M-58-653, St Petersburg IIMK RAN. Rim fr. H 3.7, WT 0.25, ø rim 13, 11%, RH 1.8. Fabric: standard, 5Y 5/1. Dull coat, ext. Gley 1 2.5/N, int. 5YR 4/2. Hard fired, reduced. Stacked in firing.

EPH-1155
Olbia, Sector NGS, О-НГС-06-483, Parutine, Olbia National Preserve storeroom. Rim fr. H 3.7 × W 2.7, WT 0.3, RH 1.8. Fabric: relatively fine and micaceous, 7.5YR 6/6. Thin lustrous coat, 5Y 2.5/1. Medium hard fired, oxidized.

EPH-1156
Olbia, Square Б5, О-Б5-76-21, Kiev, Institute of Archaeology storeroom. Rim fr. H 4 × W 7.5, WT 0.2, ⌀ rim 12.5, 20%, RH 1.4. Fabric: standard, 7.5YR 6/6. Coat with purplish metallic sheen, 2.5YR 5/2. Hard fired, oxidized.

EPH-1157*
Olbia, O-49-3326, Kiev, Institute of Archaeology storeroom. Rim fr. Dull red coat. Oxidized.

EPH-1158*
Olbia, O-38-5163, Kiev, Institute of Archaeology storeroom. Rim fr. Dull dark brown coat. Oxidized.

Vertical S-spirals

EPH-1159*
Olbia, Sector NGS, О-НГС-06-367, Parutine, Olbia National Preserve storeroom. Rim fr. H 3.6 × W 3.2, WT 0.3, RH 1.1. Fabric: relatively fine and micaceous, some small lime inclusions, 2.5YR 6/8. Thin dull coat, 2.5YR 4/8. Medium hard fired, oxidized.

Guilloche

EPH-1160*
Myrmekion, M-56-191, St Petersburg IIMK RAN. Rim fr. H 3.6, WT 0.3, ⌀ rim 12, 11%, RH 2.1. Fabric: fine, micaceous, small lime inclusions, 5YR 6/6. Thin dull flaking coat, 2.5YR 4/6. Oxidized. Rim frieze: guilloche right.

EPH-1161*
Myrmekion, Sector И, courtyard VII, M-49-678, St Petersburg IIMK RAN. Rim fr. H 3.2, WT 0.2, ⌀ rim 12, 8%, RH 1.2. Fabric: standard, 7.5YR 6/6. Thin coat with slight lustre, ext. 7.5YR 3/2, int. 7.5YR 3/1. Oxidized. Rim frieze: guilloche right.

EPH-1162
Olbia, Sector AGD, Bothros 11, О-АГД-88-212, Kiev, Institute of Archaeology storeroom. Rim fr. H 2.9 × W 2.3, WT 0.3, RH 1.7. Oxidized. Rim frieze: guilloche right.

EPH-1163*
Olbia, Sector NGS, О-НГС-05-907, Parutine, Olbia National Preserve storeroom. Fr. of rim and upper body. H 3.7 × W 4.8, WT 0.25, RH 1.8. Fabric: relatively fine and micaceous, 7.5YR 6/6. Thin coat with dull metallic sheen, 7.5YR 3/1. Medium hard fired, oxidized. Rim frieze: guilloche right. Calyx: edge of acanthus leaf preserved. On lip ext. deeply incised letters ΕΤΩ with strong serifs; perhaps same vessel as **EPH-1164***, or at least part of same dedication.

EPH-1164*
Olbia, Sector NGS, О-НГС-06-96, Parutine, Olbia National Preserve storeroom. Rim fr. H 3 × W 4, WT 0.4, RH 1.9. Fabric: relatively fine and micaceous, 5YR 6/8. Thin coat with dull metallic sheen, 5YR 3/1. Medium hard fired, oxidized. Rim frieze: guilloche right. On lip ext. deeply incised letter. Same bowl or part of same dedication as **EPH-1163***.

EPH-1165*
Olbia, O-57-462(?), Kiev, Institute of Archaeology storeroom. Rim fr. Slightly lustrous red coat. Oxidized. Rim frieze: guilloche left.

EPH-1166*
Olbia, Sector R25, О-Р25-05-1257, Parutine, Olbia National Preserve storeroom. Rim fr. H 3.1 × W 4.1, WT 0.35, RH 1.8. Fabric: relatively fine and micaceous, small voids, 7.5YR 5/4. Thin coat with slight metallic sheen ext., dull int., flaking, 7.5YR 2.5/1. Medium hard fired, oxidized. Rim frieze: guilloche left.

EPH-1167*
Pantikapaion, palace foundation trench, M-89-illegible 50, Moscow, Puškin Museum of Fine Arts. Body fr. Black coat with metallic sheen. Oxidized. Rim frieze: triple guilloche right. Main decoration: unidentified. Monogram PAR.

Wave Meander

EPH-1168*
Olbia, Sector E2, square 55, Cistern Л, О-Е2-49-446, Kiev, Institute of Archaeology storeroom. Rim fr. Oxidized. Rim frieze: meander left.

EPH-1169*
Olbia, Sector NGS, House IV-2 B 302/180, О-НГС-94-59, Parutine, Olbia National Preserve storeroom. Rim fr. H 3.5 × W 4.3, WT 0.45–0.53, ⌀ rim 13, RH 1.95. Fabric: micaceous, a few lime inclusions and small rounded brownish stones, 7.5YR 6/6, 5YR 6/6. Fine firm coat, slightly lustrous int. and blackened at lip, ext. darkened with a slight bluish metallic sheen, ext. 10YR 2/2, int. 2.5YR 4/6. Medium hard fired, oxidized. Stacked in firing. Rim frieze: meander right, incised in mould.
– Guldager Bilde 2010, 277 cat. F-10, pl. 169.

EPH-1170*
Pantikapaion, palace foundation trench, M-84-58. Moscow, Puškin Museum of Fine Arts. Rim fr. H 3.3 × W 6, WT 0.2, ⌀ rim 11, 15%, RH 1.8. Shiny black coat. Reduced. Stacked in firing. Rim frieze: meander right, with dot filling below. Frieze separators: dots. Secondarily burnt.

EPH-1171*
Olbia, Sector R25, O-P25-92-1223, Parutine, Olbia National Preserve storeroom. Rim fr. H 3.3 × W 5.3, WT 0.3, ⌀ rim 12, 12%, RH 1.9. Fabric: relatively fine and micaceous, 10YR 5/3. Thin dull coat, 10YR 3/1. Medium hard fired, oxidized. Rim frieze: meander upside-down.

Rosette 1

EPH-1172
Porthmion, П-75-389, Kerč History and Culture Reserve. Rim fr. Reduced. Menemachos.
– Grzegrzółka 2010, 186 cat. 307.

EPH-1173
Porthmion, П-75-21, Kerč History and Culture Reserve. Rim fr. Oxidized. Menemachos?
– Grzegrzółka 2010, 182 cat. 298.

EPH-1174*
Istros, His-V 19453 B, Bucharest, Institute of Archaeology storeroom. Body fr. close to rim. Oxidized. Rim frieze: rosette 1, small.
– Domăneanțu 2000, 77 cat. 370, pl. 24 (attributed to Plagiaire).

Rosette 2

EPH-1175*
Tyritake, Sector L, Л-37-139, St Petersburg IIMK RAN. Rim fr. H 3.6, WT 0.35, ⌀ rim 12, RH 1.4. Fabric: standard, 2.5YR 5/8. Slightly lustrous coat, mottled ext., dull int., ext. 2.5YR 4/6, 3/1, int. 2.5YR 4/6. Oxidized. Stacked in firing. Rim frieze: rosette 2/7. Frieze separators: dots.

EPH-1176*
Olbia, Sector NGS, O-НГС-05-61, Parutine, Olbia National Preserve storeroom. Two joining rim frs. H 3.6 × W 7.8, WT 0.2, ⌀ rim 12, 18%, RH 1.8. Fabric: relatively fine and micaceous, 7.5YR 5/6. Thin dull coat, ext. 2.5YR 4/8, 5YR 4/2, int. 2.5YR 4/8. Medium hard fired, oxidized. Stacked in firing. Rim frieze: rosette 2/7.

EPH-1177
Chersonesos, Х-1957-16, St Petersburg, State Hermitage Museum. Rim fr. H 3.2, WT 0.3, ⌀ rim 11, 17%, RH 2.1. Fabric: standard, 10YR 6/2. Dull coat, 5Y 3/1. Reduced. Rim frieze: rosette 2/7.

EPH-1178
Myrmekion, M-57-306, St Petersburg IIMK RAN. Rim fr. H 3.4, WT 0.3, ⌀ rim 12, RH 1. Fabric: standard, 5YR 5/8. Thin dull coat, 2.5YR 4/6. Oxidized. Rim frieze: rosette 2/7.

EPH-1179
Myrmekion, M-56-2062, St Petersburg IIMK RAN. Rim fr. H 4.6, WT 0.2, ⌀ rim 12, 10%, RH 1.9. Fabric: standard, 2.5Y 6/1. Thin slightly lustrous coat, Gley 1 3/N. Reduced. Rim frieze: rosette 2/7.

EPH-1180
Olbia, Sector R25, O-P25-03-2422, Parutine, Olbia National Preserve storeroom. Rim fr. H 2.3 × W 4.3, WT 0.48, ⌀ rim 12, 10%, RH 1.3. Fabric: relatively fine and micaceous, many small lime inclusions, 5YR 6/8. Thin dull coat, ext. 2.5YR 5/6, 3/1, int. 2.5YR 5/6. Medium hard fired, oxidized. Stacked in firing. Rim frieze: rosette 2/7. One repair hole.

EPH-1181*
Istros, His-917, Bucharest, Institute of Archaeology storeroom. Body fr. close to rim. Oxidized. Rim frieze: rosette 2/7.

EPH-1182
Porthmion, П-77-236, Kerč History and Culture Reserve. Rim fr. Oxidized. Rim frieze: rosette 2/8 (M). Menemachos?
– Grzegrzółka 2010, 189 cat. 315.

EPH-1183*
Pantikapaion, palace foundation trench, M-84-50[d], Moscow, Puškin Museum of Fine Arts. Rim fr. H 3.5 × W 4.7, WT 0.3, RH 1.8. Dull black coat, worn int. Reduced. Rim frieze: rosette 2/4. Secondarily burnt.

Rosette 3

EPH-1184*
Olbia, O-47-4469, Kiev, Institute of Archaeology storeroom. Rim fr. H 3.8 × W 6.4, WT 0.25, ⌀ rim 12, 17%, RH 1.8. Fabric: standard, 2.5YR 6/8. Dull coat, 10R 5/6. Relatively hard fired, oxidized.

EPH-1185*
Istros, His-884, Bucharest, Institute of Archaeology storeroom. Body fr. close to rim. Reduced.
– Domăneanțu 2000, 66 cat. 309, pl. 20.

Rosette 4 (Star Rosette)

EPH-1186*
Myrmekion, M-57-617, St Petersburg IIMK RAN. Rim fr. H 3.2, WT 0.32, ⌀ rim 12, RH 1.8. Fabric: standard, 2.5YR 5/8. Thin coat

with slight metallic sheen where darkened ext., dull int., ext. 2.5YR 3/4, 3/1, int. 2.5YR 4/6. Oxidized. Stacked in firing.

EPH-1187*
Myrmekion, M-58-831, St Petersburg IIMK RAN. Fr. of lower body. H 2.1, WT 0.25. Fabric: standard, 2.5YR 6/8. Thin coat with slight lustre, 2.5YR 4/8. Oxidized.

EPH-1188
Olbia, Sector NGS, O-НГС-06-100, Parutine, Olbia National Preserve storeroom. Rim fr. Oxidized.

EPH-1189*
Pantikapaion, palace foundation trench, M-89-illegible 33, Moscow, Puškin Museum of Fine Arts. Rim fr. Oxidized.

Rosette 5

EPH-1190*
Istros, His-V 8573 T, Bucharest Institute of Archaeology storeroom. Rim fr. Reduced.

Rosette 6

EPH-1191*
Istros, His-193, Bucharest, Institute of Archaeology storeroom. Rim fr. Oxidized. My(…).
– Domăneanțu 2000, 52 cat. 239, pl. 15 (attributed to Apollonios).

EPH-1192
Istros, His-902, Bucharest, Institute of Archaeology storeroom. Body fr. close to rim. Oxidized. My(…).

Rosette 7

EPH-1193
Olbia, Sector R25, O-P25-04-1907, Parutine, Olbia National Preserve storeroom. Rim fr. H 3.8 × W 4.9, WT 0.2, RH 1.4. Fabric: fine, micaceous, 7.5YR 6/6. Thin slightly lustrous coat, 5Y 2.5/1. Medium hard fired, oxidized.

EPH-1194*
Olbia, Sector R25, O-P25-04-2310, Parutine, Olbia National Preserve storeroom. Rim fr. H 3.4 × W 5.4, WT 0.2, ⌀ rim 12, 9%, RH 1.5. Fabric: fine, micaceous, 5Y 5/1. Dull coat, Gley 1 2.5/N. Hard fired, reduced. Six petals.

EPH-1195*
Istros, His-1927-1942-B 429, Bucharest Institute of Archaeology storeroom. Rim fr. Oxidized.

EPH-1196*
Istros, His-514, Bucharest, Institute of Archaeology storeroom. Rim fr. Oxidized.

EPH-1197
Istros, His-271, Bucharest, Institute of Archaeology storeroom. Rim fr. Oxidized.

Rosette 8

EPH-1198*
Istros, His-820[a], Bucharest, Institute of Archaeology storeroom. Rim fr. Reduced.
– Domăneanțu 2000, 66 cat. 311, pl. 20.

Rosette 9

EPH-1199*
Olbia, Sector NGS, House IV-4 B 351/206, O-НГС-92-356, Parutine, Olbia National Preserve storeroom. Rim fr. Reduced.
– Guldager Bilde 2010, 284 cat. F-93, pl. 187.

Rosette 10

EPH-1200*
Chersonesos, X-1965-65 St Petersburg, State Hermitage Museum. Rim fr. H 3.1, WT 0.32, ⌀ rim 11, 10%, RH 1.8. Fabric: standard, 5YR 6/6. Lustrous coat int., ext. 7.5YR 2.5/1, int. 10YR 2/1. Oxidized.

Sunburst Rosette

EPH-1201*
Myrmekion, M-57-348, St Petersburg IIMK RAN. Rim fr. H 3.1, WT 0.32, ⌀ rim 12, 7%, RH 1.7. Fabric: standard, 5Y 5/1. Dull coat, slightly lustrous at rim ext., ext. Gley 1 2.5/N, int. 2.5Y 3/1. Reduced. Rim frieze: sunburst rosette var.

Miniature Acanthus-Flower Scroll Left

EPH-1202
Olbia, Sector NGS, O-НГС-06-424, Parutine, Olbia National Preserve storeroom. Rim fr. H 3 × W 3, WT 0.3, RH 1.1. Fabric: relatively fine and micaceous, some small lime inclusions, 5YR 6/6. Thin slightly lustrous coat, 5YR 3/1. Hard fired, oxidized. Monogram PAR.

EPH-1203*
Tyritake, Sector L, Л-37-140, St Petersburg IIMK RAN. Rim fr. H 3.3, WT 0.4, ⌀ rim 13, RH 2. Fabric: standard, 7.5YR 5/6. Slightly lustrous coat, 7.5YR 2.5/1. Oxidized. Stacked in firing. Monogram PAR.

EPH-1204
Istros, His-956[a], Bucharest, Institute of Archaeology storeroom. Rim fr. Oxidized. Monogram PAR.

Miniature Acanthus Scroll

EPH-1205*
Myrmekion, M-55-155, St Petersburg IIMK RAN. Rim fr. H 3.5, WT 0.22, ⌀ rim 12, 10%, RH 2. Fabric: soft, finely micaceous, 5YR 6/6. Thin flaking coat, ext. 5YR 3/1, int. 2.5YR 4/6. Oxidized. Stacked in firing. Rim frieze: scroll left. Menemachos.

EPH-1206*
Istros, His-1111, Bucharest, Institute of Archaeology storeroom. Rim fr. Reduced. Rim frieze: scroll left. Frieze separators: dots. Menemachos.
– Domăneanțu 2000, 7 cat. 25, pl. 2 (attributed to Menemachos).

EPH-1207
Istros, Sector MC1 Sa, His-56-48, 49, 50, 62, Bucharest, Institute of Archaeology storeroom. Three joining rim frs. and two non-joining body frs. Oxidized. Rim frieze: scroll left. Menemachos.
– Domăneanțu 2000, 12 cat. 46, pl. 3 (attributed to NI).

EPH-1208
Istros, His-545, Bucharest, Institute of Archaeology storeroom. Rim fr. Oxidized. Rim frieze: scroll left. Menemachos. Yet more fragments of this rim pattern by Menemachos at Istros: Domăneanțu 2000, 12 cat. 47, pl. 3; 45 cat. 203, pl. 13.
– Domăneanțu 2000, 45 cat. 205, pl. 13 (attributed to Monogram PAR).

EPH-1209
Olbia, Sector NGS, O-НГС-03-398, Parutine, Olbia National Preserve storeroom. Rim fr. Reduced. Rim frieze: scroll left. Menemachos.

EPH-1210
Olbia, O-1925-81, present whereabouts unknown. Rim fr., heavily encrusted with lime, consequently identification uncertain. Rim frieze: scroll left. Menemachos.
– St Petersburg, IIMK RAN, photo archive neg. II 19396.

EPH-1211
Istros, His-419, Bucharest, Institute of Archaeology storeroom. Rim fr. Oxidized. Rim frieze: scroll left. Menemachos.

EPH-1212
Pantikapaion, area of 51 Armii Str., П-76-no.(?), Kerč History and Culture Reserve. Rim fr. Oxidized. Rim frieze: scroll left. Menemachos.
– Grzegrzółka 2010, 62–63 cat. 41.

EPH-1213
Porthmion, П-73-no.(?), Kerč History and Culture Reserve. Rim fr. Oxidized. Rim frieze: scroll left. Menemachos.
– Grzegrzółka 2010, 177 cat. 286.

EPH-1214
Porthmion, П-75-238, Kerč History and Culture Reserve. Rim fr. Oxidized. Rim frieze: scroll left. Menemachos.
– Grzegrzółka 2010, 177–178 cat. 287.

EPH-1215*
Istros, His-B 531/V 19341, Bucharest, Institute of Archaeology storeroom. Rim fr. Oxidized. Rim frieze: scroll right. Menemachos.
– Domăneanțu 2000, 45 cat. 204, pl. 13 (attributed to Monogram PAR).

EPH-1216*
Pantikapaion, palace foundation trench, M-84-49, 89-illegible 43, Moscow, Puškin Museum of Fine Arts. Two non-joining rim frs. H 3.5 × W 5, WT 0.25, RH 1.4. Dull red-brown coat. Oxidized. Rim frieze: scroll right. Menemachos.

Miniature Ultra-Stylized Scroll

EPH-1217*
Istros, Ul 1913, His-V 7527 H, Bucharest Institute of Archaeology storeroom. Fr. of rim and upper body. H 3.7 × W 4.7, WT 0.2, ⌀ rim 12, 10%, RH 1.3. Fabric: standard, Gley 1 5/10Y. Dull coat ext., slightly lustrous int., ext. Gley 1 3/N, int. Gley 1 2.5/N. Hard fired, reduced. VG Workshop/Menemachos.
– Domăneanțu 2000, 107 cat. 543, pl. 35.

EPH-1218*
Pantikapaion, palace foundation trench, M-84-52, 89-illegible 26, Moscow, Puškin Museum of Fine Arts. Rim fr. H 3.5 × W 4, WT 0.5, RH 1.8. Black coat with metallic sheen. Oxidized. VG Workshop/Menemachos.

Miniature Myrtle Wreath

EPH-1219*
Myrmekion, M-58-819, 826, St Petersburg IIMK RAN. Two non-joining rim frs. H 3.1, WT 0.3, ⌀ rim 12, 5%, RH, 1.55. Fabric:

standard, 5YR 6/6. Thin slightly lustrous coat, ext. 2.5YR 4/6, 10YR 3/1, int. 2.5YR 3/4. Oxidized. Stacked in firing. Rim frieze: miniature bound three-leaved myrtle wreath left.

Crossed Dotted Lines with Box

EPH-1220
Kepoi, no. unknown, Moscow, State Historical Museum. Rim fr. Menemachos.
– Usačeva 1978, fig. 1.22.

EPH-1221*
Myrmekion, M-57-2101, St Petersburg IIMK RAN. Fr. of rim and upper body. H 3.9, WT 0.3, RH 1.8. Fabric: standard, 10YR 5/1. Thin dull coat, 5Y 3/1. Hard fired, reduced. Main decoration: long petals?

EPH-1222*
Istros, His-798[a], Bucharest, Institute of Archaeology storeroom. Rim fr. Reduced.
– Domăneanțu 2000, 9 cat. 37, pl. 2 (attributed to Menemachos).

Crossed Dotted Lines

EPH-1223*
Porthmion, pavement of 2nd longitudinal street, with three bronze coins of Pantikapaion (first half of the 3rd century; mid-3rd century; 2nd century), П-77-257, Kerč History and Culture Reserve. Rim fr. H 3.1, WT 0.2, RH 1.8. Fabric: standard, fine, 2.5YR 6/8. Thin dull coat, slightly lustrous at rim ext., ext. 2.5YR 5/6, 5YR 3/1, int. 2.5YR 5/8. Oxidized. Stacked in firing.

EPH-1224
Istros, His-B 517, Bucharest, Institute of Archaeology storeroom. Rim fr. H 3 × W 3.7. Oxidized.
– Domăneanțu 2000, 34 cat. 141, pl. 10 (attributed to Monogram PAR).

Oblique Boxes

EPH-1225*
Istros, His-974, Bucharest, Institute of Archaeology storeroom. Body fr. close to rim. Reduced.
– Domăneanțu 2000, 20 cat. 79, pl. 6 (attributed to Comique à la canne).

EPH-1226*
Olbia, Sector R25, O-P25-03-2097, Parutine, Olbia National Preserve storeroom. Body fr. close to rim. H 3.1 × W 2.9, WT 0.3. Fabric: relatively fine and micaceous, 7.5YR 5/4. Dull coat, ext. 7.5YR 2.5/1, int. 7.5YR 4/3. Medium hard fired, oxidized.

'Paw'

EPH-1227*
Istros, His-B 538/V 19420, Bucharest, Institute of Archaeology storeroom. Rim fr. Reduced. Philon(nios).
– Domăneanțu 2000, 65 cat. 304, pl. 20.

EPH-1228
Istros, His-284, Bucharest, Institute of Archaeology storeroom. Body fr. close to rim. Reduced. Philon(nios).
– Domăneanțu 2000, 65 cat. 306, pl. 20.

EPH-1229
Istros, His-332, Bucharest, Institute of Archaeology storeroom. Rim fr. Reduced. Philon(nios).
– Domăneanțu 2000, 65 cat. 305, pl. 20.

EPH-1230
Istros, His-no no. 23, Bucharest, Institute of Archaeology storeroom. Rim fr. Reduced. Philon(nios).

EPH-1231
Istros, His-755, Bucharest, Institute of Archaeology storeroom. Body fr. close to rim. Reduced. Philon(nios).

EPH-1232
Istros, His-624, Bucharest, Institute of Archaeology storeroom. Rim fr. Reduced. Philon(nios).

EPH-1233*
Olbia, Sector Sever-Zapad, O-C3-81-66, Parutine, Olbia National Preserve storeroom. Rim fr. Reduced. Philon(nios)?

EPH-1234*
Pantikapaion, palace foundation trench, M-89-illegible 15, Moscow, Puškin Museum of Fine Arts. Rim fr. H 3 × W 4.3, WT 0.3, ⌀ rim 12, 10%. RH 1.5. Dull black coat. Reduced. Philon(nios)?

EPH-1235
Olbia, Sector R25, O-P25-05-851, Parutine, Olbia National Preserve storeroom. Rim fr. H 3.2 × W 7.3, WT 0.2, ⌀ rim 12, 22%, RH 2.1. Fabric: relatively fine and micaceous, small lime inclusions, 5Y 3/1. Thin slightly lustrous coat, Gley 1 2.5/N. Hard fired, reduced. Philon(nios)?

EPH-1236*
Volna 1, C3-98-142 St Petersburg, State Hermitage Museum. Rim fr. Reduced. Philon(nios)?

EPH-1237
Olbia, Sector R25, O-P25-05-3742, Parutine, Olbia National Preserve storeroom. Rim fr. Reduced. Philon(nios)?

Ivy-Berry Cluster

EPH-1238*
Olbia, O-1925-396. Rim fr.
– St Petersburg, IIMK RAN, photo archive neg. II 19394.

EPH-1239
Istros, His-941, Bucharest, Institute of Archaeology storeroom. Rim fr. Reduced.

Five-Rayed Sun Wheel

EPH-1240*
Istros, Sector "Pescărie", His-63-41, Bucharest, Institute of Archaeology storeroom. Rim fr. Oxidized.

Jewellery Pendants

EPH-1241*
Istros, His-191[a], Bucharest, Institute of Archaeology storeroom. Rim fr. Oxidized.
– Domăneanțu 2000, 21 cat. 82, pl. 6 (attributed to Comique à la canne).

EPH-1242*
Olbia, Sector R25, O-P25-04-2800, Parutine, Olbia National Preserve storeroom. Two non-joining rim frs. and a body fr. H 4.1 × W 5.3, WT 0.3, ⌀ rim 12, 14%, RH 1.4. Fabric: realtively fine and micaceous, many small lime inclusions, 5Y 4/1. Dull coat, Gley 1 2.5/N. Medium hard fired, reduced. Rim frieze: rosette 7, var. alternating with single pendants. Philon(nios)?

EPH-1243
Olbia, Sector R25, O-P25-04-no no.[2, 10, 22], Parutine, Olbia National Preserve storeroom. Three non-joining rim frs. Reduced. Rim frieze: rosette 7, var. alternating with single pendants. Philon(nios)?

Hatched H's

EPH-1244*
Bol'šoj Kastel', БК-86-74(?), Černomorskoe Museum of Historical Lore. Body fr. close to rim. Oxidized. Rim frieze: hatched H's with alternating orientations. Cf. Laumonier 1977, 106 cats. 640, 1939, pl. 24 (Vases gris). VG Workshop.

Small Horizontal Leaves

EPH-1245*
Bol'šoj Kastel', БК-86-75, Černomorskoe Museum of Historical Lore. Rim fr. H 2.9, ⌀ rim 14, RH 1.3. Fabric: highly micaceous, 2.5YR 5/8. Dull flaking coat, 2.5YR 4/6. Oxidized. Rim frieze: leaves with central and side veins, outlined.

H Base Fragments

EPH-1246*
Pantikapaion, M-46-4647, Moscow, Puškin Museum of Fine Art. Fr. of base and part of lower body. H 2.5 × W 5.5, ⌀ base 5. Dull red coat. Oxidized. Traces of vegetal calyx. Plain concave base on low ring foot, signed [...]NEMA[...]. Menemachos.

EPH-1247
Pantikapaion, no. unknown, present whereabouts unknown. Base fr. Signed MOIRAGEN (Moiragenes): cf. EPH-693*, EPH-786*.
– Loseva 1962, 199.

EPH-1248
Pantikapaion, M-46-6466, Moscow, Puškin Museum of Fine Art. Base fr. Remains of signature PHILO[...]. Philon(nios).
– Loseva 1962, 197 n. 11.

EPH-1249*
Istros, His-109, Bucharest, Institute of Archaeology storeroom. Fr. of base and lower body. H 3.5 × W 1.9, WT 0.38, ⌀ base 5. Fabric: standard, 5Y 6/1. Dull coat, Gley 1 3/N. Relatively hard fired, reduced. Traces of vegetal calyx. Plain concave base with false ring foot, faint traces of signature incised in vessel: [...]ONU[...] or [...]ONT[...]. One repair hole.

EPH-1250*
Myrmekion, M-56-979, St Petersburg IIMK RAN. Fr. of base and lower body. H 3.7, WT 0.3, ⌀ base 4. Fabric: standard, 2.5YR 5/8. Thin slightly lustrous coat, 2.5YR 4/6. Oxidized. Calyx: Lesbian kyma above base. Plain concave base.

EPH-1251 (see Fig. 70)
Istros, His-135, Bucharest, Institute of Archaeology storeroom. Fr. of base and part of lower body. H 4.5 × W 2, WT 0.25, ⌀ base 3. Fabric: standard with abundant lime inclusions. Coat with dull lustre, flaking on int. Relatively hard fired, oxidized. Main decoration: plastic long petals? Medallion: PAR monogram surrounded by Ionian kyma. Secondarily burnt. Monogram PAR.
– Domăneanțu 2000, 25 cat. 88, pl. 7 (attributed to Monogram PAR).

EPH-1252*
Olbia, Sector R25, O-P25-00-2016, Parutine, Olbia National Preserve storeroom. Fr. of base and lower body. Oxidized. Calyx: acanthus and long petal? Medallion: rosette A, var. 1.

EPH-1253*
Istros, His-983, Bucharest, Institute of Archaeology storeroom. Base fr. Oxidized. Medallion: rosette A (six petals).

EPH-1254
Olbia, Sector NGS, O-НГС-85-100, Parutine, Olbia National Preserve storeroom? (not found in 2009). Fr. of base and part of lower body. Reduced. Traces of vegetal calyx. Medallion: rosette A.

EPH-1255
Porthmion, П-73-31, Kerč History and Culture Reserve. Fr. of base and lower body. Oxidized. Calyx: unidentifed. Medallion: rosette A.
– Grzegrzółka 2010, 149 cat. 220.

EPH-1256*
Olbia, Sector R25, O-P25-92-2239, Parutine, Olbia National Preserve storeroom. Fr. of base and part of lower body. H 5 × W 4.1, WT 0.3, ⌀ base 3.8. Fabric: relatively fine and micaceous, small lime inclusions, 7.5YR 6/6. Dull coat, 7.5YR 2.5/1. Medium hard fired, oxidized. Traces of vegetal calyx. Medallion: rosette A, var. 3. Cf. Laumonier 1977, 85 cat. 716, 717, pl. 19.

EPH-1257
Porthmion, П-68-89, Kerč History and Culture Reserve. Fr. of base and lower body. Oxidized. Calyx: unidentified. Medallion: rosette related to rosette A.
– Grzegrzółka 2010, 156 cat. 237 (attributed to Asia Minor).

EPH-1258*
Volna 1, C3-99-3, St Petersburg, State Hermitage Museum. Fr. of base and lower body. Oxidized. Base of vegetal calyx. Medallion: rosette B.

EPH-1259
Istros, His-566[a], Bucharest, Institute of Archaeology storeroom. Fr. of base and part of lower body. H 3.5 × W 3. Oxidized. Calyx: unidentified. Medallion: rosette B.
– Domăneanțu 2000, 46 cat. 210, pl. 13 (attributed to Monogram PAR).

EPH-1260*
Istros, His-B 629/V 8570 B, Bucharest, Institute of Archaeology storeroom. Fr. of base and lower body. H 3.2 × W 3.5. Oxidized. Calyx: bottom of acanthus leaf. Medallion: rosette B.

– Domăneanțu 2000, 29 cat. 108, pl. 8 (attributed to Monogram PAR).

EPH-1261*
Olbia, Sector NGS, O-НГС-91-212, Parutine, Olbia National Preserve storeroom. Fr. of base and lower body. H 4.4 × W 5.6, WT 0.3, ⌀ base 4. Fabric: relatively fine and micaceous, 5Y 4/1. Thin firm slightly lustrous coat, Gley 1 2.5/N. Hard fired, reduced. Traces of vegetal calyx. Medallion: Rosette B, var., with 12 overlapping pointed petals

EPH-1262* (see also Fig. 79)
Istros, His-1927-1942-V 8571 N, Bucharest Institute of Archaeology storeroom. Base fr. Reduced. Medallion: rosette F surrounded by large dots.
– Domăneanțu 2000, 101 cat. 505, pl. 33.

EPH-1263
Istros, His-567, Bucharest, Institute of Archaeology storeroom. Base fr. Reduced. Medallion: rosette E.

EPH-1264*
Myrmekion, M-53-474, St Petersburg IIMK RAN. Base fr. H 4.1, WT 0.5, ⌀ base 4. Fabric: standard, 2.5YR 6/6. Lustrous coat, mottled ext., ext. 2.5YR 4/6, 3/1, int. 2.5YR 3/3. Oxidized. Stacked in firing. Medallion: rosette of six wide petals with five-rayed sun wheel at center. Menemachos?

SUPPLEMENTARY SHAPES

Small Bowl

EPH-1265*
Olbia, Sector NGS, O-НГС-94-498, Parutine, Olbia National Preserve storeroom. Fr. of rim and body. H 4.2 × W 6, WT 0.2, ⌀ rim 8, 25%, RH 1.2. Fabric: relatively fine and micaceous, small lime inclusions, 5YR 6/8. Thin dull coat int., ext. with slight metallic lustre, ext. Gley 1 3/N, int. 2.5YR 4/4. Medium hard fired, oxidized. Stacked in firing. Rim frieze: guilloche left. Calyx: straight acanthus, curved petal, male moving right (hunter?).

EPH-1266*
Olbia, Sector I, West, ash clay layer, O-И-48-2100, Kiev, Institute of Archaeology storeroom. Fr. of rim and upper body. H 4.6 × W 4.8, WT 0.3, ⌀ rim 9, 14%, RH 1.8. Fabric: relatively fine and micaceous, 5YR 6/6. Dull coat, ext. 2.5YR 4/8, int. 2.5YR 4/8, 3/2. Relatively hard fired, reduced. Rim frieze: Ionian kyma. Main decoration: mantled dancing women right.

EPH-1267
Olbia, V.I. 4954, Antikensammlung, Staatliche Museen zu Berlin (formerly Vogell collection), lost in WW II. Complete. ⌀ rim 7.9; vessel H 5.1; H:⌀ 1:1.5. Brown, almost black coat. Oxidized. Rim frieze: Ionian kyma. Main decoration: mantled dancing women right. Calyx: ovoid lotus petals alternating with incised wavy line. Medallion: small rosette with nine petals. Frieze separators: dots.
– Zahn 1908, 62 cat. 18; Boehlau 1908, 31 no. 283.

EPH-1268*
Olbia, Sector E6, squares 408s, 413n, grey clay layer, O-E6-61-52, Kiev, Institute of Archaeology storeroom. Fr. of rim and upper body. H 3.8 × W 7.1, WT 0.1, ⌀ rim 9, 25%, RH 1.4. Fabric: fine and slightly micaceous, a few minute lime particles, 2.5YR 6/8. Coat with dull lustre, ext. 2.5YR 3/1, 4/4, int. Gley 1 3/N. Hard fired, oxidized. Rim frieze: Ionian kyma. Main decoration: five actors with comic masks.

EPH-1269
Olbia, Sector NGS, O-НГС-02-136, Parutine, Olbia National Preserve storeroom. Fr. of rim and upper body. H 3.1 × W 3.3, WT 0.25–0.44, ⌀ rim 8, 10%, RH 1.6. Fabric: relatively fine and micaceous, a few minute lime particles and small voids, 5Y 5/1. Thin firm slightly lustrous coat, ext. 2.5Y 2/0, int. 2.5Y 3/0. Hard fired, reduced. Rim frieze: Ionian kyma. Calyx A (top of 'nelumbo'). One repair hole.

EPH-1270*
Olbia, Sector E6, square 413, 414, north and west of Cistern (128?), O-E6-59-2271, Kiev, Institute of Archaeology storeroom. Fabric: relatively fine and micaceous. Reduced. Calyx A (lotus petal, acanthus leaf with bent tip, sepal with turned tip). Medallion: rosette A.

EPH-1271*
Istros, His-1086, Bucharest, Institute of Archaeology storeroom. Fr. of rim and upper body. H 3.2 × W 2.2, WT 0.3, RH 1.2. Fabric: fine, slightly micaceous, a few minute lime particles, 5Y 6/1. Coat with dull lustre, Gley 1 2.5/N. Relatively hard fired, reduced. Rim frieze: Ionian kyma. Calyx: acanthus with bent tip.

EPH-1272*
Olbia, Sector NGS, House IV-2 B 302/182, O-НГС-94-116, Parutine, Olbia National Preserve storeroom. Fr. of rim and upper body. H 3.7 × W 4.2, WT 0.25–0.43, ⌀ rim 8, 13%, RH 1.6. Fabric: relatively fine and micaceous, numerous small rounded red-brown stones, some lime particles, some rather large voids, 7.5YR 6/6, 5YR 6/6. Thin firm coat with bluish metallic sheen, 10YR 3/1. Medium hard fired, oxidized. Stacked in firing. Rim frieze: Ionian kyma. Calyx: 'nelumbo' alternating with sistrum bud. Menemachos.
– Guldager Bilde 2010, 276 cat. F-6, pl. 169.

EPH-1273*
Pantikapaion, П-1902-129, St Petersburg, State Hermitage Museum. Complete. H 3.5, ⌀ rim 8.5. Fabric: relatively fine and micaceous. Oxidized. Stacked in firing. Multiple rim friezes: Ionian kyma; rosette 2/7. Calyx B2 (all petals rhomboidal). Medallion: rosette B.

EPH-1274*
Olbia, O-no no. D, Kiev, Institute of Archaeology storeroom. Fr. of rim and upper body. H 2.8 × W 4.9, WT 0.24, ⌀ rim 8, 15%, RH 1.3. Fabric: relatively fine and micaceous, Gley 1 4/N. Dull coat, Gley 1 3/N. Relatively hard fired, reduced. Rim frieze: horizontal S-spirals. Calyx: Calyx B, var? (acanthus with bent tip alternating with lotus petal). Three grooves below rim.

EPH-1275*
Olbia, Sector E, square 117, humus layer, O-E-49-143, Kiev, Institute of Archaeology storeroom. Fr. of rim and body. H 3.6 × W 4.3, WT 0.2, ⌀ rim 9, 14%, RH 1.5. Fabric: fine and slightly micaceous, a few minute lime particles, 5YR 6/8. Dull coat, 2.5YR 4/6. Relatively hard fired, oxidized. Rim frieze: Ionian kyma. Calyx: straight acanthus leaf with sistrum bud as space filler. Menemachos.

EPH-1276
Istros, His-275, Bucharest, Institute of Archaeology storeroom. Body fr. Fabric: relatively fine and micaceous. Reduced. Rim frieze: Ionian kyma. Calyx: straight palm frond enclosed in outline.

EPH-1277*
Olbia, Sector R25, O-P25-93-1363, Parutine, Olbia National Preserve storeroom. Fr. of rim and upper body. H 3.5 × W 4.6, WT 0.33, ⌀ rim 9, 12%, RH 1.8. Fabric: relatively fine and micaceous, small lime inclusions, 2.5Y 4/2. Slightly lustrous coat, Gley 1 2.5/N. Hard fired, reduced. No rim frieze. Calyx: imbricate pointed petals.

EPH-1278
Pantikapaion(?), inv. CA 2286, Paris, Louvre (formerly collection of Messaksoudy, 1920). Complete. ⌀ rim 9.3; vessel H 5.5; H:⌀ 1:1.7. Rim frieze: Ionian kyma. Calyx: imbricate pointed petals with central and side veins. Base signed PHILONOS. Philon(nios).
– Jentel 1964, 116 cat. 2, pl. XII.

EPH-1279
Chersonesos, X-1900-1, St Petersburg, State Hermitage Museum. Complete profile, but lacks a few minor fragments. WT 0.2, ⌀ rim 8.5, RH 1.9, ⌀ base 3.8; vessel H 5.5; H:⌀ 1:1.6. Fabric: relatively fine and micaceous, 5YR 4/3. Thin dull coat, ext. 5YR 4/3, int. 5YR 3/1. Oxidized. Stacked in firing. Rim frieze: Lesbian kyma. Calyx: imbricate pointed petals with central and side veins. Plain slightly concave base. Menemachos?
– IAK 2, p. 11.

EPH-1280
Tyritake, Kerč History and Culture Reserve inv. KMAK 10397 (1933?). Complete profile; two large frs. of rim, body, and base. ⌀ rim 8.8, ⌀ base 3.2; vessel H 5.4. Reduced. Rim frieze: rosette 2/7. Calyx: imbricate pointed petals with central and side veins. Plain concave base.
– Grzegrzółka 2010, 114 cat. 146.

EPH-1281*
Olbia, Sector AGD, Bothros 11, О-АГД-88-209+214, 87-893, Kiev, Institute of Archaeology storeroom. Complete profile; two joining frs. of rim and most of body; one similar non-joining fr. preserving part of base; sherds from 1987 and 1988 do not join but are from the same vessel. H 5.6 × W 8.3, WT 0.35–0.45, ⌀ rim 9, 25%, RH 1.7; vessel H 4.9; H:⌀ 1:1.8. Fabric: relatively fine and micaceous, 2.5YR 6/8. Coat with slight metallic lustre, 2.5YR 4/4, 2.5/1. Relatively hard fired, oxidized. Stacked in firing. Rim frieze: miniature acanthus-flower scroll left. Main decoration: pendent semicircles outlined by crude dots, with rosette 2/5 at centre. Medallion: three concentric circles. Monogram PAR.
– Rusjaeva & Nazarčuk 2006, pl. 193.6.

EPH-1282*
Olbia, Sector R25, O-P25-04-3260, Parutine, Olbia National Preserve storeroom. Fr. of upper body. H 3.7 × W 2.7, WT 0.4. Fabric: relatively fine and micaceous, small lime inclusions, 5YR 6/6. Thin dull coat, ext. 5YR 4/6, 2.5/1, int. 2.5YR 4/6. Medium hard fired, oxidized. Stacked in firing. Main decoration: pendent semicircles, outlined by large dots, four-rayed sun wheel at centre.

EPH-1283
Olbia, V.I. 4998, Antikensammlung, Staatliche Museen zu Berlin (formerly Vogell collection), lost in WW II. Complete. ⌀ rim 9.5; vessel H 5.7; H:⌀ 1:1.7. Fabric: fine and slightly micaceous, a few minute lime particles. Brown coat. Oxidized. Rim frieze: Ionian kyma. Main decoration: pendent semicircles outlined by large dots, five-rayed sun wheel at centre.
– Zahn 1908, 67 cat. 24; Boehlau 1908, 31 no. 282.

EPH-1284*
Olbia, Sector R25, O-P25-98-2143, Parutine, Olbia National Preserve storeroom. Fr. of rim and upper body. H 3.2 × W 3, WT 0.2, ⌀ rim 7.5, 12%, RH 1.3. Fabric: relatively fine and micaceous, 2.5Y 6/2. Slightly lustrous coat, Gley 1 2.5/N. Hard fired, reduced. Rim frieze: horizontal S-spirals. Main decoration: pendent semicircle with five-rayed sun wheel at center, row of dots above. Two grooves below rim.

EPH-1285*
Olbia, Sector R25, O-P25-93-1297, Parutine, Olbia National Preserve storeroom. Rim fr. H 2.3 × W 3.3, WT 0.2, ⌀ rim 8.5, 12%, RH 1.1. Fabric: relatively fine and micaceous, Gley 1 5/10Y. Lustrous coat, Gley 1 2.5/N. Hard fired, reduced. Rim frieze: horizontal S-spirals. Main decoration: pendent-semicircle design suggested by dots at top of wall. Two grooves below rim.

EPH-1286
Istros, His-1073, Bucharest, Institute of Archaeology storeroom. Fr. of lower body and part of base. H 2 × W 2.3, WT 0.3. Fabric: fine, slightly micaceous, a few minute lime particles, Gley 1 7/10Y. Dull coat ext., 5Y 5/1, uncoated int. Relatively hard fired, reduced. Main decoration: pendent semicircles outlined by dots, four-rayed sun wheel (?) at center. Medallion: three concentric circles.

EPH-1287
Istros, His-166, Bucharest, Institute of Archaeology storeroom. Fr. of lower body. Fabric: relatively fine and micaceous. Oxidized. Main decoration: pendent semicircles outlined by dots.

EPH-1288*
Pantikapaion, palace foundation trench, M-84-56, Moscow, Puškin Museum of Fine Arts. Fr. of rim and upper body. H 3.9 × W 5, WT 0.1, ⌀ rim 8, 18%, RH 1.8. Fabric: relatively fine and micaceous. Thin dull coat. Oxidized. Stacked in firing. Rim frieze: star rosettes. Main decoration: net pattern.

EPH-1289*
Olbia, Sector R25, O-P25-92-836, Parutine, Olbia National Preserve storeroom. Rim fr. H 2.8 × W 2.8, WT 0.25, small diameter, RH 1.35. Fabric: relatively fine and micaceous, some small voids, Gley 1 5/10Y. Slightly lustrous coat, Gley 1 2.5/N. Medium hard fired, reduced. Rim frieze: astragal. Main decoration: pendent-semicircle pattern suggested by dots at top of wall, unless they are frieze separators. Two grooves below rim.

EPH-1290*
Olbia, Sector E2, square 55, Room [Cistern] Л, western part, grey clay layer, О-E2-48-4977, Kiev, Institute of Archaeology storeroom. Rim fr. H 3.2 × W 1.8, WT 0.5. Fabric: relatively fine and

micaceous, 5Y 5/1. Slightly lustrous coat, Gley 1 3/N. Relatively hard fired, reduced. Rim frieze: Ionian kyma.

EPH-1291
Myrmekion, M-53-19, St Petersburg, IIMK RAN. Rim fr. H 2.9, WT 0.35, ⌀ rim 8, 15%, RH 1.3. Fabric: relatively fine and micaceous, 2.5YR 5/8. Thin dull coat, ext. 2.5YR 4/6, 3/1, int. 2.5YR 4/6. Oxidized. Stacked in firing. Rim frieze: Ionian kyma.

EPH-1292
Istros, His-403, Bucharest, Institute of Archaeology storeroom. Rim fr. Fabric: relatively fine and micaceous. Reduced. Rim frieze: Ionian kyma.

EPH-1293
Olbia, Sector R25, O-P25-95-111b, Parutine, Olbia National Preserve storeroom. Rim fr. H 2.7 × W 2.7, WT 0.21, small diameter, RH 1.25. Fabric: relatively fine and micaceous, small lime inclusions, 5Y 5/1. Slightly lustrous coat, ext. Gley 1 2.5/N, int. 2.5Y 3/1. Hard fired, reduced. Rim frieze: horizontal S-spirals. Two grooves below rim.

EPH-1294
Olbia, Sector NGS, O-НГС-02-399, Parutine, Olbia National Preserve storeroom. Rim fr. H 2.5 × W 3.5, WT 0.2–0.39, ⌀ rim 8, 12%, RH 1.9. Fabric: fine and slightly micaceous, a few minute lime particles, some voids, 5Y 5/1. Thin firm lustrous coat, 2.5Y 2/0. Medium hard fired, reduced. Rim frieze: horizontal S-spirals. Calyx: imbricate pointed petals with central and side veins.

EPH-1295*
Olbia, Sector NGS, O-НГС-02-738, Parutine, Olbia National Preserve storeroom. Rim fr. H 3.2 × W 5.4, WT 0.18–0.38, ⌀ rim 9, 14%, RH 1.9. Fabric: fine, micaceous, a few minute lime particles, 7.5YR 6/4. Thin slightly flaking coat with slight lustre, 10YR 3/1. Medium hard fired, oxidized. Rim frieze: guilloche left.

Juglet

EPH-1296
Olbia, Sector AGD, O-АГД-87-660, Kiev, Institute of Archaeology storeroom. Fr. of shoulder and upper part of body; attachment of band handle. H 5 × W 7, WT 0.4. Fabric: soft, very micaceous, 10YR 5/2. Thin dull coat, very worn ext., 5Y 2.5/1, uncoated int. Low fired, reduced. Rim frieze: box meander, ccw.

EPH-1297* SHA-94
Myrmekion, M-49-631, St Petersburg, State Hermitage Museum. Fr. of shoulder and body. H 4.3, WT 0.35. Fabric: no fresh break for observation. Dull black coat ext. Reduced. Rim frieze: Ionian kyma. Main decoration: Greek moving left but turned back to right, right hand raised as for spear (which is not represented). Hunt?

EPH-1298
Olbia, present whereabouts unknown (formerly Vogell collection). Complete except for handle. Vessel H 7.4. Fabric: fine, micaceous, grey. Black coat. Reduced. Rim frieze: heart guilloche left. Calyx: imbricate. Medallion: rosette.
– Boehlau 1908, 27 no. 254, pl. VII.7.

Juglet on Foot

EPH-1299*
Olbia, Sector E7, squares 783, 782s, 764s, 710s, House 12, O-E7-69-489+492, Kiev, Institute of Archaeology storeroom. Two joining frs. of base and lower body. H 3.2 × W 4.2, WT 0.35, ⌀ base 2.6. Fabric: fine, slightly micaceous, a few minute lime particles, 5Y 5/1. Slightly lustrous coat ext., Gley 1 2.5/N, uncoated int. Medium hard fired, reduced. Calyx: lotus petal, acanthus. Medallion: rosette A.

Juglet?

EPH-1300* SHA-119
Pantikapaion, palace foundation trench, M-84-33, Moscow, Puškin Museum of Fine Arts. Fr. of shoulder and upper part of body. H 4.2 × W 5.5, WT 0.5. Fabric: fine brownish grey. Dull black coat ext., uncoated int. Reduced. Main decoration: upper frieze of dolphins left; below, warrior with shield moving left, warrior with shield moving right.

Kantharos

EPH-1301*
Olbia, Sector AGD and Bothros 11, O-АГД-88-195, 208, Kiev, Institute of Archaeology storeroom. Four rim fragments (one with handle) and one body fr., all joining; one non-joining body fr. WT. 0.3–0.5, ⌀ rim 14.5, 38%; vessel H 11. Fabric: standard, 10YR 6/1, 6/2. Dull coat, 5Y 2.5/1. Not too hard fired, reduced. Rim frieze: guilloche right. Calyx: filled 'nelumbo' with kissing couple on *kline*, suspended draperies in the background. The 'nelumbo' is surrounded by lush floral work with looped stems, large acanthus flowers, and buds; large naturalistic acanthus leaf with bent tip. Frieze separators: dots. Secondarily burnt. Six repair holes, a seventh has been attempted. VG Workshop?
– Samojlova 1994, fig. 1.3.

Skyphos with Pinched Handles

EPH-1302*
Olbia, Sector I, West, ash clay layer, О-И-48-2103, 3827, Kiev, Institute of Archaeology storeroom. Two non-joining frs. of rim and upper body. H 5.5 × W 6.3, WT 0.28, ⌀ rim 13, 15%, RH 3.3. Fabric: standard, 5YR 6/8. Dull mottled coat, ext. 5YR 3/1, 2.5YR 4/8, int. 2.5YR 4/8. Relatively hard fired, oxidized. Stacked in firing. Rim frieze: box meander, cw. Above, laurel wreath painted with thin buff paint over thin incised line. Monogram PAR.

Amphora, Pergamene Type

EPH-1303* SHA-224
Pantikapaion, П-1909-140, St Petersburg, State Hermitage Museum. Joined from numerous frs., preserving almost complete profile except for base. ⌀ rim 14; vessel H 17.8. Oxidized. Multiple rim friezes: miniature acanthus-flower scroll left; rosette 2/7. Main decoration: widely spaced figures walking or facing right. Eros walking right, alternately with hand on hip or crowing himself; saluting Pan right. Calyx B1, widely spaced. Monogram PAR.

EPH-1304
Olbia, present whereabouts unknown, probably Odessa, Historical Museum. Complete. Vessel H 19. Dark coat. Oxidized. Multiple rim friezes: Ionian kyma; jewellery pendants. Main decoration: winged thunderbolts. Calyx: unknown. Medallion: rosette A. VG Workshop.
– Samojlova 1994, fig. 3.2.

Amphora, Ephesian Type

EPH-1305*
Pantikapaion, П-1850-20, St Petersburg, State Hermitage Museum. Complete. ⌀ rim 16, ⌀ base 12.4; vessel H 22.5. Reduced. Rim frieze: heart guilloche left. Main decoration, upper frieze: altar scene D, Centaur, Eros playing musical instrument(?), female holding bowl and lifting dress (dancer?). Lower frieze: alternating masks of young satyr and bearded horned 'Phonician' Pan(?). Calyx: slender bent leaves flanking ovoid petal alternating with vertical floral scroll; nine-petalled rosettes as space filler. Medallion: rosette with petal in three tiers surrounded by astragals. Frieze separators: astragal.
– Schwabacher 1941, 187 no. 16; Pochmarski 1990, RK 90.

EPH-1306*
Pantikapaion, П-1852-5, St Petersburg, State Hermitage Museum. Complete. ⌀ rim 15.8, ⌀ base 12.5; vessel H 20.9. Reduced. Rim frieze: rosette 2/10. Main decoration: rider with *gorytos* (twice), parade rider (once), lion, dog attacking stag (twice), Greek against boar, Amazon. Calyx: straight naturalistic acanthus with segmented mid-rib alternating with vertical floral scroll. Medallion: five-rayed sun wheel surrounded by heart stamp from heart guilloche. Frieze separators: dots. VG Workshop.

EPH-1307*
Pantikapaion, П-1842-41, St Petersburg, State Hermitage Museum. Complete. ⌀ rim 15.9, ⌀ base 13.4; vessel H 21.5. Reduced. Rim frieze: Ionian kyma. Main decoration, upper frieze: parade rider (three times), centaur on knees, battling Greeks, horse with turned head. Lower frieze: 18 rabbits jumping left. Calyx: straight naturalistic acanthus under every other rabbit. Medallion: rosette with eight rounded petals alternating wide and narrow. Frieze separators: dots.
– Reinach 1892, 101 pl. XLVII.1–3; Raeder 1986, 204 cat. 10.

EPH-1308
Kepoi, Ке-62-192/39, Moscow, State Historical Museum. Complete. ⌀ rim 13, ⌀ base 13.5; vessel H 17.5. Fabric: very fine, micaceous, grey. Dull black coat, not covering underside of foot. Reduced. Rim frieze: guilloche right. Main decoration: plastic long petals separated by dots. Medallion: Pan mask. Frieze separators: dots.
– Sorokina 1967, fig. 39.3–4; Usačeva 1978, 105 figs. 3.1; 4; Raeder 1986, 204 cat. 12.

EPH-1309
Olbia, present whereabouts unknown. Complete. Multiple rim friezes: Ionian kyma; eight-petalled star rosettes. Calyx: imbricate rounded petals with central vein. Medallion: rosette A.
– Farmakovskij 1906, 157, fig. 315a–b; Raeder 1986, 204 cat. 13.

Amphora, Hybrid Athenian/Ephesian/Pergamene

EPH-1310
Olbia, Odessa, Historical Museum. Complete. Vessel H 20.5. Dark coat. Oxidized. Rim frieze: Ionian kyma. Main decoration: acanthus-vine scroll left. Calyx A. Medallion: rosette A, var. 1.
– Samojlova 1994, fig. 1.1.

Amphora, Type?

EPH-1311*
Olbia, Sector R25, O-P25-92-3227, Parutine, Olbia National Preserve storeroom. Fr. of mid- and lower body. H 6 × W 6.7, WT 0.4. Fabric: relatively fine and micaceous, small lime inclusions,

some small voids, Gley 1 4/10Y. Slightly lustrous coat ext., Gley 1 2.5/N. Medium hard fired, reduced. Rim frieze: flower left. Main decoration: thunderbolt alternating with large rosette 2/8. Calyx: alternating lotus petal and acanthus flower. Very similar to EPH-1312* but not the same vessel. VG Workshop.

EPH-1312*
Olbia, Sector R25, O-P25-93-896, 990b, Parutine, Olbia National Preserve storeroom. Two non-joining frs., from shoulder and upper body. H 2.7 × W 7.8 (shoulder fr.), WT 0.31–0.36, ⌀ max. 18. Fabric: relatively fine and micaceous, Gley 1 4/10Y. Slightly lustrous coat, ext. Gley 1 2.5/N. Medium hard fired, reduced. Rim frieze: flower left. Main decoration: thunderbolt alternating with large rosette 2/8. Calyx: broad lotus petal alternating with bud (stem not preserved). Very similar to EPH-1311*. VG Workshop.

EPH-1313*
Olbia, Sector NGS, O-НГС-06-113, 471, 484, Parutine, Olbia National Preserve storeroom. Shoulder fr., two joining and two non-joining body frs. H 4.5 × W 14.7, WT 0.26, ⌀ max. 18. Fabric: relatively fine and micaceous, some small lime inclusions, 5Y 3/1. Coat with slight lustre ext., 5Y 2.5/1. Medium hard fired, reduced. Multiple rim friezes: astragal; Ionian kyma. Main decoration: two mounted figures with skirted cuirasses and flying cloaks moving left. Back legs of horse extended as in gallop, but front legs positioned as though parading, and horse turns head back. Calyx: imbricate small palmettes, upside down. Frieze separators: dots.

EPH-1314
Olbia, Sector NGS, O-НГС-88-136, Parutine, Olbia National Preserve storeroom. Shoulder fr. H 4.1 × W 6.4, WT 0.3, ⌀ ca. 20. Fabric: fine, soft, micaceous, 10YR 7/4. Thin dull coat ext., 5Y 2.5/1. Low fired, oxidized. Multiple rim friezes: Ionian kyma; faint row of small circles. Main decoration: bunch of grapes, perhaps of acanthus-vine scroll.

EPH-1315*
Pantikapaion, Zabelina 1247 26/3 [b], Moscow, State Historical Museum (Zabelina collection). Body fr. H 7 × W 9, WT 0.5. Fabric: fine, micaceous, grey (no fresh break for observation). Fine slightly lustrous black coat ext., uncoated int. Reduced. Multiple rim friezes: wave meander; small circles; Ionian kyma. Main decoration: acanthus-vine scroll right. Calyx: tips of low pointed petals with double outline preserved.

EPH-1316
Olbia, Sector NGS, O-НГС-92-240, Parutine, Olbia National Preserve storeroom. Shoulder fr. with handle attachment. H 3 × W 3.3, WT 0.4. Fabric: relatively fine, slightly micaceous, 5Y 4/1. Dull coat ext., 5Y 2.5/1. Medium hard fired, reduced. Rim frieze: ivy leaves left. Main decoration: ivy wreath. Frieze separators: dots.

EPH-1317*
Olbia, Cliff, square 285, O-70-148+149, Parutine, Olbia National Preserve storeroom. Two joining frs. of shoulder and body; scar of handle attachment. H 5.5 × W 10.5, WT 0.31. Fabric: standard, fine, 5YR 6/6. Coat with dull lustre ext., 5YR 4/6, 2.5YR 4/8, uncoated int. Relatively hard fired, oxidized. Stacked in firing. Multiple rim friezes: box meander, ccw; Ionian kyma; astragal with decorated beads.

EPH-1318
Pantikapaion, M-64-43, Moscow, Puškin Museum of Fine Arts. Fr. of base and lower body. H 6.5 × W 7. Shiny black coat ext., int. dull. Reduced. Calyx: straight acanthus leaf (acanthus X) alternating with jewelled petal and vertical floral scroll. Medallion: double rosette with broad petals. Frieze separators: astragal. VG Workshop.

EPH-1319
Olbia, Sector E7, squares 475, 495, 515, yellow clay layer, O-E7-62-152, Kiev, Institute of Archaeology storeroom. Shoulder fr. with band handle with low rotellae. Oxidized. Rim frieze: Ionian kyma. Two scraped grooves on shoulder.

EPH-1320
Olbia, O-38-796, Kiev, Institute of Archaeology storeroom. Shoulder fr. Reduced. Rim frieze: Ionian kyma.

Jug

EPH-1321*
Olbia, O-1909-2407, present whereabouts unknown. Complete except for lip and most of handle. Rim frieze: Ionian kyma. Calyx: imbricate rounded petals with central and side veins. Base/medallion not visible in photograph.
– St Petersburg, IIMK RAN, photo archive neg. III 3426.

Lagynos?

EPH-1322*
Olbia, Sector R25, O-P25-95-902.1+96-1439, 95-902.2, 3, 4, 1161 (note join across years), Parutine, Olbia National Preserve storeroom. Two joining body frs. (95-902.1+96-1439) and four non-joining body frs. H 8.7 × W 6, WT 0.42, ⌀ max. 21. Fabric: relatively fine and micaceous, small voids, 5YR 6/6. Thin coat with metallic sheen ext., 5YR 4/3. Medium hard fired, oxidized. Rim frieze: astragal. Main decoration: pendent semicircles outlined by large dots, with small five-rayed sun wheel at centre;

vertical line of large dots with same sun wheel between circles. Frs. may come from two almost identical vessels.

Situula with Everted Angular Rim

EPH-1323*
Olbia, Sector E3, O-E3-54-2014+2017, St Petersburg, State Hermitage Museum. Two joining frs. of rim and upper body. H 8, ⌀ rim 20. Reduced. Rim frieze: flower left. Main decoration: bound myrtle wreath with three leaves and flower buds left. Frieze separators: dots. Menemachos?
– St Petersburg, IIMK RAN, photo archive neg. II 57144.

EPH-1324*
Pantikapaion, M-46-89(?), 2250, Moscow, Puškin Museum of Fine Arts. Two non-joining frs. of rim and body. H 7, ⌀ rim 22, 18%. Black coat with dull lustre, covering surface well. Reduced. Multiple rim friezes: box meander, cw; horizontal S-spirals.
– Loseva 1962, fig. 3.1.

EPH-1325
Pantikapaion, M-47-3645, Moscow, Puškin Museum of Fine Arts. Two frs. of rim and upper body; a further rim fr. with heart-shaped handle attachment (not seen) must belong. H 4.7 × W 9, ⌀ rim 18, 12%. Dull worn coat. Reduced. Rim frieze: box meander, ccw. Calyx: imbricate fern-like leaves.
– Loseva 1962, fig. 3.2 (fr. with handle attachment).

EPH-1326
Olbia, inv. 23808, Odessa, Historical Museum. Complete profile, fragmentary. ⌀ rim 24, ⌀ base 10.2; vessel H 21.5. Dark coat. Reduced. Rim frieze: box meander. Main decoration: Skylla, Odysseus on ship. Calyx A with twisted stems topped by bud.
– Samojlova 1994, fig. 1.2; Samojlova & Batizat 1994, fig. 1.

EPH-1327
Chersonesos, year and no. unknown, present whereabouts unknown. Fr. of rim and upper body. ⌀ rim 22. Black coat. Reduced. Rim frieze: Ionian kyma. Main decoration: Judgement of Paris (Athena, traces of heads of other figures). One repair hole?
– Ushakov & Strukova 2009, 431 fig. 2.

Situla with Everted Angular Undercut Rim

EPH-1328*
Olbia, Cliff "B-VIII", square 285, yellow clay layer, O-70-214, Parutine, Olbia National Preserve storeroom. Fr. of rim and upper body. H 6.3 × W 11.6, WT 0.4, ⌀ rim 21, 19%, RH 3.3. Fabric: standard, fine, compact, 10YR 4/1. Slightly lustrous coat ext., dull int., 10YR 2/1. Relatively hard fired, reduced. Rim frieze: Ionian kyma. Calyx: imbricate pointed petals with central vein.
– Samojlova 1994, fig. 1.5.

EPH-1329*   SHA-322
Pantikapaion, M-46-1107, Moscow, Puškin Museum of Fine Arts. Rim fr. H 7.2 × W 8, ⌀ rim 22.5, 14%. Black coat with slight lustre. Reduced. Rim frieze: rosette 8/7.

Krater, Ephesian Type

EPH-1330*
Olbia, Sector NGS, House IV-4 B 351/218, O-НГС-92-677+93-539, 92-673, 678, 93-533, 539 (note join across years), Kiev, Institute of Archaeology storeroom. Five rim frs. and seven body frs.; three of the rim frs. and three of the body frs. join. H 7.1 × W 12.5, WT 0.5–0.6, ⌀ rim 36. Fabric: relatively fine and micaceous, 5Y 4/1. Medium hard fired, reduced. Rim frieze: rosette 5. Main decoration: Erotes playing musical instruments moving left and right. Calyx: looped tendrils alternating with acanthus(?). Frieze separators: dots. For Erotes, cf. Laumonier 1977, 39 cats. 3203, 3216bis, pl. 6; 42 cat. 3478, pls. 8, 118 (playing kithera); Jentel 1964, pl. XI; Chazidakis 2000, pl. 64 below, signed (playing aulos). Menemachos.
– Samojlova 1994, 90, fig. 2.2; Samojlova 1998; Guldager Bilde 2010, 284 cat. F-95, pl. 188.

EPH-1331*
Olbia, Sector NGS, O-НГС-06-149, Parutine, Olbia National Preserve storeroom. Rim fr. H 4 × W 5.7, WT 0.3, ⌀ rim 20, 8%. Fabric: relatively fine and micaceous, some small lime inclusions, 5Y 5/1. Slightly lustrous coat, 5Y 3/1. Medium hard fired, reduced. Relief decoration inside, at top of wall: box meander, cw, in very high relief; rope pattern above, guilloche(?) below; Ionian kyma on downturned outside face of rim.

Large Open Vessel (Krater?)

EPH-1332*
Olbia, Sector NGS, House III-3 C 331/128, O-НГС-91-676, Parutine, Olbia National Preserve storeroom. Fr. of upper body. H 6.1 × W 3.8, WT 0.52–0.61. Fabric: relatively fine, some mica and small lime particles, 5Y 5/1. Thin firm semi-lustrous black coat, 10YR 3/1. Hard fired, reduced. Rim frieze: flower, right. Main decoration: naked male hunter thrusting spear to right. Flower of rim appears as spacers between long petals on EPH-1043*. Menemachos.
– Guldager Bilde 2010, 284 cat. F-97, pl. 189.

EPH-1333*
Istros, His-B 503, Bucharest, Institute of Archaeology storeroom. Body fr. H 4.5 × W 4.5, WT 0.66. Fabric: standard, fine, rather compact, 5Y 5/1. Coat with slight lustre ext., shiny int., Gley 1 2.5/N. Relatively hard fired, reduced. Rim frieze: Ionian kyma. Main decoration: myrtle wreath with bud on dotted stem, right.

EPH-1334
Pantikapaion, palace foundation trench, M-85-40, Moscow, Puškin Museum of Fine Arts. Fr. of shoulder and upper body. H 7.1 × W 7.2, WT 0.5. Slightly lustrous black coat. Reduced. Rim frieze: Ionian kyma.

Dinos

EPH-1335*
Olbia, V.I. 5002, Antikensammlung, Staatliche Museen zu Berlin (formerly Mavrogordato collection, 1909). Complete. ⌀ rim 11, ⌀ base 11.1; vessel H 14.5. Fabric: fine, micaceous, yellowish. Dull blackish coat. Oxidized. Multiple rim friezes: astragal; Ionian kyma; box meander, cw. Main decoration: 'wreath' formed of a three-petal width of horizontally placed, slightly rounded imbricate petals, their forms alternating between petals with central vein alone and petals with central and side veins. Calyx A variant; beneath this, smaller 'nelumbo' with ribbed top repeated four times. Medallion: rosette A.

Lentoid Guttus

EPH-1336*
Olbia, Sector NGS, O-НГС-05-914, Parutine, Olbia National Preserve storeroom. Shoulder fr. with attachment of ring handle. H 3.8 × W 4.8, WT 0.15, ⌀ neck 3. Fabric: fine, micaceous, 5YR 6/6. Yellow wash ext., int. uncoated. Misfired or only partly fired? Oxidized. Rim frieze: box meander, ccw. Main decoration: bird, right, palmette(?). Frieze separators: dots, astragal.

EPH-1337
Kepoi, Moscow, State Historical Museum? Fr. of foot and lower body. Calyx: imbricate pointed petals with central and side veins, upside-down.
– Usačeva 1978, fig. 1.29.

Large Closed Vessel

EPH-1338
Istros, His-260, Bucharest, Institute of Archaeology storeroom. Body fr. H 2 × W 3, WT 0.58. Fabric: standard, Gley 1 6/10Y. Slightly lustrous coat. ext., Gley 1 2.5/N, uncoated int. Relatively hard fired, reduced. Main decoration: altar scene D (only upper part of D1 and 2 preserved).
– Domăneanțu 2000, 92 cat. 441, pl. 30.

EPH-1339
Istros, His-916, Bucharest, Institute of Archaeology storeroom. Body fr. H 2.7 × W 2.7, WT 0.5. Fabric: standard, 5Y 5/1. Dull coat ext., Gley 1 2.5/N, uncoated int. Relatively hard fired, reduced. Main decoration: altar fig. B1, Athena?
– Domăneanțu 2000, 15 cat. 59, pl. 4 (attributed to Vases gris).

EPH-1340*
Istros, His-B 499, Bucharest, Institute of Archaeology storeroom. Body fr. H 2.5 × W 2.3, WT 0.4. Fabric: standard, fine, 5Y 6/1. Slightly lustrous ext. Gley 1 2.5/N, uncoated int. Relatively hard fired, reduced. Main decoration: naked male left, playing aulos.

EPH-1341*
Olbia, Sector E2, square 55, Cistern Л, O-E2-49-623, Kiev, Institute of Archaeology storeroom. Body fr. H 4.5 × W 4.3, WT 0.32. Fabric: standard, fine, 5Y 5/1. Coat with dull lustre ext., Gley 1 3/N, uncoated int. Relatively hard fired, reduced. Main decoration: large flower with six broad petals separated by tongues; in the centre, ivy-berry cluster partly obscured by clay blob.

EPH-1342*
Pantikapaion, palace foundation trench, M-84-63, Moscow, Puškin Museum of Fine Arts. Fr. of mid-body. H 5 × W 5.5, WT 0.52. Thin dull brownish coat ext., uncoated int. Oxidized. Rim frieze: star rosettes. Main decoration: bound myrtle wreath with five leaves right, berry on stems and groups of three-dot berries. Frieze separators: guilloche.

EPH-1343*
Olbia, Sector R25, O-P25-06-647, Parutine, Olbia National Preserve storeroom. Fr. of upper body. H 2.8 × W 3.4, WT 0.38. Fabric: relatively fine and micaceous, Gley 1 4/N. Slightly lustrous coat ext., Gley 1 2.5/N. Medium hard fired, reduced. Multiple rim friezes: small circles; Ionian kyma. Main decoration: plastic long petals.

EPH-1344*
Olbia, Sector NGS, O-НГС-86-287, Parutine, Olbia National Preserve storeroom. Shoulder fr. H 2.7 × W 5.9, WT 0.23–0.4, ⌀ shoulder 16.5. Fabric: relatively fine and micaceous, abundant minute lime inclusions, 7.5YR 4/4, 6/6. Thin firm semi-lustrous coat ext., int. on upper part of sherd only, 2.5Y 3/2. Medium hard fired, oxidized. Rim frieze: wave meander right. Frieze separators: dots.

EPHESOS 427

EPH-1345
Olbia, Sector R25, O-P25-00-1707, Parutine, Olbia National Preserve storeroom. Fr. of upper body. Reduced. Plastic pine cone.

EPH-1346
Olbia, Sector NGS, O-НГС-91-592, Parutine, Olbia National Preserve storeroom. Fr. of lower body. Reduced. Main decoration: unidentified traces above single row of small leaves. Calyx: 'nelumbo' beside straight acanthus leaf with tip bent forward. Menemachos.

EPH-1347
Olbia, Sector R25, O-P25-04-3268, Parutine, Olbia National Preserve storeroom. Body fr. Oxidized. Calyx: imbricate rounded petals with central and side veins.

EPH-1348*
Olbia, O-52-2431, Kiev, Institute of Archaeology storeroom. Body fr. Reduced. Calyx: rows of imbricate rounded petals with central vein alternating with rows of rounded petals with central and side veins.

EPH-1349*
Olbia, Sector E6–7, square 474, grey clay layer, O-E6-7-62-264, Kiev, Institute of Archaeology storeroom. Body fr. H 3.7 × W 6.3, WT 0.35. Fabric: fine, soft, with many light-reflecting particles, 5YR 7/4. Good shiny coat ext., 5YR 3/1, uncoated int. Hard fired, oxidized. Rim frieze: Ionian kyma. Main decoration: plastic long petals surrounded by dots.

Large Vessel (Type?)

EPH-1350*
Olbia, O-63-1834, Kiev, Institute of Archaeology storeroom. Body fr. H 3.8 × W 5.3, WT 0.5. Fabric: standard, fine, Gley 1 6/N. Lustrouscoat, flaking int., Gley 1 2.5/N. Hard fired, reduced. Rim frieze: flower right. Frieze separators: dots. Identical rim pattern and dot separators on EPH-1351*.

EPH-1351*
Olbia, O-61-no no., present whereabouts unknown.
Two joining frs. of upper and mid-body. Rim frieze: flower right. Main decoration: satyr playing trumpet, Erotes playing syrinx and kithara. Frieze separators: dots. Identical rim pattern and dots as separator on EPH-1350*. Menemachos.
– St Petersburg, IIMK RAN, photo archive neg. II 73210.

DISTRIBUTION

Beljaus

EPH-902

Bol'šoj Kastel'

EPH-133*, EPH-233*, EPH-333, EPH-513*, EPH-540*, EPH-603*, EPH-649*, EPH-656*, EPH-705, EPH-832*, EPH-1004*, EPH-1009*, EPH-1041*, EPH-1122, EPH-1244*, EPH-1245*

Chersonesos

EPH-41*, EPH-66*, EPH-111*, EPH-117*, EPH-142*, EPH-161*, EPH-196*, EPH-214*, EPH-215*, EPH-234*, EPH-235*, EPH-245*, EPH-296*, EPH-334, EPH-337*, EPH-346*, EPH-348*, EPH-355*, EPH-374*, EPH-378*, EPH-492*, EPH-501*, EPH-573*, EPH-582*, EPH-639, EPH-747*, EPH-786*, EPH-808*, EPH-815*, EPH-834*, EPH-854*, EPH-895*, EPH-963*, EPH-979, EPH-1084*, EPH-1091, EPH-1095, EPH-1096*, EPH-1129*, EPH-1177, EPH-1200*, EPH-1279, EPH-1327

Istros

EPH-9*, EPH-10, EPH-12, EPH-18*, EPH-19*, EPH-23*, EPH-24*, EPH-39, EPH-42*, EPH-60, EPH-62, EPH-67*, EPH-69*, EPH-70, EPH-72*, EPH-79*, EPH-85*, EPH-86*, EPH-98*, EPH-107*, EPH-123*, EPH-132, EPH-134*–EPH-136*, EPH-140*, EPH-143, EPH-148*–EPH-150*, EPH-152*–EPH-154*, EPH-156–EPH-159*, EPH-232, EPH-243*, EPH-253*, EPH-265*, EPH-268*, EPH-270*, EPH-292, EPH-300, EPH-301, EPH-318*, EPH-319*, EPH-321*, EPH-323, EPH-330*, EPH-336*, EPH-339, EPH-343*, EPH-347*, EPH-391*, EPH-394*, EPH-395*, EPH-398*, EPH-401*, EPH-402, EPH-417*, EPH-425*–EPH-427*, EPH-430*, EPH-431*, EPH-450*, EPH-464*–EPH-466*, EPH-470*, EPH-475*, EPH-479*, EPH-491*, EPH-495*, EPH-514*, EPH-516*, EPH-523*, EPH-525*, EPH-528*, EPH-529*, EPH-531*–EPH-533*, EPH-537*, EPH-542, EPH-543*, EPH-545*–EPH-548*, EPH-560*, EPH-569*, EPH-581*, EPH-585*, EPH-593, EPH-594, EPH-602*, EPH-606*, EPH-640*, EPH-642, EPH-644, EPH-657*, EPH-658, EPH-672*, EPH-703, EPH-709, EPH-713*, EPH-736*, EPH-744, EPH-760*, EPH-775*, EPH-790*, EPH-798*, EPH-801*, EPH-807*, EPH-809, EPH-812*, EPH-816*, EPH-820*, EPH-823*, EPH-827*, EPH-836, EPH-840*–EPH-843*, EPH-846–EPH-849,

EPH-852*, EPH-858–EPH-861*, EPH-865, EPH-872, EPH-881*, EPH-885, EPH-887, EPH-890*, EPH-892*, EPH-893, EPH-896*, EPH-897*, EPH-899*, EPH-903*, EPH-904, EPH-906, EPH-912, EPH-915, EPH-922*–EPH-925*, EPH-927*, EPH-933, EPH-934*, EPH-938, EPH-940, EPH-945–EPH-947*, EPH-953*, EPH-964, EPH-974, EPH-990*–EPH-993*, EPH-996*, EPH-997*, EPH-1001, EPH-1003, EPH-1012*, EPH-1014, EPH-1018*–EPH-1020*, EPH-1023*, EPH-1024*, EPH-1029*, EPH-1030, EPH-1037*, EPH-1038*, EPH-1045*–EPH-1047*, EPH-1055*, EPH-1058*, EPH-1061*, EPH-1067*, EPH-1068*, EPH-1071*, EPH-1074, EPH-1078*, EPH-1090*, EPH-1092, EPH-1101*–EPH-1104, EPH-1106*, EPH-1108–EPH-1110*, EPH-1113*, EPH-1115*, EPH-1119*, EPH-1120*, EPH-1123–EPH-1125*, EPH-1127, EPH-1130, EPH-1138*, EPH-1142, EPH-1174*, EPH-1181*, EPH-1185*, EPH-1190*–EPH-1192, EPH-1195*–EPH-1198*, EPH-1204, EPH-1206*–EPH-1208, EPH-1211, EPH-1215*, EPH-1217*, EPH-1222*, EPH-1224, EPH-1225*, EPH-1227*–EPH-1232, EPH-1239–EPH-1241*, EPH-1249*, EPH-1251, EPH-1253*, EPH-1259, EPH-1260*, EPH-1262*, EPH-1263, EPH-1271*, EPH-1276, EPH-1286, EPH-1287, EPH-1292, EPH-1333*, EPH-1338–EPH-1340*

Kepoi

EPH-108*, EPH-126, EPH-188, EPH-190*, EPH-249*, EPH-276, EPH-608, EPH-609, EPH-636, EPH-782, EPH-810*, EPH-871, EPH-982, EPH-1220, EPH-1308, EPH-1337

Myrmekion

EPH-8*, EPH-11*, EPH-29*, EPH-34*, EPH-36*, EPH-37*, EPH-43*, EPH-51*, EPH-87*, EPH-119*, EPH-122, EPH-131*, EPH-151*, EPH-155*, EPH-184, EPH-219, EPH-231*, EPH-240*, EPH-271*, EPH-279*, EPH-281, EPH-282*, EPH-290, EPH-329*, EPH-335*, EPH-341, EPH-342, EPH-344*, EPH-354*, EPH-373, EPH-382*, EPH-399*, EPH-424*, EPH-428*, EPH-435*, EPH-437*, EPH-467*, EPH-476*, EPH-498, EPH-500, EPH-534*, EPH-553*, EPH-556*, EPH-589*, EPH-600*, EPH-607*, EPH-610*, EPH-613, EPH-625*, EPH-627*, EPH-628, EPH-632*, EPH-635*, EPH-637, EPH-646*, EPH-647, EPH-659*, EPH-663*, EPH-670*, EPH-674*, EPH-731*, EPH-735, EPH-789*, EPH-853*, EPH-864*, EPH-879, EPH-908*, EPH-936*, EPH-952*, EPH-976, EPH-981*, EPH-1006*, EPH-1010*, EPH-1017*, EPH-1021*, EPH-1025*, EPH-1031*–EPH-1034*, EPH-1039, EPH-1054, EPH-1076*, EPH-1083*, EPH-1085, EPH-1107*, EPH-1143, EPH-1151, EPH-1153, EPH-1154, EPH-1160*, EPH-1161*, EPH-1178, EPH-1179, EPH-1186*, EPH-1187*, EPH-1201*, EPH-1205*, EPH-1219*, EPH-1221*, EPH-1250*, EPH-1264*, EPH-1291, EPH-1297*

Olbia

EPH-3*, EPH-4, EPH-6*, EPH-7*, EPH-13*, EPH-15–EPH-17, EPH-20*–EPH-22*, EPH-25*, EPH-30–EPH-35*, EPH-44*–EPH-50*, EPH-52*, EPH-53*, EPH-55–EPH-59*, EPH-63*–EPH-65*, EPH-68*, EPH-71, EPH-73*, EPH-74*, EPH-77*, EPH-83*, EPH-84*, EPH-88*–EPH-97*, EPH-102, EPH-105*, EPH-114–EPH-116, EPH-118, EPH-120*, EPH-121*, EPH-124*, EPH-125, EPH-129, EPH-130, EPH-137–EPH-139*, EPH-144*–EPH-147*, EPH-160*, EPH-162*–EPH-164*, EPH-164 bis*, EPH-165*–EPH-179, EPH-182*, EPH-183*, EPH-185*, EPH-187*, EPH-191*–EPH-195*, EPH-197*–EPH-200*, EPH-203, EPH-204*, EPH-206*–EPH-213, EPH-216*–EPH-218*, EPH-222*–EPH-224*, EPH-228*, EPH-229, EPH-237, EPH-239*, EPH-241, EPH-242*, EPH-244*, EPH-246, EPH-248*, EPH-250*–EPH-252*, EPH-254*–EPH-264*, EPH-266*, EPH-272*–EPH-274*, EPH-277*, EPH-278, EPH-280*, EPH-284*–EPH-287*, EPH-291, EPH-293*–EPH-295*, EPH-298, EPH-299, EPH-302–EPH-304*, EPH-306*–EPH-313*, EPH-315*–EPH-317*, EPH-320*, EPH-322*, EPH-325*, EPH-328*, EPH-332, EPH-338*, EPH-340*, EPH-345, EPH-349*, EPH-351–EPH-353*, EPH-358–EPH-364*, EPH-368*–EPH-372*, EPH-375*–EPH-377*, EPH-380*, EPH-381, EPH-383*, EPH-385*, EPH-388*–EPH-390*, EPH-397*, EPH-400*, EPH-403–EPH-408*, EPH-411*–EPH-416*, EPH-418, EPH-419*, EPH-423*, EPH-434, EPH-438*–EPH-441*, EPH-443*, EPH-445*, EPH-448*, EPH-449*, EPH-451*–EPH-453, EPH-455*–EPH-457*, EPH-459*, EPH-460*, EPH-462*, EPH-463*, EPH-468*, EPH-469*, EPH-471–EPH-474*, EPH-477*, EPH-478*, EPH-480*, EPH-481*, EPH-483*–EPH-485*, EPH-487*, EPH-489*, EPH-493*, EPH-494*, EPH-496*, EPH-497*, EPH-499*, EPH-502*, EPH-504*–EPH-509*, EPH-511*, EPH-515*, EPH-518*–EPH-520*, EPH-530*, EPH-535*, EPH-538, EPH-541, EPH-544*, EPH-549–EPH-552*, EPH-554, EPH-555*, EPH-557, EPH-559, EPH-562–EPH-564, EPH-566*–EPH-568*, EPH-571*, EPH-578*, EPH-579*, EPH-588*, EPH-590, EPH-596*, EPH-598*, EPH-601*, EPH-611*, EPH-612*, EPH-614, EPH-616, EPH-618*, EPH-619*, EPH-621*–EPH-624*, EPH-626*, EPH-630*, EPH-631*, EPH-633*, EPH-634*, EPH-643*, EPH-648, EPH-650*, EPH-654*, EPH-660*–EPH-662*, EPH-664*–EPH-666, EPH-668*, EPH-673*, EPH-675*, EPH-677*, EPH-679*, EPH-680, EPH-682–EPH-684*, EPH-686–EPH-689*, EPH-691*–EPH-693*, EPH-695, EPH-697*–EPH-700*, EPH-704*, EPH-707*, EPH-708*, EPH-715–EPH-719*, EPH-721–EPH-724*, EPH-726*, EPH-728–EPH-730*, EPH-732*–EPH-734*, EPH-737*–EPH-742*, EPH-748*–EPH-752*, EPH-754*, EPH-755*, EPH-757*–EPH-759*, EPH-761–EPH-774*, EPH-776*, EPH-778*–EPH-781*, EPH-788*, EPH-792*–EPH-797*, EPH-799*, EPH-802, EPH-803, EPH-805*, EPH-811*, EPH-813*, EPH-814, EPH-817, EPH-818, EPH-821*, EPH-822*, EPH-824*, EPH-826, EPH-828, EPH-833,

EPH-835, EPH-837*, EPH-850, EPH-851, EPH-855*–EPH-857, EPH-862*, EPH-868*, EPH-870*, EPH-874, EPH-876*–EPH-878, EPH-882*, EPH-883*, EPH-886, EPH-889*, EPH-891*, EPH-894*, EPH-898*, EPH-909–EPH-911*, EPH-913*, EPH-919*–EPH-921, EPH-926, EPH-930*, EPH-932*, EPH-937*, EPH-939*, EPH-941, EPH-944*, EPH-948*–EPH-951, EPH-954*–EPH-962*, EPH-965*–EPH-973*, EPH-975*, EPH-977*, EPH-978, EPH-984, EPH-985*, EPH-987, EPH-988*, EPH-994*, EPH-1000*, EPH-1005*, EPH-1007*, EPH-1008*, EPH-1011*, EPH-1013*, EPH-1015*, EPH-1016*, EPH-1026*–EPH-1028*, EPH-1035*, EPH-1036*, EPH-1042*–EPH-1044*, EPH-1048*–EPH-1052*, EPH-1059, EPH-1063*, EPH-1065, EPH-1069, EPH-1072, EPH-1073*, EPH-1080*, EPH-1081*, EPH-1093*, EPH-1097*–EPH-1100, EPH-1105*, EPH-1111*, EPH-1112*, EPH-1114*, EPH-1126, EPH-1128*, EPH-1131, EPH-1132*, EPH-1134*, EPH-1135*, EPH-1137, EPH-1139, EPH-1140*, EPH-1144–EPH-1146*, EPH-1149*, EPH-1155–EPH-1159*, EPH-1162–EPH-1166*, EPH-1168*, EPH-1169*, EPH-1171, EPH-1176*, EPH-1180, EPH-1184*, EPH-1188, EPH-1193, EPH-1194*, EPH-1199*, EPH-1202, EPH-1209, EPH-1210, EPH-1226*, EPH-1233*, EPH-1235, EPH-1237, EPH-1238*, EPH-1242*, EPH-1243, EPH-1252*, EPH-1254, EPH-1256*, EPH-1261*, EPH-1265*–EPH-1270*, EPH-1272*, EPH-1274*, EPH-1275*, EPH-1277*, EPH-1281*–EPH-1285*, EPH-1289*, EPH-1290*, EPH-1293–EPH-1296, EPH-1298, EPH-1299*, EPH-1301*, EPH-1302*, EPH-1304, EPH-1309–EPH-1314, EPH-1316, EPH-1317*, EPH-1319–EPH-1323*, EPH-1326, EPH-1328*, EPH-1330*–EPH-1332*, EPH-1335*, EPH-1336*, EPH-1341*, EPH-1343*–EPH-1351*

Olbia?

EPH-396*, EPH-678*, EPH-756, EPH-884

Olbia or Pantikapaion

EPH-54*

Pantikapaion

EPH-1*, EPH-2*, EPH-5, EPH-27*, EPH-28, EPH-40, EPH-61*, EPH-78*, EPH-80*, EPH-81*, EPH-99–EPH-101*, EPH-103*, EPH-104*, EPH-106*, EPH-110*, EPH-112*, EPH-113, EPH-127*, EPH-141, EPH-189*, EPH-201, EPH-202, EPH-220, EPH-275, EPH-283*, EPH-289*, EPH-314*, EPH-324*, EPH-327, EPH-331, EPH-350, EPH-356*, EPH-365*, EPH-367*, EPH-379, EPH-386*, EPH-387, EPH-393, EPH-442*, EPH-446*, EPH-482, EPH-488*, EPH-490*, EPH-536, EPH-570, EPH-572, EPH-574*, EPH-580*, EPH-583, EPH-584*, EPH-587*, EPH-595*, EPH-605, EPH-615, EPH-617, EPH-638, EPH-641*, EPH-651*, EPH-669*, EPH-671*, EPH-676, EPH-696*, EPH-702, EPH-706*, EPH-712, EPH-720, EPH-725*, EPH-727*, EPH-746*, EPH-753*, EPH-777, EPH-783–EPH-785, EPH-791*, EPH-804, EPH-806, EPH-845*, EPH-863, EPH-866*, EPH-873*, EPH-875*, EPH-880, EPH-900*, EPH-901, EPH-931*, EPH-942*, EPH-943*, EPH-983, EPH-986, EPH-989*, EPH-995*, EPH-998*, EPH-999, EPH-1002*, EPH-1060*, EPH-1066, EPH-1070, EPH-1082, EPH-1094, EPH-1116, EPH-1118, EPH-1167*, EPH-1170*, EPH-1183*, EPH-1189*, EPH-1212, EPH-1216*, EPH-1218*, EPH-1234*, EPH-1246*–EPH-1248, EPH-1273*, EPH-1288*, EPH-1300*, EPH-1303*, EPH-1305*–EPH-1307*, EPH-1315*, EPH-1318, EPH-1324*, EPH-1325, EPH-1329*, EPH-1334, EPH-1342*

Pantikapaion?

EPH-109, EPH-186, EPH-1278

Porthmion

EPH-26, EPH-76, EPH-128, EPH-180, EPH-181, EPH-205, EPH-221, EPH-226, EPH-227, EPH-236*, EPH-238, EPH-247, EPH-267*, EPH-269*, EPH-288*, EPH-297, EPH-305, EPH-357, EPH-409, EPH-420–EPH-422, EPH-432, EPH-433, EPH-447*, EPH-458*, EPH-461*, EPH-510*, EPH-512, EPH-517, EPH-521, EPH-526, EPH-527, EPH-539, EPH-558*, EPH-561*, EPH-575, EPH-586, EPH-591, EPH-592, EPH-604*, EPH-629*, EPH-667, EPH-685*, EPH-701*, EPH-710, EPH-711, EPH-714, EPH-743, EPH-745, EPH-787, EPH-800*, EPH-829*, EPH-830*, EPH-838, EPH-839, EPH-844*, EPH-867, EPH-869, EPH-888, EPH-905, EPH-914, EPH-916–EPH-918, EPH-928, EPH-929, EPH-1022, EPH-1040, EPH-1053, EPH-1056, EPH-1057, EPH-1062*, EPH-1077, EPH-1079, EPH-1087–EPH-1089, EPH-1117, EPH-1121, EPH-1136*, EPH-1141*, EPH-1147*, EPH-1148*, EPH-1172, EPH-1173, EPH-1182, EPH-1213, EPH-1214, EPH-1223*, EPH-1255, EPH-1257

Ruminskoe/Za Rodinu

EPH-75*, EPH-410*, EPH-597*, EPH-907*

Tyras

EPH-694

Tyritake

EPH-14*, EPH-38, EPH-225*, EPH-384*, EPH-429*, EPH-444*, EPH-486*, EPH-524, EPH-599, EPH-653*, EPH-681, EPH-935*, EPH-980, EPH-1075, EPH-1086, EPH-1133*, EPH-1150*, EPH-1152*, EPH-1175*, EPH-1203*, EPH-1280

Volna 1

EPH-82*, EPH-230, EPH-326*, EPH-366, EPH-392*, EPH-436*, EPH-454*, EPH-503*, EPH-522, EPH-565, EPH-576*, EPH-577*, EPH-620*, EPH-645*, EPH-652*, EPH-655*, EPH-690*, EPH-819, EPH-825*, EPH-831*, EPH-1064*, EPH-1236*, EPH-1258*

CHAPTER 15

Knidos

Knidos produced and exported late Hellenistic fine pottery to an extent which has hitherto gone unrecognized. This has first of all to do with the fact that, until recently, very little Knidian material had been published; consequently, it was difficult to identify Knidian pottery when it was found outside Knidos. For some time, however, it has been recognized that bowls with exterior rouletting are in large part the products of Knidian workshops (Kögler 2010, 123–126); these have also been found in the Black Sea region. Knidian MMB, however, were almost completely unknown (Love 1967) until P. Kögler turned her attention to the Knidian fine wares (Kögler 2000a; 2010). Fragments of at least 35 moulds have been unearthed at Knidos. Most of these were found by American archaeologists in 1967 in workshop debris in the South Necropolis (Context F), but some also came to light in the North Necropolis.[1] According to Kögler, the moulds allow us to establish ca. 40 individual stamps native to this industry (2010, 298). Unfortunately, in her otherwise monumental book on the Knidian fine ware, Kögler allots only a few pages to the MMB, due to the overwhelming amount of material present (Kögler 2010, 296). Nevertheless, her publication makes it possible to identify a number of Knidian bowls found not just in the Black Sea region, but also on Delos.

Fabric

The fabric is normally fine and compact, with occasional lime inclusions and some light-reflecting particles. It is in general very hard fired and the vessels are mostly reduced, even though on the surface they may appear to be oxidized. Common colours amongst the Black Sea collection of Knidian vessels are 10YR 6/1, 2.5Y 6/1, 5Y 5/1, Gley 1 4/N, 5/N and 6/N, often with orange or pinkish margins. The vessels are covered with a dull slip fired blackish, dark greyish, or deep reddish, 10R 5/6, 10YR 3/1, 2.5Y 3/1, 5Y 3/1, Gley 1 3/N, Gley 1 4/10Y.

Shape

The shape is invariably a relatively deep bowl with a plain, straight, or slightly everted rim with a diameter of 13 to 16 cm (one measures almost 18 cm). There are normally two crude grooves below the lip. Shape, size, and the grooves reveal that the instigation for the production of MMB in Knidos most likely was through emulation of Athenian vessels, and the popularity of the heart guilloche as a rim pattern points in the same direction.

Decoration

Based on the published moulds and fragments of bowls from Knidos (Kögler 2010), the unpublished manuscript by Laumonier of 'non-Ionian' bowls in Delos (see Chapter 2), and the Black Sea assemblages, it is possible to outline the character of the Knidian decoration. Not surprisingly, the most varied decoration is found at Knidos itself. Represented there, and not elsewhere, are hunting scenes,[2] a stylized scroll,[3] plastic pine-cone design,[4] imbricate petals,[5] and net pattern.[6]

The following decoration, which can be placed in several friezes as well as cover the entire body, can be found in the Mediterranean and the Black Sea assemblages: figural scenes, myrtle wreath, garland, multiple rim friezes, imbricate palmettes, and PSC design; the most common decoration in all areas is a calyx, frequently featuring a distinctive slender palmette with branches curving in alternating directions ('Knidian palmette'). It should be noted that decoration based on a long-petal pattern is almost completely unknown in the repertoire of the Knidian MMB.

The heart guilloche and the Ionian kyma, and, in a secondary position, the astragal, are almost universal as rim patterns. A number of different base devices are employed, such as several types of rosettes with lobed petals. The Eros and Psyche kissing, found on a mould (Kögler 2010, 523 cat. F.160, pl. 31) and a bowl (Kögler 2010, 519 cat. F.115,

---

1 P. Kögler, pers. comm.

2 Kögler 2010, 520 cat. F.132, pl. 29; 521 cat. F.146, pl. 30 (mould); and probably 438 cat. C.59, pl. 6; 519 cat. F.117, pl. 27; 520 cat. F.130, pl. 29.
3 Kögler 2010, 430 cat. B.58, pl. 4; 523 cat. F.166, pl. 32 (mould); 592–593 cats. Kn.327, Kn.328, Kn.338, pl. 59.
4 Kögler 2010, 520–521 cat. F.136, pl. 29; 522 cat. F.157, pl. 31 (mould); 593 cat. Kn.331, pl. 59.
5 Kögler 2010, 437–438 cat. C.58, pl. 6; 520 cat. F.126, pl. 28; 521 cat. F.137, pl. 29; 522 cat. F.158, pl. 31 (mould); 593 cat. Kn.334, pl. 59.
6 Kögler 2010, 430 cats. B.54–B.56, pls. 3, 4; 437 cat. C.57, pl. 6; 593 cat. Kn.332, pl. 59; with dotted outline: 593 cat. Kn.335, pl. 59.

pl. 27) at Knidos (but not elsewhere), is striking. One should also note the medallion of myrtle leaves alternating with a berry on a stalk, known, again, from moulds (Kögler 2010, 523 cats. F.161, F.162, pl. 31) and bowls.[7]

The style of the decoration varies from very fine to very sloppy. Frequently, the decoration has a 'wooden' look – the rim patterns in particular often look as if they had been carved in wood.

Chronology

MMB are very rare in Knidian deposits dating before the second half of the 2nd century (Kögler 2010, 300). This suggests that, even though MMB probably began to be made there in the first half of the century (second quarter?), the main production was in its second half; a related production continued even into the early Roman period (Kögler 2010, 304–307). This corresponds well with the fact that Knidian MMB are decisively more frequent in the later assemblage of Istros than they are in the earlier one of Olbia (2.6% and 1.1% respectively), and it should be noted that at Olbia, proportionally more Knidian pieces were found in Sector R25, where in general the MMB are later than those in the other Olbian sectors (see Chapter 20).

Distribution

Kögler is of the opinion that Knidian MMB were little exported, and she quotes (in addition to the Olbian specimens I have mentioned to her) only a few pieces from Athens and one from Paphos, as well as a group of finds from Amorgos, the last-mentioned unpublished (Kögler 2010, 58). Knidian MMB are relatively well represented on Delos, though the Knidian bowls with rouletting are almost twice as common there. It should not be overlooked that Amorgos is on the direct route between Knidos and Delos, and this may explain the presence of Knidian MMB there.

In the Black Sea region, I have been able to identify Knidian MMB at Tomis (Constanta Museum inv. 12032; Ocheșeanu 1969, cat. 14), Istros, Olbia, Chersonesos, Pantikapaion, Myrmekion, Tyritake, Kepoi, and Theodosia (Moscow, State Historical Museum inv. 32733[j], collection of Berthier de la Garde). In terms of quantity, almost the same number of vessels were imported from Knidos as were imported from Athens (up to 75 and 76, respectively). We find the same proportion on Delos, where Knidian and Athenian vessels each constitute up to 0.8% (Fig. 4).[8] So Knidian MMB were certainly exported; they are just waiting to be identified.

---

7   Kögler 2010, 430 cats. B.54, B.55, pl. 3; 519 cats. F.121, F.122, pl. 28.

8   [Ed. More Athenian mouldmade bowls from Delos have now been published, upsetting this equivalence; see Rotroff 2018.]

CATALOGUE TO CHAPTER 15

BOWLS

A   Figural Decoration

Erotes

In contrast to, for example, the Ephesian production, Knidian workshops depicted Erotes only sparingly. KNI-1*, with syrinx-playing Erotes, is the only occurrence in the Black sea region, although Erotes are known on Knidian MMB from Knidos (Kögler 2010, 519, 520 cats. F.114, F.131, pls. 27, 29) and from Delos (Laumonier vol. 2, cat. 3229).

KNI-1*
Olbia, Sector NGS, О-НГС-05-215+217, Parutine, Olbia National Preserve storeroom. Two joining rim frs. and two joining body frs. H 6.8 × W 10.7, WT 0.28, ⌀ rim 14, 13%, RH 2.3. Fabric: fine, dense, non-micaceous, Gley 1 4/N, core/int. 5YR 6/6. Thin dull wash, ext. 5YR 3/1, 3/3, int. 2.5Y 4/1. Very hard fired, reduced. Rim friezes: two grooves below lip; Ionian kyma. Main decoration in two registers: Satyr masks; frontal syrinx-playing Erotes separated by long-bearded masks.

Aulos-Playing Pan

The aulos-playing Pan is also found on bowls from Knidos (Kögler 2010, 594 cat. Kn.341, pl. 59) and from Delos (Laumonier vol. 2, cat. 3434).

KNI-2*
Istros, His-B 433/V 19462, B 443, Bucharest, Institute of Archaeology storeroom. Two non-joining body frs. H 4.4 × W 4.8, WT 0.45. Fabric: relatively fine, non-micaceous(?), some minute lime inclusions, 5YR 7/8. Slightly lustrous coat, 10YR 3/2. Very hard fired, oxidized. Rim frieze: dolphin upside-down; dog running left. Main decoration: frontal aulos-playing Pan wrapped in short cloak alternating with loutrophoros with conical lid. The tall loutrophoros with conical lid is found on a number of bowls, such as KNI-2*, KNI-35*, KNI-36*, as well as on moulds and vessels from Knidos (Kögler 2010, 521 cat. F.145, pl. 30; 523 cat. F.160, pl. 31 [moulds]; 479 cat. E.252, pl. 16; 519 cats. F.112, F.113, pl. 27; 521 cat. F.143, pl. 30; 593 cat. Kn.330, pl. 59 [bowls]). It was probably copied from Kymean production (cf. KYX-15*). A related rim frieze occurs on a bowl from Delos (Laumonier vol. 2, cat. 3434).
– Domăneanţu 2000, 11 cat. 43, pl. 3 (identified as Ephesian).

KNI-3*
Istros, His-B 456/V 19455+B 495, Bucharest, Institute of Archaeology storeroom. Two joining frs. of mid- and lower body. H 6.3 × W 9.5, WT 0.43. Fabric: fine, compact, some very fine light-reflecting particles, 10YR 6/1 with orange edges. Dull mottled coat ext., partly oxidized int., ext. 10YR 3/1, 2.5YR 5/6, int. 5Y 3/1. Very hard fired, reduced with oxidized margins. Stacked in firing. Main decoration in two registers: frontal aulos-player with mantle alternating with bunches of grapes(?); suspended wreaths separated by bees. One repair hole. The bees in the lower frieze are known from a mould at Knidos (Kögler 2010, 521 cat. F.147, pl. 30), from a bowl fragment, also at Knidos (Kögler 2010, 593 cat. Kn.330, pl. 59), as well as from a fragment from Delos (Laumonier vol. 2, cat. 3082).
– Domăneanţu 2000, 132 cat. 647, pl. 46.

Masks

Frontal masks with a long beard, either Dionysos, a Satyr, or Pan, occur in a number of varieties, e.g., KNI-1*, KNI-4*–KNI-8, KNI-37, KNI-73*, KNI-74*. In the Pontic area, we also find them on a Knidian vessel from Tyras (Batizat 2002, fig. 8.1) and in the Mediterranean on moulds (Kögler 2010, 594–595 cats. Kn.348, Kn.353, pl. 60) and bowl fragments (Kögler 2010, 594 cats. Kn.342, Kn.345, pl. 60) from Knidos as well as from Delos (Laumonier vol. 2, cat. 3048).

KNI-4*
Istros, His-105, Bucharest, Institute of Archaeology storeroom. Fr. of rim and upper body. H 6.5 × W 7, WT 0.35, ⌀ rim 16, 11%, RH 2.8. Fabric: fine, compact, some very fine light-reflecting particles, 2.5Y 6/1 with orange edges. Dull coat, 2.5Y 3/1, 2.5YR 5/6. Hard fired, reduced with oxidized rim. Stacked in firing. Rim frieze: grooves. Main decoration: frontal Dionysos masks alternating with Herakles in short garment holding club.
– Domăneanţu 2000, 128 cat. 622, pl. 44.

KNI-5*
Istros, His-V 19457, Bucharest, Institute of Archaeology storeroom. Fr. of rim and upper body. H 5.5 × W 6.3, WT 0.35, ⌀ rim 14, 15%, RH 1.9. Fabric: fine, compact, occasional lime inclusions, some light-reflecting particles, 5YR 6/8. Dull mottled coat, 2.5YR 4/6, 10YR 3/2. Hard fired, oxidized. Stacked in firing. Rim frieze: grooves. Main decoration: frontal Dionysos masks.
– Domăneanţu 2000, 128 cat. 623, pl. 44.

KNI-6*
Istros, His-B 616, V 19364 B, Bucharest, Institute of Archaeology storeroom. Two non-joining body frs. H 3.8 × W 5.5, WT 0.33. Fabric: rather fine, compact, a few voids, 10YR 7/1. Dull coat, ext. 2.5Y 4/1, int. 2.5Y 3/1. Hard fired, reduced. Main decoration: frontal Dionysos masks. Calyx: 'Knidian' palmette with rosette (sloppily stamped) as space-filler.
– Domăneanțu 2000, 128 cat. 626, pl. 44.

KNI-7*
Chersonesos, X-1953–461, St Petersburg, State Hermitage Museum. Fr. of rim and upper body. H 6.4, WT 0.25, ⌀ rim 15, 20%, RH 2.2. Fabric: standard, fine, 2.5YR 7/6. Thin dull coat, ext. 10R 5/6, 7.5YR 2.5/1, int. 10R 5/6, Gley 1 4/N. Oxidized. Stacked in firing. Rim friezes: two thin grooves; astragal. Main decoration: Pan mask, bird left (peacock?).

KNI-8
Istros, His-984, Bucharest, Institute of Archaeology storeroom. Body fr. Reduced. No rim frieze. Main decoration: frontal mask. One repair hole.

Dogs

A hunting scene is hardly intended: the dogs look more like lap dogs than hunting dogs, and there is no prey.

KNI-9*
Istros, His-490, 1074, V 8575 A, Bucharest, Institute of Archaeology storeroom. Three non-joining body frs. H 5 × W 3.7, WT 0.5. Fabric: standard, fine, 5Y 6/1. Dull coat, 5Y 3/1. Relatively hard fired, reduced. Rim frieze: Ionian kyma. Main decoration: dogs right alternating with short 'Knidian' palmette. Calyx: straight acanthus leaf alternating with acanthus flower. The acanthus flower occurs on several vessels, see also **KNI-43***, **KNI-44***, **KNI-48***, Kögler 2010, 593–594 cat. Kn.339, pl. 59, and Laumonier vol. 2, cat. 3434.
– Domăneanțu 2000, 110 cats. 552 and 554, pl. 36 (identified as Pergamene).

Dolphins

KNI-10*
Kepoi, Ке-66-153, Moscow, State Historical Museum. Fr. of mid-body. Stacked in firing. Multiple rim friezes: Ionian kyma; astragal. Main decoration: heraldic(?) dolphin(s) around krater with ribbed body. The same krater can be found on a mould fragment from Knidos (Kögler 2010, 522 cat. F.152, pl. 30).
– Usačeva 1978, fig. 1.6.

Boukrania

Boukrania can be found on several bowls, mostly combined with suspended garlands (Knidos: Kögler 2010, 437 cat. C.56 [unnumbered on pl. 6]; Delos: Laumonier vol. 2, cat. 3269).

KNI-11*
Istros, His-B 502, Bucharest, Institute of Archaeology storeroom. Fr. of upper body. H 4.5 × W 3.1, WT 0.33. Fabric: rather fine, compact, minute lime inclusions, 2.5Y 6/1. Slightly lustrous coat, ext. 10YR 3/2, int. 10YR 3/1. Relatively hard fired, oxidized. Main decoration in several registers: boukrania between rosettes in negative relief functioning as phialai(?); decoration in lower register unidentified (vegetal?). The rosette in negative relief occurs on a number of bowls: **KNI-11***, **KNI-15***, **KNI-41**, and on a mould (Kögler 2010, 523 cat. F.164, pl. 32) and a bowl from Knidos (Kögler 2010, 520 cat. F.128, pl. 28), as well as on a bowl from Tyras (Batizat 2002, fig. 8.1).

Birds

Birds are depicted on a number of vessels, e.g., **KNI-12***, **KNI-13***, and **KNI-38*** as well as on a mould from Knidos (Kögler 2010, 595 cat. Kn.356, pl. 60).

KNI-12*
Olbia, Sector NGS, O-НГС-88-96, Parutine, Olbia National Preserve storeroom. Fr. of upper body. H 1.7 × W 2.5, WT 0.24–0.31. Fabric: fine, dense, slightly micaceous, some minute lime particles, many small voids, N5/. Thin dull coat, slightly diluted on top of relief, 5Y 2.5/1. Medium hard fired, reduced. Main decoration: bird flying right. An identical bird occurs on a bowl from Myrmekion (**KNI-39**).

KNI-13*
Istros, His-B 449, Bucharest, Institute of Archaeology storeroom. Fr. of upper body. H 2.8 × W 2.4, WT 0.3. Fabric: fine, compact, 5Y 5/1 with orange edges. Dull wash, 5Y 3/1. Very hard fired. Rim frieze: Ionian kyma? Main decoration: bird left between spirals.
– Domăneanțu 2000, 93 cat. 449, pl. 30.

Ear of Grain

The motif is probably intended to represent rye (*Secale cereale*). Interestingly enough, we also find an ear of grain on a fragment from Delos most likely of Knidian manufacture (Laumonier vol. 2, cat. 1386). I do not know of this motif from other production places.

KNI-14*
Olbia, O-66-1133, Kiev, Institute of Archaeology storeroom. Body fr. H 3.1 × W 4.7, WT 0.35. Fabric: fine, a few light-reflecting particles, Gley 1 5/N with light red margins. Thin dull coat, ext. 5Y 4/1, int. 10YR 4/2. Hard fired, reduced. Main decoration: ear of grain, probably rye.

Concentric Circles

Decoration with concentric circles is known from Knidos and Delos. At both sites it is employed as a space-filler in the calyx (Knidos: Kögler 2010, 429–430 cat. B.53, pl. 3; 437 cat. C.55, pl. 6. Delos: Laumonier vol. 2, cat. 947), whereas on Delos, it can also constitute the main decoration (Laumonier vol. 2, cat. 4333).

KNI-15*
Istros, His-V 19440, Bucharest, Institute of Archaeology storeroom. Fr. of base and lower body. Reduced. Main decoration: rosette in negative relief and concentric circles. Medallion: trace of petal and ray?

B   *Garlands and Wreaths*

Myrtle Wreath

The myrtle wreath is occasionally encountered on Knidian MMB: on a single vessel at Knidos, combined with U-shaped garlands suspended between boukrania (Kögler 2010, 537 cat. C.56 [unnumbered on pl. 6]), and on a few fragments from Delos (Laumonier vol. 2, cats. 1948, 3092–3093, 3103). See also **KNI-75***, where this pattern appears on a closed vessel. Myrtle leaves also appear (with the same berries on stalks) as a base medallion (Kögler 2010, 430 cats. B.54, B.55, pl. 3; 519 cats. F.121, F.122, pl. 28; 523 cats. F.161, F.162, pl. 31).

KNI-16*
Olbia, Sector NGS, House III-3 B 368/102, O-НГС-93-122, Parutine, Olbia National Preserve storeroom. Fr. of rim and body. H 6.8 × W 8, WT 0.23–0.28, Ø rim 13, 14%, RH 2.27. Fabric: relatively fine, slightly micaceous, some very small black inclusions, 5YR 6/8, 10YR 6/1, bicolour from stacking, with grey core. Thin dull firm coat, blotchy, ext. 2.5Y 3/0, 5YR 5/4, int. 10YR 4/1. Hard fired, oxidized. Stacked in firing. Rim frieze: grooves; Ionian kyma with double outline. Main decoration: myrtle wreath left with berries on stems. One repair hole.
– Guldager Bilde 2010, 283 cat. F-75, pl. 182.

KNI-17*
Istros, His-1013, Bucharest, Institute of Archaeology storeroom. Body fr. close to rim. H 3.3 × W 2.4, WT 0.25. Fabric: fine, compact, some light-reflecting particles, Gley 1 4/N. Dull wash, Gley 1 3/N. Very hard fired. No rim frieze. Main decoration: bound myrtle wreath left.

Suspended Garlands

Suspended garlands are amongst the most popular decorative patterns. Amongst the Pontic finds, two main types occur: a thick, flat garland (**KNI-18***–**KNI-22***) and a slender, more pendant one, normally with a *tainia* (**KNI-23***–**KNI-25***). At Knidos and on Delos, a third, small U-shaped garland is documented (Kögler 2010, 429 cat. B.52, pl. 3; 437 cat. C.56 [unnumbered on pl. 6]; 519 cat. F.118, pl. 27; 594 cat. Kn.350, pl. 60 [mould]; Delos: Laumonier vol. 2, cats. 1950, 3105–3107, 3269), whereas – strangely enough – the thick, flat garland is not represented. A complete bowl with the slender garland over a calyx of 'Knidian' palmettes has been found at Tomis (Constanta Museum inv. 12032; Ocheşeanu 1969, cat. 14).

KNI-18*
Olbia, O-59-1919, Parutine, Olbia Archaeological Museum. Complete. Rim frieze: grooves. Main decoration in two registers: suspended garlands in both friezes. Calyx: straight acanthus with rosettes as space-filler. Medallion: small rosette. Frieze separator: Ionian kyma.
– Levi 1964a, fig. 7.3; St Petersburg, IIMK RAN, photo archive neg. II 69083.

KNI-19*
Istros, His-B 613/V 19370, Bucharest, Institute of Archaeology storeroom. Large body fr. H 6 × W 5.7, WT 0.54. Fabric: fine, non-micaceous, a few silvery particles, 5Y 6/2. Dull worn coat, ext. 2.5YR 4/6, int. 2.5Y 3/1. Relatively hard fired, oxidized. Main decoration: suspended garland. Calyx: 'Knidian' palmette topped by ivy-berry cluster alternating with various vegetal elements. Frieze separator: Ionian kyma.

KNI-20*
Olbia, Sector R25, O-P25-04-1909, Parutine, Olbia National Preserve storeroom. Fr. of upper body. H 3.8 × W 5.5, WT 0.2. Fabric: fine, dense, non-micaceous, 5Y 5/1. Thin dull coat, ext. 5Y 3/1, int. 2.5YR 5/6. Very hard fired, reduced. Stacked in firing. Rim frieze: Ionian kyma? Main decoration: suspended garlands over vertical myrtle bunch (*bakchos*) alternating with palmette or similar.

KNI-21
Olbia, Sector E7, square 558w, yellow clay layer, O-E7-59-1151[a], Kiev, Institute of Archaeology storeroom. Fr. of upper body. Rim frieze: astragal. Main decoration: suspended garlands.

KNI-22*
Olbia, Sector D, cleaning of sector borders, О-Д-46-3122, Kiev, Institute of Archaeology storeroom. Fr. of rim and body. H 5.4 × W 6, WT 0.3, RH 2.5. Fabric: fine, minute lime inclusions, 10YR 6/1 with light red edges. Slightly lustrous coat, ext. 5YR 3/1, 2.5YR 4/8, int. 5YR 3/1. Hard fired. Stacked in firing. Rim frieze: astragal, very finicky. Main decoration: suspended garland.

KNI-23*
Istros, His-B 455a/V 19463, Bucharest, Institute of Archaeology storeroom. Fr. of upper body. H 3 × W 2.2, WT 0.25. Fabric: fine, compact, no visible inclusions, 5Y 5/1 with orange edges. Coat with dull lustre, 5Y 3/1. Very hard fired. Rim frieze: astragal. Main decoration: suspended garlands with *tainia*.
– Domăneanțu 2000, 92 cat. 443, pl. 30.

KNI-24
Istros, His-Dup-[14] In the possession of P. Dupont. Rim fr. No rim frieze. Main decoration: suspended garland with *tainia*.

KNI-25*
Istros, His-V 19433, Bucharest, Institute of Archaeology storeroom. Fr. of rim and upper body. H 4.3 × W 2.8, WT 0.2, RH 2.2. Fabric: fine, compact, 5Y 5/1 with orange edges. Dull wash, ext. 10YR 3/1, 2.5YR 5/6, int. 5Y 2.5/1. Very hard fired. Stacked in firing. Rim frieze: astragal. Main decoration: probably suspended garland with *tainia*.

C   *Multiple Rim Friezes*

Multiple rim friezes were very popular. In Knidos, a number of moulds featuring this decoration have been found (Kögler 2010, 521–522 cats. F.144, F.148–F.151, F.153, pls. 30, 31; 594 cat. Kn.349, pl. 60) together with bowl fragments (Kögler 2010, 438 cat. C.60, pl. 6; 451–452 cats. D.109, D.110, pl. 9; 520 cats. F.134, F.135, pl. 29; 593–594 cats. Kn.329, Kn.340, pl. 59). This decoration is also documented on Delos (Laumonier vol. 2, cats. 5835, 8007).

Multiple Rim Friezes Combined with Calyx

KNI-26*
Chersonesos, Tomb 232, X-1910-106, St Petersburg, State Hermitage Museum. Complete; restored from five frs. ⌀ rim 17.7, RH 3.2, ⌀ base 3; vessel H 10.4; H:⌀ 1:1.7. Fabric: no fresh break for observation. Dull coat, Gley 1 4/N. Reduced with oxidized margins. Stacked in firing. Multiple rim friezes: grooves; heart guilloche left; astragal; Ionian kyma; heart guilloche left. Calyx: slender S-curved acanthus leaves alternating with 'Knidian' palmettes; birds sitting left on tip of acanthus. Medallion: rosette with rounded petals.
– Belov 1978, 55, fig. 7.

Multiple Rim Friezes Combined with Imbricate Palmettes

KNI-27
Olbia, O-1925-371, present whereabouts unknown. Body fr. Multiple rim friezes: palmettes; Ionian kyma; heart guilloche right. Calyx: three rows of small imbricate palmettes.
– St Petersburg, IIMK RAN, photo archive neg. II 19395.

KNI-28*
Olbia, Sector R25, O-P25-96-1457.1, 2, 992, Parutine, Olbia National Preserve storeroom. Three non-joining frs. of body and base. H 3.5 × W 3, WT 0.18–0.65, ⌀ base 3.8. Fabric: fine, some light-reflecting particles, Gley 1 4/N. Thin slightly lustrous coat, 2.5Y 3/1. Very hard fired, reduced. Multiple rim friezes: Ionian kyma; Ionian kyma; astragal. Calyx: small imbricate palmettes. Medallion: rosette with eight rounded petals separated by stylized tongues.

Multiple Rim Friezes, Rim Fragments

KNI-29*
Istros, His-Dup- [1], in the possession of P. Dupont. Fr. of rim and upper body. ⌀ rim 14.5. Multiple rim friezes: Ionian kyma; astragal; Ionian kyma; astragal.

KNI-30*
Olbia, Sector E6, House E5, Room "B", yellow clay layer, O-E6-67-1231, 1231[a, b], Kiev, Institute of Archaeology storeroom. Three body frs., two joining. Above relief decoration, a frieze of painted blobs in clay ground and oblong line in white connecting the blobs. H 6.8 × W 7, WT 0.35–14.4. Fabric: fine, compact, Gley 1 4/N. Coat with dull lustre, ext. 2.5Y 3/1, 2.5/1, 2.5YR 5/6, int. 2.5Y 3/1. Hard fired, reduced. Stacked in firing. Multiple rim friezes: heart guilloche left; Ionian kyma; heart guilloche left.

KNI-31*
Chersonesos, X-1953-462, St Petersburg, State Hermitage Museum. Fr. of rim and upper body. H 5.3, WT 0.25, ⌀ rim 16, 13%, RH 3.6. Fabric: fine, compact, some particles of silvery mica, Gley 1 5/N, at rim 2.5YR 7/6. Thin slightly lustrous black coat, Gley 1 3/N. Multiple rim friezes: two grooves below lip; heart guilloche left; astragal.

KNI-32
Chersonesos, X-1952-160, St Petersburg, State Hermitage Museum. Fr. of upper body. H 1.7, WT 0.3. Fabric: fine, compact,

some lime inclusions and particles of silvery mica, Gley 1 5/N. Thin slightly lustrous coat, Gley 1 3/N. Reduced. Multiple rim friezes: Ionian kyma; heart guilloche left.

KNI-33
Istros, His-222, present whereabouts unknown. Fr. of upper body. H 3 × W 2.5. Multiple rim friezes: heart guilloche left; Ionian kyma; heart guilloche left.
– Domăneanţu 2000, 131 cat. 644, pl. 45.

D *Vegetal Decoration*

Not just amongst the vegetal designs, but in general, the calyx as the main decoration is by far the most popular design on Knidian bowls. The most common vegetal element employed in the calyx is a slender palmette with branches curving in alternating directions. The palmette, which I call the 'Knidian' palmette, is frequently topped by an ivy-berry cluster. This motif is found on **KNI-19***, **KNI-38***, and **KNI-39**, as well as on a fragment from Theodosia (Moscow, State Historical Museum inv. 32733[j]), on a fragment exhibited in the Kerč History and Culture Reserve (inv.?), and on many fragments of moulds and bowls at Knidos (Kögler 2010, 429–430 cat. B.53, pl. 3; 430 cat. B.57, pl. 4; 437 cats. C.54, C.55, pl. 6; 521 cat. F.143, pl. 30; 512 cat. F.44, pl. 30 [mould]) and on Delos (Laumonier vol. 2, cat. 1414). It is also employed in the Kymean workshops (see Chapter 11, palmettes C, D, E, and N). Not infrequently, figural elements appear as space-fillers amongst the vegetation. Loutrophoroi, as rendered on **KNI-35*** and **KNI-36***, are quite common and can be found on moulds and bowls unearthed at Knidos (Kögler 2010, 521, cat. F.145, pl. 30; 523 cat. F.160, pl. 31 [moulds]; 519 cats. F112, F.113, pl. 27; 521 cat. F.143, pl. 30 [bowls]). Other motifs found at Knidos include Erotes (Kögler 2010, 518–519 cats. F109, F.114, pl. 17), frontal masks (Kögler 2010, 549 cat. Kn.348 [mould], Kn.342 [bowl], pl. 60), kraters (Kögler 2010, 519 cat. F.119, pl. 28), dolphins (Kögler 2010, 594 cat. Kn.345, pl. 60), concentric circles (Kögler 2010, 429–430 cat. B.53, pl. 3; 437 cat. C.55, pl. 6; and at Delos, Laumonier vol. 2, cat. 947) and rosettes (Kögler 2010, 595 cat. Kn.354, pl. 60 [mould]; 518–519 cats. F.110–F.111, pl. 27; 520 cat. F.128, pl. 28 [bowls]). To my knowledge, the fine herm on **KNI-34*** is unique.

Calyx with Figural Decoration

KNI-34*
Olbia, Sector NGCentre, Hellenistic basement, О-НГЦ-68-1093+1096, Kiev, Institute of Archaeology storeroom. Two joining frs. of base and lower body. H 5 × W 9.7, WT 0.25, ⌀ base 3.8. Fabric: fine, some small voids, 5Y 7/1 with orange edges. Coat with dull lustre, ext. 2.5Y 4/1. Hard fired, reduced. Main decoration: acanthus flower growing from acanthus calyx, frontal male herm with nebris, palmettes as space-fillers. Medallion: rosette with 10(?) broad petals. The acanthus flower growing from an acanthus calyx is known from several bowls at Knidos (Kögler 2010, 519–520 cats. F.122–F.124, pl. 28) and from one on Delos (Laumonier vol. 2, cat. 611). An identical base rosette can be found on a mould fragment (Kögler 2010, 523 cat. F.165, pl. 32) and on a bowl from Knidos (Kögler 2010, 519 cat. F.118, pl. 27).

KNI-35*
Chersonesos, X-1965-63, St Petersburg, State Hermitage Museum. Fr. of large part of bowl. H 8.3, WT 0.35 16. Fabric: relatively coarse, non-micaceous, with lime inclusions, and some light-reflecting particles, 5YR 5/4. Thin dull coat, mottled ext., more uniform int., ext. Gley 1 6/N, int. 5Y 2.5/1. Very hard fired, reduced with buff margins. No rim frieze. Main decoration: tall acanthus leaf, tall loutrophoroi as space-fillers; very sloppily made.

KNI-36*
Istros, His-B 483/V 8573 M, Bucharest, Institute of Archaeology storeroom. Fr. of rim and upper body. H 5.8 × W 7, WT 0.33, ⌀ rim 14, 10%, RH 2.5. Fabric: fine, compact, Gley 1 5/N. Thin dull coat, ext. 10YR 4/1, int. 10YR 3/1. Very hard fired, reduced with oxidized margins. Rim friezes: two grooves; dots; astragal. Main decoration: loutrophoroi with conical lids alternating with slender palmettes.
– Domăneanţu 2000, 139 cat. 694, pl. 50.

KNI-37
Chersonesos, Quarter VIII 19/37102, present whereabouts unknown. Fr. of rim and upper body. Rim frieze: grooves. Main decoration: bearded mask between straight acanthus leaves.
– Chlystun 1996, 155, fig. 1.

KNI-38*
Myrmekion, M-57-256, St Petersburg, State Hermitage Museum. Fr. of base and most of body. H 10.5, WT 0.4, ⌀ base 3.3. Fabric: fine, compact with some lime inclusions and particles of silvery mica, 2.5Y 5/1. Dull coat ext., slightly lustrous int., ext. 10R 5/6, int. 7.5YR 5/6. Very hard fired, reduced with oxidized margins. Calyx: acanthus with ivy-berry cluster alternating with 'Knidian' palmette with ivy-berry cluster; between the vegetation, bird left. Medallion: several rows of small triangular leaves.

KNI-39
Myrmekion, 1957-D 294, Warsaw, National Museum. Fr. of mid- and lower body. Calyx: 'Knidian' palmette topped by ivy-berry cluster alternating with lower vegetal element; on tip of latter, bird flying right. An identical bird appears on a small fragment from Chersonesos (**KNI-12***).
– Sztetyłło 1976, fig. 81.b.

KNI-40*
Olbia, Sector NGS, О-НГС-02-631, Parutine, Olbia National Preserve storeroom. Fr. of base and lower body. H 5.3 × W 6.4, WT 0.3 0.85, ⌀ base 4. Fabric: fine, slightly micaceous, some minute lime particles, 5YR 5/8. Thin firm coat, slightly lustrous int., dull mottled ext. but slightly lustrous where blackened, ext. 10R 5/6, 10YR 3/1, int. 2.5YR 4/6. Medium hard fired, oxidized. Stacked in firing. Calyx: 'Knidian' palmettes separated by Ionic columns. Medallion: crude rosette with tongue-shaped petals encircled by crudely shaped ridge.

Calyx

KNI-41
Istros, His-1033, Bucharest, Institute of Archaeology storeroom. Fr. of lower body. Oxidized. Calyx: 'Knidian' palmette and rosette in negative relief. For the rosette, see **KNI-11***.

KNI-42*
Olbia, Sector R25, O-P25-95-999, Parutine, Olbia National Preserve storeroom. Fr. of lower body. H 3.4 × W 4.2, WT 0.3. Fabric: fine, some light-reflecting particles, Gley 1 5/10Y. Thin dull coat, Gley 1 3/N. Hard fired, reduced. Calyx: 'Knidian' palmettes.

KNI-43*
Istros, His-252, Bucharest, Institute of Archaeology storeroom. Fr. of upper body. H 3.5 × W 2.2, WT 0.4. Fabric: standard, fine, 10YR 6/3. Dull coat, 10YR 3/1. Medium hard fired, oxidized. Main decoration: narrow band with fish(?) and forelegs of animal(?). Calyx: acanthus flower. For the acanthus flower, see **KNI-9***.
– Domăneanțu 2000, 110 cat. 553, pl. 36 (identified as Pergamene).

KNI-44*
Istros, His-1023, Bucharest, Institute of Archaeology storeroom. Body fr. H 2.2 × W 4, WT 0.35. Fabric: fine, compact, Gley 1 6/10Y. Thin dull mottled coat, ext. Gley 1 6/10Y, 3/N, int. Gley 1 4/10Y. Hard fired, reduced. Main decoration: unidentified traces. Calyx: lotus petal, acanthus flower. For the acanthus flower, see **KNI-9***.
– Domăneanțu 2000, 16 cat. 64, pl. 4 (identified as Ephesian).

KNI-45
Istros, Sector Z1, His-57-12?/V 17586 B, Bucharest, Institute of Archaeology storeroom. Body fr. H 4.5 × W 6, WT 0.28. Fabric: fine, compact, some light-reflecting particles, Gley 1 6/N. Dull wash, ext. 5Y 5/1, int. 5Y 4/1. Very hard fired. Calyx: slender S-curved acanthus leaves and perhaps looped stem.
– Domăneanțu 2000, 137 cat. 682, pl. 49.

KNI-46*
Istros, His-515/B 141, Bucharest, Institute of Archaeology storeroom. Body fr. H 4.3 × W 4.7, WT 0.3. Fabric: fine, compact, some light-reflecting particles, Gley 1 6/N. Dull wash, ext. 5Y 4/2, 3/2, int. 5Y 5/1. Very hard fired. Calyx: straight acanthus leaf and tall vegetal element, perhaps slender S-curved acanthus leaf.
– Domăneanțu 2000, 138 cat. 683, pl. 49.

KNI-47*
Istros, His-925, Bucharest, Institute of Archaeology storeroom. Body fr. Reduced. Calyx: straight palm branch.

KNI-48*
Istros, His-B 600/V 19369, Bucharest, Institute of Archaeology storeroom. Fr. of lower body. H 2.2 × W 4.2, WT 0.3. Fabric: fine, compact, Gley 1 5/10Y. Thin dull coat, Gley 1 4/10Y. Hard fired, reduced. Calyx: acanthus flower, straight acanthus leaf with segmented central vein. For the acanthus flower, see **KNI-9***.
– Domăneanțu 2000, 97 cat. 474, pl. 31.

KNI-49*
Istros, Sector MC1, His-56-88, Bucharest, Institute of Archaeology storeroom. Body fr. Reduced. Main decoration: vegetal stem with berries; rosette.

KNI-50*
Istros, His-404, Bucharest, Institute of Archaeology storeroom. Body fr. Fabric: fine, non-micaceous. Oxidized. Rim frieze: astragal. Calyx: straight acanthus leaves.

KNI-51*
Myrmekion, M-57-216[b], St Petersburg, IIMK RAN. Fr. of rim and upper body. H 5, WT 0.2, ⌀ rim 16, 12%, RH 2.6. Fabric: fine, compact with some lime inclusions and particles of silvery mica, ext. 2.5YR 5/8, int. Gley 1 6/5GY. Thin dull coat, 10R 5/6. Oxidized. Rim friezes: two grooves below lip; heart guilloche left. Calyx: tip of vegetal element (type?) (omitted from drawing).

KNI-52*
Istros, His-1080, Bucharest, Institute of Archaeology storeroom. Fr. of upper body. H 3.3 × W 3.1, WT 0.35. Fabric: fine, compact, 5Y 5/1 with orange edges. Dull wash, ext. 10YR 3/1, 2.5YR 5/6, int. 2.5Y 3/1. Very hard fired. Stacked in firing. Main decoration: large palmette.

KNI-53*
Istros, His-V 19423, Bucharest, Institute of Archaeology storeroom. Fr. of base and lower body. H 4.7 × W 4.8, WT 0.25, ⌀ base 2.7. Fabric: hard, compact, some minute lime inclusions, Gley 1 4/N. Dull slip, ext. Gley 1 4/10Y, int. Gley 1 3/N. Hard fired,

reduced. Calyx: lotus sepals. Plain, slightly convex base surrounded by low ridge. Attribution to Knidos is tentative.

Imbricate

KNI-54*
Olbia, Sector R25, O-P25-04-2810, Parutine, Olbia National Preserve storeroom. Two joining frs. of base and lower body. H 3.7 × W 6.6, WT 0.4, RH 4. Fabric: relatively fine, non-micaceous, Gley 1 3/N. Thin dull coat, Gley 1 3/N. Medium hard fired, reduced. Calyx: crude imbricate palmettes. Medallion: surrounded by two ridges. Imbricate palmettes are documented on a number of moulds and bowl fragments from Knidos (Kögler 2010, 523 cat. F.161, pl. 31 [mould]; 519 cats. F.115, F.116, pl. 27; 520 cat. F.127, pl. 28 [bowls]).

KNI-55*
Olbia, Sector NGS, O-НГС-88-94, Parutine, Olbia National Preserve storeroom. Body fr. Reduced. Main decoration: small imbricate leaves.

KNI-56
Istros, His-621, Bucharest, Institute of Archaeology storeroom. Body fr. Reduced. Calyx: plastic imbricate leaves.

E   *Linear Decoration*

Pendent-Semicircle Design

This uncommon design is documented by two mould fragments (Kögler 2010, 522 cat. F.154, pl. 31; 594 cat. Kn.352, pl. 60) and perhaps a bowl fragment (Kögler 2010, 594 cat. Kn.343, pl. 60) at Knidos, as well as by KNI-57* and KNI-58*.

KNI-57*
Istros, His-963, 1131, Bucharest, Institute of Archaeology storeroom. Two non-joining frs. of rim and body. H 5.5 × W 6.5, WT 0.45, Ø rim 13, 13%, RH 2.3. Fabric: fine, compact, occasional lime inclusions, some light-reflecting particles, 10YR 6/1 with orange edges. Dull wash, ext. 10YR 4/1–4/2, 3/1, int. 2.5Y 4/1. Very hard fired. Rim frieze: astragal. Main decoration: pendent-semicircle pattern with five-rayed sun wheel in centre of semicircles.
– Domăneanțu 2000, 142 cats. 709 and 710, pl. 52.

KNI-58*
Istros, His-190, Bucharest, Institute of Archaeology storeroom. Fr. of lower body. Main decoration: field of large dots, probably of pendent-semicircle pattern.

Net Pattern(?)

Net pattern can be found on a small number of vessels from Knidos (Kögler 2010, 430 cats. B.54–56, pls. 3, 4; 437 cat. C.57, pl. 6; 593 cat. Kn.332, pl. 59; with dotted outline: 593 cat. Kn.335, pl. 59). They are all made with regular pentagons, not like KNI-59*, where the net is made of rounded elements. It is not entirely certain that KNI-59* is a Knidian product; the ascription is based on the similarity of its fabric to that of the Knidian group.

KNI-59*
Istros, His-1149, Bucharest, Institute of Archaeology storeroom. Body fr. Reduced. Main decoration: net pattern? One repair hole. Attribution to Knidos is tentative.

Long petals

Even though Knidian production belongs mainly in the second half of the 2nd century, long-petal design hardly ever occurs. There is a single example at Knidos, where stylized long petals appear below a frieze of scrolls (Kögler 2010, 593 cat. Kn.328, pl. 59). Clearly this design did not appeal to the Knidians.

KNI-60*
Tyritake, Sector L, Л-52-351+352+356+357+360+361+362+424, St Petersburg, IIMK RAN. Complete profile; one rim fr. and seven body frs. all joining. H 7.3, WT 0.3, Ø rim 16, 40%, RH 2.8. Fabric: fine, dense, non-micaceous, some fine light-reflecting particles, 5Y 5/7. Uncoated. Hard fired, reduced. Rim frieze: fine dots. Main decoration: isolated stylized long petals alternating with straight acanthus leaf with segmented central vein. Attribution to Knidos is tentative.

F   *Rim Fragments*

As already mentioned, the heart guilloche and the Ionian kyma, and, in a secondary position, the astragal, are almost the only rim patterns that occur.

Astragal

KNI-61*
Istros, His-1927-1942-V 8572 F, Bucharest, Institute of Archaeology storeroom. Fr. of rim and upper body. Fabric: fine, compact. Hard fired. Two grooves below lip. Secondarily burnt.

KNI-62
Istros, His-V 8572 U[a], Bucharest, Institute of Archaeology storeroom. Rim fr. Oxidized. Two grooves below lip.

KNI-63
Istros, His-233[a], Bucharest, Institute of Archaeology storeroom. Rim fr. Reduced. Two grooves below lip.

Ionian kyma

KNI-64*
Istros, His-874, Bucharest, Institute of Archaeology storeroom. Fr. of rim and upper body. H 3.8 × W 4, WT 0.3, RH 2.2. Fabric: fine, compact, 5Y 5/1 with orange edges. Dull wash, 10YR 3/1, 2.5YR 5/6. Very hard fired. Stacked in firing. Two grooves below lip.

KNI-65
Olbia, Sector R25, O-P25-97-2156.2, Parutine, Olbia National Preserve storeroom. Fr. of upper body. H 2.3 × W 3.8, WT 0.3. Fabric: fine, dense, Gley 1 4/10Y. Dull coat, ext. Gley 1 3/N, 2.5YR 4/8, int. Gley 1 3/N. Very hard fired, reduced. Stacked in firing.

Heart Guilloche Left

KNI-66
Istros, Sector "Pescărie", His-63-14a, 26, Bucharest, Institute of Archaeology storeroom. Two non-joining frs. of rim and upper body. H 4.1. Two grooves below lip.
– Domăneanţu 2000, 131 cat. 643, pl. 45.

KNI-67*
Myrmekion, M-57-470, St Petersburg, State Hermitage Museum. Body fr. close to rim. H 3.3, WT 0.35. Fabric: no fresh break for observation. Reduced. Two grooves below lip. Completely burnt or re-fired to a medium grey.

KNI-68
Istros, Sector Z, His-64-508, Bucharest, Institute of Archaeology storeroom. Body fr. close to rim.

KNI-69
Olbia, O-48-1730, Kiev, Institute of Archaeology storeroom. Body fr. close to rim. Reduced.

Heart Guilloche Right

KNI-70
Chersonesos, X-1952-151, St Petersburg, State Hermitage Museum. Two joining frs. of rim and upper body. H 4.2, WT 0.21, ⌀ rim 13, 22%, RH 3. Fabric: fine, compact with small oblong voids, a few particles of silvery mica, Gley 1 6/N. Thin dull coat, Gley 1 3/N. Reduced. Two grooves below lip.

KNI-71
Pantikapaion, year and number unknown, present whereabouts unknown. Rim fr. Grooves below lip.
– AGSP 1984, pl. CLIV.11 (only upper part of the illustrated 'bowl' is taken into consideration).

No Rim Pattern Preserved

KNI-72
Istros, His-519, Bucharest, Institute of Archaeology storeroom. Rim fr. Two grooves below lip.

SUPPLEMENTARY SHAPES

Kögler has documented several vessels on a low, wide foot, most likely amphorae, amongst the finds from Knidos (Kögler 2010, 479 cat. E.254, fig. 28, pl. 16; 521 cats. F.138–F.141, pls. 29, 30; 594 cat. Kn.346, fig. 63, pl. 60), but none of the shapes below.

Small Bowl

The attribution of **KNI-73*** and **KNI-74*** to Knidos is tentative. The Dionysos mask is very close to the one on **KNI-5***, but the fabric of the two pieces is not typical of Knidian production.

KNI-73*
Olbia, Sector R25, O-P25-98-2806, Parutine, Olbia National Preserve storeroom. Fr. of rim and upper body. H 5.1 × W 4.4, WT 0.3–0.4, ⌀ rim 8, 15%, RH 1.7. Fabric: relatively fine and micaceous, many voids, 7.5YR 5/4. Thin dull coat, mottled ext., ext. 7.5YR 3/1, 5YR 6/4, int. 7.5YR 3/1. Low fired, oxidized. Stacked in firing. Rim frieze: dots. Main decoration: Dionysos mask, Corinthian column. One repair hole. The execution of the rim is very sloppy, but the stamp is very fine and detailed. Perhaps from same vessel or from same mould as **KNI-74***.

KNI-74*
Olbia, Sector R25, O-P25-00-1703, Parutine, Olbia National Preserve storeroom. Fr. of upper body. H 3.8 × W 2.5, WT 0.35. Fabric: relatively fine and micaceous, 5YR 7/6. Dull mottled coat, ext. 5YR 5/4, 6/4, int. 5YR 5/4, 6/4. Medium hard fired, oxidized. Main decoration: Dionysos mask. Perhaps from same vessel or from same mould as **KNI-73***.

Closed Vessel

KNI-75*
Istros, His-V 19367 B, Bucharest, Institute of Archaeology storeroom. Fr. of shoulder and body. H 4.7 × W 4.5, WT 0.2. Fabric: fine, very compact, a few light-reflecting particles, Gley 1 6/N. Dull wash, Gley 1 4/10Y. Very hard fired, reduced. Multiple rim friezes: astragal; Ionian kyma. Main decoration: bound trefoil myrtle wreath with berries on stems right. Frieze separator: astragal.
– Domăneanţu 2000, 138 cat. 688, pl. 50.

DISTRIBUTION

Chersonesos

KNI-7*, KNI-26*, KNI-31*, KNI-32, KNI-35*, KNI-37, KNI-70

Istros

KNI-2*–KNI-6*, KNI-8, KNI-9*, KNI-11*, KNI-13*, KNI-15*, KNI-17*, KNI-19*, KNI-23*–KNI-25*, KNI-29*, KNI-33, KNI-36*, KNI-41, KNI-43*–KNI-50*, KNI-52*, KNI-53*, KNI-56–KNI-59*, KNI-61*–KNI-64*, KNI-66, KNI-68, KNI-72, KNI-75*

Kepoi

KNI-10*

Myrmekion

KNI-38*, KNI-39, KNI-51*, KNI-67*

Olbia

KNI-1*, KNI-12*, KNI-14*, KNI-16*, KNI-18*, KNI-20*–KNI-22*, KNI-27, KNI-28*, KNI-30*, KNI-34*, KNI-40*, KNI-42*, KNI-54*, KNI-55*, KNI-65, KNI-69, KNI-73*, KNI-74*

Pantikapaion

KNI-71

Tyritake

KNI-60*

CHAPTER 16

Vessels from Unidentified Production Sites

[Ed. PGB assembled a group of 455 unassigned mouldmade vessels from the 11 sites under consideration in this volume, of which the 77 entries of the following catalogue are only a small sample. All vessels referred to elsewhere in the book are included, along with a selection of others, largely unpublished elsewhere, that stand out for their good state of preservation or unusual decoration. Those that have been omitted are mostly very small fragments, none of which contribute to the arguments in the present book. About 150 of the omitted items have previously been published in Domăneanțu 2000, Grzegrzółka 2010, or Guldager Bilde 2010.]

BOWLS

Figural Decoration

XXX-1*
Olbia, inv. A 5500, Nikolaev, Historical Museum. Complete profile; lacking part of rim and medallion. ⌀ rim 14.1, RH 2.3, ⌀ base 3; vessel H 8.3; H:⌀ 1:1.7. Dull brownish coat. Oxidized. Rim frieze: Ionian kyma. Main decoration: dolphins alternating with Eros playing lyre riding dolphin, all swimming right. Calyx: tall 'nelumbo' with segmented central vein alternating with slender acanthus, tall thin lotus petal, and vertical acanthus scroll; in between, low plastic long petals, above which rests either head of boar left or bird sitting right. Medallion: Ephesian rosette A without tongues. Twelve repair holes. Probably imitation Ephesian rather than Ephesian; for the figures, cf. EPH-22 (early Ephesian).

XXX-2*
Olbia, Sector AGD, cistern, О-АГД-75-118, 119+120, Kiev, Institute of Archaeology storeroom. Two joining frs. of rim and body, one non-joining rim fr. H 6.6, WT 0.3. Fabric: 7.5YR 6/6. Dull coat, mottled ext., ext. 7.5YR 2.5/1, 2.5YR 4/4, int. 7.5YR 2.5/1. Not too hard fired, oxidized. Stacked in firing. Rim frieze: cross-hatching. Main decoration: naked male flanked by heraldic dolphins. Chubby figure resembles Eros but has no wings.

XXX-3 (see Fig. 41)
Olbia, O-1910-1242, present whereabouts unknown. Fr. of base and body. Main decoration: column(?), palmette(?). Calyx: widely spaced straight acanthus leaves with segmented vein, Eros driving biga with very large wheel and mismatched horses to right; low acanthus leaves at base of wall. Medallion: rosette with broad petals separated by tongues (very worn). For the Eros motif, see Chapter 6; for the Ephesian version of Eros stamp, see EPH-27*–EPH-53*.
– St Petersburg, IIMK RAN, archive inv. 4059.519.7 (pl. II).

XXX-4*
Myrmekion, M-57-1587, St Petersburg IIMK RAN. Three joining frs. of mid- and lower body. H 6.4, WT 0.45. Fabric: relatively fine, slightly micaceous, 2.5YR 6/3. Thin dull coat, adhering badly, 2.5YR 3/1. Low fired, oxidized. Main decoration: back and hind-leg of feline(?). Calyx A. Close imitation of Ephesian, cf. EPH-550*–EPH-558.

XXX-5*
Myrmekion, M-48-477, St Petersburg, State Hermitage Museum. Fr. of rim and large part of body. H 6.6, WT 0.43, ⌀ rim 12, RH 2.6. Fabric: relatively fine, very abundant lime and mica, 10YR 6/1, 5/1. Uncoated? Oxidized. Rim frieze: Ionian kyma. Main decoration: felines left and right in high relief (jewellery stamps?); below, acanthus scroll enclosing flower left. Birds sits on scroll, turning heads back.
– Šurgaja 1962, fig. 1.7; Kovalenko 1996, fig. 1.25–26 (wrongly attributed to workshop of Damokles).

XXX-6
Olbia, Sector NGS, House III-1 Stove 329/71, О-НГС-91-617, present whereabouts unknown. Fr. of rim and large part of body. Oxidized. Rim frieze: crude box meander, ccw. Main decoration: mantled women dancing to right. For mantled dancers, who appear regularly on Aiolian and Ephesian bowls, see Chapter 6.
– Guldager Bilde 2010, 288 cat. F-125.

XXX-7*
Olbia, Sector NGCentre, Basement 1, grey clay layer, О-НГЦ-68-2459, Kiev, Institute of Archaeology storeroom. Large fr. of rim, body, and tiny part of base. H 8 × W 9, WT 0.3, ⌀ rim 14, 14%, RH 2. Fabric: fine, non-micaceous, with some small voids, 2.5YR 6/4. Flaking coat with slight metallic lustre, ext. 10R 4/1, 5/6, int. 10R 4/1. Medium hard fired, oxidized. Rim frieze: Ionian kyma. Main decoration: row of Amazons with battle axe and shield striding right. Calyx B2. Medallion missing, surounded by low ridge. Imitation of Ephesian; for Amazon, cf. EPH-81*; Laumonier 1977, 304 cat. 2426, pls. 71, 128.

© PIA GULDAGER BILDE AND SUSAN I. ROTROFF, 2024 | DOI:10.1163/9789004680463_017

XXX-8*
Olbia, Sector NGS, O-НГС-06-541, Parutine, Olbia National Preserve storeroom. Fr. of mid-body. H 2.9 × W 4.5, WT 0.4. Fabric: relatively fine and micaceous, 5YR 5/6. Thin coat with slight metallic sheen, 5YR 3/1. Medium hard fired, oxidized. Main decoration: wing of large Nike(?), male in short chiton with legs crossed (Attis?), vertical branch, male figure repeated. One repair hole.

XXX-9*
Olbia, Sector NGS, O-НГС-08-366, Parutine, Olbia National Reserve storeroom. Body fr. H 3.8 × W 3.5, WT 0.3. Fabric: relatively fine and micaceous, 5YR 6/8. Thin dull coat, 2.5YR 5/6. Hard fired, oxidized. Calyx: elaborate, delicate flower on dotted stem, arm of figure wrapped in cloak. Edge of frond at left.

XXX-10
Art market, inv. O-12446, Römisch-Germanischen Zentralmuseum zu Mainz. Complete. Rim frieze: large hanging buds. Main decoration: *Agyieus* growing from vegetal calyx. Calyx: alternating straight acanthus and lotus petal. Medallion: double eight-petalled rosette. Imitation of Pergamene. *Agyieus* is common in Pergamene production: see PER-91*; Conze et al. 1913, Beibl. 43.16. Rosette, cf. Boehringer & Krauss 1937, pl. 58.b.10. Bud, cf. Conze et al. 1913, Beibl. 43.23.
– Kraus 1951, 11 cat. 13, fig. 4.2, pl. 3.5.

Scroll

XXX-11*
Olbia, Sector NGS, O-НГС-02-133+138+141+369, 05-276, Parutine, Olbia National Preserve storeroom. Complete profile; three rim frs. and one fr. of base and body, all joining; one non-joining rim fr. Body fr. burnt. H 4.4 × W 9, WT 0.22–0.45, ⌀ rim 11, RH 1.75. Fabric: relatively fine and micaceous, many small lime particles, a few voids, 5YR 5/8. Thin coat with slight lustre, missing in large patches, ext. 2.5YR 4/6, int. 2.5YR 4/8. Medium hard fired, oxidized. Rim frieze: guilloche left. Main decoration: full body acanthus-vine scroll right with crudely incised spiral tendrils. Calyx: two rows of imbricate rounded petals. Medallion: rosette (very worn). One repair hole. Imitates full-body scroll of early EC Belle Méduses and Monogram PAR; cf. Laumonier 1977, pls. 18, 35, 119, 124. See also EPH-171.

XXX-12*
Olbia, O-1929-1878, present whereabouts unknown. Fr. of rim and large part of body. Rim frieze: Ephesian rosette 7. Main decoration: crude acanthus-vine scroll left. Calyx B: pointed petals alternating with folded acanthus leaf. Imitates Ephesian; cf. EPH-182.
– St Petersburg, IIMK RAN, photo archive neg. II 4840.

XXX-13*
Olbia, Sector E2, square 55, Room [Cistern] Л, western part, grey clay layer, O-E2-48-4973[a], Kiev, Institute of Archaeology storeroom. Body fr. Oxidized. Main decoration: acanthus scroll left. Frieze separators: astragal.

XXX-14*
Myrmekion, M-58-2850, St Petersburg, IIMK RAN. Fr. of mid-body. H 3.5, WT 0.25. Fabric: fine, soft, highly micaceous, 5YR 5/4. Thin dull coat, 5YR 4/4, 3/1. Reduced. Stacked in firing. Rim frieze: Ionian kyma. Main decoration: fine incised acanthus scroll right, with poppies(?).

Myrtle Wreath

XXX-15*
Olbia, O-48-2099+2102, Kiev, Institute of Archaeology storeroom. Two joining frs. of rim and upper body. H 6 × W 6.6, WT 0.4, ⌀ rim 15, 8%, RH 1.8. Fabric: fine, non-micaceous, much minute lime, a few small light-reflecting particles, 7.5YR 7/3. Dull coat, almost completely missing, 7.5YR 3/1. Medium hard fired, oxidized. Rim frieze: Ephesian rosette 2/7. Main decoration: bound myrtle wreath with five leaves right, with berries on stems and groups of three-dot berries. Imitates Ephesian: cf. EPH-328*, EPH-344*.

XXX-16*
Istros, His-483, Bucharest, Institute of Archaeology storeroom. Body fr. H 3.6 × W 3, WT 0.26. Fabric: fine, non-micaceous, abundant minute lime inclusions, 5Y 7/1 with orange edges. Dull coat, 2.5Y 3/1. Relatively hard fired, oxidized. Rim frieze: unclear. Main decoration: bound myrtle wreath with five leaves right, with groups of three-dot berries.

XXX-17*
Istros, His-175[a], Bucharest, Institute of Archaeology storeroom. Body fr. Black coat. Reduced. Main decoration: bound myrtle wreath with five leaves right.

XXX-18*
Istros, His-61, Bucharest, Institute of Archaeology storeroom. Body fr. H 2.9 × W 2.8, WT 0.4. Fabric: fine, micaceous, 5YR 7/6. Thin dull coat, 2.5YR 4/6. Not too hard fired, oxidized. Rim frieze: small rosettes with six rhomboidal petals. Main decoration: myrtle wreath with berries on stems left; two of the five myrtle leaves replaced by heads of grain. For a rare instance of a grain wreath, cf. Kraus 1951, 12 cat. 15, fig. 5.1, pl. 4.1.

XXX-19*
Istros, His-216, Bucharest, Institute of Archaeology storeroom. Body fr. H 4.7 × W 6, WT 0.5. Fabric: fine, very fine mica, 5YR

7/6. Dull coat, 7.5YR 3/1. Relatively hard fired, oxidized. Rim frieze: flower left. Main decoration: stylised bound trefoil myrtle wreath left. Calyx: bent acanthus leaf and bent sepal corresponding to Ephesian calyx A.
– Domăneanțu 2000, 139 cat. 689, pl. 50.

Suspended Garland

XXX-20*
Istros, His-V 19373, Bucharest, Institute of Archaeology storeroom. Fr. of lower body. H 3.7 × W 3.7, WT 0.47. Fabric: fine, micaceous, a few lime or shell inclusions, 5YR 6/6. Dull coat, 5YR 6/6. Medium hard fired, oxidized. Main decoration: suspended garland with ends of *tainia*(?) at right. Calyx: single row of small palmettes.

Multiple Rim Friezes

XXX-21*
Olbia, Sector NGS, House III-3 B 368/102, O-НГС-93-270, Parutine, Olbia National Reserve storeroom. Body fr. H 3.7 × W 3.7, WT 0.2–0.47. Fabric: fine, a few light-reflecting particles, some small voids, 5YR 6/4. Thin firm coat, int. slightly lustrous, ext. with bluish metallic sheen, ext. 10YR 3/1, int. 2.5YR 4/6. Medium hard fired, oxidized. Multiple rim friezes: Ionian kyma; guilloche left. Calyx: top of rounded petal with ribbed interior preserved.
– Guldager Bilde 2010, 280 cat. F-55, pl. 178 (erroneously identified as Ephesian).

Calyx

XXX-22*
Pantikapaion, palace foundation trench, M-84-62[a], Moscow, Puškin Museum of Fine Arts. Base fr. H 3 × W 3.7, WT 0.26, ⌀ base 3. Dark brown coat. Oxidized. Calyx: small acanthus and small ovoid petals with segmented vein; rosette as space filler.

XXX-23*
Olbia, Sector NGS, O-НГС-05-911, Parutine, Olbia National Reserve storeroom. Body fr. H 4.4 × W 6, WT 0.4. Fabric: relatively fine and micaceous, 7.5YR 6/6. Thin dull coat, 7.5YR 4/1. Hard fired, oxidized. Multiple rim friezes: not preserved; rosette 2/8. Calyx: acanthus leaf with bent tip and acanthus flower on looped(?) stem. Perhaps imitates Pergamene; for acanthus flower, cf. de Luca 1975, cat. 413, pl. 54.12; 1990, pl. 26.1, 4.

XXX-24*
Olbia, Sector NGS, O-НГС-05-915, Parutine, Olbia National Reserve storeroom. Body fr. H 4.8 × W 5.6, WT 0.3. Fabric: relatively fine, many small lime inclusions, Gley 1 3/N. Thin slightly soapy coat, ext. 5Y 4/1, 2.5/1, int. 5Y 2.5/1. Medium hard fired, reduced. Stacked in firing. No rim frieze. Calyx: straight acanthus leaf alternating with pointed petal, flowers with rhomboidal petals on wavy stems between them.

XXX-25
Pantikapaion, M-71-204, Moscow, Puškin Museum of Fine Arts. Mid-body fr. H 4.5 × W 4. Dull red-brown coat. Oxidized. Multiple rim friezes: Ionian kyma; astragal. Calyx: vertical miniature flower scroll alternating with acanthus(?) and hatched petal.

XXX-26*
Olbia, O-1929-1115, present whereabouts unknown. Fr. of rim and large part of body. Rim frieze: large dots. Main decoration: pointed cross-hatched petals flank cross-hatched bud on stem. Possibly imitates Menemachean bud; cf. Laumonier 1977, 30 cat. 1893 et al. on pl. 2; 35 cat. 1343, pl. 116. For cross-hatched petals, cf. 111 cats. 603+1163, 1151, pl. 25 (Comique à la canne/late Menemachos).
– St Petersburg, IIMK RAN, photo archive neg. II 4828.

XXX-27*
Olbia, O-1910-822, present whereabouts unknown. Body fr. Calyx: pointed petals with segmented central vein alternating with vertical guilloche.
– St Petersburg, IIMK RAN, archive inv. 4058.519.6 (pl. III).

XXX-28*
Olbia, Sector NGS, O-НГС-06-134, Parutine, Olbia National Reserve storeroom. Fr. of lower body and tiny part of base. H 4.3 × W 3.3, WT 0.25. Fabric: fine, micaceous, 2.5YR 6/8. Thin dull coat, 2.5YR 4/8. Medium hard fired, oxidized. Calyx: ovoid petal with volutes alternating with column of dots. Medallion: rosette? May imitate Ephesian Wadjet symbol: cf. **EPH-33**.

XXX-29*
Olbia, Sector R25, O-P25-96-1493, Parutine, Olbia National Reserve storeroom. Fr. of lower body and base. H 5.5 × W 8.8, WT 0.6. Fabric: relatively fine and micaceous, many voids, 7.5YR 5/4. Thin dull coat, 7.5YR 3/1. Medium hard fired, oxidized. Calyx: straight, stylized acanthus; hind legs of animal leaping right over tip of acanthus. Medallion: rosette with rounded petals surrounded by radiating and overlapping pointed lotus petals.

xxx-30*
Olbia, Sector Sever-Zapad, O-СЗ-77-23, Parutine, Olbia National Reserve storeroom. Fr. of base and lower body. H 6.5 × W 5.5, WT 0.6, ⌀ base 3.5. Fabric: medium fine, slightly micaceous, abundant small lime inclusions, 7.5YR 5/4. Thin dull coat, 7.5YR 3/2. Not too hard fired, oxidized. Calyx: tall ovoid petals. Medallion: two frontal Erotes side by side; the one on the right reaches his arm across his chest, holding an object (ladle?) in his right hand; medallion surrounded by two ridges. For small human figures as medallion decoration, cf. Künzl 2002, 35–36, 38–39 cats. 22–24, 46, pls. 52–58, 119–121.

xxx-31*
Olbia, Sector R25, O-P25-95-1121, Parutine, Olbia National Reserve storeroom. Fr. of lower body. H 4.3 × W 4, WT 0.31. Fabric: relatively fine and micaceous, 7.5YR 7/6. Thin slightly lustrous coat, 7.5YR 4/1. Medium hard fired, oxidized. Calyx: lotus petals in several layers, one of them embellished with dots. One repair hole.

xxx-32
Porthmion, room 43, depth 1.67 m, П-75-372, Kerč History and Culture Reserve. Fr. of lower body. Oxidized. Calyx.
– Grzegrzółka 2010, 150 cat. 222 (attributed to Ionia)

Imbricate Pointed Petals

xxx-33
Olbia, O-1929-1145, present whereabouts unknown. Fr. of base and lower body. Calyx: imbricate, pointed petals with double veins. Medallion: within false ring foot, wide flat area with overlapping pointed and rhomboidal petals forming a rosette. One repair hole.
– St Petersburg, IIMK RAN, photo archive neg. II 4830.

Pendent-Semicircle Decoration

xxx-34*
Olbia, Sector AGD, Bothros 11, О-АГД-87-998[a], Kiev, Institute of Archaeology storeroom. Fr. of body and tiny part of base. H 8.3 × W 4.6, WT 0.3. Fabric: relatively coarse, slightly micaceous, abundant lime inclusions, some small rounded stones, 2.5YR 6/8. Thin dull wash, 5YR 4/3. Relatively hard fired, oxidized. Main decoration: widely spaced pendent semicircles with four-rayed sun wheel at centre and as spacer; field of irregular dots between circles. Medallion surrounded by ridge. One repair hole.
– Rusjaeva & Nazarčuk 2006, pl. 194.5.

xxx-35*
Olbia, Sector E7, squares 515w, 535w, humus layer, O-E7-60-531, Kiev, Institute of Archaeology storeroom. Fr. of rim and body. H 6.3 × W 6, WT 0.32, ⌀ rim 14, 10%, RH 2.1. Fabric: sandy, abundant small lime inclusions, some fine light-reflecting particles, many voids, 7.5YR 7/4. Thin dull coat, ext. 7.5YR 4/3, 3/1, int. 7.5YR 5/3. Low fired, oxidized. Stacked in firing. Rim frieze: Ionian kyma. Main decoration: pendent semicircles with four-rayed sun wheel at center, outlined by large dots.

xxx-36*
Olbia, Sector E2, square 55, Room [Cistern] Л, western part, grey clay layer, O-E2-48-4986, 49-123, 123[a], Kiev, Institute of Archaeology storeroom (two frs.; one fr. not found). Three non-joining(?) body frs. Reduced. Main decoration: crude pendent semicircles outlined by large dots, five-rayed sun wheel at center. Between semicircles, column of dots with sun wheel at bottom. Row of dots and two ridges at base of wall. Same design as xxx-68*.
– Levi 1964b, 251, fig. 13.2; St Petersburg, IIMK RAN, photo archive neg. I 43058 (O-49-123[a]).

xxx-37*
Olbia, Sector NGS, О-НГС-02-262, Parutine, National Olbia Reserve storeroom. Three rim and six body frs., all joining; bottom missing. H 8, WT 0.3–0.5, ⌀ rim 12.5. Fabric: relatively fine, micaceous, some small lime particles, 5YR 6/6. Semilustrous brownish black coat int, ext. duller and browner, large orangish blotches. Hard fired, finely potted but with crude design. Oxidized. Rim frieze: large hand-drawn box meander, ccw. Main decoration: shallow, hand-drawn crude pendent semicircles outlined by irregular short strokes and with strokes between some semicircles; stamped rosette at center. Frieze separators: short vertical strokes.

Net Pattern

xxx-38*
Olbia, Sector NGS, О-НГС-08-196+b+c, Parutine, National Olbia Reserve stroreroom. Fr. of base and lower body, two non-joining frs. of rim and upper body. H 8.2 × W 6.5, WT 0.35, ⌀ base 4.6. Fabric: relatively fine, some light-reflecting particles, 5YR 7/6. Thin dull coat, small areas missing, 2.5YR 3/4. Medium hard fired, oxidized. Main decoration: net pattern. Medallion: Ephesian rosette A surrounded by two ridges. Imitates Ephesian.

xxx-39*
Chersonesos, X-1959-25, St Petersburg, State Hermitage Museum. Fr. of base and lower body. H 4.4, WT 0.4, ⌀ base 4.5. Fabric:

sandy, highly micaceous, 10YR 8/4. Lustrous coat, 7.5YR 3/3. Hard fired, oxidized. Main decoration: net pattern. Medallion: Ephesian rosette B surrounded by two ridges. Imitates Ephesian.

Long Petals

XXX-40*
Olbia, O-51-24, Kiev, Institute of Archaeology storeroom. Body fr. Reduced. Main decoration: plastic long petals alternating with columns of palmettes.

XXX-41*
Istros, Sector "Pescărie", OI-0.87, His-63-40, Bucharest, Institute of Archaeology storeroom. Fr. of upper body. H 2.1 × W 2.6, WT 0.36. Fabric: similar to Ephesian, 5YR 6/6. Dull coat, ext. 2.5YR 4/4, int. 2.5YR 3/2. Relatively hard fired, oxidized. Main decoration: plastic long petals separated by dots and vertical vegetal element.

XXX-42
Porthmion, Sector G, sector 2, square 17–18, depth 0.42 m, П-87-99, St Petersburg IIMK RAN? Fr. of base and lower body. Main decoration: stylized long petals. Low ring foot with large diameter, concave underside.

Other Linear Designs

XXX-43*
Olbia, O-38-156, Kiev, Institute of Archaeology storeroom. Fr. of base and lower body. H 5 × W 3.3, WT 0.35, ⌀ base 4. Fabric: fine, non-micaceous, 5YR 6/6. Dull coat, int. flaking, 2.5YR 4/2. Relatively hard fired, oxidized. Calyx: small X's over entire lower body. Medallion: four radiating rounded petals with central vein. For lower body, cf. Kraus 1951, 4–5, no. 2, fig. 1.3, pl. 1.2, 3.

XXX-44
Porthmion, Sector V, П-77-79, present whereabouts unknown. Body fr. Oxidized. Main decoration: alternating vertical ridges and columns of dots. Cf. Laumonier 1977, 198–199 cats. 4890–4892, pl. 44.
– Grzegrzółka 2010, 166–167 cat. 260 (attributed to Asia Minor).

XXX-45*
Istros, His-A3-2, Bucharest, Institute of Archaeology storeroom. Body fr. Red coat. Oxidized. Main decoration: wavy lines overstamped with small dots.

Single Rim Frieze

XXX-46*
Porthmion, square 20, depth 0.75 m with material of the 2nd century, П-53-932, St Petersburg, IIMK RAN. Rim fr. H 4.3, WT 0.25, ⌀ rim 13, RH 2.2. Fabric: like standard Ephesian, but softer, 5YR 4/4, 2.5YR 4/1. Thin dull coat, adhering poorly int., 5YR 4/1, 4/2. Reduced. Rim frieze: vertical eyed chevron alternating with dots. Main decoration: traces of dots.

XXX-47*
Pantikapaion, palace foundation trench, M-89-illegible 42, Moscow, Puškin Museum of Fine Arts. Rim fr. Reduced. Rim frieze: faint, cannot be identified.

SUPPLEMENTARY SHAPES

Small Bowl

XXX-48*
Pantikapaion, П-1902-128, St Petersburg, State Hermitage Museum. Complete. ⌀ rim 8.9; vessel H 5; H:⌀ 1:1.8. Brownish orange coat, much missing. Oxidized. Rim frieze: wave meander, upside-down. Calyx: imbricate rounded petals with central vein. Medallion: very worn, Ephesian rosette B?

XXX-49*
Pantikapaion, П-1847-21, St Petersburg, State Hermitage Museum. Complete. ⌀ rim 8; vessel H 4.6; H:⌀ 1:1.7. Orangish brown coat. Oxidized. No rim frieze. Main decoration: crudely incised net pattern. Medallion: rosette with eight rounded petals.

XXX-50
Olbia, Giessen (formerly Vogell collection). Complete. ⌀ rim 8.8; vessel H 4; H:⌀ 1:2.2. Fabric: yellowish red, slightly micaceous. Brownish coat. Oxidized. No rim frieze. Main decoration: Kirbeis krater A. Calyx: lotus petals. Medallion: frontal head with flowing locks. Holes for mending.
– Zahn 1908, 62 cat. 17; Boehlau 1908, 29 no. 266.

XXX-51
Istros, Tumular necropolis, Tomb XXVI, His-58-V 19663, present whereabouts unknown. Complete profile; fragmentary bowl, ca. half preserved. ⌀ rim 8.4; vessel H 5.3. Multiple rim friezes; wave meander; fleur de lys left. Calyx: four straight, slender palm branches alternating with slender swaying acanthus leaves; floral tendrils between them. Medallion: eight-petalled rosette.

– Alexandrescu 1966, 190 cat. XXVI.1, pls. 79, 94; Domăneanțu 2000, 135 cat. 666, pl. 48.

XXX-52
Pantikapaion, Mithridates Hill, Kerč History and Culture Reserve inv. KMAK 2144 (1962). Five joining frs. of rim and body. ⌀ rim 8.6. Oxidized. No rim frieze. Calyx: slender lotus petals of varying heights.
– Grzegrzółka 2010, 73–74 cat. 60 (attributed to Pergamon).

XXX-53
Pantikapaion, Gagarin Str. П-77-no.(?), Kerč History and Culture Reserve inv. KMAK 1701. Complete profile; almost half preserved, joined from a number of frs. ⌀ rim 8.6. Oxidized. No rim frieze. Calyx: tall slender lotus petals. Medallion: rosette with slender petals with dots as space filler.
– Grzegrzółka 2010, 79–80 cat. 71 (attributed to Pergamon).

Small Bowl with One Handle

XXX-54*
Olbia, Sector R25, O-P25-95-1124, Parutine, Olbia National Reserve storeroom. Fr. of body with stub of band handle. H 5.2 × W 3, WT 0.3. Fabric: relatively fine and micaceous, small lime inclusions, 5YR 5/8. Dull coat, 2.5YR 4/8. Medium hard fired, oxidized. Calyx: straight naturalistic acanthus with hatched central vein alternating with lotus petal.

Juglet

XXX-55*
Olbia, O-1909-no no., present whereabouts unknown. Complete. No rim frieze. Calyx: 'Knidian' palmettes alternating with and overlapping ovoid petals. Medallion: small, plain, slightly concave.
– St Petersburg, IIMK RAN, photo archive neg. II 18228.

XXX-56
Kepoi, Moscow, State Historical Museum? Upper part of vessel, lacking handle and base. No rim frieze. Calyx: ovoid petals.
– Usačeva 1978, fig. 3.2.

Unguentarium?

XXX-57*
Olbia, Sector NGS, O-НГС-06-487, Parutine, Olbia National Reserve storeroom. Shoulder fr. Vertical wall, sharp angle to horizontal shoulder sloping up to narrow neck. H 2.1 × W 3.9,

WT 0.35, ⌀ max. 6. Fabric: fine, soft, non-micaceous, 10YR 6/2. Dull coat, 5Y 2.5/1. Medium hard fired, reduced. Rim frieze: vertical hearts alternating with vertical line. Frieze separators: dots. For shape, cf. de Luca 1968, 139 cat. 265, pl. 49.

Skyphos with Ring Handle

XXX-58*
Olbia, Sector NGS, O-НГС-91-555, Parutine, Olbia National Research storeroom. Fr. of lower body. WSl decoration on int.: vertical petals painted alternately in dilute clay and white. H 4.1 × W 4.1, WT 0.18–0.36. Fabric: fine, slightly micaceous, a few minute lime particles, some burnt-out organic material(?), 5YR 6/8–5/8. Dull worn coat, ext. 2.5Y 3/0, int. 2.5YR 5/6. Medium hard fired, oxidized. Plastic pine-cone decoration.

Stemmed Bowl

XXX-59
Olbia, O-1929–872, present whereabouts unknown. Fr. of lower body and part of base. Plastic pine-cone decoration, very detailed. Cf. de Luca 1968, 144 cat. 293, pl. 51 (Pergamon Asklepieion *Bauphase* 11); Tuluk 2001, 67 cat. 26, pl. 44 (mould from Ephesos).
– St Petersburg, IIMK RAN, photo archive neg. II 4825.

XXX-60
Pantikapaion, Cistern N 179, 96-no.(?), Kerč History and Culture Reserve. Fr. of stem and lower part of bowl. Traces of relief decoration.
– Tolstikov & Zhuravlev 2004, pl. 101.15

Cup with Shallow Body, Tall Collared Rim

XXX-61*
Olbia, Sector R25, O-P25-99-2886, Parutine, Olbia National Reserve storeroom. Fr. of lower body. H 2 × W 2.5, WT 0.38. Fabric: fine, very dense, non-micaceous, 2.5YR 5/6. Thin dull coat, ext. 2.5YR 4/3, int. 2.5YR 3/2. Hard fired, oxidized. Calyx: imbricate rounded petals with concentric incised bands. A two-handled cup from Tomis in the Constanta Museum is identical; otherwise I know of no parallels.

Amphora, Hybrid Athenian/Pergamene Type

XXX-62
Olbia, inv. 1315, Bonn, Akademisches Kunstmuseum (formerly Vogell collection). Complete. Handles with rotellae. White

and yellow WSl decoration on neck (wreath right) and shoulder (horizontal droplets). Vessel H 24.3. Fabric: micaceous, yellowish-red. Reddish and light brown coat. Oxidized. Rim frieze: two ridges. Main decoration: myrtle wreath with three petals left, with groups of three-dot berries. Calyx: 'palmettes', lotus petal, boukrania as space fillers. Underside undecorated.
– Boehlau 1908, 26 no. 248; Raeder 1986, 205 no. 17; Zimmer 2005, 103 cat. A21, fig. 16.

Amphora, Type?

xxx-63*
Olbia, Sector NGS, O-НГС-97-508, Parutine, Olbia National Preserve storeroom. Two joining frs. of lower part of neck, shoulder and upper (moulded) part of body. Handles with rotellae. WSl decoration: parallel filled oblique triangles on shoulder; white dot on rotella. H 4.9 × W 11.2, WT 0.19–0.45. Fabric: relatively fine, slightly micaceous, some small lime particles, some voids, 5YR 6/6. Thin coat with metallic sheen, largely missing, ext. 5YR 3/1, int. 5YR 3/3. Medium hard fired, oxidized. Rim frieze: Ionian kyma. Unidentifiable traces of main decoration.

xxx-64
Olbia, Sector R25, O-P25-93-169, Parutine, Olbia National Preserve storeroom. Shoulder fr. WSl decoration on shoulder: shadow of wavy line originally painted white. H 3.1 × W 3, WT 0.3. Fabric: fine with some light-reflecting particles, 5YR 6/8. Lustrous coat ext, dull int., 7.5YR 2.5/1. Hard fired, oxidized. Rim frieze: Ionian kyma.

xxx-65
Olbia, Sector E3O-E3-64-2400, present whereabouts unknown. Base fr. Reduced. Medallion: rosette surrounded by small palmettes.
– St Petersburg, IIMK RAN, photo archive neg. I 56357.

xxx-66
Pantikapaion, Cistern N 179, 96-no.(?), Kerč History and Culture Reserve. Part of neck and shoulder with attachment of band handle with rotella. Rim frieze: simple meander.
– Tolstikov & Zhuravlev 2004, pl. 101.8.

xxx-67
Olbia, O-1924-257b, present whereabouts unknown. Shoulder fr. Rim frieze: Ionian kyma.
– St Petersburg, IIMK RAN, photo archive neg. II 19333.

Lagynos

xxx-68*
Olbia, V.I. 4955, Antikensammlung, Staatliche Museen zu Berlin (formerly Vogell collection). Complete. Vessel H 23. Slightly lustrous black coat; foot and underside unglazed. Oxidized. Rim frieze: Ionian kyma, upside down. Main decoration: pendent semicircles with five-rayed sun wheel at centre; semicircles bordered by large dots. Columns of large dots with sun wheel at bottom as spacers. Row of large dots at base of wall. Medallion: small eight-rayed sun wheel. Graffito: SYMPLANOS (*scil.* lagynos).
– Zahn 1908, 68–71 cat. 32; Boehlau 1908, 27 no. 251; Leroux 1913, 67 cat. 133a; Zahn 1940, pl. 1.2.

Lagynos?

xxx-69*   SHA 304
Olbia, O-64-2498, St Petersburg, State Hermitage Museum. Lower half of vessel. H 9.5, ⌀ base 11. Reduced. Rim frieze: grooves. Main decoration: pendent semicircles outlined by dots with small four-rayed sun wheel at center, somewhat primitive. Column of dots as spacer. Row of large dots at base of wall. Plain medallion surrounded by three ridges.

Krater

xxx-70*
Olbia, Sector E6, square 247, 436, room with walls 54, 45, 41, grey clay layer, O-E6-57-262, Kiev, Institute of Archaeology storeroom. Rim fr. H 3.8 × W 4.1, WT 0.6. Fabric: fine, compact, no visible inclusions, 10YR 5/1. Dull coat, Gley 1 3/N. Medium hard fired, reduced. Rim frieze: on interior of rim, outer frieze of scroll with dot flowers; inner scroll perhaps of ivy. Traces of further relief decoration on floor.

Krater with Applied Feet

xxx-71*
Olbia, Sector NGS, O-НГС-91-185, Parutine, Olbia National Preserve storeroom. Applied foot in the shape of head (mask?) of bald Silenos. H 5.4 × W 4.9, WT 0.5–0.7. Fabric: relatively fine, dense, non-micaceous, 10YR 4/2. Dull coat, ext. Gley 1 2.5/N, int. uncoated. Medium hard fired, reduced. Cf. Ochotnikov 2006, pl. 13.1 (Leuke). Corinthian.

XXX-72*
Pantikapaion, palace foundation trench, M-85-45[f], 47, Moscow, Puškin Museum of Fine Arts. Fr. of base and lower body, non-joining body fr.; applied foot in form of astragal. H 6.5 × W 6, WT 0.4. Fabric: fine, very micaceous, soft, grey. Dull black coat ext., uncoated int. Reduced. Rim frieze: heart guilloche right. Calyx: straight acanthus with segmented central vein alternating with ovoid petals; jewelled 'nelumbo'(?). Frieze of fine dots around medallion.

Lentoid Guttus

XXX-73*
Pantikapaion, 1905-109.1, present whereabouts unknown. Complete. Rim frieze: large dots? Calyx: straight acanthus alternating with ovoid lotus petals.
– St Petersburg, IIMK RAN photo archive neg. III 9925.

Large Closed Vessel

XXX-74*
Istros, His-A 313, Bucharest, Institute of Archaeology storeroom. Fr. of shoulder and upper body. H 6.7 × W 7.1, WT 0.4. Fabric: fine, compact, slightly micaceous, 5Y 7/2. Dull coat ext. and on upper int., 2.5Y 2.5/1. Hard fired, reduced. Rim frieze: disc rosettes. Main decoration: scroll with leaf and tendrils.

XXX-75
Olbia, Sector NGCentre, squares 33se, 34s, 35s, 53ne, 54n, 55n, humus, О-НГЦ-67-180, 180[a], Kiev, Institute of Archaeology storeroom. Two joining body frs. H 6.6 × W 5.7, WT 0.4. Fabric: fine, soft, non-micaceous, a few fine light-reflecting particles, some voids. Thin wash. Not too hard fired, oxidized. Rim frieze: box meander, ccw. Calyx: imbricate, large rounded petals with central vein.

XXX-76*   SHA 564
Olbia, Sector E6, square 400, grey clay layer, O-E6-56-595, Kiev, Institute of Archaeology storeroom. Two joining frs. of mid- and lower body with tiny part of base. H 5 × W 5.5, WT 0.35. Fabric: fine, dense, non-micaceous, 5YR 5/2. Dull coat, ext. Gley 1 3/N, int. uncoated. Medium hard fired, reduced. Calyx: isolated plastic long petals set amongst acanthus scrolls, vine leaves, flowers, and bunches on grapes on stems.

XXX-77*
Olbia, Sector NGS, О-НГС-04-439, Parutine, Olbia National Preserve storeroom. Fr. of mid-body. H 3.5 × W 5.8, WT 0.35. Fabric: relatively fine and micaceous, some small lime inclusions, 5YR 6/6. Coat with metallic highlights, 5YR 5/4, Gley 1 3/N. Hard fired, oxidized. Stacked in firing. Calyx: naturalistic acanthus with segmented central vein in high relief. At right, end of trefoil bound myrtle garland left.

PART 3

Pontic Productions

∴

CHAPTER 17

Mouldmade Bowls in the Black Sea Region: Introduction

The second part of this book is devoted to an analysis of the MMB found at a number of Pontic sites of the north and west coast of this immense water basin. We shall first discuss the evidence for production of MMB in the Black Sea region. Then follows the analysis of the finds. The latter will fall into four parts: first we will examine the two largest assemblages at my disposal, which come from Olbia and Istros; next follows Chersonesos and its distant chora, located as a bridge between the northeastern and northwestern Pontic realm; and finally the Bosporan Kingdom with its capital, Pantikapaion, and a number of smaller sites in the European (Myrmekion, Porthmion, and Tyritake) and Asiatic (Kepoi, Ruminskoe, and Volna 1) Bosporos.

We shall start with Olbia, the earliest and largest of the Pontic ensembles. We shall then proceed to Istros, the second largest assemblage which I have studied, and a relatively late one, very close in overall composition to the Delian corpus. The group of material from Chersonesos and the fortified farm site at Bol'šoj Kastel' in its distant chora is small, and, as concerns Chersonesos, only a portion of a larger whole. But since so few MMB are known from this important city, I have found it worthwhile to include a brief section on the finds.

The Bosporan Kingdom with its capital at Pantikapaion, modern Kerč, is amongst the few places in the Black Sea region known to have produced MMB. Currently, a large project financed by the Demeter Foundation in Kerč is working on a complete publication of the objects in the Kerč Museum and its storerooms, including the MMB. The task of analysing the MMB in Kerč was undertaken by the Polish scholar S. Grzegrzółka. It was not possible to gain access to the museum's MMB while she was at work on the project, but her book became available in the spring of 2011, just in time for me to include her results in the present study. The vessels published by Grzegrzółka were unearthed mainly in the towns of the European Bosporos (Porthmion, Parthenion, Myrmekion, and Pantikapaion), as well as in A.A. Maslennikov's excavations in the Eastern Crimea and in I.L. Grač's and O.Ju. Sokolova's excavations at Nymphaion.

The collection of material from the minor sites in the Bosporan Kingdom which I have had access to is, with the exception of Myrmekion, of limited size. Nevertheless, it is included here, partly because the assemblages are mostly unpublished, but also because its inclusion gives us a precious opportunity to compare the composition of an assemblage from the capital with assemblages at smaller sites of the Bosporan Kingdom, and hence to draw conclusions about the respective consumption patterns and the relationships between imports and local products in these two different situations.

Before we turn to the Pontic assemblages, we shall consider some general issues concerning MMB in the Black sea region. We shall start with an overview of research on MMB in the Black Sea region.

An Overview of the History of Research

Our understanding of MMB in the Black Sea region is patchy: from large parts of the area, just a handful of sherds have been published – if any at all. This is the case first of all of the east and south coasts. Research on MMB in the remaining part of the Black Sea region has been sporadic as well and to a large extent dominated by single objects or small groups of finds from individual sites (overview in Fig. 2).[1] However, four scholars in particular merit mention. Three based their dissertation/habilitation on the MMB of the region (Chapter 2): the German E. Mahler in 1924 (unpublished), the Russian S.A. Kovalenko in 1989 (unpublished), and the Rumanian C. Domăneanţu (published in 2000). The first two produced general syntheses based on Black sea finds, whereas the last-mentioned concentrated solely on the bowls found at Istros. Of these three scholars, Kovalenko is the only one who has contributed a whole series of articles on MMB (e.g., 1987a, 1987b, 1996, 1998, 2007; Turova & Kovalenko 2005; Vnukov & Kovalenko 1998). Regrettably, he has now turned his attention to coins instead of MMB. The fourth to be mentioned is the scholar J. Bouzek, of Prague. He too has contributed significantly to our understanding of MMB in the Pontic realm (1985, 1990, 2005, 2012), in addition to his works on Mediterranean MMB, especially of Kyme (Chapter 10).

---

1 A discussion of the bibliography concerning sites included in this book can be found under the appropriate site.

Production of Mouldmade Bowls: The Evidence of Moulds

As we saw in Chapter 4, MMB were produced in most of the larger Hellenistic centres throughout the ancient world (Appendix 4). This also holds true for the Pontic region. However, actual finds of moulds are negligible. I am aware of a mould found in the debris of a Hellenistic house at Mesambria (Ognenova 1960, 228; Čimbuléva 2005, 112; perhaps the mould for a pine-cone bowl on display in the Archaeological Museum of Nessebar). Domăneanţu (2000, 144 with references) refers to a mould from Istros, and from Olbia comes a mould fragment with a long-petal pattern (unpublished), which was exhibited in the Odessa Archaeological Museum before the museum's recent refurbishment. In addition to these sparse finds from the Greek cities of the northwestern and western part of the area, we should not fail to mention the imitations crafted in the indigenous cities of the Getes (Chapter 19). At four different localities, moulds were found which in sheer numbers by far outnumber those from the Greek cities (Appendix 4).

Turning to the Bosporan Kingdom, production of MMB there is certified by the discovery of moulds (Chapter 18). Eleven mould fragments have been found to date, nine at Pantikapaion (DEM-1*, DEM-4*–DEM-11) and two at nearby Myrmekion (DEM-2, DEM-3). Even though only one of the moulds preserves his signature, consensus has it that they all belong to the production of Demetrios, and, as we shall see in Chapter 18, there is no reason to dispute this. The last mould fragment from this region was found at Phanagoreia, on the opposite side of the Kerč Strait. This is a rim fragment of a mould with a debased pine-cone pattern below two rows of crude dots (Kovalenko 1989, 405 cat. 212; fig. 29; Kovalenko 1996, 55; Žuravlev & Žuravleva 2014, 260, fig. 6.2.).

Production of Mouldmade Bowls: The Evidence of Distribution

Distribution patterns have been adduced as an argument in favour of locating a production at a site where a significant proportion of the MMB found belong to a particular group which is absent or only sparsely attested elsewhere. As explained in Chapter 13, A. Petrova (2014) has recently championed a group of bowls of uniform fabric, shape, and decoration found in significant numbers at Mesambria as candidates for local production there. The numbers are striking, with vessels of this group constituting close to a third of the MMB in one excavation sector. Petrova is to be congratulated for being the first to recognize the integrity of this group, but, as I explained in Chapter 13, there are good reasons for rejecting these bowls as local Mesambrian products. I propose instead that the vessels in question were produced in Aiolis (Aiolis B), probably in Elaia, a suggestion recently supported by archaeometric investigations (see Chapter 13).

The distribution pattern of the Meter Medallion Workshop resembles the one just mentioned – and its interpretation has been very much the same. Again, vessels of this group have been found mainly in the Black Sea region, and only a few pieces have been identified in the Mediterranean. As we saw in Chapter 11, there is a long tradition of ascribing pottery of this workshop to the Black Sea region. And because the largest corpus comes from Olbia and its environs, when publishing the MMB from the deposits of Olbia's Sector NGS in 2010, I too was inclined to view these vessels as the products of a local Olbian workshop. However, the surprising results of recent archaeometric investigations by two independent laboratories teach us that this is not the case: the bowls of the Meter Medallion Workshop too were produced in the Mediterranean, to be more specific, at Kyme.

We must conclude that the use of distribution as an indicator of production places can be a hazardous business.

One final possible production merits mention. The retrograde signature of one Damokles (DAMOKLEIOS) encircles the base of a single fragment found at Čaika (Kovalenko 1996, fig. 1.3). Kovalenko has suggested that the vessel is of Bosporan origin (1996, 55). This is followed by Rogl 2001a, 139 and Žuravlev & Žuravleva 2014, 261. The Čaika fragment has a bright red fabric with lime and a red coat, and, according to Kovalenko, the clay is similar to that of vessels produced by Demetrios. However, the bowls of Demetrios are almost never coated (see Chapter 18). Kovalenko associates the fragment from Čaika with another vessel bearing the signature Ad or Da (Šurgaja 1962, 118, fig. 4.4; Kovalenko 1996, fig. 1.2). There can be no doubt that this vessel is late Ephesian of WC1, because two complete vessels with the same signature have been found on Delos (Laumonier 1977, 309 cats. 4052 and 4266, pl. 73). Clearly, then, the potter signing Ad or Da is *not* Bosporan. Whether Damokles is a Bosporan potter, or whether he also belongs to WC1, which I find most likely, cannot be decided on the basis of the available evidence. However, I myself have not seen any fragment that I can attribute to this potter, so if he is not a phantom, his products are at any rate rare.

We shall now turn to an overall discussion of the pattern of imports into the Pontic region, as it emerges from

		Mainland		Aiolis							S Asia Minor		Pontos			
		ATH	COR	PER	KYA	KYB	KYX	AIA	AIB	AIX	EPH	KNI	DEM	GET	XXX	Total
Olbia	Sum	51	1	44	34	238	64	4	44	15	1,152	20	1		162	1,830
	%	2.8		2.4	1.9	13.0	3.5	0.2	2.4	0.8	63.0	1.1			8.9	
Olbia or Pantika-paion						4					1		2			7
Olbia?		1				4					11		2		1	19
Istros	Sum	11		39	17	95	30	31	18	10	1,093	41		3	170	1,558
	%	0.7		2.5	1.1	6.1	1.9	2.0	1.2	0.6	70.2	2.6		0.2	10.9	
Chersone-sos	Sum	2		1		11			2	1	62	7	3		7	96
	%	2.1		1.0		11.5			2.1	1.0	64.6	7.3	3.1		7.3	
Bol'šoj Kastel'	Sum										28				1	29
	%										96.6				3.4	
Kepoi	Sum					3	1				25	1	5		8	43
	%					7.0	2.3				58.1	2.3	11.6		18.6	
Myrmeki-on	Sum	1		3	2	8	2		7	4	147	4	80		21	279
	%	0.4		1.1	0.7	2.9	0.7		2.5	1.4	52.7	1.4	28.7		7.5	
Myrmeki-on?													5			5
Pantika-paion	Sum	9		5	3	30	4	1	7	3	242	1	37		46	388
	%	2.3		1.3	0.8	7.8	1.0	0.3	1.8	0.8	62.4		9.5		11.9	
Pantika-paion?						1					3				1	5
Porthmion	Sum	1		1	1	1			1	1	197		45		24	272
	%	0.4		0.4	0.4	0.4			0.4	0.4	72.4		16.5		8.8	
Rumin-skoe	Sum										6		5			11
Tyritake	Sum					3				1	49	1	20		13	87
	%					3.4				1.1	56.3	1.1	23.0		14.9	
Volna 1	Sum										34		2		1	37
	%										91.9		5.4		2.7	
Sum		76	1	93	57	398	101	36	79	35	3,050	75	207	3	455	4,666
Average %		1.6		2.0	1.2	8.5	2.2	0.8	1.7	0.7	65.4	1.6	4.4		9.8	100

FIGURE 80 Numbers and percentages of mouldmade bowls from the Pontic sites that form the basis for this study

an analysis of the 11 sites included in the present book (Fig. 80). For a more detailed discussion of the imports at the individual sites, see the following chapters.

Imports

The pattern of imports varies little from site to site. Attic vessels are scarce at any location. They are best represented at Olbia, where they constitute 2.8% of the finds. The same pattern can be observed in the Mediterranean, if we exclude localities which geographically are close to Athens (Chapter 7). One of the most interesting results of our analysis is that various Aiolian workshops are much better represented in the Black Sea region than in the Mediterranean. In fact, more than 17% of all the MMB found at the sites analysed in this book were manufactured in Aiolian workshops. Of these, by far the most common are the products of Kymean workshops, especially of the Meter Medallion Workshop. The reason for the Aiolian workshops' success in the Pontic region must be their location along the north-bound sailing route from the Mediterranean to the Black Sea.

After the middle of the 2nd century, Ephesos came to dominate the market in the Black Sea region. At some sites, Ephesian products constitute almost 100% of the MMB, and at no site are less than 50% of the finds Ephesian. Knidian MMB are as yet not very well recognized. Nevertheless, we may confidently point to Knidian MMB at most of the sites, albeit never in any large quantity.

Supplementary Shapes

In Chapter 5, we saw that supplementary shapes were relatively common in the Pontic assemblages. In total, they constitute 3.8% of all of the MMB found. However, these shapes do not appear in equal proportions at the individual sites (and at sites with small assemblages, they are not documented at all; Fig. 33, see also Fig. 31). The two shapes which are found at most sites are the small bowl and the juglet.

Olbia seems to have been a special case when it comes to the import of supplementary shapes. The number, relative proportion, and variation in shapes found there are well over the average, not just compared with other Black Sea sites, but also compared with the Mediterranean. This probably has to do with the chronological profile of the Olbia assemblage, most of which accumulated before and in the 140s.

Before we end this chapter, I should like to point to a specific feature which characterizes MMB found in the Black Sea region to such an extent that I am willing to call it a Pontic habitus, namely repairs.

Pottery Repair: A Pontic Habitus?

Repairs to ancient pottery are frequently encountered in the Black Sea region. All kinds of pottery were repaired, not just table ware, but also amphorae, cooking ware, and even handmade pottery. In an article written in collaboration with my colleague, S. Handberg, we have discussed pottery repair in general and specifically as it occurs at Olbia (Guldager Bilde & Handberg 2012). Pottery was repaired throughout the existence of the city, but it was an especially common practice in the 2nd century. We conclude that this way of prolonging the use-life of the pottery is, in fact, so common that it seems to be part of a specific Pontic habitus.

The traces left by the repair are small circular holes with a diameter of 2–5 mm drilled into vessels on either side of a break, and sometimes a lead clamp is preserved *in situ*. The standard repair found on the MMB is what has been termed by J.T. Peña the 'hole-and-clamp' type (2007, 232, 235, 242). Cracks were bridged and broken pieces were joined with a lead clamp consisting of a cylindrical bar attached to a Π-shaped bar at each side of the break. The bar lay across the surface of the vessel and was not, as in earlier periods, imbedded into the vessel with a swallow-tail clamp. Apparently no attempt was made to compensate for the rather clumsy appearance of the cylindrical bars on the inner and outer surfaces of the vessel. Adhesives were probably employed in order to stabilize the vessel prior to adding the clamp. It is even conceivable that vessels could have been joined with cord or string made of perishable materials.[2] Complete vessels with repair holes but no lead clamps found in primary depositions, e.g., in tombs, most likely attest to this practice, simply because it is not conceivable that the clamps were removed before the vessels were deposited.

A fine example of the repairing technique is found on EPH-857, where a T-shaped clamp is still preserved *in situ* (Fig. 81). The metal was pressed into place with a small oblong, concave instrument. It flowed under this instrument and out along its edges when the clamp was pressed against it.[3] The instrument itself must have been heated in order to make the clamp soft enough to fill the holes and make the lead run under its pressure.

As we can see from Fig. 82, 178 MMB from the Pontic sites under study were repaired. In terms of absolute numbers, most repairs are encountered in Olbia, constituting 6.7% of all MMB which I have recorded from the site. Similar proportions of repaired pottery are recorded at Chersonesos and Bol'šoj Kastel', but the total number of bowls from these two localities is small, so perhaps they should be disregarded. No repairs are recorded from Tyritake, Kepoi, Volna 1, and Ruminskoe, but again, the assemblages are small, so it is difficult to interpret the numbers.

If we turn to the cities where sizeable assemblages allow us to draw better-founded conclusions, it is first of all striking how few repairs are attested at Pantikapaion: only two vessels, a mere 0.5% of all the finds of MMB. As we also saw in Chapter 4, Pantikapaion did not rely on the local Bosporan products of the Demetrios workshop, but via its trade networks apparently had access to an unlimited supply of imported Mediterranean MMB. So the limited number of repairs at Pantikapaion can probably be interpreted as the effect of the city's status as the royal capital of the Bosporan Kingdom.

The issues of availability and status can also be addressed at Olbia, because the present study allows us to break down the finds from individual sectors in the city (Fig. 83). 'Barbarian' tribes put significant pressure on Olbia and its chora in the 2nd century (see Chapter 20). These strains might very well have resulted in an irregular supply of pottery – and perhaps also an increasing

---

2   Repair carried out with string and then glued is preserved in Egypt, e.g., Tomber 2011, 109, fig. 2.

3   This can also be seen on a krater from the Sabucina necropolis (Nadalini 2003, 203, fig. 18), on a West-Slope amphora with ribbed body from Olbia (Handberg et al. 2010, 227 cat. Db-325), and on an Athenian household lekane (Rotroff 2011a, 123, fig. 9).

FIGURE 81　Repair with lead clamp in place (EPH-857)
PHOTO FROM THE AUTHOR'S ARCHIVE

		Evidence category A+B			
		Number of repaired vessels	Maximum number of vessels	% of total at site
Northwest Pontic region	Olbia	122	1,830	6.7
	Istros	24	1,558	1.5
Western Crimea	Chersonesos	7	96	7.3
	Bol'šoj Kastel'	2	29	6.9
Bosporan Kingdom (European part)	Pantikapaion	2	388	0.5
	Myrmekion	6	279	2.2
	Porthmion	15	272	5.5
Sum		178	4,452	4.0

FIGURE 82　Repaired MMB in the Pontic assemblages

Sector	Number of bowls	Number of bowls with repair	%
NGS	643	56	8.7
E	215	8	3.7
R25	329	12	3.6

FIGURE 83　Repaired bowls in Olbian sectors with the largest assemblages

number of poorer people who could not afford to replace broken pottery. If we consider all the various excavation sectors where MMB have been found, it is striking that repairs are overrepresented in Sector NGS (Fig. 83). The inhabitants of this sector, which is located close to the harbour, were of relatively modest means (Kryžiskij & Lejpunskaja 2010). This is demonstrated chiefly by the implements of daily use and craft found throughout the sector, such as fishing equipment and tools for producing simple jewellery and for weaving. Sector E, on the other hand, is in the central part of the Upper City, covering the Central Temenos, the Agora's so-called East Trade Building, and the house blocks of the Central Quarter located west of the Agora. In all likelihood, the houses of the Central Quarter were the dwellings of the élite, some with peristyle courtyards, which are not attested in Sector NGS. Of the eight repaired vessels from Sector E, two were found in a cistern at the Agora (KYB-81*, KYB-243*), the remainder in the houses of the Central Quarter (ATH-46*, EPH-195*, EPH-211*, EPH-483*, EPH-776*, EPH-971*). I am not aware of the contexts of the finds from Sector R25. However, as mentioned, the material accumulated later than in the other Sectors.

There are clearly many reasons why pottery was repaired, and these may well have differed in time and place. Repair is always occasioned by a certain need and it is always the second-best solution: both from a practical and an aesthetic point of view, a repaired vessel is less useful and less attractive than an intact, pristine one. Thus, the choice to repair must reflect the reality that a new vessel could not be acquired, either because a replacement (or something similar) was not available on the market or because the person with the broken pot could not afford to replace it. It is even possible that the owner of the broken pot simply did not care whether it was repaired or not.

If we compare the figures in Fig. 82 with the number of repairs of MMB from the Mediterranean, we must conclude that the number of repairs in the Pontic region, not just in Olbia, is very high indeed. The largest corpus of MMB published to date is A. Laumonier's catalogue of the mostly Ephesian bowls from Delos (Laumonier 1977; see also Chapter 2). Amongst the almost 6,500 complete or fragmentary MMB, no more than three are furnished with drilled holes. In Laumonier's cat. 3240, two holes are drilled next to one another in the middle of the sherd (Laumonier 1977, 116, pl. 26). They could hardly have functioned as a repair, but were most probably intended for suspension, as also suggested by Laumonier (1977, 116). Cats. 1205 and 5607 (Laumonier 1977, 119, pl. 27; 193, pl. 42) preserve one drilled hole each. They were probably intended for suspension too rather than for repair, and even if not, the repair rate in Delos is negligible, being less than 0.05%. A similar conclusion is reached in a recent study of the repaired pottery from the Athenian Agora, where S. Rotroff was unable to find a single repair on a mouldmade bowl (2011a).

Comparing the Pontic region with the Mediterranean, in the former there seems to be a particular ceramic habitus which included repair of broken pottery. Whether the Pontic dwellers could not, would not, or did not care to replace broken pots with new ones we shall perhaps never know with certitude. However, as documented above, economic and social factors were of significance.

CHAPTER 18

Myrmekion and Pantikapaion: (Pontic) Demetrios

At least two different workshops producing MMB employed the signature of a Demetrios. One was located at Argos (Siebert 1978), and one in the Bosporan Kingdom by the North Pontic shore (*infra*). This has caused some confusion, because Siebert was of the opinion that some of the certainly Pontic vessels signed DEMETRIOU under the base belonged to his Argive Workshop of Demetrios-Iason (Siebert 1978, pl. 21, Metropolitan Mus. inv. 98.8.26 [DEM-69], Baltimore, Walters Art Gallery inv. 48.129 [DEM-154]). But in contrast to Pontic Demetrios, the Argive Demetrios signed very neatly on the *wall* of the bowl, not under the base, and the decoration differs so much that there can be no doubt that two completely different workshops signing with the same name existed. In this chapter, we will discuss the Workshop of Pontic Demetrios, the only Black Sea workshop producing MMB about which we are relatively well informed.

History of Research

Recognition of the Workshop of (Pontic) Demetrios is relatively recent. Courby, for example, referred to just one bowl signed Demetrios; it was found on Delos and, according to him, of 'Delian' type, and he therefore believed that the only Demetrios bowl he knew from the Pontic region, namely a bowl found in Chersonesos (DEM-76), was imported from Delos (Courby 1922, 393, 396, 412).[1] Since the Delian vessel was not illustrated, we have no means of ascertaining whether it belonged to the Pontic workshop. However, Laumonier points out that the inscription on Courby's Delian fragment is, in fact, just a graffito (Laumonier 1977, 407 n. 1), so there is no reason to include it in the present chapter. The Chersonesean bowl, on the other hand, is undoubtedly of Bosporan production.

Our knowledge of this workshop is based primarily on the Russian excavations of the 1930s–1950s at Pantikapaion and the contemporary Polish-Russian excavations at Myrmekion, even though most of the finds are still unpublished.[2] Demetrios' workshop has been discussed by a number of scholars, mostly on the occasion of finds from his workshop.[3] The first scholar to propose a typology was I.G. Šurgaja (1962, 117–119, fig. 3). Her typology is, in fact, still the one in current use. S. Kovalenko elaborated on Šurgaja's typology in his unpublished dissertation of 1989 and subsequently provided a summary of his conclusions in English (Kovalenko 1996, 51–57). J. Bouzek has touched upon the Demetrios workshop on several occasions (Bouzek 1982; 1985; 1990, 76–78; 2008), and lately, drawing almost exclusively on Bouzek 1990, the distribution of Demetrios's bowls has been discussed briefly by C. Rogl (2001a, 139). The present author has presented a brief version of this chapter at a conference devoted to Pontic grey wares in Bucharest/Constanta in 2008 (Guldager Bilde 2009).

Moulds

I have been able to identify fragments of 11 moulds, though more probably exist. V.D. Blavatskij mentions in passing that several moulds were found in Pantikapaion in 1946 (1953, 280). I have found only one mould from this year (DEM-4*); apparently they were never published, and their present whereabouts are unknown.

Half of the mould fragments are from the rim or body (DEM-2, DEM-3, DEM-5*, DEM-6*, DEM-8*, DEM-9*) and therefore do not preserve a signature, and two of the base fragments preserve so little of the base proper that no signature survives (DEM-4*, DEM-7). Only DEM-1* preserves almost the entire signature, whereas DEM-10 and DEM-11 definitely were not signed. The moulds I have studied first-hand (DEM-1*, DEM-4*–DEM-6*, DEM-8*, DEM-9*) are made of the same hard fired, relatively fine fabric with some light-reflecting particles; only DEM-1* is somewhat coarser in fabric with shell inclusions. All mould fragments are quite thick-walled, 0.5–1 cm. The rim profile is also the same, namely broad and everted. The form of the base varies: DEM-4* and DEM-10 feature a ring foot, whereas DEM-1* has a disc foot marked off by an incised groove; the base of DEM-11 is completely flat.

---

1 K. Michałowski even calls Demetrios the "famous Delian potter," with reference to Courby, though he did consider the signed bowls which he unearthed in Myrmekion to be local copies (Michałowski 1958, 79). This is repeated by Platek (1974, 48).
2 It is a great pleasure to acknowledge the help of a number of Russian colleagues, who have shared their material with me for this chapter: N. Astašova, D.E. Čistov, J.P. Kalašnik, N.Z. Kunina, S.S. Solovjov, V.P. Tolstikov, M.Ju. Vachtina, Ju.A. Vinogradov, and D.D. Žuravlev.
3 E.g., Blavatskij 1953, 280; Gajdukevič 1958, 209; Blavatskij 1959; Loseva 1962, 205; Tolstikov & Zhuravlev 2004; Kropotov & Leskov 2006.

Even though just one base is inscribed, Demetrios' production is so characteristic that it is unproblematic to ascribe even unsigned fragments to his workshop. This goes for the mould fragments as well as for fragmentary bowls. Of the 11 moulds and fragments, only two are of a style which either has not been encountered in the rest of his production (DEM-10) or is very rare (DEM-11). However, since both were found at Pantikapaion, they are included as probably belonging to Demetrios' workshop.

Nine of the 11 moulds were found at Pantikapaion (DEM-1*, DEM-4*–DEM-11), whereas two were excavated at Myrmekion (DEM-2, DEM-3). The two cities were located very close to one another, on either side of Pantikapaion Bay, 4 km as the crow flies, so Myrmekion was more or less a 'suburb' of the Bosporan capital. As far as I have been able to discover, none of the mould fragments were found together; at least, they were unearthed over a number of years, those from Pantikapaion in 1946, 1955, 1956, 1962, and 1967 and those from Myrmekion in 1949. The Myrmekion moulds belong to the earliest type of decoration (Decoration 1b), so it is likely that the production moved from Myrmekion to the capital, rather than that there were two contemporary branch workshops (see also below p. 529).

Fabric and Surface Treatment

The fabric used in the Workshop of Demetrios is medium fine with inclusions of lime. Many bowls also show inclusions of crushed shell (as do the moulds) and partially burnt-out organic material can frequently be noted. The vessels are relatively hard fired and normally fired through, though the walls are relatively thick, 0.25–0.45 cm. A dull grey surface resembling silver was probably intended, so the bowls were almost exclusively fired steel grey in the hues 3/1, 4/1, 5/1 and 6/1 of the colours 7.5YR, 10YR, 2.5Y, 5Y, Gley 1 3–6/N and 10Y. A small percentage of the vessels are oxidized (red) and probably to be regarded as 'misfired'. According to Kovalenko, oxidized vessels constitute 15% of the entire Demetrios production (1996, 51). This number is somewhat too high; according to my calculations, the percentage is ca. 10%. This finish is not known on bowls with Decoration 1, but only on bowls with Decoration 2–5 and 8.[4] This may indicate that this feature has chronological significance. However, a single oxidized specimen with Decoration 2 and base type A make the pattern slightly more complicated (DEM-67*).

In contrast to Mediterranean MMB – but like the Central Italian so-called Italo-Megarian vases – the Demetrios production was mostly left uncoated, even though a dull colour coat has occasionally been mentioned.[5]

It is to be noted that even though moulds have been found in several places, and even though the fabric shows some variation, based on macroscopic observation it is not possible to distinguish separate production places. The different variations of fabric can be found with all the types of decoration, and even the fragments with uncommon decoration, such as the pine cone, and not connected with an inscribed base, are made of exactly the same fabric as the inscribed pieces.

Shape

Demetrios' workshop produced exclusively bowls with a plain, straight or more commonly slightly inturned rim, similar to later products of Ephesian Workshop Circle 1 (see Chapter 14). The height of the rim is mostly between 1.8 and 2.4 cm, and the rim diameter is normally quite small, 11–12 cm. In contrast to this, the base diameter is generally rather large, between 4 and 6 cm (mostly between 4.5 and 5.5 cm). The bases normally have a small, low false ring foot, and the underside is either flat or slightly concave. The bowls have a height to diameter ratio ranging from 1:1.6 to 1:2.3 and they seem to undergo the same development as noted in Chapter 3, namely that they become gradually shallower (Fig. 84).

Decoration	H:Ø	
1d	1:1.7	DEM-47
	1:1.8	DEM-48
2	1:1.7	DEM-96
	1:1.9	DEM-68
3a	1:1.8	DEM-154
	1:1.9	DEM-155
	1:2	DEM-163
4a	1:1.6	DEM-182
5a	1:1.8	DEM-218
	1:1.8	DEM-219
	1:2	DEM-208
5c	1:2.3	DEM-242

FIGURE 84 Proportions of Demetrios bowls according to decoration type

---

4 Decoration 2: DEM-67*, DEM-98, DEM-117–DEM-119, DEM-123; Decoration 3a: DEM-148*, DEM-151, DEM-155, DEM-161*, DEM-163; Decoration 3b: DEM-180*; Decoration 4a: DEM-198, DEM-199; Decoration 4b: DEM-203*; Decoration 1, 2 or 4: DEM-63*; Decoration 5a: DEM-207, DEM-215*, DEM-217, DEM-235; Decoration 5c: DEM-241, DEM-242; Decoration 5(?): DEM-244*; Decoration 8a: DEM-248; Decoration 8b: DEM-249; Decoration ?: DEM-253*.

5 DEM-98, DEM-117–DEM-119, DEM-123, DEM-198, DEM-199. Grzegrzółka (2010) does not consider these Bosporan but Mediterranean.

Decoration

As already mentioned, the first scholar to propose a typology was I.G. Šurgaja, who divided the Demetrios bowls into five different types of decoration (Šurgaja 1962, 117, fig. 3):
(1) Various types of long-petal decoration
(2) Long-petal decoration alternating with slender ovoid petals
(3) Various types of decoration with acanthus leaves
(4) Imbricate
(5) Pine-cone decoration

In addition, S.A. Kovalenko has provided an overview of the stamps used by Demetrios, adding rosettes on stems (stamp 17) and birds (stamp 19) to Šurgaja's typology, as well as the pendent-semicircle pattern (stamp 20) (Kovalenko 1996, 52, fig. 1).

Overall, the decoration of the Demetrios bowls is a simple affair. It is almost without exception based on the long-petal motif, and it almost exclusively employs a single Ionian kyma as a rim pattern. We can expand the above-mentioned typologies further, however, because, in total, eight main decorative schemes can be distinguished:
(1) Calyx with bending acanthus leaves alternating with tall pointed petals (moulds, DEM-2–DEM-4*) (Decoration 1a–1e)
(2) Groups of stylised long petals alternating with tall pointed petals; all elements are separated by columns of fine dots (mould, DEM-5*) (Decoration 2)
(3) Plastic long petals separated by columns of fine dots (moulds, DEM-6* and DEM-7) (Decoration 3a–b)
(4) Stylised long petals mostly separated by columns of fine dots (moulds, DEM-8* and DEM-9*) (Decoration 4a–b)
(5) Imbricate (Decoration 5a–c) Long petals alternating with an imbricate field (mould, DEM-10) (Decoration 6)
(6) Pine cone (mould, DEM-11) (Decoration 7)
(7) Pendent semicircles (Decoration 8a–b)

Most come in two or more variants; for details, see the introductory sections of the catalogue.

Decoration types 1–5 account for 91% of the vessels (ECA+ECB), whereas Decoration types 6–8 seem to have been quite uncommon (2.7%). Nevertheless, the latter three attest to some willingness to experiment and to emulate more common Mediterranean decoration types, such as the plastic pine cone (Decoration 7) and the pendent semicircles (Decoration 8).

Decoration 1a, 1b, 2, 3a, 4, and 5a all occur on signed vessels, and all types of decoration, including variants, are present on unsigned vessels (Fig. 89). When one takes into consideration shape and fabric as well as the occurrence of decorative patterns known from signed vessels, it is not difficult to attribute unsigned vessels to Demetrios' workshop.

As already mentioned, a single rim frieze featuring an Ionian kyma is the almost exclusive rim pattern used by Demetrios, but we do find a few experiments

Base type			Sum	
			ECA+B	ECC
Signed	A	Signed DEMETRIOU around a double, eight-petalled rosette (rosette A)	34	7
	B	Signed DEMETRIOU, no rosette	24	12
	A or B	Too little of base is preserved to ascertain whether there was a rosette or not; or this has not been mentioned in publications	13	
	C	D[...] incised in vessel before firing, plain base	1	
Not signed	D	No signature, double, six-petalled rosette (rosette B)	2	
	E	No signature, rosette with four broad heart-shaped petals (rosette C)	1	
	F	No signature, no rosette	32	
	G	No signature; imbricate	1	

FIGURE 85 Base types on Demetrios bowls and their frequency

with other types of rim pattern, such as vertical combing (DEM-143*, DEM-200*) or a frieze of eight-petalled rosettes (DEM-179*), in addition to the slightly more frequent bowls without a rim pattern.[6]

The bases come in seven variants, three signed and four unsigned. They were not equally common, as Fig. 85 shows. Occasionally, the body decoration, especially the ends of the long petals, continues under the base. This attests to a somewhat sloppy finish of the mould and is not considered to be decoration.

Signatures

In overall form, Demetrios follows the conventions of Ephesian WC1, inscribing the signature in the base medallion of the mould before firing with bold letters with serifs. But how many bowls of the entire production were signed? Signed pieces may be overrepresented in publications, both because of the presence of the signature and because unsigned fragments are less easy to recognize. Kovalenko mentions that 30 of the 50 bases known to him were signed, a percentage of 60% (Kovalenko 1996, 55). According to my calculations, the number is even higher, because out of 107 bases known to me (ECA+ECB), 70 were signed, corresponding to ca. 65%. This is considerably higher than the percentage of signed vessels in WC1, which amounts to ca. 38% (Chapter 4).

Source of Inspiration

Where did Demetrios find the inspiration for his production? I have already mentioned that Demetrios followed the example of Ephesian Workshop Circle 1 in the shape of the vessel and the location and execution of the signature. In terms of decoration, however, there can be no doubt that Demetrios initially imitated the production which I have termed Aiolis B, probably to be located in Elaia (Chapter 13). In this workshop, we find the same motifs that appear in Demetrios' earliest decoration (Decoration 1a): a duck-like bird with the head turned back sitting on the tip of an acanthus leaf, as well as rosettes on stems alternating with isolated long petals (AIB-19, AIB-41*, AIB-43, AIB-44, AIB-73*–AIB-75, and especially AIB-83*, AIB-84; see Figs. 86 and 87). Since this production is known from

FIGURE 86 Bird with head turned back on curving acanthus in calyx of Aiolian bowl (AIB-83)
PHOTO BY THE AUTHOR

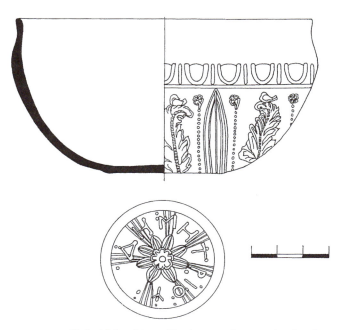

FIGURE 87 Bird with head turned back on curving acanthus in calyx of bowl of Demetrios (DEM-12), Drawing from Žuravlev & Žuravleva 2014, 260 fig. 6.3
REPRODUCED WITH THE KIND PERMISSION OF DENIS ŽURAVLEV

the Bosporan Kingdom,[7] whereas the Bosporan production, with a single exception (DEM-154), is not known from the Mediterranean, it is more likely that the production of Aiolis B inspired Demetrios than vice versa.

---

6 DEM-54*, DEM-55, DEM-166*, DEM-167, DEM-180*, DEM-184, DEM-185, DEM-187*–DEM-191, DEM-245*.

7 AIB-20, AIB-38*, AIB-40*, AIB-45, AIB-54, AIB-59*, AIB-72, AIB-73*, AIB-76*, AIB-78*, AIB-101, AIB-104, AIB-105, AIB-117, AIB-120, AIB-124*, AIB-131*.

Chronology

Relative Chronology

The decorative patterns were not equally popular (Figs. 88, 89). By far the most common is Decoration 2 (alternating long petals and tall pointed petals), occurring on around 75 specimens, and it is also the most widely distributed. Slightly less common are the acanthus leaves and tall pointed petals of Decoration 1, the only decoration employing vegetal and figural elements (acanthus leaf; duck; Decoration 1a), and therefore probably the earliest. Decorations 3, 4 and 5 (long-petal, imbricate) were less popular than Decorations 1 and 2. Decoration 4, stylized long petals, is slightly less common (28 examples) than Decoration 3 and 5 (plastic long petals, imbricate), of which around 40 specimens each are known. The distribution of Decoration 3a is as wide as that of Decoration 2; also Decoration 5a is almost as widely distributed, though in contrast to Decoration 2 and 3a, it is not found outside the Bosporan Kingdom. In terms of numbers and distribution, Decorations 2 and 3a probably mark the acme of the Demetrios production.

The place of the rare pine-cone bowls (Decoration 7) in the relative chronological sequence is unknown, but I suspect that they belong in the latter part of the production.

The relative chronology can be gleaned from a simple sequence analysis of the relationship between main decoration and base stamps (Fig. 89). Base A, with the signature surrounding a rosette, is the most common base type, recorded on at least 34 bowls. It occurs exclusively with Decoration 1a–b and 2. Base type B (the signature alone) can be found in combination mostly with Decoration 3, but also with Decoration 1b, 4, and 5. Base type C, with the signature incised in the bowl itself, is very rare, and the body decoration connected with it is unknown. Also bases of types D and E (rosettes without signature) are virtually unknown. I know only two specimens of base type D. Kovalenko mentions three, but gives no reference to find place or inventory number, so this cannot be verified. Base type D occurs with Decoration 2 and a variant of Decoration 1b. Base E is found only once, in combination with Decoration 3a. Base F, on the other hand, the flat, plain, unsigned base, is the second most common

Decoration	Sum ECA+B	Sum ECC	Decoration	Sum ECA+B	Sum ECC
1 or 2	4		3b	1	
1-2 or 4	4		4a	23	
1, 2, 4 or 5	1		4b	3	
1a	15		4?	2	
1b	18		5a	33	5
1b var.	1		5b	1	
1c	2		5c	3	
1d	4		5?	1	
1e	8		6	1	
2	75	2	7	3	
2 var.	1		8a	2	
2?	1		8b	1	
3a	38	1	?	16	

FIGURE 88 Frequency of types of decoration of Demetrios bowls

	Signed				Not signed			
	Rosette A		?		Rosette B	Rosette C		
Base	A	B	A or B	C	D	E	F	G
Decoration								
1								
1a	5							
1b	4	1	1				3	
1b var.					1			
1c							1	
1d							3	
1e							5	
2	23	1	4		1		3	
3a		16	5			1		
4a		1	1				4	
4b							1	
4?			2					
5a		5					8	
5c							1	1
6							1	
7							1	
8a							1	
?	2			1				

FIGURE 89   Correlation between base types and decoration types of Demetrios bowls. The colours denote the likely sequence of the various decoration patterns (pink → green → blue → lilac)

base, occurring on at least 32 bowls. It was employed with all decorative schemes apart from 1a and 3. Šurgaja was of the opinion that this type was the earliest (1962, 118). Kovalenko disagrees (1996, 54), and I suspect he is right. Base F is most commonly found with Decoration 1e, 4 and 5. If this base occurs later than base type A, it shows that Decorations 1c–e are most likely later developments of Decoration 1a. Nevertheless, we cannot make the sequence so tight that the base types succeed one another, because signed and unsigned bases were undoubtedly in use contemporaneously, as we also know from Ephesian Workshop Circle 1 (see Chapters 4 and 14). Decoration 2, which is the most common, can be found with most of the base types (A, B, D, and F). So even though there was a development within Demetrios' products, as sketched above, numerous types coexisted, as we can also see from some of the better contexts in which Demetrios' bowls have been found. This is especially true concerning the funerary offering trench (*trizn*) of a 'collective' burial, which was unearthed in 1957 near the village of Kriničky in the chora of Theodosia (Kropotov & Leskov 2006). The pieces in this trench must be more or less contemporary because they were deposited as part of one action. They include one vessel with Decoration 1b and base type A (DEM-29), fragments of two bowls of Decoration 3a, one with base type B (DEM-155) and one with base type A or B (DEM-163), as well as fragments of vessels with Decoration 1 or 2 (DEM-60) and Decoration 4a (DEM-191). The same combination was found in a tomb with two chambers discovered in Kerč in 1956 (Blavatskij 1959, 176): one vessel with Decoration 2 and base type A (DEM-68) and one with Decoration 4a with base type B (DEM-182). The stylistic development and the contexts together show us that the production was probably relatively short-lived.

Absolute Chronology

Demetrios' production undisputedly post-dates ca. 165, when the long-petal design which features prominently on his vessels was first introduced (see Chapter 6). Kovalenko is the first author who suggested a more precise date, namely the end of the 2nd to the first quarter of 1st century (Kovalenko 1996, 56–57; Kovalenko 1998, 71). The earliest contexts in which isolated fragments of Demetrios bowls occur are Neapolis horizon E–D (DEM-159) and a dump in Čaika (DEM-140), both well dated by Rhodian amphora stamps. In the Čaika dump, the latest stamps date to ca. 126 (Kovalenko 2007, 216) and in Neapolis to 125 (Zaytsev 2004, 11). However, both localities are outside the core area of the bowls' distribution.

Not a single scrap of Demetrios' production was found amongst the fragments of up to 118 MMB in the Pantikapaion palace foundation trench (see Chapter 24). The fill in this trench was characterized primarily by Ephesian vessels of the classical production. *Exactly* the same type of Ephesian vessels has also been found in several other contexts together with signed Demetrios bowls. This holds true for the funerary offering trench at Krinički already mentioned. An ensemble of 13 MMB was unearthed there (Kropotov & Leskov 2006). Six of these are of Demetrios' production (DEM-29, DEM-60, DEM-155, DEM-163, DEM-191, DEM-261), whereas at least five are of classical Ephesian production, including three bowls with multiple rim friezes (Kropotov & Leskov 2006, fig. 7.1, 6, 7), one with a bound myrtle wreath (Kropotov & Leskov 2006, fig. 7.5), and one with long petals under a rim frieze with 'paws' (Kropotov & Leskov 2006, fig. 7.8). Some contexts at Porthmion, however, suggest later dates: DEM-116 and DEM-196 were found in pit 18 in room T, with 'fill connected with cessation of city in mid-1st century BC', and DEM-96 and DEM-123 were found in room X with a bronze coin of Pantikapaion of the 'first half of 1st century BC'; neither was found with other vessels.

This may suggest that the production of Demetrios bowls started immediately after the rebuilding of the palace of the Bosporan king Pairisades V in Pantikapaion, which took place in the heyday of the classical Ephesian production, perhaps when he ascended the throne around 125 (Chapter 24). As we have seen in Chapter 13, the same chronological frame is also provided for vessels of the Aiolis B production, attributed to Elaia, which formed the source of inspiration for the earliest part of Demetrios' production (Decoration 1a). Based on the above, I will therefore suggest that the production of Demetrios was initiated at the end of the third quarter of the 2nd century, perhaps as late as 125, and perhaps continued until the end of the century.

Distribution

The distribution of Demetrios bowls has been discussed by several authors (e.g., Rogl 2001a, 139 with references). It is hardly surprising that they circulated mostly in the Bosporan Kingdom, where they were also produced. In Chapter 4, we have already discussed the Bosporan Kingdom's degree of self-sufficiency (Figs. 28, 29). If we consider the total distribution, the figures are telling (Fig. 90). First of all, it is interesting to note that only one Pontic Demetrios bowl has ever been identified outside the Black Sea region, namely a bowl in the Walters Art Museum in Baltimore (DEM-154), which, according to its publication, derives from Kyzikos. In fact, of the more than 400 bowls of his production known to me (ECA-ECC), at the very most, only 20 bowls or fragments, ca. 5%, have been found outside the Bosporan Kingdom. Most of them come from the neighbouring state of Chersonesos and its chora. In the northwestern corner of the Black Sea, at Olbia and Tyras, they are so few that the evidence is negligible, and further west, at Istros, they have not been found at all.

There could be several reasons why the products of this workshop are so rare at Olbia. One could be chronological. The fourth quarter of the 2nd century, when the Workshop of Demetrios was probably in operation, was a period of little activity in Olbia, and, as explained in Chapter 20, the city had just been devastated. However, if we compare the finds from Olbia with those from Istros, we obtain exactly the same picture. As I will make clear in Chapter 21, the finds from Istros by and large belong to the second half of the 2nd century; consequently, we would expect to find Demetrios bowls in this important Pontic city. C. Domăneanțu, who published the Istros fragments, identified six fragments as probably belonging to the Workshop of Demetrios (Domăneanțu 2000, 120–121 cats. 594–599, pl. 41). However, after having inspected them myself, I want to make it clear that *none* of them belong to Demetrios' production (they are all Ephesian). We must therefore conclude that chronology was not the reason why so few (at Olbia) or no (at Istros) Bosporan MMB were unearthed outside the Crimea. Instead, their absence there indicates that they were not items of trade; instances found outside their homeland most probably testify to people moving with their pots.

Let us now turn to the distribution in the Bosporan Kingdom. Within the area of production, the relatively largest number of Demetrios vessels seems to come from sites in the chora (General'skoe, Krinički, Ogon'ki, Ruminskoe); this may be a matter of the chronology of the sites. This could, at least, be the reason why so few were found at the Taman' chora site of Volna 1 (see Chapter 30). At the sites where a large body of material has been found, chiefly Myrmekion and Porthmion, the relative frequency of Demetrios bowls is almost 30% and 16.5%, respectively. In both of these two cities we also find the largest variety

		Evidence category A+B		Evidence category C		Grand total	
		Sum	% of total at site	Sum	% of total at site	Sum	% of total at site
Northwest Pontic region	Olbia	1				1	
	Olbia?	2				2	
	Olbia or Pantikapaion	2				2	
	Tyras			1		1	
Western Crimea	Chersonesos	3				3	
	Čaika	3		1		4	
	Kara Tobe	3				3	
	Kerkinitis	1				1	
	Neapolis	1		1		2	
Bosporan Kingdom (European part)	Pantikapaion	37		88		125	
	Myrmekion	80		39		119	
	Myrmekion?	5				5	
	General'skoe	4				4	
	Krinički	6				6	
	Kytaion	1					
	Ogon'ki	24	92.3			24	92.3
	Porthmion	45		5		50	
	Tyritake	20		1		21	
	Uročišče Uščel'e Ved'm	2				2	
	Location?	5				5	
Bosporan Kingdom (Asian part)	Kepoi	5				5	
	Phanagoreia			2		2	
	Ruminskoe/Za Rodinu	5	45.5			5	45.5
	Volna 1	2	5.4			2	5.4
Maiotis	Tanais	4				4	
?	Find place?	2				2	
Mediterranean	Kyzikos	1				1	

FIGURE 90 Relative and absolute frequency of Demetrios vessels

of decorations (Fig. 91). The large number of Demetrios bowls in Myrmekion should hardly surprise us, since this town was the home of its earliest production. If we consider Pantikapaion, to which the production later moved, it is obvious that neither in terms of relative (and absolute) numbers, nor in terms of richness in decorations represented can the capital match the finds from Myrmekion and Porthmion. As explained below (p. 523), the Demetrios and other non-Ephesian products are overrepresented in my catalogue of MMB from Pantikapaion, and so the relatively low frequency of Demetrios bowls in Pantikapaion is even more surprising. Chronology is hardly the explanation. It is likely that as the capital of the kingdom, Pantikapaion had access to a wider range of products brought to the city as part of its international trade, and perhaps these were preferred over the local products.

Evidence category A+B		1								2		3		4			5				6	7	8	?
	Decoration	a	b	c	d	e	?	1 or 2	1, 2 or 4	1, 2, 4 or 5	?	a	b	a	b	?	a	b	c	?			a	b
Northwest Pontic region	Olbia									1														
	Olbia?			1								1												
	Olbia or Pantikapaion									2		1												
	Tyras																							1
Western Crimea	Chersonesos					1				1		1												
	Čaika									3														
	Kara Tobe	1								2														
	Kerkinitis									1														
	Neapolis											1												
Bosporan Kingdom (European part)	Pantikapaion	3	5							7		7		4			7		1		1	1		
	Myrmekion	6	7	1		5		2	1	20	1	10		9	3		5			1		2		
	Myrmekion?		1								1	1		1			1							
	General'skoe									2		1												
	Kriniči		1			1						2		1										
	Kytaion									1														
	Ogon'ki	4						2		10		4			1									
	Porthmion		2		2	1	1	1		14		5	1	6		1	6						1	1
	Tyritake		2	1						5		1		2			6	1	1				1	1
	Uročišče Uščel'e Ved'm				2																			
Bosporan Kingdom (Asian part)	Kepoi		1							1		1					1							
	Phanagoreia																					1		
	Ruminskoe/ Za Rodinu									3							2							
	Volna 1											1					1							
Maiotis	Tanais	1								1							2							
Mediterranean	Kyzikos									1														

FIGURE 91 Frequency of the various types of decoration on Demetrios bowls and their distribution. Blue rows indicate sites with a wide range of types. Pink columns indicate types with wide distribution. The green block indicates absence of certain types at certain sites

CATALOGUE TO CHAPTER 18

All pieces are reduced in firing unless otherwise stated.

MOULDS

Base Type A

DEM-1*
Pantikapaion, M-49-168, Moscow, Puškin Museum of Fine Arts. Base fr. H 4 × W 6.5, WT 1. Fabric: relatively coarse, shell inclusions, some light-reflecting particles. Low fired. Medallion: type A; signed [...]EMETRIOU around rosette A.

Decoration 1b

DEM-2
Myrmekion, square 26, depth 2.46 m, M-49-739. Present whereabouts unknown. Fr. of rim and upper body. Rim frieze: Ionian kyma. Main decoration: stylized long petal and acanthus leaf with bent tip and segmented central vein, with column of dots in between.
– Gajdukevič 1958, fig. 66; 1959, 78, fig. 85; 1971, 157 n. 107, fig. 39; Platek 1974, 44, fig. 5; 49; Bouzek 1990, 81–82, fig. 31.10.

DEM-3
Myrmekion, Warsaw, National Museum inv. 225168. Fr. of rim and upper body. Rim frieze: Ionian kyma. Main decoration: stylized long petals alternating with acanthus leaf with bent tip and segmented central vein with column of dots in between.
– Platek 1974, 43, fig. 4; 49.

DEM-4*
Pantikapaion, M-46-84, VI/6-2608, Moscow, Puškin Museum of Fine Arts. Fr. of base and lower body; H 4.3 × W 5.5, WT 0.5, ⌀ base 6. Fabric: relatively fine with some light-reflecting particles. Hard fired. Main decoration: acanthus with small triangular petals at base alternating with three stylized long petals separated by column of dots. Secondarily burnt.
– Blavatskij 1953, 280; Blavatskij 1959, 174 cat. 1 (not illustrated).

Decoration 2

DEM-5*
Pantikapaion, M-56-747, XVI/9-1663, Moscow, Puškin Museum of Fine Arts. Fr. of rim and upper body. H 6.3 × W 5, WT 0.7, ⌀ rim 14. Fabric: relatively fine with some light-reflecting particles. Hard fired. Rim frieze: Ionian kyma. Secondarily burnt.
– Blavatskij 1959, 174 cat. 3, fig. 62.4; Loseva 1962, fig. 6.1; Cvetaeva 1966, pl. 20.2.

Decoration 3a

DEM-6*
Pantikapaion, M-62-1048, 91/5-314, Moscow, Puškin Museum of Fine Arts. Fr. of rim and upper body. H 6.2 × W 5.5, WT 0.5, ⌀ rim 14. Fabric: relatively fine with some light-reflecting particles. Hard fired. Rim frieze: Ionian kyma. Secondarily burnt.

DEM-7
Pantikapaion, M-55-no no. Kerč History and Culture Reserve? Fr. of base and lower body.
– Blavatskij 1959, 174 cat. 2, fig. 62.1–3.

Decoration 4a

DEM-8*
Pantikapaion, M-57-769, LII/2-2001, Moscow, Puškin Museum of Fine Arts. Fr. of rim and upper body. H 3.6, WT 0.55, ⌀ rim 14. Fabric: relatively coarse, shell inclusions, some light-reflecting particles. Low fired. Rim frieze: Ionian kyma. Main decoration: stylized(?) long petals separated by column of dots.

DEM-9*
Pantikapaion, M-56-748, VII/1-693, Moscow, Puškin Museum of Fine Arts. Body fr. H 2.2 × W 2.3, WT 0.8, ⌀ rim 14. Fabric: relatively fine, some light-reflecting particles. Main decoration: stylized long petals separated by column of dots. Secondarily burnt.
– Blavatskij 1959, 174 cat. 4; Loseva 1962, fig. 6.2.

Decoration 6

DEM-10
Pantikapaion, so-called *kaserma*, year and number unknown, Moscow, Puškin Museum of Fine Arts. Half preserved mould; complete profile. Rim frieze: Ionian kyma. Main decoration: two plastic long petals separated by column of dots, alternating with

panel with imbricate petals. Medallion: type F; plain, slightly concave base; no signature.
– Žuravlev & Žuravleva 2014, 261, fig, 7.

Decoration 7

DEM-11
Pantikapaion, year and number unknown, Kerč History and Culture Reserve inv.? Lower part of mould. Main decoration: pine cone. Medallion: type F; plain, slightly concave base; no signature.
– Žuravlev & Žuravleva 2014, 260, fig. 6.1.

BOWLS

Decoration 1

Decoration 1 featuring a calyx with acanthus comes in a number of variants. Common to all is an elegantly curved, somewhat naturalistic acanthus leaf with segmented central vein, its tip bending either left or right.

Decoration 1a
Acanthus leaf alternating with tall pointed petal and four-petalled rosette on dotted stem; occasionally a bird (duck?) turning its head backwards sits on the tip of the acanthus. There is frequently a small group of small triangular petals at the base of the acanthus leaf.

DEM-12 (see Fig. 87)
Pantikapaion, year and number unknown, Moscow, State Historical Museum. Complete profile; fragmentary vessel. Rim frieze: Ionian kyma. Main decoration: bird sits left on acanthus leaf. Medallion: type A; signed DEMETRIOU around rosette A. Ends of petals continue into medallion.
– Žuravlev & Žuravleva 2014, 260, fig. 6.3.

DEM-13*
Myrmekion, M-48-178, St Petersburg, IIMK RAN. Fr. of base and lower body. H 4.8, WT 0.43, ⌀ base 4. Fabric: standard, with lime inclusions, hard and compact, Gley 1 4/N. Main decoration: two small pointed petals at base of acanthus. Medallion: type A; signed [...]OU around rosette A.
– Kovalenko 1989, 402 cat. 139+140.

DEM-14*
Pantikapaion, M-57-767, XLVI/2-1020, Moscow, Puškin Museum of Fine Arts. Fr. of base and lower body. H 7, WT 0.5, ⌀ base 5. Fabric: no fresh break for observation. Main decoration: two small pointed petals at base of acanthus. Medallion: type A; signed DE[...]U around rosette A.

DEM-15
Myrmekion, year and no. unknown, Warsaw, National Museum inv. 225006 MN. Fr. of base and lower body. Main decoration: acanthus with segmented central vein alternating with tall petal. Medallion: type A; signed [...]EME[...] around rosette A.
– Platek 1974, 46, fig. 7.

DEM-16
Tanais, year and no. unknown, present whereabouts unknown. Fragmentary; complete profile. Rim frieze: Ionian kyma. Main decoration: bird sits left on tips of acanthus leaves. Four small triangular leaves at base of acanthus leaves. Medallion: type A; signed DEMETRIOU around rosette A.
– Šelov 1966, fig. XXI.1.

DEM-17*
Myrmekion, M-49-843, St Petersburg, IIMK RAN. Fr. of midbody. H 4.7, WT 0.45. Fabric: standard, fine, with lime and shell inclusions, 2.5Y 3/1. Rim frieze: Ionian kyma. Main decoration: bird sits left on top of acanthus leaf. One repair hole.
– Kovalenko 1989, 402 cat. 146.

DEM-18*
Myrmekion, M-56-12, St Petersburg, IIMK RAN. Fr. of rim and upper body. H 4.9, WT 0.25, ⌀ rim 12, 9%, RH 2.3. Fabric: standard, with much lime, 7.5YR 4/1. Rim frieze: Ionian kyma. Main decoration: bird sits left on acanthus leaf.
– Kovalenko 1989, 401 cat. 122.

DEM-19
Pantikapaion, Cistern N 179, 96-no.(?), Kerč History and Culture Reserve inv.? Two joining frs. of rim and upper body. Rim frieze: Ionian kyma. Main decoration: columns of dots (without rosettes); bird sits left on acanthus leaf.
– Tolstikov & Zhuravlev 2004, pl. 101.11.

DEM-20
Kara Tobe, K-94-353, present whereabouts unknown. Three joining frs. of rim and upper body. Rim frieze: Ionian kyma. Main decoration: bird sits left on acanthus leaf. One repair hole.
– Vnukov & Kovalenko 1998, fig. 5.6 (identified as Pergamene).

DEM-21
Ogon'ki, O-65-281, Kerč History and Culture Reserve inv. KMAK 10279. Two joining rim frs. Rim frieze: Ionian kyma. Main decoration: tall pointed petal alternating with acanthus with segmented central vein with small pointed petals at base; between

petals and acanthus, leaf with bent top separated by column of dots topped by rosettes; on the acanthus, sitting bird turning head back.
– Grzegrzółka 2010, 224–225 cat. 400.

DEM-22
Ogon'ki, O-65-no.(?), Kerč History and Culture Reserve inv. KMAK 10280. Body fr. Rim frieze: Ionian kyma. Main decoration: tall pointed petal alternating with acanthus with segmented central vein and small pointed petals at its base; between petals and acanthus, leaf with bent top separated by column of dots topped by rosettes; on the acanthus, sitting bird turning head back.
– Grzegrzółka 2010, 224 cat. 399.

DEM-23
Ogon'ki, O-65-no.(?), Kerč History and Culture Reserve inv. KMAK 10296. Fr. of base and lower body. Tall pointed petal alternating with acanthus with segmented central vein and small pointed petals at its base; between petals and acanthus, leaf with bent top separated by column of dots; on the acanthus, sitting bird turning head back.
– Grzegrzółka 2010, 223–224 cat. 398.

DEM-24
Ogon'ki, O-65-241, Kerč History and Culture Reserve inv. KMAK 10295. Body fr. Tall pointed petal alternating with acanthus with segmented central vein and small pointed petals at its base; between petals and acanthus, leaf with bent top separated by column of dots.
– Grzegrzółka 2010, 225 cat. 401.

Decoration 1b
As Decoration 1a, but with the addition of groups of one or more stylized or plastic long petals delimited by columns of fine dots. This decoration is represented by two moulds, DEM-2 and DEM-3, excavated at Myrmekion and one mould unearthed at Pantikapaion, DEM-4*.

DEM-25
Pantikapaion, 1903–20, present whereabouts unknown. Complete. Rim frieze: Ionian kyma. Main decoration: groups of three stylized long petals separated by columns of dots, alternating with tall petal flanked by acanthus leaf with bent tip and segmented central vein. Two small triangular leaves at base of each acanthus. Medallion: type F; plain, almost flat base; no signature.
– St Petersburg, IIMK RAN, photo archive neg. III 9672.

DEM-26*
Myrmekion, M-56-269, St Petersburg, State Hermitage Museum. Fr. of base and lower body. H 7.6, WT 0.47, ⌀ base 4.5. Fabric: some small lime inclusions. Hard fired. Main decoration: tall ovoid petal alternating with groups of stylized long petals and acanthus with three small triangular petals at base, all separated by columns of dots. Medallion: type A; signed DEMETRIOU around rosette A.
– Šurgaja 1962, 119, fig. 4.1.

DEM-27*
Myrmekion, M-37-797, St Petersburg, IIMK RAN. Fr. of base and lower body. H 5.6, WT 0.35, ⌀ base 4. Fabric: standard, 10YR 6/2, 5/1, 4/2. Main decoration: slender slightly curving acanthus with segmented central vein and two rows of three small pointed petals at its base, alternating with tall petals; groups separated by columns of fine dots. Medallion: type A; signed [...]ETR[...] around rosette A.
– Kovalenko 1989, 402 cat. 155.

DEM-28
Pantikapaion, temple, Čkalov Str., year and no. unknown, Kerč History and Culture Reserve? Fr. of base and lower body. Main decoration: acanthus leaf with six small pointed leaves at base, alternating with long petals and tall petal, all separated by columns of fine dots. Medallion: type A; signed [...]TRIOU around rosette A.
– Zinko 2001, 309, fig. 6.1.

DEM-29
Kriničkí, tomb, funerary meal, year and no. unknown, present whereabouts unknown. Fr. of base and lower body. Main decoration: stylized long petals separated by column of dots alternating with acanthus leaf with small pointed petals at base. Medallion: type A; signed DEME[...] around rosette A.
– Kropotov & Leskov 2006, fig. 7.12.

DEM-30*
Pantikapaion, M-58-illegible no., Moscow, Puškin Museum of Fine Arts. Fr. of base and lower body. H 5.5 × W 5, ⌀ rim 5, ⌀ base 5. Main decoration: three stylized long petals delimited by columns of fine dots alternating with acanthus leaves with dotted vein. Medallion: type B; plain, slightly concave base; signed D[...]U.

DEM-31
Myrmekion, 1956-C I 100, Warsaw, National Museum inv. 225025. Fr. of base and lower body. Main decoration: groups of three stylized long petals alternating with acanthus leaf with segmented

central vein, all separated by column of dots. Medallion: type A or B; signed [...]TRI[...]; rosette cannot be distinguished.
– Bernhard 1957, 27 cat. 101; Platek 1974, 42, fig. 2.

DEM-32*
Kepoi, Ке-66-30, Moscow, State Historical Museum. Three non-joining frs. of base and lower body. H 7.5 × W 6.5, ⌀ base 5. Main decoration: groups of stylized long petals separated by columns of dots, alternating with acanthus with bent tip and segmented central vein flanking tall petal; small pointed petals at base of acanthus. Medallion: type F; plain, slightly concave base; no signature.
– Usačeva 1978, fig. 1.31.

DEM-33*
Tyritake, Sector L, Л-47-no. missing, St Petersburg, IIMK RAN. Fr. of base and lower body. H 4.7, WT 0.25, ⌀ base 6. Fabric: fine, compact, some small lime inclusions, Gley 1 6/N, 3/N, 10R 3/4, layered. Main decoration: groups of stylized long petals, alternating with acanthus leaves with segmented central vein flanking tall petal; all separated by columns of dots. Medallion: type F; plain, almost flat base; no signature.

DEM-34*
Myrmekion, M-56-1883, St Petersburg, IIMK RAN. Fr. of rim and upper body. H 3.5, WT 0.25, ⌀ rim 12, 12%, RH 2. Fabric: standard, with organic material and shell, 10YR 4/1. Rim frieze: Ionian kyma. Main decoration: tips of stylized long petal, column of fine dots, and tip of acanthus leaf. Frieze separators: dots.

DEM-35*
Myrmekion, M-49-676, St Petersburg, IIMK RAN. Fr. of rim and upper body. H 5.1, WT 2.2, ⌀ rim 11, 14%, RH 2.3. Fabric: standard, with shell and lime, 5Y 4/1, 5/2. Low fired. Rim frieze: Ionian kyma. Main decoration: stylized long petals separated by columns of dots, acanthus with bent tip. Frieze separators: dots.
– Kovalenko 1989, 401 cat. 121.

DEM-36*
Tyritake, Sector L, Л-47-150, St Petersburg, IIMK RAN. Fr. of rim and upper body. H 4.3, WT 0.2, RH 2.6. Fabric: fine, compact, some small lime inclusions, Gley 1 6/N, 3/N, layered. Rim frieze: Ionian kyma. Main decoration: stylized long petals separated by column of fine dots; bird turning head backwards sits left on missing element. Frieze separators: dots.

DEM-37*
Myrmekion, M-57-2063, St Petersburg, IIMK RAN. Fr. of lower body. Main decoration: three stylized long petals separated by columns of dots, acanthus with segmented central vein.
– Kovalenko 1989, 403 cat. 174.

DEM-38
Myrmekion(?), year and no. unknown, present whereabouts unknown. Fr. of rim and upper and mid-body. Rim frieze: Ionian kyma. Main decoration: two groups of stylized long petals flanking pointed petal, alternating with acanthus with segmented central vein and bent tip; bird turning head back sits left on rosette.
– Šurgaja 1962, 115, fig. 3.4.

DEM-39
Pantikapaion, area of 2 Lenin Str., Kerč History and Culture Reserve inv. KMAK 6474 (1961). Fr. of rim and upper body. Rim frieze: Ionian kyma. Main decoration: acanthus leaf with bent tip alternating with stylized long petals separated by columns of dots.
– Grzegrzółka 2010, 72 cat. 58.

DEM-40
Porthmion, Sector V, П-77-76, according to M. Vachtina discarded. Fr. of rim and upper body. Rim frieze: Ionian kyma. Main decoration: acanthus leaves with segmented central vein and tips bent left and right, alternating with tall pointed petal, separated by columns of dots. Frieze separators: dots.

DEM-41
Porthmion, П-77-78, Kerč History and Culture Reserve inv. KMAK 9506. Fr. of rim and upper body. Rim frieze: Ionian kyma. Main decoration: acanthus leaves with tips bent left and right separated by slender lotus petal and stylized long petal; in between, column of dots. Frieze separators: dots.
– Grzegrzółka 2010, 208 cat. 364.

Decoration 1b var.

DEM-42*
Myrmekion, M-58-1419+1420+1421, St Petersburg, IIMK RAN. Three joining frs. of base and lower body. H 6.9, WT 0.25, ⌀ base 3.2. Fabric: standard, fine, with shell, Gley 1 6/N. Main decoration: group of (at least) three stylized long petals, acanthus leaf, two tall petals(?), all separated by column of fine dots. Calyx: one row of triangular leaves. Medallion: type D; six-petalled rosette B; no signature.
– Kovalenko 1989, 403 cat. 166.

Decoration 1c
Bent acanthus leaves alternating with long petals and buds on dotted stems.

DEM-43*
Tyritake, Sector L, Л-47-343, St Petersburg, IIMK RAN. Fr. of rim and upper body. H 4.4, WT 0.35, ⌀ rim 11, 18%, RH 2. Fabric: fine, compact, some small lime inclusions, Gley 1 5/N, 3/N. Rim

frieze: Ionian kyma. Main decoration: plastic long petals alternating with acanthus leaf with bent tip and bud on dotted stem.
– Kovalenko 1989, 404 cat. 194.

DEM-44
Myrmekion, 1956-G 1, Warsaw, National Museum. Fr. of body and part of base. Rim frieze: Ionian kyma. Main decoration: plastic(?) long petals alternating with acanthus leaf with bent tip and vertical dotted stems. Medallion: type F; plain, almost flat base; no signature.
– Bernhard 1957, 26 cat. 98; Michałowski 1958, pl. XV; Platek 1974, 47, fig. 10.

Decoration 1d
Bent acanthus leaf alternating with one or two plastic long petals; no column of dots.

DEM-45*
Porthmion, square 16, depth 1.05 m with material of the 2nd–1st century, П-53-785[c], St Petersburg, IIMK RAN. Fr. of base and lower body. H 4.3, WT 0.38. Fabric: standard, with coarse shell, Gley 1 5/N. Main decoration: acanthus leaves with segmented central vein and three small triangular leaves at base, alternating with single plastic long petals. Calyx: one row of triangular leaves. Medallion: type F; plain, slightly concave base; no signature.

DEM-46*
Porthmion, square 16, depth 1.05 m with material of the 2nd–1st century, П-53-785[a, b], St Petersburg, IIMK RAN. Two nonjoining frs. of rim and upper body. H 4.4, WT 0.35, ⌀ rim 11.5, 27%, RH 2.7. Fabric: standard, Gley 1 3/N, 2/N. Rim frieze: Ionian kyma. Main decoration: acanthus leaves with tips bent heraldically towards tall petal; isolated plastic long petals; above, pinecone scale as space-filler.
– Kovalenko 1989, 402 cat. 131.

DEM-47
Olbia(?), the first owner of the vessel stated that it came from a tomb in the vicinity of Parutine (1892), inv. 237048, Warsaw, National Museum. Complete. ⌀ rim 10, ⌀ base 4.5; vessel H 5.8; H:⌀ 1:1.7. Fabric: fine-grained dark grey. Rim frieze: Ionian kyma. Main decoration: two plastic long petals alternating with acanthus leaf with segmented central vein, its tip bent alternately left and right. Medallion: type F; plain, concave base; ends of long petals continue under base; no signature.
– Grzegrzółka 2001, 121–123 cat. 5, fig. 5 (identification: PGB).

DEM-48
Bosporan Kingdom, Kerč History and Culture Reserve inv. KMAK 384. Complete. ⌀ rim 11.7, ⌀ base 4.7; vessel H 6.6; H:⌀ 1:1.8. Rim frieze: Ionian kyma. Main decoration: acanthus leaves alternating with two and three slightly plastic long petals. Medallion: type F; flat, plain base; no signature.
– Grzegrzółka 2010, 45 cat. 15.

Decoration 1e
Bent acanthus leaf alternating with four to six parallel lines acting as stylized long petals.

DEM-49*
Myrmekion, M-58-1704, St Petersburg, IIMK RAN. Fr. of base and lower body. H 5, WT 0.45, ⌀ base 6. Fabric: standard, with inclusions of lime and small shells, 2.5Y 4/1. Main decoration: two stylized long petals alternating with straight acanthus on small 'base'. Medallion: type F; plain, slightly concave base; no signature.
– Kovalenko 1989, 403 cat. 163.

DEM-50*
Myrmekion, M-56-1736a, St Petersburg, IIMK RAN. Fr. of base and lower body. H 5.2, WT 0.33, ⌀ base 5. Fabric: standard, 2.5Y 4/1. Main decoration: two stylized long petals alternating with straight acanthus on small 'base'. Medallion: type F; plain, slightly concave base with false ring foot, lines of long petals continue under base; no signature.
– Kovalenko 1989, 402 cat. 138.

DEM-51
Myrmekion, M-57-1166, St Petersburg, IIMK RAN. Fr. of base and lower body. H 4.9, WT 0.42, ⌀ base 4.75. Fabric: standard, with many lime inclusions, 7.5YR 5/1, 4/1, 3/1. Main decoration: acanthus leaves alternating with three stylized long petals. Medallion: type F; plain, slightly concave base, the ends of the long petals continue under base; no signature.

DEM-52
Uročišče Uščel'e Ved'm, year and no. unknown, Kerč History and Culture Reserve? Fr. of base and lower body. Main decoration: acanthus on small 'base'. Medallion: type F; plain, slightly concave base; no signature.
– Maslennikov 2007, fig. 137.18.

DEM-53
Uročišče Uščel'e Ved'm, year and no. unknown, Kerč History and Culture Reserve? Fr. of base and lower body. Main decoration: acanthus on small 'base'. Medallion: type F; plain, slightly concave base; no signature.
– Maslennikov 2007, fig. 137.19.

DEM-54*
Myrmekion, M-49-715, St Petersburg, State Hermitage Museum. Fr. of rim and upper body. H 6.8, WT 0.5, ⌀ rim 11, 10%, RH 2.1. Fabric: rather coarse, abundant lime and shell inclusions, 10YR 4/1. Hard fired. No rim frieze. Main decoration: two stylized long petals flanked by acanthus leaves, the tips of which bend toward it.

DEM-55
Porthmion, П-75-236, Kerč History and Culture Reserve inv. KMAK 6066. Fr. of rim and body. No rim frieze. Main decoration: two stylized long petals flanked by acanthus leaves with tips curving in opposing directions.
– Grzegrzółka 2010, 208–209 cat. 365.

DEM-56*
Myrmekion, M-49-20, St Petersburg, State Hermitage Museum. Three joining frs. of rim and upper body. H 5.4, WT 0.4, ⌀ rim 12, 10%, RH 2.45. Fabric: rather coarse, abundant lime inclusions, 5Y 4/1, 7.5YR 7/4. Hard fired. Rim frieze: Ionian kyma. Main decoration: two stylized long petals flanked by acanthus leaf with bent tip.

Decoration 1?
DEM-57*
Porthmion, square 10, depth 0.6 m, П-53-433, St Petersburg, IIMK RAN. Fr. of mid-body. H 5.3, WT 0.45. Fabric: standard, with organic material, Gley 1 6N/10Y. Rim frieze: Ionian kyma. Main decoration: acanthus with bent tip; 'nelumbo'(?) with beaded side and central vein.

DEM-58
Porthmion, П-77-75, Kerč History and Culture Reserve inv. KMAK 9505. Fr. of rim and upper body. Rim frieze: Ionian kyma. Main decoration: stylized long petal with vertical dotted lines; low acanthus leaf(?). Frieze separators: dots.
– Grzegrzółka 2010, 208 cat. 363.

Decoration 1 or 2
DEM-59
Porthmion, П-77-123[a], Kerč History and Culture Reserve inv. KMAK 9517. Fr. of rim and upper body. Rim frieze: Ionian kyma. Main decoration: stylized long petals separated by column of dots; lotus petal or acanthus leaf? Frieze separators: dots.
– Grzegrzółka 2010, 205–206 cat. 358.

DEM-60
Krinički, tomb, funerary meal, year and no. unknown, present whereabouts unknown. Fr. of rim and upper body. ⌀ rim 12.7. Rim frieze: Ionian kyma. Main decoration: stylized long petal and column of dots under horizontal frieze of dots.

– Kropotov & Leskov 2006, fig. 7.11.

Decoration 1, 2 or 4
DEM-61*
Chersonesos, X-1965-75, St Petersburg, State Hermitage Museum. Fr. of rim and upper body. H 3.5, WT 0.35, ⌀ rim 14, 10%, RH 2.4. Fabric: no fresh break for observation. Rim frieze: Ionian kyma. Main decoration: stylized long petals.

DEM-62*
Myrmekion, M-57-563, St Petersburg, IIMK RAN. Fr. of rim and upper body. H 3.8, WT 0.32, ⌀ rim 12, 18%, RH 1.7. Fabric: standard, 5Y 5/1. Rim frieze: Ionian kyma. Main decoration: groups of three stylized long petals separated by column of fine dots.
– Kovalenko 1989, 403 cat. 175.

DEM-63*
Myrmekion, M-48-305, St Petersburg, IIMK RAN. Fr. of rim and upper body. H 4.1, WT 0.3, ⌀ rim 12, 12%, RH 2.1. Fabric: standard, 10YR 5/2, oxidized. Rim frieze: Ionian kyma. Main decoration: stylized long petals alternate with columns of dots. Frieze separators: dots.
– Kovalenko 1989, 401 cat. 129.

DEM-64
Ogon'ki, O-65-no.(?), Kerč History and Culture Reserve inv. KMAK 5591. Rim fr. Rim frieze: Ionian kyma.
– Grzegrzółka 2010, 221–222 cat. 394.

DEM-65
Ogon'ki, O-65-no.(?), Kerč History and Culture Reserve inv. KMAK 10270. Fr. of rim and upper body. Rim frieze: Ionian kyma. Frieze separators: dots.
– Grzegrzółka 2010, 222–223 cat. 396.

Decoration 1, 2, 4 or 5
DEM-66*
Myrmekion, M-no year, no no., St Petersburg, IIMK RAN. Rim fr. H 3.6, WT 0.32, RH 1.9. Fabric: standard, with lime and shell inclusions, 5Y 3/1. Rim frieze: Ionian kyma. Main decoration: trace of pointed petal.

Decoration 2

Groups of stylised long petals alternating with tall pointed petal; all elements are separated by columns of fine dots. This decoration is known from a mould fragment from Pantikapaion, DEM-5*.

DEM-67*
Myrmekion, Sector И, courtyard VII, M-49-400, St Petersburg, IIMK RAN. Three rim frs., two joining, one joining body fr., frs. of base and lower body; almost complete profile. WT 0.45, ⌀ rim 12, 18%, RH 1.8, ⌀ base 4.5. Fabric: standard, with many small inclusions of lime and larger stones, 2.5YR 4/6. Not too hard fired, oxidized. Rim frieze: Ionian kyma. Medallion: type A; signed DEME[...] around rosette A.
– Kovalenko 1989, 401 cat. 114a.

DEM-68
Pantikapaion, tomb 56/East/N 20, Kerč History and Culture Reserve inv. KMAK 1856. Complete. ⌀ rim 12.2, ⌀ base 4.8; vessel H 6.5; H:⌀ 1:1.9. Rim frieze: Ionian kyma. Medallion: type A; signed DEME[...]IOU around rosette A.
– Blavatskij 1959, fig. 62.5; Loseva 1962, fig. 5.2; AGSP 1984, pl. CLXIV.19–20?; Kovalenko 1989, 400 cat. 93; Grzegrzółka 2010, 52 cat. 21.

DEM-69
Provenance unknown, inv. 98.8.26, New York, Metropolitan Museum. Complete. Rim frieze: Ionian kyma. Medallion: type A; signed DEMETRIOU around rosette A.
– Siebert 1978, pl. 21.

DEM-70
Kara Tobe, К-88-806, present whereabouts unknown. Fragmentary bowl; complete profile. Rim frieze: Ionian kyma. Medallion: type A; exact extent of inscription is not mentioned. Frieze separators: dots.
– Vnukov & Kovalenko 1998, fig. 4.9.

DEM-71*
Pantikapaion, M-57-768, Moscow, Puškin Museum of Fine Arts. Fr. of base and lower body. H 6.2, WT 0.32. Fabric: no fresh break for observation. Medallion: type A; signed DEME[...] around rosette A. Secondarily burnt.

DEM-72*
Olbia or Pantikapaion, Buračkov 143, Moscow, State Historical Museum (Buračkov collection). Fr. of base and lower body. H 3 × W 2.5. Medallion: type A; signed [...]IOU around rosette A.

DEM-73
Myrmekion, M-48-218, St Petersburg, IIMK RAN. Five joining frs. of base and lower body; base largely missing and partly worn. H 9.7, WT 0.32, ⌀ base 4.75. Fabric: standard, 10YR 5/1, 5/3. Medallion: type A; signed DEME[...] around rosette A.
– Kovalenko 1989, 402 cats. 144 and 153.

DEM-74
Myrmekion, M-56-2242+57-1345 (join across years), St Petersburg, IIMK RAN. Two joining frs. of base and lower body. H 10, WT 0.45. Fabric: standard, with lime and shell inclusions, large voids, 2.5Y 4/1, 6/2. Medallion: type A; signed DE[...] around rosette A.
– Kovalenko 1989, 403 cat. 170.

DEM-75*
Provenance unknown, year and number unknown [a], Moscow, State Historical Museum. Base fr. H 3 × W 3.5, ⌀ base 5. Medallion: type A; signed [...]METR[...] around rosette A.

DEM-76
Chersonesos, year and no. unknown, present whereabouts unknown. Fr. of base and lower body. Medallion: type A; signed [...]METRIOU around rosette A.
– Koscjuško-Valjužinič 1901, 31, fig. 24.

DEM-77
Myrmekion, Sector И, M-56-1730, St Petersburg, IIMK RAN. Fr. of lower body. H 2, WT 0.28. Fabric: standard, with lime inclusions, 5Y 4/1. Medallion: type A; signed DEMETRIO[...] around rosette A.
– Gajdukevič 1959, 78 n. 186, fig. 86; Kovalenko 1989, 402 cat. 145.

DEM-78*
Myrmekion, M-49-410, St Petersburg, State Hermitage Museum. Fr. of base and lower body. H 7.2, WT 0.35, ⌀ base 4.5. Fabric: medium fine, compact, some organic material. Hard fired. Medallion: type A; signed [...]TRIOU around rosette A; the bowl was not centred well in the mould, leaving the name triple stamped.

DEM-79
Myrmekion, 1956-A 27, Warsaw, National Museum 225005 MN. Fr. of base and lower body. Medallion: type A; signed [...]IOU around rosette A.
– Bernhard 1957, 26 cat. 95; Michałowski 1958, pl. XIII; Platek 1974, 45, fig. 6.

DEM-80
Myrmekion, 1956-B 27, Warsaw, National Museum inv. 225016 MN. Fr. of base and lower body. Medallion: type A; signed D[...]U around rosette A.
– Bernhard 1957, 26 cat. 96; Platek 1974, 46, fig. 8.

DEM-81
Olbia, O-1929-38, present whereabouts unknown. Fr. of base and lower body. Medallion: type A; signed DE[...]OU around rosette A.
– St Petersburg, IIMK RAN, photo archive neg. II 4816.

DEM-82
Pantikapaion, year and no. unknown, Kerč History and Culture Reserve? Base fr. Medallion: type A; signed DEME[...] around rosette A.
– Loseva 1962, fig. 6.3.

DEM-83
Porthmion, courtyard A, П-77-171, Kerč History and Culture Reserve inv. KMAK 9520. Fr. of base and lower body. Medallion: type A; signed DEM[...]RIOU around rosette A.
– Grzegrzółka 2010, 204 cat. 355.

DEM-84
Porthmion, П-53-722, present whereabouts unknown. Base fr. Medallion: type A; signed [...]EMET[...] around rosette A.
– Šurgaja 1962, 119, fig. 4.3–3a; Kovalenko 1989, 404 cat. 191.

DEM-85
Tanais, Tomb 14, year and no. unknown, present whereabouts unknown. Fr. of base and lower body. Medallion: type A; signed [...]ME[...] around rosette A.
– Arsen'eva et al. 2001, pl. 63 cat. 799.

DEM-86
Ogon'ki, O-65-no.(?), Kerč History and Culture Reserve inv. KMAK 8600. Fr. of base and lower body. Medallion: type A; signed DE[...]T[...] around rosette A.
– Grzegrzółka 2010, 217–218 cat. 386.

DEM-87
Ogon'ki, O-65-182, Kerč History and Culture Reserve inv. KMAK 10278. Lower part of vessel joined from two frs. Medallion: type A; signed DEMETRIOU around rosette A. Two repair holes.
– Grzegrzółka 2010, 218–219 cat. 387.

DEM-88
Kara Tobe, К-87-879, present whereabouts unknown. Fr. of base and lower body. Medallion: type A; signed DEMETRIO[...] around rosette A.
– Vnukov & Kovalenko 1998, fig. 4.8.

DEM-89
Kytaion, year and no. unknown, present whereabouts unknown. Fr. of base and lower body. Medallion: type A; signed DEMETRIOU around rosette A.
– Molev 1985, 61, fig. 7.9 cf. Bouzek 1990, 78 n. 61; Molev 2003, 881, fig. 4.6.

DEM-90
Ogon'ki, O-65-99(?), Kerč History and Culture Reserve inv. KMAK 10387/1. Two non-joining frs. of base and lower body. Medallion: type B; plain, flat base signed DE[...].
– Grzegrzółka 2010, 215 cat. 381.

DEM-91*
Myrmekion, M-49-845, St Petersburg, IIMK RAN. Fr. of base and lower body. H 3.8, WT 0.3, ⌀ base 5. Fabric: standard, with lime inclusions, 10YR 4/2, 4/3. Medallion: type A or B; small part of signature preserved: [...]E[...].
– Kovalenko 1989, 402 cat. 152.

DEM-92*
Ruminskoe/Za Rodinu, РУМ-72-150, Moscow, State Historical Museum, inv. 103991. Fr. of base and lower body, underside mostly missing. H 3.5 × W 4. Medallion: type A or B; signed [...]T[...].

DEM-93
Ogon'ki, O-65-no.(?), Kerč History and Culture Reserve inv. KMAK 10292. Fr. of base and lower body. Medallion: type A or B; signed DE[...]; rosette cannot be distinguished.
– Grzegrzółka 2010, 219 cat. 388.

DEM-94
Čaika, Ч-71-1287+1300, present whereabouts unknown. Fr. of base and lower body. Medallion: type A or B; signed DEM[...]; rosette cannot be distinguished.
– Kovalenko 1987a, 7, fig. 1.7; Kovalenko 1989, 405 cat. 205; Kovalenko 1996, 55.

DEM-95*
Tyritake, Sector L, Л-47-127, St Petersburg, IIMK RAN. Fr. of base and lower body. H 5.5, WT 0.3, ⌀ base 4. Fabric: standard, with lime and shell inclusions, Gley 1 4/10Y. Medallion: type D; six-petalled rosette B; no signature.
– Kovalenko 1989, 404 cat. 202.

DEM-96
Porthmion, room X, pavement, П-75-371+376, Kerč History and Culture Reserve inv. KMAK 6077+6079. Complete profile; two

large joining frs. ⌀ rim 10.5, ⌀ base 4.5; vessel H 6.3; H:⌀ 1:1.7. Rim frieze: Ionian kyma. Medallion: type F; plain, slightly concave base; no signature.
– Grzegrzółka 2010, 206–207 cat. 360.

DEM-97
Myrmekion, M-58-695, St Petersburg, IIMK RAN. Fr. of base and body. H 4, WT 0.3, ⌀ base 6. Fabric: standard, fine, 2.5Y 6/1. Medallion: type F; plain, slightly concave base; no signature.
– Kovalenko 1989, 403 cat. 161.

DEM-98
Porthmion, П-75-240+242, Kerč History and Culture Reserve inv. KMAK 6071. Two joining frs. of base and lower body. Oxidized. Medallion: type F; plain, slightly concave base; no signature.
– Grzegrzółka 2010, 166 cat. 259 (attributed to Asia Minor).

DEM-99*
Myrmekion, M-48-306, St Petersburg, IIMK RAN. Fr. of rim and upper body. H 4, WT 0.4, ⌀ rim 11, 14%, RH 2.1. Fabric: standard, with organic material, long voids, 10YR 5/2. Rim frieze: Ionian kyma.
– Kovalenko 1989, 401 cat. 119.

DEM-100*
Myrmekion, M-56-1889, St Petersburg, IIMK RAN. Fr. of rim and upper body. H 4, WT 0.4, ⌀ rim 11, 8%, RH 1.8. Fabric: standard, fine, 10YR 5/1, 5/3. Rim frieze: Ionian kyma.
– Kovalenko 1989, 401 cat. 123.

DEM-101*
Myrmekion, M-49-945, St Petersburg, IIMK RAN. Fr. of rim and upper body. H 4.9, WT 0.4, ⌀ rim 12, 12%, RH 2.1. Fabric: standard, compact with much fine lime, Gley 2 7/5PB, 4/5PB. Rim frieze: Ionian kyma.

DEM-102*
Myrmekion, Sector И, courtyard VII, M-49-39, St Petersburg, State Hermitage Museum. Fr. of rim and upper body. H 6, WT 0.4, ⌀ rim 12, 15%, RH 1.9. Fabric: medium fine, compact, some organic material, 10YR 5/1. Hard fired. Rim frieze: Ionian kyma.

DEM-103*
Myrmekion, M-49-519, St Petersburg, IIMK RAN. Fr. of rim and upper body, two non-joining frs. H 4.2, WT 0.3, ⌀ rim 12, 20%, RH 1.7. Fabric: standard, compact, large shell inclusions, 10YR 3/3. Rim frieze: Ionian kyma.
– Kovalenko 1989, 401 cat. 115.

DEM-104
Pantikapaion, M-58-illegible no.[a], Moscow, Puškin Museum of Fine Arts. Fr. of mid-body. H 3 × W 5.5. Rim frieze: Ionian kyma.

DEM-105*
Porthmion, П-53-147, St Petersburg, IIMK RAN. Fr. of rim and upper body. H 4, WT 0.4, ⌀ rim 13, 8%, RH 2.1. Fabric: standard, Gley 1 4/N, core 6/N. Rim frieze: Ionian kyma.

DEM-106*
Porthmion, square 20, depth 1.4 m, П-53-987, St Petersburg, IIMK RAN. Four rim frs. and two body frs., all joining. H 5.3, WT 0.22, ⌀ rim 11.5, 35%, RH 2.4. Fabric: standard, 10YR 4/2, core Gley 1 4/N. Rim frieze: Ionian kyma. Two repair holes.

DEM-107*
Ruminskoe/Za Rodinu, Рум-72-22, Moscow, State Historical Museum, inv. 103991. Fr. of rim and upper body. H 4.5 × W 5.5, RH 2.3. Reduced. Rim frieze: Ionian kyma. Secondarily burnt.

DEM-108*
Ruminskoe/Za Rodinu, Рум-72-125, Moscow, State Historical Museum, inv. 103991. Fr. of upper body close to rim. H 3.5 × W 4. Rim frieze: Ionian kyma.

DEM-109*
Tyritake, Sector L, Л-47-112, St Petersburg, IIMK RAN. Fr. of rim and upper body. H 4.8, WT 0.35, ⌀ rim 11, 19%, RH 1.8. Fabric: standard, with shell and organic material, Gley 1 6/N. Rim frieze: Ionian kyma.
– Kovalenko 1989, 404 cat. 192.

DEM-110*
Tyritake, Sector L, Л-47-151, St Petersburg, IIMK RAN. Fr. of rim and upper body. H 5.9, WT 0.3, ⌀ rim 11, 8%, RH 2. Fabric: standard, with shell and some light-reflecting particles, Gley 1 6/N, 3/10Y, layered. Rim frieze: Ionian kyma.
– Kovalenko 1989, 404 cat. 195.

DEM-111*
Tyritake, Sector L, Л-47-47, St Petersburg, IIMK RAN. Fr. of rim and upper body. H 4.7, WT 0.35, ⌀ rim 12, 14%, RH 2. Fabric: fine, compact, some small lime inclusions, Gley 1 6/N, 3/N, 10R 3/4, layered. Rim frieze: Ionian kyma.
– Kovalenko 1989, 404 cat. 200.

DEM-112
Kepoi, year and no. unknown, Moscow, State Historical Museum? Fr. of rim and upper body. Rim frieze: Ionian kyma.
– Usačeva 1978, fig. 1.32.

DEM-113*
Myrmekion, M-49-677, St Petersburg, IIMK RAN. Fr. of midbody. H 3.8, WT 0.35. Fabric: fine, slightly soft, Gley 1 5/N. Rim frieze: Ionian kyma.
– Kovalenko 1989, 401 cat. 120.

DEM-114*
Myrmekion, M-57-622, St Petersburg, IIMK RAN. Fr. of midbody. H 3, WT 0.41. Fabric: standard, Gley 1 5/N, 3/N. Rim frieze: Ionian kyma.
– Kovalenko 1989, 403 cat. 173.

DEM-115
Myrmekion, 1956-C I 13, Warsaw, National Museum. Rim fr. Rim frieze: Ionian kyma. Frieze separators: dots.
– Michałowski 1958, pl. XVI.b.

DEM-116
Porthmion, room T, in pit 18, П-75-234, according to M. Vachtina, discarded. Complete profile; fr. from rim to base. Rim frieze: Ionian kyma.

DEM-117
Porthmion, Vachtina: room X, with bronze coin of Pantikapaion of first half of 1st century; Grzegrzółka: room 51, pavement 134, NE corner, depth 1.6 m, П-75-412, Kerč History and Culture Reserve inv. KMAK 6089. Fr. of rim and upper body. Oxidized. Rim frieze: Ionian kyma.
– Grzegrzółka 2010, 164 cat. 255 (attributed to Asia Minor).

DEM-118
Porthmion, room 51, pavement 134, NE corner, depth 1.6 m, П-75-414, Kerč History and Culture Reserve inv. KMAK 6091. Fr. of rim and upper body. Oxidized. Rim frieze: Ionian kyma.
– Grzegrzółka 2010, 164–165 cat. 256 (attributed to Asia Minor).

DEM-119
Porthmion, П-75-61, Kerč History and Culture Reserve inv. KMAK 6025. Fr. of rim and upper body. Oxidized. Rim frieze: Ionian kyma.
– Grzegrzółka 2010, 165–166 cat. 258 (attributed to Asia Minor).

DEM-120
Porthmion, П-77-123, Kerč History and Culture Reserve inv. KMAK 9516. Fr. of rim and body. Rim frieze: Ionian kyma.
– Grzegrzółka 2010, 205 cat. 357.

DEM-121
Porthmion, П-75-241, Kerč History and Culture Reserve inv. KMAK 6070. Body fr. Rim frieze: Ionian kyma.
– Grzegrzółka 2010, 207 cat. 362.

DEM-122
Porthmion, П-75-237, Kerč History and Culture Reserve inv. KMAK 6067. Fr. of rim and body. Rim frieze: Ionian kyma. Frieze separators: dots.
– Grzegrzółka 2010, 207 cat. 361.

DEM-123
Porthmion, room X, with bronze coin of Pantikapeion of first half of 1st century, П-75-415+416, Kerč History and Culture Reserve inv. KMAK 6092+6093. Two non-joining body frs. with tiny part of base. Oxidized. Rim frieze: Ionian kyma.
– Grzegrzółka 2010, 165 cat. 257 (attributed to Asia Minor).

DEM-124
Tyritake, Sector T, Kerč History and Culture Reserve inv. KMAK 8924 (1938). Fr. of rim and upper body. Rim frieze: Ionian kyma.
– Grzegrzółka 2010, 125 cat. 172.

DEM-125*
Bosporan Kingdom, year(?)-122, St Petersburg, IIMK RAN. Fr. of rim and upper body. ⌀ rim 11, 13%. Frieze separators: dots.

DEM-126
Ogon'ki, O-65-no.(?), Kerč History and Culture Reserve inv. KMAK 10294. Fr. of rim and body. Rim frieze: Ionian kyma.
– Grzegrzółka 2010, 219–220 cat. 389.

DEM-127
Ogon'ki, O-65-193, Kerč History and Culture Reserve inv. KMAK 10283. Body fr. Rim frieze: Ionian kyma.
– Grzegrzółka 2010, 220 cat. 390.

DEM-128
Ogon'ki, O-65-36(?), Kerč History and Culture Reserve inv. KMAK 10291. Body fr. Rim frieze: Ionian kyma.
– Grzegrzółka 2010, 220–221 cat. 391.

DEM-129
Ogon'ki, O-65-196, Kerč History and Culture Reserve inv. KMAK 10281. Fr. of rim and upper body. Rim frieze: Ionian kyma.
– Grzegrzółka 2010, 221 cat. 392.

DEM-130
Ogon'ki, O-65-189, Kerč History and Culture Reserve inv. KMAK 10282. Fr. of rim and upper body. Rim frieze: Ionian kyma.
– Grzegrzółka 2010, 221 cat. 393.

DEM-131
General'skoe, building 5, year and no. unknown, Kerč History and Culture Reserve? Three joining frs. of rim, body and base; almost complete profile. Rim frieze: Ionian kyma.
– Maslennikov 1997, fig. 14.5; Maslennikov 2007, fig. 93.9 and 10.

DEM-132
General'skoe, year and no. unknown, Kerč History and Culture Reserve? Fr. of rim and upper body. Rim frieze: Ionian kyma. Frieze separators: dots.
– Maslennikov 2007, fig. 72.15.

DEM-133
Ogon'ki, O-65-210, Kerč History and Culture Reserve inv. KMAK 10293. Body fr. Rim frieze: Ionian kyma. Frieze separators: dots.
– Grzegrzółka 2010, 222 cat. 395.

DEM-134
Čaika, Ч-71-1298, present whereabouts unknown. Fr. of rim and upper body. Rim frieze: Ionian kyma.
– Kovalenko 1987a, 7, fig. 1.6; Kovalenko 1989, 405 cat. 208; Kovalenko 1996, 55.

DEM-135*
Myrmekion, M-48-205, St Petersburg, IIMK RAN. Fr. of lower body close to base. H 3.7, WT 0.35. Fabric: standard, fine, Gley 1 4/N.
– Kovalenko 1989, 402 cat. 143.

DEM-136
Pantikapaion, M-58-977, Moscow, Puškin Museum of Fine Arts. Fr. of lower body and tiny part of base. H 3.5 × W 6.

DEM-137
Myrmekion, M-48-455, St Petersburg, IIMK RAN. Fr. of midbody. H 3.2, WT 0.3. Fabric: standard, fine with some fine organic material, large voids, 5Y 4/1.
– Kovalenko 1989, 402 cat. 156.

DEM-138
Myrmekion, 1956-A 15, Warsaw, National Museum. Fr. of body and part of base.
– Michałowski 1958, pl. XVI.a.

DEM-139
Pantikapaion, gift of E.B. Moiseeva, Kerč History and Culture Reserve inv. KMAK 13793. Fr. of lower body.
– Grzegrzółka 2010, 85 cat. 85.

DEM-140
Čaika, dump, Ч-82-70, present whereabouts unknown. Fr. of lower body and tiny part of base.
– Kovalenko 1987a, 7; Kovalenko 1989, 405 cat. 206; Kovalenko 1996, 55; Kovalenko 2007, fig. 19.13.

DEM-141
Kerkinitis, E-80-842, present whereabouts unknown. Fr. of rim and upper body. Rim frieze: Ionian kyma.
– Kovalenko 1989, 405 cat. 214; Kovalenko 1998, 71; Kutajsov 2004, fig. 62.13.

Decoration 2 Var.

DEM-142
Myrmekion(?), year and no. unknown, present whereabouts unknown. Fr. of rim and upper body. Rim frieze: Ionian kyma. Frieze separators: dots.
– Šurgaja 1962, 115, fig. 3.3.

Decoration 2?

DEM-143*
Myrmekion, M-56-2243, St Petersburg, IIMK RAN. Rim fr. H 3.8, WT 0.4, ⌀ rim 14, 10%, RH 2.4. Fabric: slightly coarse, lime inclusions, 2.5Y 4/1. Rim frieze: vertical combing. Main decoration: spikey vertical elements (slender lotus petals?) separated by dotted lines.
– Kovalenko 1989, 402 cat. 137.

Decoration 3

Plastic long petals.

Decoration 3a

Plastic long petals separated by columns of fine dots. Two mould fragments excavated in Pantikapaion exhibit this decoration, **DEM-6*** and **DEM-7**.

DEM-144*
Olbia or Pantikapaion, Buračkov 142, Moscow, State Historical Museum (Buračkov collection). Fr. of base and lower body. ⌀ base 4.5. Medallion: type B; plain base, signed DEMETRIOU.

DEM-145*
Myrmekion, M-47-87, St Petersburg, State Hermitage Museum. Fr. of base and lower body. H 5.6, WT 0.32, ⌀ base 4.5. Fabric: medium fine, compact, Gley 1 5/N. Hard fired. Medallion: type B; plain base signed DEMETRI[…].
– Gajdukevič 1958, 209, fig. 65c; Šurgaja 1962, 119, fig. 4.2.

DEM-146*
Myrmekion, M-47-109, St Petersburg, IIMK RAN. Fr. of base and lower body. H 5.3, WT 0.4, ⌀ base 4.5. Fabric: standard, Gley 1 4/N. Medallion: type B; plain base with false ring foot, signed DE[…]U.

DEM-147
Myrmekion, M-49-176, St Petersburg, State Hermitage Museum. Fr. of base and lower body. H 8, WT 0.3, ⌀ base 4.5. Fabric: rather coarse, abundant lime and shell inclusions, many voids, 10YR 4/1. Hard fired. Medallion: type B; plain base signed […]EMETRI[…].

DEM-148*
Porthmion, П-53-601+602, St Petersburg, IIMK RAN. Two joining frs. of base and lower body. H 5.8, WT 0.3, ⌀ base 5. Fabric: relatively fine, sandy, some lime and shell inclusions, occasional light-reflecting particles, 2.5YR 5/6. Oxidized. Medallion: type B; signed DE[…]. Three repair holes.

DEM-149*
Chersonesos, X-1965-74, St Petersburg, State Hermitage Museum. Fr. of base and lower body. H 4.3, WT 0.35, ⌀ base 4.5. Fabric: standard, Gley 1 4/N. Medallion: type B; signed […]ME[…].

DEM-150
Myrmekion, 1956-B III 24, Warsaw, National Museum inv. 225017 MN. Fr. of base and lower body. Medallion: type B; signed DEME[…].
– Bernhard 1957, 26 cat. 97; Platek 1974, 42, fig. 1.

DEM-151
Pantikapaion, П-1867-121, St Petersburg, State Hermitage Museum. Fr. of base and lower body. ⌀ base 4.5, oxidized. Medallion: type B; plain base, signed DEM[…]U.
– Kovalenko 1989, 400 cat. 92.

DEM-152
Pantikapaion, year and no. unknown, Kerč History and Culture Reserve? Base fr. Medallion: type B; plain base, signed DEM[…].
– Loseva 1962, fig. 6.4.

DEM-153
Porthmion, square 51, depth 0.75, П-75-391, according to M. Vachtina, discarded. Fr. of base and lower body. Medallion: type B; plain base, signed DEM[…].

DEM-154
Kyzikos, inv. 48.129, Baltimore, Walters Art Museum. Complete. ⌀ rim 11.2; vessel H 6.4; H:⌀ 1:1.8. Rim frieze: Ionian kyma. Medallion: type B; plain, flat base; signed DEMETRIOU.
– Siebert 1978, pl. 21; Reeder 1988, 197 cat. 99.

DEM-155
Krinički, tomb, funerary meal, year and no. unknown, present whereabouts unknown. Complete profile; fragmentary bowl. ⌀ rim 11.4; vessel H 5.9; H:⌀ 1:1.9. Oxidized. Rim frieze: Ionian kyma. Medallion: type B; plain base, signed DE[…]U.
– Kropotov & Leskov 2006, fig. 7.3.

DEM-156
Pantikapaion, year and number unknown, Kerč History and Culture Reserve inv. ? Fr. of base and lower body. Medallion: type B; plain base, signed […]EMETRIO[…].

DEM-157
Olbia(?), inv. I 1907/12.14, Leiden, Rijksmuseum van Oudheden. Complete. Rim frieze: Ionian kyma. Medallion: type B; plain base, signed DEMETRIOU.
– Rogl 2008b, 525, fig. 2.

DEM-158
General'skoe, building 4, year and no. unknown, Kerč History and Culture Reserve? Non-joining frs. of base, mid-, and upper body. Medallion: type B; plain base, signed DEM[…]U.
– Maslennikov 1997, fig. 14.6–7; Maslennikov 2007, fig. 87.13.

DEM-159
Neapolis, section 7v, horizon E–D, 170–108 BCE, year and no. unknown, present whereabouts unknown. Fr. of base and lower body. Medallion: type B; plain, slightly concave base; signed DEME[…].
– Zaytsev 2004, fig. 91.3.

DEM-160*
Tyritake, Sector L, Л-47-210, St Petersburg, IIMK RAN. Fr. of base and lower body. H 5.5, WT 0.4, ⌀ base 5.5. Fabric: standard, with lime and shell inclusions, Gley 1 3/10Y. Medallion: type A or B; clumsy base ring; remains of signature […]OU.
– Kovalenko 1989, 404 cat. 201.

DEM-161*
Myrmekion, M-53-602, St Petersburg, IIMK RAN. Fr. of base and body. Oxidized. Medallion: type A or B; signed [...]E[...]; rosette cannot be distinguished. One repair hole.
– Kovalenko 1989, 402 cat. 148.

DEM-162
Ogon'ki, O-65-192, Kerč History and Culture Reserve inv. KMAK 10285. Fr. of base and lower body. Medallion: type A or B; signed [...]EM[...]; rosette cannot be distinguished.
– Grzegrzółka 2010, 217 cat. 385.

DEM-163
Krinički, tomb, funerary meal, year and no. unknown, present whereabouts unknown. Complete profile; fragmentary. ⌀ rim 11.5; vessel H 5.7; H:⌀ 1:2. Oxidized. Rim frieze: Ionian kyma. Medallion: type A or B; plain base, signed [...]EM[...].
– Kropotov & Leskov 2006, fig. 7.4.

DEM-164
Ogon'ki, O-65-no.(?), Kerč History and Culture Reserve inv. KMAK 10277. Two non-joining frs. of rim, lower body and base. Rim frieze: Ionian kyma. Medallion: type A or B; signed [...]TRI[...]; rosette cannot be distinguished. Frieze separators: dots. Two repair holes.
– Grzegrzółka 2010, 216 cat. 382.

DEM-165*
Volna 1, C3-99-22, St Petersburg, State Hermitage Museum. Five joining frs. of base and lower body. Medallion: type E; rosette C with four broad heart-shaped petals; no signature.

DEM-166*
Myrmekion, M-57-2361, St Petersburg, IIMK RAN. Fr. of rim and upper body. H 5.2, WT 0.35, ⌀ rim 11, 12%, RH 2.8. Fabric: standard, sandy, 5YR 5/2, 4/3. No rim frieze.
– Kovalenko 1989, 403 cat. 168.

DEM-167
Pantikapaion, M-62-651, Moscow, Puškin Museum of Fine Arts. Body fr. close to rim. H 4.5 × W 5.5. No rim frieze.
– Kovalenko 1989, 399 cat. 64.

DEM-168*
Myrmekion, M-56-1892, St Petersburg, IIMK RAN. Fr. of rim and upper body. H 4.3, WT 0.25, RH 1.8. Fabric: standard, fine, slightly soft, Gley 2 5/5PB. Rim frieze: Ionian kyma. One repair hole.
– Kovalenko 1989, 401 cat. 126.

DEM-169
Myrmekion, M-56-6, St Petersburg, IIMK RAN. Fr. of mid-body. H 4.2, WT 0.25. Fabric: standard, with lime and shell inclusions, 10YR 5/4, 4/1, Gley 2 6/5PB. Rim frieze: Ionian kyma.
– Kovalenko 1989, 401 cat. 127.

DEM-170*
Myrmekion, M-56-283, St Petersburg, IIMK RAN. Fr. of rim and upper body. Rim frieze: Ionian kyma.

DEM-171*
Pantikapaion, M-58-illegible no.[b], Moscow, Puškin Museum of Fine Arts. Fr. of rim and upper body. H 4.5 × W 6, ⌀ rim 9, 14%, RH 1.4. Rim frieze: Ionian kyma.

DEM-172
Kepoi, year and no. unknown, Moscow, State Historical Museum? Fr. of lower body with tiny part of base.
– Usačeva 1978, fig. 1.30.

DEM-173
Myrmekion(?), year and no. unknown, present whereabouts unknown. Fr. of rim and large part of body. Rim frieze: Ionian kyma.
– Šurgaja 1962, 115, fig. 3.2.

DEM-174
Porthmion, П-75-387, Kerč History and Culture Reserve inv. KMAK 6081. Fr. of rim and upper body. Rim frieze: Ionian kyma.
– Grzegrzółka 2010, 210 cat. 368.

DEM-175
Porthmion, П-73-247, Kerč History and Culture Reserve inv. KMAK 6199/83. Fr. of rim and upper body. Rim frieze: Ionian kyma.
– Grzegrzółka 2010, 210 cat. 369.

DEM-176
Porthmion, П-73-247[a], Kerč History and Culture Reserve inv. KMAK 6199/65. Fr. of upper body. Rim frieze: Ionian kyma.
– Grzegrzółka 2010, 211 cat. 370.

DEM-177
Ogon'ki, O-65-no.(?), Kerč History and Culture Reserve inv. KMAK 10358. Rim fr. Rim frieze: Ionian kyma.
– Grzegrzółka 2010, 216–217 cat. 383.

DEM-178
Ogon'ki, O-65-191, Kerč History and Culture Reserve inv. KMAK 10284. Rim fr. Rim frieze: Ionian kyma.
– Grzegrzółka 2010, 217 cat. 384.

DEM-179*
Myrmekion, M-57-2065, St Petersburg, IIMK RAN. Fr. of rim and upper body. H 4, WT 0.45, ⌀ rim 12, 8%, RH 2.2. Fabric: standard, Gley 1 6/N. Rim frieze: rosettes with eight petals.

Decoration 3b
Plastic long petals without column of dots.

DEM-180*
Porthmion, square 21, depth 0.75 m, 1st longitudinal street, П-53-968, 77-226, St Petersburg, IIMK RAN. Two non-joining frs. of rim and body probably from the same vessel. H 3.3, WT 0.28, ⌀ rim 12, 8%, RH 1.8. Fabric: standard, 2.5YR 6/8. Thin dull coat, 2.5YR 5/6. Oxidized. No rim frieze.

Decoration 4
Stylized long petals.

Decoration 4a
Stylised long petals separated by columns of fine dots. Two mould fragments found at Pantikapaion preserve this decoration, DEM-8* and DEM-9*.

DEM-181*
Porthmion, square 1, depth 0.6 m, П-53-22[a], St Petersburg, IIMK RAN. Fr. of base and lower body. H 3.7, WT 0.2, ⌀ base 4. Fabric: standard, 5YR 5/8. Thin dull coat, 10R 5/6. Medallion: type A or B; remains of one letter with square apex.

DEM-182
Pantikapaion, tomb 56/East/N(?), Kerč History and Culture Reserve inv. KMAK 1858. Complete. ⌀ rim 10.7, ⌀ base 5; vessel H 6.5; H:⌀ 1:1.6. Rim frieze: Ionian kyma. Medallion: type B; plain, flat base signed DEMETRIOU.
– Blavatskij 1959, fig. 62.6; Loseva 1962, fig. 5.1; Kovalenko 1989, 400 cat. 94; Grzegrzółka 2010, 52–53 cat. 22.

DEM-183*
Myrmekion, M-58-3035, St Petersburg, IIMK RAN. Fr. of base and lower body. H 5.1, WT 0.2. Fabric: standard, 10YR 3/1. Main decoration: petals and dot columns widely spaced. Medallion: type F; slightly concave base; the ends of the long petals fill most of the space under the base; no signature.
– Kovalenko 1989, 403 cat. 162.

DEM-184
Myrmekion, year and no. unknown, present whereabouts unknown. Complete. No rim frieze. Main decoration: petals and dot columns widely spaced. Medallion: type F; plain, slightly concave base, no signature.
– Gajdukevič 1958, 209, fig. 65a.

DEM-185
Myrmekion(?), year and no. unknown, present whereabouts unknown. Fragmentary; complete profile. No rim frieze. Medallion: type F; plain, slightly concave base; no signature.
– Šurgaja 1962, 115, fig. 3.1.

DEM-186
Myrmekion, 1956-A 41, Warsaw, National Museum. Fr. of base and lower body. Medallion: type F; plain, slightly concave base; no signature.
– Platek 1974, 47, fig. 9.

DEM-187*
Myrmekion, M-58-1418, St Petersburg, IIMK RAN. Fr. of rim and upper body. H 5.6, WT 0.45, ⌀ rim 13, 8%, RH 2.5. Fabric: standard, with lime inclusions, 2.5Y 5/1. No rim frieze.
– Kovalenko 1989, 403 cat. 160.

DEM-188
Pantikapaion, M-46-4433, Moscow, Puškin Museum of Fine Arts. Body fr. H 3.8 × W 2.8. No rim frieze.

DEM-189*
Myrmekion, M-49-168, St Petersburg, State Hermitage Museum. Fr. of rim and upper body. H 5, WT 0.25, ⌀ rim 11, 20%, RH 2.3. Fabric: medium fine, compact, 10YR 4/1. Hard fired. No rim frieze.

DEM-190
Tyritake, Kerč History and Culture Reserve inv. KMAK 6411/3 (1936). Fr. of rim and upper body. No rim frieze.
– Grzegrzółka 2010, 125 cat. 171.

DEM-191
Krinički, tomb, funerary meal, year and no. unknown, present whereabouts unknown. Fr. of rim and upper body. ⌀ rim 11. No rim frieze.
– Kropotov & Leskov 2006, fig. 7.13.

DEM-192*
Myrmekion, M-49-493, St Petersburg, IIMK RAN. Fr. of rim and upper body. H 3.8, WT 0.25, ⌀ rim 11, 11%, RH 2. Fabric: standard, with organic material, long voids, 10YR 4/1, 4/2. Rim frieze: Ionian kyma. Frieze separators: dots. One repair hole.
– Kovalenko 1989, 401 cat. 125.

DEM-193*
Myrmekion, M-38-12, St Petersburg, IIMK RAN. Fr. of rim and upper body. H 5.7, WT 0.35, ⌀ rim 12, 18%, RH 2.4. Fabric: standard, 10YR 5/1, 3/3. Rim frieze: Ionian kyma.
– Kovalenko 1989, 401 cat. 116.

DEM-194*
Tyritake, Sector L, Л-47-476, St Petersburg, IIMK RAN. Fr. of rim and upper body. H 4.5, WT 0.32, ⌀ rim 10, 18%, RH 2.5. Fabric: fine, compact, Gley 1 4/N. Rim frieze: Ionian kyma. Main decoration: petals and dot columns widely spaced.
– Kovalenko 1989, 404 cat. 193.

DEM-195*
Myrmekion, M-49-7, St Petersburg, State Hermitage Museum. Fr. of rim and upper body. H 4.6, WT 0.23, ⌀ rim 12, 10%, RH 2. Fabric: medium fine, compact. Hard fired. Rim frieze: Ionian kyma. Frieze separators: dots.

DEM-196
Porthmion, room T, in pit 18 fill connected with abandonment of city in mid-1st century, П-75-235, Kerč History and Culture Reserve inv. KMAK 6065. Fr. of rim and upper body. Rim frieze: Ionian kyma. Main decoration: petals and dot columns widely spaced.
– Grzegrzółka 2010, 211 cat. 371.

DEM-197
Porthmion, П-75-388, Kerč History and Culture Reserve inv. KMAK 6171. Fr. of rim and upper body. Rim frieze: Ionian kyma.
– Grzegrzółka 2010, 211–212 cat. 372.

DEM-198
Porthmion, room 51, pavement 134, NE corner, depth 1.6 m, П-75-413, Kerč History and Culture Reserve inv. KMAK 6090. Fr. of rim and upper body. Oxidized. Rim frieze: Ionian kyma. Frieze separators: dots.
– Grzegrzółka 2010, 163 cat. 253 (identified as Ionian).

DEM-199
Porthmion, cleaning of pavement 118 N of wall 127 and E of wall 126, П-75-239, Kerč History and Culture Reserve inv. KMAK 6069. Three joining frs. of rim and upper body. Oxidized. Rim frieze: Ionian kyma. Frieze separators: dots.
– Grzegrzółka 2010, 164 cat. 254 (identified as Ionian).

DEM-200*
Myrmekion, M-49-494, St Petersburg, IIMK RAN. Two non-joining frs. of rim and upper body. H 4, WT 0.4, ⌀ rim 12, 14%, RH 2.2. Fabric: standard, compact, relatively fine, ext. Gley 1 6/N, int. 3/N. Rim frieze: vertical combing.
– Kovalenko 1989, 401 cat. 117.

DEM-201
Porthmion, П-76-223, Kerč History and Culture Reserve inv. KMAK 7090. Two joining frs. of rim and upper body. Rim frieze: Ionian kyma. Frieze separators: dots.
– Grzegrzółka 2010, 206 cat. 359.

Decoration 4b
Stylized long petals, not separated by column of dots.

DEM-202*
Myrmekion, M-56-1299, St Petersburg, IIMK RAN. Fr. of base and lower body. H 4.3, WT 0.32, ⌀ base 5.5. Fabric: standard, 2.5Y 5/14/2, Gley 1 7/N. Medallion: type F; very crude slightly concave base, with ends of long petals occupying most of underside; no signature.
– Kovalenko 1989, 402 cat. 141.

DEM-203*
Myrmekion, M-57-383, St Petersburg, IIMK RAN. Fr. of mid-body. H 3.2, WT 0.45. Fabric: standard, compact, shell and lime inclusions, 5Y 3/1.
– Kovalenko 1989, 403 cat. 165.

DEM-204*
Myrmekion, M-58-170[c], St Petersburg, IIMK RAN. Body fr. H 3, WT 0.25. Fabric: standard, fine, 2.5YR 5/8. Oxidized.

Decoration 4 Var.
DEM-205
Porthmion, Sector V, П-77-77, Kerč History and Culture Reserve inv. KMAK 9507. Fr. of base and lower body. Main decoration: groups of two stylized long petals(?) separated by column of fine dots alternating with columns of large dots. Medallion: type A or B; tiny part of signature preserved [...]10[...]; rosette cannot be distinguished.
– Grzegrzółka 2010, 205 cat. 356.

Decoration 5

Imbricate pattern, of three different types; Decoration 5a is by far the most common.

Decoration 5a
Imbricate broad triangular petals with double outline and 'teardrops' indicating veins.

DEM-206*
Bosporan Kingdom, no year-no no., St Petersburg, IIMK RAN. Fr. of base and lower body. ⌀ base 5. Medallion: type A or B; signed [...]MET[...]; rosette cannot be distinguished.

DEM-207
Pantikapaion, inv.(?) [B], Odessa, Historical Museum. Complete. Oxidized. Rim frieze: Ionian kyma. Medallion: type B; plain, slightly concave base; signed DEMETRIOU.

DEM-208
Pantikapaion, tomb in Gross's orchard, Kerč History and Culture Reserve inv. KMAK 185 (1885). Complete. ⌀ rim 11.3, ⌀ base 4.6; vessel H 5.7; H:⌀ 1:2. Rim frieze: Ionian kyma. Medallion: type B; plain, flat base signed DEMETRIOU.
– Grzegrzółka 2010, 53–54 cat. 24.

DEM-209
Myrmekion, year and no. unknown, present whereabouts unknown. Fr. of base and lower body. Medallion: type B; plain base, signed DEMETRIOU.
– Gajdukevič 1958, 209, fig. 65b.

DEM-210
Porthmion, square 51, room E, depth 1.05 m, П-75-456, according to M. Vachtina, discarded. Fr. of base and lower body. Medallion: type B; plain base, signed DE[...]RIOU.

DEM-211
Tanais, fill layer, year and no. unknown, present whereabouts unknown. Fr. of base and lower body. Medallion: type B; plain base, signed [...]EMET[...].
– Arsen'eva et al. 2001, pl. 81 cat. 1045.

DEM-212*
Pantikapaion, M-58-1506, Moscow, Puškin Museum of Fine Arts. Fr. of base and lower body. WT 0.5, ⌀ base 4.5. Medallion: type F; plain, slightly concave base; no signature.

DEM-213*
Porthmion, square 21, depth 0.65 m between walls 26 and 29 (Room J), П-53-923, St Petersburg, IIMK RAN. Fr. of base and lower body. H 3.7, WT 0.35, ⌀ base 4. Fabric: standard, 2.5Y 4/1, core Gley 1 6/N. Medallion: type F; plain, slightly concave base; no signature.

DEM-214*
Ruminskoe/Za Rodinu, Рум-72-111, Moscow, State Historical Museum, inv. 103991. Fr. of base and lower body. H 3.7 × W 6.2, ⌀ base 4.5. Medallion: type F; plain, slightly concave base; no signature.

DEM-215*
Myrmekion, M-57-844, St Petersburg, IIMK RAN. Fr. of base and body. H 5.1, WT 0.35, ⌀ base 4.8. Fabric: standard, 2.5YR 5/8. Oxidized. Medallion: type F; plain base with false ring foot; no signature.
– Kovalenko 1989, 401 cat. 113.

DEM-216
Myrmekion(?), year and no. unknown, present whereabouts unknown. Fr. of base and lower body. Medallion: type F; plain, slightly concave base; no signature.
– Šurgaja 1962, 115, fig. 3.5.

DEM-217
Pantikapaion, П-1849-7, St Petersburg, State Hermitage Museum. Complete. ⌀ rim 10.7; vessel H 5.2. Oxidized. Rim frieze: Ionian kyma. Medallion: type F; plain, slightly concave base; no signature.
– AGSP 1984, pl. CLXIV.18?

DEM-218
Bosporan Kingdom, Kerč History and Culture Reserve inv. KMAK 186. Complete. ⌀ rim 10.5, ⌀ base 4.3; vessel H 5.8; H:⌀ 1:1.8. Rim frieze: Ionian kyma. Medallion: type F; flat, plain base; no signature.
– Grzegrzółka 2010, 46 cat. 16.

DEM-219
Bosporan Kingdom, Kerč History and Culture Reserve inv. KMAK 6591. Complete. ⌀ rim 10.6, ⌀ base 4.5; vessel H 6.2; H:⌀ 1:1.8. Rim frieze: Ionian kyma. Medallion: type F; flat, plain base; no signature.
– Grzegrzółka 2010, 46–47 cat. 17.

DEM-220*
Pantikapaion, M-47-332(?), Moscow, Puškin Museum of Fine Arts. Fr. of rim and upper body. H 4.5 × W 4, RH 0.9. Rim frieze: Ionian kyma.

DEM-221*
Pantikapaion, M-62-619, Moscow, Puškin Museum of Fine Arts. Fr. of rim and upper body. H 5.5 × W 6.5, ⌀ rim 10, 19%, RH 1.7. Rim frieze: Ionian kyma.

DEM-222*
Ruminskoe/Za Rodinu, Рум-72-123, Moscow, State Historical Museum, inv. 103991. Fr. of rim and body. H 4.5 × W 4.5, ⌀ rim 10, 12%. Rim frieze: Ionian kyma.

DEM-223*
Tyritake, Sector L, Л-52-384, St Petersburg, IIMK RAN. Rim fr. H 3.4, WT 0.45, ⌀ rim 10, 10%, RH 1.8. Fabric: standard, ext. Gley 1 5/10Y. Rim frieze: Ionian kyma.
– Kovalenko 1989, 404 cat. 199.

DEM-224*
Tyritake, Sector L, Л-52-353, St Petersburg, IIMK RAN. Fr. of rim and upper body. H 4.3, WT 0.45, ⌀ rim 12, 10%, RH 2.1. Fabric: standard, Gley 1 6/N. Rim frieze: Ionian kyma.
– Kovalenko 1989, 404 cat. 197.

DEM-225*
Tyritake, Sector L, Л-52-355, St Petersburg, IIMK RAN. Rim fr. H 3.4, WT 0.45, ⌀ rim 12, 10%, RH 2.3. Fabric: standard, Gley 1 3/N. Rim frieze: Ionian kyma.
– Kovalenko 1989, 404 cat. 198.

DEM-226
Myrmekion, 1956-G 21, Warsaw, National Museum. Rim fr. Rim frieze: Ionian kyma.
– Michałowski 1958, pl. XIV.

DEM-227
Porthmion, П-75-386, Kerč History and Culture Reserve inv. KMAK 6080. Fr. of rim and body. Rim frieze: Ionian kyma.
– Grzegrzółka 2010, 212 cat. 373.

DEM-228
Porthmion, П-75-411, Kerč History and Culture Reserve inv. KMAK 6088. Fr. of rim and upper body. Rim frieze: Ionian kyma.
– Grzegrzółka 2010, 212 cat. 374 (considered to be from an unidentified production place).

DEM-229
Tyritake, Kerč History and Culture Reserve inv. KMAK 10391 (1933?). Fr. of rim and body. Rim frieze: Ionian kyma.
– Grzegrzółka 2010, 123 cat. 167.

DEM-230
Tyritake, Kerč History and Culture Reserve inv. KMAK 6411/2 (1936). Fr. of upper body. Rim frieze: Ionian kyma.
– Grzegrzółka 2010, 123–124 cat. 168.

DEM-231*
Volna 1, С3-96-23, St Petersburg, State Hermitage Museum. Fr. of rim and upper body. Rim frieze: Ionian kyma.

DEM-232
Ogon'ki, O-65-no.(?), Kerč History and Culture Reserve inv. KMAK 10290. Fr. of rim and upper body. Rim frieze: Ionian kyma.
– Grzegrzółka 2010, 225–226 cat. 402.

DEM-233
Tanais, ash hill, year and no. unknown, present whereabouts unknown. Rim fr. Rim frieze: Ionian kyma.
– Arsen'eva et al. 2001, cat. 609, pl. 48.

DEM-234
Pantikapaion, M-46-no.(?), Moscow, Puškin Museum of Fine Arts. Fr. of lower body.
– Kovalenko 1989, 400 cat. 89.

DEM-235
Myrmekion, M-58-698, St Petersburg, IIMK RAN. Body fr. H 2.3, WT 0.25. Fabric: standard, fine, 7.5YR 4/3. Thin dull coat, ext. 7.5YR 5/3, int. Gley 1 3/N. Oxidized.

DEM-236
Myrmekion, 1957-D 104, Warsaw, National Museum. Fr. of lower body and tiny part of base.
– Bernhard 1959, 44 cat. 176; Platek 1974, 43, fig. 3.

DEM-237
Porthmion, pavement outside western defensive wall near wicket, П-75-101[a], according to M. Vachtina, discarded. Fr. of lower body.

DEM-238
Porthmion, Sector V, П-77-115, Kerč History and Culture Reserve inv. KMAK 9513. Fr. of base and lower body. Calyx of small leaves around medallion.
– Grzegrzółka 2010, 213 cat. 375.

DEM-239
Tyritake, Kerč History and Culture Reserve inv. KMAK 8861. Fr. of lower body.
– Grzegrzółka 2010, 124 cat. 170.

Decoration 5b
Imbricate small pointed petals.

DEM-240*
Tyritake, Sector L, Л-47-174, St Petersburg, IIMK RAN. Fr. of rim and upper body. H 3.8, WT 0.32, ⌀ rim 12, 10%, RH 2.3. Fabric: fine, compact, Gley 1 5/N. Rim frieze: Ionian kyma. Main decoration: imbricate, pointed petals without veins.

Decoration 5c
Small pointed imbricate petals with central vein. This decoration could very well have been inspired by the Ephesian Workshop Circle 1, in which this is a common pattern and relatively late in its production (see Chapter 14).

DEM-241
Tyritake, Kerč History and Culture Reserve inv. KMAK 6411/4 (1936). Fr. of base and body. Oxidized. Rim frieze: Ionian kyma. Medallion: type F; plain, slightly concave base; no signature?
– Grzegrzółka 2010, 124 cat. 169.

DEM-242
Pantikapaion, tomb 56/East/N 19, Kerč History and Culture Reserve inv. KMAK 1854. Complete. ⌀ rim 12.4; vessel H 5.5; H:⌀ 1:2.3. Oxidized. Rim frieze: Ionian kyma. Medallion: imbrication covers base as well.
– Grzegrzółka 2010, 53 cat. 23.

DEM-243
Kepoi, year and no. unknown, Moscow, State Historical Museum? Fr. of lower body.
– Usačeva 1978, fig. 1.33.

Decoration 5, Type?

DEM-244*
Myrmekion, M-47-81, St Petersburg, IIMK RAN. Fr. of rim and upper body. H 3, WT 0.35, ⌀ rim 11, 16%, RH 1.7. Fabric: standard, 5YR 6/6. Oxidized. Rim frieze: Ionian kyma. Main decoration: imbricate, tips of pointed petals.

Decoration 6

This decoration (combined long petals and imbricate panels) is represented only by the mould DEM-10. The base is undecorated and without signature (Base type F).

Decoration 7

Plastic pine-cone decoration. This decoration is known from the lower part of a mould excavated in Pantikapaion, DEM-11. The base is undecorated and without signature (Base type F).

DEM-245*
Myrmekion, M-57-2487, St Petersburg, IIMK RAN. Fr. of rim and large part of body. H 4.9, WT 0.6, ⌀ rim 10, 22%, RH 1.6. Fabric: standard, with lime inclusions and organic material, 10YR 3/1. No rim frieze.
– Šurgaja 1962, 115, fig. 3.6; Kovalenko 1989, 403 cat. 167.

DEM-246*
Myrmekion, M-48-136, St Petersburg, IIMK RAN. Fr. of rim and upper body. H 3.8, WT 0.35, ⌀ rim 10, 18%, RH 1.8. Fabric: standard, with lime and shell inclusions, Gley 1 3/N. Rim frieze: Ionian kyma.

Decoration 8

Pendent semicircles.

Decoration 8a

Concentric semicircles surrounded by crescent-shaped dots. Over the semicircles, a rosette. This decoration is clearly inspired by Mediterranean vessels (e.g., EPH-971*, KYB-380*).

DEM-247*
Tyritake, Sector L, Л-38-69, St Petersburg, IIMK RAN. Fr. of upper body. H 2, WT 0.3. Fabric: standard, Gley 1 3/10Y. Main decoration: PSC with rosette at centre; field in between filled with crescent-shaped dots.

DEM-248
Porthmion, П-75-140, Kerč History and Culture Reserve inv. KMAK 6046. Fr. of base and lower body. Oxidized. Main decoration: PSC with rosette at centre; field in between is filled with crescent-shaped dots. Medallion: type F; plain, slightly concave base; no signature.
– Grzegrzółka 2010, 213 cat. 376.

Decoration 8b

Pendent semicircles alternating with isolated plastic long petals; over the semicircles and used as spacer, rosette with five broad petals separated by slender tongues.

DEM-249
Porthmion, Sector V, courtyard B, П-77-147, Kerč History and Culture Reserve inv. KMAK 9502+9537. Two joining frs. of rim and body. Oxidized. Rim frieze: Ionian kyma (mostly obliterated). Main decoration: slightly plastic long petals alternating with PSC with large five-petalled rosettes at centre and between motifs.
– Grzegrzółka 2010, 209 cat. 366 and 367 (mentions that they probably belong to the same vessel, but she has not noted the join).

Base Fragments, Main Decoration Unidentified

DEM-250
General'skoe, year and no. unknown, Kerč History and Culture Reserve? Base fr. Medallion: type A; signed [...]MET[...] around double rosette A.
– Maslennikov 2007, fig. 72.16.

DEM-251*
Myrmekion, M-48-354, St Petersburg, IIMK RAN. Base fr. H 3.5, WT 0.42, ⌀ base 5.5. Fabric: standard, 5Y 5/1. Main decoration:

long petals? Medallion: type C; low ring foot; under the base ends of the lines of the long petals; small D incised in vessel before firing.

Rim Fragments, Main Decoration Unidentified

All the following fragments feature a single rim frieze of Ionian kyma.

DEM-252*
Myrmekion, M-48-451, St Petersburg, IIMK RAN. Rim fr. H 3.8, WT 0.22, RH 1.9. Fabric: standard, fine with some fine organic material, large voids, 10YR 5/2, 4/2, 3/1. Main decoration: unidentified traces. Frieze separators: dots.

DEM-253*
Myrmekion, M-49-806, St Petersburg, IIMK RAN. Rim fr. H 4.1, WT 0.3, ⌀ rim 11, 21%, RH 2.2. Fabric: standard, fine with lime and shell inclusions, 7.5YR 5/2, 5/3. Oxidized. Main decoration: only columns of dots preserved. Frieze separators: dots.
– Kovalenko 1989, 402 cat. 135.

DEM-254
Myrmekion, M-58-171[b], St Petersburg, IIMK RAN. Fr. of rim and upper body. ⌀ rim 10. Main decoration: remains of pointed petal.

DEM-255*
Myrmekion, M-58-768, St Petersburg, IIMK RAN. Rim fr. H 2.8, WT 0.35, ⌀ rim 12, 10%, RH 1.6. Fabric: standard, 10YR 4/2. Not too hard fired. Main decoration: remains of column of dots.

DEM-256
Kepoi, year and no. unknown, Moscow, State Historical Museum? Rim fr.
– Usačeva 1978, fig. 1.25.

DEM-257*
Myrmekion, M-56-1373, St Petersburg, IIMK RAN. Rim fr. H 2.7, WT 0.3, RH 1.8. Fabric: very fine and soft, some light-reflecting particles, 5YR 5/3, 4/1.

DEM-258
Myrmekion, M-no year, no no. St Petersburg, IIMK RAN. Rim fr. H 6.8, WT 0.45. Fabric: 7.5YR 6/4. Thin dull coat, 5YR 5/6.

DEM-259
Porthmion, П-75-403, Kerč History and Culture Reserve inv. KMAK 6087. Rim fr.
– Grzegrzółka 2010, 214 cat. 378.

DEM-260
Porthmion, П-73-471, Kerč History and Culture Reserve inv. KMAK 6199/70. Rim fr.
– Grzegrzółka 2010, 213–214 cat. 377.

DEM-261
Krinički, tomb, funerary meal, year and no. unknown, present whereabouts unknown. Fr. of rim and upper body. ⌀ rim 12.5.
– Kropotov & Leskov 2006, fig. 7.10.

DEM-262
Ogon'ki, O-65-207, Kerč History and Culture Reserve inv. KMAK 10274. Rim fr. Frieze separators: dots.
– Grzegrzółka 2010, 223 cat. 397.

DEM-263
Ogon'ki, O-65-no.(?), Kerč History and Culture Reserve inv. KMAK 5592. Rim fr.
– Grzegrzółka 2010, 226 cat. 404.

DEM-264
Ogon'ki, O-65-no.(?), Kerč History and Culture Reserve inv. KMAK 10289. Rim fr.
– Grzegrzółka 2010, 226 cat. 403.

DISTRIBUTION (ECA+ECB)

Bosporan Kingdom, Locality?

DEM-48, DEM-125*, DEM-206*, DEM-218, DEM-219

Čaika

DEM-94, DEM-134, DEM-140

Chersonesos

DEM-61*, DEM-76, DEM-149*

General'skoe

DEM-131, DEM-132, DEM-158, DEM-250

Kara Tobe

DEM-20, DEM-70, DEM-88

Kepoi

DEM-32*, DEM-112, DEM-172, DEM-243, DEM-256

Kerkinitis

DEM-141

Krinički

DEM-29, DEM-60, DEM-154, DEM-163, DEM-191, DEM-261

Kytaion

DEM-89

Kyzikos

DEM-154

Myrmekion

DEM-2, DEM-3, DEM-13*, DEM-15, DEM-17*, DEM-18*, DEM-26*, DEM-27*, DEM-31, DEM-34*, DEM-35*, DEM-37*, DEM-38, DEM-42*, DEM-44, DEM-49*–DEM-51, DEM-54*, DEM-56*, DEM-62*, DEM-63*, DEM-66*, DEM-67*, DEM-73, DEM-74, DEM-77–DEM-80, DEM-91*, DEM-97, DEM-99*–DEM-103*, DEM-113*–DEM-115, DEM-135*, DEM-137, DEM-138, DEM-143*, DEM-145*–DEM-147, DEM-150, DEM-161*, DEM-166*, DEM-168*–DEM-170*, DEM-179*, DEM-183*, DEM-184, DEM-186, DEM-187*, DEM-189*, DEM-192*, DEM-193*, DEM-195*, DEM-200*, DEM-202*–DEM-204*, DEM-209, DEM-215*, DEM-226, DEM-235, DEM-236, DEM-244*–DEM-246*, DEM-251*–DEM-255*, DEM-257*, DEM-258

Myrmekion?

DEM-38, DEM-142, DEM-173, DEM-185, DEM-216

Neapolis

DEM-159

Ogon'ki

DEM-21–DEM-24, DEM-64, DEM-65, DEM-86, DEM-87, DEM-90, DEM-93, DEM-126–DEM-130, DEM-133, DEM-162, DEM-164, DEM-177, DEM-178, DEM-232, DEM-262–DEM-264

Olbia

DEM-81

Olbia?

DEM-47, DEM-157

Olbia or Pantikapaion

DEM-72*, DEM-144*

Pantikapaion

DEM-1*, DEM-4*–DEM-12, DEM-14*, DEM-19, DEM-25, DEM-28, DEM-30*, DEM-39, DEM-68, DEM-71*, DEM-82, DEM-104, DEM-136, DEM-139, DEM-151, DEM-152, DEM-156, DEM-167, DEM-171*, DEM-182, DEM-188, DEM-207, DEM-208, DEM-212*, DEM-217, DEM-220*, DEM-221*, DEM-234, DEM-242

Porthmion

DEM-40, DEM-41, DEM-45*, DEM-46*, DEM-55, DEM-57*–DEM-59, DEM-83, DEM-84, DEM-96, DEM-98, DEM-105*, DEM-106*, DEM-116–DEM-123, DEM-148*, DEM-153, DEM-174–DEM-176, DEM-180*, DEM-181*, DEM-196–DEM-199, DEM-201, DEM-205, DEM-210, DEM-213*, DEM-227, DEM-228, DEM-237, DEM-238, DEM-248, DEM-249, DEM-259, DEM-260

Ruminskoe/Za Rodinu

DEM-92*, DEM-107*, DEM-108*, DEM-214*, DEM-222*

Tanais

DEM-16, DEM-85, DEM-211, DEM-233

Tyritake

DEM-33*, DEM-36*, DEM-43*, DEM-95*, DEM-109*–DEM-111*, DEM-124, DEM-160*, DEM-190, DEM-194*, DEM-223*–DEM-225*, DEM-229, DEM-230, DEM-239–DEM-241, DEM-247*

Uročišče Uščeľe Veďm

DEM-52, DEM-53

Volna 1

DEM-165*, DEM-231*

Provenance?

DEM-69, DEM-75*

Getic Productions

MMB won significant popularity amongst the Thracian population, not so much in the southern part of their territory (Bozkova 1994, 230) as amongst the Geto-Dacians north of the Danube.[1] A thin but widespread sprinkling of imported MMB has been found at a number of inland sites in this area (Irimia 2006, fig. 1). But more importantly, in the same area, the bowls were emulated both in precious metal (e.g., Slej [ed.] 2004, 146 cat. 73) and in clay. Moulds have been found at at least four different places, Popești, Crăsani, Radovanu, and Zimnicea, attesting to local production, and local production is suspected at other sites on the basis of particularities of fabric and decoration (Irimia 2006, 74; Appendix 4). The Getic bowls were made in a relatively coarse fabric and mostly fired in a reducing atmosphere (**GET-1***, **GET-2***). They have a pronounced concave rim with an everted lip, perhaps inspired by the bowl shape of Aiolis B. In terms of decoration, the Geto-Dacians developed their own iconography, which, though based on the imported models, soon followed its own trajectory (e.g., Vulpe 1965; Comșa 1988). The time of production was roughly the second half of the 2nd and early 1st century, with the time of maximum production around 100.

Further north, amongst the Sarmatian tribes, the shape and decoration of MMB served as a source of inspiration for the production of so-called *phalerae*, hemispherical metal plaques which were part of the adornment of horse harnesses (see especially Mordvintseva 1999, who also notes the similarity to the MMB). With such equipment, the bowls had clearly lost their original function but acquired a completely new one, which was appropriate to the local milieu.

Getic Mouldmade Bowls in the Pontic Assemblages

It has been possible to identify three Getic bowls amongst the Pontic assemblages I have studied. Not surprisingly, all came to light in Istros, which is geographically (and culturally) close to the Getic heartland. It is difficult to form an opinion about where precisely they were produced; I have found no parallels amongst published Getic bowls, and their decoration and fabric suggest that the three fragments may come from two different sources. One (**GET-1***) follows the calyx decoration of Mediterranean bowls relatively closely, whereas two (**GET-2***, **GET-3***) are decorated with only a net of widely-spaced cross-hatched lines.

---

1 Vulpe 1965; Casan-Franga 1967; Crișan 1969; Vulpe & Gheorghiță 1976; Conovici 1978 and 1981; Morintz & Șerbănescu 1985; Comșa 1988; Irimia 2006.

CATALOGUE TO CHAPTER 19

CALYX

GET-1*
Istros, His-446, Bucharest, Institute of Archaeology storeroom. Fr. of upper body. H 3.8 × W 4.5, WT 0.5. Fabric: coarse, much sand, some white inclusions, much fine mica, 5Y 5/2. Uncoated. Low fired, reduced. Main decoration: lotus petals and long petal(?) outlined with dots. Medallion: missing; row of rounded petals around base.

NET PATTERN MADE OF CRUDE CROSS-HATCHING

The only parallel I know of for this decoration is a bowl found in a tomb in Tomis (Bucovală 1967, 52-52-54 tomb 34 cat. g; Ocheșeanu 1969, 240 cat. 25, figs. 42–43).

GET-2*
Istros, His-A 314/V 19320, Bucharest, Institute of Archaeology storeroom. Fr. of upper body. H 4.1 × W 4.2, WT 0.45. Fabric: relatively fine, much fine mica, 7.5YR 6/6. Dull coat, flaking off int., 5Y 3/1. Low fired, oxidized.
– Casan-Franga 1967, fig. 3.8.

GET-3*
Istros, His-947, Bucharest, Institute of Archaeology storeroom. Fr. of upper body. H 1.7 × W 1.7, WT 0.43. Fabric: relatively fine, much fine mica, 5YR 7/6. Uncoated. Medium hard fired, oxidized.

PART 4

Pontic Sites

∴

CHAPTER 20

Olbia Pontike

Olbia is one of the best preserved of the ancient Pontic cities, having largely escaped overbuilding in post-antique times. Only the northern part of its necropolis is partly occupied by the extended modern village of Parutine. Olbia is the only Pontic city which is characterised by extended late Hellenistic layers. One of the reasons is the fact that Olbia faced a series of destructions in the 140s and 130s. The city's demise in the 2nd century was probably an effect of continuous pressure from 'barbarian' tribes, not least the expansion of King Skiluros' Late Scythian Kingdom, which had its capital in the mountainous part of the Crimea. Clean-up operations after these destructions have preserved a number of closed deposits and other complexes in which MMB have been preserved. Thus, historical events have 'trapped' a significant amount of late Hellenistic material in a series of deposits and thus fossilized a picture of the late Hellenistic city. More than 100 years of exploration of the ancient city have contributed to the accumulation of immense amounts of material, including MMB.

Obviously it is not possible to establish a complete catalogue of the MMB found at Olbia. Many finds from the old excavations have been dispersed to collections throughout the world. Some of these I have had the good fortune to study, due to the gracious help of the current director of the Olbia expedition, V.V. Krapivina. This concerns finds from the excavations of B.V. Farmakovskij, of L.M. Slavin, A.N. Karasev, and E.I. Levi, carried out in the first half of the 20th century. Some of this material is documented by photographs or drawings in St Petersburg, and some is stored in Kiev and Parutine. However, some of the old collections are inaccessible, because they are zealously defended by their curators, who do not allow other scholars access to them, even though they have lurked unpublished in storerooms for many decades. Even so, the current book can present fragments of no less than 1,830 individual vessels found throughout the city. The largest part derives from excavations carried out between the 1970s and today. The main body of this material derives from work in Sector NGS between 1985 and 2008 (638 vessels) and in Sector R25 between 1992 and 2009 (331 vessels). This chapter also draws on the excavations in the Western Temenos between 1969 and 1992 and elsewhere in the city (see below, pp. 495–501).

Research History

The history of the investigations of Olbia has been outlined by a number of scholars, especially S.D. Kryžickij. The most thorough treatments are by Kryžickij (1985, 17–32) and Vinogradov & Kryžickij (1995, 1–11, 21–26). The brief overview below focuses on investigations particularly relevant to the present study (Fig. 92). Interest in Olbia goes back to the late 18th century, when the site was first correctly identified. During the 19th century, a number of topographical plans were created, and excavations took place sporadically from the beginning of the century. We know next to nothing about the results of these efforts, however, and the topographical plans are crude. This changed when B.V. Farmakovskij initiated his work at the end of the century.

B.V. Farmakovskij (1896–1914, 1924–1926)

Farmakovskij was a pupil of the German philologist, historian and archaeologist E. von Stern, professor at the Russian University of Odessa between 1884 and 1912 (Hausmann 1998, 276, 301, 307). He was trained in the excavations of W. Dörpfeld, and he left a significant imprint on the history of the site's investigation.

He first worked in Olbia's necropolis (1896 and 1901), turning his attention to the city in 1902 (Farmakovskij 1896, 1902, 1903a–b). During the years 1902–1903, the area of the Zeus Kurgan was excavated. This kurgan was located on top of an entire city quarter, Sectors A, B, and V, which had been destroyed as a result of the Getic invasion in the middle of the 1st century. The western necropolis was located in 1902, the western fortification wall in 1903. In 1905–1906 Farmakovskij investigated what he thought was the acropolis. In 1906 he also excavated trenches west and south of the Zeus Kurgan, and in 1907 and 1908 he investigated the northern defensive wall.

During the years 1909–1914, Farmakovskij concentrated his work in the southern part of the Lower City (Sector NGF), where he excavated two houses of the Hellenistic period as well as the remains of a Roman house. Excavations were discontinued at the outbreak of World War I and only after the October Revolution were they reopened. The first explorations were made in 1920 and 1921 by S.A. Semenov-Zuser, immediately north of

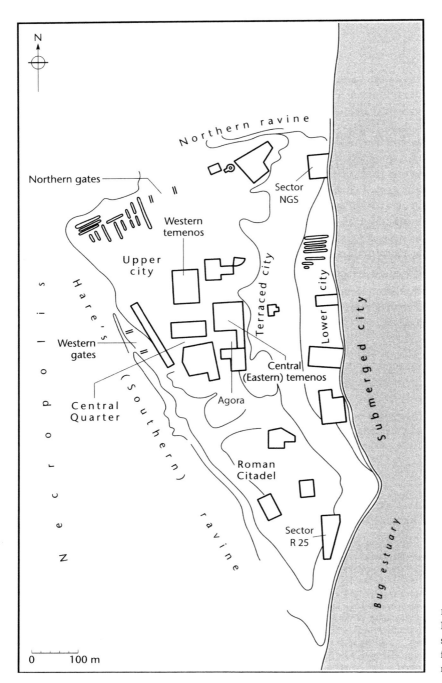

FIGURE 92
Map of Olbia with the indication of the main sectors where MMB studied in this book have been found, after Guldager Bilde & Handberg 2012 and reproduced with the permission of *AJA*

Sector NGF, but we know next to nothing about their results. Farmakovskij returned to Olbia between 1924 and 1926. In 1925 he opened the northeastern part of the city (Sector I) and in 1926 initiated excavations in Sector AGD in the central part of the Upper City, west of the Zeus Kurgan. During the last years of his excavations at Olbia, he became curator of antiquities at the State Hermitage Museum, a position he held from 1924 until his death in 1928.

The procedures established during Farmakovskij's time – the excavation of large, horizontal surfaces – are still employed today by the Olbian expedition (Vinogradov & Kryžickij 1995, 3). Farmakovskij published site plans by phase, and he thoroughly documented the site, excavations, and finds by means of photography. His records as well as the original glass negatives from his expedition are kept in the archives of the IIMK RAN in St Petersburg.[1]

---

1 I am grateful to the two archives and their director G.V. Družnevskaja for allowing me access to the archives and for permission to study and publish material from them.

After Farmakovskij, a 'scientific council' (F. Boltenko, S.S. Dloževskij, G.P. Krysin, F.T. Kaminskij, I.I. Meščaninov [1927–1932], F.A. Kozubovskij [1935]) directed the excavations. In the first years (1927–1930, 1932), work took place in Sectors A and AGD and was mainly concerned with Hellenistic houses. In 1930, Sector NR in the northern part of the Lower City was opened. Again, almost no information concerning the results of these excavations has ever been published.

Farmakovskij's Followers (1936–1974)
Then followed the decades when Farmakovskij's students and followers, L.M. Slavin (head of expedition), A.N. Karasev, E.I. Levi, T.N. Knipovič, and S.I. Kapošin, worked at Olbia (1936–1974). Excavations in Sectors A and AGD continued, and new excavations in the Lower City, in Sectors NG and NGC, were undertaken.

From 1946 onwards, excavations in the central part of the Upper City revealed the city's (central) temenos and the agora located further to the south. The residential quarters of Sector E west of the agora, as well as the defences of the Lower City, were also investigated. In the middle of the 1950s, the excavation was divided into two separate expeditions, of the Kiev Institute of Archaeology under the direction of Slavin, and of the Leningrad Institute of Archaeology, led by A.N. Karasev and E.I. Levi; both institutes were part of the Academy of Sciences of the USSR. During these years, Sector I with Hellenistic houses, Sector AGD, and Olbia's central quarter with public buildings – in addition to the temenos and agora, also the dikasterion, gymnasion and several stoas – were investigated (Levi and Karasev), whereas Slavin excavated the western part of the agora and the house blocks to the west (Sector E).

S.D. Kryžickij (1972–1996)
In the early 1970s, a new generation of Kiev-based researchers headed by S.D. Kryžickij (from 1972) took over the excavations. J.I. Kozub took charge of the excavations of the suburb and necropolis; N.A. Lejpunskaja excavated the Central Quarter, the Western Gate, and Sector NGS; A.S. Rusjaeva was in charge of the excavation of the Western Temenos and Sector AGD; V.V. Krapivina excavated Sectors R19 and R25, A.I. Kudrenko Sector R19, and N. Mazarati the northwestern sector.

The Investigation of Olbia in the New Millennium
Since 1996 the expedition has been headed by V.V. Krapivina. Today, the main areas of excavation are Sectors R25 and NGS. In 2006, the site was made a national preserve.

Excavation Contexts of Relevance for the Current Study

A complete overview of the results of the many years of excavation in Olbia is not relevant in the present context. I concentrate instead on discussion of the evidence for the period in which MMB were in use at the site, i.e., the late 3rd through the early 1st century. In most of the literature, this period is viewed as one of general decline (e.g., Vinogradov & Kryžickij 1995, 17–18). The detailed study of Sector NGS, however, has provided us with a fresh picture of this important period in the life of the city (*NGS 2010*; Lawall 2011; Lawall et al. 2014).

Sector AGD, Bothros 11
The first excavation in Sector AGD in the central part of the Upper City took place in 1926, and thus, this part of Olbia has been the object of study since Farmakovskij's time. Between 1971 and 1998, work was carried out at irregular intervals under the direction of A.S. Rusjaeva. She soon discovered that part of this sector was a second temenos, called the Western Temenos in order to distinguish it from the (now) Central Temenos excavated by the St Petersburg team of archaeologists between 1951 and 1970 (Gajdukevič [ed.] 1964). A number of deities were worshipped in the temenos, most importantly Apollo Ietros, the patron god of Olbia, but Meter also played an important role from the time of colonization onward, and the Dioskouroi, Hermes, and Aphrodite were venerated in the temenos as well. The earliest cultic installations are a modest temple, constructed of mudbricks and wood in the third quarter of the 6th century, as well as altars and a number of bothroi. Throughout classical antiquity, constructions in this temenos were simple and not at all monumental. In general, we know very little about the temenos in the late Hellenistic period, which is normally considered a time of decline (e.g., Rusjaeva 2003, 110). In 2006, Rusjaeva and a number of colleagues issued the first comprehensive publication devoted to the temenos (Ajbabin et al. [eds. 2006]; see also Rusjaeva 2003).

In 1987, the first closed complex with late Hellenistic material, called Bothros 11, was found in the temenos. This bothros or pit is part of a small, enclosed, open-air sanctuary north of the Apollo Ietros temple (Fig. 93). It is unknown to which god(s) it was devoted. The 0.7 m-deep bothros was excavated during three days in 1987 (18–20 July) and four days in 1988 (18–23 July). It was filled with ash and charcoal, and the soil contained significant amounts of fish bones and scales. Objects recovered include a few terracottas and an assortment of tableware, but unfortunately no amphora material. Of considerable

FIGURE 93 Sector AGD and the Western Temenos at Olbia. The small open air sanctuary with Bothros 11 is shaded in grey
PLAN DRAWN BY ALEXANDER V. KARJAKA AND PUBLISHED WITH HIS PERMISSION

Excavation year	1987		1988	Cat. no.
Production place	In pit	Outside pit	In pit	
Ephesos, grey			195, 208	**EPH-1301**
Ephesos	999		203	**EPH-390**
	994	594		**EPH-734**
			210	**EPH-771**
	995		199	**EPH-717**
			206	**EPH-732**
	996			**EPH-207**
	997	207	197	**EPH-204**
			200	**EPH-182**
			207	**EPH-740**
	998			**EPH-956**
	998b			**EPH-955**
		893	209+214	**EPH-1281**
			196	**EPH-1007**
			212	**EPH-1162**
Meter Medallion Workshop		925+926		**KYB-412**
			201	**KYB-206**
			204+205	**KYB-383**
Probably Meter Medallion Workshop			215	**KYB-448**
Kyme, unassigned			211	**KYX-90**
Pergamon	1000		198	**PER-72**
?	998			**XXX-34**

FIGURE 94   MMB from Bothros 11. Grey indicates that the fragments join

interest for the present study is the group of 22 MMB found there. The bothros was covered by an ashy layer (probably the same as its fill), in which a nearly complete mouldmade bowl was discovered (KYB-412*), as well as some fragments joining vessels unearthed in the bothros (Fig. 94). The majority of these have previously been published by Rusjaeva and Nazarčuk in the 2006 publication mentioned above. That treatment, however, is very summary, and, according to Rusjaeva, it was based upon drawings and photographs (pers. comm.). The following discussion is based upon personal inspection of the fragments (June 2010). With the exception of EPH-955*, which is kept in the storeroom of the Olbia Expedition in Parutine, all other fragments are currently preserved in the storerooms of the Archaeological Institute of the Ukrainian Academy of Sciences in Kiev.[2]

The contents of this pit and the ash layer covering it are very homogeneous (Fig. 94). The fragments of MMB are large, up to more than half preserved and, with the exception of the large Menemachos kantharos (EPH-1301*), they are all made in very fresh moulds and can thus can be described as in 'mint condition'. The majority of the

[2] I am grateful to A.S. Rusjaeva and to the bothros' excavator, V.I. Nazarčuk, for allowing me to work with this material. Thanks are also due to V.V. Krapivina for offering me this material as well as to N. Son, the director of the Kiev storerooms, and Tatiana Shevchenko, the director of the Parutine storerooms.

vessels belong to the early Classical Ephesian production and all are oxidized (again, except for the Menemachos kantharos). In addition to the Ephesian vessels, there is one late Kirbeis bowl (KYB-206*) and a Possis bowl (KYB-383*) with isolated plastic long petals amongst broad 'nelumbo' and ovoid petals (neither preserving a signature), a rim fragment probably from the same workshop (KYB-448*), and another unassigned Kymean rim fragment (KYX-90*). The bothros also contained a bowl probably of Pergamene production, as well as a bowl from an unknown source (PER-72, XXX-34).

Sector E2, Cistern Л East of the Central Temenos

East of the Central Temenos, in Sector E2, over two field campaigns in 1948 and 1949 Levi and Karasev excavated a reservoir called Cistern Л (Sector E2, square 55; Fig. 95).[3] It was constructed of square limestone blocks and measured 2.03 × 2.8, with a depth of 3.95 m. A selection of the finds, which included both MMB and amphora fragments, was published by Levi (1964b). In her discussion of a fragment of a Kirbeis bowl from Samothrace (KYB-240*), Rotroff (2010, 69–70) considered this deposit in the light of G. Finkielsztejn's revised chronology of Rhodian amphorae (Finkielsztejn 2001) (Fig. 96).

The vast majority of the Rhodian amphorae in the deposit can be placed within Finkelsztejn's period 3 (dating 198–161), with more than 90% confined to 3c–3e (181–161), whereas three fragments may be placed in period 4 (160–146), and one in period 5 (eponym Astymedes II, dated to 144). At least 25 MMB were found in the cistern.[4] Of these, only six have been published previously (Levi 1964b, 250–251, figs. 12–13), but a further 17 can be attributed to the reservoir on the basis of information from the excavation archives in Kiev. More than half of the 25 bowls and fragments are of the Kymean production of Kirbeis (KYB-14*, KYB-28*, KYB-81*, KYB-88*, KYB-233*, KYB-243*, KYB-301*, two of which are signed), Possis (KYB-352*, KYB-359*), as well as Workshop A (KYA-14*, KYA-37, KYA-56*), and there is one unassigned Kymean piece (KYX-56*). The reservoir also contained a fragment of an Athenian(?) bowl with 'nelumbo' with internal scales (ATH-40*), of a Pergamene bowl with a fine myrtle wreath (PER-31*), as well as seven Ephesian fragments (EPH-164 bis*, EPH-766*, EPH-773*, EPH-1146*, EPH-1168*, EPH-1290*, EPH-1341*), two by the Monogram PAR potter, one with full-body acanthus scroll. One fragment belongs to the Aiolis B production (AIB-37*) and two are of unknown production (XXX-13*, XXX-36*, the latter with PSC decoration).

It is plausible that the spread in date of the MMB mirrors the chronological spread of the Rhodian amphorae (see also Chapter 3). Since 90% of the Rhodian amphorae can be attributed to period 3c–3e, they date to the short interval of no more than 20 years between 181/179 and 161; this is probably also the date of the majority of the MMB found in the reservoir.

If we compare the contents of Bothros 11 with those of Cistern Л, it is obvious that the two assemblages are very similar. Both are primary deposits, where the contents are of a relatively compressed chronology: in short, the finds were probably in use at more or less the same time. In both we find abundant vessels of the MMW, and both contained vessels with PSC design (XXX-36* from the cistern; EPH-955*, EPH-956, EPH-1276, PER-72*, and XXX-34* from the bothros) as well as calyx designs with isolated, plastic long petals (KYX-56* from the cistern, KYB-383* from the bothros). In Cistern Л, however, we lack the large corpus of Ephesian vessels which dominates Bothros 11. Conversely, in the bothros there are many fewer vessels of the MMW and they also seem to be later, especially KYB-206*, where we find acanthus R, which is not represented in the cistern. The presence of a Zenodotos bowl (KYB-412*) in the cistern also points in this direction. It is therefore likely that the assemblage of the cistern is slightly earlier than that of the bothros. Nevertheless, fragments of a single vessel with imbricate pattern of the Monogram PAR Workshop found in both contexts are so alike that it is conceivable that they were made in the same mould (EPH-773* from the cistern and EPH-771* from the bothros). Therefore, the overlap in time between the two deposits was probably greater than the distance between them.

Sector B5

This sector is located 65 m north of Sector AGD. It was briefly investigated in 1976. In its western part, a large Hellenistic basement was excavated, in which a fair number of MMB were found.

---

3 From the field documentation kept in Kiev we learn that when the deposit was first found in 1948, it was labelled Room Л; in 1949 the appellation was changed to Cistern Л. This demonstrates that the true character of the structure is debatable. From Levi 1964b, fig. 1 it appears that the structure most closely resembles a basement, a building type of which many have been found at Olbia. However, as Levi notes, a trapezoidal stone may have served as an inlet to the reservoir (1964b, 226 and fig. 1).

4 Levi (1964b, 249) mentions "a large amount of relief bowls", but I have been able to find only the mentioned 25.

OLBIA PONTIKE

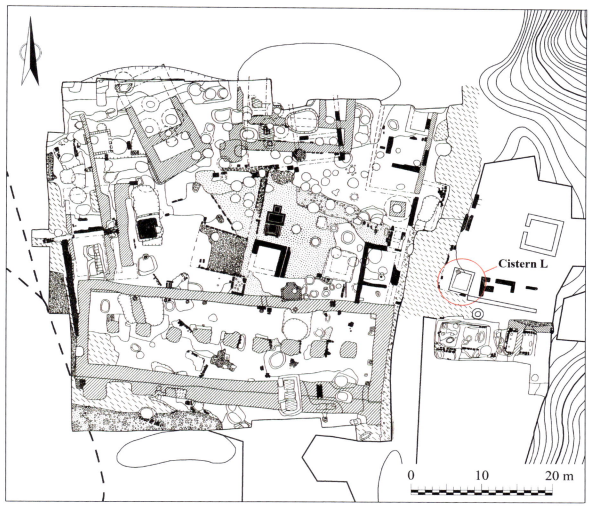

FIGURE 95 Location of Cistern Л east of the Central Temenos at Olbia
PLAN DRAWN BY ALEXANDER V. KARJAKA AND PUBLISHED WITH HIS PERMISSION

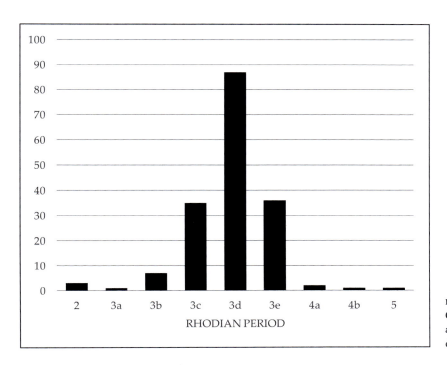

FIGURE 96
Chronological distribution of the Rhodian amphorae found in Cistern Л following the dating of Finkielsztejn 2001

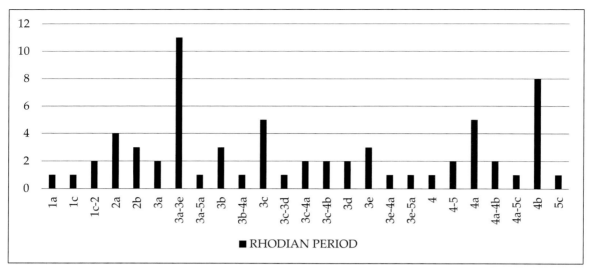

FIGURE 97 Chronological distribution of the Rhodian amphorae unearthed in Sector NGS (based on Lawall et al. 2010). Unidentified pieces are not included

Sector NGS

Sector NGS is situated in the northernmost part of the city, near the city wall. This part of the ancient city has been excavated since 1985 during annual campaigns by Kiev archaeologists directed by N.A. Lejpunskaja, assisted by T.L. Samojlova (1985–1997) and A.V. Karjaka (2000 to present) (*NGS 2010*).

Remains of eight house blocks have been identified, two of which are now fully excavated. The blocks range in size from 522 to 1,200 m^2 and each contains four to seven living units. The houses are relatively modest. They do not have any uniform plan, but they share a number of features, such as three to four rooms grouped around a central paved courtyard and one or more well-built cellars. The cellars and the foundations of the walls were constructed of more or less well-dressed stones, whereas the upper parts of the houses were built of mudbricks.

NGS was situated not far from the harbour, and it is clear from the finds in the houses that the residents were fishermen and artisans. Net weights and fishing hooks attest to this, as well as small moulds for crafting simple metal jewellery.

The earliest activity here seems to have been in the late Archaic period, attested by at least one hut dug into the ground as well as a number of pits. Abundant material of the 5th and early 4th century testifies that the area was inhabited in the Classical period, but building remains are situated beneath later houses and hence inaccessible. The main building phases belong to the late Classical and early Hellenistic periods. In 331, Alexander the Great's general, Zopyrion, besieged the city. This may be the reason for a significant drop in activity in the city as well as in NGS during the last third of the 4th century. Extended building activity took place in the early 3rd century, but this came to an abrupt end sometime in the second quarter of the century. This period was a time of crisis in the northern Black Sea region as a whole, and during the next decades, very little seems to have happened in NGS. At the end of the 3rd century, the area was partly re-inhabited. The late Hellenistic period, up to the 130s, saw the last habitation phase in Sector NGS. In the 130s, this part of the city was almost completely abandoned and the amphora stamps found in the sector document a gap in the 120s (Lawall et al. 2010). Sparse deposits of the following decades are largely connected with clean-up and filling activities. A number of furnaces and tombs attest to occasional activity in this part of the city in the Roman period.

The NGS corpus of MMB consists of fragments of about 675 vessels, and stratigraphy within some of the houses there helps to support their chronology. For example, fragments of 25 MMB were found in the stratified fill of the basement of house III-3. There, as described in more detail above in Chapter 11, excavators were able to distinguish between an upper fill of the 140s and a lower deposit that was put in place some 20 to 40 years earlier. Similar closed deposits were found in other basement structures as well; House II-2, for example, also provides a closed context probably dating no later than the 140s (*NGS 2010*, 270). Deposits such as this document the last years of habitation before the abandonment of this part of the city.

Up to 22 amphora stamps from the sector belong to period 4a and 4b,[5] but none to period 5a or 5b (Fig. 97). In fact, there is a gap in the Rhodian amphorae from 146 to 118 BCE, when the only secure stamp of period 5c appears (Lawall et al. 2010, cat. L-165). As Lawall et al. also point out (2010, 388), this pattern is surprising in that it is unrelated to the distribution pattern of Rhodian amphorae in the region and elsewhere; this gap requires a particular, site-specific explanation.

Sector R25
This sector is located in the southern part of the city. Excavations have been in progress there since the early 1990s, under the direction of V.V. Krapivina and A. Bujskich. The sector is part of Olbia's citadel, which was surrounded by a defensive wall with towers. After the decline of the 140s, the city contracted to this area, which, according to the excavators, is characterized chiefly by Roman and late antique structures and layers.

Museum Collections of Relevance for the Present Study

St Petersburg, State Hermitage Museum
Before the Russian revolution, objects excavated in Southern Russia were brought to St Petersburg by the Archaeological Commission, and most ended up in the State Hermitage Museum. I have had the opportunity to study some Olbian material in the Hermitage storerooms, but, regrettably, it has not been possible to acquire any kind of overview of the MMB from Olbia (or indeed from any other Pontic site) housed there. I am sure that the collection must be impressive and I can only urge colleagues at the Hermitage to make it known to the public.

Collection of Arnold Vogell in Nikolaev
The first corpus of MMB published from Olbia came from the large collection created by the German merchant Arnold Vogell (1857–1911), who settled in Nikolaev in 1892. He took a great interest in Olbia: he participated in its excavation, and in 1909 he wrote the 140-page *Studie über die milesische Kolonie Olbia* (Merten 1999). Over a period of 15 years, he acquired almost 1,500 objects from the site, and his collection counted as one of the most important private collections in South Russia while it was still in Nikolaev (Merten 1999, 339). From the correspondence kept in the archive of IIMK RAN in St Petersburg,

we can see that as early as 1901 Vogell was in contact with Count Bobrinskij, the chamberlain and head of the Archaeological Commission, because he wanted to sell his collection to the Hermitage Museum.[6] He provided 289 photographs of the antiquities and, in 1902, a list was made of the collection, recording a total of 818 items "deriving from the old Greek town of Olbia and from the Island of Berezan". Included in this list were 43 'relief vases', in all likelihood MMB. From the many letters that went back and forth between the parties, we can see that Vogell originally asked 115,000 roubles for his collection. The price was negotiated down to 60,000 roubles, but, even though the acquisition was endorsed by Bobrinskij, Farmakovskij, and G.E. Kizericki in 1904, no decision was made. The acquisition seemed less and less attractive as the years went by, because similar finds had now turned up in Farmakovskij's own excavations. Finally in March 1905 the collection was declined.

Disappointed, Vogell returned to Germany with his collection, and on 26–30 May 1908 it was sold at auction in Kassel. The auction catalogue (Boehlau 1908), with the list and partial illustration of 1,364 objects, is a precious source of information on Olbia. Just before the auction, R. Zahn wrote an influential article in *Jahrbuch des Instituts* on the *Hellenistische Reliefgefässe aus Südrussland* (Zahn 1908), and he included as an appendix a list of the museums that had bought the vessels he published. Vogell himself stated that the objects in his collection came from Olbia,[7] so even though Zahn more cautiously gives *Südrussland* as the provenance (a precedent followed by museums buying objects from the Vogell collection), we can be confident in attributing the Vogell collection to Olbia.

Zahn published 36 MMB, which are included in the present study. Their precise find spot in the city is unknown, but because the vases are complete, it is more than likely that they came from the necropolis. It is during the same years (in 1899) that the magnificent situla in the Hermitage was unearthed (**PER-91***).

Collection in the Nikolaev Historical Museum
The collections from Olbia in the Nikolaev Museum, together with records of excavations, were removed by the

---

5 Lawall et al. 2010, cats. L-164, L-166–L-172, L-177–L-179, L-183, L-193–L-195, L-201, L-218, L-224–L-227, L-236.

6 IIMK RAN St Petersburg, folder no. 255 concerning the Archaeological Commission from 1900 and on accessed 21 March 2007. Archival documents nos. 19 (15 January 1901); 34 (12 November 1901); 36 (29 January 1902); 38 (3 March 1902); 39 (7 March 1902); 47 (29 September 1904); 46 (11 November 1904); 48 (19 November 1904); 49 (4 February 1905); 50 (February 1905 [no date]); 51 (21 March 1905).

7 Archival documents no. 36 and especially 47 (see preceding note); see also Merten 1999, 338.

Germans during WWII and thus largely lost (Minns 1945, 111; Slavin 1947, 192–194). However, a few MMB are still kept in the museum. They mostly derive from the excavations immediately following the death of Farmakovskij. According to the inventory cards of the museum, some of them were found in tombs; others come from various excavations in the city. I was able to study this material in 2009.

Moscow, State Historical Museum

In the State Historical Museum is housed a small but fine collection acquired in Olbia before the mid-19th century by Count Aleksej Sergejevič Uvarov (1825–1884), who was a Russian archaeologist of immense importance and one of the co-founders of the State Historical Museum. All 18 pieces are gathered under the same inventory number (inv. 54791); half of them were published in Uvarov 1851, pls. XIX–XX.

Berlin

In the Berliner Antikensammlung are gathered a number of small collections which had been assembled during the late 19th and early 20th century and then acquired by the museum (Kästner et al. 2007).

Collection of Paul Becker

Paul Adam von Becker came from a German-speaking family of the Baltic part of the Russian Empire. He taught language and literature in the university of Odessa; he was knighted and became a Russian Imperial minister. During his years in Odessa, he collected antiquities from Olbia, amongst other sites (Kästner et al. 2007, 60–61), totalling ten modest fragments (ATH-16*, ATH-33*, EPH-772*, EPH-774*, EPH-776*, EPH-778*, EPH-781*, KYB-238*, KYX-84*, PER-38*). In 1862 Becker returned with his family to Dresden, where he died in 1881. The bowls are now in the Altes Museum in Berlin.

Collection of Peter Mavrogordato

Peter Mavrogordato was a Greek born in Nikolaev in 1870 to a wealthy family,[8] and later married to a Russian aristocrat, Erato. They created a large collection of antiquities, selling objects from time to time to other European collections. They acquired numerous objects from the excavations in Olbia. In 1907, a bowl by Possis from Olbia was bought by the British Museum (inv. 1907.520.60) and two years later, two Kirbeis vessels and an Ephesian dinos were acquired by the Antikensammlung in Berlin (KYB-54*, KYB-321, EPH-1335*). The London bowl was said to derive from Olbia's necropolis, and since the three Berlin bowls are complete, as is the London one, it is likely that they were also found in the necropolis.

Collection of Alexandre Merle de Massonneau

de Massonneau was a rich banker and merchant who lived in Massandra near Yalta. He also acquired antiquities in the region, but only a single base fragment from his collection has Olbia as its provenance (KYB-258*).

Archival Material

The MMB from Farmakovskij's excavations were acquired by the Archaeological Commission in St Petersburg and it must be assumed that they are now kept mainly in the storerooms of the State Hermitage Museum.

I have had the opportunity to study these vessels as documented in a small series of six plates with inked pencil drawings, kept in the archive of the IIMK RAN, St Petersburg. Fragments of 49 bowls are depicted, documenting vessels found mostly in 1910, though two fragments are numbered 1909 and two are numbered 1912. The plates are numbered I, II, III, XI, XII and XIII, so we may suspect that at least seven plates are missing. Investigations in the archive did not bring the remainder to light.

The photo archive of the IIMK RAN, St Petersburg also preserves glass negatives from the old Olbian excavations. In total, fragments of 128 different bowls and other vessels are documented. Of these, 48 fragments can be connected with Farmakovskij's excavations, whereas another 48 come from excavations in 1928 and 1929. The remainder are from Slavin's and Levi and Karasev's excavations between 1935 and 1975, mostly from Sector E. Most of these have never been published, and the same is true of the fragments recorded in the drawings mentioned above. I have identified one of the illustrated vessels in the Historical Museum, Kiev (KYB-151*) and four in the storerooms of the Archaeological Institute in Kiev (KYB-88*, KYX-56*, AIB-37*, EPH-773*), another in the Historical Museum, Nikolaev (KYB-351*), and one in the storerooms at Parutine (KNI-18*), as well as four vessels in the State Hermitage Museum (KYB-326*, KYB-363*, AIB-97, EPH-1323*). I suspect that most of the others are also in the Hermitage, but I have been granted access to only a fraction of the MMB in this museum during the years of

---

8 Kriseleit 1990, 61; Kästner 2007 et al., 63; on the Mavrogordato family, see also Herlihy 1989, 242–243. Both spouses died in 1948.

		Mainland		Aiolis							S Asia Minor		Pontos			
		ATH	COR	PER	KYA	KYB	KYX	AIA	AIB	AIX	EPH	KNI	DEM	GET	XXX	Total
Olbia	Sum	51	1	44	34	238	64	4	44	15	1,152	20	1		162	1,830
	%	2.8		2.4	1.9	13.0	3.5	0.2	2.4	0.8	63.0	1.1			8.9	
Olbia or Pantikapaion						4					1		2			7
Olbia?		1				4					11		2		1	19
Average % all Pontic sites		1.6		2.0	1.2	8.5	2.2	0.8	1.7	0.7	65.4	1.6	4.4		9.8	100

FIGURE 98   Distribution of MMB found at Olbia according to production place

my study. Nevertheless, even though I have not seen most of the fragments, I have included them in the present study in order to provide as comprehensive a picture as possible of the MMB found at Olbia.

Bowls from Farmakovskij's excavations were the point of departure for a dissertation written by one of his students, Elsa Mahler (1888–1970).[9] The dissertation, entitled *Die Megarischen Becher*, was completed under his supervision, assisted by Ernst Pfuhl and Paul Jacobsthal, and it was submitted to the University of Basel in 1924. The original manuscript is in the university library.[10] Mahler's work was based largely on unpublished material in German museums and in St Petersburg (collections of the former Archaeological Commission and of the State Hermitage Museum, probably mostly from Olbia, though this is never stated). The corpus of South Russian bowls and fragments at her disposal amounted to ca. 225 items (Mahler 1924, 19). In 1923, the year before she submitted her dissertation, Mahler had become *Lektor* in Russian language. In 1928 she defended her *Habilitation* and in 1938 she became Basel University's first *Extraordinaria* in Russian language and culture.[11] This change of career track is probably the reason she never published any of the results of her study of the MMB and why her dissertation is completely unknown today.

Mouldmade Bowls at Olbia

The overall conclusions paint a very consistant picture of the different assemblages in the city (the numbers are collected in Fig. 98).

Excavations at Olbia have recovered by far the largest collection of Athenian MMB of any Pontic site. In total, 51 complete or fragmentary vessels have been found, amounting to 67.1% of the 76 Athenian finds from the region. It is also at Olbia that we find Athenian vessels of supplementary shapes, namely two small bowls (ATH-72*, ATH-73) and three juglets (ATH-74*–ATH-76*), 6.8% of the Athenian vessels in the Black Sea and almost 10% of the Athenian vessels from Olbia. The comparatively high number of Athenian vessels recorded in Olbia must have to do with the overall chronology of the Olbian assemblage, which is earlier than all other Pontic assemblages (see p. 512). The preference for supplementary shapes corresponds to a pattern we have already discussed in Chapter 5. A grey-ware krater with applied feet in the shape of a bald Silenos mask (XXX-71*) is possibly a Corinthian import.

About one-fourth (24.3%) of the vessels found at Olbia were produced in Aiolian workshops. The city documents the highest percentages of Kymean vessels, first of all of the Meter Medallion Workshop, but also of Workshop A and unattributed Kymean workshops, in comparison to all other Pontic sites. Since these workshops were active predominantly in the second quarter of the 2nd century, this is another feature which characterizes the Olbian assemblage as early. A limited number of Pergamene MMB were unearthed at Olbia: up to 44 vessels (2.4%). Only at Istros were a similar number found. The Olbian assemblage is representative in terms of decoration, since all of the main types of decoration occur.

---

9   I am grateful to J.I. Il'ina, State Hermitage Museum, for drawing my attention to the existence of this dissertation.
10 The university library most kindly lent me the original. The manuscript contains neither bibliography nor list of figures, and, unfortunately, the plate volume could not be located. However, I suspect that the fine plates of drawings in the archive of IIMK RAN, St Petersburg may have constituted some of Mahler's study material (see p. 502).
11 https://slavistik.philhist.unibas.ch/de/fachbereich/seminar geschichte/elsa-mahler/ [accessed 10 January 2024].

Ephesian bowls are well-represented, but, in terms of numbers, they are below the average when compared with other Pontic sites. As we discussed in Chapter 6, Ephesian MMB in Olbia show a number of early features, such as PSC decoration in significant numbers (see also Fig. 57) and the common occurrence of the box meander (Fig. 72).

Knidian vessels are present, but they are rarer at Olbia than at most Pontic sites. Most likely, this has also to do with chronology, because by and large, Knidian MMB are a feature of the second half of the 2nd century (Chapter 15).

Demetrios bowls are very rare; a few can be ascribed to Olbia, but only DEM-81 can be attributed with confidence. This testifies to an almost complete lack of communication between Olbia and the Bosporan Kingdom in the last quarter of the 2nd century, when Demetrios produced his vessels (Chapter 18). In Chapter 18, I discussed whether this has to do with chronology. But since we find exactly the same pattern at Istros, where not a single fragment of a Demetrios bowl can be identified, even though Istros is certainly contemporary with the Bosporan production, a different explanation is necessary. Most likely, this is the effect of non-intersecting regional trade networks.

VESSELS FOUND AT OLBIA

Athens

Figural decoration
 ATH-1, ATH-2, ATH-4*, ATH-5*, ATH-8*, ATH-9*, ATH-11*, ATH-14*–ATH-18*, ATH-20*–ATH-23*, ATH-26*–ATH-28, ATH-32*
Pine-cone decoration
 ATH-33*
Calyx
 ATH-34*–ATH-40*, ATH-42*
Imbricate
 ATH-45(?), ATH-46*, ATH-49*, ATH-50*
Rim fragments
 ATH-51*, ATH-52*, ATH-58*–ATH-62, ATH-64*–ATH-70*
Supplementary shapes
 ATH-72*, ATH-73 (small bowls); ATH-74*–ATH-76* (juglets)

Pergamon

Figural decoration and objects
 PER-1*, PER-2, PER-16
Garlands carried by Erotes
 PER-18*–PER-20*
Unidentified figural decoration
 PER-21*, PER-22*
Calyx with figural decoration
 PER-24*–PER-27*
Acanthus scroll
 PER-28*
Myrtle wreath
 PER-31*, PER-32*, PER-34
Calyx
 PER-38*–PER-41*, PER-43–PER-46*, PER-53*, PER-54*, PER-58*, PER-62*
Imbricate
 PER-70*, PER-71*
Pendent-semicircle design
 PER-72*
Net pattern
 PER-74, PER-75*, PER-77*
Plastic long petals
 PER-80*
Stylized long petals alternating with vegetation
 PER-81*
Rim fragments
 PER-84*, PER-85

Supplementary shapes
 PER-87* (chalice); PER-88*, PER-89* (juglets); PER-91*–PER-93 (situlae)

Kyme, Workshop A

Figural decoration
 KYA-2*–KYA-4*
Calyx with figural decoration
 KYA-10*, KYA-14*, KYA-15*, KYA-17*, KYA-18*
Scroll decoration
 KYA-19*–KYA-23
Myrtle wreath
 KYA-24*, KYA-27*
Suspended garlands
 KYA-28*, KYA-31 – KYA-35*, KYA-37, KYA-41*, KYA-42*
Rim fragments
 KYA-43*–KYA-45, KYA-48
Base fragments
 KYA-50
Supplementary shapes
 KYA-51 (small bowl); KYA-52, KYA-54*, KYA-56* (skyphoi); KYA-58* (juglet)

Kyme, MMW: Kirbeis

Figural decoration
 KYB-1*(?), KYB-3, KYB-5(?), KYB-6–KYB-8*, KYB-11, KYB-13*–KYB-15, KYB-17*–KYB-19*, KYB-22*, KYB-23*, KYB-25*–KYB-30*, KYB-32*, KYB-34*–KYB-42
Suspended wreath
 KYB-43*
Flower
 KYB-44*
Calyx with figural decoration
 KYB-50–KYB-64, KYB-66, KYB-69*–KYB-71*, KYB-74*, KYB-75*, KYB-81*–KYB-89*, KYB-93*, KYB-96–KYB-102*, KYB-104*, KYB-105(?), KYB-107–KYB-111, KYB-117*, KYB-118, KYB-120*, KYB-121, KYB-127*
Scroll decoration
 KYB-128*
Suspended garlands
 KYB-129*, KYB-133*, KYB-136*–KYB-138, KYB-142*, KYB-143*, KYB-145*(?), KYB-147*, KYB-149, KYB-151*, KYB-153*, KYB-155*, KYB-156, KYB-158*, KYB-159*, KYB-162*, KYB-163*, KYB-167*, KYB-170*
Myrtle wreath
 KYB-173

Calyx
    KYB-177*–KYB-179*, KYB-181–KYB-183*, KYB-188*–KYB-190, KYB-193*, KYB-199*, KYB-202*, KYB-204*–KYB-206*, KYB-209*, KYB-210*, KYB-213*, KYB-220–KYB-223*, KYB-225*, KYB-231*, KYB-233*, KYB-235*–KYB-238*, KYB-241*, KYB-243*, KYB-245*, KYB-246*, KYB-250*

Imbricate
    KYB-251*, KYB-252, KYB-254

Net pattern
    KYB-255*

Base fragments
    KYB-259*, KYB-261*(?), KYB-264, KYB-268*

Rim fragments
    KYB-269, KYB-270, KYB-273–KYB-278*, KYB-283, KYB-285, KYB-289, KYB-290*, KYB-292, KYB-293*, KYB-301*, KYB-302, KYB-305*–KYB-308*, KYB-311*–KYB-313

Supplementary shapes
    KYB-316, KYB-317*(?), KYB-319* (small bowls); KYB-321–KYB-326*, KYB-327*(?) (amphorae); KYB-328 (closed shape)

Kyme, MMW: Possis

Calyx with figural decoration
    KYB-330*, KYB-332*, KYB-334*, KYB-336*–KYB-338*, KYB-340*–KYB-342*, KYB-344*–KYB-347*, KYB-348(?), KYB-351*, KYB-352*

Scroll decoration
    KYB-355*, KYB-357*–KYB-360

Suspended garlands
    KYB-362*

Calyx
    KYB-363*, KYB-365*–KYB-367*, KYB-370*, KYB-371*, KYB-373*, KYB-376*, KYB-378, KYB-379

Pendent-semicircle design(?)
    KYB-381*

Net pattern
    KYB-382*

Long petals with vegetal and/or figural decoration
    KYB-383*, KYB-385*–KYB-387*

Base fragment
    KYB-389

Rim fragments
    KYB-392–KYB-394*, KYB-397, KYB-398, KYB-409, KYB-410

Supplementary shapes
    KYB-411* (small bowl)

Kyme, MMW: Zenodotos

    KYB-412*, KYB-413*(?), KYB-414, KYB-420*–KYB-422*

Kyme, MMW: Unattributed

Base fragments
    KYB-424*, KYB-427*

Figural decoration
    KYB-428*

Calyx
    KYB-433*, KYB-435, KYB-438*

Rim fragments
    KYB-442*, KYB-445–KYB-448*, KYB-452*, KYB-453

Kyme, Unattributed

Figural decoration
    KYX-4*, KYX-6*, KYX-8*–KYX-14*, KYX-16*, KYX-17*, KYX-19*, KYX-20*, KYX-22*, KYX-23*–KYX-27, KYX-30*

Calyx with figural decoration
    KYX-31–KYX-34, KYX-38*, KYX-40, KYX-41*, KYX-44*, KYX-45*

Scroll decoration
    KYX-47*–KYX-51*, KYX-53

Suspended garlands
    KYX-54*, KYX-56*, KYX-57*, KYX-59*, KYX-60*, KYX-62, KYX-63*, KYX-66*

Calyx
    KYX-67*, KYX-72*, KYX-73, KYX-77*–KYX-81*

Imbricate
    KYX-84*–KYX-87

Long petals
    KYX-89*

Rim fragments
    KYX-90*–KYX-95*, KYX-98

Supplementary shapes
    KYX-101 (amphoriskos)

Aiolis, Workshop A

Myrtle wreath
    AIA-6*

Rim fragments
    AIA-18*, AIA-19*, AIA-31*

Aiolis, Workshop B

Figural decoration
    AIB-3*, AIB-4*, AIB-7*, AIB-8*, AIB-16*–AIB-18*

Calyx with figural decoration
    AIB-25*

Scroll decoration
   AIB-32*, AIB-34, AIB-35, AIB-37*, AIB-41*, AIB-50*, AIB-53*
Suspended garlands
   AIB-56*, AIB-57
Myrtle wreath
   AIB-62*–AIB-66*
Calyx
   AIB-67*, AIB-68*
Calyx with isolated long petals
   AIB-77*, AIB-82–AIB-84
Stylized long petals
   AIB-97, AIB-102*
Supplementary shapes
   AIB-115* (bowl with shell feet); AIB-118*, AIB-122*, AIB-124*, AIB-125*, AIB-128–AIB-130*, AIB-132* (shallow cups with high collared rim); AIB-133*–AIB-135* (cups with band handles); AIB-136* (cup?); AIB-137* (beaker)

Aiolis, Production Place Unknown

Figural decoration
   AIX-1*–AIX-3*, AIX-6*
Suspended garlands
   AIX-8*, AIX-9*
Calyx
   AIX-11*, AIX-12*, AIX-16*, AIX-17*
Imbricate pointed petals
   AIX-20*
Net pattern
   AIX-23*
Long petals
   AIX-24*, AIX-27*
Multiple rim friezes
   AIX-30

Ephesos

Figural decoration
   EPH-3*, EPH-4, EPH-6*, EPH-7*, EPH-13*, EPH-15–EPH-17, EPH-20*–EPH-22*, EPH-25*, EPH-30–EPH-33, EPH-35*, EPH-44*–EPH-50*, EPH-52*, EPH-53*, EPH-54(?), EPH-55–EPH-59*, EPH-63*–EPH-65*, EPH-68*, EPH-71, EPH-73*, EPH-74*, EPH-77*, EPH-83*, EPH-84*, EPH-88*–EPH-97*, EPH-102, EPH-105*, EPH-114–EPH-116, EPH-118, EPH-120*, EPH-121*, EPH-124*, EPH-125, EPH-129, EPH-130, EPH-137–EPH-139*, EPH-144*–EPH-147*
Double axes
   EPH-160*

Scroll decoration: full body
   EPH-162*–EPH-177*
Scroll decoration: frieze
   EPH-178, EPH-179, EPH-182*, EPH-183*, EPH-185*, EPH-187*, EPH-191*–EPH-195*, EPH-197*–EPH-200*, EPH-203, EPH-204*, EPH-206*–EPH-213, EPH-216*–EPH-218*, EPH-222*–EPH-224*, EPH-228*, EPH-229, EPH-237, EPH-239*, EPH-241, EPH-242*, EPH-244*, EPH-246, EPH-248*, EPH-250*–EPH-252*, EPH-254*–EPH-264*, EPH-266*, EPH-272*–EPH-274*, EPH-277*, EPH-278, EPH-280*, EPH-284*–EPH-287*, EPH-291, EPH-293*–EPH-295*, EPH-298, EPH-299, EPH-302–EPH-304*, EPH-306*–EPH-313*, EPH-315*–EPH-317, EPH-320*, EPH-322*
Myrtle wreath
   EPH-325*, EPH-328*, EPH-332, EPH-338*, EPH-340*, EPH-345, EPH-349*, EPH-351–EPH-353*, EPH-358–EPH-364*, EPH-368*–EPH-372*, EPH-375*–EPH-377, EPH-380*, EPH-381
Ivy wreath
   EPH-383*, EPH-385*, EPH-388*
Suspended garlands
   EPH-389*, EPH-390*, EPH-396*(?), EPH-397*, EPH-400*, EPH-403
Suspended wreath
   EPH-404*–EPH-406*
Multiple rim friezes
   EPH-407*, EPH-408*, EPH-411*–EPH-416*, EPH-418, EPH-419*, EPH-423*, EPH-434, EPH-438*–EPH-441*, EPH-443*, EPH-445*, EPH-448*, EPH-449*, EPH-451*–EPH-453, EPH-455*–EPH-457*, EPH-459*, EPH-460*, EPH-462*, EPH-463*, EPH-468*, EPH-469*, EPH-471–EPH-474*, EPH-477*, EPH-478*, EPH-480*, EPH-481*, EPH-483*–EPH-485*, EPH-487*, EPH-489*, EPH-493*, EPH-494*, EPH-496*, EPH-497*, EPH-499*, EPH-502*, EPH-504*–EPH-509*, EPH-511*, EPH-515*, EPH-518*–EPH-520*
Pine-cone decoration
   EPH-530*, EPH-535*, EPH-538, EPH-541, EPH-544*, EPH-549
Calyx A
   EPH-550*–EPH-552*, EPH-554, EPH-555*, EPH-557, EPH-559, EPH-562–EPH-564, EPH-566*–EPH-568*, EPH-571*, EPH-578*, EPH-579*
Calyx A with filled 'nelumbo'
   EPH-588*, EPH-590
Other calyces with 'nelumbo'
   EPH-596*, EPH-598*, EPH-601*
Calyx B
   EPH-611*, EPH-612*, EPH-614, EPH-616, EPH-618*, EPH-619*, EPH-621*–EPH-624*, EPH-626*, EPH-630*, EPH-631*, EPH-633*, EPH-634*, EPH-643*, EPH-648, EPH-650*, EPH-654*
Other calyces with folded or bent acanthus leaf
   EPH-660*, EPH-661*

Calyx C
    EPH-662*, EPH-664*–EPH-666
Other calyces
    EPH-668*, EPH-673*, EPH-675*, EPH-677*, EPH-678*(?), EPH-679*, EPH-680, EPH-682–EPH-684*, EPH-686–EPH-689*, EPH-691*–EPH-693*, EPH-695, EPH-697*–EPH-700*, EPH-704*, EPH-707*, EPH-708*, EPH-715, EPH-716
Imbricate rounded petals
    EPH-717*–EPH-719*, EPH-721–EPH-724*, EPH-726*, EPH-728–EPH-730*, EPH-732*–EPH-734*, EPH-737*–EPH-742*, EPH-748*–EPH-752*, EPH-754*, EPH-755*, EPH-756(?), EPH-757*–EPH-759*, EPH-761–EPH-774*, EPH-776*, EPH-778*–EPH-781*, EPH-788*, EPH-792*–EPH-797*, EPH-799*
Imbricate pointed petals
    EPH-802, EPH-803, EPH-805*, EPH-811*, EPH-813*, EPH-814, EPH-817, EPH-818, EPH-821*, EPH-822*, EPH-824*, EPH-826, EPH-828, EPH-833, EPH-835, EPH-837*, EPH-850, EPH-851, EPH-855*–EPH-857, EPH-862*, EPH-868*, EPH-870*, EPH-874, EPH-876*–EPH-878, EPH-882*, EPH-883*, EPH-884(?), EPH-886, EPH-889*, EPH-891*, EPH-894*, EPH-898*, EPH-909–EPH-911*, EPH-913*, EPH-919*–EPH-921, EPH-926, EPH-930*, EPH-932*, EPH-937*, EPH-939*, EPH-941, EPH-944*
Imbricate designs using other elements
    EPH-948*–EPH-951, EPH-954*
Pendant-semicircle design
    EPH-955*–EPH-962*, EPH-965*–EPH-973*, EPH-975*, EPH-977*, EPH-978
Net pattern
    EPH-984, EPH-985*, EPH-987, EPH-988*, EPH-994*, EPH-1000*, EPH-1005*, EPH-1007*, EPH-1008*
Plastic long petals
    EPH-1011*, EPH-1013*, EPH-1015*, EPH-1016*, EPH-1026*–EPH-1028*, EPH-1035*, EPH-1036*, EPH-1042*–EPH-1044*
Stylized long petals
    EPH-1048*–EPH-1052*, EPH-1059, EPH-1063*, EPH-1065, EPH-1069, EPH-1072, EPH-1073*, EPH-1080*, EPH-1081*, EPH-1093*, EPH-1097*–EPH-1100, EPH-1105*, EPH-1111*, EPH-1112*, EPH-1114*
Single rim frieze
    EPH-1126, EPH-1128*, EPH-1131, EPH-1132*, EPH-1134*, EPH-1135*, EPH-1137, EPH-1139, EPH-1140*, EPH-1144–EPH-1146*, EPH-1149*, EPH-1155–EPH-1159*, EPH-1162–EPH-1166*, EPH-1168*, EPH-1169*, EPH-1171*, EPH-1176*, EPH-1180, EPH-1184*, EPH-1188, EPH-1193, EPH-1194*, EPH-1199*, EPH-1202, EPH-1209, EPH-1210, EPH-1226*, EPH-1233*, EPH-1235, EPH-1237, EPH-1238*, EPH-1242*, EPH-1243
Base fragments
    EPH-1252*, EPH-1254, EPH-1256*, EPH-1261*

Supplementary shapes
    EPH-1265*–EPH-1270*, EPH-1272*, EPH-1274*, EPH-1275*, EPH-1277*, EPH-1281*–EPH-1285*, EPH-1289*, EPH-1290*, EPH-1293–EPH-1295 *(small bowls); EPH-1296, EPH-1298, EPH-1299* (juglets); EPH-1301* (kantharos); EPH-1302* (skyphos with pinched handles); EPH-1304, EPH-1309–EPH-1314, EPH-1316, EPH-1317*, EPH-1319, EPH-1320 (amphorae); EPH-1321* (jug); EPH-1322* (lagynos?); EPH-1323*, EPH-1326, EPH-1328* (situlae): EPH-1330*, EPH-1331*, EPH-1332*(?) (kraters); EPH-1335* (dinos); EPH-1336* (guttus); EPH-1341*, EPH-1343*–EPH-1349* (large closed vessels); EPH-1350*, EPH-1351* (large vessels)

Knidos

Figural decoration
    KNI-1*, KNI-12*
Ear of grain
    KNI-14*
Myrtle wreath
    KNI-16*
Suspended garlands
    KNI-18*, KNI-20*–KNI-22*
Multiple rim friezes/imbricate palmettes
    KNI-27, KNI-28*
Multiple rim friezes, rim fragments
    KNI-30*
Calyx with figural elements
    KNI-34*, KNI-40*
Calyx
    KNI-42*
Imbricate
    KNI-54*, KNI-55*
Rim fragments
    KNI-65, KNI-69
Supplementary shapes
    KNI-73*, KNI-74* (small bowls)

Bosporan Kingdom, Workshop of Demetrios

Decoration 1d
    DEM-47(?)
Decoration 2
    DEM-72*(?), DEM-81
Decoration 3a
    DEM-144*(?), DEM-157(?)

Production Place Unknown

Figural decoration
    XXX-1*–XXX-3, XXX-6–XXX-8*
Calyx with figural decoration
    XXX-9*
Full-body acanthus scroll
    XXX-11*
Scroll
    XXX-12*, XXX-13*
Myrtle wreath
    XXX-15*
Multiple rim friezes
    XXX-21*, XXX-23*
Calyx
    XXX-24*, XXX-26*–XXX-31*
Imbricate, pointed petals
    XXX-33
Pendent-semicircle design
    XXX-34*–XXX-37*
Net pattern
    XXX-38*
Plastic long petals
    XXX-40*
Calyx of X's
    XXX-43*
Supplementary shapes
    XXX-50 (small bowl); XXX-54* (small bowl with one handle); XXX-55* (juglet); XXX-57* (unguentarium?); XXX-58* (skyphos with ring handles); XXX-59 (stemmed bowl); XXX-61* (shallow cup with high collared rim); XXX-62–XXX-65, XXX-67 (amphorae); XXX-68*, XXX-69*(?) (lagynoi); XXX-70*, XXX-71* (kraters); XXX-75–XXX-77* (large closed vessels)

CHAPTER 21

Istros

Together with Olbia and Chersonesos, Istros is one of the most important cities of the northwestern Black Sea region. The site, which has never been built over in more recent times, has been intensively investigated by Rumanian scholars for almost 100 years.

Founded by Milesian settlers in 657 (Euseb. *Chron.* 95b) or thereafter, Istros (also Histria) was amongst the early Greek poleis in the Pontic region. The site, located on a peninsula, is named after the mighty river of the region, today the Danube, in antiquity the Istros. As an effect of the Danube's silt deposits, the site is today closed off from the sea by Lake Sinoe. In antiquity, Istros had a widely extended chora; it also served as a port of trade. Thus, the city thrived on a mixed economy consisting of farming, fishing, and trade.

The ruins of Istros were first identified in 1868 by the French archaeologist E. Desjardins. Regular archaeological excavations were initiated by V. Pârvan in 1914. Since his death in 1927, the excavations have been directed by various Rumanian archaeologists (M. and S. Lambrino 1928–1942; E. Condurachi 1949–1970; D.M. Pippidi 1971–1981; P. Alexandrescu 1982–1988; A. Suceveanu from 1989). Excavation has taken place at many different locations in and around the city, and each excavation sector has had its own field director (Fig. 99).

Thanks to the pioneering publication by C. Domăneanțu, *Les bols hellénistique à décor en relief*, Istros is the Black Sea locality where we are best informed about MMB.[1] The book, issued in 2000 as volume XI of the Histria series, is based on Domăneanțu's 1998 doctoral thesis. It provides a brief history of Rumanian research on MMB, in addition to the obligatory words on technique, name, and chronology of the group. Domăneanțu includes brief catalogue entries with photographs (but no drawings) of 711 vessels (scale 1:1).[2]

The fragments included in Domăneanțu's publication derive mainly from excavations carried out between 1927 and 1942 by M. and S. Lambrino. Regrettably, they are completely devoid of any contextual information, primarily due to the loss of the Lambrinos' diaries (Domăneanțu 2000, xvi). Domăneanțu also includes sherds from her own excavations in the 1950s, 60s, 70s, and 90s. Most of them come from layers of fill which were dug when the various defence walls of the city were investigated, but some sectors, such as the Plateau, Sector X, and Sector Z2, also revealed Hellenistic structures and layers (e.g., Oppermann 2004, 156 with references).

A sector name and/or an excavation year has been written on some of the fragments, and in a few instances the level below the surface where the fragment was found is also indicated. The numbering system employed is not altogether clear. Most fragments feature just one number, seemingly a consecutive number which was given to a large collection of sherds at some point. These numbers run from 1 to 1225, but some are missing and quite a few are duplicates. About one-third of the fragments feature a number prefaced by A-, B-, and/or V-; most of these sherds do not have the consecutive number (though some do). On some, the years 1927–1942 are indicated. But there are also V-numbers from 1957, 1958, 1959, and 1961, so we cannot assume that all sherds with V-numbers were excavated before the war. Knowledge about the numbering system was lost with Domăneanțu's untimely death. Even though the numbers may not have a contextual significance, I have nevertheless retained all numbers written on the fragments in my catalogue.

From the above we can conclude that, unfortunately, almost all of the MMB from Istros either have no context or only a very broad one. The only good, closed contexts are the two tombs in Istros' tumular necropolis (Tombs XXVI and XXXVII). In the first were found two bowls made in the Kymean Workshop A (**KYA-8***, **KYA-12***), as well as a bowl of unknown production (**XXX-51**). A late Kirbeis bowl (**KYB-123**) was unearthed in the second tomb, together with an early Ephesian WC2 bowl (Domăneanțu 2000, 143 cat. 711, pl. 53).

Currently, the vessels are stored in the Institute of Archaeology of the Rumanian Academy of Sciences, Bucharest. In March, August, and October 2010 I had the opportunity to study the collection first hand.[3] From my

---

1 The volume may be accessed on the internet: http://www.cimec.ro/Arheologie/web-histria/6bibliografie/1monografie/XI/ro/histria11ro.htm, visited on the 17th of September 2022.
2 20 of these are not MMB, but Knidian roulette bowls and cups (cats. 565–579) and horizontally grooved bowls (cats. 580–585), pls. 38–39.
3 I am much indebted to the collegiality and help of the Rumanian colleagues of the institute: head of department F. Matei-Popescu and V. Lungu. Regrettably, C. Domăneanțu died during the first day of my visit to the institute in March 2010. It was therefore impossible to solve many of the riddles of the material and its registration.

Find place	Year
Unknown	Lambrino 1927-1942
'Bothros'	year?
Plateau	year(?), two from 1974
Sector "Pescărie"	mostly 1963, but also 1966, 1969, and 1974
Sector A	1988
Sector MC1	1956
Sector MC1 Sa	1956
Sector SB	year(?), 1979
Sector SC	year(?), 1969
Sector SZ	year?
Sector X	mostly 1996, but also 1950, 1992
Sector Z	1957, 1964
Sector Z1	1951, 1957
Sector Z2	mostly 1957, but also 1956, 1959, 1964, 1965, 1966, 1969
Tumular necropolis	Tomb MVI (1955), Tomb XXVI (1958), Tomb XXXVII (1961)
UI 1913	year? (1913?)
ZOE/90	year? (1990?)

FIGURE 99   Find places of MMB at Istros

work it soon became clear that Domăneanţu had not included all the pieces in her catalogue. In fact, fewer than half of the fragments housed in Bucharest have been published. The criteria for her selection are not apparent. According to oral information from F. Matei-Popescu and V. Lungu, it seems that she had no plans to publish a second volume with the remaining material.

In her publication, Domăneanţu organizes the material by production place and workshop. Her identifications, however, are based almost exclusively on style rather than on fabric and surface treatment, and she drew heavily on Laumonier 1977. Thus, she divided (part of) the material into workshops conforming with the Ephesian workshops which Laumonier had established on the basis of the finds on Delos. As we have already discussed in Chapter 2, this is problematic in itself. Moreover, Domăneanţu's ascriptions are – to say the least – problematical as well, and many are certainly wrong. For example, she attributes to Ephesian workshops many fragments which more correctly can be ascribed to various Aiolian and Knidian workshops.[4] She also assigns a number of fragments to Pontic productions, especially Demetrios. My own study of the pottery, however, has made it clear that not a single fragment belongs to his production (see Chapter 18). In addition, a very large proportion of the catalogue has not been attributed at all.

Thus, the Istros corpus as published by Domăneanţu cannot be used to its full potential. With the permission of the Institute of Archaeology, I republish this collection and include all the fragments at hand.[5]

With the exception of the finds from the tombs, which are more or less complete, the material is very fragmentary and the vessels are reduced to quite small fragments. It is difficult to find joins, and since it is unknown precisely in which year between 1927 and 1942 the majority of the fragments were excavated, I have been very hesitant to postulate that non-joining fragments derive from the same bowl. Thus, the number of fragments almost corresponds to the estimated number of vessels. The fact that the material is so fragmentary induces me to assume that the fragments mainly derive from secondary deposits and thus that the pieces have been repeatedly shuffled around (Chapter 3). When fragments are very small, they are not so informative as to the original decoration of the vessel, because the connection between the individual elements of the decoration (rim pattern, frieze or main decoration, calyx, and base) has often been lost. Thus, the original number of vessels could well be smaller than that currently proposed.

---

4   E.g., AIA-11*–AIA-13*, AIA-16*; AIB-79; AIX-14*, AIX-15*, AIX-21*, AIX-22*; KYA-7*, KYA-40*; KYB-16, KYB-31, KYB-160, KYB-165*, KYB-168, KYB-184*, KYB-207*, KYB-208*, KYB-314*, KYB-450*; KYX-2*, KYX-5*, KYX-18*, KYX-21*, KYX-39*, KYX-65*, KYX-71*, KYX-88*; PER-7*, PER-9, PER-12*, PER-23*, PER-48*, PER-55*, PER-56*, PER-79*, PER-83*.

5   [Ed. Although PGB clearly intended to include all of the Ephesian and unattributed items, I have made a selection because of considerations of length. Thus, 305 bowls in Domăneanţu's catalogue that PGB identified as Ephesian have been omitted, along with about 500 more that are unpublished. About 160 Istrian pieces which PGB did not attribute have also been omitted, amongst them about 50 that are in Domăneanţu's catalogue.]

Mouldmade Bowls at Istros

A comparison with Olbia is very instructive for understanding the character of the Istrian assemblage, because in almost every respect the two localities represent two different overall trends (Fig. 100). At Olbia, a large percentage of the MMB can be dated before the 140s, even though, of course, material of the last third of the century is also at hand (Chapter 20). This is in contrast to Istros, where the overall picture is late; in fact, the best parallel to the composition of the Istrian assemblage is Delos (deposits mainly formed after 166).

The presence/absence of Athenian vessels is a good chronological indicator, and at Istros, the number of Athenian vessels is indeed very low. The same is true of supplementary shapes, which are also mainly (though not exclusively) an early feature. No more than 12 vases of supplementary shapes, 0.8% of the corpus, have been found at Istros; at Olbia, by comparison, 119 vessels of supplementary shapes have been unearthed, making up 6.5% of the whole (Fig. 31).

Ephesian vessels dominate the Istrian collection, with more than 70% of the finds, but it is typical that EE and EC are much less common than the late Ephesian repertoire. Thus, we find hardly any box-meander rim friezes (but many with Ionian kyma and various types of rosettes: Fig. 72), very few multiple rim friezes (Fig. 76), almost no acanthus-vine scrolls, very few vessels with PSC (but many with long petals: Fig. 57), no vessels with a calyx with 'nelumbo', and very few vessels employ dots as frieze separators. Moreover, the bichrome finish produced by stacking during firing is much less common than it is at Olbia.

Aiolian workshops are well represented at Istros; one should note, however, that the number of products of the early workshops in particular (Workshop A, the Meter Medallion Workshop) are below the Pontic average – and present in far smaller numbers than at Olbia, where they are well above the average.

If we exclude Chersonesos, it is at Istros that the largest proportion of Knidian vessels at Pontic sites has been found – and not only Knidian MMB, but also a number of Knidian roulette bowls and cups have come to light at Istros, erroneously classified with the MMB by Domăneanţu (Domăneanţu 2000, 112–115 cats. 565–579, pls. 38–39). As we saw in Chapter 15, the Knidian production is mainly a feature of the second half of the 2nd century, even though it started slightly earlier.

Finally, I have been able to identify a few fragments of Getic bowls amongst the Istrian sherds. As already mentioned in Chapter 19, it is not surprising that they have come to light here, since Istros is close to the Getic homeland both geographically and culturally.

Istros was settled uninterruptedly from the 7th century onward; it is therefore of note that MMB of the first half of the 2nd century are so poorly represented amongst the fragments I have studied from the site.

		Mainland		Aiolis							S Asia Minor		Pontos			
		ATH	COR	PER	KYA	KYB	KYX	AIA	AIB	AIX	EPH	KNI	DEM	GET	XXX	Total
Olbia	Sum	51	1	44	34	238	64	4	44	15	1,152	20	1		162	1,830
	%	2.8		2.4	1.9	13.0	3.5	0.2	2.4	0.8	63.0	1.1			8.9	
Istros	Sum	11		39	17	95	30	31	18	10	1,093	41		3	170	1,558
	%	0.7		2.4	1.1	6.1	1.9	2.0	1.2	0.6	70.2	2.6		0.2	10.9	
Average % all Pontic sites		1.6		2.0	1.2	8.5	2.2	0.8	1.7	0.7	65.4	1.6	4.4		9.8	100

FIGURE 100 Distribution of MMB according to production place; Istros compared with Olbia

ISTROS 513

VESSELS FOUND AT ISTROS

Athens

Figural decoration
   ATH-29*, ATH-31*
Calyx
   ATH-41*, ATH-43*, ATH-44*, ATH-48*
Rim fragments
   ATH-53*, ATH-54*, ATH-56, ATH-57*, ATH-63

Pergamon

Figural decoration
   PER-3*, PER-7*–PER-9, PER-11*–PER-14*, PER-17*, PER-23*
Wreaths
   PER-30*, PER-33*, PER-35*, PER-36*
Calyx
   PER-42*, PER-47*–PER-50*, PER-52*, PER-55*–PER-57, PER-59*–PER-61*, PER-63*–PER-69*
Pendent-semicircle design
   PER-73*
Net pattern
   PER-76*
Plastic long petals with figural decoration
   PER-78*
Plastic long petals
   PER-79*
Stylized long petals
   PER-83*
Supplementary shapes
   PER-90* (juglet)

Kyme, Workshop A

Figural decoration
   KYA-1*, KYA-5*, KYA-7*–KYA-9*
Calyx with figural decoration
   KYA-11*–KYA-13*
Palmettes and vases
   KYA-16*
Myrtle wreath
   KYA-25*, KYA-26*
Suspended garlands
   KYA-29*, KYA-30*, KYA-36*, KYA-40*
Rim fragment
   KYA-46*
Base fragment
   KYA-49*

Kyme, MMW: Kirbeis

Figural decoration
   KYB-10*, KYB-12*, KYB-16, KYB-20, KYB-31, KYB-45
Calyx with figural decoration
   KYB-77, KYB-91*, KYB-92*, KYB-112, KYB-113, KYB-123
Suspended garlands
   KYB-135, KYB-148*, KYB-157*, KYB-160, KYB-161, KYB-165*, KYB-166, KYB-168, KYB-169, KYB-171*
Myrtle wreath
   KYB-175, KYB-176*
Calyx
   KYB-184*, KYB-187*, KYB-191, KYB-198*, KYB-203, KYB-207*, KYB-208*, KYB-212, KYB-214*, KYB-216–KYB-219, KYB-224, KYB-226, KYB-227*, KYB-232*, KYB-239*, KYB-242*, KYB-244
Multiple rim friezes
   KYB-271*
Rim fragments
   KYB-284*, KYB-286–KYB-288, KYB-291*, KYB-294, KYB-295, KYB-297, KYB-298, KYB-300, KYB-303, KYB-310*, KYB-314*, KYB-315*

Kyme, MMW: Possis

Calyx with figural decoration
   KYB-333*, KYB-339*, KYB-343*
Ivy scroll
   KYB-353*
Calyx
   KYB-372
Pendent-semicircle design
   KYB-380*
Multiple rim friezes
   KYB-391*
Single rim frieze
   KYB-395*, KYB-399*–KYB-408

Kyme, MMW: Zenodotos

Vegetal decoration
   KYB-416*

Kyme, MMW: Unattributed

Figural decoration
   KYB-429*–KYB-432*, KYB-434*, KYB-437*, KYB-439*–KYB-441

Rim fragments
>KYB-443*, KYB-444*, KYB-449–KYB-451, KYB-454–KYB-456

Kyme, Unattributed

Figural decoration
>KYX-1*–KYX-3*, KYX-5*, KYX-18*, KYX-21*

Calyx with figural decoration
>KYX-28*, KYX-29*, KYX-35*–KYX-37*, KYX-39*, KYX-43*

Scroll decoration
>KYX-52*

Suspended garlands
>KYX-55*, KYX-58, KYX-65*

Calyx
>KYX-68–KYX-71*, KYX-74*–KYX-76, KYX-82, KYX-83

Pendent-semicircle design
>KYX-88*

Rim fragments
>KYX-96*, KYX-97

Supplementary shapes
>KYX-100* (small bowl)

Aiolis, Workshop A

Figural decoration
>AIA-1*–AIA-3:

Acanthus scroll
>AIA-5*

Myrtle wreath
>AIA-7, AIA-8*

Multiple rim friezes
>AIA-9*

Plastic pine-cone decoration?
>AIA-10*

Calyx?
>AIA-11*

Net pattern
>AIA-12*

Plastic long petals
>AIA-13*

Rim fragments
>AIA-14*–AIA-17*, AIA-20–AIA-30*, AIA-32*–AIA-36*

Aiolis, Workshop B

Figural decoration
>AIB-5*, AIB-10–AIB-13

Acanthus-ivy scroll with figures
>AIB-28*

Scroll decoration
>AIB-29*, AIB-36*, AIB-49

Calyx with 'nelumbo' and isolated long petals
>AIB-79

Calyx with isolated long petals
>AIB-86*, AIB-87*

Long petals
>AIB-93*, AIB-94, AIB-100*

Single rim friezes
>AIB-109*, AIB-110

Supplementary shapes
>AIB-127* (shallow cup with high collared rim)

Aiolis, Production Place Unknown

Plastic pine-cone decoration
>AIX-10*

Calyx
>AIX-13–AIX-15*

Imbricate
>AIX-18*, AIX-21*

Net pattern
>AIX-22*

Multiple rim friezes
>AIX-31*, AIX-32*

Single rim frieze
>AIX-33*

Ephesos

Figural decoration
>EPH-9*, EPH-10, EPH-12, EPH-18*, EPH-19*, EPH-23*, EPH-24*, EPH-39, EPH-42*, EPH-60, EPH-62, EPH-67*, EPH-69*, EPH-70, EPH-72*, EPH-79*, EPH-85*, EPH-86*, EPH-98*, EPH-107*, EPH-123*, EPH-132, EPH-134*–EPH-136*, EPH-140*, EPH-143, EPH-148*–EPH-150*, EPH-152*–EPH-154*, EPH-156–EPH-159*

Scroll decoration
>EPH-232, EPH-243*, EPH-253*, EPH-265*, EPH-268*, EPH-270*, EPH-292, EPH-300, EPH-301, EPH-318*, EPH-319*, EPH-321*, EPH-323

Myrtle wreath
>EPH-330*, EPH-336*, EPH-339, EPH-343*, EPH-347*

Suspended garlands
>EPH-391*, EPH-394*, EPH-395*, EPH-398*, EPH-401*, EPH-402

Multiple rim friezes
>EPH-417*, EPH-425*–EPH-427*, EPH-430*, EPH-431*, EPH-450*, EPH-464*–EPH-466*, EPH-470*, EPH-475*, EPH-479*, EPH-491*, EPH-495*, EPH-514*, EPH-516*, EPH-523*, EPH-525*

Pine-cone decoration
EPH-528*, EPH-529*, EPH-531*–EPH-533*, EPH-537*, EPH-542, EPH-543*, EPH-545*–EPH-548*

Calyx A
EPH-560*, EPH-569*

Calyx A with filled 'nelumbo'
EPH-581*, EPH-585*, EPH-593, EPH-594

Other calyces with 'nelumbo'
EPH-602*

Calyx B
EPH-606*, EPH-640*, EPH-642, EPH-644

Other calyces
EPH-657*, EPH-658, EPH-672*, EPH-703*, EPH-709, EPH-713*

Imbricate rounded petals
EPH-736*, EPH-744, EPH-760*, EPH-775*, EPH-790*, EPH-798*, EPH-801*

Imbricate pointed petals
EPH-807*, EPH-809, EPH-812*, EPH-816*, EPH-820*, EPH-823*, EPH-827*, EPH-836, EPH-840*–EPH-843*, EPH-846–EPH-849, EPH-852*, EPH-858–EPH-861*, EPH-865, EPH-872, EPH-881*, EPH-885, EPH-887, EPH-890*, EPH-892*, EPH-893, EPH-896*, EPH-897*, EPH-899*, EPH-903*, EPH-904, EPH-906, EPH-912, EPH-915, EPH-922*–EPH-925*, EPH-927*, EPH-933, EPH-934*, EPH-938, EPH-940, EPH-945

Imbricate designs using other elements
EPH-946*, EPH-947*, EPH-953*

Pendent-semicircle design
EPH-964, EPH-974

Network pattern
EPH-990*–EPH-993*, EPH-996*, EPH-997*, EPH-1001, EPH-1003

Plastic long petals
EPH-1012*, EPH-1014, EPH-1018*–EPH-1020*, EPH-1023*, EPH-1024*, EPH-1029*, EPH-1030, EPH-1037*, EPH-1038*

Stylized long petals
EPH-1045*–EPH-1047*, EPH-1055*, EPH-1058*, EPH-1061*, EPH-1067*, EPH-1068*, EPH-1071*, EPH-1074, EPH-1078*, EPH-1090*, EPH-1092, EPH-1101*–EPH-1104, EPH-1106*, EPH-1108–EPH-1110*, EPH-1113*, EPH-1115*

Vertical fluting
EPH-1119*, EPH-1120*

Rim fragments
EPH-1123–EPH-1125*, EPH-1127, EPH-1130, EPH-1138*, EPH-1142, EPH-1174*, EPH-1181*, EPH-1185*, EPH-1190*–EPH-1192, EPH-1195*–EPH-1198*, EPH-1204, EPH-1206*–EPH-1208, EPH-1211, EPH-1215*, EPH-1217*, EPH-1222*, EPH-1224, EPH-1225*, EPH-1227*–EPH-1232, EPH-1239–EPH-1241*

Base fragments
EPH-1249*, EPH-1251, EPH-1253*, EPH-1259, EPH-1260*, EPH-1262*, EPH-1263

Supplementary shapes
EPH-1271*, EPH-1276, EPH-1286, EPH-1287, EPH-1292 (small bowls); EPH-1333* (krater?); EPH-1338–EPH-1340* (large closed vessels)

Knidos

Figural decoration
KNI-2*–KNI-6*, KNI-8, KNI-9*, KNI-11*, KNI-13*

Concentric circles
KNI-15*

Myrtle wreath
KNI-17*

Suspended garlands
KNI-19*, KNI-23*–KNI-25*

Multiple rim friezes
KNI-29*, KNI-33

Calyx with figural elements
KNI-36*

Calyx
KNI-41, KNI-43*–KNI-50*, KNI-52*, KNI-53*

Imbricate leaves
KNI-56

Pendent-semicircle design
KNI-57*, KNI-58*

Net pattern(?)
KNI-59*

Rim fragments
KNI-61*–KNI-64*, KNI-66, KNI-68, KNI-72

Supplementary shapes
KNI-75* (closed vessel)

Production Place Unknown

Myrtle wreath
XXX-16*–XXX-19*

Suspended garlands
XXX-20*

Long petal alternating with vegetal element
XXX-41*

Dotted wavy lines
XXX-45*

Supplementary shapes
XXX-51 (small bowl); XXX-74* (large closed vessel)

Getic Production

Calyx
GET-1*

Net pattern
GET-2*, GET-3*

CHAPTER 22

Chersonesos

Chersonesos was one of the major poleis of the Black sea region. Tradition has it that the city was founded by Dorian Greeks from the South Pontic city of Herakleia Pontike in 422/1, but archaeological finds document Greek presence around 100 years earlier, and a group of *ostraka* from the late 6th and early 5th century points to a joint colonization by Pontic settlers from Ionian Sinope and Doric Herakleia (Zolotarev 1996). The Hellenistic period is among the least known phases, first of all because its remains lie buried under the Roman, Byzantine, and Medieval city. In fact, we possess very few good contexts from the Hellenistic period. Among other factors, this has contributed to an almost complete lack of knowledge of MMB in this city. In fact, no more than a handful of MMB have been published in excavation reports of the 20th century.

J. Bouzek is the only scholar who has attempted to provide an overall description of MMB found at Chersonesos. However, when he wrote his section on MMB in 1990, he was able to cite no more than eight pieces (Bouzek 1990, 75).

I know of just one article devoted fully to MMB from Chersonesos, namely Chlystun 1996. This is a very bizarre publication. The author reports the discovery of 174 fragments of MMB which came to light during excavations of Quarter VIII in 1985 (Chlystun 1996, 153). Of these s/he chooses to depict and briefly discuss nine fragments with 'mythological subjects' (Chlystun 1996, 154, fig. 1). The fragments are a mix of Attic, Ephesian, Knidian, and others. The descriptions lack basic information, nor are we provided with the fragments' contexts. Because of the poor illustrations, I have included items in my catalogue only when I am relatively certain of the identification.

Through the kindness of keeper J. Kalašnik, I have had the opportunity to study a group of fragments and complete bowls kept in the State Hermitage Museum. In total 81 bowls, they derive from excavations carried out in the city in the first half of the 20th century. A few of these have previously been published (ATH-1, KYB-4*, KYB-46*, KYB-48*, KNI-26*). Most of the fragments are devoid any contextual information. I have nevertheless found it worthwhile to include them in the present study, because so little is known about the MMB in Chersonesos.

Deposits

As already noted, Hellenistic layers in Chersonesos are scarce; therefore, most of the fragments which I have studied lack contextual information. Of 'closed deposits' with MMB, I am able to quote just the following three.

Pit 2
According to archival information in the State Hermitage Museum, this pit was excavated in 1877 not far from the 19th-century St Volodymyr cathedral which today dominates the ancient site. The pit contained fragments of two bowls of the Meter Medallion Workshop, one signed by Kirbeis and one by Possis (KYB-130* and KYB-350*), along with two almost complete Ephesian bowls of the classical production, one with a myrtle wreath and one with multiple rim friezes (EPH-348* and EPH-639). Since all four are quite well-preserved, it is likely that the deposition was a primary one (see Chapter 3).

Quarter XVIII, Room абвд
This house was excavated by G.D. Belov and A.L. Jakobson in the 1950s (Belov & Jakobson 1953). There is one context there which is of interest for us, namely Room абвд, in which were found two large fragments of Kirbeis bowls (KYB-46* and KYB-48*) in addition to black-gloss and West Slope pottery.

Kazarma
In the early 1990s, a room (the 'gallery') in the so-called *kazarma* ('barracks'), which is located in the harbour area by the 16th curtain of the defence wall, was excavated. In 2005, M.I. Zolotarev published a handful of MMB from a seemingly 'closed' context in this 'room' (Zolotarev 2005, fig. 1.28. 30–34). Zolotarev's article is primarily devoted to the discussion of a bowl with incised net pattern (which he, wrongly, refers to as 'Megarian'). According to Zolotarev, the lower layer in the room was tightly packed with ceramic material, a selection of which he publishes in his fig. 1, including the net bowl (no. 35 and fig. 2). He dates the layer "no later than the middle of the 180s BC" (2005, 55). A look at the finds in his fig. 1 tells us that this

		Mainland		Aiolis						S Asia Minor		Pontos			
		ATH	COR	PER	KYA	KYB	KYX	AIA	AIB	AIX	EPH	KNI	DEM	GET	XXX	Total
Chersonesos	Sum	2		1		11			2	1	62	7	3		7	96
	%	2.1		1.0		11.5			2.1	1.0	64.6	7.3	3.1		7.3	
Average % all Pontic sites		1.6	2.0	1.2	8.5	2.2	0.8	1.7	0.7	65.4	1.6	4.4		9.8	100

FIGURE 101 Distribution of bowls found at Chersonesos according to production place

date is too early. Indeed, a date in the 140s (or 130s) is more likely, because the finds include a Campanian black-gloss bowl (fig. 1.20) with decoration which places it securely in the 140s–130s. Amongst the MMB, we find at least one Ephesian bowl with a box meander over an imbricate body (fig. 1.31), the shape of which places it in the early Ephesian production (cf. Chapter 14), and one further Ephesian bowl of the same shape features PSC decoration under an Ionian kyma (fig. 1.33). Both would conform well to a date in the 140s–130s.

Mouldmade Bowls at Chersonesos

The assemblage of MMB in Chersonesos which I have had at my disposal is small, so it is difficult to make too much out of the statistics. Nevertheless, most of the production places discussed in this book are represented (Fig. 101). This indicates that the formation of the assemblage took place throughout the period during which the MMB were produced and used. There is no evidence of rupture, such as we saw at Olbia and Istros. This corresponds well with our understanding of Chersonesos' history in the Hellenistic period (e.g., Mack & Carter [eds.] 2003).

The composition and date of the MMB clearly mirror Chersonesos' political and geographical position. It is obvious that Ephesian vessels dominate the assemblage, with almost 65% of the finds; this corresponds to the Pontic average. However, the presence of 7.4% Knidian vessels is conspicuous. Normally, they are present in the range of 1.1 to 2.6% at any given site (see Fig. 80).[1]

Three fragments of Pontic Demetrios bowls have been found. The decoration of one cannot be identified with certainty (DEM-61*), whereas the other two represent Decoration 2 and 3a (DEM-76 and DEM-149*, respectively). These decorative patterns are the most widely distributed (Chapter 18), and their occurrence at Chersonesos is therefore hardly surprising. The relative geographical proximity of the site to the Bosporan Kingdom probably accounts for the presence of vessels of Pontic production at Chersonesos and in the Chersonesean chora. We find similar bowls at Čaika (DEM-94, DEM-134, DEM-140) and at Kara Tobe (DEM-20, DEM-70, DEM-88), both Chersonesean fortified settlements. Furthermore, a Demetrios bowl from Kerkinitis is mentioned by S. Kovalenko (Kovalenko 1989, 405 cat. 214; Kovalenko 1998, 71), and in the same general area, in the capital of the Late Scythian Kingdom, Neapolis, a single fragment of a Demetrios bowl has been unearthed (DEM-158). It is to be noted that not a single fragment of Demetrios' production has been found as far north as Bol'šoj Kastel'. This distribution pattern is, as also noted in Chapter 18, in contrast to the areas further north and west of the Black Sea region, where Demetrios bowls are inconspicuous.

---

1 One further Knidian vessel unearthed in Chersonesos can be identified in Chlystun 1996, 155, fig. 1, lower left-hand corner.

VESSELS FOUND AT CHERSONESOS

Athens

Figural decoration
 ATH-12*, ATH-13

Pergamon

Figural decoration
 PER-5*

Kyme, MMW: Kirbeis

Figural decoration
 KYB-4*
Calyx with figural decoration
 KYB-46*, KYB-48*, KYB-67*, KYB-122
Suspended garlands
 KYB-130*, KYB-131, KYB-150
Calyx
 KYB-228*, KYB-229

Kyme, MMW: Possis

Calyx with figural decoration
 KYB-350*

Aiolis, Workshop B

Suspended garlands
 AIB-60*
Supplementary shapes
 AIB-126* (shallow cup with collared rim)

Aiolis, Production Place Unknown

 AIX-19*

Ephesos

Figural decoration
 EPH-41*, EPH-66*, EPH-111*, EPH-117*, EPH-142*
Scroll decoration: full body
 EPH-161*
Scroll decoration: frieze
 EPH-196*, EPH-214*, EPH-215*, EPH-234*, EPH-235*, EPH-245*, EPH-296*
Myrtle wreath
 EPH-334, EPH-337*, EPH-346*, EPH-348*, EPH-355*, EPH-374*, EPH-378*
Multiple rim friezes
 EPH-492*, EPH-501*
Calyx A2
 EPH-573*
Calyx A with filled 'nelumbo'
 EPH-582*
Calyx B2
 EPH-639
Imbricate rounded petals
 EPH-747, EPH-786*
Imbricate pointed petals
 EPH-808*, EPH-815*, EPH-834*, EPH-854*, EPH-895*
Pendent-semicircle design
 EPH-963*, EPH-979
Stylized long petals
 EPH-1084*, EPH-1091, EPH-1095, EPH-1096*
Single rim frieze
 EPH-1129*, EPH-1177, EPH-1200*
Supplementary shapes
 EPH-1279 (small bowl); EPH-1327 (situla)

Knidos

Figural decoration
 KNI-7*
Multiple rim friezes
 KNI-26*, KNI-31*, KNI-32
Calyx with figural elements
 KNI-35*, KNI-37
Rim fragments
 KNI-70

Bosporan Kingdom, Workshop of Demetrios

Decoration 1, 2 or 4
   DEM-61*
Decoration 2
   DEM-76
Decoration 3a
   DEM-149*

Place of Production Unknown

Net pattern
   XXX-39*

CHAPTER 23

The Chersonesean chora and Bol'šoj Kastel'

During the brief interval between ca. 350 and 325, the entire western and northwestern Crimea was incorporated into the Chersonesean state as its distant chora. Thus, a number of previously independent poleis, such as Kerkinitis and Kalos Limen, were subjected to Chersonesean rule, and the territory was divided into cadastres, also known from the Chersonesean home chora. The material remains witnessing this process attest to the spread of a uniform culture in terms of building style and design as well as a common spiritual culture centred on the Dorian founder hero, Herakles (Ščeglov 1978, 125). Most of the towns and settlements in the extended Chersonesean chora suffered a severe crisis around 270, when many settlements were abandoned and the territory contracted.

In the late Hellenistic period, it is generally believed that Scythians took over the Greek settlement sites as well as Greek farms, such as Bol'šoj Kastel', turning them into coastal strongholds.

The only Chersonesean chora site where we are relatively well informed about the discovery of MMB is Čaika. During the years 1965, 1980, and 1982–1984, an ash hill with a dump of plentiful material was excavated. About 240 fragments of MMB from about 150 vessels were found; about a third have been published with illustrations (Popova 2007; Kovalenko 2007). As also noted by Kovalenko (2007, 204), the assemblage consists exclusively of Ephesian vessels. They seem to be of the classical type. The dump is well dated by amphora stamps. The latest Rhodian ones in particular cluster in the first half of the 120s (dating to 128, 126, and 125: Kovalenko 2007, 209–210). It is likely that the Ephesian MMB are more or less contemporary or immediately precede this date.

Bol'šoj Kastel'

Between 1981 and 1987, at the locality Bol'šoj Kastel' (*the large fort*), a fortified, multi-period farmhouse located on the north coast of the Tarchankut Peninsula some 13 km west of the present-day district town of Černomorskoe was excavated by a Leningrad expedition directed by A.N. Ščeglov (Ščeglov 2002, pl. 4.1.19). Regrettably, this important site has never been published. In 2007, I had the opportunity to study the MMB from the site, currently housed in the Černomorskoe Museum of Historical Lore. Fragments of up to 28 MMB had been unearthed. With the exception of two partially preserved bowls, currently exhibited in the museum, the remainder are quite small fragments. The bowls are exclusively of Ephesian production.[1] With the exception of three, all vessels were oxidized.

---

1 Four fragments are attributed to Ephesos with a question mark: EPH-1004*, EPH-1245*, and two small rim fragments appropriate for Ephesos in shape and fabric but preserving no decoration.

VESSELS FOUND AT BOL'ŠOJ KASTEL'

Ephesos

Figural decoration
    EPH-133*
Acanthus-vine scroll
    EPH-233*
Myrtle wreath
    EPH-333
Multiple rim friezes
    EPH-513*
Plastic pine-cone decoration
    EPH-540*

Calyx
    EPH-603*, EPH-649*, EPH-656*, EPH-705
Imbricate, pointed petals
    EPH-832*
Net pattern
    EPH-1004*, EPH-1009*
Plastic long petals
    EPH-1041*
Single rim frieze
    EPH-1122*, EPH-1244*, EPH-1245*

CHAPTER 24

Pantikapaion

Pantikapaion was the capital of the Bosporan Kingdom. Explorations and, later, scientific excavations have been undertaken there since at least the beginning of the 19th century. Apart from the many rich kurgans in the city's surroundings, the main focus of excavation has been Mount Mithridates, the ancient acropolis. Excavations were initiated in 1945 by the Puškin State Museum of Fine Arts in Moscow and by the Institute of Archaeology of the USSR Academy of Sciences, and they continue today. In 1984, V.S. Zabelina reported that more than 1,300 fragments of MMB had been found (Zabelina 1984, 153), and the number must have grown substantially since then.

We know relatively little about the MMB found at Pantikapaion. The only general overview is Zabelina's article, "Importnye ,megarskie' čašy iz Pantikapeia" (1984), which presents a selection of fragments found in excavations between 1947 and 1974 and kept in the Puškin Museum of Fine Arts in Moscow, where Zabelina was curator. We are not informed of their contexts, but since their inventory numbers are prefixed with the letter M, we must assume that they come from the excavations of the Puškin Museum on Mount Mithridates, even though it is not clear from which more precise context they come. The Zabelina article also formed the basis for J. Bouzek's assessment of the MMB from Pantikapaion in his book, *Studies of Greek Pottery in the Black Sea Area* (1990). Recently, V.P. Tolstikov and D. Zhuravlev have published a number of MMB from cistern N 179, excavated in 1996 (Tolstikov & Zhuravlev 2004, pls. 100–101). As they explain, the cistern was not a closed context, inasmuch as it contained unstratified material of the Classical through early Roman period (Tolstikov & Zhuravlev 2004, 269, 273). Through the kind help of its excavator, V.P. Tolstikov, I have been able to see the field documentation, so I can assert that, even though the pieces published are a selection, it is indeed a representative one. Finally, S. Grzegrzółka's 2010 book on the MMB in the Kerč Historical Museum documents a number of bowls from excavations carried out in the city before the end of the 1970s, as well as chance finds. Apart from these more general works, a number of studies focus on the local production of Demetrios (see Chapter 18).

The present chapter does not in any way pretend to be exhaustive. It nevertheless attempts to draw together published and unpublished material from the city in order at least to provide a 'profile' of the MMB found in the city. With the help of Russian colleagues, I have studied the MMB from Pantikapaion in the storerooms of the State Hermitage Museum, St Petersburg[1] as well as in the storerooms of the Puškin Museum in Moscow.[2] As mentioned in Chapter 20, objects excavated in Southern Russia in pre-Revolutionary times were brought to St Petersburg and most are now curated in the State Hermitage Museum. This is the reason why the vessels in the Hermitage are from the old excavations (1842, 1847, 1849–1850, 1852, 1864, 1867–1868, 1873, 1877, 1883, 1901–1904, 1906, 1908–1909, 1914).

In the Puškin Museum in particular there is a very large collection of MMB, left unstudied since the 1984 article of Zabelina. I have been through all the material excavated during the years 1945–1947, 1949–1950, 1956–1958, 1960–1967, 1970–1975, but, because of the extent of this collection, I have selected for study only the non-Ephesian material.[3] In the future, the entire collection will be dealt with in detail by N. Astašova of the museum.

The only context useful for the present study is a foundation trench for the construction of the late Hellenistic palace on Mount Mithridates; its excavation produced many MMB, which I discuss below; they are housed in the Puškin Museum.[4]

Palace Foundation Trench

During the years 1984–1985 and 1989, V.P. Tolstikov excavated a trench along the side of the royal palace, which was located on the acropolis. The best pieces of MMB unearthed in this trench were illustrated by Košelenko (1992, fig. 23), but they were published without any further explanation. It is therefore worth (re)considering this ensemble.

---

1 I am much obliged to D.E. Čistov and the late N.Z. Kunina, the curators of the Pantikapaion collection in the State Hermitage Museum.
2 I am grateful to N. Astašova, curator of the relief pottery, S. Kovalenko for his unfailing help, and V.P. Tolstikov, the excavator of Pantikapaion.
3 This is the reason why the Pantikapaion statistics are uncomplete.
4 I am most grateful to V.P. Tolstikov for the possibility of publishing this important context.

		Mainland		Aiolis						S Asia Minor		Pontos			
		ATH	COR	PER	KYA	KYB	KYX	AIA	AIB	AIX	EPH	KNI	DEM	GET	XXX	Total
Pantikapaion	Sum	9		5	3	30	4	1	7	3	242	1	37		46	388
	%	2.3		1.3	0.8	7.8	1.0	0.3	1.8	0.8	62.4		9.5		11.9	
Average % all Pontic sites		1.6		2.0	1.2	8.5	2.2	0.8	1.7	0.7	65.4	1.6	4.4		9.8	100

FIGURE 102   Distribution of bowls found at Pantikapaion according to production place

Fragments of up to 118 MMB were unearthed in this trench. The material is very homogenous and consists almost exclusively of Ephesian bowls (two-thirds oxidized, one-third reduced). There are also a few vessels of other productions, such as a Pergamene and a Kymean vessel (PER-51* and KYX-64*), a fine reduced bowl of the Aiolis A production (AIA-4*), which forms a bridge to the Aiolis B production, three vessels of unidentified production (XXX-22*, XXX-47*, XXX-72*), and four non-joining fragments probably of the same Knidian bowl with rouletting (M-89-no no. 1). The latter is typologically of a stage that belongs to the 2nd century, prior to its end (Kögler 2010, fig. 71.a, middle group). It is noticeable that not a single fragment of the local production of Demetrios was found in this trench. As mentioned in Chapter 18, the earliest absolutely dated contexts for fragments of Demetrios' production (DEM-140, DEM-159) were probably deposited around 125 or shortly thereafter. Not a single Athenian fragment was found in the palace trench either. Thus, the accumulation of the MMB in the trench must have taken place over a relatively short period in (the second half of?) the third quarter of the 2nd century.

This date accords well with the homogenous character of the Ephesian vessels. Their decoration is characterized primarily by multiple rim friezes, and there are many net-pattern bowls and bowls with long-petal decoration (mainly stylized). There are also significant numbers of imbricate vessels (with rounded and pointed petals) and, if imbricate petals do not decorate the lower part of the vessel, calyx B is employed. In terms of the main decoration, there is very little figural decoration; there are no examples of acanthus-vine scrolls or PSC decoration, but five vessels feature myrtle wreaths, and two are decorated with stylized acanthus scrolls. Thus, the early part of the classical Ephesian production is not represented.

Summing up the evidence from the palace foundation trench, it is likely that the palace was rebuilt when Pairisades V, the last king of the Spartokid dynasty, was installed on the throne around 125. According to the Diophantos decree (*IOSPE* I² 352), he was killed in a Scythian uprising headed by Saumakos around 108. In 107, the Scythians were defeated and the Bosporan Kingdom was incorporated into the Pontic Kingdom.

Mouldmade Bowls at Pantikapaion

As mentioned above, the statistics for the MMB found at Pantikapaion (Fig. 102) are somewhat flawed, because I have not recorded all the Ephesian vessels housed in the Puškin Museum, but only those from the palace foundation trench. Nevertheless, we can conclude for Pantikapaion as we did in Chapter 22 for Chersonesos, that vessels from all of the production places discussed in this book have been found there, so most likely the assemblage accumulated uninterruptedly during the entire 2nd century.

The production of Demetrios bowls took place in Pantikapaion, as is demonstrated by the recovery of at least nine moulds there (DEM-1*, DEM-4*–DEM-11). The most common types of decoration encountered are Decorations 2, 3a and 5a. In general, the decorative types documented in Pantikapaion are less rich than those in the assemblages from Myrmekion and Porthmion, for example. At Pantikapaion, Demetrios bowls constitute 9.7% (ECA+ECB), revealing a very limited degree of self-sufficiency, amounting to one local bowl out of 10.4 vessels (Fig. 28). This number is surprisingly low, considering the fact that these bowls were (also) produced in the city. At Myrmekion, where production also took place, the proportion of local bowls is much higher, accounting for one out of 2.3 bowls. The difference can probably be explained by Pantikapaion's position as a hub in the region's trade network, but chronology may also play a role, because whereas the MMB from Pantikapaion have a long chronological horizon, the chronology of the assemblage from Myrmekion seems to have been shorter and confined to the second half of the 2nd century (Chapter 25). The fact that, as mentioned, the Demetrios and other non-Ephesian products are overrepresented in my catalogue makes the relatively low frequency of Demetrios bowls at Pantikapaion even more astonishing.

Pantikapaion's privileged position apparently gave its inhabitants unlimited access to imported MMB. As we have seen, this is probably the reason why repairs, which are so common in the Pontic region, are next to unknown at Pantikapaion (Fig. 82).

VESSELS FOUND AT PANTIKAPAION

Athens

Figural decoration
  ATH-3*, ATH-6, ATH-10*, ATH-19*, ATH-24, ATH-25
Imbricate
  ATH-47
Rim fragments
  ATH-55*, ATH-71

Pergamon

Figural decoration
  PER-10*
Scroll
  PER-29
Calyx
  PER-51*
Stylized long petals alternating with acanthus
  PER-82
Supplementary shapes
  PER-86* (small bowl)

Kyme, Workshop A

Figural decoration
  KYA-6*
Suspended garlands
  KYA-39
Supplementary shapes
  KYA-55 (skyphos)

Kyme, MMW: Kirbeis

Figural decoration
  KYB-1*(?), KYB-33
Calyx with figural decoration
  KYB-47*, KYB-49, KYB-68*, KYB-76*, KYB-80, KYB-94*, KYB-103*, KYB-125
Suspended garlands
  KYB-134*, KYB-145*(?), KYB-146*
Calyx
  KYB-180*, KYB-197, KYB-211
Imbricate
  KYB-248*, KYB-253*
Base fragments
  KYB-261*(?), KYB-262(?), KYB-267
Rim fragments
  KYB-279–KYB-282, KYB-296*, KYB-304, KYB-309
Supplementary shapes
  KYB-318* (small bowl), KYB-327*(?) (amphora)

Kyme, MMW: Possis

Calyx
  KYB-364*
Base fragment
  KYB-390*
Rim fragment
  KYB-396

Kyme, MMW: Zenodotos

Calyx
  KYB-418*

Kyme, MMW: Unattributed

Calyx
  KYB-436*

Kyme, Unattributed

Calyx with figured decoration
  KYX-42
Suspended garlands
  KYX-61, KYX-64*
Supplementary shapes
  KYX-99 (small bowl)

Aiolis, Workshop A

Ivy-acanthus scroll
  AIA-4*

Aiolis, Workshop B

Calyx with figural decoration
　AIB-20
Acanthus-flower scroll
　AIB-40*
Calyx with 'nelumbo' and isolated long petals
　AIB-76*
Stylized long petals
　AIB-101
Multiple rim friezes
　AIB-104, AIB-105
Supplementary shapes
　AIB-123 (shallow cup with high collared rim)

Aiolis, Production Place Unknown

Suspended wreath
　AIX-5
Plastic long petals
　AIX-26
Supplementary shapes
　AIX-34* (small bowl)

Ephesos

Figural decoration
　EPH-1*, EPH-2*, EPH-5, EPH-27*, EPH-28, EPH-40, EPH-54*, EPH-61*, EPH-78*, EPH-80*, EPH-81*, EPH-99*–EPH-101*, EPH-103*, EPH-104*, EPH-106*, EPH-109, EPH-110*, EPH-112*, EPH-113, EPH-127*, EPH-141
Scroll decoration
　EPH-186, EPH-189*, EPH-201, EPH-202, EPH-220, EPH-275, EPH-283*, EPH-289*, EPH-314*
Myrtle wreath
　EPH-324*, EPH-327, EPH-331, EPH-350, EPH-356*, EPH-365*, EPH-367*, EPH-379
Ivy wreath
　EPH-386*, EPH-387
Suspended garlands
　EPH-393
Multiple rim friezes
　EPH-442*, EPH-446*, EPH-482, EPH-488*, EPH-490*
Plastic pine-cone decoration
　EPH-536
Calyx A2
　EPH-570, EPH-572, EPH-574*
Calyx A with filled 'nelumbo'
　EPH-580*, EPH-583, EPH-584*, EPH-587*
Other calyces with 'nelumbo'
　EPH-595*, EPH-605
Calyx B
　EPH-615, EPH-617, EPH-638, EPH-641*, EPH-651*
Other calyces
　EPH-669*, EPH-671*, EPH-676, EPH-696*, EPH-702, EPH-706*, EPH-712
Imbricate rounded petals
　EPH-720, EPH-725*, EPH-727*, EPH-746*, EPH-753*, EPH-777, EPH-783–EPH-785, EPH-791*
Imbricate pointed petals
　EPH-804, EPH-806, EPH-845*, EPH-863, EPH-866*, EPH-873*, EPH-875*, EPH-880, EPH-900*, EPH-901, EPH-931*, EPH-942*, EPH-943*
Net pattern
　EPH-983, EPH-986, EPH-989*, EPH-995*, EPH-998*, EPH-999, EPH-1002*
Stylized long petals
　EPH-1060*, EPH-1066, EPH-1070, EPH-1082, EPH-1094
Stylized long petals with other vegetal motifs
　EPH-1116, EPH-1118
Single rim frieze
　EPH-1167*, EPH-1170*, EPH-1183*, EPH-1189*, EPH-1212, EPH-1216*, EPH-1218*, EPH-1234*
Base fragments
　EPH-1246*–EPH-1248
Supplementary shapes
　EPH-1273*, EPH-1278, EPH-1288* (small bowls); EPH-1300* (juglet?); EPH-1303*, EPH-1305*–EPH-1307*, EPH-1315*, EPH-1318 (amphorae); EPH-1324*, EPH-1325, EPH-1329* (situlae); EPH-1334 (large open vessel); EPH-1342* (large closed vessel)

Knidos

Rim fragment
　KNI-71

Bosporan Kingdom, Workshop of Demetrios

Moulds

Decoration unknown
　DEM-1*
Decoration 1b
　DEM-4*
Decoration 2
　DEM-5*
Decoration 3a
　DEM-6*, DEM-7

Decoration 4a
 DEM-8*, DEM-9*
Decoration 6
 DEM-10
Decoration 7
 DEM-11

Bowls

Decoration 1a
 DEM-12, DEM-14*, DEM-19
Decoration 1b
 DEM-25, DEM-28, DEM-30*, DEM-39
Decoration 2
 DEM-68, DEM-71*, DEM-72*(?), DEM-82, DEM-104, DEM-136, DEM-139
Decoration 3a
 DEM-144*(?) DEM-151, DEM-152, DEM-156, DEM-167, DEM-171*
Decoration 4a
 DEM-182, DEM-188

Decoration 5a
 DEM-207, DEM-208, DEM-212*, DEM-217, DEM-220*, DEM-221*, DEM-234
Decoration 5c
 DEM-242

Production Place Unknown

Calyx
 XXX-22*, XXX-25
Rim fragment
 XXX-47*
Supplementary shapes
 XXX-48*, XXX-49*, XXX-52, XXX-53 (small bowls); XXX-60 (stemmed bowl); XXX-66 (amphora); XXX-72* (krater); XXX-73* (guttus)

CHAPTER 25

Myrmekion

Myrmekion, 'the Ant', was one of the smaller towns in the Bosporan Kingdom (Vinogradov, Butyagin & Vachtina 2003). It is located on a rocky promontory across the Bay of Kerč, just 4 km northeast of Pantikapaion as the crow flies. It covers an area of about 8 ha. During the height of the Bosporan Kingdom, Myrmekion became a suburb of the capital.

The first scientific excavations at Myrmekion took place in 1934, when the Bosporan Expedition was formed by the Institute of the History of Material Culture of the Leningrad branch of the Soviet Academy of Sciences, under the direction of V.F. Gajdukevič. Interrupted by World War II, Gajdukevič worked in Myrmekion between 1934 and 1938 and again from 1946 to 1966. During the three-year period 1956–1958, a group of Polish researchers led by K. Michałowski took part in the excavations. The results of the first two years of the Soviet-Polish excavations were published in three monographs (Michałowski 1958; Gajdukevič 1959; Sztetyłło 1976). Between 1982 and 1994, the Petersburg expedition was directed by Ju.A. Vinogradov. In 1999 the State Hermitage Museum in St Petersburg joined the expedition, and since 2000 the Hermitage has been in charge of the excavations, under the direction of A.M. Butjagin.

Most of the finds from Gajdukevič's excavations are kept in the storerooms of the IIMK RAN St Petersburg, but some came to the State Hermitage Museum and some to the Kerč Historical Museum, whereas those from the Polish excavations are conserved in the National Museum of Warsaw. S. Grzegrzółka, who published the collection in the Kerč Historical Museum in 2010, is also in charge of publishing the collection of the Polish expedition kept in the National Museum in Warsaw. This collection formed the subject of a master's thesis by S. Platek (Sztetyłło 1976, 11 n. 21): *Czarki megaryjskie z wykopalisk polskich w Mirmeki na Krymie*, which I have not seen.

With the kind permission of Ju.A. Vinogradov (IIMK RAN) and A.M. Butjagin (the State Hermitage Museum), I have been able to study and publish the MMB in the two St Petersburg collections. All of the fragments which I have examined first-hand are from Gajdukevič's excavations, but I have also included illustrated finds from the Polish excavations. It was not possible to gain access to the material in the Kerč collection during the time Grzegrzółka was studying it.

Few of the MMB from Myrmekion have been published previously (Gajdukevič 1959; Bernhard 1957; Michałowski 1958; Bernhard 1959; 1961; Šurgaja 1962; Platek 1974; Gricik 2007; Grzegrzółka 2010). Platek claims that a total of 267 MMB were excavated there (1974, 41), but the number must considerably larger, since in St Petersburg alone there are fragments of 237 vessels.

Regrettably, almost all are without a known context. The St Petersburg archaeologist K. Gricik has recently attempted to reconstruct the context of the finds from Myrmekion through a study of the archival material in the IIMK RAN, but with limited results. She succeeded in recovering just one context, a Hellenistic house which had been excavated in the mid-50s in the central part of the town (Sector И; Gricik 2007). It was covered by an ash hill (a *zol'nik*), the identification of which has been the subject of recent controversy (Čistov 2004). According to Gricik, the excavation was never completed, and it is only partially published. Of the material kept in St Petersburg, she has been able to locate the find place of just a handful of sherds, namely, seven fragments found in 1949 in courtyard VII: five of these are Ephesian (EPH-11*, EPH-43*, EPH-151*, EPH-1107*, EPH-1161*) and two are products of Demetrios (DEM-67*, DEM-102*). Even though the context of the majority of the MMB found at Myrmekion is unknown, I have found it worthwhile to include them in the present publication, because there is no published overview of this group of pottery from this town.

Mouldmade Bowls at Myrmekion

The MMB unearthed at Myrmekion (Fig. 103) fall into three large groups: imports from Ephesos (52.7%), local Bosporan products from the workshop of Demetrios (28.7%), and a miscellaneous group (18.6%). With the exception of the Aiolis B vessels, which constitute 2.5% of the whole, all other Aiolian vessels are represented in quantities far below the average. This probably has to do with the chronology of the MMB from the site, few of which date earlier than the mid-2nd century. This is also mirrored in the very low presence of Athenian vessels, of which I have recorded just one. This late date is also reflected in the small number of supplementary shapes, just 2.2%, which, again, is much below the Pontic average (Fig. 31).

		Mainland			Aiolis							S Asia Minor		Pontos			
		ATH	COR	PER	KYA	KYB	KYX	AIA	AIB	AIX	EPH	KNI	DEM	GET	XXX	Total
Myrmekion	Sum	1		3	2	8	2		7	4	147	4	80		21	279
	%	0.4		1.1	0.7	2.9	0.7		2.5	1.4	52.7	1.4	28.7		7.5	
Average % all Pontic sites		1.6		2.0	1.2	8.5	2.2	0.8	1.7	0.7	65.3	1.6	4.5		9.8	100

FIGURE 103   Distribution according to production place of bowls found at Myrmekion

Myrmekion was the home of Demetrios' production, as we can see from the two moulds found in the town (DEM-2, DEM-3). Both feature Decoration 1b, and none of the later types of decoration are represented. This is in contrast to the situation at Pantikapaion, and it is therefore likely that production shifted from Myrmekion to the capital at an early stage. Nevertheless, by far the largest body of Demetrios bowls in terms of both relative and absolute numbers has been found at Myrmekion: up to 85 bowls, almost 30% of the site assemblage (ECA+ECB). At Myrmekion (as well as at Porthmion) we also find the largest variety of decoration types (Fig. 91).

The local production of MMB in Myrmekion implies that to a large extent the town was self-sufficient in MMB. In fact, of the 11 sites included in the present publication, the largest relative proportion of Demetrios bowls has been unearthed in Myrmekion. This high degree of self-sufficiency is probably also the reason why so few vessels in Myrmekion were repaired (2.2%) when compared with other sites (Fig. 82).

VESSELS FOUND AT MYRMEKION

Athens

Rim fragment
   ATH-30

Pergamon

Figural decoration
   PER-6*, PER-15
Oak wreath?
   PER-37*

Kyme, Workshop A

Rim fragment
   KYA-47*
Supplemental shapes
   KYA-53* (skyphos?)

Kyme, MMW: Kyrbeis

Calyx with figural decoration
   KYB-114
Suspended garlands
   KYB-164
Calyx
   KYB-194, KYB-200*, KYB-201*
Base fragment
   KYB-266*
Multiple rim friezes
   KYB-272*

Kyme, MMW: Possis

Calyx
   KYB-377

Kyme, Unattributed

Figural decoration
   KYX-7*, KYX-46*

Aiolis, Workshop B

Scroll decoration
   AIB-38*, AIB-45
Suspended garlands
   AIB-59*
Calyx with 'nelumbo' and long petals
   AIB-73*, AIB-78*
Supplementary shapes
   AIB-119*, AIB-131* (shallow cups with high collared rim)

Aiolis, Production Place Unknown

Figural decoration
   AIX-4*
Long petals
   AIX-25*, AIX-29
Scroll/ivy wreath
   AIX-35* (large vessel)

Ephesos

Figural decoration
   EPH-8*, EPH-11*, EPH-29*, EPH-34*, EPH-36*, EPH-37*, EPH-43*, EPH-51*, EPH-87*, EPH-119*, EPH-122, EPH-131*, EPH-151*, EPH-155*
Scroll decoration
   EPH-184, EPH-219, EPH-231*, EPH-240*, EPH-271*, EPH-279*, EPH-281, EPH-282*, EPH-290
Myrtle wreath
   EPH-329*, EPH-335*, EPH-341, EPH-342, EPH-344*, EPH-354*, EPH-373, EPH-382*
Suspended garlands
   EPH-399*
Multiple rim friezes
   EPH-424*, EPH-428*, EPH-435*, EPH-437*, EPH-467*, EPH-476*, EPH-498, EPH-500
Plastic pine-cone decoration
   EPH-534*
Calyx A
   EPH-553*, EPH-556*, EPH-589*, EPH-600*
Calyx B
   EPH-607*, EPH-610*, EPH-613, EPH-625*, EPH-627*, EPH-628, EPH-632*, EPH-635*, EPH-637, EPH-646*, EPH-647

Calyx with acanthus and looped stem
    EPH-659*
Calyx C
    EPH-663*
Calyx with acanthus leaf and lotus petal
    EPH-670*, EPH-674*
Imbricate rounded petals
    EPH-731*, EPH-735, EPH-789*
Imbricate pointed petals
    EPH-853*, EPH-864*, EPH-879, EPH-908*, EPH-936*
Imbricate rosettes
    EPH-952*
Pendent-semicircle design
    EPH-976, EPH-981*
Net pattern
    EPH-1006*
Plastic long petals
    EPH-1010*, EPH-1017*, EPH-1021*, EPH-1025*, EPH-1031*–EPH-1034*, EPH-1039
Stylized long petals
    EPH-1054, EPH-1076*, EPH-1083*, EPH-1085
Stylized long petals and Menemachos bud
    EPH-1107*
Single rim frieze
    EPH-1143, EPH-1151, EPH-1153, EPH-1154, EPH-1160*, EPH-1161*, EPH-1178, EPH-1179, EPH-1186*, EPH-1187*, EPH-1201*, EPH-1205*, EPH-1219*, EPH-1221*, EPH-1250*
Base fragment
    EPH-1264*
Supplementary shapes
    EPH-1291 (small bowl), EPH-1297* (juglet)

Knidos

Calyx with figural elements
    KNI-38*, KNI-39
Calyx
    KNI-51*
Rim fragment
    KNI-67*

Bosporan Kingdom, Workshop of Demetrios

Moulds
Decoration 1b
    DEM-2, DEM-3

Bowls
Decoration 1a
    DEM-13*, DEM-15, DEM-17*, DEM-18*
Decoration 1b
    DEM-26*, DEM-27*, DEM-31, DEM-34*, DEM-35*, DEM-37*, DEM-38(?)
Decoration 1b var.
    DEM-42*
Decoration 1c
    DEM-44
Decoration 1e
    DEM-49*–DEM-51, DEM-54*, DEM-56*
Decoration 1, 2 or 4
    DEM-62*, DEM-63*
Decoration 1, 2, 4 or 5
    DEM-66*
Decoration 2
    DEM-67*, DEM-73, DEM-74, DEM-77–DEM-80, DEM-91*, DEM-97, DEM-99*–DEM-103*, DEM-113*–DEM-115, DEM-135*, DEM-137, DEM-138
Decoration 2 var.
    DEM-142(?)
Decoration 2?
    DEM-143*(?)
Decoration 3a
    DEM-145*–DEM-147, DEM-150, DEM-161*, DEM-166*, DEM-168*–DEM-170*, DEM-173(?), DEM-179*
Decoration 4a
    DEM-183*, DEM-184, DEM-185(?), DEM-186, DEM-187*, DEM-189*, DEM-192*, DEM-193*, DEM-195*, DEM-200*
Decoration 4b
    DEM-202*–DEM-204*
Decoration 5a
    DEM-209, DEM-215*, DEM-216(?), DEM-226, DEM-235, DEM-236
Decoration 5?
    DEM-244*
Decoration 7
    DEM-245*, DEM-246*
Decoration unknown
    DEM-251*–DEM-255*, DEM-257*, DEM-258

Production Place Unknown

Figural decoration
    XXX-4*, XXX-5*
Scroll decoration
    XXX-14*

CHAPTER 26

Porthmion

With a Contribution by M.Ju. Vachtina

The present chapter owes much to the kindness of M.Ju. Vachtina (IIMK RAN). Not only did she grant me access and publication rights to a collection of fragmentary MMB from three years of excavations in the smaller Bosporan city of Porthmion, currently in the storerooms of IIMK RAN, St Petersburg, but she has also contributed an introduction to the city (the section *Porthmion: city and excavations*) and the relevant excavations as well as found the necessary archival documentation.[1]

Porthmion: City and Excavations

The ancient Greek city of Porthmion, located in the modern village of Jukovka, is one of the smaller towns of the European part of the Bosporan Kingdom. The site is situated on a rocky plateau not far from the shores of the Kerč Strait, 14 km northeast of the modern city of Kerč, the location of the Bosporan Kingdom's ancient capital, Pantikapaion (Šurgaja 1984). The area of the Greek settlement corresponds to the size of the plateau (ca. 0.7 ha). Porthmion was founded in the middle or the third quarter of the 6th century. In the second half of the 3rd century, the old town was levelled and a new, Hellenistic town constructed. This was a small fortified settlement, rectangular in layout, with three parallel, longitudinal streets crossed at right angles by a number of lanes (Fig. 104). The city was abandoned around the middle of the 1st century and never reoccupied.

The excavation of the site has been carried out with intervals by the Bosporan Archaeological Expedition of the IIMK RAN since 1953. Building remains connected with the two main periods of Porthmion's history, the Archaic (Vachtina 2003, 40–52; 2006, 31–42) and the Hellenistic (Kastanajan 1972, 77–82; 1983, 162–168), have been unearthed.[2] Almost all the houses of the Classical period were destroyed during the rebuilding of the site in the 3rd century.

The Hellenistic remains have been investigated mostly under the direction of E.G. Kastanajan (1953–1984). Her excavations allow us to reconstruct the layout of the Hellenistic settlement. During that period, Porthmion was a small fortress with defensive walls and houses built contemporaneously (Kastanajan 1983; Fig. 104). One of the towers, the northwestern, has been explored. Porthmion consisted of 11 residential blocks, each divided into a number of dwellings. The houses typically consisted of one or more rooms around a courtyard. The rooms had earthen floors whereas the courtyards were paved with limestone slabs.

The majority of the MMB found at Porthmion are connected with the excavation of layers and structures of the Hellenistic period. Currently, the finds are kept partly in the Kerč History and Culture Reserve, partly in IIMK RAN. A further group of fragments excavated in 1975, 1977, and 1987 is documented through photographs only, since they were discarded after excavation.[3] The excavation reports employed in the following are kept in the archive of the IIMK RAN.

1953
Excavation of the site began this year under the overall direction of V.F. Gajdukevič, who headed the Leningrad expedition to a number of Bosporan sites. The data concerning these excavations, including Porthmion, can be found in Gajdukevič's excavation report.[4] More detailed excavation diaries were kept by E.G. Kastanajan.[5] See also Kastanajan 1958, 203–207.

---

1   The archival information is integrated into the catalogue.
2   See also more recently, Vinogradov, Butyagin & Vachtina 2003, 821–825.
3   This cannot be entirely the case, because most of the fragments from 1975 and 1977 are included in S. Grzegrzółka's catalogue of the fragments inventoried before 1980 in the Kerč History and Culture Reserve (Grzegrzółka 2010), see ATH-24; KYB-33; AIB-72; AIX-28; PER-4; DEM-41, DEM-55, DEM-58, DEM-59, DEM-83, DEM-96, DEM-98, DEM-117–DEM-123, DEM-174, DEM-196–DEM-199, DEM-201, DEM-205, DEM-227, DEM-228, DEM-238, DEM-248, DEM-249, DEM-259. Vachtina's information concerning their find spots supplements that of Grzegrzółka.
4   Preserved in the IIMK archive: Kratkij predvaritel'nyj otčot archeologičeskogo issledovanija antičnych gorodov na Kerčenskom poluostrove v 1953 godu,. IIMK archival reference F. 35. 1953/26.
5   Preserved in the IIMK archive: Dnevnik n. 1 raskopok gorodišča Porfmij s zarisovkami i opisjami nachodok, IIMK archival reference

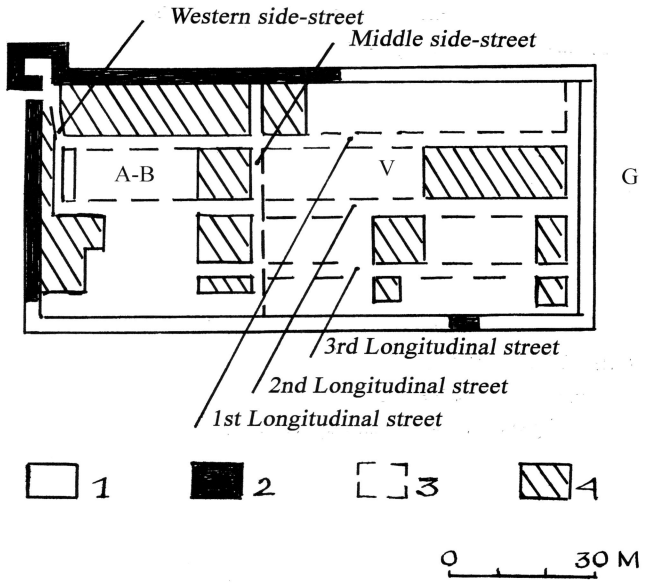

FIGURE 104   Schematic plan of Hellenistic Porthmion, after E.G. Kastanajan, redrawn by Marina Vakhtina (2009, fig. 28) and published here with her permission. 1 – Unexcavated areas. 2 – Excavated fortifications. 3 – Unexcavated dwelling structures. 4 – Excavated dwelling blocks. A–B, V, G – indications of the main excavation areas

In 1953 the excavations were concentrated in the western and northwestern areas (Sectors A–B). The northern and western parts of the Hellenistic defensive wall and the nearby areas were investigated. The excavation followed the standard methodology of Russian archaeology, with the excavation area divided into squares measuring 5 × 5 m, each furnished with a number. Discoveries were recorded according to depth, measuring from the modern surface level, employing the approximate length of the head of a spade, 20–25 cm; this too is normal Russian excavation practice.

1975
The excavations of 1975 were concentrated in Sector A, in the northwestern part of the city, along the western defensive wall, where fortifications, streets, and dwellings of the Hellenistic period were investigated. In total ca. 283 m² were excavated, reaching a depth of 3 m. The excavations are documented in the excavation report (*Otčet*)

F. 35. 1953/42; Dnevnik n. 2 raskopok gorodišča Porfmij s zarisovkami i opisjami nachodok, IIMK archival reference F. 35. 1953/43; Dnevnik n. 3 raskopok gorodišča Porfmij s zarisovkami i opisjami nachodok. IIMK archival reference F. 35. 1953/44.

by E.G. Kastanajan.[6] During the same year, excavation of the paved area outside the western defensive wall, near the wicket opened in 1974, was continued. The area was paved partly with limestone slabs, partly with pottery fragments. The area excavated in 1975 was 0.60 m wide and extended north-south for a distance of 6 m. Another context that produced MMB was Pit 18, in Room T (DEM-116, DEM-196). It dates to the end of the active of life in the city, in the middle of the 1st century. Pit 18 was oval in shape, measuring 1.17 × 1.24 m at the top and 1.55 × 1.45 m below; its depth was 2.23 m. Another room, Room X, delimited to the south by courtyard F, is situated near the city gates in the western wall, south of the northwestern Hellenistic tower. It measured about 20 m², and the walls survived to a height of 1.5 m; the floor was paved with large limestone slabs. Room X was limited by walls 137 (northern), 131 (southern), and 136 (eastern); part of the western defensive wall served as its western wall. Kastanajan supposed that this room was a guardhouse. Among the Hellenistic objects found there were fragments of Koan and Knidian amphorae, light-clay amphorae with double-barrelled handles, fragments of red-clay, black- and red-gloss pottery, fragments of Demeter protomes of the 4th–early 3rd century, and a bronze coin of Pantikapaion dating to the first half of 1st century. During the cleaning of the floor, fragments of Sinopean, Knidian, and Koan amphorae, a Sinopean louterion, a red-gloss fish-plate, red and grey ware, a fragment of a small clay altar with remains of a relief representation of an eagle, and fragments of kitchen and handmade pottery were found. Among the finds were also two fragments of black-figured pottery (a krater handle and a small body fragment) and several fragments of MMB (DEM-96, XXX-32; perhaps also DEM-117, DEM-118, and DEM-198).

1977
This year, attention was paid mainly to the layout of the dwellings in the central and eastern part of the site. The results are provided in the excavation report by E.G. Kastanajan.[7] The fragments of MMB mentioned below were found during the excavation of blocks of buildings in the eastern part of the city (Sector V).

DEM-249 was found in courtyard B, which was paved with limestone slabs and measured 11.90 m². During the clearing of the pavement, fragments of Bosporan tiles, double-barrelled amphora handles, and fragments of black- and red-gloss Hellenistic pottery were found. DEM-83 came to light in another limestone-paved court (courtyard A, measuring 7 × 11 m), which belonged to a one-room house. Other finds here were a handle of a Rhodian amphora, a coin of Pantikapaion (type Zograf 1951, pl. XLI; 2), fragments of Hellenistic jugs with twisted, channelled, ribbed and oval handles, and fragments of black- and red-gloss pottery and grey and handmade wares.

1987
In this year, the large area east of the main territory occupied by the Hellenistic city was investigated. The excavations were concentrated east of the supposed eastern Hellenistic defensive wall (Sector G). The remains of a large Hellenistic dwelling complex were unearthed, covering an area of about 160 m² (Sector 2). The remains were poorly preserved, but the structure was rather unusual compared to other contemporary buildings known within the walls of the city. It was oriented northwest-southeast, was much larger than the 'typical' Porthmion houses, and contained rather 'rich' material, including numerous fragments of MMB. Most of the finds connected with this dwelling date from the second half or end of the 3rd to the first half of the 2nd century. Among the amphora stamps, Rhodians predominate. Some of them belong to V. Grace's chronological period 3 (ending in 164, according to G. Finkielsztejn's down-dating), whereas the latest Rhodian stamp dates to ca. 150. The fragment of a Bosporan stamped tile dates to the 3rd century (M.Ju. Vachtina, Otčet o rabote Porfmijskogo otrjada Bosporskoi ekspedicii LOIA AN SSSR v 1987 g.; archive of the IIMK RAN, F. 35, 1987/97, p. 10–11).

Mouldmade Bowls at Porthmion

Until S. Grzegrzółka's recent publication of the MMB from Porthmion in the Kerč Historical Preserve (2010), just one fragment, DEM-84 had been published (Šurgaja 1962, fig. 4.3–3a; Kovalenko 1989, 404 cat. 191).[8] In order to provide an overview, the present chapter draws together the MMB kept in the IIMK RAN in St Petersburg, as well as the

---

6 Preserved in the archive of IIMK RAN: F. 35, 1975/86 (excavation report); F. 35, 1975/92 (inventory of finds).
7 Preserved in the archive of IIMK RAN: Otčot o rabotach Porfmijskogo otrjada Bosporskoi ekspedicii Leningradskogo otdelenija Instituta archeologii AN SSSR za 1977 god, archival reference F. 35. 1977/76.

8 A few fragments are included in S. Kovalenko's dissertation, but without illustration, so I have not had the opportunity to evaluate them: M-80-113 (Kovalenko 1989, 404 cat. 188), П-80-115.87 (Kovalenko 1989, 404 cat. 186), M-80-117 (Kovalenko 1989 404, cat. 189), M-80-118 (Kovalenko 1989, 404 cat. 187), M-83-36 (Kovalenko 1989, 404 cat. 190).

		Mainland		Aiolis					S Asia Minor		Pontos					
		ATH	COR	PER	KYA	KYB	KYX	AIA	AIB	AIX	EPH	KNI	DEM	GET	XXX	Total
Myrmekion	Sum	1		3	2	8	2		7	4	147	4	80		21	279
	%	0.4		1.1	0.7	2.9	0.7		2.5	1.4	52.7	1.4	28.7		7.5	
Porthmion	Sum	1		1	1	1			1	1	197		45		24	272
	%	0.4		0.4	0.4	0.4			0.4	0.4	72.4		16.5		8.8	
Average % all Pontic sites		1.6	2.0	1.2	8.5	2.2	0.8	1.7	0.7	65.3	1.6	4.5	9.8	100

FIGURE 105 Comparison of the composition of the assemblages at Porthmion and at Myrmekion

fragments documented in the photographs mentioned above and the pieces published by Grzegrzółka (Fig. 105).

Very few production places are represented in this assemblage. First of all we should note that Ephesian bowls dominate the picture: in total, more than 72% of the bowls are of Ephesian provenance (ca. one-fourth in a reduced fabric). Not surprisingly, the Bosporan workshop of Demetrios is also well represented, with what is, in fact, the second largest corpus of Demetrios bowls found: 45 bowls out of a total of 272 (16.5%). As we saw in Chapter 25, the largest number of Demetrios bowls was found at Myrmekion, where they were also produced. In Porthmion (as well as in Myrmekion) we also find the largest variety of decoration types (Fig. 91).

In contrast to the Ephesian and Pontic vessels, the number of vessels from Athenian and Aiolian workshops is negligible and does not include any supplementary shapes.

The composition of the group of MMB found in 1987 differs markedly from those found earlier, for amongst the 20 bowls unearthed in Sector G, not a single scrap of Demetrios' production was recorded, a production which otherwise dominates the Porthmion assemblage. With the possible exception of the long-petal bowl XXX-42, all the fragments seem to be of Ephesian manufacture. According to Vachtina, one part of the 1987 finds (EPH-357, EPH-667, EPH-714, EPH-743, EPH-905, XXX-42) derives from the same sub-assemblage (Sector G, sector 2, square 17–18; depth 0.42 m), whereas the context of the remainder is noted simply as 'fill in rooms'. Both assemblages contain a long-petal bowl, so both certainly date later than ca. 165. The latter group seems to be slightly earlier than the former, to judge from the presence of figural decoration (EPH-76), box meander (EPH-76, EPH-422), and calyx A (EPH-575), but this may be fortuitous. At any rate, the building in Sector G can be dated with confidence to the third quarter of the 2nd century. A third sub-assemblage (pavement of second longitudinal street), with eight Ephesian bowls, also lacks any products of Demetrios' workshop. This group seems to be relatively homogeneous and relatively early as well. Half of the fragments are of grey ware, and early elements such as the acanthus-flower scroll (EPH-267*, EPH-269*), rim friezes with box meander (Grzegrzółka 2010, 200 cat. 343), and crossed dotted lines (EPH-1223*) are represented. This assemblage too should be dated to the third quarter of the 2nd century.

Conversely, a number of other sub-assemblages contain only or mostly Demetrios bowls:
- Room T, Pit 18: DEM-116, DEM-196; Demetrios decoration 2 and 4 respectively
- Room X: DEM-96, DEM-117, DEM-123; Demetrios decoration 2
- Sector V: DEM-40, DEM-205, DEM-238 and probably DEM-249; Demetrios decoration 1b, 4 var., 5a, and 8b, respectively, in addition to a fragment of an Ephesian bowl with a folded acanthus leaf (inv. П-77-118), a fragment of a bowl of the Aiolis B production (AIB-72), and XXX-44 of unknown production place.

These assemblages can be dated to the last quarter of the 2nd century (and perhaps later).

Summing up, we can conclude that the overall composition of the Porthmion assemblage is relatively late, from the second half of the 2nd century until the town was abandoned in the middle of the 1st century. In this respect, the Porthmion assemblage corresponds to that of Myrmekion.

VESSELS FOUND AT PORTHMION

Athens

Figural decoration
ATH-7

Pergamon

Figural decoration
PER-4

Kyme, Workshop A

Suspended garlands
KYA-38

Kyme, MMW: Kirbeis

Calyx with figural decoration
KYB-115

Aiolis, Workshop B

Calyx
AIB-72

Aiolis, Production Place Unknown

Stylized long petals
AIX-28

Ephesos

Figural decoration
EPH-26, EPH-76, EPH-128
Scroll decoration
EPH-180, EPH-181, EPH-205, EPH-221, EPH-226, EPH-227, EPH-236*, EPH-238, EPH-247, EPH-267*, EPH-269*, EPH-288*, EPH-297, EPH-305
Myrtle wreath
EPH-357
Multiple rim friezes
EPH-409, EPH-420–EPH-422, EPH-432, EPH-433, EPH-447*, EPH-458*, EPH-461*, EPH-510*, EPH-512, EPH-517, EPH-521, EPH-526, EPH-527
Plastic pine-cone decoration
EPH-539
Calyx A
EPH-558*, EPH-561*, EPH-575
Calyx A with filled 'nelumbo'
EPH-586, EPH-591, EPH-592
Other calyces with 'nelumbo'
EPH-604*
Calyx B2
EPH-629*
Calyx C
EPH-667
Other calyces
EPH-685*, EPH-701*, EPH-710, EPH-711, EPH-714
Imbricate rounded petals
EPH-743, EPH-745, EPH-787, EPH-800*
Imbricate pointed petals
EPH-829*, EPH-830*, EPH-838, EPH-839, EPH-844*, EPH-867, EPH-869, EPH-888, EPH-905, EPH-914, EPH-916–EPH-918, EPH-928, EPH-929
Plastic long petals
EPH-1022, EPH-1040
Stylized long petals
EPH-1053(?), EPH-1056, EPH-1057, EPH-1062*, EPH-1077, EPH-1079, EPH-1087–EPH-1089
Stylized long petal alternating with acanthus leaf
EPH-1117
Vertical fluting
EPH-1121
Single rim frieze
EPH-1136*, EPH-1141*, EPH-1147*, EPH-1148*, EPH-1172, EPH-1173, EPH-1182, EPH-1213, EPH-1214, EPH-1223*
Base fragments
EPH-1255, EPH-1257

Bosporan Kingdom, Workshop of Demetrios

Decoration 1b
DEM-40, DEM-41
Decoration 1d
DEM-45*, DEM-46*

Decoration 1e
- DEM-55

Decoration 1
- DEM-57*, DEM-58(?)

Decoration 1 or 2
- DEM-59

Decoration 2
- DEM-83, DEM-84, DEM-96, DEM-98, DEM-105*, DEM-106*, DEM-116–DEM-123

Decoration 3a
- DEM-148*, DEM-153, DEM-174–DEM-176

Decoration 3b
- DEM-180*

Decoration 4a
- DEM-181*, DEM-196–DEM-199, DEM-201

Decoration 4a var.
- DEM-205

Decoration 5a
- DEM-210, DEM-213*, DEM-227, DEM-228, DEM-237, DEM-238

Decoration 8a
- DEM-248

Decoration 8b
- DEM-249

Decoration unknown
- DEM-259, DEM-260

Production Place Unknown

Calyx
- XXX-32

Stylized long petals
- XXX-42

Vertical lines separated by dots
- XXX-44

Single rim frieze
- XXX-46*

CHAPTER 27

Tyritake

Along with Myrmekion and Porthmion, Tyritake is among the smaller towns in the Bosporan Kingdom. It is located around 10 km south of Pantikapaion, in Kamyš-Burun (Aršintsevo), the industrial suburb of present-day Kerč. Covering an area of ca. 4.5 ha, the town is situated on a low cape on the northern shore of Lake Čurubaš and close to the Kamyš-Burun Bay. It was settled sometime in the first half of the 6th century and was inhabited at least until the 4th century CE.

The first archaeological exploration of the site took place as early as 1859, led by A. Lucenko, director of the Kerč Museum, whereas the first scientific excavations were initiated in 1932 by J. Marti of the same museum. Between 1935 and 1957, the Leningrad Bosporan Expedition headed by V.F. Gajdukevič carried out systematic excavations in the city. Later, in the 1970s and 80s, the town's territory was investigated by an expedition of the Kerč Museum (D. Kirilin and O. Ševelev), and since 2000, V.N. Zin'ko has reopened excavations in the settlement, from 2008 onward in collaboration with the National Museum in Warsaw (A. Twardecki).

The town was fortified several times, most recently in the Hellenistic period, when a wall with square towers was constructed. Tyritake had a small territory, hemmed in by Pantikapaion to the north and Nymphaion just south of the Čurubaš Lake, and was probably subordinate to Pantikapaion from early times. In the Roman period, the manufacture of fish products, e.g., fish sauce, is amply attested (overview in Højte 2005, 142–148).

Mouldmade Bowls at Tyritake

The MMB included in this chapter were excavated during the years 1933, 1936–1939 (by Marti) and 1946–1947, 1951–1952, 1954–1955 (by Gajdukevič). The first group is kept in the Kerč History and Culture Reserve and has recently been published (Grzegrzółka 2010). Material found after WWII is stored in St Petersburg, IIMK RAN. Some of it was included in Kovalenko's habilitation of 1989,[1] but most is unpublished.

The assemblage of MMB from Tyritake is limited and the number of production places represented is correspondingly small. As is the case in all Pontic assemblages, Ephesian vessels predominate. The second-largest group is constituted by MMB produced by Demetrios: 20 bowls out of 87, corresponding to 23% (ECA+ECB). The most frequent decoration types are 2 and 5a; with the exception of the earliest Decoration 1a, which has not been found, most of the remaining types are represented, even the rare Decoration 8a. As can be seen from Fig. 106, the Tyritake assemblage mirrors that of the other smaller Bosporan towns, in particular Myrmekion, but also Porthmion.

---

1 DEM-43*, DEM-95*, DEM-109*–DEM-111*, DEM-160*, DEM-194*, DEM-223*–DEM-225*: Kovalenko 1989, 404 cats. 192–202.

		Mainland		Aiolis						S Asia Minor		Pontos			
		ATH	COR	PER	KYA	KYB	KYX	AIA	AIB	AIX	EPH	KNI	DEM	GET	XXX	Total
Myrmekion	Sum	1		3	2	8	2		7	4	147	4	80		21	279
	%	0.4		1.1	0.7	2.9	0.7		2.5	1.4	52.7	1.4	28.7		7.5	
Porthmion	Sum	1		1	1	1			1	1	197		45		24	272
	%	0.4		0.4	0.4	0.4			0.4	0.4	72.4		16.5		8.8	
Tyritake	Sum					3				1	49	1	20		13	87
	%					3.4				1.1	56.3	1.1	23.0		14.9	
Average % all Pontic sites		1.6		2.0	1.2	8.5	2.2	0.8	1.7	0.7	65.3	1.6	4.5		9.8	100

FIGURE 106   Composition of the assemblage of MMB at Tyritake compared with those at Myrmekion and Porthmion

VESSELS FOUND AT TYRITAKE

Kyme, MMW: Kirbeis

Calyx
  KYB-230*, KYB-234*
Rim fragment
  KYB-299*

Aiolis, Production Place Unknown

Ivy scroll
  AIX-7

Ephesos

Figural decoration
  EPH-14*, EPH-38
Acanthus-vine scroll
  EPH-225*
Ivy wreath
  EPH-384*
Multiple rim friezes
  EPH-429*, EPH-444*, EPH-486*, EPH-524
Calyx with 'nelumbo'
  EPH-599
Calyx B
  EPH-653*
Other calyces
  EPH-681
Imbricate pointed petals
  EPH-935*
Pendent-semicircle design
  EPH-980

Stylized long petals
  EPH-1075, EPH-1086
Single rim frieze
  EPH-1133*, EPH-1150*, EPH-1152*, EPH-1175*, EPH-1203*
Supplementary shapes
  EPH-1280 (small bowl)

Knidos

Plastic long petals alternating with acanthus
  KNI-60*

Bosporan Kingdom, Workshop of Demetrios

Decoration 1b
  DEM-33*, DEM-36*
Decoration 1c
  DEM-43*
Decoration 2
  DEM-95*, DEM-109*–DEM-111*, DEM-124
Decoration 3a
  DEM-160*
Decoration 4a
  DEM-190, DEM-194*
Decoration 5a
  DEM-223*–DEM-225*, DEM-229, DEM-230, DEM-239
Decoration 5b
  DEM-240*
Decoration 5c
  DEM-241
Decoration 8a
  DEM-247*

CHAPTER 28

Kepoi

Kepoi, 'the Gardens', is an unfortified town on the Asiatic side of the Bosporos. It is currently identified with a settlement in the Taman' Peninsula, on the northern outskirts of the present-day village of Sennaja.

The town was excavated between 1957 and 1972 under the direction of N. Sokol'skij and N. Sorokina (Sokol'skij 1959; 1961a; 1961b; 1962; 1963a; 1963b); from 1984 to 1989 V. Kuznetsov was in charge of the investigations (Kuznetsov 2003). The necropoleis surrounding the settlement site were investigated between 1959 and 1970 (Sorokina 1962; 1963; Sorokina & Sudarev 2002).

Part of the site is submerged, and the preservation of the stratigraphy is in general very poor. Therefore, little is known about the town's lay-out and architecture, and even its history is known in only the broadest terms.

Kepoi was founded in Archaic times and in the Classical period became subject to the Bosporan Kingdom. According to Aischines (3.171–172), Gylon, the grandfather of Demosthenes, received Kepoi as a reward from the Spartokids for handing Nymphaion over to them. Kepoi was continuously settled until its destruction in the 4th century CE, perhaps by invading Huns.

Mouldmade Bowls at Kepoi

The small collection of 43 MMB unearthed at Kepoi (Fig. 107) is (partly?) preserved in the storerooms of the State Historical Museum in Moscow, where, with the kind help of the keeper of the collection, D. Žuravlev, I have been able to study the assemblage. All of the fragments have previously been published in small and inaccurate drawings (Usačeva 1978).

Ten of the vessels came to light in the necropolis. Three Ephesian bowls (EPH-609, EPH-782, EPH-982) were found in the assemblage belonging to the funerary meal of Kurgan 14, together with vessels for cooking, pouring, and eating (Usačeva 1978, fig. 2.5–20), and two more (EPH-608, EPH-636) made up part the assemblage of another funerary meal (square 59A), also with vessels for cooking, pouring, and eating (Usačeva 1978, fig. 3.6–19). An Ephesian amphora (EPH-1308) was found in Tomb 192, and two further Ephesian bowls came to light in Tomb 38 (EPH-871) and Tomb 373 (EPH-810*). Finally, a juglet of Kirbeis was found in Tomb 43 (KYB-320*), along with an Ephesian bowl from the early phase of the Monogram PAR Workshop, with an acanthus-vine scroll over calyx B2 (EPH-188).

The assemblage is too small to be of any statistical validity. Nevertheless, one should note the relatively low proportion of Pontic bowls of Demetrios' production. The same is true at Volna, which is also located in the Asiatic Bosporos. Because the assemblage at both sites is so small, it is difficult to decide whether this has to do with chronology or whether the distance to the production place plays a role. The Ephesian vessels which dominate the assemblage of Kepoi belong mainly to the EC phase, that is, the third quarter of the 2nd century. Among the Demetrios bowls, the most common decorative types are represented: Decoration 2 and 3a as well as Decoration 1b and 5c.

		Mainland		Aiolis						S Asia Minor		Pontos			
		ATH	COR	PER	KYA	KYB	KYX	AIA	AIB	AIX	EPH	KNI	DEM	GET	XXX	Total
Kepoi	Sum					3	1				25	1	5		8	43
	%					7.0	2.3				58.1	2.3	11.6		18.6	
Average % all Pontic sites		1.6		2.0	1.2	8.5	2.2	0.8	1.7	0.7	65.3	1.6	4.5		9.8	100

FIGURE 107   Distribution of MMB at Kepoi according to production place

© PIA GULDAGER BILDE AND SUSAN I. ROTROFF, 2024 | DOI:10.1163/9789004680463_029

VESSELS FOUND AT KEPOI

Kyme, MMW: Kirbeis

Calyx with figural decoration
 KYB-90*
Base fragment
 KYB-260*
Supplementary shapes
 KYB-320* (juglet)

Kyme, Unattributed

Figural decoration
 KYX-15*

Ephesos

Figural decoration
 EPH-108*, EPH-126
Acanthus-vine scroll/calyx
 EPH-188, EPH-190*, EPH-249*
Stylized acanthus scroll
 EPH-276
Calyx B1
 EPH-608, EPH-609
Calyx B2
 EPH-636
Imbricate rounded petals
 EPH-782
Imbricate pointed petals
 EPH-810*, EPH-871

Net pattern
 EPH-982
Single rim frieze
 EPH-1220
Supplementary shapes
 EPH-1308 (amphora); EPH-1337 (guttus)

Knidos

Figural decoration
 KNI-10*

Bosporan Kingdom, Workshop of Demetrios

Decoration 1b
 DEM-32*
Decoration 2
 DEM-112
Decoration 3a
 DEM-172
Decoration 5c
 DEM-243
Decoration unknown
 DEM-256

Production Place Unknown

Calyx
 XXX-56

CHAPTER 29

Ruminskoe (Za Rodinu)

The site is located on the Fontálovskij Peninsula in the Taman' Peninsula, near the modern settlement of Za Rodinu (Krasnodar Region, Russia). It was investigated in the course of a salvage excavation carried out prior to the construction of a local highway. The work was directed by the Moscow scholar N.I. Sokol'skij between 1970 and 1973 (Sokol'skij 1976; AGSP 1984, 86–87, pl. XLVII). Unfortunately, Sokol'skij died before the investigations were completely published. In 2010, work at the site was reopened by the Bosporan expedition of the Institute of Archaeology of the Russian Academy of Sciences, Moscow, directed by N.I. Sudarev, and the site is also included in the topographical work currently being carried out by a joint expedition of the State Historical Museum, Moscow (D. Žuravlev) and the DAI, Berlin (U. Schlotzhauer).[1]

A highly interesting suburban sanctuary was excavated at Za Rodinu in the 1970s. It was constructed in the 3rd century, and by the middle of the 2nd century it had been destroyed and abandoned. In the 120s, a fortified mansion was built over the site. Its core was a square tower located in the northwestern corner of the compound. In ground plan it was divided into four rooms and a corridor (Sokol'skij 1976, fig. 5). During the rule of Asander (47–17 BCE) it was inhabited by a certain Chrysaliskos, whose name is recorded on a base from the site (Sokol'skij 1976, fig. 30). This find has furnished the building with its popular name: the residence or mansion of Chrysaliskos. Later, in the 1st–2nd century CE, the building was further extended as a 'fort'.

Because the excavator died before the analysis of the excavation was complete, there is much that we do not understand about this highly interesting building complex. According to information from D. Žuravlev, the MMB derive from the 'western peristyle' (Sokol'skij 1976, fig. 5). In its original form, this consisted of a series of banqueting rooms in the trapezoidal stoa surrounding the tholos-shaped temple (Sokol'skij 1976, fig. 6). However, the rooms were also included in the late fortress and most likely also in the residence of Chrysaliskos and its precursor. With the exception of EPH-75*, which belongs to the EE-EC production, and which was also excavated in a different year than the others, it is likely that the MMB can be associated with the construction or use of the fortified mansion after the 120s, but undoubtedly before it became a stronghold of a Mithridatic 'governor', after the Bosporos was incorporated into the Pontic Kingdom, around the turn of the 2nd and 1st century.[2]

Mouldmade Bowls at Ruminskoe

Through the kindness of D. Žuravlev (State Historical Museum, Moscow) it has been possible to include 11 fragments from Sokol'skij's excavation in the present publication. Even though it is just a handful, I have found it worthwhile to include them, because, to date, not a single scrap of a MMB has been published from the site. With the exception of a single fragment from 1971, they were all found in 1972; irrespective of the year, they carry the same inventory number: 103991.

Even though the assemblage from Ruminskoe is small, it is striking that Demetrios' Pontic production accounts for almost half of it (Fig. 108). The two types of decoration represented are those which prove to be amongst the most common at other sites as well (see Chapter 18): Decoration 2 and 5a. All the remaining fragments are Ephesian.

---

[1] For the latter, see https://archive.is/20130414172712/http://www.dainst.org/index_679f6b74bb1f14a184730017f0000011_en.html [accessed 30 October 2023].

[2] The majority of the terracottas attributed to the residence of Chrysaliskos belong to the Mithridatic phase: Sokol'skij 1976, figs. 55–58. The same is the case of the Pergamene skyphos published several times by D. Žuravlev (1995; Zhuravlev 1998; 2000). Thus, they have nothing to do with Chrysaliskos himself.

		Mainland		Aiolis							S Asia Minor		Pontos			
		ATH	COR	PER	KYA	KYB	KYX	AIA	AIB	AIX	EPH	KNI	DEM	GET	XXX	Total
Ruminskoe	Sum										6		5			11
Average % all Pontic sites		1.6		2.0	1.2	8.5	2.2	0.8	1.7	0.7	65.3	1.6	4.5		9.8	100

FIGURE 108 Distribution of MMB at Ruminskoe according to production place

VESSELS FOUND AT RUMINSKOE

Ephesos

Figural decoration
  EPH-75*
Multiple rim friezes
  EPH-410*
Calyx with 'nelumbo'
  EPH-597*
Imbricate pointed petals
  EPH-907*

Bosporan Kingdom, Workshop of Demetrios

Decoration 2
  DEM-92*, DEM-107*, DEM-108*
Decoration 5a
  DEM-214*, DEM-222*

CHAPTER 30

Volna 1 (Severo Zelenskoe)

Volna 1 is one of the largest settlements in the Taman' peninsula, covering an area of 45 hectares. Its ancient name is unknown. Located southwest of the modern town of Taman' and about 4 km inland from Cape Panagia, it was advantageously situated at the junction of major routes to crossings of the Kuban and Kerč channels. Remains of a Greek city, founded about 575, overlie an indigenous settlement, with a large cemetery nearby. The Greek town reached its acme between the 5th and the 2nd centuries, but continued to be inhabited thereafter. Many years of excavation have uncovered remains ranging in date from the 12th c. BCE to the Medieval period (Bochkovoy et al. 2019; Dan et al. 2020).

Mouldmade Bowls at Volna 1

Bosporan MMB are a rarity at Volna: only two fragments of 37 are of Pontic origin (Fig. 109). They are of the decorative types which are amongst the most common at other sites as well (see Chapter 18): Decoration 3a and 5a.

The assemblage is completely dominated by Ephesian vessels of the EC phase. Figural decoration is rare; one bowl features an Amazonomachy (EPH-82*) and one further bowl displays figural decoration too poorly preserved for identification (EPH-565). Otherwise, the most common decorative schemes are multiple rim friezes (EPH-436*, EPH-454*, EPH-503*, EPH-522) and myrtle wreaths (EPH-326*, EPH-366), and a substantial number of bowls feature calyx B (EPH-326*, EPH-620*, EPH-645*, EPH-652*, EPH-655*).

		Mainland			Aiolis						S Asia Minor		Pontos			
		ATH	COR	PER	KYA	KYB	KYX	AIA	AIB	AIX	EPH	KNI	DEM	GET	XXX	Total
Volna 1	Sum										34		2		1	37
	%										91.9		5.4		2.7	
Average % all Pontic sites		1.6		2.0	1.2	8.5	2.2	0.8	1.7	0.7	65.3	1.6	4.5		9.8	100

FIGURE 109   Distribution of MMB at Volna 1 according to production place

VESSELS FOUND AT VOLNA 1

Ephesos

Figural decoration
 EPH-82*
Acanthus-vine scroll
 EPH-230
Myrtle wreath
 EPH-326*, EPH-366
Suspended garlands
 EPH-392*
Multiple rim friezes
 EPH-436*, EPH-454*, EPH-503*, EPH-522
Calyx A
 EPH-565, EPH-576*, EPH-577*
Calyx B2
 EPH-620*, EPH-645*, EPH-652*, EPH-655*
Calyx with funnel-shaped flowers
 EPH-690*

Imbricate pointed petals
 EPH-819, EPH-825*, EPH-831*
Stylized long petals
 EPH-1064*
Single rim frieze
 EPH-1236*
Base fragment
 EPH-1258*

Bosporan Kingdom, Workshop of Demetrios

Decoration 3a
 DEM-165*
Decoration 5a
 DEM-231*

Appendices

APPENDIX 1

Getting Started

Here I offer some tips and ideas for those planning to embark on the study of a collection of MMB. If you are new to the field, I hope you will find at least some of them useful.

Classification

First of all, don't be overwhelmed by the bewildering variety of the sherds in front of you. There is method in it, but the devil is in the details. Divide material by a combination of decoration, fabric, and shape in order to make the broad classifications. Almost every major city in the late Hellenistic world produced MMB. Most localities will contain material from two major production centres: Ephesos and the local (or perhaps regional) main production. To this group (often accounting for up to 90%) can then be added a group of sundry production places, normally represented as single pieces. Unless you work in a locality in Greece itself, Athenian production will account for about 10%. The sundry group can be dealt with when the majority of the fragments have been processed. Do not get caught up in the many rim fragments. Classification of decoration should – to my mind – first of all take its point of departure in the intended decoration of the main body zone. In the case of the Ephesian bowls, the rim pattern and type of calyx employed are secondary elements.

Recording

I normally measure the height of the fragment and its wall thickness and, in the case of rims, the outer diameter and the height of the rim over the mould (the top of the mouldmade section is usually visible as a small ridge slightly above the rim frieze). I also record the outer diameter of the base. The wall thickness is tricky, because the wall frequently varies enormously, so this measurement may not have much significance after all. In the case of the Ephesian vessels, the thinnest place is normally immediately below the point where the wall curves in. So don't measure that, even though this is where almost all rim fragments break. I try to take some kind of average measurement, which by and large will tell something of the character of the vessel. But again, I am not very confident of the usefulness of this measurement. Much more useful is the percentage of preservation, especially of the rim, because this is a good indicator of the probable accuracy of the estimate of the rim diameter; obviously, the greater the percentage preserved, the more accurate the estimate. As a matter of convention, I record the number of fragments that make up the individual vessel. But when working with the body of material, every vessel counts only as one, no matter how many fragments it consists of.

Drawing

Drawing MMB presents multiple challenges: fewest, if you work with small sherds, many if you have at your disposal complete vessels. Making the profile is easy, because the MMB is normally a very uncomplicated shape. Nevertheless, use a comb-like template (a profile gauge or contour gauge) to make the profile. These tools can be bought in most hardware stores, but not all are of the same quality. The best is the English Maco, featuring a large number of slats of a considerable height, but this is an old woodworker's instrument and almost impossible to find. I have found a good alternative, a fine Japanese steel gauge available from the company Dieter Schmid Fine Tools in Berlin (http://www.fine-tools.com/kontur.htm#ziel306930) for 13 Euro (2009; [Ed. 14.90 as of 2020]). This functions well for me. Give it a drop of acid-free oil before you start using it, so that the slats will slide more easily. It is not so difficult to crush a small sherd with a stiff template! Use transparent tracing paper – in a moment you'll understand why.

With the profile done (left or right is a matter of personal taste), the fun begins, because now you will be trying to do something that cannot be done, namely make a two-dimensional representation of an object that is not only curving vertically and horizontally, but also has figures in relief. Since this cannot be done with complete accuracy, you must choose a way that will provide the best idea of the image. Most difficult to make – and also not the most informative – is a drawing in which the draughtsman attempts to show the foreshortening. This will give a good and fairly correct impression of the rim frieze(s), but most of the decoration – especially of the lower body – will be lost in the bowl's curvature. It is better to roll out the drawing in the way attempted, e.g., by Laumonier's artist – but even this will take some compromises, because the distance between elements in the upper part of the vessel will be unrealistically wide because of the curve of the vessel (especially true for Ephesian vessels). Nevertheless, this is to be preferred when dealing with complete or near-complete vessels. With fragments, I prefer to flatten the sherd in the drawing, so again the image is not completely realistic. One should not try to compromise by, e.g., straightening the rim frieze and letting the body

© PIA GULDAGER BILDE AND SUSAN I. ROTROFF, 2024 | DOI:10.1163/9789004680463_032

decoration curve. It is better to let all elements curve. With rim fragments, the curving top will for the most part be shown over the horizontal line marking the diameter. If you want to provide a realistic depiction of the individual stamps, you will need a high degree of precision in your drawing. An eight-petalled rosette can take many forms, and since they vary from workshop to workshop, it actually matters how the individual stamp looks. In order to trace the design as precisely as possible (as well as to capture the relationship between the stamps) I have found it very useful to make a rubbing of the vessel employing small sheets of cigarette paper. Hold the paper firmly against the surface of the bowl, smear some strokes of a very soft pencil (7B or softer) onto its surface, and rub the colour with your finger into every small crevice of the surface, and voilá, you'll have a perfect image of (a small section of) the decoration. This small sheet can then be positioned under your tracing paper at its proper place. Piecing together the design from a number of small sheets will require some adjustment of the small pieces in order to make up for the vessel's convexity. This cannot be helped. No matter how hard you try, it will be an ideal drawing, not an exact representation. But at least the design will be close to perfect. Don't throw out the sheets. Give them the same number as the sherds and store them. They will eventually add up to a real stamp library much more 'true' than any drawing, and they will be an invaluable source of stamp style, size, and proportions.

APPENDIX 2

Laumonier 1977 Concordance

In order to organize the vast collection of largely undocumented and unlabeled pottery that confronted him as he began his study of the mouldmade bowls on Delos, Laumonier assigned study numbers to each of the pieces as he worked through the material. It is these 'Laumonier' numbers, rather than sequential catalogue numbers, that identify the objects in Laumonier 1977. The decision to dispense with a sequentially numbered catalogue makes it difficult to use the book, and particularly difficult to move back and forth between text and illustrations. The list below, extracted from the data base created for the study of the material presented in the present book, offers a solution to this difficulty. The data base itself includes the objects in Laumonier 1977 and much more: all of the material from the 11 Black Sea sites, along with an even larger collection of comparative material.

This concordance is based on Laumonier's "Table des nos. du catalogue répartis dans les divers ateliers, séries ou catgories" (1977, 489–513). That table lists Laumonier's numbers sequentially (as here), but refers each number only to its attribution or classification; it is a minor aid to finding the text describing the numbered object, but only a very minor one. The present concordance gives instead the page and plate numbers for each object number. Fragments without Laumonier numbers are identified by their excavation inventory numbers and appear at the end of the concordance.

[Ed. I have expanded this introduction to put the concordance in context for those not familiar with Laumonier's volume.]

1, p. 407, pl. 95
2, p. 292, pl. 67
3, p. 78, pl. 17, 131
4, p. 190, pl. 42
5, p. 221, pls. 49, 132
6, p. 191, pl. 42
7, p. 190, pl. 42
8, p. 475, pl. 110
9, p. 190
10, p. 217, pl. 48
11, p. 191, pl. 42
12, p. 474, pl. 110
13, p. 190, pls. 42, 132
13 bis, p. 191
14, p. 257, pl. 58
14 bis, p. 257
15, p. 476, pl. 110
16, p. 475, pl. 110
17, p. 293, pl. 68
18, p. 191
19, p. 191, pl. 42
20, p. 475, pl. 110
21, p. 475, pl. 110
22, p. 221
23, p. 292, pl. 67
24, p. 191, pl. 42
25, p. 468, pl. 108
26, p. 468, pl. 108

26 bis, p. 468
27, p. 292, pl. 67
28, p. 240, pl. 54
29, pp. 475–476, pl. 110
30, p. 210, pl. 17
31, p. 365
32, p. 476
33, p. 476, pl. 110
34, p. 221, pl. 49
35, p. 398
36, p. 293, pl. 68
37, p. 189
38, p. 474, pl. 110
39, p. 468, pl. 108
40, p. 190, pl. 42
41, p. 219, pl. 48
42, p. 190, pl. 42
43, p. 217, pl. 48
44, p. 217
45, p. 210, pl. 17
45 bis, p. 210
46, p. 476, pl. 110
47, p. 191, pl. 42
49, p. 293, pl. 68
50, p. 476, pl. 110
51, p. 190
52, p. 468, pl. 108
53, p. 469, pl. 108

54, p. 190, pl. 42
55, p. 189, pl. 41
56, p. 476, pl. 110
57, p. 476, pl. 110
58, p. 462, pl. 106
59, p. 475, pl. 110
60, p. 365, pl. 88
61, p. 190, pl. 42
62, p. 474, pls. 110, 134
63, p. 398, pl. 94
64, p. 398, pl. 94
65, p. 474, pl. 110
66, p. 398, pl. 94
67, p. 89, pl. 19
68, p. 387, pl. 88
69, p. 190
70, p. 469, pl. 108
71, p. 476, pl. 110
72, p. 470, pl. 108
73, p. 286, pl. 66
74, p. 190, pl. 42
75, p. 468, pl. 108
76, p. 468, pl. 108
77, p. 212, pl. 17
78, p. 212
79, p. 26, pl. 1
80, p. 468, pl. 108
81, p. 474, pl. 110

82, p. 474, pl. 110
83, p. 433, pl. 101
84, p. 187, pl. 41
85, p. 470, pl. 109
86, p. 461, pl. 106
87, p. 472, pl. 109
88, p. 258, pl. 58
89, p. 290, pl. 67
90, p. 226, pl. 50
91, p. 41, pl. 7
92, p. 193, pl. 42
93, p. 290, pl. 67
94, p. 221, pl. 49
95, p. 251, pl. 56
96, p. 251
97, p. 193
98, p. 44, pl. 8
99, p. 467, pl. 108
100, p. 189, pl. 41
101, p. 187, pl. 41
102, p. 470, pl. 109
103, p. 189
104, p. 188
105, p. 188
106, p. 189
107, p. 189, pl. 41
108, p. 188, pl. 41
109, p. 187, pl. 41

© PIA GULDAGER BILDE AND SUSAN I. ROTROFF, 2024 | DOI:10.1163/9789004680463_033

110, p. 188, pl. 41
111, p. 187, pl. 41
112, p. 472, pl. 109
113, p. 471, pl. 109
114, p. 187, pl. 41
115, p. 45, pl. 9
116, p. 45, pl. 9
117, p. 45, pl. 9
118, p. 45
119, p. 45
120, p. 187, pl. 41
121, p. 189, pl. 41
122, p. 188, pl. 41
122 bis, p. 188
123, p. 219, pl. 48
124, p. 189, pl. 41
125, p. 472, pl. 109
126, p. 472, pl. 109
127, p. 397, pl. 94
128, p. 219, pl. 48
129, p. 362, pl. 87
130, p. 470, pl. 109
131, p. 337
132, p. 337, pl. 81
133, p. 337
134, p. 338, pl. 81
135, p. 338, pl. 81
136, p. 338
137, p. 227, pl. 51
138, p. 291
139, p. 472, pl. 109
140, p. 351
141, p. 371
142, p. 476, pl. 110
143, p. 291, pl. 67
144, p. 44
145, p. 74, pl. 16
146, p. 240, pl. 54
147, p. 459, pl. 106
148, p. 472, pl. 109
149, p. 472, pl. 109
150, p. 472, pl. 109
151, p. 381, pl. 91
152, p. 432, pl. 100
153, p. 290, pl. 67
154, p. 290, pl. 67
155, p. 290
156, p. 473, pl. 109
157, p. 74, pl. 16
158, p. 193
159, p. 365, pl. 88

160, p. 469, pl. 108
161, p. 365, pl. 88
162, p. 469, pl. 108
163, p. 117, pl. 27
164, p. 377, pl. 90
165, p. 402, pls. 94, 134
166, p. 438, pl. 101
167, p. 471, pl. 109
168, p. 294, pl. 68
169, p. 384, pl. 92
170, p. 75, pl. 16
171, p. 437, pl. 101
172, p. 338, pl. 81
173, p. 338
174, p. 472
175, p. 188, pl. 41
176, p. 188
177, p. 472, pl. 109
178, p. 472
179, p. 189, pl. 41
180, p. 472, pl. 109
181, p. 471, pl. 109
182, p. 337, pl. 81
183, p. 45, pl. 9
185, p. 459, pl. 106
186, p. 26, pl. 1
187, p. 220, pl. 49
188, p. 74, pl. 16
189, p. 189, pls. 41, 132
190, p. 469, pl. 108
191, p. 190
192, p. 190
193, p. 190
194, p. 191
195, p. 469
196, p. 475, pl. 110
198, p. 474, pl. 110
199, p. 338, pl. 81
199 bis, p. 338
200, p. 294
201, p. 365, pl. 88
202, p. 365, pl. 88
203, p. 290, pl. 67
204, p. 469
205, p. 467, pl. 108
206, p. 380, pl. 91
207, p. 471, pl. 109
208, p. 338, pl. 81
209, p. 226, pl. 50
210, p. 226, pl. 50
211, p. 188, pl. 41

212, p. 190
213, p. 291, pl. 67
214, p. 398, pl. 84
215, p. 476, pl. 110
216, p. 191
217, p. 474, pl. 110
218, p. 472, pl. 109
219, p. 472, pl. 109
220, p. 290, pl. 67
221, p. 472
222, p. 290
223, p. 290, pl. 67
224, p. 189, pl. 41
225, p. 44, pl. 8
226, p. 193, pl. 42
227, p. 338
228, p. 220, pl. 49
229, p. 468, pl. 108
230, p. 475, pl. 110
231, p. 437, pl. 101
232, p. 385, pl. 92
233, p. 473, pl. 109
234, p. 380, pl. 91
235, p. 291
236, p. 475, pl. 110
237, p. 217, pl. 48
238, p. 191, pl. 42
239, p. 217, pl. 48
239 bis, p. 217
240, p. 191, pl. 42
241, p. 475
242, p. 396, pl. 93
243, p. 191
244, p. 189, pl. 41
245, p. 189, pl. 41
246, p. 191
247, p. 189, pl. 41
248, p. 475, pl. 110
249, p. 189
250, p. 189, pl. 41
251, p. 369, pl. 89
252, p. 469, pl. 108
253, p. 467, pl. 108
254, p. 187, pl. 41
255, p. 471, pl. 109
256, p. 189, pl. 41
257, p. 469, pl. 108
258, p. 370, pl. 89
259, p. 471
260, p. 471, pl. 109
261, p. 189, pl. 41

262, p. 472, pl. 109
263, p. 362, pl. 87
264, p. 45, pl. 9
265, p. 45
266, p. 472, pl. 109
267, p. 190
268, p. 292
269, p. 189, pl. 41
270, p. 45
271, p. 74, pl. 16
272, p. 193, pl. 42
274, p. 45, pl. 9
275, p. 467, pl. 108
276, p. 219, pl. 48
277, p. 472, pl. 109
278, p. 189, pl. 41
279, p. 189
280, p. 190
281, p. 396, pl. 93
282, p. 189, pl. 41
283, p. 189, pl. 41
284, p. 174, pl. 38
285, p. 293, pl. 68
286, p. 191, pl. 42
287, p. 470, pl. 109
288, p. 46, pl. 9
289, p. 292, pl. 67
290, p. 291, pl. 67
291, p. 407, pl. 95
292, p. 409, pl. 95
293, p. 409
294, p. 410, pl. 96
295, p. 257, pl. 58
296, p. 189
297, p. 330, pl. 79
298, p. 187
298 bis, p. 474, pl. 110
299, p. 226, pl. 50
300, p. 190, pl. 42
301, p. 474, pl. 110
302, p. 189, pl. 41
303, p. 56, pl. 11
304, p. 226, pl. 50
305, p. 225, pl. 50 (not labeled)
306, p. 112, pl. 25
307, p. 212, pl. 17
308, p. 83, pl. 18
310, p. 303, pl. 71
311, p. 74, pl. 16
312, p. 432, pl. 100

313, p. 83, pl. 18, 131
316, p. 193
317, p. 193
318, p. 473, pl. 109
318 bis, p. 365
319, p. 292
320, p. 226, pl. 50
321, p. 475
322, p. 92
323, p. 191, pl. 42
324, p. 103, pl. 23
325, p. 217, pl. 48
326, p. 174, pl. 38
327, p. 291, pl. 67
328, p. 291, pl. 67
329, p. 188, pl. 41
330, p. 291, pl. 67
331, p. 466
332, p. 293, pl. 68
333, p. 46, pl. 9
334, p. 473, pl. 109
335, p. 292, fig. 1, pl. 67
336, p. 469, pl. 108
337, p. 189
338, p. 227, fig. 1, pl. 50
339, p. 338, fig. 1, pl. 81
340, p. 471, pl. 109
341, p. 476, pl. 110
342, p. 192, pl. 42
343, p. 180
344, p. 469, pl. 108
345, p. 476, pl. 110
346, p. 471, pl. 109
347, p. 45
348, p. 438, pl. 101
348 bis, p. 292, pl. 67
349, p. 292, pl. 67
350, p. 330, pl. 79
351, p. 330, pl. 79
352, p. 330, pls. 79, 133
353, p. 111, pl. 25
354, p. 434, pl. 101
355, p. 67, pl. 14
356, p. 145, pl. 33
357, p. 175, pls. 38, 132
358, p. 110, pl. 25
359, p. 183, pl. 40
360, p. 359, pl. 86
361, p. 315, pl. 74
363, p. 70, pls. 15, 131
364, p. 70, pl. 15

365, p. 150, pl. 34, 132
366, pp. 105–106, pls. 24, 120, 132
367, p. 83, pls. 18, 131
369, p. 114, fig. 1, pl. 25
370, p. 110, pl. 25
371, p. 26, pls. 1, 131
372, p. 151, pl. 34
373, p. 224, pls. 50, 133
374, p. 386, pl. 92
375, p. 134, pl. 30
376, p. 136, pl. 30
377, p. 24, pl. 1
378, p. 363, pl. 87
379, p. 428, pl. 100
380, p. 371, pls. 89, 133
381, p. 301, pl. 70
382, p. 239, pl. 54
383, p. 83, pl. 18
384, p. 154, pls. 34, 124
385, p. 156, pl. 35
386, p. 429, pl. 100
388, p. 137, pl. 31
389, p. 150
390, p. 429, pl. 100
391, p. 138, pl. 31
392, p. 141, pl. 32
393, p. 232, pl. 52
394, p. 144
395, pp. 123–124, pls. 28, 132
396, p. 141, pl. 32
397, p. 145, pl. 33
398, p. 153, pl. 34
399, p. 134, pl. 30
400, p. 224, pl. 50
401, p. 152, pl. 34
402, p. 152, pl. 34
403, p. 155, pl. 35
404, p. 224, pl. 50
405, p. 153, pl. 34
406, p. 320, pl. 75
407, p. 85, pl. 19
408, p. 154, pl. 34
409, p. 429, pl. 100
410, p. 64, pl. 13
411, p. 135
412, p. 70, pl. 15
413, p. 176, pl. 38
414, p. 373, pl. 90
415, p. 361, pl. 87
416, p. 156, pl. 35

417, p. 315, pl. 74
418, p. 320, pl. 75
419, p. 303, pl. 71
420, p. 135, pl. 30
421, p. 185, pl. 40
422, p. 318, pl. 74
423, p. 239, pl. 54
424, p. 155, pl. 35
425, p. 429, pl. 100
426, p. 216, pl. 48
427, p. 142, pl. 32 (not labeled)
428, p. 31, pl. 2
429, p. 429, pl. 100
430, p. 186, pl. 40
431, p. 143. pl. 32 (not labeled)
432, p. 239, pl. 54
433, p. 320, pl. 75
434, p. 184, pl. 40
435, p. 24, pl. 1
436, p. 152
437, p. 154, pl. 34
438, p. 157, pl. 35
439, p. 111, pl. 25
440, p. 35, pl. 4
441, p. 145, pl. 33
442, p. 361, pl. 87
443, p. 224, pl. 50
444, p. 135
445, p. 210, pl. 17
446, p. 135, pl. 30
447, p. 138
448, p. 224, pl. 50
449, p. 135, pl. 30
451, p. 143, pls. 32 (not labeled), 123
452, p. 302, pl. 71
453, p. 138, pl. 31
454, p. 321, pl. 75
455, p. 134
456, p. 315
457, p. 147, pl. 33
458, p. 267, pl. 61
459, p. 376, pl. 90
460, p. 428, pl. 100
461, p. 77, pl. 17
462, p. 115, pl. 26
463, p. 186, pls. 40, 126
464, p. 224, pl. 50
466, p. 112, pls. 25, 121
467, p. 135, pl. 30
468, p. 155, pl. 35

469, p. 318, pl. 74
470, p. 124, pl. 28
471, p. 149, pl. 33
472, p. 143, pl. 32 (not labeled)
473, p. 302, pl. 71
474, p. 361, pl. 87
475, p. 330, pl. 79
476, p. 320, pl. 75
477, p. 31, pls. 2, 114
478, p. 147, pl. 33
479, p. 224, pl. 50
480, p. 367, pl. 89
481, p. 152, pl. 34
484, p. 430, pl. 100
486, p. 315, pl. 74
487, p. 32, pl. 2
488, p. 35, pl. 4
489, p. 111, pls. 25, 121, 132
490, p. 185, pl. 40
491, p. 301
492, p. 268, pl. 62
493, p. 138
494, p. 430
495, p. 135
496, p. 209, pl. 17
497, p. 137
498, p. 135
499, p. 135
500, p. 135
501, p. 134
502, p. 145, pl. 33
503, p. 144
504, p. 153, pl. 34
505, p. 153
506, p. 37, pl. 4
507, p. 429, pl. 100
509, p. 134, pl. 30
510, p. 428, pl. 100
511, p. 318, pl. 74
512, p. 367, pl. 89
513, p. 430, pl. 100
514, p. 183
515, p. 155, pl. 35
516, p. 156, pl. 35
517, p. 115, pl. 26
518, p. 299, pl. 70
519, p. 320, pl. 75
520, p. 110, pl. 25
521, p. 24, pl. 1
522, p. 23, pl. 1

523, p. 144, pl. 32
524, p. 135
525, p. 141, pl. 32
526, p. 139, pl. 31
527, p. 147
528, p. 138, pl. 31
529, p. 23, pl. 1
530, p. 176, pl. 38
531, p. 23, pl. 1
532, p. 239, pl. 54
533, p. 160, pl. 36
534, p. 361, pl. 87
535, p. 25, pl. 1
537, p. 64
538, p. 176, pl. 38
539, p. 225, pl. 50
540, p. 359
541, p. 373, pl. 90
542, p. 430, pl. 100
543, p. 267, pl. 62
544, p. 301, pl. 70
545, p. 137
546, p. 141, pl. 32
547, p. 316, pl. 74
548, p. 163, pl. 36
549, p. 112, pl. 25
550, p. 434, pl. 101
551, p. 96, pls. 21, 119
552, p. 429, pl. 100
553, p. 148, pl. 33
554, p. 433, pl. 100
555, p. 432, pl. 100
556, p. 155
557, p. 430, pl. 100
558, p. 142
559, p. 316, pl. 74
560, p. 83, pl. 18
561, p. 64, pl. 13
562, p. 360, pl. 86
563, p. 304, pl. 71
564, p. 95, pl. 21
565, p. 428, pl. 100
566, p. 137, pl. 30
567, p. 163, pl. 36
568, p. 267, pl. 61
569, p. 430, pl. 100
570, p. 210, pl. 17
571, p. 151, pl. 34
572, p. 318, pl. 74
573, p. 114, pl. 25
574, p. 428

575, p. 384, pl. 92
576, p. 359, pl. 86
577, p. 431
578, p. 113, pl. 25
579, p. 431, pl. 100
580, p. 431, pl. 100
581, p. 433, pl. 100
582, p. 433, pl. 100
583, p. 315, pl. 74
584, p. 184
587, p. 28, pl. 2
588, p. 176, pl. 38
589, p. 140, pls. 31, 132
590, p. 331, pl. 79
591, p. 110
592, p. 355, pl. 85
593, p. 110, pl. 25
594, p. 144, pl. 32
595, p. 355, pl. 85
596, p. 320, pl. 75
597, p. 134, pl. 30
598, p. 433, pl. 100
599, p. 112, pls. 25, 121
600, p. 235, pl. 53
601, p. 110, pl. 25
602, p. 144, pl. 32
603, p. 111, pl. 25
604, p. 26, pl. 1
604 (duplicate number), p. 32, pl. 2
605, p. 331, pl. 79
607, p. 384, pl. 92
608, p. 32, pl. 2
609, p. 328, pl. 78
612, p. 112, pls. 25, 121
613, p. 60, pl. 12
616, pp. 104–105, pl. 24
617, p. 105, pl. 24
618, p. 328, pl. 78
619, p. 329, pl. 79
620, p. 186
623, p. 379, pl. 91
625 bis, p. 64
626, p. 353, pl. 85
627, p. 28, pl. 2
628, p. 112, pl. 25
629, p. 186, pls. 40, 126
630, p. 154, pl. 34
631, p. 186, pl. 40
632, p. 81, pls. 18, 119
633, p. 67, pl. 14

634, pp. 266–267, fig. 1, pl. 61
635, p. 268, pl. 62
636, p. 26, pls. 1, 113
637, p. 423
638, p. 301, pl. 70
640, p. 106, pl. 24
641, p. 318, pl. 74
642, p. 329, pl. 78
643, p. 385, pl. 92
644, p. 135
645, p. 147, pl. 33
646, p. 315, pl. 74
647, p. 302, pl. 71
648, p. 27, pl. 1
649, p. 138
650, p. 23, pl. 1
651, p. 365, pl. 88
652, p. 303, pl. 71
653, p. 393, pl. 93
654, p. 301, pl. 70
655, p. 88, pl. 19
656, p. 141, pl. 32
657, p. 362, pl. 87
658, p. 239, pl. 54
659, p. 347, pls. 83, 133
660, p. 153
661, p. 317, pl. 74
662, p. 162
663, p. 221, pl. 49
664, p. 137, pl. 31
665, p. 162, pl. 36
666, p. 184, pl. 40
667, p. 27, pl. 2
668, p. 150, pl. 34
669, p. 184, pl. 40
670, p. 267, pl. 62
671, p. 144, pl. 32
672, p. 433, pl. 100
673, p. 112, pls. 25, 121
675, p. 360
677, p. 414, pl. 97
678, p. 429, pl. 100
680, p. 373, pl. 90
681, p. 35, pl. 4
682, p. 31, fig. 1, pls. 2, 114
685, p. 141, pl. 32
686, p. 164, pl. 36
687, p. 236, pl. 53
688, p. 161, pl. 36
689, p. 161
690, p. 158, pl. 36

691, p. 431
692, p. 161, pl. 36
693, p. 431
694, p. 148, pl. 33
695, p. 197, pl. 43
696, p. 149
697, p. 164
698, p. 149
699, p. 136, pl. 30
700, p. 86, pl. 19
701, p. 64, pl. 13
702, p. 434, pl. 101
703, p. 136, pl. 30
704, p. 147, pl. 33
705, p. 135
706, p. 135
707, p. 135
708, p. 135
709, p. 161, 184
710, p. 135
711, p. 158, pl. 36
712, p. 197, pl. 43
713, p. 194, pl. 43
714, p. 139, pl. 31
715, p. 136, pl. 30
716, p. 85, pl. 19
717, p. 85, pl. 19
718, p. 158, pl. 36
719, p. 117, pl. 27
720, p. 124, pl. 28
721, p. 431
722, p. 432, pl. 100
723, p. 373, pl. 90
724, p. 373, pl. 90
725, p. 113, pl. 25
726, p. 148
727, p. 459, pl. 106
728, p. 316, pl. 74
729, p. 435, pl. 101
730, p. 27
731, p. 435, pl. 101
732, p. 325, pl. 77
733, p. 299, pl. 70
734, p. 435, pl. 101
735, p. 301
736, p. 44, pl. 8
737, p. 36, pl. 4
738, p. 302, pl. 71
739, p. 184
740, p. 184
741, p. 184, pl. 40

LAUMONIER 1977 CONCORDANCE

742, p. 184, pl. 40
743, p. 401, pl. 94
744, p. 299, pl. 70
745, p. 299
746, p. 84, pl. 18
747, p. 89, pl. 19
748, p. 432, pl. 100
749, p. 405
750, p. 137
751, p. 137
752, p. 137
753, p. 155
754, p. 141, pl. 32
755, p. 427
756, p. 157, pl. 35
757, p. 316, pl. 74
758, p. 301, pl. 70
759, p. 301
760, p. 265, pl. 60
761, p. 266, pl. 61
762, p. 432, pl. 100
763, p. 145, pl. 33
764, p. 145, pl. 33
765, p. 432, pl. 100
768, p. 85, pl. 18
769, p. 82, pl. 18
770, p. 83, pl. 18
771, p. 186
772, p. 185, pls. 40, 126
773, p. 234, pl. 52
774, p. 118, pl. 27
777, p. 302
778, p. 158
779, p. 142, pl. 32
780, p. 209
781, p. 135
782, p. 137
783, p. 138
784, p. 135
785, p. 63
786, p. 209
787, p. 86
788, p. 86, pl. 19
789, p. 294, pl. 68
790, p. 153
792, p. 161, pl. 36
793, p. 432, pl. 100
795, p. 265, pl. 60
798, p. 186
799, p. 145
799 **bis**, p. 209

799 **ter**, p. 184
801, p. 28, pl. 2
802, p. 363, pl. 87
803, p. 138
804, p. 144, pl. 32
805, p. 137
806, p. 137
807, p. 187, pl. 40
808, p. 64, pl. 13
809, p. 157, pl. 35
810, p. 157, pl. 35
811, p. 155, pl. 35
812, p. 373, pl. 90
813, p. 375, pl. 90
814, p. 124, pl. 28
815, p. 124, pl. 28
816, p. 148, pl. 33
817, p. 145, pl. 33
818, p. 271, pl. 63
819, p. 63, pl. 13
820, p. 147, pl. 33
821, p. 316
822, p. 24
823, p. 145, pl. 33
824, p. 147
825, p. 149
826, p. 428, pl. 100
827, p. 135
828, p. 135
829, p. 429
830, p. 138
831, p. 135
832, p. 411, pl. 96
833, p. 64, pl. 13
834, p. 320, pl. 75
835, p. 147
836, p. 24
837, p. 142, pl. 32
838, p. 135
839, p. 363, pl. 87
840, p. 135
841, p. 149
842, p. 155, pl. 34
843, p. 373
845, p. 210, pl. 17
846, p. 430, pl. 100
847, p. 162, pl. 36
848, p. 318, pl. 74
849, p. 113, pl. 25
850, p. 186
851, p. 225, pl. 50

852, p. 164, pl. 36
853, p. 223, pl. 50
854, p. 112, pl. 25
855, p. 225, pl. 50
856, p. 303, pl. 71
857, p. 221, pl. 49
858, p. 302
859, p. 111
860, p. 271
861, p. 112
862, p. 148, pl. 33
863, p. 316
865, p. 82, pl. 18
866, p. 160, pl. 36
867, p. 111, pl. 25
868, p. 83, pl. 18
869, p. 428, pl. 100
870, p. 267, pl. 61
871, p. 267, pl. 61
872, p. 179, pl. 39
873, p. 318, pl. 75
874, p. 319, pl. 75
875, p. 267, pl. 61
877, p. 107, pl. 24
878, p. 172, pl. 38
879, p. 97, pl. 21
880, p. 137, pl. 30
881, p. 301, pl. 70
882, p. 124, pls. 28, 123
883, p. 135
884, p. 137, pl. 31
885, p. 86, pl. 19
885 **bis**, p. 383, pl. 92
886, p. 89
887, p. 138
888, p. 149
889, p. 433, pl. 100
890, p. 135
891, p. 134, pl. 30
892, p. 162
894, p. 137
896, p. 374, pl. 90
897, p. 374, pl. 90
899, p. 148, pl. 33
900, p. 142, pl. 32
901, p. 142, pl. 32
902, p. 141, pl. 32
903, p. 141, pl. 32
904, p. 135
905, p. 135
906, p. 137, pl. 30

907, p. 135
908, p. 134, pl. 30
909, p. 134
910, p. 138, pl. 31
911, p. 135, pl. 30
912, p. 135
913, p. 137, pl. 30
914, p. 138, pl. 31
915, p. 142, pl. 32
916, p. 363, pl. 87
917, p. 135, pl. 30
918, p. 138
919, p. 136, pl. 30
920, p. 137
921, p. 142, pl. 32
923, p. 360, pl. 86
924, p. 155
925, p. 155, pl. 34
926, p. 154, pl. 34
927, p. 153
928, p. 155, pl. 35
929, p. 374, pl. 90
930, p. 155, pl. 35
930 **bis**, p. 155
930 **quater**, p. 156
930 **ter**, p. 156
931, p. 150, pl. 34
932, p. 374, pl. 90
933, p. 430, pl. 100
934, p. 149, pl. 33 (not labeled)
935, p. 163, pl. 36
936, p. 152, pl. 34
937, p. 134, pl. 30
938, p. 143
939, p. 162, pl. 36
940, p. 186, pl. 40
941, p. 156
942, p. 158, pl. 36
943, p. 138, pl. 31
944, p. 146, pl. 33
945, p. 138, pl. 31
946, p. 138, pl. 31
948, p. 144, pl. 32
949, p. 64
950, p. 145, pl. 33
951, p. 147, pl. 33
952, p. 142
953, p. 124
954, p. 124
955, p. 318, pl. 75
956, p. 318

957, p. 187
958, p. 137
959, p. 110
960, p. 110, pls. 25, 121
961, p. 139, pl. 31
962, p. 135
963, p. 135
964, p. 137
965, p. 318, pl. 75
966, p. 318, pl. 75
967, p. 157, pl. 35
968, p. 145, pl. 33
969, p. 135, pl. 30
971, p. 375, pl. 90
972, p. 316, pl. 74
973, p. 224, pl. 50
974, p. 113, pl. 25
975, p. 187
976, p. 186, pl. 40
977, p. 152, pl. 34
978, p. 144, pl. 32
979, p. 124
980, p. 158
981, p. 158
983, p. 86, pl. 19
984, p. 113, pls. 25, 121
985, p. 175, pl. 38
986, p. 111, pl. 25
987, p. 63, pl. 13
988, p. 82, pl. 18
989, p. 27, pl. 1
991, p. 95, pl. 21
992, p. 300, pl. 70
993, p. 176, pl. 38
994, p. 393, pl. 93
995, p. 163, pl. 36
996, p. 160, pl. 36
997, p. 83, pl. 18
998, p. 434, pl. 101
999, p. 368, pl. 89
1000, p. 270, pl. 62
1001, p. 430, pl. 100
1002, p. 325, pl. 77
1003, p. 114, fig. 1, pl. 26
1004, p. 434, pl. 101
1005, p. 147
1006, p. 135
1007, p. 135
1008, p. 137
1009, p. 134, pl. 30
1010, p. 316

1011, p. 137, pl. 30
1012, p. 210, pl. 17
1013, p. 316, pl. 74
1014, p. 319, pl. 75
1015, p. 138, pl. 31
1016, p. 33, pl. 3
1017, p. 63, pl. 13
1018, p. 31, pl. 2
1019, p. 318, pl. 75
1021, pp. 210–211, pl. 17
1022, p. 152, pl. 34
1023, p. 374, pl. 90
1025, p. 302
1026, p. 185
1027, p. 186
1028, p. 64, pl. 13
1029, p. 431, pl. 100
1030, p. 186
1031, p. 301
1032, p. 302, pl. 70
1033, p. 73, pl. 16
1034, p. 153
1035, p. 158
1036, p. 31, pls. 2, 113
1037, p. 424, pl. 99
1038, p. 430
1039, p. 31
1040, p. 24, pl. 1
1041, p. 147
1042, p. 25
1043, p. 321
1044, p. 318
1045, p. 185
1046, p. 135
1048, p. 135
1049, p. 316, pl. 74
1050, p. 430, pl. 100
1051, p. 144
1052, p. 144
1053, p. 141, pl. 32
1054, p. 142, pl. 32
1055, p. 147
1056, p. 147
1057, p. 147
1058, p. 149
1059, p. 145, pl. 33
1060, p. 374, pl. 90
1061, p. 373
1062, p. 170
1063, p. 127, pl. 29
1067, p. 429, pl. 100

1068, p. 83, pl. 18
1069, p. 113
1070, p. 113
1071, p. 429, pl. 100
1072, p. 301, pl. 70
1073, pp. 155–156
1074, p. 225, pl. 50
1075, p. 156, pl. 35
1076, p. 85, pl. 19
1077, p. 301, pl. 70
1078, p. 302
1079, p. 124, pl. 28
1080, p. 153
1081, p. 430, pl. 100
1082, p. 209, pl. 17
1083, p. 135
1084, p. 34, pl. 3
1085, p. 138
1086, p. 153, pl. 34
1087, p. 424, pl. 99
1088, p. 153, pl. 34
1089, p. 300, pl. 70
1090, p. 208, pl. 47
1093, p. 184, pl. 40
1094, p. 114
1095, p. 111, pl. 25
1096, p. 124, pl. 28
1097, p. 149, pl. 33
1098, p. 374, pl. 90
1099, p. 147
1100, p. 363, pl. 87
1101, p. 374, pl. 90
1103, p. 113, pl. 25
1105, p. 430, pl. 100
1106, p. 267, pl. 102
1107, p. 319, pl. 75
1108, p. 320, pl. 75
1109, p. 431, pl. 100
1111, p. 115, pls. 26, 121
1112, p. 115, pl. 26
1113, p. 325, pl. 77
1114, p. 120, pls. 27, 122
1115, p. 325, pl. 77
1116, p. 325, pl. 77
1117, p. 268, pls. 62, 127
1118, p. 165, pls. 37, 125
1119, p. 327, pl. 78
1120, p. 300, pl. 70
1121, p. 385, pl. 92
1122, p. 114, pl. 26
1123, p. 376, pl. 90

1124, p. 384, pl. 92
1125, p. 344
1126, p. 300, pl. 70
1127, p. 300, pl. 70
1128, p. 173, pl. 38
1129, p. 300, pl. 70
1130, p. 300, pl. 70
1131, p. 316, pl. 74
1132, p. 148, pl. 33
1134, p. 120, pls. 27, 122
1135, p. 86, pl. 19
1137, p. 395, pl. 93
1138, p. 175, pl. 38
1139, p. 454, pl. 104
1140, p. 28, pl. 2
1141, p. 176
1142, p. 34, pl. 3
1143, p. 163, pl. 36
1144, p. 87, pl. 19
1145, p. 30, pl. 2
1146, p. 164, pl. 36
1146 bis, p. 165, pl. 36
1147, p. 327, pl. 78
1147 bis, p. 371
1148, p. 330, pl. 79
1150, p. 91, pl. 20
1151, p. 111, pl. 25
1151 bis, p. 325, pl. 77
1152, p. 327, pl. 78
1153, p. 368, pl. 89
1154, p. 393, pl. 93
1155, pp. 325–326, pl. 77
1157, p. 113, pl. 25
1158, p. 443
1159, p. 323, pl. 77
1160, p. 444, pl. 102
1163, p. 111, pl. 25
1164, p. 267, pl. 61
1165, p. 344, pl. 82
1166, p. 120, pl. 27
1167, p. 178, pl. 39
1168, p. 330, pl. 79
1169, p. 111, pl. 25
1170, p. 176, pl. 38
1171, p. 111, pl. 25
1172, p. 114, pl. 26
1173, p. 82, pl. 18
1174, p. 328, pl. 78
1175, p. 328
1176, p. 170, pl. 35
1177, p. 224, pl. 50

LAUMONIER 1977 CONCORDANCE

1178, p. 119
1179, p. 113, pl. 25
1180, p. 142, pl. 32
1181, p. 156
1182, p. 158
1183, p. 303, pl. 71
1184, p. 371
1185, p. 134, pl. 30
1186, p. 300, pl. 70
1187, p. 175, pl. 38
1188, p. 29, pl. 2
1189, p. 90, pl. 20
1191, p. 84, pl. 18
1192, p. 84, pl. 18
1194, p. 111, pl. 25
1195, p. 389, pl. 91
1196, p. 168, pl. 37
1197, p. 29, pl. 2
1198, p. 407, pl. 95
1199, p. 358, pl. 86
1200, pp. 325–326, pl. 77
1201, p. 175, pl. 38
1202, p. 424, pl. 99
1203, p. 396, pl. 93
1204, p. 327, pl. 78
1205, p. 119, pl. 27
1206, p. 439, pl. 101
1207, p. 310, pl. 73
1208, p. 91, pl. 20
1209, p. 233, pls. 52, 127
1210, p. 266, pl. 61
1211, p. 299, pl. 70
1212, p. 24, pl. 1
1213, p. 233, pl. 52
1214, p. 266, pls. 61, 128
1215, p. 327, pl. 78
1216, p. 24, pls. 1, 113
1217, p. 176, pl. 38
1218, p. 319, pl. 75
1219, p. 354, pl. 85
1220, p. 32, pl. 2
1221, p. 112, pl. 25
1222, p. 100, pl. 22
1223, p. 159
1224, p. 160, pl. 36
1225, p. 31
1226, p. 159, pl. 36
1227, p. 73, pl. 16
1228, p. 371, pl. 89
1229, p. 268, pl. 62
1230, p. 268, pl. 62

1231, p. 159, pl. 36
1232, p. 322
1233, p. 324, pl. 77
1234, p. 73, pl. 16
1235, p. 322, pl. 76
1236, p. 427
1237, p. 426, pl. 99
1238, p. 33, pls. 3, 115
1239, p. 33, pl. 3
1240, p. 33, pl. 3
1241, p. 216, pl. 48
1242, p. 216, pl. 48
1243, p. 323, pl. 77
1244, p. 323, pls. 77, 133
1245, p. 321, pl. 76
1246, p. 321, pl. 76
1247, p. 424, pl. 99
1248, p. 322, pl. 76
1249, p. 322, pl. 76
1250, p. 324, pl. 77
1251, p. 324
1252, p. 322, pl. 76
1253, p. 322, pl. 76
1254, p. 322
1255, p. 221, pl. 49
1256, p. 221, pl. 49
1257, p. 31
1258, p. 179, pl. 39
1259, p. 424, pl. 99
1260, p. 23, pl. 1
1261, p. 221, pl. 49
1262, p. 216, pl. 48
1263, p. 73, pl. 16
1264, p. 216, pl. 48
1265, p. 73, pl. 16
1266, p. 23, pl. 1
1267, p. 321, pl. 76
1268, p. 362, pl. 87
1269, p. 85, pl. 18
1270, p. 221, pl. 49
1271, p. 324, pl. 77
1272, p. 424, pl. 99
1273, p. 225, pl. 50
1274, p. 87, pl. 19
1275, p. 426, pl. 99
1276, p. 73, pl. 16
1277, p. 323, pl. 76
1278, p. 268, pl. 62
1279, p. 268, pl. 62
1279 bis, p. 268, pl. 62
1280, p. 267, pl. 62

1281, p. 160, pls. 36, 125
1282, p. 160, pl. 36
1283, p. 160, pl. 36
1284, p. 158, pls. 36, 124
1285, p. 158, pl. 36
1286, p. 158, 161
1287, p. 161
1288, p. 160
1289, p. 424, pls. 99, 134
1290, p. 427, pl. 99
1291, p. 158, pls. 36, 124
1292, p. 160, pl. 36
1293, p. 159, pl. 36
1294, p. 160, pl. 36
1295, p. 32, pl. 2
1296, p. 426, pls. 99, 134
1297, p. 186, pl. 40
1298, p. 324, pl. 77
1299, p. 72, pl. 16
1300, p. 268, pls. 62, 128
1301, p. 322, pl. 76
1302, p. 88, pl. 19
1303, p. 160, pl. 36
1304, p. 161
1305, p. 164, pl. 36
1306, p. 73
1307, p. 87, pl. 19
1308, p. 425, pl. 99
1309, p. 95, pl. 21
1310, p. 426, pl. 99
1311, p. 425, pl. 99
1312, p. 403, pl. 95
1313, p. 427, pl. 99
1314, p. 165
1315, p. 425, pl. 99
1316, p. 425, pl. 99
1317, p. 427, pl. 99
1318, p. 424, pl. 99
1319, p. 425, pl. 99
1320, p. 162, pl. 36
1321, p. 88
1322, p. 163, pl. 36
1323, p. 427, pl. 99
1324, p. 244, pl. 55
1325, p. 427, pl. 99
1326, p. 324, pl. 77
1327, p. 32, pl. 3
1328, p. 32, pls. 3, 115
1329, p. 233, pl. 52
1330, p. 233, pl. 52
1331, p. 233, pl. 52

1332, p. 233
1334, p. 233
1334 (duplicate number), p. 345, pl. 82
1335, p. 233, pl. 52
1336, p. 233, pl. 52
1337, p. 233, pl. 52
1338, p. 427, pl. 99
1339, p. 78, pl. 17
1340, p. 35, pl. 4
1341, p. 36, pl. 4
1342, p. 36, pl. 4
1343, p. 35, pls. 3, 116
1344, p. 426, pl. 99
1345, p. 34, pl. 3
1346, p. 163, pl. 36
1347, p. 24, pl. 1
1348, p. 184
1349, p. 434
1350, p. 63, pl. 13
1351, p. 427, pl. 99
1352, p. 72, pl. 16
1353, p. 88, pl. 19
1354, p. 161
1356, p. 33, pls. 3, 115
1357, p. 426, pl. 99
1358, p. 118, pls. 27, 122, 132
1359, p. 87, pls. 19, 119
1361, p. 225, pl. 50
1362, p. 376, pl. 90
1363, p. 88, pl. 19
1364, p. 63, pl. 13
1365, p. 42
1368, p. 434, pl. 101
1369, p. 437, pl. 101
1370, p. 165
1371, p. 433, pl. 100
1374, p. 326, pl. 78
1375, p. 128, pl. 29
1377, p. 30, pl. 2
1378, p. 105, pl. 24
1379, p. 175, pl. 38
1380, p. 374, pl. 90
1381, p. 165, pl. 36
1382, p. 212, pl. 17
1384, p. 300, pl. 70
1385, p. 434, pl. 101
1387, p. 400, pl. 94
1388, p. 137
1390, pp. 432, 434, pl. 100
1392, p. 124

1393, p. 439, pl. 101
1394, p. 67, pl. 14
1395, p. 28, pl. 2
1396, p. 43, pl. 8
1397, p. 429, pl. 100
1398, p. 124, pl. 28
1399, p. 147
1400, p. 176, pl. 38
1401, p. 105, pl. 24
1402, p. 328, pl. 78
1403, p. 368, pl. 89
1404, p. 328, pl. 78
1405, p. 73, pl. 16
1406, p. 233, pls. 52, 127
1407, p. 368, pl. 89
1408, p. 434
1409, p. 434
1410, p. 434, pl. 101
1411, p. 367
1412, p. 326, pl. 77
1413, p. 70, pl. 15
1416, p. 426, pl. 99
1417, p. 267
1418, p. 383, pl. 92
1419, p. 137
1420, p. 144, pl. 32
1421, p. 137, pl. 30
1422, p. 204, pl. 45
1423, p. 203, pl. 45
1424, p. 136, pl. 30
1425, pp. 24, 61, pl. 1
1426, p. 360, pl. 86
1427, p. 136, pl. 30
1428, p. 145, pl. 33
1429, p. 135, pl. 30
1430, p. 370, pl. 89
1431, p. 138
1432, p. 146, pl. 33
1433, p. 142
1434, p. 87, pl. 19
1435, p. 430
1436, p. 434
1437, p. 161
1438, p. 82, pls. 18, 119, 131
1439, p. 171, pl. 35
1440, p. 170, pls. 35, 124
1441, p. 171, pl. 35
1442, p. 171, pls. 35, 124
1443, p. 170, pl. 35
1444, p. 170, pl. 35
1445, p. 170, pl. 35

1446, p. 170, pl. 35
1447, p. 171, pl. 35
1448, p. 81, pls. 18, 119
1449, p. 82, pls. 18, 119
1450, p. 170, pl. 35
1451, p. 171, pls. 35, 124
1452, p. 170, pl. 35
1453, p. 170, pl. 35
1454, p. 82
1455, p. 225, pl. 50
1456, p. 170, pls. 35, 124
1457, p. 170, pls. 35, 124
1458, p. 170, pl. 35
1459, p. 170, pl. 35
1460, p. 170, pl. 35
1461, p. 170, pl. 35
1462, p. 170, pl. 35
1463, p. 82, pl. 18
1463 bis, p. 82, pl. 18
1464, p. 106, pl. 24
1466, p. 204
1467, p. 204
1468, p. 204, pl. 46
1469, p. 204, pls. 46, 126
1470, p. 204
1471, p. 204, pl. 46
1472, p. 204
1473, p. 204
1474, p. 204, pl. 46
1475, p. 205, pls. 46, 125
1476, p. 204
1477, p. 204, pl. 46
1478, p. 205, pl. 46
1479, p. 143, pl. 32 (not labeled)
1480, p. 143
1481, p. 143
1482, p. 205, pl. 46
1483, p. 205
1484, p. 204
1485, p. 204
1486, p. 204, pl. 46
1487, p. 204
1488, p. 204
1489, p. 204, pls. 46, 126
1490, p. 204
1491, p. 204, pl. 46
1492, p. 204
1493, p. 204
1494, p. 204, pl. 46
1495, p. 443, pl. 102

1496, p. 204
1497, p. 204
1498, p. 204, pl. 46
1499, p. 204
1500, p. 204, pl. 46
1501, p. 204
1502, p. 205, pl. 46
1503, p. 205, pl. 46
1504, p. 128
1505, p. 443, pl. 102
1506, p. 204
1507, p. 205, pl. 46
1508, p. 204
1509, p. 204, pl. 46
1510, p. 204
1511, p. 204
1512, p. 204
1513, p. 204
1514, p. 444, pl. 102
1515, p. 377, pl. 90
1516 a, p. 84, pl. 18
1516 b, c, p. 204
1516 d, p. 204
1516 f, i, p. 204
1561 g, p.161
1516 j, p. 211, pl. 17
1517, pp. 394–395, pl. 93
1518, p. 182, pl. 39
1519, p. 182, pl. 39
1520, p. 127, pl. 29
1521, p. 182, pl. 39
1522, p. 182
1523, p. 303
1524, p. 187
1525, p. 445, pl. 102
1526, p. 205, pl. 46
1527, p. 267
1528, p. 186
1529, p. 186
1530, p. 186
1531, p. 160
1532, p. 128, pl. 29
1533, p. 374
1534, p. 374, pl. 90
1535, p. 374
1537, p. 89, pl. 19
1538, pp. 438, 444, pl. 101
1539, p. 99, pl. 22
1540, p. 28, pl. 2
1541, p. 361, pl. 87
1543, p. 362, pl. 87

1544, pp. 438–439, pl. 101
1545, p. 66, pl. 12, 14 (error)
1549, p. 391, pl. 55
1550, p. 204
1551, pp. 94, 205, pl. 20
1552, p. 439, pl. 101
1553, p. 205
1554, p. 211, pl. 17
1555, p. 438, pl. 101
1556, p. 369, pl. 89
1557, p. 105, pl. 24
1558, p. 90, pl. 20
1559, p. 90
1560, p. 218, pl. 48
1561, p. 144
1562, p. 203, pl. 45
1562 bis, p. 269
1563, p. 204, pl. 45
1564, p. 240, pl. 54
1565, p. 203, pl. 45
1566, p. 156, pl. 35
1567, p. 204, pl. 45
1568, p. 203
1569, p. 204
1570, p. 203, pl. 45
1571, p. 142
1572, p. 204, pl. 45
1573, p. 443
1574, p. 204, pl. 45
1575, p. 443, pl. 102
1576, p. 222, pl. 49
1577, p. 204, pl. 45
1578, p. 204, pl. 45
1579, p. 204, pl. 45
1580, p. 204
1581, p. 269
1582, p. 269
1583, p. 204
1584, p. 203
1585, p. 218
1586, p. 218
1587, p. 93, pl. 20
1588, p. 204
1589, p. 204, pl. 45
1590, p. 93
1591, p. 443
1592, p. 203, pl. 45
1593, p. 60
1594, p. 442
1595, p. 203
1596, p. 442, pl. 102

1597, p. 443
1598, p. 443
1599, p. 443, pl. 102
1600, p. 443
1601, p. 218
1602, p. 204, pl. 45
1603, p. 228, pl. 51
1604, p. 443
1605, p. 443
1606, p. 204
1607, p. 443
1608, p. 203, pl. 45
1609, p. 204
1610, p. 204, pl. 45
1611, p. 204
1612, p. 204
1613, p. 204, pl. 46
1614, p. 443
1615, p. 443
1616, p. 143
1617, p. 143, pl. 32
1618, p. 362, pl. 87
1619, p. 204, pl. 45
1620, p. 166, pl. 37
1621, p. 269
1622, p. 204
1623, p. 170, pl. 33
1624, p. 443
1625, p. 59, pl. 12
1626, p. 443, pl. 102
1627, p. 443, pl. 102
1628, p. 204
1629, p. 443, pl. 102
1630, p. 204
1631, p. 204
1632, p. 204
1633, p. 204
1634, p. 204
1635, p. 204
1636, p. 204
1637, p. 204
1638, p. 204
1639, p. 273, pl. 105
1640, p. 311, pl. 73
1641, p. 204
1642, p. 204
1643, p. 204, pl. 45
1643, p. 204
1644, p. 204
1645, p. 443
1646, p. 237, pl. 53

1647, p. 204, pl. 45
1648, p. 443
1649, p. 187
1650, p. 443, pl. 102
1651, p. 443, pl. 102
1652, p. 442, pl. 102
1653, p. 93
1653, p. 93, pl. 20
1654, p. 136
1655, p. 196
1656, p. 203, pl. 45
1657, p. 153, pl. 34
1658, p. 153
1659, p. 443
1661, p. 443, pl. 102
1662, p. 203, pl. 45
1663, p. 203
1664, p. 204
1665, p. 32, pl. 3
1666, p. 443
1667, p. 443
1668, p. 443
1669, p. 203
1670, p. 443
1671, p. 443
1671 bis, p. 171
1672, pp. 121–122, pl. 28
1673, p. 178
1674, p. 178, pl. 39
1675, p. 178
1676, p. 242
1677, p. 442, pl. 102
1678, p. 237, pl. 53
1679, p. 269, pl. 62
1680, p. 237
1681, p. 269, pl. 62
1682, p. 269, pl. 62
1683, p. 269, pl. 62
1684, p. 333, pl. 80
1685, p. 322
1686, p. 269
1687, p. 324
1688, p. 359, pl. 86
1689, p. 90, pl. 20
1690, p. 90, pl. 20
1691, p. 395
1692, p. 233, pl. 52
1693, p. 260, pl. 59
1694, p. 204, pl. 45
1695, p. 303, pl. 71
1696, p. 204

1697, p. 93, pl. 20
1698, p. 344
1699, p. 145, pl. 33
1700, p. 154
1701, p. 206
1702, p. 206, pl. 46
1703, p. 206
1703, p. 206, pl. 46
1704, p. 206
1705, p. 206
1706, p. 206
1707, p. 180
1707 (duplicate number), p. 206
1708, p. 136
1709, p. 136
1710, p. 445
1711, p. 445
1712, p. 220, pl. 48
1713, p. 206, pl. 46
1714, p. 224, pl. 50
1715, p. 94
1716, p. 206, pl. 46
1717, p. 206
1718, p. 444, pl. 102
1719, p. 94, pl. 20
1720, p. 334
1721, p. 334
1722, p. 189
1723, p. 62, pl. 13
1724, p. 94
1725, p. 206
1726, p. 358, pls. 86, 133
1727, p. 94
1728, p. 206
1729, p. 66, pl. 14
1729 bis, p. 206
1730, p. 334, pl. 80
1731, p. 220, pl. 49
1732, p. 397, pl. 94
1733, p. 127, pl. 29
1734, p. 127
1735, p. 127, pl. 29
1736, p. 127
1737, p. 128, pl. 29
1738, p. 128, pl. 29
1739, p. 128, pl. 29
1740, p. 128
1741, p. 85, pl. 18
1742, p. 126
1743, p. 126, pl. 29

1744, p. 402, pl. 94
1745, p. 74, pl. 16
1746, p. 90, pl. 20
1747, p. 91, pl. 20
1748, p. 206, pl. 46
1749, p. 206, pl. 46
1750, p. 68, pl. 14
1751, p. 365, pl. 88
1752, p. 444, pl. 102
1754, p. 438, pl. 101
1755, p. 228, pl. 51
1758, p. 138
1759, p. 237, pl. 53
1760, p. 227, pl. 51
1761, p. 444, pl. 102
1762, p. 439, pl. 101
1763, p. 441, pl. 102
1764, pp. 203, 206, pl. 45
1765, p. 206, pl. 46
1766, p. 206
1767, p. 206, pl. 46
1768, p. 206
1769, p. 134
1770, p. 206
1771, p. 228, pl. 51
1772, p. 134
1773, p. 206, pl. 46
1774, p. 206
1775, p. 269
1776, p. 269
1777, p. 206, pl. 46
1778, p. 206, pl. 46
1779, p. 206
1780, p. 206
1781, p. 206
1782, p. 334, pl. 90
1783, p. 206
1784, p. 206
1785, p. 206
1787, p. 358
1788, p. 206, pl. 46
1789, p. 206
1790, p. 61
1791, p. 59
1792, p. 61
1793, p. 61
1794, p. 61
1795, p. 61
1796, p. 61
1797, p. 61, pl. 13
1798, p. 60, pl. 12

1799, p. 61, pl. 13
1800, p. 61, pl. 13
1801, p. 27, pl. 1
1802, p. 67, pl. 14
1803, p. 67, pl. 14
1804, p. 27, pl. 1
1805, p. 60
1806, p. 61, pl. 13
1807, p. 61
1808, p. 434, pl. 101
1809, p. 111
1810, p. 63
1811, p. 176
1812, p. 144
1812 bis, p. 24, pl. 1
1813, p. 430
1814, p. 75, pl. 16
1815, p. 75
1816, p. 362
1817, p. 79, pl. 17
1818, p. 362, pl. 87
1819, p. 362, pl. 87
1820, p. 362
1821, p. 450, pl. 103
1822, p. 362
1823, p. 362
1824, p. 78
1825, p. 59, pl. 12
1826, p. 442, pl. 102
1827, p. 208, pl. 47
1828, p. 208, pl. 47
1829, p. 208
1830, pp. 203, 204, pl. 45
1831, p. 90, pl. 20
1832, p. 193
1833, p. 203, pl. 45
1834, p. 84, pl. 18
1835, p. 441
1836, p. 119, pl. 27
1837, p. 122, pl. 28
1838, p. 442, pl. 102
1839, p. 178, pl. 39
1840, p. 178, pl. 39
1841, p. 442
1842, p. 364, pl. 88
1843, p. 171, pl. 35
1844, p. 171, pl. 35
1845, p. 204
1846, p. 229, pl. 51
1847, p. 443
1848, p. 204

1849, p. 269
1850, p. 443
1851, p. 204
1852, p. 203
1853, p. 204
1854, p. 204
1855, p. 204
1856, p. 237, pl. 53
1857, p. 93
1858, p. 269
1859, p. 269, pl. 62
1860, p. 178, pl. 39
1861, p. 178, pl. 39
1862, p. 182, pl. 39
1863, p. 205
1865, p. 204, pl. 46
1866, p. 128, pl. 29
1867, p. 444, pl. 102
1868, p. 204
1869, p. 205
1870, p. 204
1871, p. 204
1872, p. 122, pl. 28
1873, p. 119, pl. 27
1874, p. 245, pl. 55
1875, p. 220, pl. 49
1876, p. 206
1877, p. 206
1879, p. 206
1880, p. 206
1881, p. 94, pl. 20
1882, p. 228
1883, p. 228
1883 bis, p. 228
1884, p. 63, pl. 13
1886, p. 66
1887, p. 438
1888, p. 328, pl. 78
1889, p. 352
1890, p. 439
1892, p. 385, pl. 92
1893, p. 30, pl. 2
1894, p. 240, pl. 54
1895, p. 184, pl. 40
1899, p. 177, pl. 38
1900, pp. 228–229, pl. 51
1901, p. 429, pl. 100
1902, p. 303, pl. 71
1903, p. 430
1904, p. 124, pl. 28
1905, p. 459, pl. 106

1906, p. 431
1907, p. 431
1908, p. 183, pl. 40
1909, p. 183, pl. 40
1910, p. 112, pl. 25
1911, p. 426
1912, p. 35, pl. 4
1915, p. 209
1916, p. 425
1917, p. 425
1918, p. 31, pl. 2
1919, p. 31, pl. 2
1920, p. 204, pl. 46
1921, p. 204
1923, p. 207, pl. 47
1924, p. 204, pl. 46
1925, p. 204
1927, p. 444, pl. 102
1928, p. 206
1929, p. 375, pl. 90
1930, p. 328, pl. 78
1931, p. 127, pl. 29
1932, p. 348, pl. 83
1933, p. 128, pl. 29
1934, p. 204, pl. 46
1935, p. 242, pl. 54
1936, p. 65, pl. 14
1939, p. 106, pl. 24
1940, p. 427, pl. 99
1941, p. 82, pl. 18
1942, p. 146, pl. 33
1943, p. 36, pl. 4
1944, p. 144, pl. 32
1945, p. 144, pl. 32
1946, p. 142
1947, p. 36, pl. 4
1951, p. 442, pl. 102
1952, p. 138, pl. 31
1953, p. 82, pl. 18
1954, p. 445, pl. 102
1955, p. 441, pl. 102
1957, pp. 30, 60, pls. 2, 114
1958, p. 36, pls. 4, 117, 131
1960, p. 434, pl. 101
1961, p. 323, pl. 76
1962, p. 36, pl. 4
1963, p. 240, pl. 54
1964, p. 301, pl. 70
1965, p. 417, pls. 98, 134
1966, p. 183, pl. 40
1967, p. 265, pl. 61

1968, p. 345, pls. 82, 133
1969, p. 240, pl. 54
1970, p. 343, pl. 82
1971, p. 23, pls. 1, 113, 131
1972, p. 359, pl. 86
1973, p. 151, pl. 34
1974, p. 300, pl. 70
1975, p. 136, pl. 30
1976, p. 134, pl. 30
1977, p. 302, pls. 70, 133
1978, p. 184, pl. 40
1979, p. 393, pls. 93, 134
1980, p. 34, pls. 3, 116
1981, p. 26, pls. 1, 113
1982, p. 23, pl. 1
1983, p. 34, pl. 3
1984, p. 34, pl. 3
1985, p. 405, pl. 95
1986, p. 403, pl. 95
1987, p. 407, fig. 1, pl. 95
1988, p. 403, pl. 95
1989, p. 403, pl. 95
1990, p. 407, fig. 1, pl. 95
1991, p. 232, fig. 1, pl. 52
1992, pp. 232–233, pl. 52
1993, p. 381, fig. 1, pl. 91
1994, p. 224, fig. 1, pl. 50
1995, p. 224, pl. 50
1996, p. 31
1997, p. 410, pl. 96
1998, p. 410, pl. 96
1999, p. 113, fig. 1, pl. 25
2000, p. 133, pl. 30
2001, p. 133, pl. 30
2002, p. 133, fig. 1, pl. 30
2003, p. 133, pl. 30
2004, p. 271, pl. 63
2005, p. 428, pl. 100
2006, p. 82, pl. 18
2007, p. 323, pl. 76
2008, p. 204, pl. 45
2009, p. 146, pl. 33
2010, p. 264, fig. 1, pls. 60, 133
2011, p. 346, pl. 82
2012, p. 159, pl. 36
2013, p. 135
2014, p. 434, pl. 101
2015, p. 184, pl. 40
2016, p. 142
2017, p. 155, pl. 34
2018, p. 204

2019, p. 177, pl. 38
2020, p. 187, pl. 40
2021, p. 114, pl. 25
2022, p. 443, pl. 102
2023, p. 229, pl. 51
2024, p. 303, pl. 71
2025, p. 206, pl. 46
2027, p. 206
2028, p. 434
2029, p. 184
2030, p. 178, pl. 39
2031, p. 110, pl. 25
2032, p. 442, pl. 102
2033, p. 33, pls. 3, 115
2034, p. 60, pl. 12
2035, p. 203, pl. 96; see also 2065
2036, p. 203
2037, p. 268, pl. 62
2038, p. 268, pls. 62, 127
2039, p. 268, pl. 62
2040, p. 393, pl. 93
2041, p. 326, pl. 78
2042, p. 377, pl. 90
2043, p. 224, pl. 50
2044, p. 138
2045, p. 135
2046, p. 31, pl. 2
2047, p. 111, pl. 25
2048, p. 135
2049, p. 156
2050, p. 156
2051, p. 105, pl. 24
2053, p. 60, pl. 12
2054, p. 184
2055, p. 269, pl. 62
2056 bis, p. 328, pl. 78
2057, p. 63, pl. 13
2058, p. 33, pl. 3, 115
2059, p. 137
2060, p. 326, pl. 77
2061, p. 327
2062, p. 327, pl. 78
2063, p. 431
2064, p. 432
2065, p. 411, pl. 96 (mislabeled 2035)
2066, p. 227, pl. 51
2067, p. 410, pl. 96
2068, p. 82, pl. 18
2069, p. 192, pl. 42

2071, p. 202, pls. 45, 132
2074, p. 320, pl. 75
2075, p. 324
2078, p. 349
2079, p. 317, pl. 74
2080, p. 320
2081, p. 225, pl. 50
2082, p. 149, pl. 33
2083, p. 221, pl. 49
2084, p. 435, pl. 101
2085, p. 272, pl. 63
2086, p. 346, pl. 82
2087, p. 347, pl. 83
2088, p. 343, pl. 82
2089, p. 301, pl. 70
2089 bis, p. 102
2090, p. 106, pl. 24
2091, p. 152
2092, p. 153, pl. 34
2093, p. 152, pl. 34
2094, p. 111, pl. 25
2095, p. 442, pl. 102
2096, p. 115, pl. 26
2097, p. 84, pl. 18
2098, p. 128
2099, p. 84
2100, p. 84
2101, p. 245
2106, p. 345, pl. 82
2107, p. 345, pl. 82
2108, p. 62, pl. 13
2109, p. 111
2109 bis, p. 111
2110, p. 128, pl. 29
2111, pp. 438, 439, pl. 101
2112, p. 66, pl. 14
2113, p. 438, pl. 101
2115, p. 311, pl. 73
2116, p. 122, pl. 28
2117, p. 72, pl. 15
2118, p. 437, pl. 101
2119, p. 38, pl. 5
2120, p. 327, pl. 78
2121, p. 61, pl. 13
2122, p. 135
2123, p. 432, pl. 100
2125, p. 128, pl. 29
2126, p. 237, pl. 53
2127, p. 440, pl. 102
2128, p. 271, pl. 63
2129, p. 242

2130, p. 43, pl. 8
2131, pp. 271, 272
2132, pp. 271, 272
2133, p. 271, 272, pl. 63
2134, p. 440, pl. 102
2135, pp. 272, 310, pls. 63, 73
2136, p. 244, pl. 55
2136 bis, p. 310
2140, p. 106, pl. 24
2141, p. 43, pl. 8
2142, p. 310, pl. 73
2143, p. 269, pl. 62
2144, p. 346, pl. 82
2145, p. 264
2146, p. 207, pl. 47
2147, pp. 263, 269, pl. 60
2148, p. 439, pl. 101
2149, p. 353, pl. 84
2150, p. 229
2151, p. 338, pl. 81
2152, p. 122
2153, p. 338
2154, p. 473, pl. 109
2155, p. 400, pl. 94
2156, p. 437, pl. 101
2157, p. 444, pl. 102
2158, p. 271, pl. 63
2159, p. 396, pl. 93
2160, p. 271
2161, p. 237, pl. 53
2162, p. 441, pl. 102
2163, p. 338
2164, p. 207, pl. 47
2165, p. 183
2166, p. 183, pls. 39, 125
2167, p. 62
2168, p. 62
2169, p. 54
2170, p. 62, pl. 13
2171, p. 43, pl. 8
2172, p. 43
2173, p. 39, pl. 5
2174, p. 62, pl. 13
2175, p. 50
2176, p. 62
2177, p. 62
2178, p. 62, pl. 13
2179, p. 62
2180, p. 62
2181, p. 51
2182, p. 348, pl. 83

2184, p. 62
2185, p. 156, pl. 35
2186, p. 212, pl. 17
2187, p. 435
2188, p. 279
2189, p. 363, pl. 87
2191, p. 167, pl. 37
2192, pp. 34, 61, pl. 3
2193, p. 218, pl. 48
2194, p. 421
2198, p. 205, pl. 46
2199, p. 154, pl. 34
2200, p. 440, pl. 101
2202, p. 424
2203, p. 63, pl. 13
2204, p. 143, pl. 32
2205, p. 244, pl. 55
2209, p. 209, pl. 17
2210, p. 177, pl. 38
2211, p. 327
2212, p. 330, pl. 79
2213, p. 333
2214, p. 333
2215, p. 334
2216, p. 333, pl. 80
2217, p. 328, pl. 78
2218, p. 322
2219, p. 322
2220, p. 324
2221, p. 325, pl. 77
2222, p. 325, pl. 77
2223, p. 325, pl. 77
2224, p. 349, pl. 83
2225, p. 431, pl. 100
2226, p. 323, pl. 76
2227, p. 140, pl. 31
2228, p. 348
2229, p. 206
2230, p. 339, pl. 81
2231, p. 329, pl. 78
2233, p. 204
2234, p. 156, pl. 35
2236, p. 204
2237, p. 439, pl. 101
2238, p. 177
2239, p. 333, pl. 80
2240, p. 127, pl. 29
2241, p. 377, pl. 90
2242, p. 28, pl. 2
2243, p. 390, pl. 55
2244, p. 62, pl. 13

2245, p. 439, pl. 101
2246, p. 216, pl. 48
2246 bis, p. 220
2247, p. 220, pl. 49
2248, p. 267
2249, p. 399, pl. 94
2250, p. 440, pl. 102
2251, p. 344, pl. 82
2252, p. 106, pl. 24
2254, p. 440, pl. 102
2255, p. 205
2258, p. 324, pl. 77
2259, p. 319, pl. 75
2260, p. 266, pl. 61
2261, p. 326, pl. 77
2262, p. 301, pl. 70
2263, p. 240, pl. 54
2264, p. 36, pls. 4, 116
2265, p. 41, pl. 7
2266, p. 35, pl. 3
2267, p. 134, pl. 30
2268, p. 326, pl. 78
2269, p. 324
2270, p. 326
2271, p. 324, pl. 77
2272, pp. 316–317, pl. 74
2273, p. 317, pl. 74
2273 bis, p. 317
2274, p. 317, pl. 74
2275, p. 317, pl. 74
2276, p. 334
2277, p. 327, pl. 78
2278, p. 240, pl. 54
2279, p. 185
2280, p. 135
2281, p. 144
2282, p. 304, pl. 71
2283, p. 28, pl. 2
2285, p. 445
2286, p. 71, pl. 15
2287, p. 119, pl. 27
2288, p. 30, pl. 2
2289, p. 97, pl. 21
2290, p. 325, pl. 77
2291, p. 206
2292, p. 28, pl. 2
2293, p. 135
2294, p. 135
2295, p. 327
2296, p. 68, pl. 14

2298, p. 435
2299, p. 320
2301, p. 161, pl. 36
2302, p. 204
2303, p. 385, pl. 92
2304, p. 323, pl. 76
2305, p. 103, pl. 23
2306, p. 204, pl. 46
2307, p. 441, pl. 102
2309, p. 98, pl. 21
2310, p. 142
2311, p. 363, pl. 87
2312, pp. 210–211, pl. 17
2313, p. 233, pl. 52
2313 bis, p. 266, pl. 61
2314, p. 147
2315, p. 444, pl. 102
2316, p. 324
2317, p. 128, pl. 29
2318, p. 33, pl. 3, 115
2319, p. 270, pl. 62
2320, p. 384, pl. 92
2321, p. 269, pl. 62
2322, p. 204, pl. 45
2323, p. 443, pl. 102
2324, p. 334
2325, p. 122
2326, p. 431
2327, p. 272, pl. 63
2328, p. 113, pl. 25
2329, p. 228
2330, p. 98, pl. 21
2338, p. 316, pl. 74
2339, p. 146, pl. 33
2340, p. 135
2341, p. 134
2342, p. 87, pl. 19
2343, p. 25, pl. 1
2344, p. 310
2345, p. 97, pl. 21
2346, p. 162
2347, p. 431
2348, p. 164, pl. 36
2349, p. 76, pl. 16
2350, p. 425
2351, p. 328, pl. 78
2352, p. 185
2353, p. 185
2354, p. 30, pl. 2
2355, p. 205

2356, p. 435, pl. 101
2357, p. 90
2358, p. 25
2361, p. 421
2362, p. 431
2363, p. 138
2364, p. 343, pl. 82
2365, p. 377, pl. 90
2366, p. 25, pl. 1, 113
2367, p. 267, pl. 61
2368, p. 343, pls. 82, 133
2369, p. 64, pl. 13
2370, p. 221, pl. 49
2371, p. 135, pl. 30
2372, p. 95, pl. 21
2373, p. 73, pl. 16
2374, p. 73, pl. 16
2375, p. 97, pl. 21
2376, p. 331, pl. 79
2377, p. 374, pl. 90
2378, p. 63
2379, p. 63, pl. 13
2380, p. 63, pls. 13, 131
2381, p. 431, pl. 100
2382, p. 433, pl. 100
2383, p. 99, pl. 21
2384, p. 36, pl. 4
2385, p. 435
2386, p. 85, pl. 19
2387, p. 431
2388, p. 146, pl. 33
2390, p. 322, pl. 76
2391, p. 322, pl. 76
2393, p. 431
2394, p. 24
2396, p. 114
2397, p. 162, pl. 36
2398, p. 428
2399, p. 71, pl. 15
2400, p. 303, pl. 71
2401, p. 374, pl. 90
2402, p. 64
2403, p. 71, pl. 15
2404, p. 444, pl. 102
2405, p. 85, pl. 19
2405 bis, p. 85, pl. 19
2406, p. 428, pl. 100
2412, p. 349, pl. 83
2414, p. 353, pl. 85
2415, p. 355, pl. 85

2416, p. 355, pl. 85
2417, p. 34, pl. 3
2418, p. 25, pl. 1
2419, p. 64, pl. 13
2421, p. 26, pl. 1
2422, p. 111
2423, p. 113, pl. 25
2423 bis, p. 113, pl. 25
2424, p. 216, pl. 48
2425, p. 216, pl. 48
2426, p. 304, pls. 71, 128
2427, p. 304, pl. 71
2428, p. 300, pl. 70
2429, p. 302, pl. 70
2430, p. 319, pl. 75
2431, p. 179, pl. 39
2432, p. 435, pl. 101
2434, p. 142, pl. 32
2435, p. 89, pl. 19
2436, p. 395, pl. 93
2437, p. 146, pl. 33
2438, p. 148, pl. 33
2439, p. 360, pl. 86
2440, p. 134, pl. 30
2440 bis, p. 360, pl. 86
2441, p. 114, pl. 26
2442, p. 343, pl. 82
2443, p. 433, pl. 101
2446, p. 444, pl. 102
2447, p. 440, pl. 101
2448, p. 437, pl. 101
2449, p. 44, pl. 8
2450, p. 424, pl. 99
2451, p. 135
2463, p. 339
2556, p. 43
2562, p. 98, pl. 21
2785, p. 384, pls. 92, 133
3000, p. 115, pl. 26
3001, p. 115, pl. 26
3002, p. 115, pl. 26
3003, p. 329, pl. 78
3004, p. 329, pl. 78
3005, p. 384, pl. 92
3006, p. 353, pl. 84
3007, p. 413, pl. 97
3009, p. 165, pl. 37
3010, p. 165, pl. 37
3011, p. 211, pl. 17
3012, p. 165, pl. 37

LAUMONIER 1977 CONCORDANCE

3013, p. 165, pls. 37, 125
3014, p. 114, pl. 26
3015, p. 216, pl. 48
3016, p. 195, pl. 43
3017, p. 165, pl. 37
3018, p. 185, pls. 40, 126
3019, p. 196, pl. 43
3020, p. 165, pl. 37
3021, p. 165, pl. 37
3022, p. 127, pl. 29
3023, p. 127, pl. 29
3024, p. 146, pl. 33
3025, p. 413, pl. 97
3026, p. 165, pl. 37
3027, p. 165, pl. 37
3028, p. 165, pl. 37
3029, p. 148
3030, p. 165
3031, p. 165
3032, p. 377, pl. 90
3033, p. 127, pl. 29
3034, p. 127, pl. 29
3035, p. 127
3036, p. 413, pl. 97
3037, p. 413, pl. 97
3038, p. 226, pl. 50
3039, p. 226, pl. 50
3040, p. 306, pl. 72
3041, p. 226, pl. 50
3042, p. 396, pl. 93
3043, p. 166, pl. 37
3044, p. 323, pl. 76
3045, p. 323, pl. 76
3046, p. 328, pl. 78
3047, p. 323
3049, p. 185, pl. 40
3050, p. 156, pls. 35, 125
3051, p. 153, pl. 34
3052, p. 166, pl. 37
3053, p. 151, pl. 34
3054, p. 151, pl. 34
3055, p. 166, pl. 37
3057, p. 263, pl. 60
3058, p. 153, pls. 34, 124
3059, p. 179, pl. 39
3060, p. 358
3061, p. 326, pl. 78
3062, p. 327, pl. 78
3063, p. 77, pl. 16
3064, p. 37, pl. 5

3065, p. 415, pl. 97
3066, p. 414, pl. 97
3067, p. 167
3068, p. 414, pl. 97
3069, p. 414, pl. 97
3070, p. 103
3071, p. 396, pl. 93
3072, p. 414, pl. 97
3073, p. 393, pl. 93
3074, p. 394
3075, p. 394, pl. 93
3076, p. 394, pl. 93
3077, p. 394
3078, p. 394, pl. 93
3079, p. 37, pl. 5
3080, p. 103, pl. 23
3081, p. 103, pl. 23
3083, p. 414, pl. 97
3084, p. 375, pl. 90
3085, p. 343, pl. 82
3086, p. 37, pl. 5
3087, p. 38, pls. 5, 117
3088, p. 38, pl. 5
3089, p. 414, pl. 97
3090, p. 56, pl. 11
3091, p. 414, pl. 97
3094, p. 91, pl. 20
3095, p. 117, pl. 26
3096, p. 304, pls. 71, 129
3098, p. 415, pl. 97
3099, p. 415, pl. 97
3100, p. 103, pl. 23
3108, p. 192, pl. 42
3109, p. 159
3110, p. 344, pl. 82
3111, p. 149, pls. 33, 132
3112, p. 212, pl. 17
3113, p. 212, pl. 17
3114, p. 178, pl. 39
3115, p. 43, pl. 8
3116, p. 306, pl. 72
3117, p. 306, pl. 72
3118, p. 306, pl. 72
3119, p. 178, pl. 39
3121, p. 346, pls. 83, 133
3122, p. 440, pl. 102
3123, p. 346, pl. 82
3124, p. 226, pls. 50, 127
3125, p. 167
3126, p. 226, pl. 50

3127, p. 167, pl. 37
3128, p. 360, pl. 86
3129, p. 167
3130, p. 39, pl. 5
3131, p. 167
3132, p. 139, pl. 31
3133, p. 167, pls. 37, 125
3134, p. 167, pl. 37
3135, p. 167, pl. 37
3136, p. 167, pl. 37
3137, p. 153, pl. 34
3138, p. 185, pl. 40
3139, p. 184, pl. 40
3140, p. 167
3141, p. 39, pl. 5
3142, p. 167
3143, p. 167, pl. 37
3144, p. 167
3145, p. 167
3146, p. 167
3147, p. 167
3148, p. 305, pl. 71
3149, p. 167
3150, p. 167
3151, p. 167, pl. 37
3152, p. 91, pl. 20
3153, p. 167
3154, p. 167
3155, p. 216, pl. 48
3156, p. 167
3157, p. 167
3158, p. 167
3159, p. 167
3160, p. 167
3161, p. 65
3162, p. 216, pl. 48
3163, p. 65, pls. 14, 118
3164, p. 420, pl. 98
3165, p. 65
3166, p. 420
3167, p. 305, pl. 71
3168, p. 226, pl. 50
3169, p. 420, pl. 98
3170, p. 39, pl. 5
3171, p. 263, pl. 60
3172, p. 165, pl. 125
3174, p. 124, pl. 28
3175, p. 124, pl. 28
3176, p. 176, pls. 38, 125
3177, p. 178, pl. 39

3178, p. 305, pl. 71
3179, p. 146, pl. 33
3180, p. 417, pl. 98
3181, p. 164, pl. 36
3182, p. 124, pl. 28
3183, p. 417, pl. 98
3184, p. 167, pl. 37
3185, p. 417, pl. 98
3186, p. 91, pl. 20
3187, p. 417, pl. 98
3188, p. 127
3189, p. 167, pl. 37
3190, p. 305, pls. 71, 129
3191, p. 305, pl. 71
3192, p. 127, pl. 29
3193, p. 92, pl. 20
3194, p. 91, pl. 20
3195, p. 418, pl. 98
3196, p. 101, pl. 23
3197, p. 418, pl. 98
3198, p. 263, pl. 60
3199, p. 115, pl. 26
3200, p. 101, pl. 23
3201, p. 383, pl. 92
3202, p. 127, pl. 29
(mislabeled 3302)
3203, p. 39, pl. 6
3204, p. 125, pls. 29, 123
3205, p. 125, pls. 29, 123
3206, p. 125, pl. 29
3208, p. 70, pl. 15
3209, p. 167, pl. 37
3210, p. 69, pl. 15
3211, p. 69, pl. 15
3212, p. 69, pl. 15
3213, p. 418, pl. 98
3214, p. 234, pl. 53
3215, p. 115, pl. 26
3216, p. 344, pl. 82
3216 bis, p. 39, pl. 6
3217, p. 40, pl. 6
3218, p. 39, pl. 6
3219, p. 40, pl. 6
3220, p. 41, pl. 7
3221, p. 41, pl. 7
3222, p. 41, pl. 7
3223, p. 41, pl. 7
3224, p. 364, pl. 87
3225, p. 364, pl. 87
3226, p. 234, pl. 53

3227, p. 421, pl. 98
3230, p. 40, pl. 6
3231, p. 344, pl. 82
3232, p. 344, pl. 82
3233, p. 92, pl. 20
3234, p. 39, pl. 5
3235, p. 92, pl. 20
3236, p. 167, pl. 37
3237, p. 101, pl. 23
3238, p. 352, pl. 84
3239, p. 419, pl. 98
3240, p. 116, pl. 26
3241, p. 34, pl. 3
3242, p. 167, pl. 37
3243, p. 168, pl. 37
3244, p. 168, pl. 37
3245, p. 305, pl. 72
3246, p. 217, pl. 48
3247, p. 92, pls. 20, 131
3248, p. 78, pl. 17
3249, p. 41, pl. 7
3250, p. 304
3252, p. 168, pl. 37
3253, p. 263, pl. 60
3254, p. 419, pl. 98
3256, p. 116, pls. 26, 122
3257, pp. 234–235, pl. 53
3258, p. 355, pl. 85
3259, p. 92, pl. 20
3260, p. 97, pl. 21
3261, p. 419, pl. 98
3263, p. 419, pl. 98
3264, p. 116, pl. 26
3265, p. 344
3266, p. 419, pl. 98
3268, p. 107, pl. 24
3270, p. 308, pls. 73, 129
3271, p. 308, pl. 73
3272, p. 164, pl. 36
3273, p. 116
3274, p. 83, pls. 18, 131
3275, p. 42, pls. 7, 118
3276, p. 350, pl. 84
3277, p. 350, pl. 84
3278, p. 350, pl. 84
3279, p. 116, pl. 26
3280, p. 210, pl. 17
3283, p. 101, pl. 23
3284, p. 97, pls. 21, 119
3285, p. 101, pl. 23

3286, p. 116, pls. 26, 122
3289, p. 101, pl. 23
3290, p. 420, pl. 98
3291, p. 117, pls. 26, 122, 132
3292, p. 117, pl. 26
3293, p. 375, pl. 90
3294, p. 92, pl. 20
3295, p. 92, pl. 20
3296, p. 421, pl. 98
3297, p. 92, pl. 20
3301, p. 42, pl. 7
3302, see 3202
3305, p. 234, pl. 53
3306, p. 416, pl. 97
3307, p. 101, pl. 23
3308, p. 168, pl. 37
3309, p. 38, pl. 5
3310, p. 418, pl. 98
3311, p. 174, pls. 38, 125
3312, p. 177, pl. 39
3313, p. 177, pls. 39, 125
3314, p. 418, pl. 98
3315, p. 375, pl. 90
3316, p. 92, pl. 20
3317, p. 416, pl. 97
3318, pp. 101–102, pl. 23
3319, p. 346, pl. 83
3320, pp. 304–305, fig. 1, pl. 71
3321, p. 38, pl. 5
3322, p. 164, pl. 36
3323, p. 40, pls. 6, 117
3326, p. 100, pl. 22
3327, p. 305, pl. 72
3328, p. 329, pl. 78
3329, p. 167
3330, p. 305, pl. 71
3331, p. 97, pl. 21, 120
3332, p. 99, pls. 21, 120, 131
3333, p. 415, pl. 97
3334, p. 37, pls. 5, 117
3335, p. 304
3336, p. 37, pl. 5
3337, p. 418, pl. 98
3338, p. 305, pl. 71
3339, p. 347, pl. 83
3340, p. 416, pl. 97
3341, p. 76
3342, p. 38, pl. 5
3343, pp. 139–140, pls. 31, 132
3343 bis, p. 156, pl. 35

3344, p. 419, pl. 98
3345, p. 414, pl. 97
3346, p. 415, pl. 97
3347, p. 159, pl. 36
3348, p. 168, pl. 37
3349, p. 168, pl. 37
3350, p. 96, pl. 21
3351, p. 269, pl. 62
3352, p. 143, pl. 32
3353, p. 375, pl. 90
3354, p. 375, pl. 90
3355, p. 376, pl. 90
3356, p. 133, 135, pls. 30, 37
3357, p. 416, pl. 97
3358, p. 168, pl. 37
3359, p. 168, pl. 37
3360, p. 168, pl. 37
3362, p. 102, pl. 23
3363, p. 168
3364, p. 376, pl. 90
3365, p. 416, pl. 97
3366, p. 416
3367, p. 421, pl. 98
3368, p. 40, pl. 6
3369, p. 221, pl. 49
3370, p. 106, pl. 24
3371, p. 65, pls. 14, 118
3372, p. 416, pl. 97
3373, p. 416, pl. 97
3374, p. 102, pls. 23, 119
3375, p. 388, pl. 88
3376, p. 97, pl. 21
3377, p. 96, pl. 21
3378, p. 102, pls. 23, 119
3379, p. 416, pl. 97
3380, p. 169, pl. 37
3381, p. 66, pl. 14
3382, p. 38, pl. 5
3383, p. 416, pl. 97
3384, p. 65, pl. 14
3385, p. 91
3386, p. 102, pl. 23
3387, p. 416, pl. 97
3388, p. 416, pl. 97
3389, p. 102, pl. 23
3390, p. 376, pl. 90
3391, p. 415, pl. 97
3392, p. 388, pl. 88
3393, p. 37, pls. 5, 117
3394, p. 38, pl. 5

3395, p. 38, pl. 5
3396, p. 143, pl. 32
3397, p. 306, pl. 72
3398, p. 417, pl. 97
3399, p. 102, pl. 23
3400, p. 42, pl. 7
3401, p. 344, pl. 82
3403, p. 419, pl. 98
3404, p. 329, pl. 78
3406, p. 415, pl. 97
3407, p. 41, pl. 7
3408, p. 421, pl. 98
3409, p. 44, pl. 8
3410, p. 421
3411, p. 421
3412, p. 44, pl. 8
3413, p. 178, pl. 39
3414, p. 122, pl. 28
3414 bis, p. 122
3415, p. 77
3416, p. 421
3417, p. 419, pl. 98
3418, p. 326, pls. 78, 133
3420, p. 42, pl. 8
3421, p. 42, pls. 7, 118
3422, p. 43, pl. 8
3423, p. 43, pl. 8
3424, p. 40, pl. 6
3426, p. 307, pl. 72
3427, p. 411, pl. 96
3429, p. 39, pl. 5
3430, p. 413, pl. 97
3431, p. 235, pl. 53
3432, p. 165
3433, p. 169, pl. 37
3435, p. 418, pl. 98
3436, p. 348, pl. 83
3437, p. 167
3438, p. 420, pl. 98
3439, p. 416, pl. 97
3440, p. 77, pl. 16
3441, p. 140, pl. 31
3442, p. 347, pl. 83
3443, p. 116, pl. 26
3445, p. 417, pl. 97
3446, p. 418, pl. 98
3447, p. 418, pl. 98
3448, p. 417, pl. 97
3449, p. 415, pl. 97
3450, p. 420, pl. 98

3451, p. 211, pl. 17
3452, p. 166, pl. 37
3453, p. 421, pl. 98
3454, p. 421
3455, p. 369, pl. 89
3456, p. 70, pl. 15
3457, p. 78, pl. 17
3458, p. 240, pl. 54
3459, p. 413, pl. 97
3460, p. 169, pl. 37
3461, p. 165
3461 bis, p. 418, pl. 98
3462, p. 127, pl. 29
3463, p. 101
3464, p. 216, pl. 48
3465, p. 92
3466, p. 92
3467, p. 92
3468, p. 167
3469, p. 167
3470, p. 167
3471, p. 167
3472, p. 92, pl. 20
3473, p. 324, pl. 77
3474, p. 71, pls. 15, 131
3475, p. 71, pl. 15
3476, p. 263, pl. 60
3477, p. 306, pl. 72
3478, p. 42, pls. 8, 118
3479, p. 40, pl. 7
3480, p. 307, pl. 72
3481, pp. 305, 306, pls. 72, 129
3482, p. 306, pls. 72, 129
3483, p. 263, pl. 60
3484, p. 38, pl. 5
3485, p. 417, pl. 97
3486, p. 167
3487, p. 414, pl. 97
3488, p. 167
3489, p. 419, pl. 98
3490, p. 344, pl. 82
3491, p. 329, pl. 78
3491 bis, p. 333
3493, p. 41, pl. 7
3494, p. 329, pl. 78
3495, p. 415, pl. 97
3496, p. 116
3497, p. 269, pl. 62
3498, p. 413, pl. 97
3499, p. 403, fig. 1, pl. 95

3502, p. 461, pl. 106, 134
3535, p. 475, pl. 110, 134
3800, p. 291, pl. 67
3801, p. 472
3802, p. 29, pl. 2
3803, p. 189
3804, p. 44, pl. 8
3805, p. 473, pls. 109, 134
3805 bis, p. 469, pl. 108
3806, p. 191
3807, p. 189, pl. 41
3808, p. 474, pl. 110
3809, p. 338
3810, p. 338, pl. 81
3811, p. 188
3812, p. 293, pl. 68
3813, p. 291, pl. 67
4000, p. 58, pl. 12
4001, p. 307, pl. 72
4002, p. 307, pl. 72
4003, p. 307
4004, p. 307
4005, p. 477, pl. 111
4006, p. 307, pl. 72
4007, p. 308, pl. 72
4008, p. 308
4009, p. 390, pl. 55
4010, p. 200, pl. 44
4011, p. 200
4012, p. 477, pl. 111
4013, p. 390, pl. 55
4014, p. 390, pl. 55
4015, p. 200, pl. 44
4016, p. 477, pl. 111
4017, p. 245, pl. 55
4018, p. 245
4019, p. 308, pl. 72
4020, p. 200, pl. 44
4021, p. 200, pl. 44
4022, p. 477, pl. 111
4023, p. 71, pl. 15
4024, p. 72, pl. 15
4025, p. 175
4026, p. 477, pl. 111
4027, p. 106, pl. 24
4028, p. 107, pl. 24
4029, p. 308
4030, p. 308, pl. 72
4031, p. 401, pl. 94
4035, p. 308, pl. 72

4036, p. 308, pl. 72
4037, p. 308, pl. 72
4038, p. 308
4039, p. 477, pl. 111
4040, p. 200, pl. 44
4041, p. 477, pl. 111
4042, p. 78, pl. 17
4043, p. 390
4050, p. 69, fig. 1, pls. 15, 131
4051, p. 264, pl. 60
4052, p. 309, fig. 1, pl. 73
4053, p. 483, pl. 112
4054, p. 182, pl. 39
4055, p. 199, pl. 44
4056, p. 199, pls. 44, 132
4057, p. 199
4058, p. 199, pl. 44
4059, p. 199
4060, p. 199
4061, p. 199, pl. 44
4063, p. 199
4064, p. 199, pl. 44
4065, p. 401, pl. 94
4066, p. 199
4067, p. 182, pl. 39
4068, p. 308, pl. 72
4069, p. 482, pl. 112
4070, p. 332, pl. 80
4071, p. 332
4072, p. 332
4073, p. 332
4074, p. 322
4075, p. 332
4076, p. 199
4077, p. 332
4078, p. 483, pl. 112
4079, p. 483
4080, p. 199
4081, p. 218, pl. 48
4082, p. 309, pl. 72
4083, p. 483, pl. 112
4084, p. 309, pl. 72
4085, p. 264, pl. 60
4086, p. 199, pl. 44
4087, p. 483, pl. 112
4088, p. 199
4089, p. 309
4091, p. 332, pl. 80
4092, p. 199
4093, p. 199

4094, p. 182, pl. 39
4095, p. 199
4096, p. 199
4097, p. 199
4098, p. 199
4099, p. 58, pl. 12
4100, p. 184, pl. 40
4101, p. 199, pl. 44
4102, p. 236, pl. 53
4103, p. 483, pl. 112
4104, p. 199
4105, p. 199
4106, p. 199
4107, p. 120, pl. 28
4108, p. 309, pl. 72
4109, p. 199
4110, p. 199
4111, p. 199, pl. 44
4112, p. 120, pl. 28
4118, p. 368, pl. 89
4119, p. 332
4120, p. 332
4121, p. 309
4122, p. 199, pl. 44
4123, p. 332
4124, p. 182, pl. 39
4126, p. 332, pl. 80
4127, p. 309, pl. 73
4128, p. 309
4129, p. 309
4131, p. 411, pl. 96
4133, p. 332
4135, p. 58, pl. 12
4136, p. 58, pl. 12
4138, p. 66, pl. 14
4139, p. 199, pl. 44
4140, p. 199
4141, p. 199
4142, p. 199
4150, p. 57, pl. 12
4151, p. 57, pl. 12
4152, p. 57, pl. 12
4153, p. 57, pl. 12
4154, p. 236, fig. 1, pl. 53
4155, p. 403, pl. 95
4156, p. 403, fig. 1, pl. 95
4157, p. 405
4158, p. 409, pl. 95
4159, p. 410, pl. 96
4160, p. 406, fig. 1, pl. 95

4161, p. 57, pl. 12
4162, p. 57, pl. 12
4163, p. 333, pl. 80
4164, p. 385, pl. 92
4165, p. 57, pl. 12
4166, p. 228, pl. 51
4167, p. 57, pl. 12
4168, p. 480, pl. 111
4169, p. 480, pl. 111
4170, p. 480
4171, p. 480, pl. 111
4173, p. 480
4174, p. 480
4175, p. 480, pl. 111
4176, p. 478, pl. 111
4177, p. 480
4178, p. 121, pl. 28
4179, p. 264, pls. 60, 133
4180, p. 236, pl. 53
4181, p. 478, pl. 111
4182, p. 121, pl. 28
4183, p. 121, pl. 28
4184, p. 222, pl. 49
4185, p. 480
4186, p. 480, pl. 112
4187, p. 479, pl. 111
4188, p. 479
4189, p. 479, pl. 111
4190, p. 200, pls. 44, 132
4191, p. 200
4193, p. 200, pl. 44
4194, p. 200, pl. 44
4195, p. 478, pl. 111
4196, p. 478
4197, p. 200, pl. 44
4198, p. 478
4199, p. 478, pl. 111
4200, p. 479, pl. 111
4201, p. 479
4202, p. 57, pl. 12
4203, p. 57, pl. 12
4204, p. 57, pl. 12
4205, p. 222, pl. 49
4206, p. 218, pl. 48
4207, p. 57, pl. 12
4208, p. 273, pl. 105
4209, p. 479, pl. 111
4210, p. 222, pl. 49
4211, p. 200, pl. 44
4212, p. 93, pl. 20

4213, p. 479
4214, p. 479, pl. 111
4215, p. 479, pl. 111
4216, p. 368, pl. 89
4217, p. 58, pl. 12
4218, p. 58, pl. 12
4219, p. 478, pl. 111
4220, p. 173, pl. 38
4221, p. 480, pl. 111
4222, p. 200, pl. 44
4223, p. 391, pl. 55
4224, p. 220, pl. 49
4225, p. 362, pl. 87
4226, p. 78, pl. 17
4227, p. 58, pl. 12
4227 bis, p. 58, pl. 12
4228, p. 479, pl. 111
4229, p. 480
4230, p. 481
4231, p. 478, pl. 111
4232, p. 480
4233, p. 481, pl. 112
4234, p. 480
4235, p. 481, pl. 112
4236, p. 481
4237, p. 481
4238, p. 481, pl. 112
4239, p. 481
4239 bis, p. 481
4240, p. 481
4241, p. 481
4242, p. 481
4243, p. 481
4244, p. 481
4245, p. 481
4246, p. 481
4247, p. 481
4248, p. 481
4249, p. 481
4250, p. 482, pl. 112
4251, p. 200
4252, p. 479, pl. 111
4253, p. 482
4254, p. 481
4255, p. 478, pls. 111, 134
4256, p. 200, pl. 44
4257, p. 58, pl. 12
4258, p. 479, pl. 111
4259, p. 264, pl. 60
4260, p. 480, pl. 112

4261, p. 481
4262, p. 479, pl. 111
4263, p. 222
4264, p. 479
4265, p. 478
4266, p. 309, pl. 73
4267, p. 173
4268, p. 480, pl. 112
4269, p. 121, pl. 28
4270, p. 478, pl. 111
4271, p. 479, pl. 111
4272, p. 480, pl. 112
4273, p. 222, pls. 49, 133
4273 bis, pp. 391–392, pl. 86
4274, p. 218, pl. 48
4275, p. 200, pl. 44
4276, p. 200, pl. 44
4277, p. 58
4278, p. 200, pl. 44
4279, p. 482
4280, p. 482, pl. 112
4281, p. 482
4282, p. 482
4283, p. 482
4284, p. 482
4285, p. 480, pl. 112
4286, p. 479, pl. 111
4287, p. 482, pl. 112
4300, p. 351, pls. 84, 133
4301, p. 484, pls. 112, 134
4302, p. 309
4303, p. 201, pl. 45
4303 bis, p. 201
4304, p. 484, pls. 112, 134
4305, p. 201, pl. 45
4306, p. 201, pl. 45
4307, p. 201
4308, p. 402, pls. 94, 134
4309, p. 402, pl. 94
4310, p. 402, pl. 94
4311, p. 484, pl. 112
4312, p. 484, pl. 112
4313, p. 201, pl. 45
4314, p. 484, pl. 112
4315, p. 201
4316, p. 201, pl. 45
4317, p. 485
4318, p. 484, pl. 112
4319, p. 484, pl. 112
4320, p. 202, pl. 45

4321, p. 484, pl. 112
4322, p. 484, pl. 112
4323, p. 484, pl. 112
4324, p. 485, pl. 112
4326, p. 202, pl. 45
4327, p. 342, pl. 82
4328, p. 201, pl. 45
4329, p. 485, pl. 112
4330, p. 485, pl. 112
4331, p. 485, pl. 112
4332, p. 485, pl. 112
4334, p. 485, pl. 112
4335, p. 201, pls. 45, 132
4336, p. 201, pls. 45, 132
4341, p. 332, pl. 80
4342, p. 72, pl. 15
4343, p. 485
4344, p. 201
4345, p. 201
4346, p. 485, pl. 112
4347, p. 485, pl. 112
4348, p. 484, pl. 112
4348 bis, p. 484, pl. 112
4349, p. 485
4349 bis, p. 202
4350, p. 236, pl. 53
4351, p. 406, fig. 1, pl. 95
4352, p. 173, pls. 38, 132
4353, p. 173, pl. 38
4354, p. 174, pl. 38
4355, p. 258, pl. 58
4356, p. 244, pl. 55
4357, p. 448, pl. 103
4358, p. 331, pl. 79
4359, p. 175, pl. 38
4360, p. 354, pl. 85
4361, p. 411, pl. 96
4362, p. 411, pl. 96
4363, p. 411, pl. 96
4364, p. 411, pl. 96
4365, p. 242, pl. 54
4366, p. 193, pl. 42
4367, p. 53
4368, p. 53, pl. 11
4369, p. 448, pl. 103
4370, p. 180, pl. 39
4371, p. 448, pl. 103
4372, p. 258, pl. 58
4373, p. 180
4374, p. 327, pl. 78

4375, p. 173, pl. 38
4376, p. 319
4377, p. 454, pl. 104
4378, p. 449
4379, p. 177, pl. 38
4380, p. 411, pl. 96
4381, p. 447, pl. 103
4382, p. 448, pl. 103
4382 bis, p. 353, pl. 85
4383, p. 228, pl. 51
4384, p. 448, pl. 103
4385, p. 447, pl. 103
4386, p. 449, pl. 103
4387, p. 242, pl. 54
4388, p. 194, pl. 42
4389, p. 447
4390, p. 194, pl. 42
4391, p. 331, pl. 79
4392, p. 447
4393, p. 53, pl. 11
4394, p. 53, pl. 11
4395, p. 371, pl. 89
4396, p. 371
4397, p. 449
4398, p. 447, pl. 103
4399, p. 447, pl. 103
4400, p. 448, pl. 103
4401, p. 358, pl. 85
4402, p. 244, pl. 55
4403, p. 244, pl. 55
4404, p. 118, pl. 27
4405, p. 331, pl. 79
4406, p. 258, pl. 58
4407, p. 194
4408, p. 181
4409, p. 194
4410, p. 194
4411, pp. 125, 222, pl. 49
4412, p. 294, pl. 68
4413, p. 53, pl. 11
4415, p. 383, pl. 92
4416, p. 448, pl. 103
4417, p. 258
4418, p. 449
4419, p. 118, pl. 27
4420, p. 449
4421, p. 449, pl. 103
4422, p. 370, pl. 89
4423, p. 449, pl. 103
4424, p. 384, pl. 92

4425, p. 194
4426, p. 448, pl. 103
4427, p. 53, pl. 11
4428, p. 258
4429, p. 266, pl. 61
4430, p. 449, pl. 103
4431, p. 270, pl. 62
4432, p. 194, pl. 42
4433, p. 294, pl. 68
4434, p. 362, pl. 87
4435, p. 266, pl. 61
4436, p. 194, pl. 42
4437, p. 194
4438, p. 194
4439, p. 181, pl. 39
4440, p. 194
4441, p. 194, pl. 43
4442, p. 354, pl. 85
4443, p. 118, pl. 27
4444, p. 411
4445, p. 449
4446, p. 331
4447, p. 449
4448, p. 449
4449, p. 331, pl. 79
4450, p. 449
4451, p. 449
4452, p. 449
4453, p. 449
4454, p. 449
4455, p. 449
4456, p. 449
4457, p. 449
4458, p. 449
4459, p. 449
4460, p. 449
4461, p. 449
4462, p. 449
4464, p. 54, pl. 11
4465, p. 331, pl. 79
4466, p. 449
4467, p. 195, pl. 43
4469, p. 54, pl. 11
4470, p. 117
4471, p. 229, pl. 51
4472, p. 229, pl. 51
4473, p. 449
4474, p. 449
4475, p. 229, pl. 51
4476, p. 449

4477, p. 449
4478, p. 449
4479, p. 449
4480, p. 265
4481, pp. 272–273, pls. 105, 133
4482, p. 259, pl. 58
4482 bis, p. 259
4483, p. 259
4484, p. 259, pl. 58
4485, p. 259
4486, p. 259
4487, p. 259
4488, p. 259
4489, p. 259
4490, p. 259
4491, p. 259
4492, p. 451, pl. 104
4493, p. 451, pl. 104
4494, p. 241, pl. 54
4495, p. 401, pl. 94
4496, p. 294, pl. 68
4497, p. 259, pl. 59
4497 bis, p. 259
4498, p. 261, pl. 59
4499, p. 294, pl. 68
4500, p. 295, pl. 68
4501, p. 260, pl. 59
4502, p. 450, pl. 103
4503, p. 241, pl. 54
4504, p. 295, pl. 68
4505, p. 259, pl. 58
4506, p. 295, pl. 68
4507, p. 450, pl. 103
4508, p. 228, pl. 51
4509, p. 452
4510, p. 295, pl. 68
4511, p. 448, pl. 103
4512, p. 331
4513, p. 195, pl. 43
4514, p. 260, pl. 59
4515, p. 260
4516, p. 260, pl. 59
4517, p. 260, pl. 59
4518, p. 260, pl. 59
4519, p. 260, pl. 59
4520, p. 260, pl. 59
4521, p. 54, pl. 11
4522, p. 54, pl. 11
4523, p. 450, pl. 103
4524, p. 260, pl. 59

4525, p. 260
4526, p. 261, pl. 59
4527, p. 261, pl. 59
4528, p. 261, pl. 59
4529, p. 261
4530, p. 195
4531, p. 195, pl. 43
4532, p. 331, pl. 79
4533, p. 54, pl. 11
4534, p. 261, pl. 59
4535, p. 261, pl. 59
4536, p. 261, pl. 59
4537, p. 261, pl. 59
4538, p. 181
4539, p. 295, pl. 68
4540, p. 261, pl. 59
4541, p. 386, pl. 92
4542, p. 295, pl. 68
4543, p. 195, pl. 43
4544, p. 195, pl. 43
4545, p. 54, pl. 11
4546, p. 295, pl. 68
4547, p. 295, pl. 68
4548, p. 261
4549, p. 385, pl. 92
4550, p. 261, pl. 59
4551, p. 262, pl. 59
4552, p. 451
4553, p. 295, pl. 68
4554, p. 295
4555, p. 295, pl. 68
4556, p. 181, pl. 39
4557, p. 295, pl. 68
4558, p. 242, pl. 54
4558 bis, p. 181, pl. 39
4559, p. 259, pl. 58
4560, p. 259, pl. 58
4561, p. 242, pl. 54
4562, p. 295, pl. 68
4563, p. 245, pl. 55
4564, p. 54, pl. 11
4565, p. 54, pl. 11
4566, p. 242, pl. 54
4567, p. 452
4568, p. 298
4569, p. 452
4570, p. 331
4571, p. 331
4572, p. 331, pl. 79
4573, p. 262, pl. 59

4574, p. 262, pl. 59
4575, p. 452, pl. 104
4576, p. 181, pl. 39, 132
4577, p. 331, pl. 79
4578, p. 270, fig. 1, pl. 63
4579, p. 260, pl. 59
4580, p. 405, fig. 1, pl. 95
4581, p. 401, pl. 94
4582, p. 448
4583, p. 448, pl. 103
4584, p. 409, pl. 96
4585, p. 410, pl. 96
4586, p. 405, pl. 95
4587, p. 452
4588, p. 451, pl. 104
4589, p. 452
4590, p. 54
4591, p. 452
4592, p. 452
4593, p. 452
4594, p. 298
4595, p. 452
4596, p. 452
4597, p. 452
4598, p. 452
4599, p. 298
4600, p. 295
4601, p. 298
4602, p. 298
4603, p. 452
4604, p. 452
4605, p. 262
4606, p. 452
4607, p. 452
4608, p. 452
4609, p. 295, pl. 68
4610, p. 262
4611, p. 452
4612, p. 452
4613, p. 262, pl. 59
4614, p. 298
4615, p. 298
4616, p. 295, pl. 68
4617, p. 295, pl. 68
4618, p. 449
4619, p. 262, pl. 59
4620, p. 262, pl. 59
4621, p. 262, fig. 1, pl. 59
4622, p. 409, pl. 96
4623, p. 195

4624, p. 195, pl. 43
4625, p. 452
4626, p. 452, pl. 104
4627, p. 332
4628, p. 452
4629, p. 452
4630, p. 452
4631, p. 262
4632, p. 452
4633, p. 70, fig. 1, pl. 15
4634, p. 452
4635, p. 452
4636, p. 452
4637, p. 452
4638, p. 452
4639, p. 452, pl. 104
4640, p. 452
4641, p. 449, 452
4642, p. 451, pl. 104
4643, p. 451, pl. 104
4644, p. 451, pl. 104
4645, p. 271, pl. 63
4646, pp. 451, 452, pl. 104
4647, p. 262, pl. 59
4648, p. 266
4649, p. 452
4650, p. 332
4651, p. 118, pl. 27
4652, p. 260
4653, p. 452
4654, p. 229, pl. 51
4655, p. 118, pl. 27
4656, p. 118, pl. 27
4657, p. 451, pl. 103
4658, p. 83, pl. 18
4659, p. 173, pl. 38
4660, p. 380, pl. 91
4661, p. 380, pl. 91
4662, p. 300, pl. 70
4663, p. 452
4664, p. 452
4665, p. 452
4666, p. 195, pl. 43
4667, p. 295, pl. 68
4668, p. 56, pl. 11
4670, p. 454, pl. 104
4671, p. 197, pl. 43
4672, p. 454, pl. 104
4673, p. 455, pl. 104
4674, p. 30, pl. 2

4675, p. 30, pl. 2
4675 bis, p. 30, pl. 2
4676, p. 196, pls. 43, 132
4677, p. 217, pl. 48
4679, p. 196, pl. 43
4680, p. 125, pl. 29
4681, p. 452, pl. 104
4682, p. 118, pl. 27
4683, p. 196, pl. 43
4684, p. 196, pl. 43
4685, p. 454, pl. 104
4686, p. 455
4687, p. 125, pl. 29
4688, p. 55, pl. 11
4689, p. 452, pls. 104, 134
4690, p. 453, pl. 104
4691, p. 453, pl. 104
4692, p. 454, pl. 104
4693, p. 196, pl. 43
4694, p. 453, pl. 104
4695, p. 228, pl. 51
4696, p. 126, pl. 29
4697, p. 126
4698, p. 370, pl. 89
4699, p. 370, pl. 89
4700, p. 296, pl. 69
4701, p. 296, pl. 69
4702, p. 55, pl. 11
4703, p. 55, pl. 11
4704, p. 364, pl. 88
4705, p. 55, pl. 11
4706, p. 196, pl. 43
4707, p. 208
4708, p. 196, pl. 43
4709, p. 55
4710, p. 55
4711, p. 196, pl. 43
4712, p. 196, pl. 43
4713, p. 196, pl. 43
4714, p. 452, pl. 104
4715, p. 453, pl. 104
4716, p. 196, pl. 43
4717, p. 198, pl. 44
4718, p. 196, pl. 43
4719, p. 296, pl. 69
4720, p. 453, pl. 104
4721, p. 196
4722, p. 196, pl. 43
4723, p. 243, pl. 54
4724, p. 453, pl. 104

4725, p. 452, pl. 104
4727, p. 55, pl. 11
4728, p. 75, pl. 16
4728 (duplicate number), p. 453, pl. 104
4729, p. 453, pl. 104
4730, p. 35, pl. 3
4731, p. 55, pl. 11
4733, p. 197, pl. 43
4734, p. 197
4735, p. 197, pl. 43
4736, p. 197, pl. 43
4737, p. 86, pl. 19
4738, p. 197
4739, p. 197
4740, p. 197, pl. 43
4741, p. 196
4742, p. 454
4743, p. 55, pl. 11
4744, p. 454, pl. 104
4745, p. 453
4746, p. 455
4747, p. 455
4748, p. 196
4749, p. 453
4750, p. 455
4751, p. 455
4752, p. 455
4753, p. 455
4754, p. 455
4755, p. 196
4756, p. 455
4757, p. 455
4758, p. 455
4759, p. 455
4760, p. 406, pl. 95
4761, p. 296, pl. 69
4762, p. 242, pl. 54
4763, pp. 455–456, pl. 105
4764, p. 296, pl. 69
4765, p. 297, pl. 69
4766, p. 126, pl. 29
4767, p. 181
4768, p. 198, pls. 44, 132
4769, p. 181, pl. 39
4770, p. 181
4771, p. 181
4772, p. 297
4773, p. 297, pl. 69
4774, p. 297, pl. 69

4775, p. 55
4776, p. 55, pl. 11
4777, p. 126, pl. 29
4778, p. 300, pl. 70
4779, p. 297, pl. 69
4780, p. 297, pl. 69
4781, p. 455, pl. 105
4782, p. 454
4783, p. 181, pl. 39
4784, p. 297, pl. 69
4785, p. 198
4786, p. 181
4787, p. 198
4788, p. 397, pl. 94
4789, p. 455, pl. 105
4790, p. 381, pl. 91
4791, p. 219, pl. 48
4792, p. 297, pl. 69
4793, p. 391, pls. 55, 133
4794, p. 391, pl. 55
4795, p. 297, pl. 69
4796, p. 297
4797, p. 55, pl. 11
4798, p. 455, pl. 105
4799, p. 297, pl. 69
4800, p. 55, pl. 11
4801, p. 245, pl. 55
4802, p. 400, pl. 94
4804, p. 181, pl. 39
4805, p. 297, pl. 69
4806, p. 456, pl. 105
4807, p. 297, pl. 69
4808, p. 297, pl. 69
4809, p. 456
4810, p. 456, pl. 105
4811, p. 456
4812, p. 236, pl. 53
4813, p. 398, pl. 94
4814, p. 456
4815, p. 456, pl. 105
4816, p. 456, pl. 105
4818, p. 456
4819, p. 456, pl. 105
4820, p. 456
4821, p. 456
4822, p. 456
4823, p. 456
4824, p. 298
4825, p. 298
4826, p. 456

4827, p. 456, pl. 105
4828, p. 456
4829, p. 456
4830, p. 198, pl. 44
4831, p. 455, pl. 105
4832, p. 298
4833, p. 198, pl. 44
4834, p. 70, pl. 15
4835, p. 456, pl. 105
4836, p. 456
4837, p. 29, pl. 2
4838, p. 56, pl. 11
4839, p. 118, pl. 27
4840, p. 384, pl. 92
4841, p. 320, pl. 75
4842, p. 454, pl. 104
4843, p. 243, pl. 54
4844, p. 119, pl. 27
4845, p. 297, pls. 69, 133
*4850, p. 297, pl. 69
4851, p. 119, pl. 27
4852, p. 119, pl. 27
4853, p. 119
4854, p. 262, pl. 60
4855, p. 298, pl. 69
4856, p. 298, pl. 69
4857, p. 298, pl. 69
4858, p. 298, pl. 69
4859, p. 198, pl. 44
4860, p. 119
4861, p. 57, pl. 11
4863, p. 57, pl. 11
4864, p. 120, pl. 27
4865, p. 395, pl. 93
4866, p. 120, pl. 27
4867, p. 410, pl. 96
4868, p. 456, pl. 105
4869, p. 449
4870, p. 456, pl. 105
4871, p. 390
4872, p. 120, pl. 27
4873, p. 57, pl. 11
4874, p. 120, pl. 27
4875, p. 456, pl. 105
4876, p. 244, pl. 55
4877, p. 390, pl. 55
4878, p. 390
4879, p. 119, pl. 27
4880, p. 369
4881, p. 369, pl. 89

4882, p. 241, pl. 54
4883, p. 241, pl. 54
4884, p. 457, pl. 105
4886, p. 198, pl. 44
4887, p. 298, pl. 69
4888, p. 262, pl. 60
4889, p. 119, pl. 27
4890, p. 198, pl. 44
4891, p. 198, pl. 44
4892, p. 199, pl. 44
4893, p. 262, pl. 60
4894, p. 299, pl. 69
4895, p. 299, pl. 69
4896, p. 57, pl. 11
4897, p. 299
4898, p. 457, pl. 105
4899, p. 236, pl. 53
4900, p. 457
4901, p. 121, pl. 28
4902, p. 56, pl. 11
4903, p. 176
4904, p. 457
4905, p. 457, pl. 105
4906, p. 56, pl. 11
4907, p. 229, pl. 51
4908, p. 423, pl. 99
4909, p. 423, pl. 99
4910, p. 126, pl. 29
4911, p. 55, pl. 11
4912, p. 380, pl. 91
4913, p. 126, pl. 29
4914, p. 452, pl. 104
4915, p. 457, pl. 105
4917, p. 449
4920, p. 176
4921, p. 297, pl. 69
4922, p. 457
4923, p. 449, pl. 103
4924, p. 449
4926, p. 405, fig. 1, pl. 95
4927, p. 449, pl. 103
4929, p. 295, pl. 68
4930, p. 390, pl. 55
4931, p. 228, pl. 51
4932, p. 449
4933, p. 449
4934, p. 241
4935, p. 456, pl. 105
4936, p. 332, pl. 79
4937, p. 199, pl. 44

4938, p. 454
4939, p. 451, pls. 104, 134
4941, p. 448, pl. 103
4942, p. 259, pl. 59
4943, p. 262
4944, p. 260
4945, p. 332
4945 bis, p. 298
4947, p. 297, pl. 69
4948, p. 449, pl. 103
4949, p. 449
4951, p. 449
4952, p. 241
4953, p. 241, pl. 54
4954, p. 198
4955, p. 265, pl. 60
4956, p. 265, pl. 60
 (mislabeled 4986)
4957, p. 262, fig. 1, pl. 60
4958, p. 242, pl. 54
4959, p. 450, pl. 103
4960, p. 406, fig. 1, pl. 95
4961, p. 451, pl. 104
4962, p. 258, pls. 58, 133
4963, p. 295, pl. 68
4964, p. 244, pl. 55
4965, p. 452, pl. 104
4966, p. 195, pl. 43
4967, p. 258, pl. 58
4968, p. 457, pl. 105
4969, p. 296, pl. 68
4970, p. 298, pl. 69
4971, p. 455, pl. 105
4972, p. 332
4973, p. 298
4974, p. 423
4975, p. 452
4976, p. 262, pl. 59
4977, p. 53, pl. 11
4978, p. 453
4979, p. 452
4980, p. 452
4981, p. 453
4982, p. 294
4983, p. 452
4984, p. 452
4985, p. 390
4986, p. 243; see also 4956
4987, p. 72, pl. 15
4988, p. 29, pl. 2

4989, p. 196, pl. 43
4990, p. 452
4991, p. 454
4994, p. 298
4995, pp. 261, 294
4996, p. 298, pl. 69
4997, p. 298, pls. 69, 133
4998, p. 454, pl. 104
4999, p. 456, pl. 105
5001, p. 256, pl. 57
5002, p. 254, pl. 57
5003, p. 252, pl. 56
5004, p. 252, pl. 56
5005, p. 254, pl. 57
5006, p. 256, pl. 57
5007, p. 255, pl. 57
5008, p. 255, pl. 57
5009, p. 255, pl. 57
5010, p. 252, pl. 56
5011, p. 252
5012, p. 251, pl. 56
5013, p. 251, pl. 56
5014, p. 251, pl. 56
5015, p. 256
5016, p. 253, pl. 56
5017, p. 48, pl. 9
5018, p. 49
5019, p. 48, fig. 1, pl. 9
5020, p. 49, pl. 10
5021, p. 49, pl. 10
5022, p. 48, pl. 9
5023, p. 282, pl. 65
5024, p. 49, pl. 10
5025, p. 50
5026, p. 49, pl. 10
5027, p. 50, pl. 10
5028, p. 48, pl. 9
5029, p. 49
5030, p. 49
5031, p. 50, pl. 10
5031 bis, p. 50, pl. 10
5033, p. 49
5034, p. 48, pl. 9
5035, p. 463, pl. 107
5036, p. 463
5037, p. 463
5038, p. 49
5038 bis, p. 463
5039, p. 282
5040, p. 48, pl. 9

5040 bis, p. 48, pl. 9
5041, p. 48, pl. 10
5042, p. 50, pl. 10
5043, p. 48
5044, p. 463
5045, p. 48, fig. 1, pl. 10
5046, p. 49
5047, p. 48
5048, p. 463
5049, p. 37, pl. 5
5050, p. 51, pl. 10
5051, p. 51
5052, p. 50
5053, p. 51, pl. 10
5054, p. 50, pl. 10
5055, p. 283, pl. 65
5056, pp. 254, 272
5057, p. 405, fig. 1, pl. 95
5058, p. 405, pl. 95
5059, p. 466, pl. 107
5060, p. 117, pl. 27
5061, p. 117, pl. 27
5062, p. 180
5063, p. 389, pl. 55
5064, p. 180
5065, p. 180, pl. 39
5066, p. 180, pl. 39
5067, p. 180, pl. 39
5068, p. 180
5069, p. 180
5070, p. 180
5071, p. 180, pl. 39
5072, p. 371, pl. 89
5073, p. 465, pl. 107
5074, p. 180, pls. 39, 132
5075, p. 180
5076, p. 180
5077, p. 180
5078, p. 180
5079, p. 180
5080, p. 180
5081, p. 284
5082, p. 285, pl. 65
5083, p. 466
5084, p. 389, pl. 55
5085, p. 51, pl. 10
5086, p. 51
5087, p. 51, pl. 10
5088, p. 286, pl. 66
5089, p. 49, pl. 10

5090, p. 235, pl. 53
5091, p. 235, pl. 53
5092, p. 235, pl. 53
5093, p. 286, pl. 66
5094, p. 72, pl. 15
5095, p. 459, pl. 106
5096, p. 389, pl. 55
5097, p. 235, pl. 53
5098, p. 389, pl. 91
5099, p. 389, pl. 91
5100, p. 280, pl. 64
5101, p. 256, pl. 57
5102, p. 256
5103, p. 466, pl. 107
5105, p. 252, pl. 56
5106, p. 281, pl. 65
5107, p. 281, pl. 65
5108, p. 92, pls. 20, 131
5109, p. 75, pl. 16
5110, p. 51, pl. 10
5111, p. 251, pl. 56
5112, p. 358, pl. 86
5113, p. 358
5114, p. 358, pl. 86
5115, p. 358
5116, p. 256, pl. 57
5117, p. 236, pl. 53
5118, p. 236, pl. 53
5119, p. 251, pl. 56
5120, p. 27, pl. 1
5121, p. 289, pl. 67
5122, p. 47, pl. 9
5123, p. 283, pl. 65
5124, p. 459, pl. 106
5125, p. 459
5126, p. 467, pl. 108
5127, p. 46, pl. 9
5128, p. 251
5129, p. 279, pl. 64
5130, p. 280, pl. 64
5131, p. 235, pl. 53
5132, p. 252, pl. 56
5133, p. 252, pl. 56
5134, p. 252, pl. 56
5134 bis, p. 252
5135, p. 219, pl. 48
5136, p. 72, pl. 15
5137, p. 277, pl. 64
5138, p. 252, pl. 56
5139, p. 252, pl. 56

5140, p. 254, pl. 57
5141, p. 281, pl. 65
5142, p. 252, pl. 56
5143, p. 279
5144, p. 280, pl. 64
5145, p. 285, pl. 66
5146, p. 26, pl. 1
5147, p. 47, pl. 9
5148, p. 51, pl. 10
5150, p. 371, pl. 89
5151, p. 283
5152, p. 281, fig. 1, pl. 65
5153, p. 379, pl. 91
5154, p. 281, pl. 65
5155, p. 256, pl. 57
5156, p. 469, pl. 108
5157, p. 47, pl. 9
5158, p. 47, pl. 9
5159, p. 255, pl. 57
5160, p. 256, pl. 57
5161, p. 47, pl. 9
5162, p. 283, pl. 65
5163, p. 470, pl. 109
5164, p. 285, pl. 65
5165, p. 281, pl. 65
5166, p. 285
5167, p. 469, pl. 108
5168, p. 282, pl. 65
5169, p. 285, pl. 66
5170, p. 281
5171, p. 281, pl. 65
5172, p. 285, pl. 66
5173, p. 285
5174, p. 283
5175, p. 463, pl. 107
5176, p. 89, pl. 19
5177, p. 462, pl. 106
5178, p. 47, pl. 9
5179, p. 283, pl. 65
5180, p. 278
5181, p. 466
5182, p. 283
5183, p. 463
5184, p. 49
5185, p. 462, pl. 106
5186, p. 461, pl. 106
5187, p. 256, pl. 57
5188, p. 379
5189, p. 192, pl. 42
5190, p. 461, pl. 106

5191, p. 282, pl. 65
5192, p. 50
5193, p. 463
5194, p. 47, pl. 9
5195, p. 283, pl. 65
5196, p. 256, pl. 57
5197, p. 461, pl. 106
5198, p. 467, pl. 108
5199, p. 466
5200, p. 283, pl. 65
5202, p. 463
5203, p. 277
5203 bis, p. 466
5204, p. 465, pl. 107
5205, p. 459
5206, p. 463, pl. 107
5207, p. 50
5208, p. 466, pl. 107
5209, p. 284
5210, p. 335, fig. 1, pl. 81
5211, p. 465, pl. 107
5212, p. 192, pl. 42
5212 bis, p. 465, pl. 42
5213, p. 335, pl. 81
5214, p. 335, pl. 81
5215, p. 192, pl. 42
5217, p. 72, pl. 15
5218, p. 465, pl. 107
5219, p. 335, pl. 81
5220, p. 335, pl. 81
5221 bis, p. 335, pl. 81
5222, p. 335
5223, p. 465
5224, p. 355
5225, p. 355
5225 bis, p. 335
5226, p. 336, pl. 81
5227, p. 336
5228, p. 355, pl. 85
5229, p. 357, pl. 85
5230, p. 399, pl. 94
5231, p. 336, pl. 81
5232, p. 335
5233, p. 336
5234, p. 336, pl. 81
5235, p. 253, pl. 56
5236, p. 336
5237, p. 336, pl. 81
5238, p. 253, pl. 56
5239, p. 465

5240, p. 336
5241, p. 336
5242, p. 465
5243, p. 336
5244, p. 399
5245, p. 253
5246, p. 253
5247, p. 253
5248, p. 229, pl. 51
5249, p. 253
5250, p. 399, pl. 94
5251, p. 52, pl. 10
5252, p. 465, pl. 107
5253, p. 253
5254, p. 253
5255, p. 399
5257, p. 465, pl. 107
5258, p. 357, pl. 86
5259, p. 381, pl. 91
5260, pp. 459, 470, pl. 106
5261, p. 227, pl. 51
5262, p. 279, pl. 64
5263, p. 288, pl. 66
5264, p. 288, pl. 66
5265, p. 227, pl. 51
5266, p. 464, pl. 107
5267, p. 287, pl. 66
5268, p. 253, pl. 56
5269, p. 279, pl. 64
5270, p. 460, pl. 106
5271, p. 289, pl. 67
5272, p. 464
5273, p. 357, pl. 86
5274, p. 279
5275, p. 460
5276, p. 289, pl. 67
5277, p. 385, pl. 92
5278, p. 252
5279, p. 288, pl. 66
5280, p. 52, pl. 10
5281, p. 277, pl. 64
5282, p. 235, pl. 53
5283, p. 235
5284, p. 235, pl. 53
5285, p. 235, pl. 53
5286, p. 235, pl. 53
5287, p. 235
5288, p. 235, pl. 53
5289, p. 235, pl. 53
5290, p. 288, pl. 66

5291, p. 288, pl. 66
5292, p. 288, pl. 66
5293, p. 460
5294, p. 460, pl. 106
5295, p. 52, pl. 10
5296, p. 460, pl. 106
5297, p. 279, pl. 64
5298, p. 279, pl. 64
5299, p. 279, pl. 64
5300, p. 460, pl. 106
5301, p. 88, pl. 19
5302, p. 235
5303, p. 235, pl. 53
5304, p. 293, pl. 68
5305, p. 405, fig. 1, pl. 95
5306, p. 280, pl. 64
5307, p. 88, pl. 19
5308, p. 396, pl. 93
5309, p. 475, pl. 110
5310, p. 53, pl. 10
5311, p. 357, pl. 85
5312, p. 235
5313, p. 466, pl. 107
5314, p. 461, pl. 106
5315, p. 280
5316, p. 280
5317, p. 252
5318, p. 252
5319, p. 281, pl. 65
5320, p. 46, pl. 9
5321, p. 227, pl. 51
5322, p. 46
5323, p. 459, pl. 106
5324, p. 406, pl. 95
5325, p. 280, pl. 64
5326, p. 463, pl. 107
5327, p. 278, pl. 64
5328, p. 278, pl. 64
5329, p. 280, pl. 64
5330, p. 284, pl. 65
5331, p. 217, pl. 48, 132
5332, p. 217, pl. 48
5334, p. 284
5335, p. 284, pl. 65
5336, p. 293, pl. 68
5337, p. 217, pl. 48
5338, p. 281
5339, p. 49
5340, p. 256, pl. 57
5341, p. 463

5342, p. 282
5343, p. 379, pl. 91
5344, p. 256, pl. 57
5344 a, b, p. 272
5345, p. 75, pl. 16
5346, p. 75, pl. 16
5347, p. 75, pl. 16
5348, p. 193, pl. 42
5350, p. 256, fig. 1, pl. 57
5351, p. 257, pl. 58
5352, p. 257, fig. 1, pl. 57
5353, p. 48, fig. 1, pl. 10
5354, p. 52, pl. 10
5355, p. 48, pl. 10
5356, p. 227, fig. 1, pl. 51
5356 bis, p. 282, fig. 1, pl. 65
5357, p. 227, fig. 1, pl. 51
5358, p. 278, fig. 1, pl. 64
5359, p. 336, pl. 81
5360, p. 381, pl. 91
5361, p. 252, pl. 56
5362, p. 460, pl. 106
5363, p. 411
5364, p. 85, pl. 18
5365, p. 299, pl. 70
5366, p. 280, pl. 64
5367, p. 117, pl. 27
5368, p. 466, pl. 107
5369, p. 460, pl. 106
5370, p. 252, pl. 56
5371, p. 292, pl. 67
5372, p. 406, pl. 95
5373, p. 466, pl. 107
5375, p. 192, pl. 42
5377, p. 76, pls. 16, 118
5378, p. 257, 272, pl. 57
5379, p. 272, pl. 105
5380, p. 282, pl. 65
5380 bis, p. 286, pl. 66
5381, p. 282
5382, p. 227, pl. 51
5383, p. 282, pl. 65
5384, p. 254, pl. 57
5385, p. 284, pl. 65
5386, p. 284, pl. 65
5387, p. 284, pl. 65
5388, p. 254, pl. 57
5389, p. 282, pl. 65
5390, p. 49
5391, p. 463, pl. 107

5392, p. 466, pl. 107
5393, p. 257, pl. 58
5394, p. 213, pls. 17, 132
5395, p. 180
5396, p. 180
5397, p. 466, pl. 108
5398, p. 466
5399, p. 462, pl. 106
5400, p. 467, pl. 108
5401, p. 467
5402, p. 467
5403, p. 49, pl. 10, 131
5404, p. 289, pl. 67
5405, p. 287, pl. 66
5406, p. 287, pl. 66
5407, p. 287, pl. 66
5408, p. 287, pl. 66
5409, p. 287, pl. 66
5410, p. 288
5411, p. 288
5412, p. 289
5413, p. 278, pl. 64
5414, p. 463, pl. 107
5415, p. 390
5416, p. 52, pl. 10
5417, p. 52
5418, p. 390
5419, p. 390, pl. 55
5420, p. 379, pl. 91
5421, p. 465
5422, p. 465
5423, p. 289
5424, p. 289, pl. 67
5425, p. 463
5426, p. 357, pl. 85
5427, p. 288, pl. 66
5428, p. 280
5429, p. 357
5430, p. 460, pl. 106
5431, p. 336
5432, p. 284
5433, p. 464, pl. 107
5434, p. 464
5435, p. 288
5436, p. 379, pl. 91
5437, p. 50, pl. 10
5438, p. 463, pl. 107
5439, p. 278, pl. 64
5440, p. 53, pl. 10

5441, p. 391, pl. 55 (not labeled)
5442, p. 391, pl. 55
5443, p. 192, pl. 42
5444, p. 287, pl. 66
5445, p. 219, pl. 48
5446, p. 354, pl. 85
5448, p. 464
5448 bis, p. 464, pl. 107
5449, p. 465, pl. 107
5450, p. 336
5451, p. 193, pl. 42
5452, p. 336
5453, p. 252
5454, p. 253, pl. 56
5455, p. 52, pl. 10
5456, p. 465, pl. 107
5457, p. 52, pl. 10
5458, p. 253
5459, p. 253, pl. 56
5460, p. 464, pl. 107
5461, p. 465
5462, p. 253
5463, p. 465
5464, p. 52
5465, p. 461, pl. 106
5465 bis, p. 463, pl. 106
5466, p. 461, pl. 106
5467, p. 368, pl. 89
5468, p. 280
5469, p. 52
5470, p. 389, pl. 55
5471, p. 51
5472, p. 49
5473, p. 391, pl. 55 (not labeled)
5474, p. 49
5477, p. 409, pls. 96, 134
5479, p. 51, pl. 10
5479 bis, p. 466, pl. 107
5480, p. 49
5481, p. 283, pl. 65
5482, p. 49
5483, p. 180
5484, p. 180, pl. 39
5485, p. 256
5486, p. 399, pl. 94
5487, p. 283, pl. 65
5488, p. 256
5489, p. 285

5491, p. 288
5492, p. 399
5493, p. 355, pl. 85
5494, p. 288, pl. 66
5495, p. 256
5496, p. 76, pl. 16
5498, p. 51
5499, p. 286, pl. 66
5500, p. 220, pl. 49
5501, p. 289, pl. 67
5502, p. 336, pl. 81
5503, p. 281, pl. 65
5504, p. 284
5505, p. 461, pl. 106
5506, p. 464, pl. 107
5507, p. 460, pl. 106
5508, p. 252
5509, p. 285, pl. 66
5510, p. 357, pl. 85
5511, p. 357
5512, p. 461
5513, p. 252
5514, p. 235
5515, p. 385, pl. 92
5516, p. 253
5517, p. 72, pl. 15
5518, p. 49
5519, p. 283, pl. 65
5520, p. 50
5521, p. 49
5522, p. 463
5523, p. 463, pl. 107
5524, p. 49, pl. 10
5525, p. 253
5526, p. 464, pl. 107
5527, p. 252, pl. 56
5528, p. 180
5529, p. 463, pl. 107
5530, p. 52, pl. 10
5531, p. 284
5532, p. 336
5533, p. 255, pl. 57
5534, p. 257
5536, p. 284, pl. 65
5537, p. 463
5538, p. 227, fig. 1, pl. 51
5539, p. 410, pl. 96
5540, p. 465, pl. 107
5541, p. 462, pl. 106
5542, p. 255, pl. 57

5543, p. 180
5544, p. 50
5545, p. 281, pl. 65
5547, p. 467
5548, p. 467, pl. 108
5549, p. 292, pl. 67
5551, p. 476, pl. 110
5553, p. 395, pl. 93
5554, p. 278, pl. 64
5555, p. 336, pl. 81
5556, p. 278, pl. 64
5556 bis, p. 460
5557, p. 290, pl. 67
5558, p. 409, pl. 96
5559, p. 465, pl. 107
5560, p. 289, pl. 67
5561, p. 299, pls. 70, 128
5563, p. 176, pl. 38
5566, p. 283
5566 bis, p. 287
5567, p. 211, pl. 17
5568, p. 51
5570, p. 183
5573, p. 400
5574, pp. 180, 183, pl. 39
5575, p. 336, pl. 81, 133
5576, p. 254, pl. 57
5577, p. 253, pl. 56
5578, p. 462, pl. 106
5579, p. 410, pl. 96
5580, p. 465, pl. 107
5581, p. 285, pl. 66
5582, p. 285, pl. 66
5583, p. 282, pl. 65
5584, p. 285, pl. 66
5585, p. 279
5586, p. 278, pl. 64
5587, p. 290, pl. 67
5588, p. 464
5589, p. 284, pl. 65
5590, p. 278, pl. 64
5591, p. 460
5592, p. 459, pl. 106
5593, p. 466
5594, p. 462
5595, p. 75
5596, p. 180
5597, p. 46, pl. 9
5598, p. 460
5599, p. 459, pl. 106

LAUMONIER 1977 CONCORDANCE

5600, p. 46, pl. 9
5601, p. 242, pl. 54
5601 bis, p. 412, pl. 96
5602, p. 242
5603, p. 207
5604, p. 60
5604 bis, p. 412, pl. 96
5605, p. 60, pl. 12
5606, p. 60, pl. 12
5607, p. 193, pl. 42
5608, p. 207
5609, p. 207, pl. 47
5610, p. 208, pl. 47
5611, p. 310, pl. 73
5612, p. 207, pl. 47
5613, p. 200
5614, p. 207, pl. 47
5615, p. 207
5616, p. 84
5617, p. 207, pl. 47
5618, p. 218, pl. 48
5619, p. 84, pl. 18
5620, p. 445, pl. 102
5621, p. 84, pl. 18
5622, p. 142, pl. 32 (not labeled)
5624, p. 175, pl. 38
5625, p. 175, pl. 38
5626, p. 175
5627, p. 386
5628, p. 386, pl. 92
5629, p. 386, pl. 92
5630, p. 173, pl. 38
5631, p. 173, pl. 38
5632, p. 173
5633, p. 173
5634, p. 173, pl. 38
5635, p. 173, pl. 38
5636, p. 173
5637, p. 173
5637 bis, p. 207, pl. 47
5638, p. 207, pl. 47
5639, p. 207
5640, p. 62
5641, p. 62
5642, p. 272, pl. 63
5643, p. 272
5644, p. 272
5645, p. 256, pl. 57
5646, p. 272

5647, p. 272, pl. 63
5648, p. 269, pl. 62
5649, p. 272, pl. 63
5650, p. 272
5651, p. 272, pl. 63
5652, p. 272, pl. 63
5653, p. 263, pl. 60
5654, p. 272
5655, p. 261
5656, p. 272, pl. 63
5657, p. 272
5658, p. 272
5659, p. 272, pl. 63
5660, p. 330, pl. 79
5661, p. 272, pls. 63, 105
5662, p. 272
5663, p. 272
5664, p. 272, pl. 63
5665, p. 272
5666, p. 60, pl. 12
5667, p. 60
5668, p. 365, pl. 88
5669, p. 365
5670, p. 365
5671, p. 362, pl. 87
5672, p. 364, pl. 87
5673, p. 364
5674, p. 370, pl. 89
5675, p. 370, pl. 89
5676, p. 311, pl. 73
5677, p. 334, pl. 80
5678, p. 229, pl. 51
5679, p. 39, pl. 5
5679 bis, p. 62
5680, p. 62
5681, p. 62
5682, p. 62
5683, p. 151, pl. 34
5684, p. 229
5685, p. 229
5686, p. 272
5687, p. 333, pl. 80
5688, p. 388, pl. 88
5689, p. 62
5690, p. 62
5691, p. 272, pl. 63
5692, p. 62
5693, p. 62, pl. 13
5694, p. 62
5695, p. 119, pl. 27

5696, p. 122
5697, p. 122, pl. 28
5698, p. 118, pl. 27
5699, p. 122, pl. 28
5700, p. 122, pl. 28
5701, p. 121, pl. 28
5702, p. 121
5703, p. 122
5704, p. 122
5705, p. 338
5705 bis, p. 338
5705 ter, p. 338
5706, p. 271, 272
5707, p. 143, pl. 32
5708, p. 143
5709, p. 143, pl. 32
5710, p. 143
5711, p. 143
5712, p. 364
5713, p. 84, pl. 18
5714, p. 232, pl. 52
5715, p. 237, pl. 53
5716, p. 322
5717, p. 173, pl. 38
5718, p. 283
5719, p. 310
5720, p. 334, pl. 80
5721, p. 334, pl. 80
5722, pp. 228, 229, pl. 51
5723, p. 229
5724, p. 104, pl. 24
5725, p. 208
5726, p. 237, pl. 53
5727, p. 418
5728, p. 418
5729, p. 128, pl. 29
5730, p. 128
5731, p. 237, pl. 53
5732, pp. 269, 272, pl. 62
5733, p. 237, pl. 53
5734, p. 237
5735, p. 142, pl. 32
5736, p. 142
5737, p. 142
5738, p. 142, pl. 32
5739, p. 142, pl. 32
5740, p. 142
5741, p. 142
5742 (=59 S 264), p. 207
5742 (=C 62 C 2281), p. 142

5743, p. 401
5748, p. 334
5750, p. 271, pl. 63
5751, p. 333
5753, p. 386, pl. 92
5755, p. 245, pl. 55
5757, p. 128, pl. 29
5759, p. 311
5760, p. 301, pl. 70
5761, p. 333
5763, p. 271
5764, p. 352, pl. 83
5765, p. 333
5766, p. 333
5767, p. 333
5768, p. 333, pl. 80
5769, p. 333
5770, p. 333
5771, p. 333
5772, p. 333
5773, p. 333
5774, p. 333
5775, p. 333
5776, p. 333
5777, p. 334
5778, p. 333, pl. 80
5779, p. 333
5780, p. 333, pl. 80
5781, p. 333
5782, p. 333
5783, p. 319
5784, p. 334
5785, p. 334
5786, p. 334
5787, p. 334, pl. 80
5788, p. 334
5789, p. 321
5790, p. 334, pl. 80
5791, p. 357, pl. 85
5792, p. 356
5793, p. 245, pl. 55
5794, p. 334, pl. 80
5796, p. 354, pl. 85
5797, p. 355, pl. 85
5799, p. 350
5800, p. 439, pl. 101
5801, p. 333
5802, p. 333
5803, p. 333, pl. 80
5804, p. 333

5805, p. 207, pl. 47
5806, p. 207, pl. 47
5807, p. 207
5808, p. 207
5809, p. 207
5810, p. 207
5811, p. 207, pl. 47
5812, p. 207
5813, p. 207
5814, p. 207, pl. 47
5815, p. 207
5816, p. 207
5817, p. 165, 207
5818, p. 165, 207
5819, p. 207
5822, p. 377, pl. 90
5823, p. 377
5824, p. 377
5825, p. 377
5826, p. 377
5827, p. 377, pl. 90
5828, p. 377, pl. 90
5829, p. 387, pl. 88
5830, p. 357, pl. 85
5831, p. 387, pl. 88
5832, p. 94, pl. 20
5833, p. 94
5834, p. 61, pl. 13
5837, p. 61, pl. 13
5838, p. 61, pl. 13
5839, p. 61
5840, p. 61, pl. 13
5841, p. 61, pl. 13
5842, p. 61
5843, p. 62, pl. 13
5844, p. 62
5845, p. 61, pl. 13
5846, p. 61, pl. 13
5847, p. 61, pl. 13
5848, p. 62, pl. 13
5849, p. 60, pl. 12
5850, p. 210, pl. 17
5851, p. 60, pl. 12
5852, p. 50
5853, p. 60
5854, p. 60
5855, p. 39, pl. 5
5856, p. 60
5857, p. 39
5858, p. 60

5859, p. 60
5860, p. 60
5861, p. 60
5862, p. 29, pl. 2
5863, p. 377, pl. 90
5864, p. 60
5865, p. 368, pl. 89
5866, p. 252
5867, p. 386, pl. 92
5870, p. 207, pl. 47
5871, p. 78, pl. 17
5872, p. 60
5873, p. 60
5874, p. 483
5875, p. 128, pl. 29
5876, p. 128
5877, p. 370
5878, p. 128, pl. 29
5879, p. 260
5880, p. 60
5881, pp. 155, 207, pls. 35, 47
5883, p. 60, pl. 12
5884, p. 60
5886, p. 127
5887, p. 128
5888, p. 128
5889, p. 128
5890, p. 370, pl. 89
5891, p. 300, pl. 70
5892, p. 241, pl. 54
5893, p. 238, pl. 91
5894, p. 310
5895, p. 356, pl. 85
5896, p. 237
5899, p. 60, pl. 12
5900, p. 44, pl. 8
5901, p. 229
5902, p. 183, pl. 39
5903, p. 183, pl. 39
5904, p. 269
5906, pp. 271, 272, 310, pl. 63
5907, p. 237, pl. 53
5908, p. 66
5909, p. 218, pl. 48
5910, p. 67, pl. 14
5911, p. 67, pl. 14
5913, p. 470, pl. 109
5914, p. 94, pl. 20
5915, p. 333
5916, p. 310, pl. 73

5917, p. 303, pl. 71
5918, p. 327
5919, p. 77
5920, pp. 310, 311
5921, pp. 310, 311
5922, pp. 310, 311
5923, p. 310
5924, p. 364
5925, p. 385, pl. 92
5926, p. 386, pl. 92
5927, p. 385, pl. 92
5932, p. 346
5933, p. 370, pl. 89
5934, p. 416
5935, p. 416
5937, p. 291, pl. 67
5938, p. 310, pl. 73
5939, p. 311
5940, p. 334, pl. 80
5941, p. 295, pl. 68
5942, p. 60, pl. 12
5943, p. 52
5944, p. 60
5945, p. 310, pl. 73
5946, p. 237, pl. 53
5948, p. 102, pl. 23
5949, p. 224, pl. 50
5950, p. 228
5951, p. 245, pl. 55
5955, p. 287, pl. 66
5956, p. 311
5957, p. 310, pl. 73
5958, p. 296, pl. 68
5959, p. 311, pl. 73
5960, p. 356
5961, p. 356
5963, p. 128
5966, p. 128
5967, p. 128, pl. 29
5968, p. 128
5969, p. 311
5971, p. 245, pl. 55
5972, p. 94, pl. 20
5973, p. 357, pl. 85
5975, p. 238, pl. 91
5976, p. 228, pl. 51
5978, p. 238
5979, p. 60
5980, p. 228
5982, p. 388, pl. 88

5983, p. 228
5985, p. 208, pl. 47
5986, p. 208, pl. 47
5987, p. 208, pl. 47
5988, p. 208, pl. 47
5989, p. 208, pl. 47
5990, p. 208, pl. 47
5992, p. 388, pl. 88
5993, p. 208, pl. 47
5995, p. 384, pl. 92
5996, p. 142
5997, p. 418
5998, p. 236, pl. 53
5999, p. 271, pl. 63
6000, p. 66, pl. 14, 131
6002, pp. 467–468, pls. 108, 134
6003, p. 99, pls. 22, 131
6005, p. 101, pl. 23
6007, p. 392, pls. 86, 134
6008, p. 392, pls. 86, 134
6010, p. 98, pl. 21
6016, p. 406, pls. 95, 134
6020, p. 218, pl. 48
6021, p. 103, pl. 23
6026, p. 104, pl. 24
6039, p. 104, pl. 24
6040, p. 77, pl. 16
6042, p. 77, pl. 16
6049, p. 99, pl. 22
6067, p. 101, pl. 23
6075, p. 103, pl. 23
6081, p. 482, pl. 112
6082, p. 479, pls. 111, 134
6088, p. 73, pl. 16
6091, p. 101, pl. 23
6097, p. 222, pl. 49
6170, p. 104, pl. 24
6174, p. 473, pls. 109, 134
6200, p. 103, pl. 23
6201, p. 100, pls. 22, 131
8000, p. 211, pl. 17
8001, p. 271, pl. 63
8002, p. 208
8003, p. 208
8004, p. 208
8005, p. 208
8006, p. 271, pl. 63
8008, p. 242, pl. 54
8018, p. 207

8019, p. 208, pl. 47
8020, p. 207, pl. 47
8021, p. 354, pl. 85
8022, p. 356, pl. 85
8023, p. 384, pl. 92
8024, p. 207, pl. 47
8025, p. 50
8026, p. 370
8027, p. 364, pl. 88
8028, p. 310, pl. 73
8030, p. 122, pl. 28
8031, p. 212, pl. 17
8032, pp. 308, 311, pl. 73
8033, p. 362, pl. 87
8034, p. 62
8035, p. 268
8036, p. 379, pl. 91
8037, p. 388
8039, p. 311
8040, p. 242
8041, p. 77, pl. 16
8042, p. 66
8043, p. 381, pl. 91
8044, p. 310, 311
8045, p. 386, pl. 92
8046, p. 386, pl. 92
8049, p. 310
8050, p. 60, pl. 12
8051, pp. 310, 311
8052, p. 333, pl. 80
8053, p. 220, pl. 49
8054, p. 220, pl. 49
8055, p. 243, pl. 54
8056, p. 243
8057, p. 243
8058, p. 220, pl. 49
8060, p. 406, pl. 95
8061, pp. 218, 219, pl. 48
8062, p. 219
8063, p. 243, pl. 55
8065, p. 208, pl. 47
8068, p. 70, pl. 15
8069, p. 94, pl. 20
8070, p. 440
8073, p. 438, pl. 101
8074, p. 383, pl. 92
8075, p. 207, pl. 47
8077, p. 60, pl. 12
8078, p. 220, pl. 48
8079, p. 268

8081, p. 311, pl. 73
8082, p. 220, pl. 48
8083, p. 387, pl. 88
8085, p. 334
8086, p. 310, pl. 73
8087, pp. 207–208, pl. 47
8088, p. 67, pl. 14
8095, p. 400
8099, p. 303, pl. 71
8100, p. 84, pl. 18
8102, p. 287
8103, p. 397, pl. 94
8104, p. 311, pl. 73
8105, p. 304, pl. 71
8106, p. 311
8107, p. 211, pl. 17
8108, p. 201
8109, p. 201
8110, p. 311
8111, p. 70, pl. 15
8111 bis, p. 307, pl. 72
8112, p. 72
8113, p. 211
8114, p. 311, pl. 73
8115, p. 72, pl. 15
8116, p. 60, pl. 12
8117, p. 334
8118, p. 94, pl. 20
8119, p. 334
8120, p. 212, pl. 17
8122, p. 441, pl. 102
8123, p. 440, pl. 101
8124, p. 293, pl. 68
8126, p. 205
8128, p. 384, pl. 92
8129, p. 311, pl. 73
8131, p. 383, pl. 92
8134, p. 76, pl. 16
8136, p. 311
8138, p. 208
8139, p. 280
8140, p. 52, pl. 10
8141, p. 463, pl. 107
8142, p. 191
8143, p. 253
8144, p. 279, pl. 64
8145, p. 204, 207
8146, p. 207
8148, p. 311, pl. 73
8150, pp. 310, 311, pl. 73

8151, p. 60
8152, p. 464, pl. 107
8153, p. 301
8154, p. 364, pl. 88
8155, p. 240
8156, p. 431
8157, p. 139
8158, p. 272
8159, p. 65
8160, p. 272
8161, p. 128, pl. 29
8162, p. 310, pl. 73
8165, p. 153
8168, p. 31, pl. 2
8169, p. 389, pl. 91
8170, p. 66
8171, p. 103, pl. 23
8172, p. 462, pl. 106
8173, p. 66
8174, p. 271, pl. 63
8175, p. 271
8176, p. 66
8177, p. 66
8179, p. 208
8181, p. 222
8182, p. 208, pl. 47
8184, p. 208
8187, p. 222, pl. 49
8189, p. 210
8190, p. 173
8191, p. 273, pl. 105
8195, p. 60
8196, p. 128, pl. 29
8197, p. 237, pl. 53
8198, p. 401, pl. 94
8199, p. 396
8200, p. 396
8201, p. 401, pl. 94
8202, p. 396
8203, p. 396
8204, p. 396
8205, p. 396
8206, p. 401, pl. 94
8209, p. 401
8210, p. 273, pl. 105
8211, p. 237
8217, p. 272
8218, p. 303, pl. 71
8219, p. 303
8220, p. 167

8221, p. 120, pl. 28
8222, p. 329, pl. 78
8223, p. 305, pl. 71
8224, p. 437, pl. 101
8225, p. 419, pl. 98
8226, p. 280
8227, p. 289
8228, p. 287
8229, p. 460
8230, p. 227, pl. 50
8231, p. 462, pl. 106
8232, p. 26, pl. 1
8233, p. 292, pl. 67
8234, p. 98, pl. 21
8235, p. 471, pl. 109
8236, p. 128, pl. 29
8237, p. 60
8239, p. 204
8242, p. 357
8244, p. 310
8245, p. 391
8246, p. 311
8247, p. 465, pl. 107
8248, p. 395, pl. 93
8249, p. 187
8250, p. 97, pls. 21, 119
8251, p. 60
8252, p. 364, pl. 87
8253, p. 364
8256, p. 159
8259, p. 278, pl. 64
8260, p. 463, pl. 107
8261, p. 459, pl. 106
8262, p. 128, pl. 29
8263, p. 459, pl. 106
8264, p. 51, pl. 10
8265, p. 468
8266, p. 179, pl. 39
8267, p. 257
8268, p. 193
8269, p. 463
8270, p. 180
8271, p. 385
8272, p. 89
8273, p. 280, pl. 64
8274, p. 417, pl. 97
8275, p. 47, pl. 9
8276, p. 257
8278, p. 140, pl. 31
8279, p. 153

8280, p. 44, pl. 8
8281, p. 435
8282, p. 208
8283, p. 143, pl. 32 (not labeled)
8284, p. 77
8288, p. 153
8289, p. 185
8290, p. 177
8291, p. 176
8292, p. 368, pl. 89
8293, p. 218, pl. 48
8294, p. 222
8295, p. 368, pl. 89
8296, p. 153
8297, p. 143, pl. 32 (not labeled)
8298, p. 380
8301, p. 373
8302, p. 208
8303, p. 364, pl. 87
8304, p. 60
8305, p. 60
8306, p. 78, pl. 17
8308, p. 197, pl. 43
8309, p. 208
8310, p. 208
8311, p. 429, pl. 100
8312, p. 218, pl. 48
8313, p. 401
8315, p. 241
8321, p. 356, pl. 85
8325, p. 369, pl. 89
8329, p. 371, pl. 89
8331, p. 370
8332, p. 60
8334, p. 245, pl. 55
8334 (=C 63 C 1823), p. 469, pl. 108
8338, p. 356
8339, p. 311, pl. 73
8340, p. 311
8346, p. 354
8347, p. 354
8348, p. 311, pl. 73
8349, p. 72, pl. 15
8350, pp. 72, 73
8351, p. 241, pl. 54
8353, p. 357
8354, p. 380

8358, p. 380
8359, p. 208
8360, p. 208
8361, p. 208
8362, p. 208
8363, p. 60
8364, p. 208
8365, p. 126
8366, p. 208
8367, p. 305, pl. 72
8368, p. 311, pl. 73
8368 (=B 7476), p. 208, pl. 47
8369, p. 220
8370, p. 220
8371, p. 208
8372, p. 311, pl. 73
8374, p. 364, pl. 88
8375, p. 208
8376, p. 220, pl. 48
8377, p. 208
8378, p. 208, pl. 47
8379, p. 222, pl. 49
8382, p. 222
8383, p. 311
8387, p. 208
8388, p. 310, pl. 73
8390, p. 208, pl. 47
8391, p. 177, pl. 38
8393, p. 208, pl. 47
8394, p. 62, pl. 13
8395, p. 199
8396, p. 94, pl. 20
8397, p. 207, pl. 47
8398, p. 153
8401, p. 208, pl. 47
8407, p. 199
8408, p. 208, pl. 47
8409, p. 358, pl. 86
8410, p. 440
8411, p. 208, pl. 47
8412, p. 208, pl. 47
8414, p. 208
8415, p. 61, pl. 13
8416, p. 208, pl. 47
8417, p. 208
8418, p. 122, pl. 28
8419, p. 398, pl. 94 (not labeled)
8420, p. 122, pl. 28
8421, p. 122, pl. 28

8422, p. 111, pl. 25
8423, p. 44, pl. 8
8424, p. 334, pl. 80
8425, p. 100, pl. 22
8426, p. 356
8427, p. 165
8428, p. 435, pl. 101
8429, p. 389, pl. 91
8430, p. 311
8431, p. 311, pl. 73
8432, p. 310
8433, p. 352, pl. 84
8434, p. 347
8435, p. 347, pl. 83
8436, p. 225
8438, p. 206
8439, p. 228
8440, p. 441, pl. 102
8441, p. 69, pl. 15
8442, p. 205, pl. 46
8443, p. 389, pl. 91
8444, p. 242
8445, p. 419, pl. 98
8446, p. 237, pl. 53
8447, p. 90
8448, p. 375, pl. 90
8449, p. 426, pl. 99
8450, p. 232, pl. 52
8451, p. 232, pl. 52
8452, p. 329, pl. 79
8453, p. 323, pl. 76
8454, p. 330, pl. 79
8455, p. 232, pl. 52
8456, p. 376, pl. 90
8457, p. 125, pl. 28
8459, p. 165, pl. 37
8460, p. 90
8461, pp. 203, 206, pls. 45, 46
8462, p. 173
8463, p. 178, pl. 39
8464, p. 428, pl. 100
8465, p. 428, pl. 100
8466, p. 119, pl. 27
8467, p. 234
8468, p. 113
8469, p. 78, pl. 17
8470, p. 418, pl. 98
8471, p. 362, pl. 87
8472, p. 84, pl. 18
8473, p. 102, pl. 23

8474, p. 287, pl. 66
8475, p. 285, pl. 66
8476, p. 51, pl. 10
8477, p. 294
8478, p. 473, pl. 109
8479, p. 46, pl. 9
8479 **bis**, p. 46, pl. 9
8480, p. 241, pl. 54
8481, p. 347, pl. 83
8482, p. 237, pl. 91
8483, p. 344, pl. 82
8484, p. 344, pl. 82
8485, p. 396
8486, p. 212
8487, p. 438, pl. 101
8488, p. 442, pl. 102
8489, p. 442, pl. 102
8490, p. 414, pl. 97
8491, p. 415, pl. 97
8492, p. 291, pl. 67
8493, p. 254
8494, p. 253
8495, p. 259, pl. 58
8498, p. 419, pl. 98
8499, p. 98, pl. 21
8501, p. 273, pl. 105
8502, p. 380, pl. 91
8503, p. 447, pl. 103
8504, p. 54, pl. 11
8505, p. 54
8506, p. 54, pl. 11
8507, p. 56, pl. 11
8508, p. 232
8509, p. 156
8510, p. 92, pl. 20
8511, p. 53, pl. 11
8512, p. 319, pl. 75
8515, p. 216, pl. 48
8520, p. 97, pls. 21, 119
8523, p. 483, pl. 112
8524, p. 93, pl. 20
8525, p. 182
8526, p. 415, pl. 97
8527 (=C 64 C 111), p. 175
8527 (=D 64 C 1229+1059), p. 190
8528, p. 191, pl. 42
8529, p. 76, pl. 16
8530, p. 467, pl. 108
8531, p. 55

8532, p. 395, pl. 93
8533, p. 433, pl. 100
8534, p. 161
8535, p. 370, pl. 89
8535 bis, p. 461, pl. 106
8536, p. 352, pl. 84
8537, p. 98, pl. 21
8538, p. 105, pl. 24
8539, p. 103, pl. 23
8540, p. 104, pl. 24
8541, p. 195, pl. 43
8542, p. 106, pl. 24, 120
8543, p. 106, pl. 24
8544, p. 106, pl. 24
8545, p. 98, pl. 21
8546, p. 99, pl. 21
8547, p. 101, pl. 23
8548, p. 470, pl. 108
8549, p. 395, pl. 93
8550, p. 383
8551, p. 269, pl. 62
8552, p. 347, pl. 83
8553, p. 413, pl. 97
8554, p. 221, pl. 49
8555, p. 413, pl. 97
8556, p. 418, pl. 98
8556 bis, p. 418, pl. 98
8557, p. 449, pl. 103
8558, p. 353, pl. 84
8559, p. 216, pl. 48
8560, p. 167
8561, p. 71, pl. 15
8563, p. 419, pl. 98
8564, p. 418, pl. 98
8565, p. 419, pl. 98
8566, p. 414, pl. 97
8567, p. 93, pl. 20
8568, p. 92, pl. 20
8569, p. 415, pl. 97
8570, p. 388, pl. 88
8571, p. 350, pl. 84
8572, p. 417, pl. 97
8573, p. 419, pl. 98
8574, p. 71, pl. 15
8575, p. 71, pl. 15
8576, p. 420, pl. 98
8577, p. 149, pl. 33
8578, pp. 414, 418, pl. 98
8579, p. 168, pl. 37
8580, p. 166, pl. 37

8581, p. 352, pl. 84
8582, p. 464, pl. 107
8583, p. 456
8585, p. 104, pl. 23
8586, p. 439, pl. 101
8587, p. 420, pl. 98
8589, p. 237, pl. 53
8590, p. 345, pl. 82
8592, p. 439, pl. 101
8593, p. 128, pl. 29
8594, p. 150, pl. 34
8595, p. 348, pl. 83
8596, p. 440, pl. 102
8597, p. 387, pl. 88
8599, p. 56, pl. 11
8600, p. 440, pl. 102
8601, p. 439, pl. 101
8602, p. 376, pl. 90
8603, p. 444, pl. 102
8604, p. 357, pl. 85
8605, p. 468, pl. 108
8606, p. 212, pl. 17
8607, p. 440, pl. 101
8608, p. 161
8609, p. 441, pl. 102
8610, p. 451, pl. 103
8611, p. 448, pl. 103
8612, p. 350, pl. 84
8613, p. 349, pl. 84
8614, p. 349, pl. 84
8615, p. 348, pl. 83
8616, p. 350, pl. 84
8617, p. 348, pl. 83
8618, p. 345, pl. 82
8619, p. 395, pl. 93
8620, p. 351, pl. 84
8624, p. 61
8625, p. 60
8626, p. 44, pl. 8
8627, p. 61, pl. 13, 113
8628, p. 351, pl. 84
8629, p. 41, pl. 7
8630, p. 42, pl. 7
8631, p. 43, pl. 8
8632, p. 45, pl. 9
8633, p. 50, pl. 10
8634, p. 50, pl. 10
8635, p. 51, pl. 10
8636, p. 47, pl. 9
8637, p. 50, pl. 10

8638, p. 460, pl. 106
8639, p. 50, pl. 10
8640, p. 54, pl. 11
8641, p. 55
8642, p. 255, pl. 57
8643, p. 282
8644, p. 256
8645, p. 257, pl. 58
8646, p. 472, pl. 109
8647, p. 262
8648, p. 262
8649, p. 258, pl. 58
8650, p. 298, pl. 69
8651, p. 196, pl. 43
8652, p. 450, pl. 103
8653, p. 260, pl. 59
8654, p. 259
8655, p. 258, pl. 58
8656, p. 260, pl. 59
8657, p. 259
8658, p. 260
8659, p. 260
8660, p. 259, pl. 58
8661, p. 259, pl. 58
8662, p. 259, pl. 58
8663, p. 270, pl. 62
8664, p. 270, pl. 62
8665, p. 269, pl. 62
8666, p. 380, pl. 91
8667, p. 452, pl. 104 (mislabeled 8867)
8668, p. 272, pl. 63
8669, p. 271, pl. 63
8670, p. 271, pl. 63
8671, p. 271, pl. 63
8672, p. 272
8673, p. 269
8674, p. 272
8675, p. 271, fig. 1, pl. 63
8676, p. 271, pl. 63
8677, p. 455, pl. 105
8678, p. 380, pl. 91
8679, p. 457, pl. 105
8680, p. 457, pl. 105
8681, p. 460, pl. 106
8682, p. 467, pl. 108
8683, p. 462, pl. 106
8684, p. 107, pl. 24
8687, p. 471, pl. 109
8688, p. 253, pl. 56

8689, p. 253, pl. 56
8690, p. 253, pl. 56 (not labeled)
8691, p. 254
8692, p. 254
8693, p. 254, pl. 56
8694, p. 254
8695, p. 257, pl. 58
8696, p. 257, pl. 58
8697, p. 256, pl. 57
8698, p. 257, pl. 58
8699, p. 257, pl. 58
8700, p. 255, pl. 57
8701, p. 255, pl. 57
8702, p. 27, pl. 1
8703, p. 62, pl. 13
8704, p. 34, pl. 3
8705, p. 305, pl. 71
8706, p. 44, pl. 8
8706 (duplicate number), p. 50, pl. 10
8706 bis, p. 44, pl. 8
8707, p. 41, 60, pl. 7
8708, p. 41, pl. 7
8709, p. 460, pl. 106
8710, p. 53
8711, p. 47, pl. 9
8712, p. 47, pl. 9
8713, p. 180
8714, p. 180
8715, p. 370, pl. 89
8716, p. 189
8717, p. 188, pl. 41
8718, p. 189
8719, p. 180
8720, p. 47, pl. 9
8721, p. 47, pl. 9
8722, p. 47, pl. 9
8723, p. 47, pl. 9
8725, p. 61, pl. 13
8726, p. 60
8727, p. 49
8728, p. 460, pl. 106
8729, p. 49
8729 bis, p. 49
8729ter, p. 49
8730, p. 53, pl. 11
8731, p. 60
8732, p. 60
8733, p. 462, pl. 106

8734, p. 55, pl. 11
8735, p. 207, pl. 47
8736, p. 390
8737, p. 55
8738, p. 78
8739, p. 58
8740, p. 279, pl. 64
8740 bis, p. 241, pl. 54
8741, p. 61, pl. 13
8742, p. 62, pl. 13
8744, p. 101, pl. 23
8745, p. 173
8746, p. 174
8747, p. 178, pl. 39
8748, p. 178, pl. 39
8749, p. 178, pl. 39
8750, p. 114, pl. 26
8751, pp. 121, 122, pl. 28
8752, p. 116, pl. 26
8753, p. 116, pl. 26
8754, p. 116, pl. 26
8755, p. 116, pl. 26
8756, p. 117, pl. 26
8757, p. 118, pl. 27
8758, p. 118, pl. 27
8759, p. 399, pl. 94
8760, p. 118
8761, p. 120
8762, p. 120, pl. 27
8763, p. 367, pl. 89
8764, p. 399, pl. 94
8765, p. 125, pl. 28
8766, p. 125
8767, p. 292
8768, p. 60
8769, p. 278, pl. 64
8770, p. 278, pl. 64
8771, p. 285, pl. 65
8772, p. 285, pl. 65
8773, p. 286
8774, p. 282, pl. 65
8775, p. 282, pl. 65
8776, p. 278, pl. 64
8777, p. 278, pl. 64
8778, p. 284, pl. 65
(mislabeled 8878)
8779, p. 284, pl. 65
8780, p. 286, pl. 66
8781, p. 286, pl. 66
8782, p. 283, pl. 65
8783, p. 283

8784, p. 287, pl. 66
8785, p. 288, pl. 66
8785 bis, p. 288
8786, p. 290, pl. 67
8787, p. 292
8788, p. 293, pl. 68
8789, p. 291
8790, p. 293, pl. 68
8791, p. 293, pl. 68
8792, p. 293
8793, p. 294, pl. 68
8794, p. 294
8795, p. 298, pl. 69
8796, p. 296, pl. 68
8797, p. 296
8797 bis, p. 296, pl. 68
8798, p. 294, pl. 68
8799, p. 328, pl. 78
8800, p. 52, pl. 10
8801, p. 286, pl. 66
8802, p. 298, pl. 69
8803, p. 397, pl. 94
8804, p. 299, pl. 70
8805, p. 441, pl. 102
8806, p. 185, pls. 40, 126
8807, p. 388, pl. 88
8808, p. 185
8809, p. 240, pl. 54
8810, p. 240, pl. 54
8811, p. 307
8811 bis, p. 307
8812, p. 311, pl. 73
8812 bis, p. 311
8813, p. 311
8814, p. 73
8815, p. 292
8816, p. 279
8817, p. 283
8818, p. 288, pl. 66
8819, p. 288
8820, p. 279, pl. 64
8821, p. 288, pl. 66
8822, p. 285, pl. 65
8823, p. 291
8824, p. 281
8825, p. 283
8826, p. 292, pl. 67
8827, p. 292
8828, p. 235, pl. 53
8829, p. 288, pl. 66
8830, p. 353

8831, p. 290
8832, p. 287
8833, p. 310
8834, p. 259, pl. 58
8835, p. 311
8836, p. 311
8837, p. 397, pl. 94
8838, p. 311, pl. 73
8839, p. 74, pl. 16
8840, p. 75, pl. 16
8841, p. 245, pl. 55
8843, p. 61, pl. 13
8845, p. 364
8846, p. 364, pl. 87
8847, p. 79, pl. 17
8848, p. 362, pl. 87
8849, p. 66
8850, p. 228, pl. 51
8850 (duplicate number), p. 383, pl. 92
8851, p. 228, pl. 51
8854, p. 228, pl. 51
8855, p. 229
8856, p. 232, pl. 52
8857, p. 237, pl. 53
8858, p. 237
8859, p. 269, pl. 62
8860, pp. 233–234, pl. 52
8861, p. 234, pls. 52, 133
8862, p. 234, pl. 52
8863, p. 237
8864, p. 75, pl. 16
8865, p. 89, pl. 19
8866, p. 301, pl. 70
8867, p. 397, pl. 94; see also 8667
8867 (duplicate number), p. 452, pl. 104
8868, p. 397
8869, p. 241, pl. 54
8870, p. 245, pl. 55
8872, p. 455
8874, p. 128, pl. 29
8875, p. 398
8876, p. 245, pl. 55
8877, p. 370, pl. 89
8877 bis, p. 370
8878, p. 371, pl. 89; see also 8778
8879, p. 370, pl. 89
8880, p. 370, pl. 89

8881, p. 391, pl. 55
8883, p. 279, pl. 64
8884, p. 437, pl. 101
8886, p. 236, pl. 53
8887, p. 153, pl. 34
8888, p. 153
8889, p. 161
8890, p. 107, pl. 24
8891, p. 162
8892, p. 169
8893, p. 158
8894, p. 179
8895, p. 362, pl. 87
8896, p. 189
8897, p. 190
8898, p. 189
8899, p. 189
8900, p. 191
8901, p. 258
8902, p. 194, pl. 42
8903, p. 194
8904, p. 181, pl. 39
8905, p. 197, pl. 43
8906, p. 238, pl. 91
8907, p. 93, pl. 20
8908, p. 486
8909, p. 486
8910, p. 203
8911, p. 203
8912, p. 203, pl. 45
8913, p. 203, pl. 45
8914, p. 206, pl. 46
8915, p. 206, pl. 46
8916, p. 207, pl. 47
8917, p. 226, pl. 50
8918, p. 217, pl. 48
8919, p. 237
8920, p. 244, pl. 55
8921, p. 400, pl. 94
8922, p. 347
8923, p. 354, pl. 85
8924, p. 354, pl. 85
8925, p. 355
8926, p. 354, pl. 85
8927, p. 356, pl. 85
8928, p. 362, pl. 87
8929, p. 362, pl. 87
8930, p. 212, pl. 17
8931, p. 189
8932, p. 100, pl. 22
8933, p. 375, pl. 90

LAUMONIER 1977 CONCORDANCE

8934, p. 376, pl. 90
8935, p. 375, pl. 90
8936, p. 252, pl. 56
8937, p. 254
8938, p. 255, pl. 57
8939, p. 257
8940, p. 260, pl. 59
8941, p. 270, pl. 62
8942, p. 269
8943, p. 271
8943 bis, p. 271, pl. 63
8944, p. 279
8945, p. 280, pl. 64
8946, p. 293, pl. 68
8947, p. 304, pl. 71
8948, p. 149
8949, p. 92, pl. 20
8950, p. 316, pl. 74
8951, p. 316, pl. 74
8952, p. 320, pl. 75
8953, p. 320, pl. 75
8954, p. 321, pl. 76
8955, p. 322
8956, p. 322
8957, p. 322, pl. 76
8958, p. 322, pl. 76
8959, p. 324, pl. 77
8960, p. 325, pl. 77
8961, p. 326, pl. 77
8962, p. 329, pl. 79
8963, p. 330, pl. 79
8964, p. 330, pl. 79
8965, p. 329
8966, pp. 333, 334, pl. 80
8967, p. 342, fig. 1, pl. 82
8968, p. 336
8969, p. 337, pl. 81
8970, p. 337, pl. 81
8971, p. 337, pl. 81
8972, p. 338, pl. 81
8973, p. 338, pl. 81
8974, p. 338
8975, p. 339, pl. 81
8976, p. 339, pl. 81
8977, p. 406, pl. 95
8978, p. 142, pl. 32
8979, p. 470, pl. 108
8981, p. 397, pl. 94
8982, p. 393, pl. 93
8985, p. 435, pl. 101
8986, p. 418

8993, p. 407, pl. 95
8994, p. 421
8995, p. 347
8996, p. 483, pl. 112
8997, p. 451, pl. 104
8998, p. 358, pl. 85
8999, p. 317, pl. 74
9000, p. 125, pl. 28
9001, p. 454, pl. 104
9002, p. 104, pl. 24
9003, p. 421, pl. 98
9005, p. 128, pl. 29
9006, p. 188, pl. 41
9007, p. 188, pl. 41
9008, p. 243, pl. 54
9009, p. 317, pl. 74
9010, p. 148, pl. 33
9013, p. 185, pl. 40
9014, p. 345, pl. 82
9015, p. 415, pl. 97
9016, p. 161, pl. 36
9017, p. 87, pl. 19
9018, p. 449, pl. 103
9020, p. 42, pl. 8
9021, p. 440
9022, p. 271, pl. 63
9023, p. 461, pl. 106
9024, p. 380, pl. 91
9025, p. 302, pl. 70
9026, p. 353, pl. 84
9027, p. 294, pl. 68
9028, p. 306, pl. 72
9029, p. 347
9030, p. 102, pl. 23
9031, p. 98, pl. 21
9032, p. 87, pl. 19
9033, p. 194, pl. 42
9035, p. 122
9036, p. 139, pl. 31
9037, p. 98, pl. 21
9038, p. 417, pl. 97
9040, p. 212, pl. 17
9045, p. 169
9046, p. 179, pl. 39
9047, p. 228, pl. 51
9048, p. 199
9049, p. 400, pl. 94
9050, p. 236, pl. 53
9051, p. 254, pl. 57
9052, p. 257, pl. 58
9053, p. 93, pl. 20

9054, p. 27
9055, p. 191, pl. 42
9056, p. 252, pl. 56
9057, p. 291, pl. 67
9058, p. 257
9059, p. 191
9060, p. 293, pl. 68
9061, p. 390, pl. 101
9062, p. 390, pl. 55
9063, p. 399, pl. 94
9064, p. 211
9065, p. 211, pl. 17
9066, p. 60
9067, p. 283, pl. 65
9068, p. 220
9068 bis, p. 220
9070, p. 237
9071, p. 395, pl. 93
9072, p. 379, pl. 91
9073, p. 188
9074, p. 369, pl. 89
9075, p. 398, pls. 94, 127
9076, p. 469, pl. 108
9077, p. 189, pl. 41
9079, p. 190, pl. 42
9079 bis, p. 191
9080, p. 475, pl. 110
9081, p. 190, pl. 42
9083, p. 476, pl. 110
9084, p. 469, pl. 108
9085, p. 402, pl. 94
9086, p. 400, pl. 94
9087, p. 269
9089, p. 204, pl. 45
9090, p. 452, pl. 104
9091, p. 126, pl. 29
9092, p. 218, pl. 48
9093, p. 398, pl. 94
9094, p. 396, pl. 93
9095, p. 455, pl. 105
9096, p. 190
9097, p. 485, pl. 112
9099, p. 228, pl. 51
9101, p. 351, pl. 84
9102, p. 187, pl. 40
9103, p. 332, pl. 80
9104, p. 333, pl. 80
9105, p. 321, pl. 76
9106, p. 323, pl. 76
9107, p. 317, pl. 74
9108, p. 334

9109, p. 134, pl. 30
9110, p. 138, pl. 31
9111, p. 204
9112, p. 203, pl. 45
9113, p. 363
9114, p. 134
9115, p. 138, pl. 31
9116, p. 137
9117, p. 205, pl. 46
9118, p. 204
9119, p. 358, pl. 86
9120, p. 348, pl. 83
9121, p. 349
9122, p. 357, pl. 85
9123, p. 354, pl. 85
9124, p. 401, pl. 94
9125, p. 363, pl. 87
9126, p. 348, pl. 83
9127, p. 351, pl. 84
9128, p. 345
9129, p. 351, pl. 84
9130, p. 351, pl. 84
9131, p. 234
9132, p. 421, pl. 98
9133, p. 351, pl. 84
9134, p. 50, pl. 10
9135, p. 49
9136, p. 281, pl. 65
9137, p. 180, pl. 39
9138, p. 49
9139, p. 475, pl. 110
9140, p. 469, pl. 108
9141, p. 399, pl. 94
9142, p. 377, pl. 90
9143, p. 463, pl. 107
9144, p. 466, pl. 107
9145, p. 104, pl. 24
9146, p. 463, pl. 107
9147, p. 46, 61, pl. 9
9148, p. 468, pl. 108
9149, p. 229, pl. 51
9150, p. 61
9151, p. 197, pl. 43
9152, p. 126, pl. 29
9153, p. 262
9154, p. 308, pl. 72
9155, p. 308
9156, p. 58, pl. 12
9157, p. 482
9158, p. 482
9159, p. 194, pl. 42

9160, p. 198
9161, p. 435, pl. 101
9162, p. 385, pl. 92
9163, p. 88, pl. 19
9164, p. 259
9165, p. 457, pl. 105
9175, p. 418, pl. 98
9178, p. 352, pl. 83
9179, p. 444, pl. 102
9180, p. 184, pl. 40
9181, p. 417, pl. 97
9182, p. 204
9183, p. 142, pl. 32
9184, p. 234
9185, p. 432, pl. 100
9186, p. 360, pl. 86
9187, p. 148, pl. 33
9188, p. 186, pl. 40
9189, p. 302
9190, p. 107, pl. 24
9191, p. 98, pl. 21
9192, p. 177
9194, p. 107, pl. 24
9195, p. 169, pl. 37
9196, p. 167
9197, p. 149
9198, p. 376, pl. 90
9199, p. 167
9200, p. 167
9201, p. 167
9202, p. 167
9203, p. 42, pl. 7
9204, p. 166, pl. 37
9205, p. 421
9206, p. 346, pl. 83
9207, p. 347, pl. 83
9208, p. 350, pl. 83
9209, p. 345, pl. 82
9210, p. 348, pl. 83
9211, p. 294, pl. 68
9213, p. 89, pl. 19
9214, p. 485
9215, p. 107, pl. 24
9216, p. 74, pl. 16
9217, p. 441, pl. 102
9218, p. 155
9220, p. 191, pl. 42
9221, p. 147, pl. 33
9222, p. 208, pl. 47
9223, p. 207, pl. 47

9224, p. 152, pl. 34
9225, p. 161
9226, p. 149
9227, p. 147, pl. 33
9228, p. 150, pl. 33
9233, p. 486, pl. 112
9235, p. 440, pl. 101
9236, p. 235, pl. 53
9237, p. 222, pl. 49
9238, p. 158, pl. 36
9241, p. 122, pl. 28
9242, p. 428, pl. 100
9243, p. 188
9244, p. 188, pl. 41
9245, p. 191, pl. 42
9246, p. 76, pl. 16
9247, p. 298, pl. 69 (not labeled)
9248, p. 107, pl. 24
9249, p. 128, pl. 29
9250, p. 137
9251, p. 135
9252, p. 143, pl. 32
9253, p. 169
9254, p. 206, pl. 46
9255, p. 254, pl. 57
9256, p. 222, pl. 49
9257, p. 481
9258, p. 272, pl. 105
9259, p. 460, pl. 106
9260, p. 63, pl. 13
9261, p. 208, pl. 47
9262, p. 468, pl. 108
9263, p. 189, pl. 41
9266, p. 287
9267, p. 400, pl. 94
9268, p. 311
9269, p. 260
9270, p. 421
9271, p. 53
9272, p. 121, pl. 28
9273, p. 107, pl. 24
9274, p. 216, pl. 48
9275, p. 225, pl. 50
9276, p. 225, pl. 50
9278, p. 24
9279, p. 72, pl. 15
9280, p. 222, pl. 49
9281, p. 203
9282, p. 280, pl. 64

9283, p. 280
9284, p. 290, pl. 67
9285, p. 254, pl. 56
9286, p. 472, pl. 109
9287, p. 406, pl. 95
9288, p. 406, fig. 1, pl. 95
9289, p. 169, pl. 37
9292, p. 357, pl. 85
9293, p. 204, pl. 46
9294, p. 409, pl. 96
9295, p. 354
9297, p. 369, pl. 89
9298, p. 97, pl. 21
9299, p. 170, pl. 35
9300, p. 75, pl. 16
9301, p. 64, pl. 13
9302, p. 87, pl. 19, 119
9303, p. 31, pls. 2, 131
9304, p. 425, pl. 99
9305, p. 387, pl. 88
9306, p. 204, pl. 46
9307, p. 337, pl. 81
9308, p. 409, pls. 96, 134
9309, p. 58, pls. 12, 131
9311, p. 342, pl. 82
9312, p. 229, pl. 51, 133
9313, p. 473, pl. 109
9314, p. 229, pl. 51
9315, p. 72, pl. 15
9316, p. 60, pl. 12
9317, p. 86, pl. 19
9318, p. 185, pl. 40
9319, p. 167
9320, p. 125, pl. 28
9321, p. 202, pl. 45
9322, p. 70, pl. 15
9323, p. 197, pl. 43
9324, p. 221, pl. 49
9325, p. 420, pl. 98
9326, p. 395, pl. 93
9327, p. 45, pl. 9
9328, p. 289, pl. 66
9329, p. 442, pl. 102
9330, p. 380, pl. 91
9331, p. 461, pl. 106
9332, p. 148, pl. 33
9334, p. 432, pl. 100
9335, p. 332, pl. 79
9336, p. 333, pl. 80
9337, p. 50, pl. 10

9338, p. 104, pl. 23
9339, p. 460
9340, p. 259, pl. 58
9341, p. 302, pl. 71
9342, p. 302, pl. 71
9343, p. 243, pl. 55
9344, p. 410, pl. 96
9345, p. 316, pl. 74
9346, p. 319, pl. 75
9347, p. 342, pls. 82, 133
9348, p. 151, pl. 34
9349, p. 167, pl. 37
9350, p. 76, pl. 16
9351, p. 48, pl. 9
9352, p. 289, pl. 67
9353, p. 339
9354, p. 289
9355, p. 471, pl. 109
9356, p. 425, pl. 99
9357, pp. 306–307, pl. 72
9359, p. 417, pl. 97
9361, p. 166, pl. 37
9364, p. 381, pl. 91
9365, p. 381, pl. 91
9366, p. 368, pl. 89
9367, p. 368, pl. 89
9367 bis, p. 368, pl. 89
9368, p. 369, pl. 89
9369, p. 253, pl. 56
9370, p. 388, pl. 88
9371, p. 388, pl. 88
9372, p. 171, pl. 35
9373, p. 424, pl. 99
9379, p. 56, pl. 11
9380, p. 241, pl. 54
9381, p. 483, pl. 112
9382, p. 286
9383, p. 48, pl. 9
9384, p. 306, pl. 72
9385, p. 426
9386, p. 316, pl. 74
9387, p. 218, pl. 48
9388, p. 75, pl. 16
9389, p. 107, pl. 24
9390, p. 180
9391, p. 180
9392, p. 97, pl. 21
9393, p. 469, pl. 108
9394, p. 39, pl. 5
9395, p. 243, pl. 55

9396, p. 282, pl. 65
9397, p. 266
9398, p. 307, pl. 72
9399, p. 296, pl. 68
9400, p. 302, pl. 71
9401, p. 291, pl. 67
9402, p. 296, pl. 68
9403, p. 280, pl. 64
9404, p. 307, pl. 72
9405, p. 311, pl. 73
9406, p. 280, pl. 64
9407, p. 284
9408, p. 41, pl. 7
9409, p. 222, pl. 49
9410, p. 450, pl. 103
9411, p. 411, pl. 96
9412, p. 93, pl. 20
9413, p. 450, pl. 103
9414, p. 263, pl. 60
9414 bis, p. 462, pl. 106
9415, p. 451, pl. 104
9415 bis, p. 452, pl. 104
9416, p. 450, pl. 103
9417, p. 98, pl. 21
9418, p. 197, pl. 43
9419, p. 198, pl. 44
9420, p. 464, pl. 107
9421, p. 193, pl. 42
9422, p. 465
9423, p. 466, pl. 107
9424, p. 389
9425, p. 475, pl. 110
9426, p. 471, pl. 109
9427, p. 385, pl. 92
9428, p. 385, pl. 92
9429, p. 469, pl. 108
9430, p. 400, pl. 94
9431, p. 412, pl. 96
9432, p. 441, pl. 102
9433, p. 352, pl. 84
9434, p. 112, pl. 25
9437, pp. 209–210, pl. 17
9438, p. 65, pl. 14
9439, p. 116
9440, p. 444
9441 (= D 66 C 3203) p. 122
9441 (= 68 E 1843), 242, pl. 54
9442, p. 485, pl. 112
9443, p. 434, pl. 101
9444, p. 234, pl. 52

9445, p. 125
9446, p. 171, pl. 35
9447, p. 449, pl. 103
9448, p. 362, pl. 87
9449, p. 444, pl. 102
9450, p. 63
9452, p. 84, pl. 18
9453, p. 202
9454, p. 179, pl. 39
9455, p. 149, pl. 33
9456, p. 84, pl. 18
9457, p. 441, pl. 102
9459, p. 419, pl. 98
9460, p. 432, pl. 100
9461, p. 414, pl. 97
9463, p. 64, pl. 13
9465, p. 386, pl. 92
9469, p. 167
9470, p. 412, pl. 96
9472, p. 64, pl. 13
9473, p. 355, pl. 85
9474, p. 329, pl. 78
9475, p. 334, pl. 80
9476, p. 61, pl. 13
9477, p. 44, pl. 8
9478, p. 174, pl. 38
9479, p. 180
9480, p. 120, pl. 28
9481, p. 91, pl. 20
9482, p. 140, pl. 31
9483, p. 169, pl. 37
9484, p. 319, pl. 75
9485, p. 156, pl. 35
9486, p. 191, pl. 42
9487, p. 191, pl. 42
9488, p. 449, pl. 103
9489, p. 190, pl. 42
9490, p. 355, pl. 85
9491, p. 317, pl. 74
9492, p. 154
9493, p. 438, pl. 101
9495, p. 126, pl. 29
9496, p. 205
9497, p. 27, pl. 1
9498, p. 86, pl. 19
9499, p. 180
9500, p. 159, pl. 36
9501, p. 402, pl. 94
9502, p. 64, pl. 13
9503, p. 88, pl. 19

9504, p. 435, pl. 101
9505, p. 162
9506, p. 64, pl. 13
9507, p. 68, pl. 14
9508, p. 148, pl. 33
9510, p. 189, pl. 41
9511, p. 211, pl. 17
9512, p. 197
9513, p. 237
9514, p. 197, pl. 43
9515, p. 161, pl. 36
9516, p. 97, pl. 21
9517, p. 125, pl. 28
9519, p. 167
9520, p. 125
9521, p. 180
9522, p. 49
9523, p. 95, pl. 21
9524, p. 105, pl. 24
9525, p. 448, pl. 103
9526, p. 453, pl. 104
9528, p. 420, pl. 98
9530, p. 76, pl. 16
9531, p. 107, pl. 24
9536, p. 420, pl. 98
9537, p. 148, pl. 33
9538, p. 420, pl. 98
9539, p. 377, pl. 90
9542, p. 470, pl. 108
9543, p. 207, pl. 47
9544, p. 207, pl. 47
9545, p. 225, pl. 50
9547, p. 369, pl. 89
9548, p. 394, pl. 93
9549, p. 60
9550, p. 52
9551, p. 309, pl. 73
9552, p. 330, pl. 79
9553, p. 352, pl. 84
9554, p. 353, pl. 84
9555, p. 180
9556, p. 263, pl. 60
9557, p. 329, pl. 78
9559, p. 471, pl. 109
9560, p. 430, pl. 100
9561, p. 219, pl. 48
9562, p. 271, pl. 63
9563, p. 283
9564, p. 351, pl. 84
9565, p. 237, pl. 53

9566, p. 311
9567, p. 134
9568, p. 424, pl. 99
9569, p. 45, pl. 9
9570, p. 209, pl. 17
9571, p. 394, pl. 93
9572, p. 394, pl. 93
9574, p. 72, pl. 15
9575, p. 40, pl. 7
9576, p. 87, pl. 19
9577, p. 260
9579, p. 87, pl. 19
9580, p. 54, pl. 11
9581, p. 400, pl. 94
9582, p. 58
9583, p. 180
9585, p. 281, pl. 64
9586, p. 465, pl. 107
9587, p. 125, pl. 28
9588, p. 376, pl. 90
9589, p. 284, pl. 65
9590, p. 464, pl. 107
9591, p. 460, pl. 106
9592, p. 376, pl. 90
9593, p. 457, pl. 105
9594, p. 476, pl. 110
9595, p. 435, pl. 101
9596, p. 184, pl. 40
9597, p. 148, pl. 33
9598, p. 188, pl. 41
9601, p. 162, pl. 36
9602, p. 184
9603, p. 188, pl. 41
9604, p. 330, pl. 79
9605, p. 170, pl. 35
9606, p. 156, pl. 35
9607, p. 451, pl. 104
9608, p. 138, pl. 31
9609, p. 155, pl. 34
9610, p. 285, pl. 65
9611, p. 475, pl. 110
9612, p. 377, pl. 90
9613, p. 485, pl. 112
9614, p. 97, pl. 21
9615, p. 423
9616, p. 370, pl. 89
9617, p. 354, pl. 85
9618, p. 365, pl. 88
9619, p. 390, pl. 55
9620, p. 165, pls. 37, 125

9621, p. 58, 61, pl. 12
9622, p. 289
9623, p. 235
9624, p. 387, pl. 88
9625, p. 51, pl. 10
9626, p. 347, pl. 83
9628, p. 148
9629, p. 258, pl. 58
9630, p. 375, pl. 90
9631, p. 282
9632, p. 288, pl. 66
9633, p. 464, pl. 107
9634, p. 350, pl. 83
9635, p. 30, pl. 2
9637, p. 299
9640, p. 149, pl. 33
9641, p. 194
9642, p. 485, pl. 112
9643, p. 440, pl. 102
9644, p. 204
9645, p. 46, pl. 9
9646, p. 149
9647, p. 352, pl. 84
9648, p. 50
9649, p. 171, pl. 35
9650, p. 103, pl. 23
9651, p. 264, pl. 60
9652, p. 462, pl. 106
9653, p. 259, pl. 58
9654, p. 260
9655, p. 202
9656, p. 302, pl. 71
9657, p. 237, pl. 53
9658, p. 388, pl. 88
9659, p. 62, pl. 13
9660, p. 235
9661, p. 45, pl. 9
9662, p. 421, pl. 98
9663, p. 242, pl. 54
9664, p. 465, pl. 107
9665, p. 387, pl. 88
9666, p. 232, pl. 52
9667, p. 317, pl. 74
9669, p. 286, pl. 66
9670, p. 466, pl. 107
9671, p. 222, pl. 49
9673, p. 234
9674, p. 115
9675, p. 81, pl. 18
9676, p. 280

9678, p. 283, pl. 65
9679, p. 88, pl. 19
9680, p. 486
9681, p. 134, pl. 30
9682, p. 309, pl. 73
9687, p. 414, pl. 97
9690, p. 296, pl. 68
9691, p. 338
9692, p. 56, pl. 11
9693, p. 298, pl. 69
9694, p. 107, pl. 24
9695, p. 77, pl. 16
9696, p. 254, pl. 57
9698, p. 394, pl. 93
9699, p. 380, pl. 91
9700, p. 394, pl. 93
9701, p. 356, pl. 85
9705, p. 90, pl. 20
9706, p. 67
9707, p. 41, pl. 7
9708, p. 53, pl. 11
9709, p. 41, pl. 7
9710, p. 448, pl. 103
9713, p. 471, pl. 109
9717, p. 29, pl. 2
9718, p. 99, pl. 21
9720, p. 369, pl. 89
9724, p. 208, pl. 47
9725, p. 99, pl. 21
9727, p. 477, pl. 111
9728, p. 198, pl. 43
9729, p. 126, pl. 29
9730, p. 402, pl. 94
9731, p. 102, pl. 23
9732, p. 143
9733, p. 197, pl. 43
9734, p. 444, pl. 102
9735, p. 474, pl. 110
9736, p. 482, pl. 112
9737, p. 119
9738, p. 149
9739, p. 305, pl. 71
9740, p. 54, pl. 11
9741, p. 429, pl. 100
9742, p. 199, pl. 44
9743, p. 182
9744, p. 198
9745, p. 66, pl. 14
9746, p. 438, pl. 101
9747, p. 99, pl. 21

9747 bis, p. 99, pl. 21
9749, p. 102, pl. 23
9750, p. 54, pl. 11
9751, p. 180, pl. 39
9752, p. 51, pl. 10
9753, p. 322, pl. 76
9754, p. 467, pl. 108
9755, p. 65, pl. 14
9756, p. 353
9757, p. 163, pl. 36
9758, p. 98, pl. 21;
see also 9768
9759, p. 346, pl. 83
9760, p. 433, pl. 100
9761, p. 296, pl. 69
9762, p. 120, pl. 27
9763, p. 189
9764, p. 435, pl. 101
9765, pp. 146–147, pl. 33
9766, p. 346, pl. 83
9767, p. 473, pl. 109
9768, p. 265, pl. 60
(mislabeled 9758)
9769, p. 319, pl. 75
67 D 34, p. 482, pl. 112
67 D 101, p. 32
67 D 217, p. 204, pl. 45
67 E 123, p. 397, pl. 94
67 E 135, p. 228, pl. 51
67 E 142, p. 472, pl. 109
67 E 153, p. 440, pl. 102
67 E 365+371, p. 298, pl. 69
67 E 557, p. 451
67 E 572, p. 454
67 E 844, p. 471, pl. 109
67 E 981, p. 227, pl. 50
67 E 985, p. 271, pl. 63
67 E 989, p. 77
67 E 1219, p. 452, pl. 104
67 E 1328, p. 301
67 E 1653, p. 60, pl. 12
67 E 1685, p. 222, pl. 49
67 E 1859 and 1860, p. 435, pl. 101
67 E 1884 and 1799, p. 465, pl. 107
67 E 1942, p. 371
68 D 1410, p. 77, pl. 16
68 D 1431, p. 156, pl. 35
68 D 1827, p. 211, pl. 17

68 D 2122, p. 88, pl. 19
68 D 2378, p. 445, pl. 102
68 D 2379, p. 204, pl. 45
68 D 4445, p. 172, pl. 38
68 D 4470, p. 208, pl. 47
68 D 4476, p. 205, pl. 46
68 E 1575, p. 147, pl. 33
68 E 1635, p. 59, pl. 13
68 E 2469, p. 207, pl. 47
68 E 2940, p. 114, pl. 26
68 E 3226, p. 322
68 E 3290, p. 204, pl. 45
68 E 4002, p. 67, pl. 14
68 E 4145, p. 271, pl. 63
68 E 4624, p. 140, pl. 32
68 E 4625, p. 349
68 E 5217, p. 125
68 E no. illegible, p. 180, pl. 39
A 62, 891, p. 94, pl. 20
A 62, 914, p. 204, pl. 46
A 62, 915, p. 454, pl. 104
A 391, p. 103
C 62 C 2, p. 454, pl. 104
C 62 C 181, p. 310, pl. 73
C 62 C 255, p. 465, pl. 107
C 62 C 532, p. 456, pl. 105
C 62 C 733, p. 448
C 62 C 1128 and 2949, p. 461, pl. 106
C 62 C 1397 and 1761, p. 462, pl. 106
C 62 C 1420 and 1436, p. 457, pl. 105
C 62 C 1495, p. 310, pl. 73
C 62 C 1523, p. 207, pl. 47
C 62 C 1570, p. 399
C 62 C 1617, p. 450
C 62 C 1747, p. 467, pl. 108
C 62 C 1912, p. 466, pl. 107
C 62 C 2336, p. 243, pl. 55
C 62 C 2641, p. 464, pl. 107
C 62 C 2808, p. 460, pl. 106
C 62 C 2887, p. 355, pl. 85
C 62 C 2893, p. 475, pl. 110
C 62 C 3178, p. 463, pl. 106
C 62 C 5433, p. 464, pl. 107
C 62 C no.?, p. 445, pl. 102
C 63 C 545, p. 445
C 63 C 945, p. 142, pl. 32

C 63 C 1058, p. 452, pl. 104
C 63 C 1294, p. 453
C 63 C 1382, p. 245, pl. 55
C 63 C 1545, p. 60, pl. 12
C 63 C 1585, p. 476, pl. 110
C 63 C 1668, p. 60, pl. 12
C 63 C 1714, p. 59, pl. 12
C 63 C 1774, p. 464, pl. 107
C 63 C 1828, p. 476, pl. 110
C 63 C 2451, p. 332, pl. 79
C 63 C 2473, p. 453, pl. 104
C 64 C 243, pp. 218, 219, pl. 48
D 64 C 1044, p. 486
D 64 C 1408, p. 103
D 64 C 1409, p. 486
D 65 C 1628, p. 388
D 65 C 1754, p. 457, pl. 105
D 65 C 1845, p. 474, pl. 110
D 65 C 2217, p. 194
D 66 C 4529, p. 156, pl. 35
КГ 5, p. 101, pl. 23
КГ 5 (duplicate number), p. 463, pl. 106
КГ 10, p. 287
S. no, p. 31, pl. 2
S. no, p. 44, pl. 8
S. no, p. 48, pl. 9
S. no, p. 85, under 2405, pl. 19
S. no, p. 87, pl. 19
S. no., p. 94, pl. 20
S. no, p. 128, pl. 29
S. no., p. 203, pl. 45
Tr. 63, 511, p. 206, pl. 46

APPENDIX 3

Revised Attributions of Vessels in Laumonier 1977

Ed. In the data base that she prepared while studying the material, PGB entered many changes from the workshop attributions published by Laumonier. This work was probably not complete, but the two lists below gives her new attributions, providing some of the detail upon which her account of the Ephesian industry is based.

Abbreviations

/	or
3 des 5, 4 des 5	3rd and fourth of *Cinq petites séries*
6 des 6	sixth of *Six petites séries*
an.	*Annexe*
Belles Méd.	*Belles Méduses*
Com. à la c.	*Comique à la canne*
Déc. géom.	*Décor géométrique*
Ét. à 6 br.	*Étoiles à 6 branches*
Fleur.	*Fleurons, guirlandes, rinceaux*
Godr.	*Godrons*
Menem.	Menemachos
Mono. PAR	Monogram PAR
Pan mask	Pan mask medallion
Plag.	*Plagiaire*
PRSpir	*Petite rose spiralée*
Végét.	*Décor végétal*
VG	*Vases gris*
WC1	Workshop Circle 1

The order of the following list is that of Laumonier 1977

Laumonier	PGB	Laumonier 1977
Menem.	My(...)	cat. 371, p. 26, pl. 1
Menem.	My(...)	cat. 667, p. 27, pl. 2
Menem.	My(...)	cat. 801, p. 28, pl. 2
Menem.	Menem.?	cat. 428, p. 31, pl. 2
Menem.	My(...)?	cat. 9303, p. 31, pl. 2
Menem.	Menem./My(...)	cat. 1343, p. 35, pls. 3, 116
Menem.	My(...)	cat. 736, p. 44, pl. 8
Menem.	My(...)	cat. 2449, p. 44, pl. 8
Menem.	Mono. PAR	cat. 9309, p. 58, pl. 12
Menem. an.	Mono. PAR?	cat. 2380, p. 63, pl. 13
Menem. an.	Menem.	cat. 3163, p. 65, pls. 14, 118
Menem. an.	Menem.	cat. 3371, p. 65, pls. 14, 118
Menem. an.	Menem.	cat. 1802, p. 67, pl. 14
Menem. an.	Menem.	cat. 355, p. 67, pl. 14
Menem. an.	Menem.	cat. 1803, p. 67, pl. 14
NI	Menem.	cat. 5136, p. 72, pl. 15
NI	Menem.	cat. 6088, p. 73, pl. 16
NI	Menem.	cat. 8839, p. 74, pl. 16
NI	Pan mask	cat. 5377, p. 76, pls. 16, 118
NI	Menem.	cat. 3, p. 78, pl. 17
Belles Méd.	Mono. PAR	cat. 1173, p. 82, pl. 18
Belles Méd.	Menem.	cat. 1834, p. 84, pl. 18
VG an.	VG	cat. 877, p. 107, pl. 24
VG an.	VG	cat. 3268, p. 107, pl. 24
VG an.	VG	cat. 8684, p. 107, pl. 24
VG an.	VG	cat. 9190, p. 107, pl. 24
VG an.	VG	cat. 9389, p. 107, pl. 24
Com. à la c.	Menem.	cat. 1836, p. 119, pl. 27
Com. à la c.	Menem.	cat. 4851, p. 119, pl. 27
Com. à la c.	Menem., late	cat. 1114, p. 120, pls. 27, 122
Com. à la c.	My(...)	cat. 4874, p. 120, pl. 27
Com. à la c.	Com. à la c. an.	cat. 8874, p. 128, pl. 29
Mono. PAR	WC1	cat. 1185, p. 134, pl. 30
Mono. PAR.	Menem.	cat. 823, p. 145, pl. 33
Mono. PAR	VG	cat. 3272, p. 164, pl. 36
Mono. PAR	WC1	cat. 3043, p. 166, pl. 37
Mono. PAR	Mono. PAR?	cat. 3242, p. 167, pl. 37
Mono. PAR	Mono. PAR?	cat. 3244, p. 168, pl. 37
Mono. PAR	Menem.	cat. 8579, p. 168, pl. 37
Mono. PAR	Menem.	cat. 4352, p. 173, pl. 38
Mono. PAR	VG/Menem.	cat. 3311, p. 174, pls. 38, 125
Mono. PAR	Menem., late?	cat. 357, p. 175, pl. 38
Mono. PAR	Menem.	cat. 3176, p. 176, pls. 38, 125
Mono. PAR	Menem.	cat. 1899, p. 177, pl. 38
Mono. PAR	VG/Menem.	cat. 3312, p. 177, pl. 39
Mono. PAR	VG/Menem.	cat. 3313, p. 177, pls. 39, 125
Mono. PAR	VG/Menem.	cat. 1167, p. 178, pl. 39
Mono. PAR	VG/Menem.	cat. 1674, p. 178, pl. 39
Mono. PAR	VG/Menem.	cat. 1860, p. 178, pl. 39
Mono. PAR	VG/Menem.	cat. 1861, p. 178, pl. 39

REVISED ATTRIBUTIONS OF VESSELS IN LAUMONIER 1977

Mono. PAR	VG/Menem.	cat. 2030, p. 178, pl. 39	Philon(nios)	My(...)	cat. 2260, p. 266, pl. 61
Mono. PAR	VG/Menem.	cat. 3114, p. 178, pl. 39	Philon(nios)	My(...)	cat. 4429, p. 266, pl. 61
Mono. PAR	VG/Menem.	cat. 3119, p. 178, pl. 39	Philon(nios)	My(...)	cat. 4435, p. 266, pl. 61
Mono. PAR	VG/Menem.	cat. 8463, p. 178, pl. 39	Philon(nios)	My(...)	cat. 568, p. 267, pl. 61
Mono. PAR	VG/Menem.	cat. 8747, p. 178, pl. 39	Philon(nios)	My(...)	cat. 875, p. 267, pl. 61
Mono. PAR	VG/Menem.	cat. 8748, p. 178, pl. 39	Philon(nios)	My(...)	cat. 2367, p. 267, pl. 61
Mono. PAR	Menem.	cat. 3059, p. 179, pl. 39	Philon(nios)	My(...)	cat. 670, p. 267, pl. 62
Mono. PAR	Menem.	cat. 9046, p. 179, pl. 39	Philon(nios)	My(...)	cat. 1117, p. 268, pls. 62, 127
Mono. PAR	Menem.	cat. 5065, p. 180, pl. 39	Philon(nios)	My(...)	cat. 1229, p. 268, pl. 62
Mono. PAR	Menem.	cat. 2166, p. 183, pls. 39, 125	Philon(nios)	My(...)	cat. 1230, p. 268, pl. 62
Mono. PAR	Mono. PAR?	cat. 1978, p. 184, pl. 40	Philon(nios)	My(...)	cat. 1278, p. 268, pl. 62
Mono. PAR	Pan mask	cat. 772, p. 185, pls. 40, 126	Philon(nios)	My(...)	cat. 1300, p. 268, pls. 62; 128
Mono. PAR	Pan Mask	cat. 940, p. 186, pl. 40	Philon(nios)	My(...)	cat. 2037, p. 268, pl. 62
Mono. PAR	WC1	cat. 8806, p. 185, pls. 40, 126	Philon(nios)	My(...)	cat. 2038, p. 268, pl. 62 127
Mono. PAR	Pan mask	cat. 430, p. 186, pl. 40	Philon(nios)	My(...)	cat. 2039, p. 268, pl. 62
Mono. PAR	Pan mask	cat. 463, p. 186, pls. 40, 126	Philon(nios)	My(...)	cat. 1683, p. 269, pl. 62
Mono. PAR	Pan mask	cat. 1297, p. 186, pl. 40	Philon(nios)	My(...)	cat. 1679, p. 269, pl. 62
Mono. PAR	WC1	cat. 111, p. 187, pl. 41	Philon(nios)	My(...)	cat. 1681, p. 269, pl. 62
Mono. PAR	Menem.	cat. 4666, p. 195, pl. 43	Philon(nios)	My(...)	cat. 1682, p. 269, pl. 62
Mono. PAR	Menem., late?	cat. 4010, p. 200, pl. 44	Philon(nios)	My(...)	cat. 1859, p. 269, pl. 62
Mono. PAR	Mono. PAR?	cat. 4020, p. 200, pl. 44	Philon(nios)	My(...)	cat. 2055, p. 269, pl. 62
Mono. PAR	Mono. PAR?	cat. 4021, p. 200, pl. 44	Philon(nios)	My(...)	cat. 2321, p. 269, pl. 62
Mono. PAR	Menem.	cat. 8735, p. 207, pl. 47	Philon(nios)	My(...)	cat. 4578, p. 270, pl. 63
Mono. PAR an.	WC1	cat. 496, p. 209, pl. 17	Philon(nios)	My(...)	cat. 2004, p. 271, pl. 63
PRSpir.	Menem.	cat. 239, p. 217, pl. 48	Godr.	My(...)	cat. 8675, p. 271, pl. 63
PRSpir.	WC1	cat. 228, p. 220, pl. 49	Godr.	My(...)	cat. 8676, p. 271, pl. 63
Apollonios	Athenaios?	cat. 3124, p. 226, pls. 50, 127	Hera(...)	My(...)?	cat. 733, p. 299, pl. 70
Apollonios	WC1	cat. 3041, p. 226, pl. 50	Hera(...)	My(...)	cat. 1130, p. 300, pl. 70
Apollonios	WC1	cat. 3038, p. 226, pl. 50	Hera(...)	My(...)?	cat. 638, p. 301, pl. 70
			Hera(...)	My(...)?	cat. 1977, p. 302, pl. 70 133
Athenaios	My(...)	cat. 1335, p. 233, pl. 52	Hera(...)	My(...)?	cat. 2429, p. 302, pl. 70
Athenaios	Pan mask	cat. 1406, p. 233, pls. 52, 127	Hera(...)	My(...)?	cat. 9341, p. 302, pl. 71
Athenaios	Pan mask	cat. 1209, p. 233, pls. 52, 127	Hera(...)	My(...)?	cat. 738, p. 302, pl. 71
Athenaios	Pan mask	cat. 773, p. 234, pl. 52	Hera(...)	My(...)	cat. 3096, p. 304, pl. 71 129
			Hera(...)	My(...)	cat. 3330, p. 305, pl. 71
3 des 5	Menem., late?	cat. 4009, p. 390, pl. 55	Hera(...)	VG/Menem.	cat. 3116, p. 306, pl. 72
			Hera(...)	VG/Menem.	cat. 3118, p. 306, pl. 72
4 des 5	My(...)	cat. 4793, p. 391, pl. 55	Hera(...)	VG/Menem.	cat. 3477, p. 306, pl. 72
			Hera(...)	Menem.	cat. 4001, p. 307, pl. 72
Philon(nios)	Menem.	cat. 4179, p. 264, pl. 60	Hera(...)	Menem.	cat. 1207, p. 310, pl. 73
Philon(nios)	My(...)	cat. 760, p. 265, pl. 60	Hera(...)	WC1	cat. 2115, p. 311, pl. 73
Philon(nios)	My(...)	cat. 795, p. 265, pl. 60			
Philon(nios)	My(...)	cat. 4955, p. 265, pl. 60	Plag.	My(...)?	cat. 559, p. 316, pl. 74
Philon(nios)	My(...)	cat. 4956, p. 265, pl. 60	Plag.	My(...)?	cat. 1131, p. 316, pl. 74
		(mislabeled 4986)	Plag.	My(...)	cat. 2272, p. 316, pl. 74
Philon(nios)	My(...)	cat. 1967, p. 265, pl. 61	Plag.	My(...)	cat. 2273, p. 317, pl. 74
Philon(nios)	My(...)	cat. 634, p. 266, pl. 61	Plag.	My(...)	cat. 9009, p. 317, pl. 74
Philon(nios)	My(...)	cat. 761, p. 266, pl. 61	Plag.	Menem.	cat. 9667, p. 317, pl. 74
Philon(nios)	My(...)?	cat. 1214, p. 266, pls. 61, 128	Plag.	My(...)?	cat. 572, p. 318, pl. 74

Plag.	My(...)?	cat. 641, p. 318, pl. 74
Plag.	My(...)?	cat. 956, p. 318
Plag.	My(...)?	cat. 955, p. 318, pl. 75
Plag.	My(...)	cat. 1019, p. 318, pl. 75
Plag.	My(...)	cat. 2259, p. 319, pl. 75
Plag.	My(...)	cat. 9346, p. 319, pl. 75
Plag.	Menem.?	cat. 418, p. 320, pl. 75
Plag.	My(...)	cat. 874, p. 319, pl. 75
Plag.	My(...)	cat. 1014, p. 319, pl. 75
Plag.	My(...)?	cat. 1218, p. 319, pl. 75
Plag.	My(...)	cat. 8952, p. 320, pl. 75
Plag.	My(...)	cat. 8953, p. 320, pl. 75
Plag.	My(...)	cat. 9769, p. 319, pl. 75
Plag.	My(...)	cat. 454, p. 321, pl. 75
Plag.	My(...)	cat. 1245, p. 321, pl. 76
Plag.	My(...)	cat. 8954, p. 321, pl. 76
Plag.	My(...)	cat. 1253, p. 322, pl. 76
Plag.	My(...)	cat. 1248, p. 322, pl. 76
Plag.	My(...)	cat. 1249, p. 322, pl. 76
Plag.	My(...)	cat. 1252, p. 322, pl. 76
Plag.	My(...)	cat. 2390, p. 322, pl. 76
Plag.	My(...)	cat. 8957, p. 322, pl. 76
Plag.	My(...)	cat. 8958, p. 322, pl. 76
Plag.	My(...)	cat. 9753, p. 322, pl. 76
Plag.	My(...)	cat. 1277, p. 323, pl. 76
Plag.	My(...)	cat. 2007, p. 323, pl. 76
Plag.	My(...)	cat. 2226, p. 323, pl. 76
Plag.	My(...)	cat. 2304, p. 323, pl. 76
Plag.	My(...)	cat. 3044, p. 323, pl. 76
Plag.	My(...)	cat. 3045, p. 323, pl. 76
Plag.	My(...)	cat. 8453, p. 323, pl. 76
Plag.	My(...)	cat. 9106, p. 323, pl. 76
Plag.	My(...)	cat. 1159, p. 323, pl. 77
Plag.	My(...)	cat. 1113, p. 325, pl. 77
Plag.	My(...)	cat. 1115, p. 325, pl. 77
Plag.	My(...)	cat. 1116, p. 325, pl. 77
Plag.	Menem.	cat. 1155, p. 325, pl. 77
Plag.	My(...)	cat. 1233, p. 324, pl. 77
Plag.	My(...)	cat. 1250, p. 324, pl. 77
Plag.	My(...)	cat. 1271, p. 324, pl. 77
Plag.	My(...)	cat. 1298, p. 324, pl. 77
Plag.	My(...)	cat. 1326, p. 324, pl. 77
Plag.	My(...)	cat. 2258, p. 324, pl. 77
Plag.	My(...)	cat. 3473, p. 324, pl. 77
Plag.	My(...)	cat. 8959, p. 324, pl. 77
Plag.	My(...)?	cat. 732, p. 325, pl. 77
Plag.	My(...)	cat. 2221, p. 325, pl. 77
Plag.	My(...)	cat. 2060, p. 326, pl. 77
Plag.	Menem.	cat. 1119, p. 327, pl. 78
Plag.	My(...)	cat. 1147, p. 327, pl. 78
Plag.	Menem.	cat. 1204, p. 327, pl. 78
Plag.	My(...)	cat. 1215, p. 327, pl. 78
Plag.	My(...)?	cat. 2268, p. 326, pl. 78
Plag.	Menem.?	cat. 609, p. 328, pl. 78
Plag.	WCl	cat. 618, p. 328, pl. 78
Plag.	Menem.	cat. 1402, p. 328, pl. 78
Plag.	WCl	cat. 1930, p. 328, pl. 78
Plag.	WCl	cat. 9557, p. 329, pl. 78
Plag.	My(...)	cat. 619, p. 329, pl. 79
Plag.	My(...)	cat. 351, p. 330, pl. 79
Plag.	My(...)	cat. 4405, p. 331, pl. 79
Plag.	My(...)?	cat. 4572, p. 331, pl. 79
Plag.	My(...)	cat. 4577, p. 331, pl. 79
Plag.	My(...)	cat. 9335, p. 332, pl. 79
Plag.	My(...)	cat. 4126, p. 332, pl. 80
Plag.	My(...)	cat. 4070, p. 332, pl. 80
Plag.	My(...)	cat. 4091, p. 332, pl. 80
Plag.	My(...)	cat. 9103, p. 332, pl. 80
Plag.	My(...)	cat. 1684, p. 333, pl. 80
Plag.	My(...)	cat. 5555, p. 336, pl. 81
Ét. à 6 br.	Menem.	cat. 657, p. 362, pl. 87
Ét. à 6 br.	Menem.	cat. 1268, p. 362, pl. 87
Ét. à 6 br.	Menem.	cat. 1818, p. 362, pl. 87
Ét. à 6 br.	Menem.	cat. 1819, p. 362, pl. 87
Ét. à 6 br.	Menem.	cat. 8848, p. 362, pl. 87
Ét. à 6 br.	Menem.	cat. 8895, p. 362, pl. 87
Ét. à 6 br.	Menem.	cat. 8928, p. 362, pl. 87
Ét. à 6 br.	Menem.	cat. 8929, p. 362, pl. 87
Ét. à 6 br.	VG/Menem.	cat. 3225, p. 364, pl. 87
Ét. à 6 br.	VG/Menem.	cat. 3224, p. 364, pl. 87
6 des 6	WCl	cat. 1203, p. 396, pl. 93
Animés	Pan mask	cat. 3072, p. 414, pl. 97
Animés	VG/Menem.	cat. 3345, p. 414, pl. 97
Animés	VG/Menem.	cat. 3445, p. 417, pl. 97
Animés	Mono. PAR	cat. 3169, p. 420, pl. 98
CI	Athenaios/CI	cat. 1334, p. 345, pl. 82
CI	Menem.	cat. 2368, p. 343, pl. 82
CI	Menem.	cat. 2011, p. 346, pl. 82
CI	Menem.	cat. 3123, p. 346, pl. 82
CI	Menem./My(...)	cat. 9759, p. 346, pl. 83
CI	My(...)	cat. 3121, p. 346, pl. 83
CI	WCl	cat. 659, p. 347, pl. 83
CI	Menem.	cat. 3436, p. 348, pl. 83
CI	WCl	cat. 8614, p. 349, pl. 84
CI	Menem.	cat. 3276, p. 350, pl. 84
CI	Menem.	cat. 3277, p. 350, pl. 84
CI	Menem.	cat. 3278, p. 350, pl. 84
CI	WCl	cat. 8612, p. 350, pl. 84

REVISED ATTRIBUTIONS OF VESSELS IN LAUMONIER 1977

CI	Menem.	cat. 8620, p. 351, pl. 84
CI	Menem.	cat. 9127, p. 351, pl. 84
CI	WC1	cat. 1889, p. 352
CI an.	WC1	cat. 592, p. 355, pl. 85
Signât.	Gorgias	cat. 1312, p. 403, pl. 95
Signât.	Gorgias	cat. 1986, p. 403, pl. 95
Signât.	Gorgias	cat. 1988, p. 403, pl. 95
Signât.	Gorgias	cat. 1989, p. 403, pl. 95
Signât.	Gorgias	cat. 3499, p. 403, pl. 95
Signât.	Gorgias	cat. 4155, p. 403, pl. 95
Signât.	Gorgias	cat. 4156, p. 403, pl. 95
Signât.	Gorgias	cat. 4157, p. 405

The order of the following list is alphabetical by workshops, according to PGB's attributions

PGB	Laumonier	Laumonier 1977
Athenaios/CI	CI	cat. 1334, p. 345, pl. 82
Athenaios?	Apollonios	cat. 3124, p. 226, pls. 50, 127
Gorgias	Signât.	cat. 4157, p. 405
Gorgias	Signât.	cat. 1312, p. 403, pl. 95
Gorgias	Signât.	cat. 1986, p. 403, pl. 95
Gorgias	Signât.	cat. 1988, p. 403, pl. 95
Gorgias	Signât.	cat. 1989, p. 403, pl. 95
Gorgias	Signât.	cat. 3499, p. 403, pl. 95
Gorgias	Signât.	cat. 4155, p. 403, pl. 95
Gorgias	Signât.	cat. 4156, p. 403, pl. 95
Gorgias	Signât.	cat. 4586, p. 405, pl. 95
Menem.	Menem. an.	cat. 3371, p. 65, pls. 14, 118
Menem.	Menem. an.	cat. 1802, p. 67, pl. 14
Menem.	Menem. an.	cat. 355, p. 67, pl. 14
Menem.	Menem. an.	cat. 1803, p. 67, pl. 14
Menem.	Menem. an.	cat. 3163, p. 65, pls. 14, 118
Menem.	NI	cat. 5136, p. 72, pl. 15
Menem.	NI	cat. 6088, p. 73, pl. 16
Menem.	NI	cat. 8839, p. 74, pl. 16
Menem.	NI	cat. 3, p. 78, pl. 17
Menem.	Belles Méd.	cat. 1834, p. 84, pl. 18
Menem.	Com. à la c.	cat. 1836, p. 119, pl. 27
Menem.	Com. à la c.	cat. 4851, p. 119, pl. 27
Menem., late	Com. à la c.	cat. 1114, p. 120, pls. 27, 122
Menem.	Mono. PAR	cat. 823, p. 145, pl. 33
Menem.	Mono. PAR	cat. 8579, p. 168, pl. 37
Menem.	Mono. PAR	cat. 4352, p. 173, pl. 38
Menem.	Mono. PAR	cat. 3176, p. 176, pls. 38, 125

Végét.	Menem.	cat. 1325, p. 427, pl. 99
Fleur.	Menem.	cat. 1206, p. 439, pl. 101
Fleur.	Menem.?	cat. 5800, p. 439, pl. 101
Fleur.	WC1	cat. 1393, p. 439, pl. 101
Fleur.	WC1	cat. 8123, p. 440, pl. 101
Fleur.	WC1	cat. 8607, p. 440, pl. 101
Déc. géom.	Mono. PAR?	cat. 4016, p. 477, pl. 111
Déc. géom.	WC1	cat. 4022, p. 477, pl. 111
Déc. géom.	WC1	cat. 4012, p. 477, pl. 111
Déc. géom.	Mono. PAR	cat. 4231, p. 478, pl. 111
Déc. géom.	WC1	cat. 4168, p. 480, pl. 111
Déc. géom.	WC1	cat. 4169, p. 480, pl. 111
Déc. géom.	WC1	cat. 4171, p. 480, pl. 111
Déc. géom.	WC1	cat. 4285, p. 480, pl. 112
Déc. géom.	WC1	cat. 4260, p. 480, pl. 112
Déc. géom.	WC1	cat. 4272, p. 480, pl. 112
Déc. géom.	WC1	cat. 4186, p. 480, pl. 112
Menem.	Mono. PAR	cat. 1899, p. 177, pl. 38
Menem.	Mono. PAR	cat. 9046, p. 179, pl. 39
Menem.	Mono. PAR	cat. 3059, p. 179, pl. 39
Menem.	Mono. PAR	cat. 5065, p. 180, pl. 39
Menem.	Mono. PAR	cat. 2166, p. 183, pls. 39, 125
Menem.	Mono. PAR	cat. 4666, p. 195, pl. 43
Menem.	Mono. PAR	cat. 8735, p. 207, pl. 47
Menem.	PRSpir.	cat. 239, p. 217, pl. 48
Menem.	Philon(nios)	cat. 4179, p. 264, pl. 60
Menem.	Hera(...)	cat. 4001, p. 307, pl. 72
Menem.	Hera(...)	cat. 1207, p. 310, pl. 73
Menem.	Plag.	cat. 9667, p. 317, pl. 74
Menem.	Plag.	cat. 1155, p. 325, pl. 77
Menem.	Plag.	cat. 1119, p. 327, pl. 78
Menem.	Plag.	cat. 1204, p. 327, pl. 78
Menem.	Plag.	cat. 1402, p. 328, pl. 78
Menem.	CI	cat. 2368, p. 343, pl. 82
Menem.	CI	cat. 2011, p. 346, pl. 82
Menem.	CI	cat. 3123, p. 346, pl. 82
Menem.	CI	cat. 3436, p. 348, pl. 83
Menem.	CI	cat. 3276, p. 350, pl. 84
Menem.	CI	cat. 3277, p. 350, pl. 84
Menem.	CI	cat. 3278, p. 350, pl. 84
Menem.	CI	cat. 8620, p. 351, pl. 84
Menem.	CI	cat. 9127, p. 351, pl. 84
Menem.	Et. à 6 br.	cat. 657, p. 362, pl. 87
Menem.	Et. à 6 br.	cat. 1268, p. 362, pl. 87
Menem.	Et. à 6 br.	cat. 1818, p. 362, pl. 87
Menem.	Et. à 6 br.	cat. 1819, p. 362, pl. 87
Menem.	Et. à 6 br.	cat. 8848, p. 362, pl. 87
Menem.	Et. à 6 br.	cat. 8895, p. 362, pl. 87
Menem.	Et. à 6 br.	cat. 8928, p. 362, pl. 87

Menem.	Et. à 6 br.	cat. 8929, p. 362, pl. 87	My(...)	Philon(nios)	cat. 1229, p. 268, pl. 62
Menem.	Végét.	cat. 1325, p. 427, pl. 99	My(...)	Philon(nios)	cat. 1230, p. 268, pl. 62
Menem.	Fleur.	cat. 1206, p. 439, pl. 101	My(...)	Philon(nios)	cat. 2037, p. 268, pl. 62
			My(...)	Philon(nios)	cat. 2038, p. 268, pls. 62, 127
Menem.?	Menem.	cat. 428, p. 31, pl. 2	My(...)	Philon(nios)	cat. 2039, p. 268, pl. 62
Menem.?	Fleur.	cat. 5800, p. 439, pl. 101	My(...)	Philon(nios)	cat. 1278, p. 268, pl. 62
Menem., late?	Mono. PAR	cat. 357, p. 175, pls. 38, 132	My(...)	Philon(nios)	cat. 1859, p. 269, pl. 62
Menem., late?	Mono. PAR	cat. 4010, p. 200, pl. 44	My(...)	Philon(nios)	cat. 2055, p. 269, pl. 62
Menem., late?	3 des 5	cat. 4009, p. 390, pl. 55	My(...)	Philon(nios)	cat. 2321, p. 269, pl. 62
Menem.?	Plag.	cat. 418, p. 320, pl. 75	My(...)	Philon(nios)	cat. 1683, p. 269, pl. 62
Menem.?	Plag.	cat. 609, p. 328, pl. 78	My(...)	Philon(nios)	cat. 1679, p. 269, pl. 62
			My(...)	Philon(nios)	cat. 1681, p. 269, pl. 62
Menem. My(...)	Menem.	cat. 1343, p. 35, pls. 3, 116	My(...)	Philon(nios)	cat. 1682, p. 269, pl. 62
Menem./My(...)	CI	cat. 9759, p. 346, pl. 83	My(...)	Philon(nios)	cat. 4578, p. 270, pl. 63
			My(...)	Philon(nios)	cat. 2004, p. 271, pl. 63
Mono. PAR	Menem.	cat. 9309, p. 58, pl. 12	My(...)	4 des 5	cat. 4793, p. 391, pl. 55
Mono. PAR	Belles Méd.	cat. 1173, p. 82, pl. 18	My(...)	Godr.	cat. 8675, p. 271, pl. 63
Mono. PAR	Animés	cat. 3169, p. 420, pl. 98	My(...)	Godr.	cat. 8676, p. 271, pl. 63
Mono. PAR	Dec. géom.	cat. 4231, p. 478, pl. 111	My(...)	Hera(...)	cat. 1130, p. 300, pl. 70
			My(...)	Hera(...)	cat. 3096, p. 304, pls. 71, 129
Mono. PAR?	Menem. an.	cat. 2380, p. 63, pl. 13	My(...)	Hera(...)	cat. 3330, p. 305, pl. 71
Mono. PAR?	Mono. PAR	cat. 3242, p. 167, pl. 37	My(...)	Plag.	cat. 2272, p. 316, pl. 74
Mono. PAR?	Mono. PAR	cat. 3244, p. 168, pl. 37	My(...)	Plag.	cat. 2273, p. 317, pl. 74
Mono. PAR?	Mono. PAR	cat. 1978, p. 184, pl. 40	My(...)	Plag.	cat. 9009, p. 317, pl. 74
Mono. PAR?	Mono. PAR	cat. 4020, p. 200, pl. 44	My(...)	Plag.	cat. 1019, p. 318, pl. 75
Mono. PAR?	Mono. PAR	cat. 4021, p. 200, pl. 44	My(...)	Plag.	cat. 9769, p. 319, pl. 75
Mono. PAR?	Dec. géom.	cat. 4016, p. 477, pl. 111	My(...)	Plag.	cat. 2259, p. 319, pl. 75
			My(...)	Plag.	cat. 9346, p. 319, pl. 75
My(...)	Menem.	cat. 371, p. 26, pl. 1	My(...)	Plag.	cat. 874, p. 319, pl. 75
My(...)	Menem.	cat. 667, p. 27, pl. 2	My(...)	Plag.	cat. 1014, p. 319, pl. 75
My(...)	Menem.	cat. 801, p. 28, pl. 2	My(...)	Plag.	cat. 8952, p. 320, pl. 75
My(...)	Menem.	cat. 736, p. 44, pl. 8	My(...)	Plag.	cat. 8953, p. 320, pl. 75
My(...)	Menem.	cat. 2449, p. 44, pl. 8	My(...)	Plag.	cat. 454, p. 321, pl. 75
My(...)	Com. à la c.	cat. 4874, p. 120, pl. 27	My(...)	Plag.	cat. 1245, p. 321, pl. 76
My(...)	Athenaios	cat. 1335, p. 233, pl. 52	My(...)	Plag.	cat. 8954, p. 321, pl. 76
My(...)	Philon(nios)	cat. 4955, p. 265, pl. 60	My(...)	Plag.	cat. 8957, p. 322, pl. 76
My(...)	Philon(nios)	cat. 4956, p. 265, pl. 60	My(...)	Plag.	cat. 8958, p. 322, pl. 76
My(...)	Philon(nios)	cat. 760, p. 265, pl. 60	My(...)	Plag.	cat. 2390, p. 322, pl. 76
My(...)	Philon(nios)	cat. 795, p. 265, pl. 60	My(...)	Plag.	cat. 9753, p. 322, pl. 76
My(...)	Philon(nios)	cat. 1967, p. 265, pl. 61	My(...)	Plag.	cat. 1253, p. 322, pl. 76
My(...)	Philon(nios)	cat. 634, p. 266, pl. 61	My(...)	Plag.	cat. 1248, p. 322, pl. 76
My(...)	Philon(nios)	cat. 2260, p. 266, pl. 61	My(...)	Plag.	cat. 1249, p. 322, pl. 76
My(...)	Philon(nios)	cat. 4435, p. 266, pl. 61	My(...)	Plag.	cat. 1252, p. 322, pl. 76
My(...)	Philon(nios)	cat. 4429, p. 266, pl. 61	My(...)	Plag.	cat. 2007, p. 323, pl. 76
My(...)	Philon(nios)	cat. 761, p. 266, pl. 61	My(...)	Plag.	cat. 2226, p. 323, pl. 76
My(...)	Philon(nios)	cat. 2367, p. 267, pl. 61	My(...)	Plag.	cat. 2304, p. 323, pl. 76
My(...)	Philon(nios)	cat. 568, p. 267, pl. 61	My(...)	Plag.	cat. 3044, p. 323, pl. 76
My(...)	Philon(nios)	cat. 875, p. 267, pl. 61	My(...)	Plag.	cat. 3045, p. 323, pl. 76
My(...)	Philon(nios)	cat. 670, p. 267, pl. 62	My(...)	Plag.	cat. 8453, p. 323, pl. 76
My(...)	Philon(nios)	cat. 1300, p. 268, pls. 62, 128	My(...)	Plag.	cat. 9106, p. 323, pl. 76
My(...)	Philon(nios)	cat. 1117, p. 268, pls. 62, 127	My(...)	Plag.	cat. 1277, p. 323, pl. 76

My(...)	Plag.	cat. 1159, p. 323, pl. 77	Pan mask	Mono. PAR	cat. 463, p. 186, pls. 40, 126
My(...)	Plag.	cat. 3473, p. 324, pl. 77	Pan mask	Mono. PAR	cat. 940, p. 186, pl 40
My(...)	Plag.	cat. 2258, p. 324, pl. 77	Pan mask	Mono. PAR	cat. 1297, p. 186, pl. 40
My(...)	Plag.	cat. 8959, p. 324, pl. 77	Pan mask	Athenaios	cat. 1406, p. 233, pls. 52, 127
My(...)	Plag.	cat. 1298, p. 324, pl. 77	Pan mask	Athenaios	cat. 1209, p. 233, pls. 52, 127
My(...)	Plag.	cat. 1271, p. 324, pl. 77	Pan mask	Athenaios	cat. 773, p. 234, pl. 52
My(...)	Plag.	cat. 1233, p. 324, pl. 77	Pan mask	Animés	cat. 3072, p. 414, pl. 97
My(...)	Plag.	cat. 1250, p. 324, pl. 77			
My(...)	Plag.	cat. 1326, p. 324, pl. 77	VG	VG an.	cat. 877, p. 107, pl. 24
My(...)	Plag.	cat. 2221, p. 325, pl. 77	VG	VG an.	cat. 3268, p. 107, pl. 24
My(...)	Plag.	cat. 1113, p. 325, pl. 77	VG	VG an.	cat. 8684, p. 107, pl. 24
My(...)	Plag.	cat. 1115, p. 325, pl. 77	VG	VG an.	cat. 9190, p. 107, pl. 24
My(...)	Plag.	cat. 1116, p. 325, pl. 77	VG	VG an.	cat. 9389, p. 107, pl. 24
My(...)	Plag.	cat. 2060, p. 326, pl. 77	VG	Mono. PAR	cat. 3272, p. 164, pl. 36
My(...)	Plag.	cat. 1147, p. 327, pl. 78			
My(...)	Plag.	cat. 1215, p. 327, pl. 78	VG/Menem.	Mono. PAR	cat. 3311, p. 174, pls. 38, 125
My(...)	Plag.	cat. 619, p. 329, pl. 79	VG/Menem.	Mono. PAR	cat. 3312, p. 177, pl. 39
My(...)	Plag.	cat. 351, p. 330, pl. 79	VG/Menem.	Mono. PAR	cat. 3313, p. 177, pls. 39, 125
My(...)	Plag.	cat. 4577, p. 331, pl. 79	VG/Menem.	Mono. PAR	cat. 8463, p. 178, pl. 39
My(...)	Plag.	cat. 4405, p. 331, pl. 79	VG/Menem.	Mono. PAR	cat. 8747, p. 178, pl. 39
My(...)	Plag.	cat. 9335, p. 332, pl. 79	VG/Menem.	Mono. PAR	cat. 8748, p. 178, pl. 39
My(...)	Plag.	cat. 9103, p. 332, pl. 80	VG/Menem.	Mono. PAR	cat. 3114, p. 178, pl. 39
My(...)	Plag.	cat. 4126, p. 332, pl. 80	VG/Menem.	Mono. PAR	cat. 2030, p. 178, pl. 39
My(...)	Plag.	cat. 4070, p. 332, pl. 80	VG/Menem.	Mono. PAR	cat. 3119, p. 178, pl. 39
My(...)	Plag.	cat. 4091, p. 332, pl. 80	VG/Menem.	Mono. PAR	cat. 1167, p. 178, pl. 39
My(...)	Plag.	cat. 1684, p. 333, pl. 80	VG/Menem.	Mono. PAR	cat. 1674, p. 178, pl. 39
My(...)	Plag.	cat. 5555, p. 336, pl. 81	VG/Menem.	Mono. PAR	cat. 1860, p. 178, pl. 39
My(...)	CI	cat. 3121, p. 346, pl. 83	VG/Menem.	Mono. PAR	cat. 1861, p. 178, pl. 39
			VG/Menem.	Hera(...)	cat. 3477, p. 306, pl. 72
My(...)?	Menem.	cat. 9303, p. 31, pl. 2	VG/Menem.	Hera[...]	cat. 3116, p. 306, pl. 72
My(...)?	Philon(nios)	cat. 1214, p. 266, pls. 61, 128	VG/Menem.	Hera(...)	cat. 3118, p. 306, pl. 72
My(...)?	Hera(...)	cat. 733, p. 299, pl. 70	VG/Menem.	Ét. à 6 br.	cat. 3225, p. 364, pl. 87
My(...)?	Hera(...)	cat. 638, p. 301, pl. 70	VG/Menem.	Ét. à 6 br.	cat. 3224, p. 364, pl. 87
My(...)?	Hera(...)	cat. 1977, p. 302, pl. 70	VG/Menem.	Animés	cat. 3345, p. 414, pl. 97
My(...)?	Hera(...)	cat. 2429, p. 302, pl. 70	VG/Menem.	Animés	cat. 3445, p. 417, pl. 97
My(...)?	Hera(...)	cat. 9341, p. 302, pl. 71			
My(...)?	Hera(...)	cat. 738, p. 302, pl. 71	WCl	Mono. PAR	cat. 1185, p. 134, pl. 30
My(...)?	Plag.	cat. 559, p. 316, pl. 74	WCl	Mono. PAR	cat. 3043, p. 166, pl. 37
My(...)?	Plag.	cat. 1131, p. 316, pl. 74	WCl	Mono. PAR	cat. 8806, p. 185, pls. 40, 126
My(...)?	Plag.	cat. 572, p. 318, pl. 74	WCl	Mono. PAR	cat. 111, p. 187, pl. 41
My(...)?	Plag.	cat. 641, p. 318, pl. 74	WCl	Mono. PAR an.	cat. 496, p. 209, pl. 17
My(...)?	Plag.	cat. 955, p. 318, pl. 75	WCl	PRSpir.	cat. 228, p. 220, pl. 49
My(...)?	Plag.	cat. 956, p. 318	WCl	6 des 6	cat. 1203, p. 396, pl. 93
My(...)?	Plag.	cat. 1218, p. 319, pl. 75	WCl	Apollonios	cat. 3041, p. 226, pl. 50
My(...)?	Plag.	cat. 732, p. 325, pl. 77	WCl	Apollonios	cat. 3038, p. 226, pl. 50
My(...)?	Plag.	cat. 2268, p. 326, pl. 78	WCl	Hera(...)	cat. 2115, p. 311, pl. 73
My(...)?	Plag.	cat. 4572, p. 331, pl. 79	WCl	Plag.	cat. 1930, p. 328, pl. 78
			WCl	Plag.	cat. 618, p. 328, pl. 78
Pan mask	NI	cat. 5377, p. 76, pls. 16, 118	WCl	Plag.	cat. 9557, p. 329, pl. 78
Pan mask	Mono. PAR	cat. 772, p. 185, pls. 40, 126	WCl	CI	cat. 659, p. 347, pl. 83
Pan mask	Mono. PAR	cat. 430, p. 186, pl. 40	WCl	CI	cat. 8614, p. 349, pl. 84

WC1	CI	cat. 8612, p. 350, pl. 84		WC1	Déc. géom.	cat. 4168, p. 480, pl. 111
WC1	CI	cat. 1889, p. 352		WC1	Déc. géom.	cat. 4169, p. 480, pl. 111
WC1	CI an.	cat. 592, p. 355, pl. 85		WC1	Déc. géom.	cat. 4171, p. 480, pl. 111
WC1	Fleur.	cat. 1393, p. 439, pl. 101		WC1	Déc. géom.	cat. 4285, p. 480, pl. 112
WC1	Fleur.	cat. 8123, p. 440, pl. 101		WC1	Déc. géom.	cat. 4260, p. 480, pl. 112
WC1	Fleur.	cat. 8607, p. 440, pl. 101		WC1	Déc. géom.	cat. 4272, p. 480, pl. 112
WC1	Déc. géom.	cat. 4022, p. 477, pl. 111		WC1	Déc. géom.	cat. 4186, p. 480, pl. 112
WC1	Déc. géom.	cat. 4012, p. 477, pl. 111				

APPENDIX 4

Moulds as Evidence of Production Places

The following list contains references to more than 80 individual production places which are attested by one or more complete or fragmentary moulds; in addition are included the two Umbrian production places evidenced by signatures on vessels (Mevania and Ocriculum). Locations are plotted in Fig. 110.

GREEK MAINLAND

Athens

Agora

69 moulds and mould fragments, three punches: Rotroff 1982a, cats. 10–12, 40–48, 78–86, 273–281, 295–320, 347–358, 363, 411–413, pls. 2, 7, 8, 14, 54–58, 63–65, 72, 93.

Kerameikos

Four mould fragments: Schwabacher 1941, 218 cats. 1, 2; 220, pl. VIIa.11–14.

Odos Othonos (Syntagma Square)

Two moulds: Andreiomenou 1968, 80, pl. 8.4c, d; Daux 1968, 749, 753 fig. 9; Zaganiari-Phrantzi 1970, 137, fig. 1.

Pnyx

57 moulds and mould fragments: Edwards 1956, 109–110 (list with catalogue nos.).

Aigeira

Nine mould fragments: Mitsopoulos-Leon 1973, 198, fig. 6; Trummer 1990; Künzl 2002, 77 cat. 1.

Argos

11 mould fragments: Siebert 1987, cats. A121, A173, A174 (Agathokles); M27, M64, M87, M101 (Monogramist); K105, K195, K222 (Kleagoras); Kolia 2000, 391 pl. 206.d; Künzl 2002, 77 cat. 4.

Corinth

At least six mould fragments: Edwards 1975, 186 cats. 939–942, pl. 83; Siebert 1978, 73; Edwards 1981, 194 n. 26, pl. 43; Edwards 1986, 396, pl. 90; Künzl 2002, 77 cat. 21.

Elis

Four mould fragments: Siebert 1978, 104; Proskynitopoulou 1992–1993, 101 cats. 87, 89, pl. 25; 124 cat. 321, pl. 37; cat. 385 pl. 38; Rogl 1996, 141; Künzl 2002, 77 cat. 12.

Gortys (Arcadia)

One mould fragment: Siebert 1978, 95.

Koroneia

Seven minute mould fragments: Oral paper by Ph. Bes and J. Poblome given 9 March 2012 at the Round table *Late Hellenistic and Roman Tableware in the Black Sea, Eastern Mediterranean and in the West (150 BC–250 AD)*, Berlin (one Atticizing; the remainder seemingly local and probably later).

Laurion

One mould fragment: Salliora-Oikonomákou 1979, 169 pl. 74c; Künzl 2002, 77 cat. 24 (copies or imitates Bion).

Lousoi

Five mould fragments: Rogl 2008a, 102, 106, 113 cats. 24, 46, 76–78, pls. 3, 5, 8, 30, 31, 34, 46.

Olympia, Well North of Building C

Four mould fragments: Siebert 1978, 104; Hausmann 1996, 102–103 cats. 248–251, pl. 45; Künzl 2002, 78 cat. 37.

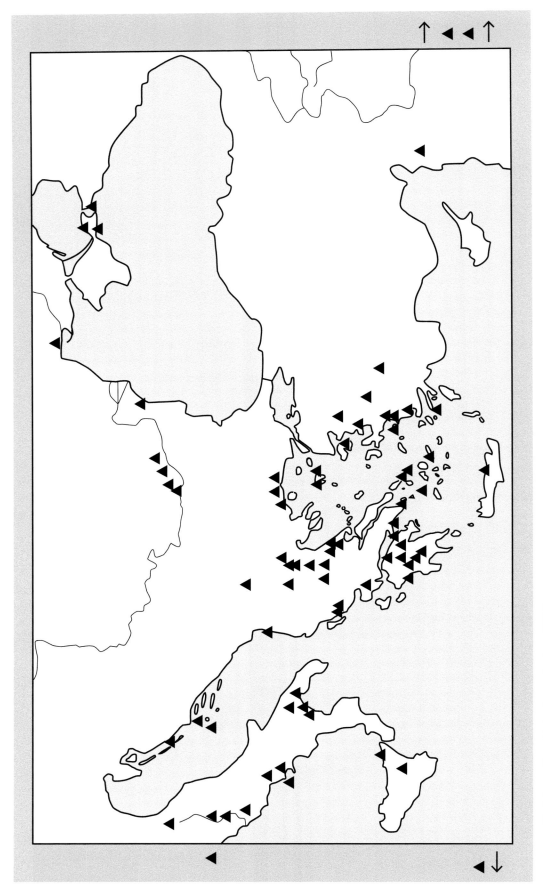

FIGURE 110 Find places of moulds for the production of MMB
MAP BY AUTHOR AND S. ROTROFF

Sparta

Five mould fragments: Hobling 1923–1925, 281–282, fig. 1.a; Siebert 1978, 83; Künzl 2002, 78 cat. 48; Zavvou 2005, 119 cat. 15, fig. 11.

THESSALY

Demetrias

Three complete and fragmentary moulds and a terracotta punch: Doulgeri-Intzesilogou 2000, 511–512, pls. 251–252; Künzl 2002, 77 cat. 10.

Gomfoi

One mould fragment: Chatziaggelakis 2004, 143–144 cat. 17, pl. 38.b.

Kierion

One mould fragment: Doulgeri-Intzesilogou 2000, 512–513, pl. 252.e; Künzl 2002, 77 cat. 18.

Larisa

One mould: Doulgeri-Intzesilogou 2000, 512 pl. 252.b; Künzl 2002, 77 cat. 23.

Pherai

At least 13 moulds and mould fragments: Kakavogiannis 1980, 274, fig. 15.a–d; Doulgeri-Intzesilogou 2000, 508–512, pl. 251; Künzl 2002, 78 cat. 42.

MACEDONIA

Abdera

Two mould fragments: Kranioti 1997, 798 (not illustrated).

Aiani

Moulds (number not mentioned): Akamatis 1993, 383.

Kavalla

One mould fragment: Bakalakis 1938, 81, fig. 8; Akamatis 1993, 343 n. 694.

Maroneia

Two mould fragments: Tsimpides-Pentazos 1971, 104, pl. 126.a; Künzl 2002, 77 cat. 25.

Pella

320 moulds and mould fragments: Akamatis 1993; Künzl 2002, 78 cat. 39.

Petres

Fragments of seven moulds: Adam Veleni 1990, pl. 41.1; Akamatis 1993, 343 n. 694; Künzl 2002, 78 cat. 41.

Stobi

11 mould fragments: Anderson-Stojanović 1992, 11–12, cats. 8–18, pls. 3, 151, 152; Künzl 2002, 78 cat. 49.

Vergina

12 mould fragments: Phaklares 1983, 211–218 cats. 1–12; Künzl 2002, 79 cat. 55.

Veroia

One mould fragment: Akamatis 1993, 343 n. 694; 383.

EPIRUS

Arta

One mould fragment: Chrysostomou 1980, 309, pl. 155.b; Künzl 2002, 77 cat. 6.

Kassope

Eight complete and fragmentary moulds: Grabani 2000, 484–485, pl. 250; Künzl 2002, 77 cat. 17.

Stratos

One mould fragment: Mastrokostas 1967, 322, pl. 231.d; Künzl 2002, 78, cat. 50.

COASTAL ASIA MINOR

Ephesos

Agora, well

One mould fragment: Meriç 2002, 34 cat. K 50, pl. 92.

Agora, location?

One mould fragment: Rogl 2008b, 528, fig. 10.

Basilica

Two mould fragments: Mitsopoulos-Leon 1985, 249, pl. XXVIII.6; Mitsopoulos-Leon 1991, 70, 74 cats. D1, D56, pls. 76, 87.

Hanghaus 2

Two mould fragments: Dereboylu 2001, 44, cat. 1, pl. 23.219, cat. 2, pl. 23.220.

Magnesia Gate

At least 62 mould fragments: Seiterle 1981, 28; 1982, fig. 3; Rogl 2001b, 106–111 cats. RB 1–24, pls. 60–69; Tuluk 2001, 67–69 cats. 26–34, pls. 44–45; Kerschner et al. 2002, cats. Ephe 105–108, figs. 2.3–6.

Prytaneion

One mould fragment: Mitsopoulos-Leon 1985, 249, pl. XXVIII.5.

Iasos

One mould fragment: Pierobon 1987, 86, fig. 8; Pierobon-Benoit 1997, 375–376, pl. 279.c; Künzl 2002, cat. 16.

Knidos

At least 35 moulds and mould fragments: Love 1967, figs. 44, 45; Kögler 2000a and b; Künzl 2002, 77 cat. 19; Kögler 2010, 521–523, cats. F.144–F.166, pls. 30–32; 594–595, cats. Kn.347–Kn.356, pl. 60.

Kyme

19 moulds and mould fragments: Horáková-Jansová 1931; Bouzek & Jansová 1974, 51–52 cats. MB 1–MB 14, Smyrna A and B, neg. Pergamon 72/87, 2; Lagona 1994, 29 fig. 5.b; Künzl 2002, 77 cat. 22.

Miletos

Four mould fragments: Kossatz 1990, cat. M 306, pl. 1, cat. M 136, pl. 4, cat. M 241, pl. 7; cat. M 508, pl. 10; Künzl 2002, 78 cat. 29.

Pergamon

Several moulds and kiln: Hepding 1952, pl. 4; Parlasca 1955, 132, fig. 1; de Luca 1968, 163 cat. 421, pl. 57; Özyǧit 1990, 96; Künzl 2002, 78 cat. 40.

Priene

At least four mould fragments: Rumscheid & Rumscheid 2007; Fenn 2011, 526, pl. 225.a; 2014, 143, fig. 2.

MOULDS AS EVIDENCE OF PRODUCTION PLACES

INLAND ASIA MINOR

Art Market

114 moulds and mould fragments: Künzl 2002 with references to older literature. The location is unknown and a number of different provenances have been given by the dealers, such as 'between Burdur and Gölhisar', 'Knidos', 'Pergamon' or 'Magnesia ad Sipylum'. There can be no doubt that the moulds come from the same production place, somewhere in the orbit of Pergamene influence.

Hierapolis

"A very large number of fragmentary moulds": d'Andria 1987, 91–93; Künzl 2002, 77 cat. 15; d'Andria 2003, 216 fig. 192.

Kibyra

At least three mould fragments: Ekinci et al. 2007, 24, fig. 3.

Sardis

62 mould fragments and one terracotta punch: Rotroff 1997b, 365 cats. 1–4, pl. 265; Rotroff 2003, 96–104 cats. 359–422, pls. 60–70.

GREEK ISLANDS

Amorgos, Minoa

Seven mould fragments: Marangou 1981, 320 fig. 7, pl. 221; 1982, 303, fig. 15; 1983, 323; 1987, 260; Pappa 1997, pls. 259–261; 2000, 112, pl. 55.g; Künzl 2002, 78 cat. 30.

Crete, Knossos

One mould fragment: Catling et al. 1981, 98 cat. V.339, fig. 9, pl. 10.c, d; Eiring 2001, 102 (KSP V339); Künzl 2002, 77 cat. 20.

Delos

Two mould fragments: Courby 1922, 333, pl. IX.d; Laumonier 1973, 254; Laumonier 1977, 2; Chatzidakis 1997, 302, pl. 223.a; Künzl 2002, 77 cat. 9.

Lemnos, Hephaistia

297 moulds and mould fragments: Massa 1992; Massa 1997, pls. 251–254; Künzl 2002, 77 cat. 14.

Lemnos, Myrina

One mould fragment: Archontidou-Argyri 1994, 233 cat. BE 11244, pl. 179.b; Künzl 2002, 78 cat. 34.

Lesbos, Mytilene

Moulds, number not mentioned: Neuru 1991, 13 and n. 32; Künzl 2002, 78 cat. 35.

Samos

Nine mould fragments: Tsakos 1990, 144; 1994, pls. 229–232; Künzl 2002, 78 cat. 45.

Siphnos

One mould fragment: Brock 1949, 61 cat. 17, pl. 21.6; Künzl 2002, 78 cat. 47.

Tenos

Two mould fragments: Etienne & Braun 1986, 224 cat. An. 9, An. 10, pl. 111; Künzl 2002, 78 cat. 51.

LEVANT

Antiochia

Three mould fragments: Waagé 1948, 29, fig. 9.1–3; Künzl 2002, 77 cat. 3.

COASTAL BLACK SEA REGION

Istros

One mould fragment: Mentioned by Lambrino 1938, 20, no illustration; Domăneanțu 2000, 144.

Mesambria

One mould fragment: Ognenova 1960, 228; Čimbuléva 1969, 177; Künzl 2002, 77 cat. 26.

Myrmekion

DEM-2, DEM-3.

Olbia

One mould fragment: unpublished; exhibited in Odessa Archaeological Museum before recent refurbishment.

Pantikapaion

DEM-1*, DEM-4–DEM-11.

Phanagoreia, Square 83/5

One mould fragment: Kovalenko 1989, 405 cat. 212, fig. 29; 1996, 55; Žuravlev & Žuravleva 2014, 260, fig. 6.2.

BLACK SEA REGION, INLAND

Piscul Crasani

One mould fragment: Casan-Franga 1967, 15, fig. 5.3; Künzl 2002, 78 cat. 43; Irimia 2006, 74.

Popești

At least nine mould fragments: Casan-Franga 1967, 15, fig. 5.1, 2, 4; Vulpe & Gheorghiță 1976, 167–177, pl. 11.1–6; Turcu 1976, pls. 9.6, 12.1, 2; Künzl 2002, 78 cat. 44; Irimia 2006, 74.

Radovanu

One mould fragment: Morintz & Șerbănescu 1985, 25, fig. 3.6; Irimia 2006, 74.

Zimnicea

One mould fragment: Casan-Franga 1967, 15, fig. 5.5.

MESOPOTAMIA

Babylon

One mould fragment: Wetzel, Schmidt & Mallwitz 1957, 57 no. 92.

AFGHANISTAN

Aï Khanoum

Mould fragments, number not specified: Gardin 1990, 189.

ITALY

Ariminum

Two mould fragments: Maioli 1979; Puppo 1995, 129, under cat. IT3; 186–187; Künzl 2002, 77 cat. 5.

Cales

One mould fragment: Paribeni 1927, 377; Morel 1976, 281, n. 26.

Cosa

Two mould fragments: Marabini Moevs 1980, 218 cats. 10, 11, pls. 1, 8; Puppo 1995, 83 cats. C1, C2, pl. XLIII; Künzl 2002, 77 cat. 8.

Herakleia (Policoro)

Moulds (number not mentioned): Guzzo et al. 1974, 539; Morel 1976, 281, n. 26.

Ischia

Mould: mentioned in Morel 1976, 281, n. 26.

Metapontum

One mould fragment: Morel 1976, 281, n. 26; Puppo 1995, 90; Künzl 2002, 78 cat. 27.

Mevania

Production place mentioned in signature, not mould: Siebourg 1897, 44 cat. 6; Jones 1958, 37 cat. 2, fig. 1; Marabini Moevs 1980, pl. 17.3; Puppo 1995, 49 cat. P9, pl. XIII; Künzl 2002, 78 cat. 28.

Monte Sannace

One mould fragment: Scarfì 1962, 280; Puppo 1995, 90, 100; Künzl 2002, 78 cat. 32.

Ocriculum

Production place mentioned in signature, not mould: Siebourg 1897, 45 cat. 8; Marabini Moevs 1980, 185, pl. 17.1; Puppo 1995, 48 cat. P7, pls. X, XI; Künzl 2002, 78 cat. 36.

Pompeii

One mould fragment: mentioned in Peña & McCallum 2009, 58.

Tarentum

Mould(?): Brusić 1999, 7 n. 29 (mentions part of a mould signed Ariston; without further references; no illustration).

Tivoli

S. Anna

25 moulds and mould fragments excavated in 1926: Paribeni 1927; Marabini Moevs 1980, pls. 22, 23; Puppo 1995, pls. XXXV–XXXIX.

Amphiteatre

104 moulds and mould fragments excavated 1991–1995 in a room in the amphitheatre: Leotta 1993; 1995; 1997; Künzl 2002, 78 cat. 52.

SICILY

Morgantina

One mould fragment: Stone 1981, 359 n. 403; Puppo 1995, 124 cat. M30, pl. LIV.

Tyndaris

One mould fragment: Lamboglia 1959, 87 fig. 1; Puppo 1995, 112 cat. S9, fig. 13; Falco 2000, 381, 384; Künzl 2002, 78–79 cat. 53.

EASTERN ADRIATIC (LIBURNIA)

Iader (Zadar)

One mould fragment: Brusić 1999, 76 cat. A119, pl. 21.

Issa (Vis Island)

One mould fragment: Brusić 1988, 37, pl. 26.12; 1999, 77 cat. A121, pl. 22.

Siculi (Resnik)

One mould fragment: Brusić 1999, 77 cat. A120, pl. 22.

SOUTHEASTERN ADRIATIC

Durrachium

Eight mould fragments: Hidri 1976, pl. III.16; 1988, pl. VII; Künzl 2002, 77 cat. 11.

SPAIN

Ampurias

One mould fragment: Vegas 1955–1956; Laumonier 1962, 44; Künzl 2002, 77 cat. 2.

Bibliography

Abbreviations

The abbreviations for journals and series of publications follow the guidelines and lists of the German Archaeological Institute (DAI), which are available online as follows:
https://www.dainst.org/en/research/publications/publishing-at-the-dai/dai-citation-style-and-abbreviations (English)
https://www.dainst.org/forschung/publikationen/publizieren/zitierstil-abkuerzungen (Deutsch)

In addition, the following abbreviations are used:

AGSP	G.A. Košelenko, I.T. Kruglikova & V.S. Dolgorukov (eds.), *Antičnye gosudarstva Severnogo Pričernomor'ja*, Archeologija SSSR 42 (Moscow 1984).
BSS	*Black Sea Studies*.
CONSPECTUS	Ettlinger, E., Hedinger, B., Hoffmann, B., Kenrick, Ph.M., Pucci, G., Roth-Rubi, K, Schneider, G., von Schnurbein, S., Wells, C. & Zabehlicky-Scheffenegger, S. (eds.), *Conspectus formarum terrae sigillatae Italico modo confectae*, Materialien zur römisch-germanischen Keramik 10 (Bonn 1990).
IAK	*Izvestija Archeologičeskoj Komissii* (News of the Archaeological Commission) (St Petersburg).
IIMK RAN	*Institut Istorii Material'noj Kul'tury, Rossiskoj Akademii Nauk* (Institute for the History of Material Culture, Russian Academy of Sciences, St Petersburg).
NGS 2010	Lejpunskaja, N.A.†, Guldager Bilde, P., Højte, J.M., Krapivina, V.V. & Kryžickij, S.D. (eds.), *The Lower City of Olbia (Sector NGS) in the 6th Century BC to the 4th Century AD*, BSS 13 (Aarhus).
OAK	Otčoty Archeologičeskoj Komissii (Reports of the Archaeological Commission) (St Petersburg).
TSP	*Terrakoty Severnogo Prichernomor'ia* (Moscow 1970).
Α' Συνάντηση	Α' Συνάντηση για την ελληνιστική κεραμική, Ιωάννινα, 6 Δεκεμβρίου 1986 (Ioannina 1989).
Β' Συνάντηση	Β' Επιστημονική Συνάντηση για την ελληνιστική κεραμεική. Χρονολογικά προβλήματα της ελληνιστικής κεραμεικής, Ρόδος, 22–25 Μαρτίου 1989 (Athens 1990).
Γ' Συνάντηση	Γ' Επιστημονική Συνάντηση για την ελληνιστική κεραμική. Χρονολογημένα σύνολα, εργαστήρια, 24–27 Σεπεμβρίου 1991 Θεσσαλονίκη (Athens 1994).
Δ' Συνάντηση	Δ' Επιστημονική Συνάντηση για την ελληνιστική κεραμική. Χρονολογικά προβλήματα, κλειστά σύνολα, εργαστήρια, Μυτιλήνη, Μάρτιος 1994 (Athens 1997).
Ε' Συνάντηση	Ε' Επιστημονική Συνάντηση για την ελληνιστική κεραμική. Χρονολογικά προβλήματα, κλειστά σύνολα, εργαστήρια, Χανιά 1997 (Athens 2000).
ΣΤ' Συνάντηση	ΣΤ' Επιστημονική Συνάντηση για την ελληνιστική κεραμική. Προβλήματα χρονολόγησης, κλειστά σύνολα, εργαστήρια, Βόλος 17–23 Απριλίου 2000 (Athens 2004).
Ζ' Συνάντηση	Ζ' Επιστημονική Συνάντηση για την ελληνιστική κεραμική, Αιγίο, 4–9 Απριλίου 2005 (Athens 2011).
Η' Συνάντηση	Η' Επιστημονική Συνάντηση για την ελληνιστική κεραμική, Ιωάννινα 5–9 Μαΐου 2009 (Athens 2014).
Θ' Συνάντηση	Θ' Επιστημονική Συνάντηση για την ελληνιστική κεραμική, Θεσσαλονίκη, 5–9 Δεκεμβρίου 2012 (Athens 2018).

Bibliography

Adamsheck, B., 1979: *The Pottery*, Kenchreai, Eastern Port of Corinth 4 (Leiden).

Adam Veleni, P., 1990: "Eine Werkstatt für Reliefgefässe in Petres, West-Makedonien", in *Akten des XIII. internationalen Kongresses für klassische Archäologie, Berlin, 24.–30. Juli 1988* (Mainz) 309–311.

Adam Veleni, P., 1993: "Χαλκινή ασπίδα από τη Βεγόρα της Φλώρινας Αρχαία Μακεδονία", in *Αρχαία Μακεδονία 5. Ανακοινώσεις κατά το Πέμπτο Διεθνές Συμπόσιο, Θεσσαλονίκη 10–15 Οκτωβρίου 1989. Ancient Macedonia, Papers Read at the Fifth International Symposium Held in Thessaloniki, October 10–15, 1989* (Thessaloniki) 17–28.

Adam Veleni, P., 1997: "Πέτρες Φλώρινας. Πρώτη προσέγγιση στην τοπική κεραμική παραγωγή", in *Δ' Συνάντηση*: 138–154.

Adam Veleni, P., Georgaki, P., Kalabria, B., Boli, K., 2000: "Κλειστά σύνολα ελληνιστικών χρόνων από την αγορά της Θεσσαλονίκης", in *Ε' Συνάντηση*: 275–297.

Adriani, A., 1967: "Un vetro dorato alessandrino dal Caucaso", *BArchAlex* 42: 105–127.

Ahrens, D., 1968: "Staatliche Antikensammlung und Glyptothek", *MüJb* 19: 229–234.

Ajbabin, A.I., et al. (eds.), 2006: *Drevnejšij temenos Ol'vii Pontijskoj*, Materialy po archeologii, istorii i etnografii Tavrii Suppl. 2 (Simferopol).

Akamatis, I.M., 1993: *Πήλινες μήτρες αγγείων από την Πέλλα. Συμβολή στη μελέτη της ελληνιστικής κεραμικής*, ADelt Suppl. 51 (Athens).

Alekseeva, E.M., 1997: *Antichnÿi gorod Gorgippia* (Moscow).

Alexandrescu, P., 1966: "Necropola tumulara. Săpături 1955–1961", in E. Condurachi (ed.), *Histria* 2 (Bucharest) 134–294.

Anderson-Stojanović, V.R., 1992: *Stobi, The Hellenistic and Roman Pottery* (Princeton).

Anderson-Stojanović, V.R., 1996: "The University of Chicago Excavations in the Rachi Settlement at Isthmia, 1989", *Hesperia* 65, 57–98.

Andreae, B., 1996: "L'immagine di Ulisse", in B. Andreae & C. Parisi Presicce, *Ulisse. Il mito e la memoria*, Roma, Palazzo delle Esposizioni, 22 febbraio–2 settembre 1996 (Rome) 42–157.

Andreiomenou, A., 1968: "Γ' εφορεία κλασσικών αρχαιοτήτων. 23. Οδός Όθονος", *ADelt B* 21 [1966]: 80.

Antiken 1973: *Antiken aus Rheinischem Privatbesitz*, Kunst und Altertum am Rhein 48 (Bonn).

Archibald, Z.H., Davies, J., Gabrielsen, V. & Oliver, G.J. (eds.), 2001: *Hellenistic Economies* (London and New York).

Archontidou-Argyri, A., 1994: "Εργαστήριο ελληνιστικής κεραμικής από τη Μύρινα Λήμνου", in *Γ' Συνάντηση*: 231–234.

Arena, M.S., 1969: "Su alcuni frammenti di ceramica italo-megarese conservati nell'Antiquarium di Ostia", *RivStLig* 35: 101–121.

Arribas, A. & De Arribas, G.T., 1959: "Ceramica de 'Megara' en Pollentia (Alcudia, Mallorca)", *AEsp* 32, 84–92.

Arsen'eva, T.M., Bezuglov, S.I., and Tolochko, I.V., 2001: *Nekropol' Tanaisa. Raskopki 1981–1995 gg.* (Moscow).

Avilés, A.F. 1957. "Cerâmica de Megara em Espanha: A propósito de um projecto de catálog", *RGuimar* 67.1–2: 47–54.

Aydin, B., 2007: "The Hellenistic Pottery and Small Finds of Kordon Tumulus at Kordon Köyö/Salihli (Manisa) 2001", *ÖJh* 76: 7–28.

Bakalakis, G., 1938: "Ανασκαφές εν Καβάλα και τοις πέριξ", *Prakt* 93: 75–102.

Batalis, M., 2004: "Πολύμυλος Κοζάνης: Ταφικά σύνολα ελληνιστικών χρόνων", in *ΣΤ' Συνάντηση*: 219–236.

Batizat, G.V., 2002: "'Megarian' Cups from the Excavations at Tyras", in P. Roman & S. Kryzickij (eds.), *Tyras. Cetatea Albă/Belhorod-Dnistrovs'kyj. I. Săpături 1996–1999* (Bucharest) 223–256.

Baur, P.V.C., 1941: "Megarian Bowls in the Rebecca Darlington Stoddard Collection of Greek and Italian Vases in Yale University", *AJA* 45: 228–248.

Beazley's Gifts 1967. *Select Exhibition of Sir John and Lady Beazley's Gifts to the Ashmolean Museum 1912–1966* (London).

Belov, G.D. 1962: "Ellenističeskij dom v Chersonese", *TrudyErmit* 7: 143–183.

Belov, G.D., 1978, "Nekropol' Chersonesa ellinisticheskoi epochi", *Archeologicheskii sbornik Gosudarstvennogo Ermitazha* 19: 45–66.

Belov, G.D. & Jakobson, A.L., 1953: "Kvartal XVII (Raskopki 1940 g.)", *MIA* 34: 109–159.

Belov, G.D., Streželeckij, S.F. & Jakobson, A.L., 1953: "Kvartal XVIII (Raskopki 1941, 1947, 1948 g.)", *MIA* 34: 160–236.

Benndorf, O., 1883: *Griechische und sicilische Vasenbilder*, Vierte Lieferung (Berlin).

Benoit, F., 1947: "Recherches archéologiques dans la région d'Aix-en-Provence (Bouches-du-Rhône)", *Gallia* 5: 81–89.

Benoit, F., 1952: "L'Archélogie sous-marine en Provence", *Revue d'etudes Ligures* 18: 237–307.

Benton, S., 1938–1939: "Excavations at Ithaca III; The Cave at Polis, 2", *BSA* 39: 1–51.

Berger, K., 1993: "Die griechischen und italischen Antiken des Archäologischen Instituts der Universität zu Köln", *KölnJb* 26: 217–319.

Berger, K., 1995a: "Griechische und italische Antiken der Sammlung C.A. Niessen im Römisch-Germanischen Museum und im Archäologischen Institut der Universität zu Köln", *KölnJb* 28: 7–124.

Berger, K., 1995b: "Griechische und italische Antiken in der Studiensammlung des RGM", *KölnJb* 28: 125–156.

Bernhard, M.L., 1957: *Katalog wystawy zabytków z wykopalisk w Mirmeki w r. 1956* (Warsaw).

Bernhard, M.L., 1959: *Pamiętnik wystawy zabytków z wykopalisk w Mirmeki w 1957 roku*, (Warsaw).

Bernhard, M.L., 1961: "La céramique hellénistique à Mirmeki", in *Atti del settimo congresso internazionale di archeologia classica III, Roma – Napoli 1958* (Rome) 73–79.

Bielefeld, D. 1995: "Zur Ikonographie attischer Sarkophage mit Eroten-Weinlese Darstellungen", *RM* 102: 397–404.

Bielefeld, D., 1997: *Die stadtrömische Eroten-Sarkophage. Weinlese- und Ernteszenen*, Die antiken Sarkophagreliefs 5.2.2 (Berlin).

Blavatskij, V.D., 1953: *Istorija antičnoj raspisnoj keramiki* (Moscow).

Blavatskij, V.D., 1959: "O proizvodstve 'Megarskich' čaš v Pantikapee", *KSIIMK* 75: 174–176.

Blech, M., 1982: *Studien zum Kranz bei den Griechen*, Religionsgeschichtliche Versuche und Vorarbeiten 38 (Berlin and New York).

Bobrinskij, A., 1904: "Notes d'archéologie russe", *RevArch* 4, 3: 1–18.

Bodzek, J. (ed.), 2006: *Skarby znad Morza Czernego. Treasures from the Black Sea Coast. Exhibition at Krakow from the Collections of the Archaeological Museum at Odessa* (Kraków).

Boehlau, J., 1908: *Griechische Altertümer südrussischen Fundorts aus dem Besitze des Herrn A. Vogell, Karlsruhe*. Versteigerung zu Cassel in der Gewerbehalle, Friedrich-Wilhelmsplatz 6, 26.–30. Mai 1908 (Kassel).

Boehringer, E. & Krauss, F., 1937: *Das Temenos für den Herrscherkult, Prinzessinen Palais*, AvP 9 (Berlin and Leipzig).

Borgeaud, Ph., 1979: *Recherches sur le dieu Pan* (Geneva).

Bounegru, O., 2003: "La production des ateliers de céramique de Pergame (vallée de Ketios): un aperçu général", in C. Abadie-Reynal (ed.), *Les Céramiques en Anatolie aux epoques hellénistique et romaine, Actes de la Table Ronde d'Istanbul, 22–24 mai 1996*, Varia Anatolica 15 (Paris) 137–140.

Bouzek, J., 1982: "Ein megarischer Becher mit Iliou Persis", in B. von Freytag gen. Löringhoff, D. Mannsperger & F. Prayon (eds.), *Praestant interna. Festschrift für Ulrich Hausmann* (Tübingen) 244–247.

Bouzek, J., 1985: "Megarian Bowls, Production Centers, Imports and Local Workshops in the West Pontic Area", in M. Lazarov (ed.), *Le littoral Thrace et son rôle dans le monde ancien, Sozopol 4–7 octobre 1982*, Tracia Pontica 2 (Sozopol) 66–73.

Bouzek, J., 1990: *Studies of Greek Pottery in the Black Sea Area* (Prague).

Bouzek, J., 2005: "Ephesier ausserhalb von Ephesos: Ephesische Keramik in Mittel- und Schwarzmeerbereich", in V. Gassner (ed.), *Synergia. Festschrift für Fritz Krinzinger* (2 vols) (Vienna) 55–65.

Bouzek, J., 2008: *Classical and Hellenistic Greek Pottery in the Black Sea Region*, http://www.ehw.gr/l.aspx?id=12224.

Bouzek, J. & Jansová, L., 1974: *Anatolian Collection of Charles University. Kyme* 1 (Prague).

Bozkova, A., 1994: "Importations grecques et imitations locales: La céramique hellénistique en Thrace. Chronologie et centres de production", in *Γ' Συνάντηση*: 223–230.

Braun, K., 1970: "Der Dipylon-Brunnen B1. Die Funde", *AM* 85: 129–269.

Bringmann, K. & Steuben, H.V. (eds.), 1995: *Schenkungen hellenistischer Herrscher an griechische Städte und Heiligtümer, 1. Zeugnisse und Kommentare* (Berlin).

Brock, J.K., 1949: "Excavations in Siphnos", *BSA* 44: 1–92.

Brughmans, T., 2010: "Connecting the Dots: Towards Archaeological Network Analysis", *OxfJA* 29: 277–303.

Brusić, Z., 1988: "Helenistička reljefna keramika u Liburniji", *Diadora* 10: 19–61.

Brusić, Z., 1999: *Hellenistic and Roman Relief Pottery in Liburnia (North-East Adriatic, Croatia)*, BARIntSer 817 (Oxford).

Bucovală, M., 1967: *Necropole elenistice la Tomis* (Constanţa).

Burn, L. & Higgins, R.A., 2001: *Catalogue of Greek Terracottas in the British Museum* 3 (London).

Byvanck-Quarles van Ufford, L., 1953: "Les bols mégariens. La chronologie et les rapports avec l'argenterie hellénistique", *BABesch* 28: 1–21.

Byvanck-Quarles van Ufford, L., 1959: "Variations sur le thème des bols mégariens", *BABesch* 34: 58–67.

Byvanck-Quarles van Ufford, L., 1970: "Les bols hellénistiques en verre doré", *BABesch* 45: 129–141.

Byvanck-Quarles van Ufford, L., 1974. " Bols 'déliens' et bols de Popilius", *BABesch* 49: 262–264.

Callaghan, P.J., 1978: "Macedonian Shields, 'Shield-Bowls' and Corinth: A Fixed Point in Hellenistic Chronology?", *AAA* 11: 53–60.

Callaghan, P.J., 1980: "The Trefoil Style and Second-Century Hadra Vases", *BSA* 75: 33–47.

Callaghan, P.J., 1981: "On the Date of the Great Altar of Zeus at Pergamon", *BICS* 28: 115–121.

Callaghan, P.J., 1982: "On the Origin of the Long Petal Bowl", *BICS* 29.1: 63–68.

Camp, J.M., 2001: *The Archaeology of Athens* (New Haven and London).

Casan-Franga, I., 1967: "Contribuţii cu privire la cunoaşterea ceramicii geto-dacice. Cupele 'deliene' getice de pe teritoriul României", *AMold* 5: 7–35.

Catling, H.W., Catling, E.A., Callaghan, P. & Smyth, D., 1981: "Minoan Paralipomena and Post-Minoan Remains", *BSA* 76: 83–108.

Chatziaggelakis, L.P., 2004: "Ανάγλυφοι σκύφοι από τη δυτική Θεσσαλία, Νομός Καρδίτσας", in *ΣΤ' Συνάντηση*: 137–148.

Chatzidakis, P., 1997: "Κτίριο νότια του Ιερού του Προμαχώνος. Μία taberna vinaria στη Δήλο", in *Δ' Συνάντηση*: 291–307.

Chatzidakis, P.I., 2000: "Οψοποιητικά σκεύη από τη Δήλο", in *Ε' Συνάντηση*: 115–130.

Chatzidakis, P., 2004: "Ειδωλιόμορφα σκεύη από τη Δήλο", in *ΣΤ' Συνάντηση*: 367–392.

Chlystun, T.G., 1996: "Mifologičeskie obrazy v relefah megarskih čaš Hersonesa", *ChSbor* 7: 153–157.

Christensen, A.P., 1971: "Les poteries hellénistiques", in A.P. Christensen & Ch.F. Johansen, *Les poteries hellénistiques et les terres sigillées orientales*, Hama, Fouilles et Recherches de la Fondation Carlsberg 1931–1938 3.2 (Copenhagen) 1–54.

Chrysostomou, P., 1980: "Άρτα. Οικόπεδο Σ. Κοτσαρίδα", *ADelt B* 35: 307–309.

Čimbuléva, J., 1969: *Trouvailles de la nécropole de Nessèbre*, Nessèbre 1 (Sofia) 165–178.

Čimbuléva, J., 2005: *La nécropole antique de Messambria. Matériaux et études*, Nessèbre 3 (Burgas) 91–117.

Čistov, D.E., 2004: "Svjatilišče Demetry v Mirmekii: popytka rekonstrukcii kompleksa", in *Bosporskij fenomen 1. Problemy chronologii i datirovki pamjatnikov*. Materialy meždunarodnoj naučnoj konferencii (St Petersburg) 131–142.

Comșa, M., 1988: "Signes solaires sur les bols gétiques imités d'après les coupes déliennes", *Thraco-Dacica* 9.1–2: 83–100.

Conovici, N., 1978: "Cupele cu decor în relief de la Crăsani și Copozu", *SCIVA* 2: 165–183.

Conovici, N., 1981: "Piese ceramice de interes deosebit descoperite la Piscu Crăsani", *SCIVA* 4: 571–579.

Conze, A., 1903: *Die Kleinfunde aus Pergamon*, Abhandlungen der Königlich Preussischen Akademie der Wissenschaften zu Berlin 1902 (Berlin).

Conze, A., Berlet, O., Philippson, A., Schuchhardt, C. & Gräber, F., 1913: *Stadt und Landschaft*, AvP 1.2 (Berlin).

Cornell, L., 1997: "A Note on the Molded Bowls", in S.C. Herbert (ed.), *The Hellenistic and Roman Pottery*, Tel Anafa 2.1 (Ann Arbor) 407–416.

Courby, F., 1922: *Les vases grecs à reliefs* (Paris).

Cremer, M., 1991: *Hellenistisch-römische Grabstelen im nordwestlichen Kleinasien 1. Mysien*, AMS 4.1 (Bonn).

Crișan, I.H., 1969: *Ceramica daco-getică. Cu specială privire la Transilvania* (Bucharest).

Cvetaeva, G.A., 1966: "Keramičeskoe proizvodstvo, Bospor", in I.B. Zeest (ed.), *Keramičeskoe proizvodstvo i anticnye keramičeskie stroitel'nye materialy*, Archeologija SSSR. Svod archeologičeskich istočnikov G1–20 (Moscow) 17–21.

Dakaris, S.I., 1968: "Ανασκαφή του ιερού της Δωδώνης", *Prakt* 124: 42–59.

D'Andria, F., 1987: "Artigianato", in D. de Bernardi Ferrero et al., *Hierapolis di Frigia, 1957–1987*, Catalogo delle mostra (Milano) 91–93.

D'Andria, F., 2003: *Hierapolis in Phrygia (Pamukkale): Ein archäologischer Führer* (Istanbul).

Daševskaja, O.D., Golencov, A.S., Mihlin, B.Ju. & Starcenko, E.V., 1976: "Raskopki na Beljause", *Arheologičeskie otkriytija 1975 goda* (Moscow) 321–322.

Daux, G., 1968: "Chronique des fouilles et découvertes archéologiques en Grèce en 1967", *BCH* 92: 711–1135.

Davies, J.K., 1984: "Cultural, Social and Economic Features of the Hellenistic World", in F.W. Walbank (ed.), *The Hellenistic World*, The Cambridge Ancient History 7.1 (Cambridge) 257–320.

Davies, J.K., 2001: "Hellenistic Economies in the Post-Finley Era", in Archibald, Davies, Gabrielsen & Oliver (eds.) 2001: 11–62.

De Decker, K., 2007–2008: "Une olpé au Musée Hongrois des Beaux Arts: La cruche de Budapest", *Boreas* 30/31: 73–103.

De Grummond, N.T., 2000: "Gauls and Giants, Skylla and the Palladion", in de Grummond & Ridgway (eds.) 2000: 255–277.

De Grummond, N.T. & Ridgway, B.S. (eds.), 2000: *From Pergamon to Sperlonga. Sculpture and Context* (Berkeley, Los Angeles and London).

De Luca, G., 1968: "Funde und Chronologie der Bauphasen", in O. Ziegenaus & G. de Luca, *Das Asklepieion 1. Der südliche Temenosbezirk in hellenistischer und frührömischer Zeit*, AvP 11.1 (Berlin) 91–174.

De Luca, G., 1975: "Die Funde", in O. Ziegenaus & G. de Luca, *Das Asklepieion 2. Der nördlichen Temenosbezirk und angrenzende Anlagen in hellenistischer und frührömischer Zeit*, AvP 11.2 (Berlin) 57–145.

De Luca, G., 1990: "Hellenistische Kunst in Pergamon im Spiegel der Megarischen Becher. Ein Beitrag zur pergamenischen Ornamentik", *IstMitt* 40: 157–166.

De Luca, G., 1997: "Tradierung von Bildthemen in den Werkstätten megarischer Becher in Pergamon", in *Δ' Συνάντηση*: 367–368.

De Luca, G., 1999: "Die feine Keramik", in de Luca & Radt 1999: 73–117.

De Luca, G., 2004: "Homer in Pergamon", *IstMitt* 54: 293–310.

De Luca, G. & Radt, W., 1999: *Sondagen im Fundament des Grossen Altars*, PF 12 (Berlin and New York).

Deonna, W., 1907: "Brûle-parfums en terre-cuite", *RevArch* 10: 245–256.

Dereboylu, E., 2001: "Weissgrundige Keramik und Hellenistische Reliefbecher aus dem Hanghaus 2 in Ephesos", in Krinzinger (ed.) 2001: 21–44.

Dickie, M.W., 1995: "The Dionysiac Mysteries in Pella", *ZPE* 109: 81–86.

Domăneanțu, C., 2000: *Les bols hellénistiques à décor en relief*, Histria XI (Bucharest).

Dothan, M., 1976: "Akko: Interim Excavation Report First Season, 1973/4", *BASOR* 224: 1–48.

Doulgeri-Intzesilogou, A., 2000: "Μήτρες για την κατασκευή ανάγλυφων σκύφων από τις Φερές και άλλες περιοχές της Θεσσαλίας", in *Ε' Συνάντηση*: 507–514.

Dragendorff, H., 1895: "Terra sigillata. Ein Beitrag zur Geschichte der griechischen und römischen Keramik", *BJb* 96–97: 18–155.

Dunand, F., 2007: "The Religious System at Alexandria", in D. Ogden (ed.), *A Companion to Greek Religion* (Malden MA) 253–263.

Ebert, M., 1913: "Ausgrabungen auf dem Gute Maritzyn, Gouv. Cherson (Süd-Russland)", *PZ* 5: 1–79.

Edgar, C.C., 1911: *Greek Vases*, Catalogue général des antiquités égyptiennes du Musée du Caire 56 (Cairo).

Edmonds, R.G., 2011: *The "Orphic" Gold Tablets and Greek Religion: Further Along the Path* (Cambridge and New York).

Edwards, C.M., 1981: "Corinth 1980: Molded Relief Bowls", *Hesperia* 50: 189–210.

Edwards, C.M., 1986: "Corinthian Moldmade Bowls: the 1926 Reservoir", *Hesperia* 55: 389–419.

Edwards, G.R., 1956: "Hellenistic Pottery", in *Small Objects from the Pnyx* 2, Hesperia Suppl. 10 (Princeton) 79–112.

Edwards, G.R., 1975: *Corinthian Hellenistic Pottery*, Corinth 7.3 (Princeton).

Eiring, L.J., 2001: "The Hellenistic Period", in J.N. Coldstream, L.J. Eiring & G. Forster, *Knossos Pottery Handbook: Greek and Roman*, British School at Athens Studies 7 (London) 91–135.

Ekinci, H.A., Özüdoğru, Ş., Dökü, E. et al., 2007: "Kibyra kazı çalışmaları 2006. Excavations at Kibyra in 2006", *Anadolu Akden* 5: 22–28.

Engelmann, H., 1976: *Die Inschriften von Kyme*, IK 5 (Bonn).

Erdemgil, S., 1980: "Kestel kurtarma kazısı", in *Kazı Sonuçları Toplantısı* II: 103–107.

Erdemgil, S., 1981: "Kestel kazisi 1980 yili calişmalari", in *Kazı Sonuçları Toplantısı* III: 63–66.

Erdemgil, S. et al., 1989: *Katalog des Ephesos Museums* (Istanbul).

Etienne, R. & Braun, J.-P., 1986: *Le sanctuaire de Poséidon et d'Amphitrite, Ténos* 1 (Paris).

Falco, G., 1999: "Tre coppe 'megaresi'", *Bulletin du Musée Hongrois des Beaux-Arts* 90/91: 29–38.

Falco, G., 2000: "La Sicilia ed il Mediterraneo orientale in età tardo ellenistica: la testimonianza della ceramica 'megarese'", *ReiCretActa* 36: 379–386.

Farmakovskij, B.V., 1896: "Raskopki nekropolja drevnej Ol'vii", *OAK* 1896: 200–212.

Farmakovskij, B.V., 1902: "Raskopki v Ol'vii", *OAK* 1900: 3–12.

Farmakovskij, B.V., 1903a: "Raskopki nekropol'ja drevnej Ol'vii v 1901 godu", *IAK* 8: 1–70.

Farmakovskij, B.V., 1903b: "Raskopki v Ol'vii", *OAK* 1901: 2–22.

Farmakovskij, B.V., 1906: "Raskopki v Ol'vii v 1902–1903 godach", *IAK* 13: 1–305.

Farmakovskij, B.V., 1909: "Olbia 1901–1908", *IAK* 33: 103–136.

Farmakovskij, B.V., 1913: "Raskopki v Ol'vii", *OAK* 1909–1910: 1–105.

[see also Pharmakowsky, Pharmakowskyi].

Fehrentz, V., 1993: "Der antike Agyieus", *JdI* 108: 123–196.

Fenn, N., 2011: "A Late Hellenistic Pottery Deposit from the Athena Sanctuary at Priene", in *Z' Συνάντηση*: 525–532.

Fenn, N., 2014: "The Hellenistic Mouldmade Bowl Production at Priene. A Case Study Concerning the Reception of Ephesian Examples" in Guldager Bilde & Lawall (eds.) 2014: 141–156.

Finkielsztejn, G., 2001: *Chronologie détaillée et révisée des éponymes amphoriques rhodiens, de 270 à 108 av. J.-C. environ. Premier bilan*, BARIntSer 990 (Oxford).

Finoguenova, S., 1991: "Les petites autels en terre cuite au nord de la Mer Noire", in R. Étienne & M.-Th. le Dinahet (eds.), *L'espace sacrificiel dans les civilisations méditerranéennes de l'antiquité, Actes du colloque tenu à la Maison de l'Orient, Lyon, 4–7 juin 1988* (Paris) 131–134.

Flashar, M., 1992: *Apollon Kitharodos. Statuarische Typen des musischen Apollo* (Köln).

Fleischer, R., 1972–1973: "Ein hellenistischer Fries aus Sagalassos", *ÖJh* 50: 117–124.

Fleischer, R., 1984: "Zur Datierung des Frieses von Sagalassos", *AA* 99: 141–144.

Fless, F., 2002: *Rotfigurige Keramik als Handelsware. Erwerb und Gebrauch attischer Vasen im mediterranen und pontischen Raum während des 4. Jhs. v. Chr.* (Rahden).

Flower of Pergamon = *Hellenistic Flower. Pergamon and the Silk Road* (ヘレニズムの華　ペルガモンとシルクロード – Herenizumu no hana. Perugamon to shirukurōdo)[in Japanese] (Tokyo 2008).

Friesländer, E., 2001: "The Mantle Dancer in the Hellenistic Period. Glorification of the Himation", *Assaph* 6: 1–30.

Gajdukevič, V.F., 1958: "Raskopki Tiritaki i Mirmekija v 1946–1952 gg.", *MIA* 85: 149–218.

Gajdukevič, V.F., 1959: *Sovjetskie raskopki v 1956 g., 1934–1956*, Mirmekij 2 (Warsaw).

Gajdukevič, V.F. (ed.), 1964: *Ol'vija. Temenos i agora* (Moscow and Leningrad).

Gajdukevič, V.F., 1971: *Das Bosporanische Reich* (Berlin).

Gajdukevič, V.F., 1981: *Bosporskie goroda* (Leningrad).

Gardin, J.-Cl., 1990: "La céramique hellénistique en Asie centrale. Problèmes d'interprétation", in *Akten des XIII Internationalen Kongresses für Klassische Archäologie, Berlin 1988* (Mainz) 187–193.

Garezou, M.-X., 1994: "Orpheus", *LIMC* VII (Zurich and Munich) 81–105.

Garnsey, P., Hopkins, K. & Whittaker, C.R. (eds.). 1983: *Trade in the Ancient Economy* (London).

Gassner, V., 1997: *Das Südtor der Tetragonos-Agora. Keramik und Kleinfunde*, FiE 13/1/1 (Vienna).

Gauvin, G., 1997: "Survey in the Costal Zone Area of the Strandja Area, South-Eastern Bulgaria", in J.M. Fossey (ed.), *Antiquitates Propontticae, Circumponticae et Caucasicae 2, Proceedings of the First International Conference on the Archaeology and History of the Black Sea, McGill University, 22–24th November 1994*, McGill University Monographs in Classical Archaeology and History 19 (Amsterdam) 67–79.

Ghali-Kahil, L., 1960: *La céramique grecque (Fouilles 1911–1956)*, Études Thasiennes 7 (Paris).

Gibbins, D., 2001: "Shipwrecks and Hellenistic Trade", in Archibald, Davies, Gabrielsen & Oliver (eds.) 2001: 273–312.

Giuliani, A. & Rogl, C., 2002: "Ephesische Töpferwerkstätten – ihre Töpfer und ihre Produkte", in B. Asamer, P. Höglinger, C. Reinholdt, R. Smetana & W. Wohlmayr (eds.), *Temenos. Festgabe für F. Felten und S. Hiller* (Vienna) 71–74.

Gjuzelev, M., 2007: "Spasitelni arheologičeski proučvanija na obekt Starata Obščina v UPI II, kv. 28, gr. Sozopol", *Arheologičeski otkritija I razkopki prez 2006*: 273–275.

Grammenos, D.V. & Petropoulos, E.K. (eds.), 2003: *Ancient Greek Colonies in the Black Sea* (Thessaloniki).

Greifenhagen, A., 1963: *Beiträge zur antiken Reliefkeramik*, JdI Ergh. 21 (Berlin).

Gricik, E.V., 2007: "Ellenističeskij dom s altarem iz Mirmekija", in *Bosporskij fenomen. Sakral'nyj smysl regiona pamjatnikov, nachodok. Materialy meždunarodnoj naučnoj konferencii* (St Petersburg) 126–132.

Grüßinger, R., Kästner, V. & Sholl, A., 2011: *Pergamon. Panorama der antiken Metropole. Begleitbuch zur Ausstellung. Eine Ausstellung der Antikensammlung der Staatlichen Museen zu Berlin* (Berlin).

Grzegrzółka, S., 2001: "Relief ('Megarian') Bowls in the National Museum in Warsaw", *BMusVars* 42: 107–123.

Grzegrzółka, S., 2010: *'Megarian' Bowls from the Collection of the Kerch History and Culture Reserve* I, BMusVars Suppl. 2 (Warsaw).

Gudenrath, W. & Tatton-Brown, V., 2003: "Monochrome and Polychrome Plaques (Inlays) in the British Museum", in *Annales du 15e Congrès de l'Association Internationale pour l'Histoire du Verre* 15, New York-Corning 2001 (Nottingham): 26–28.

Guldager Bilde, P., 1993: "Mouldmade Bowls, Centres and Peripheries in the Hellenistic World", in P. Bilde, L. Hannestad & T. Engberg-Petersen (eds.), *Centre and Periphery in the Hellenistic World*, Studies in Hellenistic Civilisation 4 (Aarhus) 192–209.

Guldager Bilde, P., 2005: "The Olbia Situla Revisited", in *Bosporskij fenomen. Problema sootnošenija pis'mennych i archeologičeskich istočnikov. Materialy meždunarodnoj naučnoj konferencii* (St Petersburg) 207–216.

Guldager Bilde, P., 2006: "Mouldmade Bowls from Olbia, Sector NGS. An Overview", in *Bosporskie čtenija* 7 (Kerch) 343–349.

Guldager Bilde, P., 2008: "Mouldmade Bowls", in P. Guldager Bilde & B. Poulsen (eds.), *The Temple of Castor and Pollux II. The Finds* (Rome) 187–192.

Guldager Bilde, P., 2009: "(Pontic) Demetrios: A Late Hellenistic Manufacturer of Mouldmade Bowls in Grey Ware", in *Pontic Grey Wares, International Conference Bucarest-Constantza September 30th–October 3rd 2008*, Pontica 42 Suppl. 1 (Constanța) 187–190.

Guldager Bilde, P., 2010: "Mouldmade bowls", in *NGS 2010*: 269–288.

Guldager Bilde, P., Bøgh, B., Handberg, S., Højte, J.M., Nieling, J., Smekalova, T. & Stolba, V. with contributions by Baralis, A., Bîrzescu, J., Gergova, D., Krapivina, V.V., Krusteff, K., Lungu, V. & Maslennikov, A.A., 2007–2008: "Archaeology in the Black Sea Region in Classical Antiquity 1993–2007", *ARepLond* 54: 115–173.

Guldager Bilde, P. & Handberg, S., 2012: "Ancient Repairs on Pottery from Olbia Pontica", *AJA* 116: 461–481.

Guldager Bilde, P., Højte, J.M. & Stolba, V.F. (eds.), 2003: *The Cauldron of Ariantas. Studies Presented to A.N. Ščeglov on the Occasion of his 70th Birthday* (Aarhus).

Guldager Bilde, P. & Lawall, M.L. (ed.), 2014: *Pottery, Peoples and Places. Study and Interpretation of Late Hellenistic Pottery*, BSS 16 (Aarhus).

Guzzo, P.G. et al., 1974: "Descrizione dei materiali", in *Sibari 4: relazione preliminare della campagna di Scavo, Stombi, Parco del Cavallo, Prolungamento Strada, Casa Bianca, 1972*, NSc 28 Suppl. (Rome) 200–527.

Habicht, Chr., 1992: "Athens and the Ptolemies", *Classical Antiquity* 11.1: 68–90.

Hadzisteliou Price, T., 1978: *Kourotrophos: Cults and Representations of the Greek Nursing Deities*, Studies of the Dutch Archaeological and Historical Society 8 (Leiden).

Hampe, R. & Winter, A., 1962: *Bei Töpfern und Töpferinnen in Kreta, Messenien und Zypern* (Mainz).

Hampe, R. & Winter, A., 1965: *Bei Töpfern und Zieglern in Süditalien, Sizilien und Griechenland* (Bonn).

Handberg, S. & Hjarl Petersen, J., with contributions by Guldager Bilde, P., Højberg Bjerg, L.M. & Samojlova, T.L., 2010: "Glossed Pottery", in *NGS 2010*: 185–260.

Harden, D.B., 1968: "The Canosa Group of Hellenistic Glasses in the British Museum", *JGS* 10: 21–47.

Hausmann, G., 1998: *Universität und städtische Gesellschaft in Odessa, 1865–1917. Soziale und nationale Selbstorganisation an der Peripherie des Zarenreiches*, Quellen und Studien zur Geschichte des östlichen Europa (Stuttgart).

Hausmann, U., 1959: *Hellenistische Reliefbecher aus attischen und böotischen Werkstätten. Untersuchungen zur Zeitstellung und Bildüberlieferung* (Stuttgart).

Hausmann, U., 1977–1978: "Eine pergamenische Werkstatt?", *IstMitt* 27–28: 213–226.

Hausmann, U., 1990: "Bemerkungen zu den mittelitalischen Reliefbechern", in *Akten des 13. Internationalen Kongresses für Klassische Archäologie, Berlin* (Mainz) 313–315.

Hausmann, U., 1996: *Hellenistische Keramik. Eine Brunnenfüllung nördlich von Bau C und Reliefkeramik verschiedener Fundplätze in Olympia*, OF 27 (Berlin and New York).

Hayes, J.W., 1972: *Late Roman Pottery* (London).

Hayes, J.W., 1985: "Sigillate Orientali", in *Atlante delle forme ceramiche II. Ceramica fine romana nel bacino mediterraneo (tardo ellenismo e primo impero)*, EAA Suppl. (Rome) 1–96.

Hayes, J.W., 1999: Review of Gassner 1997, in *JRA* 12: 715–717.

Heimberg, U., 1982: *Die Keramik des Kabirions*, Das Kabirenheiligtum bei Theben 3 (Berlin).

Heinen, H., 1972: "Die politischen Beziehungen zwischen Rom und dem Ptolemäerreich von den Anfängen bis zum Tag von Eleusis (273–168 v. Chr.)", *ANRW* I.1 (Berlin) 633–659.

Heinen, H., 1983: "Die Tryphè des Ptolemaios VIII. Euergetes II. Beobachtungen zum Ptolemäischen Herrscherideal und zu einer Römischen Gesandtschaft in Ägypten (140/39 v. Chr.)", in H. Heinen (ed.), *Althistorische Studien. Hermann Bengtson zum 70 Geburtstag dargebracht von Kollegen und Schülern*, Historia Einzelschriften 40 (Wiesbaden) 116–130 (repr. in H. Heinen, A. Binsfeld & S. Pfeiffer, *Vom hellenistischen Osten zum römischen Westen* [Stuttgart] 2006).

Hellström, P., 1965: *Pottery of Classical and Later Date, Terracotta Lamps and Glass*, Labraunda 2.1 (Lund).

Hepding, H., 1952: "Eine hellenistische Töpferwerkstatt in Pergamon", *NachrGiessen* 21: 49–60.

Herlihy, P., 1989: "The Greek Community in Odessa, 1861–1914", *Journal of Modern Greek Studies* 7: 235–252.

Hidri, H., 1976: "Gjurmë të punishteje qeramike në Dyrrah", *Iliria* 6: 245–258.

Hidri, H., 1988: "Kupa me dekor na reliev ta Dyrrahut", *Iliria* 18: 75–81.

Hobling, M.B., 1923–1925: "Excavations at Sparta, 1924–25. Greek Relief Ware from Sparta. Moulded Wares: Megarian Bowls", *BSA* 26: 277–310.

Hochuli-Gysel, A., 1977: *Kleinasiatische glasierte Reliefkeramik (50 v. Chr. bis 50 n. Chr.) und ihre oberitalischen Nachahmungen*, Acta Bernensia 11 (Bern).

Højte, J.M., 2005: "The Archaeological Evidence for Fish Processing in the Black Sea Region", in T. Bekker-Nielsen (ed.), *Ancient Fishing and Fish Processing in the Black Sea Region*, BSS 2 (Aarhus) 133–160.

Hölbl, G., 1994: *Geschichte des Ptolemäerreiches* (Darmstadt).

Hölscher, T., 2000: "Bildwerke: Darstellungen, Funktionen, Botschaften", in A.H. Borbein, T. Hölscher & P. Zanker (eds.), *Klassische Archäologie. Eine Einführung* (Berlin) 147–165.

Hopkins, K., 1983: "Introduction", in Garnsey, Hopkins & Whittaker (eds.) 1983: ix–xxv.

Horáková-Jansová, L., 1931: "Kadlup na vyrobu reliefní hellenistické keramiky", *LF* 58: 233–237.

Horden, P. & Purcell, N., 2004: *The Corrupting Sea. A Study of Mediterranean History* (Oxford).

Hübner, G., 1993a: *Die Applikenkeramik von Pergamon. Eine Bildersprache im Dienst des Herrscherkultes*, PF 7 (Berlin and New York).

Hübner, G., 1993b: "Plastischer Dekor an griechischer Keramik", *JdI* 108: 321–351.

Hübner, G., 1994: "Calices Pergami und die Scherbenfunde aus dem Grossen Altar", in *Γ' Συνάντηση*: 282–293.

Huskinson, J., 1996: *Roman Children's Sarcophagi. Their Decoration and Its Social Significance* (Oxford).

İdil, V., 1939: "Neue Ausgrabungen im Aeolischen Kyme", *Belleten (Türk Tarih Kurumu basımevi)* 3: 525–543.

Irimia, M., 2006: "Bols à decor en relief du Sud-Ouest de la Dobroudja", in S. Conrad, R. Einicke, A. Furtwängler, H. Löhr & A. Slawisch (eds.), *Pontos Euxeinos. Beiträge zur Archäologie und Geschichte des antiken Schwarzmeer- und Balkanraumes*, ZAKSSchriften 10 (Langenweißbach) 69–79.

Isler, H.P., 1978: *Das archaische Nordtor und seine Umgebung im Heraion von Samos*, Samos 4 (Bonn).

Janssen, A.J., 1957: *Het antieke tropaion* (Ledeberg-Gent).

Jentel, M.-O., 1964: "Bols à relief du Pont Euxin septentrional au Musée du Louvre", *Eirene* 3: 115–118.

Jentel, M.-O., 1968: *Bols et vases à reliefs*, CVA Louvre 15 [France 23] (Paris).

Jones, F.F., 1950: "The Pottery", in H. Goldman (ed.), *The Hellenistic and Roman Periods*, Excavations at Gözlü Kule, Tarsus 1 (Princeton) 149–296.

Jones, F.F., 1958: "Bowls by Popilius and Lapius", *Record of the Art Museum, Princeton University* 17.1: 21–40.

Kähler, H., 1965: *Der Fries vom Reiterdenkmal des Aemilius Paullus in Delphi*, Monumenta artis Romanae 5 (Berlin).

Kakavogiannis, E., 1980: "'Ομηρικοί σκύφοι' Φερών Θεσσαλίας", *AAA* 13.2: 262–284.

Kastanajan, E.G., 1958: "Raskopki Porfmija v 1953 g.", *SA* 3: 203–207.

Kastanajan, E.G., 1972: "Raskopki Porfmija v 1968 g.", *KSIA* 130: 77–82.

Kastanajan, E.G., 1983: "Porfmij", *EtTrav* 13: 162–181.

Kästner, U., Langner, M. & Rabe, B., 2007: *Griechen, Skythen, Amazonen* (Berlin).

Katsarou, C. & Mourtzini, T., 2011: "Κεραμική με ανάγλυφη διακόσμηση από την Ήλιδα", in *Z' Συνάντηση*: 747–760.

Kavvadias, G., 2012: "Other Table Ware", in N. Kaltsas, E. Vlachogianni & P. Vouyia (eds.), *The Antikythera Shipwreck. The Ship, the Treasures, the Mechanism. National Archaeological Museum, April 2012–April 2013* (Athens) 186–195.

Kawerau, G. & Wiegand, Th., 1930: *Die Paläste der Hochburg*, AvP 5.1 (Berlin and Leipzig).

Kazarow, G., 1918: "Zur Archäologie Thrakiens", *AA* 1918: 3–63.

Kenrick, Ph.M., 1985: *The Fine Pottery*. Excavations at Sidi Krebish, Benghazi (Berenice) 3.1, LibyaAnt 5 Suppl. (Tripoli).

Kenyon, K.M., 1957: "Roman and Later Wares. I. Terra Sigillata", in J.W. Crowfoot, G.M. Crowfoot & K.M. Kenyon with contributions by S.A. Birnbaum, J.H. Iliffe, J.S. Kirkman, S. Lake

& E.L. Sukenik, *The Objects from Samaria*, Samaria-Sebaste 3 (London) 281–288.

Keramopoullos, A.D., 1932: "Ἀνασκαφαὶ καὶ ἔρευναι ἐν τῇ Ἄνω Μακεδονίᾳ", *ArchEph* 1932: 48–133.

Kerschner, M., 2006: "On the Provenance of Aiolian Pottery", in A. Villing & U. Schlotzhauer (eds.), *Naukratis: Greek Diversity in Egypt. Studies on East Greek Pottery and Exchange in the Eastern Mediterranean* (London) 53–68.

Kerschner, M., Rogl, C. & Mommsen, H., 2002: "Die Keramikproduktion von Ephesos in griechischer Zeit. Zum Stand der archäometrischen Forschungen", *ÖJH* 71: 189–206.

Kleiner, G., 1975: "Zwei Formschüssel für megarische Becher", in *Wandlungen. Studien zur antiken und neueren Kunst Ernst Homann-Wedeking gewidmet* (Waldsassen) 217–219.

Klejman, I.B., 2001–2002: "Iz istorii Tiry vtoroj poloviny III – pervoj poloviny II vv. do n.è. (stroitel'nyj i veščestvennyj kompleks)", *Stratum plus* 2001–2002.3: 404–417.

Knappett, C., 2011: *An Archaeology of Interaction. Network Perspectives on Material Culture and Society* (Oxford).

Kobylina, M.M., 1956: "Fanagorija", *MatIssIA* 57: 5–101.

Kögler, P., 2000a: "Hellenistische Reliefkeramik aus Knidos", in *E' Συνάντηση*: 189–194.

Kögler, P., 2000b: "Frühkaiserzeitliche Feinkeramik aus Knidos. Die Füllung einer Zisterne in der sogenannten Blocked Stoa", *ReiCretActa* 36: 69–74.

Kögler, P., 2010: *Feinkeramik aus Knidos vom mittleren Hellenismus bis in die mittlere Kaiserzeit* (Wiesbaden).

Kolia, E., 2000: "Κλειστό σύνολο ελληνιστικής κεραμικής από το οικόπεδο Ι. Κολιγλιάτη στο Άργος", in *E' Συνάντηση*: 387–392.

Kolia, E., 2011: "Κεραμική με ανάγλυφη διακόσμηση από αποθέτη στο Αίγιο", in *Z' Συνάντηση*: 47–56.

Körpe, R., 2006: "Megarische Becher aus Assos", in R. Stupperich (ed.), *Ausgrabungen in Assos 1993*, AMS 57 (Bonn) 103–111.

Koscjuško-Valjužinič, K.K., 1901: "Izvlečenie iz otčota o raskopkach v Hersonese Tavričeskom", *IAK* 12: 1–55.

Koscjuško-Valjužinič, K.K., 1902: "Otčot o raskopkach v Chersonese v 1901 godu", *IAK* 4: 51–119.

Košelenko, G.A., 1992: *Očerki archeologii i istorii Bospora* (Moscow).

Kossatz, A.-U., 1990: *Die megarischen Becher*, Milet 5. Funde aus Milet 1 (Berlin).

Kotitsa, Z., 1998: *Hellenistische Keramik im Martin von Wagner Museum der Universität Würzburg*, Nachrichten aus dem Martin von Wagner Museum der Universität Würzburg, Antikensammlung 2 (Würzburg).

Kovalenko, S.A., 1987a: "Megarskie čaši Čaikinskogo gorodišča", in S.S. Dmitriev (ed.), *Iz istorii kul'tury i obščestvennoj mysli narodov SSSR* (Moscow) 3–13.

Kovalenko, S.A., 1987b: "K voprosu o proischoždenii rel'efnych čaš s nadpis'ju 'KIRBEI'", *Vestnik MGU* Ser. 8, *Istorija* 6: 70–80.

Kovalenko, S.A., 1989: *Antičnaja rel'efnaja keramika III–I vv. do n.e. v Severnom Pričernomor'e* (unpublished Habilitation, Moscow).

Kovalenko, S.A., 1996: "Some Notes on the Production of Hellenistic Mould-Made Relief Ware in the Bosporan Kingdom", in G.R. Tsetskhladze (ed.), *New Studies on the Black Sea Littoral*, Colloquia Pontica 1 (Oxford) 51–57.

Kovalenko, S.A., 1998: "K istorii izučenija pozdneellinictičeskoj štampovannoj rel'efnoj keramiki v Rosii", in D.V. Žuravlev, *Ellinističeskaja i rimskaja keramika v Severnom Pričernomor'je* (Moscow) 9–16.

Kovalenko, S.A., 2007: "Svalka II v. do n.e. v južnoj časti čaikinskogo gorodišča", in V.L. Janin & J.L. Sčapova (eds.), *Materialy issledovanij gorodišča "Čajka" v Severo-Zapadnom Krymu. Sbornik naučnych trudov* (Moscow) 195–251.

Kraft, J.C., Brückner, H., Kayan, İ. & Engelmann, H., 2007: "The Geographies of Ancient Ephesus and the Artemision in Anatolia", *Geoarchaeology* 22: 121–149.

Kranioti, L., 1997: "Άβδηρα. Τόπος παραγωγής ελληνιστικής ανάγλυφης κεραμεικής", in *Thrace ancienne. Époque archaïque, classique, hellénistique, romaine, Actes 2e Symposium International des Études Thraciennes, Komotini, 20–27 Septembre* (Komotini) 789–806.

Kranz, P., 1999: *Die stadtrömische Eroten-Sarkophage. Dionysische Themen mit Ausnahme der Weinlese- and Ernteszenen*, Die antiken Sarkophagreliefs 5.2.1 (Berlin).

Kraus, Th., 1951: *Megarische Becher im Römisch-Germanischen Zentralmuseum zu Mainz*, RGZM Katalog 14 (Mainz).

Krinzinger, F. (ed.), 2001: *Studien zur hellenistischen Keramik in Ephesos*, ÖJh Erg. 2 (Vienna).

Kriseleit, I. 1985: *Antike Mosaiken* (Berlin).

Kriseleit, I. 1990: "Fragmente von Ptolemäerkannen in der Antikensammlung", *FuB* 28, 61–64.

Kropotov, V.V. & Leskov, A.M., 2006: "Kurgan s 'kollektivnym pogrebeniem' u s. Krinički (po materialam rabot 1957 g.)", *Voprosy duchovnoj kultury* 84: 25–39.

Kryžickij, S.D., 1985: *Ol'vija. Istoriografičeskoe issledovanie architekturno-stroitel'nych kompleksov* (Kiev).

Kryžickij, S.D. & Lejpunskaja, N.A., 2010: "Building Remains and Accompanying Finds, 6th–1st century BC", in *NGS 2010*: 27–102.

Kunze-Götte, E. 2006. *Myrte als Attribut und Ornament auf attischen Vasen* (Kilchberg).

Künzl, S., 2002: *Ein Komplex von Formschüsseln für megarische Becher. Die "Mainzer Werkstatt"*, Kataloge vor- und frühgeschichtlicher Altertümer 32 (Mainz).

Kutajsov, V.A., 2004: *Kerkinitida v antičnuju epochu*, Kiev.

Kuznetsov, V.D., 2003: "Kepoi – Phanagoria – Taganrog", in Grammenos & Petropoulos (eds.) 2003: 895–955.

Ladstätter, S., Rogl, C., Giuliani, A., Bezeczky, T., Czurdaruth, B. & Lang-Auinger, C., 2003: "Ein hellenistischer Brunnen in

SR 9C", in B. Asamer & C. Lang-Auinger (eds.), *Hanghaus 1 in Ephesos. Funde und Ausstattung*, FiE 8/4 (Vienna) 22–80.

Lagona, S., 1993: "Kyme eolica", in F. Berti & G. Pugliese Carratelli (eds.), *Arslantepe, Hierapolis, Iasos, Kyme. Scavi archeologici italiani in Turchia*, (Venice) 248–301.

Lagona, S., 1994: "1993 yılı arkeolojik kazıları", *KST* 16, 2: 27–37.

Lagona, S., 2007: "Le terrecotte di Kyme eolica", abstract, International conference, Terracotta figurines in the Greek and Roman eastern Mediterranean (June 2–6 2007, Izmir), http://web.deu.edu.tr/terracottas/abstracts.html.

Lamboglia, N., 1959: "Una fabbricazione di ceramica megarica a Tindari e una terra sigillata siciliana?", *ArchCl* 11: 87–91.

Lambrino, M.F., 1938: *Les Vases archaïques d'Histria* (Bucharest).

Landi, M.E., 2007: "Ceramica di età ellenistica dagli scavi di Kyme eolica", in *Kyme e l'Eolide da Augusto a Costantino. Atti dell'Incontro internazionale di studio Missione archeologica italiana. Napoli, 12–13 dicembre 2005* (Napoli) 175–190.

Lang, G., 2003: *Klassische antike Stätten Anatoliens 2* (Norderstedt).

Langlotz, E., 1932: *Griechische Vasen, Martin von Wagner-Museum der Universität Würzburg* (Munich).

Laronde, A., 1987: "Recherches sous-marines dans le port d'Apollonia de Cyrénaïque", *BAntFr*: 322–332.

Latyšev, V.V., 1890: "Dopolneniya i popravki k sobraniyu drevnich nadpisey severnogo poberez'ya Chornogo morya I", *Zapiski Imperatorskogo Russkogo arheologičeskogo obščestva* 4: 120–153.

Latyšev, V.V., 1892: "Dopolneniya i popravki k sobraniyu drevnich grecheskich i latinskich nadpisey severnogo poberez'ya Chornogo morya II", *Zapiski Imperatorskogo Russkogo arheologičeskogo obščestva* 5: 361–384.

Latyšev, V.V., 1902: "K voprosu ob antičnoj posude so štempelem KIRBEI", *IAK* 4: 141.

Laumonier, A., 1962: "Bols hellénistiques à reliefs en Espagne", *REA* 64: 43–47.

Laumonier, A., 1967: "Bols grecs à reliefs à Toulouse", *Pallas* 14: 23–38.

Laumonier, A., 1973: "Bols hellénistiques à reliefs: Un bâtard gréco-italien", in *Études Déliennes*, BCH Suppl. 1 (Athens) 253–262.

Laumonier, A., 1977: *La céramique hellénistique à reliefs. Ateliers "Ioniens"*, Délos 31 (Paris).

Laumonier, A., vol. 2: "La céramique hellénistique à reliefs vol. 2", unpublished manuscript in École Française d'Athènes. Archival reference Delos 3–H (5).

Lawall, M.L., 2005: "Negotiating Chronologies. Aegean Amphora Research, Thasian Chronology, and Pnyx III", in Stolba & Hannestad (eds.) 2005: 31–67.

Lawall, M.L., 2011: "Greek Amphorae in the Archaeological Record", in Lawall & Lund (eds.) 2011: 38–50.

Lawall, M.L., Guldager Bilde, P., Bjerg, L., Handberg, S. & Højte, J.M., 2014: "The Lower City of Olbia Pontike. Occupation and Abandonment in the 2nd Century BC", in Guldager Bilde & Lawall (eds.) 2014: 29–45.

Lawall, M.L., Lejpunskaja, N.A., Diatroptov, P. & Samojlova, T.L., 2010: "Transport Amphoras", in *NGS 2010*: 355–405.

Lawall, M.L. & Lund, J. (eds.), 2011: *Pottery in the Archaeological Record. Greece and Beyond, Acts of the International Colloquium Held at the Danish and Canadian Institutes in Athens, June 20–22, 2008*, Gösta Enbom Monographs 1 (Aarhus).

Leotta, M.C., 1993: "Alcuni classi ceramiche dall'anfiteatro romano di Tivoli", *AttiSocTiburtina* 66: 13–48.

Leotta, M.C., 1995: "Ceramica ellenistica a rilievo dall'anfiteatro romano di Tivoli", *QuadAEI* 24: 453–458.

Leotta, M.C., 1997: "Fornaci tiburtine della tarda repubblica. I. Le matrici di ceramica ellenistica a rilievo", *AttiMemTivoli* 70: 13–70.

Leroux, G., 1913: *Lagynos* (Paris).

Levi, E.I., 1940: "Privoznaja grečeskaja keramika iz raskopok Ol'vii v 1935 i 1936 gg.", in S.A. Žebelev (ed.), *Ol'vija* 1 (Kiev) 105–127.

Levi, E.I., 1956: "Ol'vijskaja agora", *MatIssIA* 50: 35–118.

Levi, E.I., 1959: "Terrakoty iz cisterny Ol'vijskoj agory", *KSIA* 74: 9–19.

Levi, E.I., 1964a: "Itogi raskopok Ol'vijskogo temenosa i agory (1951–1960 gg.)", in Gajdukevič (ed.) 1964: 5–26.

Levi, E.I., 1964b: "Keramičeskij kompleks III–II vv. do n.e. iz raskopok Ol'vijskoj agory", in Gajdukevič (ed.) 1964: 225–280.

Levi, E.I., 1970: "Terrakoty iz Ol'vii", in B.A. Rybakov (ed.), *Terrakoty Severnogo Pričernomor'ja* (Moscow): 33–49.

Limberis, N.Ju. & Marčenko, I.I., 2000: "'Megarskie' čaši iz meotskich pogrebenij Prikuban'ja", in V.B. Vinogradov (ed.), *Staryj Svet. Archeologija, Istorija, Etnografija*, Sbornik naučnych statej, posvjaščonnyj 60-letiju so dnja roždenija professora N.I. Kireja (Krasnodar) 4–18.

Loeschcke, S., 1912: "Sigillata-Töpfereien in Tschandarli", *AM* 37: 344–407.

Long, L., 1987: "Les épaves du Grand Congloué", *Archaeonautica* 7: 9–36.

Long, L., 1992: "L'épave antique d'Apollonia", *DossAParis* 167: 70–77.

Lopatin, A.P. & Malyšev, A.A., 2002: "K voprosu ob antičnom keramičeskom importe v Zakuban'e v VI–II vv.do n.e.", *Istoriko-arheologičeskij al'manah* 3: 33–40.

Loseva, N.M., 1962: "Ob importe i mestnom proizvodstve 'Megarskich' čaš na Bospore", *MIA* 103: 195–205.

Love, I.C., 1967: "Knidos – Excavations in 1967", *TürkAD* 16.2: 133–140.

Lund, J., 2007: "The Circulation of Ceramic Fine Wares and Transport Amphorae from the Black Sea Region in the

Mediterranean, c. 400 BC–AD 200", in V. Gabrielsen & J. Lund (eds.), *The Black Sea in Antiquity*, BSS 6 (Aarhus) 183–194.

Lund, J., 2009: "Methodological Constraints Affecting the Precise Dating of African Red Slip Ware", in J.H. Humphrey (ed.), *Studies on Roman Pottery of the Provinces of Africa Proconsularis and Byzacena (Tunisia). Hommage à Michel Bonifay*, JRA Suppl. 76 (Portsmouth, R.I.) 65–72.

Lund, J., 2011: "Rhodian Transport Amphorae as a Source for Economic (Ebbs and) Flows in the Eastern Mediterranean in the 2nd Century BC", in Z. Archibald, J.K. Davies & V. Gabrielsen, *The Economies of Hellenistic Societies. Third to First Centuries BC* (Oxford and New York) 280–295.

Mack, G.R. & Carter, J.C. (eds.), 2003: *Crimean Chersonesos. City, Chora, Museum, and Environs* (Austin).

Mahler, E., 1924: *Die Megarischen Becher* (unpublished Dissertation, Universität Basel).

Maioli, M.G., 1979: "Una matrice di coppa italo-megarese rinvenuta a Rimini", *RivStLig* 45: 141–146.

Maiuri, A., 1932: "Monumenti di scultura del Museo archeologico di Rodi 1", in *Clara Rhodos* 2.1 (Rhodes), 7–76.

Mal'mberg, V.K., 1892: "Opisanie klassičeskich drevnostej najdennyx v Chersonese v 1888 i 1889 godach", *Materialy po archeologii Rossii* 7: 3–31.

Marabini Moevs, M.T., 1980: "Italo-Megarian Ware at Cosa", *MemAmAc* 34: 163–227.

Marangou, L.I., 1981: "Ἀνασκαφή Μινώας Ἀμοργοῦ", *Prakt* 137: 303–323.

Marčenko, I.D., 1956: "Raskopki Vostočnogo nekropol'ja Phanagorii v 1950–1951 gg.", *MIA* 57, 102–127.

Markle, M.M., 1999: "A Shield Monument from Veria and the Chronology of Macedonian Shield Types", *Hesperia* 68: 219–254.

Maslennikov, A.A., 1997: "Sel'skij temenos(?) v Vosto nom Krymu (predvaritel'naja publikacija)", *VDI* 4: 150–172.

Maslennikov, A.A., 2007: *Sel'skie svjatilišča evropejskogo Bospora* (Moscow).

Massa, M., 1992: *La ceramica ellenistica con decorazione a rilievo della bottega di Efestia* (Rome).

Massa, M., 1997: "La ceramica ellenistica con decorazione a relievo della bottega di Efestia", in *Δ' Συνάντηση*: 345–351.

Mastrokostas, E., 1967: "Ἀρχαιότητες καὶ μνημεῖα Αἰτωλοακαρνανίας", *ADelt B* 22: 318–324.

Mathisen, R.W., 1981: "Antigonus Gonatas and the Silver Coinages of Macedonia circa 280–270 B.C.", *American Numismatic Society Museum Notes* 26: 79–124.

Mercando, L., 1976: "L'ellenismo nel Piceno", in P. Zanker (ed.), *Hellenismus in Mittelitalien, Kolloquium Göttingen 5.–9. Juni 1974* (Göttingen) 160–218.

Meriç, R., 2002: *Späthellenistisch-römische Keramik und Kleinfunde aus einem Schachtbrunnen am Staatsmarkt in Ephesos*, FiE 9/3 (Vienna).

Merten, J., 1999: "Aus dem Nachlass von Erich Gose. Ein unbekanntes Werk von Arnold Vogell über das antike Olbia", *TrZ* 61: 331–342.

Metzger, I.R. 1969. *Die hellenistische Keramik in Eretria*, Eretria 2 (Bern).

Meyboom, P.G.P., 1995: *The Nile Mosaic of Palestrina. Early Evidence of Egyptian Religion in Italy*, Religions in the Graeco-Roman World 121 (Leiden, New York and Köln).

Meyer-Schlichtmann, C., 1988: *Die pergamenische Sigillata aus der Stadtgrabung von Pergamon, Mitte 2. Jh. v.Chr.–Mitte 2. Jh. n.Chr.*, PF 6 (Berlin).

Meyza, H. & Młynarczyk, J., (eds.) 1995: *Hellenistic and Roman Pottery in the Eastern Mediterranean – Advances in Scientific Studies. Acts of the II Nieborów Pottery Workshop. Nieborów, 18–20 December 1993* (Warsaw).

Michałowski, K., 1958: *Mirmeki. Wykopaliska odcinka polkiego w r. 1956* (Warsaw).

Miller, M.C., 1993: *Adoption and Adaptation of Achaemenid Metalwork Forms in Attic Black Gloss Ware of the Fifth Century* (Berlin).

Miller, S.G., 1993: *The Tomb of Lyson and Kallikles: A Painted Macedonian Tomb* (Mainz).

Minns, E.H., 1945: "Thirty Years of Work at Olbia", *JHS* 65: 109–112.

Mitsopoulos-Leon, V., 1973: "Zur Keramik aus Aigeira, 1972–1975 Grabungen", *ÖJh* 50: 17–31.

Mitsopoulos-Leon, V., 1985: "Töpferateliers in Ephesos", in *Pro Arte Antiqua. Festschrift für Hedwig Kenner*, SoSchrÖAI 18 (Vienna) 247–251.

Mitsopoulos-Leon, V., 1991: *Die Basilika am Staatsmarkt in Ephesos. Kleinfunde 1. Keramik hellenistischer und römischer Zeit*, FiE 9/2/2 (Vienna).

Mitsopoulos-Leon, V., 1996: "Krateriskoi und ein Teller mit Reliefdekor. Eine Gefässgruppe aus Lousoi", *ÖJh* 65: 187–206.

Molev, E.A., 1985: "Arheologičeskie issledovanija Kiteja v 1970–1983 gg.", in E.V. Dvoretski (ed.), *Arheologičeskie pam'jatniki jugo-vostočnoj Evropy* (Kursk).

Molev, Y.A., 2003: "Kyta", in Grammenos & Petropoulos (eds.) 2003: 841–893.

Monaco, M.C., 2000: *'Ergasteria'. Impianti artigianali ceramici ad Athene ed in Attica* (Rome).

Mordvintseva, V.I., 1999: "Starobel'skij klad", *Archeologičeskie Vesti* 6: 168–178.

Morel, J-P., 1976: "Aspects de l'artisanat dans la Grande Grèce romaine" in *La Magna Grecia nell'età romana. Atti del 15. Convegno di studi sulla Magna Grecia, Taranto 5–10 ottobre 1975* (Napoli): 263–324.

Morel, J-P., 1990: "L'apport des fouilles de Carthage à la chronologie des céramiques hellénistiques", in *Β' Συνάντηση*: 17–30.

Morintz, S. & Șerbănescu, D., 1985: "Rezultatele cercertării de la Radovanu, punctul 'Gorgana a doua' (jud. Călărași). Așezarea din epoca bronzului. Așezarea geto-dacică. Studii preliminare", *Thraco-Dacica* 6: 21–30.

Morris, I., Saller, R.P. & Scheidel, W., 2007: "Introduction", in I. Morris, R.P. Saller & W. Scheidel (eds.), *The Cambridge Economic History of the Greco-Roman World* (Cambridge) 1–12.

Myśliwiec, K., 2000a: "Researches on Hellenistic Pottery from Athribis (Lower Egypt)", in *E' Συνάντηση*: 253–258.

Myśliwiec, K., 2000b: *The Twilight of Ancient Egypt. First Millennium B.C.E.* (Ithaca, NY).

Nadalini, G., 2003: "Considerazioni e confronti sui restauri antichi presenti sulle ceramiche scoperte a Gela", in R. Panvini & F. Giudice (eds.), *Ta Attika. Veder greco a Gela. Ceramiche attiche figurate dall'antica colonia. Gela, Siracusa, Rodi 2004* (Rome) 197–205.

Nedev, D. & Draževa, C., 2007: "Spasitelni arheologičeski proučvanija v starata čast na gr. Sozopol-UPI 226, kv. 18", *Arheologičeski otkritija I razkopki prez 2006*: 356–358.

Nedev, D. & Gospodinov, K., 2007: "Spasitelni arheologičeski proučvanija na teritorijata na starata čast na gr. Sozopol (UPI XI-XII-515, kv.27; UPI XIX-525, kv. 27; UPI X-393, kv. 36)", *Arheologičeski otkritija i razkopki prez 2006*: 353–356.

Negev, A., 1986: *The Late Hellenistic and Early Roman Pottery of Nabataean Oboda*, Qedem 22 (Jerusalem).

Neugebauer, K.A., 1932: *Führer durch das Antiquarium 2. Vasen* (Berlin).

Neuru, L.L., 1991: "Megarian Relief Ware", in J.W. Hayes, *Paphos 3. The Hellenistic and Roman Pottery* (Nicosia) 13–17.

Nicorescu, P., 1924: "Scavi e scoperte a Tyras", *Ephemeris Dacoromana* 2: 378–415.

Ocheșeanu, R., 1969: "Bolurile 'megariene' din colectiile Muzeului de Archeologie Constanța", *Pontica* 2: 209–244.

Ognenova, L., 1960: "Les fouilles de Mesembria", *BCH* 84: 221–232.

Ohlenroth, L., 1955: "Zu den mittelitalischen Reliefbechern (Popilius-Ware)", *Germania* 33: 43–45.

Ohlenroth, L., 1959: "Fälschungen von Popilius-Lappius Bechern aus Originalmodeln", *RFCRActa* 11: 29–35.

Oliver, A., 1977: *Silver for the Gods. 800 Years of Greek and Roman Silver* (Toledo, Ohio).

Oppermann, M., 2004: *Die westpontischen Poleis und Ihr indigenes Umfeld in vorrömischer Zeit* (Langenweißbach).

Orton, C. & Hughes, M., 2013: *Pottery in Archaeology. Second Edition*, Cambridge Manuals in Archaeology (Cambridge and New York).

Orton, C. & Tyers, P., 1992: "Counting Broken Objects: The Statistics of Ceramic Assemblages", in A.M. Pollard (ed.), *New Developments in Archaeological Science. A Joint Symposium of the Royal Society and the British Academy, London, February 1991*, Proceedings of the British Academy 77 (Oxford) 163–184.

Orton, C., Tyers, P. & Vince, A., 1993: *Pottery in Archaeology*, Cambridge Manuals in Archaeology (Cambridge and New York).

Oxé, A., 1933: *Arretinische Reliefgefässe vom Rhein*, Materialen zur Römisch-Germanischen Keramik 5 (Frankfurt am Main).

Özyiğit, Ö., 1990: "Céramiques hellénistiques d'après les fouilles de Pergame/Kestel", in *B' Συνάντηση*: 94–97.

Özyiğit, Ö., 2000: "The Chronology of Pergamene Appliqué Ware", in *E' Συνάντηση*: 195–198.

Pagenstecher, R., 1913: *Die griechisch-ägyptische Sammlung Ernst von Sieglin*, Expedition Ernst von Sieglin 2.3 (Leipzig).

Palinkas, J.L., 2008: *Eleusinian Gateways. Entrances to the Sanctuary of Demeter and Kore at Eleusis and the City Eleusinion in Athens* (Dissertation, Emory University).

Panagopoulou, K., 2007: "Between Necessity and Extravagance. Silver as a Commodity in the Hellenistic Period", *BSA* 102: 315–343.

Pappa, V., 1997: "Εργαστήρια παραγωγής 'μεγαρικών' σκύφων στην Αμοργό", in *Δ' Συνάντηση*: 352–358.

Pappa, V., 2000: "Μινώα Αμοργού. Ελληνιστική κεραμική από την τομή στο βόρειο τοίχο του Γυμνασίου", in *E' Συνάντηση*: 105–114.

Paribeni, R., 1927: "Scarichi di una fabbrica di vasi fittili in località S. Anna (Tivoli)", *NSc* 6. ser. 5: 374–378.

Parker, A.J., 1992: *Ancient Shipwrecks of the Mediterranean and the Roman Provinces*, BARIntSer 580 (Oxford).

Parlasca, K., 1955: "Das Verhältnis der megarischen Becher zum alexandrinischen Kunsthandwerk", *JdI* 70: 122–154.

Parlasca, K., 1982: "Zur hellenistischen Reliefkeramik Kleinasiens", *BABesch* 57: 176–178.

Parlasca, K. & Boss, M., 2000: *Wechselwirkungen. Aus der Sammlung Klaus Parlasca* (Erlangen).

Parovič-Pešikan, M., 1974: *Nekropol' Ol'vii ellinističeskogo vremeni* (Kiev).

Patroni, G., 1897–1898: *Catalogo dei vasi e delle terrecotte del Museo Campano a Capua* (Caserta).

Peacock, D.P.S., 1982: *Pottery in the Roman World. An Ethnoarchaeological Approach* (London and New York).

Peña, J.T., 2007: *Roman Pottery in the Archaeological Record* (Cambridge).

Peña, J.T. & Mccallum, M., 2009: "The Production and Distribution of Pottery at Pompeii. A Review of the Evidence, Part 1. Production", *AJA* 113: 57–79.

Perdrizet, P., 1908: *Monuments figurés: petits bronzes, terrescuites, antiquités diverses*, FdD 5 (Paris).

Petrova, A., 2014: "A Pontic Group of Hellenistic Mouldmade Bowls", in Guldager Bilde & Lawall (eds.) 2014: 215–231.

Petsas, P.M., 1963: "Ανασκαφαί Κοζάνης", *Prakt* 119: 55–58.

Pfrommer, M., 1987: *Studien zu alexandrinischer und großgriechischer Toreutik frühhellenistischer Zeit* (Berlin).

Pfrommer, M., 1993: *Metalwork from the Hellenized East* (Malibu).

Pfrommer, M., 1996: "Roots and Contacts. Aspects of Alexandrian Craftmanship", in M. Greenberg (ed.), *Alexandria and Alexandrianism. Papers Delivered at a Symposium Organized by The J. Paul Getty Museum and The Getty Center for the History of Art and the Humanities and Held at the Museum, April 22–25, 1993* (Malibu, CA) 171–190.

Phaklares, P., 1983: "Πήλινες μήτρες, σφραγίδες και ανάγλυφα αγγεία από τη Βεργίνα", *ADelt A* 38: 211–239.

Pharmakowsky, B.V., 1910: "Archäologische Funde im Jahre 1909. Russland", *AA* 1910: 195–244.

Pharmakowskyi, B.V., 1929: *Rozkopuvannja Ol'bii r. 1926* (Odessa).

Pierobon, R., 1987: "La ceramica e la vita della città. Le coppe a rilievo ellenistiche", in *Studi su Iasos di Caria. Venticinque anni di scavi della missione archeologica italiana*, BdA Suppl. 31–32 (Rome) 83–92.

Pierobon-Benoit, R., 1997: "Coppe ellenistiche a rilievo da Iasos. Un bilancio", in *Δ' Συνάντηση*: 371–380.

Pinkwart, D., 1984: "Die Einzelfunde. Keramik", in D. Pinkwart & W. Stamnitz, *Peristylhäuser westlich der unteren Agora*, AvP 14 (Berlin) 123–142.

Platek, S., 1974: "Bols mégariens des fouilles polonaises de Mirmeki au Musée national de Varsovie (production locale)", *BMusVars* 45: 41–50.

Pochmarski, E., 1990: *Dionysische Gruppen. Eine typologische Untersuchung zur Geschichte des Stützmotivs*, Sonderschriften (Österreichisches Archäologisches Institut) 19 (Vienna).

Popova, E.A., 2007: "Grečeskoe poselenie na gorodišče 'Čaika' vo vtoroj polovine III-II v. do n.e.", in *Materialy issledovanij gorodišča 'Čaika' v Severo-Zapadnom Krymu* (Moscow) 4–38.

Pottier, E. & Reinach, S., 1885: "Fouilles dans la nécropole de Myrina (1)", *BCH* 9: 165–207.

Proskynetopoulou, R., 1992–1993: "Σκύφοι με ανάγλυφη διακόσμηση από την Ήλιδα, νεότερες ανασκαφές 1960–1983", *ADelt A* 47–48: 83–164.

Pucci, G., 1983: "Pottery and Trade in the Roman Period", in Garnsey, Hopkins & Whittaker (eds.), 1983: 105–117.

Puglia 1979: *La Puglia dal paleolitico al tardoromano* (Milano).

Puppo, P., 1995: *Le coppe megaresi in Italia*, Studia archaeologica 78 (Rome).

Radt, W., 1999: *Pergamon. Geschichte und Bauten einer antiken Metropole* (Darmstadt).

Rădulescu, A, Buzoianu, L., Bărbulescu, M. & Cheluţă-Georgescu, N., 1995–1996: "Reprezentări figurate in aşezarea de epocă elenistică de la Albeşti", *Pontica* 28–29: 23–71.

Raeder, J., 1986: "Hellenistische Reliefamphoren", in E. Böhr & W. Martini (eds.), *Studien zur Mythologie und Vasenmalerei. Konrad Schauenburg zum 65. Geburtstag am 16. April 1986* (Mainz) 203–208.

Reeder, E.D., 1988: *Hellenistic Art in the Walters Art Gallery* (Baltimore, MD).

Reinach, S.S., 1889: "Statues archaïques de Cybèle découvertes à Cymè (Éolide)", *BCH* 13: 543–562.

Reinach, S., 1892: *Antiquités du Bosphore Cimmérien (1854). Rééditées avec un commentaire nouveau et un index général des comptes rendus*, Bibliothèque des monuments figurés grecs et romains 3 (Paris).

Renfrew, C., 1975: "Trade as Action in Distance. Questions of Integration and Communication", in J.A. Sabloff & C.C. Lamberg-Karlovsky (eds.), *Ancient Civilization and Trade* (Albuquerque) 3–59.

Rice, P.M., 2015: *Pottery Analysis. A Source Book. Second Edition* (Chicago and London).

Ridgway, B.S., 1970: "Dolphins and Dolphin-Riders", *Archaeology* 23: 86–95.

Robert, C., 1890: *Homerische Becher*, BWPr 50 (Berlin).

Robertson, D.S., 1969: *Greek and Roman Architecture*, 2nd ed. (Cambridge).

Rogers, E.M., 2003: *Diffusion of Innovations* (New York).

Rogl, C., 1996: "Hellenistische Reliefbecher aus der Stadt Elis", *ÖJh* 65: 113–158.

Rogl, C., 1999: "Werkstätten hellenistischer Reliefbecher der Peloponnes: Bisher bekannte 'Töpfersignaturen' und ihre Bedeutung", *Forum Archaeologiae – Zeitschrift für klassische Archäologie* 11.VI (http://farch.net).

Rogl, C., 2001a: "Töpfersignaturen auf hellenistischen Reliefbechern. Eine Liste", *ÖJh* 70: 135–155.

Rogl, C., 2001b: "Eine Vorschau zu den reliefverzierten Trinkbechern der ephesischen Monogramm-Werkstätte", in Krinzinger (ed.) 2001: 99–111.

Rogl, C., 2001c: "Werkstätten hellenistischer Reliefbecher der Peloponnes", in F. Blakolmer & H.D. Szemethy (eds.), *Akten des 8. Österreichischen Archäologentages am Institut für Klassische Archäologie der Universität Wien vom 23. bis 25. April 1999*, Wiener Forschungen zur Archäologie 4 (Vienna) 59–79.

Rogl, C., 2008a: *Die hellenistischen Reliefbecher aus Lousoi. Material aus den Grabungen im Bereich Phournoi 1983–1994*, ÖJh Ergh. 10 (Vienna).

Rogl, C., 2008b: "'Drinking and Dying'. Hellenistische Reliefbecher als kulturelle und ethnische Indikatoren?", *ReiCretActa* 40: 523–530.

Rogl, C., 2011a: "Ephesische Reliefbecher-Werkstätten und ihre zeitliche Stellung", in *Z' Συνάντηση*: 541–548.

Rogl, C., 2014a: "Mouldmade Relief Bowls from Ephesos – The State of Research", in Guldager Bilde & Lawall (eds.) 2014: 113–139.

Rosenthal-Heginbottom, R., 1995: "Moldmade Relief Bowls from Tel Dor, Israel – A Preliminary Report", in Meyza & Młynarczyk (eds.) 1995: 365–396.

Rostovcev, M., 1967: *The Social and Economic History of the Hellenistic World* (Oxford).

Rotroff, S.I., 1982a: *Hellenistic Pottery. Athenian and Imported Moldmade Bowls*, Agora 22 (Princeton).

Rotroff, S.I., 1982b: "Silver, Glass, and Clay. Evidence for the Dating of Hellenistic Luxury Tableware", *Hesperia* 51: 329–337.

Rotroff, S.I., 1988: "The Long-petal Bowl from the Pithos Settling Basin", *Hesperia* 57: 87–93.

Rotroff, S.I., 1994a: "The Pottery", in G. Hellenkemper Salies, H.-H. von Prittwitz und Gaffron & G. Bauchhenß (eds.), *Das Wrack. Der antike Schiffsfund von Mahdia* (Bonn) 133–152.

Rotroff, S.I., 1994b: "The Satyr Cistern in the Athenian Agora", in *Γ' Συνάντηση*: 17–22.

Rotroff, S.I. 1996: review of Hübner 1993a, in *Gnomon* 68: 356–361.

Rotroff, S.I., 1997a: *Hellenistic Pottery. Athenian and Imported Wheelmade Table Ware and Related Material*, Agora 29 (Princeton).

Rotroff, S.I., 1997b: "Moldmade Relief Bowls from Sardis", in *Δ' Συνάντηση*: 359–366.

Rotroff, S.I. 1999: review of Gassner 1997, in *BonnJbb* 199: 613–615.

Rotroff, S.I., 2002: "A Moldmade Bowl of Argeios", *Hesperia* 71: 428–430.

Rotroff, S.I., 2003: "Relief Wares", in S.I. Rotroff & A. Oliver Jr. et al., *The Hellenistic Pottery from Sardis. The Finds through 1994*, Archaeological Exploration of Sardis Monographs 12 (Cambridge, MA) 91–178.

Rotroff, S.I., 2005: "Four Centuries of Athenian Pottery", in Stolba & Hannestad (eds.) 2005: 11–30.

Rotroff, S.I., 2006a: *Hellenistic Pottery. The Plain Wares*, Agora 33 (Princeton).

Rotroff, S.I., 2006b: "The Introduction of the Moldmade Bowl Revisited: Tracking a Hellenistic Innovation", *Hesperia* 75: 357–378.

Rotroff, S.I., 2010: "Moldmade Bowls at Samothrace", in O. Palagia & B.D. Wescoat (eds.), *Samothracian Connections. Essays in Honor of James R. McCredie* (Oxford and Oakville) 60–73.

Rotroff, S.I., 2011a: "Mended in Antiquity: Repairs to Ceramics at the Athenian Agora", in Lawall & Lund (eds.) 2011: 117–134.

Rotroff, S.I., 2011b: "The Date of the Long-Petal Bowl: A Review of the Contextual Evidence", in *Z' Συνάντηση*: 635–644.

Rubinstein, L., 2004: "Aiolis and South-Western Mysia", in M.H. Hansen & Th.H. Nielsen (eds.), *An Inventory of Archaic and Classical Poleis. An Investigation Conducted by The Copenhagen Polis Centre for the Danish National Research Foundation* (Oxford) 1033–1052.

Rumscheid, F., 1994: *Untersuchungen zur kleinasiatischen Bauornamentik des Hellenismus* I–II, Beiträge zur Erschliessung hellenistischer und kaiserzeitlicher Skulptur und Architektur 14 (Mainz).

Rumscheid, J. & Rumscheid, F., 2007: "Statt Nachkaufgarantie? Vier Formschüsseln aus dem späthellenistischen Zerstörungshorizont des Lampon-Hauses in Priene", in E. Öztepe & M. Kadıoğlu (eds.), *Patronus. Festschrift Ahmet Coşkun Özgünel* (Istanbul) 315–328.

Rusjaeva, A.S., 2003: "The Main Development of the Western Temenos of Olbia in the Pontos" in Guldager Bilde, Højte & Stolba (eds.) 2003: 93–116.

Rusjaeva, A.S. & Nazarčuk, B.I., 2006: "Rel'efnaja keramika", in A.I. Ajbabin et al. (eds.), *Drevnejšij temenos Ol'vii Pontijskoj*, Materialy po archeologii, istorii i ėtnografii Tavrii Suppl. 2 (Simferopol) 178–181.

Salles, J.-F., 1995 : "Céramiques hellénistiques de Kition-Bamboula", in Meyza & Młynarczyk (eds.) 1995: 397–414.

Salliora-Oikonomakou, M., 1979: "Αρχαία Αγορά στο Λιμάνι Πασά Λαυρίου", *ADelt A* 34: 161–173.

Samojlova, T.L, 1984: "Rel'efnaja keramika ellinističeskogo vremeni iz raskopok Tiry", in G.A. Dzis-Rajko et al. (ed.), *Severnoe Pričernomor'e (materialy po archeologii)* (Kiev) 119–129.

Samojlova, T.I., 1988: *Tira v VI-I vv. do n.e.* (Kiev).

Samojlova, T.L., 1994: "Dejaki formy ellenistyčnoj rel'efnoj keramiki z Ol'vii. Some Forms of the Hellenistic Relief Pottery from Olbia", *Archeologia Kiiv* 2: 88–93.

Samojlova, T.L., 1998: "Ellinističeskij rel'efnyj sosud iz Ol'vii", in V.N. Stanko et al. (eds.), *Drevnee Pričernomor'e. IV-e čtenija pamjati professora P.O. Karyškovskogo* (Odessa) 135–137.

Samojlova, T.L. & Batizat, G.V., 1994: "Rel'efnye sosudy iz Ol'vii s izobraženijami korablej", in *Drevnee Pričernomor'e*, Kratkie soobščenija Odesskogo Archeologičeskogo Obščestva (Odessa) 164–168.

Šapcev, M.S. 2008. "Megarskie čaši podzneskifskogo gorodišča Bulganak", *Problemy istorii, filologii i kul'tury* 21: 325–335.

Scarfi, B.M., 1962: "Gioia del Colle (Bari). L'abitato peucetico di Monte Sannace", *NSc* 16: 1–286.

Ščeglov, A.N., 1978: *Severo-Zapadnyj Krym v antičnuju ėpochu* (Leningrad).

Ščeglov, A.N., 2002: "Monumental Building U6", in L. Hannestad, V. Stolba & A.N. Ščeglov (eds.), *Panskoye* 1.1 (Aarhus) 29–98.

Schäfer, J., 1968: *Hellenistische Keramik aus Pergamon*, PF 2 (Berlin).

Schäfer, J., 1974: "Zur Topographie von Kyme", in Bouzek & Jansová 1974: 207–214.

Schauenburg, C., 1996: *Die stadtrömischen Eroten-Sarkophage. Zirkusrennen und verwandte Darstellungen*, ARS 5.2.3 (Berlin).

Schazmann, P., 1923: *Das Gymnasion. Der Tempelbezirk der Hera Basilea*, AvP 6 (Berlin).

Schiering, W., 1981: "Fragmente eines Kraters mit figürlichem Reliefdekor", in *OlBer* 10. *Frühjahr 1966 bis Dezember 1976* (Berlin) 171–191.

Schmid, S.G., 2004: "Some Reflections on Recently Found Mouldmade and Relief Decorated Pottery from Eretria", in *ΣΤ' Συνάντηση*: 495–504.

Schürmann, W., 1989: *Katalog der antiken Terrakotten im Badischen Landesmuseum Karlsruhe* (Göteborg).

Schwabacher, W., 1941: "Hellenistische Reliefkeramik im Kerameikos", *AJA* 45: 182–228.

Seiterle, G., 1981: "Die sog. ionische Gattung der 'delischen' Becher stammt aus Ephesos", *MDAVerb* 12.1: 27–28.

Seiterle, G., 1982: "Das Hauptstadttor von Ephesos", *AntK* 25: 145–149.

Šelov, D.B., 1966: "Rel'efnye ellinističeskie čaši iz Tanaisa", *Sbornik narodniho muzea v Praze* Ser. A 20.1–2: 159–162.

Šelov, D.B., 1969: "Nachodki v Tanaise 'Megarskich' čaš", *MIA* 154: 220–247.

Semenov-Zuser, S.A., 1931: "Otchot o raskopkach v Olvii v 1920–21 gg.", *Izvestiya Gosudarstvennoy akademii istorii materialnoj kultury* 10, 5: 21.

Ševčenko, A.V., 1995: "Terrakotovye altariki iz Chersonesa", *Char'kovskij istoriko-archeologičeskij ježegodnik drevnosti*: 156–166.

Sichtermann, H., 1969: "Ἔρως γλυκύπικρος", *RM* 76: 266–306.

Siebert, G., 1977: "Bols à reliefs d'ateliers grecs dans le dépot marin de Santa Sabina en Apulie", *RiStBrindisi* 10: 111–150.

Siebert, G., 1978: *Recherches sur les ateliers de bols à relief du Péloponnèse à l'époque hellénistique*, BEFAR 233 (Athens).

Siebourg, M., 1897: "Italische Fabriken 'Megarischer' Becher", *RM* 12: 40–55.

Simon, E. (ed.), 1975: *Führer durch die Antikenabteilung des Martin von Wagner Museums der Universität Würzburg* (Mainz).

Sinn, U., 1979: *Die homerischen Becher. Hellenistische Reliefkeramik aus Makedonien*, AM Beih. 7 (Berlin).

Škorpil', V.V., 1904: "Otčet' ob archeologičeskich raskopach v g. Kerči i ego okrestnostjach v 1902 godu", *IAK* 9: 73–177.

Slavin, L.M., 1938: *Ol'vija*, Kiev.

Slavin, L.M., 1947: "Rezultaty archeologicheskich issledovanij Ol'vijskoj ekspeditsii 1947–1948 gg.", *Naukovyi arkhiv instytutu arkheolohii Natsionalnoi akademii nauk Ukrainy*, 1947/9.

Slej, K. (ed.), 2004: *Guldskatter: Rumänien under 7000 år* (Stockholm).

Smirnova, T., 1967: "Poselenie rimskogo vremeni bliz Kerči", *KSIA* 109: 140–143.

Sokol'skij, N.I., 1959: "Raskopki v Kepach v 1957 g.", *KSIIMK* 78: 53–63.

Sokol'skij, N.I., 1961a: "Raboty v Kepach", *KSIA* 83: 66–72.

Sokol'skij, N.I., 1961b: "Raskopki v Kepach v 1959 g.", *KSIA* 86: 55–65.

Sokol'skij, N.I., 1962: "Raskopki v Kepach v 1960 g.", *KSIA* 91: 83–91.

Sokol'skij, N.I., 1963a: "Raskopki gorodišča Kepy v 1961 g.", *KSIA* 95: 52–59.

Sokol'skij, N.I., 1963b: "Kepy", in *Antičnyj gorod* (Moscow) 97–114.

Sokol'skij, N.I., 1976: *Tamanskij tolos i rezidencija Chrisaliska* (Moscow).

Sorokina, N.P., 1962: "Raskopki nekropolja v Kepach v 1959–1960 godach", *KSIA* 91: 98–106.

Sorokina, N.P., 1963: "Raskopki nekropolja Kep v 1961 g.", *KSIA* 95: 60–65.

Sorokina, N.P., 1967: "Raskopki nekropolja v Kepach", *KSIA* 109: 101–107.

Sorokina, N.P. & Sudarev, N.I., 2002: "Sposoby obraščenija s telami pogrebaemych v nekropole Kep", in *Bosporskij fenomen: pogrebal'nye pamjatniki i svjatilišča. Materialy meždunarodnoj naučnoj konferencii* (St Petersburg) 279–281.

Spratt, D.A., 1982: "The Analysis of Innovation Processes", *JAS* 9: 79–94.

Spratt, D.A., 1989: "Innovation Theory Made Plain", in S.E. van der Leeuw & R. Torrence (eds.), *What's New? A Closer Look at the Process of Innovation* (London) 245–257.

Stephani, L., 1879: "Erklärung einiger im Jahre 1875 im Südlichen Russland gefundener Kunstwerke", *Compte-rendu de la Commission Impériale Archéologique pour l'année 1876*: 3–228.

Stewart, A., 2000: "Pergamo ara marmorea magna: On the Date, Reconstruction, and Functions of the Great Altar of Pergamon", in de Grummond & Ridgway (eds.) 2000: 32–57.

Stolba, V.F. & Hannestad, L. (eds.), 2005: *Chronologies of the Black Sea Area in the Period c. 400–100 BC*, BSS 3 (Aarhus).

Stone, S.C., 1981: *Roman Pottery from Morgantina in Sicily* (Dissertation, Princeton University).

Strong, D.E., 1966: *Greek and Roman Gold and Silver Plate* (London).

Šurgaja, I.G., 1962: "O proizvodstve ellinističeskoj rel'efnoj keramiki na Bospore", *MASP* 4: 108–120.

Šurgaja, I.G., 1965: "K voprosu o pergamskom importe na Bospore vo II v. do n.ė.", *KSIA* 103: 41–43.

Šurgaja, I.G., 1984: "Porfmij", in *AGSP*: 69–70.

Svoronos, I.N., 1904–1908: *Τὰ νομίσματα του κράτους των Πτολεμαίων* (Athens).

Sztetyłło, Z., 1976: *Mirmeki. Wykopaliska odcinka polskiego w r. 1957*, Wykopaliska polsko-radzieckie w Mirmeki 3 (Warsaw).

Taliano Grasso, A., 2008: *Il santuario della kourotrophos a Kyme eolica*, Ricerche. Università della Calabria 1 (Arcavata di Rende).

Thompson, D.B. 1962. "Three Centuries of Hellenistic Terracottas, II C. The Satyr Cistern", *Hesperia* 31: 244–262.

Thompson, H.A., 1934: "Two Centuries of Hellenistic Pottery", *Hesperia* 3: 311–480.

Tolstikov, V. & Zhuravlev, D., 2004: "Hellenistic Pottery from two Cisterns on the Acropolis of Panticapaeum", in *ΣΤ' Συνάντηση*: 269–276.

Tomber, R., 2011: "Reusing Pottery in the Eastern Desert of Egypt", in Lawall & Lund (eds.) 2011: 107–116.

Tončeva, G., 1953: "Starograckata keramika v muzeja na gr. Stalin", *Izvestija na arheologičeskija institute* 9: 29–39.

Treister, M.Y., 1996: *The Role of Metals in Ancient Greek History*, Mnemosyne Suppl. 156 (Leyden).

Trummer, R., 1990: "Hellenistische Keramik aus Aigeira", in *Akten des XIII. internationalen Kongresses für Klassische Archäologie, Berlin, 24.–30. Juli 1988* (Mainz) 311–313.

Tsakos, K., 1990: "Σκύφοι με ανάγλυφη διακόσμηση από τη Σάμο", in *Β' Συνάντηση*: 139–144.

Tsakos, K., 1994: "Πήλινες μήτρες 'Μεγαρικών' σκύφων από τη Σάμο", in *Γ" Συνάντηση*: 294–301.

Tsimpides-Pentazos, E., 1971: "Αρχαιολογικαί έρευναι εν Θράκη", *Prakt* 127: 86–118.

Tuchelt, K., 1971: "Didyma. Bericht über die Arbeiten 1969/70" mit Beiträgen von Helga Gesche und Wolfgang Günther, *Ist-Mitt* 21: 45–108.

Tuluk, G.G., 2001: "Hellenistische Reliefbecher im Museum von Ephesos", in Krinzinger (ed.) 2001: 51–69.

Turcu, M., 1976: "Les bols à reliefs des collections du musée d'histoire du municipe de Bucarest", *Dacia* N.S. 20: 199–204.

Turova, N.P. & Kovalenko, S.A., 2005: "Megarskie čaši iz archeologičeskoj kollekcii Jaltinskogo Istoričesko-literaturnogo Museja", in *Bosporskie issledovanija – Bosporos Studies* 8 (Simferopol) 339–349.

Usačeva, O.N., 1978: "Rel'efnaja keramika iz Kep", *KSIA* 156: 100–107.

Ushakov, S.V. & Strukova, E.V., 2009: " Dve nachodki fragmentov redkich antichnych so-sudov iz Chersonesa", in *Bosporskij fenomen. Iskusstvo na periferii antičnogo mira. Materialy meždunarodnoj naučnoj konferencii* (St Petersburg) 429–433.

Uvarov, A., 1851: *Issledovanija o drevnostjach Južnoj Rossii i Čornogo Morja* (St Petersburg).

Vachtina, M.Ju., 2003: "Archaic Buildings of Porthmion", in Guldager Bilde, Højte & Stolba (eds.) 2003: 37–54.

Vachtina, M.Ju., 2006: "Ob arhaičeskom Porfmii (po materialam raskopok 1986–1990; 2002–2005 gg." *Bosporskie issledovanija* 13 (Simferopol-Kerč) 31–46.

Vachtina, M.Ju., 2009: "Porfmij – grečeskij gorod u perepravy čerez Kimmerijskij Bospor, *Boporos Studies* 22 (Simferopol-Kerč), 91–126.

Vafopoulou-Richardson, C.E., 1982: "An Unpublished Arula in the Ashmolean Museum: A Minor Contribution to Hellenistic Chronology", *JHS* 102: 229–232.

Vegas, M., 1955–1956: "Fragmento de moldo megárico de Ampurias", *Ampurias* 17–18: 252–253.

Verluste 2005: *Staatlichen Museen zu Berlin. Dokumentation der Verluste. Antikensammlung 5.1. Skulpturen, Vasen, Elfenbein und Knochen, Goldschmuck, Gemmen und Kameen* (Berlin).

Vermeule, C., 1966: "Small Sculptures in the Museum of Fine Arts, Boston", *CJ* 62: 97–113.

Vinogradov, Yu.A., Butyagin, A.M. & Vachtina, M.Yu., 2003: "Myrmekion – Porthmeus. Two 'Small' Towns of Ancient Bosporus", in Grammenos & Petropoulos (eds.) 2003: 803–840.

Vinogradov, Ju.G. & Kryžickij, S.D., 1995: *Olbia. Eine altgriechische Stadt im nordwestlichen Schwarzmeerraum*, Mnemosyne Suppl. 149 (Leiden).

Vnukov, S.Ju. & Kovalenko, S.A., 1998: "Megarskie čaši s gorodišča Kara-Tobe", in D.V. Žuravlev (ed.), *Ellinističeskaja i rimskaja keramika v Severnom Pričernomor'e I* (Moscow) 61–75.

Von Saldern, A., 2004: *Handbuch der Archäologie. Antikes Glas* (Munich).

Von Stern, E., 1899: *OAK za 1899 gg.*, 102–125.

Von Stern, E., 1902: "Vasa s rel'efnymi ukrašenijami iz Ol'vii", *IAK* 3: 93–113.

Von Vacano, O.-W., 1966–1967: "Ein Krateriskos der Popiliusgruppe", *RM* 73/74: 78–93.

Vulpe, A., 1965: "Reprezentări umane pe cupele getice de la Popești", *SCIV* 2: 341–351.

Vulpe, A. & Gheorghiță, M., 1976: "Bols à reliefs de Popești", *Dacia* N.S. 20: 167–198.

Waagé, F.O., 1937: "Vasa samia", *Antiquity* 21: 46–55.

Waagé, F.O. (ed.), 1948: *Ceramics and Islamic Coins*, Antioch-on-the-Orontes 4.1 (Princeton).

Watzinger, C., 1901: "Vasenfunde aus Athen", *AM* 26: 50–102.

Watzinger, C., 1924: *Griechischen Vasen in Tübingen* (Tübingen).

Watzinger, C., 1926: *Die griechischen Vasen des Archäologischen Instituts in Tübingen* (Tübingen).

Webb, P.A., 1996: *Hellenistic Architectural Sculpture* (Madison).

Weinberg, G.D., 1961: "Hellenistic Glass Vessels from the Athenian Agora", *Hesperia* 30: 380–392.

Weinberg, S.S., 1949: "Investigations at Corinth, 1947–1948", *Hesperia* 18: 148–157.

West, M.L. 1983: *The Orphic Poems* (Oxford).

Wetzel, F., Schmidt, E. & Mallwitz, A., 1957: *Das Babylon der Spätzeit* (Berlin).

Will, E.L., 1984: "The Spargi Wreck: A Reconsideration", *AJA* 88: 264.

Willers, D., 1986: "Typus und Motiv. Aus der hellenistischen Entwicklungsgeschichte einer Zweifigurengruppe", *AK* 29: 137–150.

Wootton, W., 2012: "Making and Meaning. The Hellenistic Mosaic from Tel Dor", *AJA* 116: 209–234.

Wroth, W., 1894: *A Catalogue of the Greek Coins in the British Museum, Troas, Aeolis, and Lesbos* (London).

Wuilleumier, P., 1929: "Brûle-parfums en terre-cuite", *MEFRA* 46: 43–76.

Wuilleumier, P., 1939: *Tarente des origines à la conquète romaine*, BEFAR 148 (Paris).

Yntema, D., 1995: "Salento and the Eastern Mediterranean in the Middle and Late Hellenistic Period: Some 'Eastern' Ceramic Evidence (Fine Wares) from Valesio, Province of Brindisi", *StAnt* 8.2: 387–404.

Zabelina, V.S., 1968: "Gruppa rel'efnoj keramiki iz Pantikapeja", *SoobMuzMoskva* 4: 119–124.

Zabelina, V.S., 1984: "Importnye 'megarskie' čaši iz Pantikapeia", *SoobMuzMoskva* 7: 153–172.

Zaganiari-Phrantzi, E., 1970: "Μεγαρικοί σκύφοι", *AAA* 3: 137–151.

Zahn, R., 1904: "Thongeschirr", in Th. Wiegand & H. Schrader, *Priene. Ergebnisse der Ausgrabungen und Untersuchungen in den Jahren 1895–1898* (Berlin) 394–468.

Zahn, R., 1908: "Hellenistische Reliefgefässe aus Südrussland", *JdI* 23: 45–77.

Zahn, R., 1940: "Makedonischer Schild, makedonischer Becher", in *Studien zur Vor- und Frühgeschichte. C. Schuchhardt zum 80. Geburtstag dargebracht* (Berlin) 48–72.

Zajceva, K.I., 1973: *Mestnaja raspisnaja keramika Ol'vii ellinističeskogo vremeni (IV-II vv. do n.e.)* (Leningrad).

Zapheiropoulou, Ph. & Chatzidakis, P., 1994: "Δήλος. Κεραμική από τον δρόμο βόρεια του Ανδήρου των λεόντων, in *Γ' Συνάντηση*: 235–248.

Zapheiropoulou, Ph. & Kolia, E.-I., 2006: "Ελληνιστική κεραμική από τη Νάξο" in *Δ' Συνάντηση*: 283–290.

Zavvou, E., 2005: "Σπάρτη. Εργαστήρια ανάγλυφων σκύφων", in S. Drougou et al. (eds.), *Ελληνιστική Κεραμική από την Πελοπόννησο* (Athens) 107–125.

Zaytsev, Y.P., 2004: *The Scythian Neapolis (2nd Century BC to 3rd century AD). Investigations into the Graeco-Barbarian City on the Northern Black Sea Coast*, BARIntSer 1219 (Oxford).

Zgusta, L., 1956: "Die Deklination der Personennamen griechischer Städte der nördlichen Schwarzmeerküste. Ein Beitrag zur koiné-Forschung", *Archiv Orientální* 24: 410–419.

Zhuravlev, D.V., 1998: "A Late Hellenistic Skyphos from Pergamon with Appliqué Reliefs from the Chrysaliskos Estate", *AncCivScytSib* 4: 254–264.

Zhuravlev, D., 2000: "A Skyphos from the House of Chrysaliskos and Pergamene Pottery Import in the Bosporan Kingdom", in *Ε' Συνάντηση*: 269–272.

[See also Žuravlev].

Zimmer, T., 2005: "Hellenistische Reliefkeramik im Akademischen Kunstmuseum Bonn", *BJb* 205: 83–135.

Zinko, V.N., 2001: "Summary of Results of the Five-Year Rescue Excavations in the European Bosporus, 1989–1993", in G.R. Tsetskhladze (ed), *North Pontic Archaeology. Recent Discoveries and Studies*, Colloquia Pontica 6: 295–317.

Zin'ko, V.N., 2006: "The Chora of Nymphaion (6th Century BC–6th Century AD)", in P. Guldager Bilde & V.F. Stolba (eds.), *Surveying the Greek Chora: The Black Sea Region in a Comparative Perspective*, BSS 4 (Aarhus) 289–308.

Zograf, A.N., 1951: *Antičnye monety*, MIA 16.

Zolotarev, M.I., 1996: "Sur la chronologie de Chersonésos à l'époque archaïque", in O. Lordkipanidze & P. Lévêque, *Sur les traces des Argonautes. Actes du 6e Symposium de Vani (Colchide) 22–29 septembre 1990*, (Besançon) 311–317.

Zolotarev, M.I., 2005: "Ob odnom tipe polusferičeskich čaš ellinističeskogo vremeni", *Bosporskie Issledovanija – Bosporos Studies* 8: 54–60.

Züchner, W., 1950–1951: "Von Toreuten und Töpfern", *JdI* 65–66: 175–205.

Žuravlev, D.V., 1995: "Pozneellinističeskij keramičeskij skifos s applikativnymi rel'efami iz 'doma Chrisaliska'", *VDI* 3: 72–79.

Žuravlev, D.V. & Schlotzhauer, U., 2011: "Greki i varvary na beregach Bospora Kubanskogo", in M.Yu. Vachtina (ed.), *Bosporskij fenomen: naselenie, jazyki, kontakty. Materialy meždunarodnoj naučnoj konferencii* (St Petersburg), 264–271.

Žuravlev, D. & Žuravleva, N., 2014: "Late Hellenistic Pottery and Lamps from Pantikapaion. Recent Finds", in Guldager Bilde & Lawall (eds.) 2014: 255–286.

Recent Bibliography on Mouldmade Bowls

Ackermann, G., 2013: "Reliefkeramik aus dem Athena-Heiligtum von Eretria. Kontakte einer Stadt Euböas zum zentralen und nördlichen Griechenland", in Fenn & Römer-Strehl (eds.) 2013: 33–40.

Ackermann, G., 2020: *La céramique d'époque hellénistique. Une chrono-typologie au service de l'histoire d'une ville grecque entre la fin du IVe et le Ier s. av. J.-C.,* Eretria 24 (Gollon).

Ackermann, G., 2022: "Pottery Production in Central Euboea during the Hellenistic Period", in Rembart & Waldner (eds.) 2022: 99–109.

Antonazzo, A., 2014: "Torre S. Sabina. I materiali da recupero subacqueo (1972–1983). Distribuzione spaziale ed ipotesi interpretative", in D. Leone, M. Turchiano & G. Volpe (eds.), *Atti del III Convegna di archeologia subacquea. Manfredonia, 4–6 ottobre 2007* (Bari) 181–198.

Antoniadis, G. & Pliakou, G., 2022: "The Archaeology of 'Dead Cities': Ceramic Evidence from Late Hellenistic and Roman Epirus", in Rembart & Waldner (eds.) 2022: 527–543.

Bernal-Casasola, D., Puppo, P., Sotelo, J.L.P., Diaz, J.J. & Florido, M.L.L., 2019: "Una copa jonio/efesia de cerámica helenística con relieves firmada por Gorgias en la Bahía de Cádiz", *Boletino Ex Officina Hispania* 10: 31–35.

Bochkovoy, V.V., Bulach, E.N. & Danilin, A.I., 2019: "Arheologičeskie raskopki severo-zapadnoj časti poselenija Volna 1 v 2017 g. (Raskop XXII)", *Drevnosti Bospora* 24: 63–71.

Bounegru, O., 2013: *Mercator. Studien zur antiken Wirtschaft im Pontosgebiet und in der Ägäis* (Kaiserslautern).

Bouzek, J., 2012: "Local Production Centres of Megarian Bowls in the Black Sea and Thrace", *Studia Hercynia* 16.2: 43–48.

Bouzek, J., 2017: "Second-in-Rank Local Producers of Megarian Bowls in the Aegean and Elsewhere", in E. Kozal, M. Akar & Y. Heffron et al. (eds.), *Questions, Approaches, and Dialogues in Eastern Mediterranean Archaeology. Studies in Honor of Marie-Henriette and Charles Gates* (Münster) 561–572.

Can, C. & Can, B., 2016: "Bilecik Ahmetler Nekropolü Geç Hellenistik – Erken Roma Dönemi Kâseleri", in E. Dundar, Ş. Aktaş, M. Koçak & S. Erkoç (eds.), *Havva İşkan'a Armağan. Festschrift für Havva İşkan* (Istanbul) 153–172.

Cappelletto, E., 2019: "Moldmade Wares from Hierapolis of Phrygia", in Peignard-Giros (ed.) 2019: 275–284.

Čargo, B. & Kamenjarin, I., 2020: "Hellenistic Mouldmade Pottery from Issa (Vis) and Siculi (Resnik – Kaštela), Croatia (A Preliminary Report)", in Kamenjarin & Ugarković (eds.) 2020: 327–341.

Carilli, L., 2014, "La ceramica fine a vernice nera: le 'pinecone mouldmade bowls'", in D. Malfitana & G. Cacciaguerra (eds.), *Archeologia classica in Sicilia e nel Mediterraneo. Didattica e Ricerca nell'esperienza mista CNR e Università. Il contributo delle giovani generazioni. Un triennio di ricerche e di tesi universitarie* (Catania) 73–77.

Civelek, A. & Taş, H.Y., 2012: "Adana Müzesi'nde Korunan kalıp yapımı kâseler", *Colloquium Anatolicum* 11: 123–150.

Dan, A., Brückner, H., Fehrke, H.J., Kelterbaum, D., Schlotzhauer, U. & Zhuravlev, D., 2020: "Coracanda, Korokondamè, Korokondamitis: Notes on the Most Ancient Names of the Cimmerian Bosporus, the Kuban Bosporus and the Southern Part of the Taman Island", in A. Belousov & C. Ilyushechkina (eds.), HOMO OMNIVM HORARVM. *Symbolae ad anniuersarium septuagesimum professoris Alexandri Podosinov dedicatae* (Moscow) 682–725.

De Luca, G., 2021: *Hellenistische Reliefbecher aus Pergamon. Die 'Megarischen Becher' von der Akropolis, aus dem Asklepieion, der Stadtgrabung und von weiteren Fundorten*, PF 18 (Wiesbaden).

De Mitri, C., 2020–2021: "Dolphins in the Ionian-Adriatic Basin. Hellenistic Moldmade Ware from Orikos, Southern Illyria (Excavations 2012–2020)", *Journal of Hellenistic Pottery and Material Culture* 5: 21–44.

Drougou, S. (ed.), 2020: *Pottery Workshops: Craftsmen and Workshops. 10th International Scientific Meeting on Hellenistic Pottery* (Athens).

Erol, A.F. & Tamer, D., 2017: "Ordu-Fatsa cıngırt kayası kazısı hellenistik dönem kalıp yapımı kabartmalı kâseleri", *Anadolu* 43: 111–145.

Erol, A.F. & Tamer, D., 2021: "Recent Finds of Hellenistic Mould-made Relief Bowls from the Ordu-Fatsa Cingirt Kayasi Excavations in the Southern Black Sea Region", in G.R. Tsetskhladze, A. Avram & J. Hargrave (eds.), *The Greeks and Romans in the Black Sea and the Importance of the Pontic Region for the Graeco-Roman World (7th Century BC–5th Century AD). 20 Years On (1997–2017). Proceedings of the Sixth International Congress on Black Sea Antiquities (Constanța, 18–22 September 2017). Dedicated to Prof. Sir John Boardman to Celebrate his Exceptional Achievements and his 90th Birthday* (Oxford 2021) 561–570.

Ersoy, A., 2013: "Smyrna/İzmir kazıları kalıp yapımı kaseleri ve kebartmalı kaplar – Moldmade Bowls and Relief Wares. Findings from Smyrna/Izmir Excavations", *TÜBA-KED* 11: 31–50.

Falco, G. 2016: "Un frammento di ceramica 'megarese' con scena di caccia al museo 'Paolo Orsi' di Siracusa", *Sicilia Antiqua* 13: 95–102.

Fenn, N., 2016: *Späthellenistische und frühkaiserzeitliche Keramik aus Priene. Untersuchungen zu Herkunft und Produktion*, Priene 4, AF 35 (Wiesbaden).

Fenn, N. & Römer-Strehl, Chr. (eds.), 2013: *Networks in the Hellenistic World According to the Pottery in the Eastern Mediterranean and Beyond*, BARIntSer 2539 (Oxford).

Gabrilaki, E., Biglaki, P. & Daskilakis, N., 2012: "Ἀνάγλυφοι σκύφοι ἀπό τὴν ἀρχαία Λάππα (Ἀργυρούπολι) στο Ῥέθυμνο", *Creta Antica* 13: 227–300.

Gamberini, A., 2016: *Ceramica fini ellenistiche da Phoinike: forme, produzioni, commerci*. Scavi di Phoinike 2, DiSCi. Archeologia 10 (Bologna).

Gamberini, A., 2018: "Indicatori di produzione artigianale a Phoinike in età ellenistico-romana", in J.-L. Lamboley, L. Përzhita & A. Skënderja (eds.), *L'Illyrie méridionale et l'Epire dans l'antiquité 6. Actes du VIᵉ colloque international de Tirana, 20–23 mai 2015* (Paris) 579–583.

Granata, A., 2019: "Ceramica a rilievo da una cisterna da Kyme Eolica", in Peignard-Giros (ed.) 2019: 109–120.

Intzesiloglou, C., 2020: "The Identity of the Pottery Workshop of the Ancient Theatre of Demetrias", in Drougou (ed.) 2020: 122–153.

Japp, S., 2013: "Pottery Production in Pergamon – A Short Overview", in Fenn & Römer-Strehl (eds.) 2013: 165–172.

Japp, S. & Kögler, P. (eds.), 2016: *Traditions and Innovations. Tracking the Development of Pottery from the Late Classical to the Early Imperial Periods. Proceedings of the 1st Conference of IARPotHP Berlin, November 2013, 7th–10th*, IARPotHP publications 1 (Vienna).

Kamenjarin, I., 2014: "Hellenistic Moldmade Relief Pottery from Siculi (Resnik)", *VjesDal* 107: 129–160.

Kamenjarin, I., 2016: "Hellenistic Pottery from Siculi (Resnik), Croatia", in Japp & Kögler (eds.) 2016: 177–185.

Kamenjarin, I., 2017: *Helenistička reljefna keramika iz Sikula. Hellenistic moldmade relief pottery from Siculi* (Kaštela).

Kamenjarin, I. & Ugarković, M. (eds.), 2020: *Exploring the Neighborhood. The Role of Ceramics in Understanding Place in the Hellenistic World, Kaštela 2017*, IARPotHP Publications 3 (Vienna).

Katsadima, I. & Papakosta, D., 2014: "Ἑλληνιστική κεραμική ἀπό οἰκία τῆς Ἀμβρακίας. Πινάκια καὶ ἀνάγλυφοι σκύφοι", in *Η' Συνάντηση*: 69–83.

Kemppainen, T. & Leone, A., 2012: "Ceramica italo-megarese", in E.M. Steinby (ed.), *Lacus Iuturnae 2. Saggi degli anni 1982–85. 2, Materiali*, ActaInstRomFin 38, 2 (Rome) 93.

Klöckl, R., 2022: "Zu einigen Reliefbechern aus Pheneos, Arkadien", in Rembart & Waldner (eds.) 2022: 595–606.

Kögler, P., 2019: "Lissos in Illyria: Two Centuries of Hellenistic Pottery and a Plea for the Publication of Contextual Material", *Journal of Hellenistic Pottery and Material Culture* 4: 79–141.

Kögler, P., 2020–2021: "Lissos in Illyria, 2: A Hellenistic Fill from the Upper Town and Some Considerations on the Importance of Ceramic Debris", *Journal of Hellenistic Pottery and Material Culture* 5: 91–137.

Lagona, S., 2016: "Le terrecotte figurate di Kyme eolica", in A. Muller, E. Laflı & S. Huysecom-Haxhi (eds.), *Figurines de terre cuite en Méditerranée grecque et romaine 1. Production, diffusion, étude*, BCH Suppl. 54 (Athens) 289–301.

Lancov, S.B. & Šapcev, M.S., 2016: "'Megarskie' čaši iz sborov i raskopok A.S. Golencova v 70–90 gg. XX v. na gorodiše Kul'čuk", *Bosporos Studies* 33: 397–410.

Landi, M.E., 2012: "Note sulla circolazione di alcune classi di ceramica fine di età ellenistica da Kyme eolica", in L.A. Scatozza Höricht (ed.), *Nuovi studi su Kyme Eolica. Produzioni e rotte trasmarine* (Naples) 71–100.

Lanzi, D., 2013: "La ceramica a vernice rossa e la ceramica italo-megarese", in F. Coarelli, G. Ghini, P. Braconi & F. Diosono (eds.), *Il santuario di Diana a Nemi. Le terrazze e il ninfeo. Scavi 1989 – 2009* (Rome) 331–337.

Lazari, K. & Tzortzatou, A., 2014: "Ἀνάγλυφη ἑλληνιστική κεραμική ἀπό τον ἀρχαιολογικό χώρο Δυμοκάστρου Θεσπρωτίας", in *Η' Συνάντηση*: 568.

Lech, P. & Stroczyńska, E., 2017: "Finds of Hellenistic Mouldmade Bowls from Polish Excavations in Tanais. Seasons 2014–2017", *Novensia* 28: 147–160.

Leotta, M.C., 2017: *La ceramica ellenistica a rilievo dell'Italia centrale. Produzione e diffusione*, Fecit te 10 (Roma).

Lilimbakis, M. & Akamati, I.M., 2020: "Pottery Production Centres in Hellenistic Macedonia. Contribution to the Study of the Pottery Production of Pella", in Drougou (ed.) 2020: 50–99.

Limberis, N. & Marčenko, I., 2020: "Rel'efnaja 'megarskaja' čaša c Elizavetinskogo gorodišča", *ANews* 29: 308–313.

Lungu, V. & Dupont, P., 2020: "Hellenistic Mould Made Relief Bowls from Celaenae (Kelainai)/Apameia Kibotos", in Kamenjarin & Ugarković (eds.) 2020: 603–614.

Martin, A., 2019: "Fragments of Molds for Hellenistic Relief Bowls from Pompeii (Reg. VIII, Ins. 7, 1)", in J. Mellnerová Šuteková, M. Bača & P. Pavúk (eds.), *Salve, Edvarde! A Toast for the Jubilee of Professor E. Krekovič, Facultas Philosophica Universitatis Comenianae Bratislavensis*, Studia Archaeologica et Mediaevalia Tomus 12 (Bratislava) 29–35.

Mermelstein, S., 2022: "Off to the Market: The Production and Movement of Hellenistic Moldmade Relief Bowls (MMBs) in the Southern Levant", in Rembart & Waldner (eds.) 2022: 805–812.

Metin, H., 2013: "An Example of the Transfer of the Decorations on the Hellenistic Mouldmade Bowls to Lamps: A Lamp from Boubon", *Colloquium Anatolicum* 12: 239–252.

Metin, H., 2014: "Boubon'dan bir grup kalıp yapımı kâse", *Colloquium Anatolicum* 13: 243–259.

Metin, H., 2015a: "Burdur Müzesi'nden bir grup kalıp yapımı kâse", *The Journal of International Social Research* 8, issue 37: 473–485.

Metin, H., 2015b: "Burdur Müzesi'nden iki kalıp ışığında Pisidialı bir kalıp yapımı kâse ustası: ΑΡΤΕΜΗΣ", *Arkeoloji ve Sanat Dergisi* 149: 146–150.

Metin, H., 2015c: "Ünik bir situala ışığında Pisidia yerel üretimli hellenistik kabartmalı kaplarda kullanılan bezemeler (Decorations Used to Hellenistic Relief Wares with Pisidia Local Production in Light of a Unique Situla)", in E. Okan & C. Atila (eds.), *Ömer Özyiğit'e Armağan – Studies in Honour of Ömer Özyiğit* (Istanbul) 307–315.

Metin, H., 2017: "Hellenistic Mouldmade Bowl Moulds from Kremna", OLBA 25: 271–295.

Morsiani, S., 2014: "Coppe megaresi", in L. Mazzeo Saracino (ed.), *Scavi di Suasa I. I reperti ceramici e vitrei dalla Domus dei Coiedii*, Studi e Scavi n.s. 39 (Bologna) 111–112.

Mosca, F. & Puppo, P., 2014: "Dinamiche commerciali nel Mediteraneo Occidentale. La ceramica megarese a Malta", in *Η' Συνάντηση*: 175–180.

Novoselova, N. & Akhmadeeva, M., 2022: "A Hellenistic Pottery Deposit from the "Archelaos" Household of Tauric Chersonessos: Evidence for Globalization", in Rembart & Waldner (eds.) 2022: 653–665.

Pascual, G. & Pliakou, G., 2022: "Transport Amphorae from the Late Hellenistic Farmstead of Episkopi, Ioannina", in Rembart & Waldner (eds.) 2022: 447–758.

Peignard-Giros, A. (ed.), 2019: *Daily Life in a Cosmopolitan World: Pottery and Culture During the Hellenistic Period*, IARPotHP Publications 2 (Vienna).

Pliakou, G., 2016: "Ανάγλυφοι σκύφοι από ελληνιστική αγροικία στην 'επισκοπή' Ιωαννίνων", in M. Giannopoulou & Chr. Kallini (eds.), *Ηχάδιν. Τιμητικός τόμος για τη Στέλλα Δρούγου* (Athens) 370–386.

Polat, R.T., 2016: "Mold-Made Bowls from Teos Hellenistic City Wall Excavations", *Colloquium Anatolicum* 15: 108–131.

Poveda Navarro, A.M. & Puppo, P., 2022: "Nuovi dati sulla diffusione della ceramica ellenistica a rilievo nelle Isole Baleari (Spagna)", in Rembart & Waldner (eds.) 2022: 781–791.

Puppo, P., 2013: "Ceramica megarese", in L. Gambaro, A. Del Lucchese & M. Rendeli (eds.) *Monte Rocche (Castellaro). Un insediamento d'altura del Ponente Ligure*, Studi e Ricerche. Collana del Museo Civico di Sanremo (Imperia) 119–122.

Puppo, P., 2014: "Recenti ritrovamenti di ceramica megarese ad Ancona", in *Η' Συνάντηση*: 381–388.

Puppo, P., 2019: "The Italo-Megarian Ware: New Data about the Production of the Potter L. Quintus", in Peignard-Giros (ed.) 2019: 357–362.

Rembart, L. & Waldner, A. (eds.), 2022: *Manufacturers and Markets. The Contributions of Hellenistic Pottery to Economies Large and Small*, IARPotHP Publications 4 (Vienna).

Rogl, C., 2014b: "Ephesos und seine Reliefbecher. Eine Analyse der Produktion und Verbreitung", in *Η' Συνάντηση*: 320.

Rogl, C., 2014c: "Multifunktionalität durch Formenwandel am Beispiel der hellenistischen Reliefbecher", in *Η' Συνάντηση*: 668.

Rogl, C., 2021: *Die hellenistischen Reliefbecher aus Ephesos. Gefäßrepertoire – Fundmaterial – Ateliers – Fundkontexte*, Hand- und Arbeitsbücher zur hellenistischen Keramik 1 (Spittal an der Drau).

Rogl, C., 2022: *Die hellenistischen Reliefbecher aus Ephesos. Die Modelabzüge zu den Formschüsseln*, Hand- und Arbeitsbücher zur hellenistischen Keramik 2 (Spittal an der Drau).

Rosenthal-Heginbottom, R., 2016: "Moldmade Bowls from Straton's Tower (Caesarea Maritima)", *Journal of Hellenistic Pottery and Material Culture* 1: 113–168.

Rotroff, S.I., 2013a: "Bion International. Branch Pottery Workshops in the Hellenistic Aegean", in Fenn & Römer-Strehl (eds.) 2013: 15–23.

Rotroff, S.I., 2013b: "A New Moldmade Bowl from Athens", in J. Bodzek (ed.), *Studies in Ancient Art and Civilization* 17 (Kraków) 151–159.

Rotroff, S.I., 2016: "Hausmann's Workshop and Innovaton in the Production of Athenian Mold-made Bowls", in Japp & Kögler (eds.) 2016: 297–305.

Rotroff, S.I., 2018: "Athenian Moldmade Bowls on Delos: Laumonier's Sample", BCH 142.2: 567–692.

Rotroff, S.I., 2019: "Drinking under the New Hellenistic Order at Sardis and Athens" in: A. Berlin and P.J. Kosmin (eds.), *Spearwon Land: Sardis from the King's Peace to the Peace of Apamea*, Wisconsin Studies in Classics (Madison) 262–279.

Rotroff, S.I. 2020. "Drinking without Handles in the Age of Alexander", in Kamenjarin and Ugarković (eds.) 2020: 61–73.

Rotroff, S.I., 2022: "An Italian in Arcadia? Moldmade Bowls of Italian Type at Mount Lykaion", in Rembart & Waldner (eds.) 2022: 793–803.

Samojlova, T., 2014: "Štampovannaja rel'efnaja keramika", in S.D. Kryžickij & N.A. Lejpunskaja (eds.), *Žilye doma Central'nogo kvartala Ol'vii*, ΜΑΙÈΤ Supplementum 13 (Simferopol-Kerch): 380–394.

Saygili, B., 2012: "Kalıp yapımı Kibyra kâseleri", in K. Dörtlük, T. Kahya, B.R. Sayhan & T. Ertekin (eds.), *Uluslarası Genç Bilimciler Buluşması I. Anadolu Akdenizi, Sempozyumu 4–7 Kasım 2009, Sempozyum Bildirileri* (International Young Scholars Conference 1. Mediterranean Anatolia, 4–7 November 2009, Symposium Proceedings) (Antalya) 397–414.

Schmid, S.G., 2014: "Imported Mould Made Bowls from Ensérune (France) and the Long Distance Trade in the Hellenistic Mediterranean", in *Η' Συνάντηση*: 181–188.

Shehi, E. & Galaty, M.L., 2013: "Gjashtë pjesë kallëpe kupash me zbukurime në relief nga Durrësi", *Iliria* 37: 185–205.

Škribljak, I.I., 2012: "Megarskie čaši iz raskopok Neapolja Skifskogo (predvaritel'nyj analiz)", in N.P. Tel'nov (ed.), *Drevnosti Severnogo Pričernomor'ja III-II vv. do n. è.* (Tiraspol): 197–206.

Shkribliak, I., 2016: "Hellenistic Mold-made Relief Bowls from Late Scythian Sites of Crimea", in Japp & Kögler (eds.) 2016: 529–537.

Stavrogiannis, L., 2015: "Σκύφοι με ανάγλυφη διακόσμηση από τη Μελιταία. Πρώτη παρουσίαση", in *Φθιωτική ιστορία. Πρακτικά 5ου Συνεδρίου Φθιωτικής ιστορίας: ιστορία – αρχαιολογία – λαογραφία, 16, 17 και 18 Απριλίου 2010* (Lamia) 115–134.

Stone, S.C., 2014: *The Hellenistic and Roman Fine Pottery*, Morgantina Studies 6 (Princeton).

Sudarev, N.I. & Kašaev, S.V. 2018: "Importnye megarskie čaši iz nekropolja u poselenija Vinogradnyj-7", *Bosporos Studies* 37: 197–224.

Tiurin, M., 2016: "Novye nahodki attičeskoj rel'efnoj èllinističeskoj keramiki iz Chersonesa i ego hory", in *Elita Bospora i bosporskaya elitarnaya kul'tura. Materialy mezhdunarodnogo Kruglogo stola* (St Petersburg) 400–406.

Tiurin, M., 2018a: "Bosporskie rel'efnye čaši iz raskopok Chersonesa i ego bližajšej okrugi", in *Bosporskij fenomen: Obščee i osobennoe v istoriko-kul'turnom prostranstve antičnogo mira*, Materialy meždunarodnoj naučnoj konferencii (St Petersburg) 113–120.

Tiurin, M., 2018b: "Dve rel'efnye čaši iz zakrytogo kompleksa na ukreplenii Masljanaja gora", in *Bosporskie čtenija – Bosporan Readings* 19 (Simferopol and Kerch) 508–514.

Tiurin, M., 2019: "Rel'efnye čaši iz zakrytogo kompleksa na ukreplenii Masljanaja gora", *Bosporskie issledovanija – Bosporos Studies* 38: 242–255.

Tiurin, M., 2020: "Neskol'ko knidskih rel'efnych čaš iz zakrytych kompleksov Chersonesskogo gorodišča", in *Bosporskie čtenija – Bosporan Readings* 21 (Simferopol and Kerch) 363–369.

Tsantila, V.K., 2012: *Η Ελληνιστική ανάγλυφη κεραμική από τους νεώσοικους των ακαρνανικών Οινιαδών. Συμβολή στη μελέτη της ελληνιστικής κεραμικής της Δυτικής Ελλάδας* (Hellenistic Pottery with Relief Decoration from the Ship-Sheds of Oiniades/Acarnania. Contribution to the Study of Hellenistic Pottery of Western Greece) (Dissertation, University of Ioannina).

Tsantila, V., 2013: "Οι εισηγμένοι 'δηλιακοί' ανάγλυφοι σκύφοι των ακαρνανικών Οινιαδών", in F. Lang, P. Funke, L. Kolonas, E.-L. Schwandner & D. Maschek (eds.), *Interdisziplinäre Forschungen in Akarnanien* 1 (Bonn) 293–302.

Tsantila, V., 2016: "Oiniadai, a Significant Akarnanian Port on the Trade Route from Asia Minor to Italy: The Evidence Provided by the Relief Pottery", in Japp & Kögler (eds.) 2016: 223–240.

Tsitsiridis, S., 2014: "Μίμος, κίναιδοι και κιναιδολόγοι (I)", *Logeion* 4: 201–226.

Ugarković, M. & Paraman, L., 2020: "Appropriation of the Hellenistic Relief Ware in Ancient Trogir (Central Dalmatia, Eastern Adriatic). Preliminary Observations", in Kamenjarin & Ugarković (eds.) 2020: 301–325.

Ushakov, S.I., Tiurin, M. & Lesnaya, K., 2016: "The New Hellenistic Assemblages from the North-East District of Tauric Chersonesos", in Japp & Kögler (eds.) 2016: 491–502.

Vachtina, M.Ju., 2018: "Dve 'megarskie' čaši iz porfmijskogo nekropolja", *Problemy istorii, filologii i kul'tury* 2018, 3: 215–224.

Yedidağ, T.Y., 2015: "Dorylaion Kalıp Yapımı Kaseleri – Dorylaion Mold Made Bowls", OLBA 23: 235–272.

Yedidağ, T.Y., 2016: "Hellenistic Moldmade Bowls from Phrygia Epiktetos: New Evidence from Dorylaion", in R.A. Stucky, O. Kaelin & H.-P. Mathys (eds.), *Proceedings of the 9th International Congress in the Archaeology of the Ancient Near East 2, Basel 2014* (Wiesbaden) 235–244.

Zarkadas, A., 2014: "Μία ανάγλυφη οινοχόη του Μουσείου Κανελλοπούλου με παράσταση του μύθου του Ακταίωνα", in P. Valavanis & E. Manakidou (eds.), *Έγραφσεν και εποίεσεν. Μελέτες κεραμικής και εικονογραφίας προς τιμήν του καθηγητή Μιχάλη Τιβέριου* (Thessaloniki) 481–492.

Index to the Text

A (Ephesian potter)   44, 293, 319
Abdera   213
acanthus flower (wall motif)   311
acanthus-flower scroll, miniature (rim motif)   300, 305, 312, 321
acanthus leaf
   agyieus growing from   120
   arrangement of in baroque calyx   28–32, 34, 36, 104, 155, 294
   combined with long petals   295, 297, 320
   on Ephesian products   289, 290, 291, 294, 295, 296, 297, 309, 535
   with 'eyes'   29–30
   form, use of for defining workshops   12, 14
   imbricate   319
   on products of Aiolian workshops   171, 269, 270, 271
   on products of Demetrios   461, 462, 463
   on products of Meter Medallion Workshop   206–208, 212
   symbolism of   106, 130
   See also calyx; 'feuille typique'; scroll decoration
acanthus stem (wall motif)   211, 271
Achaean League   35, 36, 127
Achaia   33
actor (wall motif)   118, 300, 307, 310, 323
Ad(…) or Da(…) (Ephesian potter)   44, 293, 316
aegis   311
Aemilius Paullus monument (Delphi)   125, 127
Agathopolis   272
agyieus (wall motif)   33, 35, 119, 120, 130, 169, 307
Aigina   49
Aigion   33, 36
Aiolian *koine*   123, 146, 169, 197, 271
Aiolian mouldmade vessels
   chronology   213
   decoration   33, 116, 120, 121, 123, 131, 146, 148, 310
   distribution   6, 16, 49, 148, 213, 503, 511, 512, 528, 535
   fabric   19, 193
   Pergamene influence on   x, 148, 154
   supplementary shapes   55, 56, 59, 60
   See also Aiolis, Workshop A; Aiolis, Workshop B; Kymean mouldmade vessels; Kyme, Workshop A; Meter Medallion Workshop
Aiolis   146, 147
Aiolis, Workshop A   146, 261–262, 271, 272, 512, 523
Aiolis, Workshop B
   chronology   271–272
   decoration   21, 118, 122, 123, 130, 148, 202, 269–271, 462

   distribution   272, 498, 528, 535
   double stamping   271
   fabric and shape   19, 20, 146, 267–268
   influence of on Pontic industries   261, 271, 462, 465, 489
   Pergamene influence on   153, 268, 271, 272
   place of production   267, 272, 454
   relationship to Workshop A   261, 271, 272, 523
   supplementary shapes   55–56, 57–58, 268–269
Akurgal, E.   168
Alexander the Great   125, 500
Alexandria   29, 35, 51, 60, 110, 120
   influence of on mouldmade bowls   10, 25–26, 27–36, 118, 155, 310. *See also* Egyptian elements of mouldmade-bowl decoration; Ptolemaic iconography
altar
   of precious metal   118
   in Sinadino Collection   118
   wall motif   121, 122, 124, 146, 154, 155, 205
altar scene D. *See* Dionysiac trio
altars, 'Tarentine'   x, 26, 33, 110–115, 131, 309
Amazon (wall motif)
   fighting (Amazonomachy)   50, 116, 195, 200–201, 295, 300, 307, 310, 545
   hunting   115–116, 310
Amorgos   432
Amphitrite   112
amphora
   mouldmade   53, 54, 55, 56, 58, 135, 195, 197, 287, 289, 301, 309, 323, 324, 540
   Rhodian transport   22, 24, 26, 29, 50–51, 52, 135, 156, 212, 213, 326, 464, 498, 499, 500–501, 520, 534
amphoriskos, mouldmade   53, 56, 57, 170
Amymone (wall motif)   112–114, 309
Ancona   56
Andriskos   127
An(…) or Na(…) (Ephesian potter)   44, 293
Anti(…) (Ephesian potter)   44, 293, 319
Antikythera shipwreck   23, 24
Antioch   14, 15
Antiochos IV Epiphanes   35
Aphrodite   121, 495
   wall motif   108, 117–118
Apollo and Leto (wall motif)   112
Apollo Ietros   495
Apollonia   271, 272
Apollonia B/II shipwreck   51
Apollonios (Ephesian potter)   12, 43, 44, 292
Ap(…) or Pa(…) (Ephesian potter)   44, 293, 319
Apulia   51, 59
Archaeological Commission (St Petersburg)   10, 501, 502, 503

archaeometric analysis
   of Aiolian products   146, 193, 261, 272, 454
   at Elaia   262
   of mould found at Ephesos   287
   utility of, for provenience studies   11, 18, 19
Argive mouldmade vessels   14, 15, 19, 49, 50, 60, 115, 117, 118, 128, 310
Ariadne. *See* Dionysiac trio
Ariston (potter)   61
Ariston (Rhodian eponym or fabricant)   51
Arkesialos/Arkesilaos/Arkesilas (Ephesian potter)   44, 45, 288, 292, 315, 319
Artemis (goddess)   112, 214
   Leukophryene, temple of (Magnesia)   29
Artemis (potter)   41
Astašova, N.   522
astragal (rim pattern)   110, 169, 289, 296, 298, 301, 303, 314, 431
   with decorated bead   298, 301
   with decorated reel   290, 291, 301
Athena   59, 117, 120
Athenaios (Ephesian potter)   12, 44, 293, 296, 305, 309, 316, 318, 319, 320, 325
Athenaios (Greek author)   106
Athenian mouldmade vessels
   chronology   135
   decoration   21, 29, 108, 111, 115, 116, 118, 119, 120, 124, 127, 128, 130, 196, 303, 307, 320
   distribution (Mediterranean)   6, 15, 16, 16n13, 48, 49, 50, 51, 136n6, 145, 168
   distribution (Pontic)   6, 50, 136, 213, 432, 455, 498, 503, 512, 516, 523, 528, 535
   influence of on other industries   14, 19, 21, 26–28, 108, 119, 135, 155, 172, 195, 196, 200, 203, 212, 286, 287, 290, 297–298, 431
   invention of   ix–x, 3, 22, 25–26, 135
   relationship to 'Tarentine' altars   111
   shape   135
   supplementary shapes   56–60 *passim*, 135, 503
   See also Hausmann's Workshop; Workshop A (Athens); Workshop of Bion
Athenodoros, destruction of Delos by   325
Athens
   Athenian Agora   7, 11, 55, 61, 128, 129, 135, 458
   deposits at   x, 29, 45, 55, 129, 135, 325n84
   imports to   49, 432
   Kerameikos   45, 135
   moulds found at   45, 46, 124
   Pnyx   45, 135
   repairs at   458
   Rhodian amphorae at   51
   scale of production at   46, 286
   self-sufficiency of   48

Athribis, rhyta from   36, 58, 108
Attalos II   51, 122, 123
Attalos III   153
Atticizing products   20, 26, 28, 59, 115, 119, 135
Auge. *See* Herakles and Auge
aulos-player (wall motif)   202, 271, 307

bakchos (wall motif)   121
base
    concave undecorated   40, 43, 287, 290, 291, 296, 316, 319, 320, 325, 463–464
    medallion, stamps of   109, 130, 154–155, 170, 172, 193–198, 206, 210, 269–270, 289, 295, 296, 322, 325
    medallion, surrounded by band of rim-frieze pattern   198, 296, 297, 298
beading. *See* dots, as frieze separators
beaker, mouldmade   56, 58, 268
Becker, P.A. von, collection of   502
Beljaus   272
Belles Méduses Workshop (Ephesos)   12, 288, 296–298, 303, 305, 310, 312, 319, 323, 325
Benndorf, O.   7
Berliner Antikensammlung   502
Beschi, L.   39
Bibi Hanım (tortoiseshell)   128
bicolour firing   19, 286, 325, 512
bird (wall motif)   14, 21, 25, 32, 148, 171, 172, 199, 203–204, 208, 461. *See also* duck/bird
Birds and Imbrications Workshop (Kyme)   42, 168
Black Sea, south coast of   193
boar (wall motif)   115, 173, 204
Bobrinskij, A.   501
Bol'šoj Kastel'   5, 453, 456, 517, 520
Bosporan Archaeological Expedition
    of the Institute of Archaeology (Moscow)   542
    of the Institute of the History of Material Culture (Leningrad)   528, 532, 538
Bosporan Kingdom   3, 5, 6, 272, 453, 454, 459, 462, 463, 465, 504, 517, 523, 528, 532, 538, 540
boukranion/boukephalion (wall motif)   121, 122, 124, 128, 130, 146, 154, 171, 204–205, 206, 314
Bouzek, J.   168, 192–193, 212, 213, 453, 459, 516
bowl with mouldmade feet   59
box meander (rim motif)   21, 59, 289, 290, 291, 298, 301, 303, 315, 316, 324, 504, 512, 517, 535
breakage patterns   17
Brindisi   51
Bulgaria   29, 272
bull (wall motif)   120
Butjagin, A.M.   528

caduceus (wall motif)   291, 295
Čaika   272, 454, 464–465, 517, 520

cake stamp   120
Callaghan, P.J.   10, 127, 128, 129
calyx
    baroque-style   28–36, 104, 106, 118, 155, 310, 317, 323
    botanical term   104
    cosmic meaning of   105–106
    Egyptian inspiration of   25
    on Ephesian mouldmade bowls   287, 289, 295, 300, 316–318
    on Knidian mouldmade bowls   431
    on Kymean mouldmade bowls   170, 195
    on Pontic mouldmade bowls   461
    type A   32, 291, 300, 316–318, 325, 535
    type B   122, 291, 298, 300, 308, 313, 317, 318, 325, 523, 540, 545
    type C   300, 308, 317, 318
calyx bowls   106, 154, 155
Çandarli ware   58, 262, 268–269
Canosa, gold-glass bowls from   29–30, 34
Carthage   55
Castor and Pollux, Temple of (Rome)   x, 3, 23, 326
catalogues, content of   IX, 5n2, 327, 442, 466, 511n5
centaur (wall motif)   116, 290
Central Limit Theorem   21–22
Černomorskoe Museum of Historical Lore   520
Ch [Greek X] (Ephesian potter)   44, 294, 319
chalice, mouldmade   55, 57–58, 59, 154, 268–269, 272
chariot race. *See* Eros; Nike
Charles University (Prague)   168
Chersonesos   5, 136, 157, 272, 432, 453, 456, 459, 465, 512, 516–517
chronology of mouldmade bowls   3, 10–11, 14, 22–25
    Aiolian   212–213, 261, 271–272
    Athenian   135
    Ephesian   x, 14, 324–326
    Getic   489
    Knidian   432
    Pergamene   155–156
    Pontic   463–465
Chrysaliskos   542
Cī. *See* Si(...)
coins
    Kymean   215
    Macedonian   125, 127
    of Pantikapaion   465, 534
    Ptolemaic   119, 311, 312
Coitus a tergo (wall motif)   32–33, 35, 36, 310
column (wall motif)   130, 154, 205
    as scene divider   57, 116
    supporting garlands   121, 122, 146, 206
combing (rim motif)   307, 462
comic mask
    appliqué foot   59, 60
    medallion motif   155, 170, 172, 197
    wall motif   57, 202

Comique à la canne (Ephesian workshop)   12, 292, 294, 305, 306, 311, 320, 321
Corinth   58, 60, 128, 155
    1926 reservoir   127
Corinthian mouldmade vessels   21, 33, 49, 55, 59–60, 115, 117, 118, 127, 128, 129, 503
Cosa   33, 35
Courby, F.   10, 53, 459
Crăsani   489
'Crimean workshops'   10
crossed dotted lines (rim motif)   289, 290, 291, 292, 306, 308, 535
cross-hatched lines (wall motif)   489
cup
    with band handle(s), mouldmade   56, 58, 268
    with high collared rim, mouldmade   55, 57, 268

D (Ephesian potter)   44, 293, 319
Da(...). *See* Ad(...) or Da(...)
daisy pattern (wall motif)   57, 59
Damokles (Ephesian potter)   44, 292, 454
Damokrateus (Rhodian fabricant)   156
Danube   3, 489, 510
Daskyleion   272
Delos
    assemblage of mouldmade vessels, compared to that at Istros   512
    destruction debris on   x, 23, 55, 320, 324, 326
    Ephesian mouldmade vessels found on   IX, X, 10, 16, 43–44, 50, 125, 128, 286, 288, 296, 305, 308–309, 310, 312, 313, 315–316, 320, 321
    mouldmade vessels produced on   10, 16, 60–61
    moulds found on   16, 28, 61, 135
    non-Ephesian mouldmade vessels found on   14–16, 16n13, 49, 136n6, 148, 213, 432
    repairs at   458
    supplementary shapes found on   15–16, 55, 59, 60
Délos XXXI   6, 7, 11–14, 286, 458
de Luca, G.   10, 129, 153, 154, 155
Demetrios (Pontic potter)
    chronology   261, 263–265, 523
    decoration   129, 460, 461–462, 463, 464, 467
    distribution   6, 49–50, 122, 136, 271, 465–466, 486–488, 504, 511, 518, 523–524, 526–527, 528, 535, 538, 540, 543, 545, 465–466
    fabric and shape   19, 460
    inspiration of   148, 270, 290, 462, 465
    moulds   459
    production places of   49, 454, 523, 529
    scale of production   46
    signatures   45, 462
Demetrios-Iason (Argive workshop)   15, 459

Demosthenes 540
Deonna, W. 111, 112
Desjardins, E. 510
Di(...) (Ephesian potter) 43, 44, 293, 316
Dias (Ephesian potter) 43, 44, 293, 319
Didymos 106
dinos, mouldmade 60, 324, 502
Dionysiac trio (wall motif) 33, 111, 112–114, 115, 116, 170, 309
Dionysios (Ephesian potter) 43, 44, 293
Dionysos x, 119, 120, 199, 214
　iconography of 33, 119, 120, 121, 125, 130–131, 154, 290, 291, 311
　religion of 36, 115, 131, 215
　wall motif 170, 202, 290. See also Dionysiac trio
Dionysos-Eros (wall motif) 289
Dioskouroi 495
diplomatic gifts x, 25, 35, 104, 118
dipper, mouldmade 53, 56
distribution 5, 6, 11, 17, 21, 25, 26, 46–51, 455
　of Aiolian products 148, 157, 213, 258–260, 262, 266, 272, 284–285
　of Athenian products 6, 50, 136, 145
　of Ephesian products 43, 44, 46, 290, 427–430
　as evidence of production place 18, 272, 454
　of Knidian products 432, 441
　of products of Demetrios 459, 465–466, 486–488, 517
dog (wall motif) 115, 116, 118, 203, 291, 295, 300, 309
dolphin (wall motif) 108, 119, 120, 130, 203, 300, 307, 311, 320
Domăneanţu, C. 453, 465, 510, 511
Dörpfeld, W. 493
dots
　column of (wall motif) 128, 318, 320, 461
　as frieze separators 21, 32, 172, 198, 267, 269, 287, 289, 298, 305–306, 512
　large (rim motif) 290, 292, 301, 305–306
Doubles filets épais (Ephesian workshop) 12, 294
double stamping 271
Drakontidas (Rhodian fabricant) 51
drawing, method of, for mouldmade bowls 549–550
duck/bird turning its head back (wall motif) 148, 270, 462
Dupont, P. 193, 261, 272

eagle (wall motif) 115, 116, 119, 295, 300, 309, 311, 534
Eastern sigillata C. See Çandarli ware
École française d'Athènes 11, 14
Edwards, C.M. 129
Edwards, G.R. 125, 128, 135
Egyptian bean (*aiguptios kuamos*) 106
Egyptian elements of mouldmade-bowl decoration 25, 32, 36, 107–108, 119, 120
Ei(...) (Ephesian potter) 44, 293, 319

Elaia 261–262, 272, 454, 462, 465
Eleusinian religion 121
Elis 32, 33, 49
Entremont x, 23, 24, 298, 299, 309, 326
Ephesian mouldmade vessels
　Athenian influence on 19, 21, 287, 290, 297–298
　chronology 14, 23, 50, 115, 136, 271, 286, 324–326
　decoration 21, 32, 33, 35, 108–110 *passim*, 115–119 *passim*, 122–125 *passim*, 127, 128, 130, 169, 194, 196, 200, 201, 202, 269, 286–287, 289, 290–292, 294–297, 298–322
　distribution (Mediterranean) 10, 25, 48, 49, 51
　distribution (Pontic) 6, 50, 136, 213, 261, 427–430, 455, 465, 498, 504, 510, 512, 516, 517, 520, 523, 528, 535, 538, 540, 542, 543, 545
　fabric 19, 56, 286
　found on Delos ix, x, 10, 16, 43–44, 50, 125, 128, 286, 288, 296, 305, 308–310 *passim*, 312, 313, 315–316, 320, 321. See also *Délos* XXXI
　influence of on other industries 33, 460, 462
　moulds found at Ephesos 11, 45, 122, 125, 286, 287, 288, 298, 314, 325
　moulds found on Samos 21
　Pergamene influence on 154, 287
　shape 19–20, 195, 287, 290, 298
　signatures on 12, 41, 43, 44, 45, 194, 292–294, 296, 298, 299, 315–316, 319, 454
　supplementary shapes 55, 56, 57, 58, 59, 60, 135, 289, 301, 323–324, 325
　trade in xi, 51, 52
　workshop organization and scale of production 41, 43–44, 46, 50, 286, 288
Ephesos
　agora 45, 288
　harbour xi, 51, 52
　Magnesia Gate 45, 122, 287, 288, 298, 314, 325
　mouldmade bowls found at 108, 286
　scale of production at 42–44, 46, 286
　self-sufficiency of 49
　Südtor deposit x, 287, 325, 325n82
　Tetragonos Agora 287
Erdemgil, S. 153
Eretria 53, 59
Eros (wall motif) 108–109, 130
　and Aphrodite 117
　carrying objects 170, 200, 307
　dancing or walking 270, 289, 300, 307
　and dolphin 108, 130, 307, 311
　flanking objects 120, 307, 314
　freeing bird 199, 203, 204, 208, 212
　hunting 115
　and Pan 130, 215, 309

　as phlyax 118, 200
　playing musical instrument 116, 130, 199, 200, 289, 290, 291, 300, 307, 310
　pouring wine 170
　and Psyche 32–33, 35–36, 199, 289, 431–432
　racing two-horse chariot 108–110, 130, 291, 295, 298, 300, 307, 308–309, 325
　supporting garlands 121, 122, 130, 314
Eros-Paniskos (wall motif) 168, 200, 215
Erotes Workshop (Kyme) 42, 168, 213
ethnographic parallels 38
Etruria 49
Eumenes II 122, 129, 153, 156
evidence categories 5, 192
eyed chevron (rim motif) 307

fabrics 146, 154, 170, 172, 195, 261, 267, 286, 431, 460, 489
Farmakovskij, B.V. 10, 493, 493–495, 501, 502, 503
Fayoum 28, 34
feline (wall motif) 204
'feuille typique' 318, 325
figural decoration 36, 37, 50, 104, 108–120, 136, 154, 170, 195, 212, 269, 270, 289, 291, 295, 300, 307–312, 314, 316, 318, 323, 324, 325, 463, 523, 535, 545. See also individual figural motifs
filter jug, mouldmade 14, 15, 16, 53, 55, 60–61
Finkielsztejn, G. 29, 135, 498, 534
fleur de lys (rim and wall motif) 172
flower (rim motif) 289, 290, 291, 306
flower, funnel-shaped (wall motif) 210
frieze dividers with architectural moulding 148, 169, 170, 172
funerary use, items made for 37, 53, 55, 59, 110. See also urn
funnel, mouldmade 53, 54, 58, 323, 325

Gajdukevič, V.F. 528, 532, 538
garlands, suspended (wall motif) x, 120–121, 122–124, 125, 130, 146, 154, 169, 195, 205, 206, 269, 271, 313–314, 431
Gauls, victory over 129
General'skoe 465
German Archaeological Institute (DAI) 261, 542
Getes 3, 454
　invasion of Olbia by 493
　mouldmade bowls produced by 489, 512
gilding 25, 60
glass x, 10, 25, 32, 34, 155. See also Canosa
globular vessel, mouldmade 53, 57
goat, rampant (wall motif) 33, 35, 119, 120
Golubickoe 193
Gorgias (Ephesian potter) 44, 292–293, 294, 315
gorytos (wall motif) 50, 205, 309
Grač, I.I. 453

Grand Congloué shipwreck   51, 51*n14*
grape vine (wall motif)
    bunch of grapes   211
    garland   206
    leaf   211
    See also scroll decoration
grave marker   111–112
graves/tombs, moldmade vessels found in   17, 33*n31*, 49, 53, 56, 59, 60, 61, 110, 464, 502, 510, 540
Greek mainland, productions of   5, 35, 108, 115, 116, 118, 119, 120, 124, 129
grey ware   16, 19, 32, 33, 56, 59, 60, 172, 261, 267–271, 286, 294, 295, 298, 309, 323, 324, 431, 459, 503, 523, 535
griffin (wall motif)   115, 204, 310
groove
    incised, below the lip   170, 287, 323, 431
    rim motif   170, 172, 267, 269
grotesque (wall motif)   289, 311
Gryneion   272
Grzegrzółka, S.   453, 522, 528
guilloche (rim motif)   26, 32, 289, 290, 297, 298, 301, 303. See also heart guilloche
guttus, mouldmade   53, 55, 58, 60, 61, 287, 323, 324
Gylon   540

Halios priest   22
Hampe, R.   38
Hanghaus 1, well in   325–326
harp, played by Eros   307
Hathor's crown (wall motif)   108, 118
Hausmann, U.   153, 192
Hausmann's Workshop (Athens)   135
heart bud (rim pattern)   15, 172, 195, 196, 199, 208, 211
heart guilloche (rim pattern)   170, 195, 196, 303, 431
Hebe   112
Hegesander of Delphi   106
Hephaisteion (Athens)   116
Hephaistia (Lemnos)   20, 26, 39–40, 45, 135
Hera (wall motif)   117–118, 120
Hera(…)/Hera(ios) (Ephesian potter)   12, 14, 44, 293, 294, 310, 316, 319, 325
Herakleia Pontike   516
Herakles
    and Auge (wall motif)   108
    Dorian founder hero   520
    labors of (wall motif)   116–117, 202, 289, 290, 520
Hermes   120, 495
    wall motif   118, 310
Hermitage (State Hermitage Museum) (St Petersburg)   10, 310, 494, 501, 502, 503, 516, 522, 528
Hermogenes of Priene   29
hetairai   119
Hierapolis   33
hippocamp (wall motif)   307

honey   56
Horai   116
horse (wall motif)   201
horseman (wall motif)   172, 201, 311
H's in alternating orientation (rim motif)   289, 307
hunt (wall motif)   21, 115–116, 130, 201, 289, 290, 291, 295, 309, 310, 323, 431
Huskinson, J.   130
hydra (wall motif)   116, 202
hydria, mouldmade   53, 60

İdil, V.   168
IIMK RAN   494, 501, 502, 503*n10*, 528, 532, 534, 538
imbricate decoration   14, 23, 37, 56, 106, 170, 213, 290, 291, 296, 300, 307, 313, 315, 318–319, 323, 324, 325, 326, 431, 461, 463, 498, 517, 523
incision directly into mould   40, 41, 42, 43, 120, 121, 125, 128, 194, 287, 292, 293, 294, 296
innovations, adoption of   22, 25, 26, 36
inscription, bawdy   311
Institute of Archaeology
    of Rumanian Academy of Sciences (Bucharest)   510, 511
    of Russian Academy of Sciences (Moscow)   542
    of Ukrainian Academy of Sciences (Kiev)   3, 495, 497, 502
    of USSR Academy of Sciences (Leningrad)   495, 522
Institute of the History of Material Culture, USSR Academy of Sciences (Leningrad)   528. See also IIMK RAN
invention of the mouldmade bowl   3, 5, 25–26, 135
Ionian kyma (rim motif)   26, 169, 170, 172, 195, 269, 289, 290, 294, 296, 297, 298, 301, 303, 308, 313, 315, 431, 461, 512, 517
Isis   214
Istros   3, 5
    assemblage compared to that at Olbia   122, 127–128, 129, 136, 301, 303, 314, 315, 432, 465, 512
    decoration found at   122, 127–128, 129, 315
    excavation and contexts at   510, 511
    mould found at   454
    mouldmade bowls found at   50, 136, 154, 157, 261, 262, 267, 272, 432, 465, 489, 503, 504, 512
    previous publication of mouldmade bowls from   453, 511
    river. See Danube
    self-sufficiency of   49
    supplementary shapes found at   61, 512
Italo-Megarian mouldmade vessels
    bowls   3, 10, 15, 20, 32–33, 35, 118, 119, 460
    supplementary shapes   56, 57
Ithaka   33

ivy
    bundled leaves (wall motif)   153
    leaf (wall motif)   211, 270, 271, 303
    wreath (wall motif)   120–121, 122, 130, 269, 300, 313
    See also scroll decoration, acanthus-vine-ivy scroll
ivy-berry cluster
    medallion motif   130, 155, 172, 269
    rim motif   306
    wall motif   211, 270

Jansová, L.   168, 213
jewellery pendants (rim motif)   289, 296, 300, 306
judgement of Paris (wall motif)   117–118, 290, 310
jug/juglet
    mouldmade   14, 53, 55, 56, 58, 61, 135, 136, 154, 172, 195, 323, 456, 503, 540
    wall motif   205

K (Ephesian potter)   44, 294, 319
Kaikos valley   146, 261, 272
Kalašnik, J.P.   516
kalathos, moldmade   60
Kalos Limen   520
kantharos
    mouldmade   57, 135, 290. See also Olbia kantharos
    wall motif   170, 171, 205
    wheelmade   36
Kapošin, S.I.   495
Karasev, A.N.   493, 495, 498, 502
Kara Tobe   272, 517
Karjaka, A.V.   500
Kastanjan, E.G.   532, 534
Kaystros River   51
Kazarma (Chersonesos)   516–517
Kepoi   IX, 56, 60, 61, 432, 453, 456, 540
Kerameikos. See Athens
Kerberos (wall motif)   117
Kerč   272, 453, 464, 528
    Historical Museum   453, 522, 528, 538
    History and Culture Reserve   532, 534, 535, 538
Kerkinitis   517, 520
Kerynian hind (wall motif)   117
Ketios Valley workshops   153, 156
Ketos (wall motif)   204
kiborion   7, 106–107
Kiev Historical Museum   502
kilns   39, 153
Kirbeis (Kymean potter)   6, 14, 15, 42, 45, 50, 168, 169, 172, 192–193, 195–198, 199–213 *passim*, 498, 502, 510, 516, 540
kiss   112, 114–115. See also Eros and Psyche
kithara   194, 205, 206
    played by Eros   199, 200, 307
    played by Orpheus   112, 114
Kizericki, G.E.   501
Kleagoras (Argive potter)   117

Knidian moldmade vessels
    Athenian influence on   19, 431
    chronology   432
    decoration   116, 122, 124, 125, 128, 169, 431–432
    distribution   6, 15, 16, 48, 148, 213, 432, 441, 455, 504, 511, 512, 516, 517, 523
    fabric and shape   19, 431
    moulds   125, 431
    scale of production   46
Knidian rouletted bowls/cups   15, 261, 431, 432, 510n2, 512, 523
Knipovič, T.N.   495
Kögler, P.   XI
Koroneia survey (Boiotia)   28, 135
Kovalenko, S.A.   10, 453, 459, 464, 538
Kozani   60
Kozub, J.I.   495
Kra(...) (potter)   41
Krapivina, V.V.   493, 495, 501
krater
    mouldmade   14, 16, 53, 54, 55, 57, 59–60, 117, 135, 268, 287, 289, 290, 301, 323, 324
    wall motif   33, 108, 119, 124, 130, 205, 270, 271, 290, 295, 309, 311, 314
krateriskos, moldmade   57
Krinički, funerary offering trench at   122, 136, 464, 465
krotala, played by Eros   307
Kryžickij, S.D.   495
Künzl, S.   40–42, 146
Kurgan 14, funerary meal at (Kepoi)   540
Kybele. See Meter Theon
Kyme (Amazon founder hero)   215
Kyme (city)   50, 146, 168, 213–215
Kyme, Workshop A   42, 57, 168–169, 171, 172–173, 197, 201–206 passim, 208–211 passim, 213, 258–260, 498, 503, 510, 512
Kymean mouldmade vessels   19–20, 42–43, 46, 50, 168, 170–171, 198, 213. See also Kyme, Workshop A; Meter Medallion Workshop; Paniskos Workshop
Kyzikos   50, 465

L (Ephesian potter)   44, 294
Lagona, S.   168
Lagynophoria   60
lagynos, mouldmade   14, 15, 53, 55, 56, 58, 61, 324
Lake Sinoe   510
la Marca, A.   168
Lamboglia, N.   51
Lambrino, M. and S.   510
lamps, made in same shops with mouldmade bowls   45
Larisa on the Hermos   193
Late Scythian Kingdom   493, 517
Latyšev, V.V.   192, 193
Laumonier, A.   11–13, 36, 194, 294, 511. See also Délos XXXI
Laumonier, volume 2   14–16, 60, 431

laurel wreath   121, 313, 324
Laurion   28, 119, 135
leaf (rim motif)   303
Lejpunskaja, N.A.   495, 500
Lemnos   115. See also Hephaistia; Myrina
Lerna   112, 114
Lesbian kyma (rim motif)   269, 301, 303, 314, 315
Leto (wall motif)   112
Levantine mouldmade bowls   5, 15, 19, 196
Levi, E.I.   493, 495, 498, 502
Libknechtovka village   272
Liburnia   10, 59, 116
lid, mouldmade   53, 56, 57, 60, 61
life-cycle model   23
lily (wall motif)   210
linear decoration   60, 104, 125–129, 130, 271, 292, 301, 319–320, 325
lion
    medallion motif   155
    Nemean (wall motif)   116, 290
    prey (wall motif)   115, 116
Little Eagles Workshop (Kyme)   42, 168
longevity of pottery   24–25
long-petal decoration   125, 127, 128–129
    on Aiolian mouldmade bowls   212, 269, 271
    on Athenian mouldmade bowls   135
    combined with other motifs   269, 290, 295, 297, 318, 320, 461, 462, 463, 498
    distribution (Pontic)   136, 512, 523, 535
    on Ephesian mouldmade bowls   289, 290, 292, 295, 296, 297, 301, 307, 314, 320, 325
    introduction and chronology   10, 127, 128, 155–156
    on Knidian mouldmade bowls   431
    mould for, found on Delos   16, 28
    on Pontic mouldmade bowls   461, 462, 463
    supplementary shapes with   56, 60, 61
lotus flower, parts of   104, 106
Lousoi   21, 33, 48–49, 53, 54, 60
Lucenko, A.   538
Lungu, V.   511
Ly(...) (Ephesian potter)   44, 293
Lyson and Kallikles, tomb of   127

M (Ephesian potter)   44, 294, 316
Macedonia   39, 56, 58, 60, 120, 127, 130
Macedonian mouldmade bowls   5, 7, 10, 58, 116
Macedonian shield   125–127
Macedonian-shield decoration. See Pendent-semicircle design
maenad (wall motif)   112, 114, 116, 290
Magna Graecia   115
Mahdia shipwreck   51
Mahler, E.   10, 453, 503
'Mainzer Workshop'   40, 41–42, 43, 45, 146
mantled dancing woman (wall motif)   116, 146, 154, 169, 202, 269, 294, 310, 323

manufactory   XI, 6, 38–39, 43–44, 46, 286, 288
Marabini Moevs, T.   33
Marti, J.   538
mask (wall motif)   130, 146. See also comic mask; Pan, mask of; satyr/silenos mask
Maslennikov, A.A.   453
Massa, M.   40
Massonneau, A.M. de, collection of   502
mass production   XI, 3, 37, 38, 39–40, 46, 50
Matei-Popescu, F.   511
Mavrogordato, P.A., collection of   194, 502
Mazarati, N.   495
Me(...) (Ephesian potter)   43, 44, 293
meaning and mouldmade bowls   3, 5, 6, 7, 130–131
measurement of mouldmade bowls   XVII, 549
mechanical copying   39, 41, 195–196, 197, 296–298, 325
medallion. See base, medallion
Medusa head (medallion motif)   128, 155, 205, 206, 296, 297–298
Megara   7, 25
Melidon (Ephesian potter)   43n3, 44, 293
Menemachos (Ephesian potter)   12, 43, 288, 289–292
    adoption of baroque-style calyx by   32
    chronology   X, 14, 23, 35, 324–325, 326
    decoration   116, 117, 118, 200, 286, 289, 294, 295, 298, 301, 303, 304–308 passim, 310, 313, 315, 316, 318, 319, 320, 321, 323
    influence of on Pontic Demetrios   290
    relationship to other Ephesian workshops   289, 292–296, 298
    signatures   41, 43, 44, 310, 315, 319
    supplementary shapes   59, 323, 324
    See also Olbia kantharos
Meniskou (potter's signature)   60
Mesambria, mouldmade bowls found at   108, 110, 267, 271, 272, 454
Metal bowls, ceramics as a model for   489
Metalwork, as model for ceramics   X–XI, 10, 15, 21, 25–26, 29, 32, 35–36, 39, 104, 118, 119, 128, 135, 155, 269, 316, 323–324. See also silver bowls
Meter bust (medallion motif)   42, 192, 193, 197–198
Meter Medallion Workshop (Kyme)
    chronology   50, 212–213
    decoration   108, 116, 119, 128, 170, 172, 192, 195–212
    distribution   15, 148, 192, 213, 214, 258–260, 454, 455, 503, 512, 516
    fabric and shape   19–20, 195
    influence of other production centers on   21, 196, 202, 203, 205, 212
    named potters of   192, 193–195
    place of production   10, 169, 192–193, 454
    scale of production   41, 42–43, 45
    signatures   42, 193–195

Meter Medallion Workshop (Kyme) (*cont.*)
    small bowl produced by   56
    See also Kirbeis; Possis; Zenodotos;
        Zenodoules
Meter Theon   198, 214–215, 495
Michałowski, K.   528
Miletos   29, 49, 110, 148, 213, 309, 316
Mithridates VI   61, 131
Moiragenes (Ephesian potter)   44, 45, 293
Mommsen, H.   193
Monogram PAR Workshop (Ephesos)
    chronology   x, 14, 23, 325–326
    contexts of products found at
        Ephesos   287, 288, 298, 314, 325
    decoration   32, 116, 117, 127, 298–301,
        301, 303–304, 305, 308–309, 310, 311,
        312–313, 314, 318, 319, 320, 321
    distribution (Pontic)   56, 213, 271, 326,
        498, 540
    fabric and shape   298
    products of found on Delos   12
    relationship to other Ephesian
        workshops   32, 288, 289, 292, 294,
        295, 296, 297, 298, 316
    signatures   24, 43, 298, 299
    supplementary shapes   55, 57, 58, 59,
        323, 324
Monogram potter (Argos)   117
Moragenes (Ephesian potter)   44, 45, 293
mosaics   106–107, 123
Moscow, State Historical Museum   502,
    540, 542
mould maker, identity of   40–41
moulds
    consequences of their use for
        production   24, 38, 39, 39–40, 45
    as evidence for place of production   18,
        38, 110
    found in Black Sea Region   49, 454,
        459–460, 489, 523, 529
    found on Delos   16, 28, 61, 135
    found at Ephesos   11, 45, 122, 125, 286,
        287, 288, 298, 314, 325
    found at other sites   20, 26, 28, 33, 39–40,
        45–46, 48, 49, 118, 119, 124, 125, 135, 138,
        146, 168, 170, 172, 193, 197, 270, 431, 432
    of the 'Mainzer Workshop'   40, 41–42,
        121, 146
    for supplementary shapes   53, 55–60
        passim
    taken directly from metal vessels   15, 25,
        29, 32
    trade in   20–21
    See also Appendix 4
mould/stamp generations   32, 199, 205, 208,
    210, 212, 308
Mount Mithridates   522
multiple rim friezes   104, 196, 269, 289, 290,
    291, 294, 297, 300, 301, 308, 314, 315, 316,
    318, 320, 431, 465, 512, 516, 523, 545
My(…) (Ephesian potter)   12, 43, 289,
    294–296, 304, 311, 312, 319, 321

Mycenae   49
Myrina (Aiolis)   56, 57, 60, 168, 169–170
Myrina (Lemnos)   20, 26, 28, 45, 119, 135
Myrmekion
    excavations at   459, 528
    mouldmade bowls found at   50, 108, 136,
        157, 194, 272, 432, 465–466, 523–524,
        528–529, 535, 538
    moulds found at   454, 460
    self-sufficiency of   49–50
    supplementary shapes found at   60, 323
myrtle
    leaves (medallion motif)   432
    wreath (wall motif)   10, 57, 120, 121–122,
        173, 206, 269, 291, 295, 300, 313, 324, 431,
        465, 498, 516, 523, 545
    wreath, miniature (rim motif)   305
Myrtus communis   121

N (Ephesian potter)   44, 294
Na(…). *See* An(…) or Na(…)
naja. *See* Wadjet symbol
name, ancient, for mouldmade bowl   7. *See
        also* kiborion
National Museum of Warsaw   528, 538
Neapolis   464–465, 517
necklace, 'spearhead'   306
'nelumbo' (wall motif)   28–29, 34, 36, 104,
    106, 155, 170, 209–210, 212, 270, 290, 291,
    294, 295, 316, 318, 320, 323, 498, 512
    filled   14, 28, 29, 32–33, 34, 36, 118, 119,
        120, 125, 155, 170, 269, 289, 290, 296, 310,
        315, 318, 324
Nelumbo nucifera   104–106
Neos Dionysos   130–131
net pattern (wall motif)   25, 56, 57, 125, 128,
    155, 289, 291, 292, 295, 301, 319–320,
    323, 431, 516, 523
network
    social   3, 25, 36
    pottery   36
    See also trade
network theory   21, 25
Ni(…)/NI (Ephesian potter)   12, 14, 44, 293,
    303, 305
Nikander   106
Nike
    apteros   111, 203
    racing a chariot   108–109, 291, 308
Nikolaev Historical Museum   501–502
normal distribution   21–22, 26, 27
Northern Greek mouldmade bowls   51. *See
    also* Macedonian mouldmade bowls
nymph   112, 116
Nymphaea lotus   104–106, 321
Nymphaion   453, 538, 540

Oak (wall motif)
    garland   206
    leaf   211
Oblique box (rim motif)   292, 306
Odessa Archaeological Museum   194, 454

Odessos   272
Odysseus   117, 202
Ogon'ki   50, 465
oil, perfumed   53, 61
oinochoe, mouldmade   53, 54, 56, 58
Olbia
    archives and museums   501–503
    assemblage compared to that at
        Istros   122, 127–128, 129, 136, 301, 303,
        314, 315, 432, 465, 512
    Bothros 11   x, 32, 213, 323, 326, 495–498
    chronology   325–326, 432, 503
    Cistern Л   x, 22, 24, 212, 271, 326, 498, 499
    excavations   493–495
    geography   5, 10
    House III-3   213, 500
    mould found at   49, 454
    mouldmade bowls found at   3, 5, 50, 109,
        121, 122, 127, 128, 129, 136, 157, 194, 262,
        267, 271, 272, 303, 309, 312, 314, 315, 316,
        320, 432, 455, 465, 493, 503–504, 512
    necropoleis of   59, 493, 495, 501, 502
    repairs at   456, 458
    Sector AGD   494, 495–498
    Sector B5   498
    Sector E   258, 262, 495, 502
    Sector NGF   493, 494
    Sector NGS   3, 213, 262, 454, 458, 493,
        495, 500–501
    Sector R25   267, 271, 432, 458, 493, 495,
        501
    self-sufficiency of   49
    supplementary shapes found at   53, 59,
        60, 61, 136, 323, 456, 503
    Western Temenos   32, 213, 493, 495, 496
Olbia kantharos   32, 33, 35, 36, 323–324, 497
Olbia situla   110*n*12, 111, 120, 121, 307, 501
olive wreath   121, 313
Orpheus and Persephone (wall motif)   33,
    112, 116
Orphic biography of Dionysos   120, 311
Olympia   32, 35, 36
Oriental/Semitic deities   121
owners' marks   40

Pa(…). *See* Ap(…) or Pa(…)
Pagenstecher, R.   25
Pairisades V   465, 523
palmette
    rim motif   26, 111, 171
    wall motif   119, 173, 208–209, 270, 294,
        311, 319, 324, 431
palm frond (wall motif)   171, 209
Pan (wall motif)   215, 270
    mask of   202
    saluting   21, 110, 130, 170, 215, 300, 309,
        323
Panathenaic Games   34–35
Paniskos Workshop (Kyme)   42, 168, 170, 172,
    197, 213, 215
Pan Mask Medallion Workshop
    (Ephesos)   289, 324

panther (wall motif)   289, 309
Pantikapaion
    excavations and earlier research   459, 522
    mouldmade bowls found at   110, 122, 127, 157, 272, 288, 309, 310, 432, 466, 523–524
    moulds found at   454, 459, 460, 523
    palace foundation trench   122, 136, 261, 262, 465, 522–523
    repairs at   456, 524
    self-sufficiency of   49
    supplementary shapes found at   60, 61, 323
Paphos   432
PAR. See Monogram PAR Workshop
paradeisos tes tryphes   36, 130
Parios (putative potter)   298
Paris (mythological character). See judgement of Paris
Paris (putative potter)   298
Parthenion   453
Parutine   493, 497, 502
Pârvan, V.   510
Patras   21, 33
'paw' (rim motif)   294, 296, 306, 319, 465
Pe(...) (Ephesian potter)   44, 293, 316
Peacock, D.P.S.   38, 39, 42, 43, 48
Pella, workshop at   39, 40, 45, 118
Peloponnesian mouldmade bowls   7, 10, 18, 28, 33, 48, 51, 115, 116. See also Argive mouldmade vessels; Corinthian mouldmade vessels
pendent drop (wall motif)   211
pendent-semicircle design   10, 25, 125–128, 129, 130, 155, 156, 196, 212, 213, 289, 291, 301, 305, 306, 309, 314, 319, 323, 324, 325, 431, 461, 498, 504, 512, 517, 523
Pergamene *Applikenkeramik*   118, 122, 146, 153, 156, 268, 270, 271, 272, 310
Pergamene mouldmade vessels
    Athenian influence on   19, 155
    chronology   155–156
    decoration   21, 115–125 *passim*, 127, 128, 129, 130, 154–155, 196, 197, 314
    distribution (Mediterranean)   14, 15, 49, 148
    distribution (Pontic)   108, 123, 157, 167, 213, 498, 503, 518, 523
    fabric and shape   146, 154, 268
    influence of on other industries   40, 148, 287, 321
    relationship to other Aiolian workshops   36, 148, 153, 169, 173, 195, 196, 205, 211, 269, 270, 271
    supplementary shapes   56, 57, 58, 59, 268
    See also Olbia situla
Pergamene sigillata ware   57, 146, 153
Pergamon
    Asklepieion   10, 122, 127, 129, 153n5, 156
    Athena sanctuary   122
    Great Altar   10–11, 122, 128, 129, 155–156
    gymnasium   153
    harbour   261–262
    Hera Basileia temple   123
    locations of workshops at   153
    mouldmade bowls found at   11, 272, 288
    moulds found at   146
    new designs introduced at   125, 127, 128, 129
    Palace V   123
Persephone (wall motif)   112, 114, 115, 120
Perseus   35, 126, 127
Petite rose spiralée (Ephesian workshop)   12
Petrova, A.   267, 271, 272, 454
Ph(...) [Greek Φ] (Ephesian potter)   43, 44, 293, 296
phalerae   489
phallus, feline (wall motif)   289, 297, 310–311
Phanagoreia   194, 454
Phanes/Protogonos   215
Philip V, coins of   125
Philon(nios) (Ephesian potter)   12, 14, 43, 44, 45, 293, 294, 295, 296, 305, 306, 319, 324, 325
phlyax. See Eros as phlyax
Pindaros (putative potter)   298
pine-cone decoration (wall motif)   124–125, 290, 291, 294, 296, 300, 306, 315–316, 431, 454, 460, 461, 463
Pitane   108, 261, 262, 272
Plagiaire (Ephesian potter)   12, 14, 292, 294, 325
plaque   206
plaster casts   36
plate, mouldmade   54, 60
Platek, S.   528
Plato   110
Pnyx. See Athens
Pokalkantharos   170, 171, 205
Pontic Kingdom   523, 542
Popeşti   489
Popilius, C. (Italian potter)   32–33, 35, 36, 45n5
Popillius Laenas, Gaius (Roman diplomat)   35
Porthmion   50, 136, 157, 271, 272, 453, 465, 466, 523, 529, 532–535, 538
Posei[...] (Ephesian potter)   40, 44, 194, 293
Poseidon and Amymone (wall motif)   112–114
Posi[...] (Ephesian potter)   44, 293
Posid[...] (Ephesian potter)   44, 194, 293
Possis (Kymean potter)   42, 92, 192, 193, 194, 195, 196, 197, 198, 199–213 (*passim*), 498, 502, 516
potters, travelling   26, 28, 39–40, 135
Pottier, E.   168
Praeneste, mosaic at Sanctuary of Fortuna at   106–107
Priapos   202, 271
price marks   40
Psyche. See Eros and Psyche
Ptolemaia at Athens   3, 25, 26, 135
Ptolemaic iconography   104, 119–120, 309, 310, 311
Ptolemaic ideology   x, 36, 58, 130
Ptolemy I Soter   120
Ptolemy III Euergetes   104, 311
Ptolemy IV Philopator   130–131, 311
Ptolemy VI Philometor   34, 35, 104
Ptolemy Keraunos   120
Puppo, P.   33
Puškin State Museum of Fine Arts (Moscow)   522, 523
Pydna, battle of   127, 129
pyxis(?), mouldmade   60

quantification   17, 25

rabbit (wall motif)   115–116, 128, 300, 309
Radovanu   489
Radt, W.   129, 156
Raeder, J.   53
ratio of bowl's height to diameter   19–20, 135, 195, 268, 290, 292, 294, 298, 460
red-figured pottery   24, 50
red-gloss wares   56. See also Çandarli ware; Pergamene *Applikenkeramik*; terra sigillata, Roman
reduced firing. See grey ware
Reinach, S.   168
repairs   xi, 32, 267, 456–458, 524, 529
Rhodes   35, 51, 56, 117, 213
Rhodian mouldmade bowls   117
rhyton, mouldmade   36, 53, 58, 108, 118
rim, wheelmade, height of   19, 20, 195, 261, 268, 460
rim pattern lacking   301, 308, 462
ritual preparation or scene (wall motif)   116, 154, 170, 171, 269
Rogers, E.M.   26, 36, 37
Rogl, C.   x, 40, 49, 286, 287, 301
Rome   35, 127, 153
Rosette
    frieze divider   169
    medallion motif   21, 29, 43, 130, 154–155, 170, 172, 197, 269–270, 289, 292, 295, 296, 297, 298, 300, 301, 312, 316, 319, 321, 325, 431, 463
    rim motif   26, 111, 289–292, 294, 296, 297, 298, 300, 301, 304–305, 306, 308, 314, 315, 462, 512
    wall motif   119, 125, 154, 170, 171, 203, 210, 270, 297, 311, 314, 316, 319, 320, 461, 462
Rosette échancrée (Ephesian workshop)   196
Rostovcev, M.   xi
Rotroff, S.I.   7, 24, 25, 26, 56
rouletting   269. See also Knidian rouletted bowls/cups
Ruminskoe   ix, 453, 456, 465, 542–543
Rusjaeva, A.S.   495, 497

sacred space, reference to   154, 155. See also ritual preparation or scene
Sagalassos   116
Salač, A.   168, 214
Samojlova, T.L.   53, 194, 500

Samos 21, 116, 287
Samothrace 56, 213, 498
Santa Sabina shipwreck 49, 51
Sardis
　mouldmade bowls of, inspired by Aiolian or Pergamene bowls 148
　mouldmade bowls made at 33, 109, 110, 120, 125, 128, 130, 197, 321
　moulds found at 20–21, 125
　self-sufficiency of 49
　supplementary shapes made at 54–55, 56, 61
satyr (wall motif) 32, 33, 110, 202, 290. See also Dionysiac trio
satyr/silenos mask
　appliqué 58, 59, 503
　wall motif 291
Saumakos 523
Ščeglov, A.N. 520
sceptre (wall motif) 291, 295
Schäfer, J. 10, 153, 168
Schreiber bowl 29
scroll decoration 104, 120, 130, 195, 269, 287, 291, 314, 318
　acanthus and acanthus-flower scroll (wall motif) 270, 295, 297, 312, 535
　acanthus-vine-ivy scroll (wall motif) 130, 300, 312
　acanthus-vine scroll (wall motif) 23, 297, 300, 312, 313, 316, 512, 523, 540
　full-body scroll (wall motif) 297, 300, 312, 325, 498
　miniature (rim motif) 289, 290, 291, 292, 297, 300, 305, 312, 321
　stylized scroll (wall motif) 289, 291, 300, 312, 316, 431, 523
Scythians 483, 517, 520, 523
Seleucids 34–35, 131, 153
self-sufficiency 47, 48–49, 465, 523, 529
Semele 112, 120
Semenov-Zuser, S.A. 493–494
Severo Zelenskoe. See Volna 1
shapes of mouldmade bowls 12, 19–20, 20–21, 43, 135, 146, 154, 155, 170, 172, 195, 261, 267–268, 287, 290, 294, 298, 325, 431, 460, 489
sharing of stamps 42–43, 169, 171, 198–199, 298
shell (appliqué) 59, 268
ship (wall motif) 117, 202
Si(…)/CI (Ephesian potter) 12, 14, 44, 196, 293, 294, 295, 319, 325
Siebert, G. 14, 18, 168, 172
signatures on mouldmade bowls 6, 19, 23, 33, 38, 40–45, 60, 192, 193–195, 286, 288, 289–290, 292–294, 296, 310, 315–316, 319, 320, 325, 454, 459, 462, 463
silver bowls 28–29, 31, 32, 107
single rim frieze 122, 195, 289, 294, 301, 308, 313, 314, 315, 316, 318, 461
Sinope 516

sistrum (wall motif) 291, 307
situla, mouldmade 53, 55, 58–59, 154, 287, 290, 324. See also Olbia situla
skeleton (wall motif) 128, 131, 320
Skiluros 493
Skylla (wall motif) 117, 120, 155, 202
skyphos, mouldmade 14, 53, 55, 57, 172, 301, 323, 324, 325
Slavin, L.M. 493, 495, 502
small bowl, mouldmade 53, 54, 55, 56, 61, 135, 136, 154, 172, 195, 287, 290, 301, 323, 456, 503
Smyrna 146, 193, 213
Smyrna Workshop (Kyme) 42, 168
Sokolova, O.Ju. 453
Sokol'skij, N. 540, 542
Sorokina, N. 540
Spartokid dynasty 523, 540
specialization 38, 39, 41, 45, 46, 324
Sperlonga 117
Spratt, D.A. 26
S-spirals
　rim motif 26, 111, 290, 291, 303, 308
　wall motif 320
stacking in the kiln 19, 170, 172, 195, 267, 286, 325, 512
stacking ring 19, 40
stag (wall motif) 115, 204
stamp (punch) for producing molds 33, 40, 41
stamps, copying of 21, 195, 197, 296, 325
star, eight-pointed (medallion motif) 297
stemmed bowl, mouldmade 57, 135
Strabo 51, 106–107
Stranja 272
Sudarev, N.I. 542
Südtor Workshop (Ephesos) 19, 287–288, 325
Sulla, destruction of Athens by 135
sunburst
　rim motif 292
　wall motif 311
sun wheel (wall motif) 125, 212, 289, 306, 319
supplementary shapes 7, 14, 15, 53–62, 135, 136, 172, 268–269, 287, 289, 301, 323–324, 325, 456, 503, 512, 528, 535
Šurgaja, I.G., typology of 459, 461
symplegma (wall motif) 36, 118–119, 146, 153, 269, 271, 290, 291, 307, 310, 324. See also coitus a tergo; Eros and Psyche
Syntagma Square (Athens) 45, 135
syntax, as applied to mouldmade bowl decoration 6, 21, 170, 172, 195, 298
syrinx, played by Eros or Pan 200, 215, 270, 307

tablets, gold 115
tainia (wall motif) 121, 122, 123, 124, 125, 130, 154, 197, 204–205, 206, 295, 311, 314
Taman' Peninsula 465, 540, 542, 545

Tel Dor 288
tendrils, stylized (rim motif) 269, 271
terminology 7, 104–106
terracotta figurines, made in same shops with mouldmade bowls 45
terra sigillata, Roman 58, 269, 272. See also Çandarli ware
Thasos 213
Theodosia 432, 464
Theophrastos 106
Thessaloniki 110
Thessaly 115
Third Macedonian War 127
Thompson, H.A. 129, 135
Thrace 58
thunderbolt (wall motif) 119–120, 289, 291, 295, 307, 309, 310, 311
thymiaterion (wall motif) 154
thymiaterion lid 57
Thyone 120
thyrsos-bearer (wall motif) 200, 202
Timur (cat 3272) 310
Tiryns 49
Titans 120
Tivoli 33, 35, 45–46
Tolstikov, V.P. 522
Tomis 272, 432
Torbali-Metropolis 110
torch (wall motif) 154
trade 3, 5, 11, 25, 36, 46–52, 288, 456, 504, 523
tree (wall motif) 211
trident (wall motif) 295, 311
tripod (wall motif) 154
trophy decorated by woman (wall motif) 111–112
twisted stem (wall motif) 211, 295
Tyche 198, 215
　of Antiocheia 118
tympanon 197, 198
Tyras 194, 465
Tyritake IX, 50, 127–128, 432, 453, 456, 538

Underworld 114–115, 120, 121
unguentarium, mouldmade 53, 56
urn, moldmade 55, 59, 61, 121
Uvarov, A.S. 502

Vachtina, M.Ju. 532, 535
Vases gris. See VG Workshop
vegetal decoration 104, 125, 136, 154, 270–271, 291, 300, 315–319
vertical fluting (wall motif) 56, 290, 320
VG Workshop (Ephesian) 12
　chronology 14, 289, 324, 325
　decoration 116, 196, 289, 305, 307, 309, 310, 318
　relationship to other Ephesian workshops 59, 289, 295
　supplementary shapes 289, 323
　See also Olbia kantharos

Vinogradov, Ju.A.   528
Vogell, A., collection of   324, 501
Volna 1   IX, 453, 456, 465, 540, 545
von Stern, E.   111, 112, 194, 493
Vulci   32

Wadjet symbol   107–108, 118, 270, 318
Walters Art Museum   465
wave meander (rim motif)   297, 298, 303
West Slope decoration   37, 58, 59, 125, 128, 135, 306, 324
white-ground pottery   156
Winter, A.   38
woman (wall motif)
    draped, frontal   202, 205, 206
    naked   202
    pouring liquid   202, 270, 271
    undressing   33
    with wreath   203
    See also mantled dancing woman; trophy decorated by woman
Workshop A (Athens)   24, 135, 136

Workshop Circle 1   43, 45, 50, 122, 123, 288–296, 303, 305, 310, 311, 313, 315, 316, 318, 319, 320, 326, 454, 460, 462, 464
Workshop Circle 2   43, 50, 122, 294, 296–301, 303, 316, 319, 510
Workshop of Bion (Athens)   24, 44–45, 55, 108, 135, 136
workshops
    individual   14, 38, 39, 42, 43, 44, 46, 199, 287, 290
    lifespan of   24
    means of defining   18–21
    nucleated   38, 41–43, 46, 169, 198–199, 286, 287
    organization of   38–39
wreath, encircling (wall motif)   104, 120–122, 130, 195, 287, 297, 314, 318
    See also ivy wreath; myrtle wreath
wreath, suspended
    medallion motif   197
    wall motif   124, 146, 154, 169, 206, 271, 297, 314

X [Greek Ξ] (Ephesian potter)   44, 294
Xenophantos (Rhodian eponym)   29
X's (rim motif)   307

Zabelina, V.S.   522
Zagreus   120
Zahn, R.   25, 125, 501
Za Rodinu. See Ruminskoe
Zenodotos (Kymean potter)   42, 192, 193, 194–195, 197, 198, 203, 206–213 *passim*, 498
Zenodoules (Kymean potter)   42, 192, 193, 194–195, 197, 198, 212
Zeus   112, 119, 120, 215
Zimnicea   489
Zin'ko, V.N.   538
Zoilos (Ephesian potter)   44, 293
Zolotarev, M.I.   516
Zopyrion   500
Žuravlev, D.   522, 540, 542

Plates

∴

PLATE 1   ATHENS (ATH) – FIGURAL

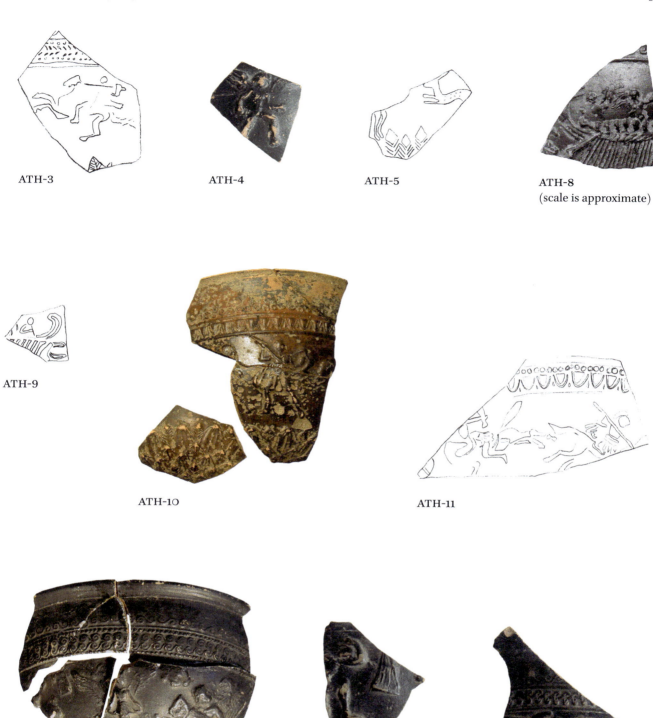

SCALE 2:3

ATH-16

ATH-17

ATH-18

ATH-19

ATH-20

ATH-21

ATH-22

ATH-23

ATH-26
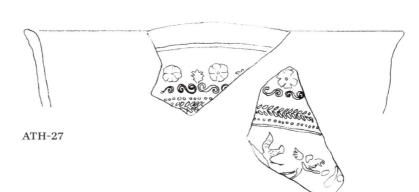
ATH-27

ATH-29

ATH-31

ATH-32

SCALE 2:3

PLATE 3   ATHENS (ATH) – PINE-CONE; CALYX

ATH-33

ATH-34   ATH-35

ATH-37

ATH-38

SCALE 2:3

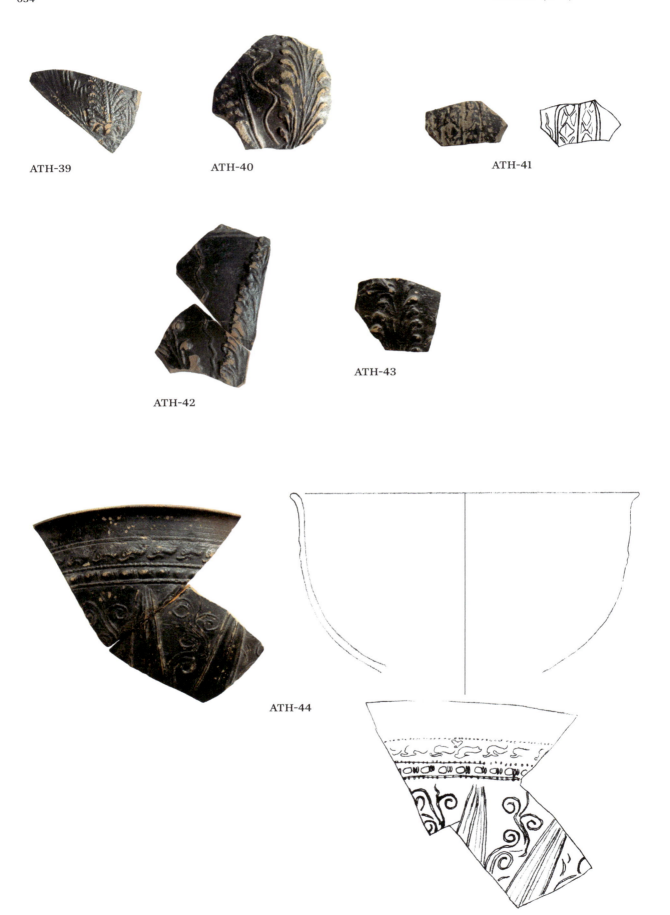

PLATE 5 ATHENS (ATH) – IMBRICATE; RIM FRAGMENTS

ATH-46

ATH-48

ATH-49

ATH-50

ATH-51

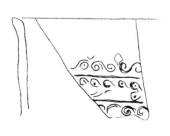
ATH-52

ATH-53

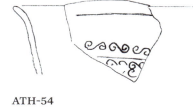
ATH-54

ATH-55

ATH-57

ATH-58

SCALE 2:3

ATH-60

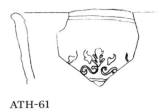

ATH-61

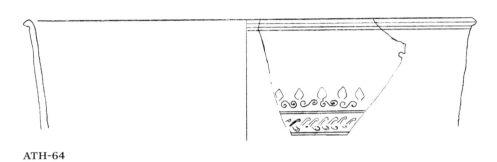

ATH-64

ATH-65

ATH-67

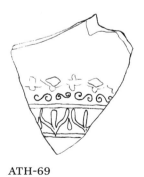

ATH-69

PLATE 7   ATHENS (ATH) – RIM FRAGMENTS; SMALL BOWL; JUGLET

ATH-70

ATH-72

ATH-74

ATH-75

ATH-76

SCALE 2:3

AIOLIS (AIX) – FIGURAL PLATE 8

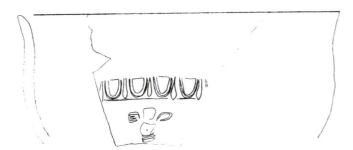

AIX-1

AIX-2

AIX-3

AIX-4

AIX-6

AIX-8

SCALE 2:3

PLATE 9   AIOLIS (AIX) – GARLANDS; VEGETAL   639

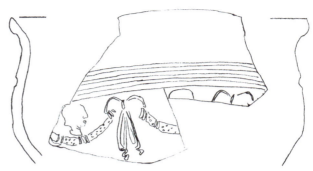

AIX-9

AIX-10   AIX-11   AIX-12

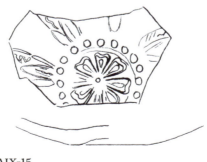

AIX-14   AIX-15   AIX-16

SCALE 2:3

AIX-17

AIX-18

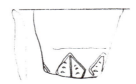
AIX-19

AIX-20

AIX-21

AIX-22

AIX-23

AIX-24

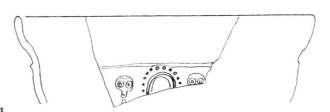

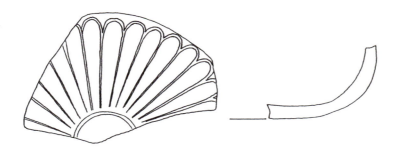
AIX-25

AIX-27

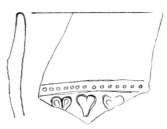
AIX-31

SCALE 2:3

PLATE 11   AIOLIS (AIX) – RIM FRAGMENTS; SMALL BOWL; LARGE CLOSED VESSEL

AIX-32

AIX-33

AIX-34

AIX-35

SCALE 2:3

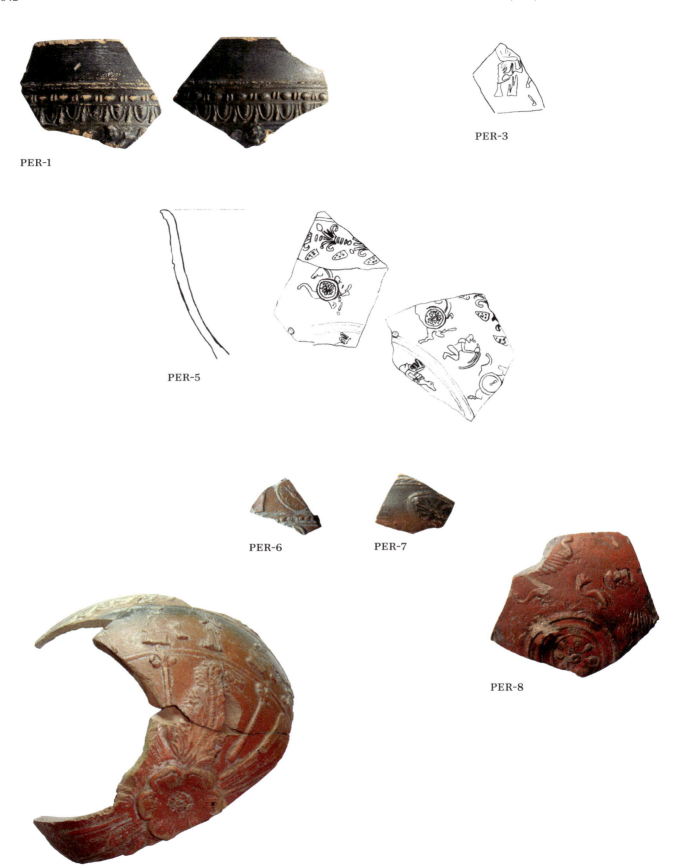

SCALE 2:3

PLATE 13   PERGAMON (PER) – FIGURAL   643

SCALE 2:3

644 PERGAMON (PER) – FIGURAL; SCROLL; MYRTLE WREATH PLATE 14

PER-23

PER-24

PER-26

PER-27

PER-28

PER-30

PER-31

SCALE 2:3

PLATE 15 PERGAMON (PER) – WREATH; CALYX

PER-32

PER-33

PER-35

PER-36

PER-37

PER-38

PER-39

PER-40

SCALE 2:3

646 PERGAMON (PER) – CALYX PLATE 16

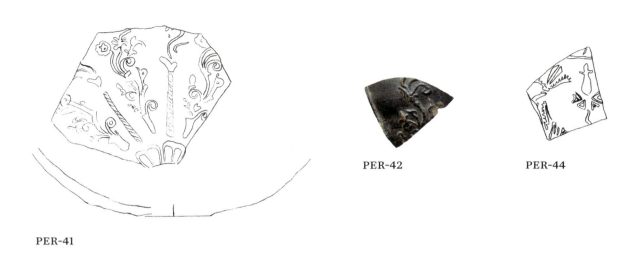

PER-41

PER-42

PER-44

PER-45

PER-46

PER-47

PER-48

PER-49

PER-50

PER-51

PER-52

SCALE 2:3

PLATE 17   PERGAMON (PER) – CALYX

PER-53

PER-54

PER-55

PER-56

PER-58

PER-59

PER-60

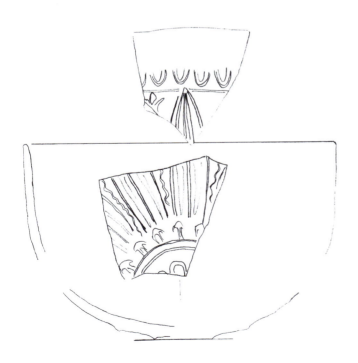
PER-61

PER-62

647

SCALE 2:3

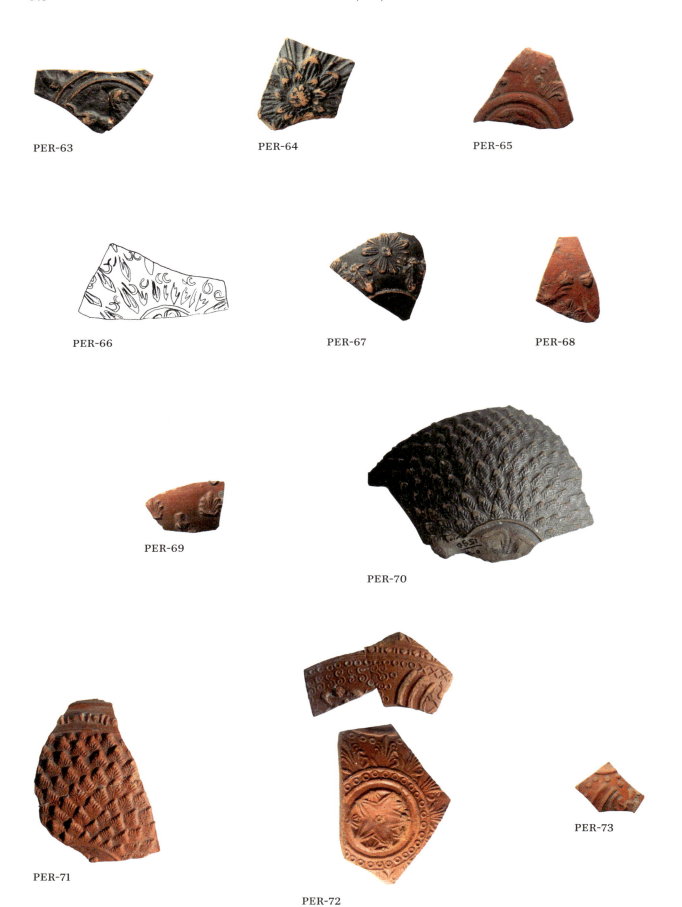

SCALE 2:3

PLATE 19   PERGAMON (PER) – NET PATTERN; LONG PETALS; RIM FRAGMENT   649

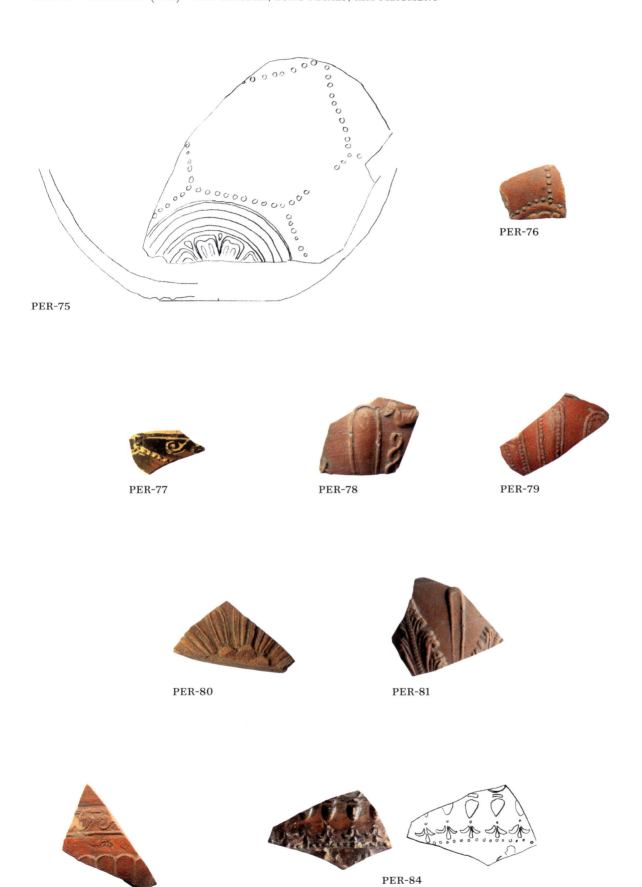

SCALE 2:3

650 PERGAMON (PER) – SUPPLEMENTARY SHAPES PLATE 20

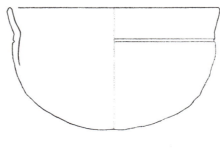

PER-86

PER-87 (scale is approximate)

PER-88

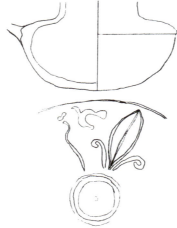

PER-89

PER-90

SCALE 2:3

PLATE 21   PERGAMON (PER) – SITULA

PER-91

PER-92

SCALE 2:3

KYA-1

KYA-2

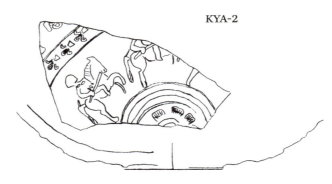

KYA-3

KYA-4

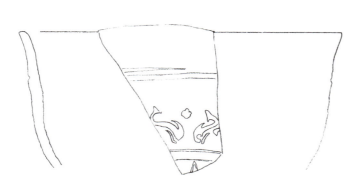

KYA-5

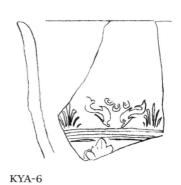

KYA-6

KYA-7

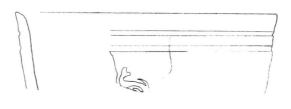

KYA-8

SCALE 2:3

PLATE 23   KYME I (KYA) – FIGURAL

KYA-9

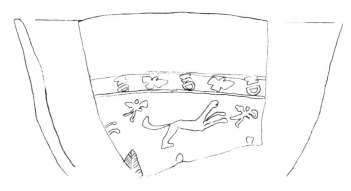

KYA-10

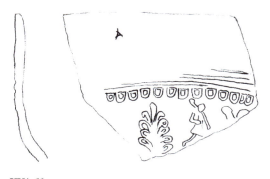

KYA-11

KYA-12

KYA-13

KYA-14

KYA-15

SCALE 2:3

KYA-16

KYA-17

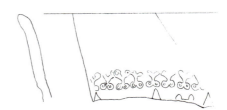
KYA-18

KYA-19

KYA-19-20-21

KYA-24

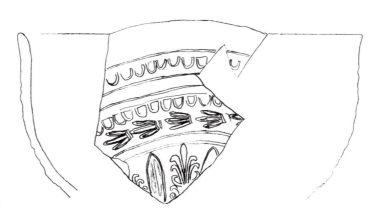

SCALE 2:3

PLATE 25   KYME I (KYA) – MYRTLE WREATH; GARLANDS   655

KYA-25

KYA-26

KYA-27

KYA-28

KYA-29

KYA-30

KYA-32

KYA-33

KYA-34

KYA-35

KYA-36

SCALE 2:3

KYA-40

KYA-41

KYA-42

KYA-43

KYA-46

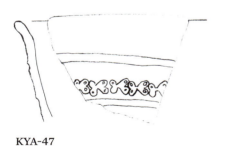

KYA-47

KYA-49

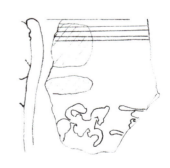

KYA-53

SCALE 2:3

PLATE 27 KYME I (KYA) – SKYPHOS; JUGLET 657

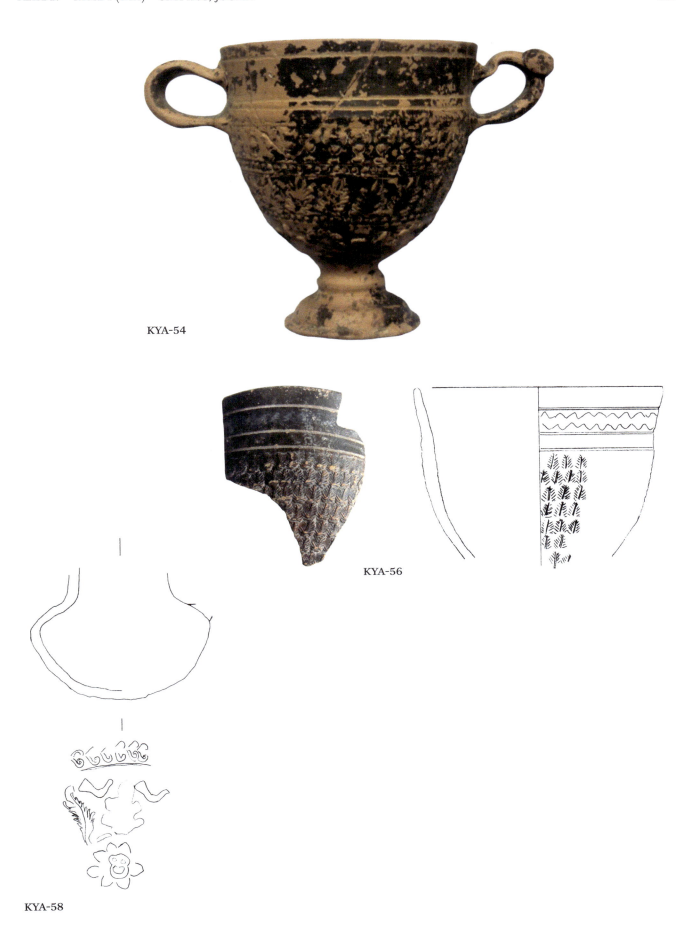

KYA-54

KYA-56

KYA-58

SCALE 2:3

KYX-1

KYX-2

KYX-3

KYX-4

KYX-5

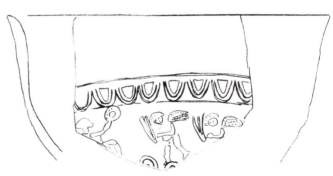

KYX-6

KYX-7

KYX-8

SCALE 2:3

PLATE 29   KYME UNATTRIBUTED (KYX) – FIGURAL   659

KYX-11

KYX-12

KYX-13

KYX-14

KYX-15

KYX-16

KYX-17

KYX-18

KYX-19

KYX-20

SCALE 2:3

KYX-21

KYX-22

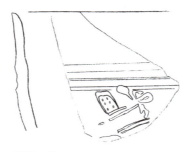
KYX-23

KYX-25

KYX-26

KYX-28

KYX-29

KYX-30

KYX-35

KYX-36

KYX-37

KYX-38

PLATE 31   KYME UNATTRIBUTED (KYX) – FIGURAL; SCROLL

KYX-39

KYX-41

KYX-43

KYX-44

KYX-45

KYX-46

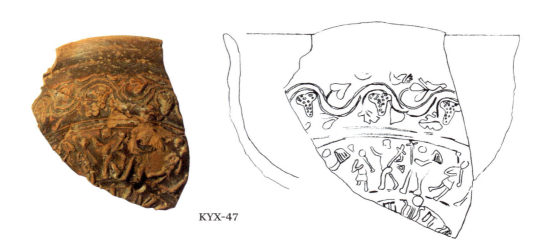
KYX-47

SCALE 2:3

KYX-49 KYX-50

 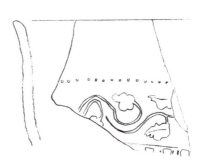

KYX-51

KYX-52

KYX-54

PLATE 33   KYME UNATTRIBUTED (KYX) – GARLANDS

KYX-56 (scale is approximate)

KYX-55

KYX-57

KYX-59

KYX-60

SCALE 2:3

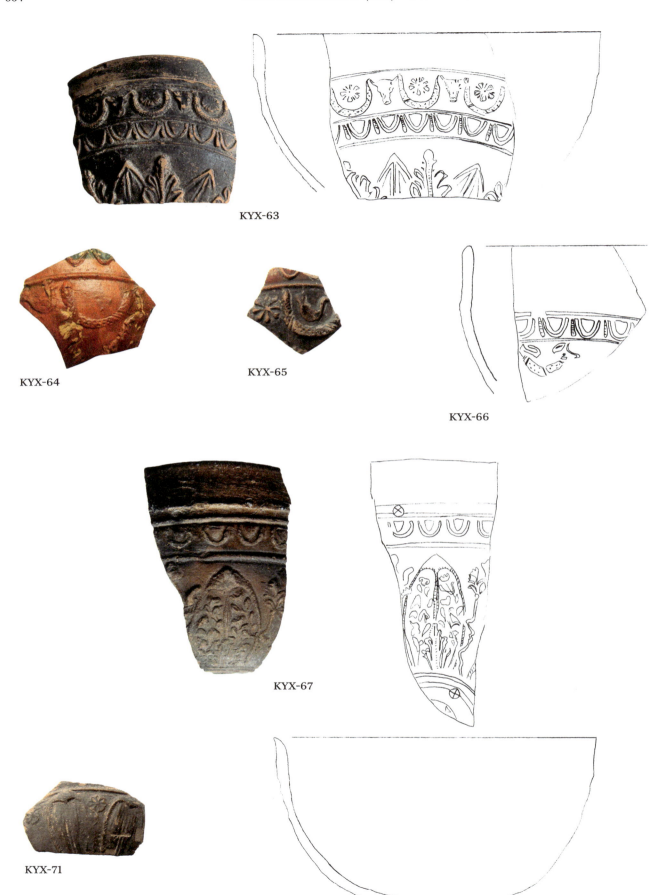

KYX-63

KYX-64

KYX-65

KYX-66

KYX-67

KYX-71

SCALE 2:3

PLATE 35   KYME UNATTRIBUTED (KYX) – CALYX   665

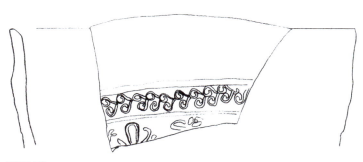

KYX-72

KYX-74

KYX-77

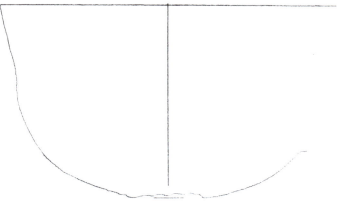

SCALE 2:3

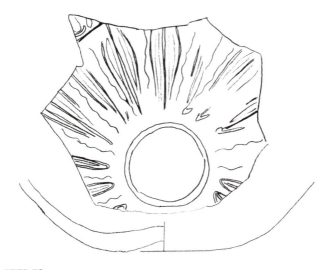

KYX-78

KYX-79

KYX-80

KYX-81

KYX-84

KYX-85

KYX-88

SCALE 2:3

PLATE 37 KYME UNATTRIBUTED (KYX) – LONG PETALS; RIM FRAGMENTS; SMALL BOWL

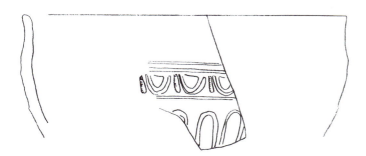
KYX-89

KYX-90

KYX-94

KYX-95

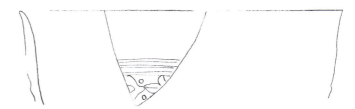
KYX-96

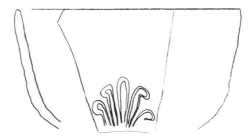
KYX-100

SCALE 2:3

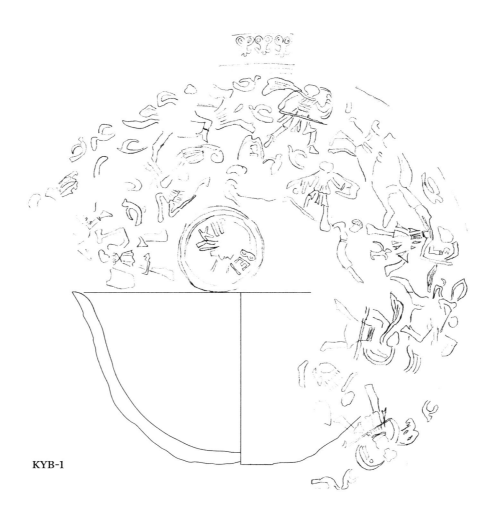

KYB-1

SCALE 2:3

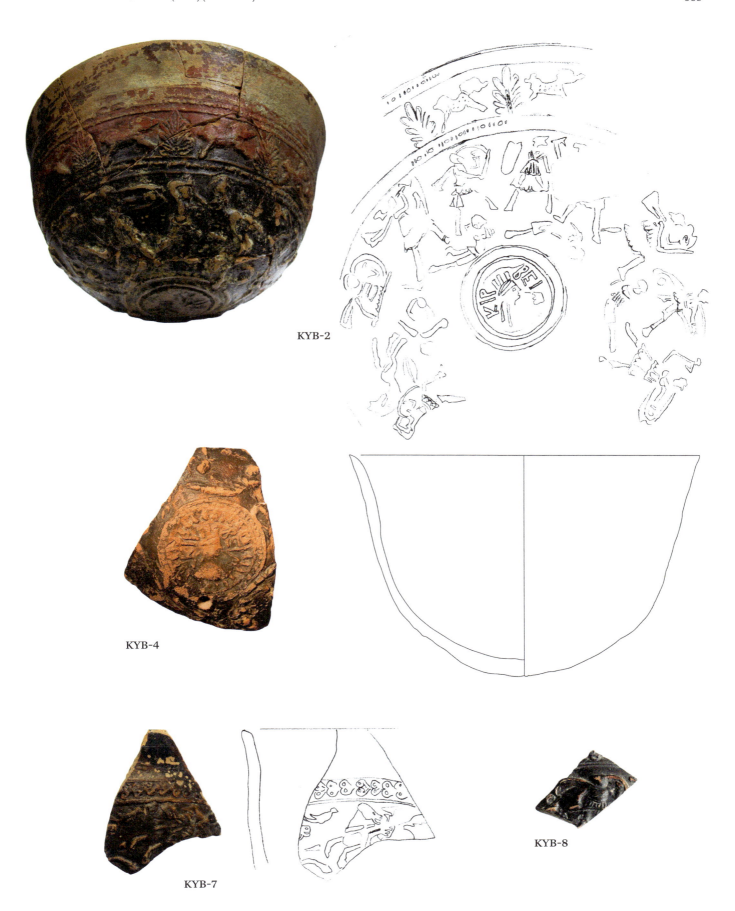

KYB-10 KYB-12

KYB-13

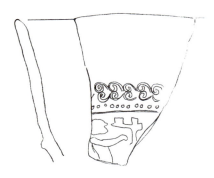

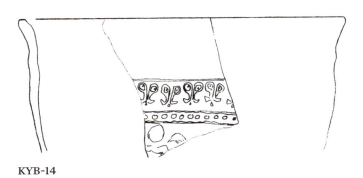
KYB-14

KYB-17

KYB-18 KYB-19 KYB-22 KYB-23

SCALE 2:3

PLATE 41   KYME, MMW (KYB)(KYRBEIS) – FIGURAL   671

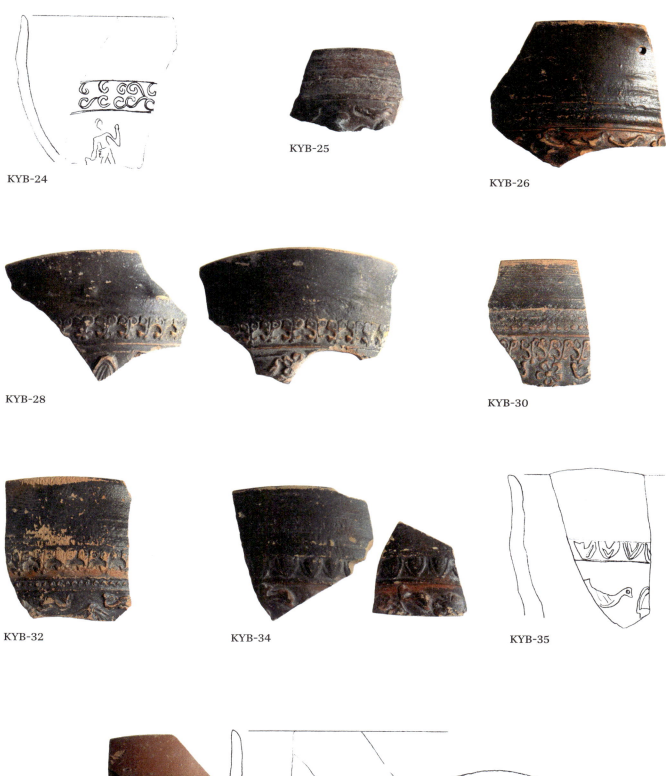

KYB-24

KYB-25

KYB-26

KYB-28

KYB-30

KYB-32

KYB-34

KYB-35

KYB-36

SCALE 2:3

KYB-37

KYB-39

KYB-40

KYB-43

KYB-44

KYB-46

SCALE 2:3

PLATE 43   KYME, MMW (KYB)(KYRBEIS) – FIGURAL   673

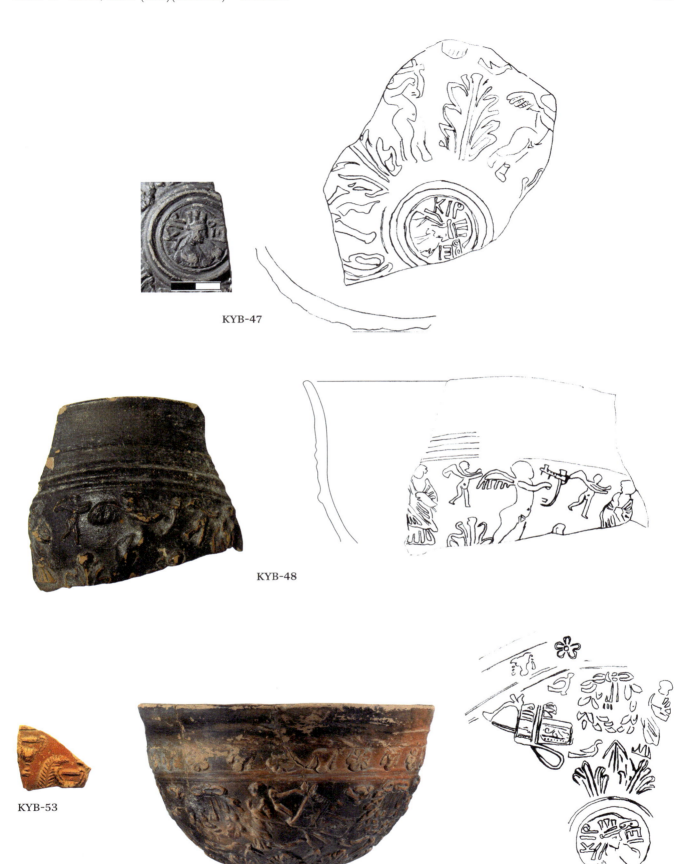

KYB-47

KYB-48

KYB-53

KYB-54

SCALE 2:3

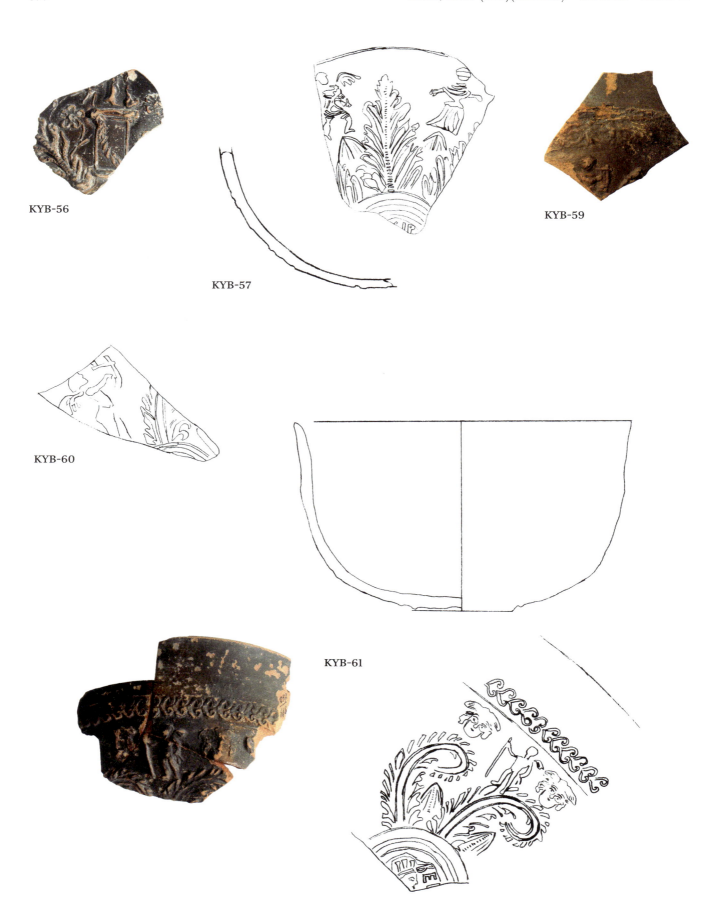

PLATE 45   KYME, MMW (KYB)(KYRBEIS) – FIGURAL

KYB-67

KYB-68

KYB-69

SCALE 2:3

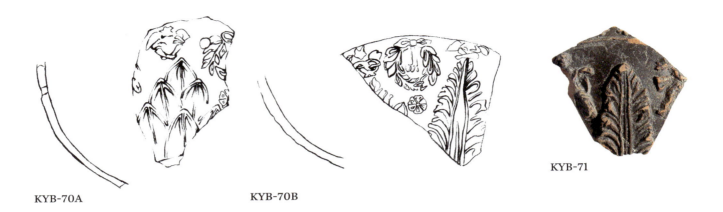

KYB-70A KYB-70B KYB-71

KYB-74 KYB-75 KYB-76

KYB-81 KYB-83 KYB-84 KYB-85

SCALE 2:3

PLATE 47   KYME, MMW (KYB)(KYRBEIS) – FIGURAL

KYB-86

KYB-87

KYB-88

KYB-89

KYB-90

KYB-91

KYB-92

KYB-93

KYB-94

KYB-97

SCALE 2:3

KYB-99

KYB-100

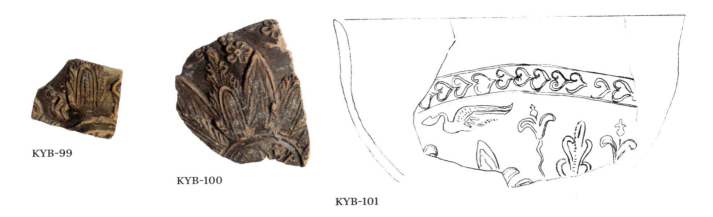
KYB-101

KYB-102

KYB-103

KYB-104

KYB-108

KYB-109

KYB-117

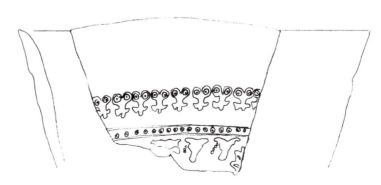
KYB-120

SCALE 2:3

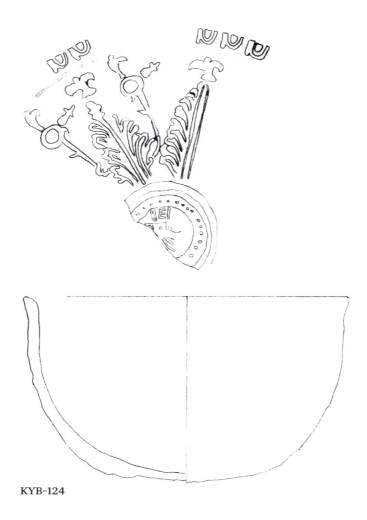

KYB-124

KYB-127

KYB-128

PLATE 51   KYME, MMW (KYB)(KYRBEIS) – GARLANDS

KYB-129

SCALE 2:3

KYB-130

KYB-132

KYB-133

KYB-134

KYB-136

KYB-137

KYB-140

KYB-142

KYB-143

KYB-145

PLATE 55   KYME, MMW (KYB)(KYRBEIS) – GARLANDS   685

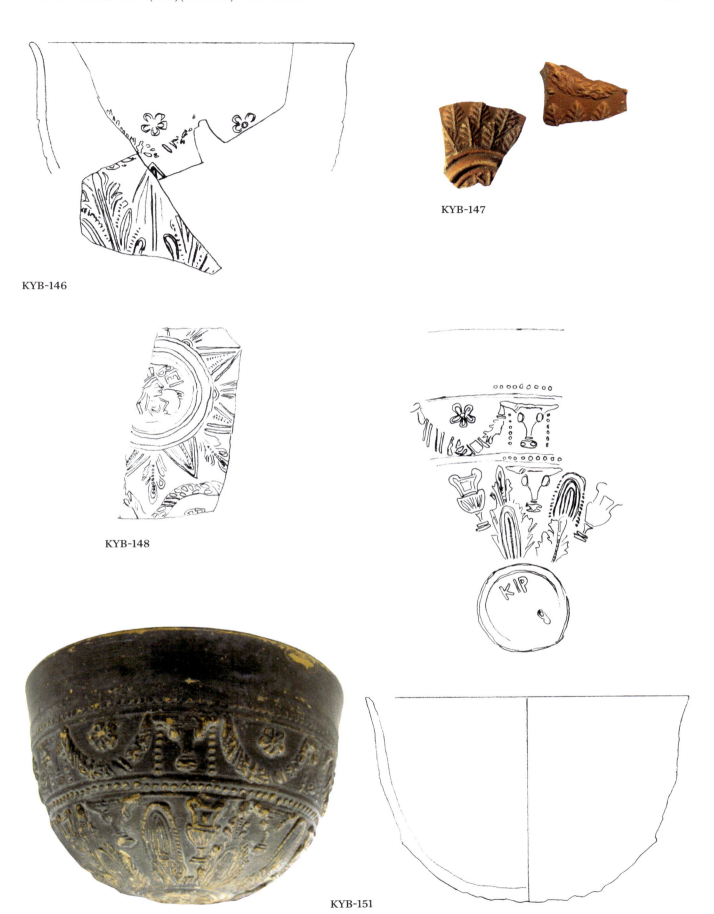

KYB-146

KYB-147

KYB-148

KYB-151

SCALE 2:3

KYB-152

KYB-153

KYB-155

KYB-157

SCALE 2:3

KYB-158

KYB-159

KYB-162

KYB-163

KYB-165

KYB-167

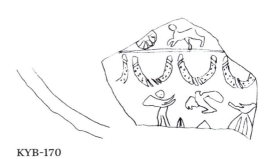

KYB-170

KYB-171

KYB-172

KYB-176

KYB-177 KYB-178

SCALE 2:3

KYB-179

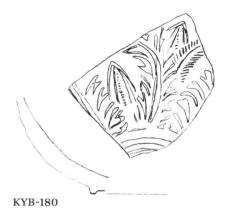

KYB-180

KYB-182

KYB-183

KYB-184

KYB-187

KYB-188

KYB-193

KYB-198

KYB-199

KYB-200

KYB-201

KYB-202

KYB-204

PLATE 61   KYME, MMW (KYB)(KYRBEIS) – CALYX

KYB-206

SCALE 2:3

KYB-207

KYB-208

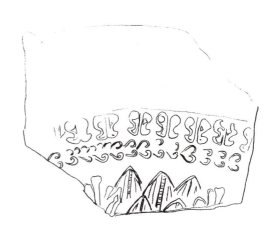
KYB-209

KYB-210

KYB-213

KYB-214

KYB-221

KYB-222

KYB-223

KYB-225

KYB-227

KYB-228

SCALE 2:3

PLATE 63   KYME, MMW (KYB)(KYRBEIS) – CALYX

KYB-230

KYB-231

KYB-232

KYB-233

KYB-234

KYB-235

KYB-237

KYB-238

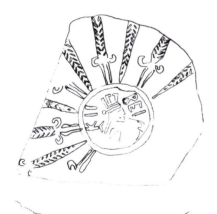
KYB-239

KYB-240

KYB-241

KYB-242

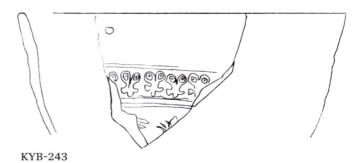
KYB-243

SCALE 2:3

PLATE 65 KYME, MMW (KYB)(KYRBEIS) – BASE AND RIM FRAGMENTS

KYB-258

KYB-259

KYB-260

KYB-261

KYB-266

KYB-268

KYB-271

KYB-272

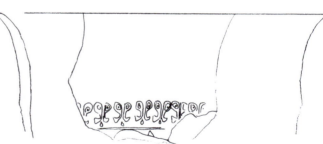
KYB-274

KYB-277

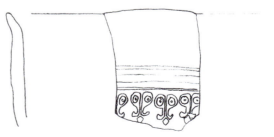
KYB-278

SCALE 2:3

KYB-284

KYB-290

KYB-291

KYB-293

KYB-296

KYB-299

KYB-301

KYB-305

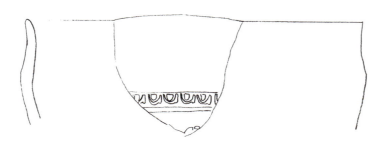
KYB-308

KYB-310

KYB-311

SCALE 2:3

PLATE 67 KYME, MMW (KYB)(KYRBEIS) – RIM FRAGMENTS; SMALL BOWL   697

KYB-312

KYB-314

KYB-315

KYB-317

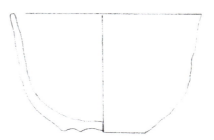

KYB-318

KYB-319

SCALE 2:3

KYB-320

KYB-322

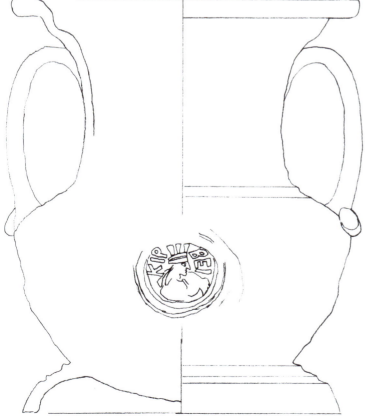

SCALE 2:3

KYB-325

PLATE 71 KYME, MMW (KYB)(KYRBEIS) – AMPHORA 701

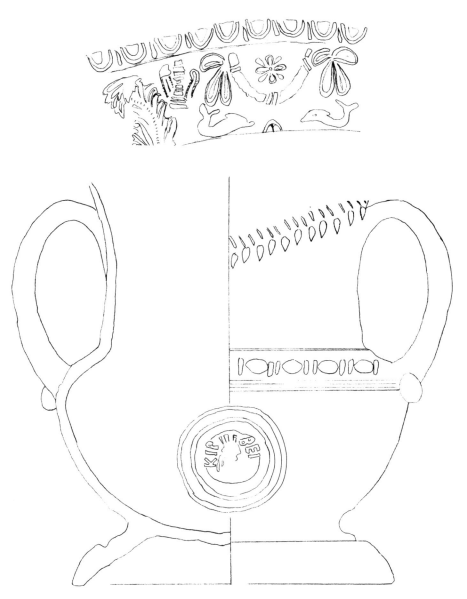

KYB-325

SCALE 2:3

KYB-326

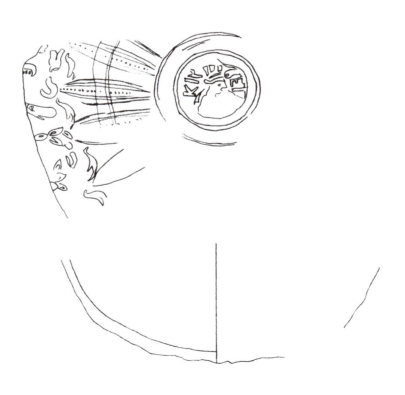

KYB-327

SCALE 2:3

PLATE 73   KYME, MMW (KYB)(POSSIS) – CALYX WITH FIGURAL DECORATION

KYB-330

SCALE 2:3

KYB-331

SCALE 2:3

PLATE 75   KYME, MMW (KYB)(POSSIS) – CALYX WITH FIGURAL DECORATION

KYB-332

KYB-333

KYB-334

KYB-336

KYB-337

KYB-338

KYB-339

KYB-340

KYB-341

KYB-342

KYB-343

SCALE 2:3

KYB-344

KYB-345

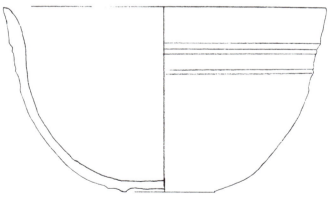

PLATE 77   KYME, MMW (KYB)(POSSIS) – CALYX WITH FIGURAL DECORATION

KYB-346

KYB-347

SCALE 2:3

KYB-348

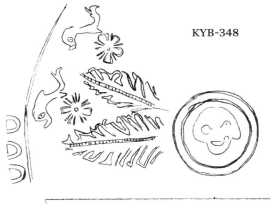

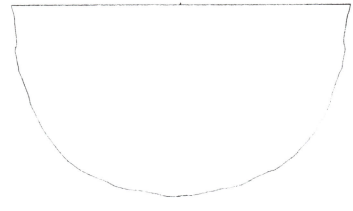

KYB-350

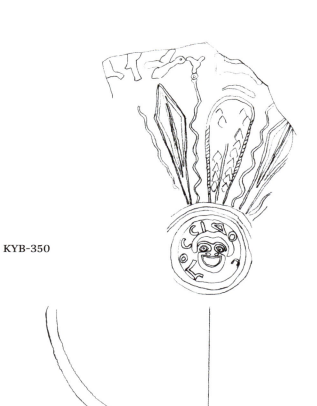

KYB-351

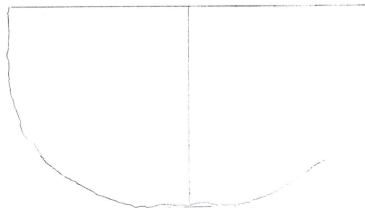

KYB-352

KYB-353

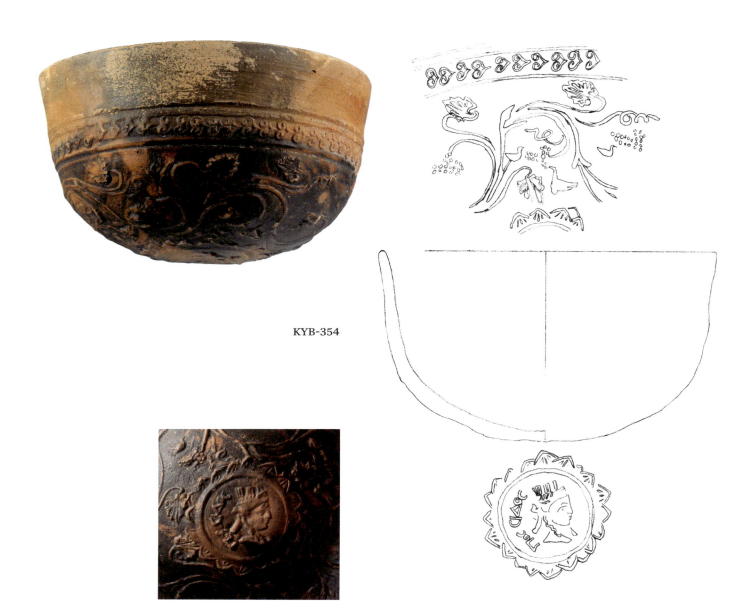

KYB-354

PLATE 81   KYME, MMW (KYB)(POSSIS) – SCROLL; GARLANDS; CALYX

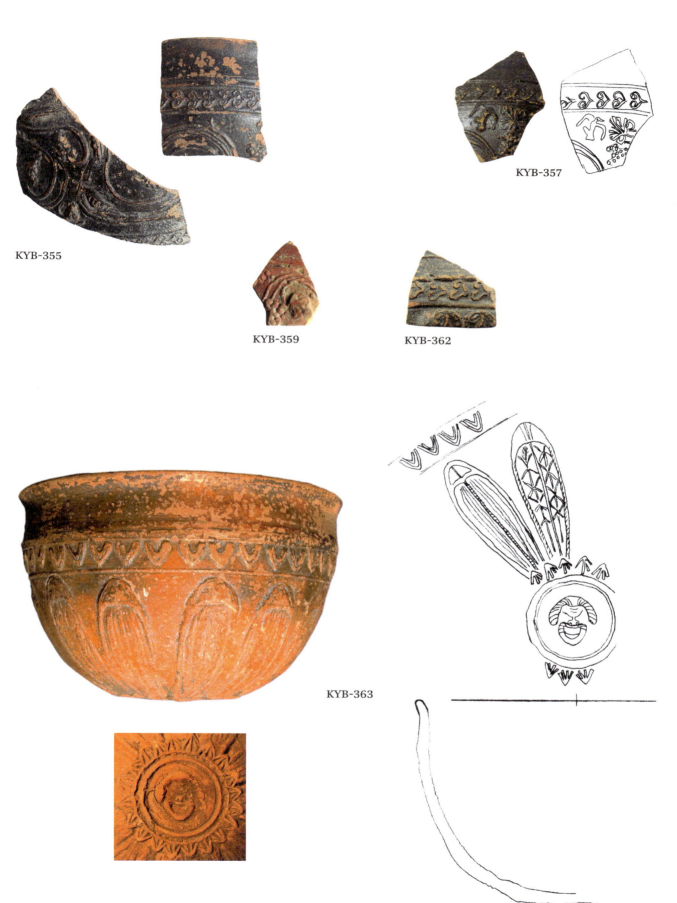

KYB-355

KYB-357

KYB-359   KYB-362

KYB-363

SCALE 2:3

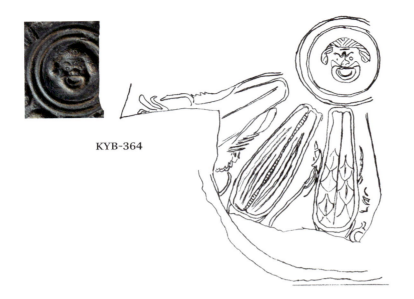

KYB-364

KYB-365

KYB-367

KYB-370

PLATE 83   KYME, MMW (KYB)(POSSIS) – CALYX

KYB-371

SCALE 2:3

KYB-373

KYB-376

KYB-380

KYB-381

KYB-382

KYB-383

KYB-385

KYB-386

SCALE 2:3

PLATE 85   KYME, MMW (KYB)(POSSIS) – LINEAR; BASE AND RIM FRAGMENTS; SMALL BOWL

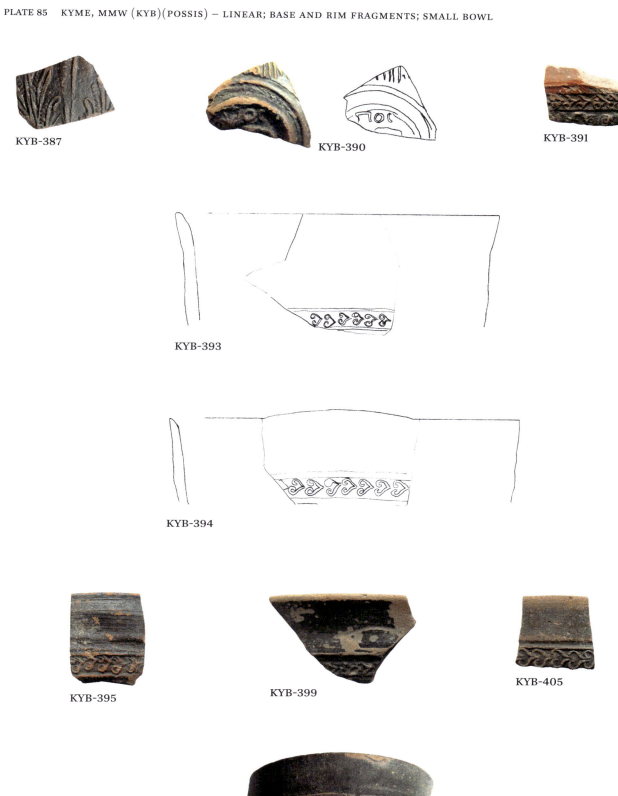

KYB-387

KYB-390

KYB-391

KYB-393

KYB-394

KYB-395

KYB-399

KYB-405

KYB-411

SCALE 2:3

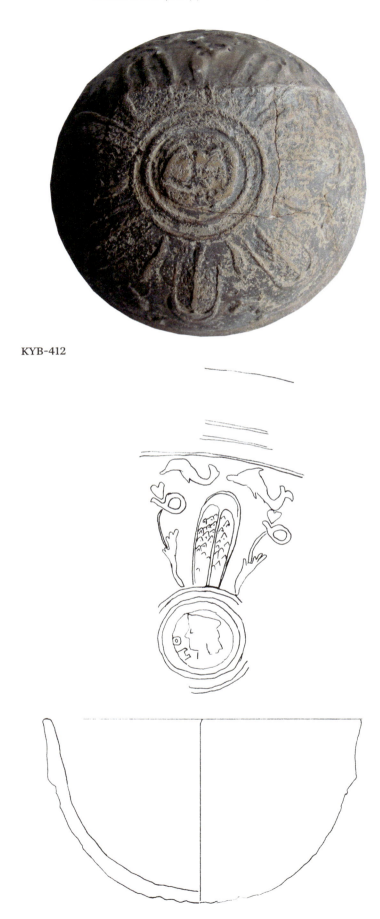

KYB-412

KYB-413

KYB-416

KYB-418   KYB-420   KYB-421

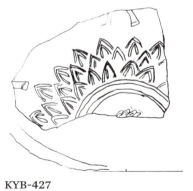

KYB-422   KYB-424   KYB-427

PLATE 89   KYME, MMW (KYB)(UNATTRIBUTED) – FIGURAL; SCROLL; CALYX

KYB-428

KYB-429

KYB-430

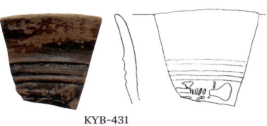
KYB-431

KYB-432

KYB-433

KYB-434

KYB-436

KYB-437

KYB-438

SCALE 2:3

KYB-439

KYB-440

KYB-442

KYB-443

KYB-444

KYB-448

KYB-450

KYB-452

KYB-455

PLATE 91   AIOLIS A (AIA) – FIGURAL; SCROLL

AIA-1

AIA-2

AIA-3

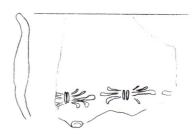

AIA-4

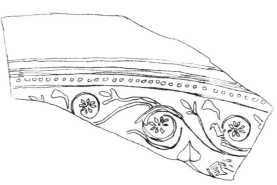

AIA-5

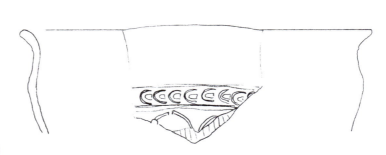

SCALE 2:3

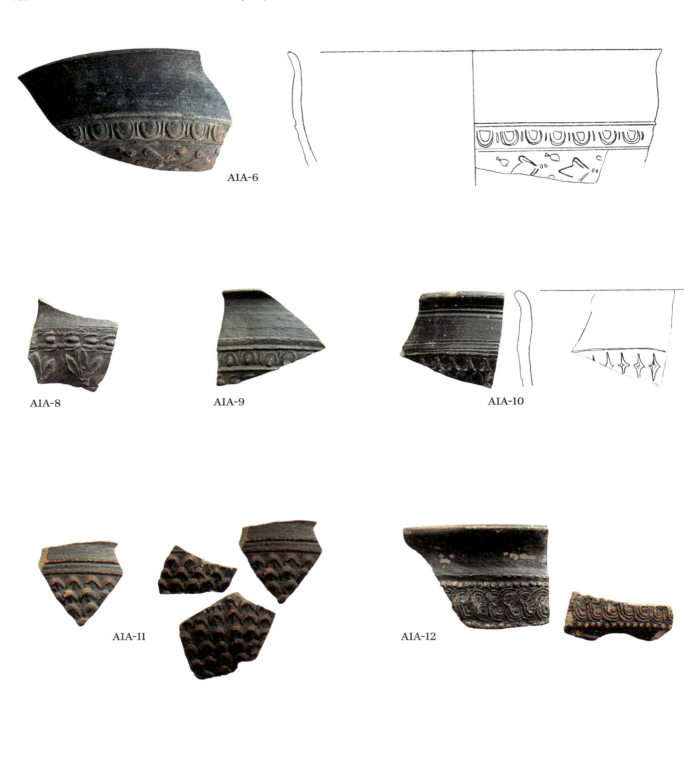

AIA-6

AIA-8　　AIA-9　　AIA-10

AIA-11　　AIA-12

AIA-13

PLATE 93   AIOLIS A (AIA) – LONG PETALS; RIM FRAGMENTS

AIA-14

AIA-16

AIA-17

AIA-18

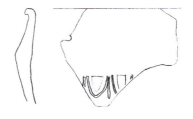

AIA-19

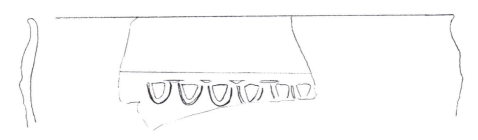

SCALE 2:3

AIA-22

AIA-24

AIA-28

AIA-29

AIA-30

AIA-31

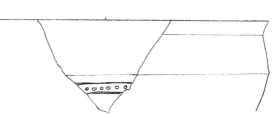

AIA-32

AIA-35

AIA-36

SCALE 2:3

PLATE 95   AIOLIS B (AIB) – FIGURAL

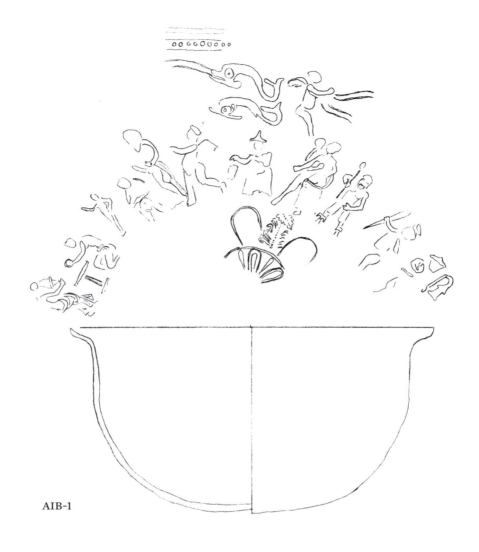

AIB-1

AIB-2

AIB-3

SCALE 2:3

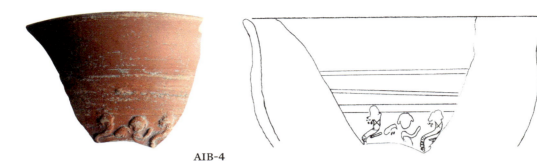

AIB-4

AIB-5

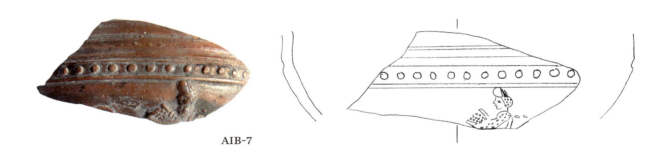

AIB-7

AIB-8

PLATE 97   AIOLIS B (AIB) – FIGURAL

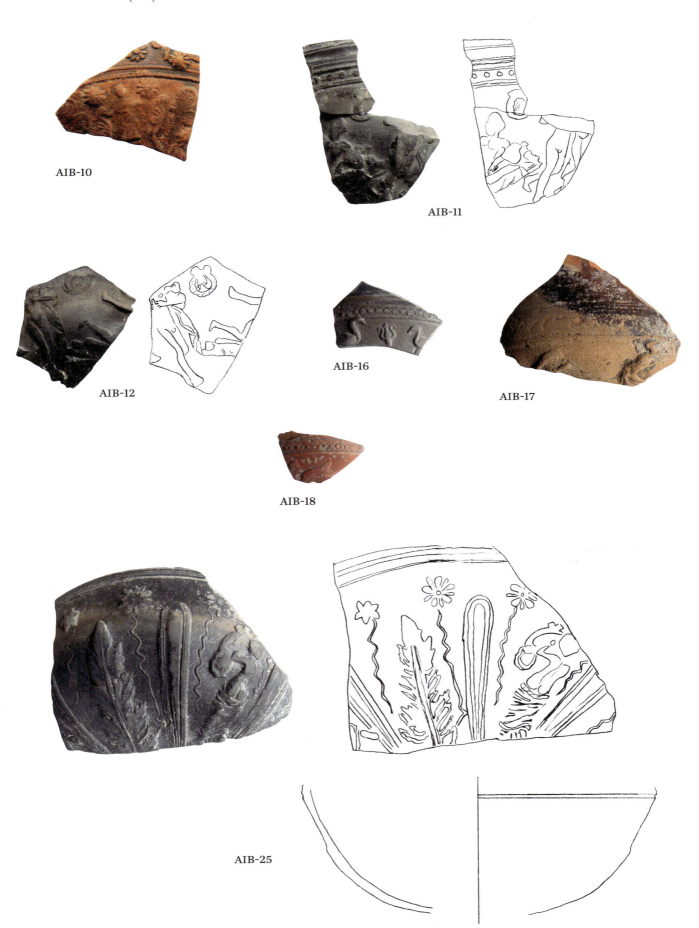

AIB-28

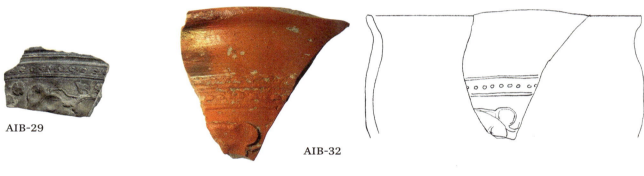

AIB-29 AIB-32

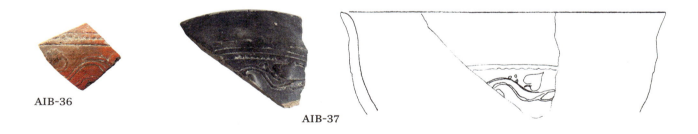

AIB-36 AIB-37

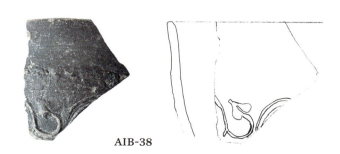

AIB-38

SCALE 2:3

PLATE 99   AIOLIS B (AIB) – SCROLL   729

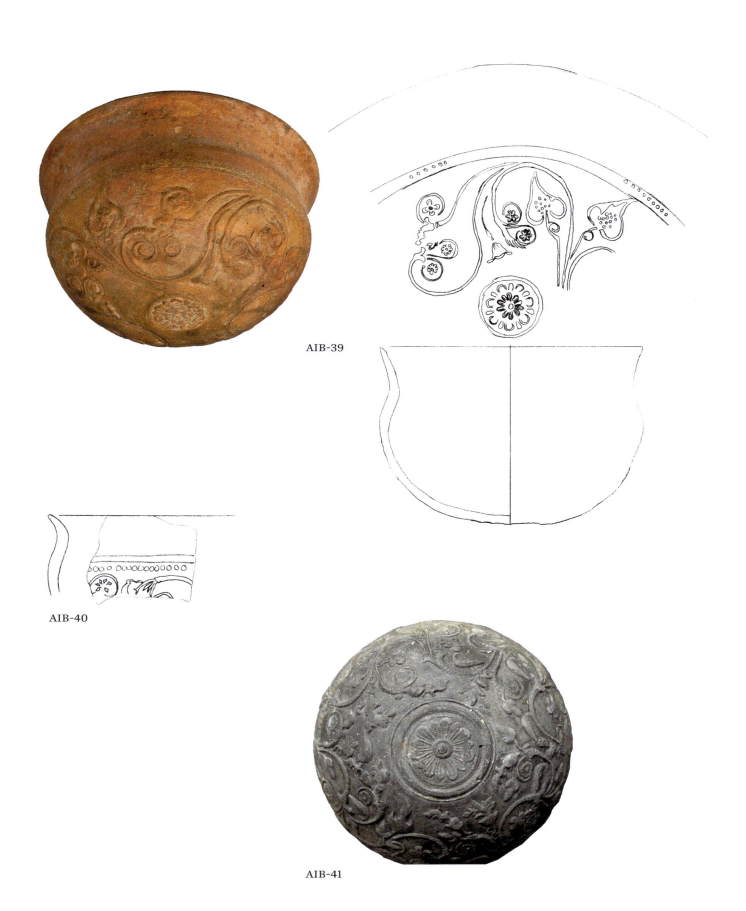

AIB-39

AIB-40

AIB-41

SCALE 2:3

730 AIOLIS B (AIB) – SCROLL; GARLANDS; WREATHS PLATE 100

AIB-50

AIB-53

AIB-56

AIB-59

AIB-60

AIB-62

AIB-63 AIB-64 AIB-65

SCALE 2:3

PLATE 101   AIOLIS B (AIB) – MYRTLE WREATH; CALYX WITH 'NELUMBO' AND LONG PETALS   731

AIB-66   AIB-67   AIB-68

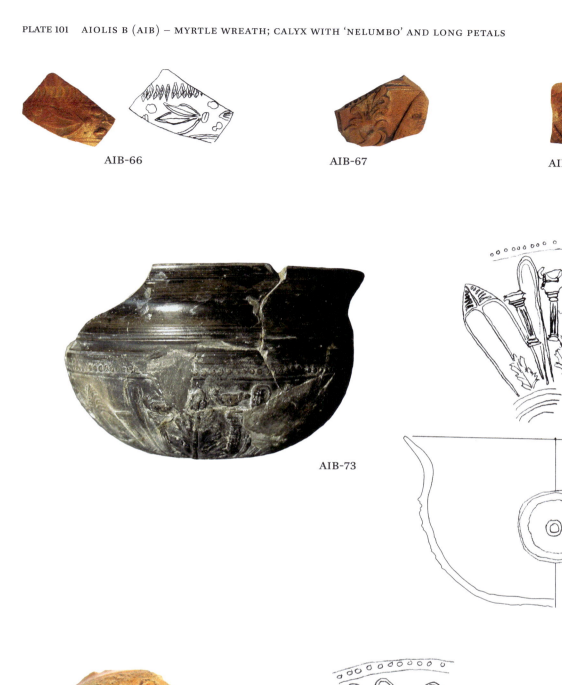

AIB-73

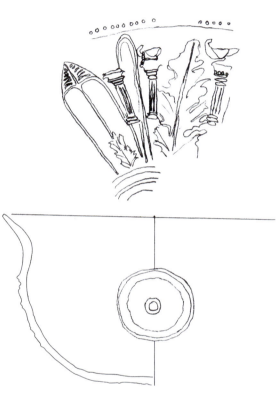

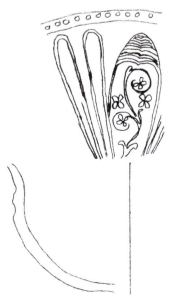

AIB-76

SCALE 2:3

AIB-77

AIB-78

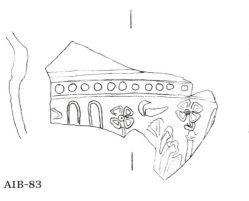
AIB-83

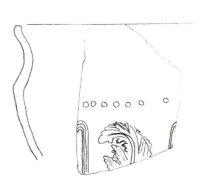
AIB-86

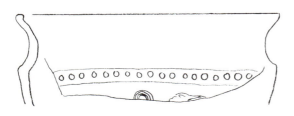
AIB-87

AIB-91

SCALE 2:3

PLATE 103   AIOLIS B (AIB) – LONG PETALS; RIM FRAGMENT; BOWL WITH SHELL FEET

AIB-93

AIB-100

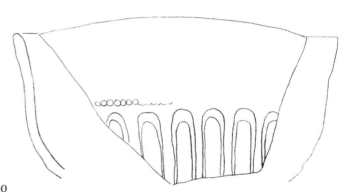

AIB-102

AIB-109

AIB-115

SCALE 2:3

734   AIOLIS B (AIB) – CHALICE   PLATE 104

AIB-116

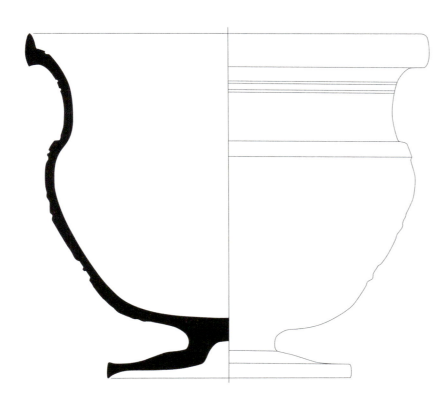

SCALE 2:3

PLATE 105   AIOLIS B (AIB) – SHALLOW BOWL WITH HIGH RIM

AIB-118

AIB-119

AIB-122

SCALE 2:3

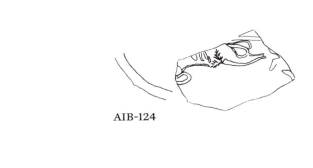

AIB-124

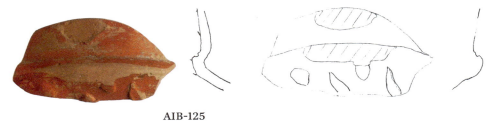

AIB-125

AIB-126

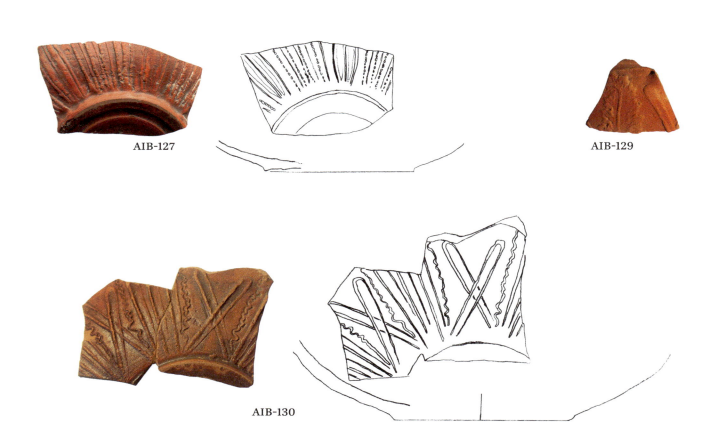

AIB-127   AIB-129

AIB-130

PLATE 107   AIOLIS B (AIB) – SHALLOW BOWL WITH HIGH RIM; CUP; BEAKER

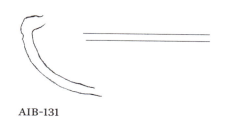

AIB-131

AIB-132

AIB-133

AIB-134

AIB-135

AIB-136

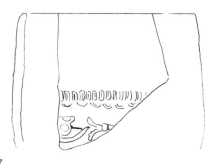

AIB-137

SCALE 2:3

738 EPHESOS (EPH) – EROTES PLATE 108

EPH-1

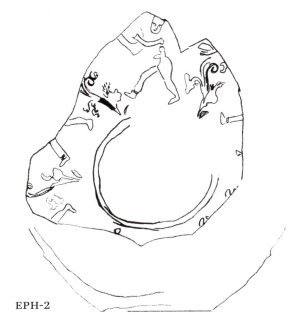
EPH-2

EPH-3

EPH-6

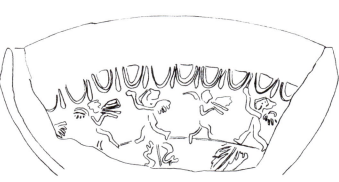

EPH-7

EPH-8

EPH-9

SCALE 2:3

PLATE 109   EPHESOS (EPH) – EROTES

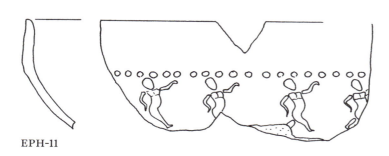
EPH-11

EPH-13

EPH-14

EPH-16

EPH-18

EPH-19

EPH-20

EPH-22

EPH-23

SCALE 2:3

EPH-24

EPH-25

EPH-27

EPH-29

EPH-34 EPH-35 EPH-36 EPH-37

EPH-41

EPH-42

EPH-43

EPH-44

EPH-45

SCALE 2:3

PLATE 111   EPHESOS (EPH) – EROS RACING CHARIOT

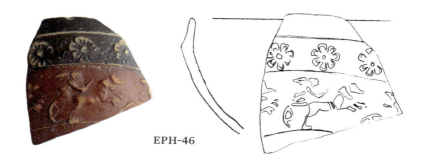
EPH-46

EPH-48

EPH-49

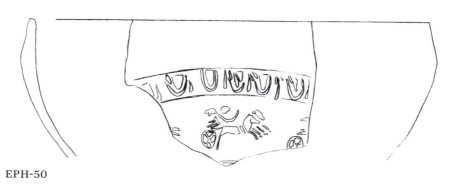
EPH-50

EPH-51

EPH-52

SCALE 2:3

EPH-53

EPH-54

EPH-57

EPH-58

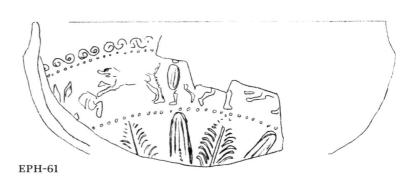
EPH-61

EPH-59

SCALE 2:3

PLATE 113   EPHESOS (EPH) – HUNT; ANIMAL FRIEZES

EPH-63

EPH-64

EPH-65

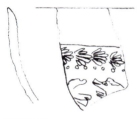

EPH-66

EPH-67

EPH-68

EPH-69

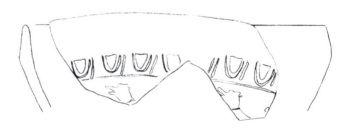

EPH-72

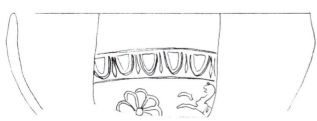

EPH-73

EPH-74

SCALE 2:3

EPH-75

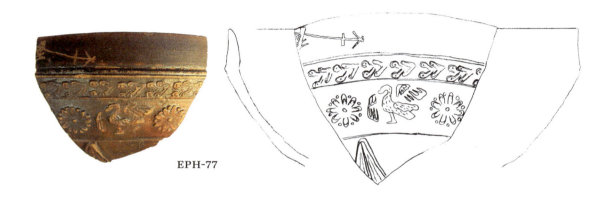

EPH-77

EPH-78   EPH-79   EPH-80

EPH-81

SCALE 2:3

PLATE 115   EPHESOS (EPH) – AMAZONOMACHY

EPH-82

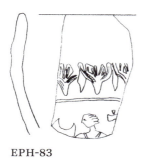
EPH-83

EPH-84

EPH-85

EPH-86

EPH-87

EPH-88

EPH-90

EPH-91

SCALE 2:3

746 EPHESOS (EPH) – BATTLE; MYTHOLOGICAL FIGURES PLATE 116

EPH-94

EPH-95

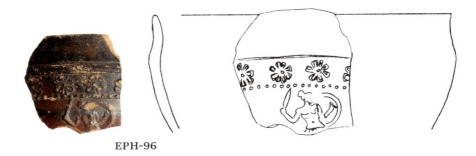
EPH-96

EPH-97

EPH-98

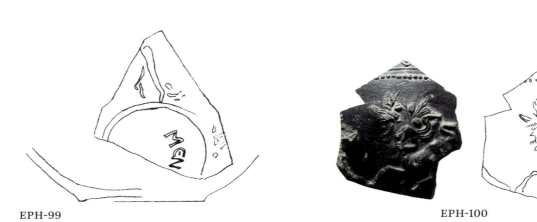
EPH-99　　　　　　　　　　　EPH-100

SCALE 2:3

PLATE 117   EPHESOS (EPH) – JUDGEMENT OF PARIS; LABORS OF HERAKLES   747

EPH-101

EPH-103

EPH-104

EPH-105

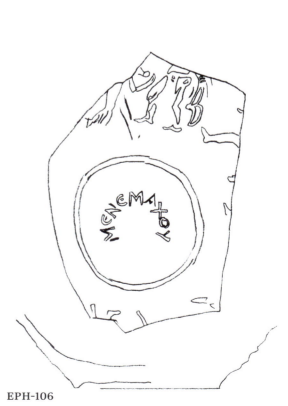

EPH-106

SCALE 2:3

EPH-107

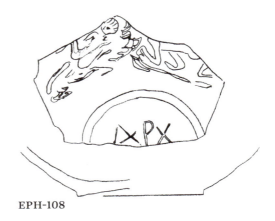

EPH-108

EPH-110

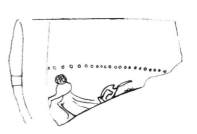

EPH-111

EPH-112

EPH-117

EPH-119

SCALE 2:3

PLATE 119   EPHESOS (EPH) – DOLPHINS; THUNDERBOLT
749

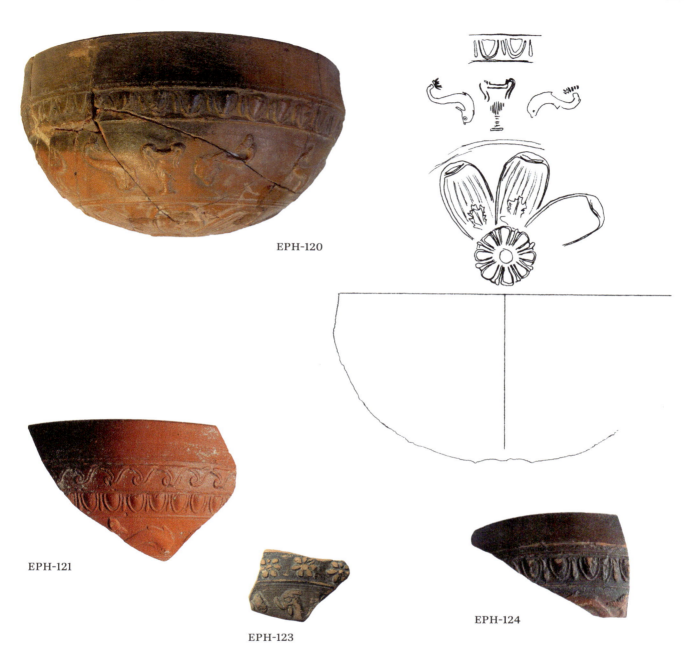

EPH-120

EPH-121

EPH-123

EPH-124

EPH-127

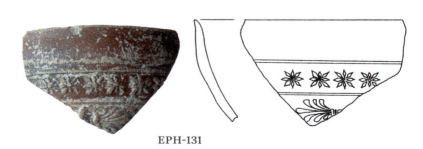

EPH-131

SCALE 2:3

750 EPHESOS (EPH) – THUNDERBOLT; MISCELLANEOUS FIGURES; INANIMATE MOTIFS PLATE 120

EPH-133

EPH-134

EPH-135

EPH-136

EPH-138

EPH-139

EPH-140

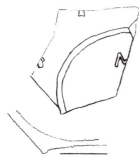
EPH-142

EPH-144

EPH-145

EPH-146

EPH-147

EPH-148

EPH-149

EPH-150

SCALE 2:3

PLATE 121   EPHESOS (EPH) – INANIMATE MOTIFS; FULL-BODY ACANTHUS SCROLL

EPH-151

EPH-152

EPH-153

EPH-154

EPH-155

EPH-157

EPH-158

EPH-159

EPH-160

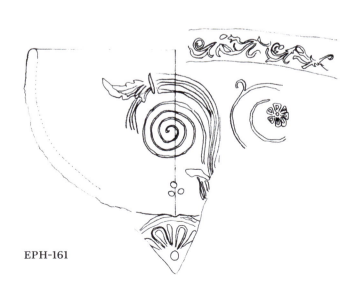
EPH-161

SCALE 2:3

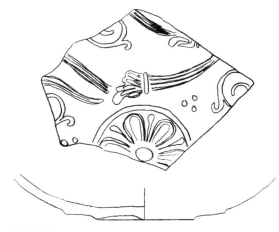

EPH-162

EPH-163

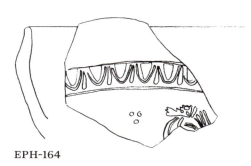

EPH-164

EPH-164BIS

EPH-165

EPH-166

EPH-167

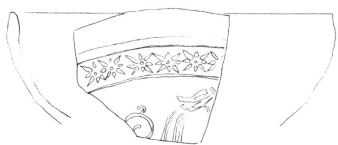

EPH-168

SCALE 2:3

PLATE 123   EPHESOS (EPH) – FULL-BODY ACANTHUS AND ACANTHUS-VINE SCROLL

EPH-169

EPH-170

EPH-172

EPH-173

EPH-174

EPH-175

EPH-176

EPH-177

SCALE 2:3

754 EPHESOS (EPH) – ACANTHUS-VINE SCROLL PLATE 124

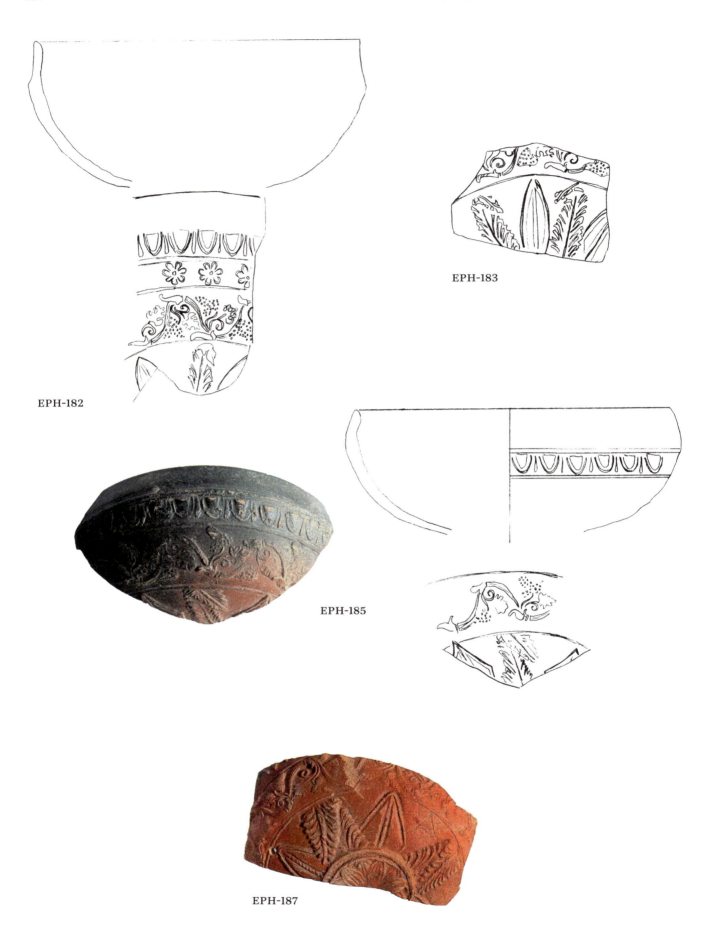

SCALE 2:3

PLATE 125 EPHESOS (EPH) – ACANTHUS-VINE SCROLL

EPH-189

SCALE 2:3

756 EPHESOS (EPH) – ACANTHUS-VINE SCROLL PLATE 126

EPH-190

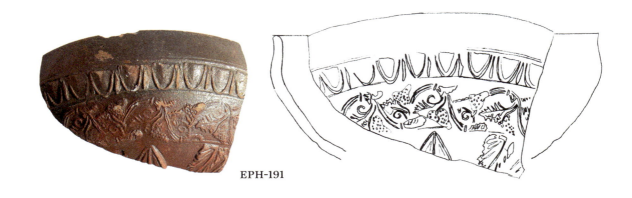

EPH-191

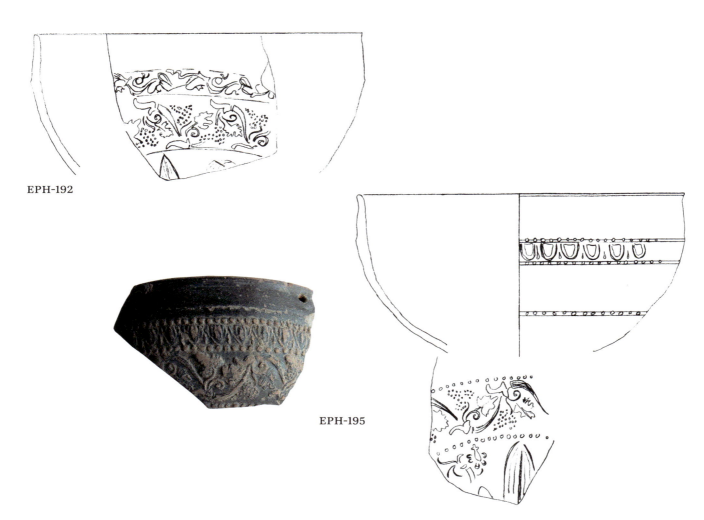

EPH-192

EPH-195

SCALE 2:3

EPH-196

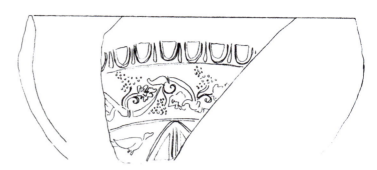

EPH-197

EPH-198

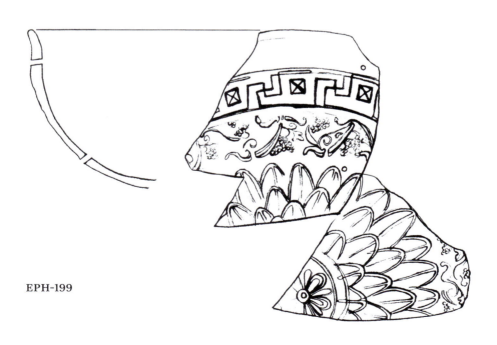

EPH-199

758   EPHESOS (EPH) – ACANTHUS-VINE SCROLL   PLATE 128

EPH-200

EPH-204

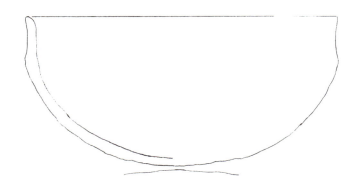

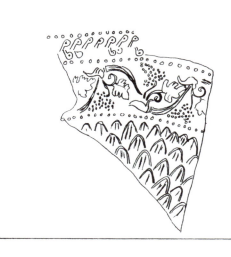

SCALE 2:3

PLATE 129   EPHESOS (EPH) – ACANTHUS-VINE SCROLL

EPH-206

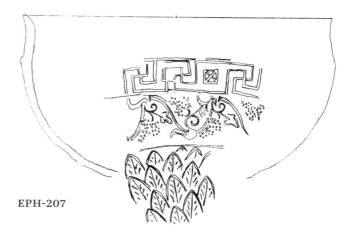
EPH-207

EPH-208

EPH-211

EPH-212

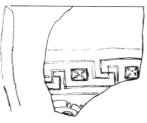
EPH-214

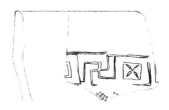
EPH-215

EPH-216

EPH-218

EPH-222

SCALE 2:3

EPH-223

EPH-224

EPH-225

EPH-228

EPH-231

EPH-233

EPH-234

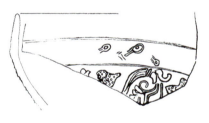

EPH-235

EPH-236

EPH-239

EPH-240

SCALE 2:3

PLATE 131   EPHESOS (EPH) – ACANTHUS-VINE AND ACANTHUS-VINE-IVY SCROLL   761

EPH-242

EPH-243

EPH-244

EPH-245

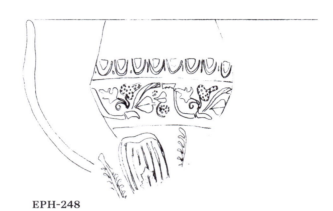

EPH-248

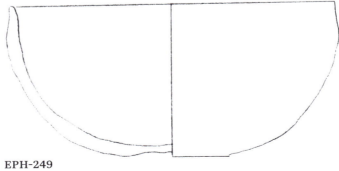

EPH-249

SCALE 2:3

EPH-250

EPH-252

EPH-253

EPH-254

EPH-255

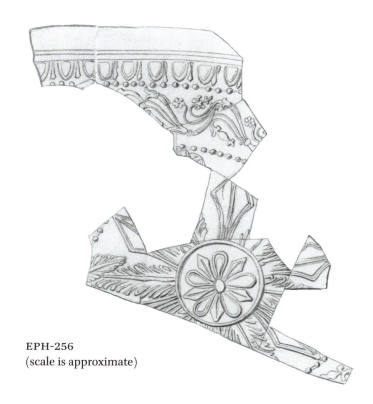
EPH-256
(scale is approximate)

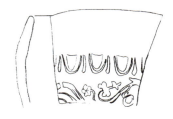
EPH-258

EPH-259

EPH-260

PLATE 133　EPHESOS (EPH) – ACANTHUS-FLOWER SCROLL

EPH-261

EPH-262

EPH-263

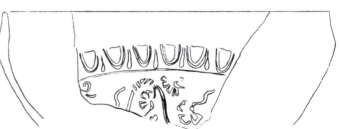

EPH-264

EPH-265

EPH-266

SCALE 2:3

EPH-267

EPH-268

EPH-269

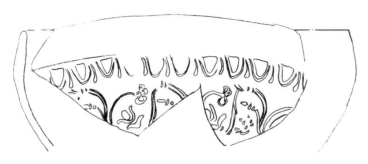
EPH-270

EPH-271

EPH-272

EPH-273

EPH-274

EPH-277

SCALE 2:3

PLATE 135 EPHESOS (EPH) – STYLIZED ACANTHUS SCROLL

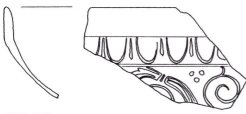

EPH-279

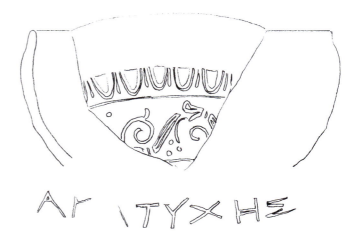

EPH-280

EPH-282

EPH-283

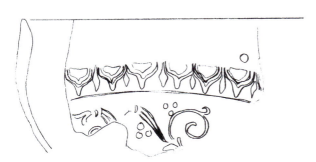

EPH-284

EPH-285

SCALE 2:3

EPH-287

EPH-288

EPH-289

EPH-293

EPH-294

EPH-295

EPH-296

EPH-304

SCALE 2:3

PLATE 137   EPHESOS (EPH) – STYLIZED ACANTHUS SCROLL   767

EPH-306

EPH-307

EPH-308

EPH-309

EPH-310

EPH-311

EPH-312

EPH-313

EPH-314

SCALE 2:3

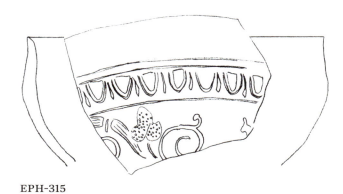

EPH-315

EPH-316

EPH-318

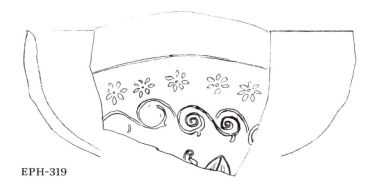

EPH-319

EPH-320

SCALE 2:3

PLATE 139   EPHESOS (EPH) – ULTRA-STYLIZED ACANTHUS SCROLL; MYRTLE WREATH   769

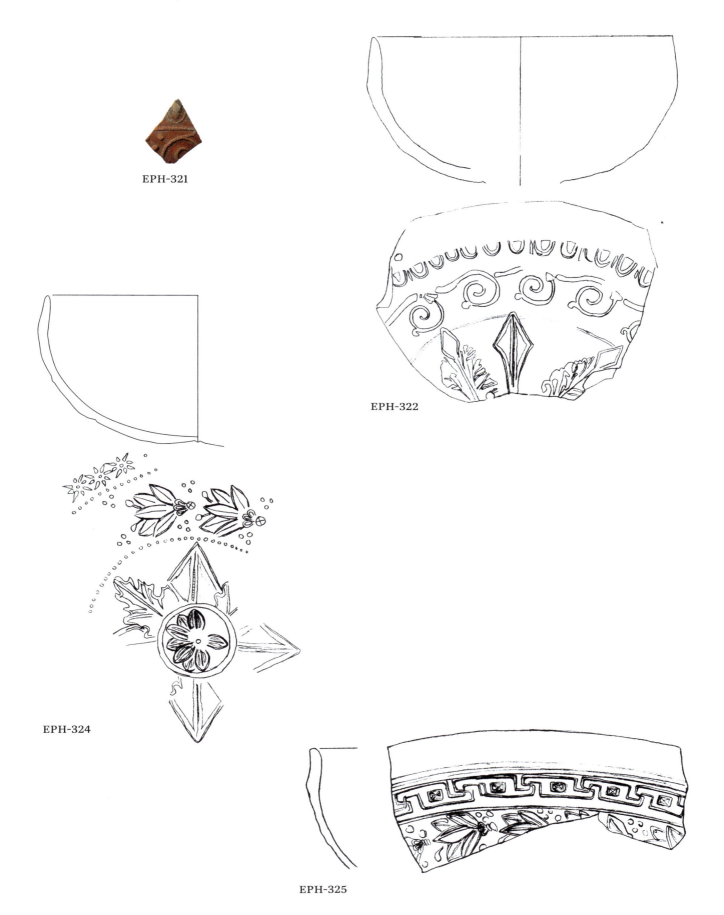

SCALE 2:3

EPH-326

EPH-328

EPH-329

EPH-330

EPH-335

EPH-336

EPH-337

EPH-338

EPH-340

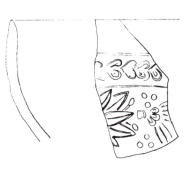

EPH-343

SCALE 2:3

PLATE 141   EPHESOS (EPH) – MYRTLE WREATH

EPH-344

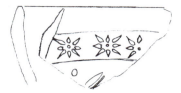

EPH-346

EPH-347

EPH-348

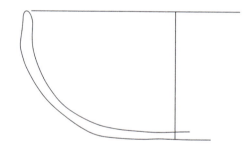

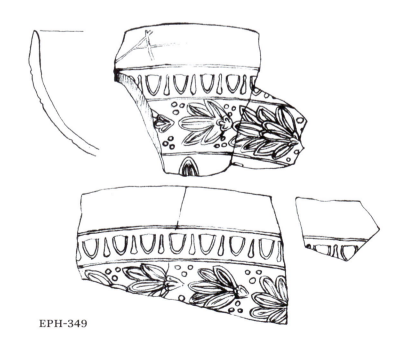

EPH-349

SCALE 2:3

EPH-352

EPH-353

EPH-354

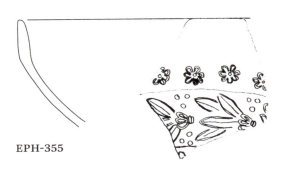
EPH-355

EPH-356

EPH-359

EPH-360

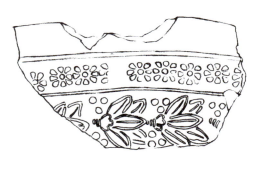

EPH-361

EPH-362

EPH-363

SCALE 2:3

PLATE 143   EPHESOS (EPH) – MYRTLE WREATH

EPH-364

EPH-365

EPH-367

EPH-368

EPH-369

EPH-370

EPH-372

EPH-374

EPH-375

EPH-376

EPH-378

EPH-380

SCALE 2:3

774 EPHESOS (EPH) – MYRTLE WREATH; IVY WREATH PLATE 144

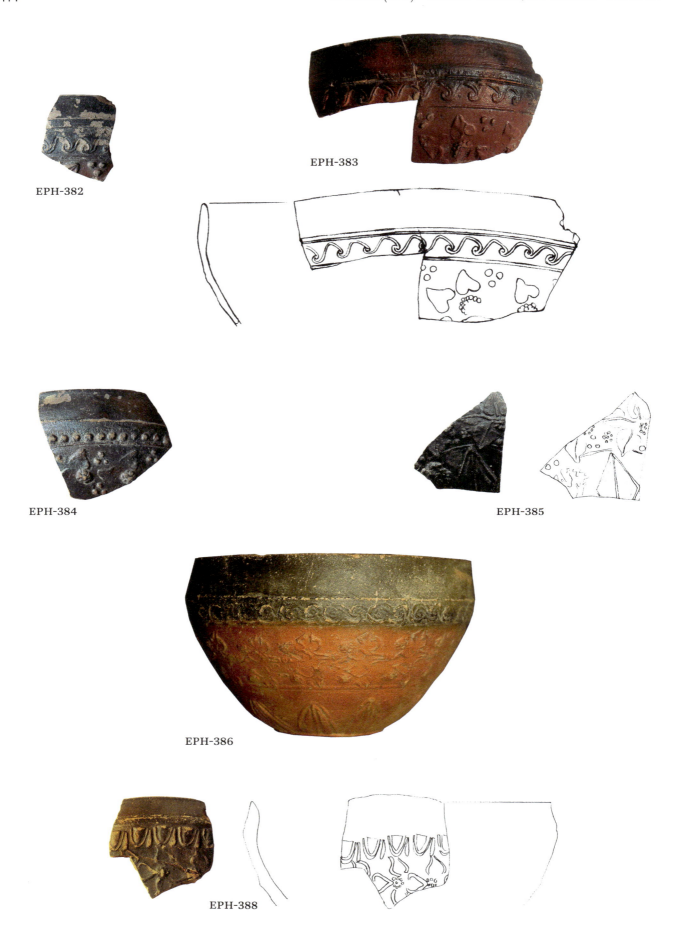

SCALE 2:3

PLATE 145 EPHESOS (EPH) – GARLANDS

EPH-389

EPH-390

EPH-391

EPH-392

SCALE 2:3

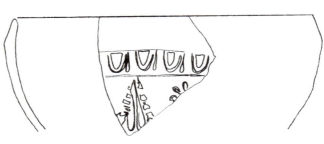

EPH-394

EPH-395

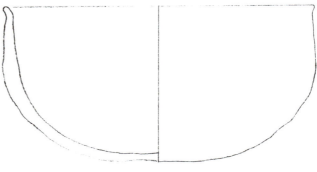

EPH-396

EPH-397 EPH-398

SCALE 2:3

PLATE 147   EPHESOS (EPH) – GARLANDS; SUSPENDED WREATH; MULTIPLE RIM FRIEZES
777

EPH-399

 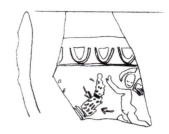
EPH-400

EPH-401

EPH-404

EPH-405

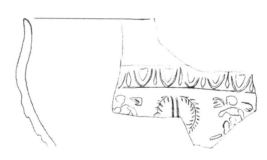
EPH-406

EPH-407

SCALE 2:3

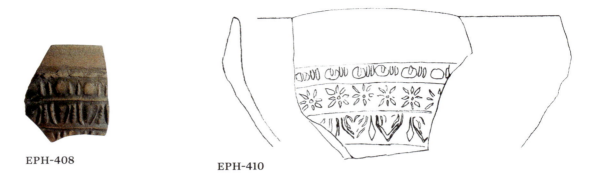

EPH-408   EPH-410

EPH-411   EPH-412

   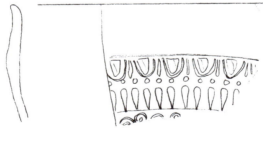

EPH-416

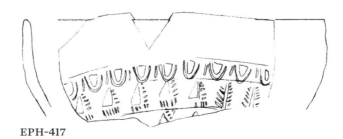

EPH-417

PLATE 149   EPHESOS (EPH) – MULTIPLE RIM FRIEZES

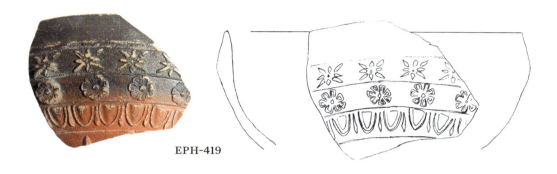
EPH-419

EPH-423

EPH-424

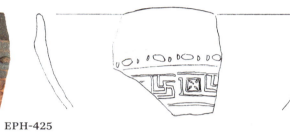
EPH-425

EPH-427

EPH-428

EPH-429

EPH-430

EPH-431

EPH-435

SCALE 2:3

780 EPHESOS (EPH) – MULTIPLE RIM FRIEZES PLATE 150

EPH-436

EPH-437

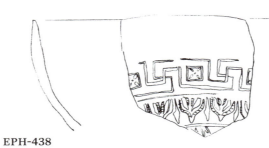
EPH-438

EPH-439

EPH-440

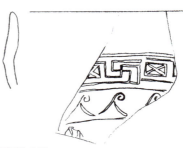
EPH-441

EPH-442

EPH-443

EPH-444

SCALE 2:3

PLATE 151 EPHESOS (EPH) – MULTIPLE RIM FRIEZES

EPH-445

EPH-446

EPH-447

EPH-448

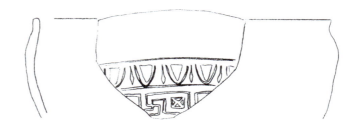

EPH-449

EPH-450

EPH-451

EPH-454

EPH-455

EPH-456

EPH-457

SCALE 2:3

782   EPHESOS (EPH) – MULTIPLE RIM FRIEZES   PLATE 152

EPH-458

EPH-459

EPH-460

EPH-461

EPH-462

EPH-463

EPH-464

EPH-465

EPH-466

EPH-467

EPH-468

EPH-469

SCALE 2:3

PLATE 153　EPHESOS (EPH) – MULTIPLE RIM FRIEZES

EPH-470

EPH-472

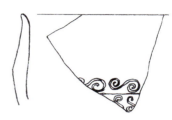
EPH-473

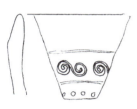
EPH-474

EPH-475

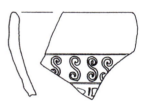
EPH-476

EPH-477

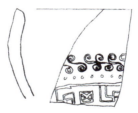
EPH-478

EPH-479

EPH-480

EPH-481

SCALE 2:3

EPH-483

EPH-484

EPH-485

EPH-486

EPH-487

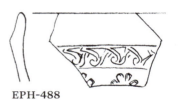
EPH-488

EPH-489

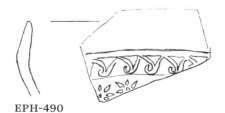
EPH-490

EPH-491

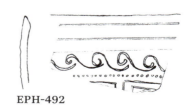
EPH-492

SCALE 2:3

PLATE 155   EPHESOS (EPH) – MULTIPLE RIM FRIEZES 785

EPH-493

EPH-494

EPH-495

EPH-496

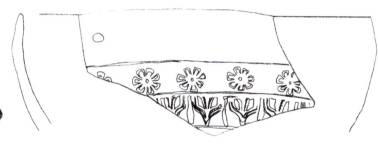
EPH-497

EPH-499

EPH-501

EPH-502

EPH-503

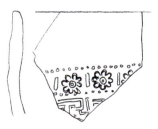
EPH-504

SCALE 2:3

EPH-505

EPH-506

EPH-507

EPH-509

EPH-510

EPH-511

EPH-513

EPH-514

EPH-515

SCALE 2:3

PLATE 157   EPHESOS (EPH) – MULTIPLE RIM FRIEZES; PINE-CONE

EPH-516

EPH-518

EPH-519

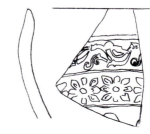
EPH-520

EPH-523

EPH-525

EPH-528

EPH-529

EPH-530

EPH-531

EPH-533

EPH-534

SCALE 2:3

EPH-535

EPH-537

EPH-540

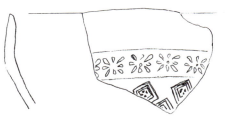
EPH-543

EPH-544

EPH-545

EPH-546

EPH-548

EPH-550

SCALE 2:3

EPH-552

EPH-553

EPH-555

EPH-556

EPH-558

EPH-560

EPH-561

EPH-566

EPH-567

EPH-568

EPH-569

EPH-571

EPH-573

EPH-574

EPH-576

EPH-577

EPH-578

EPH-579

PLATE 161   EPHESOS (EPH) – CALYX A WITH FILLED 'NELUMBO'

SCALE 1:1

EPH-580

EPH-580

EPH-581

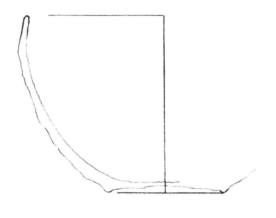

EPH-582

EPH-584

EPH-585

EPH-587

EPH-588

SCALE 2:3

EPH-589

EPH-595

EPH-596

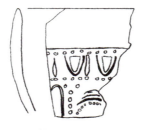
EPH-597

EPH-598

EPH-600

EPH-601

EPH-602

EPH-603

EPH-604

PLATE 163   EPHESOS (EPH) – CALYX B1 AND B2

EPH-606

EPH-607

EPH-610

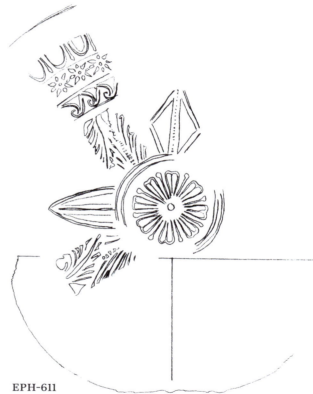

EPH-611

EPH-612

SCALE 2:3

EPH-618

EPH-619

EPH-620

EPH-621

EPH-623

EPH-624

EPH-625

EPH-626

EPH-627

EPH-629

EPH-630

PLATE 165   EPHESOS (EPH) – CALYX B2

EPH-631

EPH-632

EPH-633

EPH-634

EPH-635

EPH-640

EPH-641

EPH-643

SCALE 2:3

EPH-645

EPH-646

EPH-649

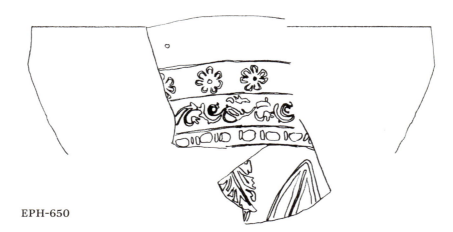
EPH-650

EPH-651

EPH-652

EPH-653

EPH-654

EPH-655

EPH-656

EPH-657

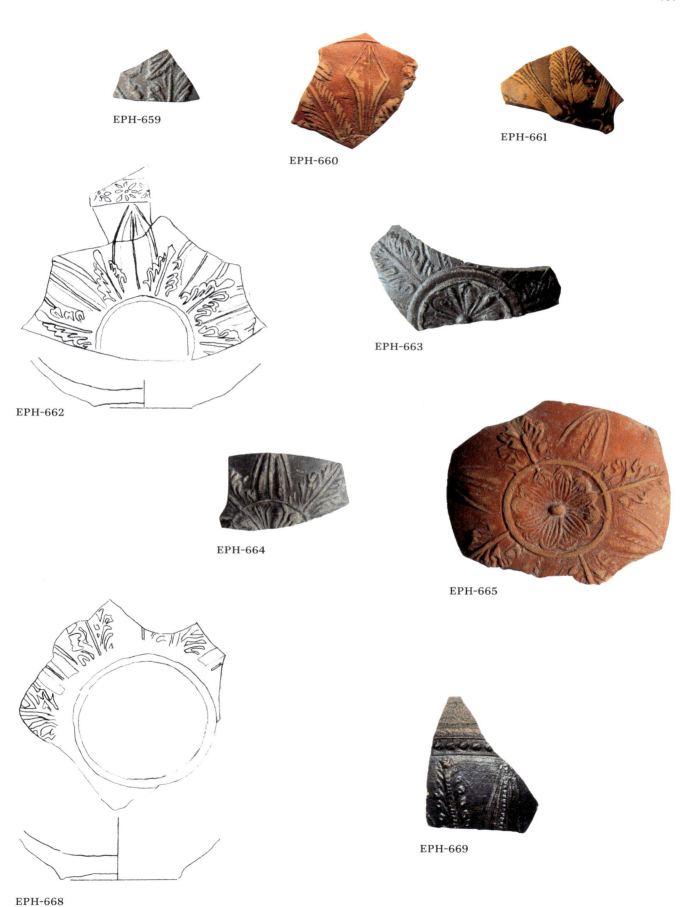

EPHESOS (EPH) – OTHER CALYCES   PLATE 168

EPH-670

EPH-671

EPH-672

EPH-673

EPH-674

SCALE 2:3

PLATE 169 EPHESOS (EPH) – OTHER CALYCES

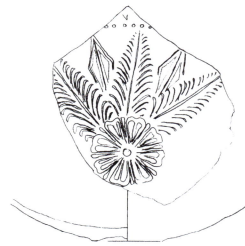

EPH-675

EPH-677

EPH-679

EPH-678

EPH-683

SCALE 2:3

EPH-684

EPH-685

EPH-687

EPH-688

EPH-689

EPH-690

EPH-691

EPH-692

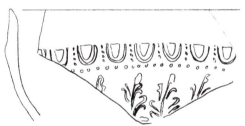

EPH-693

EPH-696

EPH-697

EPH-699

SCALE 2:3

PLATE 171   EPHESOS (EPH) – OTHER CALYCES; IMBRICATE ROUNDED PETALS   801

EPH-700

EPH-701

EPH-703

EPH-704

EPH-706

EPH-707

EPH-708

EPH-713

EPH-717

SCALE 2:3

802 EPHESOS (EPH) – IMBRICATE ROUNDED PETALS PLATE 172

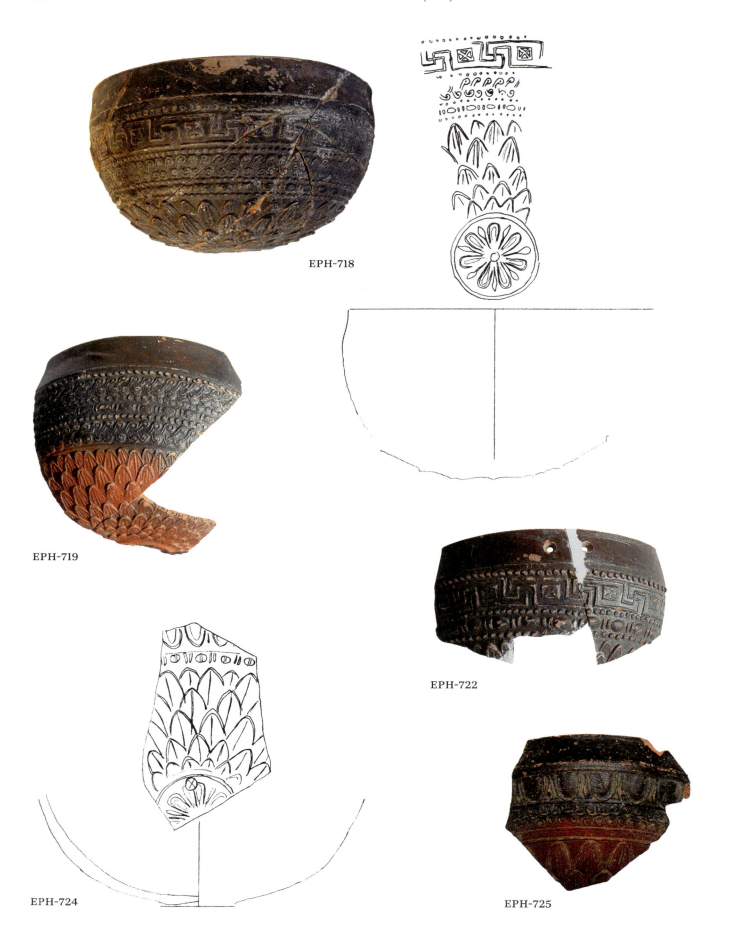

EPH-718

EPH-719

EPH-722

EPH-724

EPH-725

SCALE 2:3

PLATE 173 EPHESOS (EPH) – IMBRICATE ROUNDED PETALS

EPH-726

EPH-727

EPH-730

EPH-731

SCALE 2:3

804 EPHESOS (EPH) – IMBRICATE ROUNDED PETALS PLATE 174

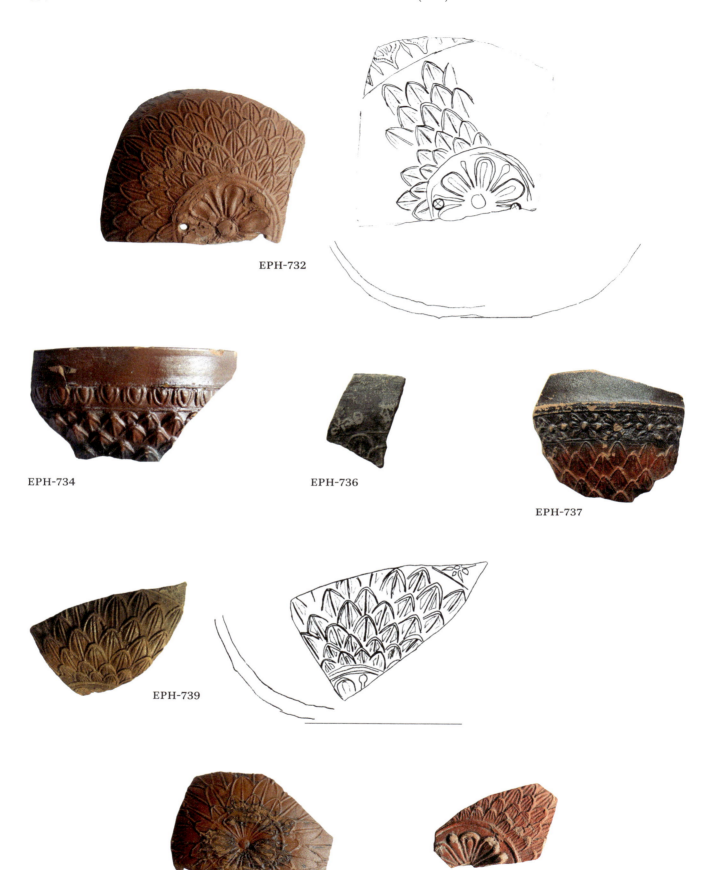

EPH-732

EPH-734　　　EPH-736　　　EPH-737

EPH-739

EPH-740　　　EPH-742

SCALE 2:3

PLATE 175 EPHESOS (EPH) – IMBRICATE ROUNDED PETALS

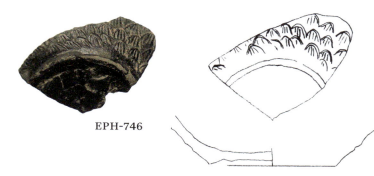

EPH-746

EPH-747

EPH-748

EPH-749

EPH-750

EPH-751

SCALE 2:3

806   EPHESOS (EPH) – IMBRICATE ROUNDED PETALS   PLATE 176

EPH-752

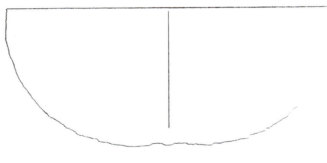

EPH-753

EPH-754

EPH-755

EPH-757

SCALE 2:3

PLATE 177   EPHESOS (EPH) – IMBRICATE ROUNDED PETALS

EPH-758

EPH-759

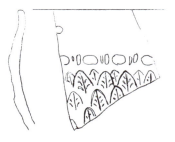
EPH-760

EPH-762

EPH-763

EPH-764

EPH-765

EPH-766

EPH-767

EPH-769

SCALE 2:3

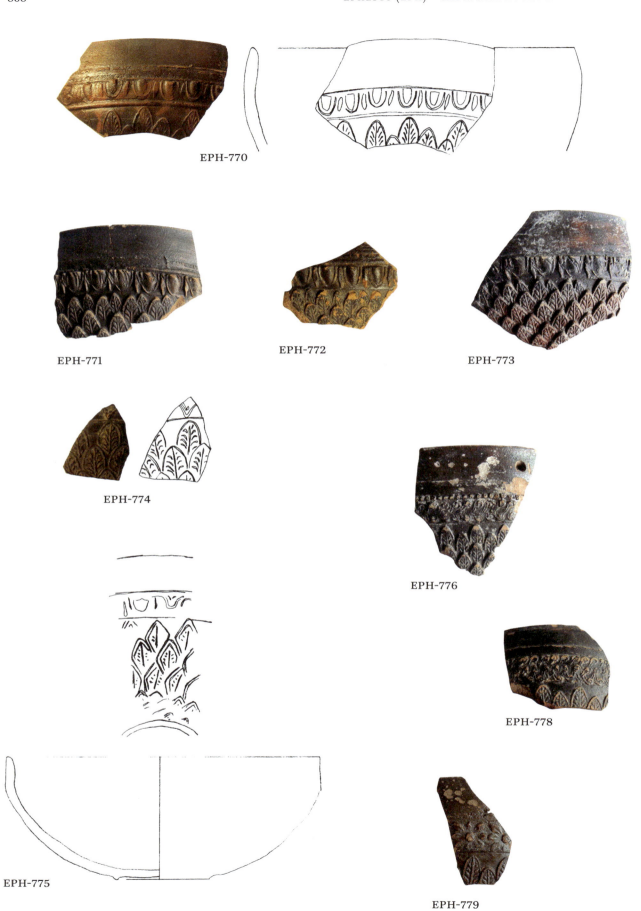

PLATE 179   EPHESOS (EPH) – IMBRICATE ROUNDED PETALS

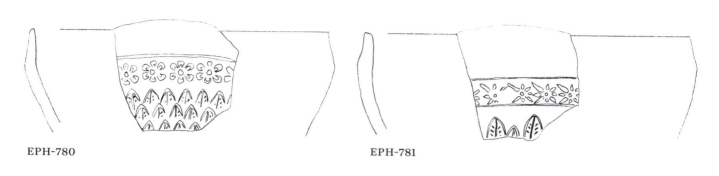

EPH-780   EPH-781

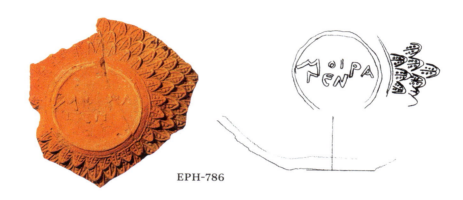

EPH-786

   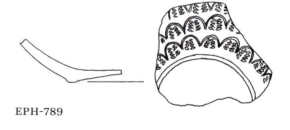

EPH-788   EPH-789

EPH-790   EPH-791   EPH-792

SCALE 2:3

810 EPHESOS (EPH) – IMBRICATE ROUNDED AND POINTED PETALS PLATE 180

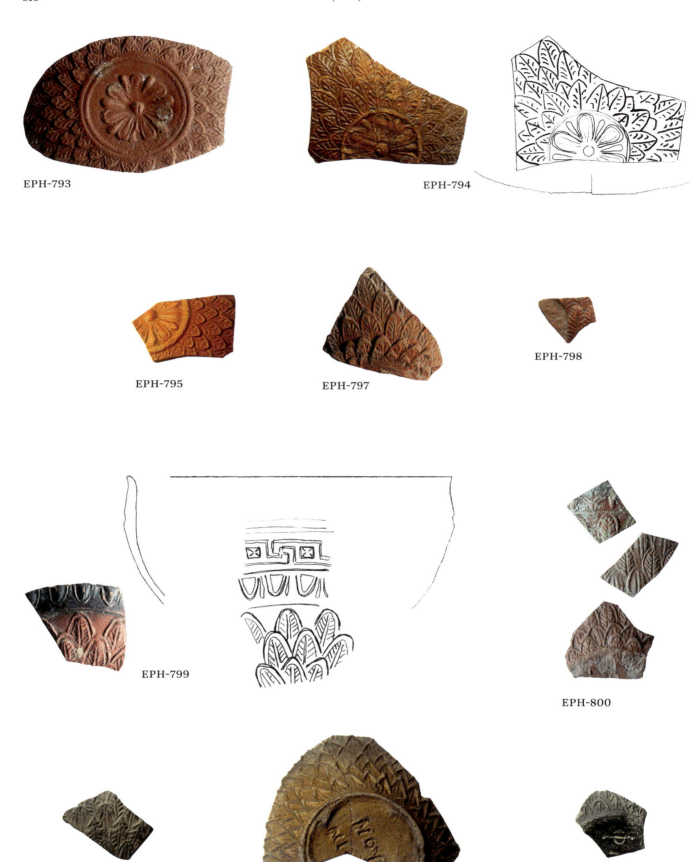

EPH-793

EPH-794

EPH-795

EPH-797

EPH-798

EPH-799

EPH-800

EPH-801

EPH-805

EPH-807

SCALE 2:3

PLATE 181   EPHESOS (EPH) – IMBRICATE POINTED PETALS

EPH-808

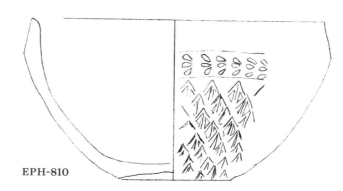

EPH-810

EPH-811

EPH-812

EPH-813

EPH-815

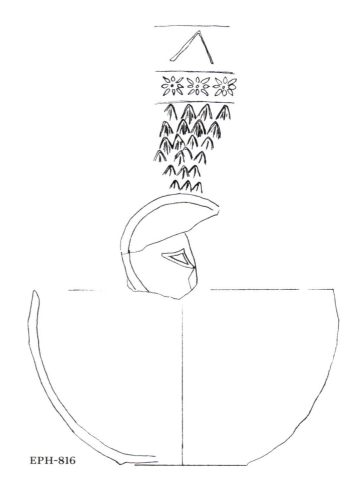

EPH-816

SCALE 2:3

EPH-820

EPH-821

EPH-822

EPH-823

EPH-824

EPH-825

EPH-827

EPH-829

EPH-830

EPH-831

EPH-832

EPH-834

EPH-837

SCALE 2:3

PLATE 183 EPHESOS (EPH) – IMBRICATE POINTED PETALS

EPH-840

EPH-841

EPH-842

EPH-843

EPH-844

EPH-845

EPH-852

EPH-853

EPH-854

EPH-855

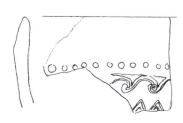
EPH-856

EPH-859

SCALE 2:3

814 EPHESOS (EPH) – IMBRICATE POINTED PETALS PLATE 184

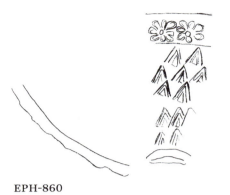
EPH-860

EPH-861

EPH-862

EPH-864

EPH-866

EPH-868

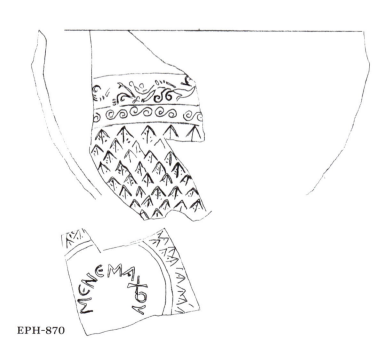
EPH-870

SCALE 2:3

PLATE 185   EPHESOS (EPH) – IMBRICATE POINTED PETALS

EPH-873

EPH-875

EPH-876

EPH-877

EPH-881

EPH-882

EPH-883

EPH-889

EPH-890

EPH-891

EPH-892

SCALE 2:3

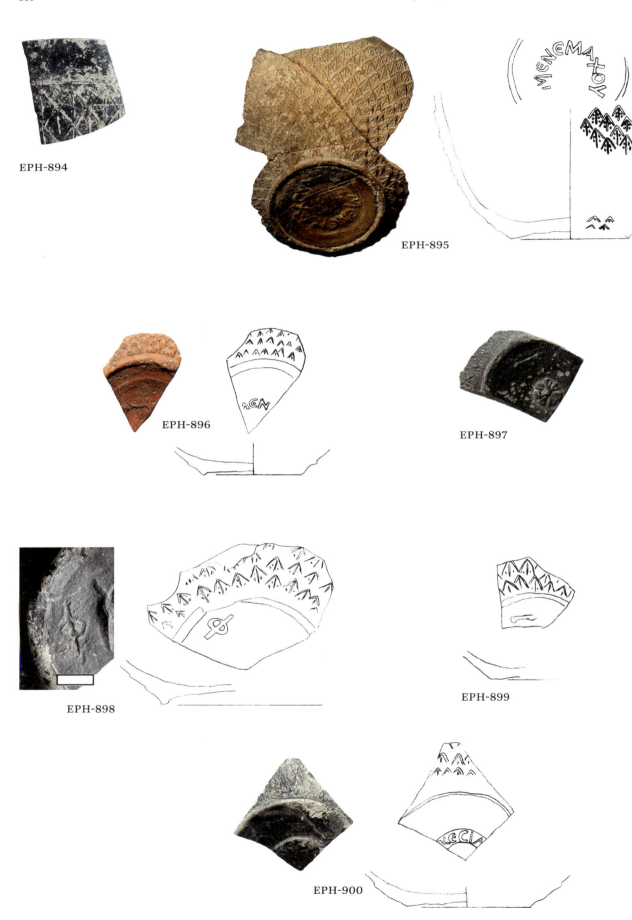

PLATE 187   EPHESOS (EPH) – IMBRICATE POINTED PETALS

EPH-903

EPH-907

EPH-908

EPH-910

EPH-911

EPH-913

EPH-919

EPH-922

EPH-925

EPH-927

EPH-930

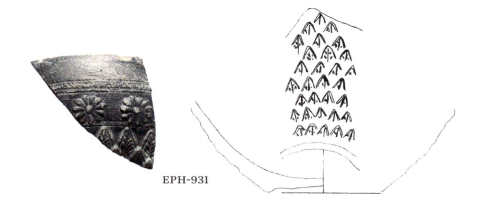
EPH-931

SCALE 2:3

818　　　　　　　　　EPHESOS (EPH) – IMBRICATE POINTED PETALS; OTHER IMBRICATE DESIGNS　　PLATE 188

EPH-932

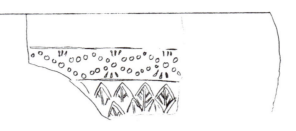

EPH-934

EPH-935

EPH-936

EPH-937

EPH-939

EPH-942

EPH-943

EPH-944

EPH-946

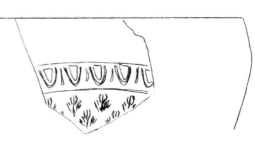

EPH-947

SCALE 2:3

PLATE 189   EPHESOS (EPH) – OTHER IMBRICATE DESIGNS; PENDENT-SEMICIRCLE

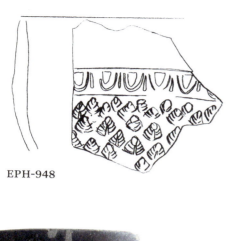
EPH-948

EPH-949

EPH-950

EPH-952

EPH-953

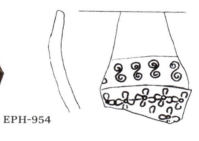
EPH-954

EPH-955

SCALE 2:3

EPH-957

EPH-959

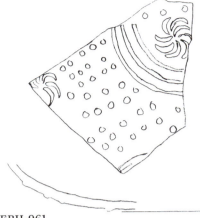
EPH-961

EPH-962

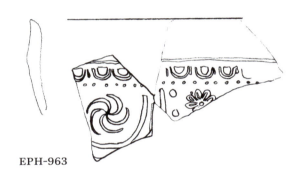
EPH-963

EPH-965

EPH-969

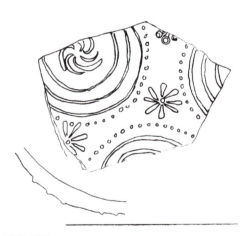
EPH-970

EPH-971

EPH-972

EPH-973

SCALE 2:3

PLATE 191   EPHESOS (EPH) – PENDENT-SEMICIRCLE; NET PATTERN

EPH-975

EPH-977

EPH-981

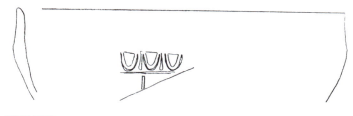
EPH-985

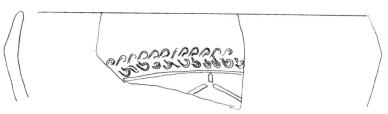
EPH-988

EPH-989

EPH-990

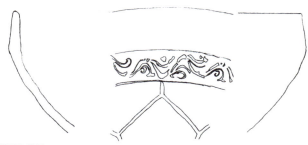
EPH-991

SCALE 2:3

822   EPHESOS (EPH) – NET PATTERN   PLATE 192

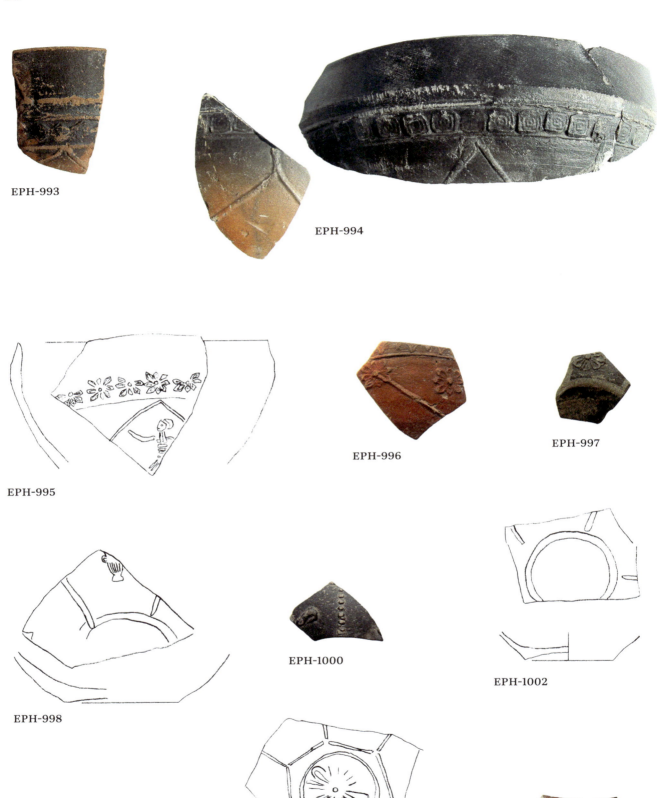

SCALE 2:3

PLATE 193 EPHESOS (EPH) – NET PATTERN; LONG PETALS

EPH-1007

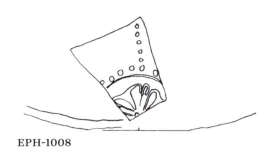
EPH-1008

EPH-1009

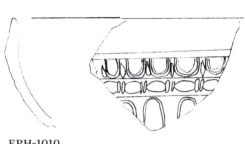
EPH-1010

EPH-1011

EPH-1012

EPH-1015

EPH-1016

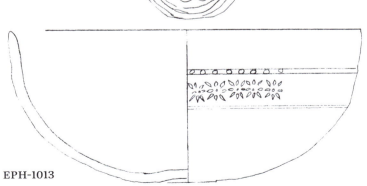
EPH-1013

SCALE 2:3

824   EPHESOS (EPH) – LONG PETALS   PLATE 194

EPH-1017

EPH-1018

EPH-1020

EPH-1021

EPH-1023

EPH-1024

EPH-1025

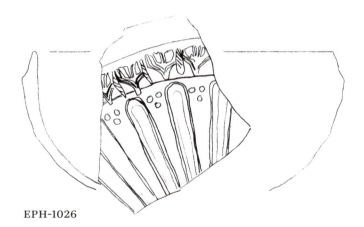
EPH-1026

EPH-1027

EPH-1028

EPH-1029

EPH-1031

EPH-1032

SCALE 2:3

PLATE 195　EPHESOS (EPH) – LONG PETALS

EPH-1033

EPH-1034

EPH-1035

EPH-1036

EPH-1037

EPH-1038

EPH-1041

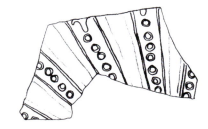
EPH-1042

EPH-1044

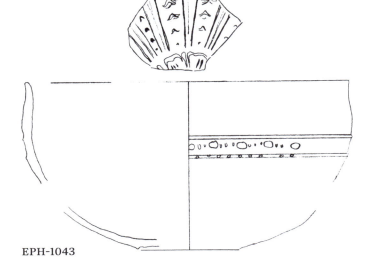
EPH-1043

EPH-1045

EPH-1046

SCALE 2:3

EPH-1047

EPH-1048

EPH-1049

EPH-1050

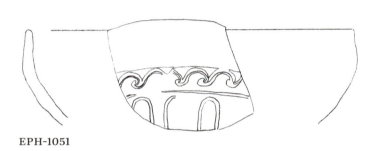

EPH-1051

EPH-1052

EPH-1055

EPH-1058

EPH-1060

EPH-1061

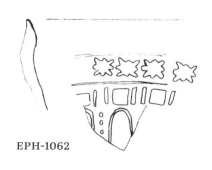

EPH-1062

SCALE 2:3

PLATE 197   EPHESOS (EPH) – LONG PETALS 827

EPH-1063

EPH-1064

EPH-1067

EPH-1068

EPH-1071

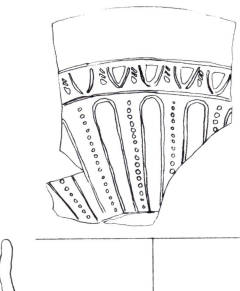

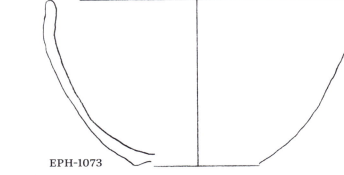
EPH-1073

EPH-1076

EPH-1078

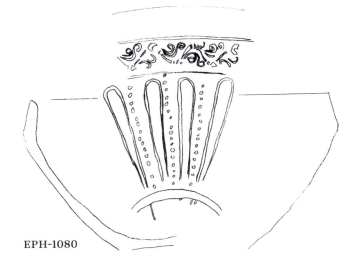
EPH-1080

SCALE 2:3

828   EPHESOS (EPH) – LONG PETALS   PLATE 198

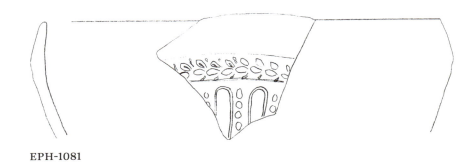
EPH-1081

EPH-1083

EPH-1084

EPH-1090

EPH-1093

EPH-1096

EPH-1097

EPH-1101

EPH-1102

EPH-1103

EPH-1105

EPH-1106

SCALE 2:3

PLATE 199   EPHESOS (EPH) – LONG PETALS; VERTICAL FLUTING; RIM FRAGMENTS   829

SCALE 2:3

830 EPHESOS (EPH) – RIM FRAGMENTS PLATE 200

EPH-1129

EPH-1132

EPH-1133

EPH-1134

EPH-1135

EPH-1136

EPH-1138

EPH-1140

EPH-1141

EPH-1146

EPH-1147

EPH-1148

EPH-1149

EPH-1150

SCALE 2:3

PLATE 201   EPHESOS (EPH) – RIM FRAGMENTS

EPH-1152

EPH-1157

EPH-1158

EPH-1159

EPH-1160

EPH-1161

EPH-1163

EPH-1164

EPH-1165

EPH-1166

EPH-1167

EPH-1168

EPH-1169

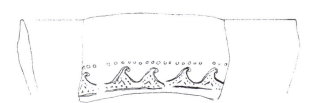
EPH-1170

EPH-1171

SCALE 2:3

EPH-1174

EPH-1175

EPH-1176

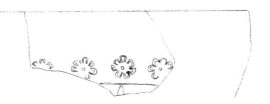
EPH-1181

EPH-1181

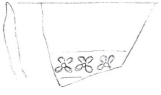
EPH-1183

EPH-1184

EPH-1185

EPH-1186

EPH-1187

EPH-1189

EPH-1190

EPH-1191

EPH-1194

SCALE 2:3

PLATE 203   EPHESOS (EPH) – RIM FRAGMENTS   833

EPH-1195

EPH-1196

EPH-1198

EPH-1199

EPH-1200

EPH-1201

EPH-1203

EPH-1205

EPH-1206

EPH-1215

EPH-1216

EPH-1217

SCALE 2:3

EPH-1218

EPH-1219

EPH-1221

EPH-1222

EPH-1223

EPH-1225

EPH-1226

EPH-1227

EPH-1233

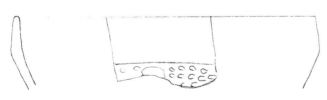
EPH-1234

EPH-1236

EPH-1238
(scale is approximate)

EPH-1240

EPH-1241

SCALE 2:3

PLATE 205 EPHESOS (EPH) – RIM AND BASE FRAGMENTS 835

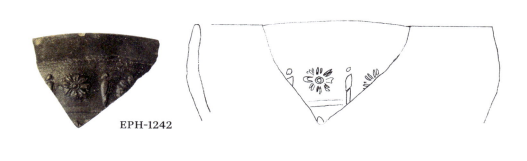
EPH-1242

EPH-1244

EPH-1245

EPH-1246

EPH-1249

EPH-1250

EPH-1252

EPH-1253

EPH-1256

EPH-1258

SCALE 2:3

EPH-1260

EPH-1261

EPH-1262

EPH-1264

EPH-1265

EPH-1266

EPH-1268

EPH-1270

EPH-1271

EPH-1273

EPH-1272

SCALE 2:3

PLATE 207   EPHESOS (EPH) – SMALL BOWL; JUGLET

EPH-1274

EPH-1275

EPH-1277

EPH-1281

EPH-1282

EPH-1284

EPH-1285

EPH-1288

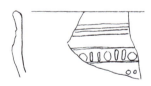
EPH-1289

EPH-1290

EPH-1295

EPH-1297

EPH-1299

SCALE 2:3

EPH-1300

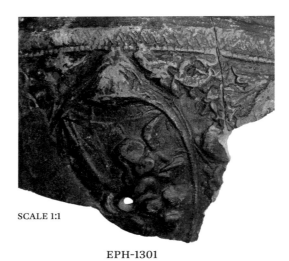

SCALE 1:1

EPH-1301

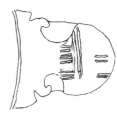

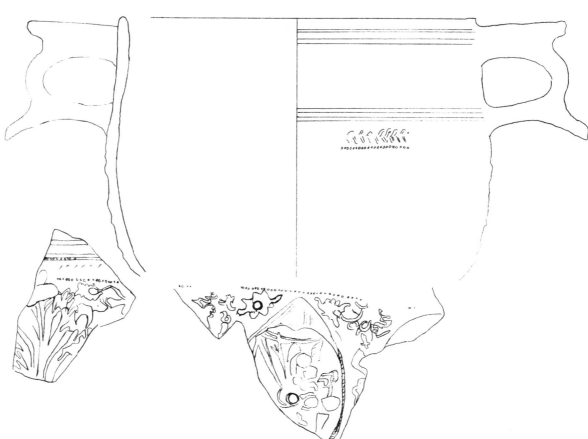

SCALE 2:3

PLATE 209   EPHESOS (EPH) – SKYPHOS; AMPHORA

EPH-1302

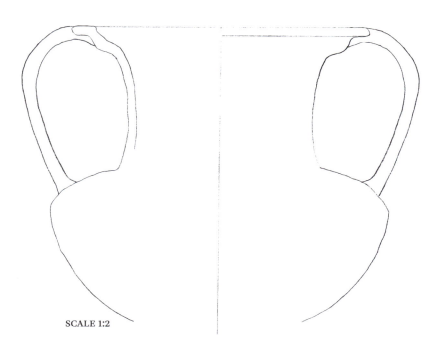

SCALE 1:2

EPH-1303

SCALE 2:3

EPH-1305

EPH-1306

SCALE 1:1

SCALE 1:2

PLATE 211   EPHESOS (EPH) – AMPHORA

SCALE 1:2

EPH-1307

SCALE 1:1 (all four of the details)

EPH-1311

EPH-1312

EPH-1313

EPH-1315

EPH-1317

EPH-1321
(SCALE 2:5)

SCALE 2:3

PLATE 213 EPHESOS (EPH) – LAGYNOS(?); SITULA

EPH-1322

EPH-1323

EPH-1324

EPH-1328

SCALE 2:3

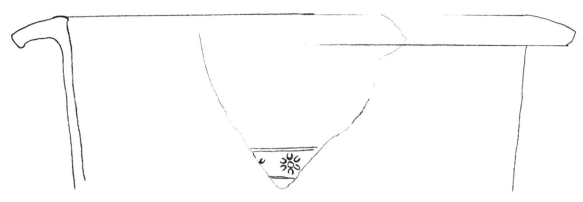

EPH-1329

SCALE 2:5

EPH-1330

SCALE 2:3

PLATE 215   EPHESOS (EPH) – KRATER; DINOS   845

EPH-1331

EPH-1332

EPH-1333

EPH-1335

SCALE 1:1

SCALE 2:3

EPH-1336

EPH-1340

EPH-1341

EPH-1342

EPH-1343

EPH-1344

EPH-1348

EPH-1349

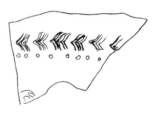
EPH-1350

EPH-1351
(scale is approximate)

SCALE 2:3

PLATE 217   KNIDOS (KNI) – FIGURAL

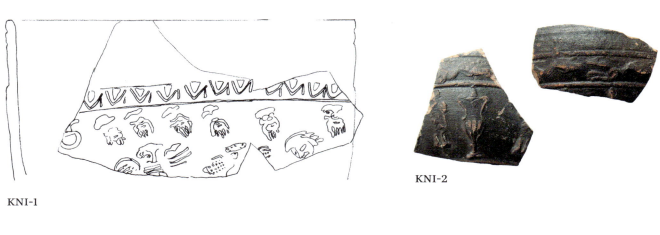

KNI-1

KNI-2

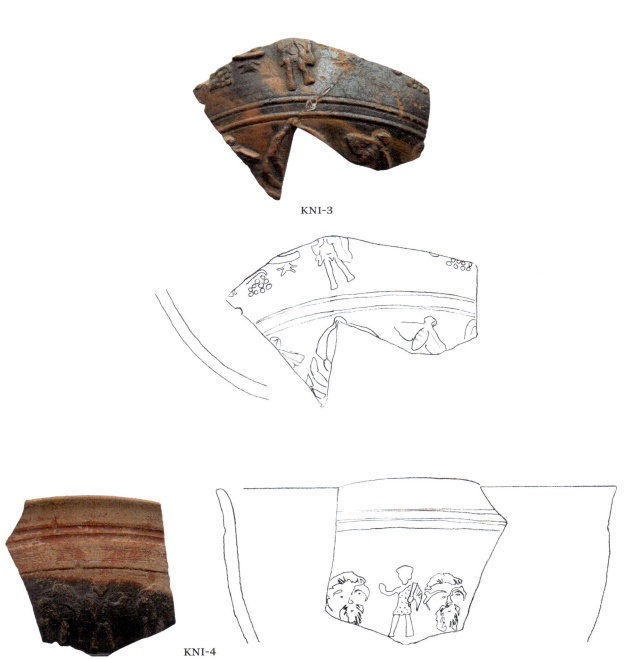

KNI-3

KNI-4

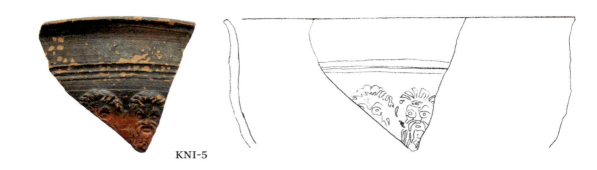
KNI-5

KNI-6

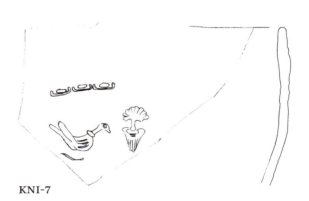
KNI-7

KNI-9

KNI-10

KNI-11

KNI-12

KNI-13

KNI-14

KNI-15

KNI-16

KNI-17

KNI-18

KNI-19

KNI-20

KNI-22

KNI-23

KNI-25

SCALE 2:3

KNI-26

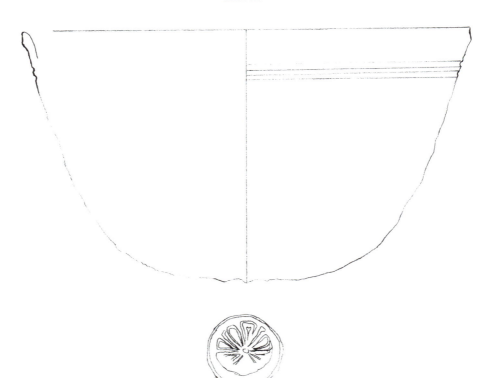

PLATE 221   KNIDOS (KNI) – MULTIPLE RIM FRIEZES

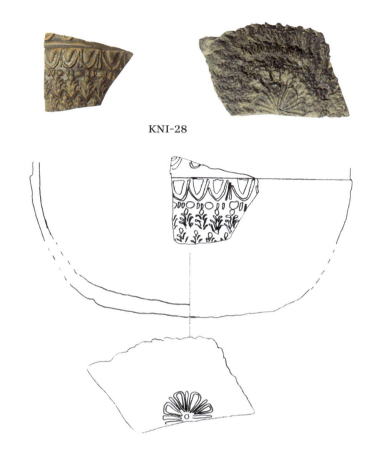

KNI-28

 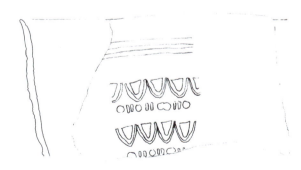

KNI-29

SCALE 2:3

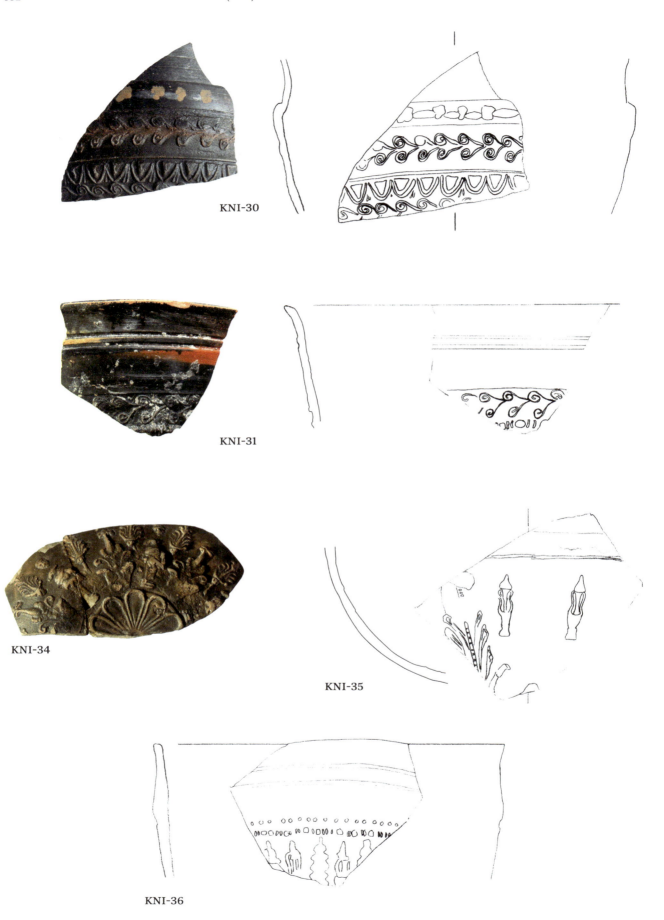

PLATE 223 KNIDOS (KNI) – CALYX WITH FIGURAL DECORATION; CALYX 853

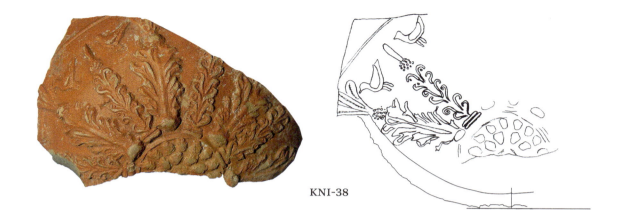
KNI-38

KNI-40

KNI-42

KNI-43

KNI-44

KNI-46

KNI-47

KNI-48

KNI-49

KNI-50

SCALE 2:3

PLATE 225   KNIDOS (KNI) – RIM FRAGMENTS; SUPPLEMENTARY SHAPES

KNI-61

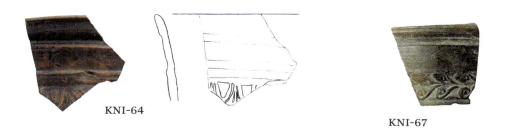
KNI-64   KNI-67

KNI-73

KNI-74

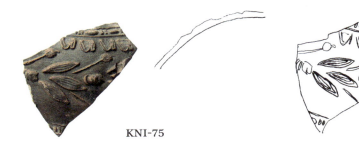
KNI-75

SCALE 2:3

XXX-1

XXX-2

XXX-4

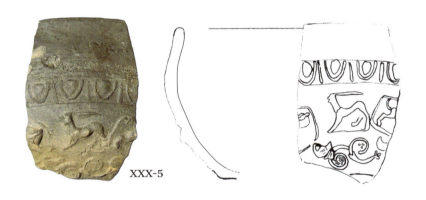

XXX-5

XXX-7

XXX-8

XXX-9

SCALE 2:3

PLATE 227 UNIDENTIFIED PRODUCTION (XXX) – SCROLL; WREATH; GARLAND; RIM FRAGMENT   857

XXX-11

XXX-12

XXX-13

XXX-14

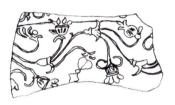

XXX-15

XXX-16

XXX-17

XXX-18

XXX-19

XXX-20

XXX-21

SCALE 2:3

358 UNIDENTIFIED PRODUCTION (XXX) – CALYX; IMBRICATE; PENDENT-SEMICIRCLE PLATE 228

XXX-22

XXX-23

XXX-24

XXX-26

XXX-27

XXX-28

XXX-29

XXX-30

XXX-31

XXX-34

SCALE 2:3

PLATE 229   UNIDENTIFIED PRODUCTION (XXX) – LINEAR; RIM FRAGMENTS   859

XXX-35

XXX-36

XXX-37

XXX-38

XXX-39

XXX-40

XXX-41

XXX-43

XXX-45

XXX-46

XXX-47

SCALE 2:3

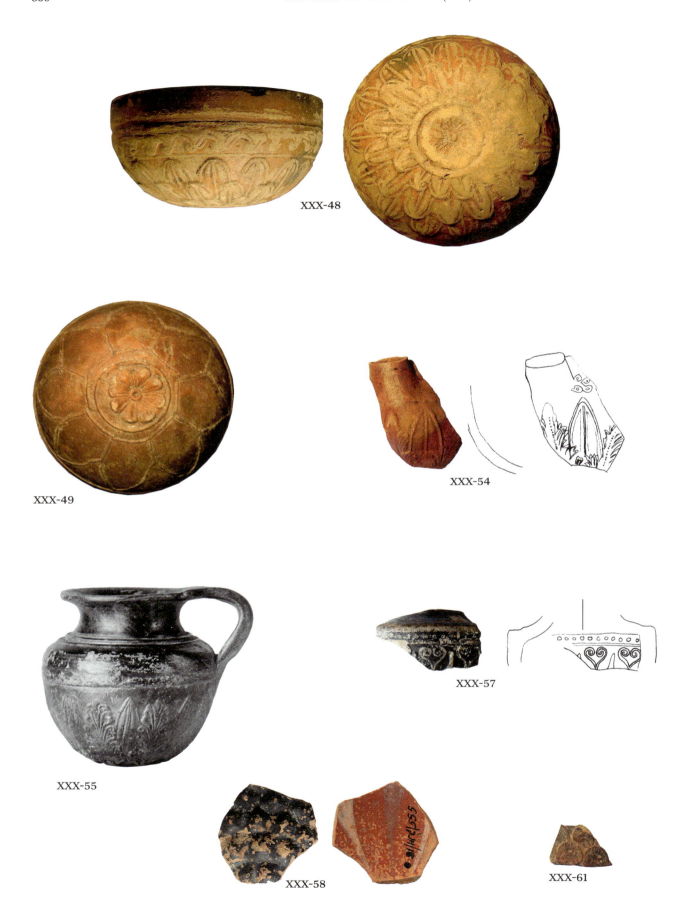

PLATE 231   UNIDENTIFIED PRODUCTION (XXX) – AMPHORA; LAGYNOS   861

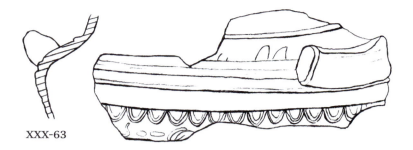

XXX-63

XXX-68

SCALE 2:3

XXX-69

XXX-70

XXX-71

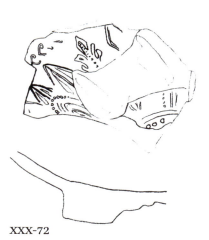

XXX-72

SCALE 2:3

XXX-73

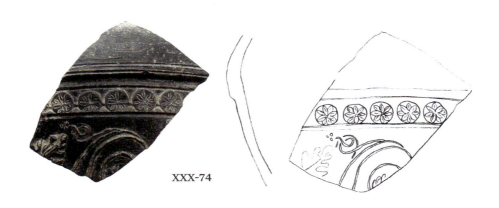

XXX-74

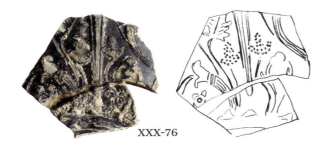

XXX-76

XXX-77

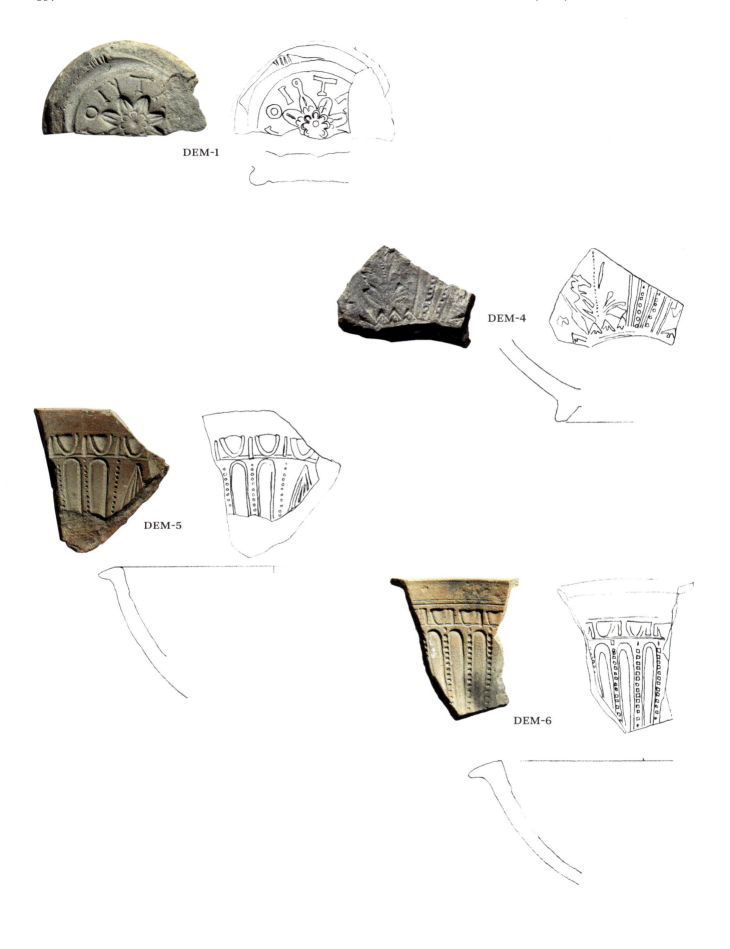

PLATE 235   DEMETRIOS (DEM) – MOULDS; DECORATION 1   865

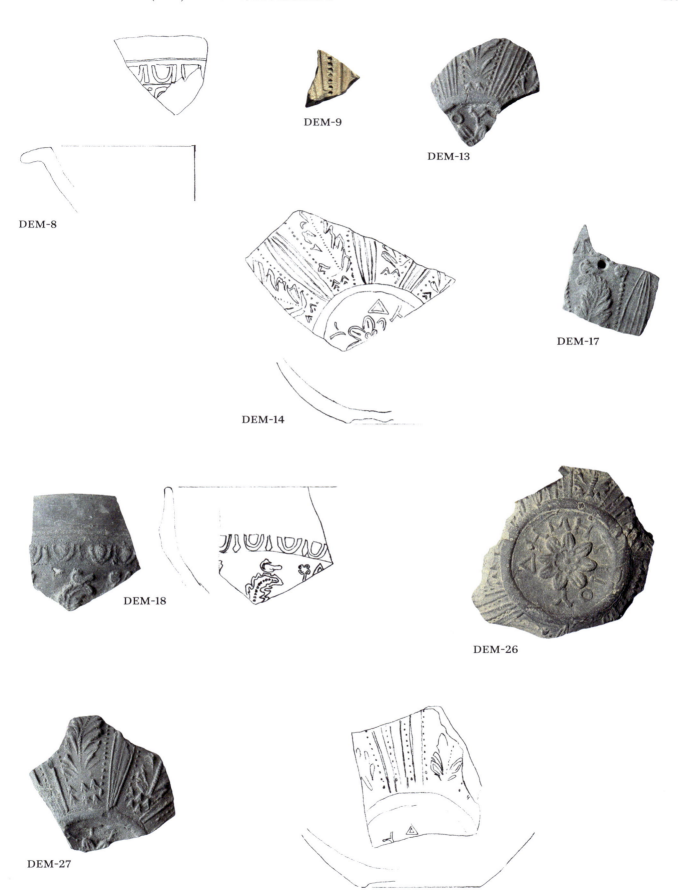

SCALE 2:3

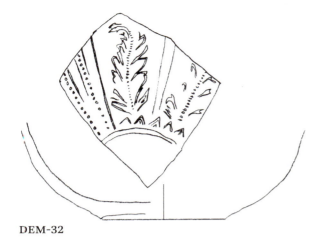
DEM-32

DEM-33

DEM-34

DEM-35

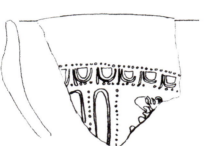

DEM-36

DEM-37

DEM-42

DEM-43

DEM-45

DEM-46

SCALE 2:3

DEM-49

DEM-50

DEM-51

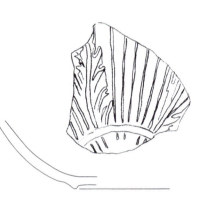

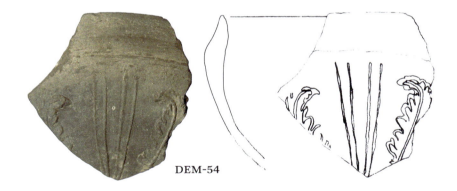
DEM-54

DEM-56

DEM-57

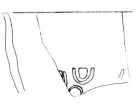
DEM-61

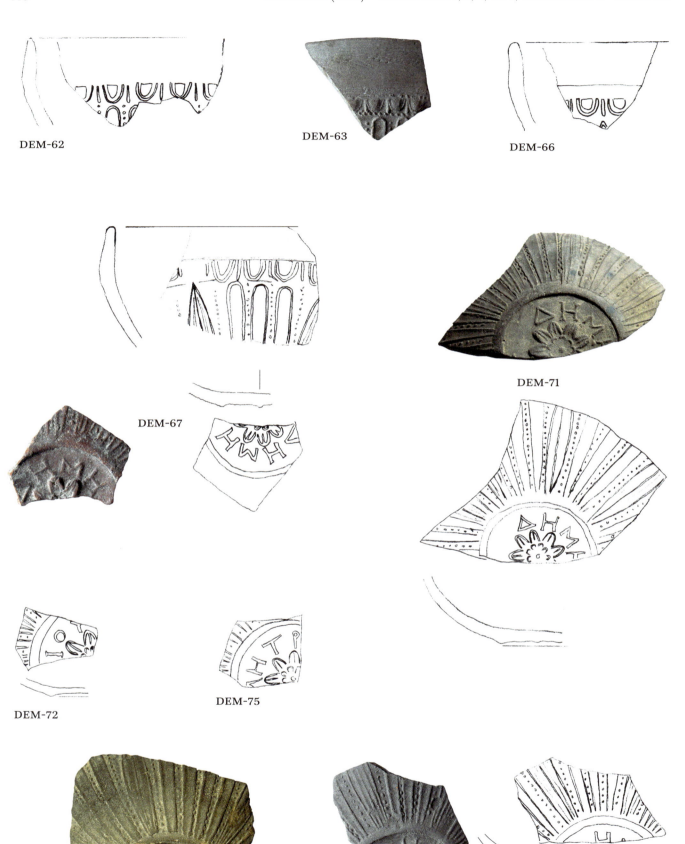

DEM-62 DEM-63 DEM-66 DEM-67 DEM-71 DEM-72 DEM-75 DEM-78 DEM-91

SCALE 2:3

PLATE 239   DEMETRIOS (DEM) – Decoration 2

DEM-92

DEM-95

DEM-99

DEM-100

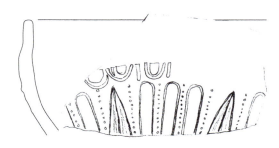
DEM-101

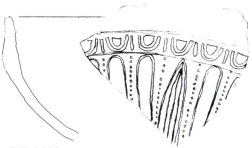
DEM-102

DEM-103

DEM-105

DEM-106

SCALE 2:3

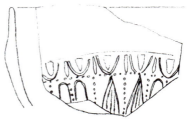
DEM-107

DEM-108

DEM-109

DEM-110

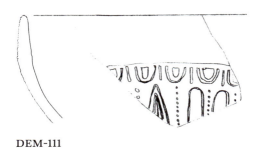
DEM-111

DEM-113

DEM-114

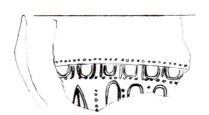
DEM-125

DEM-135

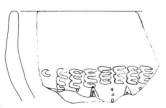
DEM-143

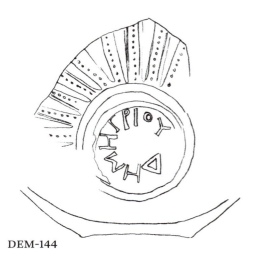
DEM-144

SCALE 2:3

PLATE 241   DEMETRIOS (DEM) – DECORATION 3

DEM-145

DEM-146

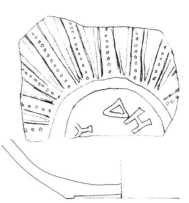

DEM-148

DEM-149...

DEM-160

DEM-161

DEM-165

DEM-166

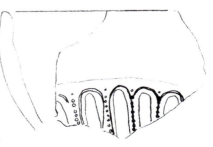

SCALE 2:3

DEM-168

DEM-170

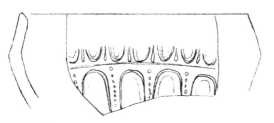
DEM-171

DEM-179

DEM-180

DEM-181

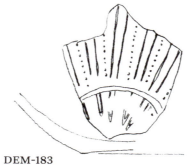
DEM-183

DEM-187

DEM-189

DEM-192

SCALE 2:3

PLATE 243   DEMETRIOS (DEM) – DECORATION 4 AND 5   873

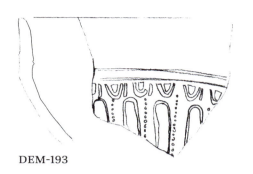

DEM-193   DEM-194   DEM-195

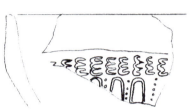

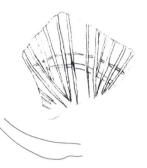

DEM-200   DEM-202

DEM-203   DEM-204   DEM-206

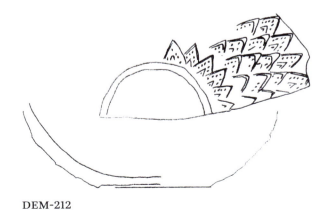

DEM-213

DEM-212

DEM-214

SCALE 2:3

DEM-215

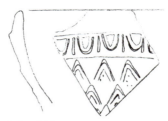
DEM-220

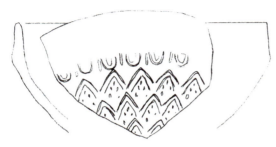
DEM-221

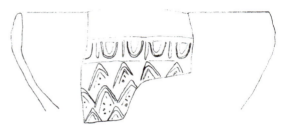
DEM-222

DEM-223

DEM-224

DEM-225

DEM-231

DEM-240

DEM-244

SCALE 2:3

PLATE 245 DEMETRIOS (DEM) – DECORATION 7 AND 8; FRAGMENTS. GETIC (GET)

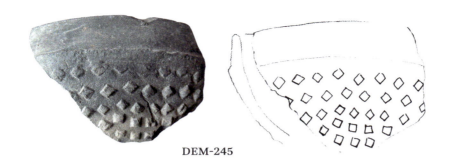

DEM-245

DEM-246

DEM-247

DEM-251

DEM-252

DEM-253

DEM-255

DEM-257

GET-1

GET-2

GET-3

SCALE 2:3